31943

THE AUTHORITARIAN PERSONALITY

STUDIES IN PREJUDICE

EDITED BY MAX HORKHEIMER
AND SAMUEL H. FLOWERMAN

THE AUTHORITARIAN PERSONALITY

By T. W. Adorno, Else Frenkel-Brunswik,
Daniel J. Levinson and R. Nevitt Sanford

DYNAMICS OF PREJUDICE

A PSYCHOLOGICAL AND SOCIOLOGICAL STUDY OF VETERANS
by Bruno Bettelheim and Morris Janowitz

ANTI-SEMITISM AND EMOTIONAL DISORDER

A PSYCHOANALYTIC INTERPRETATION
by Nathan W. Ackerman and Marie Jahoda

REHEARSAL FOR DESTRUCTION

A STUDY OF POLITICAL ANTI-SEMITISM IN IMPERIAL GERMANY
by Paul W. Massing

PROPHETS OF DECEIT

A STUDY OF THE TECHNIQUES OF THE AMERICAN AGITATOR
by Leo Lowenthal and Norbert Guterman

Other Volumes in Preparation

SPONSORED BY
THE AMERICAN JEWISH COMMITTEE
SOCIAL STUDIES SERIES: PUBLICATION NO. III

THE AUTHORITARIAN PERSONALITY

by

T. W. ADORNO
ELSE FRENKEL-BRUNSWIK
DANIEL J. LEVINSON
R. NEVITT SANFORD

in collaboration with

BETTY ARON, MARIA HERTZ LEVINSON
AND WILLIAM MORROW

Studies in Prejudice
EDITED BY MAX HORKHEIMER
AND SAMUEL H. FLOWERMAN

HARPER & BROTHERS · NEW YORK

FOREWORD TO STUDIES IN PREJUDICE

At this moment in world history anti-Semitism is not manifesting itself with the full and violent destructiveness of which we know it to be capable. Even a social disease has its periods of quiescence during which the social scientists, like the biologist or the physician, can study it in the search for more effective ways to prevent or reduce the virulence of the next outbreak.

Today the world scarcely remembers the mechanized persecution and extermination of millions of human beings only a short span of years away in what was once regarded as the citadel of Western civilization. Yet the conscience of many men was aroused. How could it be, they asked each other, that in a culture of law, order, and reason, there should have survived the irrational remnants of ancient racial and religious hatreds? How could they explain the willingness of great masses of people to tolerate the mass extermination of their fellow citizens? What tissues in the life of our modern society remain cancerous, and despite our assumed enlightenment show the incongruous atavism of ancient peoples? And what within the individual organism responds to certain stimuli in our culture with attitudes and acts of destructive aggression?

But an aroused conscience is not enough if it does not stimulate a systematic search for an answer. Mankind has paid too dearly for its naive faith in the automatic effect of the mere passage of time; incantations have really never dispelled storms, disaster, pestilence, disease or other evils; nor does he who torments another cease his torture out of sheer boredom with his victim.

Prejudice is one of the problems of our times for which everyone has a theory but no one an answer. Every man, in a sense, believes that he is his own social scientist, for social science is the stuff of everyday living. The progress of science can perhaps be charted by the advances that scientists have made over commonsense notions of phenomena. In an effort to advance beyond mere commonsense approaches to problems of intergroup conflict, the American Jewish Committee in May, 1944, invited a group of American scholars of various backgrounds and disciplines to a two-day conference on religious and racial prejudice. At this meeting, a research program was outlined which would enlist scientific method in the cause of seeking solutions to this crucial problem. Two levels of research were recommended. One was more limited in scope and geared to the recurring problems faced by educational agencies; e.g., the study of public reaction to selected current events, and the evaluation of various techniques and methods such as those involved in mass media of communication as they impinge upon intergroup relationships. The other level suggested was one of basic research, basic in that it should result eventually in additions to organized knowledge in this field. The first level frequently consists of a large number of small studies, limited in scope and focused sharply on a given issue. In practice, we have found that the "goodness" of our smaller studies was proportional to our ingenuity in so devising them that they, too, could contribute basically to knowledge. The chief difference between the two levels of research—sometimes loosely called "short-range" and "long-range" research—seems largely to be due to the immediacy of implementation of findings as program-related or unrelated, rather than to differences in methodology, skills and techniques. On both levels, it is necessary to pursue an interdisciplinary approach to research problems.

To further research on both levels, the American Jewish Committee established a Department of Scientific Research, headed in turn by each of us. The department saw its responsibility not only in itself initiating fundamental studies in the phenomenon of prejudice, but also in helping to stimulate new studies.

The present series of volumes represents the first fruits of this effort. In a sense, the initial five volumes constitute one unit, an integrated whole, each part of which illuminates one or another facet of the phenomenon we call prejudice. Three of the books deal with those elements in the personality of modern man that predispose him to reactions of hostility to racial and religious groups. They attempt answers to the question: What is there in the psychology of the individual that renders him "prejudiced" or "unprejudiced," that makes him more or less likely to respond favorably to the agitation of a Goebbels or a Gerald K. Smith? The volume on *The Authoritarian Personality* by Adorno, Frenkel-Brunswik, Levinson and Sanford, based upon a combination of research techniques, suggests one answer. It demonstrates that there is a close correlation between a number of deep-rooted personality traits, and overt prejudice. The study has also succeeded in producing an instrument for measuring these traits among various strata of the population.

Within a more limited range of inquiry, the same question was asked with respect to two specific groups. The study on *Dynamics of Prejudice* by Bettelheim and Janowitz, considers the connection between personality traits and prejudice among war veterans. Here the investigators were able to examine the impact of the war experience, with its complex anxieties and tensions, as an added factor of major significance affecting tens of millions of people. *Anti-Semitism and Emotional Disorder* by Ackerman and Jahoda, is based upon case histories of a number of individuals, from different walks of life, who have received intensive psychotherapy. The special significance of this study lies precisely in the analytical source of the material, in the availability of a body of evidence dealing with phenomena beneath the realm of the conscious and the rational, and illuminating the correlation established in more general terms in the basic investigation of the authoritarian personality.

The other important factor in prejudice is of course the social situation itself, i.e., the external stimuli to which the predispositions within the individual have reacted and continue to react. Nazi Germany is the vivid example of the effect of the social situation, and it is to the understanding of the roots of Nazi anti-Semitism and thence to the present task of democratic reorientation in Germany that *Rehearsal for Destruction* by Massing is directed.

In *Prophets of Deceit* by Lowenthal and Guterman the role of the agitator is studied. The agitator's technique of persuasion, the mechanism of mediation that translates inchoate feeling into specific belief and action make up the theme of that volume. As mediator between the world and the individual psyche, the agitator molds already existing prejudices and tendencies into overt doctrines and ultimately into overt action.

It may strike the reader that we have placed undue stress upon the personal and the psychological rather than upon the social aspect of prejudice. This is not due to a personal preference for psychological analysis nor to a failure to see that the cause of irrational hostility is in the last instance to be found in social frustration and injustice. Our aim is not merely to describe prejudice but to explain it in order to help in its eradication. That is the challenge we would meet. Eradication means re-education, scientifically planned on the basis of understanding scientifically arrived at. And education in a strict sense is by its nature personal and psychological. Once we understand, for example, how the war experience may in some cases have strengthened personality traits predisposed to group hatred, the educational remedies may follow logically. Similarly, to expose the psychological tricks in the arsenal of the agitator may help to immunize his prospective victims against them.

Since the completion of these studies the Department of Scientific Research of the American Jewish Committee has moved ahead into areas of research in which the unit of study is the group, the institution, the community rather than the individual. Fortified by a better knowledge of *individual* dynamics, we are now concerned with achieving a better understanding of *group* dynamics. For we recognize that the individual *in vacuo* is but an artifact; even in the present series of studies, although essentially psychological in nature, it has been necessary to explain individual behavior in terms of social antecedents and concomitants. The second stage of our research is thus focused upon problems of group pressures and the sociological determinants of roles in given social situations. We seek answers to such questions as: Why does an individual behave in a "tolerant" manner in one situation and in a "bigoted" manner in another situation? To what extent may certain forms of intergroup conflict, which appear on the surface to be based upon ethnic difference, be based upon other factors, using ethnic difference as content?

The authors of the volumes and the many colleagues upon whose experience and assistance they have been able to draw have widely differing professional interests. This is immediately reflected in the various techniques they have used, even in the way they write. Some of the books are more technical, others more "readable." We have not sought uniformity. A search for the truth conducted in accordance with the best techniques of the contemporary social sciences was our sole aim. Yet through all this diversity of method and technique a significant measure of agreement has been achieved.

The problem requires a much more extensive and much more sustained effort than any single institution, or any small group such as ours, could hope to put forth. It was our hope that whatever projects we could undertake would not only be contributions in themselves, but would also serve to stimulate active interest in continued study by other scholars. With deep satisfaction we have watched the steady increase in scientific publications in this field in the past few years. We believe that any study that bears upon this central theme, if carried out in a truly scientific spirit, cannot help but bring us closer to the theoretical, and ultimately to the practical, solution of the problem of reducing intergroup prejudice and hatred.

This foreword to *Studies in Prejudice* would not be complete without a tribute to the vision and leadership of Dr. John Slawson, Executive Vice-President of the American Jewish Committee, who was responsible for calling the conference of scholars and for establishing the Department of Scientific Research. Both editors owe Dr. Slawson a debt of gratitude for the inspiration, guidance, and stimulation which he gave them.

MAX HORKHEIMER
SAMUEL H. FLOWERMAN

PREFACE

This is a book about social discrimination. But its purpose is not simply to add a few more empirical findings to an already extensive body of information. The central theme of the work is a relatively new concept—the rise of an "anthropological" species we call the authoritarian type of man. In contrast to the bigot of the older style he seems to combine the ideas and skills which are typical of a highly industrialized society with irrational or anti-rational beliefs. He is at the same time enlightened and superstitious, proud to be an individualist and in constant fear of not being like all the others, jealous of his independence and inclined to submit blindly to power and authority. The character structure which comprises these conflicting trends has already attracted the attention of modern philosophers and political thinkers. This book approaches the problem with the means of sociopsychological research.

The implications and values of the study are practical as well as theoretical. The authors do not believe that there is a short cut to education which will eliminate the long and often circuitous road of painstaking research and theoretical analysis. Nor do they think that such a problem as the position of minorities in modern society, and more specifically the problem of religious and racial hatreds, can be tackled successfully either by the propaganda of tolerance or by apologetic refutation of errors and lies. On the other hand, theoretical activity and practical application are not separated by an unbridgeable gulf. Quite the contrary: the authors are imbued with the conviction that the sincere and systematic scientific elucidation of a phenomenon of such great historical meaning can contribute directly to an amelioration of the cultural atmosphere in which hatred breeds.

This conviction must not be brushed aside as an optimistic illusion. In the history of civilization there have been not a few instances when mass delusions were healed not by focused propaganda but, in the final analysis, because scholars, with their unobtrusive yet insistent work habits, studied what lay at the root of the delusion. Their intellectual contribution, operating within the framework of the development of society as a whole, was decisively effective.

I should like to cite two examples. The superstitious belief in witchcraft was overcome in the seventeenth and eighteenth centuries after men had come more and more under the influence of the results of modern science. The impact of Cartesian rationalism was decisive. This school of philosophers demonstrated—and the natural scientists following them made practical use of their great insight—that the previously accepted belief in the immediate effect of spiritual factors on the realm of the corporal is an illusion. Once this scientifically untenable dogma was eliminated, the foundations of the belief in magic were destroyed.

As a more recent example, we have only to think of the impact of Sigmund Freud's work on modern culture. Its primary importance does not lie in the fact that psychological research and knowledge have been enriched by new findings but in the fact that for some fifty years the intellectual world, and especially the educational, has been made more and more aware of the connection between the suppression of children (both within the home and outside) and society's usually naive ignorance of the psychological dynamics of the life of the child and the adult alike. The permeation of the social consciousness at large with the scientifically acquired experience that the events of early childhood are of prime importance for the happiness and work-potential of the adult has brought about a revolution in the relation between parents and children which would have been deemed impossible a hundred years ago.

The present work, we hope, will find a place in this history of the interdependence between science and the cultural climate. Its ultimate goal is to open new avenues in a research area which can become of immediate practical significance. It seeks to develop and promote an understanding of social-psychological factors which have made it possible for the authoritarian type of man to threaten to replace the individualistic and democratic type prevalent in the past century and a half of our civilization, and of the factors by which this threat may be contained. Progressive analysis of this new "anthropological" type and of its growth conditions, with an ever-increasing scientific differentiation, will enhance the chances of a genuinely educational counterattack.

Confidence in the possibility of a more systematic study of the mechanisms of discrimination and especially of a characterological discrimination-type is not based on the historical experience of the last fifteen years alone, but also on developments within the social sciences themselves during recent decades. Considerable and successful efforts have been made in this country as well as in Europe to raise the various disciplines dealing with man as a social phenomenon to the organizational level of cooperation that has been a tradition in the natural sciences. What I am thinking of are not merely mechanical arrangements for bringing together work done in various fields of study, as in symposia or textbooks, but the mobilization of different methods and skills, developed in distinct fields of theory and empirical investigation, for one common research program.

Such cross-fertilization of different branches of the social sciences and psychology is exactly what has taken place in the present volume. Experts in the fields of social theory and depth psychology, content analysis, clinical psychology, political sociology, and projective testing pooled their experiences and findings. Having worked together in the closest cooperation, they now present as the result of their joint efforts the elements of a theory of the authoritarian type of man in modern society.

They are not unmindful that they were not the first to have studied this phenomenon. They gratefully acknowledge their debt to the remarkable psychological profiles of the prejudiced individual projected by Sigmund Freud, Maurice Samuel, Otto Fenichel, and others. Such brilliant insights were in a sense the indispensable prerequisites for the methodological integration and research organization which the present study has attempted, and we think achieved to a certain degree, on a scale previously unapproached.

Institutionally, this book represents a joint undertaking of the Berkeley Public Opinion Study and the Institute of Social Research. Both organizations had already made their mark in efforts to integrate various sciences and different research methods. The Berkeley Public Opinion Study had devoted itself to the examination of prejudice in terms of social psychology and had hit upon the close correlation between overt prejudice and certain personality traits of a destructive nihilistic nature, suggested by an irrationally pessimistic ideology of the intolerant. The Institute of Social Research was dedicated to the principle of theoretical and methodological integration from its earliest days at the University of Frankfurt, and published several studies growing out of this basic approach. In one volume, on authority and the family, the concept of the "authoritarian personality" was put forward as a link between psychological dispositions and political leanings. Pursuing this line of thought further, the Institute formulated and published in 1939 a comprehensive research project on anti-Semitism. Some five years later, a series of discussions with the late Dr. Ernst Simmel and Professor R. Nevitt Sanford of the University of California laid the basis for the present project.

As finally organized, the research staff was headed by four senior members, Dr. R. N. Sanford of the Berkeley Public Opinion Study and Dr. T. W. Adorno of the Institute of Social Research, who were the directors, and Dr. Else Frenkel-Brunswik and Dr. Daniel Levinson. Their collaboration was so close, perhaps I should say democratic, and the work so evenly divided among them that it became clear at an early stage that they ought to share equally in the responsibility and the credit for the present publication. The main concepts of the study were evolved by the team as a whole. This is true above all of the idea of the indirect measurement of antidemocratic trends, the F scale. Some division of labor could not be avoided, however, and it proved advisable to have the various chapters signed by individual staff members. The actual writing process necessarily involves a more intimate occupation with the materials under consideration and thus a measure of more specific responsibility. Nevertheless, the fact remains that each of the four senior members contributed to every chapter and hence that the work as a whole is thoroughly collective.

It may be of interest to note the primary assignments of each of the senior staff members during the actual research process. Dr. Sanford conceived the way the various techniques should be combined and planned the research procedures. Much of his time was devoted to detailed case studies, with special reference to the dynamic etiology of the prejudiced personality. Dr. Adorno introduced sociological dimensions related to personality factors and characterological concepts concomitant with authoritarianism. He also analyzed the ideological sections of the interviews by means of categories of social theory. Dr. Brunswik formulated some of the first personality variables of the research. On the basis of her earlier work, she carried through the systematic, dynamically oriented categorization and quantification of the interview material. Dr. Levinson had primary responsibility for the AS, E, and PEC scales, for the analysis of ideology in psychological terms, for the Projective Question analysis, and for the statistical design and procedure.

Three monographic chapters, one an over-all presentation of the methodology and results of one of the main techniques, the Thematic Apperception Test, and two dealing with "critical" groups were written by Betty Aron, Maria Levinson, and William Morrow. All three were permanently on the staff of the study and completely familiar with its progress.

The project could not have been realized without the generous and intelligent support of the American Jewish Committee. In 1944 the Committee, feeling the need for a sound research basis for the financial and organizational support it planned to give to cooperative studies, of a type which this book exemplifies, decided to create a Department of Scientific Research. From the first the Department was conceived as a scientific center to stimulate and co-ordinate the work of leading scientists in the sociology and psychology of prejudice and, at the same time, as a laboratory for evaluating action programs. Though the members of the Department's research staff are constantly under pressure to solve problems set up for them by the day-to-day work of an extensive organization fighting for democratic rights on several broad fronts, they have never shirked the responsibility of furthering basic research programs. This volume symbolizes that link between democratic education and fundamental research.

MAX HORKHEIMER,
Director, Institute of Social Research

ACKNOWLEDGMENTS

The authors wish to express their indebtedness to the American Jewish Committee for the grants which sustained their research during a period of two and one-half years. They owe a special debt of gratitude to Dr. Max Horkheimer, Director of the Department of Scientific Research of the American Jewish Committee at the time the present study was undertaken. Dr. Horkheimer played the crucial role in the initiation of the study, and he remained closely identified with it until the end; he contributed ideas, guidance, encouragement and untiring activity in support of our aims. We wish to thank him, further, for contributing the preface to this volume. To Dr. Samuel Flowerman, who succeeded Dr. Horkheimer as Director of the Department of Scientific Research of the American Jewish Committee, the authors are likewise heavily indebted. Dr. Flowerman's interest, advice, and tangible help in practical matters were invaluable in bringing about the publication of this volume.

Our collaborators, Betty Aron, Maria Levinson, and Dr. William Morrow, are to be thanked not only for their special studies which contribute so substantially to the content of this volume but for their participation in all phases of the study as a whole. For extended periods during the course of the study each of them contributed to the development of theory and to the collection, analysis and interpretation of data in areas other than those covered by their special studies. Dr. Suzanne Reichard, who conducted a special investigation of the Rorschach records of some of our subjects, likewise participated in the various phases of the study; she devoted most of her time to administering the Thematic Apperception Test, interviewing subjects and assisting in the analysis and interpretation of the interview material.

In conducting interviews with our subjects in the San Francisco Bay Area we had the able assistance of Dr. Merle Elliott, Virginia Ives, Dr. Mary Cover Jones, Sheila Moon and Rose Segure. Rose Segure also assisted, as did Jack Danielson, in making the arrangements whereby certain groups of subjects filled out our questionnaires. Dr. Winfield Wickham generously cooperated by administering the Thematic Apperception Test to a large group of our subjects, and Roger Bardsley assisted in the analysis of Thematic Apperception Test records.

Numerous colleagues and friends read all or parts of the manuscript, took the time to discuss it with us, and made many corrections, suggestions, and helpful criticisms. We wish to express our appreciation to Dr. Egon Brunswik, Frederick Carpenter, Dr. William R. Dennes, Dr. Ernst Kris, Dr. Calvin Hall, Dr. David Krech, Dr. Boyd McCandless, Dr. Robert Merton, Dr. Donald MacKinnon, Dr. Gardner Murphy, Dr. Lois B. Murphy, Dr. Milton Rokeach, Richard Seymour, and Dr. Edward Tolman. Dr. Rheem Jarrett and Dr. George Kuznets deserve special thanks for their valuable advice in statistical matters.

Chapters XVI, XVII, XVIII and XIX, were prepared in continuous collaboration with members of the Institute of Social Research. Particular thanks are due Dr. Leo Lowenthal and Dr. Frederick Pollock. The latter also participated in organizing a small staff to carry on our research in Los Angeles. The gathering of data was here supervised by Dr. J. F. Brown, who also contributed important theoretical concepts. The distribution and collection of questionnaires and the interviewing of subjects in Los Angeles was in the hands of Emily Gruen and Carol Creedon, assisted by Ida Malcolm and James Mower. Grace Berg and Margaret Weil served ably as secretaries, and Margot von Mendelssohn, permanent secretary of the Institute of Social Research, devoted a large part of her time to this project. Dr. Frederick Hacker, Dr. Ernest Lewy, and Dr. Marcel Frym participated in the seminars which were held regularly in Los Angeles while the research was in progress there; their devotion to the study is particularly appreciated.

The mountainous task of scoring, tabulating and performing innumerable statistical operations upon the material gathered by means of some 2000 questionnaires was performed with patience and care by Ellan Ulery and Anne Batchelder Morrow. They were assisted in no small way by Lionel Whitnah, Jack Danielson, Frank Vanasek, and Nannette Heiman. Ellan Ulery and Anne Batchelder Morrow also deserve much credit for their scoring of the material elicited by the "projective questions" described in Chapter XV. Dr. Alfred Glixman is to be thanked for performing a special correlational analysis of our attitude scales—work which is described in Chapters IV and VII.

At different periods during the course of the study, Marjorie Castagnetto, Anne Vollmar and Zelma Seidner had charge of the secretarial work in Berkeley. Each in turn, with complete loyalty and superior competence, assumed the enormous burden of typing records and manuscripts and, in addition, took responsibility for the innumerable small but crucially important tasks incident to keeping in motion a research involving numerous workers and subjects. Our most heartfelt thanks go to Anne Vollmar who, in addition to performing the secretarial work described above, labored with endless patience and devotion to make something relatively uniform and presentable out of the manuscripts of all shapes and sizes which we handed her—an editorial job of enormous proportion—and whose serenity and wisdom in practical matters were relied upon and deeply appreciated by all members of our staff. Alice Wilson, Alice Davis, Ruth Gay, Betty

Cummings, and Edna Sexias also helped with the typing of records and manuscript; we greatly appreciate their willingness to be called upon when needed.

If we were to mention here all the people who cooperated by making arrangements for us to administer our questionnaires to the groups with which they were associated, and other people who assisted in particular aspects of the study, the list would be very long indeed. Acknowledgments are made at appropriate places in the chapters that follow.

To complete a special project lying within the scope of our study and to meet unexpected expenses connected with preparation of the manuscript for publication it was necessary to seek financial aid in addition to that described above. We are indebted to the Social Science Research Council for the Grant-in-Aid which made possible the correlational analysis described in Chapters IV and VII, and to the Rosenberg Foundation, the Research Board of the University of California, the Institute of Social Sciences of the University of California and the Graduate Division of Western Reserve University for their support in time of special need.

Finally, we are grateful to Dr. Felix J. Weil of the Institute of Social Research. He contributed many helpful criticisms of the manuscript, undertook the arduous task of coordinating all the proof reading, and performed invaluable services of an editorial nature.

THE AUTHORS

CONTENTS

PART III

PERSONALITY AS REVEALED THROUGH PROJECTIVE MATERIAL

PART IV

QUALITATIVE STUDIES OF IDEOLOGY

PART V

APPLICATIONS TO INDIVIDUALS AND TO SPECIAL GROUPS

TABLES AND FIGURES

The stimulus pictures used for the Thematic Apperception Tests in Chapter XIV are reproduced
on the insert opposite page 508.

CHAPTER I

INTRODUCTION

A. THE PROBLEM

The research to be reported in this volume was guided by the following major hypothesis: that the political, economic, and social convictions of an individual often form a broad and coherent pattern, as if bound together by a "mentality" or "spirit," and that this pattern is an expression of deeply-lying trends in his personality.

The major concern was with the *potentially fascistic* individual, one whose structure is such as to render him particularly susceptible to anti-democratic propaganda. We say "potential" because we have not studied individuals who were avowedly fascistic or who belonged to known fascist organizations. At the time when most of our data were collected fascism had just been defeated in war and, hence, we could not expect to find sub-jects who would openly identify themselves with it; yet there was no difficulty in finding subjects whose outlook was such as to indicate that they would readily accept fascism if it should become a strong or respectable social movement.

In concentrating upon the potential fascist we do not wish to imply that other patterns of personality and ideology might not profitably be studied in the same way. It is our opinion, however, that no politico-social trend imposes a graver threat to our traditional values and institutions than does fascism, and that knowledge of the personality forces that favor its accept-ance may ultimately prove useful in combating it. A question may be raised as to why, if we wish to explore new resources for combating fascism, we do not give as much attention to the "potential antifascist." The answer is that we do study trends that stand in opposition to fascism, but we do not conceive that they constitute any single pattern. It is one of the major findings of the present study that individuals who show extreme susceptibil-ity to fascist propaganda have a great deal in common. (They exhibit numerous characteristics that go together to form a "syndrome" although typical variations within this major pattern can be distinguished.) Indi-viduals who are extreme in the opposite direction are much more diverse. The task of diagnosing potential fascism and studying its determinants required techniques especially designed for these purposes; it could not be asked of them that they serve as well for various other patterns. Neverthe-less, it was possible to distinguish several types of personality structure that seemed particularly resistant to antidemocratic ideas, and these are given due attention in later chapters.

If a potentially fascistic individual exists, what, precisely, is he like? What goes to make up antidemocratic thought? What are the organizing forces within the person? If such a person exists, how commonly does he exist in our society? And if such a person exists, what have been the determinants and what the course of his development?

These are questions upon which the present research was designed to throw some light. Though the notion that the potentially antidemocratic individual is a totality may be accepted as a plausible hypothesis, some analysis is called for at the start. In most approaches to the problem of polit-ical types two essential conceptions may be distinguished: the conception of ideology and the conception of underlying needs in the person. Though the two may be thought of as forming an organized whole within the individual, they may nonetheless be studied separately. The same ideological trends may in different individuals have different sources, and the same personal needs may express themselves in different ideological trends.

The term ideology is used in this book, in the way that is common in current literature, to stand for an organization of opinions, attitudes, and values—a way of thinking about man and society. We may speak of an indi-vidual's total ideology or of his ideology with respect to different areas of social life: politics, economics, religion, minority groups, and so forth. Ideol-ogies have an existence independent of any single individual; and those which exist at a particular time are results both of historical processes and of contemporary social events. These ideologies have for different individ-uals, different degrees of appeal, a matter that depends upon the individual's needs and the degree to which these needs are being satisfied or frustrated.

There are, to be sure, individuals who take unto themselves ideas from more than one existing ideological system and weave them into patterns that are more or less uniquely their own. It can be assumed, however, that when the opinions, attitudes, and values of numerous individuals are examined, common patterns will be discovered. These patterns may not in all cases correspond to the familiar, current ideologies, but they will fulfill the defi-nition of ideology given above and in each case be found to have a function within the over-all adjustment of the individual.

The present inquiry into the nature of the potentially fascistic individual began with anti-Semitism in the focus of attention. The authors, in common with most social scientists, hold the view that anti-Semitism is based more largely upon factors in the subject and in his total situation than upon actual characteristics of Jews, and that one place to look for determinants of anti-Semitic opinions and attitudes is within the persons who express them. Since this emphasis on personality required a focusing of attention on psychology rather than on sociology or history—though in the last analysis the three can be separated only artificially—there could be no attempt to account for the existence of anti-Semitic ideas in our society. The question was, rather, why is it that certain individuals accept these ideas while others do not? And since from the start the research was guided by the hypotheses stated above, it was supposed (1) that anti-Semitism probably is not a specific or isolated phenomenon but a part of a broader ideological framework, and (2) that an individual's susceptibility to this ideology depends primarily upon his psychological needs.

The insights and hypotheses concerning the antidemocratic individual, which are present in our general cultural climate, must be supported by a great deal of painstaking observation, and in many instances by quantification, before they can be regarded as conclusive. How can one say with assurance that the numerous opinions, attitudes, and values expressed by an individual actually constitute a consistent pattern or organized totality? The most intensive investigation of that individual would seem to be necessary. How can one say that opinions, attitudes, and values found in groups of people go together to form patterns, some of which are more common than others? There is no adequate way to proceed other than by actually measuring, in populations, a wide variety of thought contents and determining by means of standard statistical methods which ones go together.

To many social psychologists the scientific study of ideology, as it has been defined, seems a hopeless task. To measure with suitable accuracy a single, specific, isolated attitude is a long and arduous proceeding for both subject and experimenter. (It is frequently argued that unless the attitude is specific and isolated, it cannot properly be measured at all.) How then can we hope to survey within a reasonable period of time the numerous attitudes and ideas that go to make up an ideology? Obviously, some kind of selection is necessary. The investigator must limit himself to what is most significant, and judgments of significance can only be made on the basis of theory.

The theories that have guided the present research will be presented in suitable contexts later. Though theoretical considerations had a role at every stage of the work, a beginning had to be made with the objective study of the most observable and relatively specific opinions, attitudes, and values.

Opinions, attitudes, and values, as we conceive of them, are expressed more or less openly in words. Psychologically they are "on the surface." It must be recognized, however, that when it comes to such affect-laden questions as those concerning minority groups and current political issues, the degree of openness with which a person speaks will depend upon the situation in which he finds himself. There may be a discrepancy between what he says on a particular occasion and what he "really thinks." Let us say that what he really thinks he can express in confidential discussion with his intimates. This much, which is still relatively superficial psychologically, may still be observed directly by the psychologist if he uses appropriate techniques—and this we have attempted to do.

It is to be recognized, however, that the individual may have "secret" thoughts which he will under no circumstances reveal to anyone else if he can help it; he may have thoughts which he cannot admit to himself, and he may have thoughts which he does not express because they are so vague and ill-formed that he cannot put them into words. To gain access to these deeper trends is particularly important, for precisely here may lie the individual's potential for democratic or antidemocratic thought and action in crucial situations.

What people say and, to a lesser degree, what they really think depends very largely upon the climate of opinion in which they are living; but when that climate changes, some individuals adapt themselves much more quickly than others. If there should be a marked increase in antidemocratic propaganda, we should expect some people to accept and repeat it at once, others when it seemed that "everybody believed it," and still others not at all. In other words, individuals differ in their *susceptibility* to antidemocratic propaganda, in their readiness to exhibit antidemocratic tendencies. It seems necessary to study ideology at this "readiness level" in order to gauge the potential for fascism in this country. Observers have noted that the amount of outspoken anti-Semitism in pre-Hitler Germany was less than that in this country at the present time; one might hope that the potentiality is less in this country, but this can be known only through intensive investigation, through the detailed survey of what is on the surface and the thorough probing of what lies beneath it.

A question may be raised as to what is the degree of relationship between ideology and action. If an individual is making antidemocratic propaganda or engaging in overt attacks upon minority group members, it is usually assumed that his opinions, attitudes, and values are congruent with his action; but comfort is sometimes found in the thought that though another individual expresses antidemocratic ideas verbally, he does not, and perhaps will not, put them into overt action. Here, once again, there is a question of potentialities. Overt action, like open verbal expression, depends very largely upon the situation of the moment—something that is best described in socio-economic and political terms—but individuals differ very widely with respect to their readiness to be provoked into action. The study of this potential is a part of the study of the individual's over-all ideology; to know what kinds and what intensities of belief, attitude, and value are likely to lead to action, and to know what forces within the individual serve as inhibitions upon action are matters of the greatest practical importance.

There seems little reason to doubt that ideology-in-readiness (ideological receptivity) and ideology-in-words and in action are essentially the same stuff. The description of an individual's total ideology must portray not only the organization on each level but organization among levels. What the individual consistently says in public, what he says when he feels safe from criticism, what he thinks but will not say at all, what he thinks but will not admit to himself, what he is disposed to think or to do when various kinds of appeal are made to him—all these phenomena may be conceived of as constituting a single structure. The structure may not be integrated, it may contain contradictions as well as consistencies, but it is *organized* in the sense that the constituent parts are related in psychologically meaningful ways.

In order to understand such a structure, a theory of the total personality is necessary. According to the theory that has guided the present research, personality is a more or less enduring organization of forces within the individual. These persisting forces of personality help to determine response in various situations, and it is thus largely to them that consistency of behavior —whether verbal or physical—is attributable. But behavior, however consistent, is not the same thing as personality; personality lies *behind* behavior and *within* the individual. The forces of personality are not responses but *readinesses for response;* whether or not a readiness will issue in overt expression depends not only upon the situation of the moment but upon what other readinesses stand in opposition to it. Personality forces which are inhibited are on a deeper level than those which immediately and consistently express themselves in overt behavior.

What are the forces of personality and what are the processes by which they are organized? For theory as to the structure of personality we have leaned most heavily upon Freud, while for a more or less systematic formulation of the more directly observable and measurable aspects of personality we have been guided primarily by academic psychology. The forces of personality are primarily *needs* (drives, wishes, emotional impulses) which vary from one individual to another in their quality, their intensity, their mode of gratification, and the objects of their attachment, and which interact with other needs in harmonious or conflicting patterns. There are primitive emotional needs, there are needs to avoid punishment and to keep the good will of the social group, there are needs to maintain harmony and integration within the self.

Since it will be granted that opinions, attitudes, and values depend upon human needs, and since personality is essentially an organization of needs, then personality may be regarded as a *determinant* of ideological preferences. Personality is not, however, to be hypostatized as an ultimate determinant. Far from being something which is given in the beginning, which remains fixed and acts upon the surrounding world, personality evolves under the impact of the social environment and can never be isolated from the social totality within which it occurs. According to the present theory, the effects of environmental forces in moulding the personality are, in general, the more profound the earlier in the life history of the individual they are brought to bear. The major influences upon personality development arise in the course of child training as carried forward in a setting of family life. What happens here is profoundly influenced by economic and social factors. It is not only that each family in trying to rear its children proceeds according to the ways of the social, ethnic, and religious groups in which it has membership, but crude economic factors affect directly the parents' behavior toward the child. This means that broad changes in social conditions and institutions will have a direct bearing upon the kinds of personalities that develop within a society.

The present research seeks to discover correlations between ideology and sociological factors operating in the individual's past—whether or not they continue to operate in his present. In attempting to explain these correlations the relationships between personality and ideology are brought into the picture, the general approach being to consider personality as an agency through which sociological influences upon ideology are mediated. If the role of personality can be made clear, it should be possible better to understand which sociological factors are the most crucial ones and in what ways they achieve their effects.

Although personality is a product of the social environment of the past, it is not, once it has developed, a mere object of the contemporary environment. What has developed is a *structure* within the individual, something which is capable of self-initiated action upon the social environment and of selection with respect to varied impinging stimuli, something which though always modifiable is frequently very resistant to fundamental change. This conception is necessary to explain consistency of behavior in widely varying situations, to explain the persistence of ideological trends in the face of contradicting facts and radically altered social conditions, to explain why people in the same sociological situation have different or even conflicting views on social issues, and why it is that people whose behavior has been changed through psychological manipulation lapse into their old ways as soon as the agencies of manipulation are removed.

The conception of personality structure is the best safeguard against the inclination to attribute persistent trends in the individual to something "innate" or "basic" or "racial" within him. The Nazi allegation that natural, biological traits decide the total being of a person would not have been such a successful political device had it not been possible to point to numerous instances of relative fixity in human behavior and to challenge those who thought to explain them on any basis other than a biological one. Without the conception of personality structure, writers whose approach rests upon the assumption of infinite human flexibility and responsiveness to the social situation of the moment have not helped matters by referring persistent trends which they could not approve to "confusion" or "psychosis" or evil under one name or another. There is, of course, some basis for describing as "pathological" patterns of behavior which do not conform with the most common, and seemingly most lawful, responses to momentary stimuli. But this is to use the term pathological in the very narrow sense of deviation from the average found in a particular context and, what is worse, to suggest that everything in the personality structure is to be put under this heading. Actually, personality embraces variables which exist widely in the population and have lawful relations one to another. Personality patterns that have been dismissed as "pathological" because they were not in keeping with the most common manifest trends or the most dominant ideals within a society, have on closer investigation turned out to be but exaggerations of what was almost universal below the surface in that society. What is "pathological" today may with changing social conditions become the dominant trend of tomorrow.

It seems clear then that an adequate approach to the problems before us must take into account both fixity and flexibility; it must regard the two not as mutually exclusive categories but as the extremes of a single continuum along which human characteristics may be placed, and it must provide a basis for understanding the conditions which favor the one extreme or the other. Personality is a concept to account for relative permanence. But it may be emphasized again that personality is mainly a potential; it is a readiness for behavior rather than behavior itself; although it consists in dispositions to behave in certain ways, the behavior that actually occurs will always depend upon the objective situation. Where the concern is with antidemocratic trends, a delineation of the conditions for individual expression requires an understanding of the total organization of society.

It has been stated that the personality structure may be such as to render the individual susceptible to antidemocratic propaganda. It may now be asked what are the conditions under which such propaganda would increase in pitch and volume and come to dominate in press and radio to the exclusion of contrary ideological stimuli, so that what is now potential would become actively manifest. The answer must be sought not in any single personality nor in personality factors found in the mass of people, but in processes at work in society itself. It seems well understood today that whether or not antidemocratic propaganda is to become a dominant force in this country depends primarily upon the situation of the most powerful economic interests, upon whether they, by conscious design or not, make use of this device for maintaining their dominant status. This is a matter about which the great majority of people would have little to say.

The present research, limited as it is to the hitherto largely neglected psychological aspects of fascism, does not concern itself with the production of propaganda. It focuses attention, rather, upon the consumer, the individual for whom the propaganda is designed. In so doing it attempts to take into account not only the psychological structure of the individual but the total objective situation in which he lives. It makes the assumption that people in general tend to accept political and social programs which they believe will serve their economic interests. What these interests are depends in each case upon the individual's position in society as defined in economic and sociological terms. An important part of the present research, therefore, was the attempt to discover what patterns of socioeconomic factors are associated with receptivity, and with resistance, to antidemocratic propaganda.

At the same time, however, it was considered that economic motives in the individual may not have the dominant and crucial role that is often ascribed to them. If economic self-interest were the only determinant of opinion, we should expect people of the same socioeconomic status to have very similar opinions, and we should expect opinion to vary in a meaningful way from one socioeconomic grouping to another. Research has not given very sound support for these expectations. There is only the most general similarity of opinion among people of the same socioeconomic status, and the exceptions are glaring; while variations from one socioeconomic group to another are rarely simple or clear-cut. To explain why it is that people of the same socioeconomic status so frequently have different ideologies, while people of a different status often have very similar ideologies, we must take account of other than purely economic needs.

More than this, it is becoming increasingly plain that people very frequently do not behave in such a way as to further their material interests, even when it is clear to them what these interests are. The resistance of white-collar workers to organization is not due to a belief that the union will not help them economically; the tendency of the small businessman to side with big business in most economic and political matters cannot be due entirely to a belief that this is the way to guarantee his economic independence. In instances such as these the individual seems not only not to consider his material interests, but even to go against them. It is as if he were thinking in terms of a larger group identification, as if his point of view were determined more by his need to support this group and to suppress opposite ones than by rational consideration of his own interests. Indeed, it is with a sense of relief today that one is assured that a group conflict is merely a clash of economic interests—that each side is merely out to "do" the other— and not a struggle in which deep-lying emotional drives have been let loose. When it comes to the ways in which people appraise the social world, irrational trends stand out glaringly. One may conceive of a professional man who opposes the immigration of Jewish refugees on the ground that this will increase the competition with which he has to deal and so decrease his income. However undemocratic this may be, it is at least rational in a limited sense. But for this man to go on, as do most people who oppose Jews on occupational grounds, and accept a wide variety of opinions, many of which are contradictory, about Jews in general, and to attribute various ills of the world to them, is plainly illogical. And it is just as illogical to praise all Jews in accordance with a "good" stereotype of them. Hostility against groups that is based upon real frustration, brought about by members of that group, undoubtedly exists, but such frustrating experiences can hardly account for the fact that prejudice is apt to be generalized. Evidence from the present study confirms what has often been indicated: that a man who is hostile toward one minority group is very likely to be hostile against a wide variety of others. There is no conceivable rational basis for such generalization; and, what is more striking, prejudice against, or totally uncritical acceptance of, a particular group often exists in the absence of any experience with members of that group. The objective situation of the individual seems an unlikely source of such irrationality; rather we should seek where psychology has already found the sources of dreams, fantasies, and misinterpretations of the world—that is, in the deep-lying needs of the personality.

Another aspect of the individual's situation which we should expect to affect his ideological receptivity is his membership in social groups—occupational, fraternal, religious, and the like. For historical and sociological reasons, such groups favor and promulgate, whether officially or unofficially, different patterns of ideas. There is reason to believe that individuals, out of their needs to conform and to belong and to believe and through such devices as imitation and conditioning, often take over more or less ready-made the opinions, attitudes, and values that are characteristic of the groups in which they have membership. To the extent that the ideas which prevail in such a group are implicitly or explicitly antidemocratic, the individual group member might be expected to be receptive to propaganda having the same general direction. Accordingly, the present research investigates a variety of group memberships with a view to what general trends of thought—and how much variability—might be found in each.

It is recognized, however, that a correlation between group membership and ideology may be due to different kinds of determination in different individuals. In some cases it might be that the individual merely repeats opinions which are taken for granted in his social milieu and which he has no reason to question; in other cases it might be that the individual has chosen to join a particular group because it stood for ideals with which he was already in sympathy. In modern society, despite enormous communality in basic culture, it is rare for a person to be subjected to only one pattern of ideas, after he is old enough for ideas to mean something to him. Some selection is usually made, according, it may be supposed, to the needs of his personality. Even when individuals are exposed during their formative years almost exclusively to a single, closely knit pattern of political, economic, social, and religious ideas, it is found that some conform while others rebel, and it seems proper to inquire whether personality factors do not make the difference. The soundest approach, it would seem, is to consider that in the determination of ideology, as in the determination of any behavior, there is a situational factor and a personality factor, and that a careful weighing of the role of each will yield the most accurate prediction.

Situational factors, chiefly economic condition and social group memberships, have been studied intensively in recent researches on opinion and attitude, while the more inward, more individualistic factors have not received the attention they deserve. Beyond this, there is still another reason why the present study places particular emphasis upon the personality. Fascism, in order to be successful as a political movement, must have a mass basis. It must secure not only the frightened submission but the active cooperation of the great majority of the people. Since by its very nature it favors the few at the expense of the many, it cannot possibly demonstrate that it will so improve the situation of most people that their real interests will be served. It must therefore make its major appeal, not to rational self-interest, but to emotional needs—often to the most primitive and irrational wishes and fears. If it be argued that fascist propaganda fools people into believing that their lot will be improved, then the question arises: Why are they so easily fooled? Because, it may be supposed, of their personality structure; because of long-established patterns of hopes and aspirations, fears and anxieties that dispose them to certain beliefs and make them resistant to others. The task of fascist propaganda, in other words, is rendered easier to the degree that antidemocratic potentials already exist in the great mass of people. It may be granted that in Germany economic conflicts and dislocations within the society were such that for this reason alone the triumph of fascism was sooner or later inevitable; but the Nazi leaders did not act as if they believed this to be so; instead they acted as if it were necessary at every moment to take into account the psychology of the people—to activate every ounce of their antidemocratic potential, to compromise with them, to stamp out the slightest spark of rebellion. It seems apparent that any attempt to appraise the chances of a fascist triumph in America must reckon with the potential existing in the character of the people. Here lies not only the susceptibility to antidemocratic propaganda but the most dependable sources of resistance to it.

The present writers believe that it is up to the people to decide whether or not this country goes fascist. It is assumed that knowledge of the nature and extent of antidemocratic potentials will indicate programs for democratic action. These programs should not be limited to devices for manipulating people in such a way that they will behave more democratically, but they should be devoted to increasing the kind of self-awareness and self-determination that makes any kind of manipulation impossible. There is one explanation for the existence of an individual's ideology that has not so far been considered: that it is the view of the world which a reasonable man, with some understanding of the role of such determinants as those discussed above, and with complete access to the necessary facts, will organize for himself. This conception, though it has been left to the last, is of crucial importance for a sound approach to ideology. Without it we should have to share the destructive view, which has gained some acceptance in the modern world, that since all ideologies, all philosophies, derive from non-rational sources there is no basis for saying that one has more merit than another.

But the rational system of an objective and thoughtful man is not a thing apart from personality. Such a system is still motivated. What is distinguishing in its sources is mainly the *kind of personality organization* from which it springs. It might be said that a mature personality (if we may for the moment use this term without defining it) will come closer to achieving a rational system of thought than will an immature one; but a personality is no less dynamic and no less organized for being mature, and the task of describing the structure of this personality is not different in kind from the task of describing any other personality. According to theory, the personality variables which have most to do with determining the objectivity and rationality of an ideology are those which belong to the ego, that part of the personality which appreciates reality, integrates the other parts, and operates with the most conscious awareness.

It is the ego that becomes aware of and takes responsibility for nonrational forces operating within the personality. This is the basis for our belief that the object of knowing what are the psychological determinants of ideology is that men can become more reasonable. It is not supposed, of course, that this will eliminate differences of opinion. The world is sufficiently complex and difficult to know, men have enough real interests that are in conflict with the real interests of other men, there are enough ego-accepted differences in personality to insure that arguments about politics, economics, and religion will never grow dull. Knowledge of the psychological determinants of ideology cannot tell us what is the *truest* ideology; it can only remove some of the barriers in the way of its pursuit.

B. METHODOLOGY

1. GENERAL CHARACTERISTICS OF THE METHOD

To attack the problems conceptualized above required methods for describing and measuring ideological trends and methods for exposing personality, the contemporary situation, and the social background. A particular methodological challenge was imposed by the conception of *levels* in the person; this made it necessary to devise techniques for surveying opinions, attitudes, and values that were on the surface, for revealing ideological trends that were more or less inhibited and reached the surface only in indirect manifestations, and for bringing to light personality forces that lay in the subject's unconscious. And since the major concern was with *patterns* of dynamically related factors—something that requires study of the total individual—it seemed that the proper approach was through intensive clinical studies. The significance and practical importance of such studies could not be gauged, however, until there was knowledge of how far it was possible to generalize from them. Thus it was necessary to perform group studies as well as individual studies, and to find ways and means for integrating the two.

Individuals were studied by means of interviews and special clinical techniques for revealing underlying wishes, fears, and defenses; groups were studied by means of questionnaires. It was not expected that the clinical studies would be as complete or profound as some which have already been performed, primarily by psychoanalysts, nor that the questionnaires would be more accurate than any now employed by social psychologists. It was hoped, however—indeed it was necessary to our purpose—that the clinical material could be conceptualized in such a way as to permit its being quantified and carried over into group studies, and that the questionnaires could be brought to bear upon areas of response ordinarily left to clinical study. The attempt was made, in other words, to bring methods of traditional social psychology into the service of theories and concepts from the newer dynamic theory of personality and in so doing to make "depth psychological" phenomena more amenable to mass-statistical treatment, and to make quantitative surveys of attitudes and opinions more meaningful psychologically.

In the attempt to integrate clinical and group studies, the two were carried on in close conjunction. When the individual was in the focus of attention, the aim was to describe in detail his pattern of opinions, attitudes, and values and to understand the dynamic factors underlying it, and on this basis to design significant questions for use with groups of subjects. When the group was in the focus of attention, the aim was to discover what opinions, attitudes, and values commonly go together and what patterns of factors in the life histories and in the contemporary situations of the subjects were commonly associated with each ideological constellation; this afforded a basis on which to select individuals for more intensive study: commanding first attention were those who exemplified the common patterns and in whom it could be supposed that the correlated factors were dynamically related.

In order to study potentially antidemocratic individuals it was necessary first to identify them. Hence a start was made by constructing a questionnaire and having it filled out anonymously by a large group of people. This questionnaire contained, in addition to numerous questions of fact about the subject's past and present life, a variety of antidemocratic statements with which the subjects were invited to agree or disagree. A number of individuals who showed the greatest amount of agreement with these statements—and, by way of contrast, some who showed the most disagreement or, in some instances, were most neutral—were then studied by means of interviews and other clinical techniques. On the basis of these individual studies the questionnaire was revised, and the whole procedure repeated.

The interview was used in part as a check upon the *validity* of the questionnaire, that is to say, it provided a basis for judging whether people who obtained the highest antidemocratic scores on the questionnaire were usually those who, in a confidential relationship with another person, expressed antidemocratic sentiments with the most intensity. What was more important, however, the clinical studies gave access to the deeper personality factors behind antidemocratic ideology and suggested the means for their investigation on a mass scale. With increasing knowledge of the underlying trends of which prejudice was an expression, there was increasing familiarity with various other signs or manifestations by which these trends could be recognized. The task then was to translate these manifestations into questionnaire items for use in the next group study. Progress lay in finding more and more reliable indications of the central personality forces and in showing with increasing clarity the relations of these forces to antidemocratic ideological expression.

2. THE TECHNIQUES

The questionnaires and clinical techniques employed in the study may be described briefly as follows:

a. THE QUESTIONNAIRE METHOD. The questionnaires were always presented in mimeographed form and filled out anonymously by subjects in groups. Each questionnaire included (1) factual questions, (2) opinion-attitude scales, and (3) "projective" (open answer) questions.

1. The *factual questions* had to do mainly with past and present group memberships: church preference and attendance, political party, vocation, income, and so on. It was assumed that the answers could be taken at their face value. In selecting the questions, we were guided at the start by hypotheses concerning the sociological correlates of ideology; as the study progressed we depended more and more upon experience with interviewees.

2. *Opinion-attitude* scales were used from the start in order to obtain quantitative estimates of certain surface ideological trends: anti-Semitism, ethnocentrism, politico-economic conservatism. Later, a scale was developed for the measurement of antidemocratic tendencies in the personality itself.

Each scale was a collection of statements, with each of which the subject was asked to express the degree of his agreement or disagreement. Each statement concerned some relatively specific opinion, attitude, or value, and the basis for grouping them within a particular scale was the conception that taken together they expressed a single general trend.

The general trends to which the scales pertained were conceived very broadly, as complex systems of thought about wide areas of social living. To define these trends empirically it was necessary to obtain responses to many specific issues—enough to "cover" the area mapped out conceptually—and to show that each of them bore some relation to the whole.

This approach stands in contrast to the public opinion poll: whereas the poll is interested primarily in the distribution of opinion with respect to a particular issue, the present interest was to inquire, concerning a particular opinion, with what other opinions and attitudes it was related. The plan was to determine the existence of broad ideological trends, to develop instruments for their measurement, and then to inquire about their distribution within larger populations.

The approach to an ideological area was to appraise its grosser features first and its finer or more specific features later. The aim was to gain a view of the "over-all picture" into which smaller features might later be fitted, rather than to obtain highly precise measures of small details in the hope that these might eventually add up to something significant. Although this emphasis upon breadth and inclusiveness prevented the attainment of the highest degree of precision in measurement, it was nevertheless possible to develop each scale to a point where it met the currently accepted statistical standards.

Since each scale had to cover a broad area, without growing so long as to try the patience of the subjects, it was necessary to achieve a high degree of efficiency. The task was to formulate items which would cover as much as possible of the many-sided phenomenon in question. Since each of the trends to be measured was conceived as having numerous components or aspects, there could be no duplication of items; instead it was required that each item express a different feature—and where possible, several features—of the total system. The degree to which items within a scale will "hang together" statistically, and thus give evidence that a single, unified trait is being measured, depends primarily upon the surface similarity of the items—the degree to which they all say the same thing. The present items, obviously, could not be expected to cohere in this fashion; all that could be required statistically of them was that they correlate to a reasonable degree with the total scale. Conceivably, a single component of one of the present systems could be regarded as itself a relatively general trend, the precise measurement of which would require the use of numerous more specific items. As indicated above, however, such concern with highly specific, statistically "pure" factors was put aside, in favor of an attempt to gain a dependable estimate of an over-all system, one which could then be related to other over-all systems in an approach to the totality of major trends within the individual.

One might inquire why, if we wish to know the intensity of some ideological pattern—such as anti-Semitism—within the individual, we do not ask him directly, after defining what we mean. The answer, in part, is that the phenomenon to be measured is so complex that a single response would not go very far toward revealing the important differences among individuals. Moreover, anti-Semitism, ethnocentrism, and politico-economic reactionism or radicalism are topics about which many people are not prepared to speak with complete frankness. Thus, even at this surface ideological level it was necessary to employ a certain amount of indirectness. Subjects were never told what was the particular concern of the questionnaire, but only that they were taking part in a "survey of opinions about various issues of the day." To support this view of the proceedings, items belonging to a particular scale were interspersed with items from other scales in the questionnaire. It was not possible, of course, to avoid statements prejudicial to minority groups, but care was taken in each case to allow the subject "a way out," that is to say, to make it possible for him to agree with such a statement while maintaining the belief that he was not "prejudiced" or "undemocratic."

Whereas the scales for measuring surface ideological trends conform, in general, with common practice in sociopsychological research, the scale for measuring potentially antidemocratic trends in the personality represents a new departure. The procedure was to bring together in a scale items which, by hypothesis and by clinical experience, could be regarded as "giveaways" of trends which lay relatively deep within the personality, and which constituted a *disposition* to express spontaneously (on a suitable occasion), or to be influenced by, fascist ideas.

The statements in this scale were not different in form from those which made up the surface ideology scales; they were direct expressions of opinion, of attitudes, or of value with respect to various areas of social living—but areas not usually touched upon in systematic presentations of a politico-socioeconomic point of view. Always interspersed with statements from other scales, they conveyed little or nothing to the subject as to the nature of the real question being pursued. They were, in the main, statements so designed as to serve as rationalizations for irrational tendencies. Two statements included in this scale were the following: (a) "Nowadays with so many different kinds of people moving around so much and mixing together so freely, one has to be especially careful to protect himself against infection and disease" and (b) "Homosexuality is an especially rotten form of delinquency and ought to be severely punished." That people who agree with one of these statements show a tendency to agree with the other, and that people who agree with these two statements tend to agree with open antidemocratic statements, e.g., that members of some minority group are basically inferior, is hardly to be explained on the basis of any obvious logical relation among the statements. It seems necessary, rather, to conceive of some underlying central trend which expresses itself in these different ways.

Different people might, of course, give the same response to a statement such as the above for different reasons; since it was necessary to give the statements at least a veneer of rationality, it was natural to expect that the responses of some people would be determined almost entirely by the rational aspect rather than by some underlying emotional disposition. For this reason it was necessary to include a large number of scale items and to be guided by the general trend of response rather than by the response to a single statement; for a person to be considered potentially antidemocratic in his underlying dynamic structure, he had to agree with a majority of these scale items.

The development of the present scale proceeded in two ways: first, by finding or formulating items which, though they had no manifest connection with open antidemocratic expressions, were nevertheless highly correlated with them; and second, by demonstrating that these "indirect" items were actually expressions of antidemocratic potential within the personality as known from intensive clinical study.

3. *Projective Questions*, like most other projective techniques, present the subject with ambiguous and emotionally toned stimulus material. This material is designed to allow a maximum of variation in response from one subject to another and to provide channels through which relatively deep personality processes may be expressed. The questions are not ambiguous in their formal structure, but in the sense that the answers are at the level of emotional expression rather than at the level of fact and the subject is not aware of their implications. The responses always have to be interpreted, and their significance is known when their meaningful relations to other psychological facts about the subject have been demonstrated. One projective question was, "What would you do if you had only six months to live, and could do anything you wanted?" An answer to this question was not regarded as a statement of what the subject would probably do in actuality, but rather an expression having to do with his values, conflicts, and the like. We asked ourselves if this expression was not in keeping with those elicited by other projective questions and by statements in the personality scale.

Numerous projective questions were tried in the early stages of the study, and from among them eight were selected for use with most of the larger groups of subjects: they were the questions which taken together gave the broadest view of the subject's personality trends and correlated most highly with surface ideological patterns.

b. CLINICAL TECHNIQUES.   1. *The interview* was divided roughly into an ideological section and a clinical-genetic section. In the first section the aim was to induce the subject to talk as spontaneously and as freely as possible about various broad ideological topics: politics, religion, minority groups, income, and vocation. Whereas in the questionnaire the subject was limited to the topics there presented and could express himself only by means of the rating scheme offered, here it was important to know what topics he would bring up of his own accord and with what intensity of feeling he would spontaneously express himself. As indicated above, this material afforded a means for insuring that the questionnaire, in its revised forms, more or less faithfully represented "what people were saying"—the topics that were on their minds and the forms of expression that came spontaneously to them—and provided a valid index of antidemocratic trends. The interview covered, of course, a much wider variety of topics, and permitted the expression of more elaborated and differentiated opinions, attitudes, and values, than did the questionnaire. Whereas the attempt was made to distill from the interview material what seemed to be of the most general significance and to arrange it for inclusion in the questionnaire, there was material left over to be exploited by means of individual case studies, qualitative analyses, and crudely quantitative studies of the interview material by itself.

The clinical-genetic section of the interview sought to obtain, first, more factual material about the subject's contemporary situation and about his past than could be got from the questionnaire; second, the freest possible expressions of personal feelings, of beliefs, wishes, and fears concerning himself and his situation and concerning such topics as parents, siblings, friends, and sexual relationships; and third, the subject's conceptions of his childhood environment and of his childhood self.

The interview was conducted in such a way that the material gained from it would permit inferences about the deeper layers of the subject's personality. The technique of the interview will be described in detail later. Suffice it to say here that it followed the general pattern of a psychiatric interview that is inspired by a dynamic theory of personality. The interviewer was aided by a comprehensive interview schedule which underwent several revisions during the course of the study, as experience taught what were the most significant underlying questions and what were the most efficient means for evoking material bearing upon them.

The interview material was used for estimation of certain common variables lying within the theoretical framework of the study but not accessible to the other techniques. Interview material also provided the main basis for individual case studies, bearing upon the interrelationships among all the significant factors operating within the antidemocratic individual.

2. The *Thematic Apperception Test* is a well-known projective technique in which the subject is presented with a series of dramatic pictures and asked to tell a story about each of them. The material he produces can, when interpreted, reveal a great deal about his underlying wishes, conflicts, and mechanisms of defense. The technique was modified slightly to suit the present

purposes. The material was analyzed quantitatively in terms of psychological variables which are found widely in the population and which were readily brought into relation with other variables of the study. As a part of the case study of an individual an analysis in terms of more unique personality variables was made, the material here being considered in close conjunction with findings from the interview.

Though designed to approach different aspects of the person, the several techniques actually were closely related conceptually one to another. All of them permitted quantification and interpretation in terms of variables which fall within a unified theoretical system. Sometimes two techniques yielded measures of the same variables, and sometimes different techniques were focused upon different variables. In the former case the one technique gave some indication of the validity of the other; in the latter case the adequacy of a technique could be gauged by its ability to produce measures that were meaningfully related to all the others. Whereas a certain amount of repetition was necessary to insure validation, the main aim was to fill out a broad framework and achieve a maximum of scope.

The theoretical approach required in each case either that a new technique be designed from the ground up or that an existing one be modified to suit the particular purpose. At the start, there was a theoretical conception of what was to be measured and certain sources—to be described later—which could be drawn upon in devising the original questionnaire form and the preliminary interview schedule. Each technique then evolved as the study progressed. Since each was designed specifically for this study, they could be changed at will as understanding increased, and since an important purpose of the study was the development and testing of effective instruments for diagnosing potential fascism, there was no compulsion to repeat without modification a procedure just in order to accumulate comparable data. So closely interrelated were the techniques that what was learned from any one of them could be applied to the improvement of any other. Just as the clinical techniques provided a basis for enriching the several parts of the questionnaire, so did the accumulating quantitative results indicate what ought to be concentrated upon in the interview; and just as the analysis of scale data suggested the existence of underlying variables which might be approached by means of projective techniques, so did the responses on projective techniques suggest items for inclusion in the scales.

The evolution of techniques was expressed both in expansion and in contraction. Expansion was exemplified in the attempt to bring more and more aspects of antidemocratic ideology into the developing picture and in the attempt to explore enough aspects of the potentially antidemocratic personality so that there was some grasp of the totality. Contraction took place continuously in the quantitative procedures as increasing theoretical clarity permitted a boiling down so that the same crucial relationships could be demonstrated with briefer techniques.

C. PROCEDURES IN THE COLLECTION OF DATA

1. THE GROUPS STUDIED

a. THE BEGINNING WITH COLLEGE STUDENTS. There were enough practical reasons alone to determine that the present study, which at the beginning had limited resources and limited objectives, should start with college students as research subjects: they were available for the asking, whether singly or in groups, they would cooperate willingly, and they could be reached for retesting without much difficulty. At the same time, other considerations favored the use of college students in a study of ideology. In the first place, the intellectual and educational level is high enough so that there needed to be relatively little restriction with respect to the number and nature of issues that might be raised—a very important matter in a study that emphasized breadth and inclusiveness. One could be fairly certain that college students *had* opinions about most of the various topics to be considered. In the second place, there could be relative certainty that all the subjects understood the terms of the questions in the same way and that the same responses had uniform significance. In the third place, however large a population one might be able to sample he would probably find that most of his generalizations had in any case to be limited to various relatively homogeneous subclassifications of the total group studied; college students form one group that is relatively quite homogeneous with respect to factors that might be expected to influence ideology. And they represent an important sector of the population, both through their family connections and through their prospective leadership in the community.

It is obvious, however, that a study which used only college students as subjects would be seriously limited in its general significance. Of what larger population could a group of students at a state university be regarded as an adequate sample? Would findings on this sample hold for all the students at this university? For college students generally? For young people of the middle class? It depends upon what kind of generalization is to be made. Generalizations about the distribution of particular opinions or about the average amount of agreement with this or that statement—the kind of information sought in poll studies—could hardly go beyond the students at the university where the survey was made. Results from an Eastern university or from a privately endowed institution might be quite different. The present concern, however, was not so much with questions of distribution as with questions of relationship. For example, there was less interest in what per cent of the general population would agree that "labor unions have grown too powerful" and that "there are too many Jews in government agencies" than in whether or not there was a general relationship between these two opinions. For the study of how opinions, attitudes, and values are organized within the individual, college students had a great deal to offer, particularly in the early stages of the work where the emphasis was upon improving techniques and obtaining first approximations of general relationships. This work could proceed without hindrance so long as the factors to be studied were present, and varied sufficiently widely from one individual to another. In this regard, the limitations of the college sample were that the relatively high intellectual and educational level decreased the number of extremely prejudiced individuals, and that some of the factors which were presumed to influence prejudice were rarely or never present.

These considerations made it necessary to study various other groups of subjects. As it turned out, the *strength* of the various ideological trends was found to vary widely from one group to another, while the *relationships* found in the college group were very similar to those found elsewhere.

b. The General Noncollege Population from Which Our Subjects Were Drawn. When it became possible through increased resources to expand the scope of the study, there began an attempt to obtain as subjects a wide variety of adult Americans. The aim was to examine people who possessed in different degrees as many as possible of the sociological variables presumed to be relevant to the study—political, religious, occupational, income, and social group memberships. A list of all the groups (college and noncollege) from whom questionnaires were collected is given in Table 1(I).

The group within which a subject was functioning at the time he filled out the questionnaire was, of course, not necessarily the most important or representative of the various groups to which he belonged. The questionnaire itself was relied upon to give information about the group memberships deemed most relevant to the study, and subjects could be categorized on this basis regardless of the group through which the questionnaires were collected.

The emphasis throughout was upon obtaining different *kinds* of subjects, enough to insure wide variability of opinion and attitude and adequate coverage of the factors supposed to influence ideology. The subjects are in no sense a random sample of the noncollege population nor, since there was no attempt to make a sociological analysis of the community in which they lived, can they be regarded as a representative sample. The progress of the study was not in the direction of broadening the basis for generalization about larger populations, but rather toward the more intensive investigation

TABLE 1(I)
Groups From Whom Questionnaires Were Collected[a]

	No. of Cases
I. *Form 78* (January to May, 1945)	
University of California Public Speaking Class Women	140
University of California Public Speaking Class Men	52
University of California Extension Psychology Class (adult women).	40
Professional Women (public school teachers, social workers, public health nurses) (San Francisco area)	63
Total	295
II. *Form 60* (Summer, 1945)	
University of Oregon Student Women	47
University of Oregon and University of California Student Women.	54
University of Oregon and University of California Student Men	57
Oregon Service Club Men (Kiwanis, Lions, Rotary Clubs) (Total questionnaire)	68
Oregon Service Club Men (Form A only)[b]	60
Total	286
III. *Forms 45 and 40* (November, 1945, to June, 1946)	
A. *Form 45*	
University of California Extension Testing Class (adult women)..	59
Psychiatric Clinic Patients (men and women) (Langley Porter Clinic of the University of California)	121
San Quentin State Prison Inmates (men)	110
Total	243
B. *Both Forms 45 and 40*	
Alameda School for Merchant Marine Officers (men)	343
U.S. Employment Service Veterans (men)	106
Total	449

C. *Form 40*
Working-Class Women:

California Labor School	19
United Electrical Workers Union (C.I.O.)	8
Office Workers	11
Longshoremen and Warehousemen (I.L.W.U.) (new members)	10
Federal Housing Project Workers	5

53

[a] In most cases each group taking the questionnaire was treated separately for statistical purposes, e.g., San Quentin Prison Inmates, Psychiatric Clinic Men. However, some groups were too small for this purpose and were therefore combined with other sociologically similar groups. When such combinations occurred, the composition of the overall group is indicated in the table.

[b] *Form A* included the scale for measuring potentially antidemocratic trends in the personality and half of the scale for measuring politico-economic conservatism.

Working-Class Men:
United Electrical Workers Union (C.I.O.)   12
California Labor School   15
Longshoremen and Warehousemen (I.L.W.U.) (new
    members)   26
United Seamen's Service   8
                                                        ────
                                                                 61

Middle-Class Women:
Parent-Teachers' Association   46
California Labor School (middle-class members)...   11
Suburban Church Group   29
Unitarian Church Group   15
League of Women Voters   17
Upper Middle-Class Women's Club   36
                                                        ────
                                                                154

Middle-Class Men:
Parent-Teachers' Association   29
Suburban Church Group   31
California Labor School (middle-class members)...   9
                                                        ────
                                                                 69

California Service Club Men:
Kiwanis Club   40
Rotary Club   23
                                                        ────
                                                                 63

George Washington University Women Students   132
Los Angeles Men (classes at University of California and Univer-
    sity of Southern California, fraternity group, adult evening class,
    parents of students, radio writers group)   117
Los Angeles Women (same groupings as above)   130
                                                        ────
                        Total   779
                Total Forms 45 and 40   1,518
                Overall Total of All Forms   2,099

of "key groups," that is, groups having the characteristics that were most crucial to the problem at hand. Some groups were chosen because their sociological status was such that they could be expected to play a vital role in a struggle centering around social discrimination, e.g., veterans, service clubs, women's clubs. Other groups were chosen for intensive study because they presented extreme manifestations of the personality variables deemed most crucial for the potentially antidemocratic individual, e.g., prison inmates, psychiatric patients.

Save for a few key groups, the subjects were drawn almost exclusively from the middle socioeconomic class. It was discovered fairly early in the study that the investigation of lower classes would require different instruments and different procedures from those developed through the use of college students and, hence, this was a task that had best be postponed.

Groups in which there was a preponderance of minority group members were avoided, and when minority group members happened to belong to an organization which cooperated in the study, their questionnaires were excluded from the calculations. It was not that the ideological trends in minority groups were considered unimportant; it was rather that their investigation involved special problems which lay outside the scope of the present study.

The great majority of the subjects of the study lived within the San Francisco Bay area. Concerning this community it may be said that the population increased rapidly during the decade preceding the outbreak of World War II, so that a large proportion were newcomers from all parts of the nation. During the war, when the area took on the aspect of a boom town, the influx was greatly intensified and, hence, it is probable that a large number of the present subjects were people who had recently come from other states.

Two large groups were obtained in the Los Angeles area, several smaller groups in Oregon, and one group in Washington, D. C.

Unless a person had at least a grammar school education, it was very difficult, if not impossible, for him to fill out the questionnaire properly—to understand the issues set forth in the scales and the instructions for marking the forms. The average educational level of the subjects in the study is about the twelfth grade, there being roughly as many college graduates as there were subjects who had not completed high school. It is important to note that the present samples are heavily weighted with younger people, the bulk of them falling between the ages of twenty and thirty-five.

It will be apparent that the subjects of the study taken all together would provide a rather inadequate basis for generalizing about the total population of this country. The findings of the study may be expected to hold fairly well for non-Jewish, white, native-born, middle-class Americans. Where the same relationships appeared repeatedly as different groups—e.g., college students, women's clubs, prison inmates—came under scrutiny, generalizations may be made with the most certainty. When sections of the population not sampled in the present study are made the subjects of research, it is to be expected that most of the relationships reported in the following chapters will still hold—and that additional ones will be found.

2. THE DISTRIBUTION AND COLLECTION OF QUESTIONNAIRES

In approaching a group from whom questionnaires were to be collected, the first step was to secure the cooperation of the group leadership. This was never difficult when the leader was liberal in his outlook, e.g., the instructor of a class in public speaking, the psychologist at a Maritime School, a minister in the inner councils of a men's service club. The purposes and procedures of the study were explained to him fully, and he then presented the project of filling out the questionnaires to his group. When the group leadership was conservative, the procedure was more difficult. If it were made known that the study had something to do with social discrimination, it was not unusual for great interest in this "important problem" to be expressed at first and then for one delay to follow another until hope of obtaining responses from the group in question had to be abandoned. Among people of this type there appeared to be a conviction that it was best to let sleeping dogs lie, that the best approach to the "race problem" was not to "stir up anything." A more successful approach to conservative leaders was to present the whole project as a survey of general public opinion, "like a Gallup poll," being carried forward by a group of scientists at the University, and to count upon the variety and relative mildness of the scale items to prevent undue alarm.

In collecting questionnaires from classes of students, whether in regular sessions of the University, in summer school, or in university extension, it was usual for the instructor of the class to handle the whole proceeding himself. In other instances it was usually necessary to combine the administration of the questionnaire with a talk to the group by a member of the Study staff. He gave the instructions for filling out the questionnaires, aided in their collection, and then gave a talk on "Gauging Public Opinion," coming only as close to the real issues of the study as he judged possible without arousing the resistances of his audience.

Whether the group was judged to be liberal or not, the questionnaire was always presented to it as a public opinion inventory—not as a study of prejudice. The instructions given to the groups follow:

SURVEY OF GENERAL PUBLIC OPINION: INSTRUCTIONS

We are trying to find out what the general public feels and thinks about a number of important social questions.

We are sure you will find the enclosed survey interesting. You will find in it many questions and social issues which you have thought about, read about in newspapers and magazines, and heard about on the radio.

This is *not* an *intelligence test* nor an information test. There are no "right" or "wrong" answers. The best answer is *your personal opinion*. You can be sure that, whatever your opinion may be on a certain issue, there will be many people who agree, many who disagree. And this is what we want to find out: how is public opinion really divided on each of these socially important topics?

It must be emphasized that the sponsors of this survey do not necessarily agree or disagree with the statements in it. *We have tried to cover a great many points of view.* We agree with some of the statements, and disagree with others. Similarly, you will probably find yourself agreeing strongly with some statements, disagreeing just as strongly with others, and being perhaps more neutral about still others.

We realize that people are very busy nowadays, and we don't want to take too much of your time. All that we ask is that you:

(a) Read each statement carefully and mark it according to your first reaction. It isn't necessary to take a lot of time for any one question.
(b) *Answer every question.*
(c) *Give your personal point of view.* Don't talk the questions over with anyone until you have finished.
(d) Be as *sincere, accurate,* and *complete* as possible in the limited time and space.

This survey works just like a Gallup Poll or an election. As in any other secret ballot, the "voters" who fill it out do not have to give their names.

The cooperation of the groups, once they were presented with the questionnaire, was excellent, at least 90 per cent of those present usually handing in completed questionnaires. Some members of each group were, of course, absent on the day the questionnaire was administered, but since there was never any advance notice about this part of the program, there is no reason to believe that the responses of these absentees would have been generally different from those of the rest of the group. Subjects who were present but failed to hand in completed questionnaires fall almost entirely into two classes: those who made no attempt to cooperate and those who handed in incomplete questionnaires. It is to be suspected that the former were more antidemocratic than the average of their group, while the slowness or carelessness of the latter is probably of no significance for ideology.

There was one attempt to collect questionnaires by mail. Over 200 questionnaires with complete instructions were mailed to teachers and nurses, together with a letter soliciting their cooperation and covering letters from their superintendents. The return was a disappointing 20 per cent, and this sample was strongly biased in the direction of low scores on the scales for measuring antidemocratic trends.

3. THE SELECTION OF SUBJECTS FOR INTENSIVE CLINICAL STUDY

With a few exceptions, the subjects from a given group who were interviewed and given the Thematic Apperception Test were chosen from among the 25 per cent obtaining the highest and the 25 per cent obtaining the lowest scores (high and low quartiles) on the Ethnocentrism scale. This scale, it seemed, would give the best initial measure of antidemocratic tendencies.

If the group from which subjects were to be selected was one which held regular meetings, as was usually the case, the procedure was to collect the questionnaires at one meeting, to obtain the scale scores and decide upon suitable interviewees, and then to solicit further cooperation at the next meeting. In the few cases where the use of a second meeting was impossible, the request for interviewees was made at the time of administering the questionnaire, those willing to be interviewed being asked to indicate how they might be reached. In order to disguise the basis of selection and the purpose of the clinical study, the groups were told that the attempt was being made to carry on a more detailed discussion of opinions and ideas with a few of their number—about 10 per cent—and that people representing the various kinds and degrees of response found in the group were being asked to come for interviews.

Anonymity was to be insured for the interviews as well as for the group survey, if the subject so desired. In order to arrange this, subjects desired for individual study were referred to by the birth date which they had entered on their questionnaires. This could not be done, however, in those cases where subjects were asked to signify at the time of filling out the questionnaire whether or not they were willing to be interviewed. This may have been one reason why the response in these instances was poor. But there were other reasons why subjects of these groups were difficult to interview, and it is to be noted that the great majority of those secured under the birth date arrangement showed no concern about anonymity once their appointments had been made.

Subjects were paid $3.00 for the two to three hours they spent in the clinical sessions. In offering this inducement at the time of the request for interviewees, it was pointed out that this was the only way to insure that the staff of the Study would not be conscience-stricken for taking so much valuable time. The arrangement did indeed have this effect, but what was more important, it was a considerable aid to securing suitable subjects: most of those who scored low on the Ethnocentrism scale would have co-operated anyway, being somewhat attracted to psychology and willing to give their time in a "good cause," but many of the high scorers made it plain that the money was the determining consideration.

In selecting subjects for clinical study the aim was to examine a variety of high and low scorers. Considerable variety was assured by the device of taking a few from most of the different groups studied. Within a given group it was possible to achieve further variety with respect to group memberships and scores on the other scales. There was no attempt, however, to arrange that the percentage of the interviewed subjects having each of various group memberships was the same as that which held for the group from which they were drawn. The question of how well the high and low scorers who were interviewed represent all those who scored high or low on the Ethnocentrism scale is taken up in Chapter IX.

Very few "middle" subjects—the 50 per cent whose scores fall between the high and the low quartiles—were interviewed. It was believed that for the understanding of antidemocratic trends the most important first step was to determine the factors which most clearly distinguished one extreme from the other. In order properly to compare two groups it is necessary to have a minimum of thirty to forty subjects in each group, and since men and women, as it turned out, presented somewhat different problems and had to be treated separately, the study of high- vs. low-scoring men and the study of high- vs. low-scoring women involved four statistical groupings totaling

150. To conduct more interviews than this was for practical reasons impossible. The intensive study of representative middle scorers should form a central part of any future research along the lines of the present study. Since they are more numerous than either extreme, it is especially important to know their democratic or antidemocratic potentialities. The impression gained from a few interviews with middle scorers, and from the examination of many of their questionnaires, is that they are not indifferent or ignorant with respect to the issues of the scales, or lacking in the kinds of motivation or personality traits found in the extremes. In short, they are in no sense categorically different; they are, as it were, made of the same stuff but in different combinations.

PART I

The Measurement of Ideological Trends

CHAPTER II

THE CONTRASTING IDEOLOGIES OF TWO
COLLEGE MEN: A PRELIMINARY VIEW

R. Nevitt Sanford

A. INTRODUCTION

Although the present research is concerned primarily with the organization of ideological trends within the individual, the reader will soon note that the bulk of this volume is concerned not with individuals as such but with variables and their general relationships. This is unavoidable, for although each variable is but an abstraction when lifted out of the total context in which it operates, the study of individuals can proceed only by analysis into components, and the relations of these components can be regarded as significant only if they can be, to some extent at least, generalized. Nevertheless, every effort will be made to keep the individual constantly in mind as the analysis of components proceeds.

The verbatim interview protocols of two extreme scorers—one high (prejudiced) and one low (against prejudice)—on the Ethnocentrism scale will, in the present chapter, picture these subjects as they might appear to the casual observer during, let us say, an evening's discussion, among friends, of current social issues. Only the interview discussions of minorities, politics, religion, vocation, and income are given, the more personal clinical-genetic material being left for later sections. That the distinction between "ideological" and "personal" is artificial—though often useful—is indicated by the fact that in the subject's spontaneous discussion of ideology some references to personal matters such as family and childhood repeatedly crop up. The aim is to set forth in a preliminary way that which is to be studied, to give a general impression of the totality which is to be analyzed and, in so far as possible, generalized. As the various components are taken up in turn in the following chapters, each is related to what has gone before, until a point is reached where each can be related to the whole. The value of the analysis can be measured in terms of how much the formulations arrived at in the end contribute to an understanding of the individuals whose protocols are presented here.

31

A special advantage of having actual cases in view at the start is that it becomes possible to state research problems in concrete terms. The reader will probably find that the kinds of discussion presented below are familiar; he may even have asked himself after listening to such a discussion, "Why does he talk that way?" This is one way of putting the major question of the present research. In order to approach an answer it is necessary first to describe as precisely as possible *how* the subject talks, to have terms in which the manner and content of his thought may be compared with that of others. In the present chapter, therefore, the interviews are used to illustrate the derivation of the descriptive concepts of the study. These concepts are then employed in framing research questions and formulating explanatory hypotheses.

The protocols which follow do not represent the most extreme cases found in the study (if the total population were sampled they probably would not be extreme at all); nor can they be said to be typical, in any strict sense of the word, of subjects falling into the high or the low quartiles on the Ethnocentrism scale. There are other types of extremes than these, but at the least they belong to the types found most commonly among the high and low scorers. Lack of space makes it impossible to consider in this chapter examples of women with extreme scores; studies of individual women are, however, presented in later sections.

Much of the interview material given below may, at first glance, impress the reader as rather unimportant, and quite unrelated to prejudice. The analysis to follow, however, will show that nearly everything these subjects say makes some contribution to the general picture and has meaning when viewed in relation to it.

B. MACK: A MAN HIGH ON ETHNOCENTRISM

This subject is a twenty-four year old college freshman who intends to study law and hopes eventually to become a corporation lawyer or a criminal lawyer[1]:
His grades are B— on the average. After graduating from high school and attending business school for a year, he worked in the Civil Service in Washington, D. C. His brief sojourn in the Army was terminated by a medical discharge—because of a stomach condition—when he was attending Officer Candidate School.

He is a Methodist, as was his mother, but he does not attend services and he thinks religion is not important to him. His political party affiliation

[1] Most of the material of this brief introduction to the subject was contained in his questionnaire, though a few pertinent facts are from his interview. In later sections all of his responses on the questionnaire will be considered in relation to the clinical material, but here the aim is merely to identify him, as it were, before proceeding with the discussion of his ideology.

is, like his father's, Democratic. He "agrees" with the political trends expressed by the Anti-New Deal Democrats and "disagrees" with the New Deal Democrats; he "disagrees" with the traditional Republicans but "agrees" with the Willkie-type Republicans.

The subject is of "Irish" extraction and was born in San Francisco. Both of his parents were born in the United States. He states in his questionnaire that his father is a retired lumberman who owns his own home and has a retired income of $1,000. It is learned in the interview that the father was a worker in the woods and in the mills and it is to be inferred that his income derives mainly from a pension. The mother died when the subject was six. He has a sister four years his senior.

The protocol of his interview follows:[2]

Vocation: This student has decided to make law his vocation. He says he has been out of school three years and is now a freshman at the University. However, he went for two years to business school and in addition has attended night school; but he has to start at the beginning here. He had a Civil Service job in Washington, being for a time principal clerk in one of the sections of the War Department. (What made you decide to be a lawyer?) "I decided when I was in Washington. Of course, I was half decided when I was at business school, where business law was emphasized. When I was in high school, my financial means were such that I figured I had better get a general business education and then go to work. (In what ways does law appeal to you?) Well, it seems to me to unlock an awful lot of doors. In any profession, you go so far and then you bump up against it. It is the fundamental basis of our government. It is really the foundation of our enterprise. Sometime I have hopes of making it available to people without funds, so that they can have equal sittings in the court. I want to go in for a general practice at the start and then maybe corporate law and then maybe criminal law. Law will be more important in the future than ever before. There is a trend toward more stringent laws, more regimentation. This will be true whether the form of government alters or not. Economists have determined that for the good of everybody there has to be central control. (What does your father think of the law?) My father is quite interested in it. Of course, he wanted business for me. He has business ability but he is a very retiring fellow. He wouldn't meet people. He owned some lumber land, but mostly he preferred working for other people. He is very unassuming; he worked in the woods and in the mills. His $1,000 income now is from investments, stocks and bonds. He hasn't worked for thirty years. At the time he worked, the wage was around $75 a month. He had stomach trouble. Yes, he owns his own home in a little town. We have our own cistern and an electric pump that I helped install. He built the old house himself and he has all the modern conveniences. He can get by all right on $1,000 a year."

Income: (You want to earn $5,000 per year?) "Well, $5,000 sounds like a lot of money right now. It depends on where you live and how. In ordinary circumstances you could live comfortably on it. The opportunities for a lawyer in a small town are limited, but I do like the small town. Especially those that are adjacent

[2] The interviewer wrote as rapidly as he could, in a "shorthand" of his own, throughout the interview and then immediately used a dictaphone to record all that he had written. In this way it was possible to approach a verbatim recording of what the subject had said. Throughout the book, the interviewer's report of the interview is given in small type. Quotation marks within this material indicate a verbatim record of the subject's statements.

to the mountains. I enjoy hunting, fishing, and camping. But I like the conveniences of the city. In the city you have finer houses and the theaters. I haven't found any place I like better than California, and I have traveled quite a lot. I'm going to travel to Alaska. My father's brother died there in the Yukon. There are great possibilities there in the future. If a person studies it carefully and locates properly, he goes up with a town. I worked with some men lumbering last summer who worked on the Alaska highway. They found it pretty tough going. But these difficulties can be overcome if big capitalists get interested. There is a huge pool of oil up there, you know, and that ought to be developed."

Politics: "I voted for Dewey. In previous times I would have voted for FDR, but I worked there in Washington and saw things I would put a stop to. There is a concentration of power in the bureaus. People who work there have different attitudes. In the Civil Service you are paid according to how many people are under you, so they want people to come in. They think of themselves only. I'm not mercenary enough to understand it. I would simplify things by a competent administration. There is too much overlapping and bungling. I was the right-hand man of the General there when the OWI was introduced. They put up this building for $600,000 with little purpose in mind. They did the same thing that the Army monitoring service was already doing. The OWI wanted to take it over. Even after the OWI took it over, the War Department still helped prepare the communiques; but the OWI wanted credit. All that duplication at a tremendous outlay of money for no purpose. And all the time our department was crying for personnel. I worked many hours overtime for no pay because I was in the Civil Service. I was there from September, 1940, to September, 1942. I was there when war was declared. I worked then for thirty-seven hours straight. It was quite a day in Washington. I liked living in Washington very much. I like being close to the center of things. You can learn a lot about how the government functions. There are daily events at your fingertips that by the time it gets here have changed somehow. It was fun knowing about the background, knowing about the secret committees. My salary was $2,000 a year. Living conditions, of course, were terrible. (What did you like about Dewey especially?) I liked Dewey's background, his frankness, honesty, his clear-cut way of presenting his case. I think that at heart he is a very honest man, interested in maintaining the old government traditions. (How do you see things shaping up for the future?) If we maintain our present system of government, and I think we will for a time, some things will have to be altered. The system in Washington has outgrown the limits of one man to control. We have got to eliminate confusion. The man who runs it must pick his lieutenants carefully. The way it is now, there is no clear authority. You have to consult a half a dozen agencies to get anywhere. This will recede very little after the war. Eventually the President will have to appoint a strong Cabinet to run things for him. There is no doubt that the system is becoming more centralized. I doubt that President Roosevelt will be reelected. It depends on the way the war goes. From his speeches, one seems to see that he feels he is necessary to the United States. He has control of the Party and will run as long as he is physically able. The popular vote in the last election was very close. It was skilful politics that enabled the old guard to win. Considering his obstacles, Dewey did very well. In ordinary times, he would have had a landslide. People who had sons in the war effort felt that taking the President out might prolong the war. That was wrong. The Army and the Navy were prepared for the war ten years in advance. General Marshall would have had a lot to say, whoever was elected. I have sat beside him and heard him talk. Nobody could alter his position. A change of presidents might have altered our relations to England, but not to Russia. Recently there has been a lot of opposition to Churchill. He has been OK in war, but how he will be in peace is a question. There is, of course, close feeling between Roosevelt and Churchill. But Roosevelt would come out second-best in a contest with Winnie. Of course, a lot of Roosevelt's ideas came from Hoover. (Would there be a difference in our relations with Russia?) No, there would be no difference in our relations with Russia. I think Joe Stalin would play pretty fair with us. And Dewey is honest to the death. He has a good background, though not of the wealthy class, and he would think of the average people. His honesty and straightforwardness appeal to me greatly. But a man has to use some underhandedness to get across the highest ideals."

Religion: "On my father's side, my folks were Catholic. My father and his brothers and sisters were Catholic. Father was never deeply religious, but he was a good man. He drank but little, and he never smoked. He was very honest and strict in his dealings. He followed the church rules without going to church. It stems back to his not wanting to meet people. He was very retiring, and I can't understand it. The other members of his family were not that way. His sisters are very average. My mother was a Methodist and quite strict up until her death. I was sick much of the time. She brought us up very strictly under this guidance. Her aunt took us in hand when Mother died and saw that we attended Sunday School with her children. That was up until I was twelve or thirteen. Then I got out of the habit. I like church OK, though I disagree with some of its doctrines. I like the music and singing in church. I was so busy since high school that I stopped going. I have gone in for social things in spite of a great dread of them. But I looked at my father and saw that I had to do differently. Yes, the teachings of Sunday School did mean something. But the arbitrary beliefs were too much. I grew up quickly. My father has allowed me to do as I pleased, although he forced some decisions upon me. About smoking, he said I must do it in front of him, if I must. He also provided wines and liquors in the ice chest. I soon tired of smoking and never took much to drinking. I have a stubborn nature, and if he had tried to stop me, I probably would have taken it up. (Under what conditions might you turn to religion?) Yes, under some conditions I might. I have had a lot of sickness, stomach trouble ever since I was twelve. I was in the hospital once for three months. During those periods, I like to turn to the Bible. I like the history and sayings of Christ, principally. I like to consider them and analyze them and figure out how they affect me. I'm not so interested in the apostles' sayings—that's not first-hand, so I don't accept it entirely. I have to be assured of it factually. I have always tried to live according to His Ten Commandments. I like to receive just treatment and to give it to others. (What about your conception of God?) Well, I have none especially. The closest conception I got was when I was in the service, that is, God as strictly man, greater than any on this earth, one that would treat us as a father would his son. I don't think God is terrible in His justice. If one lives justly, his laxness will be overlooked. The thing is to make things happier and juster on the earth."

Minorities: "My mother comes from an Irish-English-German background. I think of myself as Irish—perhaps because my father is definitely so, and proud of it. He likes the thought of St. Patrick's Day. I have a quick temper like the Irish. If there is a lot of Irish in people, they are very enjoyable. They are easy spenders, even though they never have much. They have the ability to make other people happy. They are often witty. I wish I were more like that. But there is too much of the lackadaisical and laziness in some classes of Irish. (Which groups would you contrast with the Irish?) The Irish are most different from the Germans or Dutch or maybe the Scandinavians—perhaps Polish or White Russians, where you find a more stolid person in thought and action. The types that I have encountered have a solid build and are not very excitable. (Question about Irish assimilating.) I like to think of an Irish strain; it is enjoyable. Yet in some people the Irish seems to predominate. It depends on the individual. I don't have any desire to be Irish, but I like people who are. I never met an Irishman I didn't like. My brother-in-law is very definitely Irish. (What about groups of people you dislike?) Principally those I don't understand very well. Austrians, the Japanese I never cared for; Filipinos—I don't know—I'd just as soon leave them as have them. Up home there were Austrians and Poles, though I find the Polish people interesting. I have a little dislike for Jewish people. I don't think they are as courteous or as interested in humanity as they ought to be. And I resent that, though I have had few dealings with them. They accent the clannish and the material. It may be my imagination, but it seems to me you can see their eyes light up when you hand them a coin. I avoid the Jewish clothiers because they have second-rate stuff. I have to be careful about how I dress. I mean, I buy things so seldom I have to be careful I get good things. (Can you tell that a person is a Jew?) Sometimes; usually only after I get their ideas. Like one of the girls in Public Speaking. She had all the characteristics, but she left a favorable impression on me, even though her ideas I disagree with. (You mean there are certain ideas which characterize the Jews?) Yes, to stick together, no matter what; to always be in a group; to have Jewish sororities and Jewish organizations. If a Jew fails in his business, he's helped to get started again. Their attention is directed very greatly toward wealth. Girls at the Jewish sorority house all have fur coats, expensive but no taste. Almost a superiority idea. I resent any show of superiority in people, and I try to keep it down myself. I like to talk with working people. (Do you think the dislike of Jews is increasing?) No, I think this war has made people closer together in this country. I've come across Jewish soldiers and sailors; they would be liked and accepted if they would be willing to mix, but they would rather be alone, though I would have accepted them the same as anybody. I think they have interesting ideas, but they have to have something in return. (Do you think the Jews have done their part in the war effort?) Perhaps they have, but they are businessmen, and they have been fully repaid. (Do you think the Jews are a political force in this country?) Yes, in New York there is an organization for Jewish immigration and comfort of Jews. They are very well organized. This should not be allowed. (What do you think is the danger?) I don't believe it is a danger except in a concentration of wealth in a certain class. I hate to see people in this country take on the burdens of people who have been misfits in other countries. We have enough problems at home without helping the oppressed of other countries. The Jews won't intermingle. So they are not a great contribution to our country—though Jewish scientists and doctors have contributed a great deal. I checked on the immigration. Three-quarters of those leaving Europe arrive here. They are very thorough in it. They are businessmen and they will bring pressure to bear on Congress. We ought to prevent further immigration and concentrate on trying to get them to mingle and become a part of our people. (Do you think they would mingle more if they felt there was no prejudice against them?) If they would mingle more, there would be more willingness to break down the barriers on the part of other people. Of course, they have always been downtrodden, but that's no reason for resentment. (I notice you stated you wouldn't marry a Jew.) I certainly wouldn't. I would date that girl in Public Speaking, but she doesn't emphasize her Jewishness. She was accepted by the whole class. I would marry her if she had thrown off her Jewishness, but I wouldn't be able to associate with her class."

C. LARRY: A MAN LOW ON ETHNOCENTRISM

This subject is a twenty-eight year old college sophomore, a student of Business Administration, with a B– average. Like Mack, his choice of a career was made after he had been out of school for a number of years—working part of the time and spending part of the time in a tuberculosis sanitarium.

He is of "American" extraction and was born in Chicago. Both parents were born in the United States. His father is a café and bar owner (a small businessman, working in his own business), whose income is now $12,000 as compared with a prewar $3,000. The father owns his own home and some other real estate.

The subject, like his parents, is a Methodist, though he attends church seldom. He is a Republican—again like his parents. He "agrees" with the Willkie-type Republicans and "disagrees" with the traditional Republicans; he "disagrees" with the New Deal Democrats, while "agreeing" with the Anti-New Deal Democrats. This pattern of response, on the questionnaire, is the same as that of Mack, the high-scoring man. It will be especially interesting therefore to note the contrast in the political ideologies of these two men as given in the interview. It will show how great, sometimes, is the discrepancy between the political party or the "official" ideology of a subject and his actual political tendencies.

Vocation: "I have definite plans; I want to go into real estate and finance. I want to own my own business as an executive. I want to combine real estate and finance, that is lending money, and if successful, I would go into a brokerage business, buying and selling stocks and bonds. (Money?) Several of my relatives and my father have money, and will support me. I worked for them, as assistant manager for my father who is in a café and bar business, and he is also in real estate. Then I worked for CPA accounting firms, for several, and I have taken courses where I could pick things up, in accounting and business. I had one year of junior college, but I didn't take my work seriously. I got fairly good grades, but not as good as I should have gotten. I got a disease; I was in the hospital for four years. (It took several questions to learn that the subject had tuberculosis and was in a sanitarium.) But I never lost hope. I always planned to return to college. I took correspondence courses during my last two years in the hospital. (Larry always calls it a hospital, never a sanitarium.) In accounting, business management, etc., I did reading to improve my mind. I almost memorized Dale Carnegie's *How to Win Friends* . . . because I thought it would help me in business contacts. I planned my whole life, even where I'd settle down, in Los Angeles. That was all I had to do, lying there in bed, was plan my whole future, what I would do, and how I would do it. (What do you like about your planned business?) My grandmother had a rather successful restaurant; she was a very efficient businesswoman, and I admired her. My whole environment was about business; it glorified it, and I learned the same attitude. Being in business for yourself gives independence, more money, vacations whenever you want, the freedom you don't get in a 365-days-a-year job. I never cared for sciences like chemistry, zoology, dentistry, and stuff like that. (Medicine?) That would be all right if I thought I could go to the top; but the average one is holed up in a top-floor office, not making more than $200 a month very often. That's nothing compared to a businessman who hasn't had any education or worked to prepare himself as a doctor has. It's not only the money, but also the general way of living. (However, the money seems to be clearly and focally important.) I returned to school for three reasons: (1) knowledge—to be able to philosophize and understand things; (2) security—to get an adequate living; (3) social prestige." (This is a good example of Larry's tendency to make everything organized and explicit. He knows just what he wants to do and why he wants to do it, and has even tried to make psychological explanations for this tendency. He enumerated 1, 2, 3 on his fingertips.)

Income: "I'd like to earn at least $25,000 a year and have a personal capital of $100,000, that is to say, my own money apart from the business, so I could travel, do whatever I want, whatever I see other people do, go to Europe, attend the Kentucky Derby, or whatever. I would travel first class, go by air, see South America, go nearly any place. I've traveled only a little so far. Or, go to a convention in the East if I want to. Not a millionaire, just enough to do these things with full security for the future. (How optimistic or pessimistic are you?) I'm very optimistic. I don't know exactly how much, but I'll be at least fairly successful, probably as I said before. I've already had a little success. Last year in Chicago I had an opportunity to go into business with some men in the cabaret and bowling-alley business, along that line. But they didn't offer enough money, and I didn't like the bowling business anyway. Besides, I wanted to come back to school, lay a basis for my final plans, and having my own business. (What if you fail?) I wouldn't commit suicide or get terribly depressed. That sickness (he never calls it by name) taught me to philosophize, to take things as they come with a smile, to start again fresh after every difficulty. (What about your family?) During the depression my father had a good job, as always; not wealthy, but better than average, about $3,000 a year, I guess; but we had a large family, six children; I'm in the middle. Then he went into business and did very well; he now has a gold-mine bar. He makes more in a year than he ever expected to make in a lifetime. He has also bought some property on the side and is making a lot at that. He is like his mother, my grandmother. She and he just love their business. He doesn't want vacations, or social prestige, or wealth as such. He just wants to be an efficient, successful businessman, and all his pleasure comes from that. I guess it's wanting to have satisfied customers, having them come in for years and be satisfied and to have well-coordinated employees. (What kind of a boss is he?) He is kind but firm. He bought homes for two employees; he lets them pay it off to him gradually. He gives them a Christmas bonus, stuff like that, but he also demands efficiency and output. He is an ideal employer. In fact, I don't think I'd be as good to my employees as he is, like risking money on their homes and not knowing whether they might run out on me or not."

Politics: "My father and mother are Republicans. They never voted for Roosevelt. I have voted in two elections, and I voted Republican. But our relatives are Democrats and our friends too. The whole family has been Republican for years and I guess that's why I am, and that's why my father is too. Also because businessmen generally don't like the taxes, restrictions, and bureaus, the red tape. Roosevelt is too much of a politician; he hasn't enough principles. Like the way he threw over Wallace in the last election. I prefer Jones to Wallace as Secretary of Commerce, because Jones is a better businessman and would be more efficient; in general I like Wallace and Willkie, though I don't like Wallace's farm program. (Who is the best Republican?) Willkie. I voted for Dewey mostly as a protest against Roosevelt. But Dewey is too young and not experienced enough. (Dewey vs. Wallace?) Wallace is the better man, and I usually vote for the better man, but I guess I put politics ahead of the man this time, to get the Republicans back. I think it's time for a change of party."

Minorities: (What do you think about the minority problem in this country?) "I can say that I haven't any prejudices; I try not to. (Negroes?) They should be given social equality, any job they are qualified for; should be able to live in any neighborhood, and so on. When I was young, I may have had prejudices, but since the war I've been reading about the whole world, and our minority problems seem so petty compared with the way other countries have worked things out. (Example?) Like Russia; I don't like their share-the-wealth economics, but I think they are unified and fighting so wonderfully because everyone is equal. (He then gives a discourse on France, England, the Dutch, etc., and shows good knowledge of imperialism, exploitation of colonies, and so on, in the minorities aspect. He is less clear about the economics.) I believe in life, liberty, and the pursuit of happiness for all. We aren't unified and we don't know what we're fighting for, and the discrimination is at the root of it. Racial and economic questions are at the root of war. I don't believe in the suppression of anyone. I think the Japs are taken off the coast for undemocratic reasons. It's just that a lot of people wanted their farms and businesses. There was no real democratic reason for it. The segregation of one nationality just leads to more segregation, and it gets worse. The discrimination toward Negroes is because they aren't understood and because they are physically different. Towards Jews it's because of their business ability—the fear that they'll take over business control of the country. There should be education in Negro history, for instance, the part Negroes have played in the development of the country; and education in the history of other minorities, too. How the Jews came to be persecuted, and why some of them are successful."

Religion: "I'm Methodist, and my family is Methodist, except for one brother who is going to be a Catholic priest. He's fifteen. He just likes it—he got into it by himself. Well, my mother was Catholic as a girl, but she became a Methodist when she married, and she didn't try to make any of us Catholics. (Value of religion?) It teaches the morals of right and wrong; that's the main value. But I question lots of religious teachings, after studying science and philosophy—like Darwin's evolution theory and the fact that man's history goes back to before the Bible. I go to church, I try to believe in religion, but I sometimes question much of it. I enjoy church, a good sermon on morals and good living, and how to progress. That's what's most important about religion (Parents?) They were church attenders, fairly religious; they sent us to Sunday School; they still say blessing before each meal. But they don't discuss religion or think much about it outside of church."

D. ANALYSIS OF THE TWO CASES

Before we turn to the analysis of these two interviews, a few words concerning their significance for our major research problem may be injected. It will probably be granted that each of these protocols gives a total impression. Though each contains some contradictions, each appears to be relatively organized and relatively self-consistent psychologically. What is the importance for prejudice or potential fascism of such overall patterns? It may be argued that overt behavior in specific situations forms the crux of social discrimination, and that the most pressing need is for information concerning how many people today will, under given conditions, engage in this or that discriminatory practice. This kind of information is important, but it is not the particular concern of the present research. The major concern here is with the potential for fascism in this country. Since we do not have fascism, and since overt antidemocratic actions are officially frowned upon, surveys of what people actually do at the present time are likely to underestimate the danger. The question asked here is what is the degree of *readiness* to behave antidemocratically should social conditions change in such a way as to remove or reduce the restraint upon this kind of behavior? This readiness, according to the present theory, is integral with the total mental organization here being considered.

Though each ideological pattern may be regarded as a whole, it is a complex whole, one that embraces numerous features with respect to which individuals may differ significantly. It is not enough to say that the one man is "prejudiced" and the other "unprejudiced," and on this basis to make value judgments and to plan for action. What are the distinguishing features? How is their presence within the individual to be accounted for? What is their role within his over-all adjustment? How do they interact with other features to form an organized totality?

In order to arrive at answers to these questions, the first task, it appears, is one of description. It is necessary to inquire, first, what are the trends or themes which run through an individual's discussion of each ideological area and through his discussion of ideology in general and, second, in what respect are these contents (variables) similar to and how do they differ from those found in another subject.

The following examination of the interview protocols just presented is designed to illustrate the kinds of descriptive concepts used in the present study, and to show the manner of their derivation. The analysis was guided by a theoretical approach, and it is to be recognized that another approach might draw attention to other aspects of the cases; there seems little reason to doubt, however, that the features here distinguished are among the most important ones.

As the descriptive concepts are brought forward, it will be possible to raise concrete questions for research. These questions concern (a) the determinants of consistent trends within the individual and of differences from one individual to another, and (b) the *generality* in larger populations of the variables and the explanatory relationships formulated on the basis of a few case studies.

The order of topics in the interview protocols was determined by considerations of interviewing technique: one should start with what the subject finds it easiest to talk about and leave the more affect-laden questions, such as those concerning minorities, until the end. It is convenient here, however, to take up the topics in an order which is more in keeping with the development of the study and the general plan of the present volume: anti-Semitism, then ethnocentrism, and then ideology in general.

1. IDEOLOGY CONCERNING THE JEWS

Mack's accusations against the Jews may be grouped under three main headings: (a) violations of conventional values, (b) ingroup characteristics (clannish and power-seeking), and (c) burdens and misfits. The Jews are said to violate conventional values in that they are "not courteous or interested in humanity" but, instead, are materialistic and money-minded. As businessmen they have "second-class stuff" and are given to cheating; in social contacts the accent is on what is expensive but lacking in taste.

The Jews as a whole are conceived of as constituting a closely knit group, the members of which are blindly loyal and stick together for mutual comfort and help. They have their own organizations because they are unwilling to mix with Gentiles. By sticking together they accumulate wealth and power which will be used to benefit no one but themselves.

But if there is Jewish power there is also Jewish weakness, for among them are burdens and misfits, and as a group, they have always been downtrodden. Why this should be true, in view of their capacity to stick together and accumulate wealth, remains unexplained by the subject. He seems to feel that it is their own fault, for they "should not resent" what has befallen them. Weak Jews are left in a particularly hopeless position; it is not only that non-Jews cannot be expected to help them but strong Jews should use their wealth and power, not to support weak members of their group, but to help non-Jews. Strong Jews could thus escape the accusation of clannishness and lack of interest in humanity. In general, Jews should throw off their Jewishness and mix with the rest of the population; then the social distance between the subject and them may be diminished. (It may be suggested, however, that there is probably nothing the girl in the public speaking class could do to bring complete acceptance by the subject. Her Jewishness would probably remain as something to intrigue as well as to repel him.)

Whereas Mack spent most of his time talking about "what's wrong with the Jews" and "what the Jews should do about it," Larry spent most of his time talking about "what's wrong with non-Jews" and "what non-Jews should do about it." Larry opposes the idea that Jews want power and control; he wants to educate people about what Jews are really like. One of the most important differences between the two subjects is that Larry focuses on *why* these problems exist, while Mack does not seriously consider this question. Larry says he believes in completely open interaction with everybody equal. Discrimination is at the root of war; it is a threat for all groups and a problem they must all attack.

These discussions afford suitable examples of what is meant by *ideology* concerning Jews. It seems plain that what one has to deal with here is not a single specific attitude but a *system* that has content, scope, and structure.

It may be noted at once that Mack expresses negative *opinions* concerning what the Jews are like (they are clannish, materialistic, etc.), hostile *attitudes* toward them (it is up to them to do the changing), and definite *values* (for courtesy, honesty, good taste, etc.) which shape the opinions and justify the attitudes. In contrast, Larry reveals no negative opinions about Jews, expresses attitudes that are favorable to them (nondiscrimination, understanding), and speaks of different values (freedom from prejudice, social equality, etc.).

Questions for research immediately come to mind. How common in larger populations are the kinds of accusations made by Mack? What other kinds of accusations may be found and with what frequency? What, within our society, are the most characteristic features of imagery concerning Jews? How general is the readiness to accept negative opinions, that is to say, to what extent would an individual who, like Mack, expresses spontaneously a set of negative opinions, agree with others that were proposed to him? In what sense, and to what extent, is anti-Semitic ideology irrational? (For example, are there other irrational features similar to those exhibited by our prejudiced subject: to speak of Jews as if they were all alike and then to ascribe to them traits which could not possibly coexist in the same person, to insist that the thing for them to do is to assimilate and then to make it clear that he cannot accept them if they do? Are these irrational trends typical of high scorers?) Are the attitudes toward Jews expressed by the present subjects typical of prejudiced and unprejudiced individuals? What are the main attitudes to be found in our society? Do people with negative opinions usually have hostile attitudes as well? Is there a general readiness to accept or oppose a broad pattern of anti-Semitic attitudes and opinions?

All of the above questions concern the *content* of anti-Semitic ideology; questions may likewise be directed to its intensity. If there is in each individual a general readiness to accept or oppose anti-Semitic opinions and attitudes, is it not possible roughly to rank individuals on a dimension ranging from extreme to mild anti-Semitism, to a middle point representing indifference, ignorance or mixed feelings, to mild and then to extreme *anti*-anti-Semitism? The belief that this was possible led to the construction of a scale for measuring anti-Semitism, a scale that was at the same time broad enough to include most of the main content of anti-Semitic ideology. And the success of this scale made it possible to investigate quantitative relations of anti-Semitism and numerous other variables, including factors conceived to have a determining role.

Various explanations for such talk against the Jews as that found in Mack's interview have been suggested: that this is largely a true appraisal of the Jews, that he has had specific unpleasant experiences from which he has overgeneralized, that he is merely repeating what is common talk among his associates, particularly those who have prestige for him, that he feels more or less frustrated in his economic, social, and professional aspirations and takes it out on the Jews, that he seeks to rationalize his own failures and weaknesses by placing responsibility on a suitable outgroup, and so on. While giving due attention to these hypotheses, the procedure in the present study was to postpone questions of determination and, instead of asking why he talks this way about Jews, to discover first how he talks about other people. The aim was to understand as fully as possible the nature of the readiness in the subject before inquiring into its sources. If the features found in his discussion of anti-Semitism are not found in his discussion of other groups, then his anti-Semitism has to be explained in and of itself. If, on the other hand, trends found in his thinking about Jews are found also in his thinking about other groups, then it is these trends which have to be accounted for, and any theory which explained only the anti-Semitism would be inadequate.

2. GENERAL ETHNOCENTRISM

It was noted in Mack's discussion of Jews that he tends to think in ingroup-outgroup terms: he seems to think of the Jews as constituting a relatively homogeneous group that is categorically different from the group to which he feels that he belongs. A logical next step was to explore further his conception of his own group, and to inquire into his opinions and attitudes concerning various other groups.

In the interview with this man the general topic of imagery and attitudes concerning minority groups was introduced by inviting him to discuss his own ingroup belongingness. Most striking in this discussion is the *stereotyped* way in which he speaks of the Irish and of the groups with which they are contrasted. Each ethnic group is regarded as a homogeneous entity, and little mention is made of exceptions. There is no attempt to explain how the groups came to be as they are, beyond the assumption of different "blood strains." What a person is like depends on how much "Irish" or other "strain" he has in him. The Irish have certain *approved traits*—quick temper, easy spending, ability to make people laugh and be happy—and certain traits which he regards as *faults*—lackadaisicalness and laziness.

It is interesting to compare this ingroup appraisal with his appraisal of the Jews, who are described in the same terms but who are conceived of as lacking the good traits of the Irish. Also noteworthy is the contradiction in his attitude toward ambition and power: whereas he criticizes it in the outgroup, he regrets its lack in the ingroup. The problem for him is not how to eliminate an unequal distribution of power, but how to make sure that the bulk of power is in the right (ingroup) hands. Whereas a major fault of the Jews as noted above is their "clannishness" and their failure to assimilate, the existence of an unassimilated Irish strain is "enjoyable." Once again, something for which Jews are blamed is seen as a virtue in the ingroup. Both ingroups and outgroups are thought of in the same general terms; the same evaluative criteria are applied to groups generally, and a given characteristic, such as clannishness or power, is good or bad depending on what group has it.

Unfortunately, there was not time to explore the subject's ideas concerning the other groups which he mentions among his dislikes—Austrians, Japanese, Filipinos—nor to inquire how far this list might have been expanded. Even by itself, however, the fact that the subject rejects other groups just as he rejects the Jews is important.

Larry's first remark calls attention to the fact that views about people and groups may be distorted or at least influenced by personal factors. Mack, on the other hand, shows little such self-orientation or self-awareness; he does not suggest that his confident generalizations might have any of the possible inaccuracies of personal opinions, nor does he feel obliged to account for them on the basis of real experience. One might ask whether such differences in the degree of *intraception,* i.e., the inclination to adopt a subjective, psychological, human approach to personal and social problems, do not as a general rule distinguish nonethnocentric from ethnocentric individuals.

Characteristics notable in Mack's ideology concerning minorities but relatively lacking in that of Larry might be described as follows: (a) *Stereotypy*—the tendency mechanically to subsume things under rigid categories. (b) The idea that groups are *homogeneous units* which more or less totally determine the nature of their numbers. This places the responsibility for intergroup tensions entirely on outgroups as independent entities. The only question asked is how outgroups can change in order to make themselves acceptable to the ingroup; there is no suggestion that the ingroup might need to modify its behavior and attitudes. Larry, in contrast, places the responsibilities primarily on the ingroup and urges understanding and education within the ingroup as the basis for solving the problem. (c) The tendency to explain group differences in terms of "blood strain"—how quick a temper a man has depends on how much Irish he has in him. This is in contrast to Larry's attempt at explanation in social, psychological, and historical terms. (d) Mack favors total assimilation by outgroups, as well as total *segregation* of those outgroup members who refuse to assimilate. Larry, for his part, seems neither to threaten segregation nor demand assimilation.

He says he wants full "social equality" and interaction, rather than dominance by the ingroup and submission by outgroups. (e) Since he is relatively free of the stereotypes about ingroups and outgroups, and since groups are not his units of social description, Larry stands in opposition to Mack's tendency to think of groups in terms of their coherence and in terms of a *hierarchical arrangement* with powerful ingroups at the top and weak outgroups at the bottom.

The question, raised earlier, of whether an individual who is against Jews tends to be hostile to other minority groups as well is answered in the case of one man at least. Mack rejects a variety of ethnic groups. And Larry, for his part, is opposed to all such "prejudice." The first question for research, then, would be: Is it generally true that a person who rejects one minority group tends to reject all or most of them? Or, is it to be found more frequently that there is a tendency to have a special group against which most of the individual's hostility is directed? How broad is the ethnocentric rejection, that is to say, how many different groups are brought within the conception of outgroup? Are they extranational as well as intranational? What are the main objective characteristics of these groups? What traits are most commonly assigned to them by ethnocentric individuals? What imagery, if any, applies to all outgroups, and what is reserved for particular outgroups? Is the tendency, found in Mack but not in Larry, to make a rigid distinction between the ingroup and the outgroup, common in the population at large? Are Mack's ways of thinking about groups—rigid categories, always placing blame on the outgroup, and so forth—typical of ethnocentric individuals?

If ethnocentrism is conceived of as the tendency to express opinions and attitudes that are hostile toward a variety of ethnic groups and uncritically favorable to the group with which the individual is identified, then is it possible to rank individuals according to the degree of their ethnocentrism, as was proposed in the case of anti-Semitism? This would make it possible to determine the quantitative relations of ethnocentrism to numerous other factors—in the contemporary social situation of the individual, in his history, and in his personality. But, to pursue the general approach outlined above, it seems best first to explore further the outlook of the ethnocentric individual before raising fundamental questions of determination. What of his opinions and attitudes concerning other groups than ethnic or national ones? How does he approach social problems generally?

3. POLITICS

In his discussion of politics Mack deals at considerable length with the attributes of what for him is the outgroup. The structure and dynamics of the outgroup are conceived as follows. It is closely cohesive and power-seeking. Power is sought as an end in itself, and to attain it any means may be employed, no matter how wasteful or harmful to others. Selfishness and money-mindedness are important aspects of this power drive. At the same time, however, he ascribes to the outgroup characteristics which are the opposite of powerful: it is inefficient (shows bungling and confusion), wasteful and poorly organized; this inadequacy is attributed to the "fact" that the power arrangements within it are inadequate, with no clear authority and with lieutenants who are both too few and too carelessly selected. In addition to organizational weakness there is also physical weakness. (The reference to Roosevelt's physical ability brings to mind the argument of his political opposition that he was physically too weak to carry the burdens of a wartime president.) A further attribution of weakness to the New Deal is the idea of Roosevelt's submissiveness toward more powerful leaders—"he would come out second-best in a contest with Winnie," his ideas came from Hoover, and it is implied that he would lose out with Stalin if the latter did not play fair with us.

Parenthetically, it may be noted that there is an apparent inconsistency between Mack's general ethnocentrism and his acceptance of Stalin. This apparent discrepancy may possibly be explained in terms of our subject's attitude toward power: his admiration for power is great enough so that he can accept and momentarily ally himself with a distant outgroup when that group is not seen as a direct threat to himself. It is probably a safe guess that like many who supported cooperation with Russia during the war, this man's attitude has now changed, and Russia is regarded as a threat to the ingroup.

Mack's conception of the relations between the outgroup and the ingroup is simple: the outgroup with its selfish, materialistic, power-seeking drives, on the one hand, and its inefficiency and weakness on the other, is out to control and exploit the ingroup—to take power from it, to take over its functions, to grab all the credit, to seduce people into its fold by skillful manipulation, in short, to weaken the ingroup and run everything itself, for its own narrow, selfish ends.

When he comes to the political ingroup, Mack speaks only of admired characteristics, and the only political agencies discussed are the man, Dewey, and the army. The ingroup characteristics fall in exactly the same dimensions as do those ascribed to the outgroup, sometimes being identical and sometimes the exact opposite. Whether there is identity or reversal seems to follow a simple rule: those outgroup characteristics which have an aspect of *power* are kept intact in the ingroup, only now they are regarded as good, whereas for each outgroup characteristic signifying *weakness* or *immorality* there is an ingroup characteristic signifying the opposite.

To consider the reversals first, the inefficiency of the New Deal is in direct contrast to Dewey's clear-cut, straightforward approach. Roosevelt's "skillful politics" is the opposite of Dewey's frankness and honesty-to-the-death. Roosevelt's submission to stronger leaders is in contrast to Dewey's determined overcoming of obstacles and to General Marshall's indomitable firmness. The organizational confusion of the outgroup is to be corrected by the concentration of power in a small, closely knit organization having clearly defined levels of authority with a strong leader at the top and a cabinet of carefully chosen lieutenants.

It becomes clear, then, that the only real difference between the ingroup and the outgroup is the greater weakness of the latter. Leaving aside the weaknesses of the outgroup, we find that in all other respects the conceptions of outgroup and ingroup are identical: both seek to concentrate power in a small, cohesive organization the only purpose of which is to maintain itself. While the outgroup is accused of selfishness and materialism, the only virtues of the ingroup are the honesty and efficiency of its methods; there is no reference to its ends.

Whatever the ingroup aims might be, however, they will presumably benefit the ingroup, for Mack tells us that one of the reasons for supporting Dewey is that "he would think of the *average* people," with whom the subject seems to be identified. We know from Mack's discussion of ethnic groups that "average" is not an all-inclusive conception, but rather an ingroup from which he excludes a large proportion of the population. We see also that wealthy people are excluded from his concept of average. That this latter is not typical equalitarianism, however, is shown by his desire to become a corporation lawyer, and by his favoring a form of stratified social organization which in the economic sphere would—far from averaging things out—perpetuate the present distribution of wealth. This would seem to place the subject on the conservative side. Certainly, he quotes with approval many of the slogans of contemporary American conservatism, and he tells us that Dewey is to be supported because he is "interested in maintaining the old government traditions." Yet there is reason to believe that his conservatism is not of the traditional kind. The type of centralized control which he favors is certainly out of keeping with traditional conservative principles of free competition and restriction of government's functions. Indeed, there is a suggestion that his apparent conservatism is in reality a kind of anticonservatism. We may note his remark "if we maintain our present system of government, and I think we will for a time, some things will have to be altered." Why should he suggest that our system of government might *not* be maintained, and why does he think that at best it will be maintained only *for a time*? He seems to give us the answer himself, for the changes which he suggests as a means of maintaining the conservative tradition are actually changes which would overthrow it entirely.

The main points considered so far are Mack's attribution of both power and weakness to the outgroup and of only power to the ingroup. It must be noted, however, that weakness, too, is thought of as existing in the ingroup, though in a different form. Thus, when Mack describes the OWI as a power-seeking behemoth, the War Department is pictured in a situation of distress: "And all the time our department was crying for personnel." Again, Dewey's campaign is seen as a sort of struggle between David and Goliath, in which the clean-cut, straightforward younger man loses only because of the over-whelming power and lack of scruple which opposes him: "It was skilful politics that enabled the old guard to win. Considering his obstacles, Dewey did very well. In ordinary times he would have had a landslide." This im-agery of persecution is expressed not only in Mack's political thinking but also in his discussion of himself and his life in Washington. There is a clear note of self-pity in his remarks that he "worked many hours overtime for no pay," that when war was declared he "worked for thirty-seven hours straight," and that "living conditions were terrible."

It is important to note that weakness in Mack and his group is only implied in these statements. What he seems to be trying to tell us is that in so far as the ingroup might appear to be weak at any time, this is due only to persecu-tion by an outgroup that is momentarily—and unfairly—stronger. It is im-portant to note further that his feelings of being persecuted do not lead to sympathy for other persecuted people nor to any inclination to eliminate persecution generally, but only to the thought that justice would consist in his group becoming the powerful one. Here, as is typical of people with persecution fantasies, Mack believes that he (his group) is essentially strong but is at the same time in a weak position; he can solve this dilemma only by attributing evil (dishonesty, unfairness, and so on) and undeserved power to his opponent. His desire to be attached to the same kind of power which he decries in the outgroup is expressed in his wanting to be "close to the center of things," and "know about the background" of important daily events, to be in on "the secret committees."

Turning now to Larry, it may be noted that perhaps the most striking aspect of his remarks about politics is their lack of organization and of con-viction. This is in contrast to his ideas in other ideological areas, such as minority questions, which show a relatively high degree of organization and firmness. However, even in his brief, casual utterances about politics we can see a different orientation from that found in Mack. True, there is here, as in their preferences for political labels, a certain amount of surface similarity—both men show general conservatism and the usual conservative accusations against the New Deal. But it is precisely this superficial similarity that makes the differences stand out.

The main over-all difference lies in the absence from Larry's thinking of those features which led us to question Mack's conservatism. Thus, Larry's thinking does not revolve around the ingroup-outgroup distinction: there is no conception of the ingroup as a static homogeneous entity which is beyond any criticism; nor is the outgroup conceived of as an aggregation of weak and evil people who through plotting and conniving are able to use their undeserved power in persecuting the ingroup. Indeed, he can even identify himself with a man, Wallace, who not only belongs to the outgroup but is, according to the prevalent propaganda, "inefficient" to boot.

As the second main difference between the two men, there is more positive evidence that Larry's conservatism is genuine, in the sense that it is a means for furthering his admitted material motives. Since he intends to become a businessman, he supports the political party which seems to offer the most help to business. This is in contrast to Mack, who stresses the conventional ideal of unselfishness in order, we may suppose, to disavow his underlying interest in power.

Larry finds difficulty, to be sure, in reconciling this "realism" with the idealism which he expresses in other areas. But he is aware of this difficulty—and here again he differs from Mack. The latter speaks as if his utterances were sufficiently objective, so that there need be no reference to himself or to the possibility of personal determinants of opinion. Larry, on the other hand, is aware that his views reflect things within himself as well as external reality, and that consequently they are tentative, approximate, and possibly self-contradictory. He feels it necessary to explain the origins of his views, he can admit some inner conflict, and consider the possibility that he may not have acquired his views in the most intelligent way. While these features may prevent this subject from being very militant about anything, they would seem to insure him against reactionism.

If two men whose ideas about politics are as different as those of Mack and Larry nevertheless have the same political alignment (they both agree with the Willkie-type Republicans and the Anti-New Deal Democrats), and if they understand what these party labels mean, then it might be inquired whether political alignment bears any relationship to ethnocentrism. Or, if the two are related, what ideology concerning minority groups is more typical of the Willkie-type Republicans and the Anti-New Deal Democrats, that of Mack or that of Larry?

And what of those who favor the New Deal Democrats or the traditional Republicans? According to theory, we should expect political liberalism to go with relative freedom from prejudice, and political conservatism, at least the extreme form of it, i.e., reaction, to go with ethnocentrism. Indeed, considerable evidence that this is true already exists. A natural step in the present study, therefore, was to conceive of a continuum extending from extreme conservatism to extreme liberalism and to construct a scale which would place individuals along this continuum. This would permit the determination of the quantitative relations of conservatism to anti-Semitism and to general ethnocentrism. It is apparent from consideration of what Mack and Larry have to say, however, that (a) conservatism is not a simple, unidimensional attitude but a complex ideological pattern, and (b) that the relations of conservatism to ethnocentrism are by no means one to one.

It cannot be supposed, of course, that all the aspects of conservatism-liberalism have been touched upon in the spontaneous remarks of these two subjects. It will be the task of research not only to determine whether the features expressed here—conservative values, pro-business attitudes, and the like—commonly go together, but to inquire what other opinions, attitudes, and values might belong to an over-all conservative or liberal pattern. What, in other words, is the composition of conservative (or liberal) politico-economic ideology? Is there a coherent pattern that is broad enough to include what Mack and Larry have in common and at the same time to permit a delineation of such differences as exist between them? And which is more important for the problem of potential fascism, conservatism in general, or the special kind of conservatism seen in Mack but not in Larry?

It could well be argued that Mack's position is not conservative at all but rather *pseudoconservative*. Although, as noted above, he professes belief in the tenets of traditional conservatism, it is clear that he considers it "time for a change," and there is a strong implication that the kind of change he desires is one which would abolish the very institutions with which he appears to identify himself. It has frequently been remarked that should fascism become a powerful force in this country, it would parade under the banners of traditional American democracy. Thus, the slogan "rugged individual-ism" which apparently expresses the liberal concept of free competition among independent and daring entrepreneurs, actually refers more often to the uncontrolled and arbitrary politics of the strongest powers in business—those huge combines which as a matter of historical necessity have lowered the number of independent entrepreneurs. It is clear that an investigation of antidemocratic trends must take this phenomenon into account. Is it possible to define pseudoconservatism in objective terms, to diagnose it in the individual and to estimate its strength within a population? Is it true that pseudoconservatism is generally to be found, as in the case of Mack, associated with ethnocentrism and other antidemocratic trends?

On any ordinary scale for measuring conservatism, the pseudoconservative would probably obtain a high score; he would agree with the usual statements of conservative opinions, attitudes, and values. How to frame scale items that will reflect the conservative façade and at the same time induce the subject to reveal his underlying readiness for radical change is a particularly challenging technical problem. We are confronted here with a clear instance of those different *levels* of expression which were discussed earlier. The only recourse, it would appear, is to employ clinical techniques that go more or less directly to the deeper tendencies, and give sufficient understanding of them, so that it becomes possible to formulate scale items which permit the indirect expression, on the surface, of these deeper tendencies.

The Politico-Economic Conservatism (PEC) scale described in Chapter V is designed to give an estimate of the individual's general readiness to express conservative ideology and at the same time to distinguish the pseudo-conservative from the others. For a fuller description of the different patterns of conservative ideology, however, other scales and other techniques have in addition to be relied upon. With this approach it becomes possible to investigate the relations of pseudoconservatism to "genuine conservatism" —if, indeed, the distinction can be maintained. The question may be raised as to whether there is any deeply ingrained conservatism, within the individual, that does not derive its energy in large part from the personal need to curb one's own rebellious tendencies.

In any case, it is clear that Mack's political ideology is different from Larry's. The differences stand out with particular clarity when Mack's discussion of politics is considered in relation to what he has to say about Jews and other ethnic groups. Just as his anti-Semitism could not be understood or evaluated until his ideas about other groups had been examined, so did his politics come into focus when seen against the background of his ethnocentrism. It seems particularly significant that he talks about the New Deal, the Civil Service, and the OWI in the same way that he talks about Jews. This seems strongly to suggest that we are faced here not with a particular set of political convictions and a particular set of opinions about a specific ethnic group but with a *way of thinking* about groups and group relations generally. Is the manner of this thinking—in rigid categories of unalterable blacks and whites—usually to be found in people who are prejudiced against minority groups? Is there any group, save those with which the subject is identified, that is safe from the kind of total rejection and potential hostility that is found here? Is there a general relationship between the manner of thinking and the *content* of thinking about groups and group relations? In Mack the stereotyped thinking is accompanied by imagery of power versus weakness, moral purity versus moral lowness, and hierarchical organization. Are these trends commonly associated in the general population? If so, is the relationship a dynamic one, and what might be its nature?

It would appear that the more a person's thinking is dominated by such general tendencies as those found in Mack, the less will his attitude toward a particular group depend upon any objective characteristics of that group, or upon any real experience in which members of that group were involved. It is this observation that draws attention to the importance of personality as a determinant of ideology. And if personality has this crucial role in the broad areas of attitude and opinion that have been considered, might we not expect it to influence a subject's thinking in *all* areas that are important to him? It would be impossible to know what Mack thinks about everything, but we may examine his ideas about religion, income, and vocation and see if something approaching a total view emerges.

4. RELIGION

The interviewer, in questioning Mack about religion, took into consideration the following statement which he had made on his questionnaire. In response to the question, "How important, in your opinion, are religion and the church?" Mack wrote, "Especially important for people who need sustenance or who are highly erratic. I have had to rely too much on my own ability for the necessities of life to devote a great deal of time to the spiritual." Larry, for his part, wrote, "Very important as the center of moral teachings."

The question may be raised at once whether rejection of religion is usually associated with an antidemocratic outlook as is the case with Mack, while acceptance of religion, as in Larry, usually goes with relative freedom from prejudice. There would appear to be some reason to expect that the general trend would be the other way around, that freedom from religious dogmas would go with political "liberalism" and hence with freedom from prejudice, while acceptance of religion would go with conservatism and authoritarianism and, hence, probably with ethnocentrism. In all likelihood the problem is not so simple. It may be that the mere acceptance or rejection of religion is not so important as *how* the individual accepts or rejects it, that is to say, the pattern of his ideas about religion. This is a matter upon which the interviews ought to throw some light.

It may be noted in the interviews of Mack and Larry that both men were subjected to a rather usual type of conventional pressure, that in both cases the application of this pressure was mainly a maternal function, and that in the background of both cases there is a mixture of Methodist and Catholic influences. Mack makes more of a distinction between father and mother roles than does Larry, and it seems important to Mack that his father was good without going to church. In the mind of the latter subject, church and mother seem to be rather closely identified and to stand for that which weak or dependent people turn to when they need sustenance. But it may be asked whether, in turning away from the church, Mack has not had to substitute something else in its stead; and that is authority, as represented first by the father and later by a "God who is strictly a man." It can be supposed that the kind of religious feeling which this "great man" arouses in the subject is like that he experienced when he sat next to General Marshall and heard him talk. Similar deference toward sufficiently high authority can be noted in Mack's respect for the sayings of Christ, which are contrasted with the "not first hand" words of the apostles.

But Mack's respect for authority comes into conflict with his explicit value of independence. How to reconcile the two is the problem with which his religious ideology is mainly concerned. Apparently he can get some feeling of independence by asserting that he is stubborn and hard-headed, and by rejecting people who "need sustenance." And if the authority is sufficiently powerful, it becomes possible to submit without losing altogether the sense of independence. If dependence and passivity are to be accepted, it must be in circumstances that are beyond his control, e.g., when he is sick.

It is strongly suggested that as much as Mack would like to be independent he would also like to be dependent. He does admit to liking the music and singing in church; he seems to make a point of telling us how much sickness he has had, and when he emphasizes that he has had to rely upon himself since an early age, we may detect not only a note of pride but a note of self-pity. An underlying need for dependence (passivity, sympathy, comfort), in conflict with the desire to maintain masculine pride and self-respect, could give rise to an exaggerated value for independence; and it could at the same time receive a measure of gratification, in a somewhat disguised form, through submission to a powerful authority. This would seem to be a fairly clear instance in which a deeper-level need operates to affect manifest strivings, openly expressed values, and ideas about God and man.

Since Mack does not belong to any organized religious sect, he does not speak of his group versus various religious outgroups. It is to be noted, however, that he seems to regard all religious people as constituting an outgroup, ascribing to them some of the same features—weakness, dependence—which he sees in Jews and in the New Deal.

Larry, for his part, regards religion as a valued part of everyday living rather than something that is called for in a particular situation. For him it has the general function of promoting high ethical standards, good living, and progress rather than the limited function of offering relief in times of acute distress. Moreover, in contrast with Mack, who identifies morals with "the man," Larry conceives that the moral values of religion reside in the church as an institution. A further contrast between the two men lies in the fact that Larry accepts religion in general yet is able to criticize it, while Mack generally rejects it without offering specific criticisms. In criticizing the content of religion on intellectual grounds, Larry shows that he will not be likely to use it for reactionary aims. Mack exhibits his characteristic all-or-nothing approach to ideological matters, and without any analysis of content concentrates on people—Christ, the apostles, God the man—who are to be totally accepted or totally rejected.

Regardless of whether or not the general acceptance or the general rejection of religion should be found in a larger population to be associated with antidemocratic trends, it will be necessary to inquire whether the distinguishing features in the thought of Mack and Larry are generally significant.

No attempt was made in the present research to measure any variables in the area of religious ideology (although, as noted above, subjects did state in their questionnaires how important they considered religion and the Church); instead, effort was directed to the discovery of patterns of religious thought in the interview discussions of the subjects. How common in our society are the patterns found in Mack and Larry? Do these patterns generally bear the same kinds of relations to thought in other areas as they do in these two cases? What other patterns of religious thought may be discovered and what is their significance for democracy or its opposite? Do the different religious sects represent systems of belief that are related to prejudice? Do "racial" and "religious prejudice" go together and have the same significances, as has been so frequently supposed?

In the case of Mack, a deep-lying personality need, dependence, comes into prominence when religion is under discussion. Is it possible to demonstrate dynamic relationships between such needs and ideological systems? In other areas as well as in the area of religion? Also in the case of Mack, there appears to be a close connection between religious ideology and the pattern of family relations. Is this generally the case? It may be that the pattern of family relations is an important determinant not only of religious thought but of ideology in general.

5. VOCATION AND INCOME

The previous discussion has shown that Mack tends to think of the structure of any group as a hierarchy of power. It is not surprising therefore to find that he thinks of our total society as being organized along the same lines. In government he sees increasing centralization and regimentation, i.e., more and more control vested in fewer and fewer people, and in economics, important developments will continue to be in the hands of the big capitalists. However much objective truth there may be in this view, the significant point is that Mack considers the state of affairs he describes as, if not desirable, inevitable. Given this kind of social organization, then the thing to do is to "go up," "to open doors," to be "on the inside," and this is the main trend in his vocation-income ideology. He wants to belong to or be "in with" the ruling group. It is not so much that he himself wants to dominate, but rather that he wants to serve powerful interests and so *participate in their power*. It was seen in his discussion of politics that the power attributes of the ingroup and of the outgroup were, in his mind, the same; it is not too much to hypothesize now that the reason he accuses the Jews, the Civil Service, the OWI, the New Deal of wishing to establish a closely cohesive and selfishly exploitive ingroup is that he wishes to do the same thing himself. It is necessary to add, of course, that he cannot fully justify to himself such an antidemocratic wish and so, under its sway but unable to admit it, he sees it as existing not in himself but in the world around him.

Larry, it appears, is also identified with business and would like to go up in the world, but there the similarity between the two subjects ends. Whereas for Larry, going up means improving his lot in the ordinary sociological sense, for Mack it means changing his status in a hierarchy; in other words, Larry thinks of climbing primarily in its individual sense, while Mack thinks of it more in its class sense. Larry does not seem to mind competing, once he has been given support at the start, while Mack would get there by submitting to those who are going to win. Larry is frankly interested in money and a lot of it while Mack is moralistically temperate in this regard; Larry wants pleasure, Mack seems more interested in power; Larry feels that the main object of work and efficiency is that one might the sooner take a vacation and enjoy life; Mack appears to regard these things as ends in themselves. In general, both subjects express ideas that are closely in accord with their political ideologies.

Another difference between the two men, which may be of considerable importance, lies in Larry's greater awareness of his motivation: he is entirely open about his desire for money and pleasure, his willingness to accept support, his susceptibility to influence by his family, his interest in social prestige. There is little reason to doubt that these motives are just as strong, if not considerably stronger, in Mack, but it is plain that he does not fully accept them as parts of his self. It might be inquired whether this tendency to keep important personality needs out of consciousness, to allow them to remain *ego-alien*, is not a regular feature of the potential fascist.

In the present area of vocation-income, perhaps more than in any of the others, the subjects' discussion of what they *believe* is closely bound up with discussion of what, more or less explicitly, they *want*. Personality needs, in other words, have a central place in the whole picture. To climb socially, to be independent, to have pleasure and security, to attain a sense of power by submitting to those who have it—these are personality needs. The moralistic depreciation of money, the oversolicitous but unrealistic attitude toward poor people—these may be regarded as defense mechanisms, devices whereby needs which conflict with the stronger need to maintain self-respect are held in check. It is plain that with respect to a number of these variables Mack and Larry are widely different; and it was one of the main hypotheses of the present research that there are numerous such variables with respect to which prejudiced and unprejudiced individuals differ generally and which in individuals at either extreme go together to form a psychologically meaningful pattern. In proceeding to test this hypothesis the interview protocols of numerous ethnocentric and anti-ethnocentric subjects—as well as other sources—were combed for just such distinguishing features, and these were then put into the form of questionnaire scale-items for testing with groups of subjects. A liking for "nice equipment," a fondness for hunting and fishing, a preference for living in a small town—numerous such small but suggestive items were given consideration. On the assumption that potential antidemocracy at the personality level is a general trend with respect to which individuals differ quantitatively, a scale for the measurement of this trend was constructed in the manner of those described above. This supplied the means for demonstrating on a mass basis some of the relationships which appear to exist in the two individuals under discussion.

Even if factors of personality did not come explicitly to the fore at particular points in the interviews with these two men, the conception of personality would be forced upon us by observation of the *consistency* with which the same ideas and the same modes of thought recur as the discussion turns from one ideological area to another. Since no such consistency could conceivably exist as a matter of sociological fact, we are bound to conceive of central tendencies *in the person* which express themselves in various areas. The concept of a dynamic factor of personality is made to order for explaining the common trend in diverse surface manifestations. For example, a need for power in the personality is ready to express itself in any area of social relations. It may be suggested, in this connection, that where social psychologists have not so far given a great deal of attention to personality it is because they have not studied total ideology. Specific social attitudes if adequately measured will undoubtedly be found to correlate with a variety of external and contemporary factors, and if one studies only specific attitudes he may easily be led to the belief that this is all there is to it. Consistent trends in the person can only be revealed by subjecting him to a variety of stimuli, or placing him in a number of different situations, or questioning him on a wide array of topics; but if this is done, then, according to the present hypothesis, consistent trends, i.e., personality, will always be revealed.

The varied stimuli to which subjects of the present study were subjected were not limited to questions of attitude, opinion, and value; there were the clinical techniques designed especially for bringing the factors of personality to light. The aim was to go as far as possible toward demonstrating the covariation of personality factors and the ideological trends discussed above, toward discovering as many as possible of the features which distinguished the potentially antidemocratic individual. Given a relationship between a personality variable and an ideological trend, it was usually assumed that the causal sequence was from the former to the latter—on the grounds that the formation of personality was genetically earlier, the most important structures going back to childhood. This led to an attempt to learn something about the determination of the potential fascist in childhood, through investigation of the early social environment. But this is a subject which cannot be considered until much later; not until the several areas of ideology have been analyzed in detail.

CHAPTER III

THE STUDY OF ANTI-SEMITIC IDEOLOGY

Daniel J. Levinson

A. INTRODUCTION

One of the most clearly antidemocratic forms of social ideology is prejudice, and within this context anti-Semitism provides a fruitful starting point for a social psychological study. As a social movement, organized anti-Semitism presents a major threat to democracy: it is one of the most powerful psychological vehicles for antidemocratic political movements and it provides, for reasons which are largely politico-economic and beyond the scope of this discussion, perhaps the most effective spearhead for a frontal attack on our entire social structure.

From a psychological viewpoint as well, anti-Semitism is particularly important and revealing. Much that psychologically oriented writers have already said about anti-Semitism and about fascism suggests that the deeper psychological sources of these ideologies are very similar. The irrational quality in anti-Semitism stands out even in casual everyday discussions. The fact that people make general statements about "the Jew," when the Jews are actually so heterogeneous—belong to every socioeconomic class and represent every degree of assimilation—is vivid evidence of this irrationality. This striking contrast between the Jews' actual complexity and their supposed homogeneity has suggested the hypothesis that what people say against Jews depends more upon their own psychology than upon the actual characteristics of Jews. For example, when the belief that Jews possess financial power out of all proportion to their numbers persists in the face of overwhelming evidence to the contrary, one is led to suspect not only that the individual holding this belief has an unusual preoccupation with power but also that he might himself wish to assume the kind of power which he supposes Jews to have. It is clear that research into the emotional sources of ideology is required for the understanding of such phenomena as these.

These considerations, which suggest the advantage of making anti-Semitism a point of departure for research, were also some of the hypotheses that guided the research as a whole. The study of anti-Semitism may well

57

be, then, the first step in a search for antidemocratic trends in ideology, in personality, and in social movements.

Anti-Semitism is conceived here as an ideology, that is, as a relatively organized, relatively stable system of opinions, values, and attitudes concerning Jews and Jewish-Gentile relations. More specifically, it involves *negative opinions* regarding Jews (that they are unscrupulous, clannish, power-seeking, and so on); *hostile attitudes* toward them (that they should be excluded, restricted, kept subordinate to Gentiles, and so on); and *moral values* which permeate the opinions and justify the attitudes.

Numerous questions concerning the structure and content of anti-Semitism were raised in Chapter II. These and other questions guided the construction of an opinion-attitude scale for the measurement of anti-Semitic ideology. The source material for the scale included: the writings of virulent anti-Semites; technical, literary, and reportorial writings on anti-Semitism and fascism; and, most important, everyday American anti-Semitism as revealed in parlor discussion, in the discriminatory practices of many businesses and institutions, and in the literature of various organizations which are trying, with small success, to counter numerous anti-Semitic accusations by means of rational argument.

This scale, like the others used in the present research, had several functions. It yielded a quantitative measure which could be correlated with measures of other, theoretically related, variables. It provided a basis for the selection of criterion groups of extreme high and low scorers, who could then be subjected to intensive clinical study. It permitted, as part of a larger questionnaire, a relatively detailed, quantifiable study of large groups of subjects. Finally, it was constructed in such a way that statistical analysis of its properties might reveal much of the structure, scope, and content of anti-Semitic ideology.

B. CONSTRUCTION OF THE ANTI-SEMITISM (A-S) SCALE

An opinion-attitude scale is a series of statements dealing with a given topic, in this case anti-Semitic ideology. The subject is asked to respond to each item by agreeing or disagreeing. His responses are converted into scores in such a way that a high score indicates a great amount of what is being measured—for this scale, anti-Semitism—a low score the opposite. The scoring procedure is discussed below (Section C).

The Likert method of scaling (73, 84) was used. It is easier to apply and requires fewer items than the Thurstone method (118), but yields equally high reliabilities and generally comparable results (22, 84). It was desired to avoid the assumptions and difficulties in the use of judges which the latter method entails. Also, since it was anticipated that in further stages of the research the items might be modified in wording, it was highly desirable to avoid the repeated use of judges. A measure of intensity of opinion and attitudes is obtained, in the Likert method, by having the subject indicate the degree of his agreement or disagreement with each item; this makes possible a more adequate determination of subtle group and individual differences, and facilitates the qualitative analysis of individual response patterns. This method also permits the covering of a wider area of opinions and attitudes. Finally, the Likert technique of item analysis (see below) was particularly suited to the general theoretical approach of this research.

1. GENERAL RULES IN ITEM FORMULATION

The procedure used for selecting and formulating items, in contrast to a frequent practice, did not involve the testing of several hundred items as a basis for selection of a final short scale. Rather, fifty-two items were formulated and all of these were used throughout the statistical analysis of the preliminary form of the scale. (To anticipate a result presented below, only a few items were statistically inadequate, and this inadequacy is interesting in its own right.) In successive stages of the research there were, however, no qualms about modifying, deleting, or adding items.

The present scale differs from most opinion-attitude scales in that it contains only negative items, that is, they all state the anti-Semitic position regarding the issue in question. The reasons for the use of negative items only and an answer to some possible criticisms, presented in detail in a previous publication (71), may be summarized here. One advantage of negative items is that they tend to be more discriminating. Also, negative items can be so phrased that they express subtle hostility without seeming to offend the democratic values which most prejudiced people feel they must maintain. Since the scale attempts to measure receptivity to anti-Semitic ideology, it seemed reasonable to use only anti-Semitic statements in the scale. The main argument against the present procedure is that it might produce a "set" or mechanical tendency consistently to agree or to disagree. This argument is answered on the ground that (a) most individuals show variability of response, as indicated by item intercorrelations averaging .3–.4; (b) there is a tendency to vary in order to avoid an extreme position; (c) very similar results have been obtained in later stages of the present research when an all-negative scale is inserted randomly into a longer series containing positive items; and, most important, (d) since the "set" argument implies that high scorers are not necessarily anti-Semitic nor lows anti-anti-Semitic, the final test is the validity of the scale, that is, the demonstration that high scorers are significantly different from low scorers in a variety of meaningful characteristics. The scale does, as will be shown later, have considerable validity.

Since the A-S scale, like the others, was intended not only to provide a *quantitative* measure of an ideology but also to aid in the *qualitative* description of that ideology (and of individual ideological patterns), its construction followed certain general rules. These rules had to do with (a) the formulation of individual items, and (b) the division of the total scale into subscales.

Since the scale should not, for practical reasons, include more than about fifty items (preferably fewer in later forms), each item should be maximally rich in ideas and there should be a minimum of duplication in wording or essential content of items. While the items are therefore often more complex than those of many other scales, this is not considered a fault. At the same time, they should be clear and unambiguous in meaning, so that agreement is ordinarily an expression of anti-Semitism, disagreement an expression of its opposite. It is important to avoid "double-barreled" items, that is, items with two parts such that a subject might agree with one part and disagree with the other, and thus not know how to respond.

Extreme prejudice of a violent and openly antidemocratic sort does not seem to be widespread in this country, especially in the middle class.[1] Since the present scale is intended to measure everyday, "garden variety" anti-Semitism, the items were formulated in such a way as to reflect the prevalent forms in which anti-Semitism now appears.

Most prejudice as one finds it in business, housing, and general social interaction is *pseudodemocratic* rather than *openly antidemocratic;* this distinction plays an important role in the analysis of anti-Semitic ideology which guided the construction of the scale and the formulation of items. An idea may be considered openly antidemocratic when it refers to active hatred, or to violence which has the direct aim of wiping out a minority group or of putting it in a permanently subordinate position. A pseudodemocratic idea, on the other hand, is one in which hostility toward a group is somewhat tempered and disguised by means of a compromise with democratic ideals. Pseudodemocratic statements about Jews are often introduced by qualifying phrases which deny hostility or which attempt to demonstrate the democratic attitude of the speaker, e.g., "It's not that I'm prejudiced, but. . . ."; "Jews have their rights, but. . . ."

This pseudodemocratic façade is probably relatively untouched by most of the current literature attacking prejudice as "race hatred," "un-American," "un-Christian intolerance," and the like. There is no hatred in the surface content of these attitudes and they have been squared with certain democratic values in such a way that the individual holding them apparently feels little if any sense of antidemocracy. And, of course, merely to label this way of thinking as un-American will not change it, first, because labeling is not enough, and second, because such thinking falls within one of the main streams of American social history and can be found to some extent in most sections of American life. It is necessary, rather, to understand its

---

[1] This is shown by various public opinion polls and reportorial studies although comprehensive and rigorously obtained data are lacking. It is also indicated by results from the present study.

external sources in American culture and tradition as well as the inner sources which make certain individuals particularly receptive to these cultural pressures.

It is probably an error to regard the pseudodemocratic compromise as a mere surface disguise used deliberately and skillfully by prejudiced people to camouflage their actual, conscious antidemocracy. The person whose approach to social problems is pseudodemocratic is actually different *now* from one whose approach is now openly antidemocratic. For various reasons —perhaps because he has internalized democratic values, perhaps out of conformity to present social standards—the pseudodemocrat does not now accept ideas of overt violence and active suppression. The concern with democratic values, and the resistance to antidemocratic ones, must be considered as psychologically and socially important facts in any attempt to understand prejudice, American variety. Undoubtedly very many people who are now pseudodemocratic are potentially antidemocratic, that is, are capable in a social crisis of supporting or committing acts of violence against minority groups. Nevertheless, it is important to understand the attempted compromise with democratic values: because it may reveal a democratic potential which might, if supported and strengthened, ultimately gain the upper hand; because it colors the whole fabric of pseudodemocratic social thinking; and, since this compromise reflects the prevalent forms of overt discrimination in this country—quotas, segregation, exclusion, denial of opportunities—to understand the former may help to combat the latter.

If patterns of ideology are conceived as falling on a dimension ranging from democratic to antidemocratic, then the pseudodemocratic ones probably stand somewhere between the center and the antidemocratic extreme. This is, of course, not a simple dimension: there are diverse approaches falling into each of these broad categories, and the dimension is not a simple quantitative one like length or weight. A change of certain trends in an individual may produce a qualitative reorganization and ideological change from one extreme of this dimension to the other. The task is to understand the total individual and, especially in the case of the pseudodemocrat, to gauge the psychological potential for both democracy and open antidemocracy.

Most of the items of the A-S scale have been formulated as pseudodemocratically as possible. This consideration was, in fact, one of the main reasons for the use of negative items only. The following rules have been followed in general: Each item should be made appealing and "easy to fall for" by avoiding or soft-pedaling or morally justifying ideas of violence and obvious antidemocracy. Much use is made of qualifying phrases such as "One trouble with Jewish . . ."; "There are a few exceptions, but . . ."; "It would be to the best interests of all if . . . ," in order to avoid a categorical, aggressive condemnation. Items are worded so that the person can add at the end: "but I am not anti-Semitic." Seeming tentativeness is introduced by qualifications such as "it seems that," "probably," "in most cases." Finally, an attempt is made to give each statement a familiar ring, to formulate it as it has been heard many times in everyday discussions.

To the extent that the above rules have been followed, pseudodemocratic subjects are likely to make scores on this scale as high, or nearly as high, as those of the antidemocratic ones. It will be the task of later techniques, both questionnaire-style and clinical, to provide further information concerning the distinctions between these two groups of subjects.

2. MAJOR SUBDIVISIONS OR AREAS: THE SUBSCALES

The general rules of item formulation just described refer primarily to the formal structure of items and can be applied to each item irrespective of the *content* of the ideas expressed in it. The content of the items was largely determined by the general conception of anti-Semitic ideology and the specific hypotheses discussed above. Several subscales were formed in order to insure systematic coverage of the various aspects conceived and in order to test certain hypotheses. The subscales cannot be thought of as dealing with *components* of anti-Semitism in any statistical sense; they are not based on statistical treatment of prior results, nor was any intensive correlational analysis of the present items made. The subscales are, rather, convenient ways of conceiving and grouping items.

The anti-Semitism scale contains five subscales dealing respectively with imagery (opinions) of Jews as personally *offensive* and as socially *threatening*; with *attitudes* concerning what should be done to or against Jews; and with the opposing views that Jews are *too seclusive* or *too intrusive* (assimilative). These subscales are probably not entirely independent either in a statistical sense or with respect to the actual content of the items; indeed, there is some question as to whether certain items may not equally well have been placed in a different subscale than the one to which they were assigned. Nevertheless, each subscale as a whole seems to deal with a fairly definite and definable phase of anti-Semitism. The subscales will now be discussed in order.

a. SUBSCALE "OFFENSIVE" (S_O). This subscale is presented in Table 1(III). (The items are numbered as they appeared in the total scale, which was given in two parts, I and II, with twenty-six items in each part; thus, I–4 is Item 4, part I.) The items describe various "Jewish traits" which are offensive, unpleasant, and disturbing. Stereotypy is implicit in items ascribing faults to "Jews"—implicitly, "all" or "most" Jews—without recognition of individual differences. It is explicit in item I–13, which specifically states that "Jews are pretty much alike" and which indicates an image of "the Jews" as a stereotyped model of the entire group.

What are the characteristics of this stereotyped image? If the other items offer an adequate description, "the Jew" is extravagant, sensual, conceited, and overaggressive; but he is also "smelly," shabby, and unconcerned with his personal appearance. Jews are accused of being excessively Jewish, so to

TABLE 1 (III)
ANTI-SEMITISM SUBSCALE "OFFENSIVE"

I-1. Jews seem to prefer the most luxurious, extravagant, and sensual way of living.

I-4. A major fault of the Jews is their conceit, overbearing pride, and their idea that they are a chosen race.

I-7. No matter how Americanized a Jew may seem to be, there is always something basically Jewish underneath, a loyalty to Jewry and a manner that is never totally changed.

I-10. Districts containing many Jews always seem to be smelly, dirty, shabby, and unattractive.

I-13. There are a few exceptions, but in general Jews are pretty much alike.

I-16. The Jews shoud not pry so much into Christian activities and organizations nor seek so much recognition and prestige from Christians.

II-1. The Jews should make sincere efforts to rid themselves of their conspicuous and irritating faults if they really want to stop being persecuted.

II-4. There is something different and strange about Jews; one never knows what they are thinking or planning, nor what makes them tick.

II-7. The trouble with letting Jews into a nice neighborhood is that they gradually give it a typical Jewish atmosphere.

II-10. I can hardly imagine myself marrying a Jew.

II-13. One general fault of Jews is their overaggressiveness, a strong tendency always to display their Jewish looks, manners, and breeding.

II-16. Jews should be more concerned with their personal appearance, and not be so dirty and smelly and unkempt.

speak, but their attempts to assimilate into "Christian" activities are regarded as prying. Jewish faults are considered the main cause of anti-Semitism (Item II–1), which would be eliminated if the Jews made sincere efforts to improve. However, there is some doubt that Jews can ever quite manage to be fully Americanized (Item I–7). Item II–10, "I can hardly imagine myself marrying a Jew," is included here because it seems to refer more to an unpleasant image than to a clear-cut, hostile attitude. It represents a pseudodemocratic equivalent to Item I–15 in the "Attitude" subscale (see below). Are people consistent in their general agreement (or disagreement) with these items? This will be seen in the results presented below.

b. SUBSCALE "THREATENING" (S_T). These items, presented in Table 2 (III), describe the Jews as a dangerous, dominating, corrupting social group. They are asserted to have great power economically and politically, and to be unscrupulous and conniving in their dealings with Gentiles. They do not like hard work (Item II–11) but at the same time they lower the general standard of living by doing menial work and by living under low standards (Item I–14). In addition to being simultaneously rich and poor, powerful and parasitic, they are also at once capitalists and revolutionaries. In their lack of patriotism they are a threat to the nation, and in general they are a threat to civilization.

Apart from the enormous complexity of "the Jew" so described, there is something fantastic in the idea that a group so small numerically can be so

TABLE 2 (III)
ANTI-SEMITISM SUBSCALE "THREATENING"

I-2. The Jews must be considered a bad influence on Christian culture and civilization.

I-5. One trouble with Jewish businessmen is that they stick together and connive, so that a Gentile doesn't have a fair chance in competition.

I-8. Jewish power and control in money matters is far out of proportion to the number of Jews in the total population.

I-11. There are too many Jews in the various federal agencies and bureaus in Washington, and they have too much control over our national policies.

I-14. Jews tend to lower the general standard of living by their willingness to do the most menial work and to live under standards that are far below average.

II-2. War shows up the fact that the Jews are not patriotic or willing to make sacrifices for their country.

II-5. Jews may have moral standards that they apply in their dealings with each other, but with Christians they are unscrupulous, ruthless, and undependable.

II-8. The Jew's first loyalty is to Jewry rather than to his country.

II-11. Jews seem to have an aversion to plain hard work; they tend to be a parasitic element in society by finding easy, nonproductive jobs.

II-14. There seems to be some revolutionary streak in the Jewish make-up as shown by the fact that there are so many Jewish Communists and agitators.

powerful and so basic a social threat. This imagery in extreme cases seems to be an ideological expression of underlying paranoid trends; in *Mein Kampf*, for example, the Jews are regarded not only as "base and inferior" but also as having "germicidal potency" and "devilish cunning." However, most American anti-Semites are undoubtedly not psychotic or paranoid in the usual psychiatric sense. The personality trends related to this kind of imagery in Americans will be dealt with in later chapters.

c. SUBSCALE "ATTITUDES" (S_A). All the attitudes contained in this subscale (see Table 3(III)) are regarded as negative or hostile to the Jews as a group, and this hypothesis is generally borne out by the statistical results. These attitudes were intended to represent varying degrees of discrimination ranging from simple avoidance to suppression and attack, with intermediate actions of exclusion, quotas (partial exclusion), and segregation. In order to cover many forms of discrimination, a list of the major social areas in which it occurs was used in the formulation of items. These areas are: employment, residence (neighborhoods, apartment houses, hotels), education and professions, marriage, social organizations, politics, the nation. Item II–21 is a good example of pseudodemocracy: it assumes that the Jews are actually a threat (imagery: powerful, offensive, etc.) and suggests that the Jews solve "their own problem"—implicitly, that if they do not limit themselves voluntarily, the Gentiles may be forced to more drastic action. A person can agree to this, and many have, in the name of tolerance and democracy. It is, nevertheless, essentially an anti-Semitic idea: first, because as a matter of fact, it correlates well with the scale as a whole, and second, because it is based on hostile imagery, suppressive attitudes, and the assumption that anti-

TABLE 3 (III)
ANTI-SEMITISM SUBSCALE "ATTITUDES"

I-3. In order to maintain a nice residential neighborhood it is best to prevent Jews from living in it.

I-6. Colleges should adopt a quota system by which they limit the number of Jews in fields which have too many Jews now.

I-9. A step toward solving the Jewish problem would be to prevent Jews from getting into superior, profitable positions in society, for a while at least.

I-12. The Jewish problem is so general and deep that one often doubts that democratic methods can ever solve it.

I-15. It is wrong for Jews and Gentiles to intermarry.

I-18. It is best that Jews should have their own fraternities and sororities, since they have their own particular interests and activities which they can best engage in together, just as Christians get along best in all-Christian fraternities.

I-21. It is sometimes all right to ban Jews from certain apartment houses.

I-24. Anyone who employs many people should be careful not to hire a large percentage of Jews.

II-3. It would hurt the business of a large concern if it had too many Jewish employees.

II-6. The best way to eliminate the Communist menace in this country is to control the Jewish element which guides it.

II-9. In order to handle the Jewish problem, Gentiles must meet fire with fire and use the same ruthless tactics with the Jews that the Jews use with the Gentiles.

II-12. It is not wise for a Christian to be seen too much with Jews, as he might be taken for a Jew, or be looked down upon by his Christian friends.

II-15. One of the first steps to be taken in cleaning up the movies and generally improving the situation in Hollywood is to put an end to Jewish domination there.

II-18. Most hotels should deny admittance to Jews, as a general rule.

II-21. Jewish leaders should encourage Jews to be more inconspicuous, to keep out of professions and activities already overcrowded with Jews, and to keep out of the public notice.

II-24. It would be to the best interests of all if the Jews would form their own nation and keep more to themselves.

Semitism is merely a rational reaction of Gentiles to the intrinsic badness of Jews.

d and e. SUBSCALES "SECLUSIVE" (S_S) AND "INTRUSIVE" (S_I). It is often stated that the cause of anti-Semitism lies in the fact that "Jews are different," and it has often been suggested that assimilation is the only solution to "the Jewish problem." Indeed, many Jews have taken the same point of view, attempting in every way possible to take over the prevalent culture of their local American community, and becoming anxious over all signs of "foreign Jewishness" in their family and friends. This is not the place to discuss the problem of the adjustment of Jews and other minorities to American culture. The question raised here concerns instead the psychology of anti-Semites: Is Jewish assimilation what they really want? If Jews behaved in a thoroughly conforming manner, would this satisfy the anti-Semites? One indication that these questions will receive negative answers lies in the fact that highly assimilated Jews usually meet the same sort of discrimination that others do. Another sign in the same direction is the stereotypy so common in anti-Semitism. To the extent that a person is reacting to his self-created label or image of "the Jew" rather than to the *particular Jewish individual* with whom he is dealing, it matters but little what the Jew in question is like. The sign "no Jews wanted" is entirely insensitive to the virtues or faults of the specific individual applying for a job.

TABLE 4 (III)
ANTI-SEMITISM SUBSCALES "SECLUSIVE *vs.* INTRUSIVE"
A. *"Seclusive"*

I-5. One trouble with Jewish businessmen is that they stick together and connive, so that a Gentile doesn't have a fair chance in competition.

I-17. Much resentment against Jews stems from their tending to keep apart and to exclude Gentiles from Jewish social life.

I-20. The Jews should give up their un-Christian religion with all its strange customs (kosher diet, special holidays, etc.) and participate actively and sincerely in the Christian religion.

I-23. Jews tend to remain a foreign element in American society, to preserve their old social standards and to resist the American way of life.

II-13. One general fault of Jews is their overaggressiveness, a strong tendency always to display their Jewish looks, manners, and breeding.

II-17. The Jewish districts in most cities are results of the clannishness and stick-togetherness of Jews.

II-20. Jewish millionaires may do a certain amount to help their own people, but little of their money goes into worthwhile American causes.

II-23. The Jews keep too much to themselves, instead of taking the proper interest in community problems and good government.

B. *"Intrusive"*

I-11. There are too many Jews in the various federal agencies and bureaus in Washington, and they have too much control over our national policies.

I-16. The Jews should not pry so much into Christian activities and organizations nor seek so much recognition and prestige from Christians.

I-19. One thing that has hindered the Jews in establishing their own nation is the fact that they really have no culture of their own; instead, they tend to copy the things that are important to the native citizens of whatever country they are in.

I-25. Jews go too far in hiding their Jewishness, especially such extremes as changing their names, straightening noses, and imitating Christian manners and customs.

II-3. It would hurt the business of a large concern if it had too many Jewish employees.

II-7. The trouble with letting Jews into a nice neighborhood is that they gradually give it a typical Jewish atmosphere.

II-19. The true Christian can never forgive the Jews for their crucifixion of Christ.

II-25. When Jews create large funds for educational or scientific research (Rosenwald, Heller, etc.), it is mainly due to a desire for fame and public notice rather than a really sincere scientific interest.

In an attempt to quantify attitudes regarding assimilation, two subscales representing opposing sides on this issue were included in the A-S scale (Table 4(III)). Subscale "Seclusive" (S_S) takes the stand that Jews are too foreign and unassimilated; it accuses them of being clannish, of keeping apart, and of not being sufficiently concerned with other groups and other ways. The implication of these items is that Jews ought to assimilate more, that they could solve the problem of anti-Semitism themselves by entering more actively into American life and by conforming more closely with American conventions and standards. (Two of these items were also included in other subscales, Item I–5 being also in S_T, and II–13 in S_O).

Subscale "Intrusive" (S_I), on the other hand, accuses the Jews of over-assimilation and overparticipation. When Jews seem to be conforming in social behavior they are actually just "imitating" and "hiding their Jewishness" (Item I–25). Their attempts to join organizations are based on prestige-seeking and the desire to pry (Item I–16). Their admission into the government or into neighborhoods only leads to attempts by them at control and domination of non-Jews (Items I–11, II–7). Their seeming philanthropy is based on selfish motives (Item II–25). And finally, they lack a culture of their own and must therefore copy or "sponge on" the culture of the country in which they live (Item I–19). The implication of these items, in direct contrast to those in the "Seclusive" subscale, is that Jews ought to keep more to themselves and to develop a culture, preferably even a nation, of their own. (Four of these items were also included in other subscales, Item I–11 being also in S_T, I–16 and II–7 in S_O, and II–3 in S_A.)

f. "NEUTRAL" ITEMS NOT IN A SUBSCALE (TABLE 5(III)). Four items in the A-S scale were not included in any of the five subscales. This illustrates

TABLE 5 (III)

"NEUTRAL" ITEMS IN THE ANTI-SEMITISM SCALE

I-22. One big trouble with Jews is that they are never contented, but always try for the best jobs and the most money.

I-26. There is little doubt that Jewish pressure is largely responsible for the U. S. getting into the war with Germany.

II-22. There is little hope of correcting the racial defects of the Jews, since these defects are simply in their blood.

II-26. On the whole, the Jews have probably contributed less to American life than any other group.

the fact that the subscales represent "components" of anti-Semitism only in a general prestatistical sense. A correlational analysis of the scale would very probably indicate components containing these four items, since they deal with significant aspects of anti-Semitic ideology and since they correlate well with the total scale.

Item II–22 is worth noting in particular; it takes a hereditarian-racist stand concerning the "defects" of the Jews and, like all hereditarian approaches, is pessimistic regarding improvement of group relations along democratic lines. To the person who feels that Jews have special and basic faults which cannot be changed, all talk about ending discrimination, about improving Jewish-Gentile relations, and about "what Jews can do to help themselves" is meaningless and irrelevant. The fact that many people who take this "Jewish immutability" viewpoint also tend to tell the Jews how they must change is another sign of the illogicality of anti-Semitism. This idea of the insolubility of the problem is also expressed in Items I–7 and I–12.

3. THE TOTAL ANTI-SEMITISM (A-S) SCALE

The total anti-Semitism scale consists of fifty-two items and comprises all the items in the five subscales as well as the four neutral items discussed above. Both parts of the scale are present in Table 6(III), with instructions to subjects, just as it was administered.

TABLE 6 (III)
The Total Anti-semitism Scale
Public Opinion Questionnaire A

This is an investigation of general public opinion concerning Jewish people. The following are statements with which some people agree and others disagree. Please mark each one in the left margin, according to the amount of your agreement or disagreement, by using the following scale:

+1: slight support, agreement   −1: slight opposition, disagreement
+2: moderate support,   "   −2: moderate opposition,   "
+3: strong support,   "   −3: strong opposition,   "

_____ 1. Jews seem to prefer the most luxurious, extravagant, and sensual way of living.

_____ 2. The Jews must be considered a bad influence on Christian culture and civilization.

_____ 3. In order to maintain a nice residential neighborhood it is best to prevent Jews from living in it.

_____ 4. A major fault of the Jews is their conceit, overbearing pride, and their idea that they are a chosen race.

_____ 5. One trouble with Jewish businessmen is that they stick together and connive, so that a Gentile doesn't have a fair chance in competition.

_____ 6. Colleges should adopt a quota system by which they limit the number of Jews in fields which have too many Jews now.

_____ 7. No matter how Americanized a Jew may seem to be, there is always something basically Jewish underneath, a loyalty to Jewry and a manner that is never totally changed.

_____ 8. Jewish power and control in money matters is far out of proportion to the number of Jews in the total population.

_____ 9. A step toward solving the Jewish problem would be to prevent Jews from getting into superior, profitable positions in society, for a while at least.

_____ 10. Districts containing many Jews always seem to be smelly, dirty, shabby, and unattractive.

_____ 11. There are too many Jews in the various federal agencies and bureaus in Washington, and they have too much control over our national policies.

_____12. The Jewish problem is so general and deep that one often doubts that democratic methods can ever solve it.

_____13. There are a few exceptions, but in general Jews are pretty much alike.

_____14. Jews tend to lower the general standard of living by their willingness to do the most menial work and to live under standards that are far below average.

_____15. It is wrong for Jews and Gentiles to intermarry.

_____16. The Jews should not pry so much into Christian activities and organizations nor seek so much recognition and prestige from Christians.

_____17. Much resentment against Jews stems from their tending to keep apart and to exclude Gentiles from Jewish social life.

_____18. It is best that Jews should have their own fraternities and sororities, since they have their own particular interests and activities which they can best engage in together, just as Christians get along best in all-Christian fraternities.

_____19. One thing that has hindered the Jews from establishing their own nation is the fact that they really have no culture of their own; instead, they tend to copy the things that are important to the native citizens of whatever country they are in.

_____20. The Jews should give up their un-Christian religion with all its strange customs (kosher diet, special holidays, etc.) and participate actively and sincerely in the Christian religion.

_____21. It is sometimes all right to ban Jews from certain apartment houses.

_____22. One big trouble with Jews is that they are never contented, but always try for the best jobs and the most money.

_____23. Jews tend to remain a foreign element in American society, to preserve their old social standards and to resist the American way of life.

_____24. Anyone who employs many people should be careful not to hire a large percentage of Jews.

_____25. Jews go too far in hiding their Jewishness, especially such extremes as changing their names, straightening noses, and imitating Christian manners and customs.

_____26. There is little doubt that Jewish pressure is largely responsible for the U. S. getting into the war with Germany.

THE TOTAL ANTI-SEMITISM SCALE
Public Opinion Questionnaire S

This is an investigation of general public opinion concerning Jewish people. The following are statements with which some people agree and others disagree. Please mark each one in the left margin, according to the amount of your agreement or disagreement, by using the following scale:

+1: slight support, agreement   −1: slight opposition, disagreement
+2: moderate support, "   −2: moderate opposition, "
+3: strong support, "   −3. strong opposition, "

_____ 1. The Jews should make sincere efforts to rid themselves of their conspicuous and irritating faults, if they really want to stop being persecuted.

_____ 2. War shows up the fact that the Jews are not patriotic or willing to make sacrifices for their country.

_____ 3. It would hurt the business of a large concern if it had too many Jewish employees.

_____ 4. There is something different and strange about Jews; one never knows what they are thinking or planning, nor what makes them tick.

_____ 5. Jews may have moral standards that they apply in their dealings with each other, but with Christians they are unscrupulous, ruthless, and undependable.

_____ 6. The best way to eliminate the Communist menace in this country is to control the Jewish element which guides it.

_____ 7. The trouble with letting Jews into a nice neighborhood is that they gradually give it a typical Jewish atmosphere.

_____ 8. The Jew's first loyalty is to Jewry rather than to his country.

_____ 9. In order to handle the Jewish problem, Gentiles must meet fire with fire and use the same ruthless tactics with the Jews that the Jews use with the Gentiles.

_____ 10. I can hardly imagine myself marrying a Jew.

_____ 11. Jews seem to have an aversion to plain hard work; they tend to be a parasitic element in society by finding easy, nonproductive jobs.

_____ 12. It is not wise for a Christian to be seen too much with Jews, as he might be taken for a Jew, or be looked down upon by his Christian friends.

_____ 13. One general fault of Jews is their overaggressiveness, a strong tendency always to display their Jewish looks, manners, and breeding.

_____ 14. There seems to be some revolutionary streak in the Jewish make-up as shown by the fact that there are so many Jewish Communists and agitators.

_____ 15. One of the first steps to be taken in cleaning up the movies and generally improving the situation in Hollywood is to put an end to Jewish domination there.

_____ 16. Jews should be more concerned with their personal appearance, and not be so dirty and smelly and unkempt.

_____ 17. The Jewish districts in most cities are results of the clannishness and stick-togetherness of Jews.

_____ 18. Most hotels should deny admittance to Jews, as a general rule.

_____ 19. The true Christian can never forgive the Jews for their crucifixion of Christ.

_____ 20. Jewish millionaires may do a certain amount to help their own people, but little of their money goes into worthwhile American causes.

_____ 21. Jewish leaders should encourage Jews to be more inconspicuous, to keep out of professions and activities already overcrowded with Jews, and to keep out of the public notice.

_____ 22. There is little hope of correcting the racial defects of the Jews, since these defects are simply in their blood.

_____ 23. The Jews keep too much to themselves, instead of taking the proper interest in community problems and good government.

_____ 24. It would be to the best interests of all if the Jews would form their own nation and keep more to themselves.

_____ 25. When Jews create large funds for educational or scientific research (Rosenwald, Heller, etc.) it is mainly due to a desire for fame and public notice rather than a really sincere scientific interest.

_____ 26. On the whole, the Jews have probably contributed less to American life than any other group.

The scale is intended to measure the individual's readiness to support or oppose anti-Semitic ideology as a whole. This ideology consists, according to the conception on which the scale was based, of *stereotyped negative opinions describing the Jews as threatening, immoral, and categorically different from non-Jews, and of hostile attitudes urging various forms of restriction, exclusion, and suppression as a means of solving "the Jewish problem."* Anti-Semitism is conceived, then, as a general way of thinking about Jews and Jewish-Gentile relations.

Can one legitimately speak of a readiness in the individual to accept anti-Semitic ideology *as a whole?* More concretely, can it be expected that people will respond relatively consistently to such varied scale items? These are questions which must be answered empirically. The content and generality of anti-Semitic ideology, and the adequacy with which it is measured by the present scale are indicated below by a statistical analysis of scale results. The validity of the scale will be indicated by correlations of the scale with measures of other, theoretically related, variables, and by analysis of the responses of the two subjects discussed in Chapter II.

C. RESULTS: STATISTICAL ANALYSIS OF THE SCALE

The procedure used for all scales in the present research was to allow six choices of response for each item: slight, moderate, or strong agreement, and the same degrees of disagreement, with no middle or neutral category. Each subject indicated the degree of his agreement by marking $+1$, $+2$, or $+3$, disagreement by -1, -2, or -3.

It seemed likely that three degrees of agreement or disagreement could easily be distinguished by the subjects, and that three degrees gave them the best chance to record clearly felt differences in strength of agreement or disagreement. Certainly the data indicate that all six response categories were used. The "don't know" category has been a source of difficulty and controversy in many fields of psychological research (121). In techniques which permit its use, it tends to be the most frequent choice. Without it, the subject must take a stand one way or the other, although the categories of slight agreement and slight disagreement permit him to be nearly neutral. If a subject is unable to decide, he can, of course, omit the item; but there were never more than 2 to 3 per cent omissions among subjects taking the questionnaire, and never more than 1 per cent of the group to which it was administered failed to fill it out adequately. Furthermore, the frequency with which the "moderate" and "strong" categories were used indicates that the items were relatively unambiguous.

The *responses* were converted into *scores* by a uniform scoring system. Since higher scores were intended to express increasing anti-Semitism, all responses were scored as follows:

$$-3 = 1 \text{ point} \qquad +1 = 5 \text{ points}$$
$$-2 = 2 \text{ points} \qquad +2 = 6 \text{ points}$$
$$-1 = 3 \text{ points} \qquad +3 = 7 \text{ points}$$

It will be noted that the scoring skips from 3 to 5 points between -1 and $+1$. Four points represented the hypothetical neutral response, and was assigned when the item was omitted. It probably makes little difference statistically that this scheme was used rather than a six-point one in which $+1$ would receive 4 points. This scheme was used mainly because there seemed to be a greater psychological gap between -1 and $+1$ responses than between any other two adjacent responses. It was also convenient in marking the omissions.

A person's scale score is simply the sum of his scores on the single items. For the 52 items the scores can range between 52 points (1 point on each item, indicating strong opposition to anti-Semitism) and 364 points (7 points on each item, strong anti-Semitism). When the scale score is divided by 52 we obtain the mean score per item; thus, a total score of 78 can also be stated as a score per item of 1.5.

The initial results obtained with the A-S scale have been published elsewhere (71). The present discussion will deal with the second administration of the scale; on this occasion the questionnaire administered contained, in addition to the A-S scale, most of the other techniques which were used in subsequent stages of the research. The questionnaire was administered in April, 1944, to a class in Introductory Psychology at the University of California. It was given as a routine class activity in two parts, separated by an interval of one week; Part I (Questionnaire A) of the A-S scale was given in the first session, Part II (Questionnaire S) in the second. The class was designed for nonmajors in psychology and was rather heterogeneous with respect to major subject and year in school.

In view of a possible sex difference, the questionnaires of men and women were separated for statistical purposes. Due to wartime conditions, however, there were fewer than thirty men in the group, so that no statistics on men were computed. The data presented here are based on the questionnaires of the 144 women subjects, including nineteen members of major minorities: Jews, Negroes, Chinese, and foreign-born. In all subsequent groups the statistical analysis was limited to the questionnaires of native-born, white, non-Jewish Americans.

1. RELIABILITY

The reliability and related statistical properties of the A-S scale and its subscales are presented in Table 7(III). The total-scale reliability of .92 meets rigorous statistical standards, especially in view of the fact that Part II was administered a week after Part I. (The reliability of the scale on the

TABLE 7 (III)

RELIABILITY OF THE ANTI-SEMITISM SCALE AND ITS SUBSCALES

Property	Total Scale	Part I	Part II	Subscale[a]				
				S_O	S_T	S_A	S_S	S_I
Reliability[b]	.92	.94	.91	.84	.89	.89	.71	.84
Number of items	52	26	26	12	10	16	8	8
Mean (total)[c]	2.70	2.74	2.66	3.08	2.59	2.47	3.28	2.55
Mean (odd half)	2.74	2.94	2.86	3.52	2.84	2.48	3.00	2.60
Mean (even half)	2.66	2.54	2.46	2.65	2.34	2.46	3.55	2.50
S.D. (total)[c]	1.11	1.21	1.12	1.33	1.23	1.18	1.26	1.24
S.D. (odd half)	1.21	1.31	1.19	1.55	1.34	1.21	1.35	1.30
S.D. (even half)	1.12	1.15	1.15	1.30	1.32	1.25	1.45	1.35
Range[c]	1.0-5.5	1.0-5.7	1.0-5.8	1.0-6.5	1.0-5.7	1.0-5.8	1.0-6.3	1.0-5.9

[a] The subscales are abbreviated as follows: subscale "Offensive" (S_O), "Threatening" (S_T), "Attitudes" (S_A), "Seclusive" (S_S), "Intrusive" (S_I).

[b] The reliability of the total scale was obtained by correlating scores on Part I (the half administered first) with scores on Part II (in second half of questionnaire). All other reliabilities are based on correlations between the odd items and the even items. The correlations were corrected by the Spearman-Brown formula to give the reliability values in the table.

[c] The values of the means, S.D.'s and ranges are given in terms of mean score per item. If multiplied by the number of items in the scale or subscale in question, they are converted into values representing mean per total scale or subscale.

first group studied, as previously published, was .98.) The two parts were equated in terms of the subscales, so that an equal number of items from each subscale appeared in each part. Parts I and II are also roughly equivalent in terms of mean and standard deviation. In view of the high correlation between Parts I and II, as well as their equivalence and their high reliabilities (.94 and .91), it would appear that either of them alone provides as good a quantitative measure as does the total scale.

It will be noted that the over-all mean is relatively low (140.2 as compared with a theoretical neutral point of 208) and that the obtained range includes extremely low scores but does not include the highest possible scores. The item analysis, as will be seen below, suggests the reason for this: despite our attempt to limit the scale to pseudodemocratic statements numerous items were still too openly or crudely prejudiced and had extremely low means (below 3.0). The present group of students was, however, less anti-Semitic on the average than the one studied earlier, the latter having a mean of 158 and a range of 52–303. The distribution of scores in both cases was fairly symmetrical but platykurtic, with very little clustering of scores around the mean.

The reliabilities of the total scale and of the two parts are almost matched by the high reliabilities of the subscales. Reliabilities of .8 to .9 are very satisfactory even for scales three or four times their length.

With regard to reliability, equivalence of halves, and form of distribution, then, it seems safe to conclude that the A-S scale (as well as the subscales) provides an adequate measuring instrument. It ranks the subjects with a relatively small error of measurement along a continuum or dimension. That this dimension may be called general anti-Semitism must still be demonstrated by the data on item analysis and validity which follow. No claim is made that the dimension is "pure" or homogeneous. To the extent that the scale is valid, it provides a measure of anti-Semitism in most of its generality and complexity. More specifically, it may be claimed that the higher an individual's score, the greater his acceptance of anti-Semitic propaganda and the greater his disposition to engage in anti-Semitic accusations and programs of one form or another.

2. INTERCORRELATIONS OF THE SUBSCALES

The above reliability data indicate that people are relatively consistent in their responses to the A-S scale and to the individual subscales dealing with relatively specific kinds of imagery and attitudes. Correlations among the subscales are shown in Table 8(III).

Intercorrelations of .74 to .85 are of considerable significance. The fact that they involve subscales dealing with so great a variety of opinions and attitudes is an important source of support for the hypothesis that anti-

TABLE 8 (III)

INTERCORRELATIONS[a] OF THE A-S SUBSCALES

Subscale	"Threatening"	"Attitudes"	"Seclusive"	Total A-S
"Offensive"	.85	.83	.75	92
"Threatening"		.84		.93
"Attitudes"			.74	.94
"Intrusive"			.74	

[a]These are the raw correlation coefficients. If they were corrected for attenuation to give the maximal value theoretically obtainable (with perfectly reliable instruments), they would all be well over .90.

Semitism is a general frame of mind, a way of viewing Jews and Jewish-Gentile interaction. Imagery of Jews as personally offensive and as socially threatening, attitudes of restriction, exclusion and the like, the view that Jews are too assimilative and yet too clannish—these seem to be various facets of a broad ideological pattern. An individual's stand with regard to one of these issues tends to be very similar in direction and degree to his stand with regard to the others.

The correlations of .92 to .94 between each of the three major subscales and the total anti-Semitism scale are high enough so that knowing an individual's score on any one subscale permits one to predict with considerable accuracy his score on the total A-S scale. In short, while almost every subject varies somewhat in his responses to the individual items (as will be shown below), almost every subject demonstrates a general degree of support or rejection of anti-Semitism which is relatively consistent from one type of accusation or attitude to another. This is not to say that all the ideas contained in the scale are of equal importance emotionally to each anti-Semite. It is more probable—and this view is supported by the interviews—that for each high scorer there are a few central opinions (imagery of Jews as cunning, power-seeking, sensual, etc.) and attitudes of primary importance; but these "pet" ideas seem to provide a basis or general readiness for the acceptance of almost any anti-Semitic idea. The fact that this generality is not complete suggests that various patterns of anti-Semitic ideology may exist and might profitably be studied (as variations within the general framework described here).

The correlation of .74 between subscales "Seclusive" and "Intrusive" reveals a deep contradiction in anti-Semitic ideology. As a matter of simple logic, it is impossible for most Jews to be both extremely seclusive and aloof and at the same time too intrusive and prying. This categorical, self-contradictory rejection of an entire group is, however, more than a matter of faulty logic. Viewed psychologically, these results suggest a deep-lying ir-rational hostility directed against a stereotyped image to which individual Jews correspond only partially if at all.

The illogical manner in which the hostility operates is illustrated by a comparison of related items from these two subscales. Thus, "Seclusive" Item II–20 states that rich Jews help "their own people" but not "American causes." However, "Intrusive" Item II–25 takes care of any exceptions: Jews donate money not out of generosity but rather out of desire for prestige and fame. Similarly, either Jews do not take enough interest in community and government (Seclusive), or when they do, they have too much control over national politics (Intrusive). Anti-Semitic hostility leads, then, either to a denial of demonstrable facts (Jewish philanthropy, smallness of number, etc.) or to an interpretation of them which finds the Jews at fault.

The same self-contradictions and the same implications are evident in the high correlation (.74) between subscales "Seclusive" and "Attitudes." It is indeed paradoxical to accuse the Jews of being clannish and aloof, and at the same time to urge that they be segregated and restricted. It would seem, then, that a general hostility and readiness to accept negative imagery are an essential part of the psychological functioning of anti-Semitic individ-uals, who can regard a great variety of specific accusations, often mutually contradictory, as valid.

The reliabilities and subscale intercorrelations, taken together, permit several conclusions regarding the nature and inner sources of anti-Semitism. It is a general way of thinking in which hostile attitudes and negative opinions toward Jews predominate. Several patterns of imagery brought out by the subscales seem to be partial facets of a single broad ideological framework. While these ideas are relatively common today, it would appear that those individuals (the high scorers) who take them over most easily are different in their psychological functioning from those who do not. One major char-acteristic of anti-Semites is a relatively blind hostility which is reflected in the stereotypy, self-contradiction, and destructiveness of their thinking about Jews.

3. INTERNAL CONSISTENCY: STATISTICAL ANALYSIS OF THE INDIVIDUAL ITEMS

A critical reader of the A-S scale may feel that certain items are unsatis-factory in one way or another: that they do not measure what the others measure, that everyone agrees with the ideas expressed, that certain items are too ridiculous to be supported by anyone, and so on. He may like a few items particularly and wonder how successful they were. Or he may be con-cerned with shortening and improving the scale and want a statistical basis for item selection and improvement. For these and other reasons a statistical analysis of the items has considerable value.

The problem can be posed in statistical terms as follows. If an item is good, in terms of the total scale, then item scores ought to correlate well with total scale scores. Since few high scorers agree with all items, and since some low scorers agree with several items, a statistical technique is necessary to determine the closeness of the relationship between item score and scale score. The most extensive technique for item analysis is the computing of *correlations* between item scores and scale scores, especially if some sort of factor analysis is planned. The Likert "Discriminatory Power" technique, although statistically more limited, has a great time-saving advantage. Furthermore, Murphy and Likert (84), obtaining both Discriminatory Powers and item-total scale correlations for a single scale, found a correlation of .91 between these two measures of item value. In other words, the order of goodness of the items, as determined by the Discriminatory Power technique, is practically the same as the order determined by the correlation technique. The Likert technique was therefore used in the present study.

The Discriminatory Power (D. P.) of each item is obtained by the following procedure. Subjects whose total scores fall in the highest 25 per cent of the distribution are considered high scorers, while those whose scores fall in the lowest 25 per cent of the distribution are considered the low scorers.

The mean of the high scorers is obtained for each item and found to vary from item to item. Similarly for the low scorers. If an item measures anti-Semitism well, then anti-Semites (high scorers), as determined by the total scale score, will make higher scores on it than will those who are opposed to anti-Semitism (low scorers). The greater the difference between the item mean for the high scorers and that for the low scorers, the greater the Discriminatory Power of that item, and the better the measure of anti-Semitism it gives. A positive D. P. indicates that the item is anti-Semitic, in the sense that anti-Semites as determined by the total scale agree with the item to a greater degree than do unprejudiced subjects. If an item has a negative D. P., it has apparently been scored in reverse, since low scorers agree with it more than high scorers do. All items in the present scale have positive D. P.'s.

The data on the item analysis of the A-S scale are presented in Table 9 (III). Each item is identified by a key phrase, and the letters O, T, A, S, and I refer to the subscales Offensive, Threatening, Attitudes, Seclusive, and Intrusive respectively.

The most important data on each item are the group mean and the D. P. The group mean reflects the general group tendency toward agreement or disagreement. A mean near 4.0 indicates that the group was pretty evenly divided pro and con on the issue. Group means between 3.0 and 5.0 are likely to involve scores covering well the entire range from 1 to 7. Means below 3.0 indicate a strong group tendency toward disagreement,

TABLE 9 (III)

ANTI—SEMITISM SCALE: ITEM MEANS AND DISCRIMINATORY POWERS
UNIVERSITY OF CALIFORNIA WOMEN

Part I

No.	Item	Mean H.Q.	Mean L.Q.	D.P.	Mean for Total Group
1.	(O: luxurious)	4.44	2.03	2.41	3.11
2.	(T: bad influence)	2.75	1.11	1.64	1.85
3.	(A: keep Jews out)	4.25	1.03	3.22	2.30
4.	(O: conceit)	4.50	1.30	3.20	2.71
5.	(S,T: businessmen)	5.86	1.38	4.48	3.45
6.	(A: quota)	2.89	1.00	1.89	1.67
7.	(O: basically Jewish)	5.78	1.99	3.79	3.59
8.	(T: power and control)	5.33	2.30	3.03	3.80
9.	(A: suppress Jews)	3.61	1.05	2.56	1.84
10.	(O: dirty districts)	2.94	1.24	1.70	1.98
11.	(I,T: Washington)	4.55	1.24	3.31	2.56
12.	(A: democratic methods)	4.75	1.13	3.62	2.76
13.	(O: all alike)	5.50	1.67	3.83	3.64
14.	(T: low living standards)	3.00	1.24	1.76	2.05
15.	(A: wrong to intermarry)	4.19	1.19	3.00	2.57
16.	(I,O: prying)	3.89	1.03	2.86	2.24
17.	(S: Jews exclude Gentiles)	4.22	2.11	2.11	3.53
18.	(A: fraternities)	5.89	2.13	3.76	3.84
19.	(I: no culture)	4.86	1.73	3.13	3.19
20.	(S: give up religion)	3.03	1.30	1.73	2.66
21.	(A: apartment houses)	4.47	1.30	3.17	2.52
22.	(N: never contented)	5.42	1.22	4.20	3.17
23.	(S: foreign element)	4.28	1.38	2.90	2.88
24.	(A: don't hire Jews)	5.30	1.19	4.11	2.84
25.	(I: hide Jewishness)	4.33	1.62	2.71	2.87
26.	(N: war with Germany)	2.86	1.05	1.81	1.69
	Mean:	4.34	1.42	2.92	2.74

ANTI-SEMITISM SCALE: ITEM MEANS AND DISCRIMINATORY POWERS
UNIVERSITY OF CALIFORNIA WOMEN

Part II

No.	Item	Mean H.Q.	Mean L.Q.	D.P.	Mean for Total Group
1.	(O: own fault)	5.89	2.51	3.38	4.31
2.	(T: unpatriotic)	2.97	1.05	1.92	1.75
3.	(I,A: too many employees)	4.89	1.30	3.59	2.95
4.	(O: different and strange)	4.17	1.19	2.98	2.23
5.	(T: unscrupulous)	4.47	1.16	3.31	2.45
6.	(A: Communists)	3.39	1.05	2.34	2.08
7.	(I,O: typical atmosphere)	5.28	1.32	3.96	3.23
8.	(T: first loyalty)	5.05	1.81	3.24	3.10
9.	(A: Gentiles ruthless)	3.22	1.00	2.22	1.84
10.	(O: marry a Jew)	6.58	2.30	4.28	4.22
11.	(T: parasitic)	4.36	1.27	3.09	2.19
12.	(A: avoid Jews)	3.89	1.13	2.76	2.09
13.	(S,O: overaggression)	4.97	1.73	3.24	3.44
14.	(T: revolutionary)	4.28	1.35	2.93	2.69
15.	(A: Hollywood)	3.94	1.13	2.81	2.47
16.	(O: dirty)	3.78	1.24	2.54	2.30
17.	(S: clannish)	5.78	2.32	3.46	4.57
18.	(A: hotels)	2.22	1.05	1.17	1.46
19.	(I: crucifixion)	2.69	1.08	1.61	1.66
20.	(S: millionnaires)	3.97	1.32	2.65	2.44
21.	(A: Jewish leaders)	4.64	1.62	3.02	3.07
22.	(N: racial defects)	3.86	1.08	2.78	2.40
23.	(S: Jews keep apart)	4.03	1.94	2.09	3.21
24.	(A: form own nation)	4.78	1.70	3.08	3.23
25.	(I: Rosenwald)	2.89	1.16	1.73	1.74
26.	(N: contributed least)	2.89	1.19	1.70	1.97
	Mean:	4.19	1.42	2.77	2.66
	Means for total scale:	4.27	1.42	2.85	2.70

Number: Total group = 144; H.Q. = 36; L.Q. = 37.
Range of total scores: Total group: 52–286; H.Q.: 183–286; L.Q.: 52–89.

with few scores of 6 or 7 (+2 and +3 responses). And group means of over 5.0, conversely, indicate relatively uniform agreement.

The Discriminatory Power, on the other hand, is a measure of the variability of the high and low scorers around the group mean, and of their average difference in response. How large must a D. P. be in order to indicate almost no overlap between highs and lows? This depends on the form of the distribution and the size of the group mean. An item with a group mean of 2.0, a low quartile mean of 1.0, a high quartile mean of 3.0, and a D. P. of 2.0, is undoubtedly very discriminating; the low scorers responded unanimously with —3, and the high scorers probably varied but little around the —1 response. In general, the more extreme the group mean (especially below 3.0 or above 5.0) the lower the D. P. can be and still adequately separate the low from the high scorers. From a broader point of view, however, the best items should have means nearer to 4.0; when the item mean is above 5.0 or below 3.0, the item should be reworded so that fewer people or more people, respectively, will agree.[2]

For items with group means in the approximate range 3.0 to 5.0, Discriminatory Powers may be evaluated according to the following general standards: a D. P. of over 4.0 is very high and indicates almost uniform agreement by the high scorers, disagreement by the low scorers, with almost no overlap. D. P.'s of 3.0–4.0 are very satisfactory and indicate a clear-cut difference between high and low scorers. D. P.'s of 2.0–3.0, while statistically significant, indicate greater variability in the responses of low and high scorers and a fair amount of overlap. A D. P. between 1.0 and 2.0 involves considerable agreement by the low scorers and disagreement by the high scorers, but it still indicates a statistically significant difference between the low mean and the high mean.[3] As the D. P. decreases below 1.0, the possibility of significance decreases rapidly.

With these considerations in mind we can examine the data in Table 9. In general the Discriminatory Powers are quite satisfactory, averaging 2.85 for the entire group.[4] For the 52 items, 5 D. P.'s are over 4.0, 21 are between

[2] A minimum item mean of 2.5 ought probably to be set for this group, since various studies have shown college students to be less prejudiced than the general population. For other groups studied in the present research, many item means were as much as a point higher.

[3] While standard deviations have not been obtained for all items, it can be shown that (with group N = 100 to 150) the standard error of the difference between the means for low and high scorers is almost never above .50, seldom below .25. In terms of the critical ratio, then, a D.P. of over 1.0 is statistically significant, that is, the means are different though the distributions are partially overlapping.

[4] While correlations between items or between each item and the total scale have not been computed for this group, later data on similar scales suggest that the average inter-item correlation is about .4, while between each item and the sum of the remaining items the average correlation is about .6. (See Chapter IV.)

3.0 and 3.9, and 15 are between 2.0 and 2.9. Only 11 D. P.'s are between 1.0 and 1.9, the lowest being 1.2.

All of the D. P.'s are therefore above a minimum standard of acceptability. The 26 items with D. P.'s of over 3.0 are statistically very satisfactory. Why were the other items less adequate? The answer is indicated by the group means on these items. Of the 11 items with D. P.'s of less than 2.0, 10 have means below 2.1. Conversely, almost all of the items with means of over 3.0 have D. P.'s of over 3.0. The mean for the low quartile is very low (below 2.0) on almost every item. The mean of the high quartile, on the other hand, varies greatly from item to item. *The items with low D. P.'s were, in almost every case, statements with which the high quartile tended predominantly to disagree.* This result seems to be due partly to a lack of pseudodemocratic coloring in these items, partly to their obvious illogicality or lack of truth, and partly to a lack of extreme anti-Semites among these subjects. Thus, the mean of the high quartile on all 52 items averages 4.3 and varies from 2.2 to 6.6. For the 10 items with the highest D. P.'s, however, the high quartile means average well over 5.0.

The dependability of the item means and D. P.'s is indicated by a comparison of the present group with the group of college students previously tested and reported on. The latter group responded to the entire scale (and other questionnaire material) at one sitting; the reliability was .98 and the subscale intercorrelations were also slightly higher than in the present group. The group mean per item was 3.0 as compared with 2.7 for the present group, and the average D. P. was 3.4 as compared with 2.85 here. The main difference between the two groups seems to lie in the greater number of high scorers in the first group tested. The over-all mean of the low quartile was almost identical for the two groups: 1.39 then, 1.42 now. But the high quartile averaged 4.80 then as compared to 4.27 now. In noncollege groups a larger number of high scorers, and larger D. P.'s, have been found (see pp. 76, 140). Despite the over-all scale differences between the two groups, however, the adequacy of the individual items was very similar. Thus, the rank-order correlation between the D. P.'s was .78, while the item means correlated .92. In short, the most discriminating items for one group were also the best for the other group, and similarly for the poor items. The general conclusions about item means and discriminabilities to be drawn from the present group, then, are generally true for the previous group as well.

Table 9(III) reveals that the best items pertain to a variety of topics. *Stereotypy* in anti-Semitic imagery is shown in the tendency to overgeneralize Jewish faults, and in the fact that Item I–13 ("Jews are all alike") is one of the most discriminating, with a D. P. of 3.83. The idea of Jews as a *political threat* (radicalism: Items II–6, –14) was much less prevalent than the idea of Jews as an *economic threat* (wealth and power: Items I–5, –8, –22,

II–5, –11) or as a *moral threat* (immorality: Items I–1, II–1, –7, –13). Accusations on *religious* grounds were seldom supported,[5] as shown by the low group means and D. P.'s on Items I–20 and II–19. A variety of *discriminatory attitudes* (exclusion, restriction, suppression: most items in the "Attitude" subscale) found considerable support and were very discriminating.

The importance of careful formulation of items is shown by a comparison of good with poor items. The most discriminating items are usually the most pseudodemocratic ones according to criteria discussed above (Section B, 1). Consider, for example, the two items dealing with intermarriage. Item II–10 ("I can hardly imagine myself marrying a Jew") has a group mean of 4.2 and a D. P. of 4.3, with a high quartile mean of 6.6 (almost all +2 and +3 responses). On the other hand, Item I–15 ("It is wrong for Jews and Gentiles to intermarry") has a group mean of only 2.6, a D. P. of 3.0, and a high quartile mean of 4.2. The higher mean and discriminability of the former item are probably due to its greater indirectness and distance from crude anti-Semitism. By what criterion is this item anti-Semitic? The criterion is the fact that it correlates well with the total scale, that is, it differentiates very well between subjects who score high and subjects who score low on the total scale. (The fact that the correlation is not perfect indicates that response to any single item is not a clear-cut sign of anti-Semitism nor of its opposite; the criterion must be the total scale score).

Similar reasoning applies to items dealing with housing restrictions. The following items had very low group means (1.5 to 2.5): Item II–18 (consistent exclusion from hotels), I–3 (exclusion from neighborhoods), I–21 (occasional exclusion from apartment houses). Item II–7 (Jews give a neighborhood a "typical Jewish atmosphere"), which is more indirect and pseudodemocratic, had a higher mean (3.2) and D. P. (4.0). It would appear that many individuals who are not now willing actively to support anti-Semitic programs have nevertheless a negative imagery and an underlying hostility that constitute a definite potentiality for such action. Even the more open and crude items on housing had significant D. P.'s, and the high quartile means of 4.3 and over (except on II–18), seem to indicate only weak resistance to these ideas.

The same considerations hold for the items dealing with occupations. Items which urge explicit policies of suppression and restriction of Jews (I–6, –9, II–9, –15) tend to have low means. But items which emphasize gen-

---

[5] It is frequently held that Sunday School training is a major cause of anti-Semitism, which is then regarded as a form of "religious prejudice." In this group, at least, rejection on religious grounds was infrequent. From the generality and irrationality of anti-Semitic ideology, it is clear that many diverse accusations are almost always involved, and that there are many sources for the underlying hostility which makes a given individual receptive to anti-Semitism. For a discussion of the role of religion in prejudice see Chapters VI and XVIII.

eralized Jewish faults and which introduce subtly discriminatory practices tend to have higher means; thus, Jewish businessmen are regarded as unfair and conniving (Item I–5), and they have too much financial power (I–8). While active suppression is not so desirable (low mean on I–9), it is unwise for an employer to hire many Jews (higher mean on I–24, II–3). The simplest solution—one that eliminates the need for suppression—would be for Jews to form their own nation (II–24).

The pessimism of the high scorers regarding the solution to this problem is brought out by a number of items. On the one hand, they take the view that anti-Semitism has been entirely or primarily brought by the Jews on themselves and that any solution of the problem is a matter of Jewish responsibility (Items II–1, II–21). Non-Jews are simply the victims of Jewish faults; if Jews would improve, become as good as "other people," anti-Semitism would be eliminated. On the other hand, the Jews seem to be incorrigible, and any apparent change only masks the Jewishness beneath (Items I–7, –13, II–4, –8, –22). The contradiction is therefore complete: anti-Semitism is due to Jewish faults, but the Jews are unable to improve; the Jews should make sincere efforts to change, but their "basic Jewishness" is unchangeable. For the antidemocratic anti-Semite the only answer is open and direct suppression; for the pseudodemocrat it is subtle exclusion and "resigned tolerance" toward a bad state of affairs. The pseudodemocrats seem to betray a sense of threat and some antidemocratic potential by their doubts that democratic methods can solve the problem (Item I–12).

D. THE SHORT FORM OF THE A-S SCALE

It was a regular policy of the present research to contract the proven techniques in order to introduce new ones measuring additional trends of theoretical importance. In line with this policy, and in view of the high reliability and internal consistency of the original 52-item A-S scale, a short form of ten items was used in the first revision of the questionnaire.

The short form is presented in Table 10(III). The ten items were selected from the original fifty-two on the basis of both statistical and theoretical considerations. Since statistical adequacy (Discriminatory Power) was a necessary—but not sufficient—condition for inclusion, the new items were selected from the fifteen or twenty which had been most discriminating on the two administrations of the long form. Among these, selection was determined by the following qualitative considerations. Each item should be as rich in meaning as possible. There should be a minimum of duplication of meaning or content among items. They should cover most of the subscales and most of the areas of accusation and discrimination. These desiderata have not been realized entirely; there were other items that seemed to merit inclusion, and for certain

TABLE 10 (III)
THE TEN-ITEM A-S SCALE (Form 78)

Old No.	New No.[a]	
I-24	11.	Anyone who employs many people should be careful not to hire a large percentage of Jews.
I-5	16.	One trouble with Jewish businessmen is that they stick together and connive, so that a Gentile doesn't have a fair chance in competition.
II-17	21.	The Jewish districts in most cities are results of the clannishness and stick-togetherness of Jews.
II-1	26.	Persecution of the Jews would be largely eliminated if the Jews would make really sincere efforts to rid themselves of their harmful and offensive faults.
II-21	33.	Jewish leaders should encourage Jews to be more inconspicuous, to keep out of professions and activities already overcrowded with Jews and to keep out of the public notice.
II-10	40.	I can hardly imagine myself marrying a Jew.
II-7	49.	The trouble with letting Jews into a nice neighborhood is that they gradually give it a typical Jewish atmosphere.
I-7	62.	No matter how Americanized a Jew may seem to be, there is always something different and strange, something basically Jewish underneath.
I-13	69.	There may be a few exceptions, but, in general, Jews are pretty much alike.
I-11	72.	There are too many Jews in the various federal agencies and bureaus in Washington, and they have too much control over our national policies.

[a] "New number" refers to the numbering of the items in Form 78.
"Old number" refers to numbering in the long form discussed previously. Slight revisions will be noted in the wording of several items.

purposes they would probably be superior. The high internal consistency of the long form indicates that several statistically adequate short forms might be constructed. Nevertheless, the present form was expected to provide an adequate tool for most purposes of measurement. The slight revisions in the wording of some items were intended to make them simpler and clearer in meaning. The manner of presentation of this form was different from that previously used. Whereas previously each scale had been presented "all of a piece," on a page or pages of its own, in this and all successive forms of the questionnaire the various scales were presented interspersed with each other, so that no single scale was particularly prominent or focal, and adjacent items dealt with widely varying topics.[6]

The new questionnaire, identified as Form 78 (on the basis of its having

[6] The other scales in this form, to be discussed in the chapters that follow, deal with general prejudice (Negroes, other minorities, patriotism), with politico-economic liberalism and conservatism, and with potentially antidemocratic personality trends. There were 78 items in all. This form of the questionnaire, like all the other forms, contained in addition other questions dealing with group memberships, personality, and so on.

78 scale items), was administered in the spring of 1945 to the following groups. Two of the groups comprise undergraduate students at the University of California: the full membership, save for absentees, of the introductory Public Speaking class. Here, as in all groups, men and women were separated in the statistical treatment and analysis was limited to native-born, white, non-Jewish Americans. The first two groups, then, are the Public Speaking Women (N = 140) and the Public Speaking Men (N = 52). The third group comprised forty women, the entire feminine membership of an Extension Division class in Psychology at the University of California. Most subjects of this group were in their thirties and late twenties, and hence were somewhat older on the average than those of our college sample. The fourth group, Professional Women (N = 63), is actually a combination of three smaller groups: (a) Twenty-four public health nurses, the entire nursing staff of a nearby health department (the director of this department was generally liberal in his outlook and had tried to select younger nurses with more advanced ideas about public health); (b) public school teachers; and (c) social workers, who were reached through the mails. In the latter two cases, only about 20 per cent of those appealed to sent in their questionnaires, and this sampling technique was not tried again.

The reliability data for the short A-S scale are presented in Table 11(III). Reliabilities of .89–.94 are extremely satisfactory, especially for a 10-item scale, and they are similar to those obtained on the long form.[7] The means of 3.3 to 3.4 for University and Extension Class students are substantially the same as the mean of 3.55 on these ten items for the previous class taking the long form of the scale. However, the mean of 2.6 for the Professional Women is significantly lower than the others (above the 1 per cent level statistically). This difference may be due partly to sampling errors; the teachers and social workers responded voluntarily by mail, and the tendency to cooperate in filling out a questionnaire dealing with prejudice and with personal feelings is probably correlated with lack of prejudice.[8] The slightly greater reliability (.94) of the scale for this group may reflect a greater ideological consistency in older age groups.

The Discriminatory Power method of item analysis was again carried out, and the results are presented in Table 12(III). The average D. P. of 3.68 is very satisfactory and indicates that on most items there were very few low-quartile members who agreed, few high-quartile members who disagreed.

---

[7] The fact that these reliabilities are similar to those obtained on the long form argues against the hypothesis that the high reliability of the latter was due to a "set" for all-negative items.

[8] This hypothesis is supported by questionnaire and clinical material on personality trends (opposition to "prying" and to "being analyzed" in the prejudiced subjects). Also, fewer high-scoring than low-scoring subjects in the groups tested were willing to be interviewed.

TABLE 11 (III)

RELIABILITY OF THE A-S SCALE (FORM 78)

Property[c]	Gr.A[a]	Gr.B[a]	Gr.C[a]	Gr.D[a]	Over-all[b]
Reliability	.89	.93	.90	.94	.92
Mean (total)	3.33	3.36	3.40	2.57	3.16
Mean (odd half)	2.98	3.30	3.20	2.34	2.96
Mean (even half)	3.66	3.42	3.63	2.83	3.38
S.D. (total)	1.43	1.48	1.36	1.37	1.41
S.D. (odd.half)	1.42	1.51	1.38	1.27	1.40
S.D. (even half)	1.62	1.56	1.48	1.58	1.56
Range	1.0-7.0	1.1-6.3	1.2-6.1	1.0-6.2	1.0-7.0

[a]The four groups on which these data are based are: *Group A*, U. C. Public Speaking Class Women (N = 140); *Group B*, U. C. Public Speaking Class Men (N = 52); *Group C*, U. C. Adult Extension Class Women (N = 40); *Group D*, Professional Women (nurses, teachers, social workers, N = 63).

[b]In obtaining the over-all means, the individual group means were not weighted by N.

[c]The values of the means, Standard Deviations, and ranges are given in terms of mean/person/item. If multiplied by 10 (the number of items), they are translated into values representing total scale score per person.

The best items deal with such varied topics as conniving businessmen, Jews being all alike, intermarriage, exclusion from neighborhoods.

How much influence did the form of presentation of the items have on their individual means and D. P.'s? Does it matter whether the items are presented in a solid block, as in the first form, or randomly dispersed through a longer series of extremely varied items, as in Form 78? Evidence bearing on this question was obtained by comparing the results on these ten items for the two types of presentation. The mean for the Psychology Class women on these ten items (first form, excluding the remaining forty-two items) was 3.55, as compared with 3.32 for the Public Speaking Class women, the most comparable group taking Form 78, and the average D. P.'s were 3.76 and 3.68 respectively. The differences are not statistically significant. Furthermore, the rank-order correlations between the individual item means for these two groups was .62, while the D. P.'s correlated .90. These correlations seem even more significant when one considers that the wording of some items was changed, and that the two groups were not systematically equated. The results on the first form were also compared with the over-all averages for all four groups taking Form 78. The individual item means correlated .88,

TABLE 12 (III)

ITEM MEANS AND DISCRIMINATORY POWERS[a]

A-S SCALE — FORM 78

No.	Item	Group A Mean	D.P.	Group B Mean	D.P.	Group C Mean	D.P.	Group D Mean	D.P.	Over-all[b] Mean	D.P.	Rank D.P.
11.	(Hire Jews)	2.76	4.25	3.10	3.69	3.40	4.13	1.71	2.36	2.74	3.61	(6)
16.	(Businessmen)	3.79	4.58	3.62	4.10	3.58	4.35	2.63	4.35	3.40	4.34	(1)
21.	(Jewish districts)	3.46	2.97	3.81	3.17	3.92	3.35	2.86	2.00	3.51	2.87	(9)
26.	(Get rid of faults)	3.41	3.20	3.42	3.96	3.92	3.83	3.16	4.58	3.48	3.89	(5)
33.	(Jewish leaders)	2.29	2.28	2.96	3.09	2.12	1.25	2.10	2.86	2.37	2.37	(10)
40.	(Marry a Jew)	4.44	4.60	3.92	4.67	4.42	4.09	3.04	3.77	3.96	4.28	(3)
49.	(Nice neighborhood)	3.03	3.57	3.31	4.35	3.15	3.88	2.29	4.70	2.94	4.12	(4)
62.	(Basically Jewish)	3.54	3.85	3.31	3.29	3.60	2.76	2.94	4.12	3.35	3.50	(7)
69.	(All alike)	3.44	4.02	3.19	4.20	3.22	4.24	2.73	4.76	3.14	4.30	(2)
72.	(Federal agencies)	3.07	3.49	2.81	3.50	2.60	2.63	2.27	4.30	2.69	3.48	(8)
	Mean/person/item	3.32	3.68	3.35	3.80	3.39	3.45	2.57	3.78	3.16	3.68	

[a]The four groups on which these data are based are: *Group A*, U.C. Public Speaking Class Women (N = 140); *Group B*, U.C. Public Speaking Class Men (N = 52); *Group C*, U.C. Adult Extension Class Women (N = 40); *Group D*, Professional Women (nurses, teachers, social workers, (N = 63).

[b]In obtaining the over-all means, the individual group means were not weighted by N.

and the D. P.'s correlated .80. It would therefore appear that the relative discriminability (D. P.) and level of acceptability (mean) of the items is due mainly to the nature of the items themselves rather than to their form of presentation in the questionnaire.

Although no correlations were computed among the four groups taking Form 78, the great variability of the over-all means and D. P.'s indicates considerable consistency of item mean and D. P. from group to group. The best items for one group tend to be the best for other groups, and similarly for the worst items. This consistency in rank order of means and D. P.'s holds even for the Professional Women, despite the fact that the absolute values of the item means were considerably lower for this group than for the others.

Further evidence on these issues is given by results obtained in September, 1945, from a group of 153 students, preponderantly women, at George Washington University, Washington, D. C.[9] The ten A-S items were presented in a solid block, on a sheet containing no other scales, the instructions duplicating those given for the long form of the scale. The obtained reliability was .91, a value almost identical with those for the other groups. The group mean per item was 4.52 and the average D. P. was 4.02. The mean is significantly different (above the 1 per cent level) from the University of California means, and suggests, as have other independent studies, that significant sectional differences in anti-Semitism exist (the Far West being, apparently, less prejudiced than the East). While the Washington students obtain consistently higher scores, the item means show a rank-order correlation of .84 between the Washington group and the average of the four California groups, indicating a marked similarity in the relative acceptability of the items. This group also gives evidence that extremely high scorers do exist, and that the restricted range of the groups taking Form 78 is due mainly to a lack of extremely anti-Semitic members. The individual scores in the Washington group covered the entire range of possible scores, 10–70, with a mean per item of 6.27 for the high quartile, 2.25 for the low quartile.

The Discriminatory Powers for the Washington group correlated .54 with the average D. P.'s for the four California groups. The smallness of this value, in contrast to that for the item means, is due primarily to a change in the rank of item 72, which asserts that "there are too many Jews in Washington agencies." The D. P. for this item had a rank of 8 in the California groups, but a rank of 2 for the Washington group (the D. P. being 4.5). While the rank of the mean on this item was identical in the two groups (9 in both cases), the difference between low and high scorers was relatively much greater in Washington than in California. Living in Washington should provide, one might expect, a reality basis on which to respond to this

9 We wish to thank Dr. G. H. Smith, then teaching at George Washington University, for his cooperation. These results were not incorporated in the main body of data because this group was not given the remaining sections of the questionnaire.

item and thus minimize the differences between otherwise low and high scorers. This does not seem to be the case. It would seem, rather, that how an individual assimilates and interprets social reality is to a large extent determined by his pre-existing ideology. Living in Washington appears to have mainly a polarizing rather than a homogenizing effect, especially on the "Jews in government" issue.

From the above discussion the following conclusions may tentatively be drawn.

a. The item means and D. P.'s are not appreciably changed by changes in the form of presentation (from 52 consecutive anti-Semitic items to 10 consecutive anti-Semitic items to ten items randomly interspersed among a series totalling 78 in all).

b. While over-all mean and average D. P. vary considerably from group to group, relative discriminability and level of acceptability of each item (rank D. P. and mean) tend to remain fairly constant, with the exception of certain sectional differences (as in Item 72, regarding Washington agencies). That is, certain items tend consistently to have relatively high D. P.'s, others to have low D. P.'s, and similarly for the item means.

c. The item means and particularly the D. P.'s were statistically very satisfactory. For eight of the ten items the D. P.'s averaged 3.5 to 4.3 (these values would be even higher were the Washington group included), and even the lowest average D. P.'s of 2.4 and 2.9 are adequate.

d. The most discriminating items deal with Jewish businessmen, stereotyped imagery, marriage, exclusion from neighborhoods, and Jewish responsibility for anti-Semitism. It is interesting that items stating the most frequently heard accusations and the more openly antagonistic attitudes usually had lower means and D. P.'s.

e. In view of its high reliability and internal consistency, the short form of the A-S scale can be used for most research purposes in place of the original, longer form.

E. VALIDATION BY CASE STUDIES: THE RESPONSES OF MACK AND LARRY ON THE A-S SCALE

One meaning of the concept of validity as applied to a psychological test is that the test, which involves only a small sample of the individual's responses, tells us something that is generally true of that individual as judged by an intensive study of him. The A-S scale may be said to have validity of this kind to the degree that the subjects, in their responses to the scale, reveal the same tendencies which come out in their interviews. It will be worth while, therefore, to compare the responses of Mack and Larry to the A-S scale with what they have to say about Jews when they are invited to speak spontaneously.

In Table 13(III) are shown the scores of Mack and Larry, the group
mean and the D. P. for each of the ten items in the short form of the A-S

TABLE 13 (III)

RESPONSES OF MACK AND LARRY ON THE A–S SCALE

Item		Mack	Larry	Group[a] Mean	Group[a] D.P.
11.	(Hire Jews)	3	1	2.74	3.61
16.	(Businessmen)	6	1	3.40	4.34
21.	(Jewish districts)	5	1	3.51	2.87
26.	(Get rid of faults)	6	1	3.48	3.89
33.	(Jewish leaders)	3	1	2.37	2.37
40.	(Marry a Jew)	7	3	3.96	4.28
49.	(Nice neighborhood)	5	1	2.94	4.12
62.	(Basically Jewish)	5	1	3.35	3.50
69.	(All alike)	3	1	3.14	4.30
72.	(Federal agencies)	3	1	2.69	3.48
	Over-all mean	4.6	1.2	3.16	3.68

[a]The group means and D.P.'s are based on all four groups taking Form 78.

scale (Form 78). Mack's mean score, 4.6, is definitely, but not extremely
far, above the over-all group mean of 3.16. He was just barely inside the
high quartile for the group of Public Speaking Men of which he was a member. This is in keeping with the moderation which characterized the whole
ideological section of his interview, and it forms part of the basis for the
statement, in Chapter II, that he is a relatively mild case. His anti-Semitism
is fairly general, in that he agrees with six of the ten statements and scores
above the group mean on all but one of them; but a study of the responses
to individual items reveals a clear pattern, one that can be distinguished from
other patterns of anti-Semitism. In disagreeing slightly, and thereby scoring
close to the group mean, in the case of Items 11 (Hire Jews), 33 (Jewish
leaders), and 72 (Federal agencies), he is saying that he would have no
serious objection if Jews should participate more fully in American life,
that this indeed is what they ought to do. The main trouble, as seen in the
positive responses to Items 16 (Businessmen) and 21 (Jewish districts), is
that they would rather stick together and accumulate wealth and power for
their own group. Although persecution would be largely eliminated if they
should rid themselves of their faults (Item 26), they cannot really become
"Americanized" (Item 62) and would still have to be kept at some distance
personally and socially (Items 40 and 49).

This is almost exactly what Mack tells us in his interview. It is the main point that he tries to make. "They accent the clannish and the material. . . . If a Jew fails in business, he's helped to get started again. . . . They would be liked and accepted if they would be willing to mix. . . . The Jews won't intermingle. . . . I certainly wouldn't (marry a Jew). . . . I would date that girl in Public Speaking, but she doesn't emphasize her Jewishness. She was accepted by the whole class. I would marry her if she had thrown off her Jewishness, but I wouldn't be able to associate with her class."

It is interesting that Item 40 (Marry a Jew) is the one about which Mack feels most strongly and on which he deviates most markedly from the group mean. It would appear that he feels safe in saying, in the interview, that he would marry the Jewish girl "if she had thrown off her Jewishness," because he does not really believe that she ever can do this; there would always be "something basically Jewish underneath" (Item 62).

The item on which Mack obtains a score that is slightly below the group mean is 69 (All alike). Here there is a real discrepancy between scale and interview. The analysis of the interview seemed to show that stereotypy was an outstanding characteristic of this subject's thinking, and yet when it comes to the item which pertains most directly to this characteristic, he fails to agree. This is not because the item is a poor one, for its D. P. was next to the highest obtained with this short form of the A-S scale; nor do there appear to be any special features of Mack's stereotypy that would render Item 69 inapplicable. Perhaps it is too much to expect that scale and interview will agree in every particular; these instruments are not that precise, or perhaps most subjects are not that consistent.

It may be noted that Mack, in the interview, where he is allowed free scope, brings into his discussion of the Jews certain ideas, e.g., Jewish "weakness," that are not touched upon in any of the ten statements which comprise the A-S scale. This outcome would have been considerably less likely, it seems, if he had responded to the 52 items of the original A-S scale. It is claimed for the short form of the scale that for most research purposes it can be substituted for the long form. In Mack's case there appears to be no reason for dissatisfaction with the measure of the degree of his anti-Semitism which the short form yields; concerning the content of his anti-Semitic ideology it is noteworthy that the pattern which appears in his responses to the scale corresponds to what is central and seemingly most important in his spontaneous discussion. That the ten-item scale should at the same time reveal the more incidental and individualistic features of a subject's ideology concerning Jews would be too much to ask.

Larry's responses to the A-S scale are true to form. He obtains the lowest possible score on every item except 40 (Marry a Jew), and even here he disagrees slightly. When it was stated in Chapter II that Larry was not an extreme example of low-scoring men, the reference was to what was known of him from all the diagnostic devices employed in the research. He made it clear enough in his interview that he was strongly opposed to prejudice against minority groups, and had he not come out with an extremely low score on the A-S scale we would have had cause for serious doubt of its validity. That he did not obtain the lowest possible score on Item 40 is evidence that he did not respond to the A-S items in an automatic way. It seems that at this point his impulse toward complete social interaction with Jews collided with his conventionalism, a trait which we have seen to be well developed in him, and he could not in honesty go beyond slight disagreement with the item.

In general, the responses of these two subjects on the A-S scale are consistent with what they say about Jews in their interviews. This consistency appears not only in the degree of anti-Semitism expressed but in the content of the subjects' thinking about Jews. To the extent that these results may be generalized, the A-S scale is a valid index of ideology concerning Jews.

F.   DISCUSSION: THE STRUCTURE OF ANTI-SEMITIC IDEOLOGY

Perhaps the first conclusion to be drawn from the results presented above is that anti-Semitism is best conceived psychologically not as a specific aversion but as an ideology, a general way of thinking about Jews and Jewish-Gentile interaction. This is demonstrated by the high reliability of a scale dealing with so varied a set of ideas, by the reliabilities and intercorrelations of the subscales, and by the high internal consistency of the scale as revealed by the item Discriminatory Powers. The statistical results indicate that a quantitative measure of total anti-Semitic ideology has been obtained. Any individual can be assigned, with a relatively small margin of error, a rank along a dimension ranging from strong support of anti-Semitic ideology at one (high) extreme, to strong opposition at the other (low) extreme. The meaning of middle scores on this dimension is ambiguous, since they may represent indifference, ignorance, or an ambivalent combination of partial support and partial rejection of anti-Semitism. It is noteworthy, however, that individuals making middle scores on one subscale tend to make middle scores on the other subscales as well. Despite item-by-item variability, individuals tend to be highly consistent in their responses to the several subscales.

The fact that an individual's stand on one set of items is similar to his stand on all others does not necessarily imply that all anti-Semitic ideas are of equal psychological importance to each individual. The spontaneous discussions of anti-Semites, whether in an interview or in everyday social life, suggest that for each individual there are certain "nuclear ideas"—imagery of Jews as conniving, or sexual, or radical, and the like, and corresponding primary attitudes—which have primary emotional significance. However, these central ideas apparently make the individual receptive to a great variety of other ideas. That is, once the central or nuclear ideas are formed, they tend to "pull in" numerous other opinions and attitudes and thus to form a broad ideological system. This system provides a rationale for any specific idea within it and a basis for meeting and assimilating new social conditions.

This conception of anti-Semitism aids in the understanding of the present results. It also offers an explanation of why an anti-Semitic rumor that is entirely new in its specific details (for example, the wartime accusations that only Jews could get tires or draft exemptions or officer status) is easily believed by anti-Semites: because of a receptivity to negative imagery generally and by means of an ideological system within which the new idea is easily assimilated.

This conception of the *inclusiveness* of anti-Semitic ideology stands in sharp contrast to numerous theories which conceive of anti-Semitism in terms of certain specific accusations or motives. The notion of anti-Semitism as a form of "racial" prejudice, for example, seems to be based on the idea that the main accusations against Jews involve their "racially inherited" traits (faults). Another common view, that anti-Semitism is a form of "religious" prejudice, is based on the explicit or implicit assumption that religious differences, and thus accusations on religious grounds, are the central issues in anti-Semitism. A third "specifistic" view is that anti-Semitism is based primarily on distortions of facts which some individuals have mistakenly accepted as true; for example, that Jews are unusually rich, dishonest, radical, and so on. This last theory has led to numerous attempts to fight anti-Semitism by giving the "true facts"—attempts which are distinguished for their lack of success. What this theory has overlooked is the *receptivity* of many individuals to any hostile imagery of Jews, and the emotional *resistance* of these individuals to a less hostile and less stereotyped way of thinking. Finally, anti-Semitism is sometimes explained in terms of financial motives and accusations: many people, it is asserted, oppose the Jews on the simple grounds of economic competition and financial self-interest. This theory ignores the other accusations (of power seeking, immorality, and the like) which are made with equal or greater emotional intensity. It also fails to explain why anti-Semites so often violate their own material self-interest in maintaining their prejudices. None of these conceptions of anti-Semitism has adequately grasped its generality, its psychological complexity, and its function in the emotional life of the individual. Nor can they suggest why many individuals oppose anti-Semitism despite their having economic situations, religious backgrounds, sources of information, and so on, which are similar to those of anti-Semites. What is required, in our opinion, is a psychological approach which seeks to grasp both anti-Semitic ideology and *anti*-anti-Semitic ideology in their full complexity and scope, and which then attempts to discover the various sources of each viewpoint in the psychological development and social background of the individuals holding it.[10]

Before discussing the major ideas comprising anti-Semitic ideology, a few words regarding the scale and the scale data are necessary. It is believed that most of the major facets of everyday American anti-Semitism have been represented in the scale, though no claim is made that it contains all the anti-Semitic ideas currently in vogue. The scale data provide an empirical basis for the following discussion in the sense: (a) that each of the ideas to be discussed is supported by most anti-Semites (subjects who fall within the highest 25 per cent of scorers on the scale), opposed by most *anti*-anti-Semites, the differences being statistically significant; and (b) that each anti-Semite supports most of these ideas, while each low scorer opposes most of them. Thus, one can speak of a broad framework of anti-Semitic ideology which is held in its entirety by relatively few individuals but which is supported in varying degrees by many more.

What, then, are the major opinions, values, and attitudes comprising anti-Semitic ideology, how are they organized or systematized, and how is this system different from other, non-anti-Semitic points of view?

One striking characteristic of the imagery in anti-Semitic ideology is its *stereotypy*, which takes several forms. There is, first, a tendency to over-generalize single traits, to subscribe to statements beginning "Jews are . . ." or "The Jews do not . . ." Second, there is a stereotyped negative image of the group as a whole, as if "to know one is to know all," since they are all alike. Third, examination of the specific characteristics comprising the imagery reveals a basic contradiction in that no single individual or group as a whole could have all these characteristics.

Another aspect of stereotypy which is implied by the scale items and brought out more directly in the interviews may be termed "stereotypy of interpersonal relationships and experiences." It involves an inability to experience Jews as individuals. Rather, each Jew is seen and reacted to as a sort of sample specimen of the stereotyped, reified image of the group. This form of stereotypy is expressed very clearly in Mack's discussion of Jews (see Chapter II); while no statistics are available, the other interviews as well as everyday conversations indicate that his approach is not uncommon.

This limitation in the experience of individuals has certain implications

---

[10] It may again be emphasized that the present approach is a psychological one. The sociologist, at least during this stage in the development of social science, tends to proceed along other, perhaps parallel, lines. Thus, a psychological approach in terms of purely religious or purely economic *motives* is inadequate. However, a sociological approach in terms of religious or politico-economic *structures* and their relation to anti-Semitism as a sociocultural trend is, in our opinion, both valid and of great significance. What must be opposed, as we see it, is the tendency mechanically to subsume psychology under sociology and to confuse basic economic or religious social forces with superficial economic or religious motives in the individual. Sociological forces are considered in Chapters XVI, XVII, XVIII, XIX.

for the theory that contact with "good Jews" lessens anti-Semitism. The effectiveness of social contact would seem to depend in large part on the individual's *capacity for individuated experience*. This capacity is certainly not hereditarily determined, but it may often be difficult to change in adults. When it is lacking, new social experiences are likely to lead, not to new learning and development, but merely to the mechanical reinforcement of established imagery.

Further analysis of stereotypy and other characteristics of anti-Semitic thinking, as well as concrete examples from the interview material, are presented in Chapter XVI.

These considerations raise several questions which are dealt with in later sections of this research. Do anti-Semites express the same stereotypy of thought and experience in relation to other groups and issues, that is, are stereotypy and rigidity aspects of their general psychological functioning? Why is it so important for anti-Semites to reject Jews on any and all grounds? Are the contradictions and oversimplifications primarily surface signs of a deeper-lying anxiety and hostility? If so, what are the personality trends involved, and how are they different from those found in non-anti-Semites?

Let us consider the deeper psychological meaning of the stereotyped negative imagery of Jews. While the specific surface opinions cover a great variety of topics, there seem nevertheless to be certain unifying ideas or themes underlying the opinions and giving them coherence and structure. Perhaps most central is the idea that Jews are *threatening*. Certainly this idea is present, explicitly or implicitly, in almost all the scale items. It is expressed in the subscale "Offensive," where Jews are described as a *moral threat*, that is, as violators of important standards and values. These values include: cleanliness, neatness, and conformity; also opposition to sensuality, extravagance, prying, social aggressiveness, exhibitionism. The imagery of Jews as value-violators makes them not only offensive but also very disturbing. The anxiety becomes almost explicit in item II–4: "There is something different and strange about Jews . . ."

These values are, of course, not limited to anti-Semites. Indeed, many of them are among the currently prevailing conventional middle-class values—and most Americans are *psychologically* middle class. It may be that anti-Semites and non-anti-Semites differ regarding certain values such as sensuality or conformity. However, it is likely that many unprejudiced individuals have substantially the same values as the anti-Semites do. Why, then, do these values become the basis for anti-Semitic accusations in one group but not in the other? One hypothesis would be that the non-anti-Semites are more flexible in their support of these values, less disturbed by value-violators and less inclined to stereotypy and overgeneralization.

Moreover, these values tend, as will be shown later, to be held very strongly by the high-scoring subjects, and they appear frequently in these individuals' thinking about themselves, other people, and social issues generally. In view of the emotional support given these values, and the intensity with which supposed value-violators are rejected, it is reasonable to ask whether the surface opinions and attitudes are motivated by deeper emotional dispositions. It is possible, for example, that anti-Semites are unconsciously struggling to inhibit in themselves the same tendencies that they find so unbearable in Jews. Jews may be a convenient object on which they can project their unconscious desires and fears. It is difficult otherwise to explain why anti-Semites feel so threatened by violations of their moral values, and why they develop exaggerated, stereotyped imagery of the "morally impure" Jews as a threat to the "morally pure" Gentiles. It will be significant in this connection whether the categorical distinction between *value-violators* (ego-alien, morally threatening groups) and *value-supporters* (ego-syntonic, morally pure groups) appears generally in the thinking of these individuals regarding the various other ideological areas to be considered in the following chapters. To the extent that this and other themes underly and unify the entire social thinking of anti-Semites, their specific opinions and attitudes must be regarded in part as expressions of deeper-lying personality needs, anxieties, and conflicts.

The idea of Jews as a *social threat* is expressed directly in the subscale "Threatening," where they are described as having harmful effects in various areas of social life. This concern with supposed Jewish *power* is a recurrent theme in the sources from which our scale items were taken and in the later interviews of our subjects as well as in the A-S scale itself. In the case of the moral values mentioned above, it is implied that non-Jews are the opposite of Jews: clean, conforming, modest, and the like. It would seem that power, however, while threatening in Jews, is justified and even valued in non-Jews.[11] For example, the attitudes of segregation and exclusion are based on the assumption that Gentiles should be more powerful than Jews in order to enforce these policies. Why does the concern with power recur so often and in so many forms? Why is the Jewish group, which is actually small and relatively weak, regarded as so threatening, while the really powerful and dominating groups in the *status quo* are supported rather than feared? Is it actually the weakness of the Jews which is most disturbing to the anti-Semite? If the concern with power and the fear of weakness in the high scorers represent deeper personality trends, these trends should be revealed by the clinical techniques and they should be expressed in the other ideological areas.

The issues of Jewish group loyalty and Jewish assimilation, viewed psychologically, reveal several central themes in anti-Semitic ideology. At first glance the criticisms of Jews and the demands on them seem both simple and reasonable. The Jews are, it is asserted, too clannish: they either keep apart in a kind of snobbish seclusion, or, if they do enter community affairs

[11] Cf. the "usurper complex" described in Chapter XVII.

they stick together and take advantage of other people. Therefore, the Jews must overcome their pride and clannishness, and their attempts to control other groups. When they have thoroughly assimilated, when they have lost their foreign ways and their clannish, conniving methods of gaining money and power at the expense of others, they can be liked and accepted. Until they change, they can hardly be surprised to find themselves excluded or limited in certain ways. The essential demand is that the Jews liquidate themselves, that they lose entirely their cultural identity and adhere instead to the prevailing cultural ways. Related to this narrowness is a punitive rather than an understanding approach to value-violators; the Jews deserve whatever hardships they may sometimes undergo since they have brought it on themselves. In this vindictive approach there is no room for more complex explanation, no way of considering discrimination as primarily a cause rather than an effect of Jewish traits. There is an aversion to the idea that the basis for resolution of Jewish-Gentile conflict lies primarily in the total social organization—and therefore in the dominant groups in the society—and only secondarily in Jews themselves.

But this demand for assimilation is not as simple as it seems at first glance. Jews who attempt to assimilate are apparently even more suspect than the others. Accusations of "prying," "power-seeking," and "imitation" are made, and seemingly generous acts by Jews are attributed to hidden selfish motives (subscale "Intrusive"). There is no logical basis for urging on the one hand that Jews become like everyone else, and on the other hand, that Jews be limited and excluded in the most important areas of social life.

It need not be denied by non-anti-Semites that there are extremely clannish and power-seeking individuals in the Jewish as well as in the Gentile group. But why do the high scorers not oppose *all* individuals who seek power for themselves or their narrow groups and who would take advantage of others? It is a remarkable fact that most individuals who see clannishness, prying, and power-seeking as "Jewish traits" value the same things, under other names, in Gentiles. It is accepted as "human nature" that each individual will stand by his group, that "blood is thicker than water," and that each group is therefore unified in its material interests. As long as there is any trace of a Jewish group, therefore, it is expected that each Jew will have primary loyalty to it. While this "clannishness" is deplored, the anti-Semites tend to hold in contempt anyone who lacks "loyalty and pride" in his group, and to put great value on these traits in their own groups.

The imagery described above seems to characterize the thinking of most anti-Semites. Individual differences in the pattern of *attitudes* (programs of action) supported depend primarily on the strength of adherence to democratic values. Openly antidemocratic individuals have a direct and clear-cut program: violent attack on the Jews leading to total liquidation or to permanent suppression and restriction. What to do is, however, a greater psychological problem for those who have the same imagery, but who at the same time want to support democratic values of equality, nonviolence, and the like.

The negative imagery of Jews, and the accompanying sense of threat, involve two main fears which form the basis for attitudes. There is, first, the fear of *contamination*: the fear that Jews may, if permitted intimate or intensive contact with Gentiles, have a corrupting or degenerating influence. Various forms of corruption may occur: moral, political, intellectual, sensual, and so on. Among the many ideas which have been attributed to "Jewish contamination" are free love, radicalism, atheism, moral relativism, modern trends in art and literature. Gentiles who support ideas such as these tend to be regarded as unwitting victims who have been psychologically contaminated in the same way that one may be organically infected by a disease. The notion that one Jew can "infect" many Gentiles is very useful in rationalizing many apparent contradictions. It permits one to attribute great influence to the Jews and thus to blame most social problems on them, despite their relatively very small number. It justifies one's hostile feelings and discriminatory actions. Furthermore, an idea or social movement can be called "Jewish" even when most of its supporters are Gentile, since the latter are regarded as merely dupes or victims of Jewish contamination. An individual who accepts this reasoning feels compelled, no matter how great his value for tolerance, to protect the Gentile group by restricting the activities of the Jewish group.

Viewed psychologically, this way of thinking raises several questions. Why is it necessary for anti-Semites to regard Jews as the source of all these ideas, that is, why do they regard these ideas as *imposed* on Gentile but *originating* in Jews? One hypothesis is that this represents an attempt on the part of the prejudiced individual to resolve an inner moral conflict by externalizing or projecting his own immoral tendencies; the inner conflict is replaced by a new conflict between groups: the sterotypically moral "we" and the stereotypically immoral "they." That the inner conflict persists unconsciously in full force is shown by emphasis on external immorality and by the fear that this immorality will corrupt all who are exposed to it. The investigation of this and other hypotheses is reported in later chapters.

In addition to the fear of contamination there is the *fear of being overwhelmed*. This anxiety is related to the imagery of Jews as prying and power-seeking. If Jews are given the opportunity of free participation in community affairs then, granted that they have these tendencies, they will form a small sectarian clique interested only in their own power and material interests. To gain these aims they will shrewdly use even the most ruthless and dishonest methods. There is thus great danger that the Gentile group will be persecuted, victimized, exploited—in short, overwhelmed.

It is difficult indeed, for a person with such hostile imagery and such anxiety, to have entirely democratic attitudes regarding Jewish-Gentile interaction. Most pseudodemocratic attitudes represent attempts, conscious or unconscious, at compromise between the tendency to express the underlying hostility directly (aggressive attack) and the tendency to conform to democratic values (tolerance, equality). The demand for total Jewish assimilation represents one such compromise, since total assimilation is, so to speak, a nonviolent way of liquidating the Jews. If there were *no* Jews then at least one source of anxiety and one object of hostility would be removed. Unfortunately, partial assimilation (the phase in which some Jews attempt to assimilate while others do not) seems to be more disturbing to anti-Semites than none at all. As long as the anti-Semites have some sense of the presence of a Jewish group—and thus an image of "the Jew" which can be applied stereotypically to all individual Jews—those Jews who seem to be assimilating will be suspected of evil motives. It is an oft-repeated historical paradox that those who demand total assimilation do the most to prevent it, since their hostility and discrimination tend on the one hand to increase Jewish nationalism and pride, and on the other hand to provide external barriers repelling those Jews who attempt assimilation into the dominant group. Conversely, Jewish assimilation has proceeded most rapidly in those communities which have accepted them without totalitarian demands for submission and all-out assimilation.

A second way of nonviolently eliminating the Jews, and thus of solving the problem of interaction by simply not having any, is for them to "stay on their side of the fence and we stay on ours." If they cannot be entirely absorbed—and, despite their demand for total assimilation, most anti-Semites seem to feel that the "basic Jewishness" is permanent—then they should be totally separate. The separation could be made complete if the Jews would "form a nation of their own and keep more to themselves" (Item II–24).[12]

Some individuals, including Jews, have supported the idea of separation (fraternal organizations, neighborhoods, and the like) on grounds of differences in interests and culture. There can be no objection, from a democratic point of view, to an organization devoted primarily to Jewish culture and conducted in the Yiddish language, nor to one concerned mainly with Chris-

---

[12] The idea of a Jewish nation, particularly the important issue of Jewish settlement in Palestine, has been supported by various ideological camps. Much support in America has come from open or pseudodemocratic anti-Semites who wish that all Jews would settle there and who are afraid that, if the doors of Palestine are closed, America would have to open its doors to the refugees.

Many non-anti-Semites have also supported the idea of a Jewish homeland, but not for reasons of separation and exclusion. The main democratic reasoning, in general, is that there should be a geographical-political unit in which Jewish culture can be the primary one, that this nation should be a part of the family of nations, and that all individuals should be free to settle in whatever nation they choose, without the demand for total assimilation or the threat of exclusion. Since the Jewish group contains the same diversity of ideologies and personalities as any other major grouping, it is not surprising that there is much disagreement on this issue among Jews. In the present discussion, however, the main concern is with non-Jews.

tian religion or any other cultural form. But consistency with democratic values does require that, once the primary aims and functions of the organization are laid down, membership be open to *any* individual who accepts its principles and meets its requirements. It is undemocratic to exclude any group as a whole, that is, to be unwilling to consider any applicant on the basis of his *individual* merits and faults. The exclusionism of some Jewish groups, while understandable as a defensive "pride" reaction, is no more justified than the equivalent policy in other groups. The total exclusion of one group by another, whether on ethnic, religious, social class, skin color, or other grounds, is necessarily based on stereotypy, hostility and anxiety, conscious or not. It is sometimes said that "a Jew (or Negro or Catholic) would not be comfortable here." This usually means that he would be exposed to some degree of prejudice, subtle or crude, and it is the others who would be uncomfortable.

Discrimination takes a variety of other forms, all designed to limit Jewish-Gentile interaction by restricting the full participation of Jews in community and national affairs. All forms of discrimination (exclusion, segregation, suppression, and so forth) against all groups have the double function of restricting intergroup contact and of maintaining the dominant social position of the group doing the discriminating.

There are many economic, political, religious, and other institutional forces involved in the subordination of various American groups. These broader social forces were, however, beyond the scope of this research. We were concerned, as stated in Chapter I, with the problem of the *consumption* of ideology by the individual: granted that various ideologies are present in the social environment, why is it that some individuals consume (assimilate, accept) the more undemocratic forms while others consume the more democratic forms? The general assumption made was that, granted the possibility of choice, an individual will be most receptive to that ideology which has most psychological meaning for him and the most significant function within his over-all adjustment. Accordingly, there was much concern with the psychological content of anti-Semitic ideology in an attempt to form hypotheses regarding the deeper psychological trends, if any, which underlie and motivate the surface opinions and attitudes.

Numerous trends underlying anti-Semitic ideology are suggested by the present scale results: stereotypy; rigid adherence to middle-class values; the tendency to regard one's own group as morally pure in contrast to the immoral outgroup; opposition to and exaggeration of prying and sensuality; extreme concern with dominance and power (fear of Jewish power and desire for Gentile power); fear of moral contamination; fear of being overwhelmed and victimized; the desire to erect social barriers in order to separate one group from another and to maintain the morality and the dominance of one's own group.

Can it be demonstrated that these personality trends are actually present in anti-Semitic individuals? In the chapters which follow, there are several lines of evidence bearing on this question: (a) If these trends are present, then they should also be found in various other ideological areas. (b) These trends should be expressed in nonideological forms as well, that is, in ways of thinking about people and life generally. (c) Intensive clinical study should reveal these and other trends directly, as well as their organization and function in the total personality, and their course of development.

CHAPTER IV

THE STUDY OF ETHNOCENTRIC IDEOLOGY

Daniel J. Levinson

A. INTRODUCTION

Our attention turns now to the problem of prejudice, broadly conceived. The term "prejudice" is not entirely adequate, since it has numerous meanings and connotations which might obscure or distort the ideas guiding this research. The term "ethnocentrism" is preferable because its traditional meaning comes much closer to that used here. First introduced and used descriptively by Sumner (115) in 1906, the term had the general meaning of provincialism or cultural narrowness; it meant a tendency in the individual to be "ethnically centered," to be rigid in his acceptance of the culturally "alike" and in his rejection of the "unlike."

The traditional conception of ethnocentrism, from which the present one is derived, differs in several important respects from the usual notion of prejudice. Prejudice is commonly regarded as a feeling of dislike against a specific group; ethnocentrism, on the other hand, refers to a relatively consistent frame of mind concerning "aliens" generally. Usually, in discussions of prejudice against groups there is specific reference to "race prejudice" or "prejudice against racial and religious minorities." This terminology is used even by people who know that "race" is a socially harmful idea as ordinarily understood, and who know that many groups (zootsuiters, "Okies," and so forth) are discriminated against on neither racial nor religious grounds. Ethnocentrism refers to group relations generally; it has to do not only with numerous groups toward which the individual has hostile opinions and attitudes but, equally important, with groups toward which he is positively disposed.

A theory of ethnocentrism offers a starting point for the understanding of the psychological aspect of group relations—why individuals are inclined toward competition, or conflict, or harmonious interaction, and so on. It is concerned with such questions as: What kinds of general attitudes do individuals have about their own and other groups? What underlying ideas or themes run through an individual's thinking about groups and group rela-

102

tions? How do these ideas develop? How are they related to trends in the individual's thinking about other social processes? What personality trends, if any, are they related to, and in what way? How are they related to membership in class, church, political party, and so forth?

The term "ethnocentrism" shifts the emphasis from "race" to "ethnic group." The everyday use of the term "race" has been criticized from many sides and on many grounds. It was originally suggested as one type of broad classification of human beings on the basis of skin color. Other anthropometric measures such as head shape and blood type were also suggested. Each of these organic bases of classification divides human beings (also known as the human "race") into groups which are mixed with respect to the other organic characteristics. Thus, the Negroes, a "race" according to the skin color criterion, are mixed with respect to head shape and blood type. But, apart from the arbitrariness of the organic basis of classification, the greatest dangers of the race concept lie in its hereditarian psychological implications and in its misapplication to cultures. Psychologically, the race theory implies, whether or not this is always made explicit, that people of a given race (e.g., skin color) are also very similar psychologically because they have a common hereditary family tree. This notion has been controverted in the past few decades by work in psychology on the problem of "heredity vs. environment" and by work in cultural anthropology on the tremendous psychological variations within any given culture. Furthermore, the term "race" is often applied to groups which are not races at all in the technical sense. Sometimes this term is applied to nations, e.g., "the German race" or even "the American race." Sometimes it is misused in connection with American ethnic minorities, such as Italians or Greeks. There is no adequate term, other than "ethnic," by which to describe cultures (that is, systems of social ways, institutions, traditions, language, and so forth) which are not nations, that is, which do not form politico-geographical entities. This confusion, which is more than merely terminological and which permeates much thinking on social problems, has plagued the Jews particularly; they are a good example of an ethnic group which is neither a formal nation nor a race. From the point of view of sociology, cultural anthropology, and social psychology, the important concepts are not race and heredity but social organization (national, regional, subcultural, communal) and the interaction of social forms and individual personalities. To the extent that relative uniformities in psychological characteristics are found within any cultural grouping, these uniformities must be explained primarily in terms of social organization rather than "racial heredity." The use and development of the concept of "ethnic group," as part of a broad educational program dealing with individual development and social change, can do much to clarify everyday thinking about social processes and problems.

The conception of ideology presented in earlier chapters has been utilized here. Ethnocentrism is conceived as an ideological system pertaining to groups and group relations. A distinction is made between *ingroups* (those groups with which the individual identifies himself) and *outgroups* (with which he does not have a sense of belonging and which are regarded as antithetical to the ingroups). Outgroups are the objects of negative opinions and hostile attitudes; ingroups are the objects of positive opinions and uncritically supportive attitudes; and it is considered that outgroups should be socially subordinate to ingroups.

The basic questions for research were raised in Chapter II. They concern the inclusiveness of ideas regarding a given group, the *generality* of outgroup rejection, the *content* of ideas about ingroups and outgroups, and the amount of *stereotypy* in thinking about groups generally.

There were numerous indications that some generality of ingroup and outgroup ideology within the individual would be found (13, 25, 85, 90). Sumner found such consistency in his anthropological studies. Fascistic social movements have shown consistent tendencies to oppose a variety of minority groups. Many historians, literary men, and political analysts have, in a nontechnical, nonquantitative way, had this conception of ideology (21, 69, 72, 92, 93, 95, 101). One meets consistent outgroup rejection in everyday parlor and street-corner discussions.

A quantitative indication of consistency was found in a previous study of anti-Semitism (71). Increasing degrees of anti-Semitism were shown to be closely related to increasing opposition to labor unions and racial equality, and to increasing support of Father Coughlin. Members of college sororities —which tend to have a strong ingroup ideology—were significantly more anti-Semitic on the average than nonmembers. And subjects reporting some ideological friction with parents—indicating ability to criticize the family, a major ingroup—were significantly less anti-Semitic than those reporting no such friction.

To obtain a more conclusive answer to the questions raised in Chapter II, it seemed that the best method—in terms of rigor and quantification—was an opinion-attitude scale for the measurement of ethnocentrism. The construction of this scale was, therefore, the first step taken. It was constructed in such a way that an analysis of its statistical properties and internal relationships might help to answer the major questions concerning the structure of ethnocentric ideology.

B. CONSTRUCTION OF THE ETHNOCENTRISM (E) SCALE

The procedure followed in the construction of the E scale was the same as that for the anti-Semitism scale (Chapter III). Once again, and by the same reasoning, the Likert method of scaling was used. Again, all items were negative, that is, hostile to the group in question, and finally, the same general rules of item formulation were followed.

1. MAJOR SUBDIVISIONS OR AREAS: THE SUBSCALES

Subscales were used in order to insure broad coverage of the total field and to permit statistical analysis of certain relationships with ethnocentric ideology. Since one of the primary research questions concerned the generality of ethnocentrism, each subscale dealt with a different set of ingroup-outgroup relations. Within each subscale an attempt was made to cover a variety of common pseudodemocratic—and a few openly antidemocratic—opinions and attitudes.

The E scale in its initial forms did not include items about Jews; rather, the initial anti-Semitism scale was included separately in the questionnaire

TABLE 1 (IV)
ETHNOCENTRISM SCALE
Negro Subscale (N)

2. If there are enough Negroes who want to attend dances at a local dance hall featuring a colored band, a good way to arrange this would be to have one all-Negro night, and then the whites could dance in peace the rest of the time.

5. The Negroes would solve many of their social problems by not being so irresponsible, lazy, and ignorant.

8. Negro musicians are sometimes as good as white musicians at swing music and jazz, but it is a mistake to have mixed Negro-white bands.

11. It would be a mistake to have Negroes for foremen and leaders over whites.

14. Negroes may have a part to play in white civilization, but it is best to keep them in their own districts and schools and to prevent too much intermixing with whites.

16. Manual labor and menial jobs seem to fit the Negro mentality and ability better than more skilled or responsible work.

19. In a community of 1,000 whites and 50 Negroes, a drunken Negro shoots and kills an officer who is trying to arrest him. The white population should immediately drive all the Negroes out of town.

22. The people who raise all the talk about putting Negroes on the same level as whites and giving them the same privileges are mostly radical agitators trying to stir up conflicts.

25. An occasional lynching in the South is a good thing because there is a large percentage of Negroes in many communities and they need a scare once in a while to prevent them from starting riots and disturbances.

28. It would be best to limit Negroes to grammar and trade school education since more schooling just gives them ambition and desires which they are unable to fulfill in white competition.

31. There is something inherently primitive and uncivilized in the Negro, as shown in his music and his extreme aggressiveness.

34. Most Negroes would become officious, overbearing, and disagreeable if not kept in their place.

so that correlations between the two scales might be obtained. The development of a more complete E scale, including items about Jews, will be reported later in this chapter.

The initial E scale consists of thirty-four items arranged in three subscales dealing respectively with Negroes, various other minorities, and patriotism (extranational outgroups). These will now be discussed.

a. NEGROES. Since Negroes are a large and severely oppressed group and since imagery of "the Negro" has become so elaborated in American cultural mythology, they merited a subscale of their own. The twelve items presented in Table 1(IV) constitute the Negro subscale. (The items are numbered as they appear in the total scale.)

These items attempt to cover most of the current ideology regarding Negroes and Negro-white relations. Negroes are described as lazy and ignorant (Item 5) and as not really wanting equality with whites (Item 22: it is "radical agitators" who stir them up). Do individuals with the opinion that

TABLE 2 (IV)
ETHNOCENTRISM SCALE
Minority Subscale (M)

1. The many political parties tend to confuse national issues, add to the expense of elections, and raise unnecessary agitation. For this and other reasons, it would be best if all political parties except the two major ones were abolished.

4. Certain religious sects whose beliefs do not permit them to salute the flag should be forced to conform to such a patriotic action, or else be abolished.

6. Any group or social movement which contains many foreigners should be watched with suspicion and, whenever possible, be investigated by the FBI.

9. Although women are necessary in the armed forces and in industry, they should be returned to their proper place in the home as soon as the war ends.

15. One main difficulty with allowing the entire population to participate fully in government affairs (voting, jobs, etc.) is that such a large percentage is innately deficient and incapable.

17. It is a mistake to allow any Japanese to leave internment camps and enter the army where they would be free to commit sabotage.

21. The many faults, and the general inability to get along, of the Oklahomans ("Okies") who have recently flooded California, prove that we ought to send them back where they came from as soon as conditions permit.

24. A large-scale system of sterilization would be one good way of breeding out criminals and other undesirable elements in our society and so raise its general standards and living conditions.

27. Filipinos are all right in their place, but they carry it too far when they dress lavishly, buy good cars, and go around with white girls.

29. Zootsuiters demonstrate that inferior groups, when they are given too much freedom and money, just misuse their privileges and create disturbances.

30. The most vicious, irresponsible, and racketeering unions are, in most cases, those having largely foreigners for leaders.

32. We are spending too much money for the pampering of criminals and the insane, and for the education of inherently incapable people.

Negroes are "naturally" lazy or unambitious also have the attitude that when Negroes do strive for higher status they should be "kept in their place" (Item 34) and prevented from having positions of leadership (Item 11)? Is the attitude that Negroes should be segregated (Items 2, 8, 14) held by the same persons who regard Negroes as threatening and inferior and who favor more active subordination of Negroes? These are some of the questions underlying this subscale, and the statistical results should offer at least a partial answer to them.

b. MINORITIES. The second subscale (see Table 2(IV)) contains twelve items dealing with various American minority groups (other than Jews and Negroes) about which negative opinions and imagery often exist and toward which attitudes of subordination, restriction of social functioning, segregation, and the like are often directed. Included are *organized groups* such as minority political parties and religious sects as well as social movements and labor unions "containing many foreigners"; also *ethnic* minorities such as Japanese-Americans, Oklahomans (in California), and Filipinos.[1] Zootsuiters, criminals, the insane, "inherently incapable people" and "undesirable elements," which constitute *moral* minorities or outgroups, are also objects of hostile opinions and attitudes.

Although prejudice is usually thought of as directed against minorities—in the sense of small numbers, and as opposed to a vague "majority"—one may ask if prejudice is not sometimes directed against a group containing more than half of the population. The phenomena of "contempt for the masses" and the subordination of women were considered examples of ethnocentrism of this type; Items 9 and 15 were included to determine how closely such attitudes are correlated with the others. Can the attitude that "women's place is in the home" be considered a prejudice? It would appear that it is, to the extent that people with this attitude have others which are more obviously ethnocentric. A more conclusive proof would require a detailed study of ideology regarding women, oriented within a general theory of ethnocentric vs. nonethnocentric approaches.

c. PATRIOTISM. This subscale (see Table 3(IV)) contains ten items dealing with international relations and viewing America as an ingroup in relation to other nations as outgroups. The term "patriotism" as used here does not mean "love of country." Rather, the present concept involves blind attachment to certain national cultural values, uncritical conformity with the prevailing group ways, and rejection of other nations as outgroups. It might better be termed *pseudopatriotism* and distinguished from *genuine* patriotism, in which love of country and attachment to national values is based on critical understanding. The genuine patriot, it would appear, can appreciate the values and ways of other nations, and can be permissive

---

[1] During the war at least, the status of the last-named groups was a focal issue in California—more so than in most other states.

TABLE 3 (IV)
ETHNOCENTRISM SCALE
Patriotism Subscale (P)

3. Patriotism and loyalty are the first and most important requirements of a good citizen.

7. There will always be superior and inferior nations in the world and, in the interests of all concerned, it is best that the superior ones be in control of world affairs.

10. Minor forms of military training, obedience, and discipline, such as drill, marching and simple commands, should be made a part of the elementary school educational program.

12. The main threat to basic American institutions during this century has come from the infiltration of foreign ideas, doctrines, and agitators.

13. Present treatment of conscientious objectors, draft evaders, and enemy aliens is too lenient and mollycoddling. If a person won't fight for his country, he deserves a lot worse than just prison or a work camp.

18. In view of the present national emergency, it is highly important to limit responsible government jobs to native, white, Christian Americans.

20. European refugees may be in need, but it would be a big mistake to lower our immigration quotas and allow them to flood the country.

23. It has become clear that the Germans and Japanese are racially war-minded and power-seeking, and the only guarantee of future peace is to wipe out most of them and to keep the rest under careful control.

26. Mexico can never advance to the standards of living and civilization of the U. S., due mainly to the innate dirtiness, laziness, and general backwardness of Mexicans.

33. There will always be wars because, for one thing, there will always be races who ruthlessly try to grab more than their share.

toward much that he cannot personally accept for himself. He is free of rigid conformism, outgroup rejection, and imperialistic striving for power.

Ingroup opinions and attitudes are expressed in Items 3, 7, and 10. They are intended to express a general value for obedience and discipline, the opinion that nations are arranged hierarchically from superior to inferior, and the attitude that the superior ones should be dominant—with the assumption that we are one of the superior nations. The rigidity of the value for obedience is shown by the punitive attitude toward those who disobey (Item 13: Punishment of conscientious objectors and draft evaders).

The glorification of the national ingroup is shown further in the tendency to regard other nations as inferior when they are distant (Item 26), and threatening when they come too close (Items 12, 20, and 23). We are therefore morally justified in excluding refugees, in "wiping out" the Germans and Japanese,[2] in excluding foreigners and others from government jobs,

[2] This item (23), so relevant during the war, can of course no longer be used. (It should be pointed out that one could actively support the war without such a destructive attitude toward the enemy or such national smugness.) If these attitudes are correlated with rejection of most other nations, then the people who made high (ethnocentric) scores on this scale may be the ones who now show similar attitudes toward our wartime allies and support militaristic, imperialistic, "tough-minded policies guaranteeing American sovereignty and interests."

and in maintaining our dominant position as a nation. The cynicism about peace and the moralistic attribution of war to "ruthless, grabbing races" also indicate the sense of threat from outgroups and the moral righteousness of the ingroup. The fact that this theory of the cause of war is held by many college students who have been exposed to sociological explanations in terms of socioeconomic organization and conflicts raises the question: What are the inner barriers in some individuals which make them unreceptive to non-moralistic explanations? This problem, to be taken up in later chapters, concerns the personality dynamics underlying ethnocentric ideology.

If people who make high scores on this subscale are also high on the others, then it would appear that although they hold America to be superior and inviolable, they actually reject the great majority of the people in this country. Item 18 brings this out directly: it is only the native, white, Christian Americans who can be trusted. And various items from the "Minorities" subscale indicate that large sections of this population are also in the outgroup category.

2. THE TOTAL ETHNOCENTRISM (E) SCALE

The total E scale is intended to measure the individual's readiness to accept or oppose ethnocentric ideology as a whole. The scale consists of 34 items[3] and comprises the three subscales N, M, and P. It is presented in Table 4 (IV), with instructions to subjects, just as it was administered.

C. RESULTS: STATISTICAL ANALYSIS OF THE SCALE

The subjects were allowed the same six choices of response for each item (+3 to −3, with no neutral response), and the responses were converted into scores in the same way (−3 = 1 point, −2 = 2 points, etc.) as was the case with the A-S scale. All the items were regarded as pro-ethnocentric. For the 34 items, then, the total scores can range between 34 points (1 point on each item, indicating strong anti-ethnocentrism) and 238 points (7 points on each item, strong ethnocentrism). When the total score is divided by 34 we obtain the mean score per item; thus, a total score of 51 can also be stated as a mean per item of 1.5.

This scale was administered as part of the questionnaire which also contained the initial (52 item) A-S scale. As reported in Chapter III, this questionnaire was given in April, 1944, to a class in Introductory Psychology at the University of California. The data presented here are based on the questionnaires of the 144 women subjects, including nineteen members of major minorities.

[3] Items 1, 3, 4, 7, 9, 10 of the present scale were taken, in some cases with slight modifications, from the "Unlabelled Fascist Attitudes" Scale of Edwards (24). Both Edwards' study and the present one have profitted from previous studies by Gundlach (46), Katz and Cantril (17), and Stagner (112, 113). Several of the "Negro" items have been taken from Murphy and Likert (84).

TABLE 4 (IV)
The Total Ethnocentrism Scale
Public Opinion Questionnaire E

The following statements refer to opinions regarding a number of social groups and issues, about which some people agree and others disagree. Please mark each statement in the left-hand margin according to your agreement or disagreement, as follows:

+1: slight support, agreement   —1: slight opposition, disagreement
+2: moderate support,   "   —2: moderate opposition,   "
+3: strong support,   "   —3: strong opposition,   "

_____ 1. The many political parties tend to confuse national issues, add to the expense of elections, and raise unnecessary agitation. For this and other reasons, it would be best if all political parties except the two major ones were abolished.

_____ 2. If there are enough Negroes who want to attend dances at a local dance hall featuring a colored band, a good way to arrange this would be to have one all-Negro night, and then the whites could dance in peace the rest of the time.

_____ 3. Patriotism and loyalty are the first and most important requirements of a good citizen.

_____ 4. Certain religious sects whose beliefs do not permit them to salute the flag should be forced to conform to such a patriotic action, or else be abolished.

_____ 5. The Negroes would solve many of their social problems by not being so irresponsible, lazy, and ignorant.

_____ 6. Any group or social movement which contains many foreigners should be watched with suspicion and, whenever possible, be investigated by the FBI.

_____ 7. There will always be superior and inferior nations in the world and, in the interests of all concerned, it is best that the superior ones be in control of world affairs.

_____ 8. Negro musicians are sometimes as good as white musicians at swing music and jazz, but it is a mistake to have mixed Negro-white bands.

_____ 9. Although women are necessary now in the armed forces and in industry, they should be returned to their proper place in the home as soon as the war ends.

_____10. Minor forms of military training, obedience, and discipline, such as drill, marching and simple commands, should be made a part of the elementary school educational program.

_____11. It would be a mistake to have Negroes for foremen and leaders over whites.

_____12. The main threat to basic American institutions during this century has come from the infiltration of foreign ideas, doctrines, and agitators.

_____13. Present treatment of conscientious objectors, draft-evaders, and enemy aliens is too lenient and mollycoddling. If a person won't fight for his country, he deserves a lot worse than just a prison or a work camp.

_____14. Negroes may have a part to play in white civilization, but it is best to keep them in their own districts and schools and to prevent too much intermixing with whites.

_____15. One main difficulty with allowing the entire population to participate fully in government affairs (voting, jobs, etc.) is that such a large percentage is innately deficient and incapable.

16. Manual labor and menial jobs seem to fit the Negro mentality and ability better than more skilled or responsible work.

17. It is a mistake to allow any Japanese to leave internment camps and enter the army where they would be free to commit sabotage.

18. In view of the present national emergency, it is highly important to limit responsible government jobs to native, white, Christian Americans.

19. In a community of 1,000 whites and 50 Negroes, a drunken Negro shoots and kills an officer who is trying to arrest him. The white population should immediately drive all the Negroes out of town.

20. European refugees may be in need, but it would be a big mistake to lower our immigration quotas and allow them to flood the country.

21. The many faults, and the general inability to get along, of the Oklahomans ("Okies"), who have recently flooded California, prove that we ought to send them back where they came from as soon as conditions permit.

22. The people who raise all the talk about putting Negroes on the same level as whites and giving them the same privileges are mostly radical agitators trying to stir up conflicts.

23. It has become clear that the Germans and Japanese are racially warminded and power-seeking, and the only guarantee of future peace is to wipe out most of them and to keep the rest under careful control.

24. A large-scale system of sterilization would be one good way of breeding out criminals and other undesirable elements in our society and so raise its general standards and living conditions.

25. An occasional lynching in the South is a good thing because there is a large percentage of Negroes in many communities and they need a scare once in a while to prevent them from starting riots and disturbances.

26. Mexico can never advance to the standards of living and civilization of the U. S., due mainly to the innate dirtiness, laziness, and general backwardness of Mexicans.

27. Filipinos are all right in their place, but they carry it too far when they dress lavishly, buy good cars, and go around with white girls.

28. It would be best to limit Negroes to grammar and trade school education since more schooling just gives them ambitions and desires which they are unable to fulfill in white competition.

29. Zootsuiters demonstrate that inferior groups, when they are given too much freedom and money, just misuse their privileges and create disturbances.

30. The most vicious, irresponsible, and racketeering unions are, in most cases, those having largely foreigners for leaders.

31. There is something inherently primitive and uncivilized in the Negro, as shown in his music and his extreme aggressiveness.

32. We are spending too much money for the pampering of criminals and the insane, and for the education of inherently incapable people.

33. There will always be wars because, for one thing, there will always be races who ruthlessly try to grab more than their share.

34. Most Negroes would become officious, overbearing, and disagreeable if not kept in their place.

1. RELIABILITY

Data indicating the reliability and related statistical properties of the E scale and its subscales are given in Table 5(IV).

TABLE 5 (IV)

RELIABILITY OF THE ETHNOCENTRISM (E) SCALE AND ITS SUBSCALES

Property	Total E Scale	Negroes	Subscales Minorities	Patriotism
Reliability[a]	.91	.91	.82	.80
Number of items	34	12	12	10
Mean (total)[b]	3.17	2.72	3.32	3.53
Mean (odd half)	3.02	2.65	3.23	3.88
Mean (even half)	3.32	2.78	3.40	3.18
S.D. (total)[b]	1.15	1.25	1.21	1.26
S.D. (odd half)	1.17	1.25	1.37	1.26
S.D. (even half)	1.21	1.42	1.28	1.46
Range[b]	1.2–5.6	1.0–5.6	1.0–6.0	1.0–6.1

[a]The split-half reliability of each scale was obtained by correlating the sum of the scores on the odd items with the sum of the even items, and correcting this value by the Spearman-Brown formula.

[b]The means, S.D.'s, and ranges are given in terms of mean score per item on the scale or subscale in question. If this value is multiplied by the number of items in the scale or subscale, it is converted into mean total score.

The split-half reliability of the total E scale is .91, a value which meets accepted statistical standards.[4] The odd and even halves were roughly equivalent in the sense that they contained about equal numbers of items from the three subscales. The lower mean of the odd half seems due to the slight overweighting with low-mean Negro items. The obtained range covered most of the possible range, with the exception of the extremely high end. The absence of very high scores (averages of over 6 points per item) is also reflected in the relatively low group mean of 3.17, as compared with the neutral point of 4.0 per item. The distribution of scores is very symmetrical—the mean divides the range in half, and the median is 3.2—but platykurtic, with very little clustering of scores around the mean.

The high reliabilities of the subscales are noteworthy, especially in view of the small number of items in each.

In terms of reliability, equivalence of halves, and form of distribution,

[4] On the chance that the 19 minority group members might be atypical in some way, a separate reliability was computed for the 125 remaining subjects. The obtained value was .91, identical with that for the total group.

then, it seems safe to conclude that the E scale and its subscales provide adequate measuring instruments. To the extent that the scale is valid, it provides a measure of ethnocentrism, in most of its generality and complexity. It may be claimed that the higher an individual's score, the greater his acceptance of ethnocentric propaganda and the greater his disposition to engage in ethnocentric accusations and programs of one form or another.

2. INTERCORRELATIONS AMONG THE SUBSCALES

The reliability data support the hypothesis that there is such a thing as general ethnocentric ideology and that people can be roughly ranked according to the strength of their acceptance or rejection of it. Support for this hypothesis is also given by the high intercorrelations among the subscales, as shown in Table 6(IV).

TABLE 6 (IV)

CORRELATIONS OF THE E SUBSCALES WITH EACH OTHER AND WITH THE TOTAL E SCALE[a]

	Negroes	Minorities	Patriotism	Total E
Negroes	---	.74	.76	.90
Minorities	.74	---	.83	.91
Patriotism	.76	.83	---	.92

[a]These are the raw correlation coefficients. If they were corrected for attenuation to give the maximal value theoretically obtainable (with perfectly reliable instruments), they would all be .9 or over.

The subscale intercorrelations, which range from .74 to .83, are of considerable significance. The fact that they involve items dealing with so great a variety of groups and ideas suggests again that ethnocentrism is a general frame of mind, that an individual's stand with regard to one group such as Negroes tends to be similar in direction and degree to his stand with regard to most issues of group relations.

The intercorrelations of .90 to .92 between each subscale and the total E scale make the same point; an individual's score on any one subscale permits one to predict very closely his score on the entire E scale. Or, to put it in another way: While almost every subject shows some variability in his responses to the individual items (as will be shown below), almost every one demonstrates a general degree of pro- or anti-ethnocentrism which is relatively consistent from one group or type of group to another. And ethnocentric hostility toward outgroups is highly correlated with ethnocentric idealization of ingroups.

3. INTERNAL CONSISTENCY: STATISTICAL ANALYSIS OF THE INDIVIDUAL ITEMS

The functions of item analysis, and the procedures involved, have been discussed in the previous chapter. The data on the item analysis of the E scale are presented in Table 7(IV). Each item is identified by a key word or phrase, and the letters N, M, and P refer to the subscales Negroes, Minorities, and Patriotism respectively. It will be recalled that the Discriminatory Power (D. P.) equals the mean for the high quartile minus the mean for the low quartile. The total group mean is, of course, based on all four quartiles.

In general the D. P.'s in Table 7(IV) are very satisfactory,[5] averaging 2.97. For the 34 items, 5 D. P.'s are over 4.0, 13 are between 3.0 and 3.9, and 10 are between 2.0 and 2.9; only 3 are between 1.0 and 1.9, and 3 less than 1.0. Furthermore, all 6 items with D. P.'s of less than 2.0 have group means of less than 3.0, so the D. P. is more significant than it appears.[6]

The three least discriminating items are 19, 25, and 28, all in subscale N. They are also the only three items with group means of less than 2.0. Their low means indicate almost unanimous disagreement by all subjects. This is to be expected, since the items are particularly violent and repressive: Negroes should be driven out of town, lynched, kept ignorant and uneducated. But these data show the advantage of permitting three degrees of agreement and of disagreement, and they also reveal a subtle receptiveness in the high-scoring subjects to openly antidemocratic programs. Of the 36 low scorers only one responded with −2 (on Item 28), all other responses on all three items being a firm −3 (and thus a low mean of 1.00). The high quartile, on the other hand, had a mean of 1.8 on each of the three items; nearly half of them responded with −2 or above. One might ask if this is an indication of potential response during a period in which fascism had become a real power. Not all those who score high on E, certainly, are receptive to violent antidemocracy; the task of determining the deeper psychological forces which make for potential receptiveness or opposition to fascism—the ultimate in ethnocentrism—is one which follows the first task of measuring ethnocentrism in its presently existing form.

The item analysis indicates that the N, M, and P subscales contributed about equally to the total differentiation between the high and low quartiles on the total scale, the average D. P. being 3.0, 2.9, and 3.1 respectively. Apart from items 19, 25, and 28, discussed above, the Negro items were highly discriminating. Ethnocentrists and anti-ethnocentrists, as measured by the total scale, are clearly differentiated with respect to most of the ideas contained

[5] The D. P.'s would be even higher if the "range of talent" in this group included more extreme ethnocentrists. This is shown by results on subsequently tested groups.

[6] While correlations between items or between each item and the total scale have not been computed for this group, later data on similar scales suggest that the average correlation between single items is about .4, while between each item and the sum of the remaining items the average correlation is about .6.

TABLE 7 (IV)

MEANS AND DISCRIMINATORY POWERS OF THE E-SCALE ITEMS

No.	Item	Mean		D.P.	Mean for Total Group
		High Quartile	Low Quartile		
1.	(M: political parties)	3.72	2.17	1.55	2.85
2.	(N: dance)	6.17	1.97	4.20	4.04
3.	(P: patriotism)	6.48	3.86	2.62	5.21
4.	(M: religious sects)	5.08	1.61	3.47	3.26
5.	(N: lazy)	3.10	1.53	3.19	3.19
6.	(M: foreign groups)	4.50	1.69	2.81	3.02
7.	(P: superior nations)	3.67	1.25	2.42	2.54
8.	(N: bands)	5.08	1.25	3.83	2.77
9.	(M: women)	5.86	3.75	2.11	4.76
10.	(P: military training)	5.06	2.47	2.59	3.83
11.	(N: foremen)	6.05	1.69	4.36	3.99
12.	(P: foreign ideas)	4.86	1.22	3.64	3.13
13.	(P: conscientious objectors)	4.64	1.44	3.20	2.90
14.	(N: districts)	6.33	1.72	4.61	4.08
15.	(M: voting)	5.06	2.33	2.73	3.71
16.	(N: menial jobs)	5.22	1.58	3.64	3.17
17.	(M: Japs in army)	5.86	1.92	3.94	3.87
18.	(P: native white Americans)	4.75	1.08	3.67	2.80
19.	(N: drive out)	1.86	1.00	.86	1.26
20.	(P: refugees)	6.39	3.50	2.89	5.28
21.	(M: Okies)	5.39	1.81	3.58	5.70
22.	(N: agitators)	4.53	1.08	3.45	2.51
23.	(P: Germans and Japs)	5.28	1.50	3.78	3.07
24.	(M: sterilize)	3.11	2.03	1.08	2.71
25.	(N: lynch)	1.81	1.00	.81	1.32
26.	(P: Mexico)	3.69	1.06	2.63	2.15
27.	(M: Filipinos)	5.64	1.22	4.42	3.68
28.	(N: grammar schools)	1.86	1.03	.83	1.30
29.	(M: zootsuiters)	5.58	1.39	4.19	3.62
30.	(M: foreigners, unions)	4.08	1.17	2.91	2.42
31.	(N: primitive)	3.72	1.17	2.55	2.42
32.	(M: pamper criminals)	3.22	1.53	1.69	2.20
33.	(P: always war)	5.89	2.64	3.25	4.37
34.	(N: overbearing)	4.75	1.06	3.69	2.67
Means:	Total scale	4.70	1.73	2.97	3.17
	Subscale N	4.34	1.34	3.00	2.72
	Subscale M	4.76	1.89	2.87	3.32
	Subscale P	5.07	2.00	3.07	3.53

Number: Total group = 144
        H. Q.   = 36
        L. Q.   = 36

Range of scores: Total group = 1.2-5.6
                H. Q.   = 4.2-5.6
                L. Q.   = 1.2-2.2

in the Negro items. The mean for the low quartile is invariably below 2.0, indicating that the low scorers seldom agree with these items and usually disagree strongly. The high scorers are not so outspoken in their stand; their most frequent responses are in the range of −1 to +2; but the frequency of the agreements overshadows the slight disagreements.

The means are somewhat higher on the Minorities subscale but once again, despite the great variety of groups represented, the highs and lows are clearly differentiated on most items. Three Minorities items (1, 24, 32) had group means below 3.0 and Discriminatory Powers between 1.1 and 1.7. These D. P.'s indicate statistically significant trends but do not establish clear-cut differentiations. The high scorers apparently did not fall for the suggestions in these items that minority political parties be suppressed— perhaps because these parties were not described as immoral or threatening (suppression of religious sects was accepted in Item 4)—that undesirables be sterilized, and that less money be spent on criminals, the insane and the "inherently incapable." The idea that "woman's place is in the home" is apparently accepted by most women (Item 9; mean = 4.76). While the low quartile is almost equally divided on this issue, the high scorers are definitely in favor of it; the D. P. of 2.1 is clearly significant. One wonders whether this item would be better correlated with ethnocentrism in men. The most discriminating items in this subscale deal with a variety of groups: religious sects (Item 4), foreign ideas (Item 12), Japanese (Item 17), Oklahomans in California (Item 21), Filipinos (Item 27), and zootsuiters (Item 29).

The Patriotism subscale differentiates high and low scorers as well as do the other subscales and on as great a variety of groups. The Discriminatory Powers range from 2.42 to 3.78, with an average D. P. of 3.07. Again the major hypotheses underlying the items are substantiated. Other nations (Japanese, Mexicans, refugees, and "inferior nations" generally) are regarded as backward, immoral, and threatening. The superiority of the American nation justifies a policy of destruction and subordination of others. Submissiveness and obedience to the ingroup are regarded as primary virtues, and a punitive attitude—so characteristically taken toward extranational and intranational outgroups—is taken toward conscientious objectors. It is also interesting that Item 33, concerning the inevitability of war, is highly differentiating (D. P. = 3.25). It is as if the ingroup-outgroup distinction, and the intergroup hostility underlying it, are woven into the fabric of ethnocentric thinking; given a conflict with no conceivable possibility of resolution, there is nothing to do but make sure that the ingroup is on top and prepared to maintain itself.

4. SECOND FORM OF THE E SCALE (FORM 78)

In line with the general policy of contracting proven techniques in order to include new ones which might broaden the framework of the research, the original 34-item E scale was shortened to 14 items in the next version of the questionnaire, Form 78. This questionnaire, described more fully in Chapter III, included four separate scales whose items, 78 in all, were interspersed randomly in a single series. The revised E scale is presented in Table 8(IV).

TABLE 8 (IV)
THE SECOND FORM OF THE E SCALE (FORM 78)

Old No.	New No.[a]	
___	4.	All forms of racial and religious discrimination should be made illegal and punishable.
29.	7.	Zootsuiters demonstrate that inferior groups, when they are given too much freedom and money, just misuse their privileges and create disturbances.
12.	18.	The main threat to basic American institutions during this century has come from foreign ideas, doctrines, and agitators.
___	25.	If and when a new world organization is set up, America must be sure that she loses none of her independence and full sovereignty as a separate nation.
14.	29.	Negroes have their rights, but it is best to keep them in their own districts and schools and to prevent too much contact with whites.
9.	34.	Women, if they work at all, should take the most feminine positions, such as nursing, secretarial work, or child care.
5.	37.	If Negroes live poorly, it's because they are just naturally lazy, ignorant, and without self-control.
___	41.	America may not be perfect, but the American Way has brought us about as close as human beings can get to a perfect society.
11.	45.	It would be a mistake to have Negroes for foremen and leaders over whites.
23.	48.	The only full guarantee of future peace is to wipe out as many as possible of the Germans and Japs, and to keep the rest under strict control.
___	51.	Most of our social problems would be solved if the immoral, corrupt, and defective people could somehow be removed from the scene.
15.	54.	One main difficulty with allowing the entire population to participate fully in government affairs is that such a large percentage is innately deficient and incapable.
22.	57.	The people who raise all the talk about putting Negroes on the same level as whites are mostly radical agitators trying to stir up conflicts.
17.	64.	Citizen or not, no Jap should be allowed to return to California.

[a] "New number" refers to the numbering of the items in Form 78. "Old number" refers to numbering in the initial form discussed previously. Slight revisions will be noted in the wording of several items.

The general rules guiding contraction of the longer form were the same as those described previously in connection with the A-S scale. Statistical adequacy was again a necessary but not sufficient condition for retention of an item. It was deemed necessary to maintain broadness of coverage and to ensure nonduplication as well as significance of ideas. Revisions in the word-

ing of some items were made, especially in the direction of brevity and simplification. Item 9 of the initial form, suggesting that "woman's place is in
the home," was entirely revised (present Item 34) in an attempt to improve
its discriminability. In view of changing issues, former Item 17, which opposed the entrance of Japanese-Americans into the army, was changed in
the new form to Item 64, which opposes their return to California.

There are four new items in the short form. Item 4 proposes legislation
against discrimination; it is the first and only positive E item, that is, one
in case of which agreement is given a low score. Number 25, a "patriotism"
item, was intended to appeal both to the open isolationist and to the kind of
pseudointernationalist who, while more or less accepting the idea of a world
organization, wanted nevertheless to maintain complete American sovereignty and control. Item 41, which replaces several previous items, was
intended to express an uncritically idealizing relation to America as a national
ingroup. Finally, Item 51 refers to moral outgroups; it suggests that immorality is a cause of our social problems (rather than a concurrent symptom), and it contains implicitly a punitive attitude against such people, although punitive action is not explicitly proposed. Also worth noting is this
item's stereotypic distinction between "good" people and "bad" people—
the latter being the cause of the misfortunes of the former. This way of
thinking often includes the "contempt for the masses" expressed in Item 54.

The three subscales of the initial E scale are represented proportionately
in the new form. There are four Negro items (29, 37, 45, 57), four Patriotism
items (18, 25, 41, 48), and six Minority items (4, 7, 34, 51, 54, 64).

It will be recalled from the preceding chapter that Form 78 was administered in the spring of 1945 to four groups: Public Speaking Class Women
(N = 140), Public Speaking Class Men (N = 52), Extension Psychology
Class Women (N = 40), all from the University of California; and the Professional Women (nurses, social workers, teachers; N = 63).

The reliability data for the E scale (Form 78) are presented in Table
9(IV). The average reliability of .80 is at the lower level of significance in
terms of precise measurement of the individual, but it is quite satisfactory
for the group comparisons and correlations for which it was used.[7] This is
perhaps all that could be expected of so short and diversified a scale. Hope
of improvement is held out, however, by the possibility of eliminating or
revising poorly discriminating items, and by the fact that the absence of

---

[7] There are no absolute standards concerning what is an adequate reliability, as this
varies with the variables measured, the uses to which the instrument will be put, and so
forth. In the present study the following approximate standards of reliability have been
used. (a) Above .85: permits relatively precise measurement of the individual. (b) From
.75 to .85: permits rough ordering of individuals into, say, a quartile series of "low," "low
middle," "high middle," and "high." Quite satisfactory for statistical analysis of group
data. (c) From .60 to .75: lower level of adequacy, but sufficient for determining general
relationships and for comparing extreme scorers.

TABLE 9 (IV)

RELIABILITY OF THE E-SCALE (FORM 78)

Property[a]	Group[b]				Over-all[c]
	A	B	C	D	
Reliability	.80	.74	.80	.88	.80
Mean (total)	3.44	3.33	3.68	2.72	3.29
Mean (odd half)	3.36	3.11	3.68	2.56	3.18
Mean (even half)	3.55	3.52	3.68	2.87	3.40
S.D. (total)	1.07	1.04	1.13	1.21	1.11
S.D. (odd half)	1.16	1.12	1.29	1.22	1.20
S.D. (even half)	1.15	1.18	1.25	1.37	1.24
N	140	52	40	63	295
Range	1.4–5.9	1.2–5.9	1.2–6.1	1.0–5.9	1.0–6.1

[a]The values of the means, S.D.'s, and ranges are given in terms of mean per item. If multiplied by 14 (the number of items), they are converted into values representing total scale score per person.

[b]The four groups on which these data are based are:
Group A: U.C. Public Speaking Class Women
Group B: U.C. Public Speaking Class Men
Group C: U.C. Extension Psychology Class Women
Group D: Professional Women

[c]In obtaining the over-all means, the individual group means were not weighted by N.

extremely high scorers (restriction of "range of talent") in these groups tends to depress the reliabilities somewhat. As in the case of the A-S scale, the Professional Women obtained the lowest mean and the highest reliability, being thus the least prejudiced and the most consistent group on both scales. The E scale means and ranges of all four groups indicate, on the average, slight disagreement with ethnocentric ideology, a sizable minority being strongly opposed and relatively few expressing strong support.

The item analysis of the scale is presented in Table 10(IV). The average D. P. of 2.90 is quite satisfactory for a scale of this length. Only one D. P. is below 2.1, and even this one (Item 4) is well above the minimum level of statistical significance. As in the initial, longer E scale, the items dealing with segregation and suppression of Negroes, opposition to "foreign infiltration" and zootsuiters, desire to "wipe out the Germans and Japs," and so on, were highly discriminating. Two of the four new items also worked very well: Item 25, placing American sovereignty above world organization, had an over-all rank D. P. of 4; and Item 41, an expression of ethnocentric conservatism in idealizing the "American Way," ranked 7 in terms of over-all D. P.

Among the poorest items are several which, only fairly successful in the initial form, were revised for Form 78 in an attempt at improvement. Thus,

TABLE 10 (IV)

MEANS AND DISCRIMINATORY POWERS OF THE E-SCALE ITEMS (FORM 78) [a]

No.	Item	Group A Mean	D.P.	Group B Mean	D.P.	Group C Mean	D.P.	Group D Mean	D.P.	Over-all[b] Mean	D.P.	Rank D.P.
4.	(Discrimination illegal)	3.99	0.17	3.44	2.29	4.30	1.45	4.06	2.12	3.95	1.51	(14)
7.	(Zootsuiters)	3.73	3.94	3.29	2.93	3.58	4.07	2.90	5.12	3.38	4.02	(1)
18.	(Foreign ideas)	3.36	3.01	3.69	2.15	3.32	3.95	2.30	3.92	3.17	3.26	(5)
25.	(World organization)	4.89	2.76	3.90	3.35	5.60	2.29	4.02	4.74	4.60	3.28	(4)
29.	(Negroes have rights)	3.69	4.54	3.12	3.29	4.52	4.04	2.30	4.12	3.41	4.00	(2)
34.	(Feminine positions)	2.66	1.89	4.42	2.36	2.00	1.91	1.89	2.57	2.74	2.18	(12)
37.	(Negroes lazy)	2.06	2.85	1.75	1.86	2.35	2.34	1.50	1.60	1.92	2.16	(13)
41.	(American Way)	4.11	2.38	3.69	3.14	5.22	2.69	4.33	3.98	4.34	3.05	(7)
45.	(Negro foremen)	4.26	3.76	3.60	3.58	5.28	3.54	3.21	3.06	4.09	3.48	(3)
48.	(Germans – Japs)	2.49	2.27	2.56	2.00	2.90	4.72	2.03	3.33	2.50	3.08	(6)
51.	(Remove corrupt people)	3.59	2.70	3.37	1.50	3.22	1.95	2.43	3.21	3.15	2.34	(11)
54.	(Population incapable)	4.44	2.44	4.33	1.86	3.95	3.11	3.17	3.22	3.97	2.66	(10)
57.	(Radicals pro-Negro)	2.51	2.52	2.75	2.21	2.98	3.65	2.14	3.05	2.60	2.86	(8)
64.	(No Japs in California)	2.52	2.96	2.46	2.93	2.25	1.87	1.75	3.00	2.24	2.69	(9)
	Mean per item	3.45	2.73	3.31	2.53	3.68	2.97	2.72	3.36	3.29	2.90	

[a] The four groups on which these data are based are: Group A, U.C. Public Speaking Class Women (N = 140). Group B, U.C. Public Speaking Class Men (N = 52). Group C, U.C. Extension Psychology Class Women (N = 40). Group D, Professional Women (N = 63).

[b] In obtaining the over-all means, the individual group means were not weighted by N.

Item 34, stating that women should be restricted to "feminine positions" such as nursing, ranked 12 out of 14. It is interesting that the women's groups (A, C, D in Table 10(IV)) tended predominantly to disagree with this item, obtaining means of only 1.9 to 2.7, while the group of college men showed a slight tendency to agree, having a mean of 4.4. Despite the similar Discriminatory Powers for men and women, the D. P. for women is probably more significant statistically, since their mean is so much lower. It would appear that the ethnocentric women are more bound, at least on the surface, to the traditional imagery of femininity, while the nonethnocentrists wish to emancipate women, occupationally and otherwise, from their traditionally imposed limitations. While the relationship is far from perfect, it suggests that different patterns of ideology regarding masculinity and femininity may exist in the two groups. This general problem is investigated more fully in later chapters.

The attempted improvements in Items 37 and 54 were also relatively unsuccessful. Item 37, which makes the Negroes entirely responsible for their own poverty, was apparently too strongly worded to receive much agreement (mean = 1.92). The low mean indicates that the D. P. of 2.16 is very significant; there is very little overlapping between low and high scorers, the former tending almost uniformly to disagree strongly (-3), while the latter disagree on the average only slightly (-1). Similarly, the relatively low D. P. of 2.7 and mean of 2.2 on Item 64 (No Japs in California) might have been higher had the item been given a pseudodemocratic coloring, thus allowing the ethnocentrists more moral justification for agreeing with it. Item 54, rejecting the bulk of the people as "innately deficient and incapable," has a more ambiguous relation to ethnocentrism. The subjects were evenly divided on this issue, and the D. P. of 2.7, while indicating a significant difference between the high and low quartiles, nevertheless permits considerable agreement by low scorers, disagreement by high scorers.

Of the four entirely new items, two were among the least discriminating. Item 51, which suggests that our social problems could be solved by eliminating "bad" people (rather than by changing the underlying social forces and institutions), had a D. P. of 2.3, rank 11, indicating a clear-cut difference between the high and the low quartiles, but numerous exceptions as well.

The poorest item, with a D. P. of 1.5, was number 4 (urging that discrimination be made illegal). The subjects were apparently evenly divided on this issue, and relatively few were willing to take an extreme stand either way. The fact that the Professional Women had a mean of 4.1 on this item, as compared with their scale mean of 2.7, was perhaps a straw in the wind to indicate that the attempted California Fair Employment Practices Law (referendum) of 1946 would receive far less than majority support. In their interview discussions many strongly anti-ethnocentric subjects—who clearly recognized the crucial role of discrimination in maintaining ingroup-outgroup conflicts—were nevertheless political pacifists in the sense of being unwilling militantly to oppose discrimination. Some of the psychological sources of this point of view will be considered in later chapters.

The E scale (Form 78), while adequate for its intended uses, was revised in the light of the results just discussed. The revision also took account of the correlations now to be considered, between the E and A-S scales.

D. THE INCLUSION OF ANTI-SEMITISM WITHIN GENERAL ETHNOCENTRISM

It will be recalled that the E scale contained no items referring to Jews; rather, the independent A-S scale was included within the total questionnaire. We may now consider the correlations between these scales.

The initial form of the questionnaire, administered in 1944 to the University of California Psychology Class Women, contained the 52-item A-S scale and the 34-item E scale. Correlations of the A-S scale with the E scale and its subscales are presented in Table 11(IV).

TABLE 11 (IV)

CORRELATIONS BETWEEN THE A-S AND E SCALES (INITIAL FORMS) [a]

		E Subscale		
	Total E Scale	"Negroes"	"Minorities"	"Patriotism"
A-S	.80	.74	.76	.69

[a]The reliabilities of these scales, as presented previously, are as follows: A-S = .92; E = .91; "Negroes" = .91; "Minorities" = .82; "Patriotism" = .80.

The correlation of .80 between E and A-S permits a further broadening in the conception of ethnocentrism. The correlations of .69–.76 between A-S and the E subscales are only slightly lower than the correlations of .74–.83 among the E subscales (see Section C, above). These values indicate once again the generality of the ethnocentric approach to group relations. Anti-Semitism is best regarded, it would seem, as one aspect of this broader frame of mind; and it is the total ethnocentric ideology, rather than prejudice against any single group, which requires explanation. The fact that A-S correlates slightly less with the E subscales than the latter correlate among themselves may be due in part to the shortened range of A-S scores (absence of extreme highs); however, it appears likely that there are certain specific determinants of anti-Semitism apart from those which hold for general ethnocentrism.

The correlations between the A-S and E scales in Form 78, presented in

Table 12(IV), provide a further indication of the generality of ethnocentrism. The average correlation, .68, is lower than that of .80 obtained in the initial form. This difference is due partially to the decreased reliability of the shortened E scale. However, it suggests once again that anti-Semitism,

TABLE 12 (IV)

CORRELATIONS BETWEEN THE A-S AND E SCALES (FORM 78)

Group	N	Correlation
Public Speaking women	140	.71
Public Speaking men	52	.75
Extension women	40	.63
Professional women	63	.63
Mean r[a]	295	.68

[a]The mean r is unweighted for N and not based on Z_r.

while it is essentially a facet of a broader ethnocentric pattern, may nevertheless have certain independent determinants of its own.

1. THE THIRD FORM OF THE E SCALE (FORM 60)

The close, though imperfect, relationship between the A-S and E scales in Form 78 led, in the construction of Questionnaire Form 60, to their contraction into an inclusive 12-item E scale. This scale, presented in Table 13 (IV), contains 4 A-S items (numbers 8, 21, 38, 47), 3 Negro items (14, 28, 42), and 5 items dealing with other minorities and with patriotism. Once again slight revisions in the wording have frequently been made, particularly in the direction of simplicity and brevity. Again items were selected on the basis both of statistical adequacy and theoretical significance. Two items (42, 55) were included, despite their previous low means and D. P.'s, because they seemed to express significant ideas and because the means, and thus the D. P.'s, were expected to go up in some of the groups to be tested. Item 59 ("Okies") was recovered from the initial E scale.

a. THE GROUPS STUDIED. Questionnaire Form 60 was administered in the summer of 1945 to the following groups:

1. Summer session students in psychology classes at the University of Oregon (one of us taking advantage of his summer teaching position there).

2. Summer session students in an education class at the University of California.[8] Whereas the Oregon students were almost entirely of college age, the members of this particular education class at the University of California were somewhat older (age range about 25–45), the most common occupation

---

[8] We wish to express our thanks to Dr. Harold Carter for the administration of the questionnaires to his class.

TABLE 13 (IV)
THE THIRD FORM OF THE E SCALE (FORM 60)

3. Zootsuiters prove that when people of their type have too much money and freedom, they just take advantage and cause trouble.

8. One trouble with Jewish businessmen is that they stick together and prevent other people from having a fair chance in competition.

14. Negroes have their rights, but it is best to keep them in their own districts and schools and to prevent too much contact with whites.

21. I can hardly imagine myself marrying a Jew.

28. It would be a mistake ever to have Negroes for foremen and leaders over whites.

33. If and when a new world organization is set up, America must be sure that she loses none of her independence and complete power in matters that affect this country.

38. There may be a few exceptions, but in general, Jews are pretty much alike.

42. If Negroes live poorly, it's mainly because they are naturally lazy, ignorant, and without self-control.

47. The trouble with letting Jews into a nice neighborhood is that they gradually give it a typical Jewish atmosphere.

51. The worst danger to real Americanism during the last 50 years has come from foreign ideas and agitators.

55. Citizen or not, no Jap should be allowed to return to California.

59. For the good of all, the Oklahomans ("Okies") who recently flooded California ought to be sent back home as soon as possible.

being that of teacher, although other, particularly semiprofessional, occupations were well represented.

3. Men's service clubs (Kiwanis, Lions, Rotary) in the vicinity of the University of Oregon.

In order that separate data for men and women might be obtained, the above groups were divided and recombined for statistical purposes. The first University of Oregon class obtained included enough women to form a statistical group (Group I, N = 47). However, the second class at Oregon was too small to be divisible into statistically adequate subgroups of men and women, and so was the class at California. Accordingly, statistical Group II contains the combined Oregon and California Student Women (N = 54), Group III the combined men (N = 57). Finally, Group IV contains the Oregon Service Club Men (N = 68).

b. RELIABILITY. The reliability data for the E Scale (Form 60) are presented in Table 14(IV). The reliabilities, ranging from .82 to .88 and averaging .86 for the four groups, are entirely adequate in terms of currently accepted standards. The obtained scores cover most of the possible range (1.0–7.0) with the exception of the extremely high end; there are few scores of over 6.0. A slight predominance of low scores is also indicated by the group means, which are well below the neutral point of 4.0.

The differences among the various groups are of some interest. The highest degree of ethnocentrism was expressed by the Oregon Service Club Men.

TABLE 14 (IV)

RELIABILITY OF THE E SCALE (FORM 60) [a]

Property	Group				Over-all
	I	II	III	IV	
Reliability	.88	.88	.86	.82	.86
Mean (total)	3.43	3.25	2.96	3.55	3.30
Mean (odd half)	3.48	3.24	2.95	3.72	3.35
Mean (even half)	3.38	3.26	2.97	3.43	3.26
S.D. (total)	1.38	1.29	1.26	1.11	1.26
S.D. (odd half)	1.63	1.77	1.38	1.21	1.50
S.D. (even half)	1.30	1.53	1.23	1.17	1.31
N	47	54	57	68	226
Range	1.0-6.3	1.1-5.9	1.0-6.3	1.3-5.8	1.0-6.3

[a]The four groups on which these data are based are:
Group I: University of Oregon Student Women.
Group II: University of Oregon and University of California Student Women.
Group III: University of Oregon and University of California Student Men.
Group IV: Oregon Service Club Men.

Their mean of 3.55 is significantly higher (1 per cent level) than the lowest mean, 2.96, obtained by the University Student Men. We may note that the group of Service Club Men was also the most constricted in its range of scores (1.3–5.8) and in its internal variability (S. D. = 1.11); that is, its members tended to cluster around the middle position so that there are few extreme high or low scorers. These considerations help to explain why the E scale has the lowest reliability in this group and why the average D. P. is, as will be shown below, also lower for this group than for the others. That this group should exhibit a clustering around a modal "point of conformity" is perhaps not surprising, since conformity is one of its central values. It may, however, be surprising to some that the mode should be in a middle rather than a more extreme position.

It is also of some interest that the California subjects are slightly less ethnocentric than the Oregonians. Thus, Group I, composed entirely of Oregon students, has a slightly higher mean than Group II (3.43 to 3.25), which is more than half Californian in make-up. The likelihood of a regional difference is given greater weight by the fact that at least two items (55, "Japs," and 59, "Okies," and perhaps also 3, "Zootsuiters") refer specifically to conditions in California. A slight, though also not statistically significant difference is found between comparable sex groups, the University Student Women (Group II) having a higher mean than the University Student Men (Group III) (3.25–2.96). No consistent, significant difference between com-

TABLE 15 (IV)

MEANS AND DISCRIMINATORY POWERS OF THE E-SCALE ITEMS (FORM 60)[a]

No.	Item	Group I		Group II		Group III		Group IV		Over-all		Rank D.P.
		Mean	D.P.	Mean	D.P.	Mean	D.P.	Mean	D.P.	Mean	D.P.	
3.	(Zootsuiters)	3.34	2.31	3.41	3.06	2.77	3.07	4.06	3.11	3.40	2.89	(9)
8.	(J. businessmen)	4.11	3.47	3.65	3.87	3.40	3.47	3.78	2.22	3.74	3.26	(7)
14.	(Negro rights)	3.79	4.55	3.70	5.26	3.46	3.93	4.57	2.28	3.88	4.00	(2)
21.	(Marry a Jew)	4.94	4.15	4.50	2.87	3.61	3.60	4.47	3.22	4.38	3.46	(5)
28.	(Negro foreman)	4.00	4.69	3.87	4.46	3.53	3.67	4.31	4.05	3.93	4.22	(1)
33.	(World organization)	4.49	4.23	4.54	2.73	3.91	3.80	4.32	4.00	4.32	3.69	(4)
38.	(Jews alike)	3.70	4.38	3.15	3.33	2.93	3.66	3.99	3.89	3.44	3.82	(3)
42.	(Negroes lazy)	1.81	1.46	2.04	1.93	1.86	1.80	2.82	2.87	2.13	2.02	(11)
47.	(Jewish neighbors)	3.30	4.00	3.07	3.07	3.00	3.93	3.38	2.54	3.19	3.38	(6)
51.	(Foreign ideas)	2.74	3.54	2.56	3.13	2.75	2.27	3.25	3.61	2.82	3.14	(8)
55.	(No Japs)	2.34	2.69	2.13	1.87	1.93	1.13	2.00	1.50	2.10	1.80	(12)
59.	(Okies)	2.62	2.39	2.41	2.86	2.19	2.26	1.81	0.84	2.26	2.09	(10)
	Mean per item	3.43	3.49	3.25	3.20	2.95	3.05	3.56	2.84	3.30	3.15	

aThe four groups on which these data are based are:

Group I: University of Oregon Student Women (N = 47).
Group II: University of Oregon and University of California Student Women (N = 54).
Group III: University of Oregon and University of California Student Men (N = 57).
Group IV: Oregon Service Club Men (N = 68).

parable groups of men and women has been found, as may be noted below in the results on additional groups (p. 133 ff.).

c. ITEM ANALYSIS. The results of the item analysis of the E scale (Form 60) are presented in Table 15(IV). The average D. P. of 3.15 is very satisfactory. The three lowest D. P.'s (1.8–2.1) were obtained by the items having the lowest means (2.1–2.3). Two of these items, numbers 42 and 55, obtained similar means on previous forms of the scale. They were included here, slightly revised, with the expectation that the present groups might agree more strongly. This expectation was not borne out. In view of the relatively strong rejection of Oklahomans in California, the low mean and D. P. of Item 59 are probably due more to faults in formulation than to the inadequacy of the idea which we intended to express. Even the three poorest items, however, differentiate significantly and with a minimum of overlap between the high and low quartiles, the low scorers being strongly opposed (almost uniform responses of −3), the high scorers tending to disagree only slightly.[9]

The rank order of goodness of items is, on the whole, consistent with previous results. The five best items (14, 21, 28, 33, 38) include two referring to Negroes, two to Jews, and one to world organization; these items ranked similarly in earlier forms. Item 3 (Zootsuiters) has a rank of 9, as compared with a rank of 1 on Form 78. The drop may well be due to the fact that the zootsuiter issue was less focal, and therefore less likely to produce extreme agreement or disagreement, in Oregon than in California. The groups taking Form 60 agree quite well among themselves regarding the relative level of acceptability (mean) and level of discriminability (D. P.) of the items. While rank-order correlations between the groups were not computed, it appears from inspection of Table 15(IV) that the mean or D. P. rank of each item is fairly stable from group to group.

2. THE FOURTH FORM OF THE E SCALE (FORMS 45 AND 40)

The fourth and final form of the E Scale (see Table 16(IV)), as used in Form 45, involved the deletion of two items ("Japs" and "Okies") from the previous form, the other ten items remaining intact. It was understood that this contraction of the E scale would eliminate many of its qualitative functions and would probably lower its reliability to the minimum required by the present research purposes. Nevertheless, the intention to distribute the questionnaire to a wide variety of groups, many of whom would have very little time for filling it out, made every reduction in size seem desirable. The entire Questionnaire Form 45 could, accordingly, be filled out in approximately thirty minutes—short enough so that, for example, a club or

---

[9] The group mean for each item is usually about midway between the means for the high and low quartiles. It is therefore legitimate to infer the quartile means from the item mean and D. P.

TABLE 16 (IV)
The Fourth Form of the E Scale (Forms 45 and 40)[a]

E_A 5. Zootsuiters prove that when people of their type have too much money and freedom, they just take advantage and cause trouble.

E_A 10. Negroes have their rights, but it is best to keep them in their own districts and schools and to prevent too much contact with whites.

E_A 15. The worst danger to real Americanism during the last 50 years has come from foreign ideas and agitators.

E_A 20. It would be a mistake ever to have Negroes for foremen and leaders over whites.

E_B 24. One trouble with Jewish businessmen is that they stick together and prevent other people from having a fair chance in competition.

E_B 28. I can hardly imagine myself marrying a Jew.

E_B 32. If Negroes live poorly, it's mainly because they are naturally lazy, ignorant, and without self-control.

E_B 36. There may be a few exceptions, but in general, Jews are pretty much alike.

E_B 40. The trouble with letting Jews into a nice neighborhood is that they gradually give it a typical Jewish atmosphere.

E_A 45. If and when a new world organization is set up, America must be sure that she loses none of her independence and complete power in matters that affect this country.

[a] The five E_A items constitute the entire E scale in Form 40. The total ten-item scale was given, numbered as it appears above, in Form 45. The reliability of Form 45 was obtained by correlating the 5 E_A items with the remaining 5 E_B items. It will be noted that there are no items about Jews in E_A, it being desired as a practical aim to construct a questionnaire which would give an index of anti-Semitism without mentioning Jews at all.

organization could take it during a meeting, just before hearing a talk not directly related to the questionnaire.

Demands of practicality and expediency forced an additional compromise. Questionnaire Form 40 was even shorter than Form 45; in addition to contractions of other techniques, the E scale in this form was reduced to five items (as shown in Table 16(IV)). A primary reason for Form 40 was that certain groups might be unable to spare even the thirty minutes required by Form 45. An additional consideration in the contraction of the E scale, however, was the possibility that, in certain groups at least, the items referring to Jews might be too "controversial" or might focus attention too directly on the issue of prejudice. Accordingly, the five E_A items in Form 40 contain no direct reference to Jews. They deal, rather, with Negroes, zootsuiters, foreigners, and "world organization." (In Form 45 the E scale contains, in addition to these, five E_B items, four referring to Jews, one to Negroes.) It was recognized that these five items do not constitute a scale in the more technical sense, but this loss seemed justified by the gain in applicability to various groups.

Our conclusions regarding the advantage of using Form 40 ought perhaps to be noted for those faced with similar problems. Although it avoided focusing attention on Jews, the loss in terms of research aims was not sufficiently compensated for by the small gain in time nor by elimination of resistance. Indeed, the resistance encountered seemed to be based as much on the other phases of the questionnaire as on the E scale. Probably the basic opposition psychologically was to being "investigated" at all in an intensive way. Unlike the usual several-question poll, this questionnaire seemed, to many a subject, to *identify* him as a total individual even though he knew that his anonymity was preserved. In some cases this was highly anxiety-producing despite our careful attempts at reassurance and at explaining the entire procedure in terms of an impersonal, public opinion, nonindividual approach. In some cases it was impossible to gain the cooperation of the leadership of a group; in other cases cooperative leaders were unable to put the idea across or to have it carried out. Difficulties of this sort were as great with Form 40 as with Form 45. Once a group was induced to cooperate, there were very few omissions of questions or scale items in either form. In short, resistance was related more to the general nature of the questionnaire than to any specific individual items. Form 45 might therefore have been used on practically all of the groups tested. When it is absolutely necessary to delete certain items—e.g., if one were testing groups with a large Jewish or Negro membership and items referring to these groups might cause friction—probably the best procedure would be to have alternative items to replace those deleted.

While the number of groups which were actively but unsuccessfully approached is not large, there is some indication that resistance of the type mentioned above is correlated positively with ethnocentrism. For example, among the "Middle-Class Women" (Table 15(V)) there was an exclusive club which "just barely" decided to cooperate and which refused even to consider our request for volunteers to be interviewed. This group obtained one of the highest E means of all groups tested. Such resistance was seldom encountered in less ethnocentric groups. This difficulty might have been expected on the basis of the ethnocentrists' tendency toward self-deception and concern with prying, which was expressed indirectly in the responses on the A-S and E scales, and which is brought out more directly in the chapters that follow.

Considerations of this type are of great importance in any attempt to generalize from a research sample to a broader population. Thus, because of the greater resistance of ethnocentrists to psychological investigation, it is likely that the average degree of ethnocentrism (over-all mean E score) in our total sample is somewhat lower than that which would be found in a truly random or truly representative sample. Even in the more customary public opinion polls, where population areas are often mapped out in advance (stratification or other attempt at representative sampling), an adequate sample may not be achieved because, in their door-to-door polling, interviewers cannot reach those subjects who are unreceptive to the idea of being "tested."[10]

[10] The common assumption that "any 50 people" within a given area or income level will do, and that errors of sampling on an individual level will cancel each other out, overlooks the likelihood that *receptivity* may correlate with what is being polled.

It seems necessary, therefore, in describing the groups on whom data were obtained, to mention briefly the nature and adequacy of the sampling procedure.

a. THE SAMPLE AND THE SAMPLING PROCEDURE.   The distribution of Forms 45 and 40 took place during the latter part of 1945 and the first half of 1946, a period of about nine months in all. Form 45 was given to the following groups:[11]

1. *Testing Class Women* (N = 59). This was an adult evening class given by the Extension Division of the University of California. Since it was a class in Psychological Tests, it probably attracted a more diversified group than does the usual adult class in psychology. It was expected to contain not only individuals seriously interested in understanding themselves better—individuals who, as we shall see later, are not likely to be extremely ethnocentric—but also persons interested in psychology more as a means of manipulating others. The class was also varied with respect to age (range about 20–50), income, and previous education. Therefore, despite the desire to get away from the university groups which predominated in our previous samples, we could not resist taking the opportunity to test this marginal university group. The questionnaire was administered during a class meeting, all members being present. The men were too few to constitute a separate statistical group, and our policy of separating the sexes—perhaps too strictly adhered to—prevented us from combining them.

2. *San Quentin State Prison (California) Inmates* (N = 110). Since these men constitute a particularly important group, psychologically and sociologically, they were studied more intensively than the others; the sampling procedures and results are discussed in detail in Chapter XXI. It may suffice here to say that the sample was well randomized.

3. and 4. *Psychiatric Clinic Patients* (71 women, 50 men). This group, like the San Quentin group, was considered to have special importance both practically and for a full theoretical understanding of our problem. As a "key group," it seemed to merit thorough study and analysis (Chapter XXII). The questionnaires were administered individually (each subject filling out the questionnaire by himself) as part of the clinic routine, and there appeared to be no systematic bias operating in the selection of cases.

5. *Working-Class Men and Women.* A number of small groups were combined to form the "working-class" sample on which statistics were computed. Of the 53 women in this sample, 19 were from the California Labor School (an extremely liberal school for working people which has classes in a variety of fields, from trade unionism to arts and crafts), 8 were members of the United Electrical Workers, C.I.O., 10 were new members of the International Longshoremen and Warehousemen's Union (I.L.W.U., C.I.O.), and 16 were office workers obtained

[11] The collection of questionnaires from these groups would have been impossible without the generous cooperation of numerous people. We wish to express our gratitude to Dr. Merle H. Elliott, who obtained questionnaires from his class in the Extension Division of the University of California, Dr. David G. Schmidt, who made the necessary arrangements for the San Quentin Group, Dr. Karl Bowman and Dr. Robert Harris, who made it possible for us to obtain subjects at the Langley Porter Clinic, Dr. Barbara Kirchheimer, who made the arrangements, and Mrs. Emily Moulton, who collected questionnaires at the U.S. Employment Service, Captain Malcolm E. Crossman, who gave his support, and Dr. Boyd R. McCandless, who gave freely of his time in obtaining questionnaires at the Alameda School for Merchant Marine Officers.

through the employers. The 61 men were obtained similarly: 15 were from the California Labor School, 12 from the United Electrical Workers, 26 from the I.L.W.U., and 8 from the United Seamen's Service. All groups were obtained in the San Francisco Bay area. The Labor School subjects constitute the total membership of various classes, the questionnaire being administered in class.[12] The 20 Electrical Workers were obtained in the union hall as they came in on business matters. The 36 I.L.W.U. members were given the questionnaire at the beginning of a class for new members before any indoctrination had started. While the female office workers took the questionnaire at the request of interested employers, it was understood that they maintained their anonymity, and no systematic selective factors appear to have entered in. Less reliance can be placed on the male sample from the Seamen's Service, since the 8 subjects are but a small percentage of those passing in and out of the center. The working-class sample as a whole does not appear to reflect, in either a random or a representative manner, the actual working-class population, and any generalizations from the data must be drawn tentatively and with great caution.

The bulk of the working-class sample was given Form 40, only 19 women and 31 men receiving Form 45. Therefore, for the statistical purpose of relating the E scale to the other scales and measures (see Chapters V through VII), all questionnaires were treated as if they were Form 40, that is, only E_A was statisticized in Form 45. In consequence there are results on Form 40 for *Working-Class Women* (N = 53) and *Working-Class Men* (N = 61).

However, when additional data were desired on the total Form 45 E scale, it was decided to combine the 19 women and 31 men into a single sample,[13] the *Working-Class Men and Women* (Form 45) (N = 50). This sample is, then, actually a part of the larger Form 40 sample (see below). The men in the Form 45 sample were obtained from the groups mentioned above in almost exactly the same proportions as those taking Form 40. However, the Form 45 women are preponderantly from the Labor School and the United Electrical Workers' Union, and may consequently differ systematically from the others with respect to E.

Form 40 was given to a number of groups forming the following statistical samples:

6. *George Washington University Women* (N = 132). This group comprises the total female membership of several day and evening classes in psychology at George Washington University, Washington, D.C.[14] (There were so few men that their questionnaires were not statisticized.) It was included out of an interest in regional differences between California and the East, even though only limited generalizations can be drawn from so selected a sample.

7. *California Service Club Men* (N = 63). Two service clubs, Kiwanis and Rotary, comprise this sample. Questionnaires were filled out during a customary luncheon meeting (procedure not previously announced) just prior to the featured talk, given by a member of our staff.

---

[12] It appeared necessary to distinguish "middle-class" from "working-class" members of the Labor School, and to place the former in the broader "middle-class" sample. (See the discussion of the middle-class sample, Form 40.) The present figures refer only to working-class members.

[13] This sample was used only for getting the reliability data on the Form 45 E scale; no statistics were computed on the other scales.

[14] As mentioned previously, while the questionnaire was administered to all present, only the native-born, white, non-Jewish, American subjects were included in the statistical treatment. The N's reported refer to the number of cases treated statistically.

8. *Middle-Class Men* (N = 69) and 9. *Middle-Class Women* (N = 154). These two samples represent the combination, for statistical purposes, of the following groups: The membership at a meeting of the Parent-Teachers' Association in a "solid" middle-class section of Berkeley, California (46 women, 29 men). Again, the questionnaire was administered just before the featured talk on child training. The membership of a Protestant church in a small town just outside of San Francisco (29 women, 31 men). The 15 women in a local Unitarian Church group. The members of the California Labor School who appeared to be "middle class" in terms of occupation (lawyer, engineer, independent businessman, etc.) and income (11 women, 9 men); in case of doubt the individual remained in the "working-class" sample discussed above. The 17 women in one division or panel of the local League of Women Voters. Finally, the 36 members of an exclusive, upper middle-class women's club. It would appear, then, that these two samples, particularly the women, represent diverse elements of the middle class.

10. *Working-Class Men* (N = 61) and 11. *Working-Class Women* (N = 53). These groups have been described above in connection with the Form 45 sample of Working-Class Men and Women.

12. *Los Angeles Men* (N = 117) and 13. *Los Angeles Women* (N = 130).[15] In an attempt to obtain greater regional diversity for the total sample, a group of men and women was tested in the Los Angeles area. Because of time limitations the sampling procedure was not thoroughly controlled, and exact figures are not available on the number of subjects in each of the groups comprising the sample. Subjects were obtained from the following groups (not more than 25 per cent of the total N from any one group): parents of college students (volunteers), high school teachers, veterans at a counseling center, Radio Writers Guild (tested during a meeting), League of Women Voters, Boy Scout leaders, members of an anti-Semitic organization (12 responders out of some 100 questionnaires mailed out), and several small local clubs and neighborhood groups. The sample is primarily middle class in composition, although it cannot be considered clearly representative of the middle-class population. Moreover, its mean may be systematically lowered by the relatively high educational level and by the fact that many of the subjects were obtained on a volunteer basis. It was suitable for the present research purposes, however, since it appeared highly diverse with respect to ethnocentrism and with respect to the social and psychological characteristics whose relations to ethnocentrism were being investigated.

In addition to the above groups, the following two groups received both Forms 45 and 40:

14. *Employment Service Men Veterans* (N = 106). It seemed likely, early in 1946, that the questionnaire, particularly the F scale (see Chapter VII) and the projective questions (Chapter XV) could reveal much that was of interest to the clinician and the vocational counselor. Thus, when the questionnaire was given to veterans seeking vocational guidance at the local U. S. Employment Service, it was with the thought that it would be an aid to the agency as well as to the research. With a few exceptions, all (white, Christian) male veterans coming in for counseling during a several-month period starting early in 1946 were given the questionnaire, the first 51 receiving Form 45, the next 55, Form 40. The exceptions were men who seemed not to have enough education to handle the questionnaire and men in whose case a convenient time could not be arranged. This group can thus be considered a relatively random sample of the counselees. However,

---

[15] These questionnaires were collected by Dr. J. F. Brown with the assistance of Emily Gruen and Carol Creedon.

it may well be that counselees as a group are not representative of the veteran population. Thus, our sample is above average in socioeconomic level (see Chapter V) and in education and intelligence (see Chapter VIII). Furthermore, on the basis of evidence to be presented in later chapters, particularly Chapter XI, it appears likely that willingness to seek guidance, and especially to accept the mild psychotherapy going with it, is more common in nonethnocentrists than in others. How serious a sampling bias this produces depends in part on other factors which might impel ethnocentric individuals to seek help (e.g., external pressures, or a tendency to conceive of the Service as benevolent authority). At any rate, it is not unlikely that the mean E score for this sample may be somewhat lower than for the veteran population generally.

15. *Maritime School Men* (N = 343). This group comprises the entire membership of a government training school for Merchant Marine officers. The school is located in Alameda (San Francisco Bay area), but its students come from all parts of the country. Upon admission all of them must have had at least fourteen months of active service as unlicensed seamen. The questionnaires were administered during the study periods, under well-controlled conditions, by members of the Psychology staff who seemed to be on excellent terms with the men. Half of the study sections received Form 45, the other half Form 40, the halves being roughly equated in terms of ability and time in school. This group, like the one described immediately above, cannot be considered a fully representative sample of the armed services population. It is selected in at least the following ways: predominantly lower middle-class background, relatively few members coming from the lower socioeconomic strata or from the upper middle class or above; above average in upward social mobility—in the desire to "raise oneself socially and financially"; above average in intelligence, this being a primary qualification for admission (mean AGCT score of 126.2, range of 102–153).[16] Despite these relative uniformities, the group is extremely diverse in most other ways.

b. RELIABILITY AND GROUP DIFFERENCES. The reliability data for Forms 45 and 40 are presented in Table 17(IV). As noted above, the 5-item E_A scale in Form 40 contained no items referring to Jews; Form 45 contained these five items plus five E_B items, four of which are from the former A-S scale. Since the small number of items in Form 40 made it unfeasible to compute a reliability coefficient, it was decided to determine the reliability of the total scale by correlating E_A with E_B rather than by correlating odd-even or equivalent halves. This procedure gave some indication of the degree of equivalence between scores on Form 40 and scores on Form 45; it provided, for example, a partial answer to the question: of a group scoring in the low quartile on the E_A scale, what percentage would score in the low quartile on $E_{A + B}$? The average reliability of .79 for the seven groups taking Form 45 (Table 17(IV) A, C) indicates that the overlap is relatively great—although it also brings out the advantage of using the longer scale.

The present method of computing reliability, while it was helpful in determining the degree of relationship between E_A and $E_{A + B}$, and in showing

[16] No detailed description of the social and psychological properties of the various groups will be presented in this chapter. Instead, each set of properties will be presented and discussed in the appropriate chapter, e.g., politico-economic properties in Chapter V, religion in Chapter VI, and so on.

the great, though incomplete, unity in ethnocentric ideology, had nevertheless the disadvantage of yielding lower reliabilities than would have been obtained by a division into odd-even or equivalent halves. Two halves equated
for content are certainly likely to intercorrelate more highly than two halves,
such as E_A and E_B, which differ in content. This hypothesis was tested on
two groups. In the case of the San Quentin Men, who obtained an $E_A - E_B$
reliability of .65, the lowest of any group tested, the reliability rose to .79
when odd-even halves were used. In a group of 517 women, students at the
University of California,[17] the reliability based on E_A vs. E_B was .79, while
the odd-even reliability was .87. Since in its usual meaning "reliability"
refers to the relation between "'equivalent measures of the same thing,"
the reliability of the total E scale is probably around .85 on the average, a
value which meets current testing standards.

In view of the shortness of the E scale (Form 40), it was not feasible to
compute reliabilities on it. Instead, the mean Discriminatory Power (D. P.)

TABLE 17 (IV)

RELIABILITY OF THE E SCALE (FORMS 45 AND 40)

A. Groups Taking Form 45 (E_{A+B})

Property	Group[a]					Over-all[b]
	I	II	III	IV	V	
Reliability[c]	.82	.65	.84	.75	.91	.79
Mean (total)	3.41	4.61	3.65	3.67	3.34	3.74
Mean (A half)	3.77	5.33	4.23	3.92	3.62	4.17
Mean (B half)	3.06	3.86	3.06	3.42	3.07	3.29
S.D. (total)	1.40	1.28	1.60	1.59	1.78	1.53
S.D. (A half)	1.68	1.31	1.81	1.78	1.91	1.70
S.D. (B half)	1.35	1.60	1.64	1.70	1.77	1.61
N	59	110	71	50	50	340
Range	1.0–6.1	1.6–7.0	1.0–7.0	1.0–6.2	1.0–7.0	1.0–7.0

[a]The groups taking this form are as follows:
Group I: Extension Testing Class Women
Group II: San Quentin Men Prisoners
Group III: Psychiatric Clinic Women
Group IV: Psychiatric Clinic Men
Group V: Working Class Men and Women

[b]In obtaining the over-all means, the individual group means were not
weighted by N.

[c]The reliabilities for Form 45 are not based on odd-even or equivalent
halves but on E_A vs. E_B; they are therefore slightly lower than they
would be had equivalent halves been used (see text).

[17] This group was not included in the over-all sample because the proportion of students
in the sample was already too great. This group was obtained for the primary purpose of
making a correlational analysis of the Form 45 scales, particularly the F scale (see Chapter
VII).

TABLE 17 (IV) (CONT'D.)

RELIABILITY OF THE E SCALE (FORMS 45 AND 40)

B. Groups Taking Form 40 (E_A)[a]

Property	Group[b]								Over-all[c]
	VI	VII	VIII	IX	X	XI	XII	XIII	
Mean	4.04	4.31	3.89	3.64	3.92	3.91	3.82	3.71	3.90
S.D.	1.58	1.73	2.08	1.96	1.71	2.25	1.89	1.78	1.87
Mean D.P.	4.10	4.54	5.28	5.11	4.53	5.64	5.08	4.67	4.87
N	132	63	69	154	61	53	117	130	779
Range[d]									

[a] The E scale in Form 40 contained only 5 items, referred to as the E_A items and identical to the E_A items in Form 45.

[b] The groups taking this form are as follows:

Group VI: George Washington University Women
Group VII: California Service Club Men
Group VIII: Middle-Class Men
Group IX: Middle-Class Women
Group X: Working-Class Men
Group XI: Working-Class Women
Group XII: Los Angeles Men
Group XIII: Los Angeles Women

[c] In obtaining the over-all means, the individual group means were not weighted by N.

[d] The range in every case was 1.0–7.0.

TABLE 17 (IV) (CONT' D.)

RELIABILITY OF THE E SCALE (FORMS 45 AND 40)[a]

C. Groups Taking both Forms 45 and 40

Property	Group		Over-all
	Employment Service Men Veterans	Maritime School Men	
Form 45:			
Reliability	.86	.73	.80
Mean (total)	4.26	4.34	4.30
Mean (A half)	4.67	4.82	4.74
Mean (B half)	3.85	3.85	3.85
S.D. (total)	1.60	1.25	1.42
S.D. (A half)	1.63	1.40	1.52
S.D. (B half)	1.71	1.36	1.54
N	51	179	230
Range	1.1–6.6	1.2–6.6	1.1–6.6
Form 40:			
Mean (E_A)	4.21	5.08	4.64
S.D. (E_A)	1.75	1.47	1.61
N	55	164	219
Range	1.0–7.0	1.2–7.0	1.0–7.0

[a]The total number of cases on Forms 45 and 40 is as follows:

	Form 45	Form 40	Total
N	570	998	1568

is reported for each group in Table 17 (IV)*B*. The over-all mean D. P. of 4.87 suggests what the total E reliability also suggests: that the subjects show a relatively high degree of consistency in response to all items. The mean D. P. in four of the eight groups is over 5.0; this suggests that the distribution of scores is bimodal, that is, that the subjects tend either to agree strongly or to disagree strongly (in contrast to the more common result in which scores cluster around the "uncertain" neutral point). The high S. D.'s and wide range of scores indicate the same thing.

The group differences in average degree of ethnocentrism are of some interest. Among the groups taking Form 45, the three which stand clearly at the head of the list in terms of mean E score are the San Quentin Men (4.61), the Maritime School Men (4.34), and the Employment Service Men Veterans (4.26), these means being significantly higher than the others (3.34–3.67). That the San Quentin Men are so ethnocentric makes it clear that being in a subordinate group is not a guarantee against ethnocentrism. The results for the San Quentin group, and the psychological affinity between criminality and fascism, are considered in detail in Chapter XXI.

It is unclear why, in the Veteran and Maritime School groups, the E_A

means should be so different in Form 40 as compared with Form 45 (Table 17(IV) C). Thus, for the Veterans, the E_A mean drops from 4.67 to 4.21, while for the Maritime School it increases from 4.82 to 5.08. Although these differences are not statistically significant (at the 5 per cent level), they might, if they were both in the same direction, suggest a general systematic difference between the two Forms. It might he hypothesized, for example, that the presence of the anti-Semitic items in E_B makes some people defensive and thus lowers the mean on the entire scale in Form 45. This hypothesis is opposed, however, by the facts that neither difference is significant, that in the Maritime School the E_A mean is higher in Form 40 than in Form 45, and that the E_A means in the other Form 40 groups (Table 17(IV) B) are of the order of magnitude as in the Form 45 groups. It would appear, in short, that the presence of the E_B items in Form 45 produces no systematic increase or decrease in scores on the other items.

The mean E score of 3.7, as well as the wide range and the large S. D., for the Psychiatric Clinic patients indicates that no simple relationship exists between psychological ill health and ethnocentrism. The degree of ethnocentrism in this group of neurotic and psychotic—primarily the former—individuals just about equals the average of all groups tested. It would appear incorrect, therefore, to assume that there is on the average more pathology, psychologically speaking, in ethnocentrists than in nonethnocentrists or conversely.[18] Evidence to be presented later, however (Chapter XXII), will show that high and low scorers differ significantly with respect to type of pathology. The least ethnocentric groups taking Form 45 and 40 are the Testing Class Women and the Working-Class Men and Women. The low mean for the former group is consistent with previous results on University groups in California and Oregon. The E_A mean for the Form 45 group of Working-Class subjects is slightly but nonsignificantly lower than for the larger Working-Class group taking Form 40. This difference is apparently due to the fact that the Form 45 sample contains a greater proportion of subjects from the California Labor School, a subgroup with an extremely low E mean. Further discussion of the relation of economic class and politico-economic ideology to ethnocentrism is reserved for Chapter V. From the results in Table 17(IV), particularly for the groups taking Form 40, it would appear that socioeconomic class, as such, is not a major determinant of differences in ethnocentrism. The means for the Middle-Class groups are almost identical with those for the Working-Class groups. This is not to

---

[18] This conclusion depends, of course, on the representatives of our sample. What can be stated unequivocally is that every quartile on E contains some psychologically disturbed individuals. We may suspect, however, that a truly random sample of seriously disturbed individuals would show a higher average degree of ethnocentrism than is shown by the present sample, which includes, for the most part, individuals who recognize their problems as primarily psychological and who are willing to undergo psychological treatment—personality trends associated, as later chapters will show, with lack of ethnocentrism.

say that economic forces play no role in ethnocentrism, or that class membership is unimportant. However, the *average* amount of ethnocentrism in the
two classes appears to be the same, to the extent that the measuring instrument is valid and the sample adequate. Moreover, there are wide variations
within each class, some groups being very high in ethnocentrism, others very
low. Thus, within the middle class, the service clubs are significantly more
ethnocentric than the university groups. Individual and group differences in
E score within each class are associated with differences in *ideology* (political,
religious, and so forth) and in *personality* as shown by the chapters which
follow.

c. ITEM ANALYSIS: FORMS 45 AND 40.   The item means and D. P.'s for the
groups taking Forms 45 and 40 are presented in Table 18(IV). While the
item means for men average slightly higher than those for women, the rank
orders of the individual item means and D. P.'s are similar for the two sexes.
Furthermore, the wide range of the over-all item means and D. P.'s suggests
that similar consistency exists among the various groups of men and women
comprising the total sample. In other words, the relative level of acceptability
(mean) and "goodness" (D. P.) of the items is fairly stable from group to
group.

The best items in Form 45 deal with Negroes, Jews, zootsuiters, and
foreigners. For the women two items, 32 (Negroes' own fault) and 40 (Jewish neighborhoods), had means of below 3.0 and D. P.'s ranking 10 and 9
respectively. Even the lowest D. P. for men and for women (3.0 in each
case) is sufficient to differentiate high from low scorers with a minimum of
overlap. The only item in Form 45 with a mean of over 5.0 for both men
and women is number 45 (World organization). While this item discriminates very well between low and high scorers on the total scale, the
low scorers are apparently less sure of themselves on the issue of national
sovereignty than on the other issues; the high scorers almost uniformly rate
this item +3, but the low scorers are less emphatic and more divided.

The significantly higher means for men than for women on both forms
may not reflect a true sex difference since they are not based on *comparable
groups* of men and women. Thus, the four highest men's groups (San Quentin, Veterans, Maritime School, Service Clubs) have no high-scoring counterparts among the women. The absence of a significant sex difference is
also suggested by the very similar means obtained by comparable sex groups
(see Table 17(IV) *B*): Working-Class, Middle-Class, and Los Angeles
Men and Women. Significant differences between comparable groups of
men and women might, of course, be found on various individual items; this
problem has not been systematically explored.

The differences in means and D. P.'s between Forms 45 and 40 may also
be less significant than they appear at first glance. That the mean D. P.
is almost one point higher for both sexes on Form 40 than on Form 45 is

TABLE 18 (IV)

MEANS AND DISCRIMINATORY POWERS OF THE E-SCALE ITEMS (FORMS 45 AND 40)

No.	Item	MEN'S GROUPS[a] (N = 969)						WOMEN'S GROUPS[b] (N = 599)					
		Form 45 (N=440)			Form 40 (N=529)			Form 45 (N=130)			Form 40 (N=469)		
		Mean	D.P.	Rank D.P.	Mean	D.P.	Rank D.P.	Mean	D.P.	Rank D.P.	Mean	D.P.	Rank D.P.
5.	(Zootsuiters)	4.14	3.57	(7)	4.10	4.26	(5)	3.64	4.05	(4)	3.48	4.50	(4)
10.	(Negro rights)	4.57	4.58	(1)	4.25	4.92	(2)	3.93	4.91	(1)	3.96	5.21	(1)
15.	(Foreign ideas)	3.81	3.34	(9)	3.64	4.44	(3)	3.26	3.99	(5)	3.25	4.49	(5)
20.	(Negro foremen)	4.32	4.54	(2)	4.07	4.93	(1)	4.00	4.60	(2)	3.86	5.15	(2)
24.	(J. businessmen)	4.11	4.04	(4)				3.48	3.88	(6)			
28.	(Marry a Jew)	3.25	3.49	(8)				3.24	3.50	(7.5)			
32.	(Negroes live)	3.10	3.82	(5)				2.42	2.99	(10)			
36.	(Jews alike)	4.03	4.35	(3)				3.20	4.24	(3)			
40.	(Jewish Neighb.)	3.55	3.71	(6)				2.96	3.26	(9)			
45.	(World org.)	5.54	3.01	(10)	4.97	4.38	(4)	5.16	3.50	(7.5)	4.58	5.07	(3)
	Mean-per item[c]	4.04	3.84		4.20	4.59		3.53	3.89		3.83	4.88	

[a] The data were obtained from the following groups of men: San Quentin Men Prisoners (N = 110). Employment Service Men Veterans (N = 106). Maritime School Men (N = 343). California Service Club Men (N = 63). Psychiatric Clinic Men (N = 50). Middle-Class Men (N = 69). Working-Class Men (N = 61). Los Angeles Men (N = 117). The Working-Class Men and Women (N = 50) were also included here since 34 of these 50 subjects were men.

[b] The data were obtained from the following groups of women: Extension Testing Class Women (N = 59). George Washington University Women Students (N = 132). Psychiatric Clinic Women (N = 71). Middle-Class Women (N = 154). Working-Class Women (N = 53). Los Angeles Women (N = 130).

[c] In obtaining the over-all means and D.P.'s, the individual group values were not weighted by N.

due in part to the smaller number of items in Form 40 (each item therefore contributing a larger portion of the total score). It is also partly due to sampling factors: the composition of the various samples taking Form 40 was more heterogeneous, resulting in larger S. D.'s (Table 17(IV)), more extreme scorers, and thus higher D. P.'s. Both men and women had slightly lower E_A means on Form 40 than on Form 45 (4.48–4.20 for men, 4.00–3.83 for women). For reasons discussed earlier, these differences in means may be attributed mainly to sampling differences (both systematic and random) rather than to the nature of the forms themselves.

d. CORRELATIONAL ANALYSIS: FORM 45. It was possible, using the group of 517 University of California student women mentioned above, to make a correlational analysis of the E scale (Form 45).[19] Only the highlights of these results need be presented here. The group was near the average of the total sample with respect to mean (3.64), S. D. (1.52), and reliability (.79 for E_A vs. E_B, .87 for odd vs. even halves). For the single items the means ranged from 2.25 for Item 32 (Negroes' own fault) to 5.00 for Item 45 (World organization), while the S. D.'s ranged from 1.77 for Item 32 to 2.47 for Item 28 (Marry a Jew). The average of the interitem correlations was .42. The lowest interitem r's, .25 and .26, were between Item 15 (Foreign ideas) and Items 40 (Jewish neighborhoods) and 32 (Negroes' own fault), respectively. The highest r's, .61 and .62, were between Items 24 (Jewish businessmen) and 36 (Jews alike), and between Items 10 (Negro rights) and 20 (Negro foremen), respectively. The correlations between each item and the sum of the remaining items averaged .59; the two lowest values, .43 and .46, were for Items 15 and 45, the two highest, .67 and .69, for Items 10 and 36. Six of the ten items correlated .60 or higher with the sum of the remaining ones. These results, including the rank order of goodness of items and the general level of magnitude of the correlations, are consistent with the results for the other groups. While there is a tendency for items referring to a given group to cluster somewhat, the predominant trend is toward broad internal consistency. That the consistency is incomplete is shown by the fact that the correlations are far from perfect. In terms of statistical rigor, the scale shows about the same degree of unidimensionality (consistency) as the standard intelligence tests.

e. AGE AND ETHNOCENTRISM. The total sample from which the above data were obtained was not randomly distributed with respect to age. Its members were predominantly in their twenties and thirties, a disproportionately small number being in their forties or older. It was hypothesized that younger people tend to be less conservative and less ethnocentric than their elders, and that the mean E scores for the present sample might consequently

[19] We wish to express our thanks to the Social Science Research Council for the funds which made this aspect of the research possible.

be lower than for the population at large. As a partial check on this hypothesis, correlations between age and E score (Form 45) were computed for the Psychiatric Clinic Men and Women (N = 121). This group, despite its atypicality with respect to psychological health, appeared to be the most diverse group taking Form 45, and its E-scale results (mean, reliability, internal consistency, and correlations with other scales) were fairly representative of the total sample. Approximately 80 per cent of this group was between 18 and 40 years old, the mean (and median) being 34 years. The figures for men were very similar to those for women.

The correlation between age and E score for both men and women was .19. This value for men and women combined is significantly above zero at the 5 per cent (lowest acceptable) level of confidence. It suggests that there is a slight but consistent tendency for younger adults to be less ethnocentric than those of middle or old age. That the correlation is not likely to be higher for the general population is indicated by the fact that very high E-scale means were made by such young adult groups as the Employment Service Veterans and the Maritime School Men. The sampling bias in favor of younger age levels appears, then, to be of minor importance in our final results: the average degree of ethnocentrism found is slightly but significantly lower than would be found in a more representative sample.

3. A SUGGESTED FINAL E SCALE

The above data indicate that even the brief ten-item E scale in Form 45 can be used as a dependable measure of ethnocentrism. Whenever possible, however, it would appear advantageous to use a longer form which is likely to be more reliable and which can cover in a more systematic fashion various aspects of ethnocentric ideology. Table 19 (IV) contains a suggested final E scale of 20 items—short enough to meet most demands of practicality, yet sufficiently long to meet theoretical and statistical requirements. These items were selected, on the basis of both statistical adequacy and theoretical significance, from previous forms of the Ethnocentrism and Anti-Semitism scales. The wording of several items has been shortened and simplified. Subscales have been reinstated: six items dealing with Jews, six with Negroes, and eight with other Minorities and Patriotism.

In some cases the demands of time or administrative expediency may require that the scale be shortened or that certain items be deleted. From the experience of the present research it would appear that such changes can be made without seriously damaging the effectiveness of the scale in providing an adequate index of ethnocentrism. From a broader point of view, however, it is desirable to have further data on the internal structure of ethnocentric ideology, as revealed by the total scale, and on the social and psychological structures with which this ideology is associated.

TABLE 19 (IV)
ETHNOCENTRISM SCALE: SUGGESTED FINAL FORM
A. Jews

1. One trouble with Jewish businessmen is that they stick together and prevent other people from having a fair chance in competition.
2. I can hardly imagine myself marrying a Jew.
3. There may be a few exceptions, but in general Jews are pretty much alike.
4. The trouble with letting Jews into a nice neighborhood is that they gradually give it a typical Jewish atmosphere.
5. To end prejudice against Jews, the first step is for the Jews to try sincerely to get rid of their harmful and irritating faults.
6. There is something different and strange about Jews; it's hard to tell what they are thinking and planning, and what makes them tick.

B. Negroes

1. Negroes have their rights, but it is best to keep them in their own districts and schools and to prevent too much contact with whites.
2. It would be a mistake ever to have Negroes for foremen and leaders over whites.
3. Negro musicians may sometimes be as good as white musicians, but it is a mistake to have mixed Negro-white bands.
4. Manual labor and unskilled jobs seem to fit the Negro mentality and ability better than more skilled or responsible work.
5. The people who raise all the talk about putting Negroes on the same level as whites are mostly radical agitators trying to stir up conflicts.
6. Most Negroes would become overbearing and disagreeable if not kept in their place.

C. Other Minorities and Patriotism

1. Zootsuiters prove that when people of their type have too much money and freedom, they just take advantage and cause trouble.
2. The worst danger to real Americanism during the last 50 years has come from foreign ideas and agitators.
3. Now that a new world organization is set up, America must be sure that she loses none of her independence and complete power as a sovereign nation.
4. Certain religious sects who refuse to salute the flag should be forced to conform to such a patriotic action, or else be abolished.
5. Filipinos are all right in their place, but they carry it too far when they dress lavishly and go around with white girls.
6. America may not be perfect, but the American Way has brought us about as close as human beings can get to a perfect society.
7. It is only natural and right for each person to think that his family is better than any other.
8. The best guarantee of our national security is for America to have the biggest army and navy in the world and the secret of the atom bomb.

E. VALIDATION BY CASE STUDIES: THE RESPONSES OF MACK AND LARRY ON THE E SCALE

In order to throw some light upon the validity of the E scale, we may compare the responses of Mack and Larry on the scale with their ideas about groups and group relations as brought out by the interview. The scores of these two subjects for each of the items of the E scale (Form 78), together with the group means and D. P.'s, are shown in Table 20(IV).

TABLE 20 (IV)

RESPONSES OF MACK AND LARRY ON THE E SCALE

No.	Item	Mack	Larry	Group[a] Mean	Group[a] D.P.
4.	(Discrimination illegal)	5	1	3.95	1.51
7.	(Zootsuiters)	6	1	3.38	4.02
18.	(Foreign ideas)	5	1	3.17	3.26
25.	(World organization)	7	7	4.60	3.28
29.	(Negroes have rights)	6	1	3.41	4.00
34.	(Feminine positions)	3	1	2.74	2.18
37.	(Negroes lazy)	5	1	1.92	2.16
41.	(American way)	5	2	4.34	3.05
45.	(Negro foremen)	6	1	4.09	3.48
48.	(Germans and Japs)	6	1	2.50	3.08
51.	(Remove corrupt people)	5	1	3.15	2.34
54.	(Population incapable)	3	5	3.79	2.66
57.	(Radicals pro-Negro)	6	1	2.60	2.86
64.	(No Japs in California)	6	1	2.24	2.69
	Over-all mean	5.3	1.8	3.29	2.90

[a]The group means and D.P.'s are based on all four groups taking Form 78.

In the analysis of Mack's interview, in Chapter II, it was shown that he exhibited in a clear-cut fashion all of the trends which, according to the present theory, are most characteristic of ethnocentrism. That he should score near the top of the high quartile on the E scale may therefore be taken as evidence of its validity. He agrees with 12 of the 14 scale items, thus presenting a picture of very general ethnocentrism. His idealization of the ingroup is as marked as his hostility toward outgroups. His rejection of Negroes, zootsuiters, and Japanese is particularly pronounced, and decidedly more extreme than his rejection of Jews. (His mean score on the five items pertaining to the former minority groups is 5.8 as compared with his mean score of 4.6 on the A-S scale.) It may be recalled that Mack's ideology concerning Jews has a somewhat special quality. He wishes to make the point that Jews ought to participate more fully in American life and that they would be accepted and liked were it not for the fact that they would rather stay apart. In order to make this point, it is necessary for him to disagree with statements pertaining to the exclusion of Jews, and this lowers his mean score. It seems that he is impressed by what he conceives to be Jewish power. The interview, unfortunately, concentrating as it did upon anti-Semitism, did not explore Mack's imagery of other minority groups. It is fairly safe to assume, however, that he considers Negroes, zootsuiters, and Japanese weaker and more submerged than the Jews, and hence more suitable objects of hostility; certainly his scale responses express strong opposition to the idea of these groups participating more fully in American life.

Mack's failure to agree with Item 34 (Feminine positions) may have to do with the fact that he is engaged to be married to a school teacher; this is a matter that will be discussed more fully later on. The other item with which he disagrees, and the one on which he scores below the group mean is 54 (Population incapable); some light may be shed upon this inconsistency by considering that Item 54 is an unusually strong statement, one that includes no pseudodemocratic rationalization, and that Mack in his interview does not make extremely aggressive statements. It will be seen later that on other scales also he fails to agree with the more openly aggressive antidemocratic statements, a fact that is considered to be in keeping with the general picture of him as a potential follower rather than a potential leader in a fascist movement.

Larry's mean E-scale score of 1.8 is extremely low. This is consistent with the fact that in the interview he makes every effort to place himself squarely on the side of democratic internationalism and social equality for minorities. He disagrees strongly with 12 of the 14 scale items, his total score being raised by agreement with Items 25 (World organization) and 54 (Population incapable). Although the group mean for item 25 is high, indicating that strong sentiment in favor of national sovereignty is probably characteristic of the country as a whole, the item nevertheless discriminates very significantly between high and low scorers on the total scale. That Larry should agree strongly with the item may be due, not to concern with power as seemed to be the case with Mack, but to his conservatism and to his linking world organization with Roosevelt's economic policies, which he generally opposes. This interpretation is supported by the interview material, as will be shown later.

It is interesting that both subjects show inconsistency in the case of Item 54. Although this statement was intended to be strongly ethnocentric, the prejudiced subject disagrees with it while the unprejudiced subject agrees. This is in keeping with the fact that the item has one of the lowest D. P.'s of any in the scale. The reason might well be that some low scorers interpret the statement not in a cynical, antihuman way, imputing the incapability to outgroups (the high scorers show clearly, in their responses to other E items, who they think are the incapable people), but rather in the sense that there are too many people in all groups who have not, because of social conditions, developed sufficiently. This explanation probably holds for Larry.

F. CONCLUSIONS: THE STRUCTURE OF ETHNOCENTRIC IDEOLOGY

On the basis of the various scale results presented above and of supporting evidence from interviews, we can now attempt to formulate a more detailed theory of ethnocentric ideology. Such a theory should indicate the generality of the ethnocentric frame of mind, should permit various patterns of surface opinions and attitudes to be viewed as alternative expressions of the same underlying point of view, and should show how the ethnocentric approach to groups and group relations differs from other approaches.

A word may first be said regarding the implications of the data presented above for such a theory. To what extent can ethnocentrism be considered a consistent, organized system of ideas? From the scale statistics the following points can be made. On an *item-by-item* basis most people are not entirely consistent in their agreement or disagreement with ethnocentric ideas. This is indicated by the correlations, about .4 on the average, between individual items. Also, inspection of the scale responses of individuals in the high and low quartiles shows that even extreme scorers vary somewhat around a generally ethnocentric or anti-ethnocentric position. Thus, to know that a person is ethnocentric in terms of total E-scale score permits only fair prediction of his stand on any single item in the scale (correlations between single items and total E scale averaging about .6).

On the other hand, there is much greater consistency on a *subscale-by-subscale* basis. The high reliability of the initial E scale and of its relatively short subscales indicates that, whatever the item-by-item fluctuation, each subscale measures a rather consistent trend. Furthermore, the correlations among the initial Negro, Minorities, Patriotism, and Anti-Semitism scales indicate that these trends are closely related, that people are notably consistent in their acceptance or rejection of *general* ethnocentrism. To attempt to measure this ideology as a totality, however, is not to deny that it has components with respect to which individuals may vary. Indeed, the assumption that each trend *is* complex underlies the formulation of subscales and the attempt to make each subscale as complex and inclusive as possible.

A person is considered ethnocentric when his total score (average agreement with items) is high enough to indicate that he has accepted most of the ideas expressed in the scale. Whenever in the text a reference is made to "generality" or "consistency," it is always on a subscale or scale basis and with a recognition of item-by-item variability. And whenever there is a reference to any specific idea in ethnocentric ideology it is understood that most, though usually not all, ethnocentrists have this idea; that is to say, *each facet of ethnocentric ideology as here conceived is accepted by most high scorers, rejected by most low scorers.*[20] Ethnocentric ideology is held in its entirety by only the most extreme high scorers on the E scale. The less extreme members of the high quartile have accepted most, though not all, of the ethnocentric ideas described below. It would be erroneous, then, to regard high scorers as "all alike"; they have in common a general way of thinking about groups, but there are wide individual differences in the imagery and attitudes regarding various groups. Similar reasoning applies to the low scorers.[21]

We may now return to a consideration of the preliminary definition of ethnocentrism as an ideology concerning ingroups and outgroups and their interaction.

The term "group" is used in the widest sense to mean any set of people who constitute a psychological entity for any individual. If we regard the individual's conception of the social world as a sort of map containing various differentiated regions, then each region can be considered a group. This sociopsychological definition includes sociological groups such as nations, classes, ethnic groups, political parties, and so on. But it also includes numbers-of-people who have one or more common characteristics but who are not formal groups in the sense of showing organization and regulation of ways. Thus, it is legitimate in a sociopsychological sense to consider as groups such sets of people as criminals, intellectuals, artists, politicians, eccentrics, and so on. Psychologically, they are groups in so far as they are social categories or regions in an individual's social outlook—objects of opinions, attitudes, affect, and striving.

"Ingroup" and "outgroup" are sociopsychological rather than purely sociological concepts, since they refer to identification and, so to speak, contraidentification, rather than to formal membership in the group. A person may be identified with groups to which he does not formally belong. This is exemplified by the type of socially upward mobile person who is identified with groups of higher status and power (class, profession, political faction) than those to which he now belongs; also by the person with motivated downward mobility[22] who identifies with lower status and power groups such as Negroes, Jews, "the proletariat," "the weak and suffering."

---

[20] The difference between high and low scorers is shown statistically for each item by the Discriminatory Power and the item-total scale correlations; for the subscales it is shown by the subscale-subscale and the subscale-total scale correlations.

[21] Various patterns of "high" and "low" ideology, as found in the interview material, will be considered later, in Chapter XIX.

[22] The word "motivated" is used to distinguish this type of downward mobility—which is psychologically desired and sought—from a loss of status which is externally imposed by depression or economic failure (and in which the individual usually remains identified with the higher status group). Similarly, a person may want to rise in economic status primarily because of the desire for comfort, leisure, and so on; this is psychologically different from that upward mobility in which the desire for status and power, and identification with powerful groups, are primary motivating forces.

An individual may, of course, be concerned with many groups which are neither ingroups nor outgroups for him. One may feel sympathetic towards Negroes or the Catholic Church without actually identifying with them. Conversely, one may be opposed to many groups in the sense of feeling a difference in interest or values, or merely of feeling that their aims and existence are irrelevant to him; but these are not outgroups if there is not the sense of contraidentification, of basic conflict, of mutual exclusiveness, of violation of primary values.

A primary characteristic of ethnocentric ideology is the *generality* of outgroup rejection. It is as if the ethnocentric individual feels threatened by most of the groups to which he does not have a sense of belonging; if he cannot identify, he must oppose; if a group is not "acceptable," it is "alien." The ingroup-outgroup distinction thus becomes the basis for most of his social thinking, and people are categorized primarily according to the groups to which they belong. The outgroups are usually entirely subordinate (Negroes, Mexicans), or groups with relatively low status and power who are struggling to better their position in society. The major outgroups in America today appear to be Jews, Negroes, the lower socioeconomic class, labor unions, and political radicals, especially Communists. Other groups whose outgroup status varies somewhat are Catholics, artists, intellectuals; Oklahomans and Japanese (in the West); pacifists, Filipinos, Mexicans, homosexuals. Most other nations, especially the industrially backward, the socialistic, and those most different from the "Anglo-Saxon," tend to be considered outgroups. While there are probably considerable sectional, class, and individual differences regarding which groups are regarded as outgroups, it would appear that an individual who regards a few of these groups as outgroups will tend to reject most of them. An ethnocentric individual may have a particular dislike for one group, but he is likely nonetheless to have ethnocentric opinions and attitudes regarding many other groups.

Another general characteristic of ethnocentric ideology is the *shifting* of the outgroup among various levels of social organization. Once the social context for discussion has been set, ethnocentrists are likely to find an outgroup-ingroup distinction. Thus, in a context of international relations ethnocentrism takes the form of pseudopatriotism; "we" are the best people and the best country in the world, and we should either keep out of world affairs altogether (isolationism) or we should participate—but without losing our full sovereignty, power, and economic advantage (imperialism). And in either case we should have the biggest army and navy in the world, and atom bomb monopoly.

However, the superior American "we" breaks down when the context shifts to intranational affairs. In a religious context the ingroup-outgroup distinction may shift in various ways: religious-nonreligious, Christian-Jewish, Protestant-Catholic, among Protestant sects. Similar outgroup-ingroup distinctions can be found in various other phases of American life.

It seems, then, that the individual who has a pseudopatriotic conception of America in relation to other nations actually regards most of America as an outgroup: various religions, non-whites, "the masses," too-educated people and too-uneducated people, criminals, radicals, and so on, tend largely to fall in the outgroup category. This is not to say that nonethnocentrists regard all these groups as ingroups; rather, the nonethnocentrist can take a supportive attitude without necessarily identifying, and he can be critical without a sense of alien-ness and of categorical difference.

The social world as most ethnocentrists see it is arranged like a series of concentric circles around a bull's-eye. Each circle represents an ingroup-outgroup distinction; each line serves as a barrier to exclude all outside groups from the center, and each group is in turn excluded by a slightly narrower one. A sample "map" illustrating the ever-narrowing ingroup would be the following: Whites, Americans, native-born Americans, Christians, Protestants, Californians, my family, and finally—I.

The ethnocentric "need for an outgroup" prevents that identification with humanity as a whole which is found in anti-ethnocentrism. (This lack in identification is related to the ethnocentrists' inability to approach individuals *as* individuals, and to their tendency to see and "prejudge" each individual only as a sample specimen of the reified group. Their experience of interpersonal relations involves, so to speak, the same stereotypy as their opinions regarding groups generally.) The inability to identify with humanity takes the political form of nationalism and cynicism about world government and permanent peace. It takes other forms, all based on ideas concerning the intrinsic evil (aggressiveness, laziness, power-seeking, etc.) of human nature; the idea that this evil is unchangeable is rationalized by pseudo-scientific hereditarian theories of human nature. The evil, since it is unchangeable, must be attacked, stamped out, or segregated wherever it is found, lest it contaminate the good. The democratic alternative—humanitarianism—is not a vague and abstract "love for everybody" but the ability to like and dislike, to value and oppose, *individuals* on the basis of *concrete specific experience;* it necessarily involves the elimination of the stereotypical ingroup-outgroup distinction and all that goes with it.

What is the *content* of ethnocentric ideology regarding outgroups? There are, of course, individual differences here, and the same individual has different conceptions of, and attitudes toward, different outgroups. Nevertheless, certain common trends seem to exist, and these are generally the same as those found in anti-Semitic ideology. Most essentially, outgroups are seen as *threatening* and *power-seeking*. Accusations against them tend to be moralistic and, often, mutually contradictory. One of the main characteristics of most outgroups is that they are objectively *weaker* than the groups whom they supposedly threaten. Sometimes this weakness is perceived by the ethnocentrist, but this does not seem to lessen his sense of being threatened. The conflict as he sees it is between an ingroup trying to maintain or recapture its justly superior position, and an outgroup, resentful of past hurts, trying to do to others what they have done to it. But the conflict is seen as permanent and unresolvable; the only alternatives are dominance and submission; justice requires dominance by the superior ingroup, and the subordinate group will always remain resentful and rebellious. Because he considers hierarchy and power conflict "natural" he has difficulty in grasping a conception of group relations in which power considerations are largely eliminated and in which no group can control the lives of other groups.

The moralistic accusations against outgroups are similar to those that were seen in the case of anti-Semitism; again we find stereotypy, an absence of theories—save simple hereditarian ones—to explain why groups are as they are, and a readiness to place all the blame for group conflict upon outgroups.

The general outlook just described must, it would seem, have to do primarily with psychological trends within the ethnocentrist rather than with the actual characteristics of the outgroups. For one thing, many people who have had bad experiences with members of minority groups—and most of us have had unhappy experiences with members of most groups including ingroups—or who have heard derogatory remarks about these groups, do not have ethnocentric imagery and attitudes. It is not the experience as such that counts, but the way in which it is assimilated psychologically. Also, the prejudiced individual is prepared to reject groups with which he has never had contact; his approach to a new and strange person or culture is not one of curiosity, interest, and receptivity but rather one of doubt and rejection. The feeling of difference is transformed into a sense of threat and an attitude of hostility. The new group easily becomes an outgroup. The stereotypy, the illogicality, the large number of outgroups, the consistency of outgroup imagery—all these point to things in the psychological functioning of ethnocentrists which differentiate them from anti-ethnocentrists.

Ethnocentric ideology regarding ingroups shows similar trends, though often in an opposite direction, to that regarding outgroups. The ingroups are conceived of as superior in morality, ability, and general development; they ought also to be superior in power and status, and when their status is lowered or threatened the ethnocentrist tends to feel persecuted and victimized. Attempts by subordinate groups to improve their status are regarded as threats; he cannot imagine that they are struggling for equality and mutual interaction because he does not think in these terms. The ingroup is idealized and blindly submitted to. Obedience and loyalty are the first requirements of the ingroup member. What is called power-seeking and clannishness in the outgroup is transformed into moral righteousness, self-defense, and loyalty in the ingroup. In all other respects the ingroup is regarded as the opposite of the outgroup: clean, unaggressive, hard-working and ambitious, honest, disciplined, well-mannered. The same values, then, are applied to both ingroups and outgroups, and in the same stereotyped way.

The interaction of ingroups and outgroups, and indeed all social interaction, is conceived in hierarchical and authoritarian terms. Groups as well as individuals must "find their level," and the greatest danger is that certain groups will attempt to rise above their natural position. The same conceptions are applied to ingroup structure and functioning. As in the army, there should be a series of levels, and individuals on a given level should submit to those above and dominate those below. The conception of the ideal family situation for the child is similar: uncritical obedience to the father and elders, pressures directed unilaterally from above to below, inhibition of spontaneity and emphasis on conformity to externally imposed values.

We can now consider the ethnocentric solution to problems of group conflict. The ingroup must be kept pure and strong. The only methods of doing this are to *liquidate* the outgroups altogether, to keep them entirely *subordinate,* or to *segregate* them in such a way as to minimize contact with the ingroups. The first method represents politicalized ethnocentrism— fascism and the dissolution of democratic values. This method so obviously violates traditional American values of nonviolence, fairness, and equal opportunity that it has found relatively little support in this country. The second and third methods are supported, however, by large numbers of ordinary citizens.

Attitudes that the main outgroups should be subordinated and segregated are characteristic of American ethnocentrism because, it would seem, they combine so well ethnocentric imagery and sense of threat on the one hand, and certain democratic values which still prevail even in ethnocentrists, on the other. The democratic values often prevent more drastic action, but they may also serve to permit discrimination and oppression behind a pseudo-democratic front.

From these considerations the following general statement emerges. *Ethnocentrism is based on a pervasive and rigid ingroup-outgroup distinction; it involves stereotyped negative imagery and hostile attitudes regarding outgroups, stereotyped positive imagery and submissive attitudes regarding ingroups, and a hierarchical, authoritarian view of group interaction in which ingroups are rightly dominant, outgroups subordinate.*

CHAPTER V

POLITICO-ECONOMIC IDEOLOGY AND GROUP MEMBERSHIPS IN RELATION TO ETHNOCENTRISM

Daniel J. Levinson

A. INTRODUCTION

That political and economic forces play a vital role in the development of ethnocentrism, in both its institutional and individual psychological forms, is no longer questioned by social scientists or even by most laymen. In modern industrial societies ethnocentric ideology has been utilized by a great variety of sociopolitical movements which can be broadly characterized as fascist, prefascist, reactionary, imperialistic, chauvinistic. It is not within the scope of the present research to investigate directly the social movements and structures—monopoly, the concentration of power and wealth, labor unions, changing government functions, the declining middle class, and so on—which are crucial for the elimination of ethnocentrism or for its further development in such forms as war and rigid socioeconomic stratification. We are concerned, however, with the ideologies of these social groupings, with the organization of ideologies in the individual, and with some of the factors responsible for these broad ideological patterns.[1]

What patterns of politico-economic ideology are related to ethnocentric and anti-ethnocentric "group relations" ideology? There is good reason to believe that the "right-left" dimension politically is correlated with ethnocentrism. Fascism, which represents the most extreme right-wing political and economic structure and ideology, is also the most virulent antidemocratic form of ethnocentrism. The emphasis in ethnocentrism on a static, rigid stratification of groups finds its politico-economic analogue in the fascist

[1] Since the term "ideology" has acquired many negative connotations, particularly in the realm of political thought, we wish again to emphasize that this concept is used here in a purely descriptive sense: "ideology" refers to an "organized system of opinions, values, and attitudes." Any body of social thought may, in this sense, be called an ideology, whether it is true or false, beneficial or harmful, democratic or undemocratic.

corporate state. Conversely, left-wing, socialistic ideology stresses the elimination of economic classes (that is, of social stratification based on unequal distribution of economic power) as a condition for the complete removal of stratification and outgroup exploitation.

While fascist and socialist-communist (Marxist) ideologies represent the extreme right and left, respectively, with regard to political economy and group relations, neither point of view has as yet found much active, open support on the American political scene. The focus of the present study was, therefore, on liberalism and conservatism, the currently prevalent left- and right-wing political ideologies—with an eye, to be sure, on their potential polarization to the more extreme left and right.

There is considerable evidence suggesting a psychological affinity between conservatism and ethnocentrism, liberalism and anti-ethnocentrism. In a preliminary study by Levinson and Sanford (71) anti-Semitism correlated significantly with opposition to labor unions and socialistic institutions (socialized medicine, government ownership of utilities, etc.). Also, Republicans were, on the average, more anti-Semitic than Democrats. The researches of Newcomb (91), Lenz (67, 68), Murphy and Likert (84), Edwards, Stagner, and others (63) have yielded similar results. Unpublished data from the present study indicate that both conservatism and ethnocentrism are significantly correlated with support of the un-American Activities Committee, Hearst, the American Legion, and militarization (postwar increases in our army and navy).

The right-left dimension (reactionary-fascist, conservative, liberal, socialist-communist) is, of course, an extremely complex one. Crucial qualitative differences can be found not only among various degrees of left-ness or right-ness, but also among various ideological camps falling at approximately the same point on the right or left. Furthermore, there exists today a great deal of ideological heterodoxy, not to speak of simple confusion, so that a cutting across of formal political categories may be expected in many individuals.

Despite these complicating factors an attempt was made, by means of an opinion-attitude scale similar to those discussed previously, to measure politico-economic ideology along a liberalism-conservatism dimension. We shall be concerned, in the sections which follow, with the construction of this scale and the results obtained; with the relation of ethnocentric ideology to politico-economic ideology, and with the relation of ethnocentrism to membership in various political and economic groupings. In addition to these quantified group results, systematic but nonquantified observations on the political views of ethnocentric and nonethnocentric subjects, as expressed in the interviews, will be presented later (Chapter XVII).

B. CONSTRUCTION OF THE POLITICO-ECONOMIC CONSERVATISM (PEC) SCALE

Quantitative study began with the construction of a politico-economic conservatism (PEC) scale, on which a high score would represent extreme conservatism, a low score, extreme liberalism. The procedure followed was similar to that used in constructing the Anti-Semitism and Ethnocentrism scales (Chapters III, IV). The PEC scale differs from the others in having positive as well as negative items and in lacking formal subscales. The same method of scaling was used and similar rules of item formulation were followed. As in the case of the other scales, a preliminary analysis of major trends within this ideological area was made. This analysis was intended to provide the basis both for the formulation of widely inclusive scale items and for the interpretation of individual patterns of response.

1. SOME MAJOR TRENDS IN CONTEMPORARY LIBERALISM AND CONSERVATISM[2]

No attempt was made, in the construction of the PEC scale, to cover all the forms in which conservatism and liberalism are currently expressed. The main focus was, rather, on some of the more underlying—and therefore more stable—ideological trends which appear to characterize conservatism and liberalism as *contrasting approaches* to politico-economic problems. While specific issues such as the OPA, rent control, Dumbarton Oaks, the TVA are always changing, most issues as they arise find liberals and conservatives taking opposing stands. The problem was to get behind the specific issues, to move, so to speak, from a purely political to a more psychological level, as a means of differentiating these two broad patterns of social thought.

Conservatism and liberalism appeared to differ markedly with regard to the following ideological trends. (These trends are conceived as interrelated and as separable only for the purposes of analysis; indeed, one principle of item formulation was that each item should, whenever possible, express more than one underlying trend.)

a. SUPPORT OF THE AMERICAN *Status Quo*. Perhaps the definitive component of conservatism is an attachment, on the surface at least, to "things as they are," to the prevailing social organization and ways. Related to the idea that "what is, is right," is a tendency to idealize existing authority and to regard the "American Way" as working very well. Social problems tend either to be ignored or to be attributed to extraneous influences rather than to defects intrinsic in the existing social structure. One way of rationalizing

---

[2] It is symptomatic of the present political situation that terms like "liberalism" and "conservatism" are given numerous definitions and are used as shibboleths rather than as aids in description or analysis. We have therefore tried to make our meanings as explicit as possible.

chronic problems is to make them "natural"; for example, "Depressions are like occasional headaches and stomach aches; it's natural for even the healthiest society to have them once in a while" (Item 5). Or, as a prominent ultraconservative radio commentator observed recently: "There is nothing wrong with our American system. It is as good as it ever was, but we must do all we can in the New Year to get rid of the charlatans, fakers and agitators who are responsible for so many problems." It is clear from the other speeches of this commentator that his "charlatans" are for the most part leaders of the labor movement or of liberal political groupings—men who, in his eyes, threaten the existing order. The following scale item expresses a similar idea, namely, that personal maturity requires conformity and the overcoming of "rebellious" tendencies: "Young people sometimes get rebellious ideas, but as they grow up they ought to get over them and settle down" (Item 27).

To be "liberal," on the other hand, one must be able actively to criticize existing authority. The criticisms may take various forms, ranging from mild reforms (e.g., extension of government controls over business) to complete overthrow of the *status quo*. As noted above, the scale attempts mainly to distinguish the political right and left rather than to identify the numerous varieties of left- and right-wing ideology.

b. RESISTANCE TO SOCIAL CHANGE.   Another aspect of traditionalism is the tendency to oppose innovations or alterations of existing politico-economic forms. If things are basically good now, then any change is likely to be for the worse. Underlying resistance to change is sometimes expressed in the form of an emphasis on caution and an antipathy to being "extreme." For example: "The best way to solve social problems is to stick close to the middle of the road, to move slowly and to avoid extremes" (Item 15).

The opposition to change is often rationalized by an elaborate mythology of human nature according to which psychological man and capitalist social order are ideally suited to each other. According to this view, liberals are "utopian dreamers" who do not see man as he really is. Man is conceived as governed by economic self-interest and the profit motive. "In general, full economic security is harmful; most men would not work if they didn't need the money for eating and living" (Item 61). Major social problems such as war and depression are regarded primarily as expressions of human nature rather than as products of the existing social structure. The person who wants to change the social structure is, therefore, either an impractical idealist or an agitator making trouble in order to gain his own selfish ends. In short, basic improvement of our politico-economic forms is not possible, man being what he is, and social change is therefore undesirable.

c. SUPPORT OF CONSERVATIVE VALUES.   As in the other areas of ideology, values play a central role in organizing and giving meaning to the total pattern of politico-economic ideology. One of the primary value systems underlying conservative ideology is concerned with practicality, ambition, and upward class mobility. Success tends to be measured in financial terms, and business is accorded very high prestige as an occupation. These values are reflected in the raising and indoctrination of children, who "should learn early in life the value of a dollar" (Item 1). They are also expressed in the selection of men who represent models of success: "Whether one likes them or not, one has to admire men like Henry Ford or J. P. Morgan, who overcame all competition on the road to success" (Item 71).

The values for practicality and rugged competitiveness stand in rather marked contrast to other, psychologically related, values for charity and community service. On the one hand, it is assumed that "most people get pretty much what they deserve" (Item 78), that ability will find its socio-economic rewards, and that those who end up on the low end of the social ladder—since they did not have what it takes—are hardly to be pitied. On the other hand, our religious tradition is one of charity and tolerance; if one cannot excuse the poor, one can at least soften their plight—with Christmas parties, Thanksgiving bazaars, orphanages, and the like. Industrialists like Carnegie and Rockefeller are examples of this combination of weekday toughness and Sunday charity, which Item 8 was intended to measure: "Every adult should find time or money for some worthy service organization (charity, medical aid, etc.) as the best way of aiding his fellow man."

From the "liberal" point of view charity is mainly a soothing of conscience and a means of maintaining an unjust state of affairs. The causes of poverty are seen, not in the innate stupidity of the poor, but in the politico-economic organization which, by virtue of its concentration of economic power, creates poverty as a symptom. And the answer is seen, not in ineffectual though often well-intentioned charity, but in the elimination of poverty through modification of its societal causes.

It would appear, then, that liberals tend to view social problems as symptoms of the underlying social structure, while conservatives view them as results of individual incompetence or immorality. This difference is expressed also in the evaluation of political candidates. Conservative politicians tend to base their election campaigns largely on qualities of personal character and moral standing. To be a good family man and a leading figure in the community are judged more important than to know social science or to understand the actual politico-economic problems of the community. A district attorney or a businessman has a great initial advantage over a college professor or a labor leader. In short, political problems tend to be seen in moral rather than sociological terms. Item 22 was intended to measure this trend. "A political candidate, to be worth voting for, must first and foremost have a good character, one that will fight inefficiency, graft and vice." The liberal alternative is not to reject "good character," but to make it secondary, in political affairs, to the understanding of issues and the desire to do what is best for the most people.

d. IDEAS REGARDING THE BALANCE OF POWER AMONG BUSINESS, LABOR, AND GOVERNMENT. This is the most technical and the most confused aspect of contemporary political thought. The confusion has multiple causes: the fact that most Americans are, politically, relatively uneducated and uninformed; the very technicality and abstractness of the basic issues involved; the factionalism in both major political parties as well as in the minority left- and right-wing groups; American antipolitical, anti-intellectual tradition; and so on. The semantic confusion is especially great. Thus, "laissez-faire," originally a characteristic of liberalism, is nowadays called "conservatism." Because of this confusion, it is necessary to make explicit the conception of conservatism used here, and to contrast it with other viewpoints.

Conservatism is taken to mean traditional economic laissez-faire individualism, according to which our economic life is conceived in terms of the free (unregulated) competition of individual entrepreneurs. Business, accorded such great prestige by conservative values, is regarded as deserving great social power in relation to labor and government. Unions are regarded as threatening, power-seeking, interfering with the traditional functions of management, and promoting radical changes. Unions are likely to be accepted only when their actual power is less than that of business: this means virtual elimination of the right to strike, of a voice in determining company policy, and of political functions—in short, of the possibility of changing to any significant degree the existing balance of politico-economic power. A liberal viewpoint regarding unions is expressed in Item 68: "Labor unions should become stronger by being politically active and by publishing labor newspapers to be read by the general public."

Conservative ideology has traditionally urged that the economic functions of government be minimized. Fear of government power (like union power) is emphasized, and great concern is expressed for the freedom of the individual, particularly the individual businessman. (The issue here is greatly complicated by the fact that our economy has changed from a large number of competing entrepreneurs to a small number of powerful economic units; more about this will be said in Subsection 5.) For example, "It is a fundamental American tradition that the individual must remain free of government interference, free to make money and spend it as he likes" (Item 63). This way of thinking assumes that the individual has "freedom" economically to the extent that there are no government restrictions on him; it overlooks the fact that economic freedom for most people today is limited to the greatest degree by economic forces originating in business monopoly. The attempt to minimize government functioning extends also to the sphere of social security, socialized medicine, and various other programs designed to help the "common man."

There are numerous patterns of left-wing ideology regarding these issues. What characterizes the left and distinguishes it from the right is the desire for a change, slight or great, in the balance of power. Support for slight change is exemplified by New Deal liberalism, which would increase the functions of government so as to reduce the power of business, increase the power of labor, and diminish somewhat the extreme class differences that now exist. The more extreme left-wing ("radical") ideologies support more basic changes in the politico-economic structure; their thesis is that capitalism, no matter how it is modified by reforms, must necessarily produce social problems such as depression, war, and mass poverty. What they want is not merely controls on business, but nationalization of industry, planned production, and production for use rather than for profit. Only when the process of production is organized on a socialist basis, they argue, can there be true economic democracy, equality of management and labor, and a high national standard of living.

This is not the place to consider in detail the differences among the various left-wing or the various right-wing ideologies. The PEC scale attempted to measure only a general right-left dimension (with the hope that the individual's pattern of response might reveal more precisely the nature of his liberalism or conservatism). It was intended that a high score should indicate a high degree of the above-mentioned trends: support of the *status quo* and particularly of business; support of conservative values; desire to maintain a balance of power in which business is dominant, labor subordinate, and the economic functions of government minimized; and resistance to social change. Conversely, a low score was intended to reflect support of trends common to most left-of-center viewpoints: opposition to the *status quo*; a tendency to think in sociological rather than moral-hereditarian terms; a tendency to identify with labor and the "common man" and to oppose the power of business; support for extension of the political and economic functions of government. Further differentiation of various liberal and conservative patterns can be attempted after the empirical findings have been presented.

2. THE INITIAL PEC SCALE (FORM 78)

The Form 78 PEC Scale is presented in Table 1(V). Eleven of the 16 items took the "conservative" position, so that agreement was given a high score ($+3 = 7$ points, $-3 = 1$ point); on the five "liberal" items the scoring was reversed. The items were, as can be seen from the numbering, distributed randomly throughout the 78-item series. The questionnaire was administered in the spring of 1945 to three groups at the University of California: Public Speaking Class Women (N = 140) and Men (N = 52), and Adult Extension Psychology Class Women (N = 40); and to a group of 63 Professional Women (teachers, nurses, social workers).[3]

---

[3] For a more detailed discussion of the groups and the sampling problems involved in Form 78 as well as in the later forms, see Chapter IV (Ethnocentrism).

TABLE 1 (V)
The Initial Politico-Economic Conservatism Scale (Form 78)

1. A child should learn early in life the value of a dollar and the importance of ambition, efficiency, and determination.

5. Depressions are like occasional headaches and stomach aches; it's natural for even the healthiest society to have them once in awhile.

8. Every adult should find time or money for some worthy service organization (charity, medical aid, etc.) as the best way of aiding his fellow man.

13. The businessman, the manufacturer, the practical man—these are of much greater value to society than the intellectual, the artist, the theorist.

15. The best way to solve social problems is to stick close to the middle of the road, to move slowly and to avoid extremes.

22. A political candidate, to be worth voting for, must first and foremost have a good character, one that will fight inefficiency, graft, and vice.

27. Young people sometimes get rebellious ideas, but as they grow up they ought to get over them and settle down.

36.[a] It is the responsibility of the entire society, through its government, to guarantee everyone adequate housing, income, and leisure.

44.[a] The only way to provide adequate medical care for the entire population is through some program of socialized medicine.

52.[a] It is essential after the war to maintain or increase the income taxes on corporations and wealthy individuals.

61. In general, full economic security is harmful; most men wouldn't work if they didn't need the money for eating and living.

63. It is a fundamental American tradition that the individual must remain free of government interference, free to make money and spend it as he likes.

68.[a] Labor unions should become stronger by being politically active and by publishing labor newspapers to be read by the general public.

71. Whether one likes them or not, one has to admire men like Henry Ford or J. P. Morgan, who overcame all competition on the road to success.

76.[a] The government must play an even greater part in the economic and business life of the nation after the war than it has before.

78. Character, honesty, and ability will tell in the long run; most people get pretty much what they deserve.

[a] These five items are "liberal," the others are "conservative." A high score is given for agreement with the conservative items, disagreement with the liberal items.

The reliability data for the PEC scale are given in Table 2 (V). The average reliability of .73 is considerably lower than those of the Anti-Semitism and Ethnocentrism scales (.8–.9); while inadequate for the precise measurement of the individual, this reliability is sufficient for the present purposes of group comparison and correlation with other measures. There are probably several major reasons for the relatively low reliability values. Several items may not have worked out as planned, because of either poor formulation or erroneous guiding hypotheses; this possibility is investigated in the item analysis below. It is also possible that the absence of extreme scorers is due in part to a real constriction in the "range of talent"—something that would tend to lower the obtained reliability—rather than to the intrinsic unreliability of the scale. This hypothesis is supported by the fact that the

TABLE 2 (V)

RELIABILITY OF THE PEC SCALE (FORM 78)

Property	Group[a]				Over-all[b]
	A	B	C	D	
Reliability	.74	.64	.72	.81	.73
Mean (total)	4.30	4.18	4.29	3.91	4.17
Mean (odd half)	4.39	4.23	4.34	3.96	4.23
Mean (even half)	4.24	4.12	4.26	3.85	4.11
S.D. (total	.81	.75	.83	1.10	.87
S.D. (odd half)	.96	.88	.86	1.28	1.00
S.D. (even half)	.86	.84	.96	1.09	.94
Range	1.5-5.9	2.3-6.0	1.6-5.6	1.5-6.4	1.5-6.4

[a]The four groups are:
  Group A: U.C. Public Speaking Class Women (N = 140)
  Group B: U.C. Public Speaking Class Men (N = 52)
  Group C: U.C. Extension Psychology Class Women (N = 40)
  Group D: Professional Women (N = 63)

[b]In obtaining the over-all means, the individual group means were not weighted by N.

Professional Women, probably the most heterogeneous of the four groups, had the highest reliability (.81) as well as the largest Standard Deviation and range. Finally, and most basic, is the likelihood that American political thinking shows an actual lack of consistency and pattern. The lack of extreme scorers may thus reflect an ideological reality, namely the absence of a well-developed and articulate political left and political right in contemporary America. To the extent that this is true, it is doubtful that any scale measuring diverse trends in politico-economic ideology could obtain an average reliability of much over .80.

It is interesting that for all groups the PEC means were almost a point higher than the A-S and E means, and that once again the Professional Women were significantly lower than the others. Thus, while the *rank order* of conservatism is similar to that of ethnocentrism, the general *level* of conservatism is considerably higher. People are, so to speak, more conservative than ethnocentric, at least as measured by these scales. The relation of conservatism to ethnocentrism will be considered more fully below (Section C).

An item analysis was made according to the procedure described in Chapter III. Table 3(V) presents the item means and Discriminatory Powers for the Form 78 PEC scale. The average D. P. of 2.14 is, like the reliability, lower than the corresponding values obtained from the previous scales. The low

TABLE 3 (V)

MEANS AND DISCRIMINATORY POWERS OF THE PEC SCALE ITEMS (FORM 78)[a]

No.	Item	Group A		Group B		Group C		Group D		Over-all[b]		Rank D.P.
		Mean	D.P.	Mean	D.P.	Mean	D.P.	Mean	D.P.	Mean	D.P.	
1.	(Value of dollar)	6.20	1.69	5.94	0.81	6.25	0.88	6.02	1.27	6.10	1.16	(15)
5.	(Depressions)	3.23	2.09	3.75	1.86	3.40	3.36	2.95	3.73	3.33	2.76	(4.5)
8.	(Charity)	5.66	1.35	5.06	1.17	5.73	1.18	5.37	2.20	5.46	1.48	(14)
13.	(Businessmen, artists)	2.24	1.73	2.54	1.25	2.05	1.94	2.32	1.87	2.29	1.70	(12)
15.	(Middle of the road)	4.03	2.60	4.44	2.45	4.60	2.71	4.32	3.86	4.35	2.90	(2)
22.	(Political candidate)	6.44	0.31	6.17	0.39	6.50	-0.03	6.41	0.60	6.38	0.32	(16)
27.	(Rebellious ideas)	3.71	2.90	3.62	2.05	4.30	2.06	3.83	4.33	3.86	2.84	(3)
36.	(Gov't. responsibility)	3.46	2.73	3.35	2.41	3.65	3.82	2.43	3.07	3.22	3.01	(1)
44.	(Socialized medicine)	2.49	1.64	2.58	1.72	2.45	1.39	1.98	2.00	2.38	1.69	(13)
52.	(Taxes, corporations)	3.73	2.02	3.69	2.58	3.78	1.76	3.43	2.80	3.66	2.29	(9)
61.	(Economic security)	4.19	2.05	3.94	2.44	3.78	2.85	3.10	3.40	3.75	2.68	(6)
63.	(Gov't. interference)	4.11	1.81	3.95	1.34	4.43	2.02	3.56	4.40	4.01	2.39	(7)
68.	(Unions stronger)	5.11	2.36	4.83	1.75	4.48	1.74	3.90	3.33	4.58	2.30	(8)
71.	(Ford, Morgan)	5.42	1.89	5.21	1.67	5.45	1.46	5.13	3.00	5.30	2.00	(10)
76.	(Gov't. activity)	3.69	2.32	3.35	4.07	3.05	1.11	3.21	3.53	3.32	2.76	(4.5)
78.	(Ability will tell)	5.14	1.96	4.42	1.52	4.80	2.74	4.62	1.73	4.74	1.99	(11)
	Mean per item	4.30	1.97	4.18	1.84	4.29	1.94	3.91	2.82	4.17	2.14	

[a]The four groups are: Group A, U.C. Public Speaking Class Women (N = 140); Group B, U.C. Public Speaking Class Men (N = 52); Group C, U.C. Extension Psychology Class Women (N = 40); Group D, Professional Women (N = 63).

[b]In obtaining the over-all means, the individual group means were not weighted by N.

average D. P. (and thus the low reliability) is not due to the counterbalancing of several very good items by several very poor ones; the best item has a D. P. of 3.0—not extremely high by previous standards—and the values diminish very gradually. It is noteworthy that the best items deal with a variety of trends: acceptance of depressions as natural (Item 5); values for the "middle of the road" and slow social change (Item 15); and for conformity to existing authority (Item 27); and "liberal" items supporting economic security, increased government functioning, and unions (Items 36, 61, 68, 76).

Of the seven items with the lowest D. P.'s, six had means greater than 5.3 or less than 2.4; that is, these items tended to evoke almost uniform responses of agreement or of disagreement. (None of the 9 best items had such extreme means.) In view of the greatly reduced variability of response to these items, the D. P.'s are more significant than they at first appear. Only the lowest D. P. of 0.32 (for Item 22) can be considered clearly insignificant. For the other low D. P. items the difference between the high and low quartiles is statistically significant. For a given item the difference is not that one quartile consistently agrees while the other disagrees; it lies rather in the fact that one quartile consistently obtains an extreme score while the other tends to be more neutral in its stand. Thus, with regard to the importance of teaching a child the value of a dollar (Item 1), the extreme conservatives most frequently responded with a +3, while the extreme liberals tended to respond +1, a difference in emphasis rather than an actual opposition. There were four such items (1, 8, 22, 71), all dealing with conventional values, on which very few subjects made extremely low scores, and two (13, 44) on which there were few high scores. Some of these items were reformulated in the succeeding form of the scale, with the intention of eliminating possible ambiguities and thus increasing the D. P.'s. The possibility remains, of course, that the relative uniformity of response to these items reflects an actual uniformity of belief on the part of these groups of subjects.

Since most of the 78 items in this series are agreed with by the high scorers on the various scales (A-S, E, PEC, F), disagreed with by the low scorers, the question of a mechanical "set" to agree or to disagree may be raised. For instance, once an individual gets set consistently to disagree, is he not likely to continue disagreeing regardless of the content of the items? The "set" factor was considered, and found to play a negligible role, in the previous scales. By way of further evidence, we may consider the five "liberal" items, that is, those which tend to be agreed with by individuals who usually disagree with the other items. The 5 rank D. P.'s range from 1 to 13, and average 7.1, or slightly better than the scale average of 8.5. Furthermore, the extreme liberals tended, as noted above, to agree even with some of the "conservative" items. The great variability of the item means is also a sign of selective response to each item. It seems safe to conclude that set is not a major determinant of response, although it may enter as a minor complicating factor.

The item means in Table 3(V) are also worthy of note. The highest means are on items expressing conventional values (1, 8, 22, 71). The very high mean (6.38), as well as the negligible D. P., on Item 22 is probably due in part to inadequate formulation; but also to the actual tendency of most Americans to regard the good politician as a fighter against vice rather than as one who understands the political and economic problems of democratic government. In contrast to this, the two "conventional values" items which discriminated very well and whose means were near the neutral point of 4.0 are particularly important. These items, 15 (Middle of the road) and 27 (Rebellious ideas), seem to reflect a primary personality trend underlying ideological conservatism, namely the surface acceptance of authority and the overcoming of rebellious tendencies. It seems possible that the rebellious tendencies have not actually been outgrown but have rather been inhibited, so that the emphasis on conformity now serves as a defense against underlying hostility toward accepted authority. This hypothesis, which arose previously in the case of the ethnocentrists' uncritical submission to ingroup authority, will be considered in detail in the chapters which follow.

Among the more directly ideological items, the highest mean, 4.58, was made on Item 68 (Unions stronger). This result may indicate a fear of union strength, and perhaps a sense of alienation from the working class, among numerous middle-class individuals who are "liberal" with respect to the other political trends expressed in the scale. For example, the means on the several items (36, 44, 52, 61, 76) dealing with social security and extension of government functions are all well below 4.0, indicating considerable support for the liberal viewpoint.

The low means on the "government" items raise another question: Why do many individuals who are otherwise conservative support an increase in government activity? In some cases this inconsistency probably reflects ideological confusion or the beginnings of change from right to left or vice versa. However, this apparent contradiction may reflect something much more basic, namely a shift from traditional laissez-faire conservatism, whose economic unit was the individual competitive businessman, to a new type of conservatism whose economic unit is organized big business. As was pointed out earlier in this chapter, the assumption of liberalism-conservatism as a simple quantitative dimension holds only in the most general sense. It was for this reason, among others, that the theory guiding scale construction was presented in some detail. It is possible, then, for an individual to make a moderately high rather than a very high score, not because of any true liberal tendency, but because of a change in the nature of his conservatism. He is now willing to extend the functions of government for reasons that are the opposite of liberal, for he conceives of government as a tool of business rather than as a means of controlling corporate capital and of preventing concentrations of economic power. We shall return again to this question after considering the relation between the PEC and E scales.

3. THE SECOND PEC SCALE (FORM 60)

In Form 60 the PEC Scale (see Table 4(V)) was shortened to 14 items, and numerous changes were made in content and wording. Items 27 and 60,

TABLE 4 (V)
THE SECOND FORM OF THE POLITICO-ECONOMIC CONSERVATISM (PEC) SCALE (FORM 60)

4.[a] Labor unions should become stronger and have more influence generally.

9.[a] Most government controls over business should continue after the war.

13. America may not be perfect, but the American Way has brought us about as close as human beings can get to a perfect society.

15.[a] If America had more men like Henry Wallace in office, we would get along much better.

20.[a] The artist and the professor are of just as much value to society as the businessman and the manufacturer.

26. It would be dangerous for the U.S. to cooperate too closely with Russia.

27. The best political candidate to vote for is the one whose greatest interest is in fighting vice and graft.

31.[a] No one should be allowed to earn more than $25,000 a year.

37.[a] It is up to the government to make sure that everyone has a secure job and a good standard of living.

43.[a] The government should own and operate all public utilities (transportation, gas and electric, railroads, etc.).

48.[a] Depressions can be prevented by proper government planning.

54.[a] Poverty could be almost entirely done away with if we made certain basic changes in our social and economic system.

56. Men like Henry Ford or J. P. Morgan, who overcome all competition on the road to success, are models for all young people to admire and imitate.

60. In general, the best way of aiding our fellow men is to give time or money to some worthy charity.

[a] These nine items are "liberal," the other five are "conservative." A high score is given for agreement with the conservative items, disagreement with the liberal items.

referring to political candidates and the importance of charity, respectively, are reformulations of items that were unsuccessful in Form 78; the present formulations are, presumably, more clear-cut expressions of the trends initially hypothesized. Two items which worked relatively well in Form 78, numbers 27 (Rebellious ideas) and 61 (Security is bad), were placed in the Form 60 F scale (see Chapter VII) because they seemed on theoretical grounds to fit better there.

Several totally new items have been added. Item 13 (The American Way) was taken from the Form 78 E scale (see Chapter IV); it is transitional between conservatism and ethnocentrism in that it expresses both conservative support of the politico-economic *status quo* and ethnocentric idealization of the ingroup. Taken literally, however, it seemed to fall more within the sphere of political ideology. Correlational analysis is required before this item can properly be placed within one scale or the other.

Three of the new items provide vivid reminders of the speed of historical change. Item 15 (Wallace) was formulated when the confirmation of Henry Wallace as Secretary of Commerce was the issue of the day. Item 26 (Russia) reflected the atmosphere of the initial postwar period, when cooperation rather than containment was the prevailing attitude toward Russia. Item 31 referred to President Roosevelt's wartime suggestion of a $25,000 limit on yearly incomes. It will be noted that the Form 60 scale contains fewer generalizations and more concrete references to specific issues than did Form 78.

Form 60 was administered in the summer of 1945 to several groups which were combined for statistical purposes as follows. (a) University of Oregon Student Women (N = 47), undergraduate students attending summer session courses in psychology. (b) Combined University of Oregon and University of California Student Women (N = 54), the Oregon group being obtained too late to be included in (a); the California group was a summer session education class containing mostly teachers and others of above college age. (c) University of Oregon and University of California Student Men (N = 57), from the same classes as the (b) women. (d) Oregon Service Club Men (N = 68), obtained at luncheon meetings of service clubs (Kiwanis, Lions, Rotary).[4]

The last three groupings received the total Form 60 questionnaire in one sitting. However, the first group of Oregon Student Women received the questionnaire in two parts, A and B. Part A included the F scale and half of PEC, while Part B contained the E scale and the remaining half of PEC. The purpose of this division was to help determine whether the presence of the E items had any effect on the responses to the F items; the results will be discussed in Chapter VII.

The reliability data for the Form 60 PEC Scale are presented in Table 5(V). The average reliability of .70 is substantially the same as that of .73 for the initial form, and indicates that the changes in wording and content did not improve this property of the scale. The fact that the reliabilities, S. D.'s, and ranges vary so little among these four groups, as well as among those taking the first form (Form 78), suggests that a scale of this length and this degree of inclusiveness can hardly be expected to obtain an average reliability greater than .7–.8. The main reason for the relatively low reliability of PEC, as compared with E, appears to lie in the fact that political ideology is intrinsically less organized and less consistent in the individual today than is ideology concerning group relations.

Once again the group means on PEC are significantly higher than those on

[4] For a discussion of the sampling problems involved, see Chapter IV.

TABLE 5 (V)

RELIABILITY OF THE PEC SCALE (FORM 60)

Property	Group[a]				Over-all[b]
	I	II	III	IV	
Reliability	.73	.69	.69	.70	.70
Mean (total)	3.72	3.82	3.77	4.40	3.92
Mean (odd half)	3.86(A)[c]	3.60	3.55	4.06	3.74[d]
Mean (even half)	3.58(B)[c]	4.03	3.99	4.68	4.23[d]
S.D. (total)	.90		.80	.92	
S.D. (odd half)	.97(A)[c]		.78	.95	
S.D. (even half)	1.02(B)[c]		1.05	1.14	
Range	1.2–5.6	1.0–5.5	1.2–5.0	1.6–6.1	1.0–6.1

[a]The four groups are:
Group I: University of Oregon Student Women (N = 47)
Group II: University of Oregon and University of California Student Women (N = 54)
Group III: University of Oregon and University of California Student Men (N = 57)
Group IV: Oregon Service Club Men (N = 68)

[b]In obtaining the over-all means, the individual group means were not weighted by N.

[c]The signs (A) and (B) refer to the two parts of the questionnaire given to Group I; half of PEC was in part (A), the other half in part (B). The reliability for this group is based on the correlation between the A and B halves.

[d]The Over-all mean (odd) (even), and S.D. (odd) (even) include only the three groups taking the total form since the (A) and (B) halves of the split form do not correspond to the odd and even halves of the total form.

E (Chapter IV), suggesting that the level of conservatism is higher than the level of ethnocentrism. Again, the rank order of group means on PEC tends to follow that on E, with the Service Club Men being significantly more conservative (beyond the 1 per cent level) than the combined university groups. These facts would lead us to expect a significant correlation between PEC and E (see Section C). While the Service Club Men are quite conservative on the average (mean of 4.4), the lowest score being 1.6, this group can by no means be considered ideologically homogeneous; indeed, it shows about the same degree of internal variability (range and S. D.) as do the other groups. We are given another warning against stereotypy in thinking about groups and about group memberships as determinants of ideology. This is not to say that service clubs are not "conservative groups" in terms of actual policy. Rather, it would appear that group policy and leadership, in this case at least, reflect the average degree of conservatism, the conservative tradition, and frequently the immediate business interests of the group. However, to say that such-and-such is a conservative group, in terms of actual policy, is not necessarily to imply that all members are strongly conservative. Similarly, not all individuals who call themselves "New Deal Democrats" are thoroughly liberal in their personal ideologies; not all Catholics support the political program of the policy-makers of the Catholic Church; and so on. This is one of the main problems in bringing together the psychological and the sociological approaches; it is an especially great problem for that theory of social psychology which regards the individual adult as merely a product or sum of his various group memberships.

The data on item analysis are presented in Table 6(V). The over-all D. P. of 2.08 is almost identical with that of 2.14 on the initial PEC scale, as might be expected from the similar reliabilities. The best items deal for the most part with government functioning; ownership of utilities, controls over business, limitations on income. Item 4 (Unions) worked out relatively well (rank order 6) despite its having the highest over-all mean, 5.35; even in the university groups the mean did not fall below 5.0. Item 15 (Wallace) came out similarly; it had the third best D. P. despite a mean of 5.00. Other items with D. P.'s of over 2.0 include 13 (American Way), 54 (Poverty), and 56 (Ford and Morgan).

The five poorest items are also of some interest. Three of these, 20 (Artists, businessmen), 27 (Political candidate), and 60 (Charity), are reformulations of poor items in Form 78. Almost none of these subjects disagreed with the idea that the artist and professor are as important as the businessmen, although the liberals agreed more emphatically than the conservatives (the difference being statistically significant only in the Service Club Men). The D. P. of 1.06 on Item 27, while statistically significant, indicates considerable overlap between the high and low quartiles. Further exploratory research is required in order to determine possible differences between liberals and conservatives with respect to underlying imagery of "the good political candidate." Item 48 (Depressions) is an example of not leaving well enough alone. In the initial form this item had a D. P. rank of 4.5; in this form, after drastic revision, its rank was 12. Both the mean and D. P. on Item 26 (Dangerous to cooperate with Russia) are somewhat surprising. The mean of 2.57 indicates that very few individuals agreed with this item. The D. P. of 1.60 is more significant than it at first appears, because of the low mean, but it shows that even conservatives were divided on the Russian issue at the close of the war. This is shown most dramatically by the Service Club Men who, although strongly conservative on most domestic issues, obtained on the Russian item a mean of 2.51 and a D. P. of .93. How and why slight support has, within less than two years, changed to bitter antagonism, is a problem beyond the scope of the present study.

TABLE 6 (V)

MEANS AND DISCRIMINATORY POWERS OF THE PEC SCALE ITEMS (FORM 60)[a]

No.	Item	Group I		Group II		Group III		Group IV		Over-all[b]		Rank D.P.
		Mean	D.P.	Mean	D.P.	Mean	D.P.	Mean	D.P.	Mean	D.P.	
4.	(Unions)	5.43	2.65	5.06	2.64	5.26	1.60	5.65	2.76	5.35	2.41	(6)
9.	(Gov't. controls)	4.43	3.54	4.81	2.26	4.39	2.94	5.87	2.82	4.88	2.89	(2)
13.	(American Way)	4.15	1.97	4.91	2.22	3.77	3.08	4.68	2.16	4.38	2.36	(7)
15.	(Wallace)	4.79	3.00	4.72	2.64	4.65	2.33	5.84	2.51	5.00	2.62	(3)
20.	(Artists and professors)	1.17	0.03	1.22	0.38	1.51	0.14	1.87	1.15	1.44	0.41	(14)
26.	(Russia)	2.94	2.49	2.54	1.47	2.30	1.52	2.51	0.93	2.57	1.60	(10.5)
27.	(Political candidate)	4.00	0.74	3.30	0.34	3.44	1.19	3.21	1.99	3.49	1.06	(13)
31.	($25,000/yr.)	4.51	2.22	4.74	1.98	5.17	3.42	5.56	2.12	5.00	2.44	(5)
37.	(Gov't. and jobs)	4.21	2.46	4.72	3.72	4.67	1.27	5.38	2.99	4.74	2.61	(4)
43.	(Utilities)	4.47	3.94	4.93	2.77	4.61	3.48	5.82	3.23	4.96	3.36	(1)
48.	(Depressions)	2.87	1.90	2.76	0.85	3.09	1.30	4.41	1.94	3.28	1.50	(12)
54.	(Poverty)	4.02	2.69	3.63	2.02	4.21	1.86	4.31	2.38	4.04	2.24	(8)
56.	(Ford, Morgan)	2.77	1.13	3.22	2.12	3.00	1.75	3.34	3.13	3.08	2.03	(9)
60.	(Charity)	2.38	1.54	2.87	1.73	2.47	0.91	2.88	2.22	2.65	1.60	(10.5)
	Mean per item	3.72	2.16	3.82	1.94	3.77	1.91	4.40	2.31	3.92	2.08	

aGroup I: University of Oregon Student Women (N = 47)
Group II: University of Oregon and University of California Student Women (N = 54)
Group III: University of Oregon and University of California Student Men (N = 57)
Group IV: Oregon Service Club Men (N = 68)

bIn obtaining the over-all means, the individual group means were not weighted by N.

These groups are more conservative on specific issues than the over-all scale mean of 3.92 indicates. The over-all means on the items (4, 9, 15, 31, 37, 43) dealing with unions, business, and government functions range from 4.74 to 5.35, and these items are also the most discriminating. It would appear, then, that with regard to what is most definitive in liberalism and conservatism—mainly ideas regarding power relations among labor, business, and government—the liberal position is as yet less crystallized and less militantly held than is the conservative position. There is some question as to how far these results can be generalized beyond the present sample.[5] They are, however, in general accord with numerous other findings and observations regarding the contemporary political scene. What is more difficult, and also more important, to gauge is the psychological *potential* for future ideological development in various directions in the face of changing political and economic conditions. Perhaps the other components of political ideology, when systematically measured and psychologically understood, would provide a basis for the solution of this problem.

4. THE THIRD PEC SCALE (FORMS 45 AND 40)

The construction of Forms 45 and 40 was, as has been discussed in the previous chapter, influenced greatly by considerations of practicality and of administrative expediency. In view of these considerations, and in order to make room for the inclusion of other material, the PEC scale was cut literally to the bone. It was identical in both forms of the questionnaire and contained only five items—not enough to obtain an adequate measure of reliability, and hardly enough to be called a "scale." The reasoning behind the use of a five-item E scale was discussed and criticized in Chapter IV; the same criticisms apply to the present PEC scale. It appears now that it would have been wiser to have used a 10-item form; the short form used did, however, make possible the comparison of various groups and the study of relationships between this scale and the others.

The Form 45–40 PEC scale is presented in Table 7(V). It will be seen that the five items were not selected solely on statistical grounds; rather an attempt was made to include items whose D. P.'s were above a minimal level and, more important, which covered as many as possible of the ideological trends previously discussed. The first four items are taken, with occasional slight revisions, from Form 60. Item 17 (Economic security), has a history of transiency; originally in the Form 78 PEC scale, it was moved to the F scale in Form 60 (see Chapter VII); it has been returned to PEC in an attempt to rid the F scale of all items which might be connected fairly directly with

---

[5] The representativeness of this sample with respect to political party and other group memberships will be considered later in this chapter (Section E). That the university groups are not unusually conservative is suggested by the fact that E-scale means are relatively low in comparison with other middle-class groups (see Chapter IV). Their PEC means can be compared with those for the groups taking Forms 45 and 40, below.

TABLE 7 (V)
THE THIRD FORM OF THE POLITICO-ECONOMIC CONSERVATISM
(PEC) SCALE (FORMS 45-40)

3.[a] Labor unions should become stronger and have more influence generally.

7. America may not be perfect, but the American Way has brought us about as close as human beings can get to a perfect society.

11.[a] Most government controls over business should be continued even though the war is over.

14. Men like Henry Ford or J. P. Morgan, who overcame all competition on the road to success, are models for all young people to admire and imitate.

17. In general, full economic security is bad; most men wouldn't work if they didn't need the money for eating and living.

[a] These items are "liberal," the others are "conservative." A high score is given for agreement with the conservative items, disagreement with the liberal items.

existing ideologies regarding politico-economic or minority groups. Item 17, as well as several others, might be included in any of several scales; proper placement must ultimately be based on statistical analysis.

Forms 45 and 40 were administered late in 1945 and in the first part of 1946. The sampling methods and problems, as well as the composition of the groups and their combination for statistical purposes, have been discussed in Chapter IV. It will suffice here to list the groups comprising this sample.

The Form 45 sample contains four groups: (a) Extension Testing Class (adult) Women (N = 59) at the University of California; (b) San Quentin Men (N = 110), inmates at the California State Prison; (c) and (d) Psychiatric Clinic Women (N = 71) and Men (N = 50), mostly outpatients at a community clinic in San Francisco.

The following groups are included in the Form 40 sample: (e) George Washington University Women (N = 132), members of day and evening classes in psychology; (f) California Service Club Men (N = 63), obtained at luncheon meetings of San Francisco Bay Area Kiwanis and Rotary clubs; (g) and (h) Middle-Class Men (N = 69) and Women (N = 154), members of various local groups such as church, P. T. A., women's clubs, etc.; (i) and (j) Working-Class Men (N = 61) and Women (N = 53), members of local groups such as United Electrical Workers Union, Warehousemen's Union (I. L. W. U.), California Labor School, etc.; (k) and (l) Los Angeles Men (N = 117) and Women (N = 130), a heterogeneous but largely middle-class sample of various local groups in Los Angeles. Data on some of the subgroupings within these statistical units will be considered in Section E, below.

In addition, there were two groups which were given both Forms 45 and 40. First, the School for Merchant Marine Officers (to be referred to as "Maritime School") (N = 343), half of which was given Form 45, the other half Form 40, the two halves being equated for intelligence (AGCT), time in school, and planned function as officer (deck or engine). Second, veterans

TABLE 8 (V)

MEANS AND STANDARD DEVIATIONS OF PEC SCALE SCORES FOR
GROUPS TAKING FORMS 45 AND 40

Group	Statistical Property					
	N	Mean	Rank	S.D.	Mean E_A	Rank
a. *Groups taking Form 45*						
Extension Testing Class						
Women	59	4.33	(4)	1.28	3.77	(12)
San Quentin Men	110	4.68a	(2)	0.96	5.33	(1)
Psychiatric Clinic Women	71	4.12a	(11)	1.53	4.23	(5)
Psychiatric Clinic Men	50	4.14a	(10)	1.40	3.92	(7.5)
Over-allb	290	4.32		1.29	4.31	
b. *Groups taking Form 40*						
George Washington						
University Women	132	4.30	(6.5)	1.13	4.04	(6)
California Service Club						
Men	63	4.83	(1)	1.31	4.31	(4)
Middle-Class Men	69	4.30	(6.5)	1.52	3.89	(10)
Middle-Class Women	154	4.26	(8)	1.62	3.64	(14)
Working-Class Men	61	3.39	(13)	1.58	3.92	(7.5)
Working-Class Women	53	3.25	(14)	1.53	3.91	(9)
Los Angeles Men	117	3.91	(12)	1.49	3.82	(11)
Los Angeles Women	130	4.16	(9)	1.41	3.71	(13)
Over-allb	779	4.05		1.45	3.91	
c. *Groups taking both forms*						
Maritime School Men						
Form 45	179	4.31)	(5)	(1.08	4.95	(2)
Form 40	164	4.32)		(		
Employment Service Men						
Veterans						
Form 45	51	4.35)	(3)	(1.28	4.43	(3)
Form 40	55	4.37)		(		
Over-allb	449	4.34		1.18	4.69	
d. Totals for all groups	1518	4.19		1.37	4.13	

aThe use of two forms for the Psychiatric Clinic groups complicated the
PEC scale results somewhat. The data above are based on 45 women and 29
men taking the Form 45 PEC scale. For the remaining 26 women taking the
Form 60 PEC scale (14 items) the mean was 4.05, and for 21 men the mean
was 4.04. For the combined 47 men and women taking this scale, the
reliability was .77 and the Standard Deviation was 1.05-- values comparable to those of the other groups taking Form 60.

bIn obtaining the over-all values, the individual group means were not
weighted by N.

coming for vocational guidance to the U.S. Employment Service over a period of several months, the first 51 receiving Form 45, the next 55, Form 40. This procedure had mainly to do with determining possible effects of the presence of certain E items on the F-scale responses and will be discussed in more detail in Chapter VII.

In view of the shortness of the PEC scale, no reliabilities were computed. However, means and S. D.'s were obtained for each group and are given in Table 8 (V). The group means appear to fall into three main levels of magnitude. The two most conservative groups are the California Service Club Men (4.83) and the San Quentin Men (4.68). At an intermediate level, with PEC means of 3.91 to 4.37 (significantly lower than the first level and higher than the third) is the bulk of the total sample: University groups, Psychiatric Clinic Patients, the Middle-Class and Los Angeles groups. Finally, the most liberal groups—although the means of 3.25 and 3.39 are far from extreme, and the variability within each group is large—are the Working-Class Men and Women.

That the Service Club Men make the highest mean is not so much a new discovery as a partial indication that the scale provides a valid measure of conservatism. The program and tradition of these groups are fairly explicit in their support of numerous trends in conservative ideology. It will be recalled that similar results were found with the Oregon Service Club Men (Form 60). Once again, however, we must emphasize the variability within this and the other groups.

The great conservatism of the San Quentin Men may come as a surprise to those who conceive of criminals as conscious foes of the social order and to those who assume a psychological affinity between criminality and radicalism. It might have been expected that those who violate prevailing laws regarding property and morality would tend to oppose the prevailing social ideology and social authority. Yet this does not appear to be the case. Criminals accept the basic premises of the capitalistic system while at the same time engaging in a pseudorebellion against the formal rules and technicalities. The criminal does not oppose the principles of rugged individualism; he simply carries them *ad absurdum*. The San Quentin material and the relation of criminality to antidemocracy are considered further in Chapter XXI.

The problem of class differences in conservatism is raised by the fact that the Working-Class Men and Women make a significantly lower PEC mean than do the Middle-Class Men and Women and the Los Angeles group (which is largely middle class). There are several reasons for questioning whether these differences can be generalized to the broad middle- and working-class populations. For one thing, the Working-Class group shows a distinct sampling bias in a liberal direction: almost half the members of this group are from the United Electrical Workers (C.I.O.), a militant union, or from the California Labor School, a strongly left-wing institution. The

Middle-Class groups are more varied and probably more representative in membership. Furthermore, several groups with PEC means similar to those of the Middle-Class groups contain a large proportion of working-class individuals; these groups are the San Quentin Men (almost entirely working class), the Psychiatric Clinic Patients, and the Maritime School and Employment Service Veteran Men. In view of the intergroup as well as the intragroup variability, it seems safe to conclude that over-all class differences in political ideology are not extremely large, and that individual and group differences within each class are so great that they become the primary problem requiring explanation. How does it happen, for example, that the same working-class background produces a law-abiding conservative worker, a politically conservative criminal, a company union leader, a C.I.O. leader, a Communist? Why does one middle-class individual join a service club while another becomes a supporter of Henry Wallace? Why is it that some, perhaps most, workers identify with the middle class or with the economic *status quo*, and some individuals with middle-class background identify with what they conceive to be the true interests of the working class? These may be not so much questions of actual class or group *membership* as questions of class or group *identification*—and "identification" is a psychological variable. An individual, in making his social identification, is determining not only his ideology, but also what he is to be like as a person. We shall have occasion to consider further, in the chapters that follow, the deeper emotional trends that help to determine the individual's group memberships and identifications.

How close is the relation between conservatism and ethnocentrism in the various groups studied? A means for obtaining a preliminary answer to this question is to compare group means on PEC and on E (see Table 8(V)). Since most groups took the short E_A scale, the E_A means were used even for those groups which took the total E_{AB} scale (see Chapter IV). The rank-order correlation between the PEC means and E_A means for the fourteen groups was $+.50$, indicating a statistically significant but not very close relationship. In general, as the degree of group conservatism increases, the degree of ethnocentrism also increases. The four groups with conspicuously high E_A means are the San Quentin Men (5.33), the Maritime School Men (4.95), the Employment Service Men Veterans (4.43), and the California Service Club Men (4.31). These groups ranked 2, 5, 3, and 1, respectively, on PEC. No groups were conspicuously low on E, the eight lowest groups having no means within the fairly narrow range of 3.64–3.92; the most liberal groups were among the least ethnocentric. The over-all E_A mean was 4.13, almost identical to the over-all PEC mean of 4.19. (The E_{AB} mean is somewhat lower, partly because of sampling differences and partly because the E_B items—four on Jews and one on Negroes—had lower means.)

The correlation of ranks does not, however, tell the whole story. Many groups made a significantly higher mean on PEC than on E, or *vice versa*.

Whether the group mean on PEC is higher than on E, or lower, seems to depend in large measure on the socioeconomic class of the group: the predominantly middle-class groups tend to be lower on E than on PEC, while the working-class groups are, it appears, more ethnocentric than conservative. Consider the middle-class groups: the PEC and E means, respectively, for the Extension Testing Class Women are 4.33 and 3.77; for the George Washington University Women, 4.30 and 4.04, for the California Service Club Men, 4.83 and 4.31; and similarly for the Middle-Class and Los Angeles Men and Women. Only one of these PEC-E differences is below the 5 per cent level of statistical significance. It will be recalled that in the Form 78 and Form 60 samples, largely middle class, the level of conservatism was greater than the level of ethnocentrism. The opposite trend is found in the working-class (or marginal middle-class) groups. Thus the PEC and E means, respectively, are: for the San Quentin Men, 4.68 and 5.33; Working-Class Men, 3.39 and 3.92; Working-Class Women, 3.25 and 3.91; Maritime School Men, 4.32 and 4.95; Employment Service Men Veterans, 4.36 and 4.43. This leaves only the Psychiatric Clinic Men and Women, who are heterogeneous with respect to class and whose PEC and E means differ only slightly (0.1–0.2).

Several factors—not mutually exclusive—may help to explain these class differences. First, open prejudice is more accepted on a verbal level in the working class than in the middle class. The higher E means of the former may therefore reflect, in part, the verbal atmosphere rather than a difference in basic outgroup hostility. (This factor would not hold for the pro-ingroup items.) Then there is the previously discussed "pseudodemocratic façade," which is more characteristic of the middle than of the working class, and which the E-scale items probably only partially circumvented. Also, certain trends in liberal ideology may appeal to some workers not on a truly liberal basis but on a "class-ethnocentric" basis which is an aspect of general ethnocentrism. For example, some workers are strongly prounion and resentful of "bosses," yet at the same time are anti-Negro, anti-foreigner, and conservative regarding many political issues.

All in all, the group data lead us to investigate further the relationship between ethnocentrism and conservatism, with an eye both to what makes the correlation relatively high and to what keeps it from being higher. These problems will be pursued further when we consider the correlations between the PEC and E scales, and the psychological connection between conservatism and ethnocentrism in the individual. But first we must complete the presentation of the PEC-scale data.

Table 9(V) gives a summary of the item analysis of the Form 45–40 PEC scale. Data for the men and the women are summarized separately. The over-all mean for the women, 4.07, is significantly lower than that of 4.25 for the men. The women were also, as noted in Chapter IV, slightly but sig-

TABLE 9 (V)

MEANS AND DISCRIMINATORY POWERS OF THE PEC SCALE ITEMS
(FORMS 40 AND 45)

No.	Item	MEN'S GROUPS[a] (N 869)[b]			WOMEN'S GROUPS[c] (N 573)[d]		
		Mean	D.P.	Rank	Mean	D.P.	Rank
3.	(Labor unions)	4.51	3.16	(4)	4.67	3.49	(4)
7.	(American Way)	4.90	3.33	(3)	4.57	3.98	(1)
11.	(Government controls)	4.19	3.08	(5)	3.92	2.97	(5)
14.	(Ford and Morgan)	3.75	3.58	(1)	3.56	3.90	(2)
17.	(Economic security)	3.93	3.46	(2)	3.62	3.77	(3)
Mean per item[e]		4.25	3.32		4.07	3.62	

[a]The individual groups of men in this sample are as follows: San Quentin Men Prisoners (N = 110). Employment Service Men Veterans (N = 106). Maritime School Men (N = 343). California Service Club Men (N = 63). Middle-Class Men (N = 69). Working-Class Men (N = 61). Los Angeles Men (N = 117).

[b]The over-all N for the PEC scale (men) is 100 less than that for the E scale because two groups were omitted: (1) Of the 50 Psychiatric Clinic Men, only 29 took the regular Form 45; the others took a form equated for E and F, but not for PEC. Because of the small N, no PEC scale analysis was made on this group. (2) The 50 Working-Class Men and Women were used as a statistical group for analysis on the E scale because additional data on the total E scale were desired; but their F and PEC scales were not analyzed statistically.

[c]The individual groups of women in this sample are as follows: Extension Testing Class Women (N = 59). George Washington University Women Students (N = 132). Psychiatric Clinic Women (N = 45). Middle-Class Women (N = 154). Working-Class Women (N = 53). Los Angeles Women (N = 130).

[d]This N is 26 less than the over-all N for women on the E and F scales because only 45 of the 71 Psychiatric Clinic Women took the regular Form 45. The remaining 26 took a form which was equated to Form 45 for E and F, but not for PEC.

[e]In obtaining the over-all means, the individual group means were not weighted by N.

nificantly less ethnocentric than the men. This may, however, be a difference in the sample rather than in the total population, since we have no female groups comparable to the high-scoring San Quentin, Service Club, and Maritime School male groups. Moreover, as shown in Table 8(V), for all comparable sex groups (Psychiatric Clinic, Middle Class, Working Class, Los Angeles) the means for men and women are almost identical. Since the sampling methods used were not primarily designed to determine the average intensity of any opinions or attitudes in broader populations, it is perhaps safest not to draw inferences about the total male and female population. It can be said, however, that for groups of the general type represented here, no sex differences of practical significance seem to exist; and that differences *among* male groups and *among* female groups are much greater than the differences *between* males and females.

The male and female subsamples are also very similar with regard to means and D. P.'s on the individual items. While the scale mean was lower in women, the relative standing of the item means was almost identical for the two sexes, the rank-order correlation being .90. Women were more conservative than men on only one item (unions). A similar relation holds also for the D. P.'s, the rank-order correlation being .70.

The general level of D. P.'s would, other things being equal, be slightly greater for a 5-item than for a 14-item scale, since each item contributes more to the total score. Therefore, the average D. P. of 3.4–3.5 for Forms 45 and 40 is comparable or slightly superior to that of 2.1 for Forms 78 and 60. All of the present items seem statistically adequate. Item 11 (Government controls over business) had the lowest D. P., but in view of the greater success of the "government function" items in earlier forms, improvement should not be difficult. While the five items can hardly claim to be considered a "scale," they show sufficient internal consistency so that one may meaningfully speak of "total PEC score" and one may determine the relations between this and various other measures.

The level of internal consistency of the PEC scale is indicated also by a correlational analysis made on a group of 517 University of California women students.[6] A mean r of $+0.26$ was found between each item and the sum of the remaining items, the range of r's being $+0.10$ to $+0.33$. The rank order of these items, according to the size of the item's correlation with the sum of the others, was identical to the rank order of item D. P.'s for the combined women's groups above (Table 9(V)). The correlations among individual items averaged $+0.14$, the range being $+0.02$ to $+0.30$. The highest correlation, 0.30, was between Item 7 (American Way ideal) and Item 14 (Ford and Morgan). Only three r's were below .10 (the 1 per cent level of significance), and all of them involved Item 11 (Government controls). These correlations, while far below those for the E scale, indicate that the PEC scale meets the minimum requirements for its present uses, and that a scale of 20 or 30 such items might, without loss of breadth, achieve a reliability in the neighborhood of .8.

5. DISCUSSION: SOME PATTERNS OF CONTEMPORARY LIBERALISM AND CONSERVATISM

The reliability and internal consistency of the PEC scales suggest, on the one hand, that liberalism and conservatism are relatively organized and measurable patterns of current politico-economic thought; and, on the other

[6] The group and procedure are discussed more fully in Chapters IV and VII.

hand, that within each of these broad patterns there is considerable subpat-
terning, inconsistency, and simple ignorance. To ignore either the relative
generality or the relative inconsistency would, it seems, lead to serious misunderstanding of the problem. More detailed exploration of the nature and
deeper psychological meaning of these ideological trends, as expressed in
the interviews, will be made in Chapter XVII, following presentation of the
clinical material. However, at this point we ought briefly to consider, on
the basis of the scale data and of some individual patterns of scale response,
certain variations within liberalism and within conservatism.

Liberalism was conceived not as a single, unitary attitude, but as an ideological system containing a number of trends or components. The reliability
and internal consistency of the initial forms of the scale show that these
trends are interrelated significantly but imperfectly in the individual. The
prototypic "liberal" is, according to our guiding conception, an individual
who actively seeks progressive social change, who can be militantly critical
(though not necessarily totally rejective) of the present *status quo*, who
opposes or de-emphasizes numerous conservative values and beliefs regarding business success, rugged individualism, human nature, and the like, and
who would diminish the power of business by increasing the power of labor
and the economic functions of government.

It is clear, however, that many individuals who are generally liberal do
not exhibit some of the above trends. While some of the inconsistency—
perhaps the largest part—is due to confusion resulting from lacks and distortions in the press and other media of mass communication, part of it seems
also to reflect deep-lying emotional trends of considerable intensity and
resistance to change. The individual's pattern of thought, whatever its content, reflects his personality and is not merely an aggregate of opinions picked
up helter-skelter from the ideological environment.

One variant, particularly common in the groups tested, might be called
the *politically pacifistic* liberal. The guiding idea here seems to be fear of
concentration of social power. This individual, who feels keenly the injustice of the present social order and who sympathizes with labor and other
subordinate groups, nevertheless cannot militantly support their strivings for
greater power. He feels that "powerful unions are as dangerous as powerful
business." He is prone to emphasize the idea that unions are no longer
weak in relation to organized industry, and he is likely therefore to accept,
in one form or another, the conservative argument that unions are all right
but their power must be limited. He would like to decrease the power of
business but finds difficulty in directly opposing it—"we might, after all, be
as bad as they are." He believes in extending the economic functions of government, perhaps even in some degree of nationalization of industry, but
fear of government power often leads him to oppose liberal measures or to

support halfway measures which accomplish little. Opposed to force, he tends to confuse force with militancy and to be indecisive, critical of both sides, overly compromising, inept at political action, shocked by the realities of political affairs. He is likely to make a middle rather than low score on the PEC scale, not out of true conservatism but rather out of inhibited liberalism; he has, one might say, a "liberal" utopia but he cannot fight for the social changes necessary to realize it. Critical of things as they are, yet afraid of change—hating to submit, yet unable to rebel—he cannot actively support the *status quo*, but he can do little to oppose it.

We were not able to attempt a quantitative study of various types of left-wing ideology. In addition to militant and politically pacifistic liberalism, we should also have been interested in determining the existence and nature of other patterns such as "disillusioned liberalism," "stereotyped (ticket) liberalism," "revolutionary socialism," and so on. Some leads for future study derived from the interview material are presented in Chapter XIX.

The political right requires similar differentiation and study. The prototypic "conservative," in terms of the present scale, is one who supports the *status quo* and resists changes in existing politico-economic power arrangements, who supports conservative values and traditions, who believes that labor is properly subordinate to employer or management, and who wishes to minimize the economic functions of government in order that individual businessmen can, in free and equal competition, provide goods of maximum quality at minimum cost to the consumer.

While this "traditional conservative" *ideology* is not uncommon today, the actual politico-economic *situation* has changed considerably from the one, of fifty or more years ago, to which the ideology refers. The individual small businessman or entrepreneur is no longer the primary economic unit; big business and group management have replaced the individual employer; the production process is more complex, organized, and impersonal; specialization and mechanization threaten the individuality and the job satisfaction of worker and manager. As both labor and industry become more organized and more clear-cut social forces, the role of government becomes increasingly an issue. The traditional conservative is in a dilemma. Shall he oppose the monopolistic trend of big business and want a return to rugged individualistic competition, with government having few economic functions (laissez-faire conservatism)? Shall he favor increased government functioning as a means of preventing monopolistic practices, even though it mean increasing the power of labor (move toward liberalism)? Or shall he, basing everything on his allegiance to the symbol "business," want government to be a force in the service of business as opposed to labor (move toward fascism)? Most conservatives seem still to be in the process of ideological adjustment along these and other lines. Much research remains to be done concerning new patterns of conservatism and concerning the psychological dispositions making some individuals more receptive to one pattern, others to another.

It is proposed, then, that the PEC scale results can best be understood in terms of both general and specific factors. The general factors—over-all liberalism and conservatism—account for the significant reliability or consistency obtained, while the specific variations within the left and the right prevent the scale from attaining higher statistical standards.

C. THE RELATION BETWEEN ETHNOCENTRISM AND CONSERVATISM

The correlations of the Anti-Semitism and Ethnocentrism scales with the PEC scale are presented in Table 10(V). The correlations range in value from .14 for the San Quentin Men to .86 for the Working-Class Women, but they fall for the most part at the level of .5–.6. Of the 29 correlation coefficients obtained, there are only 4 below .40, 5 above .70. These correlations of individual scores are consistent with the rank-order correlation of .50 between the group means on PEC and E (Forms 45 and 40).

The data in Table 10 (V) indicate that PEC is less closely related to A-S than to the other components of E. Thus, in Form 78, PEC correlates significantly higher with E (exclusive of A-S) than with A-S (.59 to .43). In Form 60, where 4 of the 12 E-scale items deal with A-S, the average r is .52, midway between the two for Form 78. The results for the two groups taking both Forms 45 and 40 (Maritime School Men and Employment Service Men Veterans) show the same thing: PEC correlates higher with E_A than with E_{A+B} (.60 to .49, and .41 to .38). It will be recalled that E_A contains no A-S items, while 4 of the 5 E_B items refer to Jews. Finally, the highest PEC-E correlations were obtained on Form 40, which contained only E_A. The average r of .66 on Form 40 is especially significant in view of the brevity of the two scales (5 items each). The explanation would seem to lie in the fact that these items represent the most general trends in their respective ideologies: in PEC, support of the *status quo* and conservative values; in E, generalized ingroup idealization and outgroup rejection. It is probably in broad trends such as these that conservatism and ethnocentrism overlap the most, because these ideological trends are rooted in the same deep-lying emotional dispositions (see Chapter VII). The specific factors which lower the correlation of A-S with PEC constitute an important problem for future research.

There appear to be no consistent sex or class differences in the E-PEC correlation. In the University, Middle-Class and Working-Class groups (with presumably comparable male and female samples in each), the value of r is about 0.1 lower for men than for women; but in the Los Angeles group this trend is reversed, while in the Psychiatric Clinic Patients the difference is

TABLE 10 (V)

CORRELATIONS OF THE A-S AND E SCALES WITH THE PEC SCALE (ALL FORMS)

		N	Correlation	
			E: PEC	A-S: PEC
A.	*Groups taking Form 78:*			
	Public Speaking Class Women	140	.52	.49
	Public Speaking Class Men	52	.55	.32
	Extension Psychology Class Women	40	.52	.23
	Professional Women	63	.76	.69
	Mean r[a]	295	.59	.43
B.	*Groups taking Form 60:*[b]			
	University of Oregon Student Women	47	.48	
	University of Oregon and University of California Student Women	54	.62	
	University of Oregon and University of California Student Men	57	.48	
	Oregon Service Club Men	68	.52	
	Mean r[a]	226	.52	
C.	*Groups taking Form 45:*[c]			
	Extension Testing Class Women	59	.60	
	San Quentin Men	110	.14	
	Psychiatric Clinic Women	71	.53[d]	
	Psychiatric Clinic Men	50	.55[d]	
	Working-Class Men and Women·	50	.75	
	Mean r[a]	340	.51	
D.	*Groups taking Form 40:*[c]			
	George Washington University Women	132	.48	
	California Service Club Men	63	.64	
	Middle-Class Men	69	.67	
	Middle-Class Women	154	.76	
	Working-Class Men	61	.74	
	Working-Class Women	53	.86	
	Los Angeles Men	117	.61	
	Los Angeles Women	130	.52	
	Mean r[a]	779	.66	
E.	*Groups taking Forms 40 and 45:*			
	Employment Service Men Veterans			
	(Form 40)	55	.60[e]	
	(Form 45)	51	.49	
	Maritime School Men (Form 40)	164	.41[e]	
	(Form 45)	179	.38	
	Mean r[a]	449	.47	
	Mean r for all groups taking Forms 40 and 45	1568	.57	

[a]In obtaining the over-all means, the individual group means were not weighted by N, and Z_r was not used.

[b]It will be recalled that in Form 60 the E scale contained 4 A-S items, there being no separate A-S scale.

[c]PEC is correlated with E_A in groups taking Form 40, with total E_{A+B} scale in groups taking Form 45.

[d]For the PEC scale in the Psychiatric Clinic groups, the number of women was 45, the number of men 29, due to a substitution of forms.

[e]These correlations are based on the E_A scores of subjects taking Form 45 as well as those taking Form 40.

negligible. The same holds for class differences: in the Working-Class Men and Women the correlations are very high (.74 and .86), but in other groups which draw heavily upon the working class, notably San Quentin and the Maritime School, the correlations are very low (.14 and .4). The reasons for the variations in the size of r seem to lie more in the specific nature of the group than in its sex or class status. It is interesting in this connection that two groups in which the E-PEC correlation was very high, the Working Class Men (.74) and Women (.86) also had the two lowest PEC means (see Table 8(V)). We may hypothesize that the E-PEC correlation will be highest when, other things such as the S. D. being equal, the group contains a sizeable minority of strong liberals. Judging from some of the other groups, the number of strong conservatives has less influence on the correlation. We shall return to this question shortly.

The general level of the E-PEC correlations demonstrates that ethnocentrism and conservatism, as measured by the present scales, are significantly but imperfectly related.[7] In everyday terms, we may say that conservatives are, on the average, significantly more ethnocentric than liberals are. The more conservative an individual is, the greater the likelihood that he is ethnocentric—but this is a probability and not a certainty. Since the existence of an affinity between these ideological patterns has often been observed previously, the present correlations are perhaps less a startling discovery than an indication of the validity of the scales. To those who have been unaware of the E-PEC relationship, the significance of the correlations must be stressed. To those who tend to equate conservatism and ethnocentrism as psychological trends in the individual, it must be pointed out that the correlations are far from perfect. Even with a much more reliable measure of PEC, the correlation with E could hardly average over .70—a value inadequate for predictive purposes. It becomes necessary, then, to understand what produces the close association between these ideological patterns in the individual, as well as what systematic factors—apart from ignorance or misinformation—make the E-PEC correlation less than 1.0.

A theoretical basis for the close tie between conservatism and ethnocentrism is suggested by certain similarities in their major underlying trends. Support of the prevailing politico-economic ideology and authority is, apparently, often a part of the generalized ethnocentric tendency to submit to accepted authority in all areas of social life. Similarly, ethnocentric rejection of outgroups is expressed in the politico-economic sphere by resistance to social change and by the tendency to subsume progressive political ideologies under the general heading of "foreign" outgroups and ideas (threats to ingroup authority). The interconnection between the two ideologies and the difficulty of separating them even for purposes of study are revealed by a

[7] These results are, on the whole, consistent with those of the other studies mentioned at the start of this chapter.

number of scale items. For example: "America may not be perfect, but the American Way has brought us about as close as human beings can get to a perfect society." To support this idea is, it would seem, to express both politico-economic conservatism and the ingroup idealization so character-istic of ethnocentrism. The item, "The worst danger to real Americanism during the last 50 years has come from foreign ideas and agitators," is another example of politicalized ethnocentrism: again we find moral stereotypy and externalization of blame for social problems onto the threatening outgroup.

There are also theoretical reasons for expecting a relationship between liberalism and anti-ethnocentrism. Both tend to involve a critical attitude toward prevailing authorities and traditions. The identification with the masses (workers, "the common man," "the weak and downtrodden") so often a central theme in left-wing political ideology, finds expression also in opposition to ethnocentrism and outgroup suppression. Indeed, the forma-tion of leftist political views in youth often begins with a sense of the injus-tice of anti-Semitism or anti-Negroism; when sympathetic imagery of sub-ordinate groups is extended to include the working class, the transition from "group relations" to "politico-economic" ideology has begun. The further development of liberal-radical views is ordinarily based on imagery and atti-tudes identical to those underlying anti-ethnocentric ideology: opposition to hierarchy and to dominance-submission, removal of class and group barriers, emphasis on equalitarian interaction, and so on.

We have also to consider the "correlation-lowering" factors. Why, in view of the theoretical argument above, is the E-PEC correlation not higher? The present data suggest, but are not adequate to test, several hypotheses. The correlation charts (scattergrams) for each sample reveal that extreme liberals (low scorers on PEC) are for the most part low as well on E. But the "middles" on PEC are extremely diversified with respect to standing on E. It is possible that the group which is low on E but middle on PEC consists largely of the "politically pacifistic" liberals discussed previously. Practically none of the subjects were low on PEC and high on E (ethnocentric liberals); such individuals would, however, be well worth intensive study.

The high scorers on PEC are more variable on E than are the low scorers. While most of those high on PEC are also high on E, a considerable number are middle and a small but consistent percentage low on E (nonethnocentric conservatives). In other words, strong political liberalism is a pretty good indicator of anti-ethnocentrism, but political conservatism is less consistently related to ethnocentrism.

In attempting to explain the variability of conservatives with respect to ethnocentrism, we are reminded of the distinction between "genuine" and "pseudo-" previously drawn with respect to patriotism and traditional-conventional values (Chapter IV). One can be politically conservative, just as one can be patriotic (in the sense of firm attachment to American culture and tradition), without being ethnocentric. We should like to use the term *"genuine conservative"* to refer to the individual with this broad pattern of thought. He is "genuine" because, whatever the merits of his political views, he is seriously concerned with fostering what is most vital in the American democratic tradition. He believes, for example, in the crucial importance of the profit motive and in the necessity of economic insecurity; but he wants the best man to win no matter what his social background. He is resistant to social change, but he can be seriously critical of the national and political ingroups and—what is more important—he is relatively free of the rigidity and deep-lying hostility characteristic of ethnocentrism.

The ethnocentric conservative is the *pseudoconservative*, for he betrays in his ethnocentrism a tendency antithetical to democratic values and tradition. He is the E-PEC "correlation raiser" because, as discussed above, his politico-economic views are based on the same underlying trends—submission to authority, unconscious handling of hostility toward authority by means of displacement and projection onto outgroups, and so on—as his ethnocentrism. It is indeed paradoxical that the greatest psychological potential for antidemocratic change should come from those who claim to represent democratic tradition. For the pseudoconservatives are the pseudo-democrats, and their needs dispose them to the use of force and oppression in order to protect a mythical "Americanism" which bears no resemblance to what is most vital in American history.

An additional hypothesis may be proposed regarding individuals high on E but middle on PEC. These may well be pseudoconservatives who have kept up with changes in the actual politico-economic situation by making changes in traditional (individualistic) conservative ideology. They emphasize competitiveness as a value, yet they support the concentration of economic power in big business—the greatest single threat at present to the individual competing businessman. They emphasize economic mobility and the "Horatio Alger" myth, yet they support numerous forms of discrimination that put severe limitations on the mobility of large sections of the population. They may also believe in extending the economic functions of government, not for humanitarian reasons but as a means of limiting the power of labor and other groups.

This is not merely a "modern conservatism." It is, rather, a totally new direction: away from individualism and equality of opportunity, and toward a rigidly stratified society in which there is a minimum of economic mobility and in which the "right" groups are in power, the outgroups subordinate. Perhaps the term "reactionary" fits this ideology best. Ultimately it is fascism. While certainly not a *necessary* sequel to laissez-faire conservatism, it can be regarded as a possible (and not uncommon) distortion of conservatism—a distortion which retains certain surface similarities but which changes the basic structure into the antithesis of the original. Since most

Americans are "middle on PEC," it becomes crucial to understand the psychological dispositions which help to determine new ideological directions in the individual.

The above distinction regarding ideological patterns within the political left and right are presented as hypotheses to help explain the scale results.[8] If these hypotheses are not borne out, others will be needed. For it is clear that political ideologies do not fall neatly along a simple liberalism-conservatism dimension; that the relation between ethnocentrism and "conservatism" is extremely complex; and that the individual's receptivity to political ideology, as to "group relations" ideology, is based to a large extent on deeplying personality trends.

D. VALIDATION BY CASE STUDIES: THE RESPONSES OF MACK AND LARRY ON THE PEC SCALE

In an attempt to judge the validity of the PEC scale we may here, as in Chapters III and IV, compare the scale responses of Mack and Larry and consider them in relation to material from their interviews (Chapter II). The PEC-scale scores of these two subjects, the group mean, and the D. P. for each of the 16 PEC items included in Form 78 are shown in Table 11(V).

TABLE 11 (V)

RESPONSES OF MACK AND LARRY ON THE PEC SCALE

No.	Item	Mack	Larry	Group[a] Mean	Group[a] D.P.
1.	(Value of dollar)	6	7	6.10	1.16
5.	(Depressions)	5	1	3.33	2.76
8.	(Charity)	3	7	5.46	1.48
13.	(Businessmen, artists)	1	1	2.29	1.70
15.	(Middle of the road)	7	5	4.35	2.90
22.	(Political candidate)	7	7	6.38	0.32
27.	(Rebellious ideas)	5	6	3.86	2.84
36.	(Gov't. responsibility)	2	1	3.22	3.01
44.	(Socialized medicine)	2	6	2.38	1.69
52.	(Taxes, corporations)	2	3	3.66	2.29
61.	(Economic security)	6	6	3.75	2.68
63.	(Gov't. interference)	5	1	4.01	2.39
68.	(Unions stronger)	6	2	4.58	2.30
71.	(Ford, Morgan)	7	6	5.30	2.00
76.	(Gov't. activity)	2	2	3.32	2.76
78.	(Ability will tell)	7	6	4.74	1.99
	Mean per item	4.56	4.19	4.17	2.14

[a]The group means and D.P.'s are based on all four groups taking Form 78.

[8] Further hypotheses, plus supporting evidence, are presented in Chapter XVII, which deals with the interview material.

The two men are much more similar in their PEC-scale scores than was the case with their A-S and E scores. Larry's mean score, 4.19, is at the group mean and Mack's, 4.56, is not very far above. When the group of Public Speaking Men to which these subjects belonged is considered by itself, Mack is just inside the high quartile, Larry is just below it. On 11 of the 16 items the scores of the two men do not differ by more than one point. Attention to the individual items, however, shows that the similarities are confined to certain areas of politico-economic ideology; in other areas there are sharp differences.

Mack and Larry are most similar in their consistent support of general conventional-conservative values. Both agree, usually rather strongly, with Items 1 (Value of a dollar), 15 (Middle of the road), 22 (Political candidate), 27 (Rebellious ideas), 71 (Ford, Morgan), and 78 (Ability will tell). This seems to be in keeping with the interviews, in which both men expressed the usual conservative criticisms of the New Deal. Both men, it appears, accept the view that a man's getting ahead depends most of all upon his living according to the values of thrift, determination, work, honesty, conformity, and the like.

Examination of the scores on other items, however, indicates that Mack and Larry differ with respect to the context in which their conservative values occur. For Mack the context appears to be one of upward social mobility on a class-ingroup basis, for Larry it appears to be one of nineteenth-century liberalism. This seems to be expressed in their wide disagreement on Items 5 (Depression) and 68 (Unions stronger). Mack's belief that depressions are "only natural" can be interpreted as an expression of the broader idea that, in the nature of things, the benefits to be had in our society are insufficient to go around and that it is no more than proper that the major portion of them should go to the "right people," that is, to an ingroup. This ingroup does not seem to include organized labor (Item 68) nor the various minority groups which he rejected in his responses on the E scale. This would appear to be another manifestation of Mack's tendency, so marked in his interview, to make rigid ingroup-outgroup distinctions in his thinking about politico-economic matters as well as about social relations generally. For Larry, on the other hand, the value for getting ahead does not exclude the possibility of various other kinds of people getting ahead, for he seems to be thinking in terms of an expanding economy in which working men can have a strong role (Item 68) and in which depressions are unnecessary (Item 5). The absence of any ingroup-outgroup distinction, and optimism with respect to the possibilities of economic abundance were outstanding features of Larry's interview.

Neither man shows the usual conservative opposition to the government's participation in the economic life of the nation: for Items 36 (Government responsibility), 44 (Socialized medicine), 52 (Taxes, corporations), 63 (Government interference), and 76 (Government activity) the two men have the same low mean score of 2.60. Their reasons, however, seem to be different. When the responses to the total scale are considered, it appears that Mack deviates from true, laissez-faire conservatism by taking a stand further to the political right. The fact that he rejects labor unions and believes in the inevitability of depressions suggests that the strong central control which he favors is not to have as its function economic planning to benefit all of the people; rather, it seems, he is thinking of rule by an ingroup from which the majority of the population would be excluded. That he does reject the majority of the population has been seen in his responses to the E scale. When it is considered that he is antigovernment only when it comes to interference with the individual's freedom "to make money and spend it as he likes" (Item 63) we are led to the conclusion that his idea of central control is a combination of government and the most powerful business interests. Thus it appears that Mack comes as close as he can, within the confines of the 16-item PEC scale, to expressing that pattern of pseudoconservatism which emerged from the analysis of his interview.

Larry, on the other hand, deviates from the usual conservative position by moving further to the left. Not only does he insist upon the social obligations of government (Items 36 and 76) but he would accept limitations upon the profits of individuals and corporations (Items 52 and 63). These views can be reconciled with his strong conservative values and pro-business senti-ments, it seems, only by means of the belief that there is plenty for all, that it is the task of government to see to it that no one has too little or too much, and that this situation will permit people who, like himself, are willing to work hard, to get as much as they really need without causing others to suffer.

It would appear from this analysis, and from the analysis of Mack's and Larry's interviews in Chapter II, that the difference of 0.37 in their PEC-scale means is not great enough to represent the actual distance between them on a right vs. left dimension of politico-economic ideology. However, as the discussion in the preceding section has shown, the differences between pseudoconservatism, which we find in Mack, and genuine conservatism as represented by Larry are qualitative as well as quantitative, and it is to the credit of the PEC scale that it pointed out these differences while indicating at the same time that Mack is somewhat more extreme in a quantitative sense.

E. THE RELATION BETWEEN ETHNOCENTRISM AND MEMBERSHIP IN VARIOUS POLITICAL AND ECONOMIC GROUPINGS

We have considered in previous sections the nature of political ideologies as measured by the PEC scales, and the relation of these ideologies to ethno-centrism. The data also revealed numerous group differences in degree of ethnocentrism. It was therefore natural to ask next: How do various political and economic groupings differ with respect to ethnocentrism? Information on such groupings (political party preference, parents' preference, organization memberships, income level, etc.) was obtained on the front page of the questionnaire, so that it was possible to compute the mean (average) E score for each group.[9]

We may consider first the relation between ethnocentrism and political group preference.

Political group preference was determined by means of several questions. First: "What political party or group do you like best?" Second: "How do you feel about each of these political groups? Democrats (Anti-New Deal), Democrats (New Deal), Willkie-type Republicans, Traditional Republicans." In each case the subject was asked to check one of four choices: agree much, agree, disagree, disagree much. On the basis of his pattern of response to these questions, each subject was assigned a single "group preference" by two raters working together (semi-independent judgments). Each subject could be placed with relative ease into one or another of the following categories: (1) "Total" Democrats (supporting both factions within the party); (2) Anti-New Deal Democrats; (3) New Deal Democrats; (4) Willkie Republicans; (5) Traditional Republicans; (6) "Total" Republicans (supporting both factions); (7) New Deal Democrats, Willkie Republicans (supporting these two groupings and opposing the others, without indicating specific party preference; (8) Communists; (9) Socialists; (10) P.A.C. (National Citizens and C.I.O. Political Action Committee); (11) Undecided (wrote in "undecided" to first question, omitted the second); (12) Anti-all parties; (13) None, nonpartisan (gave this answer to first question, omitted the second); (14) Self-contradictory (e.g., supported Traditional Republicans and New Deal Democrats, gave no over-all party preference); (15) Blank.

Table 12(V) gives the number of cases (N) and the average A-S or E score for each political grouping, as well as for each sample tested and for the group of samples taking each form of the questionnaire. It is thus possible to compare, say, the New Deal Democrats in one sample with the other political groupings in that sample, or with the over-all totals for all New Dealers tested, or with the over-all totals for all subjects tested.[10]

The N's and means in the bottom row (horizontal) may be examined first. The ratio of Democrats (columns 1–3) to Republicans (columns 4–5) is roughly 10 to 7, a value which approximates the registration figures in the 1944 California elections. However, the proportion of New Deal Democrats and of "combined liberal groups" (column 17) is unduly large. It seems safe to conclude that the present sample shows a slight but significant bias

[9] It would have been an important additional validation of the PEC scales to show differences among these groups with respect to PEC. Unfortunately, limitations of time prevented this further step.

[10] It will be noted that group-membership data was not statisticized for several of the groups tested (approximately one-third of the total N), due to time limitations. However, the groups in Table 12 (V) appear to be a fairly representative selection of the total sample.

in a liberal direction—a sampling factor which tends to lower the over-all E mean.

The various groupings appeared to fall into two clearly differentiated categories on the basis of average degree of ethnocentrism. First, the "*conservative*" category (column 16: Total Democrats, Anti-New Deal Democrats, Traditional Republicans, Total Republicans), with E means ranging from 4.17 to 4.72 and averaging 4.39. Second, the "*liberal*" category (New Deal Democrats, Willkie Republicans, New Deal-Willkie combined, Communists, Socialists, P.A.C.), with E means ranging from 1.25 to 3.60 and averaging 3.41. The difference of 0.98 between the liberal and conservative categories is statistically very significant (far above the 1 per cent level).[11]

The rank order of the individual groupings, in terms of E mean, is similar to their rank order on a right-left political dimension. The traditional wings of the Democratic and Republican parties are the most conservative as well as the most ethnocentric (E means of 4.2 to 4.7). The New Deal Democrats and the Willkie Republicans, representing in the main a slightly left-of-center political position, have a similar stand on ethnocentrism (means of 3.6 and 3.5). Interestingly enough, those who support both the New Deal and Willkie, without making an over-all party choice, have a much lower E mean of 2.4—an indication perhaps that greater political sophistication in liberals is accompanied by greater militancy regarding democratic group relations. The Socialists (those who gave this as their party preference, regardless of their views on the other groupings) were similar to the previous group with a mean of 2.6. The most militantly anti-ethnocentric groups were the P.A.C. and the Communists, with E means of 2.0 and 1.25 respectively.

The great difference between the "liberal" and "conservative" categories, as well as the rank order of the individual groupings, offer important evidence for the validity of the E scale and the E-PEC correlations reported above. The relationship between ethnocentrism and liberal-conservative group membership is very similar to that between ethnocentrism and liberal-conservative ideology in the individual. There is, on the average, a systematic relation between E, PEC, and political group preference, to the extent of a correlation of approximately .5.

Once again, both the group trend and the individual differences must be emphasized. The relationships, though significant, are far from perfect. There is, for one thing, considerable individual variability within each group-

[11] Critical ratios have not been computed for the various group differences discussed here. The following rules of thumb may be used in estimating the significance of the differences: Assume that the Standard Deviation for any grouping is equal to the S. D. for the sample containing it. This estimate is a maximal one so that any errors will tend to lower spuriously the value of the C. R. obtained. For groups with N's of about 50 each, differences of 0.6 are likely to be significant at the 5 percent level; when the N's are 100, a difference of 0.4 is adequate. These approximate standards hold for all tables in this section. An additional argument for the significance of these differences is their relative consistency from group to group.

TABLE 12 (V)

MEAN A-S OR E SCORES[a] FOR GROUPS SHOWING VARIOUS OVER-ALL POLITICAL PARTY PREFERENCES

Group	1. "Total" Democrat N Mean	2. Anti-New Deal Democrat N Mean	3. New Deal Democrat N Mean	4. Wilkie Republican N Mean	5. Traditional Republican N Mean	6. Total Republican N Mean	7. New Deal Democrat, Wilkie Republican N Mean	8. Communist N Mean
Groups taking Form 78:								
U.C. Public Speaking Class Women	6 3.63	4 3.83	28 3.11	39 3.00	13 4.19	34 3.66	0 --	0 --
U.C. Public Speaking Class Men	0 --	3 5.07	17 3.25	11 3.33	4 4.18	6 3.88	8 2.10	0 --
Extension Psychology Class Women	1 3.80	6 3.70	11 2.57	7 3.39	4 3.30	2 5.35	0 --	0 --
Professional Women	0 --	1 6.00	30 2.06	12 3.43	3 2.63	8 3.43	0 --	0 --
Totals	7 3.66	14 4.19	86 2.70	69 3.17	24 3.84	50 3.72	8 2.10	0 --
Groups taking Form 60:								
Univ. of Oregon Student Women	2 3.32	2 3.24	14 2.73	6 3.14	4 4.46	13 4.28	3 2.77	0 --
Univ. of Oregon and Univ. of California Student Women	3 4.59	4 4.15	19 2.95	9 3.26	1 2.49	14 3.24	2 2.37	0 --
Univ. of Oregon and Univ. of California Student Men	2 2.78	2 3.07	12 2.95	9 2.08	6 3.45	10 3.67	7 2.32	0 --
Totals	7 3.71	8 3.70	45 2.88	24 2.79	11 3.73	37 3.72	12 2.44	0 --
Groups taking Form 45:								
Maritime School Men	17 4.41	16 4.49	74 4.32	12 3.88	13 5.08	12 4.54	3 3.23	1 1.30
Psychiatric Clinic Men	6 4.12	0 --	20 3.97	2 3.55	7 4.27	3 3.70	1 1.30	1 1.30
Psychiatric Clinic Women	7 4.74	3 4.07	26 3.51	2 4.20	5 4.54	5 3.28	2 1.80	1 1.00
San Quentin Men[b]	19 4.44	5 4.74	45 4.60	6 4.83	3 5.90	3 4.50	0 --	0 --
Totals	30 4.43	19 4.42	120 4.08	16 3.88	25 4.74	20 4.10	6 2.43	3 1.20
Groups taking Form 40:								
Geo. Washington Univ. Women	13 4.37	17 4.86	44 3.83	5 3.48	9 5.49	14 4.14	1 3.80	0 --
Maritime School Men	21 5.10	15 5.11	69 4.95	4 3.85	5 4.84	15 5.60	2 5.80	0 --
Middle-Class Women	0 --	4 3.35	43 2.76	28 4.36	11 6.00	32 4.51	10 1.50	2 1.10
Middle-Class Men	4 6.30	0 --	16 2.51	9 4.07	10 4.34	10 4.96	3 2.73	1 1.20
Working-Class Men	8 4.52	0 --	25 3.70	1 4.20	0 --	3 4.87	2 3.70	3 1.40
Totals	46 4.90	36 4.79	197 3.86	47 4.17	35 5.63	74 4.73	18 2.56	6 1.27
Over-all totals	90 4.55	77 4.48	448 3.60	156 3.49	95 4.72	181 4.17	44 2.43	9 1.25

[a]The following scales were used in the various forms: Form 78: A-S scale (10 items); Form 60: E scale (12 items); Form 45: E scale (10 items); Form 40: E scale (5 items).

[b]The San Quentin group was not included in obtaining the totals. The means for this group were so much larger than those of the others, for reasons which seemed to have little to do with party preference, that their inclusion would distort the over-all picture.

ing, and there is much variation in group mean from one sample to the next. The New Deal Democrats, for example, obtained E means ranging from 2.06 to 4.95 in the various samples tested. Moreover, political preference is much more closely related to ethnocentrism in some groups than in others. In the middle-class groups the relation is much closer than in working-class groups such as the Maritime School Men or San Quentin Men. Indeed, the San Quentin data were so atypical that they were not included in the over-all totals; for further discussion see Chapter XXI. The great variability obtained is a warning against stereotypy in thinking about groups. Members

9. Socialist		10. P.A.C.		11. Undecided		12. Anti-all parties		13. None, nonpartisan		14. Self-contradictory		15. Blank		16. Combined conservative groups: 1, 2, 5, 6		17. Combined liberal groups: 3, 4, 7, 8, 9, 10				
N	Mean	N	Mean	N	Mean	N	Mean	N	Mean	N	Mean	N	Mean	N	Mean	N	Mean	N	Mean	S.D.
2	1.15	0	--	4	3.05	0	--	8	2.88	0	--	2	3.70	(57)	3.79	(69)	2.99	140	3.32	1.43
3	3.67	0	--	0	--	0	--	0	--	0	--	0	--	(13)	4.25	(39)	3.07	52	3.34	1.48
0	--	0	--	2	5.15	0	--	4	2.30	0	--	5	4.24	(13)	3.84	(18)	2.89	42	3.40	1.36
2	1.40	0	--	2	2.25	0	--	3	2.40	0	--	2	1.65	(12)	3.44	(44)	2.40	63	2.57	1.37
7	2.30	0	--	8	3.38	0	--	15	2.63	0	--	9	3.54	(95)	3.82	(170)	2.85	297	3.18	1.46
1	1.16	0	--	0	--	0	--	2	3.74	0	--	0	--	(21)	4.13	(24)	2.77	47	3.42	1.38
1	1.83	0	--	0	--	0	--	1	4.57	0	--	0	--	(22)	3.56	(31)	2.97	54	3.24	1.29
2	3.03	0	--	0	--	0	--	7	3.17	0	--	0	--	(20)	3.45	(30)	2.55	57	2.93	1.25
4	2.26	0	--	0	--	0	--	10	3.42	0	--	0	--	(63)	3.71	(85)	2.76	158	3.18	1.31
3	3.20	0	--	7	4.86	1	3.30	0	--	13	4.47	6	4.35	(58)	4.61	(93)	4.16	178	4.36	1.60
2	1.65	0	--	3	2.40	2	2.70	0	--	2	4.05	1	4.60	(16)	4.11	(26)	3.55	50	3.67	1.59
1	1.80	1	1.00	5	3.34	5	3.20	0	--	2	3.65	6	4.57	(20)	4.23	(33)	3.25	71	3.65	1.60
1	2.80	0	--	7	4.64	5	4.52	0	--	4	3.05	12	5.11	(30)	4.64	(52)	4.59	110	4.61	1.28
6	2.45	1	1.00	15	3.86	8	3.09	0	--	17	4.32	13	4.47	(94)	4.44	(152)	3.86	299	4.07	1.63
1	2.80	3	1.13	9	3.04	0	--	12	3.93	0	--	4	4.10	(53)	4.66	(54)	3.63	132	4.04	1.58
1	5.60	1	3.40	10	5.28	5	5.64	0	--	10	5.44	6	4.60	(56)	5.21	(77)	4.90	164	5.08	1.76
3	2.07	2	2.40	1	2.80	2	3.70	9	2.51	4	5.15	3	4.73	(47)	4.76	(88)	3.06	154	3.64	1.96
1	5.98	2	1.00	2	3.50	2	4.80	7	4.57	1	1.20	1	1.20	(24)	4.92	(32)	2.94	69	3.89	2.08
4	2.45	2	3.90	1	5.00	0	--	5	4.56	2	5.50	3	3.47	(11)	4.62	(37)	3.40	59	3.83	1.72
10	3.02	10	2.14	23	4.13	9	5.02	33	3.78	17	5.13	17	4.11	(191)	4.88	(288)	3.69	578	4.19	1.90
27	2.60	11	2.04	46	3.91	17	4.11	58	3.42	34	4.73	39	4.10	(443)	4.39	(695)	3.41	1332	3.82	

ᶜN for several of the present groups is different, by one or two subjects from the N given for the same groups in Tables 1-11 (V). If an N in Tables 12-20 (V) is smaller than the N for the corresponding group in Tables 1-11 (V), it is because one or two subjects who responded to the PEC scale left blank the whole of page 1 of the questionnaire. In one instance (Extension Class Women), two more subjects were available for the analysis of group membership than for the analysis of scale responses; their questionnaires came in late, after the statistics on scale responses were completed, but still in time to figure in the analysis of group memberships.

of any given political group are not "all alike"; and the fact that an individual belongs to a particular political group is, in most cases, an insufficient basis for predicting his standing on E.

These intra- and intergroup variations suggest that group membership is not in itself the major determinant of ideology in the individual. It would appear, rather, that different individuals support a political group for different reasons, and that we must understand why an individual *chooses* to support one group rather than another one. It is incorrect, or at least inadequate, to say that an individual is prejudiced *because* he is an Anti-New Deal

Democrat. He may be an Anti-New Dealer because he was ethnocentric to start with, or, more likely, both the ideology and the group membership must be explained in terms of more basic psychological and social factors. Consideration of these factors may help to explain why some anti-New Deal Democrats are not ethnocentric, and why some New Dealers are.

What of those who profess no preference for any political group (Table 12 (V), columns 11–15)? The results for these groups are difficult to interpret, but they are suggestive for further inquiry. Four of these groups, the "undecided," "against all parties," "self-contradictory" and "blank," with means of 3.9 to 4.7, are above the over-all mean of 3.8, while those who consider themselves "nonpartisan" are relatively low on E, with a mean of 3.4. Perhaps the most general conclusion to be drawn is that political confusion and indifference, as well as opposition to "politics," are associated with greater-than-average ethnocentrism. Since these subjects constitute some 10–15 per cent of the present sample, and at least that percentage of the American population, they merit more thorough study.

It was possible indirectly to approach the question of parental influence on subject's ideology by asking for the political party preference of father and of mother. In Table 13(V) the subjects are arranged in groups according to father's political party preference, and the E mean for each group is shown.[12] The offspring of Republicans are, on the average, slightly less ethnocentric than the offspring of Democrats, the E means being 3.41 and 3.68, respectively. Assuming an S. D. of 1.5 for each group, this difference is significant at the 5 per cent level.

These data suggest what everyday observation has often seemed to indicate, namely, that people do not necessarily believe what their parents tell them. This hypothesis is neither original nor profound—although we believe that it has profound implications for the understanding of the formation of ideology. It contradicts another commonly held theory, namely that one learns mainly by *imitation*. The "imitation" theory expects a high correlation between parents' ideology and offspring's ideology, on the assumption that one "naturally" (that is, imitatively) takes over parental ideology relatively intact. The present data, however, as well as those of many previous studies, e.g., those discussed by Murphy, Murphy and Newcomb (85), suggest that the formation of ideology in the individual is a selective, dynamic process, in which any ideological pressure from the environment will be accepted or rejected on the basis of the needs and strivings of the individual. Approaching ideological learning in this way, we ask, for example: What kinds of personalities take over intact the views of their parents or other

---

[12] Similar data were obtained in terms of mothers' political preference. These data are not presented here since identical trends were revealed. A theoretical reason for focusing on the father is that politics in the United States seems still to be largely a "paternal" concern, just as religion is for the most part the function of the mother in the home.

TABLE 13 (V)

MEAN A-S OR E SCORES[a] FOR GROUPS WHOSE FATHERS HAVE VARIOUS POLITICAL PARTY PREFERENCES

Group	Political Preference of Father														Over-all		
	Democrat		Republican		Socialist		Communist		Other		None		Blank				
	N	Mean	N	Mean	N	Mean	N	Mean	N	Mean	N	Mean	N	Mean	N	Mean	S.D.
Groups taking Form 78:																	
U.C. Public-Speaking Class Women	48	3.12	80	3.53	1	5.90	0	--	0	--	4	2.73	7	2.34	140	3.32	1.43
U.C. Public-Speaking Class Men	20	3.59	26	3.45	0	--	1	2.30	0	--	2	2.50	3	1.77	52	3.34	1.48
Extension Psychology Class Women	17	3.25	19	3.64	0	--	0	--	1	1.30	0	--	5	3.36	42	3.40	1.36
Professional Women	16	2.12	30	2.56	1	2.40	0	--	0	--	1	1.10	15	3.20	63	2.57	1.37
Totals:	101	3.08	155	3.34	2	4.15	1	2.30	1	1.30	7	2.43	30	2.88	297	3.18	1.46
Groups taking Form 60:																	
Univ. of Oregon Student Women	18	2.93	24	3.74	0	--	0	--	2	2.53	0	--	3	4.40	47	3.42	1.38
Univ. of Oregon and Univ. of California Student Women	19	3.39	28	3.19	0	--	0	--	3	3.32	0	--	4	2.80	54	3.24	1.29
Univ. of Oregon and Univ. of California Student Men	21	3.24	27	2.88	0	--	0	--	2	1.41	2	2.16	5	3.20	57	2.93	1.25
Totals:	58	3.19	79	3.25	0	--	0	--	7	2.55	2	2.16	12	3.37	158	3.18	1.31
Groups taking Form 45:																	
Maritime School Men	95	4.39	42	4.16	2	4.70	0	--	0	--	7	4.23	32	4.51	178	4.36	1.60
Psychiatric Clinic Men	20	4.10	21	3.26	1	2.70	0	--	0	--	1	5.00	7	3.60	50	3.67	1.59
Psychiatric Clinic Women	31	4.06	23	3.27	0	--	0	--	0	--	1	1.70	16	3.53	71	3.65	1.60
Totals:	146	4.28	86	3.70	3	4.03	0	--	0	--	9	4.03	55	4.11	299	4.07	1.63
Over-all totals:	305	3.68	320	3.41	5	4.08	1	2.30	8	2.39	18	3.20	97	3.64	754	3.53	--

[a]The following scales were used in the various forms: Form 78: A-S Scale (10 items) Form 60: E Scale (12 items) Form 45: E Scale (10 items)

authorities and under what psychological conditions do we find various forms of change or rebellion?

Questions such as those above were raised by the tendency for Republican fathers (presumably more ethnocentric) to have less ethnocentric offspring than did the Democratic fathers. This suggested the hypothesis that "disagreement with father" is related to anti-ethnocentrism, regardless of father's political views (see also Levinson and Sanford (71); Murphy, Murphy and Newcomb (85)). The hypothesis was tested by comparing subject's and father's political preference. The results are presented in Table 14(V). The group of subjects whose political preference was the same as their fathers', regardless of party, had a much higher mean (4.05) than the group of subjects who differed from their fathers (mean of 3.04). The difference is extremely significant; indeed, it is almost identical with the difference between groups based on liberal vs. conservative party preference (Table 12(V)). In other words, *a person's standing on E can be predicted as closely on the basis of his agreement or disagreement with his father's political party preference (without knowing subject's or father's politics) as it can on the basis of the subject's actual party preference.*[13] This is important indirect evidence in favor of hypotheses raised previously (Chapters III and IV), namely, that ethnocentrists tend to be submissive to ingroup authority, anti-ethnocentrists to be critical or rebellious, and that the family is the first and prototypic ingroup. The individual's relation to parental authority, particularly his disposition to be submissive or critically independent, appears to be a basic personality trend which partially determines his political party preference and his ideology about group relations.

Data on the average degree of ethnocentrism in various organizations taking Form 40 are presented in Table 15(V). The low-scoring groups, with E means of 1.20 to 2.41, are the Labor School men and women, the League of Women Voters, and the Unitarian Church. It is interesting that the working-class Labor School members have an E mean which is considerably higher than that for the middle-class members (2.4 to 1.2), and slightly higher than that for the (middle-class) League of Women Voters and the Unitarian Church. Apparently the middle-class leftists have identified not only with the working class (in their political ideology) but also with subordinate groups generally. There is, however, some likelihood that working-class individuals may support left-wing political groups without a full acceptance of the underlying social ideology; that is to say, they may

---

[13] The difference would probably have been even greater had we known the fathers' party-faction preference rather than the simple party preference. Thus, all New Deal Democratic subjects who gave father's preference as "Democrat" were grouped under "same preference as father." It is likely, however, that in many of these cases the father was an anti-New Deal Democrat and that thus a real difference between father and son—one which we should expect to accompany lower E scores—was concealed. This inadequacy in measurement makes the obtained differences all the more impressive.

TABLE 14 (V)

MEAN A-S OR E SCORES[a] FOR GROUPS SHOWING VARIOUS RELATIONS BETWEEN SUBJECT'S AND FATHER'S POLITICAL PREFERENCE

Relation between Subject's and Father's Political Preference	Same		Different		F None S Has		F Has S Blank		F Blank S Has		Both None or Blank		Over-all		
	N	Mean	N	Mean	N	Mean	N	Mean	N	Mean	N	Mean	N	Mean	S.D.
Groups taking Form 78:															
U.C. Public Speaking Class Women	99	3.49	19	3.10	2	2.50	11	3.07	6	2.25	3	2.93	140	3.32	1.43
U.C. Public Speaking Class Men	37	3.63	12	2.76	2	2.50	0	----	1	1.50	0	----	52	3.34	1.49
Extension Psychology Class Women	21	3.51	9	2.99	0	----	7	3.61	3	2.73	2	4.30	42	3.40	1.36
Professional Women	24	2.59	23	2.16	1	1.10	2	2.35	9	3.92	4	2.30	63	2.57	1.37
Totals:	181	3.40	63	2.68	5	2.20	20	3.19	19	3.08	9	2.96	297	3.18	1.46
Groups taking Form 60:															
University of Oregon Student Women	29	3.70	13	2.45	0	----	0	----	3	4.62	2	3.74	47	3.42	1.38
Univ. of Oregon and Univ. of California Student Women	33	3.48	18	2.81	0	----	0	----	2	2.45	1	4.57	54	3.24	1.29
Univ. of Oregon and Univ. of California Student Men	29	3.07	13	2.67	2	2.16	7	3.17	6	2.85	0	----	57	2.93	1.25
Totals:	91	3.42	44	2.66	2	2.61	7	3.17	11	3.26	3	4.01	158	3.18	1.31
Groups taking Form 45:															
Maritime School Men	107	4.32	20	4.16	4	4.58	14	4.49	20	4.51	13	4.52	178	4.36	1.60
Psychiatric Clinic Men	24	4.08	12	3.15	1	5.00	6	2.90	5	3.46	2	3.95	50	3.67	1.59
Psychiatric Clinic Women	27	4.29	18	2.80	1	1.70	9	3.86	3	3.39	9	3.63	71	3.65	1.60
San Quentin Men[b]	53	4.62	8	4.86	5	4.18	13	4.01	16	4.60	15	5.10	110	4.61	1.28
Totals:	158	4.28	50	3.43	6	4.17	29	3.96	32	4.10	24	4.14	299	4.07	1.63
Groups taking Form 40:															
George Washington University Student Women	78	4.28	12	3.85	6	3.33	13	3.66	10	3.86	13	3.62	132	4.04	1.58
Maritime School Men	94	5.17	26	4.64	2	5.07	22	5.41	14	4.86	5	4.80	164	5.08	1.76
Middle-Class Women	71	3.88	47	2.90	1	1.60	9	3.09	16	4.94	10	3.98	154	3.64	1.96
Middle-Class Men	34	4.75	19	2.07	0	----	9	3.82	4	3.80	4	5.50	69	3.89	2.08
Working-Class Men	22	4.26	17	2.71	0	----	4	5.20	9	4.09	7	4.06	59	3.83	1.72
Totals:	299	4.52	121	3.21	10	3.68	57	4.38	52	4.50	39	4.14	578	4.19	1.90
Over-all totals:	729	4.05	278	3.04	23	3.39	113	3.99	114	4.03	75	3.79	1332	3.82	----

[a]The following scales were used in the various forms:
Form 78: A-S Scale (10 items)   Form 45: E Scale (10 items)
Form 60: E Scale (12 items)   Form 40: E Scale (5 items)
[b]The San Quentin group was not included in the over-all total.

engage in liberal group activity more on the basis of economic self-interest than on that of a complete anti-ethnocentric point of view. This is also shown by the fact that the members of the United Electrical Workers, a militant C.I.O. union, had an E mean of 3.45, a value slightly higher than that (3.12) for the Parent-Teachers' Association group containing mostly middle-class members with a relatively high education level. These results suggest that union membership and college education are in themselves important forces, but by no means guarantees, against ethnocentrism. The basic question, it

TABLE 15 (V)

MEAN E SCORE FOR VARIOUS ORGANIZATIONS IN
THE FORM 40 SAMPLE

Middle-Class Women		
Group:	N	Mean
1. Parent-Teachers' Association	46	3.13
2. Labor School (middle-class membership)	11	1.20
3. Suburban Church Group	29	5.23
4. Unitarian Church Group	15	2.32
5. League of Women Voters	17	2.06
6. Upper Middle-Class Women's Club	36	5.05
Over-all totals	154	3.64
Standard Deviation		1.96

Middle-Class Men		
Group:	N	Mean
1. Labor School (middle-class membership)	9	1.27
2. Parent-Teachers' Association	29	3.12
3. Suburban Church Group	31	5.38
Over-all totals	69	3.89
Standard Deviation		2.08

Working-Class Men		
Group:	N	Mean
1. United Electrical Workers (CIO) (old members)	12	3.45
2. Labor School	15	2.41
3. International Longshoremen's and Warehousemen's Union (CIO) (new members)	26	4.60
4. United Seamen's Service	8	4.74
Over-all totals	61	3.83
Standard Deviation		1.72

would seem, is whether the individual has been able to assimilate the broader democratic ideology supplied by the group environment—and here again we find wide individual differences in receptiveness to democratic thinking.

That the union has been at least partially successful in its educative effort is suggested by the fact that the New Members Class of the International Longshoremen's and Warehousemen's Union (I.L.W.U.) has an E mean of 4.60 (Table 15(V)). Because of the small number of cases, the large difference of 1.15 between the new I.L.W.U. members and the old U.E.W. members is probably not statistically significant; but if it should be borne out in further studies, it would indicate that certain unions, at least, are doing a great deal to combat ethnocentrism.

The highest scoring groups, with E means of 5.05 to 5.38 (significantly higher than any other middle-class groups), are the Suburban Church men and women,[14] and the Upper Middle-Class Women's Club. Since neither of these groups is organized primarily or explicitly on the basis of ethnocentric ideology, their relative uniformity in this respect supports the hypothesis that ethnocentrism is correlated with patterns of ideology in other areas. The striking difference of 3.0 points between the E means of the Unitarian and Suburban Churches suggests that similar differences might well be found in the content of their religious ideologies; but these issues must await consideration of the over-all material on religion (Chapter VI). Similarly, what characterizes the Women's Club as compared, for example, with the League of Women Voters, is not its actual class or educational level, but psychological trends such as upper-class identification, upward economic mobility, conservative values, and the like. Moreover, it is not likely that membership in the group caused deep-lying personality trends such as these in the members, but rather that individuals with such dispositions gravitate toward this group—or, indeed, organize it in the first place—rather than toward the League of Women Voters or the Oakland Labor School. While no intensive case studies could be obtained from the Women's Club, because of resistance to such "investigation," the relation of the above and similar trends to ethnocentrism was studied in other groups and is reported in the chapters which follow.

Mean E scores for the various maritime unions, as represented in the Maritime School, are presented in Table 15(V) These results should probably be regarded as suggestive rather than conclusive, in view of the small N in each group and the fact that this sample is above the maritime union average in intelligence (AGCT score) and educational level, and probably in class level and economic aspiration. Among the well-represented unions, the lowest E mean (4.12) is made by the National Maritime Union (C.I.O.), which is also the most militantly left-wing. The most ethnocentric of the larger groups are the Sailor's Union of the Pacific (A.F.L.) and the Sailor's International Union (A.F.L.), with means of 4.97 and 4.81 respectively; both of these unions tend to be politically conservative and to be strongly anti-

[14] This interdenominational church is in a small town near Berkeley, California. It has several suburban features: it contains a number of small industries; many residents commute to Berkeley and San Francisco, and it is not culturally or economically isolated.

C.I.O. and anti-Communist. The Marine Firemen, Oilers and Wipers (Independent), with a mean of 4.24 is only slightly higher than the National Maritime Union; that this finding is valid is suggested by the fact that the M.F.O.W. actively joined with the C.I.O. a few years ago during a period of waterfront labor-management strife.

When the various union groups are combined into major categories, the following order is obtained (from most to least ethnocentric): blank or "none" (4.94), combined A.F.L. (4.79), combined C.I.O. (4.41), and combined Independent (4.30). While union membership, particularly in a C.I.O. or independent union, appears to play a significant role in decreasing ethnocentrism, there is clearly much that remains to be done. The National Maritime Union, for example, can take pride in having the lowest of the obtained means, but the value of 4.12 indicates only a 50–50 balance around the neutral point—still a long way from the democratic principles of its educational program and its constitutional regulations. It would be of considerable social as well as theoretical significance to understand why intensive anti-prejudice programs such as that of the N.M.U. are not more successful, and to determine how they might be improved.

The Form 40 data in Table 16(V) differ from the Form 45 data in two important respects: the over-all E mean is higher (5.08 to 4.34), and the differences among the various unions are smaller. The differences are due in part to the fact that the Form 45 data are based on the 10-item E_{AB} scale, while Form 40 contained the 5-item E_A scale. The E_A mean for the Form 45 sample was 4.82 (Chapter IV, Table 17, C), a value slightly but not significantly lower than the Form 40 E_A mean of 5.08. However, the Form 45 E_B subscale (of which four items deal with anti-Semitism) had a mean of only 3.85, and the E_A-E_B correlation, corrected by the Spearman-Brown formula, was only .73. It would appear, then, that the two samples are similar with respect to the opinions and attitudes in E_A (Negroes, foreigners, zootsuiters, patriotism). Moreover, the greater interunion differences on Form 45 than on Form 40 are probably due to the E_B items in Form 45; that is, the unions differ more with respect to anti-Semitism than with respect to other forms of prejudice. For example, the N.M.U. mean for Form 45 is 3.76, conspicuously lower than the sample mean of 4.34; but the N.M.U. Form 40 mean of 4.87 is only slightly lower than the sample mean of 5.08. While sampling differences and other uncontrolled factors probably influenced these results, the possibility is raised that the N.M.U. educational program has been less successful in combating some forms of prejudice (E_A) than others (E_B).[15]

Our attempts to determine income-class level and background of the subjects were relatively unsuccessful for several reasons. It was not possible to

[15] Had time permitted, it would have been worthwhile to obtain separate E_A and E_B means for each union group in the Form 45 sample, and to compare these with the Form 40 data.

TABLE 16 (V)

MEAN E SCORE FOR GROUPS HAVING VARIOUS MARITIME
UNION AFFILIATIONS[a]
(Maritime School Sample)

	Union	Form 45[b]		Form 40[b]		Over-all	
		N	Mean E_{AB}	N	Mean E_A	N	Mean
1.	Sailor's Union of the Pacific (AFL)	26	4.79	26	5.15	52	4.97
2.	Sailor's International Union (AFL)	20	4.52	12	5.30	32	4.81
3.	"AFL" only	7	4.10	9	4.26	16	4.19
4.	Marine Firemen, Oilers, Wipers (Independent)	16	4.11	23	4.34	39	4.24
5.	Master Mates and Pilots (Independent)	0	----	1	6.80	1	6.80
6.	Marine Engineers' Beneficial Association (CIO)	2	3.85	4	5.95	6	5.25
7.	National Maritime Union (CIO)	29	3.76	14	4.87	43	4.12
8.	"CIO" only	8	4.88	7	5.00	15	4.93
9.	"Union" only	17	4.07	12	5.45	29	4.64
10.	Combined AFL (1,2,3)	(53)	4.60	(47)	5.02	(100)	4.79
11.	Combined CIO (6,7,8)	(39)	3.99	(25)	5.08	(64)	4.41
12.	Combined Independent (4,5)	(16)	4.11	(24)	4.44	(40)	4.30
13.	All Unions Combined (1-9)	(125)	4.27	(108)	4.95	(233)	4.58
14.	Combined "None" and Blank	(53)	4.55	(56)	5.31	(109)	4.94
15.	"None"	17	4.89	21	5.25	38	5.08
16.	Blank	36	4.38	35	5.35	71	4.85
	Over-all totals	178	4.34	164	5.08	342	4.70
	Standard Deviation		1.60		1.76		

[a]These data are based on answers to the question: "What groups or organizations do you belong to (union, political, fraternal, etc.)?" In administering the questionnaire, it was stressed that the men should record their union affiliation.

[b]As discussed in Chapter IV, the Maritime School population was divided into two roughly equated halves, one of which received Form 45, the other Form 40.

ask the number of questions required to give an adequate index of socio-economic class level. Also, the several questions included were often left blank, out of defensiveness or lack of knowledge (e.g., of father's or husband's income). Many subjects had no current income, due to momentary unemployment or to student or military status. Income had in some cases increased during the war period without a corresponding increase in actual class level. For these and other reasons, the data below must be interpreted only tentatively and with great care.

Table 17(V) presents mean E scores for groups based on present income.

TABLE 17 (V)

MEAN E SCORES[a] FOR GROUPS WHO HAVE VARIOUS PRESENT YEARLY INCOMES[b]

Group	Present Income																		Over-all		
	Below $2,000		$2,000-2,900		$3,000-3,900		$4,000-4,900		$5,000-10,000		Above $10,000		Blank		None						
	N	Mean	N	Mean	N	Mean	N	Mean	N	Mean	N	Mean	N	Mean	N	Mean	N	Mean	S.D.
Groups taking Form 60:																			
Univ. of Oregon Student Women	13	3.21	15	3.87	0	--	0	--	0	--	0	--	11	3.14	8	3.29	47	3.42	1.38
Univ. of Oregon and Univ. of California Student Women	11	3.15	23	3.27	15	3.28	0	--	1	1.74	0	--	4	3.55	0	--	54	3.63	1.29
Univ. of Oregon and Univ. of California Student Men	14	2.91	10	3.06	16	2.83	5	3.42	4	2.26	0	--	4	3.59	4	2.53	57	2.93	1.25
Totals:	38	3.08	48	3.41	31	2.99	5	3.42	5	2.16	0	--	19	3.32	12	3.04	158	3.18	1.31
Groups taking Form 45:																			
Psychiatric Clinic Men	6	2.90	14	3.58	9	4.07	1	4.60	2	4.00	1	3.70	8	3.28	9	4.08	50	3.67	1.59
Psychiatric Clinic Women	12	3.51	4	3.03	3	4.37	0	--	0	--	0	--	27	3.20	25	4.21	71	3.65	1.60
Totals:	18	3.31	18	3.46	12	4.14	1	4.60	2	4.00	1	3.70	35	3.22	34	4.17	121	3.66	1.62
Groups taking Form 40:																			
Middle-Class Women	22	2.80	19	3.00	8	2.92	1	1.00	3	3.27	1	6.40	17	3.42	83	4.13	154	3.64	1.96
Middle-Class Men	11	4.49	3	4.87	9	4.04	12	4.27	25	2.89	1	4.00	0	--	8	5.10	69	3.89	2.08
Working-Class Men	7	4.20	26	4.11	8	2.80	7	2.71	3	4.67	0	--	1	4.80	7	4.20	59	3.83	1.72
Totals:	40	3.51	48	3.72	25	3.29	20	3.56	31	3.10	2	5.20	18	3.50	98	4.21	282	3.74	2.10
Over-all totals:	96	3.30	114	3.55	68	3.30	26	3.57	38	3.02	3	4.70	72	3.32	144	4.10	561	3.57	--

[a] The following scales were used in the various forms: Form 60: E Scale (12 items); Form 45: E Scale (10 items); Form 40: E Scale (5 items).

[b] These groupings are based on answers to the following question: "What is your present income (to nearest $500 per year) _____."

It will be noted that some 25 per cent of the total sample reported "no income," while 13 per cent left the question blank. The majority of reported incomes were below $3,000 per year, only three individuals reporting incomes of over $10,000. Among the incomes below $5,000 there are no appreciable differences in E mean (3.30 to 3.57), and no consistent trend of increase or decrease. However, the $5,000–$10,000 group has a conspicuously low E mean of 3.02, while the "above $10,000" group is highest in ethnocentrism, with a mean of 4.70. The large but heterogeneous group—mostly women—with no income is also relatively high on E (4.10). Among the Working-Class Men (Form 40), E mean decreases as income increases up to $5,000, after which the E mean goes up again. Among the Middle-Class Men (Form 40) and the University of Oregon and University of California Student Men (Form 60), on the other hand, the $5,000–$10,000 group is by far the lowest on E. Thus, *there is no simple relation between income and ethnocentrism*, and the relation between income and ideology may well be different for the middle class as compared with the working class. It is of some interest that in the two groups of nonstudent women (Psychiatric Clinic and Middle Class) those with no income were considerably more ethnocentric on the average than those with some income. The lower E mean in women who work may be due to their economic position; it is more likely, however, that the personality trends which lead to nonethnocentrism tend to produce also the willingness or desire to have gainful work.

It seemed that *expected* income might yield a better measure of economic aspirations (and perhaps of class identification) than did present income. The mean E scores for groups divided on the basis of expected income (ten years from now) are presented in Table 18 (V). The two largest groups are those expecting $5,000–$10,000 and $3,000–$3,900, in that order. The over-all totals for all samples combined show that E mean gradually increases as expected income increases. However, the data for individual samples reveal a more complex state of affairs. The E mean for the three highest income groupings ($4,000 and above) is greater than that for the low income groupings mainly because the ethnocentric Maritime School samples (Forms 45 and 40) form the bulk (50–70 per cent) of these groupings. It will be noted that within each Maritime School sample there is no clear-cut relationship between expected income and E mean. Similarly, there are no consistent trends in the other samples. Thus, for Form 78 the $4,000–$10,000 levels are slightly but not significantly more ethnocentric than the lower levels, but the lowest E mean is for the "above $10,000" level. For Form 60, on the other hand, the variations in E mean are small (2.97 to 3.34) and unrelated to income. Differences among samples are, therefore, much greater than differences among actual or expected income levels.[16] These results have little if any bearing

[16] Similar negative results were obtained in preliminary (unpublished) studies of E in relation to *desired* income.

TABLE 18 (V)

MEAN A-S OR E SCORES[a] FOR GROUPS HAVING VARIOUS LEVELS OF EXPECTED YEARLY INCOME

| | Expected Income | | | |
| | Below $2,000 | | $2,000-2,900 | |
Group	N	Mean	N	Mean
Groups taking Form 78:				
U.C. Public Speaking Class Women	6	3.08	26	2.99
U.C. Public Speaking Class Men	0	----	5	3.74
Extension Psychology Class Women	0	----	4	3.80
Professional Women	14	2.91	11	2.65
Totals:	20	2.97	46	3.06
Groups taking Form 60:				
University of Oregon Student Women	2	2.99	9	3.27
Univ. of Oregon and Univ. of California Student Women	6	3.90	9	3.30
Univ. of Oregon and Univ. of California Student Men	2	1.99	2	3.07
Totals:	10	3.34	20	3.27
Groups taking Form 45:				
Maritime School Men	3	5.17	9	4.16
Psychiatric Clinic Men	0	----	3	3.30
Totals	3	5.17	12	3.94
Group taking Form 40:				
Maritime School Men	1	5.20	16	5.22
Over-all totals:	34	3.34	94	3.37

on the theory that *economic forces* play a basic role in creating a setting for the development of ethnocentrism; but they provide evidence against the hypothesis that economic level and economic motives *per se* operate as major *psychological forces* impelling the individual in an ethnocentric or anti-ethnocentric direction.

A further hypothesis to be considered is that prejudice is determined by the economic level of the parents. Stated most simply: "A person growing up in a rich family is more likely to be prejudiced than one growing up in a middle- or low-income family." In order to make a partial test of this hypothesis, a question regarding father's income was included in the questionnaire, and the mean A-S or E score was obtained for groups representing several income levels. The data are presented in Table 19(V). The number of cases

					Expected Income								
$3,000-3,900		$4,000-4,900		$5,000-10,000		Above $10,000		Blank		None		Over-all	
N	Mean	N	Mean	N	Mean	N	Mean	N	Mean	N	Mean	N	Mean	S.D.
21	3.18	6	4.32	11	3.62	0	----	56	3.45	14	3.11	140	3.32	1.43
9	3.00	10	3.52	22	3.55	1	1.20	5	2.76	0	----	52	3.34	1.48
4	2.10	1	3.80	4	2.35	0	----	29	3.66	0	----	42	3.40	1.36
14	2.84	3	2.07	4	2.10	3	3.07	14	2.04	0	----	63	2.57	1.37
48	2.95	20	3.56	41	3.31	4	2.60	104	3.28	14	3.11	297	3.18	1.46
6	3.54	1	2.66	1	2.82	0	----	19	3.50	9	3.55	47	3.42	1.38
16	2.91	4	4.03	3	1.91	0	----	8	3.71	8	2.95	54	3.24	1.29
12	2.75	7	2.70	24	3.12	4	3.03	6	3.03	0	----	57	2.93	1.25
34	2.97	12	3.14	28	2.98	4	3.03	33	3.47	17	3.27	158	3.18	1.31
27	4.57	14	4.52	70	4.46	12	4.38	2	3.95	41	3.98	178	4.36	1.60
8	3.59	3	4.73	10	3.45	1	3.40	0	----	25	3.70	50	3.67	1.59
35	4.34	17	4.55	80	4.34	13	4.30	2	3.95	66	3.87	228	4.20	1.62
28	5.23	20	5.05	44	5.06	10	5.60	0	----	45	4.84	164	5.08	1.76
145	3.73	69	4.16	193	4.09	31	4.34	139	3.33	142	4.03	847	3.82	----

[a]The following scales were used in the various forms:

Form 78: A-S Scale (12 items)
Form 60: E Scale (10 items)
Form 45: E Scale (10 items)
Form 40: E Scale (5 items)

in the various income levels provides another indication of the largely middle-class character of the total sample. The $5,000–$10,000 group was the largest, with 205 cases. The $2,000–$2,900 and $3,000–$3,900 groups, which during 1944–46 would probably have been the largest in the general population, had 154 and 186 cases, respectively. A disproportionately large number, 55, were in the "$10,000 and above" group. The interpretation of these data is complicated by the fact that the father's income now may not be what it was

TABLE 19 (V)

MEAN A-S OR E SCORES[a] FOR GROUPS WHOSE FATHERS HAD VARIOUS INCOMES

	Below $2,000		$2,000-2,900	
	N	Mean	N	Mean
Groups taking Form 78:				
U.C. Public Speaking Class Women	8	2.94	17	3.35
U.C. Public Speaking Class Men	2	5.45	6	3.33
Extension Psychology Class Women	1	4.20	2	4.25
Professional Women	2	5.65	6	2.30
Totals:	13	3.84	31	3.20
Groups taking Form 60:				
University of Oregon Student Women	5	3.45	7	3.08
Univ. of Oregon and Univ. of California Student Women	0	----	9	3.17
Univ. of Oregon and Univ. of California Student Men	6	2.60	11	3.28
Totals:	11	2.99	27	3.19
Groups taking Form 45:				
Maritime School Men	12	3.88	26	4.09
Psychiatric Clinic Men	6	3.62	4	2.88
Psychiatric Clinic Women	5	4.36	4	3.70
Totals:	23	3.92	34	3.90
Groups taking Form 40:				
George Washington University Student Women	2	4.80	7	3.20
Maritime School Men	6	5.57	34	5.48
Middle-Class Women	7	3.46	9	3.29
Middle-Class Men	3	2.87	8	3.35
Working-Class Men	5	4.00	4	5.40
Totals:	23	4.16	62	4.62
Over-all totals:	70	3.84	154	3.92

during the subject's childhood. It should also be noted that almost half of the subjects left this question blank; it is not possible to say how much this has influenced the results.

The E means in Table 19(V) do not vary consistently in relation to father's income. They show negligible and unsystematic variations (from 3.77 to 3.92) among the various levels below $10,000. However, the group whose fathers earned $10,000 per year and above is significantly *less* ethnocentric than the combined lower income levels (means of 3.35 and 3.84

$3,000-3,900		$4,000-4,900		$5,000-10,000		Above $10,000		Blank		Over-all		
N	Mean	N	Mean	N	Mean	N	Mean	N	Mean	N	Mean	S.D.
28	2.99	9	3.97	22	3.32	11	3.83	45	3.34	140	3.32	1.43
10	3.18	5	3.42	13	3.39	5	3.34	11	3.03	52	3.34	1.48
7	3.17	0	----	4	2.63	1	4.70	27	3.43	42	3.40	1.36
3	2.40	0	----	10	2.23	5	2.34	37	2.59	63	2.57	1.37
48	3.02	14	3.77	49	3.06	22	3.42	120	3.10	297	3.18	1.46
8	3.17	0	----	10	3.03	1	5.31	16	3.80	47	3.42	1.38
9	3.14	4	3.13	11	3.34	0	----	21	3.28	54	3.24	1.29
8	3.17	5	2.56	8	2.66	2	2.49	17	3.01	57	2.93	1.25
25	3.16	9	2.81	29	3.05	3	3.43	54	3.35	158	3.18	1.31
31	4.48	12	4.68	28	4.68	8	3.54	64	4.40	178	4.36	1.60
6	3.03	2	3.25	7	2.97	0	----	25	4.18	50	3.67	1.59
5	1.66	2	3.95	6	2.75	1	1.60	48	3.92	71	3.65	1.60
42	3.94	16	4.41	41	4.11	9	3.32	134	4.19	299	4.07	1.63
13	4.11	10	3.64	35	4.14	7	3.97	58	4.12	132	4.04	1.58
30	5.01	14	4.73	29	5.13	5	4.60	46	4.89	164	5.08	1.76
10	3.30	5	1.84	9	2.64	5	1.72	109	3.96	154	3.64	1.96
6	4.63	5	4.56	10	4.12	4	2.40	33	4.00	69	3.89	2.08
12	4.00	0	----	3	5.67	0	----	35	3.41	59	3.83	1.72
71	4.40	34	3.96	86	4.37	21	3.29	281	4.08	578	4.19	1.90
186	3.77	73	3.88	205	3.82	55	3.35	589	3.84	1332	3.82	-

aThe following scales were used in the various forms:
Form 78:   A-S Scale (10 items)
Form 60:   E Scale (12 items)
Form 45:   E Scale (10 items)
Form 40:   E Scale (5 items)

respectively). Whether this lower mean holds for *all* individuals whose fathers are in this income group, or only for those individuals who get into organized groups such as those tested, is not clear. Further study may reveal that the lower E mean characterizes those individuals who were born in wealthier families but who tend—presumably for emotionally important reasons—to gravitate toward middle- or working-class groups, occupations, and ideologies. We are led to suspect, on the basis of results in numerous areas, that upward class mobility and identification with the *status quo* correlate positively with ethnocentrism, and that downward class mobility and identification go with anti-ethnocentrism.

A final "socioeconomic background" factor studied was father's occupation. Table 20(V) gives the mean E score for various groups based on occupation of father. The most common occupations (N = 136–169) were: Labor (skilled and unskilled), white collar, and big business-managerial. Small business and professional groups were next in size (N = 95 and 90), and in order of decreasing size we find farmers, engineers, government officials, and religious (ministers, etc.). With regard to E mean, there are only three groups which deviate more than 0.3 points from the over-all mean of 3.86. The offspring of engineers are significantly above average, with a mean of 4.36. On the other hand, the offspring of fathers with religious or government occupations are well below average (3.20 and 3.25). For all other occupations differences are minor and even smaller than the differences from sample to sample for any one occupation. No occupational grouping is consistently high or consistently low in every sample. Even in the case of fathers with big business and managerial occupations, the E mean varies considerably; it is sometimes below, sometimes above that for the test group from which it was taken. Thus, we find particularly low E means for this occupational group in the Extension Psychology Class and Professional Women, and a relatively high mean for the George Washington University Women (relative to the other occupational groupings in each sample). These variations suggest, as do the data above, that ethnocentrism in the individual is not significantly correlated with many of the socioeconomic groupings which are commonly assumed (by many social scientists as well as by laymen) to be direct, immediate determinants of ethnocentrism. It is the *meaning* of the group to the individual rather than membership *per se*, that helps us to predict his stand on ethnocentrism and other issues.

On the basis of the group membership data presented in this section (Tables 12(V)–20(V)), certain hypotheses can tentatively be drawn. Perhaps the first lesson to be learned concerns the danger of stereotyped thinking about groups. *No broad grouping in this study showed anything approaching ideological homogeneity.* This is not presented as a startling discovery but rather as a sober reminder to those who assume a close relation

TABLE 20 (V)

MEAN A-S OR E SCORES[a] FOR GROUPS WHOSE FATHERS HAVE VARIOUS OCCUPATIONS

Groups	Labor (skilled and unskilled) N	Mean	White collar (including foreman) N	Mean	Small independent businessmen N	Mean	Farmer N	Mean	Religious N	Mean	Professional N	Mean	Engineer N	Mean	Big business and managerial N	Mean	Government official N	Mean	Noncategorized (sick, dead, retired, miscellaneous) N	Mean	Blank N	Mean	Over-all N	Mean	S.D.
Groups taking Form 78:																								
U.C. Public Speaking Class Women	23	2.93	25	3.16	12	3.76	9	3.08	3	2.20	16	3.28	10	4.31	36	3.38	0	----	6	3.67	0	----	140	3.32	1.43
U.C. Public Speaking Class Men	16	3.65	5	2.96	10	2.35	0	----	1	2.60	6	3.70	2	4.80	8	3.96	0	----	4	2.78	0	----	52	3.34	1.48
Extension Psychology Class Women	1	4.00	8	3.23	2	4.55	3	4.10	0	----	4	3.13	2	3.20	6	2.72	0	----	16	3.53	0	----	42	3.40	1.36
Professional Women	6	2.80	12	2.23	6	2.75	4	3.05	0	----	9	1.63	1	2.00	10	2.34	0	----	15	3.32	0	----	63	2.57	1.37
Totals:	46	3.19	50	2.92	30	3.15	16	3.26	4	2.30	35	2.91	15	4.07	60	3.22	0	----	41	3.40	0	----	297	3.18	1.46
Groups taking Form 60:																								
Univ. of Oregon Student Women	5	2.94	8	3.37	3	3.54	6	4.08	0	----	4	3.30	0	----	13	3.20	0	----	8	3.58	0	----	47	3.42	1.38
Univ. of Oregon and Univ. of California Student Women	1	2.32	14	3.45	4	3.44	8	3.05	0	----	5	3.10	2	1.95	13	3.66	0	----	7	2.80	0	----	54	3.24	1.29
Univ. of Oregon and Univ. of California Student Men	8	3.24	7	3.69	6	2.35	11	2.54	0	----	7	1.99	0	----	7	2.58	0	----	11	3.34	0	----	57	2.93	1.25
Totals:	14	3.07	29	3.49	13	2.96	25	3.07	0	----	16	2.66	2	1.95	33	3.25	0	----	26	3.27	0	----	158	3.18	1.31
Groups taking Form 45:																								
Maritime School Men	48	4.16	29	4.29	17	4.32	9	4.82	1	6.30	9	6.40	5	5.22	18	4.58	0	----	30	4.45	12	4.08	178	4.36	1.60
Groups taking Form 40:																								
George Washington University Student Women	14	3.83	20	4.28	10	4.34	1	2.20	5	3.20	25	4.03	9	3.78	18	4.79	12	3.25	18	3.71	0	----	132	3.95	1.58
Maritime School Men	47	5.22	16	4.76	25	5.01	10	5.72	1	3.70	5	5.30	12	5.18	7	5.00	0	----	26	5.09	15	4.53	164	5.08	1.76
Totals:	61	4.90	36	4.49	35	4.82	11	5.40	6	3.28	30	4.16	21	4.58	25	4.85	12	3.25	44	4.53	15	4.53	296	4.13	1.78
Over-all totals:	169	4.07	144	3.70	95	3.95	61	3.81	11	3.20	90	3.62	43	4.36	136	3.71	12	3.25	141	3.95	27	3.95	929	3.86	

[a] The following scales were used in the various forms:

Form 78: A-S Scale (10 items)
Form 60: E Scale (12 items)
Form 45: E Scale (10 items)
Form 40: E Scale (5 items)

between prejudice and membership in certain groups. While certain average differences have been found, the Standard Deviations are large and the overlapping between groups considerable. This does not mean that group memberships and social forces are unimportant in the formation and in the expression of ethnocentrism; indeed, there is a wealth of sociological literature to show that they are. Rather, it would appear that sociological factors play an essential but *complex and indirect* psychological role. Social psychology must, therefore, advance beyond its initial stage of seeking—and expecting to find—simple relationships between ideology and group memberships; it must go on to study the complex processes by which the individual *selectivity assimilates* the manifold pressures from his socio-ideological environment.

While no ideologically homogeneous groupings were found, there were significant relations between ethnocentrism and certain group memberships. The groups which are most differentiated with respect to ethnocentrism—that is, which tend to be predominantly high or predominantly low—have two main properties: They involve membership by choice rather than membership by birth, and they show relatively great homogeneity with respect to various other psychological characteristics. Thus, the political preference or the income-occupation grouping of the father shows no consistent relation to ethnocentrism in the offspring. But the subject's personal political preference (membership by choice), like his socioeconomic aspirations and his tendency to accept or reject his father's political views, is more closely related to E score. Similarly, membership in the exclusive Women's Club or the Labor School is more significant in terms of E than membership in the United Electrical Workers Union or the Parent-Teachers' Association, the latter groups being less homogeneous in all ideological areas.

The group memberships having the greatest significance for ethnocentrism are, then, those which have the greatest *psychological significance* for the individual. They are, it seems, groups which the individual chooses to join because they permit the further development and fuller expression of dispositions existing prior to joining. We are forced to reexamine the notion that the group membership determines the ideology—that, for example, a man is prejudiced *because* he is a Republican or a member of a snobbish club. Not only is the ideology likely to have preceded (in at least a primitive form) the joining of the group but, more important, both the ideology and the group membership seem to express deeper trends in the individual. An example of such a trend is "independence" versus "submission" in relation to parental authority. Thus, high scorers on E demonstrated greater submission and conformity than did the low scorers, both in the content of their ideology (E and PEC) and in their choice of political party (Table 14(V)). The individual's choice of group, like his choice of ideology, appears to be not merely a matter of chance or of simple imitation, but in large part an expression of important emotional dispositions. Before turning to these issues in more detail we shall, in the next chapter, consider religious ideology and groupings in relation to ethnocentrism.

F. CONCLUSIONS

The study of politico-economic ideology and group memberships has led to a broadening in our conception of the antidemocratic individual. The Anti-Semitism and Ethnocentrism scales, our primary measures of antidemocratic trends, show statistically significant relationships with the right-left dimension of politico-economic ideology. There appears to be an affinity between conservatism and ethnocentrism, liberalism and anti-ethnocentrism. The relationship is, however, quantitatively imperfect ($r =$ approximately .5) and qualitatively complex. It is proposed, in further studies, to break down the right-left dimension into numerous ideological patterns. One of these—perhaps the most significant in terms of potential antidemocracy—is the *pseudoconservative*.

In previous chapters we have seen that anti-Semitism or anti-Negroism, for example, are not isolated attitudes but parts of a relatively unified ethnocentric ideology. The present chapter suggests that ethnocentrism itself is but one aspect of a broader pattern of social thinking and group functioning. Trends similar to those underlying ethnocentric ideology are found in the same individual's politico-economic ideology. In short, ideology regarding each social area must be regarded as a facet of the total person and an expression of more central ("subideological") psychological dispositions.

CHAPTER VI

ETHNOCENTRISM IN RELATION TO SOME
RELIGIOUS ATTITUDES AND PRACTICES

R. Nevitt Sanford

A. INTRODUCTION

In approaching the topic of religion, the general question was similar to that raised in connection with politico-economic ideology: What trends in religious thought and practice can be distinguished and what, if any, is their significance for prejudice or its opposite? Categories for the analysis of religious thought were not, however, ready to hand. It seemed that a qualitative study of interview material had to precede any attempt to quantify trends in religious ideology. Such a study was made, and it is reported in Chapter XVIII,[1] but since the collection of interviews and of questionnaires proceeded simultaneously, it was not possible to make use of a completed qualitative analysis in preparing measuring instruments for use with groups of subjects. Only a few hypotheses, suggested during the early stages of the study, were represented in the content of the questionnaire. The present chapter is concerned solely with results obtained through the use of the questionnaire. These results were derived from data on the religious affiliations of the subjects and their parents as set forth on the first page of the questionnaire, from answers to an open-ended question about religion and the church which was used in a preliminary form of the questionnaire, and from responses to three scale items which belong in the general area of religion.

B. RESULTS

1. RELIGIOUS GROUP MEMBERSHIPS

a. ACCEPTANCE OR REJECTION OF RELIGION. Data on religious affiliation were obtained by means of the question, "What is your religion?" which

---

[1] Interview material bearing on certain religious attitudes also appears in Chapters XI and XXI.

appeared on page one of the questionnaire in all four of its forms. In answering this question, subjects gave the name of some religious sect or wrote "none" or left the question blank. The answer "none" is taken as an indication that the subject rejects religion, while answering with the name of some religious group is taken as evidence that he somehow accepts religion. When the question is left blank, no inferences can be made. The data obtained by means of this question from the four forms of the questionnaire are summarized in Table 1(VI).

Attention may first be called to the fact that subjects who answer "none" (last column but one in Table 1(VI)) obtain an over-all mean A-S or E score, 2.71 (last row in Table 1(VI)), that is notably lower than the means for most of the religious groups.[2] The only exceptions appear in the case of the Unitarians, whose over-all mean is 1.99, and the Combined Minor Protestant Sects, whose over-all mean is 2.49. For all the other religious denominations the means are in the range 3.41 (Congregational) to 4.38 (Lutheran). These trends appear in the data for each form of the questionnaire as well as in the over-all totals. If all subjects who professed to some religious affiliation were placed in one group for statistical purposes, their mean score would be very much higher than that of those who claim no religious affiliation. There seems to be no doubt that subjects who reject organized religion are less prejudiced on the average than those who, in one way or another, accept it.

Subjects with religious affiliations are not, however, generally ethnocentric. Although the nonreligious subjects are clearly nonethnocentric on the average, the mean scores for the various religious denominations are, on the whole, very close to the neutral point.

The overwhelming majority of our subjects do profess to some religious affiliation. The nonreligious, nonethnocentric group is relatively small in number and, probably, not very important socially. The variability among the religious subjects seems to be almost as great as it is for our over-all sample. This means that among our religious subjects both extreme high and extreme low scorers are to be found. We must also take note of the fact that among the nonreligious subjects, high as well as low scorers appear. In this latter connection a possible sex difference is to be noted. Nonreligious women seem to obtain lower scores on the average than do nonreligious men. (Note, in the "none" column of Table 1(VI), the means for the groups of women and for the groups of men.) The nonreligious women almost always score definitely low while the nonreligious men are much more variable.

b. ETHNOCENTRISM IN DIFFERENT RELIGIOUS DENOMINATIONS. If we ask why some religious people score high and others low on ethnocentrism, we

[2] The estimation of the significance of differences between means in this chapter follows the same rule that was used in Chapter V. Cf. the footnote 12 to Chap. V. If the N's for the groups in question are as large as 50, then a difference of .6 is likely to be significant, at least at the 5 per cent level. Most of the differences discussed in this chapter are much larger than .6 and seem well above the minimum requirements of statistical significance.

TABLE 1 (VI)

MEAN A-S OR E SCORES OF VARIOUS RELIGIOUS GROUPS

	I. Catholic		II. Protestant[a]		III. Combined Major Protestant Sects		Presby- terian		Methodist		Lutheran	
	N	Mean	N	Mean	N	Mean	N	Mean	N	Mean	N	Mean
Groups taking Form 78:												
Public Speaking Class Women	23	3.15	24	3.35	(80)	(3.52)	18	3.69	19	3.70	6	4.03
Public Speaking Class Men	9	3.66	14	3.73	(18)	(3.04)	5	2.98	4	2.60	1	3.70
Extension Class Women	8	4.38	13	3.99	(9)	(2.80)	2	1.80	1	2.50	0	--
Professional Women	10	2.44	17	2.64	(22)	(3.09)	1	5.10	1	4.80	0	--
Total: Form 78	50	3.29	68	3.37	(129)	(3.33)	26	3.46	25	3.52	7	3.99
Groups taking Form 60:												
Univ. of Oregon Student Women	3	3.36	4	1.85	(26)	(4.12)	8	3.63	4	4.08	1	5.25
Univ. of Oregon and Univ. of California Student Women	5	3.40	18	3.15	(20)	(3.60)	3	3.83	3	3.25	2	2.58
Univ. of Oregon and Univ. of California Student Men	4	3.98	13	3.15	(19)	(3.11)	2	3.92	3	2.86	2	4.50
Total: Form 60	12	3.58	35	3.05	(65)	(3.66)	13	3.72	10	3.47	5	3.88
Groups taking Form 45:												
Maritime School Men	25	4.36	77	4.59	(46)	(4.51)	3	5.23	12	4.65	9	4.42
Psychiatric Clinic Men	11	3.46	18	3.94	(6)	(4.32)	2	3.30	1	5.50	0	--
Psychiatric Clinic Women	18	4.55	15	4.58	(18)	(3.53)	5	3.58	6	2.90	3	3.80
San Quentin Men	24	4.67	38	4.49	(29)	(4.65)	4	4.35	7	4.83	4	4.98
Total: Form 45[c]	54	4.24	110	4.48	(70)	(4.24)	10	4.02	19	4.14	12	4.27
Groups taking Form 40:												
Geo. Washington Univ. Women	16	4.51	15	3.99	(81)	(4.16)	15	4.53	12	4.52	4	4.15
Maritime School Men	35	5.15	59	5.24	(42)	(5.07)	7	4.09	9	5.07	4	5.80
Middle-Class Women	6	4.57	60	3.98	(61)	(3.59)	9	4.20	3	5.60	1	6.40
Middle-Class Men	3	6.20	29	4.28	(20)	(4.15)	3	4.00	5	4.48	1	5.00
Working-Class Men	14	4.67	16	3.75	(13)	(4.15)	0	--	5	4.12	5	4.20
Total: Form 40	74	4.92	179	4.42	(217)	(4.18)	34	4.31	34	4.69	15	4.81
Over-all total: four forms	190	4.21	392	4.13	(481)	(3.89)	83	3.92	88	4.10	39	4.38

[a]*Protestant* here refers to subjects who answered "Protestant" but did not give the name of any denomination.

[b]The following denominations of sects were combined: Bible, Brethren, Christian, Disciple, Evangelical, Humanist, Moral Rearmament, Natural Law, Nazarene, Quaker, Adventist, Unity, Universalist. The designations of these sects are those employed by the subjects in filling out their questionnaires. The division into major and minor Protestant sects does not conform in every particular with the actual membership figures for the whole United States; it was

naturally turn our attention first to the question of what role the particular religious denomination or sect has to play. Examination of Table 1(VI) shows that there are no differences of any significance between Catholics and Protestants, and this regardless of whether we place in one category those subjects who answered "Protestant" or whether we combine the largest Protestant denominations. Among the Protestant denominations which have been classed as "major," only one group distinguishes itself: the Unitarians[3] have a lower mean score than any of the others. This seems to be in keeping with the generally liberal outlook of this group. The minor Protestant denominations taken together obtain a lower mean score than do any of the other religious groups save the Unitarians. Unfortunately, none of

[3] In terms of membership figures for the United States this body probably should not be classed as "major."

Congregational		Episcopalian		Baptist		Christian Science		Mormon		Unitarian		IV. Combined Minor Protestant Sects[b]		V. None		VI. Blank	
N	Mean	N	Mean	N	Mean	N	Mean	N	Mean	N	Mean	N	Mean	N	Mean	N	Mean
2	2.25	21	3.30	5	3.18	5	3.46	3	4.30	1	1.10	(0)	(--)	10	2.49	0	--
0	--	4	2.60	1	5.60	2	4.00	0	--	1	1.80	(3)	(2.27)	7	3.16	1	5.10
0	--	1	4.70	2	4.50	1	1.60	1	2.60	1	1.20	(0)	(--)	6	1.95	5	3.22
1	2.90	11	3.46	3	1.87	0	--	1	2.70	4	2.18	(0)	(--)	9	1.28	2	1.95
3	2.47	37	3.31	11	3.28	8	3.36	5.	3.64	7	1.83	(3)	(2.27)	32	2.19	8	3.14
0	--	8	3.90	2	5.42	2	5.13	1	4.17	0	--	(0)	(--)	3	1.17	1	1.67
1	1.75	7	4.05	1	3.25	3	4.11	0	--	0	--	(0)	(--)	5	2.30	0	--
1	2.08	2	2.71	3	2.97	2	4.00	4	2.31	0	--	(0)	(--)	10	2.27	1	1.58
2	1.92	17	3.82	6	3.83	7	4.37	5	2.68	0	--	(0)	(--)	18	2.09	2	1.63
0	--	4	3.83	10	4.62	4	4.13	4	4.50	0	--	(0)	(--)	23	3.65	5	2.62
0	--	0	--	1	5.70	1	4.50	1	3.60	0	--	(2)	(1.50)	8	3.38	3	3.67
1	3.00	2	3.60	1	6.60	0	--	0	--	0	--	(0)	(--)	15	1.91	2	3.45
0	--	4	5.00	2	5.90	5	4.02	3	3.90	0	--	(0)	(--)	12	4.22	5	5.82
1	3.00	6	3.75	12	4.88	5	4.20	5	4.32	0	--	(2)	(1.50)	46	3.04	10	3.10
3	3.67	30	4.00	10	4.24	4	4.40	1	4.60	2	1.10	(4)	(2.85)	10	2.94	2	2.40
1	1.40	4	6.50	7	5.45	6	4.80	4	5.30	0	--	(0)	(--)	18	4.76	3	4.53
8	4.48	17	2.58	4	5.70	5	3.96	1	6.20	13	2.25	(2)	(2.60)	14	1.37	4	3.50
1	2.40	5	2.92	1	6.60	1	6.60	2	5.90	1	1.60	(0)	(--)	14	2.49	1	1.20
0	--	1	4.60	1	4.20	1	3.60	0	--	0	--	(1)	(3.40)	11	2.24	3	4.00
13	3.89	57	3.67	23	4.99	17	4.49	8	5.52	16	2.06	(7)	(2.86)	67	2.89	13	3.51
19	3.41	117	3.58	111	3.94	37	4.18	23	4.23	23	1.99	(23)	(2.49)	163	2.71	33	3.18

influenced somewhat by the representation of these sects within our over-all sample.

[c]The San Quentin Group was not included in obtaining any of the over-all values: their means were so much higher than those of any other group, for reasons which seemed to have little to do with religion (see Chapter XXI), that the inclusion of this large group would throw the general picture out of focus.

these minor groups was represented by enough subjects to warrant separate statistical treatment, and we have undoubtedly combined groups which have little in common. There is, however, the suggestion that belonging to a minor denomination expresses some measure of dissent or nonconformity, or at least some lack of identification with the *status quo,* and that this is something which works against ethnocentrism. An interesting project would be to obtain representative samples of these groups and to study the specific contents of their beliefs in relation to patterns of response on the present scales.

c. CHURCH ATTENDANCE. Another type of difference among people with religious affiliations, a difference that might be significant for prejudice, is in the matter of frequency of church attendance. It might be supposed that those who attend regularly participate more fully in those aspects of formalized religion which seem to favor ethnocentrism, and hence will obtain higher A-S or E scores than those who attend less frequently. The data

TABLE 2 (VI)

MEAN A-S OR E SCORES FOR GROUPS SHOWING VARIOUS FREQUENCIES OF CHURCH ATTENDANCE

	1. Regular		2. Often		3. Seldom		Combined 1,2,3		Never		Blank		Over-all		
	N	Mean	N	Mean	N	Mean	N	Mean	N	Mean	N	Mean	N	Mean	S.D.
Groups taking Form 78:															
Public Speaking Class Women	45	3.09	39	3.71	47	3.28	131	3.34	6	3.20	3	4.70	140	3.32	1.43
Public Speaking Class Men	11	3.43	10	3.28	23	3.55	44	3.45	7	2.87	1	1.90	52	3.34	1.48
Extension Psychology Class Women	6	4.47	7	3.09	24	3.21	37	3.39	4	3.70	1	2.50	42	3.40	1.36
Professional Women	14	2.70	11	3.04	24	2.76	49	2.81	13	1.76	1	1.70	63	2.57	1.37
Totals:	76	3.20	67	3.47	118	3.21	281	3.27	30	2.37	6	3.37	297	3.18	1.46
Groups taking Form 60:															
Univ. of Oregon Student Women	11	3.36	11	3.59	25	3.39	47	3.45	0	--	0	--	47	3.43	1.38
Univ. of Oregon and Univ. of California Student Women	17	3.39	10	3.59	24	3.87	51	3.18	3	4.42	0	--	54	3.25	1.29
Univ. of Oregon and Univ. of California Student Men	15	2.99	14	3.30	20	2.97	49	3.07	8	2.19	0	--	37	2.95	1.26
Totals:	43	3.24	35	3.47	69	3.09	147	3.23	11	2.80	0	--	158	3.20	1.32
Groups taking Form 45:															
Maritime School Men	14	4.74	29	4.36	100	4.46	143	4.46	32	3.82	3	4.77	178	4.36	1.60
Psychiatric Clinic Men	7	2.60	9	3.89	22	4.24	38	3.86	10	2.98	2	3.50	50	3.67	1.59
Psychiatric Clinic Women	12	4.35	13	3.65	29	4.20	54	4.10	16	2.28	1	1.30	71	3.65	1.60
Totals:	33	4.15	51	4.09	151	4.38	235	4.28	58	3.25	6	3.77	299	4.07	1.63
Groups taking Form 40:															
Geo. Washington Univ. Women	47	4.34	42	4.43	36	3.44	125	4.11	5	2.32	2	4.20	132	4.04	1.58
Maritime School Men	17	4.67	45	5.42	82	5.09	144	5.14	16	4.66	4	4.40	164	5.08	1.76
Middle-Class Women	35	4.14	38	3.61	57	3.92	130	3.89	17	1.56	7	4.06	154	3.64	1.96
Middle-Class Men	9	3.56	12	5.37	27	4.26	48	4.40	19	2.60	2	3.90	69	3.88	2.08
Working-Class Men	8	4.50	13	4.72	27	3.72	48	4.14	9	2.40	2	3.60	59	3.83	1.72
Totals:	116	4.27	150	4.62	229	4.28	495	4.38	66	2.78	17	4.08	578	4.19	1.90
Over-all Totals:	268	3.79	303	4.14	567	3.94	1138	3.96	165	2.87	29	3.87	1332	3.82	--

obtained by means of the question, "How often do you attend services?" which appeared in all forms of the questionnaire are given in Table 2(VI). Our supposition with respect to those who attend regularly is not borne out. The mean score for subjects in this category is not significantly different from the means of those who attend often or of those who attend seldom. If, however, we combine these three categories, "regularly," "often," "seldom," and compare the mean score of subjects in this broader category with that of subjects who say they never attend, then it appears that the latter score very notably lower. Once again, it appears that those who reject religion have less ethnocentrism than those who seem to accept it. What it is among the latter that makes for high or for low scores has still to be discovered.

d. RELIGIOUS AFFILIATIONS OF PARENTS. It may be inquired whether religious subjects do not differ, in a way that is significant for prejudice, with respect to the manner in which religious pressures have been applied and the manner in which they have been accepted. It has been pointed out earlier that a group membership which the subject chooses for himself may have a different significance than a group membership which he has by virtue of having grown up within it. It may be suggested also that the homogeneity of the religious pattern to which the subject was subjected during his formative years and the consistency with which religious pressures have been applied have a bearing upon prejudice. Some light may be shed upon these matters by examining the data obtained by asking the subjects to state on their questionnaires what was or is the religion of their father and of their mother. This made it possible to consider various relations between father's religion and that of the mother as possible correlates of ethnocentrism score.

The results of this proceeding are shown in Table 3(VI). Here it is worth noting that, with each form of the questionnaire, A-S or E score is slightly higher on the average in those subjects whose father and mother had the same religion than in those whose parents had different religions.[4] The difference which appears in the over-all totals probably approaches statistical significance. In groups taking Forms 78 and 60 the mean score is slightly lower for subjects neither of whose parents was religious than for subjects in either of the first two categories; in the case of the three groups taking Forms 40 and 45 whose responses were analyzed, the number of subjects in the category "neither religious" is so small as to be negligible. These results suggest that ethnocentrism may be higher in subjects whose parents presented

[4] Calculations of this relationship were performed on only one group taking Form 45 and two groups taking Form 40. The relationships with which we were concerned had appeared so consistently in all groups examined up to the time Form 60 was revised, that it seemed we might economize merely by sampling the remaining groups. This, as it turned out, was not very fortunate, in as much as some of the relationships found with Forms 78 and 60 are not confirmed in the groups selected for analysis from among those taking Forms 40 and 45.

TABLE 3 (VI)

MEAN A-S OR E SCORES FOR GROUPS SHOWING VARIOUS RELATIONS BETWEEN FATHER'S RELIGION AND MOTHER'S RELIGION

Relation Between Father's and Mother's Religion

	Same Religion N	Mean	Different Religion N	Mean	M Religious F Not N	Mean	F Religious M Not N	Mean	Neither Religious N	Mean	Blank N	Mean	Over-all N	Mean	S.D.
Groups taking Form 78:															
Public Speaking Class Women	75	3.42	38	3.53	14	2.89	2	1.40	5	2.66	6	3.00	140	3.32	1.43
Public Speaking Class Men	36	3.40	7	3.19	5	3.66	0	--	2	1.20	2	4.30	52	3.34	1.48
Extension Psychology Class Women	25	3.43	10	3.20	2	4.55	0	--	2	2.80	3	3.47	42	3.40	1.36
Professional Women	35	2.73	15	2.37	9	2.37	0	--	2	1.05	2	3.75	63	2.57	1.37
Totals:	171	3.28	70	3.20	30	2.97	2	1.40	11	2.13	13	3.42	297	3.18	1.46
Groups taking Form 60:															
Univ. of Oregon Student Women	22	3.47	9	3.69	8	3.72	2	2.00	2	3.54	4	2.71	47	3.43	1.38
Univ. of Oregon and Univ. of California Student Women	37	3.54	7	2.66	3	3.47	1	3.00	2	2.88	4	1.71	54	3.25	1.29
Univ. of Oregon and Univ. of California Student Men	41	3.17	6	2.94	5	2.10	0	--	2	2.21	3	1.78	57	2.95	1.26
Totals:	100	3.38	22	3.16	16	3.17	3	2.33	6	2.88	11	2.09	158	3.20	1.32
Groups taking Form 45:															
Maritime School Men	120	4.36	30	4.24	9	4.94	0	--	1	4.60	18	4.21	178	4.36	1.60
Groups taking Form 40:															
Geo. Washington Univ. Women	78	4.29	45	3.84	3	2.67	0	--	1	3.40	5	2.96	132	4.04	1.58
Maritime School Men	115	5.20	19	4.80	12	4.47	0	--	2	5.20	16	4.99	164	5.08	1.76
Totals:	193	4.83	64	4.12	15	4.11	0	--	3	4.60	21	4.51	296	4.61	
Over-all Totals:	584	4.03	186	3.68	70	3.51	5	1.96	21	2.81	63	3.78	929	3.87	--

a united religious front than in subjects in whose case the religious influence from the parents was inconsistent, partial, or nonexistent. It may be that in the ethnocentric subjects whose mother and father were both religious, we are dealing with submission to ingroup authority and that the effects are the more pronounced the more consistent that authority has been.

But regardless of what might have been the relation between the father's religion and that of the mother, the subject may or may not have accepted the religious pressures of his family. Going on the assumption that in America religion is most largely a "maternal" matter, we have brought together in Table 4(VI) the mean A-S or E scores of groups showing various relations between the subject's religion and the mother's religion. Here it appears that, in general, subjects professing the same religion as the mother have a higher score on A-S or E than do subjects professing a religion different from that of the mother. Where the mother is religious but the subject not, or the subject is religious while the mother is not, the prejudice score is still lower and as we should expect, the lowest means appear when neither the subject nor the mother is religious. Concerning these results as a whole, one might say that whereas religious affiliation goes with higher scores on the scales, this is less likely to be the case if the religion is "one's own," that is to say, if it has been accepted independently of or in revolt against the main carrier of religious influence in the family. Where this has been the case, the chances are that the religion has been fairly well internalized. More than this, we have reason to believe that submission to and dependence upon parental authority is an important determinant of ethnocentrism; subjects, particularly women, who profess a religion that is different from that of the mother have probably been able to free themselves from these attitudes and hence, to a considerable degree, from prejudice.

The results just presented are much more pronounced in women than in men. The explanation here might be that for men the mother is not usually a center of conflict with respect to authority and that men who side with the mother in the matter of religion may gain thereby something of that Christian humanism which works against prejudice.

These results on family relationships in relation to religion and ethnocentrism suggest that in order to understand why some religious people are prejudiced and others are not, it is necessary to explore the deeper psychological aspects of the problem rather than limit ourselves to gross sociological factors.

2. "IMPORTANCE" OF RELIGION AND THE CHURCH

One approach to the psychological aspects of religion was to ask subjects directly, "How important in your opinion are religion and the Church?" This question appeared on the questionnaire form used just prior to Form 78. Answers were obtained from 123 women students in an Introductory Psy-

TABLE 4 (VI)

MEAN A-S OR E SCORES FOR GROUPS SHOWING VARIOUS RELATIONS BETWEEN SUBJECT'S RELIGION AND MOTHER'S RELIGION

| | Relation Between Subject's and Mother's Religion | | | | | | | | | | | | | Over-all | | |
| | Same | | Different | | M Religious S Not | | S Religious M Not | | Neither Religious | | Blank | | | | | |
	N	Mean	N	Mean	N	Mean	N	Mean	N	Mean	N	Mean	N	Mean	S.D.
Groups taking Form 78:															
Public Speaking Class Women	82	3.50	41	3.32	9	2.47	6	2.23	0	--	2	3.45	140	3.32	1.43
Public Speaking Class Men	38	3.37	5	3.48	7	3.71	1	1.20	1	1.20	0	--	52	3.34	1.48
Extension Psychology Class Women	19	3.90	10	3.23	10	2.62	1	4.00	1	1.60	1	4.70	42	3.40	1.36
Professional Women	31	2.74	21	2.95	9	1.48	0	--	2	1.05	0	--	63	2.57	1.37
Totals:	170	3.37	77	3.22	35	2.51	8	2.33	4	1.23	3	3.87	297	3.18	1.46
Groups taking Form 60:															
Univ. of Oregon Student Women	21	4.22	16	3.00	1	1.17	4	2.85	2	1.17	3	3.33	47	3.43	1.38
Univ. of Oregon and Univ. of California Student Women	28	3.45	18	3.18	4	2.29	2	3.21	1	2.33	1	2.50	54	3.25	1.29
Univ. of Oregon and Univ. of California Student Men	25	3.15	22	3.11	5	1.60	1	1.67	1	2.75	3	2.78	57	2.95	1.26
Totals:	74	3.57	56	3.10	10	1.83	7	2.79	4	1.85	7	2.98	158	3.19	1.32
Groups taking Form 45:															
Maritime School Men	129	4.56	16	4.13	22	3.61	0	--	1	4.50	10	3.72	178	4.36	1.60
Psychiatric Clinic Men	24	4.16	14	2.94	6	3.17	0	--	0	--	6	3.88	50	3.67	1.59
Psychiatric Clinic Women	40	4.25	11	3.75	9	2.22	0	--	4	1.18	7	3.30	71	3.65	1.60
Totals:	193	4.44	41	3.62	37	3.20	0	--	5	1.84	23	3.64	299	4.07	1.63
Groups taking Form 40:															
Geo. Washington Univ. Women	85	4.27	33	3.88	8	3.08	0	--	1	3.40	5	2.92	132	4.04	1.58
Maritime School Men	128	5.10	15	5.43	12	4.33	0	--	2	5.20	7	5.17	164	5.08	1.76
Middle-Class Women	84	4.22	47	3.38	10	1.22	1	1.40	1	1.20	11	2.95	154	3.64	1.96
Middle-Class Men	40	4.49	13	3.75	13	2.60	0	--	1	1.00	2	2.70	69	3.89	2.08
Working-Class Men	33	4.16	7	3.83	11	2.62	5	5.00	1	1.00	2	3.40	59	3.83	1.72
Totals:	370	4.56	115	3.86	54	2.80	6	4.40	6	2.83	27	3.53	578	4.19	1.90
Over-all Totals:	807	4.19	289	3.51	136	2.76	21	3.07	19	2.03	60	3.53	1332	3.82	--

chology Class at the University of California.[5] The responses of the subjects
were categorized according to the following scheme:

1. Generally and without qualification against both religion and the Church.
2. "Not important," with no qualifications given.
3. Agnostic; emphasis on values, ethics, way of living fostered by religion and
   the Church.
4. Emphasis on religion as a source of inner strength and satisfaction.
5. Acceptance of religion but rejection of the Church; emphasis on such concepts as faith and God.
6. "Mildly important," with no qualifications given.
7. Religion and the Church both important; acceptance of prayer, church
   attendance, religious rituals.

Mean A-S score for subjects giving each of these categories of response
was calculated. Means for categories 6 and 7 were relatively high, means for
all the other categories relatively low. These results were not, however, satis-

TABLE 5 (VI)

MEAN A-S SCORES OF GROUPS GIVING DIFFERENT CATEGORIES OF RESPONSE TO THE QUESTION: "HOW IMPORTANT ARE RELIGION AND THE CHURCH?"

Categories of Response	N	Mean A-S Score	S. D.
"High" categories 6 and 7 combined	65	180.7	54.5
"Low" categories 1, 2, 3, 4, and 5 combined	58	115.4	41.8

factory from a statistical point of view, mainly because several of the categories were represented by very few subjects. It seemed justifiable to combine categories 6 and 7, on the basis that both described a favorable attitude
toward religion and the church while making no distinction between the
two; similarly, all the remaining categories could be combined on the basis
that they represented something other than uncritical acceptance of formalized religion. The means for these two higher-order categories appear in
Table 5(VI). Subjects who believe that religion and the church are both
important have a mean A-S score of 180.7, and the other subjects, those who
are against religion and the church generally, those who accept religion
but not the church, and those who emphasize the personal, ethical, and rational aspects of religion, have a mean of 115.4. The difference between these
two means is 65.3 and the C. R. is 7.3.

[5] The over-all data for this group were presented in Chapter III.

These data may be taken to mean that for subjects high on A-S, religion is important primarily as a matter of convention. Subjects who are low on A-S may either be against religion or have a religion that is relatively personal and internalized. The fact of acceptance or rejection of religion is not as important as the *way* in which it is accepted or rejected.

3. SCALE ITEMS

Three items pertaining to religious ideology were included in the scale which attempted to measure potentially fascistic trends in the personality. This scale will be described in the next chapter but it seems appropriate to consider here those items which touch upon the topic of religion. The first item was the following: "The modern church with its many rules and hypocrisies, does not appeal to the deeply religious person; it appeals mainly to the childish, the insecure, and the uncritical." The hypothesis here was that disagreement with the item would indicate uncritical acceptance of the church and, hence, ethnocentrism, and that agreement with the item would indicate either an antireligious attitude or a genuinely religious but more intellectual point of view from which the church might be criticized—something which we should expect to go with low scores on the scales for measuring prejudice. The results were disappointing. The mean score on the item for the 295 subjects taking Form 78 of the questionnaire was 4.67 and the D. P.$_{AS}$ was —1.18. It appeared in retrospect that the statement was too complex and awkward, and hence, frequently misunderstood. More than this, the high mean score indicates that relatively few people were ready to criticize the church in this way; this, of course, would lower the chances of the item's being discriminating. Needless to say, the item was not retained in the questionnaire after its first trial.

Another item in the scale was the following: "Every person should have a deep faith in some supernatural force higher than himself to which he gives total allegiance and whose decisions he does not question." The hypothesis was that agreement with this statement, which expresses very firm belief in the supernatural and an attitude of submission toward it, would be associated with prejudice. The mean score for the 295 subjects taking Form 78 was 3.97 and the D. P.$_{AS}$, 1.26. When the item, slightly revised, was used in Form 60 of the questionnaire (N = 226) the mean score was 3.60 and the D. P.$_E$, 1.38. These D. P.'s are large enough to indicate that the relation of this item to ethnocentrism approaches statistical significance. The item was significantly correlated with the remainder of the scale in which it appeared, and this total scale was highly correlated with ethnocentrism.

The third item was as follows: "Sciences like chemistry, physics, and medicine have carried man very far but there are many important things that can never possibly be understood by the human mind." It was considered that subjects in agreeing with this item conceived of a mysterious spiritual realm of things with respect to which investigation was taboo and toward which their attitude was one of reverence. This outlook was expected to correlate with ethnocentrism. The mean in the case of Form 78 was 4.35 and the D. P.$_{AS}$, .97. In the case of Form 60, where the item appeared in a slightly revised version, the mean was 4.98 and the D. P.$_E$, 1.32. Here, once again, is evidence of a relationship between a particular religious idea and ethnocentrism. This item, like the "supernatural force" item discussed above, was significantly correlated with the remainder of the scale for measuring implicit antidemocratic trends and it was employed throughout the course of the study.

These results suggest that had it been possible to express a variety of religious beliefs, ideas, and sentiments in the form of scale items, more impressive quantitative results bearing on the relations of religious ideology to ethnocentrism would have been obtained. This is a matter which might well be the topic of future research.

C. DISCUSSION

Belonging to or identifying oneself with a religious body in America today certainly does not mean that one thereby takes over the traditional Christian values of tolerance, brotherhood, and equality. On the contrary, it appears that these values are more firmly held by people who do not affiliate with any religious group. It may be that religious affiliation or church attendance is of little importance one way or the other in determining social attitudes, that the great majority of middle-class Americans identify themselves with some religious denomination as a matter of course, without thinking much about it. This would be in keeping with the facts that the mean scores and the variability for the large religious denominations are very similar to those found in our sample as a whole. It may be argued, however, that this conventional approach to religion expresses enough identification with the *status quo*, submission to external authority, and readiness to emphasize moralistically the differences between those who "belong" and those who do not, to differentiate, in terms of E score, members of the large denominations from the nonreligious and from the members of those minor groups which actually stand for trends of an opposite character. At the same time, members of the major denominations seem to differ widely among themselves with respect to trends of this kind, and where there are signs that the acceptance of religion has been determined primarily by conventional or external considerations, E score tends to go up. Thus it is that agreement between the parents in the matter of religious affiliation, a circumstance that might lessen the chances of an awakening on the part of the subject to the issues involved, and sameness of the subject's religion and that of the mother, something that might be indicative of submissiveness toward authority, tend to be associated with ethnocentrism. But among the members of the major denominations there are many subjects whose religion would appear to be "genuine," in the sense that it was arrived at more or less independently of external pressure and takes the form of internalized values. These subjects, it seems, tend to score low, often very low, on ethnocentrism. Subjects with this same outlook probably predominate in the low-scoring Protestant denominations and often, no doubt, they profess to no religious affiliation at all.

It seems that we can approach an understanding of the relations between religion and ethnocentrism by paying attention to what the acceptance or the rejection of religion means to the individual. When the problem is approached from this point of view the psychological factors which appear as most important are much the same as those which came to the fore in the preceding chapters: conformity, conventionalism, authoritarian submission, determination by external pressures, thinking in ingroup-outgroup terms, and the like vs. nonconformity, independence, internalization of values, and so forth. The fragmentary data on religious ideology afforded by the scale items lend themselves to the same mode of interpretation. An attitude of complete submissiveness toward "supernatural forces" and a readiness to accept the essential incomprehensibility of "many important things" strongly suggest the persistence in the individual of infantile attitudes toward the parents, that is to say, of authoritarian submission in a very pure form. Psychological variables of the kind discussed here are investigated directly in the next chapter.

D. SUMMARY AND CONCLUSION

Subjects who profess to some religious affiliation express more prejudice than those who do not; but mean A-S or E scores for all the large denominations are close to the theoretical neutral point. The vast majority of our subjects do identify themselves with some religious group, and the variability with respect to ethnocentrism among these subjects is almost as great as it is in our sample as a whole. The factor of religious denomination does not prove to be very significant. Among the largest denominations no differences of any significance appear; but Unitarians, who seem to be distinguished by their liberalism, and a group of minor Protestant groups, in the case of which there might be some spirit of nonconformity or some lack of identification with the *status quo*, score lower than the others. Frequency of church attendance is also not particularly revealing; however, the finding that those who never attend obtain lower E scores than those who do attend is added evidence that people who reject organized religion are less prejudiced than those who accept it.

When the religious affiliation of the subject is considered in relation to that of his parents, it appears that ethnocentrism tends to be more pronounced in subjects whose parents presented a unified religious front than in cases where the religious influence from the parents was inconsistent, partial, or nonexistent. Furthermore, there is an indication that agreement between the subject and his or her mother in the matter of religion tends to be associated with ethnocentrism, disagreement with its opposite. These results suggest that acceptance of religion mainly as an expression of submission to a clear pattern of parental authority is a condition favorable to ethnocentrism.

A quantitative approach to religious ideology was made by including in one form of the questionnaire an open-ended question concerning the importance, in the subject's mind, of religion and the church. When a categorization of the answers to this question was made and mean A-S scores calculated, it turned out that the subjects who considered both religion and the church important were very considerably more anti-Semitic than were subjects who considered neither important or emphasized the ethical aspects of religion or differentiated between the church and "real" religion and, while rejecting the former, stressed the more personal and the more rational aspects of the latter.

Two scale-items pertaining to religious ideology appeared to be slightly correlated with prejudice. The more agreement with statements to the effect that people should have "complete faith in some supernatural force" and that "there are some things that can never be understood by the human mind," the higher did the A-S score tend to be.

In general, it appeared that gross, objective factors—denomination and frequency of church attendance—were less significant for prejudice than were certain psychological trends reflected in the way the subject accepted or rejected religion and in the content of his religious ideology. These trends —conventionalism, authoritarian submission, and so forth—were generally the same as those which came to the fore in preceding chapters, and we turn now to our attempt to investigate them directly.

CHAPTER VII

THE MEASUREMENT OF IMPLICIT
ANTIDEMOCRATIC TRENDS

R. Nevitt Sanford, T. W. Adorno, Else Frenkel-Brunswik, and
Daniel J. Levinson

A. INTRODUCTION

At a certain stage of the study, after considerable work with the A-S and E scales had been done, there gradually evolved a plan for constructing a scale that would measure prejudice without appearing to have this aim and without mentioning the name of any minority group. It appeared that such an instrument, if it correlated highly enough with the A-S and E scales, might prove to be a very useful substitute for them. It might be used to survey opinion in groups where "racial questions" were too "ticklish" a matter to permit the introduction of an A-S or E scale, e.g., a group which included many members of one or another ethnic minority. It might be used for measuring prejudice among minority group members themselves. Most important, by circumventing some of the defenses which people employ when asked to express themselves with respect to "race issues," it might provide a more valid measure of prejudice.

The PEC scale might have commended itself as an index of prejudice, but its correlations with the A-S and E scales did not approach being high enough. Moreover, the items of this scale were too explicitly ideological, that is, they might be too readily associated with prejudice in some logical or automatic way. What was needed was a collection of items each of which was correlated with A-S and E but which did not come from an area ordinarily covered in discussions of political, economic, and social matters. The natural place to turn was to the clinical material already collected, where, particularly in the subjects' discussions of such topics as the self, family, sex, interpersonal relations, moral and personal values, there had appeared numerous trends which, it appeared, might be connected with prejudice.

At this point the second—and major—purpose of the new scale began to take shape. Might not such a scale yield a valid estimate of antidemocratic tendencies at the personality level? It was clear, at the time the new scale was being planned, that anti-Semitism and ethnocentrism were not merely matters of surface opinion, but general tendencies with sources, in part at least, deep within the structure of the person. Would it not be possible to construct a scale that would approach more directly these deeper, often unconscious forces? If so, and if the scale could be validated by means of later clinical studies, would we not have a better estimate of antidemocratic *potential* than could be obtained from the scales that were more openly ideological? The prospect was intriguing. And experience with clinical techniques and with the other scales gave considerable promise of success. In attempting to account for the generality of A-S and of E, to explain what it was that made the diverse items of these scales go together, we had been led to the formulation of enduring psychological dispositions in the person —stereotypy, conventionalism, concern with power, and so forth. Study of the ideological discussions of individuals, e.g., Mack and Larry, had had the same outcome: there appeared to be dispositions in each individual that were reflected in his discussion of each ideological area as well as in his discussion of matters not ordinarily regarded as ideological. And when clinical-genetic material was examined, it appeared that these dispositions could frequently be referred to deep-lying personality needs. The task then was to formulate scale items which, though they were statements of opinions and attitudes and had the same form as those appearing in ordinary opinion-attitude questionnaires, would actually serve as "giveaways" of underlying antidemocratic trends in the personality. This would make it possible to carry over into group studies the insights and hypotheses derived from clinical investigation; it would test whether we could study on a mass scale features ordinarily regarded as individualistic and qualitative.

This second purpose—the quantification of antidemocratic trends at the level of personality—did not supersede the first, that of measuring anti-Semitism and ethnocentrism without mentioning minority groups or current politico-economic issues. Rather, it seemed that the two might be realized together. The notion was that A-S and E would correlate with the new scale because the A-S and E responses were strongly influenced by the underlying trends which the new scale sought to get at by a different approach. Indeed, if such a correlation could be obtained it could be taken as evidence that anti-Semitism and ethnocentrism were not isolated or specific or entirely superficial attitudes but expressions of persistent tendencies in the person. This would depend, however, upon how successful was the attempt to exclude from the new scale items which might have been so frequently or so automatically associated with anti-Semitism or ethnocentrism that they might be regarded as aspects of the same political "line." In any case, however, it seemed that the discovery of opinions and attitudes, in various areas other than the usual politico-socioeconomic one, that were associated with anti-Semitism and ethnocentrism, would give a more comprehensive grasp of the prejudiced outlook on the world. The new instrument was termed the F scale, to signify its concern with implicit prefascist tendencies.

On theoretical grounds it was expected that the correlations of F with A-S and E would not approach unity. It was hoped that the F scale would catch some of the antidemocratic potential that might not be expressed when subjects responded to items which dealt directly with hostility toward minority groups. True, the items of the present A-S and E scales were, for the most part, so formulated as to allow the subject to express prejudice while maintaining the feeling that he was being democratic. Yet it was recognized that a subject might score relatively low on A-S or E and still, in the interview, where a confidential relationship was established and the interviewer was very permissive, reveal that he was prejudiced. More than this, it had to be admitted that a subject might refuse altogether to express hostility against minority groups and yet reveal features, e.g., a tendency to think of such groups in a stereotyped way or a tendency moralistically to reject social groups other than ethnic ones, which had to be taken as susceptibility to antidemocratic propaganda. If the F scale were to be regarded as a measure of antidemocratic potential—something which might or might not be expressed in open hostility against outgroups—then it could not be perfectly correlated with A-S or E. Rather, the demand to be made of it was that it single out individuals who in intensive clinical study revealed themselves to be receptive to antidemocratic propaganda. Although it was not possible within the scope of the study to use the F scale alone as the basis for selecting interviewees, it was possible to relate F scale score to various other indices of antidemocratic personality trends as brought to light by other techniques. Such trends, it seemed, could exist in the absence of high A-S or E scores.

However, the distinction between potential and manifest should not be overdrawn. Given emotionally determined antidemocratic trends in the person, we should expect that *in general* they would be evoked by the A-S and E items, which were designed for just this purpose, as well as by the F scale and other indirect methods. The person who was high on F but not on A-S or E would be the exception, whose inhibitions upon the expression of prejudice against minorities would require special explanation.

B. CONSTRUCTION OF THE FASCISM (F) SCALE

1. THE UNDERLYING THEORY

The 38 items of the original F scale are shown in Table 1 (VII), numbered in the order of their appearance on Form 78. If the reader considers that most of what has gone before in this volume was either known or thought about before construction of the F scale began, it will be apparent that in devising the scale we did not proceed in a strictly empirical fashion. We did not consider starting with hundreds of items chosen more or less at random and then seeing by trial and error which ones might be associated with A-S and E. For every item there was a hypothesis, sometimes several hypotheses, stating what might be the nature of its connection with prejudice.

The major source of these hypotheses was the research already performed in the present study. Available for the purpose was the following material: results, such as those given in preceding chapters, from the A-S, E, and PEC scales; numerous correlates of E derived from questionnaire studies, that is, from responses to factual and short essay questions pertaining to such topics as religion, war, ideal society, and so forth; early results from projective questions; finally, and by far the most important, material from the interviews and the Thematic Apperception Tests. Another important source of items was research in fields allied to the present one in which the authors had previously had a part. Principal among these were several studies performed at the University of California on personality in relation to war morale and ideology (19, 20, 102, 107, 108, 109), and researches of the Institute of Social Research such as content analyses of speeches of anti-Semitic agitators and a study on anti-Semitic workers (2, 3, 56, 57, 57A, 57B). Finally, there was the general literature on anti-Semitism and fascism, embracing both empirical and theoretical studies.

It will have been recognized that the interpretation of the material of the present study was guided by a theoretical orientation that was present at the start. The same orientation played the most crucial role in the preparation of the F scale. Once a hypothesis had been formulated concerning the way in which some deep-lying trend in the personality might express itself in some opinion or attitude that was dynamically, though not logically, related to prejudice against outgroups, a preliminary sketch for an item was usually not far to seek: a phrase from the daily newspaper, an utterance by an interviewee, a fragment of ordinary conversation was usually ready at hand. (As will be seen, however, the actual formulation of an item was a technical proceeding to which considerable care had to be devoted.)

As to what kinds of central personality trends we might expect to be the most significant, the major guide, as has been said, was the research which had gone before; they were the trends which, as hypothetical constructs, seemed best to explain the consistency of response on the foregoing scales, and which emerged from the analysis of clinical material as the likely sources of the coherence found in individual cases. Most of these trends have been mentioned before, usually when it was necessary to do so in order to give meaning to obtained results. For example, when it was discovered that the anti-Semitic individual objects to Jews on the ground that they violate conventional moral values, one interpretation was that this individual had a

TABLE 1 (VII)
THE F SCALE: FORM 78

2. Although many people may scoff, it may yet be shown that astrology can explain a lot of things.

3. America is getting so far from the true American way of life that force may be necessary to restore it.

6. It is only natural and right that women be restricted in certain ways in which men have more freedom.

9. Too many people today are living in an unnatural, soft way; we should return to the fundamentals, to a more red-blooded, active way of life.

10. It is more than a remarkable coincidence that Japan had an earthquake on Pearl Harbor Day, December 7, 1944.

12. The modern church, with its many rules and hypocrisies, does not appeal to the deeply religious person; it appeals mainly to the childish, the insecure, and the uncritical.

14. After we finish off the Germans and Japs, we ought to concentrate on other enemies of the human race such as rats, snakes, and germs.

17. Familiarity breeds contempt.

19. One should avoid doing things in public which appear wrong to others, even though one knows that these things are really all right.

20. One of the main values of progressive education is that it gives the child great freedom in expressing those natural impulses and desires so often frowned upon by conventional middle-class society.

23. He is, indeed, contemptible who does not feel an undying love, gratitude, and respect for his parents.

24. Today everything is unstable; we should be prepared for a period of constant change, conflict, and upheaval.

28. Novels or stories that tell about what people think and feel are more interesting than those which contain mainly action, romance, and adventure.

30. Reports of atrocities in Europe have been greatly exaggerated for propaganda purposes.

31. Homosexuality is a particularly rotten form of delinquency and ought to be severely punished.

32. It is essential for learning or effective work that our teachers or bosses outline in detail what is to be done and exactly how to go about it.

35. There are some activities so flagrantly un-American that, when responsible officials won't take the proper steps, the wide-awake citizen should take the law into his own hands.

38. There is too much emphasis in college on intellectual and theoretical topics, not enough emphasis on practical matters and on the homely virtues of living.

39. Every person should have a deep faith in some supernatural force higher than himself to which he gives total allegiance and whose decisions he does not question.

42. No matter how they act on the surface, men are interested in women for only one reason.

43. Sciences like chemistry, physics, and medicine have carried men very far, but there are many important things that can never possibly be understood by the human mind.

46. The sexual orgies of the old Greeks and Romans are nursery school stuff compared to some of the goings-on in this country today, even in circles where people might least expect it.

47. No insult to our honor should ever go unpunished.
50. Obedience and respect for authority are the most important virtues children should learn.
53. There are some things too intimate or personal to talk about even with one's closest friends.
55. Although leisure is a fine thing, it is good hard work that makes life interesting and worthwhile.
56. After the war, we may expect a crime wave; the control of gangsters and ruffians will become a major social problem.
58. *What* a man does is not so important so long as he does it well.
59. Human nature being what it is, there will always be war and conflict.
60. Which of the following are the most important for a person to have or to be? *Mark X the three most important.*

> artistic and sensuous
> popular, good personality
> drive, determination, will power
> broad, humanitarian social outlook
> neatness and good manners
> sensitivity and understanding
> efficiency, practicality, thrift
> intellectual and serious
> emotional expressiveness, warmth, intimacy
> kindness and charity

65. It is entirely possible that this series of wars and conflicts will be ended once and for all by a world-destroying earthquake, flood, or other catastrophe.
66. Books and movies ought not to deal so much with the sordid and seamy side of life; they ought to concentrate on themes that are entertaining or uplifting.
67. When you come right down to it, it's human nature never to do anything without an eye to one's own profit.
70. To a greater extent than most people realize, our lives are governed by plots hatched in secret by politicians.
73. Nowadays when so many different kinds of people move around so much and mix together so freely, a person has to be especially careful to protect himself against infection and disease.
74. What this country needs is fewer laws and agencies, and more courageous, tireless, devoted leaders whom the people can put their faith in.
75. Sex crimes, such as rape and attacks on children, deserve more than mere imprisonment; such criminals ought to be publicly whipped.
77. No sane, normal, decent person could ever think of hurting a close friend or relative.

particularly strong and rigid adherence to conventional values, and that this general disposition in his personality provided some of the motivational basis for anti-Semitism, and at the same time expressed itself in other ways, e.g., in a general tendency to look down on and to punish those who were believed to be violating conventional values. This interpretation was supported by results from the E and PEC scales, where it was shown that items expressive of conventionalism were associated with more manifest forms of prejudice. Accordingly, therefore, *adherence to conventional values* came to be thought of as a *variable* in the person—something which could be approached by means of scale items of the F type and shown to be related functionally to various manifestations of prejudice. Similarly, a consideration of E-scale results strongly suggested that underlying several of the prejudiced responses was a general disposition to glorify, to be subservient to and remain uncritical toward authoritative figures of the ingroup and to take an attitude of punishing outgroup figures in the name of some moral authority. Hence, *authoritarianism* assumed the proportions of a variable worthy to be investigated in its own right.

In the same way, a number of such variables were derived and defined, and they, taken together, made up the basic content of the F scale. Each was regarded as a more or less central trend in the person which, in accordance with some dynamic process, expressed itself on the surface in ethnocentrism as well as in diverse psychologically related opinions and attitudes. These variables are listed below, together with a brief definition of each.

   a. *Conventionalism.* Rigid adherence to conventional, middle-class values.
   b. *Authoritarian submission.* Submissive, uncritical attitude toward idealized moral authorities of the ingroup.
   c. *Authoritarian aggression.* Tendency to be on the lookout for, and to condemn, reject, and punish people who violate conventional values.
   d. *Anti-intraception.* Opposition to the subjective, the imaginative, the tenderminded.
   e. *Superstition and stereotypy.* The belief in mystical determinants of the individual's fate; the disposition to think in rigid categories.
   f. *Power and "toughness."* Preoccupation with the dominance-submission, strong-weak, leader-follower dimension; identification with power figures; overemphasis upon the conventionalized attributes of the ego; exaggerated assertion of strength and toughness.
   g. *Destructiveness and cynicism.* Generalized hostility, vilification of the human.
   h. *Projectivity.* The disposition to believe that wild and dangerous things go on in the world; the projection outwards of unconscious emotional impulses.
   i. *Sex.* Exaggerated concern with sexual "goings-on."

These variables were thought of as going together to form a single syndrome, a more or less enduring structure in the person that renders him receptive to antidemocratic propaganda. One might say, therefore, that the F scale attempts to measure the potentially antidemocratic personality. This does not imply that *all* the features of this personality pattern are touched upon in the scale, but only that the scale embraces a fair sample of the ways in which this pattern characteristically expresses itself. Indeed, as the study went on, numerous additional features of the pattern, as well as variations within the over-all pattern, suggested themselves—and it was regretted that a second F scale could not have been constructed in order to carry these explorations further. It is to be emphasized that one can speak of personality here only to the extent that the coherence of the scale items can be better explained on the ground of an inner structure than on the ground of external association.

The variables of the scale may be discussed in more detail, with emphasis on their organization and the nature of their relations to ethnocentrism. As each variable is introduced, the scale items deemed to be expressive of it are presented. It will be noted, as the variables are taken up in turn, that the same item sometimes appears under more than one heading. This follows from our approach to scale construction. In order efficiently to cover a wide area it was necessary to formulate items that were maximally rich, that is, pertinent to as much as possible of the underlying theory—hence a single item was sometimes used to represent two, and sometimes more, different ideas. It will be noted also that different variables are represented by different numbers of items. This is for the reason that the scale was designed with first attention to the whole pattern into which the variables fitted, some with more important roles than others.

a. *Conventionalism*

12. The modern church, with its many rules and hypocrisies, does not appeal to the deeply religious person; it appeals mainly to the childish, the insecure, and the uncritical.

19. One should avoid doing things in public which appear wrong to others, even though one knows that these things are really all right.

38. There is too much emphasis in colleges on intellectual and theoretical topics, not enough emphasis on practical matters and on the homely virtues of living.

55. Although leisure is a fine thing, it is good hard work that makes life interesting and worthwhile.

58. *What* a man does is not so important so long as he does it well.

60. Which of the following are the most important for a person to have or to be? *Mark X the three most important.*
    artistic and sensuous
    popular, good personality
    drive, determination, will power
    broad, humanitarian social outlook
    neatness and good manners
    sensitivity and understanding
    efficiency, practicality, thrift
    intellectual and serious
    emotional expressiveness, warmth, intimacy
    kindness and charity

It is a well-known hypothesis that susceptibility to fascism is most characteristically a middle-class phenomenon, that it is "in the culture" and, hence, that those who conform the most to this culture will be the most prejudiced.

Items referring to the holding of conventional values were included in order to gather data bearing on this hypothesis. Many of the early findings of the present study, however, gave evidence that the matter was not quite so simple. The correlation between conventional values and prejudice seemed to be positive but not very high; whereas unconventional people tended to be free of prejudice, it was clear that some conventional people were prejudiced while others were not. It seemed that, among the conventional group, what might make the difference was the deeper source of the conventionality, or rather the type of broader personality structure within which it had a functional role. If the adherence to conventional values was an expression of a fully established individual conscience, then we should expect no necessary connection between these values and antidemocratic potential. The same standards which render the individual easily offended by what he conceives to be the morally loose behavior of unassimilated minority group members or of "lower-class" people, would—if they are well internalized—cause him to resist the violence and delinquency which characterize the advanced stages of fascism. If, on the other hand, adherence to conventional values is determined by contemporary external social pressure, if it is based upon the individual's adherence to the standards of the collective powers with which he, for the time being, is identified, then we should expect a close association with antidemocratic receptivity. It is this latter state of affairs that we wish to call conventionalism—and to distinguish from mere acceptance of conventional values. The conventionalistic individual could in good conscience follow the dictates of the external agency wherever they might lead him and, moreover, he would be capable of totally exchanging one set of standards for another quite different one—as in a conversion from official Communism to Catholicism.

The scale items listed under *Conventionalism* afford the subject an opportunity to reveal whether or not his adherence to conventional values is of the rigid, absolutist character just described. For example, this would seem to be indicated by a mark of $+3$ on the item, "Obedience and respect for authority are the most important virtues children should learn." However, a sound decision on this matter would depend on the individual's responses to items in the other categories. For example, extreme conventionalism going with a strong inclination to punish those who violate conventional values is a different thing from conventional values associated with a philosophy of live and let live. In other words, the meaning of a high score on this variable, as on any of the others, is to be known from the broader context within which it occurs.

b. *Authoritarian Submission*
   20. One of the main values of progressive education is that it gives the child great freedom in expressing those natural impulses and desires so often frowned upon by conventional middle-class society.

23. He is indeed contemptible who does not feel an undying love, gratitude, and respect for his parents.

32. It is essential for learning or effective work that our teachers or bosses outline in detail what is to be done and exactly how to go about it.

39. Every person should have a deep faith in some supernatural force higher than himself to which he gives total allegiance and whose decisions he does not question.

43. Sciences like chemistry, physics, and medicine have carried men very far, but there are many important things that can never possibly be understood by the human mind.

50. Obedience and respect for authority are the most important virtues children should learn.

74. What this country needs is fewer laws and agencies, and more courageous, tireless, devoted leaders whom the people can put their faith in.

77. No sane, normal, decent person could ever think of hurting a close friend or relative.

Submission to authority, desire for a strong leader, subservience of the individual to the state, and so forth, have so frequently and, as it seems to us, correctly, been set forth as important aspects of the Nazi creed that a search for correlates of prejudice had naturally to take these attitudes into account.[1] These attitudes have indeed been so regularly mentioned in association with anti-Semitism that it was particularly difficult to formulate items that would express the underlying trend and still be sufficiently free of logical or direct relations to prejudice—and we cannot claim to have been entirely successful. Direct references to dictatorship and political figures were avoided for the most part, and the main emphasis was on obedience, respect, rebellion, and relations to authority in general. Authoritarian submission was conceived of as a very general attitude that would be evoked in relation to a variety of authority figures—parents, older people, leaders, supernatural power, and so forth.

The attempt was made to formulate the items in such a way that agreement with them would indicate not merely a realistic, balanced respect for valid authority but an exaggerated, all-out, emotional need to submit. This would be indicated, it seemed, by agreement that obedience and respect for authority were the *most important* virtues that children should learn, that a person should *obey without question* the decisions of a supernatural power, and so forth. It was considered that here, as in the case of conventionalism, the subservience to external agencies was probably due to some failure in

[1] E. Fromm (42), E. H. Erikson (25), A. Maslow (79), M. B. Chisholm (18), and W. Reich (96) are among the writers whose thinking about authoritarianism has influenced our own.

the development of an inner authority, i.e., conscience. Another hypothesis was that authoritarian submission was commonly a way of handling ambivalent feelings toward authority figures: underlying hostile and rebellious impulses, held in check by fear, lead the subject to overdo in the direction of respect, obedience, gratitude, and the like.

It seems clear that authoritarian submission by itself contributes largely to the antidemocratic potential by rendering the individual particularly receptive to manipulation by the strongest external powers. The immediate connection of this attitude with ethnocentrism has been suggested in earlier chapters: hostility against ingroup authorities, originally the parents, has had to be repressed; the "bad" aspects of these figures—that they are unfair, self-seeking, dominating—are then seen as existing in outgroups, who are charged with dictatorship, plutocracy, desire to control, and so forth. And this displacement of negative imagery is not the only way in which the repressed hostility is handled; it seems often to find expression in authoritarian aggression.

   c. *Authoritarian Aggression*

     6. It is only natural and right that women be restricted in certain ways in which men have more freedom.

  23. He is indeed contemptible who does not feel an undying love, gratitude, and respect for his parents.

  31. Homosexuality is a particularly rotten form of delinquency and ought to be severely punished.

  47. No insult to our honor should ever go unpunished.

  75. Sex crimes, such as rape and attacks on children, deserve more than mere imprisonment; such criminals ought to be publicly whipped.

The individual who has been forced to give up basic pleasures and to live under a system of rigid restraints, and who therefore feels put upon, is likely not only to seek an object upon which he can "take it out" but also to be particularly annoyed at the idea that another person is "getting away with something." Thus, it may be said that the present variable represents the sadistic component of authoritarianism just as the immediately foregoing one represents its masochistic component. It is to be expected, therefore, that the conventionalist who cannot bring himself to utter any real criticism of accepted authority will have a desire to condemn, reject, and punish those who violate these values. As the emotional life which this person regards as proper and a part of himself is likely to be very limited, so the impulses, especially sexual and aggressive ones, which remain unconscious and ego-alien are likely to be strong and turbulent. Since in this circumstance a wide variety of stimuli can tempt the individual and so arouse his anxiety (fear of punishment), the list of traits, behavior patterns, individuals, and groups that he must condemn grows very long indeed. It has been suggested before that this mechanism might lie behind the ethnocentric rejection of such groups as zootsuiters, foreigners, other nations; it is here hypothesized that this feature of ethnocentrism is but a part of a more general tendency to punish violators of conventional values: homosexuals, sex offenders, people with bad manners, etc. Once the individual has convinced himself that there are people who ought to be punished, he is provided with a channel through which his deepest aggressive impulses may be expressed, even while he thinks of himself as thoroughly moral. If his external authorities, or the crowd, lend their approval to this form of aggression, then it may take the most violent forms, and it may persist after the conventional values, in the name of which it was undertaken, have been lost from sight.

One might say that in authoritarian aggression, hostility that was originally aroused by and directed toward ingroup authorities is *displaced* onto outgroups. This mechanism is superficially similar to but essentially different from a process that has often been referred to as "scapegoating." According to the latter conception, the individual's aggression is aroused by frustration, usually of his economic needs; and then, being unable due to intellectual confusion to tell the real causes of his difficulty, he lashes out about him, as it were, venting his fury upon whatever object is available and not too likely to strike back. While it is granted that this process has a role in hostility against minority groups, it must be emphasized that according to the present theory of displacement, the authoritarian *must*, out of an inner necessity, turn his aggression against outgroups. He must do so because he is psychologically unable to attack ingroup authorities, rather than because of intellectual confusion regarding the source of his frustration. If this theory is correct, then authoritarian aggression and authoritarian submission should turn out to be highly correlated. Furthermore, this theory helps to explain why the aggression is so regularly justified in moralistic terms, why it can become so violent and lose all connection with the stimulus which originally set it off.

Readiness to condemn other people on moral grounds may have still another source: it is not only that the authoritarian must condemn the moral laxness that he sees in others, but he is actually driven to see immoral attributes in them whether this has a basis in fact or not. This is a further device for countering his own inhibited tendencies; he says to himself, as it were: "I am not bad and deserving of punishment, he is." In other words the individual's own unacceptable impulses are *projected* onto other individuals and groups who are then rejected. Projectivity as a variable is dealt with more fully below.

Conventionalism, authoritarian submission, and authoritarian aggression all have to do with the moral aspect of life—with standards of conduct, with the authorities who enforce these standards, with offenders against them who deserve to be punished. We should expect that, in general, subjects who score high on one of these variables will score high on the others also, inasmuch as all three can be understood as expressions of a particular kind of structure within the personality. The most essential feature of this structure is a lack of integration between the moral agencies by which the subject lives and the rest of his personality. One might say that the conscience or superego is incompletely integrated with the self or ego, the ego here being conceived of as embracing the various self-controlling and self-expressing functions of the individual. It is the ego that governs the relations between self and outer world, and between self and deeper layers of the personality; the ego undertakes to regulate impulses in a way that will permit gratification without inviting too much punishment by the superego, and it seeks in general to carry out the activities of the individual in accordance with the demands of reality. It is a function of the ego to make peace with conscience, to create a larger synthesis within which conscience, emotional impulses, and self operate in relative harmony. When this synthesis is not achieved, the superego has somewhat the role of a foreign body within the personality, and it exhibits those rigid, automatic, and unstable aspects discussed above.

There is some reason to believe that a failure in superego internalization is due to weakness in the ego, to its inability to perform the necessary synthesis, i.e., to integrate the superego with itself. Whether or not this is so, ego weakness would seem to be a concomitant of conventionalism and authoritarianism. Weakness in the ego is expressed in the inability to build up a consistent and enduring set of moral values within the personality; and it is this state of affairs, apparently, that makes it necessary for the individual to seek some organizing and coordinating agency outside of himself. Where such outside agencies are depended upon for moral decisions one may say that the conscience is externalized.

Although conventionalism and authoritarianism might thus be regarded as signs of ego weakness, it seemed worthwhile to seek other, more direct, means for estimating this trend in personality, and to correlate this trend with the others. Ego weakness would, it seemed, be expressed fairly directly in such phenomena as opposition to introspection, in superstition and stereotypy, and in overemphasis upon the ego and its supposed strength. The following three variables deal with these phenomena.

d. *Anti-intraception*

28. Novels or stories that tell about what people think and feel are more interesting than those which contain mainly action, romance, and adventure.

38. There is too much emphasis in colleges on intellectual and theoretical topics, not enough emphasis on practical matters and on the homely virtues of living.

53. There are some things too intimate or personal to talk about even with one's closest friends.

55. Although leisure is a fine thing, it is good hard work that makes life interesting and worthwhile.

58. *What* a man does is not so important so long as he does it well.

66. Books and movies ought not to deal so much with the sordid and seamy side of life; they ought to concentrate on themes that are entertaining or uplifting.

Intraception is a term introduced by Murray (89) to stand for "the dominance of feelings, fantasies, speculations, aspirations—an imaginative, subjective human outlook." The opposite of intraception is extraception, "a term that describes the tendency to be determined by concrete, clearly observable, physical conditions (tangible, objective facts)." The relations of intraception/extraception to ego weakness and to prejudice are probably highly complex, and this is not the place to consider them in detail. It seems fairly clear, however, that *anti*-intraception, an attitude of impatience with and opposition to the subjective and tender-minded, might well be a mark of the weak ego. The extremely anti-intraceptive individual is afraid of thinking about human phenomena because he might, as it were, think the wrong thoughts; he is afraid of genuine feeling because his emotions might get out of control. Out of touch with large areas of his own inner life, he is afraid of what might be revealed if he, or others, should look closely at himself. He is therefore against "prying," against concern with what people think and feel, against unnecessary "talk"; instead he would keep busy, devote himself to practical pursuits, and instead of examining an inner conflict, turn his thoughts to something cheerful. An important feature of the Nazi program, it will be recalled, was the defamation of everything that tended to make the individual aware of himself and his problems; not only was "Jewish" psychoanalysis quickly eliminated but every kind of psychology except aptitude testing came under attack. This general attitude easily leads to a devaluation of the human and an overevaluation of the physical object; when it is most extreme, human beings are looked upon as if they were physical objects to be coldly manipulated—even while physical objects, now vested with emotional appeal, are treated with loving care.

e. *Superstition and Stereotypy*

2. Although many people may scoff, it may yet be shown that astrology can explain a lot of things.

10. It is more than a remarkable coincidence that Japan had an earthquake on Pearl Harbor Day, December 7, 1944.

39. Every person should have a deep faith in some supernatural force higher than himself to which he gives total allegiance and whose decisions he does not question.

43. Sciences like chemistry, physics, and medicine have carried men very far, but there are many important things that can never possibly be understood by the human mind.

65. It is entirely possible that this series of wars and conflicts will be ended once and for all by a world-destroying earthquake, flood, or other catastrophe.

Superstitiousness, the belief in mystical or fantastic external determinants of the individual's fate, and stereotypy,[2] the disposition to think in rigid categories, have been mentioned so frequently in the foregoing chapters and are so obviously related to ethnocentrism that they need little discussion here. A question that must be raised concerns the relations of these trends to general intelligence—and the relations of intelligence to ethnocentrism. Probably superstition and stereotypy tend to go with low intelligence, but low intelligence appears to be correlated with ethnocentrism to only a slight degree (see Chapter VIII). It appears likely that superstition and stereotypy embrace, over and above the mere lack of intelligence in the ordinary sense, certain dispositions in thinking which are closely akin to prejudice, even though they might not hamper intelligent performance in the extraceptive sphere. These dispositions can be understood, in part at least, as expressions of ego weakness. Stereotypy is a form of obtuseness particularly in psychological and social matters. It might be hypothesized that one reason why people in modern society—even those who are otherwise "intelligent" or "informed"—resort to primitive, oversimplified explanations of human events is that so many of the ideas and observations needed for an adequate account are not allowed to enter into the calculations: because they are affect-laden and potentially anxiety-producing, the weak ego cannot include them within its scheme of things. More than this, those deeper forces within the personality which the ego cannot integrate with itself are likely to be projected onto the outer world; this is a source of bizarre ideas concerning other peoples' behavior and concerning the causation of events in nature.

Superstitiousness indicates a tendency to shift responsibility from within the individual onto outside forces beyond one's control; it indicates that the ego might already have "given up," that is to say, renounced the idea that it might determine the individual's fate by overcoming external forces. It must, of course, be recognized that in modern industrial society the capacity of the individual to determine what happens to himself has *actually* decreased, so that items referring to external causation might easily be realistic and hence of no significance for personality. It seemed necessary, therefore, to select items that would express ego weakness in a nonrealistic way by making the individual's fate dependent on more or less fantastic factors.

[2] Although no items pertaining specifically to stereotypy appear in Form 78 of the F scale, several such items do find a place in the later forms; hence, it seems well to introduce this concept into the discussion at this point.

f. *Power and "Toughness"*

9. Too many people today are living in an unnatural, soft way; we should return to the fundamentals, to a more red-blooded, active way of life.

35. There are some activities so flagrantly un-American that, when responsible officials won't take the proper steps, the wide-awake citizen should take the law into his own hands.

47. No insult to our honor should ever go unpunished.

70. To a greater extent than most people realize, our lives are governed by plots hatched in secret by politicians.

74. What this country needs is fewer laws and agencies, and more courageous, tireless, devoted leaders whom the people can put their faith in.

This variable refers, in the first place, to overemphasis upon the conventionalized attributes of the ego. The underlying hypothesis is that overdisplay of toughness may reflect not only the weakness of the ego but also the magnitude of the task it has to perform, that is to say, the strength of certain kinds of needs which are proscribed in the subject's culture. The relations of ego and impulse, then, are at least as close as the relations of ego and conscience. Nevertheless, they may be separated for purposes of analysis, and other variables of the F scale refer to the deeper strata of the individual's emotional life.

Closely related to the phenomenon of exaggerated toughness is something which might be described as a "power complex." Most apparent in its manifestations is overemphasis on the power motif in human relationships; there is a disposition to view all relations among people in terms of such categories as strong-weak, dominant-submissive, leader-follower, "hammer-anvil." And it is difficult to say with which of these roles the subject is the more fully identified. It appears that he wants to get power, to have it and not to lose it, and at the same time is afraid to seize and wield it. It appears that he also admires power in others and is inclined to submit to it—and at the same time is afraid of the weakness thus implied. The individual whom we expected to score high on this cluster readily identifies himself with the "little people," or "the average," but he does so, it seems, with little or no humility, and he seems actually to think of himself as strong or to believe that he can somehow become so. In short, the power complex contains elements that are essentially contradictory, and we should expect that sometimes one feature and sometimes another will predominate at the surface level. We should expect that both leaders and followers will score high on this variable, for the reason that the actual role of the individual seems to be less important than his concern that leader-follower relations shall obtain. One solution which such an individual often achieves is that of alignment with power figures, an arrangement by which he is able to gratify both his need for power and his need to submit. He hopes that by submitting to power he can participate in it. For example, a man who reports that the most awe-inspiring experience for him would be "to shake hands with the President" probably finds his gratification not in submission alone but in the idea that some of the big man's power has, as it were, rubbed off onto him, so that he is a more important person for having "shook his hand" or "known him" or "been there." The same pattern of gratification can be obtained by acting in the role of "the lieutenant" or by functioning in a middle position in some clearly structured hierarchy where there is always somebody above and somebody below.

The power complex has immediate relations with certain aspects of ethnocentrism. An individual who thinks of most human relations in such terms as strong versus weak is likely to apply these categories in his thinking about ingroups and outgroups, e.g., to conceive of "superior" and "inferior races." And one of the psychologically least costly devices for attaining a sense of superiority is to claim it on the basis of membership in a particular "race."

g. *Destructiveness and Cynicism*

3. America is getting so far from the true American way of life that force may be necessary to restore it.

9. Too many people today are living in an unnatural, soft way; we should return to the fundamentals, to a more red-blooded, active way of life.

14. After we finish off the Germans and Japs, we ought to concentrate on other enemies of the human race such as rats, snakes, and germs.

17. Familiarity breeds contempt.

24. Today everything is unstable; we should be prepared for a period of constant change, conflict, and upheaval.

30. Reports of atrocities in Europe have been greatly exaggerated for propaganda purposes.

35. There are some activities so flagrantly un-American that, when responsible officials won't take the proper steps, the wide-awake citizen should take the law into his own hands.

42. No matter how they act on the surface, men are interested in women for only one reason.

56. After the war, we may expect a crime wave; the control of gangsters and ruffians will become a major social problem.

59. Human nature being what it is, there will always be war and conflict.

67. When you come right down to it, it's human nature never to do anything without an eye to one's own profit.

According to the present theory, the antidemocratic individual, because he has had to accept numerous externally imposed restrictions upon the satisfaction of his needs, harbors strong underlying aggressive impulses. As we have seen, one outlet for this aggression is through displacement onto out-groups leading to moral indignation and authoritarian aggression. Undoubtedly this is a very serviceable device for the individual; yet, the strong underlying aggression seems at the same time to express itself in some other way—in a nonmoralized way. It was assumed, of course, that primitive aggressive impulses are rarely expressed with complete directness by adults, but must instead be sufficiently modified, or at least justified, so that they are acceptable to the ego.

The present variable, then, refers to rationalized, ego-accepted, nonmoralized aggression. The supposition was that a subject could express this tendency by agreeing with statements which though thoroughly aggressive were couched in such terms as to avoid his moral censorship. Thus, some items offered justifications for aggression, and were formulated in such a way that strong agreement would indicate that the subject needed only slight justification in order to be ready for all-out aggression. Other items dealt with contempt for mankind, the theory being that here the hostility is so generalized, so free of direction against any particular object, that the individual need not feel accountable for it. Still another guiding conception was that a person can most freely express aggression when he believes that everybody is doing it and, hence, if he wants to be aggressive, he is disposed to believe that everybody *is* doing it, e.g., that it is "human nature" to exploit and to make war upon one's neighbors. It goes without saying that such undifferentiated aggressiveness could easily, by means of propaganda, be directed against minority groups, or against any group the persecution of which was politically profitable.

h. *Projectivity*

46. The sexual orgies of the old Greeks and Romans are nursery school stuff compared to some of the goings-on in this country today, even in circles where people might least expect it.

56. After the war, we may expect a crime wave; the control of gangsters and ruffians will become a major social problem.

65. It is entirely possible that this series of wars and conflicts will be ended once and for all by a world-destroying earthquake, flood, or other catastrophe.

70. To a greater extent than most people realize, our lives are governed by plots hatched in secret by politicians.

73. Nowadays when so many different kinds of people move around so much and mix together so freely, a person has to be especially careful to protect himself against infection and disease.

The mechanism of projection was mentioned in connection with authoritarian aggression: the suppressed impulses of the authoritarian character tend to be projected onto other people who are then blamed out of hand. Projection is thus a device for keeping id drives ego-alien, and it may be taken as a sign of the ego's inadequacy in carrying out its function. Indeed, in one sense most of the items of the F scale are projective: they involve the assumption that judgments and interpretations of fact are distorted by psychological urges. The subject's tendency to project is utilized, in the present group of items, in an attempt to gain access to some of the deeper trends in his personality. If the antidemocratic individual is disposed to see in the outer world impulses which are suppressed in himself, and we wish to know what these impulses are, then something may be learned by noting what attributes he most readily, but unrealistically, ascribes to the world around him. If an individual insists that someone has hostile designs on him, and we can find no evidence that this is true, we have good reason to suspect that our subject himself has aggressive intentions and is seeking by means of projection to justify them. A notorious example is Father Coughlin's referring to anti-Semitism as a "defense mechanism," i.e., a protection of Gentiles against the supposed aggressive designs of the Jews. Similarly, it seemed that the greater a subject's preoccupation with "evil forces" in the world, as shown by his readiness to think about and to believe in the existence of such phenomena as wild erotic excesses, plots and conspiracies, and danger from natural catastrophes, the stronger would be his own unconscious urges of both sexuality and destructiveness.

i. *Sex*

31. Homosexuality is a particularly rotten form of delinquency and ought to be severely punished.

42. No matter how they act on the surface, men are interested in women for only one reason.

46. The sexual orgies of the old Greeks and Romans are nursery school stuff compared to some of the goings-on in this country today, even in circles where people might least expect it.

75. Sex crimes, such as rape and attacks on children, deserve more than mere imprisonment; such criminals ought to be publicly whipped.

Concern with overt sexuality is represented in the F scale by four items, two of which have appeared in connection with authoritarian aggression and one other as an expression of projectivity. This is an example of the close interaction of all the present variables; since, taken together they constitute a totality, it follows that a single question may pertain to two or more aspects of the whole. For purposes of analysis, sex may be abstracted from the totality as well as any of the other variables. Which of these variables are most basic must be determined by clinical study. In any case, it seemed that countercathexis (repression, reaction formation, projection) of sexual wishes was well qualified for special study.

The present variable is conceived of as ego-alien sexuality. A strong inclination to punish violators of sex mores (homosexuals, sex offenders) may be an expression of a general punitive attitude based on identification with ingroup authorities, but it also suggests that the subject's own sexual desires are suppressed and in danger of getting out of hand. A readiness to believe in "sex orgies" may be an indication of a general tendency to distort reality through projection, but sexual content would hardly be projected unless the subject had impulses of this same kind that were unconscious and strongly active. The three items pertaining to the punishment of homosexuals and of sex criminals and to the existence of sex orgies may, therefore, give some indication of the strength of the subject's unconscious sexual drives.

2. THE FORMULATION OF SCALE ITEMS

The considerations which guided the formulation of items in the scales described in previous chapters held as well for the F scale. There were several principles which, though a part of our general approach to scale construction, had particular significance for the present scale. In the first place, the item should have a maximum of *indirectness*, in the sense that it should not come close to the surface of overt prejudice and it should appear to be as far removed as possible from our actual interest. From this point of view, items such as 2 (Astrology) and 65 (Flood) were regarded as superior to items such as 74 (Tireless leaders) and 3 (Force to preserve). The latter two items, admittedly, could very well express certain aspects of an explicit fascist ideology, yet, as indicated above, statements touching upon the leader idea and the idea of force were definitely called for on theoretical grounds. More than this, there was a question of whether the aim of constructing a scale to correlate with E would be better served by the most indirect items or by the more direct ones, and in this first attempt it seemed the better part of wisdom to include some items of both kinds.

A second rule in item formulation was that each item should achieve a proper balance between irrationality and objective truth. If a statement was so "wild" that very few people would agree with it, or if it contained so large an element of truth that almost everyone would agree with it, then obviously it could not distinguish between prejudiced and unprejudiced subjects, and hence was of no value. Each item had to have some degree of rational appeal, but it had to be formulated in such a way that the rational aspect was not the major factor making for agreement or disagreement. This in many cases was a highly subtle matter; e.g., social historians might conceivably agree that Item 46 (Sex orgies) is probably quite true, yet it was here regarded as a possible index of projected sexuality, the argument being that most subjects would have no basis on which to judge its truth and would respond in accordance with their feelings. Since each item contained an element of objective truth or rational justification, an individual's response to a particular item might conceivably be determined by this fact alone. Hence, no item taken by itself could be regarded as diagnostic of potential fascism. The item's worth to the scale would have to be judged mainly in terms of its discriminatory power, and the meaning of an individual's response to it would have to be inferred from his total pattern of response. If a man marks +3 on Item 46 (Sex orgies) but marks —3 or —2 on Items 31 (Homosexuality) and 75 (Sex Crimes), it might be concluded that he is a man of knowledge and sophistication; but a +3 on Item 46, accompanying agreement with Items 31 and 75 would seem to be a fairly good indication of concern with sexuality.

Finally, it was required of each item that it contribute to the structural unity of the scale as a whole. It had to do its part in covering the diverse personality trends that entered into the broad pattern which the scale purported to measure. While it was granted that different individuals might give the same response to a given item for different reasons—and this apart from the matter of objective truth—it was necessary that the item carry sufficient meaningfulness so that any response to it could, when responses on all items were known, be interpreted in the light of our over-all theory.

C.   RESULTS WITH SUCCESSIVE FORMS OF THE F SCALE

1.   STATISTICAL PROPERTIES OF THE PRELIMINARY SCALE (FORM 78)

The preliminary F scale, made up of the 38 items listed above, was administered as a part of questionnaire Form 78 to four groups of subjects in the spring of 1945. These groups were described in Chapter III, and they are listed in Table 11 (III).

The scoring of the scale followed the procedures used with the A-S, E, and PEC scales. Except in the case of negative items, a mark of +3 was scored 7, +2 was scored as 6, and so on. Items 12, 20, and 28 are negative (they state the unprejudiced position), and here, of course, a mark of +3 was scored 1, and so on. Table 2 (VII) gives the reliability coefficients, mean scores per item, and Standard Deviations for these four groups. The mean reliability of .74 is within the range ordinarily regarded as adequate for group comparisons, but well below what is required of a truly accurate instrument. It might be said that, considering the diversity of elements that went into the F scale, the degree of consistency indicated by the present figure is all that could be expected of this preliminary form of the scale. The question was whether by revision of the scale it might be possible to attain the degree of reliability that characterizes the E scale, or whether we might be dealing here—as seemed to be the case in the PEC scale—with areas of response in which people are simply not very consistent.

It may be noted that the Professional Women show considerably more consistency than do the other groups of subjects, their reliability coefficient of .88 being in the neighborhood of that regularly obtained with the E scale. Since these women are considerably older, on the average, than our other subjects, it may be suggested that the higher reliability is due to their greater consistency of personality.

There appears to be no ready explanation for the low reliability found in the case of the Public Speaking Men. It may be noted that the Standard Deviation and the range for this group were also unusually small. Adequate explanation would require data from a larger sample of men and from an improved F scale.

Examination of Table 2 (VII) shows that there are no extremely high and no extremely low scores in any of the groups and that the obtained

TABLE 2 (VII)

RELIABILITY OF THE F SCALE (FORM 78) [a]

Property	Group				Over-all [b]
	A	B	C	D	
Reliability	.78	.56	.72	.88	.74
Mean (total)	3.94	3.72	3.75	3.43	3.71
Mean (odd half)	3.80	3.59	3.60	3.22	3.55
Mean (even half)	4.08	3.87	3.91	3.64	3.88
S.D. (total)	.71	.57	.70	.86	.71
S.D. (odd half)	.87	.71	.85	.94	.84
S.D. (even half)	.69	.65	.76	.84	.74
N	140	52	40	63	295
Range	2.12-5.26	2.55-4.87	2.39-5.05	1.68-5.63	1.68-5.63

[a]The four groups on which these data are based are:
Group A: U. C. Public Speaking Class Women.
Group B: U. C. Public Speaking Class Men.
Group C: U. C. Extension Psychology Class Women.
Group D: Professional Women.

[b]In obtaining the over-all means, the individual group means were not weighted by N.

means are near the neutral point. The relatively narrow distribution of scores—narrow as compared with those obtained from the other scales—may be in part a result of lack of consistency within the scale: unless the items are actually expressive of the same general trend, we could hardly expect an individual to respond to the great majority of them with consistent agreement or consistent disagreement. On the other hand, it is possible that the present sample does not contain subjects who are actually extreme with respect to the pattern which the F scale was designed to measure. This circumstance (lowered "range of talent") would tend to lower the reliability coefficients.

The F scale correlated .53 with A-S and .65 with E, in Form 78.

2. ITEM ANALYSIS AND REVISION OF THE PRELIMINARY SCALE

Data obtained from the initial four groups of subjects were used in attempting to improve the F scale—to increase its reliability and to shorten it somewhat, without loss in its breadth or meaningfulness. As with the other scales, the Discriminatory Power of an item provided the major statistical basis for judging its worth. Since it was intended that the F scale should not only have internal consistency but should also correlate highly with overt prejudice, attention was given both to the item's relation to the total F scale and to its ability to discriminate between high and low scorers on the A-S scale. An item's Discriminatory Power in terms of A-S (D. P.$_{A-S}$) is simply the difference between the mean score of the high A-S quartile on that item and the mean score of the low A-S quartile on the item. Table 3 (VII) gives for each item the mean score, the Discriminatory Power in terms of high vs. low scorers on F (D. P.$_F$), the D. P.$_F$'s order of merit, the D. P.$_{A-S}$, the latter's order of merit and, finally, the item's rank in a distribution of the sums of the D. P.$_F$ plus the D. P. $_{A-S}$. This final rank order was a convenient index of the item's statistical "goodness" for our over-all purpose.

The average D. P.$_F$, 1.80, is considerably below that found in the case of the A-S or E scales. Yet it indicates that, in general, the items yield statistically significant differences between the high and the low quartiles. Sixteen D. P.'s are above 2, 18 fall in the range 1–2, and only 4 are below 1. The means are, in general, fairly satisfactory; they average 3.71, which is near the neutral point of 4.0, and only 9 means are definitely too extreme, i.e., above 5.0 or below 3.0. As is to be expected, only 2 of the items with extreme means yield D. P.'s as great as 2.0.

The D. P.'s in terms of A-S are, of course, much lower; yet there are 17 items which appear to be significantly related to A-S, i.e., have a D. P.$_{A-S}$ greater than 1.0. Since it is the total F pattern that we expect to correlate with A-S and E, it is not necessary that each single F item by itself be significantly related to the latter. In general, items which are most discriminating in terms of F tend to discriminate best in terms of A-S, though there are some striking exceptions. In deciding whether to retain an item for use in a revised scale most weight was given to the D. P.$_F$ and to the general principles guiding our scale construction; these things being equal, the greater an item's D. P.$_{A-S}$, the greater its chances of being included in the revised scale.

TABLE 3 (VII)

MEANS AND DISCRIMINATORY POWERS OF THE F-SCALE ITEMS (FORM 78)[a]

Item	Mean	D.P.$_F$[b]	Rank D.P.$_F$	D.P.$_{AS}$[c]	Rank D.P.$_{AS}$	Final Rank[d] (D.P.$_F$+D.P.$_{AS}$)
2. (Astrology)	2.60	1.74	(22)	1.24	(11)	(18)
3. (Force to preserve)	3.04	1.98	(18)	1.05	(17)	(15)
6. (Women restricted)	2.93	1.75	(21)	0.41	(32)	(26)
9. (Red-blooded life)	3.99	2.04	(15)	-0.08	(35)	(29)
10. (Pearl Harbor Day)	2.22	2.20	(9)	1.37	(6)	(8)
12. (Modern church)	4.67	0.19	(38)	-1.18	(38)	(38)
14. (Rats... germs)	4.44	1.60	(26.5)	0.85	(24)	(23.5)
17. (Familiarity)	3.33	1.86	(19)	1.56	(4)	(10)
19. (One should avoid)	3.63	0.76	(36)	0.70	(27)	(35)
20. (Progressive education)	3.28	1.07	(33)	-0.25	(37)	(37)
23. (Undying love)	3.62	2.61	(4)	1.17	(13)	(5)
24. (Things unstable)	5.01	0.79	(35)	0.88	(22)	(33)
28. (Novels or stories)	3.02	1.29	(30)	0.76	(26)	(27)
30. (Reports of atrocities)	4.20	0.43	(37)	0.66	(28)	(36)
31. (Homosexuals)	3.22	2.16	(10)	1.18	(12)	(13)
32. (Essential for learning)	3.31	1.67	(24)	1.10	(16)	(20)
35. (Law in own hands)	2.50	1.42	(29)	0.62	(29.5)	(28)
38. (Emphasis in college)	3.91	1.20	(31)	1.14	(15)	(25)
39. (Supernatural force)	3.97	2.54	(6)	1.26	(9.5)	(4)
42. (For one reason)	2.06	1.05	(34)	0.59	(31)	(34)
43. (Sciences like chemistry)	4.35	2.79	(3)	0.97	(18)	(6)
46. (Sex orgies)	3.64	2.11	(12.5)	0.93	(20)	(14)
47. (Honor)	3.00	2.09	(14)	1.65	(3)	(7)
50. (Obedience and respect)	3.72	3.09	(1)	1.55	(5)	(2)
53. (Things too intimate)	4.82	1.99	(17)	-0.23	(36)	(32)
55. (Leisure)	5.20	2.11	(12.5)	1.26	(9.5)	(11)
56. (Crime wave)	4.60	1.16	(32)	0.62	(29.5)	(31)
58. (What a man does)	3.48	1.70	(23)	0.87	(23)	(22)
59. (Always war)	4.26	2.59	(5)	1.91	(2)	(3)
60. (Important values)	4.17	1.60	(26.5)	0.31	(34)	(30)
65. (World catastrophe)	2.58	1.55	(28)	0.90	(21)	(23.5)
66. (Books and movies)	4.10	2.48	(7)	0.38	(33)	(19)
67. (Eye to profit)	3.71	2.21	(8)	0.78	(25)	(17)
70. (Plots by politicians)	3.27	1.85	(20)	1.15	(14)	(16)
73. (Infection and disease)	4.79	2.02	(16)	1.34	(8)	(12)
74. (Tireless leaders)	5.00	1.66	(25)	0.94	(19)	(21)
75. (Sex crimes)	3.26	2.81	(2)	2.07	(1)	(1)
77. (No sane person)	4.12	2.12	(11)	1.36	(7)	(9)
Mean/Person/Item	3.71	1.80		0.89		

[a]The four groups on which these data are based are: *Group A*: U.C. Public Speaking Class Women (N = 140); *Group B*: U.C. Public Speaking Class Men (N = 52); *Group C*: U.C. Extension Psychology Class Women (N = 40); *Group D*: Professional Women (N = 63). In obtaining the over-all means, the individual group means were not weighted by N.

[b]D.P.$_F$ is based on the difference between the high quartile and the low quartile on the F scale distribution.

[c]D.P.$_{AS}$ is based on the difference between the high quartile and the low quartile on the A-S scale distribution. E.g., the D.P.$_{AS}$ of 1.24 on Item 2 indicates that the mean of the low quartile on A-S was 1.24 points lower than the mean of the high quartile on A-S.

[d]For each item the sum of D.P.$_F$ + D.P.$_{AS}$ is obtained. The final rank of an item is the rank of this sum in the distribution of sums for the whole scale.

We may now inquire what it is that distinguishes the items which turned out well statistically from those that turned out poorly. Can any general statements be made about each of these two groups of items that can serve as guides in the formulation of new items? The first question concerns the nine groups of items chosen to represent the variables that entered into the conceptualization of F. Do most of the items with high D. P.'s pertain to a few of the variables? Are there some variables which simply do not belong to the pattern we are considering? Three of the clusters, Sex, Authoritarian Aggression, and Authoritarian Submission, had mean D. P.'s above 2.0, the remaining clusters having mean D. P.'s in the range 1.26–1.80. Projectivity (1.70), Destructiveness and Cynicism (1.56), and Conventionalism (1.26) were the least satisfactory. However, it is to be noted that every cluster has within it at least one item with a D. P. above 2.0. At this stage, therefore, it seemed best not to eliminate any of the variables but to give attention to improving or replacing the poorer items found in each cluster.

Turning to a consideration of items which proved to be outstandingly good in the statistical sense, we note that Item 75 (Sex crimes) leads all the rest, i.e., has the highest sum of D. P.$_F$ plus D. P.$_{A-S}$. This item represents rather well the ideal to which we aspired in formulating items for the F scale. Not only is there a wide distribution of responses, with a mean fairly near the neutral point, but the item combines, apparently in a very effective way, several ideas which according to theory have crucial roles in prejudice: the underlying interest in the more primitive aspects of sex, the readiness for all-out physical aggressiveness, the justification of aggression by an appeal to moralistic values. More than this, the item seems to be sufficiently free of any logical or automatic connection with overt prejudice. That the next best item, 50 (Obedience and respect), should be outstandingly differentiating is not surprising since this kind of authoritarianism is a well-known aspect of the fascist outlook. The device of putting the authoritarianism in a context of child training seems to remove it from the surface of ethnocentrism; but whether or not this is true, the item pertains to an aspect of the fascist philosophy that could in no case be left out of account.

Third in the rank order of goodness is Item 59, "Human nature being what it is, there will always be war and conflict." This item, from the Destructiveness and Cynicism cluster, expresses several ideas which are particularly important in the F syndrome. In addition to an element of overt antipacifist opinion, there is contempt for men and acceptance of the "survival of the fittest" idea as a rationalization for aggressiveness. The next item, 39 (Supernatural force), seems to express very well the tendency to shift responsibility to outside forces beyond one's own control. This is a manifestation of what has been termed ego weakness; the item has also been placed in the Authoritarian Submission cluster on the ground that faith in a supernatural force is related to faith in ingroup authorities. It was not expected that the presence of religious feeling and belief would by itself be significant for prejudice; the aim in devising the present item was to compose a statement which was so extreme that not too many subjects would agree with it and which placed enough emphasis upon "total allegiance" and obedience "without question" so that the uncritically submissive person could distinguish himself. The mean of 3.97 and the D. P.$_F$ of 2.54 indicate that this aim was largely realized. Item 23 (Undying love), which ranked fifth in order of goodness, expresses extreme moral conventionality and ingroup feeling related to the family. It has a place in both the Authoritarian Submission and the Authoritarian Aggression clusters, because it includes both allegiance to the ingroup and a punishing attitude ("He is indeed contemptible") toward those who violate this value. The statement is so exaggerated, so expressive, as it seems, of the "protesting too much" attitude that we may wonder if strong agreement with it does not mask underlying but inhibited rebellious hostility against parents and parent figures.

Concerning all five of these items it may be said that they are highly diverse in their surface content, that they pertain to various aspects of the underlying theory—superego, ego, and id are expressed—and that with the possible exception of Item 50 (Obedience and respect) they are highly indirect in the present sense of the term. Indeed, as one examines further the ranking of the items in terms of their Discriminatory Powers—(Sciences like chemistry), (Honor), (Pearl Harbor Day), (No sane person), (Familiarity), (Leisure), (Infection and disease)—he may note that, in general, items which are best in the statistical sense are those which seem best in their formulation and in terms of our over-all theory and method of approach.

Items which turned out to be poor in the statistical sense are, in retrospect, easy to criticize. In some instances there was a failure in formulation: the statement was so unclear or ambiguous that many of the subjects, apparently, drew from it different implications from those intended. This would seem to have been true particularly of Items 12 (Modern church) and 20 (Progressive education). In other instances, e.g., Items 24 (Things unstable), 74 (Tireless leaders), and 58 (Crime wave), the statements contained too large an element of truth or rational justification and so appealed, as shown by the high mean scores, to both high and low scorers. Again, some of the items were too crude or openly aggressive, so that most of the high scorers as well as the low scorers tended to disagree. For example, Items 42 (For one reason) and 35 (Law in own hands) have both low means and low D. P.'s.

3. THE SECOND F SCALE: FORM 60

In preparing the new form of the questionnaire, the E and PEC scales were shortened so drastically that a comparatively long F scale (34 items) could still be used without allowing the total number of scale items to go above 60. Since we were still faced with the task of producing a reliable F scale, with-

TABLE 4 (VII)
THE F SCALE: FORM 60

a. *Conventionalism:* Rigid adherence to conventional, middle-class values.

  1. Obedience and respect for authority are the most important virtues children should learn.

  6. A person who has bad manners, habits, and breeding can hardly expect to be liked and accepted by decent people.

  53. One main trouble today is that people talk too much and work too little.

b. *Authoritarian Submission:* Submissive, uncritical attitude toward idealized moral authorities of the ingroup.

  1. Obedience and respect for authority are the most important virtues children should learn.

  7. Science has carried man very far, but there are many important things that can never possibly be understood by the human mind.

  11. Every person should have complete faith in some supernatural power whose decisions he obeys without question.

  23. Young people sometimes get rebellious ideas, but as they grow up they ought to get over them and settle down.

  29. No sane, normal, decent person could ever think of hurting a close friend or relative.

  32. What this country needs most, more than laws and political programs, is a few courageous, tireless, devoted leaders in whom the people can put their faith.

  44. In order for us to do good work, it is necessary that our bosses outline carefully what is to be done and exactly how to go about it.

c. *Authoritarian Aggression:* Tendency to be on the lookout for, and to condemn, reject, and punish people who violate conventional values.

  6. A person who has bad manners, habits, and breeding can hardly expect to be liked and accepted by decent people.

  17. An insult to our honor should always be punished.

  19. What the youth needs most is strict discipline, rugged determination, and the will to work and fight for family and country.

  22. The trouble with letting everybody have a say in running the government is that so many people are just naturally stupid or full of wild ideas.

  34. Sex crimes, such as rape and attacks on children, deserve more than mere imprisonment; such criminals ought to be publicly whipped, or worse.

  39. There is hardly anything lower than a person who does not feel a great love, gratitude, and respect for his parents.

  49. Most of our social problems would be solved if we could somehow get rid of the immoral, crooked, and feebleminded people.

  53. One main trouble today is that people talk too much and work too little.

  58. Homosexuals are nothing but degenerates and ought to be severely punished.

d. *Anti-intraception:* Opposition to the subjective, the imaginative, the tender-minded.

    16. When a person has a problem or worry, it is best for him not to think about it, but to keep busy with more cheerful things.

    30. Some cases of feeblemindedness are caused by overstudy.

    45. Nowadays more and more people are prying into matters that should remain personal and private.

    53. One main trouble today is that people talk too much and work too little.

e. *Superstition and Stereotypy:* The belief in mystical determinants of the individual's fate; the disposition to think in rigid categories.

    7. Science has carried man very far, but there are many important things that can never possibly be understood by the human mind.

    11. Every person should have complete faith in some supernatural power whose decisions he obeys without question.

    18. It is more than just chance that Japan had an earthquake on Pearl Harbor Day, December 7, 1944.

    24. Some people are born with the urge to jump from high places.

    30. Some cases of feeblemindedness are caused by overstudy.

    35. People can be divided into two distinct classes: the weak and the strong.

    40. Some day it will probably be shown that astrology can explain a lot of things.

    46. It is possible that wars and social troubles will be ended once and for all by an earthquake or flood that will destroy the whole world.

    50. It's a mistake to trust anybody who doesn't look you straight in the eye.

f. *Power and "Toughness":* Preoccupation with the dominance-submission, strong-weak, leader-follower dimension; identification with power figures; overemphasis upon the conventionalized attributes of the ego; exaggerated assertion of strength and toughness.

    2. No weakness or difficulty can hold us back if we have enough will power.

    5. Any red-blooded American will fight to defend his property.

    17. An insult to our honor should always be punished.

    19. What the youth needs most is strict discipline, rugged determination, and the will to work and fight for family and country.

    32. What this country needs most, more than laws and political programs, is a few courageous, tireless, devoted leaders in whom the people can put their faith.

    35. People can be divided into two distinct classes: the weak and the strong.

    57. Most people don't realize how much our lives are controlled by plots hatched in secret by politicians.

g. *Destructiveness and Cynicism:* Generalized hostility, vilification of the human.

    10. Human nature being what it is, there will always be war and conflict.

25. Familiarity breeds contempt.
41. The true American way of life is disappearing so fast that force may be necessary to preserve it.

h. *Projectivity:* The disposition to believe that wild and dangerous things go on in the world; the projection outward of unconscious emotional impulses.

36. Nowadays when so many different kinds of people move around so much and mix together so freely, a person has to be especially careful to protect himself against infection and disease.
45. Nowadays more and more people are prying into matters that should remain personal and private.
46. It is possible that wars and social troubles will be ended once and for all by an earthquake or flood that will destroy the whole world.
52. The wild sex life of the old Greeks and Romans was tame compared to some of the goings-on in this country, even in places where people might least expect it.
57. Most people don't realize how much our lives are controlled by plots hatched in secret by politicians.

i. *Sex:* Exaggerated concern with sexual "goings-on."

34. Sex crimes, such as rape and attacks on children, deserve more than mere imprisonment; such criminals ought to be publicly whipped or worse.
52. The wild sex life of the old Greeks and Romans was tame compared to some of the goings-on in this country, even in places where people might least expect it.
58. Homosexuals are nothing but degenerates and ought to be severely punished.

out sacrificing breadth or meaningfulness, it seemed the better part of wisdom not to undertake much shortening of it at this stage.

The 19 items from the F scale (Form 78) that ranked highest in order of goodness were retained, in the same or slightly revised form, in the new scale. Thus, statistical differentiating power of the item was the main basis of selection. As stated above, however, the items which came out best statistically were, in general, those which seemed best from the point of view of theory, so that retaining them required no compromise with the original purpose of the scale. Of these items, 5 were changed in no way; revision of the others involved change in wording but not in essential meaning, the aim being to avoid too much uniformity of agreement or disagreement and, hence, to produce mean scores as close as possible to the neutral point.

Given 19 items of known dependability, the task was to formulate 15 additional ones which, singly, met the requirements of good items and which, taken together, covered the ground mapped out according to our theory. Here, criteria other than statistical ones played an important role. In attempting to achieve a maximum of *indirectness* we not only eliminated items which were too openly aggressive (they had low D. P.'s anyway) but retained, in

a slightly revised form, Item 65 (World catastrophe) despite its relatively
low D. P. (R. O. 23.5), because it expressed a theoretically important idea
and appeared on the surface to be almost completely removed from "race"
prejudice and fascism. In the name of *breadth*, Item 67 (Eye to profit),
whose D. P. was not low (R. O. 21), was eliminated because of its too great
similarity to the highly discriminating Item 59 (Always war). To cover a
great variety of ideas as efficiently as possible, two or more of them were
combined in the same statement, e.g., "Any *red-blooded American* will *fight*
to defend his *property*" or ". . . people *think* too much and *work* too little."
With attention to these criteria, and to *meaningfulness, contribution to the
structural unity of the scale*, and proper degree of *rational justification*, 4
items from the F scale (Form 78) whose D. P. rank orders were lower than
19, were revised and 11 new items were formulated to complete the new
form. The 34 items, grouped according to the variables which they were
supposed to represent, are shown in table 4 (VII).

Reliability of the scale, mean score per item, S. D., and the range of scores
for each of the five groups to whom the F scale (Form 60) was given are
shown in Table 5 (VII). The reliability of the scale is a considerable improvement over that obtained with Form 78 (.87 as compared with .74); it

TABLE 5 (VII)

RELIABILITY OF THE F SCALE (FORM 60) [a]

Property	Group					Over-all [b]
	I	II	III	IV	V	
Reliability	86	.91	.89	.87	.81	.87
Mean (total)	3.32	3.39	3.82	3.74	3.25	3.50
Mean (odd half)	3.41	3.42	4.09	3.78	3.19	3.58
Mean (even half)	3.24	3.36	3.56	3.73	3.28	3.43
S.D. (total)	.86	.96	.93	.81	.71	.85
S.D. (odd half)	.97	1.03	.99	.77	.83	.92
S.D. (even half)	.75	.96	.97	.93	.76	.87
N	47	54	57	68	60	286
Range	1.00-5.50	1.24-5.50	1.82-4.38	2.24-5.62	1.97-5.35	1.82-5.62

[a]The five groups on which these data are based are:
   Group I: University of Oregon Student Women.
   Group II: University of Oregon and University of California Student Women.
   Group III: University of Oregon and University of California Student Men.
   Group IV: Oregon Service Club Men.
   Group V: Oregon Service Club Men (A Part only).

[b]In obtaining the over-all means, the individual group means were not weighted
   by N.

is as high as that of the shortened E scale (.87 as compared with .86) and much better than the reliability of .70 for the shortened PEC scale. The mean scores are not quite so close to the neutral point as was the case with Form 78 (over-all mean of 3.5 as compared with 3.7); the range and the variability, however, are somewhat greater.[3]

Inspection of the Discriminatory Powers of the items, as shown in Table 6 (VII), shows once again considerable improvement over Form 78. The mean D. P.$_F$ is now 2.15 as compared with 1.80 for Form 78. Three D. P.'s are above 3.0, 18 fall in the range 2.0–3.0, 12 are in the range 1.0–2.0, and only 1 is below 1.0. The mean D. P. in terms of E, 1.53, is notably greater than the mean D. P.$_{A-S}$, .89, found with Form 78. There are 28 items with a mean D. P.$_E$ greater than 1.0; these F items are significantly related to ethnocentrism at the 5 per cent level of confidence or better. Each of the variables that entered into the F scale—Conventionalism, Superstition, etc.— is represented by items that are satisfactorily differentiating.   •

The correlation between the F scale (Form 60) and E is, on the average, .69. This is a considerable improvement over the results obtained with Form 78, where F correlated .53 with A-S and .65 with E, though it is still not quite as high as its intended functions require.

4. THE THIRD F SCALE: FORMS 45 AND 40

Although the F scale (Form 60) might be described as a fairly adequate instrument, it still had some obvious shortcomings, and it was hoped that these might be removed before the scale was used with numerous groups of subjects. It still contained a number of items so poor statistically that they contributed almost nothing to the purpose of the scale. Also, there were two items (numbers 12 and 18) which, despite their ranking 1 and 9 in order of

---

[3] It may be reported here that in the case of the University of Oregon Student Women Form 60 of the questionnaire was administered in two parts: Part A contained the F scale and one half of the PEC scale and Part B, administered a day later, contained the E scale and the other half of the PEC scale. The purpose of this proceeding was to test whether responses to the items of one scale were affected by the presence within the same questionnaire of items from other scales. Apparently this variation in the manner of administration made little or no difference. When the results for the University of Oregon Student Women (Group 1) are compared with those for the University of Oregon and University of California Student Women (Group 2)—a fairly similar group—the differences in reliability, mean score, and S.D. appear to be insignificant. The same is true in the cases of the E and PEC scales, and reference to Table 14 (IV) and to Table 5 (V) will show. The mean for the group of Oregon Service Club Men (Group V) who received only the A part of Form 60 does seem to be somewhat lower than that of the other group of Oregon Service Club Men. This difference cannot, however, be attributed to the difference in the form of the questionnaire. More important, probably, is the fact that Group V, in contrast to the other group, received the questionnaire *after* having listened to a talk on "What to do with Germany." There was at least an implicit connection between the content of the talk and the content of the F scale; as one of the subjects who sensed this connection said afterwards to our staff member, "You should have given the questionnaire before your talk."

TABLE 6 (VII)

MEANS AND DISCRIMINATORY POWERS OF THE F-SCALE ITEMS (FORM 60) [a]

Item	Mean	D.P.$_F$ [b]	Rank D.P.$_F$	D.P.$_E$ [c]	Rank D.P.$_E$	Final Rank [d] (D.P.$_F$+D.P.$_E$)
1. (Obedience & respect)	4.86	2.39	(14)	1.52	(17)	(13)
2. (Will power)	4.44	2.50	(11)	1.46	(19)	(12)
5. (Red blooded American)	5.49	1.46	(29.5)	1.18	(25.5)	(27)
6. (Bad manners)	5.30	1.80	(23)	1.56	(13.5)	(22)
7. (Science)	4.98	1.71	(24)	1.32	(23)	(25)
10. (War & conflict)	4.46	1.67	(26)	1.70	(10)	(21)
11. (Supernatural power)	3.60	2.91	(4)	1.38	(21)	(10)
12. (Germans & Japs)	3.71	3.16	(3)	2.83	(1)	(1)
16. (Cheerful things)	3.15	2.08	(20.5)	1.18	(25.5)	(23)
17. (Honor)	3.14	2.46	(12)	2.34	(4)	(7)
18. (Pearl Harbor Day)	2.19	2.51	(10)	1.83	(9)	(9)
19. (Discipline & determination)	3.68	3.17	(2)	2.28	(6.5)	(3)
22. (Not everybody in gov't.)	2.74	1.46	(29.5)	1.17	(27)	(28)
23. (Rebellious ideas)	4.30	2.70	(7)	2.29	(5)	(5)
24. (Born with urge)	2.87	2.60	(8)	2.28	(6.5)	(6)
25. (Familiarity)	3.30	2.08	(20.5)	1.33	(22)	(20)
29. (No sane person)	3.55	2.82	(6)	1.95	(8)	(8)
30. (Feebleminded)	1.84	1.43	(32.5)	0.91	(30)	(30)
32. (Devoted leaders)	4.49	2.42	(13)	1.43	(20)	(15)
34. (Sex crime)	3.43	2.83	(5)	2.52	(3)	(4)
35. (Two classes)	1.44	0.73	(34)	0.38	(34)	(34)
36. (Infection & disease)	4.80	1.68	(25)	1.03	(28)	(26)
39. (Love for parents)	3.16	3.28	(1)	2.56	(2)	(2)
40. (Astrology)	2.56	2.15	(17)	1.66	(11)	(16)
41. (Force to preserve)	2.48	2.31	(15)	1.56	(13.5)	(14)
44. (Bosses outline)	2.46	1.60	(27)	0.50	(33)	(33)
45. (Prying)	3.48	2.52	(9)	1.56	(13.5)	(11)
46. (Flood)	2.15	1.43	(32.5)	0.94	(29)	(29)
49. (Rid of immoral people)	2.74	2.12	(19)	1.56	(13.5)	(18)
50. (Mistake to trust)	2.12	1.45	(31)	0.84	(31)	(31)
52. (Sex life)	3.18	2.13	(18)	1.50	(18)	(19)
53. (Talk too much)	3.87	1.83	(22)	1.24	(24)	(24)
57. (Plots)	4.24	1.55	(28)	0.63	(32)	(32)
58. (Homosexuals)	2.29	2.20	(16)	1.54	(16)	(17)
Mean/Person/Item	3.42	2.15		1.53		

[a] The four groups on which these data are based are:
Group I: University of Oregon Student Women (N = 47)
Group II: University of Oregon and University of California Student Women (N=54)
Group III: University of Oregon and University of California Student Men (N = 57)
Group IV: Oregon Service Club Men (N = 68)

In obtaining the over-all means, the individual group means were not weighted according to N.

[b] D.P.$_F$ is based on the difference between the high quartile and the low quartile of the F scale distribution.

[c] D.P.$_E$ is based on the difference between the high quartile and the low quartile of the E scale distribution. e.g., the D.P.$_E$ of 1.52 on Item 1 indicates that the mean of the low quartile on E was 1.52 points lower than the mean of the high quartile on E.

[d] For each item the sum of D.P.$_F$+D.P.$_E$ is obtained. The final rank of an item is the rank of this sum in the distribution of sums for the whole scale.

goodness, had to be dropped in the early fall of 1945 because they had lost their war-period timeliness. More than this, experience had shown that when it came to working with highly diverse groups outside the University, a questionnaire shorter than Form 60 was highly desirable. The other scales having already been reduced to an absolute minimum, the F scale had now to bear some of the pruning. Yet, such pruning had to be extremely judicious if the scale was not to lose in comprehensiveness and if, as was hoped, its reliability and its correlation with E were to be raised. Thirty was the number of items decided upon.

Revision consisted mainly in discarding seven items and adding three new ones. Two excellent items were discarded because, as mentioned above, they were no longer timely. Five items were taken out because they had relatively very low D. P.'s and because other items seemed to fulfill the same functions better: 44 (Bosses outline, R. O. 33), 50 (Mistake to trust, R. O. 31), 30 (Feebleminded, R. O. 30), 22 (Not everybody in government, R. O. 28), and 5 (Red-blooded American, R. O. 27). Several items which ranked low in terms of D. P. were thoroughly revised and kept in the new scale: 35 (Two classes, R. O. 34), 57 (Plots, R. O. 32), and 46 (Flood, R. O. 29).

One of the three new items was the following: "The businessman and the manufacturer are much more important to society than the artist and the professor." This is a slightly revised version of an item which appeared in the earlier forms of the PEC scale, where it had proved to be discriminatory both in terms of PEC and in terms of E. Since this item expresses rather well both conventionalism and anti-intraception, it appeared to be a promising addition to the F scale.

A second new item was, "It is best to use some prewar authorities in Germany to keep order and prevent chaos." At the time this item was formulated —late summer 1945—General Patton had been accused of using German Nazis and extremely conservative bigwigs to help carry out certain phases of the occupation. His critics argued that this was a poor way to secure the cooperation of democratic elements in Germany; his defenders pointed to the necessity for promoting efficiency and preventing chaos. The issue was a lively one; and it appeared that an item bearing upon it might give the high scorer a chance to express his admiration for military authority, his means-centeredness, his preoccupation with order vs. chaos. (That the item did not work very well is probably due to inadequate wording: we had not dared to be sufficiently explicit about *which* prewar authorities were to be used, so that "prewar" could be taken to mean "pre-Nazi.")

"Nobody ever learned anything really important except through suffering," was the third of the new items. Here the temptation—constantly present during each revision of the F scale—to test a new hypothesis, or better, to obtain quantitative data bearing upon a phenomenon which in clinical study had appeared in relation to the general pattern of potential fascism, became

TABLE 7 (VII)
F-Scale Clusters: Forms 45 and 40

a. *Conventionalism:* Rigid adherence to conventional, middle-class values.

1. Obedience and respect for authority are the most important virtues children should learn.

12. A person who has bad manners, habits, and breeding can hardly expect to get along with decent people.

37. If people would talk less and work more, everybody would be better off.

41. The business man and the manufacturer are much more important to society than the artist and the professor.

b. *Authoritarian Submission:* Submissive, uncritical attitude toward idealized moral authorities of the ingroup.

1. Obedience and respect for authority are the most important virtues children should learn.

4. Science has its place, but there are many important things that can never possibly be understood by the human mind.

8. Every person should have complete faith in some supernatural power whose decisions he obeys without question.

21. Young people sometimes get rebellious ideas, but as they grow up they ought to get over them and settle down.

23. What this country needs most, more than laws and political programs, is a few courageous, tireless, devoted leaders in whom the people can put their faith.

42. No sane, normal, decent person could ever think of hurting a close friend or relative.

44. Nobody ever learned anything really important except through suffering.

c. *Authoritarian Aggression:* Tendency to be on the lookout for, and to condemn, reject, and punish people who violate conventional values.

12. A person who has bad manners, habits, and breeding can hardly expect to get along with decent people.

13. What the youth needs most is strict discipline, rugged determination, and the will to work and fight for family and country.

19. An insult to our honor should always be punished.

25. Sex crimes, such as rape and attacks on children, deserve more than mere imprisonment; such criminals ought to be publicly whipped, or worse.

27. There is hardly anything lower than a person who does not feel a great love, gratitude, and respect for his parents.

34. Most of our social problems would be solved if we could somehow get rid of the immoral, crooked, and feebleminded people.

37. If people would talk less and work more, everybody would be better off.

39. Homosexuals are hardly better than criminals and ought to be severely punished.

d. *Anti-intraception:* Opposition to the subjective, the imaginative, the
    tender-minded.

    9. When a person has a problem or worry, it is best for him not to
    think about it, but to keep busy with more cheerful things.

   31. Nowadays more and more people are prying into matters that
    should remain personal and private.

   37. If people would talk less and work more, everybody would be
    better off.

   41. The businessman and the manufacturer are much more important
    to society than the artist and the professor.

e. *Superstition and Stereotypy:* The belief in mystical determinants of
    the individual's fate; the disposition to think in rigid categories.

   4. Science has its place, but there are many important things that
    can never possibly be understood by the human mind.

   8. Every person should have complete faith in some supernatural
    power whose decisions he obeys without question.

  16. Some people are born with an urge to jump from high places.

  26. People can be divided into two distinct classes: the weak and the
    strong.

  29. Some day it will probably be shown that astrology can explain
    a lot of things.

  33. Wars and social troubles may someday be ended by an earth-
    quake or flood that will destroy the whole world.

f. *Power and "Toughness":* Preoccupation with the dominance-submis-
    sion, strong-weak, leader-follower dimension; identification with
    power figures; overemphasis upon the conventionalized attributes
    of the ego; exaggerated assertion of strength and toughness.

   2. No weakness or difficulty can hold us back if we have enough
    will power.

  13. What the youth needs most is strict discipline, rugged deter-
    mination, and the will to work and fight for family and country.

  19. An insult to our honor should always be punished.

  22. It is best to use some prewar authorities in Germany to keep order
    and prevent chaos.

  23. What this country needs most, more than laws and political pro-
    grams, is a few courageous, tireless, devoted leaders in whom the
    people can put their faith.

  26. People can be divided into two distinct classes: the weak and the
    strong.

  38. Most people don't realize how much our lives are controlled by
    plots hatched in secret places.

g. *Destructiveness and Cynicism:* Generalized hostility, vilification of
    the human.

   6. Human nature being what it is, there will always be war and
    conflict.

  43. Familiarity breeds contempt.

h. *Projectivity:* The disposition to believe that wild and dangerous things go on in the world; the projection outwards of unconscious emotional impulses.

18. Nowadays when so many different kinds of people move around and mix together so much, a person has to protect himself especially carefully against catching an infection or disease from them.

31. Nowadays more and more people are prying into matters that should remain personal and private.

33. Wars and social troubles may someday be ended by an earthquake or flood that will destroy the whole world.

35. The wild sex life of the old Greeks and Romans was tame compared to some of the goings-on in this country, even in places where people might least expect it.

38. Most people don't realize how much our lives are controlled by plots hatched in secret places.

i. *Sex:* Exaggerated concern with sexual "goings-on."

25. Sex crimes, such as rape and attacks on children, deserve more than mere imprisonment; such criminals ought to be publicly whipped, or worse.

35. The wild sex life of the old Greeks and Romans was tame compared to some of the goings-on in this country, even in places where people might least expect it.

39. Homosexuals are hardly better than criminals and ought to be severely punished.

too strong. The item was taken from an editorial in a prominent picture magazine, where it had appeared in a context of political reaction. It seemed well adapted to bring out the sado-masochistic theme believed to be prominent in the personality of the high scorer: he believes that he *has* suffered and, therefore, knows the important things and that those who have not succeeded in raising their status, i.e., the underprivileged, should suffer more if they hope to improve their lot. The item did not work very well, its rank in order of goodness for men being 29. (Its D. P., 1.70, is still significant at the 5 per cent level, however.) It seems that this was partly because many subjects thought it unreasonable (the mean was 2.54), and partly because, where it was agreed with, it probably appealed to different subjects for different reasons: if it tapped the deep-lying sado-masochistic structures in some high scorers, it also appealed to the surface masochism, and perhaps to the intraceptiveness, of some low scorers.

The final F items, grouped according to the variables to which they pertain, are presented in Table 7 (VII).

Reliability of the scale, mean score per item, S. D., and range for each of the fourteen groups (total N = 1518) taking Form 40 and/or 45 are given in Table 8 (VII). The average of the reliability coefficients is .90, their range .81 to .97. Not only is there a slight improvement in reliability over Form 60 (av. $r = .87$) and a very marked improvement over the original Form 78

TABLE 8 (VII)

RELIABILITY OF THE F SCALE (FORMS 40 AND 45)

Group	N	Reliability	Mean	S.D.	Range
Form 40:					
George Washington Univ. Women	132	.84	3.51	.90	1.2 – 5.4
California Service Club Men	63	.94	4.08	1.03	1.8 – 7.0
Middle-Class Men	69	.92	3.69	1.22	1.3 – 6.7
Middle-Class Women	154	.93	3.62	1.26	1.1 – 6.7
Working-Class Men	61	.88	4.19	1.18	1.8 – 6.9
Working-Class Women	53	.97	3.86	1.67	1.3 – 6.6
Los Angeles Men	117	.92	3.68	1.17	1.1 – 6.0
Los Angeles Women	130	.91	3.49	1.13	1.2 – 5.8
Mean[a]	779	.91	3.76	1.20	1.3 – 6.4
Form 45:					
Testing Class Women	59	.89	3.62	.99	1.3 – 5.9
San Quentin Men Prisoners	110	.87	4.73	.86	2.0 – 6.8
Psychiatric Clinic Women[b]	71	.94	3.69	1.30	1.0 – 6.3
Psychiatric Clinic Men[b]	50	.89	3.82	1.01	1.7 – 5.9
Mean	290	.90	3.96	1.04	1.5 – 6.2
Form 40 and Form 45:					
Employment Service Men Veterans	106	.89	3.74	1.04	1.2 – 5.8
Maritime School Men	343	.81	4.06	.77	1.6 – 6.1
Mean[a]	449	.85	3.90	.90	1.4 – 5.9
Over-all mean	1518	.90	3.84	1.10	1.4 – 6.3

[a]In obtaining the combined group means, the individual group means were not weighted by N.

[b]Due to a substitution of forms, the F scale for the Psychiatric Clinic subjects contained only 28 items.

(av. $r = .74$), but the scale has now been developed to a point where it meets rigorous statistical requirements. A reliability of .90 may be interpreted to mean that the scale can place individuals along a dimension—in this case a broad and complex dimension—with a small margin of error. In other words, the score attained by an individual can be relied upon in the sense that chance errors of measurement have been minimized, so that in a repetition of the scale, at a time when political-socioeconomic conditions were generally the same as before, his new score would either be the same as his first or fall within narrow limits above or below it. The degree of reliability attained here is within the range which characterizes acceptable intelligence tests.

The means, though they vary from one group to another (a matter to be discussed later), are fairly close, on the whole, to the neural point. As is to be expected from administration of the scale to a great variety of subjects, the range and the S. D. are greater than in previous forms. While no distribution curves have actually been made, the scatter diagrams indicate that they would be fairly normal in form (symmetrical but slightly platykurtic).

a. INTERNAL CONSISTENCY. The Discriminatory Powers of the scale items, as shown in Table 9 (VII), are considerably higher on the average (2.85) than in the case of Form 60 (2.15). All of the items differentiate significantly between the high and the low quartiles. It is to be noted that numerous items taken over without change from Form 60 work much better here than in that instance. This is probably due in part to the fact that the diverse groups given Form 45-40 included more extreme scorers and in part to improvement of the scale as a whole: a good item differentiates the more sharply between the upper and lower quartiles the more successfully the total scale distinguishes individuals who are actually extreme with respect to the trends being measured.

The fact that the D. P.'s are somewhat higher, on the average, for women than for men is deserving of some comment. This phenomenon would seem to be connected with the fact that there were three groups of men—Maritime School, San Quentin Inmates, and Working-Class Men—in whose cases the reliability of the scale was relatively low (.81–.88). Since these groups of men were less educated than most of our subjects, there is considerable likelihood that they failed to understand some of the scale items, a circumstance that would work against high D. P.'s as well as against reliability. Moreover, these are the three groups who, of all those studied, obtained the highest mean scores. It can be inferred from this that there was too much general agreement with some of the items, something which, as we have seen, tends to lower the D. P. This raises the question of whether we did not encounter in these groups not only more extreme manifestations of potential fascism than had been anticipated but also patterns of prefascist personality trends that the F scale did not adequately cover. Most of the work that went into the construction and revision of the scale was performed with groups of subjects in which the high scorers were, in the main, highly conventional. The procedure of retaining items which differentiated best within these groups was probably not the best one for constructing an instrument which would work with maximum efficiency in groups where tendencies to psychopathy and delinquency were much more pronounced. This is a matter to be discussed in more detail later.

Despite the absolute differences in the D. P.'s between men and women,

TABLE 9 (VII)

MEANS AND DISCRIMINATORY POWERS OF THE F-SCALE ITEMS (FORMS 40 AND 45)[a]

Item	Men's Groups			Women's Groups			Men and Women Combined			
	Mean	D.P.	Rank	Mean	D.P.	Rank	Mean	Rank	D.P.	Rank
1. (Obedience & respect)	5.41	2.70	(1)	4.67	3.91	(4)	5.04	(2)	3.31	(6.5)
2. (Will power)	5.16	2.48	(4)	4.94	2.67	(1)	5.05	(1)	2.58	(22)
4. (Science)	4.20	2.55	(15)	4.32	2.89	(6)	4.26	(11)	2.72	(17)
6. (War and conflict)	4.69	2.32	(7)	4.26	2.98	(8)	4.48	(6)	2.65	(19)
8. (Supernatural power)	3.47	3.19	(22)	3.43	3.92	(18)	3.45	(20)	3.56	(4)
9. (Cheerful things)	3.80	2.52	(18)	3.71	3.14	(15)	3.76	(17)	2.83	(16)
12. (Bad manners)	5.22	1.77	(2)	4.80	2.60	(3)	5.01	(3.5)	2.19	(26.5)
13. (Discipline & determination)	4.59	3.60	(8)	4.03	4.03	(11)	4.31	(10)	3.82	(2)
16. (Born with urge)	3.75	2.54	(19)	3.25	2.47	(19)	3.50	(19)	2.51	(24)
18. (Infection and disease)	4.53	2.82	(10)	4.13	3.52	(10)	4.33	(9)	3.17	(8.5)
19. (Honor)	3.50	2.74	(21)	3.11	3.12	(25)	3.31	(22)	2.93	(14)
21. (Rebellious ideas)	4.71	3.04	(6)	4.14	3.72	(9)	4.43	(7)	3.38	(5)
22. (Germany)	4.26	1.98	(14)	3.74	2.40	(14)	4.00	(14.5)	2.19	(26.5)
23. (Devoted leaders)	5.18	2.32	(3)	4.84	2.87	(2)	5.01	(3.5)	2.60	(21)
25/24. (Sex crimes)	4.54	3.68	(9)	4.29	4.32	(7)	4.41	(8)	4.00	(1)
26/25. (Weak and strong)	3.05	2.94	(26)	2.48	3.39	(29)	2.77	(26)	3.17	(8.5)
27/26. (Undying love)	4.09	3.76	(16)	3.21	3.66	(20)	3.65	(18)	3.71	(3)
29/27. (Astrology)	3.31	2.79	(24)	3.16	3.33	(22.5)	3.24	(24)	3.06	(11)
30/28. (Force to preserve)	2.92	2.54	(27)	2.47	2.73	(27.5)	2.70	(27)	2.64	(20)
31/29. (Prying)	4.34	2.98	(12)	3.66	3.02	(16)	4.00	(14.5)	3.00	(12)
33/30. (Earthquake)	2.58	1.76	(28)	2.59	2.19	(26)	2.59	(28)	1.98	(29)
34/31. (Immoral people)	3.38	2.90	(23)	3.16	2.85	(22.5)	3.27	(23)	2.88	(15)
35/32. (Wild sex life)	4.04	2.48	(17)	3.60	2.93	(17)	3.82	(16)	2.71	(18)
37/33. (Talk less)	4.88	2.84	(5)	4.59	3.10	(5)	4.74	(5)	2.97	(13)
38/34. (Plots)	4.32	1.97	(13)	3.99	2.54	(12)	4.16	(12)	2.26	(25)
39/35. (Homosexuals)	3.10	3.25	(25)	2.67	3.36	(24)	2.89	(25)	3.31	(6.5)
41/36. (Artists-businessmen)	2.36	1.58	(30)	1.88	1.88	(30)	2.12	(30)	1.73	(30)
42/37. (No sane person)	4.42	3.13	(11)	3.85	3.18	(13)	4.14	(13)	3.16	(10)
43/38. (Familiarity)	3.56	2.20	(20)	3.20	2.90	(21)	3.38	(21)	2.55	(23)
44/39. (Suffering)	2.54	1.70	(29)	2.47	2.29	(27.5)	2.51	(29)	2.00	(28)
Mean/person/item	4.00	2.64		3.63	3.08		3.81		2.85	

[a]These data are based on all fourteen groups taking Forms 40 and 45 (see Table 8 (VII)).

items which work well for one sex tend, in general, to work well for the other. The correlation between the D. P. rank orders for the men and those for the women is .84. This is sufficient justification for averaging the D. P.'s of the two groups to obtain an over-all "order of goodness" for each item. Since the differences between men and women, in the present context, are probably as great as the differences between any two groups of the same sex in the present sample, it is highly probable that a correlation between the D. P. rankings of any two such groups would be in the neighborhood of .84. There appear to be no general or systematic differences between the items which work better for men and those which work better for women.

Mean scores for the men's groups are somewhat higher on the average than mean scores for the women's groups. This phenomenon would seem to be due primarily to the three male groups discussed above whose scores are particularly high. If men and women of the same socioeconomic class are compared, the means are not significantly different. Moreover, items which appeal most strongly to the men are much the same as those which appeal most strongly to the women, the rank-order correlation between the means for men and those for women being .95.

b. CORRELATIONAL ANALYSIS. As a part of an independent investigation, the E, PEC, and F scales (from Forms 40 and 45) were administered to 900 students in an Elementary Psychology Class at the University of California. It was decided not to include the data from this new college group among the general results of the present study because the total sample of subjects was already weighted too heavily on the side of young and relatively well-educated people. However, the 517 women from this psychology class constitute the only group in whose case the scales were subjected to an item-by-item correlational analysis.[4] The results of this analysis will be summarized here.

Each item of the F scale was correlated with every other item. The average of the 435 coefficients was .13, the range —.05 to .44.[5] In addition, each item was correlated with the remainder of the scale, the mean r here being .33, the range .15 to .52. In the case of the E scale the mean interitem r was .42, and the mean item-total score r, .59. Whereas the E scale has about the same degree of unidimensionality as do acceptable intelligence tests (in the case of the 1937 Stanford-Binet Revision the average interitem r is about .38, the average item-total score r, .61), the F scale rates considerably lower in this regard. Despite the scale's relative lack of surface homogeneity, however, we are justified in speaking of an F pattern or syndrome, for the items do "hang together" in the sense that each is significantly correlated with the

[4] This analysis was made possible by a Grant-in-aid from the Social Science Research Council.

[5] Fisher's Z_r was used in computing the average r.

scale as a whole. It will be recalled in this connection that in constructing the F scale two purposes were held in mind: (a) to seek over a wide area for diverse responses that belonged to a single syndrome, and (b) to construct an instrument which would yield a reliable prediction of scores on E. It is clear that the first purpose has been in large part realized, although the search for additional items that would help characterize the F syndrome could be continued with profit. The fact that the individual F items correlate .25 on the average with the total E scale augurs well for the fulfillment of the second purpose—a matter to which we shall turn in a moment.

Proof that the variables or groups of items used in thinking about the F scale are not clusters in the statistical sense, is contained in the data from the present group of 517 women. Although the items within each of the Form 45 F-clusters tend to intercorrelate (.11 to .24), the items in any one cluster correlate with one another no better than they do with numerous items from other clusters. We are justified in using these clusters, therefore, only as *a priori* aids to discussion.

D.　CORRELATIONS OF THE F SCALE WITH E AND WITH PEC

Correlations of F with the E and PEC scales, based on the three question-naire forms and derived from all the groups used in the study, are shown in Table 10 (VII). The major result expressed in this table is that the correlation between E and F has increased with the successive revisions of the scale until it has reached a point (about .75 on the average in Forms 40, 45) where scores on the former can be predicted with fair accuracy from scores on the latter.

The correlation between F and E varies rather widely from one group to another, a matter that seems to depend mainly upon the reliability of the scales themselves.[6] Thus, in the San Quentin group, where the reliability of F is .87 and that of E only .65, the correlation between the two scales is at the lowest, .59; while in the case of the Working-Class Women, where the reliability of F climbs to .97,[7] the correlation is at its maximum, .87. It is obvious, therefore, that if the reliabilities of the two scales were increased (which can be done by increasing the number of items within each) the

[6] The correlation between E and F does not seem to depend upon whether the two scales are administered at different times, or at the same time with items from the one scale interspersed among those of the other. The correlation obtained in the case of the Universiy of Oregon Student Women, who were given Form 60 in two parts, is not only similar to that obtained, with the use of the regular Form 60, in the case of the University of Oregon and University of California Student Women, but it is virtually the same as the mean E.F correlation for all groups of subjects.

[7] The reliability of the "A" half of the E scale, which was given as a part of Form 40 to that group, was not calculated.

TABLE 10 (VII)

CORRELATIONS OF THE F SCALE WITH THE A-S, E, AND PEC SCALES IN THE SEVERAL FORMS OF THE QUESTIONNAIRE

	N	F.A-S	F.E	F.PEC
Groups taking Form 78:				
Public Speaking Class Women	140	.55	.58	.52
Public Speaking Class Men	52	.52	.56	.45
Extension Class Women	40	.49	.74	.54
Professional Women	63	.57	.73	.65
Over-all[a]: Form 78	295	.53	.65	.54
Groups taking Form 60:				
Univ. of Oregon Student Women	47		.72	.29
Univ. of Oregon and Univ. of California Student Women	54		.78	.49
Univ. of Oregon and Univ. of California Student Men	57		.58	.43
Oregon Service Club Men	68		.69	.29
Oregon Service Club Men[b]	60			.22
Over-all: Form 60	286		.69	.34
Groups taking Form 45:				
Testing Class Women	59		.79	.54
San Quentin Men Prisoners	110		.59	.23
Psychiatric Clinic Women	71		.86	.62[c]
Psychiatric Clinic Men	50		.76	.57[c]
Working-Class Men and Women	50		.85	.70
Employment Service Men Veterans	51		.67	.62[d]
Maritime School Men	179		.56	.39[d]
Over-all: Form 45	570		.73	.52
Groups taking Form 40[e]:				
George Washington Univ. Women	132		.69	.53
California Service Club Men	63		.80	.59
Middle-Class Men	69		.81	.71
Working-Class Men	61		.76	.60
Middle-Class Women	154		.83	.70
Working-Class Women	53		.87	.72
Los Angeles Men	117		.82	.58
Los Angeles Women	130		.75	.61
Employment Service Men Veterans	55		.72	.62
Maritime School Men	165		.62	.39
Over-all: Form 40	999		.77	.61
Over-all: All Forms	2150	.53	.73	.52

[a] In obtaining the over-all group means, the individual group means were not weighted by N.

[b] This group of Oregon Service Club Men received a short questionnaire form containing only the F scale and half of the PEC scale.

[c] For the correlations of F with PEC in the Psychiatric Clinic groups, the number of women was 45, the number of men 29, due to a substitution of forms.

[d] These F-PEC correlations are based on both Forms 40 and 45. Since it was considered highly unlikely that the presence or absence of 5 E items would affect the correlation of F and PEC, the two forms are taken together in order to have the advantage of the larger N's. The total N is 106 for the Employment Service Men Veterans, 343 for the Maritime School Men.

[e] In Form 40, it will be recalled, only the "A" half of the 10-item E scale was used.

correlation between E and F would be very high indeed.[8] This is not to say, however, that E and F for all practical purposes measure the same thing. A correlation of .775 means that about two-thirds of the subjects who score in the high quartile on the one scale, score in the high quartile on the other, and that there are practically no reversals, i.e., cases in which a subject is high on one scale but low on the other. If one wished to use the F scale alone in order to single out subjects who were practically certain to be highly ethnocentric, i.e., in the high quartile on the present E scale, it would be necessary for him to limit himself to those scoring at the very highest extreme on F, perhaps the top 10 per cent. As pointed out earlier, there are reasons why some discrepancy between the two scales should be expected. Surely there are some individuals who have the kind of susceptibility to fascist propaganda with which the F scale is concerned but who for one reason or another tend to inhibit expressions of hostility against minority groups (subjects high on F but low on E). And we have good reason to believe that there are other people who rather freely repeat the clichés of ethnocentrism—perhaps in accordance with the climate of opinion in which they are living—without this being expressive of deep-lying trends in their personalities (subjects high on E but low on F). Such "exceptions" will be taken up in more detail later.

It is to be noted that the correlation between F and E is slightly higher on the average in the case of groups taking Form 40 than for groups taking Form 45. This means that F correlates slightly better with the A half of the E scale than with the total E scale, and that the correlation must be still lower in the case of the B half of the scale. In several groups taking Form 45 the correlations of E_A and of E_B with F were calculated, in addition to the correlation of total E with F. The results appear in Table 11 (VII). In each

TABLE 11 (VII)

CORRELATIONS OF THE F SCALE WITH EACH HALF AND WITH THE WHOLE OF THE E SCALE

Group	N	Correlations		
		$E_A \cdot F$	$E_B \cdot F$	$E_{A+B} \cdot F$
San Quentin Men Prisoners	110	.56	.45	.59
Employment Service Men Veterans	51	.66	.61	.67
Maritime School Men	179	.61	.40	.56
Testing Class Women	59	.77	.66	.79
Mean		.65	.53	.65

[8] The correlation coefficient which, theoretically, would result if two scales were perfectly reliable, i.e., if the average obtained r were corrected for attenuation, is about .9. This indicates a striking correspondence, though not a complete identity, of what is measured by the two scales.

group $E_A.F$ is notably higher than $E_B.F$, and about the same as $E_{A+B}.F$. It may be recalled that the A half of the scale refers to highly generalized ethnocentrism and contains no A-S items, while the B half is made up of four A-S items and one Negro item. It happened that this Negro item was a relatively poor one in the statistical sense (rank order, 5 for men, 10 for women), but this is not enough to account for the superiority of the $E_A.F$ correlations. It seems, rather, that the F syndrome is actually more closely related to general ethnocentrism than to anti-Semitism. This is in keeping with the finding, reported earlier, that in Form 78 the F scale correlated more highly with the E scale than with the A-S scale. Although anti-Semitism is still to be understood primarily as an aspect of general ethnocentrism, there can be no doubt but that it has some special features of its own. Some of these features are described in Chapter XVI.

The F syndrome bears only a moderately close relation to politico-economic conservatism, the average correlation for Forms 45 and 40 being .57. Our interpretation is that high scores on PEC may proceed either from genuine conservatism or from pseudoconservatism, and that it is the latter which is most expressive of the personality trends which the F scale measures. This is in keeping with the finding that E, which is closely related to F, also shows only moderate correlation with PEC. The E.PEC correlation is about the same as the F.PEC correlation. It would appear that general ethnocentrism, as measured by the present scales, is mainly an expression of those personality structures which the F scale measures; politico-economic conservatism, while it may have this same source, may be more dependent than E upon factors in the individual's contemporary situation.

E. DIFFERENCES IN MEAN F-SCALE SCORE AMONG VARIOUS GROUPS

We may turn now to a consideration of the mean F-scale scores of different groups. These means have been set forth in Table 12 (VII). It is well to recall here what was stated at the beginning (Chapter I, C), that since no steps were taken to insure that each group studied was actually representative of a larger section of the population, we are in no position to generalize from the present results on mean scores, however suggestive they might be. (A large-scale community study would be necessary in order to produce a sound estimate of the relative amounts of fascist potential in different sections of the general population. The F scale, we believe, is worthy to be used in such a study, though it would have to be modified somewhat in order to be suitable for groups with little education.) It seems well to recall, too, that the group with which a subject filled out the questionnaire does not necessarily represent a group membership that is significant for the present study. The differences with which we are here concerned are not very large,

TABLE 12 (VII)

MEAN F-SCALE SCORES OF GROUPS
TAKING THE SEVERAL FORMS OF THE QUESTIONNAIRE

Group	N	Mean	S. D.
Form 78:			
Public Speaking Class Women	140	3.94	.71
Public Speaking Class Men	52	3.72	.57
Extension Class Women	40	3.75	.70
Professional Women	63	3.43	.86
Over-all mean, Form 78	295	3.71	.71
Form 60:			
Univ. of Oregon Student Women	47	3.32	.86
Univ. of Oregon and Univ. of California Student Women	54	3.39	.96
Univ. of Oregon and Univ. of California Student Men	57	3.82	.93
Oregon Service Club Men	68	3.74	.81
Oregon Service Club Men (A Form only)	60	3.25	.71
Over-all mean, Form 60	286	3.50	.85
Form 45:			
Testing Class Women	59	3.62	.99
San Quentin Men Prisoners	110	4.73	.86
Psychiatric Clinic Women	71	3.69	1.30
Psychiatric Clinic Men	50	3.82	1.01
Over-all mean, Form 45	290	3.96	1.04
Form 40:			
George Washington Univ. Women	132	3.51	.90
California Service Club Men	63	4.08	1.03
Middle-Class Women	154	3.62	1.26
Middle-Class Men	69	3.69	1.22
Working-Class Women	53	3.86	1.67
Working-Class Men	61	4.19	1.18
Los Angeles Women	130	3.49	1.13
Los Angeles Men	117	3.68	1.17
Over-all mean, Form 40	779	3.76	1.20
Forms 40 and 45:			
Employment Service Men Veterans	106	3.74	1.04
Maritime School Men	343	4.06	.77
Over-all mean, Forms 40 and 45	449	3.90	.90
Over-all mean, Four Forms (78, 60, 45, 40):	2099	3.78	

while the variability within each group is marked. Only rarely is the difference between two groups greater than one S. D. In our view, we should find large group differences in mean F score only when membership in a group has some psychological significance, and this does not seem to be true of most of the present groups. (A study of the F-scale score in relation to group membership factors such as those covered by page 1 of the questionnaire [income, religion, etc.] would probably be rewarding. In view of the high correlation between F and E we should expect results generally similar to those found in the case of the latter scale, but discrepancies would be particularly interesting.) Nevertheless, some important sociological and psychological differences among the present groups are known to exist—indeed some of these groups have been described as "key" groups—and, if the F scale is valid, we should expect differences in mean score that are intelligible in the light of our general theory.

Of all the fourteen groups taking Form 40-45, the San Quentin Inmates obtained the highest mean score, 4.73. This mean is significantly different (C. R. = 3.2) from that of the next highest scoring group, the Working-Class Men, whose mean is 4.19. Between the San Quentin group and the lowest scoring group of men (Los Angeles Men, M = 3.68) the difference is very marked (C. R. = 7.8). In view of all that has been written concerning the close affinity of criminality and fascism, these results should not be surprising. Since the findings on the "key" San Quentin group are analyzed in detail in Chapter XXI, further discussion here is unnecessary.

Service Club Men and Working-Class Men do not differ significantly in mean F score. This will come as a surprise only to those who have become accustomed to explaining all important differences in social attitudes on the basis of socioeconomic group membership, and who look to the working man as the main carrier of liberal ideas. It is true, of course, as a matter of economic and social fact, that the crucial role in the struggle against increasing concentration of economic power will have to be played by the working people, acting in accordance with their self-interest, but it is foolhardy to underestimate the susceptibility to fascist propaganda within these masses themselves. For our part, we see no reason to suppose that the authoritarian structures with which we are concerned would be any less well developed in the working class than in other segments of the population. If it be argued that our sample of working-class men might be an unusually reactionary one, the answer is that approximately half of this sample come either from the militantly "liberal" United Electrical Workers Union (C.I.O.) or from classes at the California Labor School, and that there is no reason to suppose that men from the United Seaman's Service or new members of the I.L.W.U. —who constitute the remainder of the sample—are more conservative than working men generally. For that matter, the extremely high scoring San Quentin Inmates come in very large part from the working class, and there is good reason to suppose that their general outlook depends upon their background as well as upon the circumstance of their being in prison.

It appears that differences among the present groups of men depend more upon the factor of contact with liberal organizations and liberal thought than upon socioeconomic group membership. This is the basis on which we would explain the relatively low means of the Middle-Class Men (3.69) and the Los Angeles Men (3.68), both of which are significantly different (beyond the 5 per cent level) from that of the Service Club Men (4.08). The Middle-Class Men and the Service Club Men are quite similar with respect to economic and occupational status; the difference between them that is reflected in their F-scale mean lies, most probably, in whatever it is that disposes the former to appear at a meeting of the P.T.A. or the layman's league of a Presbyterian Church or at evening classes at the California Labor School, and the latter at a Service Club luncheon. This, in our opinion, is primarily a psychological matter; the difference lies in the degree of something which may be labeled, for the moment, a disposition toward liberalism or progressivism or humanitarianism. The Los Angeles Men, it will be recalled, were recruited primarily from the University and the movie communities. Thus, though their socioeconomic status was certainly no lower than that of the Service Club Men in the San Francisco area, the setting in which they were found was one of greater liberalism. The Maritime School Group, made up predominantly of men with working-class and lower middle-class antecedents who are out to raise their status, belongs on the basis of its mean (4.06) with the Service Club Men and the Working-Class Men, while the Psychiatric Clinic Men (M = 3.82) and the Employment Service Veterans (M = 3.74), who probably are more heterogeneous with respect to either class status or liberal affiliations, have intermediate positions in the rank order of means.

It has been pointed out that the fact of the men in our total sample having a higher mean than the women is due primarily to the presence in the male sample of the outstandingly high scoring groups that have just been considered. The present data show that where social group membership is constant, the means for men are not significantly different from those of women. Thus, in the case of the Working-Class Women and the Working-Class Men, the C. R. is only 1.22, while the differences between men and women in the Psychiatric Clinic, the Los Angeles and the Middle-Class groups are practically negligible. It is to be noted, however, that in each case the men are slightly higher, and that in a larger sample the difference might become significant.

Among the women's groups, the only difference that approaches significance is that existing between the Working-Class Women (M = 3.86), on the one hand, and the George Washington University Women (M = 3.51) and Los Angeles Women (M = 3.49) on the other. If a true difference exists, the explanation would seem to be the same as that advanced in the case of some of the men's groups: that the latter groups of women have been in closer touch with liberal trends.

It is of some interest to consider group differences in mean F score in relation to the mean E score of these same groups. In general, groups that score highest on F tend to score highest on E also. The most notable discrepancies occur in the cases of the George Washington Women, who are relatively much higher on E ($M = 4.04$) than on F ($M = 3.51$), and the Working-Class Men, who are slightly higher on F ($M = 4.19$) than on E ($M = 3.92$). It seems probable that in the case of this group of women, we have to deal with a regional difference: many observers have noted that there is more prejudice in the East than in the West. It may be, therefore, that although these college women were relatively liberal as a group, they were led by the prevailing climate of opinion to go fairly high on E. This is in keeping with the fact that the correlation between F and E in this group was one of the lowest obtained.

The group of Working-Class Men is the only one in which the mean E score is lower than the mean F score. This is probably attributable to the success of indoctrination in antidiscrimination which occurs in the "liberal" unions to which a majority of these subjects belong. Apparently, however, this indoctrination did not go so far as to modify those attitudes centering around authoritarianism, which are more pronounced in this group than in most others. One might say that if this indoctrination were dispensed with, or if propaganda having an opposite direction were substituted for it, then the results from this group would fall into line with all the others.

It has often been suggested that working-class people are relatively uninhibited in expressing the prejudice that they have and that this does not go very deep, while middle-class people are more restrained in giving vent to their—often deeper—prejudice. That nothing to support this formulation is to be found in the present data may be due most largely to the fact that our ethnocentric statements were for the most part fairly restrained, i.e., formulated in such a way that a pseudodemocratic person could agree with them and still maintain the illusion that he was not prejudiced.

F. VALIDATION BY CASE STUDIES: THE F-SCALE RESPONSES OF MACK AND LARRY

The responses of Mack and Larry on the F scale may now be compared with their remarks in the interview. In Table 13 (VII) are shown the scores of Mack and Larry, the group mean, and the D. P. for each of the 38 items in the F scale (Form 78), the items having been grouped according to the scheme of F-scale variables.

The mean F-scale scores of the two men seem to be in keeping with the

TABLE 13 (VII)

RESPONSES OF MACK AND LARRY ON THE F SCALE (FORM 78)

Item	Mack	Larry	Group Mean[a] (N = 295)	Group D.P.[a]
Conventionalism				
12.　(Modern church)	5	7	4.67	0.19
19.　(One should avoid)	2	1	3.63	0.76
38.　(Emphasis in the colleges)	5	2	3.91	1.20
55.　(Leisure)	7	6	5.20	2.11
58.　(What a man does)	6	1	3.48	1.70
60.　(Important values)	5	5	4.17	1.60
Cluster mean	5.00	3.66	4.18	1.26
Authoritarian Submission				
20.　(Progressive education)	3	1	3.28	1.07
23.　(Undying love)	6	7	3.62	2.61
32.　(Essential for learning)	7	6	3.61	1.67
39.　(Supernatural force)	1	1	3.97	2.54
43.　(Sciences like chemistry)	1	1	4.35	2.79
50.　(Obedience and respect)	6	2	3.72	3.09
74.　(Tireless leaders)	2	1	5.00	1.66
77.　(No sane, normal person)	6	5	4.12	2.12
Cluster mean	4.00	3.13	3.96	2.19
Authoritarian Aggression				
6.　(Women restricted)	2	1	2.93	1.75
23.　(Undying love)	6	7	3.62	2.61
31.　(Homosexuals)	6	6	3.22	2.16
47.　(Honor)	5	2	3.00	2.09
75.　(Sex crimes)	6	1	3.26	2.81
Cluster mean	5.00	3.40	3.21	2.28
Anti-intraception				
28.　(Novels or stories)	5	1	3.02	1.29
38.　(Emphasis in colleges)	5	2	3.91	1.20
53.　(Things too intimate)	3	5	4.82	1.99
55.　(Leisure)	7	6	5.20	2.11
58.　(What a man does)	6	1	3.48	1.70
66.　(Books and movies)	6	2	4.10	2.48
Cluster mean	5.33	2.83	4.09	1.80
Superstition				
2.　(Astrology)	5	6	2.60	1.74
10.　(Pearl Harbor Day)	1	1	2.22	2.20
39.　(Supernatural force)	1	1	3.97	2.54
43.　(Sciences like chemistry)	1	2	4.35	2.79
65.　(World catastrophe)	1	1	2.58	1.55
Cluster mean	1.80	2.20	3.78	1.70

TABLE 13 (VII) (CONT'D)

Item		Mack	Larry	Group Mean[a] (N = 295)	Group D.P.[a]
Power and "Toughness"					
9.	(Red-blooded life)	1	2	3.99	2.04
35.	(Law in own hands)	1	1	2.50	1.42
47.	(Honor)	5	2	3.00	2.09
70.	(Plots)	7	2	3.27	1.65
74.	(Tireless leaders)	2	1	5.00	1.66
	Cluster mean	3.20	1.60	3.55	1.77
Destructiveness and Cynicism					
3.	(Force to restore)	3	5	3.04	1.98
9.	(Return to fundamentals)	1	2	3.99	2.04
14.	(Rats...germs)	6	5	4.44	1.60
17.	(Familiarity)	3	1	3.33	1.86
24.	(Things unstable)	5	5	5.01	0.79
30.	(Reports of atrocities)	6	5	4.20	0.43
35.	(Law in own hands)	1	1	2.50	1.42
42.	(For one reason)	1	1	2.06	1.05
56.	(Crime wave)	5	5	4.60	1.16
59.	(Always war)	7	1	4.26	2.59
67.	(Eye to profit)	7	3	3.71	2.21
	Cluster mean	4.09	3.09	3.74	1.56
Projectivity					
46.	(Sex orgies)	5	2	3.64	2.11
56.	(Crime wave)	5	5	4.60	1.16
65.	(World catastrophe)	1	1	2.58	1.55
70.	(Plots)	7	2	3.27	1.65
73.	(Infection and disease)	5	1	4.79	2.02
	Cluster mean	4.60	2.20	3.78	1.70
Sex					
31.	(Homosexuality)	6	6	3.22	2.16
42.	(For one reason)	1	1	2.06	1.05
46.	(Sex orgies)	5	2	3.64	2.11
75.	(Sex crimes)	6	1	3.26	2.81
	Cluster mean	4.50	2.50	3.05	2.03
Over-all mean[b]		4.31	2.95	3.71	1.80

[a]The group means and D.P.'s are based on all four groups taking Form 78 (see Table 3 (VII), note[a])

[b]Over-all means are based on the sum of the 38 individual items, with no overlap.

earlier observation that they do not represent the most extreme cases found in the study. Mack's mean score, 4.31, is just inside the high quartile for the group of Public Speaking Men in which he was tested; it is only slightly above the average score of the Working-Class Men (4.19) and well below that of the San Quentin Group (4.73). Larry's mean score, 2.95, is barely low enough to be included in the low quartile for the Public Speaking Men. It is, however, well below any of the group means obtained in the study.

Turning to the 9 variables within the scale, it may be noted that on 7 of them Mack's mean score is above the group mean. He deviates from the group most markedly in the case of Authoritarian Aggression. This is consistent with what was set down as one of the outstanding features of his interview, that is, his tendency to blame and to condemn on moral grounds a wide variety of individuals, groups, and agencies—F.D.R., the New Deal, the O.W.I., the Civil Service, in addition to various ethnic minorities. That homosexuals, sex criminals, those who insult "our honor," and anyone who does not have undying love for his parents should be regarded in the same way is not surprising. It is to be noted, however, that he does not agree that "women should be restricted in certain ways." This inconsistency may be interpreted in the light of the following quotation from the clinical section of his interview:[9]

"I hope to get married to the girl I'm going with now. She is an awfully nice companion. Most girls are interested only in a good time and want fellows with lots of money to spend. I didn't have the money for giving them a swell time. The girl I'm in love with now lived nine miles from me. She attended a rival high school. I dated her once in high school. When I got back from the army, I worked in a lumber mill. This girl had graduated from _____ and started teaching. Her uncle is the vice-president of the bank. I talked to him about buying an automobile that she was interested in. I looked it over for her, since I knew something about cars, and told her it was in good condition. I got started going with her that way. I found out that she wasn't interested in money, but was interested in me in spite of my discharge from the army, my poor health, and prospects. She's just very good —not beautiful, but a tremendously nice personality. She is French with some Irish in her. She has a nice figure and is very wholesome. When we get married depends on circumstances. It's quite a responsibility. She wants to get married now; she is teaching in _____. I'm under the GI Bill. If I get assurance of four years in college, I might get married this spring. We're well suited; I know she's interested in me, because I have so little to offer. We're both at the proper age. I intend to work part time. I don't like her teaching; I like to support my wife. I've always had that idea. But maybe under the circumstances, that won't be fully possible. She is a good cook and that is an asset, what with my stomach condition. When I tell her that you approve of our marriage, she will be pleased, but, of course, I'm always a man to make my own decisions."

It seems that Mack does believe that "a woman's place is in the home," but

[9] Throughout the book, the interviewer's report of the interview is given in small type. Quotation marks within this material indicate a verbatim record of the subject's statements.

was prevented by the logic of his situation at the time from saying so in his questionnaire.

Sex, Anti-intraception, Conventionalism, and Projectivity, in the order named, are the other variables on which Mack is well above the group mean. Sex was not mentioned in the interview protocol given in Chapter II. The following quotation from the clinical part of Mack's interview may, however, throw some light on his responses to the Sex items in the scale:

(Where did you get your sex instruction?) "I never had any from my parents, though I did get some suggestions from my aunt; no real instruction. What I know I have picked up from reading. I've listened to men talk, but accepted little of it; I weighed it in the light of what I have read."

(What was your first sex experience?) "It was in 1940–'41, the aftermath of a New Year's party in Washington. There was liquor. I was always a backward boy."

According to well-supported theory, it is precisely the kind of sexual inhibition and "backwardness" described here, and further expressed in the extreme conventionalism of the passage about plans for marriage, that lies behind the moralistic and punitive attitude toward the supposed sexuality of other people which is the main theme of the Sex items in the scale. The inconsistency seen in Mack's disagreement with the statement that "men are interested in women for only one reason" might be explained in the same way as was his response to Item 6 (Women restricted): agreement would contradict too sharply the facts of his present situation. It is to be noted, however, that the item (For one reason) has a very low group mean and a low D. P.

Mack's interview could serve well as a model of Anti-intraception. His emphasis upon practicality, efficiency, and diligence as ends in themselves, his tendency to ignore social and psychological determinants of human characteristics and human events, his failure to take into account possible inner sources of his opinions, the discrepancies between his expressed values and what appear to be his real motives, were outstanding features of his interview. The several Anti-intraception items of the F scale seem to have afforded him an excellent opportunity to express these same tendencies. An interesting discrepancy occurs in the case of Item 53 (Things too intimate), where his score of 3 is well below the group mean. This response is not very consistent with the pattern of values that he sets forth in his interview, but it seems quite consistent with what he *does* in the interview: as the above passage in which he discusses his approaching marriage well illustrates, he is able within the space of an hour to come to a rather free discussion of certain intimate matters with a stranger. True, his generally deferential behavior in the interview is probably an aspect of his Authoritarian Submission, but, more than this, there is a strong indication that however much Mack may assert his independence he is really a rather lonesome and troubled young man who would like to talk with someone who understood him.

One familiar with Mack's interview might have expected him to go higher on Conventionalism. One of his major reasons for rejecting so many groups is that they violate conventional values, and his positive evaluations of ingroups are in the same terms—honesty, charity, thrift, diligence, etc. His ideas about work and about love and marriage seem to be utterly conventional. True, his mean score for Conventionalism is as high as it is for any other variable save Anti-intraception, and one reason why he does not stand out more sharply from the group is that the group mean itself is high—higher than for any of the other variables. Furthermore, the Conventionalism items, as a group, were not very discriminating, the mean D. P., 1.26, being the lowest of those obtained for the several variables. Item 19 (One should avoid), on which Mack's score is below the group mean, does not discriminate between the high and low quartiles; that he should not agree with it seems consistent with his expressed value for independence. It is interesting that despite his rejection of religion in the interview, he refuses to criticize the modern church when invited to do so by Item 12. His conventionalism will not allow him to attack so well-established an institution.

From Mack's interview (Chapter II) we inferred that one reason he accuses various groups and agencies of wishing to establish a closely cohesive and selfishly exploitive ingroup was that he wished to do the same thing himself; unable to justify such antisocial wishes, he sees them as existing not in himself but in the world around him. This is projectivity in a rather extreme form, and if Mack had not gone above the group mean on this variable, in his scale responses, we should have had to conclude that something was radically wrong with the scale. His score of 7 on Item 70 (Plot) seems perfectly in keeping with what he had to say about politics in his interview. His responses to Items 46 (Sex orgies) and 73 (Infection and disease) are consistent with the picture of sexual inhibition given above. That he is well below the group mean on Item 65 (World catastrophe) seems attributable to the value for hard-headed scientificness which he expressed both in his interview and in his response to items under the heading of Superstition. It is notable that his scientific "realism" does not insure that he keeps his feet on the ground when it comes to interpreting social events. (Indeed, it seems to have the opposite effect, and one might inquire if this is not generally true.)

Mack stands only slightly above the group mean on Destructiveness and Cynicism. This is a reminder of the fact that his interview leaves the impression of a relatively "mild case"; he makes no rabid statements, nor does he show any taste for violence. Attention to the individual items of the Destructiveness and Cynicism group shows that it is those pertaining to open or all-out aggression on which he scores at or below the mean, while he goes well above the mean on items that have to do primarily with cynicism. It is interesting to recall, in this connection, his outstandingly high score on

Authoritarian Aggression. One might say that Mack cannot express aggression directly unless it is done in the name of some moral authority or unless it is against some group that has been rejected on moral grounds.

It might be suggested that another way in which Mack handles aggression is by means of cynicism. There was certainly no want of cynicism in his interview—the bureaus grab power, the civil servants think only of themselves, Roosevelt selfishly seeks a fourth term, etc.—and he obtains top scores on the items most expressive of this trend: 30 (Reports of atrocities), 59 (Always war), 67 (Eye to profit). This is, of course, hypothesizing that Mack has unconscious aggressive tendencies which are projected onto human nature and the world. Something like a high-water mark in cynicism is reached by Mack when he agrees, rather emphatically, with both Item 30 (Reports of atrocities are exaggerated) and Item 48 (Germans and Japs should be wiped out) of the E scale: in agreeing with the former he is saying that the Germans were not as bad as they were pictured; in agreeing with the latter he is saying that nevertheless we ought to wipe out as many of them as possible.

On the strength of Mack's interview, we should expect him to obtain one of his highest mean scores on Authoritarian Submission. Glorification of such ingroup authorities as General Marshall, the War Department, the big capitalists, and God as "strictly a man," was one of the interview's outstanding features. Yet his scale score on this variable (4.0) is at the group mean. Consideration of the items which pertain to this variable can effect some reconciliation of scale and interview, but it also reveals certain weaknesses in the Form 78 scale. The items on which Mack scores well above the mean —23 (Undying love), 32 (Essential for learning), 50 (Obedience and respect), and 77 (No sane, normal person)—are those which express Authoritarian Submission in its purest form: three of them have to do with family loyalty and the third with authoritarian education. When it comes to the items which have to do with religion, however—39 (Supernatural force) and 43 (Sciences like chemistry)—and in which ideas and feelings first experienced, presumably, in relationships with parents are now represented on a cosmic plane, his value for the objective-scientific comes to the fore and his scores are as low as they could be. One might say that Mack's submissive tendencies are insufficiently sublimated to permit their expression in abstract religious terms; the forces which are important for him are more tangible; they have concrete existence either in men or in physical objects. In this light, it is surprising that he does not agree with Item 74 (Tireless leaders). This item, be it noted, has a very high group mean and a relatively low Discriminatory Power. It seems likely that for some of the truly submissive subjects, like Mack, the item is too open, comes too close home, so that in responding they go contrary to their strongest feeling, while the great majority of the subjects, for whom the item was not emotionally involving, responded in accordance with the element of objective truth in the statement. Rephrasing of this item in later forms seems to have improved it by minimizing the rational aspect and by putting the emphasis more squarely on leadership. Another poor item, it seems, is 20 (Progressive education). Liberals and potential fascists alike, very probably, are attracted by the word "progressive." That Mack is no real supporter of progressive education is attested to by his enthusiastic endorsement of Item 32 (Essential for learning) which is about as clear a statement of educational reactionism as could be found.

Mack is below the group mean on the rather unsatisfactory Power and "Toughness" cluster. All the items of this cluster have been discussed above. The correspondence between interview and scale lies in the fact that in neither place does he show any strong inclination to be a tough and aggressive fellow. It is in his admiration for power and in his willingness to submit to it, rather than in any wish to be an aggressive leader, that his potentiality for fascism lies.

Enough has been said about Mack's extraceptive outlook, as seen both in his interview and in the scale responses discussed above, so that his very low score on Superstition is no more than is to be expected. The surprising thing, perhaps, is that he should agree with Item 2 (Astrology), when the great majority of the subjects do not. His agreement here suggests that his relative lack of superstition is not based upon a genuine identification with science as a way of life, but rather upon his general need to appear hard-headed and realistic and unlikely to be "taken in."

In general, there is rather close correspondence between Mack's interview and his scale responses. Discrepancies appear chiefly when the scale, which concentrates upon things thought to be generally significant, fails to catch something which is relatively specific and unique, and, more commonly, when the particular scale item is deficient and fails to discriminate between high and low scorers. There is reason to believe that the latter difficulty has been largely overcome in the revisions of the scale.

Turning to a consideration of Larry's case, it may be noted first, that he scores below the group mean on all the F scale variables save one, Authoritarian Aggression. He deviates most widely from the mean, in the low direction, on Power and "Toughness," Projectivity, and Anti-intraception; then come Superstition and Authoritarian Submission; and he comes close to the mean on Destructiveness and Cynicism, Sex, and Conventionalism.

Less can be said about the relative lack of these tendencies in Larry than about their operation in Mack. Larry agrees with none of the statements in the Power and "Toughness" cluster, and this accords with the interview's picture of him as a rather soft and agreeable young man. He agrees with only one of the Projectivity statements, Item 56 (Crime wave), and even here his score is barely above the group mean on a statistically poor item. His lack of this tendency was commented upon in the discussion of his interview, where his willingness to admit his—not too lofty—motives and his inclination to find the origins of his own views were noteworthy. A low score on Anti-intraception is certainly to be expected from a man who gives considerable attention to his own feelings, makes a positive value of pleasure, says he likes to "philosophize," and discusses psychological determinants of prejudice—as Larry did in his interview. Inconsistencies appear in the case of Items 55 (Leisure) and 53 (Things too intimate), where he goes somewhat above the mean; the former may be taken as an expression of his conventionality, while the latter would appear to be connected with his special problem—"that disease" (tuberculosis) that he had.

There was nothing in Larry's interview to suggest that he was superstitious and, hence, it is to be expected that he should obtain a low score on the Superstition variable. Why he should agree with the astrology item is a question. Perhaps it should not be surprising to find an element of mysticism in this weak and rather passive character. Authoritarian Submission was rather prominent in Larry's interview. He made it clear that he has a great deal of respect for his family and that he has had little occasion to rebel against'them either in deed or in thought. That he is still below the mean makes it clear that in order to be high on this variable something more than ordinary respect for proper authority is required: the submission must be exaggerated or overdone, and it must be generalized to include other objects besides family members. Two of the three items on which Larry goes above the mean—23 (Undying love) and 77 (No sane, normal person)—refer specifically to ingroup feelings in regard to the family; the third, 32 (Essential for learning), gives him an opportunity to express his conventionality.

Larry is below the group mean on Destructiveness and Cynicism, but the naive optimism and friendliness toward the world which he showed in his interview is enough to raise the question of why he is not still lower. One thing to note is that the items on which he goes up have, in general, high group means and low D. P.'s. It seems that these items approach close enough to being clichés so that most people agree with them, and Larry is enough of a conformist to go along.

In connection with Larry's score on Sex, which is .55 below the group mean, the following quotation from the clinical section of his interview is enlightening.

(Sex?) "No great problem. I thought about girls all the time, as boys will, and I looked at them. I started out with them at about 15. I liked them a lot and associated with them at school and in the neighborhood. You know, you have the usual sexual desires, but you don't let them bother you."

(Sex morals?) "I feel a girl should remain a virgin until 21 or 22 anyway. If she expects to marry soon after that, she should wait until after marriage, but if she is a career girl or doesn't want to get married, then an affair with an unmarried man is OK if they keep it quiet and secluded so the moral standards of others are not lowered. She should pick out one fellow to have a sex relation with, not carry on with several."

(You?) "Not until after I came out of the hospital, when I was 23 or 24. Since then I've had several affairs, lasting a few weeks or a month. I won't marry until I have more security. She almost has to be a virgin, though not necessarily. I lost respect for the women I slept with. I know that's selfish, but I guess that's the way most fellows are."

Although this is conventional enough—"the way most fellows are," as Larry says—it does not bespeak the kind of inhibition which we conceive to lie behind high scores on the Sex items. Actually, Larry's score on this variable would have been very low were it not for his score of 6 on Item 31 (Homosexuality). It is possible that he is not free of worry in this area—but this is a matter that had best be left until it is time to discuss the clinical material itself.

Enough has been said about Larry's conventionalism to make it appear reasonable that he should be close to the mean on this variable. A problem is presented by the fact that he is actually above the mean on Authoritarian Aggression. True, his score is still far below that of Mack, but Larry's interview gave the impression of a young man who would hardly want to punish anybody, and it is a criticism of the scale that it fails to confirm this impression. The two items on which his score goes up are 31 (Homosexuals), which was discussed above, and 23 (Undying love). This latter item, though it has an element of punishment in it, also expresses Authoritarian Submission, and Larry's response is probably to be explained on the basis of his family loyalty. The group means and D. P.'s of the Authoritarian Aggression items are, relatively, quite satisfactory. It seems that in regard to the present variable, the F scale was not a fine enough instrument to give the true picture in Larry's case.

The differences between Larry and Mack seem to be reflected fairly well in their F-scale responses. Mack scores higher than Larry on all the variables save one, Superstition. Mack is more than 2 points higher on Anti-intraception, Projectivity, and Sex, more than 1 point higher on Power and "Toughness," Authoritarian Aggression, and Conventionalism, and 1.00 and .87 higher, respectively, on Destructiveness and Cynicism, and Authoritarian Submission. It is particularly interesting that the variables which are most differentiating, that is, Anti-intraception, Projectivity, and Sex, are those which seem to be at the greatest distance from the overt content of fascist ideology. They are variables that seem to have their sources deep within the personality and to be relatively impervious to superficial changes in the external situation. It will remain for later chapters to show that as we go deeper into the person the differentiation between high and low scorers becomes more clear-cut and dependable.

G. CONCLUSION

The attempt to construct a scale that would measure prejudice without appearing to have this aim and without mentioning the name of any minority group seems to have been fairly successful. The correlation of .75 between the E and the F scale means that scores on the former may be predicted with fair accuracy from scores on the latter. That we have achieved the second purpose underlying the F scale—to construct an instrument that would yield an estimate of fascist receptivity at the personality level—has still to be demonstrated.

Numerous variables in areas not ordinarily covered by studies of political, economic, and social ideology have been attacked directly; and they have been found to form a syndrome and to correlate significantly with antidemocratic trends in areas covered by the A-S, E, and PEC scales. This means, at the least, that the conception of a potentially fascistic pattern can be considerably extended, and that the hypothesis of central personality dispositions which give rise to this pattern is lent considerable support. It remains to be shown conclusively, however, that the variables with which the F scale has been concerned are, in reality, variables of personality. If it is true that they are, then they will be exposed directly as we consider findings from procedures designed especially for the investigation of personality and in which the individual is allowed to express himself spontaneously. If our major hypothesis is correct, then the clinical investigations soon to be reported should not only substantiate the findings of the present chapter, but give a deeper understanding of the potentially fascistic pattern and of its development within the individual.

CHAPTER VIII

ETHNOCENTRISM IN RELATION TO
INTELLIGENCE AND EDUCATION

Daniel J. Levinson

There are several reasons why one might expect intelligence and education to be related to ethnocentrism. One reason is primarily methodological: since all of the E-scale items (and most of the items in the E-F-PEC series) are negative, i.e., agreement represents a pro-ethnocentric stand, perhaps some of the less intelligent individuals make high scores not out of real conviction but simply out of suggestibility and lack of discernment. In answer to this point, it may be noted that we were primarily interested in measuring both active receptivity as well as a more passive suggestibility to antidemocratic ideology. Nevertheless, we should expect suggestibility to be but one—and far from the most important one—of the many factors showing some association with high scores on the E scale.

Various hypotheses and interpretations presented in other chapters have implied, directly or indirectly, that intelligence and ethnocentrism are negatively correlated, i.e., that the high scorers on E are somewhat less intelligent on the average than the low scorers. Thus, the analysis of the ideological as well as of the clinical material has suggested that ethnocentrism is related to stereotypy, rigidity, and concreteness in thinking (also see Rokeach (98)), to narrowness of the ego bounds, and to difficulty in grasping psychosocial explanations of social phenomena. Since these variables are at best only partial components of intelligence, and since they are only imperfectly (though significantly) related to ethnocentrism, we might expect a relatively low but consistent negative correlation between intelligence and ethnocentrism.

The correlation may be brought closer to zero by the operation of another factor: it has often been observed that an individual may function in a highly complex, abstract, and flexible manner in one area of life (e.g. in his occupation as a physical scientist, mechanic, or businessman), and in a completely contrasting—less intelligent—manner in his social outlook or in his family life. It is as if the basic intellectual capacity can express itself only in accordance with certain emotional-motivational principles; it is free, indeed stimulated, to act along certain lines, impeded and distorted to varying degrees along other lines. Whatever the reasons, it is a matter of fact that many individuals are inconsistent in their actual intellectual performance, and may show certain "nonintelligent" (stereotyped, rigid) qualities in their social thinking despite having a relatively high intelligence as it is ordinarily measured. Conversely, individuals of moderate or low "basic" intelligence may be able to function realistically and flexibly in their social thinking. To the extent that intelligence tests measure something more basic—unfortunately it is not entirely clear what specific psychological functions they do measure—their correlation with ethnocentrism may be lower than initially expected. If the correlation were very high, above .4–.5, say, we should be inclined to suspect that the scales are inadequate; it does not seem likely, on theoretical grounds, that intelligence per se plays so large a role in ideology.

The relation between ethnocentrism and education is also likely to be significant but low. One of the main stated aims of our educational system is the teaching of democratic values as expressed in our Constitution and in other great documents. To the extent that we are succeeding in aims such as these, ethnocentrism and years of education ought to be negatively correlated, that is, the more the education the less the ethnocentrism.

The above hypotheses are consistent with the results of previous studies of prejudice and general liberalism-conservatism.[1]

On the average, "liberals" (with respect to ideology regarding group relations, politics, religion, etc.) have been shown to be slightly more intelligent, to receive better grades in college, to read more and to have greater intellectual curiosity. While the differences are significant, there is of course much overlap between the two extreme groups.

It was not feasible within the scope of the present research to administer intelligence tests to the groups taking the questionnaire. Fortunately, such tests had already been administered to some or all of the members of four groups: Maritime School Men, Employment Service Men, Psychiatric Clinic Men and Women, and San Quentin Men. No information was obtained in our questionnaire regarding years of education; this question was omitted partly because of the probable unreliability of the answers and partly because of the fear that it might make the less educated subjects defensive about the entire questionnaire. In some cases, e.g., the college students and the professionals, the amount of schooling was relatively constant for the entire group. For two groups, the Psychiatric Clinic patients and the Maritime School, the years of schooling had been determined in a way that seemed fairly (though not entirely) reliable.

The data on intelligence are presented in Tables 1–3 (VIII), on education in Tables 4 (VIII) and 5 (VIII). We may consider intelligence first.

[1] For reports and summaries see: Murphy, Murphy and Newcomb (85); Kerr (63).

For all three groups in Tables 1–3(VIII), namely the Maritime School Men, Employment Service Men, and Psychiatric Clinic Men and Women, the average IQ is significantly above the general population average (usually by about one sigma); indeed, even the lowest scorer is, except in the third group, above the population mean. This fact, namely the restriction in the "range of talent," must be considered in evaluating the results. The correlations for the Maritime School Men, obtained with the AGCT (Army General Classification Test), are very similar to those obtained with the Otis Higher Form A Intelligence Test on the Employment Service Veteran Men. The correlations of these tests with the Ethnocentrism scale, Forms 45 and

TABLE 1 (VIII)

CORRELATIONS OF THE E AND F SCALES WITH
VARIOUS ABILITY TESTS (MARITIME SCHOOL MEN)

Ability Test	Test Properties			Correlation with:[b]			
	Mean[a]	S.D.	Range	AGCT	E_A	E_{A+B}	F
AGCT	126.7	8.98	102–153	--	-.02	-.20	-.20
Mechanical Comprehension	126.5	14.61	66–166	.25	-.17	.00	-.13
Reading Comprehension	92.5	13.04	57–121	.55	-.08	-.06	-.20
Arithmetical Comprehension	81.2	8.88	61–105	.59	-.06	-.16	-.16

[a]The present means may be compared with the following population means: For the general population, the AGCT and Mechanical Comprehension Tests have means of 100. For the "high school graduate" population the Reading Comprehension and Arithmetical Comprehension Tests have means of 79. On all but the last-named test, therefore, the present sample is considerably above average.

[b]The number of cases (N) involved in the correlations are as follows: Of the 343 subjects in the total sample, 342 received all of the ability tests, with the exception of four individuals who omitted the Reading Comprehension Test. The correlations involving AGCT and F, then, are based on an N of 342. The E_A Scale, contained in Form 40, has an N of 168, while E_{A+B} has an N of 178.

40, range between —.02 and —.32, averaging above —.2. The correlations of E with the Mechanical, Reading and Arithmetical Comprehension Tests[2] (Table 1 (VIII)) are slightly lower, averaging about —.1. These correlations, taken together, are statistically significant, that is, dependably above zero, at the 5 per cent level. It may be noted also that there are no positive correlations. Table 3 (VIII) gives the mean (Wechsler-Bellevue Intelligence

[2] The Bennett Mechanical Aptitude Test, the Iowa Silent Reading Test, the Stanford Adult Arithmetical Reasoning Test.

TABLE 2 (VIII)

CORRELATIONS OF THE E, F, AND PEC SCALES WITH THE OTIS HIGHER FORM A INTELLIGENCE TEST
(EMPLOYMENT SERVICE VETERAN MEN)

	Otis Test Properties		Correlation of Otis with:[c]	
	Mean[a]	Range		
Otis Raw Score	56.5	34–75	E_A:	-.32
Otis IQ	114.5	92–133	E_{A+B}:	-.22
Stanford-Binet	129.5	108–140	F:	-.48
IQ[b]			PEC:	-.16

[a]The mean Otis IQ of 114.5 is significantly above the population average of 100.0 (population S.D. is 10.0).

[b]The conversion of the Otis scores into Stanford-Binet IQ scores was done by means of a table prepared by Dr. E. E. Ghiselli. For the general population the Stanford-Binet has a mean of 100, an S.D. of 16.

[c]Otis Test data were available for 104 of the 105 cases in this sample. The N is, then, 104 for the correlations with F and PEC. The N is also 104 for E_A, since the E_A scores of the subjects taking Form 45 as well as of those taking form 40 were used. The N is 50 in the case of E_{A+B} (Form 45).

TABLE 3 (VIII)

MEAN WECHSLER-BELLEVUE IQ SCORE FOR EACH QUARTILE[a] OF THE ETHNOCENTRISM SCALE
(PSYCHIATRIC CLINIC MEN AND WOMEN)

Form 45 E-Scale Quartiles	Range on E	N	Mean IQ
Low quartile	10–24	8	125.3
Low middle quartile	25–36	5	117.8
High middle quartile	37–50	13	113.9
High quartile	51–70	11	107.3
		37	114.9

[a]The subjects represent only a part of each quartile. In all, 15 of the 50 men, and 22 of the 71 women, had received Wechsler-Bellevues. The men and women were similar with respect to proportion in each quartile, identical with respect to mean IQ. It is not clear why more upper-half than lower-half subjects have been tested. The mean of 114 approximates that for the patients generally.

Test) IQ for the four E scale quartiles, and we find the equivalent of a low negative correlation.

Tables 1–3 (VIII) indicate that, for individuals with IQ's of approximately 100 and above, there is a very low but dependable negative relationship between intelligence and ethnocentrism: *the most ethnocentric subjects are, on the average, less intelligent than the least ethnocentric, while the middle scorers on E are intermediate in IQ.*

Data on the San Quentin Men, not presented in the above tables, suggest a similar relation between E and IQ in groups having a wider intellectual range. Wechsler-Bellevue Test Scores were available on 77 of the 110 subjects in the San Quentin sample. This subsample had a mean E score of 4.68 and a Standard Deviation of 1.28, as compared with the total-sample mean of 4.61 and S. D. of 1.28. The mean Wechsler-Bellevue IQ (full scale) was 109.0, the S. D. 13.8, and the range 78–132. This subsample is, then, almost identical with the total (questionnaire) sample in E mean and S. D.; it is slightly more intelligent than the total prison population, whose mean IQ is just under 100. The obtained r between E and IQ was —.28. This value is of the same order of magnitude as those reported above for samples in which the IQ range was more constricted. It is, of course, not conclusive, since the tested sample may have been systematically biased in its selection. In addition, other factors such as educational and class level are probably contributing to this correlation, since they seem to be at least slightly related to both E and IQ. A conclusive study of the relation between IQ and E would have to partial out, or to keep constant, these other factors. Nevertheless, the series of negative r's, on a variety of groups and by means of a variety of intelligence tests, provides substantial evidence of a significant relation between E and IQ. That the correlation is greater than zero, and in a negative direction, is in keeping with previous studies as well as with the results of the present study regarding the role of stereotypy and rigidity in ethnocentrism. That the correlation is only moderately close—apparently in the range of —.2 to —.4—is evidence that intelligence is only one of many variables which determine E-scale scores.

Correlations between the Ability Tests and the F scale were computed for the Maritime School Men (Table 1 (VIII)) and the Employment Service Veterans (Table 2 (VIII)). In the former group the correlations range between —.13 and —.20 while in the latter the extremely high value of —.48 was obtained. It appears, then, that IQ is more closely related to F than to E although, except for the Veterans, the correlation is relatively small. Further study is required to determine whether or not the r of —.48 is spurious or exceptional. The higher correlations with F than with E might be explained on the basis of certain of the F clusters, e.g., superstition and stereotypy; correlations between IQ and the individual F items might well be obtained in future research. The correlation of —.16 between IQ and the PEC scale (Table 2 (VIII)) is consistent with other findings.

That the relation between intelligence and ethnocentrism is not very close is suggested also by the over-all group data. Thus, while the three groups in Tables 1–3 (VIII) are very similar in average IQ, they vary greatly in average E score. The Psychiatric Clinic patients have an E mean of 3.7, a full point below the means for the Maritime School and Veteran Men. Moreover, the latter groups, while extremely high in average IQ, are also among the most ethnocentric of all groups tested. It would seem, therefore, that high tested intelligence is no guarantee against the overall authoritarian pattern of ideology and personality.

Data on the relation of ethnocentrism to amount of education are presented in Tables 4 (VIII) and 5 (VIII). One of the most striking results is

TABLE 4 (VIII)

MEAN NUMBER OF YEARS OF EDUCATION FOR EACH
QUARTILE OF THE ETHNOCENTRISM SCALE
(PSYCHIATRIC CLINIC MEN AND WOMEN)

Form 45 E Scale Quartiles	Range on E	N[a]	Mean Yrs. Education[b]
Low quartile	10–24	29	13.8
Low middle quartile	25–36	28	12.7
High middle quartile	37–50	27	11.8
High quartile	51–70	28	11.2
		112	12.4

[a]These data are based on 45 of the 50 men, 66 of the 71 women. The means for men and women separately were so similar that they were combined in order to increase the N.

[b]One year has been added to the number of years of education in five cases where the individual had specialized training such as secretarial or accounting school.

that these two variables are much more closely related in the Psychiatric Clinic group than in the Maritime School group. The average number of years of education drops gradually but consistently (from 13.8 to 11.2) in the Clinic group as score on the E scale increases (Table 4 (VIII)). However, in the Maritime School data, computed in another manner, the changes are not so consistent. On the basis of the combined Forms 45 and 40 data, subjects with less than 12 years of education (i.e., not high school graduates) have the highest E mean, 4.9, while those with 12–14 years (there were no college graduates) had almost identical E means of about 4.6. However,

TABLE 5 (VIII)

MEAN E SCORE FOR GROUPS HAVING VARIOUS YEARS
OF EDUCATION (MARITIME SCHOOL MEN)

Years Education	Form 45 (E_{A+B})		Form 40 (E_A)		Total Group	
	N	Mean	N	Mean	N	Mean
Less than 12	36	4.38	60	5.21	96	4.90
12 years	104	4.28	91	5.04	195	4.63
13 years	13	4.75	7	4.40	20	4.63
14 years	18	4.34	6	5.17	24	4.55
Blank	7	4.63	0	--	7	4.63
Over-all	178	4.36	164	5.08	342	4.68

there is some question as to whether the results for the two Forms should be combined, since the results for each Form separately are not so clear-cut. In the Form 45 group there is no consistent trend, the subjects with 13 years of education having the highest E mean and the other educational levels varying only within a range of 0.1 points. In the Form 40 group, on the other hand, the 13-year level is the least ethnocentric, while the 14-year group vies with the less-than-12 for the most ethnocentric position. The only difference that holds up for both Forms is that between the 12 and the less-than-12 year levels, and this difference borders on the 5 per cent level of statistical significance.

Why is the relation between ethnocentrism and education more consistent in the Psychiatric Clinic group? One possibility is that the Maritime School members who had one or two years of college and then dropped out are systematically atypical, and that an unselected group of college students might be less ethnocentric. To the extent that this is true, a clear-cut relationship between ethnocentrism and education does exist. However, the relation in the case of the Psychiatric Clinic may be spuriously high, since the college students and college graduates in this sample are not a random sample of these educational levels. It is possible—though not yet demonstrated—that the college-trained patients are, to a greater degree than those who did not attend college, selected for willingness to recognize the need for, and to seek, psychological aid. To the extent that this is true, the relationship between ethnocentrism and education is less clear-cut than these results indicate.

One might venture the hypothesis that ethnocentrism is at least as closely related to the *desired* amount of education as to the *actual* amount. Thus the two Extension Classes (Forms 78 and 45), most of whose members were adults having only 12 years or less of schooling, but trying to "learn some-thing on the side" and perhaps even to obtain a college degree, had E means as low as those of the University of California students. There is also some clinical evidence to support this hypothesis. At any rate, examination of the various group means shows that two groups may have similar educational levels and very different E means, as well as similar E means and very dif-ferent educational levels. For example, the University of California students and the George Washington University Students, with similar educational levels, are significantly different in E means (Form 78, A-S scale, and Form 40, E scale). Again, the Working-Class group, though similar in socioeco-nomic and educational background to the San Quentin group, is significantly less ethnocentric (Form 45).

We may tentatively conclude that ethnocentrism shows a slight negative correlation with amount of education. It is likely, though far from a demon-strated fact, that college graduates are less ethnocentric than high school graduates, who are in turn less ethnocentric than those who did not complete high school. It is not clear which is more important: that the correlation is greater than zero, or that it is at best not far from zero. To those who urge education per se as a kind of panacea, the smallness of the correlation ought probably to be stressed. But this is not to deny the importance of education. It is, rather, to emphasize that our educational system, college as well as public school, is still far from realizing its potential strength as a social force in the service of democratic values. The reasons for this are outside the scope of the present research. It may also be pointed out that, even under the best educational conditions, *exposure* to the classroom is not enough, and that motivation to learn and receptivity to new ideas provide the only psycho-logical soil in which democratic education can develop effectively.

In summary, ethnocentrism seems to have a low but statistically significant relation to both intelligence and education, the most educated and intelligent subjects being, on the average, the least ethnocentric. However, these varia-bles were studied only secondarily in the present research, and convincing determination of their relation to ethnocentrism requires more extended sampling, particularly of the lower educational and intellectual levels. It is also necessary to control more adequately the operation of other variables such as class level, educational opportunity and educational motivation. Nevertheless, the present results do contradict seriously one of the com-monly held theories of prejudice and fascism, namely, that they are sup-ported out of simple stupidity, ignorance or confusion. It would seem, rather, that an autocratic social structure is best suited to the particular type of ra-tionality exercised by the authoritarian personality. A promising field of future research is the study of what might be called "the dynamics of in-telligence." For example, the intellectual functioning of ethnocentric indi-viduals, even those with above-average IQ's, seems to be relatively *rigid*, to work better in relation to *things* than to people, to be primarily *extra-ceptive*, and to become disrupted when required to deal with more psychological issues, especially those involving personal needs and emotions (*anti-intraceptive*).

As has been noted elsewhere (particularly in Chapter IV), the average IQ and the educational level of the entire sample used in the present research are probably somewhat above those of the general population, or, rather, above those of the urban middle class (our primary reference population). This sampling bias, together with that of age—our sample being somewhat younger than a representative sample would be—has probably resulted in our obtaining over-all means for the various scales which are slightly biased in the direction of being too low. However, the error seems to be less than might have at first been suspected. In addition, it is not likely that such sampling factors have distorted to any appreciable degree the relationships among the variables of ideology, personality, and group membership under investigation. Since we were primarily concerned with the causes and correlates of antidemocratic trends, that is, with correlations and differences, rather than with the average amount of any single trend *per se*, the diverse groups comprising the total sample provide, it would seem, an adequate basis for study.

PART II

Personality as Revealed through Clinical Interviews

CHAPTER IX

THE INTERVIEWS AS AN APPROACH
TO THE PREJUDICED PERSONALITY

Else Frenkel-Brunswik

A. INTRODUCTION: COMPARISON OF GROUPS

Reference to the interviews has so far been limited to the discussion of two individual cases, with emphasis mainly on the pattern of social and political issues (Chapter II). A series of five chapters beginning with the present will show the purpose and value of the interviews in their own right, covering in a systematic fashion a variety of topics; furthermore, analysis will be in terms of groups rather than of single individuals (Chapters IX to XIII). Some special individuals or groups as well as some special issues will be taken up once more in later chapters, bringing in additional material from the interviews (Chapters XX to XXII). The problem of ideology as revealed through the interviews is not being considered in the series of chapters which makes up the present Part II; this problem will be taken up in Chapters XVI to XIX.

The major advantage of the interview technique lies in the scope and freedom of expression it offers to the person being studied. Thus we may learn what he thinks about himself, about his hopes, fears and goals, about his childhood and his parents, about members of the other sex, and about people in general. It is through careful and critical evaluation of sources of this kind that an adequate view of the total personality can perhaps best be approximated.

Rather than making an attempt to establish the dynamic interrelationships of the significant factors for each single individual, however, we shall look for a basis of generalizations within groups which will permit us, it is hoped, to come to grips with the social and psychological trends typical of the highly prejudiced and of the unprejudiced. Does the family constellation differ in the typical prejudiced home as compared with the typical unprejudiced home? Do prejudiced individuals tend to have different images of their parents than do unprejudiced ones? How does the handling of discipline vary in this respect? Do prejudiced and unprejudiced individuals differ in their sex life, their way of choosing friends, their values, their general cognitive and emotional approach to life? These are some of the questions which will be the prime concern of the present series of chapters. By virtue of its specificity and unique character, the interview may be called upon to yield, in the first place, information of this broader kind on the personality of those scoring high or low on anti-Semitism.

In fact, it was a preliminary review of some of the crucial factors of this kind in a set of exploratory interviews which led to the construction of the F scale (Chapter VII). However, it was this and other scales, consisting of given statements calling for indications of agreement or disagreement only, upon which group comparisons between the personalities and the attitudes of prejudiced and unprejudiced subjects—now to be extended to the richer and more flexible type of evidence as given by an interview—have been thus far exclusively based in the present volume. On this comparatively limited basis, marked differences between these two groups were established.

Questions as to the specific meaning and connotation of the various statements for the individuals concerned, however, had to be left open to a considerable extent. Further validation of the questionnaire data can be effected by probing in greater detail into the spontaneous elaborations a subject may be willing to make on the topics covered by the questionnaire. To obtain such additional information on results gathered by other techniques is a further goal in the subsequent analysis of the interviews.

While the importance of the interview as source material is generally agreed upon in the social sciences, there are specific difficulties in evaluating such material. This is due mainly to the fact that interview material is highly diversified and unstructured. At the same time, the richness, flexibility, and spontaneity of this material are the features which constitute its major asset; room is left for unanticipated variations. To preserve all of this uniqueness and flavor, we should have to reproduce all, or at least the most outstanding, protocols in full—allowing the reader to form his own impressions and draw his own conclusions.

Presentation in full, though doing maximal justice to the material, has its serious drawbacks. It would not be easy to survey and would of necessity leave to the reader much of the burden of interpretation, or else introduce a potentially arbitrary distribution of emphasis in the process of interpretation. In the same manner, if we were to limit presentation itself to a few select protocols we might easily be criticized on grounds of possible arbitrariness in selection.

For these reasons it was decided to attempt some kind of quantification within groups, rather than to present only clinical results based on intensive but more impressionistic case studies as was originally planned. For the kind of evaluation chosen, hypotheses were already formulated on an empirical basis, giving "hunches" for potential validation. The procedure consisted of a careful evaluation of the interview material in terms of an extensive set of scoring categories. These categories had been designed to encompass as much as possible of the richness and intricacy of the material at hand. (See E. Frenkel-Brunswik (31, 32, 36).) They were a product of intensive study of the interviews with full consideration of all the other evidence obtained from the individuals in question, especially their standing on the prejudice scales. The result was establishment of a Scoring Manual comprising about ninety categories and subcategories (see below).

Evaluation of the interview protocols was by raters unfamiliar with the specific ideology of the subject, the Scoring Manual serving as a guide for ratings in terms of the various categories.

In order to offer to the reader as much direct contact with the raw material of the interviews as possible, numerous quotations are inserted into the subsequent chapters. The raw material is arranged through the medium of the scoring categories, and the relationship of the latter to, or even their dependence on, the original material will become evident there. Many of the quotations presented were directly instrumental in designing the categories employed in their evaluation. Actually, the system of scoring categories reflects the theory or the interrelationships between personality and prejudice which was empirically developed in the course of the exploratory study of the bulk of the interviews, individual by individual. This exploratory study preceded the more elaborate checking procedure in which the individual lost his identity in a mass of statistical evidence organized in terms of the scoring categories and evaluated in terms of larger groups. It is only through such a statistical procedure that the original hypotheses can be, and in fact have to a considerable extent been, verified.

It was hoped that use of the variables defined by the scoring categories would help to bridge the existing gap between the studies of groups and of individuals and perhaps contribute to the establishment of a mutual give and take of facts and concepts. Indeed, some of the variables and relationships which were originally conceived of in the course of the generalized, statistical establishment of personality patterns in samples of prejudiced vs. unprejudiced people, were at the same time found to be crucial in the intensive study of single individuals or small groups (see Chapters XX, XXI, XXII).

The subject's view of his own life, as revealed in the course of the interview, may be assumed to contain real information together with wishful —and fearful—distortions. Known methods had to be utilized, therefore, and new ones developed to differentiate the more genuine, basic feelings, attitudes, and strivings from those of a more compensatory character behind which are hidden tendencies, frequently unknown to the subject himself, which are contrary to those manifested or verbalized on a surface level. To cope with such distortions cues are available or may be developed to guide interpretations. The methodological safeguarding of such interpretations is one of the central problems in the approach to the interviews. The subsequent analysis of the interview data will include discussion of this point. In general, it endeavors to add to our knowledge of the relationship of surface cues and underlying strivings, with special reference to the problems raised by the personality of the ethnically prejudiced.

In the present chapter the securing of the interview material and the technical aspects of its analysis will be discussed. The sample of the subjects interviewed as compared with the total sample will be described first. A characterization of the interviewers in terms of their background, training, and psychological point of view will also be given. Next, the Interview Schedule used and the technique employed in interviewing will be presented. This will be followed, in the concluding sections of this chapter, by a discussion of the methods used in the evaluation of the interview data.

In the four following chapters a statistical analysis and discussion of the results gained from the study of the interviews will be presented, first in terms of a detailed set of rating categories (Chapters X to XII), and then in terms of over-all ratings and comprehensive description (Chapter XIII).

B. SELECTION OF SUBJECTS FOR THE INTERVIEWS

1. BASIS OF SELECTION

The selection of the subjects to be interviewed was determined, in the first place, by their responses on the A-S or the E scale. With few exceptions (see below), all interviewees belonged either to the uppermost or to the lowermost quartile in this respect, the proportions of high-scoring and low-scoring subjects being approximately equal.

Secondly, consideration was given to the response to the three scales of the questionnaire. Thus, an effort was made to include in the sample interviewed not only the most "typical" high scorers and low scorers, i.e., subjects with correspondingly high or low scores on the PEC and F scales, but also some of those more atypical subjects who obtained a high score on the first scales but a relatively low score on one or both of the others.

Thirdly, an effort was made to balance our samples of high-scoring and low-scoring subjects in terms of age, sex, political and religious affiliation, as well as national or regional background.

Of the thirty to forty different socioeconomic groups to which the questionnaire had been administered (see Chapter IV), subjects for interviews were selected from the following twelve: Psychiatric Clinic Patients from the Langley Porter Clinic of the University of California (men and women, abbreviated *LPC*); University of California Public Speaking Class (men and women, *PSM* and *PSW*); Alameda School for Merchant Marine Officers (men, *Maritime*); San Quentin State Prison Inmates (men, *SQ*); University of California Extension Testing Class (men and women, *TC*); University of California Extension Psychology Class (men and women, *EG*); University of California Summer Session Education Class (men, *EdPs*); Students at the Pacific School of Religion (men, *PSR*); Employment Service Veterans (men, *Vets*); Professional Women—public school teachers, social workers, public health nurses (*N* and *RW*); University of Oregon Summer Session Students (women, *OG*); Students at the University of California Medical School (women, *Med*).

In all, approximately one hundred persons were interviewed. Some of the interviews could not be used in the final scoring, however. One reason for this was that some of the subjects scoring at the very extreme ends of the F scale distribution had been used by the scorers in a last checkup on the scoring manual and had therefore to be excluded later from the main analysis which was to be a "blind" one (see below). Other records had to be discarded because of their brevity or barrenness.

The results to be reported in the subsequent chapters are based on the records of 80 interviewees, 40 men and 40 women. Of the men, 20 were high extremes on the E scale; and 20 were low extremes. For the women, the corresponding numbers were 25 and 15. The survey presented in Tables 1 (IX) and 2 (IX) shows for each interviewee the code number, group extraction, standing on responses to the various scales of the questionnaire, with parentheses used to designate membership in one of the middle quartiles.

The rater's "blind" diagnosis of the interview responses makes up the right half of the tables. It is to receive full discussion in Chapter XIII.

2. REPRESENTATIVENESS OF THE INTERVIEWEES

A breakdown with respect to further characteristics of the interviewees, and a comparison of the samples interviewed—approximately one-tenth of the total of the groups mentioned above—with the entire upper and lower quartiles of our over-all samples, will show that our interview samples are fairly representative of the extreme quartiles defined in terms of overt anti-Semitism or ethnocentrism. A quantitative comparison is given in Table 3 (IX). Inspection of the means of all the subjects falling into the upper and lower quartiles with those of corresponding groups of interviewees reveals a sufficiently close agreement. The interviewee samples are, more often than not, somewhat farther to the extreme end of the scale than the corresponding total extreme quartiles. This trend holds in spite of the fact that, as seen from Tables 1 (IX) and 2 (IX), in a few instances interviewees had to be taken from the extreme ends of the middle quartiles of the E scale.

A further breakdown has been undertaken with respect to age, religion,

TABLE 1 (IX)

SURVEY OF 20 PREJUDICED AND 20 UNPREJUDICED MEN INTERVIEWED[a]

Code No.	Group[b]	Standing on Questionnaire[c]				Interview Scores[d]		Composite Standing on 72 Categories	Intuitive Over-all Rating of Interviews
		A-S	E	F	PEC	"High"	"Low"		
M1	LPC	h	h	(h)	l	27	1	H	H
M4	PSM	h	h	l	h	47	2	H	H
M6	PSM	h	h	h	h	41	2	L	L
M7	PSM	h	h	(l)	l	6	32	L	L
M11	PSM	h	h	h	h	52	2	H	H
M13	PSM	h	h	h	(h)	52	1	H	H
M14	PSM	h	h	(h)	(l)	8	32	L	L
M17	PSM	h	(h)	l	h	25	4	H	H
M18	LPC	h	h	h	h	33	3	H	H
M20	Maritime	-	h	l	l	5	40	L	L
M40	SQ	h	h	(h)	h	55	2	H	H
M41	SQ	h	h	h	h	49	2	H	H
M43	SQ	h	h	h	l	43	3	H	H
M45	SQ	h	h	h	h	48	2	H	H
M46	TC	h	h	l	h	42	6	H	H
M47	SQ	h	h	h	h	44	2	H	H
M51	SQ	h	h	h	h	36	5	H	H
M52	SQ	h	h	h	h	51	4	H	H
M57	SQ	h	h	h	h	56	0	H	H
M58	TC	h	h	h	h	54	2	H	H
Means of 20 prejudiced men interviewees						38.7	7.3		
M2	EG	l	l	l	l	5	52	L	L
M3	PSM	l	l	(l)	l	0	53	L	L
M5	PSM	l	l	l	l	3	34	L	L
M8	PSM	l	(l)	l	h	5	44	L	L
M9	PSM	l	l	l	(h)	39	2	H	H
M10	EdPs	l	l	l	l	33	7	H	H
M12	EdPs	l	l	l	l	2	45	L	L
M15	LPC	l	l	l	l	2	43	L	L
M16	LPC	l	l	l	l	6	44	L	L
M19	PSM	l	l	(l)	(h)	35	0	L	H
M42	Maritime	-	l	l	l	1	57	L	L
M44	PSR	l	l	l	l	2	54	L	L
M48	Vets	l	l	l	l	6	37	L	L
M49	TC	l	l	l	l	4	42	L	L
M50	SQ	l	l	l	h	10	34	L	L
M53	Vets	l	l	l	l	1	52	L	L
M54	SQ	l	l	l	h	12	24	L	L
M55	TC	l	l	l	l	4	56	L	L
M56	SQ	l	l	l	l	5	41	L	L
M59	SQ	l	l	l	h	14	39	L	L
Means of 20 unprejudiced men interviewees						9.4	38.0		

[a]For discussion of the evaluation of the interviews and of the results shown in this table, see Section F of the present chapter, and Chapter XIII.
[b]For key to abbreviations, see text, p. 294/95.
[c]The upper and lower middle quartiles are indicated by the use of parentheses with the letters h and l.
[d]Number of ratings other than "Neutral." Number of Neutrals is obtained by subtracting that of "High" and of "Low" from 72 (on Table 1 (IX)) or 65 (on Table 2 (IX)). For selection of categories, see p. 335.

TABLE 2 (IX)[a]

SURVEY OF 25 PREJUDICED AND 15 UNPREJUDICED WOMEN INTERVIEWED

Code No.	Group	Standing on Questionnaire				Interview Scores		Composite Standing on 65 Categories	Intuitive Over-all Rating of Interviews
		A-S	E	F	PEC	"High"	"Low"		
F22	PSW	h	(h)	h	(h)	28	1	H	H
F24	PSW	h	h	h	h	37	4	H	H
F25	LPC	h	h	h	h	20	7	H	H
F26	N	h	h	(l)	h	9	22	L	L
F28	RW	h	h	h	h	19	7	H	H
F31	PSW	h	h	(h)	h	51	0	H	H
F32	N	h	h	h	h	34	3	H	H
F33	TC	h	h	h	h	3	32	L	L
F36	TC	h	h	(h)	(l)	27	5	H	H
F37	EG	h	(h)	h	h	21	10	H	H
F38	PSW	h	h	h	h	25	14	H	H
F39a	N	h	h	h	(l)	24	5	H	H
F60	RW	h	h	h	(h)	30	6	H	H
F61	LPC	h	h	l	l	23	8	H	H
F64	RW	h	h	h	h	0	26	L	L
F66	PSW	h	h	h	l	35	7	H	H
F67	RW	h	h	h	h	3	28	L	L
F68	N	h	(h)	l	h	32	4	H	H
F69	PSW	h	h	h	h	37	7	H	H
F71	PSW	h	h	h	h	47	2	H	H
F72	LPC	h	h	h	h	17	26	H	L
F74	PSW	h	h	h	h	45	4	H	H
F77	LPC	h	h	h	l	37	4	H	H
F78	PSW	h	h	h	(h)	44	1	H	H
F79	OG	h	h	h	(h)	36	4	H	H
Means of 25 prejudiced women interviewees						27.4	9.5		
F21	PSW	l	l	l	h	24	0	H	H
F23	TC	l	l	(l)	l	2	46	L	L
F27	PSW	l	(l)	l	l	0	53	L	L
F29	LPC	l	l	l	l	7	36	L	L
F30	RW	l	l	l	l	3	44	L	L
F34	PSW	l	l	(l)	l	1	49	L	L
F35	TC	l	l	l	l	1	42	L	L
F39	PSW	l	l	l	l	38	5	H	H
F62	PSW	l	l	l	h	1	44	L	L
F63	LPC	l	l	l	l	4	42	L	L
F65	PSW	l	l	h	l	6	44	L	L
F70	Med	l	l	l	l	0	38	L	L
F73	PSW	l	(l)	l	l	1	35	L	L
F75	PW	l	(l)	(h)	l	3	43	L	L
F76	PSW	l	(l)	(h)	(l)	14	22	L	L
Means of 15 unprejudiced women interviewees						7.0	36.2		

[a]See footnotes to Table 1 (IX).

TABLE 3(IX)

REPRESENTATIVENESS OF INTERVIEWEES IN TERMS OF SCORES ON THE ETHNOCENTRISM SCALE[a]

Questionnaire form	Total of all subjects taking Forms 78 or 45			High-quartile Mean	High-scoring interviewees		Low-quartile Mean	Low-scoring interviewees	
	Range	Mean	N		Mean	N		Mean	N
78: Men	17-82	46.4	52	64.6	66.5	7	29.1	30.3	6
78: Women	14-86	46.2	243	69.5	70.6	18	28.2	33.6	10
45: Men	10-70	43.2	390	59.7	58.6	12	25.0	15.8	11
45: Women	10-70	35.4	130	54.8	59.0	6	15.6	13.6	5

[a]Since 75 out of the 80 interviewees are from among the subjects tested by Form 78 or Form 45, comparisons are here limited to these two groups.

and politics. To maintain anonymity, these data are not included in the tables just mentioned which deal with individual subjects, but are presented in a statistical manner in Tables 4 (IX) to 6 (IX). For men, a few data on religion and politics are missing; hence the discrepancies in the sums relating to the total quartiles.

On the whole, the distributions of the interviewees and of corresponding extreme quartiles are not at too great odds with one another, considering the difficulties in finding subjects with the exact combination of qualifications. The more striking deviations from close correspondence may be listed as follows:

With respect to age (Table 4 (IX)), there are no low-scoring women interviewees in the age bracket of "46 and over"; the share of this bracket

TABLE 4 (IX)

AGE DISTRIBUTION IN TOTAL EXTREME QUARTILES AND INTERVIEWEES
(NUMBERS OF THE LATTER ARE SPECIFIED IN PARENTHESES)

Age Groups	High Quartile				Low Quartile			
	Men		Women		Men		Women	
16 – 22	59	(6)	70	(8)	60	(4)	60	(9)
23 – 30	88	(8)	55	(5)	90	(10)	61	(3)
31 – 45	78	(5)	59	(6)	93	(4)	75	(3)
46 and over	53	(1)	51	(6)	36	(2)	49	(0)
Sums	278	(20)	235	(25)	279	(20)	245	(15)

is added to the youngest age group. Furthermore, there is only one high-scoring male interviewee in this highest age bracket. Our interviewee sample is therefore on the younger side when compared with all the subjects.

The major deviation with respect to religion (Table 5 (IX)) is that three (i.e., 20 per cent) of the low-scoring women interviewees are Catholics while the corresponding figure for the "low" women in our total sample is only

TABLE 5 (IX)

RELIGIOUS AFFILIATION IN TOTAL EXTREME QUARTILES AND INTERVIEWEES
(NUMBERS OF THE LATTER ARE SPECIFIED IN PARENTHESES)

Religious Affiliation	High Quartile				Low Quartile			
	Men		Women		Men		Women	
Catholic	47	(7)	40	(7)	29	(1)	10	(3)
Protestant	185	(11)	184	(17)	156	(14)	156	(7)
None	15	(2)	9	(0)	65	(5)	70	(5)
Blank	13	(0)	2	(1)	11	(0)	9	(0)
Sums	260	(20)	235	(25)	261	(20)	245	(15)

10 (4 per cent). On the positive side, we may single out for special mention the fact that there is close agreement of corresponding figures for both high scorers and low scorers when the categories "None" and "Blank" are pooled; it may thus be said that both high-scoring and low-scoring interviewees are representative of their extreme quartiles with respect to indifference to or rejection of religion.

As to politics (Table 6 (IX)), "liberal" women are more numerous among the interviewees than among the corresponding quartiles, especially so far

TABLE 6 (IX)

POLITICAL OUTLOOK IN TOTAL EXTREME QUARTILES AND INTERVIEWEES
(NUMBERS OF THE LATTER ARE SPECIFIED IN PARENTHESES)

Political Outlook	High Quartile				Low Quartile			
	Men		Women		Men		Women	
Liberal	99	(7)	98	(17)	156	(14)	173	(12)
Conservative	112	(10)	109	(5)	45	(2)	23	(0)
Leftist	0	(0)	0	(0)	22	(3)	21	(2)
Misc. and blank	49	(3)	28	(3)	38	(1)	28	(1)
Sums	260	(20)	235	(25)	261	(20)	245	(15)

as the high scorers are concerned (98 to 17, i.e., 68 to 42 per cent). This latter fact, however, does not hold for men. The comparatively small group of leftists or radicals (covering those who gave their attitude as "socialist" or as "communist") is represented with relatively greater frequency among interviewees (two women and three men, all low scorers).

3. APPROACHING THE INTERVIEWEES

An effort was made to maintain anonymity for all those interviewed as well as to convince them of the fact that they would remain unidentified. Pains were taken to conceal from the interviewee the true basis of selection.

In particular, the following procedure was adopted in securing the cooperation of the prospective interviewee: After the questionnaire responses had been evaluated, the person who had administered the questionnaire appeared at one of the next meetings of the group in question and announced that further information was required of some of those who had answered the questionnaire. Those selected were identified in terms of their birthdates only and asked to arrange for an appointment after the meeting.

At the beginning of the actual interview they were told that they had been selected on the basis of age and regional origin. The interviewers gained the impression that in this way the anxiety as to the basis of selection was successfully removed. Actually, not one of even the highest scorers ever showed signs of knowing the true reason for his or her selection, although some of them showed signs of suspiciousness of a more general nature. The reason for this naiveté seems to lie primarily in the fact that most high scorers do not think of themselves as particularly prejudiced.

In most cases an invitation to be interviewed was readily accepted. The motivation seemed to be primarily the desire to talk about oneself and the implicit hope of receiving some advice in the process. To some of the subjects the added incentive of a remuneration ($3 per test or interview) seemed not unimportant.

The interviews lasted from one and a half to three hours and were usually conducted in one session. As a rule they were held in one of the offices of the Berkeley Public Opinion Study, in an atmosphere of comfort and quiet. When it was impractical or impossible for the subject to come to the office (as was the case especially with the prison group) the interviewer went to see the subject.

C. THE INTERVIEWERS

Certain specifications were also maintained as far as those conducting the interviews were concerned. Men were always interviewed by men, women only by women. All high-scoring subjects were interviewed by American-born Gentiles.

There were altogether nine interviewers. Although all were college graduates and psychologically trained, their backgrounds varied to a considerable extent. More than half of them had special experience and training in clinical psychology and considerable familiarity with the basic concepts of psychoanalysis. Four of them had undergone psychoanalysis, and one of these is a practicing psychoanalyst. Two of the remaining interviewers had primarily a social psychological rather than a clinical orientation. Another two had the traditional rather than the dynamic clinical approach. In consequence, some difference of emphasis in the collection of data had to be anticipated. This probably made for greater variety of scope in the interviews as a whole, although at the sacrifice of strict uniformity of procedure.

In order to secure a reasonable amount of uniformity, a detailed Interview Schedule, described in Section E, was worked out in advance. Not all the questions could be asked of all subjects, but an effort was made to cover all the major points with each interviewee. A relative preponderance of the ideological or of the clinical aspects was found to exist in accordance with the background of the interviewer.

All interviewers had a copy of the Interview Schedule together with a special instruction sheet, both to be discussed in detail below. In preliminary conferences all interviewers clarified every point of inquiry before seeing any of the interviewees.

D. SCOPE AND TECHNIQUE OF THE INTERVIEW

1. GENERAL PLAN FOR THE INTERVIEW

As was the case in the preparation of the questionnaire, the Interview Schedule was developed on the basis of theoretical considerations as to what is relevant with respect to the topic under investigation. We can roughly differentiate two types of hypotheses underlying the schedule, the "directed" ones and the "categorical" ones. The former are based on specific expectations in regard to the relationships to be obtained (e.g., it was tentatively assumed that a positive relationship would be found between "rigidity" and prejudice). This relationship can be hypothetically deduced from general psychological considerations and, besides, it was tentatively supported by preliminary studies. In contrast to this type of directed hypothesis, the categorical ones assume that there will be some relationship between a certain category and prejudice without its being possible to anticipate its direction.

The Schedule was revised on the basis of the evidence gained in exploratory interviewing. As the Interview Schedule is described, the reader should keep in mind that not all of the dimensions there proved equally discriminating. The idea was to study the major fields of sociopsychological development in relation to the establishment of social and political beliefs. In the present chapter the entire Interview Schedule is reported, but it will not become evident until the results are discussed in the subsequent chapters which dimensions are the crucial ones in differentiating prejudiced and unprejudiced subjects.

The major areas covered in the interviews are: 1. Vocation; 2. Income; 3. Religion; 4. Clinical Data; 5. Politics; 6. Minorities and "Race." Each of these headings has been covered in part by previous techniques. The interviews, however, went considerably beyond the information gathered by the other techniques.

In each case the interview was preceded by the study, on the part of the interviewer, of the information gathered previously, especially a detailed study of the questionnaire responses.

Our selection of the particular categories listed seems justified in view of the fact that we are dealing with patterns of political and social beliefs in relation to personal and environmental factors, the latter being regarded as potential determiners of a choice on the part of the subject between alternative ideologies offered by our culture.

There was no rigid adherence by the interviewer to any particular order of topics. The rationale for the suggested order—that in which the topics are taken up in the discussion which follows—was that it might be well to start with something relatively peripheral, like vocation. People like to talk about their vocation and are often looking for advice in this matter. This provides the necessary warming up for the interviewee. Income comes next, since it is also considered relatively peripheral, though in some cases there is considerable sensitivity about this matter. The interview then could turn to religion and from there proceed to the more intimate clinical data. It usually concluded with questions about politics and minorities in the hope of getting, at the end of the interview, more personalized reactions on these topics which are so crucial for our major problem. At the same time, these topics lead back, at the end of the interview, to more external issues.

2. "UNDERLYING" AND "MANIFEST" QUESTIONS

In preparing the Interview Schedule, an analysis was made of the relevant psychological and social factors in each of the main areas to be covered. This analysis was based both on general social and personality theory and on findings from the exploratory interviews. As a result of these considerations, a number of so-called "underlying questions" were formulated to indicate for the interviewer which psychological aspects of the particular topic should be covered. These underlying questions were meant only as a guide for the interviewer. They had to be concealed from the subject in order that undue defenses might not be established through recognition of the real focus of the interview.

A set of direct, "manifest" questions, on the other hand, gave the interviewer suggestions as to the kind of questions that should actually be asked in order to throw light on the "underlying" issues. It was not intended, however, that the interviewer should rigidly adhere to the questions suggested. Depending on the subject's personality structure and on what topics he brought up himself, the interviewer formulated manifest questions as he went along, bearing in mind constantly, however, the underlying questions. As experience accumulated, more suitable manifest questions were formulated in advance of the interviews and used in a more uniform manner.

3. GENERAL INSTRUCTIONS TO THE INTERVIEWERS

The general instructions which were given to the interviewers are as follows:

The careful and rather minute detail of the present Interview Schedule should not mislead the new interviewer. We do not intend that he should follow this schedule literally, in fact, we are definitely against this. Rather, the Interview Schedule should be regarded as providing a general orientation for the interviewer. It lists kinds of things we hope to obtain from the subject as well as suggestions as to how these things might indirectly be obtained by questioning. Not all of the kinds of things are relevant to each subject nor should all of the questions be asked each subject; in many cases an entirely original line of questioning will be necessary.

Different types of interviews can be thought of as varying between two extremes: on the one hand, a completely "controlled" interview in which the interviewer follows a rigidly defined set of questions for all subjects; and on the other hand, an extremely "free" interview in which the interviewer asks only the most general questions, the sequence of questions being determined primarily by the subject's answers.

Our prototypic interview falls between these two extremes but is somewhat closer to the latter. There are six broad areas which must be covered: Vocation, Income, Religion, Clinical Material, Politics, and Minority Groups. Within each area we make a basic distinction between *Underlying Questions* and *Suggested Direct Questions*. (Note that within each area in the interview schedule, we first list the Underlying Questions, and then the Suggested Direct Questions.) The Underlying Questions are those which the interveiwer *asks himself* about the subject; they are the variables by means of which we want to characterize the subjects; but you don't ask a person "Do you really libidinize your work?" or "What is your underlying image of the Jew?" The procedure here is methodologically the same as our procedure with the indirect items of the F scale; we ask questions the answers to which give insights regarding hypotheses which are never explicitly stated in the interview. Clearly, the Direct Questions used to get answers to a given Underlying Question will vary greatly from subject to subject, depending in each case on the subject's ideology, surface attitudes, defenses, etc. Nevertheless, we have been able to formulate for each underlying question a number of direct questions, based on our general theory and experience. The list of direct questions, as stated above, should be regarded as tentative and suggestive only. The suggested direct questions, like other surface techniques used by the study, should be changed from time to time in the light of new theory and experience.

The interview should be related closely to the subject's questionnaire. As a result of the coordination of interview and questionnaire, the latter contains items bearing on each of the six broad areas of the interview. For the convenience of the interviewers, an initial section within each of the six areas contains references to the relevant questionnaire items. It must be emphasized that *careful study of the questionnaire beforehand* is essential for an adequate interview. The questionnaire by itself reveals many important points under each topic; it also suggests hypotheses which can be verified in the interview. Pre-interview study of the questionnaire, then, gives the interviewer a more structured approach to the interview and should be done in all possible cases.

(Some further general directions are given below as parenthetic comments to the headings of the sections listing the underlying and the direct questions where they first appear in the Schedule.)

E.   THE INTERVIEW SCHEDULE[1]

A detailed description of each section of the Interview Schedule will help to clarify the procedure described.

1. VOCATION

By means of the questionnaire, information was obtained about the present and the desired occupation of the subject and about attitudes toward work in general. Over and above that, the main function of the underlying

[1] While the responsibility for the analysis of the interview material rested mainly with the author of the present and the subsequent chapters, the Interview Schedule presented here is a joint product of the entire staff of this project.

questions guiding the interview in this area was to find out (a) the meaning which vocation has for the subject, in its work and social aspects, and (b) the determinants of the choice of his vocation.

More specifically, it was relevant to our problem to find out how much genuine interest and libido the subject has for his work. Does his work represent for him a gratifying and constructive form of self-expression and achievement or does he consider his work as "drudgery" and as a mere means to some end such as attaining money, status, or power? Keeping in mind that the importance of success is a generalized pattern in our culture, we still expected that our material would differentiate people who are oriented primarily toward the subject matter of their work and toward real achievement from those for whom only the peripheral aspect of the work is meaningful, e.g., as a means for placing them within a hierarchy (leader or follower, an adjutant to the boss). Vocation can thus be viewed from the angle of its possibilities as a means to group identification and especially to identification with higher social circles. The wish to be a link in a hierarchical chain seems of importance to many of our subjects. The emphasis on the constructive content or the social values of work as contrasted with emphasis on mastery of technology and manipulation of resources and people is relevant in this connection. As an illustration of the background elements continually entering into the construction of the Interview Schedule, the well-known connection between Nazi ideology and emphasis on technology may be mentioned here.

In the attitude toward work, however, as in all of our material, the possibility of orientation on different levels has to be kept in mind. The wish to escape a kind of work which is experienced as drudgery often goes hand in hand with a superficial emphasis on the importance of "hard work," both for reasons of success and for reasons of morality. A very general emphasis on the importance of work is often associated with an absence of concrete and specific ideas about the content of work. On the other hand, a more libidinized attitude toward work is often both more relaxed and more specific, and it differentiates less between work and pleasure. The role of the social aspects of work, e.g., intergroup feeling, or general sociability and friendship, has also been explored. Attention of the interviewer has been directed, further, toward other personality needs as expressed in special cases.

The problem of how far identification with, or rebellion against, the parents determined the choice of vocation, was the starting point for further inquiry.

After listing the underlying questions which seemed relevant to the problem of vocation, a set of manifest, direct questions was suggested after the fashion described above. The part of the Interview Schedule dealing with vocation is presented here in full. Since most of the direct questions are self-explanatory in their purpose and rationale, no further explanations will be made. (In order to structure the somewhat lengthy Interview Schedule when in use by the interviewer, key words and phrases which were intended especially to catch his or her attention were underscored or capitalized. All such matters are left intact in the entire presentation of the schedule so as to reflect all shades of emphasis, using *italics* for underscoring.)

INTERVIEW SCHEDULE

1. *VOCATION*

Underlying Questions (What it is that we want to find out):
a. *Meaning* of vocation to subject (in work and social aspects):
　　1. *Work-libido:* subject-matter interest, relatedness to work, integration of work, and leisure activities. Genuine *Sublimations.*
　　2. *Aspirations: Real Achievement* drive *versus* interest in "*Success,*" *Status,* Prestige, Money, Power.
　　3. Technological-*Manipulative* attitudes?
　　4. *Hierarchical* thinking (leader-follower; the "lieutenant," etc.).
　　5. *In-group* feeling.
　　6. Concern with "*Social Value*" of the work.
　　7. Role of *Sociability* and friendship on the job. (Distinguish superficial gregariousness versus genuine friendship.)
　　8. Attitudes re *Wife working.*
　　9. *Other* special personality needs.
b. *Determinants* of choice:
　　1. *Parental* identification or rebellion.
　　2. *Other.*

Suggested Direct Questions:
(It is understood that in no interview can all of these questions be asked. The interviewer proceeds with his attention fixed primarily upon the underlying questions, using whatever direct questions seem most promising in the context of the moment. Moreover, it is not expected that the interviewer will always use the phraseology set down here. It is our belief, however, that all of these questions are good; they are being used frequently by the interviewers at the present time, and as experience accumulates, there will be more and more subjects who have been asked exactly the same question.)

Appeal
　　a. In what ways does _____ Appeal to you? (N.B., *Don't* ask automatically, "How does the job appeal": if subject is a janitor, e.g., find out first *Whether* subject's job appeals to him; if appropriate, find out what *Would* appeal to him and inquire about this instead.)
　　　What does _____ offer you?
　　　What are the main Advantages of (being a) _____? Satisfactions?
　　　What it is like to be a _____?
　　b. What are the Less Attractive aspects of (being a) _____? Disadvantages?
　　c. What does the Future look like in this field?

Alternatives

    d. Do you feel that you are "cut out" for this type of work (or profession)?

    What Other Things do you feel you might be "cut out" for?

    Have you ever seriously considered other Vocations? Had Other dreams?

    Under what conditions might you Change (i.e., from present vocation)?

History

    e. When did you Decide to be a _____?

    How did you come to be interested in _____?

    What made you decide to be a _____?

    What did your Parents (father, mother) want you to be?

    What do your Parents think of _____?

    How has your father liked his work?

    (Get work history if striking jobs, or many changes.)

Wife

    f. Does your Wife Work? (If subject is woman: Have you worked since your marriage?) How do you feel about that? (How does your husband?)

2. INCOME

Here, as in the case of vocation, some gross information, e.g., size of income, was gained by means of the questionnaire. The function of the interview was to find out the degree of "money-mindedness," the aspirations and fantasies centering around money. Is money per se important, or is it important for what it can give? Of relevance here is the emphasis on status as narcissistic enhancement of one's own person, own power, or own security, which can be realistic or exaggerated. There can be a realistic emphasis on a good life or on exaggerated craving for luxuries; the latter is often observed in those of our subjects who are not rooted in the constructive task of daily living but whose repressed anxieties, aggressions, and infantile cravings call for an escape into a living that is full of excitement. Here again the orientation toward different levels is important. An extreme money-mindedness as revealed in more concrete and specific contexts often goes hand in hand with denial of the importance of money on a superficial level and often even with an emotional rejection of the "rich."

The attitude toward charity was also explored in this connection as a possible manifestation of atonement which, in turn, is known to be a reaction to aggression. From a social point of view, charity often has the function of keeping the underprivileged in their place, kindness acting in effect as a humiliating factor.

Another important factor leading to a group of underlying questions is realism vs. autism with respect to thinking and to goal behavior in this field. A considerable discrepancy between fantasies and reality in the attitude toward economic goals, combined with lack of a structured path and lack of readiness to work and to postpone pleasure, might make one susceptible to the use of socially destructive behavior as a means of attaining, by a short cut, fulfillment of one's infantile dreams and gratifications. Again, lack of a real readiness to work can be hidden behind general emphasis or overemphasis on work, especially since work in these cases represents an unpleasant duty. Over and above this, psychoanalysts have claimed that the attitude toward money reveals early instinctual fixations and anxieties and the way of dealing with them, e.g., anal retention or expulsion, or money as a symbol of potency.

Of particular theoretical importance is the set of questions which deals with socioeconomic background, especially the changes in economic level in the family of the subject. Sudden changes either upward or downward might be followed by a lack of adaptation in the whole socioeconomic sphere and might make this sphere similar to a "weak organ," especially susceptible to becoming a medium for the acting out of difficulties. This is what H. Hartmann has called the "compliance of social factors," in analogy to Freud's concept of the "compliance of organs" in the occurrence of physical disease. Inquiry was also made into the ways financial matters were handled by the parents. The role of economic frustrations was followed up.

A final question of interest is whether a certain personality structure alone is sufficient to establish a selection from among existing ideologies, e.g., prejudice, or if, in addition to that, a special socioeconomic history and condition of the family is required for, or especially conducive to, the acting out of difficulties in the social sphere.

The underlying and manifest questions in the sphere of income are contained in the following part of the Interview Schedule.

INTERVIEW SCHEDULE

2. *INCOME*

Underlying Questions:
a. *Money-Mindedness.*
b. *Aspirations and Fantasies:*
  1. Status (narcissistic).
  2. Power, Manipulation.
  3. Security (Realistic versus Neurotic).
  4. Charity-Nurturance-Guilt Fantasies.
  5. Lavish Living, Excitement. (Q. Is a subject with "live dangerously— win a lot or lose a lot"—attitudes *really* willing to take chances?
c. *Realistic versus Autistic Thinking.*
  1. How much distance separates present from aspired status?
  2. How well is the path to the goal structured for subject?
  3. What are subject's Real Chances of reaching the goal?

4. Is there a Discrepancy between subject's Fantasies and his Actual Expectations?
d. *Determinants in Social Background.*
  1. Parental Attitudes toward money.
  2. Parental Socioeconomic Level (including changes) during subject's childhood and adolescence.
  3. How much Status-Change has (an older) subject experienced since youth?
  4. What Economic Frustrations has subject experienced?

Suggested Direct Questions:
Present Frustrations
  a. How do you Get Along on (present income)?
     Do you have a Car? (What make, model, and year?)
     What do you Miss Most that your present income doesn't permit?
Aspirations and Fantasies
  b. What would you Do with (Expected Income)? With Desired Income?)
     What would it Make Possible (Enable you to do?)
     What would it Mean to you?
  c. What is the Most Important Thing Money can Give a person?
     Some people say that the best things in life are free; others say that when you come right down to it, money is really important. How Important is Money Really?
     How much is an adequate income for, say, a family of four?
     There's an old saying, "A penny saved is a penny earned"; but then again, some people prefer the idea of "Easy come, easy go." How do you feel about that?
     Some people like to take Chances: "Win a lot, lose a lot"; then other people are more Cautious about money. What's your attitude?
Realism
  d. What's the Likelihood of your making _____ ten years from now?
     How good are your Chances of making _____? How do you expect to Reach that income?
     What are your Plans for Attaining that income?
History
  e. How did you Get Along during the Depression? (If necessary to get a clear picture, inquire as to specific details of living.)
     Were you Out of a Job for any length of time?
     What's the Highest Income you've ever had? When was that?
     How much did you make on your First Job? (i.e., the first full-time job after leaving school.)
  f. (If he chooses, the interviewer may obtain at this point—rather than later under Clinical—information re Parental Socioeconomic Level during subject's childhood and adolescence. Ask specific questions to get information re type of home, number of rooms, neighborhood, vacations, cars, servants, recreation, entertaining, allowances for children versus necessity for children to work, whether worked, whether father ever out of a job, etc. Get subject's reactions to this—especially to changes in level.)

g. (Get at Parental Policies and Attitudes re spending—casualness; display; etc.—saving, consistency of policies, any differences between mother and father, etc., by special inquiry in connection with discussion of subject's own attitudes, especially those elicited by questions under (c) above. Or, some of the above questions—especially those not asked of subject—may be repeated for the parents.)

3. RELIGION

Religion, perhaps more than the preceding areas, seems to lie at the point of interaction of social and personal factors. The purposes of the underlying questions in this category was to find out whether religion represents to the subject a further effort toward belonging to a privileged group and the explicit acceptance of a set of conventionalized mores and rules of behavior prevalent in a majority group, or whether religion represents a system of more internalized, genuine experiences and values. In the former case religion tends to assume the function of an external authority deciding what is good and what is bad, thus relieving the individual from making his own decisions and assuring him at the same time of membership in a privileged group. The rejection of outgroup religions goes hand in hand with this attitude.

The manifest questions on religion were designed to find out which of the attitudes just described is dominant in the subject. Furthermore, they were aimed at various subtle aspects of these different attitudes. Questions such as that inquiring into the concept of God were introduced to reveal whether God is conceived more directly after a parental image and thus as a source of support and as a guiding and sometimes punishing authority or whether God is seen more as an abstract entity representing general values and principles. In the former case an attempt was made to ascertain whether the emphasis is more on the punitive or on the nurturant qualities.

An effort was also made to inquire into the reasons for rejection of religion. A rejection of religion on rational and scientific grounds belongs in a different syndrome from rejection of religion out of an attitude of sober cynicism and manipulative opportunism. Questions as to the history of the conflict, in the subject, between science and religion were also asked. Areas in which there was a readiness to follow a rational approach were noted, as well as those in which irrational explanations were preferred.

It is of interest for our purposes to ascertain further whether the attitude toward religion is simply taken over from the parents or whether any change has occurred in the direction of rebellion against religious attitudes prevalent in the family or in the direction of an increase and deepening of religious feelings as compared with those of the parents. How did agreement or difference of opinion in the parents with respect to religion influence the outlook of the subject?

The underlying and manifest questions about religion are as follows:

INTERVIEW SCHEDULE

3. *RELIGION*

Underlying Questions:

a. *Ingroup-Outgroup feelings* (including moralism). (Does subject have idea of "Good enough for my fathers, so good enough for me"?)

b. Attitudes toward *Organized Religion* and the Church.

c. *Internalization.*

d. *Philosophical Pattern* (personalization; concern re "Beginning," etc.; degree of dogmatism and fundamentalism; nature and crudity of wish-satisfactions).

e. Nature and degree of *Supernaturalism.* (Including attitudes toward irrational experiences and toward unusual coincidences.)

f. Role of *Ethics* (degree of internalization). (Get subject to go into detail on Christianity, and bring up later in discussing race.)

g. *Role of Superego:* Internalized Conscience vs. Externalized Authority.

h. *Special* Personality Meanings.

Suggested Direct Questions:

General Importance

a. What are your Views on religion?
  What does your religion Offer you?
  What Appeals to you most in religion?
  What is the Most Important Thing in Religion?
  How Important Should Religion be in a person's life?

Philosophy

b. What is your conception of God?
  What is your attitude toward (do you think about) Prayer, the Bible, Immortality?
  Do you believe there is conflict between Science and Religion?
  Has there been such a conflict in the past?
  Is there likely to be in the future? (If No: Inquire whether subject accepts (1) a rationalized system of belief; (2) a dichotomy between science as physical, religion as spiritual; (3) a fundamentalist rejection; or what.)

Ingroup

c. What are the main (most important) differences between your religion and others?
  How important are the differences among the various sects?
  What do you think of Atheists?

Ethics

  What does it Mean to be a Christian?
  How can you Tell a Christian?
  What is the Main Difference between Christians and Other People?
  What is the Most Important of Christ's Teachings?

History

d. What was the nature of your early Religious Training?
  What was the Religious Atmosphere in your Home?
  In what ways do you differ from Your Parents in Religion? From your Wife (Husband)?

In what ways did your Parents Differ in Religious Matters? (If subject broke away from parental teachings: Get history; also get reactions to differences with spouse.)

Have you ever Questioned your religious beliefs?

Since data on religion and political ideology had to be excluded from the material presented to the interview raters (see below, Section F, 3), the part of the interview based on the preceding questions will not be taken up for discussion until later in this volume (Chapter XVIII).

4. CLINICAL DATA

In the clinical section of the interview an attempt was made to obtain as much personal data relevant to our problem as was possible in a single sitting and without producing anxieties in the subject. With respect to this area, even more than in the case of the others, the subject had to be unaware of the direction intended by the interview. Care was taken to avoid offering interpretations to the subject for which he was not ready and the effect of which could not be followed up and worked out. Here, as in the other sections, the almost general desire of the subjects to talk about themselves in a professional and confidential situation was of great help to the interviewer.

A variety of personal data had been collected by previous techniques. This material, as pointed out above, was at the disposal of the interviewer, who studied it before starting the interview. The first two sheets of the questionnaire brought out some gross information about the subject's personal life. Above and beyond that, the type of information which had to be obtained by the interviewer was based on hypotheses as to what aspects of personal life might be expected to influence the pattern of social beliefs and attitudes.

The information gained in the entire clinical area by previous methods is represented in the Schedule below. In view of the length of the clinical part of the interview schedule, the questions are presented and discussed under six major headings, as follows: (a) Family Background: Sociological Aspects; (b) Family Figures: Personal Aspects; (c) Childhood; (d) Sex; (e) Social Relationships; (f) School.

a. FAMILY BACKGROUND: SOCIOLOGICAL ASPECTS. The sociological aspects of the family background seem of particular relevance in the present context. The national origin of parents was explored in order to find out whether relative "purity" or mixture of national origin is related to prejudice. Although this problem was considered important, there was no specific expectancy as to the direction of the results.

The group memberships of the parents were to be taken as an indication of how much stress was placed by the family on the idea of "belonging" and of how much the parents considered themselves as individuals or mainly as members of different groups and organizations. The whole socioeconomic picture of the parents, and possibly of the grandparents, the status achieved as well as that aspired to, had to be understood in order to throw light on the security or the tensions existing, in this area, within the family.

The underlying and direct questions on the sociological aspects of the family background are presented here.

INTERVIEW SCHEDULE

4a. *FAMILY BACKGROUND: SOCIOLOGICAL ASPECTS*

Underlying Questions:
a. *National Origins* of father and mother (not just racial; e.g., third generation Polish, German immigrant, etc.).
b. Important *Ingroup Memberships* of father and mother (e.g., unions, Masons, etc.).
c. Picture of *Socioeconomic Status* of Parents and Grandparents (as reflected in occupation, education, way of life, etc.), with special attention to Social Mobility.

Suggested Direct Questions:
Background
a. Father's and mother's National Antecedents, occupation, education, politics, religion.
Economic
b. Actual Standard of Living of father and mother (Ask specific questions to get clear: cars, servants, housing, entertaining, etc.; enough to eat, on relief, have to work as child, etc.).
Ingroups
c. Who were your father's (mother's) Friends mostly?
What Organizations did your father (mother) belong to?
How did your father (mother) spend his (her) Spare Time?

b. FAMILY FIGURES: PERSONAL ASPECTS. After the inquiry into the sociological aspects of the family background, the personal conception of the family figures by the subject was recorded. The subject's conception of the parent figures could reveal, among other things, whether the picture was dominated by the authoritarian aspects of the parent-child relationship or by a more democratic type of relationship. In this connection the attention of the interviewer was further focused on the ability of the subject to appraise his parents objectively—whether on the more critical or on the more loving side—as contrasted with an inclination to put the parents on a very high plane, exaggerating their strength and virtuousness.

The conceptions concerning the siblings were likewise made the topic of a special inquiry. This was done with the idea in mind that the rivalries connected with sibling situations are an important source of the establishment of interpersonal relationships. An attempt was made to record the existing hierarchies in the sibling situation, the attitudes toward older and younger siblings, as well as the preferences, resentments, and envies arising in this connection.

The power-relationship between the parents, the domination of the subject's family by the father or by the mother, and their relative dominance in specific areas of life also seemed of importance for our problem. The sources within the family of satisfactions and tensions in general were also explored.

In this area, dealing with various personal attitudes, especially careful thought was given to the formulation of the manifest questions regarding which the subject was likely to be sensitive and in conflict. One of the primary functions of these questions was to encourage the subject to talk freely. This was attempted by indicating, for example, that critical remarks about parents were perfectly in place, thus reducing defenses as well as feelings of guilt and anxiety. But since it was obvious that we could by this method never be sure of having obtained a true answer, especially in the case of some individuals—due more often to unintended than to deliberate camouflage— a number of less conspicuous, very specific matter-of-fact questions were also designed to catch general attitudes with as little distortion as possible.

The underlying and manifest questions in this area are as follows:

Interview Schedule

4b. *FAMILY FIGURES: PERSONAL ASPECTS*

Underlying Questions:
a. *Subject's Conception of Parent-Figures and Actuality* (i.e., get basis for inferring latter): Degree of Critical Objectivity of subject.
b. Same for any important *Siblings* (Domination by older sibs? Displacement by younger sibs? Which is most important?)
c. Pattern of *Power-Relations between Father and Mother* (domination-submission, activity-passivity, etc.).

Suggested Direct Questions:
Images of Father and Mother
    a. What sort of Person is your father? (Mother?)
    What things do you Admire most in your Father? (Mother?) (Require subject to illustrate stereotypes by specific traits and situational examples.)
    Assuming most people aren't perfect, what Human Frailties do your father (mother) have?
    Which Parent do you Take After; are you most Like; Influenced you Most?
    What were his (her) ideals, etc.?
Power-Relations of Father and Mother
    b. How did your parents Get Along together?
    In what ways were your Parents most Alike?
    In what ways are they Different from each other?
    Who Made the Decisions usually? (Get specific information e.g., re finances, recreation, discipline of children, residence, etc.).
    Disagreements arise in every family from time to time; what Bones of Contention did your parents sometimes have?

Siblings
>   c. Same initial questions for any Important Siblings. Also:
>   Who was your Favorite Brother (Sister)?
>   What did you Like About him (her)?
>   What did he (she) Mean to you?
>   What things did you sometimes Quarrel about?

c. CHILDHOOD.   Some attempt was also made to obtain information about the earlier phases of childhood. It has to be kept in mind, however, that in view of the type of inquiry used in this study, no differentiation can be made between real childhood events and present tendencies projected into childhood. The assumption was that both types of material are psychologically relevant as long as the possible duality of sources is not overlooked in the interpretation of the material. Thus, the manifest question, "What were you like as a child?" was asked to get either the subject's idea about himself as a child or the possible description of the type of child he might have been. It was observed that the subject, especially if he were a prejudiced one, often attributed to himself as a child characteristics which at the present time he seemed eager to repress.

The inquiry regarding early memories, wishes, fears, dreams, and so forth had the purpose of getting material which stood out for the subject in connection with his childhood and seemed relevant as a basis for inference. Among the underlying questions, the structure of the emotional attachment to the parents seemed of paramount importance. Here we were specifically interested in the parents as objects of cathexis as well as of identification. In the case of a man, it was important to learn whether there was at any time an explicit rebellion against the father, and against what sort of father, or whether there was only passive submission. The assumption behind this question, later proved correct, was that the pattern developed in the relationship to the father tends to be transferred to other authorities and thus becomes crucial in forming social and political beliefs in men. In this connection it is of importance to know not only about rebellion against the father but also how far such rebellion is conscious and accepted as such.

Rebellion against, or submission to, the father is only one part of the picture. Another part deals with the question of identification, or the lack of identification, with the father, and thus with the masculine role in general.

The establishment of masculinity in the boy is, of course, also closely connected with the boy's attitude toward the mother. To what degree was there love for the mother and to what degree identification with the mother? Was such an identification, in its turn, sublimated and accepted by the ego, or was it rejected on the conscious level because the mother symbolized not only something "admirable" but at the same time something weak and therefore contemptible? How did the boy defend himself against the rejected and feared passivity? A compensatory display of "toughness" and ruthlessness is, according to findings from the F scale, correlated with antidemocratic social and political beliefs.

Considerations analogous to those made in the preceding paragraphs were also applied to women.

An attempt was also made to probe into pre-Oedipal fixations, that is, to pay attention to the "orality" and "anality" of the subject and especially to the defense mechanisms with which these and other instinctual problems had been handled. The problem of homosexual tendencies, their degree, and the subject's acceptance or rejection of them was also given consideration. It will be seen to be of rather crucial importance for the social and political orientation of the individual how much passive striving there is in men, and even more important, how much countercathectic defense is built up against it, and how much acceptance and sublimation of masculine identification there is in women. The problem of homosexuality relates to the different ways of failure in resolving the Oedipal conflict and the resultant regression to earlier phases.

Since, as earlier chapters have indicated, the attitude toward authority is crucial for psychological syndromes related to social and political attitudes, an attempt was made further to find out as much as possible about the type of discipline to which the subject was exposed, and about his reactions to it. Was the discipline consistent or capricious, strict or lenient? Did both parents handle discipline in a similar way or was there much difference between the parents in this respect? Was the matter in question explained to the child and was he included in the discussion of it or did the discipline appear to the child as unintelligible, arbitrary, or overwhelming? Did the parents adhere rigidly to the conventionalized values of their class, with great intolerance toward disobedience and any deviations, especially when the deviations seemed to the parents to be manifestations of lower-class behavior, or were the values the parents tried to transmit less conventional and more in the nature of internal and humanitarian values for which the child's understanding and cooperation could be secured? Was the reaction of the subject mostly fear of authority, which could be met only by acquiescence, or could the child grasp the issues involved and feel that the consideration of certain convincing social values would assure him of his parents' love? In case of failure, did the child feel that everything was lost and that something very bad might happen, or did he feel that renewed efforts would regain for him the love of his parents, only temporarily lost? It was hypothesized that the parents' emotional attitude toward the child, their permissiveness toward his weakness and immaturity, furnished the model for his future behavior toward objects which he considered as weak.

Since the way in which the parents transmit social values to the child, and the punishment and rewards with which they reinforce them, are decisive for the establishment of the superego, we are led from highly personal problems back to problems of social conscience. The effects are mirrored in interpersonal relationships, on a smaller scale in one's private life and on a larger scale in one's public function as a citizen. A person with a mature, integrated, and internalized conscience will certainly take a different stand on moral and social issues than a person with an underdeveloped, defective or overpunitive superego, or a person who still, as in childhood, clings to a set of rules and values only as they are reinforced by an external authority, be it public opinion or be it a leader.

The underlying and manifest questions under the heading of Childhood History and Attitudes follow.

INTERVIEW SCHEDULE

4c. *CHILDHOOD*

Underlying Questions:
a. *Structure of the Oedipus-Complex:* major identifications, loves, hates in relationships to parent-figures and -surrogates. (Formulated especially for men; adapt for women.)
   Has there been an underlying trend of rebellion and hostility against the father, or of submission and passivity?
   Has the hostility against the father been admitted into the ego?
   Was there real identification with the father? (If not, why not? E.g., was the parent too strong, too weak, not at home, etc.?)
   Was there genuine satisfaction in the relationship with the mother?
   Was the early attachment with her secure or insecure?
   Were there early signs of ambivalence?
   Was she a real love-object?
   Did subject ever conceive of himself as her champion, or protector, or ally? Or did he ever feel that she was unworthy, or untrustworthy, etc.?
   Was there identification with the mother?
   Femininity? How handled: by sublimation, or by overcompensation and reaction-formations, etc.?
b. What were the main *Pre-Oedipal Fixations,* and How Handled? Sublimations versus Reaction-Formations, projections, etc.
   Homosexuality? Its level?
c. *Passivity:* Accepted in the Ego, or Repressed and Overcompensated?
d. *Reaction to Punishment.*
   1. Fear of loss of love, leading to introspection, understanding, psychology, etc., versus:
   2. Fear of authority and of capricious discipline, etc. (Get detailed picture of punishment-and-discipline.)
e. How much *Internalization of Superego?* Is the dominant trend toward neurosis or normality—or toward psychopathic-delinquent attitudes?

Suggested Direct Questions:
Pre-Oedipal
a. What were you Like as a Child?
   What things about your Childhood do you Remember with most Pleasure?

With most Satisfaction?

What is your Earliest Memory?

What things did you Worry about most as a child?

Almost everybody has had some recurrent Bad Dreams; what kinds of bad dreams did you have as a child?

Oedipal Phase

   b. Which Parent did you feel Closer To when you were, say, about 6?

Superego and Reaction to Discipline

What about when you were 10? 16? 25? Now? (If there was a shift: What led to this change in your esteem?)

What were your main Satisfactions in your relationship with your father?

With your mother?

What were the chief Bones of Contention?

Which Parent do you think had More To Do with your Becoming the kind of person you are?

Which Parent Exercised the Discipline in your Family?

Whose Discipline did you Fear most? Why? (N.B., fear of physical punishment versus fear of loss of love.)

What Kind of Discipline did your Parents use?

What Things did They Discipline you for mainly?

   c. What Other People were Influential in your development?

d. 'SEX. It is well known that the pattern of sexuality mirrors in great detail the state of the entire psychosexual development. A lack of adequate heterosexual adjustment on the physical level is usually found together with inadequate object-relationships on the psychological level; it is manifested in a lack of fusion of sex and love, or in promiscuity, or in inhibition, or in a dependent and exploitative attitude toward the other sex. A lack of warmth and "inwardness" will lead to degradation of the other sex and/or an over-glorification which often turns out to be disguised hostility. As mentioned before, the conception of the masculine and feminine role, by men and women, the rigidity versus flexibility of the conception of these roles, and the intolerance versus tolerance toward tendencies of the opposite sex in oneself are of crucial importance for our problem since these attitudes tend to become generalized and projected into the social sphere. The questions concerning this issue are as follows:

INTERVIEW SCHEDULE

4d. SEX

Underlying Questions:

What is the *Major Pattern of Sexuality?*

   a. Mature, Heterosexual Attitudes?

   b. If not, What (promiscuity, exploitation of other sex, dependence on other sex, degradation of other sex, or putting other sex on pedestal, rejection of opposite sex, homosexuality, etc.)?

   c. In Heterosexual Relationships: degree of inhibition, degree of "innerness" in relationships, degree of hostility and disrespect, degree of emotional warmth in sex relations, degree of fusion of love-and-sex?

Suggested Direct Questions:
Pattern of Sexuality
>   Where did you get your sex instruction?
>   What is the earliest sex experience you can remember?
>   How important is sex in marriage?
>   What main difficulties have you found in married life?
>   Have you met many homosexuals in your travels?

e.   SOCIAL RELATIONSHIPS.   Some aspects of interpersonal relationships were considered under the preceding headings. Here the more generalized pattern of social relationships is in the focus of attention. Again the question concerns the degree of social libido invested in personal relationships as contrasted with emphasis on utilitarian and manipulative aims. The degree of rejection of other people or of superficial sociability is contrasted with genuine acceptance of others. The history of the sociability and of the social security of the subject had also to be included here. How far was the subject accepted or rejected by the groups in which he participated? Under what conditions does the fact of being rejected lead to identification with, or to hostility toward, the underdog? Participation in boyhood gangs very often shows the first clear manifestation of participation in a "group superego," a state which often continues into adulthood. What, on the other hand, are the effects of being relatively isolated during the formative years of early school life? What are the early manifestations of an internalized superego?

In particular, the questions on Social Relationships are as follows:

INTERVIEW SCHEDULE

4e. *SOCIAL RELATIONSHIPS*

Underlying Questions:
a. Degree of *Rejectiveness:* Moral, Arrogant-Individualistic.
b. Role of *Utilitarian* considerations (status, power, conventionality, manipulativeness and exploitiveness, leader-follower attitudes, etc.).
c. *Degree of Social Libido:* Warmheartedness, Group-Involvement versus being "Outside," etc. (Any history of being rejected or teased or scapegoated, etc.? Any important boyhood (fascistic) gangs, producing a "group-superego" attitude? Rituals, blood-brotherhood, secrecy, hierarchy, etc. How much genuine feeling versus detached insight?)
Type of Social-Libido: Deeper ("inner") relationships versus Superficial Sociability?

Suggested Direct Questions:
Utilitarianism
a. How Important are Friends in a person's life?
   What is the main thing Friends have to offer (can give) a person?
Social Libido
   What attracts you in a Friend?

How do you Choose your Friends?

What do you Enjoy Doing with your Friends? (Get enough details to reveal the meaning; e.g., if "talk," what about?)

Are you the sort of person who has a Few Close Friends, or do you tend to have a Lot of Friends, or . . . .

Rejectiveness

b. What things do you find most Offensive, Annoying, Objectionable, Irritating in other People?

c. Did you belong to any Boyhood Gangs? (If so, get details.)

f. SCHOOL. In connection with the school history, emphasis of the inquiry was placed on the direction of the interests manifested during this period. Had there been interest in the academic aspects of school; and was such interest more directed toward intellectual topics dealing with human problems and often requiring introspection, or was it mainly in mechanical and technological subjects?

The questions pertaining to School History are:

INTERVIEW SCHEDULE
4f. SCHOOL

Underlying Questions:
Predominant Interests and Values: Degree of Acceptance of *Sensuous and Intellectual* (especially Intraceptive) Values and interests versus Anti-Pleasure, Anti-Intellectualism, and emphasis on *Mechanical-Manipulative, Power* values?

Suggested Direct Questions:
Values
How did you Get Along in School?
How was your school record?
What Subjects were you Best in? Which did you like most?
In what ways did they appeal to you?
What Subjects were you Poorest in? Which did you like the least?
What did you dislike about them?

5. POLITICS

Information about the subject's attitudes in the area of politics was gathered rather systematically by means of the questionnaire. The party preference of the subject and of his parents was established on the first two sheets of the questionnaire, and an indication as to where the subject stood on the radicalism-liberalism-conservatism-reactionism dimension was afforded by the PEC scale. Moreover, the presence or absence of a tendency toward projection of personal needs onto the political sphere was noted in the responses on the questionnaire. As mentioned before, the interviewer was thoroughly acquainted with the subject's responses to the questionnaire before starting the interview.

The underlying questions taken up in this section of the Interview Schedule were designed to follow up directly some of the questionnaire material in order to get the subject's expanded and spontaneous reactions to these topics. Thus the problem of conservatism-liberalism was taken up in greater detail in order to get the more subtle shades of the subject's beliefs. The conception of the relationships among labor, business, and government was a good indicator of the subject's tendency toward liberalism or laissez-faire conservatism or fascism or radicalism. The manifest questions listed below were aimed at finding the degree to which the political beliefs of the subject were merely projections of his personal needs and anxieties and the degree to which they were based on information and objective situational require-ments. The need for a strong leader, for an external guiding authority, can be found again in this sphere, as transferred from the more personal sphere discussed in the clinical section. Internal anxieties not faced as such may be projected, and experienced as fears and threats arising out of the political scene.

For the history of the political opinions of the subject it was of special interest to know whether these were taken over from the parents, uncritically or critically, or whether they were established despite the fact, or because of the fact, that they were bound to lead to disagreement with the parents.

The questions in this area were:

INTERVIEW SCHEDULE

5. POLITICS

Underlying Questions:
a. *Reactionism-Conservatism-Liberalism-Radicalism; Attitudes toward Labor-Business-Government; Democratic-Antidemocratic trends.*
b. Personalization.
c. Amount of *Information and Interest.*
d. *Parental* Identification versus Rebellion in political Attitudes.

Suggested Direct Questions:
General
a. What do you think about the Political Trends in America Today?
What are the Major Problems facing the country today?
What is the Outlook for the future?
How do you feel things are shaping up for the Future in America?
In world affairs?
What is your understanding of Democracy?
What would an Ideal Society be like?
b. What do you think of (Where do you stand on; How do you feel about): Labor Unions? (Get elaboration with specific questions, prefer-ably on current issues: e.g., 30 per cent wage increase demand; current strikes; PAC; labor leaders; American Business; Free Enterprise; etc. $25,000 limitation.)
Government Control? (E.g., OPA; Unemployment Compensation;

Full-Employment Bill; Public Health Insurance; antitrust; etc. Also anti-PAC; antistrike, etc.)

Personalization

    c. What is it about a man that Makes him Worth Voting for (e.g., in presidential choice in last election)?

    d. What Ought to be Done about (any group or movement objected to)? What Groups have the Most Influence on political affairs? How do they work? What do you consider the Most Dangerous Threats to our present form of government? What ought to be done about it?

6. MINORITIES AND "RACE"

Since this topic has been given detailed consideration in previous chapters, we may be brief in outlining the underlying and manifest inquiry concerning it. As far as *opinions* are concerned, it was of interest to find the cognitive and emotional line drawn by the subject between ingroup and outgroup and the characteristics he specifically ascribed to each. How stereotyped and how automatic is the attribution of traits to outgroups? A comparison of this part of the interview with the previous ones, especially the clinical, made it possible to ascertain to what degree a subject's innermost preoccupations, such as sex, dependency, "anality," are projected into the social sphere. How far are the accusations against the minority group completely generalized stereotypes and how far is the specific content of these accusations conditioned by the personal problems of the accuser? Is there a special negative or positive affinity between the subject and one particular outgroup? Does the subject believe in social and psychological determination of individual and ethnic characteristics and does he feel his personal responsibility in this respect, or does he think of these characteristics as "inborn" and thus not flexible? The degree of realism in thinking about minority groups belongs here.

The amount of awareness of hostility, the readiness to act against outgroups, are among the major problems concerning *attitudes* toward outgroups. Of relevance in this connection is the degree of inner conflict resulting from being prejudiced. Does the subject feel the need of reconciling his prejudice with democratic and Christian ideals and with respectability, and so forth, or is he ready to act in a straight antidemocratic fashion? In the first case, what are the conditions under which he could lose his inhibitions and act antidemocratically?

The sources of opinions and attitudes were approached by inquiry into parental beliefs, into religious and educational training, and into group memberships. The question was posed as to what degree prejudice may be a function of specific experiences with minority groups.

Occasionally some attempt was made, at the conclusion of the interview, to influence prejudice by argument, by making prejudice disreputable, or by other means, in order to gain information about effective methods of combating prejudice.

The questions in this area follow:

6. MINORITIES AND "RACE"

Underlying Questions:

a. *Opinions.*

1. How *General* or how *Specific* is the Prejudice? (What outgroups are rejected? What outgroups have peculiar Fantasy-value? How does this group differ from other outgroups?)

2. What are the *Main Stereotype Characteristics* of the main outgroups (e.g., power, acquisition, sex, dirty, lazy)?

3. How Stereotyped and how Automatic is the attribution of traits to outgroups (i.e., phrasing, assurance and categoricalness, recurrence of similar projections, etc.; exceptions)?

4. Is there an "Essential" Race Theory (i.e., can those faults be eliminated, or are they "basic"; whose responsibility is it to make the change)?

b. *Attitudes.*

1. Degree and Form of Hostility (or attraction) toward outgroup(s)? How much is Conscious? Unconscious?
   How Openly is this Expressed to Others? To the Self? (i.e., how much veiling by pseudodemocratic façade?)

2. Degree and Form of *Aggressiveness* (or willingness to act aggressively) toward outgroup(s)?
   Is the attitude essentially one of Persecution—or Active Discrimination—or Segregation (with "equality")—or Exclusion only?
   Check specific readiness to support Antidemocratic measures; and type and degree of Pseudodemocratic Façade.

3. Degree and Nature of *Inner Conflicts* re prejudice?
   What forces oppose prejudice (e.g., rationality, respectability or ingroup feelings, Christian antiaggression)?

c. *History:* Sources of opinions and attitudes.

1. *Parental* opinions, attitudes, and teachings (also relatives and siblings).

2. *Religious, Educational Training.*

3. Significant *Group Memberships.*

4. *Experience* with minority group members; to what extent is the prejudice a function of frustrations and "Surface Resentments"?

d. *Ingroup Feelings:* Meaning?

e. *Therapy:* What therapeutic techniques are most effective in combating prejudice?

Suggested Direct Questions:

a. *Opinions.*

General

1. What do you think about the problem of Minority Groups in this country? Jewish problem? Negro problem?

What do you think is (are) the most important Minority Problem(s)?

What minority group(s) present(s) the Biggest Problem in this country?

What racial groups do you find the Least Attractive? Which do you like the Least?

(For any group about which subject shows a particular concern, get his ideas of what it is like, and what ought to be done. If he mentions Jews first, get this information on other groups later.)

Stereotype

2. (How) Can you tell a person is a Jew? A Jew from other people? What are the most Characteristic Traits of Jews? Their principal characteristics?

Do you think Dislike of the Jews is Increasing? (If Yes: Why?)

Influence

Do you think the Jews are more of a menace or just a nuisance?

Some people think the Jews have too much influence in this country; what do you think? In what areas? How did they obtain it? How do they use it?

Do you think the Jews have done their part in the War Effort?

Do you think the Jews are a Political Force in America?

"Exceptions"

3. Are there any Exceptions to the general rule? Where do you find them?

Are there some good Jews?

"Basic-ness"

4. Do you think the Jew(s) will Ever Change? Or will there always be something basically Jewish about them (him)? (If the Jew will change:) How might that be done (come about)?

What do you think the Jew(s) ought to do?

b. *Attitudes.*

General

What ought to be done about the Jews? (About the particular problem conceived by subject?)

(In general, if subject is mild at first, see how aggressive he can be induced to be. If he is extreme at first, see how readily he can agree to milder courses.)

Persecution

What action is being taken by people or groups that you know of? How extensive is this? Are they justified?

What do you think about what Hitler did?

What would you have done if you had had Hitler's problem?

What might lead to the same thing happening here?

What might have to be done as a Last Resort if the Jews continue (doing whatever subject emphasizes as a menace)?

What might Justify taking more Extreme Steps to solve this problem?

What steps might have to be taken?

Some people think the Jews ought to be Sent Back where they came from; how do you feel about this? Should their property be Confiscated, to make sure of putting an end to this problem?

Should their money be divided up?

Discrimination

How about keeping Jews out of Important Positions?

Would that perhaps solve the problem—essentially?

What about Educational Quotas to keep Jews from taking over certain professions?

Segregation

What about keeping Jews out of Gentile Neighborhoods?

Exclusion

Should Gentiles and Jews Mingle socially?

Do you think Gentiles should Intermarry with Jews?

"Exceptions"

(Concerning any proposed measure:) Should this be done to *all* the Jews? How to distinguish?

   c. *History*.

Where did you First Learn about the Jews?

What Personal Experiences have you had with Jews?

Have you had any Contrary Experiences?

What were your Parents' Attitudes toward the Jews, as you were growing up?

Have you Ever Felt Differently about the Jews?

As was the case with interview data on religion, interview material on political and racial attitudes is being postponed for discussion in some of the later portions of the book (Chapters XVI and XVII).

F. THE SCORING OF THE INTERVIEWS

1. QUANTIFICATION OF INTERVIEW DATA

Systematic treatment of interview material presents special problems inherent in the nature of the data. On the one hand, the interviewee has to be given as much freedom as possible for the spontaneous expression of his attitudes and needs. Guidance by means of the Interview Schedule had thus been made as noninterfering as it could be, in view of the definite direction of emphasis that was to be maintained. Material obtained under such circumstances, although contained within a common general frame, is, on the other hand, characterized by a good deal of uniqueness and personal flavor to which only presentation in the manner of case description can do full justice.

In view of the fact that the focus of this study is on group trends rather than on the single case, it seemed possible, as anticipated in the introduction to this chapter, to effect a certain compromise between case study and statistical approach and thus to gain in comprehensiveness and conclusiveness far more than is being lost in immediacy and directness. A kind of crude quantification of the interview material was achieved by counting, in terms of a number of specially designed interview scoring categories, the occurrence of certain characteristics in the interviews of those scoring extremely high and those scoring extremely low on overt anti-Semitism or ethnocentrism. Since this procedure has intrinsic shortcomings, to be discussed below, the numerical results are not meant to yield conclusive evidence for the validity of the personality differences found between our high and low scorers. They do, however, describe in a relatively systematic, organized, and controlled way the impressions formed about these personality differences in the course of intensive studies of individual cases.

This agreement between interview scoring and case studies justifies increased confidence in the figures presented in the next four chapters. The entire approach should be considered, however, as an initial attempt to combine the study of variables on a group basis with the study of individuals.

2. BROAD OUTLINE OF CATEGORIES IN THE INTERVIEW SCORING MANUAL

The list of categories as well as the more formal part of the explanations accompanying each of them, which together make up the Scoring Manual, will be presented in full, together with the discussion of the specific results, in Chapters X, XI, and XII. There are sixty-two main classifications. Subdivisions of some of them bring the total number of scoring categories used for women to ninety, the total being slightly less for men. These categories cover (1) predominantly factual material such as childhood events or family structure, along with (2) data dealing with attitudes toward oneself, one's parents, the opposite sex, or people in general, and (3) highly interpretative dimensions exemplified by technical psychodynamic terms (such as "counter-cathectic rejection" of certain drives) or else by more "formal" characterizations (such as "rigidity," "intolerance of ambiguity," "anti-intraceptive-ness," and so forth).

The factual material and the evidence on attitudes are presented under the four headings of "Family" (Chapter X) and of "Sex," "People," and "Self" (Chapter XI).

The dynamic and formal categories are especially emphasized in a fifth and concluding part of the scoring scheme, under the heading of "Character Structure and Personality Organization" (Chapter XII). Although these categories were to a considerable extent inspired by psychoanalysis, they should not be considered as psychoanalytic in the narrower sense of the word, since classification of our material is done primarily on the basis of present personality structure rather than on the basis of psychogenetic data. The entire framework, length, and condition of our interviews made it impossible directly to obtain material of a depth-level comparable to that of genuine psychoanalytic material. At the same time, however, there was enough spontaneous material at hand to make it possible for raters trained in dynamic psychology to infer some of the major structural problems and types of defense mechanisms in our subjects, in accordance with the categories provided by the Scoring Manual.

A certain parallelism, although by no means an exact duplication, between the Interview Schedule and the Scoring Manual will be noted when comparing the two in detail.

3. THE INTERVIEW RATING PROCEDURE AND THE RATERS

Since our major purpose in analyzing the interview material was to gain additional evidence concerning the relationship of prejudice to personality, it was important to conceal from the rater the explicit stand of the subject with respect to ethnic tolerance or prejudice as well as with respect to political ideology in general. All references to these topics throughout the interview were thus carefully deleted before the protocols were handed to the raters. The diagnosis of the subjects' personality was thus rendered "blind." The raters did know, of course, that their subjects had scored either high or low on the scales for measuring prejudice, but they did not know which were the high and which the low scorers.

In all other respects the interview protocols remained unchanged.

a. RATING BY CATEGORIES. The rating of the interviews was done for each of the categories separately. The score for the category in question, however, was obtained in a synoptic rather than a piecemeal fashion. The major source for the assignment of a score was the clinical part of the interview, but evidence was utilized from any part of the interview which might be brought to bear on each category.

Scores were in terms of a three-point scale. Since, as was mentioned above, a careful study of the interviews had preceded the construction of the Scoring Manual, certain more or less definite expectations as to what might constitute the personality aspects of a prejudiced as contrasted with an unprejudiced subject had been developed in the way of advance hypotheses. In view of this, the two opposites within each category were tentatively designated as the *presumably* "High" and "Low"[2] variants or alternatives, i.e., those expected to be typical of prejudiced and of unprejudiced persons, respectively. In the Manual the left column was used for the presumably high and the right column for the presumably low variant.

The third rating, "Neutral," comprised two distinct possibilities: (1) the existing evidence was too colorless or self-contradictory within the category in question to warrant assignment to either the "High" or the "Low" alternative; or (2) there was no evidence at all pertinent to this category. The former case is much less frequent among the "Neutral" ratings actually given than one might expect beforehand. In some of the protocols possibilities (1) and (2) were scored separately; their proportion was found to be about three to seven. In particular, factual questions were somewhat more likely to yield

---

[2] Note that the initial letter of the terms "High," "Low," (and "Neutral") is capitalized when referring to interview ratings in order to distinguish these ratings from the actual "high" or "low" scores of the subjects on prejudice and on the other scales of the questionnaire.

"no evidence" than interpretative categories, but even in the case of the group of categories subsumed under character structure the number of cases in which the material was too ambiguous to make a decision possible remained within comparatively low limits.

In absolute terms the number of "Neutrals" is considerable, especially in the case of some of the categories dealing with childhood events (see Chapters X to XII). For many variables lack of information is by no means always due to the impossibility of gathering evidence but rather to the spottiness of either the spontaneous responses of the subject or of the inquiry on the part of the interviewer who, as stated above, could not possibly cover the entire ground in each case. Both the Interview Schedule and the Scoring Manual make an attempt to cover systematically as many as possible of the very numerous areas, but it could not be hoped that each case would furnish material on all of the questions involved.

b. INTUITIVE OVER-ALL RATINGS. Besides the ratings on each of the categories, the raters were asked also to make intuitive over-all ratings. They were instructed, that is, to give their conclusive impression as to whether the subject involved was prejudiced or not. One of two alternatives, "High" (H) or "Low" (L), had to be chosen (for data see final column of Tables 1 (IX) and 2 (IX); discussion in Chapter XIII).

c. THE INTERVIEW RATERS. The ratings were made by two members of the staff of the study, here to be called M and R, one of them male and the other female. Both are well-trained psychologists and were thoroughly familiar with the nature of the categories and the underlying implications as to personality theory. These raters had participated actively in numerous conferences at which the scoring procedure was thoroughly discussed, prior to making the ratings.

Each of the raters scored approximately half of the men and half of the women, high and low scorers being distributed at random in about equal proportions within each group. (Concerning added duplicate ratings to check on reliability, see below.)

In particular, the interviews of cases M1 to M20 and F22 to F39a among those scoring high, and of cases M2 to M19 and of F29 to F39 among the low-scoring interviewees were evaluated by rater M, and those of the remaining interviewees, listed farther down in the respective subdivisions of Tables 1 (IX) and 2 (IX), were evaluated by rater R. It should be added that the code numbers used were distributed at random among the various groups so that each rater rated not only men and women, low scorers and high scorers, but also approximately equal proportions of subjects who had been given Forms 78 and 45 of the questionnaire (see also Table 3 (IX)).

4. RELIABILITY OF THE INTERVIEW RATINGS

There were three ways in which some light was thrown upon the difficult question of the reliability of the interview ratings, although only the second of these deals directly with reliability in the technical sense of the term. The other two refer to aspects which are merely more or less closely related to this problem.

a. PROPORTIONS OF RATINGS GIVEN.   First, the proportion of High, Low, and Neutral ratings within each category was compared for the two raters and found to be in fairly good agreement. One method used in computing an index for this agreement was the following: the frequencies of "High" responses, as scored by the first of the raters on each of the variables was plotted on a scatter diagram against the frequencies of such responses as scored by the second rater. In this comparison, the two raters are represented by the different nonoverlapping groups they were assigned to rate. Similar scattergrams were obtained for "Low" and "Neutral" ratings, and in each of the three cases men and women were plotted separately. With one exception, the correlation coefficients computed from the six scattergrams were between .70 and .82. This indicates that the two raters tended to concur fairly well in giving either a relatively large or a relatively small number of "High," or of "Low," or of "Neutral" ratings within any of the approximately ninety categories, showing a certain uniformity at least for one aspect of the rating policy.

(It may be added that in absolute terms there is also good agreement, the range of frequencies of "High" scores being 0 to 12, and 0 to 14, for the two raters, respectively, the various categories being considered for each of the sexes separately. For "Low" scores the corresponding ranges were 0 to 11 and 0 to 13. Thus, while both the raters neglect to use some of the alternatives offered by the Manual (as indicated by "0"), neither of them uses the opposite alternatives indiscriminately, i.e., in the characterization of all or nearly all the interviews analyzed by them.)

In view of the fact that the two staff members rated different samples of subjects, the coefficients and other data given above suggest that the character and distribution of ratings given for the various categories are to a considerable degree intrinsic to the category in question, at least within our specific combination of raters.

b. INTERRATER AGREEMENT.   Secondly, we turn to reliability proper. Nine interviewees in the group assigned to rater M were, in an additional checking procedure not used for the main analysis or for the survey in Tables 1 (IX) and 2 (IX), also rated by rater R under the identical detailed set of aspects. Two of these nine subjects were deliberately chosen from the relatively small group—12 of the 80 interviewees, i.e., 15 per cent—of those for whom the composite standing based on the detailed ratings of the original rater had missed the correct diagnosis as to prejudice. These subjects were M_{19} and F_{39}. As may be further seen from Tables 1 (IX) and 2 (IX), the remaining seven are likewise mostly not from among the clearest cases as far as interview ratings are concerned.

A comparison of the gross results of the two rating procedures is shown

TABLE 7 (IX)

RELIABILITY OF INTERVIEW RATINGS:
INTERRATER AGREEMENT ON NINE SUBJECTS

Interviewees	Prejudice score (from questionnaire)	Percentage of High ratings on interview		Composite standing on interview		Intuitive rating on interview	
		Rater M	Rater R	Rater M	Rater R	Rater M	Rater R
M3	low	19.2	36.1	L	L	L	L
M4	high	77.3	78.1	H	H	H	H
M5	low	31.4	31.7	L	L	L	L
M6	high	72.7	74.4	H	H	H	H
M19	low	70.4	31.1	L	H	H	H
F24	high	70.5	70.0	H	H	H	?
F29	low	33.3	34.4	L	L	L	H
F31	high	79.4	77.7	H	H	H	H
F39	low	72.2	27.2	H	L	H	L

in Table 7 (IX). The prejudice scores based on the questionnaire are taken from Tables 1 (IX) and 2 (IX). However, the numerical scores appearing on these tables for the subjects listed here, as based on the ratings of rater M, are limited to a selection of the more discriminating categories (see below, Section 6). The figures in Table 7 (IX) are based upon the ratings on all categories and are further given as percentages of "High" ratings relative to the possible maximum of ratings as given by the total number of categories. Thereby the number of Neutral ratings—easily obtained by subtracting both "High" and "Low" ratings from the total number of categories, 86 for men and 90 for women (see below)—has been added half and half to the "High" and the "Low" ratings. Composite standing as indicated by a percentage score of over, or of under, 50, and finally intuitive over-all ratings of the interview make up the remainder of the table.

Percentage scores show excellent interrater agreement for six of the nine subjects. Of the remaining three, those with really striking discrepancies are the same two mentioned above as having been misjudged by the original rater, M, namely $M19$ and $F39$. In both cases, the second rater has rectified the error very clearly by establishing percentage scores in the neighborhood of 30 which contrast sharply with those in the neighborhood of 70 as obtained from the first rater. The correlation coefficient between the columns representing the two raters—not very meaningful under the circumstances—is .61. It would be raised to about .8 if one of the two "controversial" cases just mentioned were eliminated so as to adjust the proportion of such cases more closely to that referred to above as existing in the total sample of interviewees, namely 15 per cent. Such a figure, if verified on a broader basis, would be quite satisfactory for the kind of material involved.

In terms of composite standing and intuitive ratings, agreement is perfect save for the two cases mentioned. (Intuitive ratings on one of the controversial subjects, $M19$, is incomplete due to the fact that rater R, contrary to instructions, declared herself as unable to make up her mind in this particular case.)

It may be added that the means of the percentage scores for the two raters are quite close to one another as well as to the ideal value of 50. They are 58.4 for M and 50.9 for R. This augments the evidence brought forward above under (a) with respect to the proportion of ratings given by the two raters. The slight preponderance of "High" ratings in rater M is also reflected in his intuitive over-all ratings. In fact, it is concentrated in the two cases where he makes his mistakes and where the second rater evens out the score.

A breakdown for the six major areas covered by the Scoring Manual, namely family patterns (see Chapter X), attitude toward sex, other people, and self (see Chapter XI), and dynamic character structure and cognitive personality organization (see Chapter XII) is given in Table 8 (IX). The number of categories for each area is also indicated. Considering the smallness of these numbers, pairs of averages from raw scores in terms of number

TABLE 8 (IX)

INTERRATER AGREEMENT ON INTERVIEW RATINGS FOR SIX MAJOR AREAS

Areas in Scoring Manual	Number of categories	Average number of ratings[b] received by four high scorers[c]		Average number of ratings[b] received by five low scorers[c]	
		Rater M H-L	Rater R H-L	Rater M H-L	Rater R H-L
Family pattern (parents, etc)	28	6.8-1.3	9.3-1.3	3.8-5.6	3.0-8.6
Attitude toward sex	7	4.5-0.3	5.3-0.3	1.8-2.2	1.0-3.4
Attitude toward other people	11	6.3-0.0	6.3-0.3	2.2-3.2	0.4-5.0
Attitude toward self	16	9.3-1.3	9.5-1.5	3.0-6.6	1.0-9.8
Dynamic character structure	22	15.3-0.3	14.5-0.5	5.8-6.2	1.6-8.8
Cognitive personality organization	6	5.0-0.0	5.0-0.5	2.0-2.8	0.4-5.0
Totals	90[a]	47.2-3.2	49.9-4.4	18.6-26.6	7.4-40.6

[a]For men the total is only 86; no adjustment to this slight difference has been made in the present table in the case of the men subjects.

[b]Rounded to one decimal place

[c]See Table 7 (IX)

of "High" and "Low" ratings (H-L) are given for the four high scorers as contrasted with the five low scorers listed in Table 7 (IX). No indices of reliability were computed here; but comparison of the first with the second and of the third with the fourth pair of figures in each row of Table 8 (IX) reveals a good deal of agreement between the two raters. The fact that this agreement is less pronounced in the case of the low scorers as shown in the columns containing the third and fourth pairs of figures, and that, furthermore, the values of H and L within these pairs often show less clear-cut differentiation than they do in the left part of the table, is due—as was revealed in more detailed analysis not presented here—to the fact that both cases with controversial diagnosis, $M19$ and $F39$, happen to be in this group. Perhaps with the exception of family pattern and attitude toward self, this lack of differentiation for the group of low scorers, especially in rater M, and the ensuing disagreement with rater R, is about evenly distributed over the various areas; for high scorers differentiation and agreement is about equally good for all the areas, and the "totals" are in excellent agreement with one another.

Discounting the controversial cases, i.e., the 15 per cent in our total sample of interviewees for which the original rater arrived at a diagnosis opposite to that given by the defining score on the prejudice scales, the results of this fragmentary analysis of reliability are quite encouraging. In fact, if the trend as discussed for Table 7 (IX) should be representative of the entire sample, interrater agreement for the remaining 85 per cent of the interviewees would be close to .9. For the other 15 per cent one may contemplate challenging the validity of the defining prejudice score along with doubting the validity of the interview rating. The "questionnaire-high" may after all be considered the product of an approach that is by definition less concerned with underlying dynamics than is the diagnosis of the "personality-high."

Further data on interrater agreement on the interview will be presented in Chapter XIII.

The problem of agreement of various types of ratings among themselves, such as in our present context especially of composite standing and intuitive over-all rating, will be discussed in Chapter XIII. In a broader sense such aspects are also included within the general concept of reliability.

A third avenue of scrutiny somewhat akin to reliability problems is through the study of "halo-effects," to be discussed next.

5. MINIMIZING HALO-EFFECTS IN RATING THE INTERVIEWS

We return now to the problem of the carry-over from one category to another, much in the way of the "halo-effect" known in social and educational psychology. One way of preventing or minimizing the halo-effect would have been to use designations other than "(presumably) High" and "(presumably) Low" to characterize the two opposites within the various categories. But such a procedure would have prevented only raters unfamiliar with the underlying hypotheses from succumbing to halo-effects. Such raters, on the other hand, would have been undesirable from other, more crucial points of view. It was thus decided to leave control of halo-effects to special analytical attitudes the raters were asked to maintain, and to ascertain the degree of relatedness in a statistical analysis of the completed ratings. It must be noted that—as in all cases of halo-effects—a certain amount of correlation may be fully justified by fact, i.e., by existing correlation of real traits. Exactly how much of the halo is realistic would require further intensive study for all combinations of categories involved.

Both the variability of the discriminatory power of the single categories (see below) and the variability of the proportion of "High" and "Low" ratings ascribed to the various subjects seem to indicate that the raters succeeded, at least in part, in keeping the halo-effect within reasonable bounds in rating the subjects. Evidence on the second of these points is contained in Tables 1(IX) and 2(IX) in the first two of the columns relating to ratings of the interviews. As is readily seen, hardly any of the subjects are classified as "High" or as "Low" on all categories even when the "Neutral" ratings are excluded from consideration, and for some of them there is an approximately equal number of "High" and "Low" ratings. This shows that the raters were quite capable of separating the various issues involved, and of rating a person as "High" in one respect and as "Low" in another.

6. TABULATION OF INTERVIEW RATINGS BY CATEGORIES: STATISTICAL SIGNIFICANCE

A tabulation of interview ratings by single categories was obtained simply by counting the instances of High (H), of Low (L), and of Neutral (N) ratings, on a given category, among subjects of each of four groups—high-scoring men, low-scoring men, high-scoring women, and low-scoring women (scoring, that is, extremely high or low on the direct prejudice questionnaire).

Analysis of the figures for a given category, with a view to their bearing upon the underlying hypotheses, could have any one of four outcomes—two "positive" and two "negative." The "positive" instances are confirmatory of the original hypothesis. They include "High" ratings—i.e., those designating reactions *presumed* to occur more frequently in the prejudiced person—when given to subjects scoring high on the prejudice scales, as well as "Low" ratings given to relatively unprejudiced, i.e., our so-called "low-scoring," subjects, in short, the hH and lL combinations. The remaining two figures, indicating the frequency of prejudiced subjects receiving a "Low" and of unprejudiced subjects receiving a "High" rating, in short, the hL and the lH combinations, constitute the "negative," nonconfirmatory instances.

The series of tables in Chapters X to XII (Tables 1(X) to 2(XII)) presents, for the two sexes separately, the numbers of prejudiced and of unprejudiced interviewees who give the presumably "High" and the presumably "Low" responses in the interviews, for each of the scoring categories. The number of "Neutrals" may be obtained by subtraction of their sums from the total number of subjects in the respective prejudiced or unprejudiced groups. The four raw figures are followed by two sums which contrast the total number of positive with the total number of negative instances. All "positive," i.e., confirmatory, evidence is *italicized*. Whenever a category is defined in the Scoring Manual by only one variant, H or L, rather than by an opposition of an H with an L, only the presence of the trait in question is registered in the tables and the remaining space is left blank.

The final column of the tables indicates the level of statistical significance of the difference, on the category in question, between prejudiced and unprejudiced extremes as defined in the present study. It thus refers to the "discriminatory power" and the importance of the category as a personality correlate—and therefore as a potential measure—of overtly expressed ethnic prejudice. Indications of significance are given in terms of whether or not the 5 per cent (satisfactory), the 2 per cent, or the 1 per cent level (highly satisfactory, since in this latter case there is a 99 per cent probability that the obtained difference is not due to chance factors) has been reached *or* surpassed, without specifying whether or by how much they have been surpassed. Significance was computed after evenly dividing the "Neutrals" among the "High" and the "Low" ratings. It must not be forgotten, in this connection, that dividing the Neutral ratings tends to lower the index of significance, the more so the larger the proportion of these ratings. Thus, in treating the Neutral ratings as we do, we are keeping on the safe side, since, as was pointed out above, the Neutral scorings are based, in a considerable proportion of the cases, on lack of information rather than on lack of actual discriminability.

Wherever the proportion of Neutrals for the total sample of interviewees is larger than 50 per cent, the statistical significance of the category in question was not computed and therefore there was no entry under any circumstances in the last column of the tables. The category was also omitted from the survey of interview scores in Tables 1 (IX) and 2 (IX). For men the total number of categories is 86, somewhat less than for women, in whose case a few more subdivisions were introduced into the Scoring Manual. Of these 86 categories, 72 yielded less than 50 per cent Neutrals, and thus remained for full treatment. For women only 65 of the original 90 categories yielded less than 50 per cent Neutrals and were thus retained for full treatment. The fact that the categories were generally somewhat more discriminatory in the case of the men than in the case of the women may be accounted for by the fact that most of the men were interviewed at a later stage of the study and that therefore their records were more complete.

All the calculations discussed above were performed separately for men and women. Corresponding figures for each appear closely adjacent to one another in the tables, those for men (M) in the upper left-hand and those for women (W) in the lower right-hand area of each of the "cells" that one may imagine at the intersection of vertical columns with horizontal rows, the latter defined by the various categories.

CHAPTER X

PARENTS AND CHILDHOOD AS
SEEN THROUGH THE INTERVIEWS

Else Frenkel-Brunswik

A. INTRODUCTION

In turning to the specific results of the interviews we begin with the organization of the family. Many of the attitudes and underlying needs discussed in this volume must be assumed to originate, as far as the individual is concerned, in the family situation. Here the growing child learns for the first time to handle interpersonal relations. Some of the members of the family are in an authoritative, others in an equalitarian or in a weaker position than himself. Some are of the same, others are of the opposite sex. It soon becomes evident to the youngster what kind of behavior is considered appropriate and will lead to reward and what kind of behavior will be punished. He finds himself confronted with a certain set of values and certain expectations which he has to meet.

Within the general common framework of the white American population, families vary greatly as to the rigidity or flexibility of the roles defined within the family, as well as to values in general. We shall encounter families in which considerably more emphasis is placed on obedience than it is in others. In some cases discipline is harsh and threatening, in others intelligible and mild. Or there may be rigorous adherence to conventional rules and customs rather than to more flexible and more intrinsic values which lead to greater tolerance for individual variations. Or smooth functioning within the family may depend either more on exchange of well-defined obligations and "goods," or else on an exchange of genuine affection. These and other differences in the organization of the family are under scrutiny in the light of their possible implications with respect to the personality structure of the individual and his social and political beliefs.

Although no striking relations between these patterns and gross economic factors have been uncovered in the present study, systematic investigations of a more distinctly sociological nature would undoubtedly reveal broader

337

cultural and subcultural determinants of these differences, say, the greater frequency of one or the other type of family organization in different national subgroups, or a dependence on the relative stability or instability of the socioeconomic family history.

While this goes to press, data from a separate project (Frenkel-Brunswik, for an advance report see 30)[1] seem to indicate that parents of extremely prejudiced children are relatively often the children of foreign-born parents or show preoccupation as to social and national insecurity.

Specific rating categories from the Interview Scoring Manual in the area of family organization, followed by tabulation of quantitative results and eventually by a discussion and the presentation of pertinent quotations from the interviews themselves, are given in Sections B to D.

B. ATTITUDES TOWARD PARENTS AND CONCEPTION OF THE FAMILY

1. DEFINITION OF RATING CATEGORIES AND QUANTITATIVE RESULTS

In line with the over-all subject matter of the present volume, the discussion concerning attitudes toward parents will, among others, center about the following questions: Is the general tendency toward glorification and lack of critical evaluation of ingroups on the part of the ethnically prejudiced also mirrored in their attitudes toward their parents? Is there a tendency toward submission, and how are the problems of rebellion, hostility, and guilt handled in our two opposite groups? How are the feelings of genuine love related to conformity as contrasted with independence?

The definitions of the specific categories of the Scoring Manual dealing with problems of this nature are listed here in the form in which they were used by the raters. It should be remembered, however, that the Manual represents merely a summary of what was developed, and discussed with the two raters, in extended conferences preceding the actual rating procedure. The subsequent text makes occasional use of the more prominent of the connotations thus established which were not formally incorporated in the Manual in order not to overload it in actual use.

Before starting the presentation of the various parts of the Interview Scoring Manual, attention must be called to the fact that strict opposi-

[1] The study on social discrimination in children referred to here is being carried out at the Institute of Child Welfare of the University of California. The project was initiated by the present writer, in cooperation with Harold E. Jones and T. W. Adorno, and sponsorship was at first by the Scientific Department of the American Jewish Committee. In developing the tests and experiments the present writer was aided primarily by Claire Brednor, Donald T. Campbell, Joan Havel, Murray E. Jarvik, and Milton Rokeach.

tion or near-opposition of the presumably "High" and the presumably "Low" variants is to be assumed only where the numbers or number-letter combinations appearing on the right side of the page are identical with those on the left. Thus Category 2, "victimization," stands in a somewhat oblique relation to Categories 2a to 2c. In some cases pairings of this kind reflect the fact that there is more than one opposite to a given variant. Beginning with Section C of this chapter, different sets of letters are sometimes used on the two sides to stress an absence of one-by-one correspondence of a series of alternatives listed on the right with a series of items on the left, although the lists in their entirety define a more clear-cut pattern of opposition. (Concerning the lopsided evaluation of asymmetrical categories in the tables to follow, see the concluding pages of the preceding chapter.)

The first subdivision of the Interview Scoring Manual follows. As in the Interview Schedule, *italics* are used to represent key phrases which had been emphasized to the raters by underscoring.

INTERVIEW SCORING MANUAL: ATTITUDES TOWARD PARENTS AND CONCEPTION OF FAMILY
(to Table 1(X)).

Presumably "High" Variants	Presumably "Low" Variants
1. *Conventional idealization* of parent(s): Overestimation of qualities and status, expressed in behavioral (essentially external), conventionalized generalities, or undifferentiated "all's well" attitude	1. *Objective appraisal* of parents
2. *Victimization* (quasi-persecutory) by parent(s): Neglect, including failure to give proper discipline, unjust discipline; "picked on"; unfair: resents preferring of rival sib or spouse (or foster-sib or step-spouse); etc.	2a. *Principled open rejection*
	2b. *Genuine positive affect:* some reference to (positive) psychological qualities; individualized characterizations
	2c. *Blocked affect* (Presumably mutually exclusive with 2a)
3a. *Submission* to parental authority and values: respect based on fear	3. *Principled independence*
3b. *Capricious rebellion* against parents; delinquency	
4a. *Ego-alien dependence-for-things* and support on parents: essentially exploitive-manipulative-"getting"; an externalized relationship	4. *Love-seeking succorance-nurturance-affiliation* toward parents
4b. *Sense of obligation-and-duty* to	

parents: Desire to "make it up to them"

5. *Ingroup orientation* to family as a whole; e.g., emphasis on family heredity and "background"; homogeneous-totalitarian family vs. rest of world; aristocratic superiority of family, etc.	5. *Individualized* approach to members of the family

In Table 1(X), the results for both men and women interviewees are presented in the manner described in the concluding section of the preceding chapter. Abbreviated formulations of the categories just listed are presented, along with category numbers, for purposes of easier identification.

2. IDEALIZATION *VS.* OBJECTIVE APPRAISAL OF PARENTS

In view of their general tendency toward conventionality and submission toward ingroup members, it is not surprising to find in the prejudiced subjects a tendency toward *"idealization of the parents."* This idealization is expressed characteristically in generalized and undifferentiated, conventionalized terms which primarily glorify external features of physical appearance or overt behavioral conduct rather than involving the more internal aspects of their personality. *"Objective appraisal"* of parents, referring to an ability for critical evaluation of the parents in specific and psychologically conceived terms, on the other hand, is predominant in the unprejudiced subjects.

The detailed results presented in Table 1(X) (under Category 1) reveal the striking fact that none of the low-scoring women interviewed shows the glorification of the parents just described; instead, 11 of them show objective, critical appraisal. Of the high-scoring women, 9 show glorification and 6 objective appraisal of parents. For the total group of women, there are 20 "positive" as contrasted with 6 "negative" instances in the sense defined at the end of the preceding chapter. The statistical significance of the difference between the positive evidence (i.e., that confirming the original hypothesis underlying the distinction between the "High" and the "Low" variant) and the negative (nonconfirmatory) evidence cited is found to be at the "1 per cent level," and thus highly satisfactory (see Chapter IX, Section F, 6).

A good illustration of the "High" attitude in women is given by the following quotation from the interview of one of the high scorers: "Mother— she amazes me—millions of activities—had two maids in _____ years ago, but never since—such calmness—never sick, *never*—beautiful woman she really is." The reference to external dimensions, both behavioral ("million activities") and physical ("never sick, beautiful"), can be seen clearly in the foregoing record. It must be emphasized that the subjects were asked, in this connection, "What kind of person is your father (mother)?" without further

TABLE 1 (X)

INTERVIEW RATINGS ON ATTITUDE TOWARD PARENTS AND CONCEPT OF FAMILY FOR 80 SUBJECTS SCORING EXTREMELY "HIGH" OR "LOW" ON THE ETHNIC PREJUDICE QUESTIONNAIRE SCALE

Interview rating categories (abbreviated from Manual)	Sex	Number of "High"(H) and "Low"(L) ratings received by 20 men and 25 women "high scorers"		20 men and 15 women "low scorers"		Sums of instances		Level of statistical significance reached (percentage)
		H	L	H	L	"positive"	"negative"	
1. Conventional idealization(H) vs. objective appraisal(L) of parents	Men	11	1	2	13	24	3	1
	Women	9	6	0	11	20	6	1
2. Victimization by parents (H) vs. a. Principled open rejection of parents (L)	Men	6	4			6	4	1
	Women	8	4			8	4	2
b. c. Genuine affection or blocked affect for parents(L)	Men	1		1	2	3	1	
	Women	2		2	1	3	2	
3a. Submission to parents(H) vs. principled independence(L)	Men	14	2	2	10	24	4	1
	Women	9	0	2	8	17	2	2
3b. Capricious rebellion(H)	Men	9	4			9	4	
	Women	6	1			6	1	
4a. Dependence for things on parents (H) vs. love-seeking affiliation(L)	Men	13	1	1	14	27	2	1
	Women	13	5	2	8	21	7	5
4b. Sense of obligation and duty(H)	Men	5	1			5	1	
	Women	1	1			1	1	
5. Ingroup conception of family(H)	Men	6	2			6	2	
	Women	7	1			7	1	

specification (see the Interview Schedule as presented in the preceding chapter).

The overestimation of parents in more general terms is especially clear in the record of another prejudiced woman interviewee *(F24)*: "Father—he is wonderful; couldn't make him better. He is always willing to do anything for you. He is about _____ years old, six feet tall, has dark brown hair, slim build, young-looking face, good-looking, dark green eyes." The same subject gives further evidence of the stereotypical conception of parents in the high scorers by repeating the same description for her mother, differentiating only the physical characteristics. After repeating the first two sentences she continues: "She is about 5 feet 5 inches, neither slim nor stocky. She's reducing. She has dark hair, blue eyes, is nice looking. She is _____ years old." These illustrations are quite typical of the responses of our high-scoring subjects.

It should be added that none of the 6 high-scoring women who show "objective appraisal" of parents was considered to manifest "positive affect" toward the parents (Category 2). This will be discussed below.

Very characteristic of high-scoring subjects is an initial statement of great admiration for parents, followed by some criticism which is not, however, recognized as such by the subject. The comparison of reactions to general questions with reactions to specific questions proved especially fruitful, e.g., when parents were characterized in general positive terms but the specific episodes and traits referred to were mostly of a negative character. (Regarding related mechanisms of self-deception, see 33, 34.) The subject is aware only of admiration toward the parents, and the reservations seem to enter the picture against "better" intention and knowledge, thus injecting into the statement an element of ambivalence.

Examples of this attitude from the protocols of high-scoring women are quoted in the following. It should be mentioned here that throughout Chapters X to XII the special code numbers used in rating the interviews are retained for greater anonymity; for the same reason, localities, occupations and related personal data are either left out or disguised.

F31: (Father?) "He has a marvelous personality and gets along well with people. He has a hot temper."

Or *F79:* "Mother was, of course, a very wonderful person. She was very nervous. Irritable only when overdoing."

Or again, *F74:* "Father is quiet and calm. He never shows irritation. He is very intelligent, and his opinions are very valid. He is very sincere and very well liked by friends and employees. He rarely puts himself out for people, but people love him. He is exceptionally good looking, dresses well, has gray hair, and is _____ years old."

Glorification of parents is equally or even more pronounced in our high-scoring men than it is in the high-scoring women. Of the 20 interviewees in this group, 11 show this feature whereas only one has been rated as giving evidence of "objective appraisal"; and the entire category is again significant at the 1 per cent level. One of the high-scoring men describes his father as a "very, very fine man—intelligent, understanding, excellent father, in every way." Another says that his father "is always good to his family. Naturally, a kid would not think their parents had any weaknesses in them." Use of such terms as "naturally" or "of course"—the latter in the protocol of F_{79} quoted above—reveals the element of conventionalism inherent in the mechanism of glorification. Another high-scoring man says:

M_{47}: (What sort of person was your mother?) "Well, best in the world. . . . She's good, in fact, the best. In other words, she's just tops with me. She's friendly with everybody. Never has no trouble. Does anything for me she can. Writes me all the time. (What do you admire most about her?) Just about everything. When father went away, mother took care of me all her life, where she could have put me in a home some place if she had wanted to. She always stayed with me in trouble."

Or, M_{52}: (What have you admired most about your father?) "Well, let's see. . . . Well, there's really no particular point that I admire most. . . . I've always been very proud to be his son. (What sort of person was your mother?) Most terrific person in the world to me. (Shortcomings of mother?) Well, I don't really think she has any, except maybe too wound up in her home, and didn't take more interest in social affairs. . . . I truthfully can't say she has any definite shortcomings."

Or, M_{51}: (Going back to your father, you say you didn't accept him as a shining example when you were a child?) "He was always with me except when I was in boarding school, that is, always at home. I just took him for granted, that's all. I never analyzed him . . . when I was *very* small. Instead of asking *why* does the sun shine, how are babies made, etc., etc., my father says I took everything for granted. . . . I wonder why that was. . . ."

One of the outstanding features in the above quotations from high scorers is the use of superlatives in the description of parents, such as "excellent man in every way," "best in the world," "most terrific person," etc. If more detailed and specific elaborations are made at all, they refer to material benefits or help given by the parents. Where there is no readiness to admit that one's parents have any weakness in them it is not surprising to find later an indication of repressed hostility and revengeful fantasies behind the mask of compliance. Some evidence on this point has already been presented above.

The high scorers' emphasis on more obvious rather than on subtle and internalized characteristics cannot be traced to a lower level of education or of intelligence (see Chapter VIII). Rather it must be seen as in line with their general tendency toward greater shallowness and stereotypy and a diluted diffuseness of inner experiences.

The objective appraisal of one's parents, manifested primarily by the low scorers, has a very different quality. Instead of an apparent overestimation of the parents which, as will be seen, goes hand in hand with a fearful submission to them, we find in the typical unprejudiced subject an evaluation of the parents on terms of equality. In the following records, all taken from interviews of low-scoring subjects, we find the parents described as real people with real assets and shortcomings. The emphasis in the description is on internal rather than external and physical characteristics. Concomitant with a more critical attitude, we often find in these records a closer and warmer relationship with the parents. It also becomes clear that the parents have often been a source of comfort and love for these subjects, who, in their turn, are more secure in their feelings toward their parents. They are thus able to face and to express conflicts in the areas where there is or was disagreement. Often we get the impression that the low scorers talk in a benevolently condescending way about their parents, critically and at the same time lovingly.

Thus low-scoring women are found to describe their parents as follows:

F65: "My mother is very much interested in people; she is practical and sensible, but she gets too much interested in fads. On some points I disagree with my mother very much. Mother wants me to be more social. She wants me to wear lipstick, go out to parties, etc. I am too lazy to do all those things. She is very good, nice and does the right thing, but I don't like her temperament. She is mad one minute and the next one she isn't. She gives me too much advice."

F62: "Father tries to be rational, but he is not always so. He is a dominant person, though my mother was master of the house."

F70: (What kind of person is your father?) "Father was never much in the picture; he paid more attention to me between the ages of one and six than later. I think he wanted a boy, so he paid little attention to me, so probably has not influenced my attitudes very much. Describing father is easier. He's a more definite kind of person than mother. He's a person of great intolerance; he is 'a great authority on all subjects' (spoken with some irony) including medicine and physiology."

F23: "Father was very dominating in the home, like all European men, and mother submitted to him. I almost think she enjoyed 'being a martyr'!" (It then became very clear that her mother's submissive and self-sacrificing attitude were unacceptable to the subject. The mother never got what she wanted. The things she wanted were like dreams, and she seemed satisfied to keep them as dreams. For example, she would have liked to redecorate the house or to buy a summer place, but the father would never let her.)

F26 feels that her father did not understand her point of view. She thinks he is sensitive, but does not sense other people's feelings. The mother is described as a pal, and as having a sense of humor. Subject thinks that, unlike her father, her mother understood what she was feeling.

Examples of "objective appraisal" of parents in low-scoring men follow. As is to be expected in our culture, there sometimes is a word or two of exaggerated praise at the beginning; but this is usually followed up by some more specific qualifiation of a less stereotyped, more vivid and direct kind.

M42: (What sort of person is your mother?) "Well, I think she is a wonderful woman . . . been very good to me . . . never put too many restrictions on my activities . . . her rules were few and far between, but what rules there were, had to be obeyed and not to be monkeyed with. . . . As a woman, she might seem to be a little hard to get acquainted with . . . and, at first, might seem a little 'uppitish,' but . . . she tends to have relatively few friends, and comes to know them pretty well . . . quiet, listens more than she talks, very fair. (What do you admire most about her?) I don't know. I've never given it much thought. I don't think of any one trait . . . she is very fair. . . . I don't think you could talk her into cheating . . . if she feels something is right, she'll stick up for it no matter what."

M44: (What sort of person is your father?) "Oh, he's the kind of guy who never has been very happy working for somebody else. He's always had a little difficulty, especially with a very large company (laughs). He just has a venomous hatred for any big outfit. . . . He has a very vital sense of justice and honesty, and he just can't stand pressure practices. . . ."

M50: (What sort of person is your mother?) "An intellectual and a very well-educated person. Her principal gift seems to be that of perception. And a musician (piano) . . . not by trade but certainly by nature. (What do you admire most about her?) Her intellectual ability."

M53: (What sort of person was your mother?) "Well, sort of an average person, a rather happy person, quite a happy person. I think she was fairly intelligent, and there again was conditioned to mother-wife sort of thing. Always maintained a pleasant home, I mean really pleasant. (Weaknesses?) Well, I would say a certain unworldliness. (How do you mean?) Perhaps, a perfect product of her age, in a way. Kind of a respectable, average, God-fearing sort of person (laughs). . . . Didn't know much about finances . . . clinging-vine type of female, but a very pleasant person. Made not a desperate attempt, but maintained a very pleasant home . . . very pleasant, reasonable sort of person. Certain possessiveness (towards subject)."

M3: "I like my father. He is more a taciturn type, a quiet Frenchman, keeps out of trouble. I don't particularly respect my mother. She is intellectually shallow, wishy-washy—vacillating is the word. That's a hell of a thing to say about mother, but . . . . (Q) "Like I'll tell her what I want to do, and she'll agree enthusiastically. Then father will come along with his ideas against mine, and she'll agree with him. You can only take so much of that. . . . I admire father for his ability to keep his mouth shut. He just says nothing and looks dignified and everyone admires and respects him. I wish I could do that. Of the two, I'd rather be alone with him. (What is your mother like?) Kindly, generous, always wishing well, seeing the bright side of things, fairly jolly, cracking jokes. Gets along with people fairly well, they like her and she likes them. Her geniality may be just practice because she's been teaching so long . . . principal of a local grammar school . . . she knows how to be amusing, hail-fellow-well-met, you might say. But slightly moralistic, morals of about 1910. For example, she is against Errol Flynn; doesn't moralize, just makes critical remarks in a joking way."

M15: "Father was born in 1890 on a farm in _____, mother in 1889 on an _____ farm. (Subject describes his father as having a bad temper and being very strict, punishing the children severely; such as beating them with a strap.) Father did not attend high school. He had many friends. Played football. Father started out as a game feeder at _____ University, also became a good carpenter and painter. In the 1920's the family moved to _____ and father became a minister in the _____ Church. The only prerequisite for that was to be able to read the Bible. His sermons are all hell-fire and brimstone." (Subject thinks that father had an 'inferiority complex,' doesn't know just how to explain it.)

Not only do low-scoring subjects express disagreement with their parents more freely, but there is evidence in the records that when they disagree they have the strength to follow their own way, though often not without paying the price of conflict and guilt.

It is with respect to the following aspects that the unprejudiced subjects are most often critical of their parents: pressure to sociability, parents giving too much advice, too much dominance or possessiveness, lack of understanding, religious conflicts. Often hand in hand with these resentments real appreciation of the parents is expressed in specific terms by pointing to their abilities, their independence of conventions, generosity, perceptiveness, happiness.

Since typical low scorers do not really see their parents as any too overpowering or frightening, they can afford to express their feelings of resentment more readily. Being able to mobilize rebellion, unprejudiced subjects thus learn to conceive of equality as an alternative to the relationship of dominance-submission. Ambivalence toward the parents can be openly faced and worked out on this basis, preventing the crippling effect of too much repression and submission. It is in this manner that expression of rebelliousness seems to go with increased ability to give as well as to receive genuine affection while repression of resentment is associated with a more stereotypical glorification of parents that seems devoid of real feeling.

3. GENUINENESS OF AFFECT

Manifestations of *genuine positive affect* toward the parents as revealed, among other things, by references to (positive) psychological qualities, were found mainly in low-scoring subjects (Category 2b). It can be understood readily that positive affect toward parents should be found more often where there is an objective evaluation of the parents rather than where there is resentment toward them. In addition to the illustrations of positive affect given previously, we quote here one example of a very intensive expression of positive feeling for the father on the part of a low-scoring woman:

F63: "But I remember when my father left, she came to my room and said, 'You'll never see your Daddy again.' Those were her exact words. I was crazy with grief and felt it was her fault. I threw things, emptied drawers out of the window, pulled the spreads off the bed, then threw things at the wall."

The finding that positive affect toward parents is present more often in low scorers must be seen in conjunction with the results on glorification versus objective appraisal as discussed above. In fact, 6 out of the 25 high-scoring women interviewees (as against 11 out of the 15 lower scorers, to be sure) were rated as manifesting objective appraisal. From the present data, however, it is evident that the objectivity of the high-scoring women must be regarded as more hostile than positive. None of them was rated as having "genuine positive affect." Being basically an attitude of libidinized interest, true objectivity seems to be primarily the domain of the low scorers, at least in the present context. This is far from saying that all or nearly all the unprejudiced extremes exhibit this trait. In fact, low scorers sometimes display distortions all their own, caused mainly by feelings of guilt and remorse and often leading to an obsessive rather than a genuine type of objectivity (see Chapter XII).

There is some evidence of what may be called *blocked affect* in the low scorers (Category 2c). An example is given by one of the men in this classification who answered the question, "What were your parents like?" by simply saying "normal parents" without being able to elaborate on this topic when questioned further.

It was expected, on the basis of the generally greater openness of the low scorers, that if parents were rejected by low-scoring subjects, this rejection would tend to be open and based on disagreement with respect to basic principles. *Principled open rejection* (Category 2a) did not, however, prove to be statistically differentiating. This may well be due to the fact that only a few cases manifested this attitude.

4. FEELINGS OF VICTIMIZATION

Somewhat more often than open rejection of the parents, a feeling of *victimization by the parents* (Category 2) is found in the high-scoring women interviewees. These feelings include complaints about being neglected, unjustly disciplined, picked on or otherwise unfairly treated, especially in rivalry situations within the family. Eight of the high-scoring women interviewees showed this attitude, often in conjunction with a glorification of the parents. The subsequent record of a high-scoring woman interviewee gives an example of admiration for the father in general terms, as expressed by the initial phrase, "a grand person," combined with resentment and a feeling of being neglected in favor of the brothers which is brought out after encouragement by the interviewer to describe the father's faults:

F32: Altogether she thinks her "father is a grand person." When asked whether, since no one is perfect, there were any little faults that she could name, she said that she couldn't think of any. He never drank; well, he swore a little bit. And he was argumentative. (However, in discussing her vocation, subject had mentioned that the father had been willing to finance the education of the boys, but that he expected the girls to stay home and be ladies, so what the girls got they got on their own. In another connection, subject remarked that she had got nothing out of her father. He provided them with the necessities of life, but would not give them anything extra. He never allowed the girls to entertain boys at home. Nevertheless, subject stated that she was closer to her father than to her mother.) When the interviewer broached the topic of her brothers and sisters, subject replied, "I'm right in the middle—don't they say middle children are forgotten children!" When asked if she thought that was so, subject closed up, merely remarking that her parents showed no partiality.

Some of the other high-scoring women are resentful against their parents because of a feeling that their brothers were preferred by virtue of their being boys. Envy, resentment, and depreciation of the brother by high-scoring women, in conjunction with the sense of being victimized by the parents, is exemplified by the following report:

F39: "I had to get up early with mother and bake and clean all day long. I used to say that it was especially unfair because my brother would play. Mother said, well, he was a boy, and that really made me mad."

It must be emphasized that these feelings of resentment against the parents, especially when they appear in the records of high-scoring subjects, are usually not ego-accepted. Thus *F39*, whose record was just quoted above, states that her mother was "terribly strict with me about learning to keep house. . . . I am glad now, but I resented it then." The feelings of resentment are considered "bad" and therefore projected onto childhood and not accepted as present feelings.

Such strictness and the general idea of being treated as a "child" at home are often the source of feelings of victimization. At the same time there is, as will be discussed in greater detail below, submission to the demands of the parents. One high-scoring girl complains about her father: "Can't say I don't like him . . . but he wouldn't let me date at 16. I had to stay home. . . ." Another girl in this group says, "Father and mother were so anxious to adjust that they forgot us. They treated us as 16-year-olds when we were actually 18." Prejudiced subjects generally tend to feel themselves "forgotten," the victims of injustice who did not "get" enough of the things they deserved. They thus tend to resent other people, especially outgroups, of whom they readily conceive as unjustifiably threatening, as intruding on their rights, and as attempting to take privileges away from them.

As was pointed out in previous publications (E. Frenkel-Brunswik, 35, 38) and as will be shown in detail in Chapter XIV, high-scoring women tend to express a great deal of hostility toward mother figures in their responses to the Thematic Apperception Test. In their interviews, however, we find mainly admiration for the mother, although this is frequently intermingled with nonaccepted feelings of hostility and resentment. In those relatively rare cases in which there is an open expression of hostility toward the mother in the interview of a high-scoring woman, one is likely to find this hostility very intense and of an almost paranoid character. The following example is characteristic of this:

F36: Subject describes her mother variously as domineering, dictatorial, and self-centered. Her mother is good at social relationships; she knew how to get along with people. After her divorce, she worked as a traveling ——— saleswoman until subject graduated from high school. When on the road, she was very popular with the other salesmen. She worked just long enough to see subject through school, then expected subject to support her, and so quit work. When subject was in high school, she used to make all the clothes for her mother and herself. Once her mother cut out a dress wrongly and when subject criticized what she had done, her mother cried, "You don't want to do anything for your mother!" To this, subject retorted, "I never will make anything for you again!" And she never did. In ———, subject shared an apartment with her mother; her mother wanted to run her life and made it impossible for her to have friends at home. She expected her to give in to her for everything. She practically pushed subject out of the apartment; so subject told her finally that she would have to get a place of her own. Her mother asked her how much money she was making and subject replied, "None of your business!" This was what her mother had often said to her. Her mother figured out how much she was making and then asked subject to increase her allowance. Subject retorted, "What would you do if I didn't support you!" This shut her up. Things finally became so unbearable that subject broke with her mother completely and has not seen her for years. However, she has continued to support her mother and still sends her a check regularly.

The foregoing record is atypical of the interview material but would be typical of the stories that high-scoring women tell about mother figures in the Thematic Apperception Test. In the stories told by prejudiced women about mother figures the pressure which such women exert upon their daughters is usually revealed alongside the fantasies of revenge. In the more direct descriptions of their mothers in the interviews there is, in most cases, nothing but expressions of admiration.

The intensity of hostility, once such an attitude breaks through in the interview, points toward the fact that strong defenses against it are necessary and indicates once again the source and meaning of the attitude of "glorification." In spite of the fact that the subject quoted above openly faces her hostility toward her mother, she still often feels obliged to submit to the mother although she really cannot accept this kind of dependency. Typically, the quarrel with the mother centers about material benefits and problems of exploitation.

Feelings of victimization were also found in 4 low-scoring women. However, in the low-scoring cases such feelings differ somewhat in kind from those of subjects who score high. For example, $F63$, whose intense expressions of despair have been quoted above, experiences the divorce of her parents as desertion by her father. There, the feeling of resentment has a different quality in that it seems a reaction to loss of love rather than a dissatisfaction with not "getting" enough. In other cases the feelings of resentment toward the parents in low-scoring subjects are similar to those of the high scorers, except for the fact that they are more readily accepted and therefore do not appear in the same context with glorification of the parents.

In men, feelings of "victimization" as such are still less differentiating than in women. Four low scorers and 6 high scorers, out of the 20 men interviewees in each group, show this attitude. There is again, however, a different quality in the two groups in this respect. In the high scorers, reference is usually made to the parent as a disciplinarian. One man complains of having had to work too much, another of not having been slapped enough.

M51: "Usually got my way. In fact, all I ever had to do was cry about anything and he'd do whatever it was that upset me (sic!). . . . I think if I'd been slapped around a little more as a child, I might not need to be slapped around now that I'm grown up. . . . Not only that, but my selfishness is something I can almost blame him for. His attitude and that of the whole family led me to believe that I was . . . the whole universe . . . I know now. I'm not selfish now. But I had to learn that for myself. . . . My playing cops and robbers: that was because I felt stepped on. . . ."

On the other hand, the feelings of victimization found in low-scoring men give the impression of being more directly based on reality, and tend to refer to not receiving love or some substitute for it. The following is an illustration of this:

M55: "For example, he would take a delicacy like candy, pretend to offer us some and then eat it himself and laugh uproariously. . . . Makes him seem sort of a monster, though he's not really."

5. SUBMISSION *VS.* PRINCIPLED INDEPENDENCE

Related to glorification of parents is an attitude to be characterized as *submission to parental authority* and values out of respect based on fear. Its opposite has been designated as *principled independence*. The importance of this aspect (incorporated here as Category 3a) has been stressed several times before in this volume, on the grounds that submission to parental authority may be closely related to submission to authority in general. And submission to authority, in its turn, has the broadest implications for social and personal behavior both toward those with power and those without it. It is therefore interesting to note that this category shows marked differences between prejudiced and unprejudiced interviewees. The percentage of high-scoring men who manifest this attitude (as well as the index of significance on this category for men) is greater than that of the high-scoring women. This gives some support to the hypothesis that high-scoring men are faced with a more serious submission problem than high-scoring women. Their longing for submission as well as their "toughness," described on previous occasions as a reaction to precisely this submission, will be traced below in greater detail to factors in the family constellation.

Examples of submission to parental authority in high-scoring men are the following:

M41: (Discipline?) "Well, there wasn't much to exercise. We just did what they said. Children didn't run wild in those days like they do nowadays."

M43: "Sun-up to sun-down. (How did you take that?) We did what the elders told us to. (Ever question it?) Well, I never questioned."

M47: "Well, to tell the truth, I don't think she was strict enough with us. . . . I'd get out and run around, come home later than supposed to. She never licked me. Just bawled me out, which was worse. Only licked me once, for stealing my brother's watch when I was 10. (What were you disciplined for?) Schoolwork, and doing what I was told to do. She was pretty strict about that being home on time. (How did you respond?) It just hurt. I never sassed her back or said a mean thing to her. . . ."

M57: (How did you react when you were spanked?) "I just didn't do it any-more."

M58: "But, you know, I never held that against my father—I had it coming. He laid the law down, and if I broke it, there was punishment, but never in uncontrolled anger."

From the foregoing protocols it is evident that many of the high-scoring men not only submit to discipline and punishment because there is no other choice left, but often find themselves in complete agreement with the ad-ministration of harsh punishment. They identify themselves with the punisher and even seem to enjoy punishment. Not only do they appear to have had this attitude as children, but during their adult life the idea of punishment and the fear of it stays with them, often preventing them from transgressing a narrow path of seeming virtue. This holds only for the genuinely conserva-tive type of prejudiced person, not for the delinquent or psychopathic vari-ant (see Chapter XXI).

Examples of submission to parental authority from the protocols of high-scoring women are:

F66: "He never spanked me; mother always did that. You always did what he said, but it was right; there was no question about it."

F78: Her parents definitely approve of the engagement. Subject wouldn't even go with anyone if they didn't like him.

These short examples may suffice to illustrate that submission to author-ity is not only less frequent in high-scoring women than in men, but also that it has a less intense quality.

The opposite of submission to authority we designated as *principled inde-pendence.* It is found more often in our low scorers. Eight of the 15 low-scoring women interviewees and none of the 25 high-scoring ones show this trait. Correspondingly, 10 of the 20 low-scoring men interviewees and only 2 of the like number of high scorers display this attitude in their interviews. In particular, the protocols of low-scoring subjects rated as showing prin-cipled independence contain references to "being independent," to "argu-ing with parents on certain issues," etc. As with submission toward parents, principled independence is more outspoken in the records of men.

M44: (You talked with your mother a lot?) "Yeah (laughs), though we often dis-agreed. But she was very good to talk with. . . . Now I've almost quit writing about religious things to my mother . . . to avoid disturbing her. . . . She was willing to accept my ideas about things even if she didn't like them. She'd go her way and I'd go mine. I think she was very wise in that. . . ."

This record further illustrates the fact that independence in relation to parents is easily combined with tender feelings of love for them, feelings of which the low-scoring subjects are, generally, more capable (see above).

Another example of independence—here concerning religious issues— which does not disturb the basic good relationship to parents, is the following:

M55: (Reactions to Sunday School?) Older sister (one and a half years older) is more rebellious and influenced subject rather strongly, although "I really don't think I needed much influence. (Conflict with parents?) Surprisingly, it didn't; they'd get awfully angry sometimes ... mainly over Sunday School. Didn't ever discuss the theology. When I was younger, father read the Bible, which I enjoyed a lot (age eight to eleven, about). I liked the stories, though not as religion. When went to Sunday School, then began to rebel against religion."

Unprejudiced subjects seem less in need of complete approval by their parents. The record of *M55* also points up the fact that the occasional expression of mild aggression is not detrimental to, but has a positive effect on, the basic good relationships with parents or interpersonal relationships in general. Indications in the interviews, and especially findings from the Thematic Apperception Test (see Chapter XIV), suggest that the inability of the typical high-scoring subject to express aggression toward, or independence from, parents is due to the overpitched intensity of these feelings, so that the fear of punishment is too great to allow their being openly expressed.

Still a further illustration of independence in the sphere of religion—a frequent occurrence in the low-scoring subjects—is the following:

M16: "My mother takes her religion very seriously. But I never wanted to go to church. By the time I was 6 years old I had developed ways of getting around it. There were some hills behind the town—you know the country around there in southern _____? On Sunday morning I'd be gone at dawn and wouldn't come home until evening. Just to be out of church. (Why?) I guess it was mostly boredom. I didn't want to sit there and listen to all that nonsense—salvation, Jesus Christ most of all. My mother always used to pray over me."

This record also manifests the benevolently condescending attitude of low scorers, especially the men, toward their parents in general and toward the mother in particular. It stands in clear opposition to submission; and characteristically the mother, instead of being angry, is seen as praying over her disobedient son. In some cases the strivings for independence in the unprejudiced subjects seem to be connected with the feelings of guilt and anxiety lest the intensity and warmth of the relationship with the parents might be lost in disagreement.

Though we do not find, in the high-scoring subjects, much of real rebellion based on "principled independence," there is sometimes an indication of *capricious rebellion* against the parents (Category 3b), through which resentment is expressed without any real independence being gained. Six of the high-scoring and only 1 of the low-scoring women interviewees show this trait. In men the difference is less pronounced, the rating appearing in 9 high scorers and 4 low scorers.

In high-scoring women capricious rebellion takes the form primarily of temper tantrums, which they tend to indulge in when punished or restricted by the parents. Afterwards they usually submit even more fully than before without having made any progress toward independence.

Especially high-scoring men, when dissatisfied with their parents, sometimes leave home; truancy or becoming delinquent in some other form is more frequent than fighting it out. One of the high-scoring men tells that he took to thievery because his father did not understand him.

6. DEPENDENCE FOR THINGS *VS.* DEPENDENCE FOR LOVE

The attitude of submission to and the absence of real rebellion against the parents, found primarily in high-scoring subjects, appears to be connected with a kind of materialistic dependence on them which is not recognized as such. It may thus be termed *ego-alien* dependence for things and support. This dependence is essentially an exploitive-manipulative, externalized relationship. It is in contrast with what we have called *love-seeking succorance-nurturance-affiliation* toward the parents (Category 4a).

The assumption was that typical prejudiced subjects want to be taken care of like children; that they want to exploit their parents as they want to exploit other people; and that, not being self-reliant, they need support and comfort, first from the parents and then from parent-substitutes. This dependence, however, is neither focused nor conscious; it is rather a need for the help of others in getting things; the persons from whom things can be gotten may equally well be parents, or the "leader," or anyone else who seems capable of offering tangible support. The kind of dependence on the parents expected to be characteristic of unprejudiced subjects, on the other hand, is the kind of dependence which people with an ability to love direct toward those for whom an object cathexis has been established. The first type of person is more dependent—for benefits and "things"—but at the same time he is less dependent on specific persons because of the ready exchangeability of objects.

The difference between these two types of dependence proved highly significant in the direction expected. As many as 13 of the 25 high-scoring women interviewees were considered to have displayed in their interviews evidence of marked ego-alien dependence for things, as contrasted with 2 of the 15 low scorers. Even more strikingly, 13 of the 20 high-scoring men and only 1 of the 20 low scorers show the presumedly "High" type of dependence. Conversely, 14 of the low-scoring men interviewees but only 1 of the corresponding high scorers show evidence of love-oriented dependence in the interview. The affection-seeking kind of dependence in men is oriented mainly toward the mother.

The fact that in women this difference is somewhat less pronounced than in men is probably due to the fact that in spite of the existing differences between prejudiced and unprejudiced women the orientation toward dependence tends to be stronger in women than in men.

Examples of the ego-alien dependence for things in high-scoring women and men follow:

F68: "I always say my mother is still taking care of me. You should see my closets —stacked with fruits, jams, pickles—and every couple of weeks there is chicken, eggs, cream, everything you can think of. She just loves to do things for people."

F71 writes about her father: "Right now I'm his favorite . . . he'll do anything for me—takes me to school and calls for me."

The utilitarian approach of our high-scoring subjects is shown in the record of *F79:* "Yes, as I said on my questionnaire, I was closer to my mother at 6, 9, and 12, but now I have switched to my father—that is, since I was about 20. He holds the money bags. If I want to do anything, I have to go to him."

Records of high-scoring men show the same kind of dependence for things:

M41: "Well, kids always think more of their mother than their father. They look more to their mother for things."

Or *M43:* (How do you mean?) "Good to the children—clothed, fed, took care of when sick."

M47 says about his mother: "Well, I guess her being so good and friendly to everybody, especially me. (For example?) Well, always trying to do everything for me. Very seldom go uptown without bringing something back for me."

M51 shows the dependent, parasitic attitude: "I never saw any virtue in work." Subject lived on his father's insurance policy after his father's death and before that on his father. Was never really self-supporting and when "I tried to (support myself) I landed here (prison)."

M52 evaluates his father only in terms of what he got from him: "I haven't had everything I might have wanted from him. I would have liked to have a nicer home, better position, but all in all, I was very happy to be one of his boys. . . . Father was very proud of me."

Along similar lines is the record of *M57:* (What were you disciplined for?) "Well, when I wanted to go to a dance and take the car, used to make me mad if I couldn't get it. . . . (Did you have an allowance?) $15 or $20 a week, up. Always had plenty of money to spend." Subject spontaneously mentioned that his father would commonly give him $50 or so to go to a rodeo, and that in adolescence started giving him money for prostitutes. He adds that his father would often leave money out on the table for him for various purposes, even before subject had asked for it.

The wish for guidance is expressed in the record of *M58:* "Father wanted me to go to college, but his death interrupted this. If I'd had someone to guide me. . . ." Subject's father wanted him to be an architect, and talked about it all the time.

M13 shows appreciation of the father because he gives everything to his children: (What things did you admire especially in your father?) "Mostly, his attention to us kids was very admirable. He's very honest, so much so that he won't condone charge accounts. He's known throughout the country as a man whose word is as good as his bond. His greatest contribution was denying himself pleasure to take care of us kids."

A blatant opportunism is revealed in the foregoing appraisal of parents on the part of prejudiced subjects, by the undisguised references to the food, money, and other goods they received. Most crudely, however, it is expressed by the subject who tells us she "switched to father. He holds the money bags now."

An example of the affection-seeking attitude, from the record of a low-scoring subject follows:

F62: "We have all been very close. We were like one person. We liked the same things. We were always doing things for each other."

This record shows the intimacy and loving dependence of the family members on each other. Low-scoring men show a similar affection-oriented attitude. *M44* describes his home background: "Pleasantness isn't a very good word. Simplicity and *real* affection."

In the records of low-scoring men, there are quite often affectionate remarks about the mother: "On the whole we were quite fond of her," says *M55* about his mother. As will be pointed out in Chapter XXI, some of the delinquent low-scoring men even commit crimes because of a mother fixation. In one such case the motive was to rescue the mother who was in debt; in others the desire to receive love from a mother substitute had been frustrated.

The relatively pronounced emphasis on getting love, in low-scoring subjects, as compared with a more distinct orientation toward getting power and material benefits, in the high-scoring subjects, is a basic differentiation, the far-reaching consequences of which will be discussed later.

In spite of this difference, evident all through the interview material, it is noteworthy that orientation toward love and affection is less elaborately and pronouncedly expressed by our subjects than are opportunistic sentiments of the sort just quoted. The cultural trends seem, to a certain degree, to discourage affection, or at least its overt expression.

The orientation toward "getting things" may be seen in relation to an attitude of "*exchange*." When this general attitude predominates, human relationships come to be regarded as one form of "making a deal." In the attitude toward parents this is sometimes manifested in a vague feeling of obligation, of having to return in terms of material goods what one has received from the parents. The idea of having to "give" seems generally very painful to most of the high-scoring subjects, but at the same time theirs seems to be the conception, "You scratch my back and I'll scratch yours," if not "An eye for an eye and a tooth for a tooth."

Such have been the considerations behind the introduction into the evaluation of the interviews of the aspect of *sense of obligation and duty* to parents (Category 4b). It is further defined as desire to "make it up to them." According to our expectation this attitude should be characteristic of the high scorers. However, the category did not prove discriminating in women, responses of this kind being generally few. In men, there were 5 high scorers

as compared with 1 low scorer in whom this response was found. Thus *M47*
feels he has to make recompense to his mother because he got a lot of things,
including money, from her:

M47: (Main satisfactions with her?) "Well, that's hard to say. I guess I haven't
made her very happy, but ... when I'm out there and going straight, I'll always take
care of my mother. ... I feel I've never treated her like I really should."

The orientation of low-scoring men toward gaining affection primarily
from the mother was mentioned above. High-scoring men, in contrast, seem
more oriented toward the father. This orientation and the idea of making up
to the father is illustrated in the following record:

M51: "My father is very unemotional. He never says what he is thinking, anyway.
(Did you miss him a lot when he was away?) I missed him very much when I was at
the boarding house. ... I've saved all my letters to him. ... He very dramatically
returned all my letters, like to an old love. I loved my father very much. (Q) Yeah,
I wished even before he died that I could get on my feet before he did die. When I
was sick, I used to ... daydream about his coming to see me. ... (Q) I wanted to be
more what he wanted me to be. ... "

The idea that one has to "make it up" to the parents is illustrated directly by *M6:*
"The depression had more influence on my life than on other people my age. My
parents really had a bad time. I hope to make it up to them. My father was on relief
at the same time I had to see the doctors."

Some of the other records indicate that the prejudiced person considers
that the surest way to find favor with his parents is to do something for them,
in the sense of offering them material pleasures or support.

Starting from this discussion of family relationships, subsequent presentation will show the very pronounced consistency, in the typical high-scoring
subject, with respect to a materialistic, utilitarian view of interpersonal and
social relationships. On the surface this may seem a kind of realism; actually
it is pseudorealism, since it ultimately leads to an impoverishment and to
hostilities in human relationships. The low scorer is of course by no means
free of such trends although they are on the whole less pronounced in him.

7. INGROUP ORIENTATION TO THE FAMILY

As to the conception of the family as a whole, high-scoring subjects were
expected to tend toward an *ingroup orientation*, as exemplified by emphasis
on family heredity and background, a setting off of a homogeneous totalitarian family against the rest of the world and a stressing of aristocratic
superiority of the family. This is contrasted with thinking in terms of
individuals within the family, expected in the low-scoring subjects. Seven
high-scoring and only 1 low-scoring woman, and 6 as against 2 of the men
interviewees display the presumedly "High" conception of the family.

Thus *F68* is proud of the prestige the family of her father enjoyed: "We lived up
in the mountains, _____ County. His folks were pioneers—gold settlers and quite
wealthy. Everyone knows the _____'s of _____ County up that way. My

father was the spoiled darling of the family. My mother was a German girl, proud, hard working, thrifty."

In a similar vein, $F79$ describes her family: "I am Pat _____ (giving her family name)." She made it clear that she could find nothing about herself in which she could take pride except the fact that she belonged to the _____ family.

A high-scoring man, $M46$, tells that his wife was brought up "by aristocratic parents with patriarchal setup."

One of the prison inmates, $M51$, says about his mother, "She came out in Capitol society, that's where she met my father."

The same tendency to overemphasize the socioeconomic status of his family could be seen in the record of $M4$, where the mother's family status seems to be exaggeratedly described and an effort is made to conceal embarrassment about the status of the father's family: "Family on both sides have been here for several generations. Mother came from a quite well-to-do family; her grandfather was a millionaire, her father independently wealthy and never worked. There were 6 children, all devout Catholics. Grandmother was a very well trained artist; Mother herself went to high school, then married when she was about 18. Father came from a family less well-to-do." Subject couldn't quite say this, but the grandfather ran a small grocery store in _____, sold out somewhere around _____, came to California, worked in the shipyards. "Father himself went to high school, afterwards went to a _____ school, started his _____ business, which he sold later on to work for a large corporation."

A mixture of pride and embarrassment about family status is also seen in the description of $M11$: "My father's first father was named _____. His second father was named _____, and he took that name. His father, _____, worked, or still works, as _____ on the railroads. My mother's mother was _____ from _____. Her father was Spanish, born in this country."

The high-scoring subjects show a tendency to magnify the status of their families in a way which enters and essentially modifies their entire conception of their families. We find both an insecure concern about status and an ardent wish to transmit the impression that their families had repute and prestige.

In an attempt to summarize the attitudes toward parents thus far discussed, the following may be said: The prejudiced subjects show little evidence of genuine love toward their parents. On the surface theirs is a stereotyped, rigid glorification of the parents, with strong resentment and feelings of victimization occasionally breaking through on the overt level in the interview material. Usually, however, only admiration for the parent is accepted by the subject. The underlying hostility has to be kept ego-alien for several reasons: it is too strong to be fully admitted; and it interferes with the desire to be taken care of by the parents. This conflict leads to a submission to parental authority on the surface and a resentment underneath which, although not admitted, is the more active under the guise of mechanisms of displacement.

There is evidence, on the other hand, that the unprejudiced subjects received more love and therefore have basically more security in their relationships to their parents. Disagreement with, and resentment against, the parents are openly worked out, resulting in a much greater degree of independence from them. This independence is carried over into the subject's attitude toward social institutions and authorities in general. At the same time, there is more love-oriented dependence on people, which prevents the individual from too much manipulation and exploitation of others. In spite of the conflicts these subjects carry with them, this type of relationship remains for them one of their important sources of gratification.

C. CONCEPTIONS OF CHILDHOOD ENVIRONMENT

1. DEFINITION OF RATING CATEGORIES AND QUANTITATIVE RESULTS

In this section discussion will center about the subject's conception of childhood events, including especially also the recollection and image of parental figures and their handling of discipline. The preceding section was concerned with the attitude toward the parents in general; now we proceed to describe the specific images of father and mother in the prejudiced and the unprejudiced. As stated in Chapter IX, it is difficult to say how much the image of a parent corresponds to reality and how much it is a subjective conception. However, this distinction may be of less importance when, as is the case here, personality structure rather than its genesis is the major concern. The notions our subjects have of their parents are psychologically relevant in the discussion of the parent-child relationship whether they are true or not. In a separate project, parents of prejudiced and unprejudiced children were actually studied, substantiating in kind many of the statements our present interviewees make about their own childhood (preliminary report by E. Frenkel-Brunswik, 30).

We will first consider the traits ascribed to the father by both the male and female interviewees. Since the categories under this heading in the Scoring Manual are rather specific, the total of responses in each category is not very large. Not all subjects described their parents spontaneously in such terms. The differences are, therefore, less significant here than elsewhere. The list of categories relating to the image of the parents is as follows:

INTERVIEW SCORING MANUAL: CONCEPTIONS OF
CHILDHOOD ENVIRONMENT
(to Table 2(X))

Presumably "High" Variants	Presumably "Low" Variants
6M. Traits ascribed to father by Men:	
a. *Distant*, stern, bad temper, "a barrier between us"	a. *Some demonstrativeness*
b. *A moral-model*	b. *Principled puritanism*
c. *Pseudomasculine:* Determination, worked his way up, a "success"	c. *Relaxed*, mild

6W. *Traits ascribed to father by Women:*

a. *Hardworkingprovider:*"Will do anything for me" (externalized), works fingers to bone for family; or psychopath

b. *A moral-model*

c. *Warm,* sociable, lovable

d. *Understanding*

e. *Intellectual-aesthetic*

7M. *Traits ascribed to mother by Men:*

a. *Sacrificing,* "kind," submissive

b. *A moral-model*

c. *Warm,* sociable, lovable

d. *Understanding*

e. *Intellectual-aesthetic*

7W. *Traits ascribed to mother by Women:*

a. *Restricting*

b. *A moral-model*

c. *"Sweet," pseudofeminine*

d. *Some demonstrativeness*

e. *Understanding*

f. *Intellectual-aesthetic*

8. Denial of parental conflict—except "mild-normal" disagreements

8. Objective verbalization of parental conflict

9M. *Power relationship, Man* (Score a *or* b, not both):

a. *Father* was *dominant,* more influential

b. *Henpeckingly dominant* mother

a. *Mother-centered* (Love-nurturance) *home*

b. *Equalitarian home*

9W. *Power relationship, Women* (Score a *or* b, not both):

a. *"Perfect division of labor":* Mother, home; father, work

b. *Mother stronger,* dominant

a. *Father more important,* stronger

b. *Equalitarian home*

10. *Discipline* for violation of *rules,* primarily moralistic

10. *Discipline* for violation of *principles,* primarily rationalized

11. *Discipline threatening,* traumatic, overwhelming (castration-threat)

11. *Discipline assimilable* (non-egodestructive)

In keeping with the preliminary study of the interviews which always preceded the definition of categories, categories for men and women are not always symmetrical or analogous, and distinctions appearing as a pair of opposites within one and the same subcategory in the case of one of the sexes, may be separated for the other.

Quantitative results are given in Table 2(X) in the manner established in Section F of the preceding chapter, and in Table 1(X).

2. IMAGE OF THE FATHER IN MEN: DISTANT AND STERN *VS.* RELAXED AND MILD

We begin with the conception, in men, of a *distant, stern father,* with bad temper, and a barrier between father and son, as opposed to the picture of a *warm, demonstrative father* (Category 6Ma). Twelve high- and 5 low-scoring men interviewees conceive of their father as stern; 7 low- and only 1 high-scoring men refer to the father as demonstrative. The entire category for men is statistically significant, but only at the 5 per cent level.

The "high" conception can best be understood from the actual statements of high-scoring men.

M51 declares: "My father died five years ago—he was very—I've judged him with so much prejudice. I thought he was so strict . . . actually he was just the opposite . . . not the least demonstrative . . . he disapproved of any show of emotion of *any* kind. If I ever did anything wrong, it was the Latin in me, which is the side I have more of an affinity for—my mother's side. I look more like them."

The foregoing record shows the extent to which the subject felt the (true or imaginary) coldness and remoteness of his father. At the same time he does not dare really to criticize his father; he blames himself but—characteristically—without feeling guilty; "it is the Latin strain" in him which relieves him from any real responsibility.

The barrier between parents and children in the families of high-scoring subjects is indicated by the answer of a high-scoring man, *M57*, to the question, Did you confide in your parents? "No, never had any problem to talk about." The barrier between father and son goes to the point of not talking to each other. The relationship seems to be barren of any affect. Rather than blame the parents, the subject denies the existence of any problems. After a few admiring sentences about his father, another subject says:

M11: "Maybe—well, in ways he isn't even tempered. He's as stubborn as an ox. He'd rather start a fight or an argument than do something he doesn't want to. And he can fly off the handle. We kid him out of it now. (What have you disagreed with your father about?) I have gone days without talking to him or weeks without asking any favors. . . . Well, we are lazy about such things; we are not mechanically minded, and we hate gardening. We have some trouble because he's too stubborn to ask me for help but yet he gets mad because I won't. . . . Earlier he got mad because I wouldn't wear enough clothes."

On the other hand, reference to friendliness on the part of the father is characteristic of the records of low-scoring men:

M16: (What was your father like?) "He was a very *kind* man, gentle, was always very good to us, that is, as much as was possible under the circumstances. (Strict about some things?) No, not very. He liked us kids a lot. (Q) I'm the youngest of five."

M42 gives an affectionate description of his father. We get the impression of a relaxed person who has the ability to enjoy his life deeply.

Or *M50:* "He champions my causes . . . told the other children that I had more sense in my little finger than all the other children put together. He was always in my corner . . . and of course he was fostering any latent art ability I had. . . . Curiously enough, I don't think I have any particular art ability. I think I could have become a good musician, pianist. . . ."

M53: (Pleasant memories of father?) "Lots of pleasant memories, because he spoiled us when he was home, always cooking up wonderful ideas for things to do."

M59: (How did you and your father get along?) "Well, a very friendly relationship. He was pretty much of a pal. We liked to go places together, fishing, play cards, etc. We had a lot of good times."

It is quite convincingly evident from the last three records that the fathers of these men possessed, as well as displayed, a good deal of affection for their sons. In general, the fathers of the unprejudiced men seem to have spent a great deal of time playing and "doing things" with their sons. It is interesting also to note the reference of *M50* to his father's interest in art. From all our evidence it seems likely that many of the fathers of our prejudiced men would have considered such an interest, in themselves or in their sons, as effeminate or "sissy."

A further possibility is to see the father primarily as a *moral-model*. This may be contrasted with a view of the father as an example of what may be called *principled puritanism* (Category 6Mb). This pair of opposites is intended to characterize orientation toward, and acceptance of, a set of conventional values (externalized superego, i.e., social anxiety) *vs.* an upholding of real ethical principles (internalized superego). As was expected, prejudiced men tend to describe the father as a moral-model, whereas the unprejudiced refer more often to the "puritanism" of their fathers. There is a high proportion of Neutral ratings so that the statistical significance of this difference has not been established; to be sure, there also is the difficulty in deciding, in each instance, whether we have a case of a moral model or of genuine conscientiousness before us.

A passage in the record of *M13*, a high scorer, reads as follows: "He drank but little, and he never smoked. He was very honest and strict in his dealings. He followed the church rules without going to church." It shows the emphasis on external virtue, such as abstinence from smoking, drinking, etc.

Another subject in this group, *M41*, says about his father: "He'd tell us what we should do, what he wanted us to do, and what he expected us to do. He always asked the blessings at the table and prayed at night before bedtime."

The somewhat different quality that is manifested in the records of low-scoring men in their descriptions of the puritanism of their fathers is exemplified as follows:

M56: (What sort of person is your father?) "Hard man to describe; he is a puritan really. His father is a drunkard, he reacted to that ... very strict, but human."

When there is moral strictness in the fathers of low-scoring men, it often tends to be characterized by a definite "human" touch, rather than by an emphasis on strict conformity to custom—the wish to be a shining example in the community—that appears in the fathers of high-scoring men.

TABLE 2 (X)

INTERVIEW RATINGS ON CONCEPT OF CHILDHOOD ENVIRONMENT FOR 80 SUBJECTS SCORING EXTREMELY "HIGH" OR "LOW" ON THE ETHNIC PREJUDICE QUESTIONNAIRE SCALE

Interview rating categories (abbreviated from Manual)	Sex	Number of "High"(H) and "Low"(L) ratings received by				Sums of instances		Level of statistical significance reached (percentage)
		20 men and 25 women "high scorers"		20 men and 15 women "low scorers"		"positive"	"negative"	
		H	L	H	L			
6M. Conception of father in men:								
a. Distant, bad temper(H) vs. some demonstrativeness(L)	Men	12	1	5	7	19	6	5
b. Moral-model(H) vs. principled puritanism(L)	"	5	1	1	4	9	2	
c. Pseudomasculine(H) vs. relaxed, mild(L)	"	6	1	4	9	15	5	
6W. Concept of father in women:								
a. Hardworking provider; or psychopath(H)	Women	6		4		6	4	
b. Moral-model(H)	"	4		4		4	4	
c. Warm, sociable, lovable(L)	"		2		5	5	2	
d. Understanding(L)	"		1		1	1	1	
e. Intellectual-aesthetic(L)	"		0		6	6		
7M. Concept of mother in men:								
a. Sacrificing, submissive(H)	Men	9		2		9	2	
b. Moral-model(H)	"	6		2		6	2	
c. Warm, lovable(L)	"		0		9	9	0	
d. Understanding(L)	"		2		4	4	2	
e. Intellectual-aesthetic(L)	"		0		5	5	0	

7W. Concept of mother in women:							
a. Restricting(H) — Women	10	3	2	6	10	2	
b. Moral-model(H) — "	6	5	1	4	6	1	
c. Sweet, pseudofeminine(H) — "	2	4	1	3	2	1	
d. Warm, demonstrative (L) — "					6	3	
e. Understanding(L) — "					4	5	
f. Intellectual-aesthetic(L) — "					3	4	
8. Denial(H) vs. verbalization(L) of parental conflict — Men	6	4	7	8	14	11	5
— Women	8	5	1	5	13	6	
9Ma.b. Father-dominated(H) vs. mother-oriented(L) home; or henpecking mother (H) vs. equalitarian home(L) — Men	12	1	3	10	22	4	
9Wa.b. Division of labor(H) vs. father more important(L); or henpecking mother(H) vs. equalitarian home(L) — Women	7	4	2	6	13	6	5
10. Discipline for: violation of rules(H) vs. violation of principles(L) — Men	14	1	6	5	19	7	
— Women	12	2	2	2	14	4	
11. Discipline: Threatening, traumatic(H) vs. assimilable(L) — Men	13	0	4	9	22	4	1
— Women	9	3	4	4	13	7	

It is interesting to find that a further conception, that of a *determined and successful father* with an element of pseudomasculinity (Category 6Mc), does not differentiate much between high- and low-scoring men. Obviously, the successful man who worked his way up is so much a part of our culture that he may be found in any context of patterns. Nonetheless, reference to a father who is *relaxed and mild* is frequent in, and almost exclusive with, the interviews of low-scoring men; 9 of these, but only 1 of the high-scoring men, describe their fathers in these or related terms. Examples from the records of low-scoring men are the following:

M42, asked about his father, says: "I can't tell you exactly. I was only thirteen when he left. He's quick tempered . . . might say he is inclined to be a little slovenly . . . might go for a long time without a haircut or cleaning his nails. He is poorly educated but he is very smart. His folks are farmers . . . they never had money . . . he would send them money. I knew he never liked his dad."

This record presents the picture of a relaxed man who does not live up to the ideals and customs of his community, such as cleanliness and liking his father. He follows, however, his own principles by sending money to his parents.

In the same record there are signs of the subject's relaxation about the status of his own family and that of his father. Being relaxed about one's social status apparently parallels the psychological relaxation which is a crucial condition for absence of prejudice. "Casualness" is emphasized in the following quotation from the protocol of another low scorer, commenting about his father:

M53: "Quite a bit older than mother. I was very fond of him. A very casual sort of person, by no means a disciplinarian."

M54 tells about his father's work, bookkeeper. (How did he like it?) "Crazy about it. Worked there for thirty years. Of course, in the same old groove, can't get up or down, but pretty contented."

M59: "Well, he is not very polished. He is a little crude socially. He is very happy-go-lucky."

See also the remarks on the "easy-going low" in Chapter XIX.

In the same vein, some of the other low-scoring men describe their fathers as gentle and relaxed and not too concerned about status. Reference to libidinization of work rather than of status in one of the above quotations should likewise be noted; it seemed to be quite typical of the unprejudiced on the basis of our material.

For the establishment of the psychology of the unprejudiced man a non-threatening father figure may indeed be of great importance. It makes it possible for the son to include in his conception of masculinity some measure of passivity. Not feeling greatly threatened by the father, the unprejudiced man is apparently less afraid of losing his masculinity. He thus does not have to overcompensate for such fear by an overly rigid ego-ideal of aggressive toughness. The unprejudiced man did not as a rule have to submit to stern authority in his childhood; in his later life, therefore, he neither longs for strong authority nor needs to assert his strength against those who are weaker.

3. IMAGE OF THE FATHER IN WOMEN: THE ROLE OF PROVIDER

Let us now turn to the traits ascribed to the father by our women interviewees. Since our data on women are, by and large, less complete than those on the men, there will be even fewer cases in each of these categories than were found for men. Significance in the statistical sense has not been established for any of the categories used. A few illustrations will be given to illuminate the meaning of our concepts, but less emphasis will be placed upon the discussion of quantitative results.

The opportunism found in high-scoring women, together with their underlying hostility towards men, discussed later, made us expect that they would tend to see their fathers mainly as sources of provision. It was statements like the following which led to this assumption: "Father was extremely devoted to family—will work his fingers to the bone for them—never has done any drinking" ($F71$). Another of the prejudiced extremes, $F24$, in stressing how "wonderful" her father is, explains: "He is always willing to do anything for you." Another subject in this group, $F69$, describes her father as follows: "Works hard—very serious—gets no fun out of life at all."

Six of the high- and only 1 of the low-scoring women stress the provider quality in their fathers (Category 6Wa). It is this quality that high-scoring women seem to value primarily in men and which, rather than affection, is often the source of their dependency on men. There is indeed little evidence of a genuine positive relation of prejudiced women toward their fathers. The exploitive attitude toward men in general on the part of high-scoring women will be discussed again later in connection with attitudes toward the other sex.

The notion of the father as a moral-model did not differentiate between high- and low-scoring women (Category 6Wb).

The families of our high-scoring subjects often seem to be highly conventional and respectable; however, reference is sometimes made to a *psychopathic* background. But even in the latter case—as will be seen in the material about delinquents in Chapter XXI—there is often a great deal of conventionality and stress on middle-class values in the same context with delinquent behavior.

A few of our high-scoring women describe their fathers in such terms as to make it appear that they were psychopaths. Whether this description corresponds to fact, or is merely gross exaggeration or the result of the underlying contempt many of these women seem to have for men, is difficult to decide offhand. Our best course is probably to assume a combination of these trends. In the accusations made by these subjects against the father, the main reproach is usually directed against his not having provided enough for the family.

F66 says: "My father could not stay put. We lived in ＿＿＿＿, ＿＿＿＿, ＿＿＿＿, and I don't know how many other places."

F68 relates that her father "never worked in his life. He was a gambler, an adventurer who broke his family's heart."

This may serve as an example of the fact that once the high scorer turns against the parents—which happens only rarely—there is a tendency to make them out as real villains.

For the presumedly "Low" alternatives to the above traits ascribed to the father by women, namely the conception of a warm, lovable, and understanding father, the absolute number of responses was small. Discussion of them may therefore be omitted.

However, as many as 6 of the low-scoring as against only 1 of the high-scoring women described their fathers as *intellectual-aesthetic* (Category 6We). Interest in intellectual and artistic endeavor is usually more pronounced in low-scoring persons, a fact that is in line with the "intraceptive" quality found to be more characteristic of the unprejudiced.

4. IMAGE OF THE MOTHER: SACRIFICE, MORALISM, RESTRICTIVENESS

The list of traits ascribed by our subjects to their mothers was constructed somewhat similarly to their counterparts referring to the father; and the results tend to be analogous. However, while the conception of the father by high-scoring men was, on the basis of our exploratory analysis of the interviews, expected to be best characterized by the term "stern," the corresponding image of the mother was expected to be that of a *sacrificing, kind, submissive* person. And likewise, as prejudiced women tend to refer to the provider role in their fathers, they also tend to look at their mothers primarily from the point of view of what she gives them or how well she took care of them when they were children.

Nine of the high- and only 2 of the low-scoring men had this conception of their mothers. Among the former, *M57* says about his mother: "She was a hard working lady, took care of us kids; she never did mistreat us in any way." The idea of a mother giving everything to the child is expressed especially clearly in the following quotation from the protocol of another high-scoring man, *M13*: "Mother was sick in bed a great deal of the time. She devoted her last strength to us kids." Emphasis on "devoting" the last strength carries the connotation of a limitless sacrifice devoid of healthy mutuality.

M13 further describes his mother as "a Methodist and quite strict up until her death. I was sick much of the time. She brought us up very strictly under this guidance."

A total of 6 high- and 2 low-scoring men consider the mother as a *moral-model* (Category 7Mb).

Thus another of the high-scoring men, *M47*, says of his mother: "She always taught me the difference between right and wrong, the things I should do and shouldn't."

This latter record also illustrates the absolute certainty with which many of the high-scoring subjects and their parents view "what is right and what is wrong"—the usual yardstick, however, being social approval or disapproval. This view is frequently accompanied by a good deal of intolerance toward deviations from what is "right." When present in parents, this attitude may well lead to rigid identifications and repressions in the children, thus leaving parts of their personality unmodifiable and unsublimated.

The general orientation toward affection in the low-scoring subjects, and the impression that they actually had received more love, led to the expectation that low-scoring men would conceive of their mothers as *warm, sociable, lovable*, as *understanding*, and as *intellectual-aesthetic* (Categories 7Mc-e). Of these three traits the first was the most differentiating: 9 low-scoring and none of the high-scoring men described the mother in terms similar to "warm, sociable, lovable." The warmth of the relationship between mother and son in the low-scoring men seems crucial for the development of their general concern with love (in contradistinction to power) and of their other humanitarian attitudes. The quality of "understanding" in the image of the mother did not differentiate very well; however, 5 of the low- and none of the high-scoring men mention intellectual-aesthetic inclinations in their mothers. An example of the latter attitude from the records of low-scoring men follows:

M50 says about his mother: "An intellectual and a very well educated person. Her principal gift seems to be that of perception. And an artist not by trade but certainly by nature."

Similar passages, referring to the mother's interest in music or painting, are found in the protocols of the other low-scoring men in this classification.

The woman's conception of the mother is covered by a somewhat different list of traits (Category 7W). Again, the data here are rather incomplete, due to the specificity of the categories involved and the comparative incompleteness of the women's interviews. However, 10 high- and only 2 low-scoring women describe their mothers by what may be summarized under the term *restricting*. Thus *F36*, the high scorer who was quoted above as displaying drastic rejection of, as well as submission toward, her mother, described the latter as being "domineering, dictatorial, and self-centered."

Other records are more subtle, emphasizing dominance and social success in their mothers. Unfortunately only one of the two raters scored this latter trait which thus does not appear in Table 2(X); she found 5 out of 13 mothers of high-scoring daughters described as a *social success*. On the other hand, none of the low-scoring women emphasized this quality in her mother.

The admiration that high-scoring women are inclined to have for their socially successful, dominant mothers is being offset by hate against mother figures in the stories of the Thematic Apperception Test (see Chapter XIV). Instead of admiring the successful mother, the pressure which such mothers exert upon their daughters leads some of them in their stories to conceive of maternal figures as witches (see 31, 32). Here one is reminded of Wylie's theory of "momism" in his book, *Generation of Vipers*.

The assumption that high-scoring women would tend to see their mothers as *sweet* or (*pseudo-*) *feminine* in their interviews, that is, on the conscious level, was not borne out by our material. This quality is stressed by very few of the women interviewees. The high-scoring women probably see through the pseudofeminine façade of their mothers to a greater extent than they are ready to admit, and feel rather clearly the press of domination. As far as their picture of themselves is concerned, however, they tend to believe firmly, as will be discussed later, in their own "femininity."

Six of the high- and only 1 of the low-scoring women describe their mothers as a *moral-model*, while more low-scoring than high-scoring women speak directly about their mothers as demonstratively warm and lovable.

The remaining aspects, referring to understanding and intellectual-aesthetic qualities, showed little differentiation in women. There are two possible reasons for this. One may be that the data in question are few, the other that the hostility of the high-scoring women toward their mothers is indirect rather than direct. As pointed out above, there are some clear indications of such disguised hostility in the interviews, and direct evidence of hostility in the reactions to the Thematic Apperception Test.

5. PARENTAL CONFLICT

We now turn our attention to the subjects' notions concerning the relationship between the parents. *Denial of parental conflict* as contrasted with *open and objective verbalization of parental conflict* (Category 8) will be discussed first. This pair of opposites was not enough differentiated in the Scoring Manual; it did not provide for the distinction between absence of real conflict and denial of existing conflict. Furthermore, differentiation between absence of conflict due to "smooth functioning," on the one hand, and due to real love, on the other, was likewise not considered. Either for this, or for other, still more intrinsic reasons, there was practically no difference in the denial of serious conflict between parents in high- and low-scoring men. Overt admission of such conflicts, however, occurs somewhat more often in the records of low-scoring men, but the entire category still does not differentiate significantly between the prejudiced and the unprejudiced.

In a few of those cases in which the raters, proceeding in accordance with the Manual, scored "denial of conflict" as the "High" variant in subjects who were later identified as low scorers, they added as a comment: "real love." This is quite in line with what was said above about the unsatisfactory formulation of Category 8.

Typical examples of denial of parental conflict by high-scoring men are:

M41, in answer to the question, How did your parents get along together, says: "Fine, never did hear no quarreling."
Or *M58*: "If there were any conflicts between mother and father I didn't know."

Examples of admission of parental conflicts from the records of low-scoring men are:

M15: "Mother accuses father of 'keeping her down.' She talks about her ambitions too much. Mother thinks of herself first. She doesn't want to settle down in any church. Keeps suspecting father lets another singer get ahead of her. There are many quarrels between them, which upset me. Father sometimes threatened to leave."
Or *M50*: "Father was temperamental and father and mother had considerable domestic strife. I didn't like it and I didn't like my father as champion. Preferred my mother as champion. . . . My sister became psychologically against my mother . . . nothing very definite, nothing you could put your finger on—very subtle. . . . I didn't realize it then. . . ."
M55: "Mother went along with him on all the moralizing, though not as harsh as he was, not really a very good marriage. Mother should have married someone a lot more human and he probably would have been a lot better off . . . well, it's hard to imagine him with anyone with whom he would get along."
M59: "Well, just the usual family quarrels. Maybe raise her voice a bit. (What bones of contention?) Well, the fact that in the first ten years of my mother's married life, my dad used to get drunk quite often and he would beat her physically and later on, as the children were growing up, she resented my father's influence, though he contributed to our support. . . . He used to come about twice a week, sometimes oftener."

The foregoing records illustrate the frankness and the greater insight into the marital conflicts of the parents, characteristic of low-scoring men. In addition, they show the tendency, mentioned above, of men to side with the mother.

In the records of women, on the other hand, denial of parental conflict differentiates between high scorers and low scorers in a proportion of 8 to 1. The fact that denial of parental conflict is more often found in female than in male high scorers is perhaps due to the fact that our sample of high-scoring women is, on the whole, more conventional than that of the high-scoring men. Examples of denial of parental conflict are:

F24: "Parents get along swell—never quarrel—hardly ever. Just over nonsense if they do. They quarrelled once after drinking wine over who got the last. Silly stuff like that."

F31: "My parents get along very well with each other, so far—knock on wood. They have their arguments, but they're never serious because of my mother's easy-going personality. Father teases her terrifically. She takes his jokes, but not too well. They have no serious arguments, just sort of silly things."

The foregoing records show that for some of the high-scoring women it seems important to assert that there was a good marital relationship between their parents, minimizing conflicts by presenting them as "silly little things."

6. FATHER-DOMINATED *VS.* MOTHER-ORIENTED HOME

As far as the *power relationship between parents* is concerned, 10 of the high-scoring and only 3 of the low-scoring men see the father as the more dominant and more influential; 2 additional high-scoring men think the mother is "henpeckingly dominant," bringing the number of "High" ratings up to 12 (Category 9M). Some of the high-scoring men who conceive of the home as father-dominated speak of their fathers' having made all the decisions, and of the submissiveness of their mothers.

An example is the record of *M52:* (Who made the decisions usually?) "My father. (Any bones of contention?) Well, I don't think there were any to speak of.... I've often tried in later years to analyze my father's wanderlust.... Apparently seeking business success.... My mother has remarked that I am just the opposite of him...."

Conversely, only 1 high-scoring but 10 low-scoring men interviewees think of theirs as a mother-centered (love-nurturance) home, or as an equalitarian home. The entire category differentiates to a statistically high degree between prejudiced and unprejudiced men.

If the conceptions of our subjects can be taken to represent reality—and to a certain degree they probably can—there appears to be a tendency toward *father-domination*, or just "domination," in the families of the high-scoring, and toward *mother-orientation*, in contradistinction to mother-"domination," in the families of the low-scoring men. This finding, if substantiated and found crucial in a larger sample, would have far-reaching sociological and psychological implications. It would then be more understandable why the German family, with its long history of authoritarian, threatening father figures, could become susceptible to a fascist ideology. The son of such a father figure can apparently never quite establish his personal and masculine identity; he thus has to look for it in a collective system where there is opportunity both for submission to the powerful and for retaliation upon the powerless (see G. W. Allport, 10; O. Fenichel, 26; E. Fromm, 42; E. H. Erikson, 25). It must be emphasized that looking at a fascist society from the point of view of the needs of the individual does not exclude recognition of larger socioeconomic determinants which may well be responsible both for the organization of society and for that of the family.

Following up for a moment this line of psychological reasoning, could it then be inferred that, because of the predominant mother-orientation of the American home there is less danger of fascism here? To answer this question, sociological and economic factors beyond the scope of this project would have to be considered. It might, however, be important to remember in this connection the 2 cases of high-scoring men who refer to a henpeckingly dominant mother. In both these cases it seemed evident the mother had taken over the threatening function of punishment in the family as a whole. By contrast, the family of the typical low-scoring man seems to be centered about a mother whose primary function is to give love rather than to dominate, and who is not too weak or submissive.

On the basis of their dichotomous conception of sex roles and their antagonism toward men it was expected that high-scoring women would have the following conception of the power relations between the parents: strict division of labor, mother home and father works, or else "mother stronger and dominant." On the other hand, it was expected that in the case of the records of low-scoring women the father would be experienced as more important and stronger, or that there would be an equalitarian home.

Actually, 7 high-scoring women displayed one of the first two alternatives (mostly the second), as contrasted with only 2 of the low-scoring women. The second pair of alternatives was found with only slightly greater frequency in the low-scoring group, probably because the data on this issue are not complete and because some of the high-scoring women report a dominant father.

In consequence, for women as contrasted with men, the category as a whole is not statistically significant. The data do, however, lend some further support to the original assumption that prejudiced men tend to experience the father, prejudiced women the mother, as the major figure of the family. It perhaps may be said that prejudiced women tend to have a stronger though more ambivalent tie to the mother, conversely the prejudiced man to the father. A greater inclination toward latent or overt homosexuality may be connected with this (see Chapters XI and XXI).

7. DISCIPLINE: HARSH APPLICATION OF RULES
VS. ASSIMILATION OF PRINCIPLES

How parents, being the first authorities in the life of a child, handle the problems of discipline must be assumed to be of crucial importance in the establishment of attitudes toward authority. Was the issue in question explained to the child and was he included in the discussion of it, or did it appear to the child as unintelligible, arbitrary, and overwhelming? Did the parents in their application of discipline adhere to a rigid set of conventional rules, or were they guided by more intrinsic values? These are some of the questions for which data were collected from our interviews.

In particular, discipline for violation of *rules*, primarily "moralistic," was contrasted with discipline for violation of *principles*, primarily "rationalized" (Category 10). As the first of two variables to be considered in this context, the choice between these two opposite alternatives on the part of the parents would seem to be crucial for the establishment of the child's attitude toward what is considered right or wrong: it probably decides the externalization vs. internalization of values. These two types of discipline further imply different resultant attitudes toward authority.

In the first case, discipline is handled as *"vis major,"* as a force outside of the child, to which at the same time he must submit. The values in question are primarily the values of adult society: conventions and rules helpful for social climbing but rather beyond the natural grasp of the child. At the same time this type of value lays the foundation for an attitude of judging people according to external criteria, and for the authoritarian condemnation of what is considered socially inferior.

The second type of discipline invites the cooperation and understanding of the child and makes it possible for him to assimilate it.

Fourteen of the high- and 6 of the low-scoring men interviewees report having been submitted to discipline for violation of rules whereas 5 low-scoring men and only 1 high-scoring man report discipline for violation of principles. With respect to violation of rules the difference is even greater for the women interviewees: 12 high scorers and only 2 low scorers report this type of discipline in their home. Discipline for violation of principles is reported by only 4 women, and this in even proportion among high and low scorers. On the whole, discipline for violation of rules is more characteristic of high scorers than discipline for violation of principles is of low scorers. The latter report an altogether smaller number of incidents of being disciplined.

Related to the distinction just described is the differentiation between a *threatening*, traumatic, overwhelming discipline, and an *assimilable*, and thus non-egodestructive, discipline (Category 11). The first type of discipline forces the child into submission and surrender of his ego, thus preventing his development. The second type contributes to the growth of the ego; it is similar to a therapy in which the therapist becomes an ally of the patient's ego, helping him to master his id. This second type of discipline seems an important condition for the establishment of an internalized superego, and thus crucial for the development of an unprejudiced personality. This category proved differentiating at a high level of significance. In men, 13 of the high scorers had the "threatening," none the "assimilable," type of discipline (7 received a Neutral rating due to lack of data). This finding is highly important since it seems to uncover a source of the basic fear so frequently exhibited by high-scoring men—and so often compensated for by sadistic toughness.

Furthermore, 9 of the low-scoring men—as contrasted with none of the high scorers (see above)—received the assimilable non-egodestructive type of discipline. Four of the low-scoring men were disciplined in a threatening manner.

Since discipline is of particular importance for our general theory concerning the genesis of the prejudiced personality, a series of examples from the records of high-scoring men is given herewith:

M45 reports that his father "did not believe in sparing the rod for stealing candy or someone's peaches off the tree."

M51: "My father spanked me on rare occasions, did it solemnly and it didn't hurt; and when he did it everybody cried. . . . But mother had a way of punishing me— lock me in a closet—or threaten to give me to a neighborhood woman who she said was a witch. . . . I think that's why I was afraid of the dark."

A similar psychologically cruel way of punishment is reported by *M44:* "Father picked upon things and threatened to put me in an orphanage."

M52 who, as quoted above, was struck on the finger with a knife at the table for being a bit too hungry, also reports that he "got a whipping (with a razor strop) that I thought was a little unreasonable." He tells a story about a friend who at the friend's home, in playing around, accidentally shoved subject through a window. When his father learned about it the same day, subject "got a whipping without a chance to explain. . . ."

M58, asked which parent he was closest to, answers: "I think my father. Although he beat the life out of me." He continues to emphasize that his father always gave everyone, including himself, "a square deal."

A good example of how some men in this group were frightened into obedience and submission is the following:

M57, asked about spanking, reports, "Not after 17. . . . Father had to give us one look and we knew what he meant."

An example of delayed punishment experienced as meaningless and cruel is given in the following quotation:

M20: (Nature of discipline?) "She would hold me back in. Never let me play if I'd done something wrong. . . . If I did anything wrong during the day, they couldn't spank me in public, in the hotel; they would spank me at night when I had maybe forgotten what it was for and resented it. Too delayed." Subject says he usually cried when he was spanked in order to get it over sooner, because when he started to cry, his grandmother would usually stop shortly. "It hurt my pride. . . . Just another restriction. . . . Or, sometimes, they would take away a movie." Subject says he resented this particularly since movies were few and far between for him anyway. "Grandfather never spanked me. . . ." About 10 or 12, subject says, he started running around more . . . "and they sort of lost their grip on me. I just stayed away from home. More school activities and work. . . ."

Another high-scoring man expresses his own ideas about the necessity for harsh punishment as follows:

M41: "If they have to whip them, I believe in whipping them. I don't believe in sparing the rod and spoiling the child; though I don't believe in abusing them. . . . Go down the street and hear a mother (threaten a spanking), the child says, 'Oh, mother, you know you don't mean that.' If I'd have said that to my mother, I wouldn't be able to sit down."

Further examples of the "High" type of discipline, taken from the records of high-scoring men and containing, among other things, deference to the emphasis on "being told" in terms of "petty" rules or "laws" lacking sufficient explanations, are the following:

M43: (Who gave the discipline?) "Uncle. (What kind?) Whip us. (How often?) Two or three times a month. (What for?) Going off without asking, not doing things we were told. (Was he always fair?) Well, after you'd think it over, you had it coming. (Ever question whether he was right about it?) No."

To the question whether he has been often punished, *M45* answers: "Often, and the hard part about it was that my stepmother would tell him (father) that my brother or I had done things and he wouldn't give us a chance to explain. . . . (What was your reaction?) Well, I ran off twice. . . . It didn't cause me to hate him. I held it mostly against her. (Did he exercise most of the discipline?) He did. (Did she sometimes punish you?) Yes, but not often. (For what?) Oh, things that seemed so trivial, like getting home late from school to do my chores."

M47: (What was the usual nature of the discipline?) ". . . . just bawl us out. (Q) She made it seem like it was hurting her more than it did us. . . . I think I'd rather have a licking than a good bawling out. (Q) She'd look hurt. (What were your feelings?) . . . Make me feel hurt . . . ashamed of myself. (Example?) One time I stayed out pretty late one night. When I got home, why she bawled me out, just little things like that. . . . Or going some place where she told me not to go . . . like some kid's house she told me not to play with."

Similarly, to the question, for what sort of things have you been punished, *M51* answers, "Usually something petty, stealing fudge off a shelf or something like that."

M58: "Well, my father was a very strict man. He wasn't religious, but strict in raising the youngsters. His word was law, and whenever he was disobeyed, there was punishment. When I was 12, my father beat me practically every day for getting into the tool chest in the back yard, and not putting everything away . . . finally he explained that those things cost money, and I must learn to put it back."

Another high-scoring man, *M6*, reports: "My father left the discipline to my mother, though he was the law when you came right down to it. I don't mean to say that either of them dominated us, but they kept us on the right track. I always had more respect for my mother than most. It was just the idea that she wanted me to do things that kept me on the right path. She spanked me sometimes. Father laid the strap on rarely; the last time was when I was 12 or 13 for talking back to my mother."

There is much reference to cruel punishment such as "whipping," "not sparing the rod," or "beating the life out of me" in the records of high-scoring subjects. Furthermore, the above quotations show that the discipline in the home is experienced as something arbitrary. Often it is implied that the punishment was unjust or "unreasonable" and that the subject had to submit to it without being given a "chance to explain" the situation. This is especially evident in the use, without further comment, of delayed punishment, an example of which was given above: "They would spank me at night, when I had maybe forgotten what it was for and resented it."

Furthermore, there is in these records a great deal of stress upon the fact that punishment was administered for something which seemed petty to the subject, for the violation of an external rule rather than of a basic principle.

Quite different are the reports of low-scoring men about the type of discipline they received:

Asked as to how discipline was enforced, *M16* relates: "Father lectured a good deal about honesty and integrity, etc."

A relaxed type of discipline with few restrictions is clearly indicated in the protocols of the following two low-scoring women:

F75: (Family training?) "Mother was in charge although they handled us well, I think. We were good, almost too good—and we were punished only rarely. Then it was a little spanking or scolding. There were never problems about going out. We could have had more freedom than we took."

F70: (What kind of things did she stress in your upbringing?) "She seems to me thoroughly liberal; there were not many restrictions anywhere. She accepted practically anything I did."

As is true in the case of many of the other categories, the material in the interviews on the issue of discipline of the women is not very complete. Thirteen of the high-scoring women received a Neutral rating; of the remaining 12, 9 report the threatening, and only 3 the non-egodestructive type of discipline. The following are quotations from the records of high-scoring women:

F66 relates: "I was kind of temperamental when I was little. I had temper tantrums if I didn't get my way. My mother cured them—she dunked me under the water faucet until I stopped screaming."

F36 reports a type of punishment psychologically quite cruel: Subject's mother criticized all her friends and interfered with all her friendships. In _____, subject had a boy friend eight years older than herself with whom she dated. Her mother scolded about the time she came home—said it was one or two o'clock in the morning, although it was never later than eleven P.M. Her mother said that everybody in town was talking about subject's relationship with this fellow and that she would not be allowed to teach next year (in a small town). This worried her so that she finally went to the vice principal of the school board, who had got her the job, and asked if he had heard anything about her. He said, no, that everybody liked her and liked Gus too. So that's how she knew her mother was making it all up. Her mother no doubt thought she would never check up on it.

The difference in the type of discipline found in the families of our high-scoring as compared with those of our low-scoring subjects, in conjunction with the difference in the family structure and the personality of the parents (stern vs. relaxed) may be considered part of the foundation for an authoritarian vs. democratic approach to interpersonal relationships. Evidence from the present study as well as from others (see Lasswell, 66; Fromm, 42; Erikson, 25) supports the psychoanalytic axiom that the first social relationships to be observed within the family are, to a large extent, formative of attitudes in later life.

D. CHILDHOOD EVENTS AND ATTITUDES TOWARD SIBLINGS

1. DEFINITION OF RATING CATEGORIES AND QUANTITATIVE RESULTS

The rating categories under the heading of "Childhood Events and Attitudes toward Siblings" fall into three groups: First, concern of the family with social status (Category 12), second, factual data on death, impairment of health, or divorce of the parents as well as sibling distribution (Categories 13 to 19), and third, psychological aspects of the relationship to the siblings (Categories 20a to 21c). The respective portions of the Scoring Manual are as follows:

INTERVIEW SCORING MANUAL: CHILDHOOD EVENTS AND ATTITUDES TOWARD SIBLINGS
(To Table 3(X))

Presumedly "High" Variants	Presumedly "Low" Variants
12. *Family status-concerned*	12. *Family relaxed re status*

13. *Death of father:*
   a. *In childhood* (age 1–6)
   b. *In prepuberty* (age 7–12)
   c. *In adolescence* (age 13–19)

14. *Death of mother:*
   a. *In childhood* (age 1–6)
   b. *In prepuberty* (age 7–12)
   c. *In adolescence* (age 13–19)

15. *Invalidism of father:*
   a. *In childhood* (age 1–6)
   b. *In prepuberty* (age 7–12)
   c. *In adolescence* (age 13–19)

16. *Invalidism of mother:*
   a. *In childhood* (age 1–6)
   b. *In prepuberty* (age 7–12)
   c. *In adolescence* (age 13–19)

17. *Divorce of parents:*
   a. *In childhood* (age 1–6)
   b. *In prepuberty* (age 7–12)
   c. *In adolescence* (age 13–19)

  d. *In whose care* was subject placed?
   (Father? Mother? Other relative (specify)?)
   Other (specify)?
18. *Sibling distribution:*
 a. Only child
 b. Youngest child.
 c. Eldest child
 d. Middle child
19. *Older sibling influence predominantly:*
 a. Masculine
 b. Feminine

20a. *Conventional idealization* of siblings   20a. *Objective appraisal*
20b. *Feelings of vicitimization* by siblings

        21a. *Principled open rejection*
        21b. *Genuine positive affect*
        21c. *Blocked affect*

Quantitative results are given in Table 3(X). Since on the factual aspects of childhood covered by the second group of categories little differentiation was found between the prejudiced and the unprejudiced (see below), tabulation has been omitted for these categories. The three topics will now be discussed in reverse order. Since the last of these, attitudes toward siblings, follows most logically the preceding discussion on parents, it will be discussed first.

2. ATTITUDES TOWARD SIBLINGS

Differentiations similar to those applying to the parents were expected for psychological sibling relationships. Thus *conventional idealization* (Category 20a) as well as *feelings of victimization* (Category 20b) were expected primarily in high-scoring subjects, whereas *objective appraisal* (Category 20a) as well as *genuine affect* (Category 21b), *blocked affect* (Category 21c), and *principled open rejection* (Category 21a) were expected to be present more often in the typical low scorer.

In the categories dealing with attitude toward siblings there is an unusual proportion of Neutral ratings, so that possible trends are to a large extent obscured. In the interviews this topic was often thought of as relatively less crucial, and the interviewers skipped it altogether when time ran short. In spite of this, the results, on the whole, show some interesting trends.

Since siblings are considered a part of the intimate ingroup, we find some glorification of them by our high-scoring subjects. The fact, however, that siblings are not authorities, or at least not authorities in the same sense as parents, probably accounts for the lesser absolute frequency of idealization manifested toward them. Thus only 4 high-scoring and 1 low-scoring male interviewees idealize their siblings.

An example of glorification of siblings from the record of a high-scoring man is *M52's* description of his brother: "Well, he's a wonderful kid. . . . Has been wonderful to my parents. . . . Now 21. Always lived at home. . . . Gives most of his earnings to my parents. . . ."

Again, as in the attitude toward the parents, low-scoring subjects tend to give a realistic, insightful, and openly affectionate picture of their siblings, whereas high-scoring subjects tend to repeat the stereotypical clichés that have been observed in their descriptions of the parents. The parallelism is manifested not only in the use of such terms as "a wonderful kid," but also in the opportunistic flavor of the evaluation as exemplified by the phrase "gives most of his earnings to my parents."

Neither "victimization" nor "open rejection (on grounds of general principles)" proved differentiating between the two groups of men. In women, however, there is some trend in the direction anticipated.

"Objective appraisal" of siblings, however, is much more clearly differentiating, with 12 low-scoring and 1 high-scoring men showing this attitude. Examples of objective appraisal from the records of low-scoring men follow:

M60 tells about his sister:. "My father represented authority in my house. When he died my sister lost her only authority and became quite a problem. Now has a happy, average home. . . . She was raised without adequate supervision."

The description of his sister by *M55* is along similar lines: "She's quite an amazing character, gotten to be a haphazard person now, careless . . . my parents ruined her, she's really quite bright, but has no initiative. However, a delightful person to live with because of her lackadaisical, I-don't-give-a-damn attitude . . . she's aware that she wasn't happy in her childhood. Parents were much more severe with her because she was more rebellious. She is extremely lenient with her own children."

"Genuine or blocked affect" responses, grouped together for certain purposes, were more differentiating in men than in women. Only 1 of the male high scorers but 11 of the male low scorers displayed this variant, due mostly to the presence of "genuine affect" toward siblings in low-scoring men. Examples of manifestations of real affection toward siblings from the protocols of low-scoring men are:

M59 says about his sister: "A lot of common trends. . . . Used to get a lot of pleasure in taking her out to shows, etc. because she was naive and used to get so much pleasure out of it. I used to help her with her schoolwork. She was more or less a tomboy when she was young and we had a lot of fun." Subject adds that he, and to a lesser extent her other brothers, taught her how to fight with her fists and comments that this has stood her in good stead, for example, as a professional ice-skater. "None of her competitors try any funny stuff with her because they know she can take care of herself."

M56 says about his young brother: "A good kid. A little inclined to be undiscriminating about his friends." Subject played big brother to him and made the decisions usually. (Satisfactions with brother?) "Oh, things shared together. (Q) Hunt, fish, both like people, as business partners got along swell."

M16 (answering the question, What about your brothers and sisters?): "The

TABLE 3 (X)

INTERVIEW RATINGS ON CHILDHOOD EVENTS AND ATTITUDE TOWARD SIBLINGS

FOR 80 SUBJECTS SCORING EXTREMELY "HIGH" OR "LOW" ON THE ETHNIC PREJUDICE QUESTIONNAIRE SCALE

| Interview rating categories (abbreviated from Manual) | Sex | Number of "High"(H) and "Low"(L) ratings received by | | | | Sums of instances | | Level of statistical significance reached (percentage) |
		20 men and 25 women "high scorers" H	L	20 men and 15 women "low scorers" H	L	"positive"	"negative"	
12. Family status-concerned(H) vs. status-relaxed(L)	Men	10	1	4	12	22	5	2
	Women	12	3	1	3	15	4	
20a. Conventional idealization(H) vs. objective appraisal(L) of siblings	Men	4	1	1	12	16	2	
	Women	6	3	0	7	13	3	
20b. Victimization by siblings(H)	Men	4		4		4	4	
	Women	7		3		7	3	
21a. Principled open rejection of siblings(L)	Men		3		3	3	3	
	Women		0		3	3	0	
21b. Genuine affection(L) or blocked affect(L) toward siblings	Men		1		11	11	1	
	Women		7		2	2	7	

brother fifteen years older; I was very close to him, we were good companions. (See him now?) I go to see him once in a while. Oh yes, we go into the garden together and look at his things, discuss things, philosophize. He thinks about the same way I do. He's a very intelligent sort of fellow; his IQ must be about in the genius range. (What are his interests?) Well, he's a _____; he plays in churches and different bands and he also has designed a new _____ with a different key that is easier to play. When he was fourteen, he built a steam engine for the shop." Subject describes very eagerly and seems very proud of his brother's achievements. (What is his occupation now?) "He putters around, shingles houses when he needs money and raises _____. He was interested in horticulture for a while. He likes shingling houses; he can sit up on the roof, think and philosophize. He's pretty poor, that is, he has some property, his house and another house that he rents, but he enjoys doing what he's doing. (What about your sisters?) Well, I have a sister two years older. I was sort of a pal of hers. And then one sister thirteen years older. She took care of me as a child. She was sort of a second mother to me. I'm not very close to either sister although I always got along with them alright. (Did your parents have any favorites among the children?) I don't think so. Well, probably I was the favorite of my mother because I was the baby. And my brother, the one six years older, he was so different from mother, she felt he was different, she didn't understand him. Father didn't know how to handle him."

The foregoing records give good illustrations of the way low-scoring men often display nurturant affection for their sisters, giving them support and love. The same may hold for the brothers, but mainly if there is a large age difference, with the subject being the older. Some of the records give evidence of the "fun" and pleasure they had with their sisters. Brothers near the age of the subject are often talked of in a way which indicates rivalry feelings. High-scoring men, on the other hand, tend to carry their feelings of rivalry into every relationship, and this often prevents them from having affectionate feelings toward any of their siblings.

A similar trend can be seen in women. Seven low scorers show "objective appraisal" of siblings, but none show "conventional idealization," whereas 6 of the high-scoring women interviewees do give evidence of the shallow glorification of siblings covered by the latter term. Since the number of Neutral ratings is even larger for the women interviewees than it is for men, the question of statistical significance was not approached.

An example of objective appraisal of siblings is demonstrated in the record of the following low-scoring woman:

F65 says: "One (sister) is fifteen. She thinks she resembles my mother's family. She is original and writes very cleverly, yet she is very naive and unconsciously funny. She is friendly and more social than I. She reforms everybody. My youngest sister is eight. She is very active, much more so than me. She is different than we. We are more quiet. We are 'drippy' in contrast to her. (Q) I used to have fights with my first sister."

Again we find, as so often in the case of the unprejudiced subjects, an imaginative, intraceptive quality in the description of other people, in this case of siblings. "Originality," "clever writing," being "unconsciously funny" are the characteristics appreciated in the sister. A certain self-critical tendency on the part of the subject is expressed by her reference to herself as "drippy" in comparison with her younger sister.

On the other hand, the following record of a high-scoring woman shows glorifying admiration for a sibling side by side with feelings of victimization, a combination discussed in connection with attitudes toward parents:

F69: (Parents?) "Everything was fine until my brother came into the world—Albert was such a sweet child, the whole family adored him—even grandparents. He's blond, nice looking, sickly as a child, but not now. Short nose."

Typical in this protocol also is the emphasis on physical features which is similar to that found in the high scorers' descriptions of their parents.

There is, furthermore, on the whole a greater, though not statistically significant tendency in high-scoring interviewees to manifest feelings of being victimized by siblings. The record of *F69*, quoted before, was an example of this tendency. Another example from the interview of a high-scoring woman is:

F32: "The situation with the youngest sister is very different." Not only did subject take care of this sister after the mother's death, but she gave her financial aid. Because of their father's policy of giving the children only the necessities and none of the extras, the young sister would have had to go without evening dresses and other things that a girl really has to have in high school, if these had not been supplied by subject. The interviewer asked if subject also heard regularly from this sister. With much bitterness, subject replied that she was lucky if she heard from her sister once in three months. She feels that this sister has the family characteristic of being self-sufficient and independent, and that she has never really shown any gratitude for all that subject has done for her.

This record shows clearly that the subject resents both mother and sister, without daring to criticize them.

In all, only 3 of our low-scoring and none of our high-scoring women interviewees show "open rejection" of siblings. One example may suffice as an illustration of this attitude:

F29: "Sister aged 19 years. She is in Hollywood getting into the movies. We are not particularly good friends. First real hate was my sister. Intensely jealous of one another." Subject hasn't been near her for years. After high school, sister had little money. Met a fellow who supported her. "She sort of ruled him. She went to dramatic school. Is a very beautiful girl—not conventionally beautifully—beautiful in a masculine way." Subject does not think her sister was the mistress of the man. Sister has had homosexual affairs.

Having genuine, or else blocked, affect did not differentiate significantly between the two groups; again there was a scarcity of ratable material.

It is interesting to note that low-scoring men show more "genuine affect" for siblings in their interviews than low-scoring women. This fact may be due to a greater inclination toward envy in women as compared to men, a trend noted by Freud and others.

3. CHILDHOOD EVENTS

Under the heading of "Childhood Events" the Interview Scoring Manual contained provisions for the registration of such facts as death of father or mother, divorce of parents, sibling distribution, etc. Since, as expected, the prejudiced and the unprejudiced showed, on the whole, little differentiation with respect to these categories, they were omitted in Table 3(X). A few remarks will be made here in a more informal way.

There is but little difference between the numbers of low and high scorers, women and men alike, who lost their fathers through death. The same holds true as far as the death of the mother in the case of women subjects is concerned, but the absolute number of those involved is very small in this case (2 out of the 25 high scorers and 1 out of the 15 low scorers).

However, 7 out of the 20 high-scoring men interviewees lost their mothers through death in their childhood or pre-adolescence, while all of the mothers of the 20 low-scoring men are still living. This objective finding gives support to the hypothesis, set forth above, that the relationship with the mother is important for the development of humanitarian values in the son. Early death of the mother may, it seems, contribute to the establishment of intolerant attitudes in the son.

The proportions of divorces of parents are very similar for men and women, high scorers and low scorers.

The position within the sibling distribution was likewise not found to be differentiating between the prejudiced and unprejudiced subjects.

4. STATUS CONCERN

The only aspect relating to "childhood events" which is explicitly listed in Table 3(X) (Category 12) is less palpably "objective" than those just mentioned. Yet it proved highly discriminatory. It deals with *social status*, the parents and family being classified either as "status-concerned" or as "status-relaxed" on the basis of the interview with the subject. Ten of the high- and only 1 of the low-scoring men describe a status-concerned attitude within their family. Conversely, 12 of the low-scoring men and only 4 of the high-scoring men describe their families as status-relaxed. The entire category is significant for men at the 2 per cent level.

An example of hierarchial thinking in the attitude toward work from the interview of one of the high-scoring men is the following:

M13 reports that, in spite of the fact that his father had to be careful with money, he would not let the subject work because he thought "it was beneath me."

Another of the prejudiced men interviewees gives a striking example of looking at marriage and children solely as a means to conserve possessions:

M51: "The only thing I really want—I have been paying storage on my mother's things. . . . I want a home and I want to get married, not because I want a wife, but because I want a child. I want the child because I want someone to pass my things on to—I suddenly have become very conscious of my background that I forget about. (How do you mean?) Family background. . . . And another thing is, if I have no issue, father's money will go to father's relatives. I want it to go to mother's side."

Another subject in this group shows the relationship between home discipline and aspirations to climb into "higher classes":

M57: (What were you disciplined for?) "Well, they didn't want me to run with some kind of people—slummy women—always wanted me to associate with the higher class of people."

The relaxed attitude toward status, with some tendency toward understatement, as found in unprejudiced interviewees is exemplified in the record of:

M53: (Parent's feelings about money?) "Well, kind of hard to answer. You see, my father died in. . . . I grew up in _____ (middle-class town). Neither extremes of poverty or wealth. Pretty typical middle-class community. (Did you have to work as a child?) Didn't have to. I did work in high school. (How did parents get along economically?) Well, they were lucky. Father left enough of an estate that mother didn't have to worry." Always a nice home, car, etc. "We always had Buicks (laughs) . . . which I think is typical of. . . ."

Another subject in this group displays even a lack of knowledge about the family's background:

M59: (How important was money to your parents?) "Well, I don't believe it was overemphasized or too important, was a means of providing food and shelter . . . but they found their happiness in work and little pleasures on weekends, etc." Both of subject's parents were born in this country. Mother's father was also born here. Father's father was born in Germany. "My father's father was born in Germany, I believe. . . . We didn't know very much about his family. . . . My mother's mother was born in this country. . . . Father's mother, I don't know."

The absence of a greedy attitude toward money also reflected in this protocol is further exemplified in the interview of another low-scoring man:

M12: "You know what George Bernard Shaw said? (What?) He says we ought to shoot everybody who wants to earn more than three thousand dollars a year and also those who can't make that much (laughs). I guess that's about right. (Family?) My mother had and accepted a very simple way of living. She had no envy or desire for more. I guess we all felt that way. We had sort of scorn for people who wanted too much. I guess there were just two worlds; theirs (the rich world) and ours; ours was fine—it didn't need any improvement. Our whole family felt that way, I think."

References to finding one's "happiness in work and little pleasures" or "in simple ways of living without desire or envy for more" are characteristic in this respect since the status-concern of the high scorers is often connected with an antipleasure attitude as discussed in other contexts within the interview material.

Of the high-scoring women's families, 12 are status-concerned whereas only 3 seem to be relaxed on this issue. The following quotation may suffice as an example of a status-concerned family background in the case of a high scorer:

F79: At the present time the father is the owner of a mill and logging camp and he also has interests in _____. "It's a medium sized mill but I have no idea of his income. Of course, we children have always been to private schools and lived in exclusive residential sections. In _____ we had tennis courts and horses. We had more or less to start over again when we came to this country. We lived in a nice house but really couldn't afford it. It was quite an effort to get into social circles. In _____ we felt secure and fitted in. Back here, we have lived at the same level but with anxiety about it. Mother and daddy have climbed socially . . . and I don't care so much. Yes, we have always had servants. It was easy in _____, but it's hard to get them here."

As will be discussed in the next (concluding) section of this chapter, the great concern about status characteristic of the families of our prejudiced subjects may be instrumental in the establishment of many of the attitudes shown so far as predominant in high scorers.

E. SUMMARY AND CONCLUDING REMARKS ON FAMILY PATTERNS

The quantitative data just presented give evidence that presence or absence of extreme ethnic prejudice in individuals of our culture tends to be related to a complex network of attitudes within, and relating to, the family. Lasswell, in his pioneer study (66), found that the interrelationships of his subjects with their parents and siblings were of paramount importance in determining their future political activities.

In the following summary a composite picture of the prejudiced and unprejudiced trends as based on our material is presented.[2] As stated before, most of the high-scoring and low-scoring individuals exhibit "High" as well as "Low" personality traits in varying proportions. In fact, single individuals may display any kind of configuration of traits. What is attempted in the present context is no more than a schematic outline of prevalent group trends. Such a picture must of necessity do injustice to all the many existing exceptions.

It also must be reiterated that our composite picture deals with groups scoring *extremely* high or low on the prejudice questionnaire rather than with groups that are more average in this respect.

[2] Although the results discussed in this summary are primarily based on the statements of our subjects about their families, direct evidence gathered in a separate study on social discrimination in children and their parents substantiate our inferences about the differences in the family constellation of high scorers and low scorers (see Else Frenkel-Brunswik, 30).

Prejudiced subjects tend to report a relatively harsh and more threatening type of home discipline which was experienced as arbitrary by the child. Related to this is a tendency apparent in families of prejudiced subjects to base interrelationships on rather clearly defined roles of dominance and submission in contradistinction to equalitarian policies. In consequence, the images of the parents seem to acquire for the child a forbidding or at least a distant quality. Family relationships are characterized by fearful subservience to the demands of the parents and by an early suppression of impulses not acceptable to them.

The goals which such parents have in mind in rearing and training their children tend to be highly conventional. The status-anxiety so often found in families of prejudiced subjects is reflected in the adoption of a rigid and externalized set of values: what is socially accepted and what is helpful in climbing the social ladder is considered "good," and what deviates, what is different, and what is socially inferior is considered "bad." With this narrow path in mind, the parents are likely to be intolerant of any manifestation of impulses on the part of the child which seems to distract from, or to oppose, the desired goal. The more urgent the "social needs" of the parents, the more they are apt to view the child's behavior in terms of their own instead of the child's needs.

Since the values of the parents are outside the child's scope, yet are rigorously imposed upon him, conduct not in conformity with the behavior, or with the behavorial façade, required by the parents has to be rendered ego-alien and "split off" from the rest of the personality (see Chapter XII), with a resultant loss of integration. Much of the submission to parental authority in the prejudiced subject seems to be induced by impatience on the part of the parents and by the child's fear of displeasing them.

It is in the area of social and political attitudes that the suppressed yet unmodified impulses find one of their distorted outlets and emerge with particular intensity. In particular, moral indignation first experienced in the attitude of one's parents toward oneself is being redirected against weaker outgroups.

The lack of an internalized and individualized approach to the child, on the part of the parents, as well as a tendency to transmit mainly a set of conventional rules and customs, may be considered as interfering with the development of a clear-cut personal identity in the growing child. Instead, we find surface conformity without integration, expressing itself in a stereotyped approach devoid of genuine affect in almost all areas of life. The general, pervasive character of the tendency, on the part of prejudiced individuals, toward a conventional, externalized, shallow type of relation will be demonstrated further in subsequent chapters. Even in the purely cognitive domain, ready-made clichés tend to take the place of spontaneous reactions. Whatever the topic may be, statements made by the prejudiced as contrasted with the unprejudiced are apt to stand out by their comparative lack of imagination, of spontaneity, and of originality and by a certain constrictive character.

Faithful execution of prescribed roles and the exchange of duties and obligations is, in the families of the prejudiced, often given preference over the exchange of free-flowing affection. We are led to assume that an authoritarian home régime, which induces a relative lack of mutuality in the area of emotion and shifts emphasis onto the exchange of "goods" and of material benefits without adequate development of underlying self-reliance, forms the basis for the opportunistic type of dependence of children on their parents, described in the present chapter.

This kind of dependence on the parents, the wish to be taken care of by them, coupled with the fear ensuing from the same general pattern, seems firmly to establish the self-negating submission to parents just described. There are, however, certain cues which seem to indicate the presence, at the same time, of underlying resentment against, and feelings of victimization by, the parents. Occasionally such attitudes manage to break through to the overt level in the interview material. But they are seen more directly, more consistently, and in more intense form in the fantasy material gathered from the same individuals.

Resentment, be it open or disguised, may readily be understood in view of the strong parental pressures to enforce "good" behavior together with the meagerness of the rewards offered. As a reaction against the underlying hostility, there is often rigid glorification and idealization of the parents. The artificiality of this attitude may be recognized from the description of the parents in exaggerated, superlative (and at the same time stereotypical and externalized) terms.

Usually it is only this admiration which is admitted and ego-accepted. The resentment, rendered ego-alien, is the more active through the operation of mechanisms of displacement. The larger social implications of this displaced hostility are discussed in various contexts throughout the present volume.

The superficial character of the identification with the parents and the consequent underlying resentment against them recurs in the attitudes to authority and social institutions in general. As will be seen, we often find in our high-scoring subjects both overconformity and underlying destructiveness toward established authority, customs, and institutions. A person possessed by such ambivalence may easily be kept in check and may even behave in an exemplary fashion in following those external authorities who take over the function of the superego—and partly even those of the ego. On the other hand, if permitted to do so by outside authority, the same person may be induced very easily to uncontrolled release of his instinctual tendencies, especially those of destructiveness. Under certain conditions he will even join forces with the delinquent, a fusion found in Nazism.

The orientation toward power and the contempt for the allegedly inferior and weak, found in our typical prejudiced subjects, must likewise be considered as having been taken over from the parents' attitude toward the child. The fact that his helplessness as a child was exploited by the parents and that he was forced into submission must have reinforced any existing antiweakness attitude. Prejudiced individuals thus tend to display "negative identification" with the weak along with their positive though superficial identification with the strong.

This orientation toward the strong is often expressed in conscious identification with the more powerful parent. Above all, the men among our prejudiced subjects tend to report having a "stern and distant" father who seems to have been domineering within the family. It is this type of father who elicits in his son tendencies toward passive submission, as well as the ideal of aggressive and rugged masculinity and a compensatory striving for independence. Furthermore, the son's inadequate relation to his mother prevents him from adopting some of the "softer" values.

In line with the fact that the families of the prejudiced, especially those of our male subjects, tend to be father-dominated, there is a tendency in such families toward a dichotomous conception of the sex roles and a relative separation of the sexes within the family (see Chapter XI).

In view of the fact that, depending upon his sex, the personality structure of a parent will have a different effect on that of a child, the same family constellation may make either the son or the daughter more susceptible to nondemocratic ideology. Thus, under certain conditions, a boy may become tolerant when his mother is tolerant and his father not, while the daughter in the same family may become intolerant. This is, perhaps, one of the reasons why siblings sometimes tend toward different political ideologies. Unfortunately, no systematic investigation of siblings could be made in the framework of the present study.

By and large, the prejudiced man has more possibilities available to him to compensate for underlying weaknesses. He may do so by demonstrating his independence, or by implicit or explicit assertion of his superiority over women. Prejudiced women, with fewer outlets at their disposal for the expression of their underlying feelings, show, as will become evident later, stronger underlying hostilities and more rigid defenses than their male counterparts.

In the case of the individuals extremely low on ethnic prejudice the pattern of family relationships differs at least in the degree of emphasis that is placed upon the various factors just listed. One of the most important differences as compared with the family of the typical high scorer is that less obedience is expected of the children. Parents are less status-ridden and thus show less anxiety with respect to conformity and are less intolerant toward manifestations of socially unaccepted behavior. Instead of condemning they tend to provide more guidance and support, thus helping the child to work out his instinctual problems. This makes possible a better development of socialization and of the sublimation of instinctual tendencies.

Comparatively less pronounced status-concern often goes hand in hand with greater richness and liberation of emotional life. There is, on the whole, more affection, or more unconditional affection, in the families of unprejudiced subjects. There is less surrender to conventional rules, and therefore relations within the family tend to be more internalized and individualized. To be sure, this sometimes goes to the extreme of falling short of the acceptance of normal standards and customs.

Additional evidence will be offered in the next chapter for the fact that unprejudiced individuals often manifest an unrealistic search for love in an attempt to restore the type of early relations they enjoyed within their family. Exaggerated cravings in this direction are often a source of dissatisfaction and open ambivalence.

The unprejudiced man, especially, seems oriented toward his mother and tends to retain a love-dependent nurturance-succorance attitude toward women in general which is not easily satisfied. Such an orientation toward the mother, together with the conception of the father as "mild and relaxed," makes it possible for the unprejudiced man to absorb a measure of passivity in his ideal of masculinity. No compensation through pseudo-toughness and antiweakness attitudes is thus necessary. The humanitarian approach can then be adopted on the basis of identification both with the mother and with the father.

The unprejudiced woman, on the other hand, seems to have more often a genuine liking and admiration for the father, for, say, his intellectual-aesthetic abilities. This often leads to conscious identification with him.

Since the unprejudiced subjects on the whole received more love and feel more basically secure in relation to their parents, they more easily express disagreement with them without fear of retaliation or of a complete loss of love. As is to be expected, such expressions of disagreement will nonetheless often lead to internal conflict, guilt, and anxieties. This is the more to be understood since in this group the relations to the parents tend to be intensive and often highly gratifying. There is certainly a great deal of ambivalence in this type of love-oriented family attachment. Ambivalence is here more openly faced, however, than in the case of the prejudiced.

In spite of the conflicts just mentioned, unprejudiced subjects often succeed in attaining a considerable degree of independence from their parents, and of freedom in making their own decisions. Since hostility toward the parents, when present, tends to be more open, it often takes the form of rebellion against other authorities or, more generally, against objects nearer to the original objects of aggression than are the really, or presumably, weak which serve as favorite objects of aggression in the case of the prejudiced. It is often in this form that the unprejudiced man expresses his hostility against his father.

On the whole, this type of independence recurs in the unprejudiced subjects' attitude toward social institutions and authorities in general. At the same time, the existing identification with the parents is often accompanied by a more basic identification with mankind and society in general.

The next chapter will present concrete evidence of the fact that the general attitude toward the parents, the greater ability to love, the richer and more libidinized object-cathexis, and the greater independence found in the unprejudiced recur as general traits in their interpersonal relations. Further quotations of actual statements from interviews will confirm the impression gained so far that the ethnically unprejudiced in our culture tend to be more creative and imaginative than the prejudiced and that they are characterized by a fuller integration of their personalities. The concluding chapters of Part II will round out the picture. It must be stressed, however, that the unprejudiced by no means emerges as an unmitigated ideal. Nor must, on the other hand, the prejudiced be blamed as an individual for his or her bias. Rather, the "high" character-structure must largely be considered the outcome of our civilization. The increasing disproportion of the various psychological "agencies" within the total personality is undoubtedly being reinforced by such tendencies in our culture as division of labor, the increased importance of monopolies and institutions, and the dominance of the idea of exchange and of success and competition. This may help to explain the impression the reader may have gained from a detailed perusal of the material presented in this chapter, namely, that all in all the character of the extremely unprejudiced is less clearcut and pronounced than that of the extremely prejudiced, so that one may perhaps say that the high-scorer has more "high" traits than the low-scorer has "low" traits. Of course, a full picture of our civilization will also have to account for the characteristics of the typical low-scorer. A more detailed discussion of all this will be given in Chapter XIII.

The next chapter will take up in greater detail some of the general attitudes toward the parents, the greater anxiety in love, etc., and more particularly the greater facility in love and more generally in the unprejudiced record, as general traits in their interpersonal relations. Further impressions of actual sexual relations will confirm the impression gained so far that the otherwise unprejudiced in our culture tend to be more overt and open in the expression of their personalities. The evaluation represents ...

CHAPTER XI

SEX, PEOPLE, AND SELF AS SEEN THROUGH THE INTERVIEWS

Else Frenkel-Brunswik

In the preceding chapter, family patterns have been described with the focus on the difference between the descriptions given by prejudiced as compared with unprejudiced individuals. Discussion has centered especially upon the following: authoritarian as contrasted with equalitarian approach, conventionality and stereotypy vs. genuineness and richness of affect, degree and type of dependence, love-orientation as contrasted with opportunistic orientation, openness and admission of hostility, differentiation in attitudes toward the parent of the same sex and of the opposite sex.

Similar themes will now be taken up in a consideration of the subjects' evaluation of, and contact with, the other sex and people in general, and, finally, their self-evaluation. It will be of special interest to investigate in these areas the recurrence or the modifications of the patterns found within the family.

A. ATTITUDE TOWARD SEX

1. DEFINITION OF RATING CATEGORIES AND QUANTITATIVE RESULTS

The aspects to be covered in this section can best be seen from the list of categories used in rating the interview material pertaining to the area of sex adjustment. As is the case throughout the presentation of the Interview Scoring Manual used by the interview raters, the categories are presented in their skeleton form only, omitting the bulk of the extensive oral commentary and discussion offered to the raters. Some of these further specifications are presented together with the subsequent analysis and discussion of the results by categories.

INTERVIEW SCORING MANUAL: ATTITUDE TOWARD SEX

(to Table 1(XI))

PRESUMABLY "HIGH" VARIANTS

22. *Status via sex:* E.g., "conquests," emphasis on "dates"; rationalization of any failure or shortcoming

23a. *Rejection of id:* Anti-id moralism; rejection of sex, or continued attachment to a frigid or impotent partner

23b. *Promiscuity* as a prominent pattern (no extended love relationship)

24. *Dichotomous sex attitudes:* Sex vs. affection and object-relations; pure vs. low women (in men); depersonalized sex relations or interests. Reference to specified practices

25. *Underlying disrespect-resentment* toward opposite sex, typically combined with externalized, excessive pseudo-admiration

26. *Power orientation:* Exploitive-manipulative (concrete benefits). In women: surface-submission plus aggression-castration

27. *Values conventionally determined*

Traits desired:
  Men in Women:
    Giving (kind, generous)
    Pure (wholesome, "good personality")
    Submissive, "sweet"
  Women in Men:
    Hardworking, energetic, go-getting
    Moral model, clean-cut
    Deferent

PRESUMABLY "LOW" VARIANTS

22. *Open admission of inadequacy without rationalizing*

23a. *Acceptance of id*

23b. *Conscious inhibitions without moralism*

24. *Fusion of sex and affection:* Personalized sex orientation or relations

25. *Genuine respect-fondness* for opposite sex, often with conflict about one's sex role and open ambivalence toward the other sex

26. *Love-seeking* (warmth and affection)

27. *Values individualized*

Emphasis on:
Companionship, common interest
Warmth, sociability
Sexual love
Understanding
Liberal values

As can be seen from Table 1(XI), five out of the seven differences studied in comparing the attitudes toward sex of low-scoring and high-scoring men are statistically highly significant. For women three categories are sig-

TABLE 1 (XI)

INTERVIEW RATINGS ON ATTITUDE TOWARD SEX
FOR 80 SUBJECTS SCORING EXTREMELY "HIGH" OR "LOW" ON THE ETHNIC PREJUDICE QUESTIONNAIRE SCALE

Interview rating categories (abbreviated from Manual)	Sex	Number of "High"(H) and "Low"(L) ratings received by				Sums of instances		Level of statistical significance reached (percentage)
		20 men and 25 women "high scorers" H	L	20 men and 15 women "low scorers" H	L	"positive"	"negative"	
22. Status via sex(H) vs. admission of inadequacy(L)	Men	8	2	1	8	16	3	5
	Women	10	1	1	12	22	2	1
23a. Rejection(H) vs. acceptance(L) of id	Men	17	2	6	4	21	8	
	Women	9	4	4	8	17	8	
23b. Promiscuity(H) vs. conscious inhibitions(L)	Men	0	0	1	0	0	1	
	Women	7	0	2	1	8	2	
24. Dichotomy(H) vs. fusion(L) of sex and affection	Men	11	4	3	6	17	7	
	Women	16	2	4	6	22	6	1
25. Underlying disrespect(H) vs. genuine fondness of opposite sex(L)	Men	13	4	2	7	20	6	5
	Women	12	2	1	11	23	3	1
26. Exploitive power-orientation(H) vs. love-seeking(L)	Men	13	4	2	10	23	6	1
	Women	9	2	2	14	23	4	1
27. Conventional(H) vs. individualized(L) values	Men	12	4	3	6	18	7	1
	Women	10	2	2	11	21	4	

nificant; the remaining ones likewise show the expected trend though in a somewhat less pronounced fashion.

2. STATUS VIA SEX

High-scoring individuals tend to view *sex as a means of obtaining status*, and to *rationalize failures or shortcomings* in this area (Category 22). Ten high-scoring and only 1 of the low-scoring men manifest this attitude. Similar is the proportion for women (8 to 1). These results also illustrate the general tendency of high scorers to speak well of themselves.

The typical high-scoring man apparently has a particularly strong need to conceive of himself as an ideal of masculinity, and so high-scoring men tend either to boast of their sexual conquests or to justify their lack of sexual experience or success by explanations in terms of moral restraint or unfortunate external circumstances. Embarrassment is shown about facts which might point toward a less glorious masculine role, e.g., about what is considered a late sexual start. In women a similar attitude is revealed mainly by reports about popularity with men. There is evidence both of excessive moralism (see below) and of crude promiscuity in the records of the high scorers; sex relations tend to be isolated and depersonalized and thus to become peripheral rather than being integrated with the ego. All this must be seen in the context of the general cultural confusion, and the breakdown of values in general and of sex values in particular in Western civilization; low scorers, although on the whole on better terms with their sex life, are by no means entirely free from this confusion (see below).

Examples from the protocols of interviewees scoring extremely high on the overt ethnocentrism questionnaire follow.

M45, a high-scoring man, boasts a great deal about his ability to seduce girls: (Where get sex instruction?) "In a parked automobile. (Q) I guess when I was about fourteen or fifteen.... Oh, wait a minute, I'll have to go back further than that. First time was when I was about eight years old. Of course, I didn't know what I was doing. It was my cousin ... (by mutual agreement). It made me sick though. ... (First intercourse?) Well, must have been fifteen. (Q) Girl I hardly knew. She must have been about twenty years old, out riding, two couples in the car, a Model A. She and I went off by ourselves. ... A one-night relationship. I don't think I ever saw her again. (Did you have many intercourses before you married?) Yes. (All momentary relationships?) Yes, that's all. (What about second wife?) I was with her twice. I was twenty. The second time didn't last long. I always get married spectacularly. We got married in a taxi cab. ... We had intercourse before we were married, after four months' acquaintance. She was a virgin."

M46 tells that "I have a peculiar characteristic which causes women to open up on short acquaintance and tell all about themselves."

M18 states that, since the age of 14, he has been "woman crazy" and expressed many fantastic ideas of his sexual power. States that he proposed matrimony many times, but was always repulsed because he could not support the girls. This subject seems to believe in his "sexual power," and the fact that he has been rejected by all girls to whom he proposed marriage is completely rationalized on the grounds of his economic insufficiency.

Embarrassment about what is felt as an overly late first sex experience is shown in the record of *M11:* (What was your first sex experience?) "At the age of 17, I'm sorry to admit. I mean, it was so late."

F32, a high-scoring woman, remarks that she had always had "scads of boy friends." When she was in the fourth grade there was a boy who used to carry her books home and they remained friends for many years. There was no kissing or anything of that kind. Her father had a farm in _____ and the family spent their summers there for many years. One summer when she was about 18 something very dramatic happened. One night a farmhand who had been interested in her came around to the front door and told her parents that he would shoot himself if she would not marry him. When asked how far their relationship had gone, she denied that there had even been any kissing; "he was only a farmhand."

Our low-scoring interviewees, on the other hand, are mostly frank in their *open admission* without rationalizing, of whatever is thought to be an inadequacy or undue delay with respect to sexual attractiveness, development, or adjustment. The differences on the entire Category 22 are highly significant (at the 1 per cent level) in men and satisfactory (at the 5 per cent level) in women.

Examples from the records of low-scoring men are:

M15, a low scorer, is a good example of the men who frankly admit lack of sexual experience without feeling the necessity to rationalize on moral or other grounds: Picked up all his knowledge from older boys. Remembers some sex play with neighborhood children, but denies active participation. Felt guilty, afraid gang's activities would be discovered.

M49 is frank about the sexual difficulties in his marriage: "We don't—we used to have quite a bit of difficulty, but we're getting along much better now . . . after this operation, I didn't have much desire . . . for about 6 months. . . . I feel now that we're not too close to the peak . . . but it's so much better now."

M53 describes his earliest sex experience: "Oh, I think it was about 15 or 16. (Q) With a gal that was not very satisfactory. (Q) Someone I knew fairly well." Subject indicates later that this was intercourse, although not very successful.

M55: "Oh, about 14, though I wasn't very successful. . . . So clumsy, I don't know whether you'd call it experience, but imagine when I was about seventeen, in the back seat of an automobile." (Other sex experiences before marriage?) Subject mentions several incidental relationships, none of which led to affairs. . . . "I think that probably contributed to my feeling of not being successful and not being able to . . . afraid of being clumsy. . . ."

M56 tells that he has "always been rather inhibited about sex."

M59 admits that his girl left him for another man: "At 16 about a year and a half. I felt pretty bad about it when we split up. I got a job and she started going out with another man."

Likewise frank are the low-scoring women in their admission of difficulties in adjusting to a feminine role, or of a lack of attraction for men.

Thus *F62,* asked about her boy friends, reports: "I am avoided by the male sex perhaps because I am too heavy. I only have speaking acquaintances with boys. When I meet boys I immediately try to be witty and clever and this is a great mistake. I never go on dates; sometimes I am glad of it because I have more time for reading—and sometimes I am sorry."

F27 reports: (After you began to get acquainted with boys, were you at ease with them?) "Not for a long time. At first I didn't even enjoy a date. I was so busy worrying if he would ask me for another. I can't say I ever did enjoy boys very much. It is just the idea that they are boys. I never got all thrilled like some girls do. I never cared a lot about anyone until I met my husband."

F30 has no difficulties in admitting that she never had a date: "We became engaged without ever having a date. In fact, I never had dates. . . . We often laugh now about the fact that we got engaged and knew we wanted to spend our lives together without ever having had a date."

F63 tells about her difficulty in accepting the feminine role: "Can't make myself do anything. Never have been willing to accept my role as a woman. This is just one of a long series of depressions which have resulted from having my ambitions blocked. I really love my present husband, would like to get myself straightened out while he is at sea. If I don't I'll lose him too."

Generally, one of the most outstanding characteristics of our low-scoring subjects is their ability to admit shortcomings in themselves (see Section C). The above quotations show clearly that low-scoring men can admit sexual insufficiency, "awkwardness," and "clumsiness" without further rationalization. Similarly the low-scoring women are ready to face their lack of success in this field as well as their difficulties in accepting a feminine role. Especially in the last of the records there is clear indication of conflict between love for the husband and having one's "ambitions blocked" by marriage. At the same time, sex seems to be much more integrated with social relations in unprejudiced individuals, and much more oriented toward specific persons.

3. MORALISTIC REJECTION OF INSTINCTUAL TENDENCIES

It appears, furthermore, that high scorers tend to manifest what may be called a *moralistic rejection of the id* (Category 23a). The restricted type of prejudiced person manifests, in the main, explicit anti-id moralism; the less restricted—but often not less inhibited—type of high scorer, to be found primarily in our prison sample, manifests the same tendency though often more indirectly, e.g., by attachment to a frigid woman and often in context with promiscuity. If high-scoring subjects think of sex primarily in terms of success and failure, it is not surprising to find that they tend to reject the purely erotic or sensual.

Our low scorers, on the other hand, tending in general to be less repressed, seem to manifest more *acceptance of the id*. The results on the entire Category 23a show the expected trend without, however, reaching statistical significance. There are 17 positive as contrasted with 8 negative instances in men, and a similar and slightly higher ratio in women.

Examples of high-scoring men who are attached to a frigid partner are:

M40: In the past year subject has been very much in love with a married woman.

"She doesn't like her husband, but has a false loyalty to him because he is in the army, and makes herself miserable. I never met the man. I got fed up from her sheer stupidity! When I went East, I was to send her money to get her divorce and I wrote her daily and she never replied; and I came out to find out what had happened and she re-discovered her loyalty to him and she actually wouldn't let me touch her. He hurt her physically and she couldn't enjoy sex. She had a doctor treating her and she would say to me, 'I am only half a woman.' All that was a part of it all. I was prepared to take care of everything and I had arranged to take care of her younger brother and sister."

M45: (What sort of person was she?) "The type of person that you see a lot of. Wise and dumb, both. . . . Knows a lot about business, nothing about people. . . . She trusts everyone (subject gives an example). . . . We didn't get on too good sexually because she was kind of on the frigid line, but still in all I was in love with her and I still am. I'd like nothing better than to go back to her. . . . I don't think there's much chance of it though. . . ."

M51: (Marriage?) "She was 12 years older than me. (Q) She's a very literary person. We did have a lot of things in common. She's cold as a clam sexually (Did you have intercourse with her?) Yes, lots of times and I used especially . . . in the evening getting ready to go out. . . ."

M52: "She tried very hard to make me happy. . . . The thing that eventually broke us up was (proximity of her parents). She could always run home. . . . Another drawback was the sexual relationship. . . . She was the type that didn't care much for it. . . . She never had any desire for it."

Although rejection of the id, in the foregoing records of high-scoring men, is manifested mainly in the choice of, and attachment to, a frigid woman, it is interesting to note that some of the men at the same time show signs of crude and unsocialized sex impulses (see below). In these cases the inability to accept genuine sexuality leads to both a frequent change of the sex object without personal involvement, and involvement without sex.

Anti-id moralism is more clearly manifest in the statements of prejudiced women, who often have very definite ideas of what is to be considered as wrong. Examples from their interviews follow.

F22: "Sex isn't uppermost in my mind by any means. . . . I'm more for having a good time with the exclusion of sex interest. (Q) I've been shocked by the conduct of my girl friends. I didn't think they were that type."

F31: "I think a girl should be friendly, but I don't like necking in the back of a show. A boy and a girl should be just friends."

F74: "When at high school was first kissed." Subject didn't like it. She was frightened.

F71: (Proper?) "I don't believe in parking—no matter what you're doing. I believe in kissing. I've done my share of it, but I've never parked. . . . (A girl who did) I'd stick with, but wouldn't think much of her. . . . Mother says 'a boy admires a girl who admires herself.' "

Low-scoring subjects, on the other hand, show more acceptance of sex in general, though not without evidence of conflict.

Acceptance of instinctual tendencies is shown in the following records of low-scoring subjects:

M56: (Importance of sex in marriage?) "Very high. I was fortunate in being perfectly mated to my wife, sexually, that is."

M55: (Sex adjustment with her?) "Very well, took quite a long time, though."

M16: Subject was in love several times—some of the times the girls were married or did not want to marry him. Once during the depression he had an affair with one girl for several years but did not want to get married because of financial circumstances. Subject married in _____ after living with his present wife for several years. "We get along pretty well, never quarrel. (How did you get along sexually?) Pretty well."

4. "PURE" *VS.* "BAD" WOMEN

It is probably the predominance of surface adulation of, and underlying resentment against, the mother, found in high-scoring men, that leads to what is here called their *dichotomous sex attitudes* as defined by the separation of sex and affect, or by the sharpness of the distinction between a "bad" and a "pure" woman. On the other hand, *fusion of sex and affect,* a tendency to more personalized sex relations, is found more often in low-scoring men (Category 24). The difference is significant at the 1 per cent level as defined at the end of Chapter IX.

In our sample of women we find the same trend, but the difference is not statistically significant.

Examples of the dichotomous conception of "good" vs. "bad" women, taken from the records of high-scoring men, follow.

M51: (Other relations with women?) "Well, yes, three or four, all older than me and they weren't anything but physical."

M52: "She taught me something that stuck with me all my life, that a woman is the most perfect thing in the world, that is, the right kind of woman."

M6: "I like a girl who is level-headed and can talk on several topics. I don't like the Maizie and Flo type or the sex boxes. Yes, I have been out with the latter, but you have to be careful. There's always the danger of disease."

The records of the following two high scorers show the kind of characteristics these men value most in the girls they would like to marry:

M14: (What about girls?) "Well, there is nothing definite yet, though I have known a lot. I never have found one I'd like to marry. I want a girl whose sole interest is in the home. I think a woman's place should not be in the business world. So many women have lost the sense of home. . . ."

M20: "They're (Indians) a reckless lot, careless about marriages and divorce. . . . (Q) Yes, I went through high school with one girl. . . . Very religious. Got with her around the church. . . . Never took each other very seriously, more or less, just accepted one another." The subject left and when he returned, she had gotten married. "She was more or less what I was looking for. Very religious. . . ."

The conception of marriage as a rather external affair not involving common interests, and also demonstrating conventional moralism, is given by the record of the following high scorer:

M41: (What was your wife like?) "A nice person. A nurse, before I married her.

(Q) Well, I liked her looks and manners. (In what ways were you most alike?) Well, we weren't much alike in any way. We got along all right. . . . Her mother was Christian Science. (What about her?) She was Christian Science. (Any children?) No. (In what ways most different?) Well, a little different in tastes about things. (Q) Most anything. I liked flowers and she didn't care much for flowers. (Main difficulties?) I didn't have any. We got along good. I let her have her own way. Takes two to start an argument. (Have her way in what things?) In most anything. Well, if we was going anywhere, if I went to buy a suit of clothes, I let her pick it out. If we wanted anything for the house, I let her pick it. (Childhood sex experiences?) Well, I don't remember any. When I was a kid, such things weren't taught. . . . Such things weren't mentioned by parents or anyone else. If you met a girl on the street, you'd blush. . . . I don't think it's a very good subject to teach. They learn it soon enough."

The lack of integration of sex and affection found in high-scoring men is likewise illustrated by some of these quotations. Quite commonly, in the girls they would like to marry, they require, above all, moral standards; often this is the only requirement. Frequently their marriages do not seem to be based on companionship or love. As far as their reports about premarital sexual relationships are concerned, they usually manifest contempt for the women involved. In both marriage and the more casual sex relationships there seems to be little concern with common interest and comradeship.

The difference in the attitude toward sexual relationships in high-scoring as compared with low-scoring men can perhaps best be exemplified by two records describing extramarital relationships. In both cases there is evidence of sexual and marital maladjustment. The differences, however, are characteristic of the two groups, respectively.

M58, a high-scoring man, reports: "And if you're not satisfied it might become uppermost in your mind, even above work, etc. . . . I believe I've seen where it is necessary for emotional stability, to relieve yourself regardless of marriage. (How do you mean?) First thing you know you're looking around . . . find something somewhere and relieve . . . then can go back and concentrate. . . . (What main difficulties have you found in your marriage?) My wife and I have always been thoroughly compatible . . . (only trivial daily problems) . . . can't think of anything . . . only one particular thing: I got to chasing around with another woman (although my wife had nothing to do with it; there was no conflict with her) it was in me entirely alone. . . ."

M10, a low-scoring man: "We have not enjoyed our sexual relationships almost since the first day of our marriage. I don't want it, and we often go for months without coitus . . . is that the word? My wife always takes the initiative in our relationships; she is very passionate. So am I—I have had three affairs since my marriage. I am having one now and she knows it."

The first of these men, a high scorer, talks about sex as though it were an ego-alien tension which has to be "relieved" for hygienic reasons. Thus, in the most intimate interpersonal relationships, he displays a utilitarian and (pseudo-)realistic outlook. The depersonalized attitude in this subject is drastically expressed by referring to his sexual partner as "something," and in the phrase "find something somewhere and relieve." On the other hand, the low-scoring subject, in a somewhat evasive, unperceptive effort to integrate his extramarital relationships into his total life-pattern, exemplifies the inhibited and at the same time impulse-ridden maladjustment sometimes found in those scoring low on ethnocentrism.

5. EGO-ALIEN AMBIVALENCE *VS.* "FONDNESS"

The isolation of sex experience in the typical high scorers is connected with an ambivalent *underlying disrespect for, and resentment against, the opposite sex*, often hidden behind an externalized and excessive *pseudoadmiration*. Low scorers, on the other hand, manifest more often *genuine respect and fondness* for the opposite sex (Category 25). The difference is highly significant (1 per cent level) for men, and satisfactorily significant (5 per cent level) for women.

An example of the "High" type of ambivalence toward women is the following statement:

M81: "I don't think men respect women or anything about women, the way they ought to. . . . In other words, women aren't inferior to men. If anything, they are superior. After all, they are the hands that rock the cradle." His admiration of women goes hand in hand with his conception of women as weak. Subject argues strongly at this point that restrictions should be removed on women, but still expresses his disapproval of women in business on the grounds that it would spoil the dependent (i.e., the home type) woman's chances.

More open lack of appreciation is shown in the following description of his stepmother by a high scorer:

M40: (What sort of person was your stepmother?) "Pretty hard to describe, just another woman, I guess . . . nothing glaringly outstanding. (In what ways was she like your father?) She wasn't. (How different?) In every way. She wasn't his equal in anything—intellectually. More matter of convenience than anything else."

Undisguised contempt for girls is displayed by another high scorer:

M11: "But I can't stand being around a bunch of girls, a lot of senseless chatter. They are all the same. Sororities are the cliquiest and the snottiest."

One of the high-scoring prison inmates blames his fate on his wife:

M57: "This last one I married was really a corker. . . . She just got her divorce. . . . I found out she was married all the time to another man. . . . She got me in here, I guess I got pussy-simple."

Correspondingly, contempt for men is expressed in the following records of high-scoring women:

F24: "Of course, now if you pick a boy as a friend, right away they want to get juicy. You have to be careful about boys."
F31: "I wouldn't want to be a factory worker, either. It's not very good to say now, when they need everybody that's working in factories, but I can't see a girl

working in jeans and around grease and putting themselves on the same level with men."

Low-scoring subjects, on the other hand, in seeking companionship with the opposite sex, more often manifest some measure of fondness. This attitude, shown by the following protocols, tends to increase in longer and more intimate relationships, as indicated by the statement of M42 that "a successful marriage certainly leads to familiarity but not to contempt."

The necessity of frankness in marriage is emphasized by M59: "When I do meet the one girl for me, I shall explain all my past life to her, because I do not believe that happiness can be based on lies." The frankness but also the compulsive feature in this statement are characteristic of the type of low scorer with neurotic features (see below).

Another low scorer shows love and respect for a woman in spite of the fact that the marriage did not work out:

M50: "At that time I was too self-centered to be in love with anyone. . . . I did admire and respect and like her . . . but we never should have gotten married. . . . Today I think we could have a better chance of making a go of it . . . because I have grown up sufficiently."

This record further shows the inclination toward self-blame and intrapunitiveness often found in low scorers.

Real love and common interest with her husband is stressed by:

F30: "I thought _____ was wonderful. He was so brilliant and his ideas and aspirations and mine were just alike. . . . We were all good companions and chums, and _____ and I had settled all the world's problems but we had never really talked about ourselves."

6. EXPLOITIVE MANIPULATION FOR POWER

In their relations to the opposite sex as in other interpersonal relationships, high scorers tend toward an *exploitive-manipulative type of power orientation*. There is more of a *warm and affectionate "love-seeking"* attitude in the low scorers. Differences with respect to this pair of opposites (Category (26) are statistically highly significant (1 per cent level) for both men and women.

Thus, the traits which high-scoring men tend to emphasize in women are the giving of material benefits and submissiveness ("sweet," "kind and generous"), along with purity ("wholesome") and conventionality. They expect to get something from women often without giving much in return. As in the attitude toward their parents, it is again a dependence oriented primarily toward material benefits rather than a dependence stemming from the wish to give or to receive love, although the latter tendencies are by no means completely squelched. Examples are:

M40: (What sort of woman would you like to marry?) "Wealthy woman. Other requirements?) Well, I'd like her to be maximum 35, preferably anywhere between 28 and 30. (Any other specifications?) I'll take that as it comes."

M45: "Was married three times. The first time in _____ at eighteen. It lasted six weeks. My partner in a dance walkathon. Married on the floor, no love, but received money for it from the spectators. . . . Sex relationship was more enjoyable than with either of my other wives."

In line with this, the traits which the typical high-scoring woman tends to desire in men are likewise primarily instrumental in getting the things she wants. They are: hard-working, "go-getting," energetic, "a good personality," (conventionally) moral, "clean-cut," deferent toward women. The next record shows clearly the two-sided nature of the demands high-scoring women tend to make upon a man. On the one hand, he must have a strong drive in order to get things for her; on the other, he must be deferent and "thoughtful."

F71: (Q) "Fine boy. Father a writer; grandfather secretary of _____ Canal; very wealthy family but he doesn't have the drive and ambition that I want; I just have to have more drive; somebody who doesn't have to lean on me. I had the feeling that if I walked away he would collapse. (War changed him?) He has more ambition but not the drive—I haven't seen him for a long time; that's why I haven't made any decision. Here you mingle with boys who have so much push and drive; another boy here has everything except that he isn't thoughtful like. . . . I've got to have someone who isn't selfish. I'm not critical—I know I'm not."

This as well as the next two records of other high-scoring women illustrate the inherently opportunistic point of view, the looking at men from the standpoint, above all, of social status and the ability to furnish support:

F22: "I'm going to look (among other things) for the fellow's views on supporting me. I'd like to marry someone, for instance, who is going into a profession—maybe a doctor. (Engagement?) It didn't take me long to get over it. His father died when he was 3; his mother was 40 when he was born. Father left mother lots of money. He was a playboy, worked but borrowed money from his mother. He was pretty much attached to his mother's apron strings. We were engaged 7 or 8 months. I'm not demanding, but he was selfish. We argued more and more, broke up by mutual consent. I learned a lot from it—not to go into things blindly."

F31: "But there is one thing that is bothering me. Saturday night I had a blind date, and I liked him a lot; only he is a sailor and my boy friend is an officer. It's not that I'm conscious of gold braid. . . . (Marriage?) Well, I'd like someone . . . with a good personality who mixes well with people. Someone who at the same time is serious about the future. My boy friend is an engineer."

By contrast, low-scoring subjects tend to emphasize as desired traits companionship, common interest, warmth, sociability, sexual love, understanding, presence of liberal values. Sometimes their quest for love is so intense and unrealistic that it becomes a source of disappointment to them. This search for the "great romantic love" seems to be based on a wish to restore a successful early relation with a parent, based on nurturance and succorance. As they were found to be for parents, expressions of passionate love for sex partners are generally infrequent in our interview material, however.

Two records may suffice to illustrate, each in its own way, the different quality of what low-scoring subjects expect from their partners as well as a certain pervasive tendency toward self-blame.

F34: She talks of looking forward to marriage and children eventually, but she has modest financial requirements for a husband. She has had many boy friends and is the "romantic type." "I always want to feel this is my great love—and then it isn't. That sort of thing is all right when you are in school. But nowadays when your boy friend goes away to war and you write letters and build up a lot of things that may not even be there—it isn't fair to either person." She has been "sort of engaged" for two years to a boy she knew in school. He has been overseas in the navy and they have written regularly—romantic letters. She goes out with other boys and he knows this and doesn't object. She hasn't fallen in love with anyone else, but her worry is that her feeling for him is not love. He came home on furlough, and his family, who live in _____ now, had her come down to their home and stay there for several days while he was there. She feels that he sensed that she did not feel the same, and yet she could not bring herself to say anything. She believes this was very cowardly of her and shows an absence of character. She thinks it is quite possible the boy's feelings have changed too, "but why can't people be honest about things like that? And now he is gone and nothing is settled."

M44: Subject says that in visiting someone at the hospital, his wife seems to know naturally just how to act toward the person, or, at a public meeting knows just what kind of questions to ask to draw the person out further instead of shutting him up. "And she is a helper, she is the helpingest person, the most willing and helping person that I've ever known."

7. CONVENTIONALITY *VS.* INDIVIDUALISM

Again, as in other areas of life, the values of high-scoring subjects with respect to sex tend to be *conventionally determined* as opposed to the more *individualized* values of low-scoring subjects (Category 27). This variable differentiates significantly (at the 1 per cent level) between high- and low-scoring men; a similar trend, 18 positive and 7 negative instances, is found in women; because of the large proportion of "Neutrals," however, the difference is not statistically significant.

The following records show that in the choice of their mates high-scoring subjects tend to place a great deal of emphasis on socioeconomic status, church membership, and conformity with conventional values. The accent is on what is generally socially approved and accepted. Thus the men expect their future wives to stay home, take care of house and children, and attend church. This tendency is often found in the same men who show evidence of primitive and crude sex experience, outside of marriage (see above).

The conventional approach to marriage is best illustrated by the following records of high-scoring women:

F32: "Well, I think that because of the society in which we live, young people miss a great deal by not being married in the church of their faith. They lose the reverence for marriage and don't learn the true meaning of the marriage vows, when it is done so commercially (in a public office). I think that when people are married in church—by that I don't mean a large wedding necessarily—they have one of the most beautiful experiences of their lives. . . . The thing which the church can teach youth is 'to choose.' " By this, she means principally the choice between right and wrong, but also to choose one's friends. "In a church group one meets the right kind of young people; not the kind who hang around the lake shore at night."

F78: "It was just love at first sight. He has brown hair, brown eyes, white teeth, not handsome, but good clean-cut looking; beautiful smile; mixes well, easy to get along with but has a will of his own. He's lots of fun, interested in everything. He's a high school graduate, now a mechanic in the ground crew of the Naval Air Transport. He wants to go into something in the mechanical line. Before the war he was an apprentice in the auto industry. . . ." The vocation of her husband really wouldn't matter. She thinks boy friend has good chances of getting along, definitely. She would like a profession—"sort of middle class."

F74: "Too much emotional feeling involved under these conditions." (Desirable traits?) Boy friend should be about the same socioeconomic status. They should enjoy doing the same things and get along without too many quarrels.

Or in high-scoring men:

M58: (Wife like?) "Very good person. She has gone to church, and has continued to . . . ever since the child was born. A very good wife, good mother, and darned good cook. Considerate of my folks . . . helped my mother with money, of her own accord. (What do wife and subject offer each other?) Well, I'll be doggoned if I know. Doesn't seem as if any bonds at all. Just she belongs there and so do I."

M20: "In my mind, there's no doubt about it. Woman's place is in the home. . . . To keep up a home and make it right and a man should be able to provide for the family. . . . A woman has no business working whatsoever."

In contrast with the stereotyped and conventional description of their desired or real mates given by the high-scoring subjects, the typical low-scoring subject takes a much more individualized attitude, as shown in the following quotations:

M53: (What sort of girl appeals to you?) "I don't know. . . . I think I like the ones with more independent spirit. (Q) Well, looks, charm (laughs), humor and a certain freedom of spirit. In thought, I think, more than in action. . . . (Present fiancée?) Awfully hard to say when you're sold on a girl. . . . Seems to have all the things I like . . . fun to be with, brains, pretty. She likes me, which is important. We share things together. Music, reading, swimming, dancing. Most of the things we do don't require too much energy, which makes it good."

M50: (What about your first wife?) "She was an artist also and a really thorough-going individual. She had a tremendous amount of scope, both intellectually and individually. She is looking for something too. Not as serious as my case, just the case of a girl marrying the wrong person."

M44: (What sort of person is your wife?) (laughs) "She's a little bit easy to hurt or touchy about some things. . . . The most admirable thing, the most attractive thing about her is her hands. She has very small, delicate hands. She uses them very well and they're very expressive . . . and she also does things very fast, adept, sews very well, very domestic, very much the mother. She was never really herself until she had this child, never really complete."

M2: (Ideal woman?) "She has to be (1) intelligent, (2) mature, (3) emotionally stable, (4) have adequate physiological characteristics, as well as have (5) culture and personality that goes with this. She should have at least as broad an interest and experience as my own, if not broader. She should have a maximum of femininity, since we're all bisexual. You can think of it in terms of a polyfactorial setup (subject then quotes Rosanoff's theory of four factors in sex)."

The preceding descriptions by low-scoring subjects of their real or ideal mates reveal a conception of real people and an expectation of finding a person with "independent opinions" and "independent spirit."

8. SUMMARY

Summarizing the attitude of the typical high-scoring subject toward members of the opposite sex, the following may be said: A lack of individuation and of real object relationship can be found in the field of sex as it was previously found in the attitude toward the parents. It is this lack which may be called upon to explain the attitudes described above, such as the relative isolation of sexual impulses from the rest of the personality, the paucity of affection, and the somewhat exploitive, manipulative approach in the choice of a mate. Much of this may be understood in terms of disappointments which apparently had been experienced by many of the extreme high-scorers in their first love-relations, those with their parents.

The same ambivalence which was found in the attitude toward parents can be found again in the sexual domain. Again there is surface admiration, coupled with underlying resentment against the other sex. Ambivalence also tends to be handled by establishing two separate images, one positive and one negative (good and bad women), without, however, being able really to love either of them.

Status-concern and conventionalized values again become predominant and take the place of a genuine and individualized approach. The expectations of qualities in oneself and in one's mate are quite stereotyped and rigid. Shortcomings in these respects are faced as little as they are in other fields. Thus, as pointed out above, high-scoring subjects often think of themselves as the ideal representation of the conventional conception of their sex role.

The attitudes of the low-scoring subjects reveal a rather different picture, though it is much less clear-cut than that of the high scorers. In other words, the "High" variants of the categories in question are often more typical for the high-scoring subjects than the "Low" variants are for the low-scoring subjects. On the whole, our low scorers tend toward a more individualized, more internalized, more love-oriented approach toward their mates. (See also Chapter X.)

This does not mean, however, that in most of the cases their problems in this field are readily solved. On the contrary, some of the records of low-scoring subjects quoted above reveal a great deal of conflict in this area. Such subjects refer rather frankly to their inadequacies, inhibitions, and failures in sex adjustment. There also is evidence of ambivalence toward one's own sex role and toward the opposite sex although this ambivalence is of a different, more internalized kind from the combination of overt admiration and underlying disrespect characteristic of high scorers. Its clearest representation is the conflict of the man about his passivity and of the woman about her tendency to follow masculine interests. Ambivalence toward the other sex seems in low scorers often to be the consequence of an overly intense search for love that is not easily satisfied.

Low-scoring men sometimes seem to long for a restoration, in a close relationship with a woman, of the type of love they received from the mother, and this may become a source of dissatisfaction. As Krout and Stagner (65) have shown, male liberals claim less difficulty in expressing their affection for women and show preference for women of equal status. At the same time they experience more frustration in their love relations.

Low-scoring women, on the other hand, sometimes develop a conflict between the satisfactions derived from emotional dependence on the man and a striving for independence that leads to competition with men.

However, in spite of these conflicts, retardations, and ambivalences, there seems to be more actual or potential heterosexuality in low scorers. The interview material reveals a more genuine and more personalized relationship to members of the other sex, more fondness and ability to love in sexual relationships, more ego-accepted sensuality. Conflicts and inadequacies, being faced more openly, have a greater chance of being worked out successfully.

Since the typical low-scoring man more readily accepts his own femininity than the high scorer, and the low-scoring woman her masculine strivings, one important source of hidden aggression toward the opposite sex—and toward other people generally, as it seems—is reduced.

B. ATTITUDE TOWARD PEOPLE

1. DEFINITION OF RATING CATEGORIES AND QUANTITATIVE RESULTS

The part of the Scoring Manual covering social attitudes toward people in general is as follows:

INTERVIEW SCORING MANUAL: ATTITUDE TOWARD PEOPLE
(to Table 2(XI))

Presumably "High" Variants	Presumably "Low" Variants
28. *Moralistic condemnation*	28. *Permissiveness* toward individuals; rejections rationalized by reference to principles.

29a. *Extrapunitiveness*

29a. *Impunitiveness*

29b. *Intrapunitiveness;* excessive guilt - feelings and self - reproach

30. *Distrust-suspicion,* people as threatening; *victimization;* survival of fittest idea, world as jungle

30. *Trustingness.* Openness; people essentially "good" until proved otherwise

31a. *Hierarchical conception* of human relations

31a. *Equalitarianism-mutuality*

31b. *Hero worship* of acquaintances

32a. *Diffuse, ego-alien dependence;* non-love-seeking

32a. *Focal, love-seeking succorance*

32b. *Exploitive - manipulative opportunism*

32b. *Personalized nurturance*

32c. *Genuine object-cathexis*

33. *Traits desired in friends:*

a. *Status* acceptable or admirable (economic or social)

a. Acceptable on grounds of *intrinsic worth;* companionship and common interests; intellectual-aesthetic approach; "easy-going" traits; social awareness and insight; liberal values

b. *Moral-conventional:* clean-cut, good manners, emphasis on honesty, poise, control

As can be seen from Table 2(XI), the eleven categories in this area differentiate satisfactorily, on the whole, the two extreme groups that make up our sample of interviewees.

2. MORALISTIC CONDEMNATION *VS.* PERMISSIVENESS

High-scoring individuals were found to tend toward a *moralistic condemnation* of other people while *permissiveness toward individuals* is more common in our low scorers (Category 28). For both men and women this difference is quite significant (1 per cent level). For men there are 30 positive instances as contrasted with only 4 negative ones ("positive" and "negative" in the sense defined in the last section of Chapter IX); for women, the proportion is 24 to 6.

It is easy to understand why condemnation of people, based on an external and conventional set of values, should be closely connected with prejudice; in fact, such an attitude seems close to being the very essence of prejudice.

The records, quoted below, of subjects scoring high on overt ethnocentrism illustrate a readiness to condemn others on such external bases as absence of good manners, uncleanliness, "twitching the shoulders," saying "inappropriate" things (inappropriate, as will be seen, on a superficial level only), and so forth.

The statements show a great deal of indulgence in what is seen as "righteous indignation" about people considered as inferior. This indignation seems to serve the double purpose of externalizing what is unacceptable in oneself,

TABLE 2 (XI)

INTERVIEW RATINGS ON ATTITUDE TOWARD PEOPLE

FOR 80 SUBJECTS SCORING EXTREMELY "HIGH" OR "LOW" ON THE ETHNIC PREJUDICE QUESTIONNAIRE SCALE

Interview rating categories (abbreviated from Manual)	Sex	Number of "High"(H) and "Low"(L) ratings received by				Sums of instances		Level of statistical significance reached (percentage)
		20 men and 25 women "high scorers"		20 men and 15 women "low scorers"		"positive"	"negative"	
		H	L	H	L			
28. Moralistic condemnation(H) vs. permissiveness(L)	Men	14	1	3	16	30	4	1
	Women	14	3	3	10	24	6	1
29a. Extrapunitiveness(H) vs. impunitiveness(L)	Men	17	1	1	9	26	2	1
	Women	15	2	2	3	18	4	1
29b. Intropunitiveness(L)	Men	1	1	1	7	7	1	
	Women	1	2	2	6	6	2	
30. Distrust-suspicion(H) vs. trustingness	Men	14	2	3	14	28	5	
	Women	19	4	3	9	28	7	
31a. Hierarchical conception(H) vs. equalitarianism-mutuality(L)	Men	12	1	2	11	23	3	
	Women	13	2	1	11	24	3	
31b. Hero worship of acquaintances(H)	Men	1	1	1		1	1	
	Women	1	1	0		1	0	
32a. Dependence, diffuse, ego-alien (H) vs. focal, love-seeking(L)	Men	14	3	3	10	24	6	1
	Women	10	3	1	7	17	4	5
32b. Exploitive-manipulation(H) vs. personalized nurturance(L)	Men	6	3	1	9	15	4	
	Women	3	3	0	8	11	3	5
32c. Genuine object-cathexis(L)	Men		1	1	13	13	1	
	Women		3	3	8	8	3	
Traits desired in friends:								
33a. Status(H) vs. intrinsic worth(L)	Men	7	2	2	16	23	4	5
	Women	10	3	0	10	20	3	
33b. Moral-conventional(H)	Men	11	4	4	11	11	4	
	Women	11	3	3	11	11	3	

and of displacing one's hostility which otherwise might turn against powerful "ingroups," e.g., the parents.

Furthermore, the subsequent records presented in the following contain statements referring to a positive ideal of how one should behave, the essence of which is expressed by one of the subjects in this group who demands that everybody should have a "set of rules"; these rules turn out to be determined either by convention or by a shallow interpretation of church dogma. The emphasis on conventional values is found in the respectable as well as in the delinquent high scorer (prison inmate; see also Chapter XXI).

Examples, for the various aspects listed, from the records of high-scoring male prison inmates follow:

M40: (What things offend you most in other people?) "Just that they're people. (Meaning?) Oh, the majority are ignorant, close to animals as anything else. I mean *dumb* animals. (Q) They haven't got sense enough to see things as they are; they are easily swayed, crude, uncouth; they are like a pack. Show 'em a leader and they will go anywhere. (Are most people like this?) Records show it. (What records?) Statistics. (Q) Like in here (prison). The average IQ is something around 50 or 60. Very, very low.... They carry a knife and cut some poor son-of-a-bitch, and think they're tough...."

M41: (What do you find most offensive in others?) "Well, some people are more attractive than others. Some people have no attraction. Don't take care of themselves. Don't keep *clean.* Don't have *manners....*"

M45: (What do you find most irritating in others?) "Petty habits. (What do you mean?) I've noticed some people have a habit of snorting or as if their nose is always running or twitching their shoulders or my wife's habit of picking at things with her fingernails. (Others?) Not being able to tend to their own business, not having sense enough to understand, to know when they're imposing on you.... It's changed around here (in prison) now, getting so many of these young kids, zootsuiters, don't have any tact at all.... (What else?) Greed, I can't stand anyone who will take something without thinking about the other person ... without any politeness.... You'd be surprised. You can find some of the politest people in the world right in here.... I believe in helping your fellow man regardless."

A positive ideal of behavior as derived primarily from religious convention is stated in the following records of high scorers:

M52: (Main differences between Christians and other people?) "Christians are people that at all times strive to do what is right and abide by God's word."

M58: "... and the person who has lived according to Christianity will live forever—those who have not will perish at that time."

M4: (Importance of religion?) "It's very important. It gives people an opportunity to utilize some of their extra energy, also helps to set a standard for behavior and conduct. Without religion, there would be a lot more crime and delinquency in the world. (Is the world getting better or worse?) It's getting worse—the younger generation is wilder, 17-year-old boys go out and get drunk; and science is responsible for all this, that is, provides motor cars for them to get out in, they start drinking."

In the records of high-scoring women there is a similar condemnation of people on moralistic and conventional grounds. Sometimes we find a general condemnation and contempt for an assumed inferiority of people which is quite similar to the statement of one of the high-scoring men, quoted above, to the effect that the "majority (of people) are ignorant, close to animals. . . I mean dumb animals." While rejection of other people is more common in high scorers, low scorers tend more toward self-rejection.

Illustrations from records of high-scoring women follow.

F66: (Why not social welfare?) "Well, some of the people you see—I just don't like them. I don't think I'd have enough patience to help them. . . . (Why not social activities?) I didn't like the people. We had just moved there and they just weren't my kind. (Q) They were too cliquish and infantile. They were silly, always giggling, wore jeans and dirty old plaid shirts. . . ."

F24: (Low income group?) "They don't think fast enough—can't make it. They haven't educated themselves for any line. Most people are like that all their lives. (Maybe they haven't had opportunities?) There's a way—there's always a way if they care enough. Maybe it's tough, but eventually you can get there."

F22: "I don't go in for petting; I can't see necking for hours either. (Q) I've been shocked by the conduct of my girl friends. I didn't think they were that type of girl."

By contrast, low-scoring subjects tend to be permissive and tolerant toward individuals (although not necessarily toward institutions). Or at least they make an attempt to understand behavior from a common sense (if not professional) psychological or sociological point of view; and they show generally more empathy. Whenever rejection of individuals occurs, an attempt is usually made to explain or to rationalize this rejection on the basis of violation of fundamental principles and social values rather than for surface reasons.

3. EXTRAPUNITIVENESS

Another attitude, quite directly akin to prejudice, is that of *extrapunitiveness*, to use Rosenzweig's term (16), i.e., a tendency to blame other people rather than oneself. As has been repeatedly pointed out in this volume, lack of insight into one's own shortcomings and the projection of one's own weaknesses and faults onto others is often found in high-scoring subjects. It probably represents the essential aspect of the mechanism of scapegoating.

An opposite variant to extrapunitiveness is *impunitiveness*, i.e., the tendency to refrain from blaming altogether, be it others or oneself.

The differential distribution of this pair of opposites (Category 29a) with respect to overt ethnocentrism is quite significant for men (1 per cent level)—26 positive and only 2 negative instances. For women there is a distinct trend in the same direction—18 positive as contrasted with 4 negative instances—but it is not statistically significant.

An "extrapunitive" attitude is manifested in the descriptions given by the following high-scoring women about their co-workers, fellow students or teachers:

F60: Subject just doesn't care for her fellow workers. "Some have all the PDQ's (degrees) but no common sense." She wouldn't like to mention names, but she'd like to tell me what goes on. "Some just spend their time gossiping together." She doesn't believe she should do more than just speak to her fellow workers. Very scornful of them, feels superior and aloof. They don't know her at all—no, indeed—implies she's a very special somebody and could reveal her gifts to them, but doesn't. She describes how she treated masturbation. The others were afraid to stop the children. But she just "popped" the little boys' and girls' hands and said, "Now, don't do that. It isn't good for you."

F71: Sister president of sorority in high school and of interclub council; thinks high school sororities "stupid and silly—dirty rushing, girls misplaced in clubs. Nothing as selfish and cruel as a little high school girl growing up. Noisy—no attention to business—it was just too much." Talks about high school teacher—thinks her aspiration level too high. "Too much screaming and yelling—has theateritis—polished and professional—too many students broke down—you have to be *stone* to take it."

F77, although talking about her mother, reveals her general attitude toward people in the following quotation: "This wouldn't have happened if I hadn't gone down. She's mean and inconsiderate and doesn't give a darn about anyone else but herself. I helped her with so many things. She hasn't helped me with one little thing—I can't stand it."

The foregoing statements illustrate the tendency of high scorers to blame others for difficulties that arise in their contact with other people or their work.

As was pointed out above, low-scoring subjects tend either not to blame at all (impunitiveness); or they may show exaggerated self-blame, *intrapunitiveness* (Category 29b). The latter tendency was found in 7 low-scoring men and 6 low-scoring women, while only 1 high-scoring man and 2 high-scoring women manifested this attitude. The tendency toward exaggerated self-blame in the low-scoring subjects must be interpreted as an expression of an internalized, and rather strict, superego of the sort that often leads to neurotic symptoms.

The following is a good example of a low scorer with good work adjustment who does not blame others for the difficulties which arise in co-operative work situations:

F63: "Money has never meant much to me. . . . Maybe it is stupid and unrealistic. But it is the work itself that gives me satisfaction. I work best by myself—have difficulty working with other people. I get along with them all right, but it's a strain on me. I'm rather shy and don't like competition, at least not directly with the people you work with."

The following 2 low-scoring men are described by their interviewer as suffering from excessive guilt feelings.

M42: He verbalized readily and spontaneously, and shows no reluctance to discuss any given topic. At the same time, however, he repeatedly deprecates himself, particularly as to his ability to express himself. He is quite abusive and appears to have no little moral masochism. His thinking and actions seem to be pervaded by doubt, hesitation, and indecision.

M55: Subject has a rather pervasive sense of humor which is often directed against himself. He seems to have a great deal of conscious feelings of inadequacy and inferiority and guilt.

The record of another low scorer gives evidence, over and above the absence of conventional moralism, and a stressing of intrinsic values, of a tendency not to think very highly of oneself:

M3: (Ideal wife?) "Attractive, at least average. I can't ask for too much there, with my looks. At least as much intelligence as I have. Fairly intelligent, in other words. I don't care about religion and morals, as long as they are not too bad. Her own damn business whether she is a virgin or not. . . . Essential that she be a good companion, keep me well amused; companionship includes everything from conversation to sex, with emphasis on congeniality."

Some of the low scorers come close to a tendency toward obsessional rumination about their faults and the mistakes they have made. The exaggerated feelings of guilt and self-deprecation constitute some of the major neurotic features common in low scorers. They are frequently accompanied by depressions. Instead of aggressive self-assertion, there is often an unhealthy trend toward withdrawal in the face of difficulties.

4. WORLD AS JUNGLE

Projection of one's inner impulses, particularly of aggression, onto others will naturally lead to a conception of a dangerous and hostile world and consequently to a general suspiciousness of others. Thus, it was found that typical high-scoring subjects tend to manifest *distrust and suspicion* of others. Theirs is a conception of people as threatening in the sense of an oversimplified survival-of-the-fittest idea. Feelings of victimization are often connected with such notions. The opposite variant was defined as *trustingness and openness*, as manifested by seeing people as essentially "good" until proved otherwise; it was expected to be found predominantly in the low-scoring subjects.

For both men and women, differentiation in terms of this pair of opposites (Category 30) was found to be highly significant (1 per cent level of confidence).

Emphasis on the "jungle-character" of the world[1] as just described, a world in which one has to destroy others to prevent them from destroying oneself, is best expressed by a quotation from *M41*, a high scorer: "Nowadays it's 'get the other fellow before he gets you.'"

---

[1] This, as well as many other findings reported in this chapter, is in perfect agreement with the description of the authoritarian character given by Fromm (42) and Maslow (79).

Another high-scoring man, $M57$, says: "Hell, you can't have real friends in here (prison), stab you in the back. Can't trust any of them."

Distrust in, and dislike of, other people is further manifested in the following records of high-scoring men.

$M45$: "Not being able to attend to their own business, not having sense enough to understand to know when they're imposing on you. . . ."

$M47$: (What dislike in others?) "Well, their actions, the way they talk. (How do you mean?) I don't know how to explain it. . . . Maybe a fellow comes up and gives me a couple of knick-knacks just to make up to me. I don't go for that. Some of these guys shove up in lines, go to the show and holler like little kids. (What do you find most offensive?) A guy trying to butt into my business."

$M51$: (You mentioned once before that as a child you didn't accept your father as a shining example which he was held up to you as. Tell me about your feelings towards your father as a child.) "Well, I resented a lot of things. I loved him. I always said I did. I used to have a kind of fit if I was ever taken away from him. . . . I always accused him of being harsh. . . . I never understood him. . . . And apparently this all falls in with Darwin's theory too."

The fact that the high-scoring subjects, more often than the low scorers, made inquiries as to the purpose of the interviews, as to the basis of selection of the subjects, and as to the publication of the material seemed to reflect the greater suspiciousness of the former. The general resistance to "being questioned" is clearly expressed in the records of the following high-scoring woman:

$F72$: (What kinds of things make you mad?) "Well, for instance, my sister. When I come home and she starts asking me questions about what happened and what did you do, I don't want to have to give accounts. Not that I've anything to hide. I don't have anything to hide, but I don't like being questioned. I don't like prying."

By comparison, the records of low-scoring subjects frequently reveal genuine liking of, and warm interest and concern for, people, along with belief in their essential "goodness." Examples are:

$M42$: (How did you come to be a service station operator?) "Just by accident. . . . I worked part time in school . . . another thing, I like to meet people . . . most people as a rule are pretty nice to me. . . ."

$F30$: "I would even be content to call 'evolution' my religion. When it comes to attending or working in a church I prefer the Methodist. However, that is not important. What is important is that people believe in humanity, in each other, and that the force of goodness, of progress, is the strongest force in the world."

$F34$: "I always made it a point to sit next to different people on the bus and get into conversation with them. Lots of people think that everybody is getting along fine now and making lots of money. Actually, people have a very hard time. And they are worried about the future. Everyone is under a terrible strain."

As may be suspected from the last of these records, many of the low-scoring individuals tend to be "worriers." Thus they assume that other people suffer too. However, such feelings tend to be rather structured and specific (e.g., worry about the father) when compared with the vague and diffuse anxieties about a generally threatening environment or a lack of support which are typical of high scorers.

5. HIERARCHICAL VS. EQUALITARIAN CONCEPTION OF HUMAN RELATIONS

As mentioned above, the distrust of others displayed by the typical high-scoring subject may probably be ascribed to his conception of people as seeking only power and material benefits, and his assumption that, in this struggle and competition, the more ruthless must necessarily win out. His orientation in interpersonal relationships is thus toward getting power by associating with the powerful and influential, or at least toward participating in the power of those who have it. Admiration for the strong and contempt for the weak accompany this attitude. Thus, high-scoring subjects show predominantly what may be called *hierarchical conception of human relationships* whereas those who score low conceive of an *equalitarian mutuality* in such relationships (Category 31a).

There is a highly significant difference (at the 1 per cent level) for both men and women with respect to this pair of opposites. Examples of a hierarchical conception of human relationships are found in the following reports of high-scoring subjects:

M52: (How important is money really?) "I don't think the best things in life are free. I don't believe people would be happy if they worked for nothing. . . . Every man has a certain ego that he has to satisfy. You like to be on top. If you're anybody at all, you don't like to be on the bottom. . . . I believe in the Bible. I believe there is someone a lot bigger and stronger than anyone on this earth."

M51: "Well, there are the weak and the strong. I can't elaborate on it. (What about you?) I suppose I'm one of the weak ones (said somewhat hesitantly and reluctantly)."

M58: (What would money make possible?) "Would raise our standard of living; probably buy better or higher priced automobile; move into better residential section; associations with business and fraternal groups to be raised. . . . To those in a bracket higher, except for a few staunch friends which you keep always; naturally associate with people on a higher level—with more education and more experience. After you get there, and associate with those people . . . that fires you on to the next step higher, etc."

M4: Subject likes to mingle with people, likes big parties, used to have an inferiority complex, but now is at ease. Likes to associate and talk with famous people, to be in the "upper crust." "Well, I've met a lot of people since I've been up here; it certainly made a difference to me. I've set my goal, and I want to be one of them (mentions army and navy people, a lot of wealthy and socially prominent people)."

M13: "There are great possibilities there (in Alaska) in the future. If a person studies it carefully and locates properly, he goes up with a town."

F79: "In the SPARS I liked the training and the discipline and I would make a good officer. But the girls of my type had college educations and I was thrown with waitresses, etc. I wanted to apply for officership. I admired the officers although all the other girls were interested only in boys. . . . It made me furious to see the great advantage of those who had had college education. Those I associated with were not my type."

F22: "In the first place, there have to be the ditch diggers. They can get what they want out of life. Certain people were cut out for certain things. People who are unhappy are the ones who have wasted their chances or are held back by lack of finances."

The foregoing records show how preoccupied these subjects are with social mobility, with the dichotomy of the "weak and the strong," "the bottom and the top," and with the idea of "moving upwards" through the help of the powerful and the influential. There is evidence of an almost compulsive acquisitiveness and striving for success. All this is in line with the picture of Western civilization generally presented by its students (e.g., Kardiner, 60; Mead, 82; Fromm, 43), although it appears here in a grossly exaggerated manner.

Fromm (42) states that the most important feature of the authoritarian character is its attitude toward power and its division of people into two groups: the strong and the weak. Love, admiration, and readiness for submission are automatically aroused by power of persons or institutions, while contempt is equally aroused by powerless persons or institutions. The very sight of a powerless person may lead to the urge to attack, dominate, or humiliate him.

Hero worship of acquaintances (Category 31b) which was expected to be a characteristic primarily of high scorers, yielded only a negligible number of ratings and is thus omitted from consideration as far as our material is concerned. As in other doubtful cases, one may also question the validity of our hypothesis underlying the definition of the category.

6. DEPENDENCE FOR THINGS

The orientation toward getting material benefits, predominant in the high scorers, tends to make for dependence on people, since they are used as a means for advancement. In the discussion of attitudes toward parents a distinction was made between "dependence for things"—found primarily in the high scorers—as contrasted with a "love-oriented dependence" found in the typical low scorers. A similar distinction has also been made in the case of the attitude toward people in general, setting off a *diffuse, ego-alien dependence* which is not really love-seeking against a *focal, love-seeking succorance* (Category 32a). The difference between high and low scorers with respect to this category is highly significant (1 per cent level) for men, and satisfactorily significant (5 per cent level) for women.

The examples given above for the hierarchical conception of human relationships illustrate one aspect of the utilitarian approach of the typical high-scoring subjects toward other people. Here we are dealing with another aspect of utilitarianism, namely their orientation toward getting things and help in general. In the quotations from high-scoring subjects which follow we find friendship conceived of as a means of getting things rather than as a relationship based on mutuality in giving and taking.

M43: "Oh, help in lots of needs, sickness, money, well, a friend can just help in most any way."

M45: (What do you look for in friends?) ". . . even though there is no conversation between you, know that he's there at all times and if you need any help at any time. . . ."

In line with this, high scorers tend to be oriented toward persons in positions of authority or power, or toward support; low scorers tend to be longing for someone who will really love them without reservation the way they happen to be and "in spite of shortcomings." Low-scorers also tend to place emphasis more on expectations of receiving love, understanding, and companionship from their friends. Examples from the interview protocols of men scoring extremely low on the ethnocentrism questionnaire follow:

M48: (What do friends offer a person?) "Well, offer you an understanding—they understand you and make allowances for your shortcomings . . . and like you in spite of it."

M56: (What do friends offer us?) "That's another thing—I have always been so discriminating in choice that haven't had many friends . . . my friends have always been people I could confide in—faith, companionship."

M59: ". . . . A person has very few friends in a lifetime. A friend will overlook your faults . . . and stand by you."

The longing for intensive, personalized relations, in which there is complete mutual acceptance and overlooking of faults is evident in these records. At the same time, however, one gets the impression that a tendency to preoccupation with oneself, sometimes expressed in overcriticism, is characteristic of low scorers.

7. MANIPULATION *VS.* LIBIDINIZATION OF PEOPLE AND GENUINE WORK ADJUSTMENT

A similar differentiation was made between an *exploitive-manipulative-opportunistic attitude* as opposed to one of *personalized nurturance* (Category 32b). Differences between high scorers and low scorers here show the expected trend without being statistically significant. Nonetheless, there are 15 positive instances but only 4 negative ones for men, and 11 positive as compared with 3 negative for women.

An extreme example of a manipulative orientation toward people in general, and toward sex partners in particular, is given in the record of a high-scoring prison inmate:

M51: (Why pick on an older woman?) "Well, I forgot. She had money and I didn't. . . . I never had any relations with anyone that didn't have money connected with it, even those homosexual affairs. . . . I ran away from home and that's mainly the way I supported myself." Subject quotes Dr. _____ as saying that he was only interested in men for their pocketbooks and he didn't know if he would be safe with a mule. (Preference in type of homosexual partner?) "Yes, I always had preferences, but I never let the preference stand in the way of—only thing I was ever interested in was the rent. I wasn't faithful, in other words, I wasn't expected to be. I was alone so much, I got bored. (Did any men attract you aside from the money aspect?) Oh, yes, but I never let love, so called, stand in the way. . . ." Subject emphasizes that if he were a woman, he would not let any love aspect stand in the way of marrying for as much money as possible and getting all he could in the way of money out of the sex relationship.

This statement not only shows a particularly drastic form of opportunistic attitude but also the view that affect should not be allowed to interfere with one's advantage: "I never let love, so called, stand in the way."

A narrowly opportunistic, externalized attitude toward work and the persons connected with it is illustrated in the records of the following high scorers:

M40: (Advantages of designing?) "Fairly decent, remunerative enough, and contacts are better than that of an ordinary worker. (Else?) You got a better chance to get what you want. (How do you mean?) You're constantly being thrown in with people who are up there . . . if can't get anything in theater work, legitimate stage, voice, I'll go in for that."

M58: "They come to me and say, 'Can you do this and that for me?' To keep good will, you'll do a lot of things. And then I go to work—and that's a source of dissatisfaction, to think that I help those people who can hardly read or write . . . kinda gets me down—doing their work, and then I've got to go out and do shift work—something wrong there . . . it's disheartening. Wife says to get out of the ration board work, but I feel eventually it might give me the push I need to get into something different. . . . I don't know how to go out and look for work. . . . I've just done this kind of work, no education, can't offer anything definite other than oil. . . ."

F68: "This is a nine-to-five job and when I am through I am through. You don't have to worry about personal things on this kind of a job."

Fromm (42) emphasizes that for the authoritarian character the relationship with his fellow men has lost its direct, human character and has assumed a spirit of manipulation and instrumentality.

By contrast, the following records of low-scoring subjects illustrate their need to do something for people, to help them, to give, and to receive affection in return. They also show their tendency to libidinize their relations with people and to view their work from the standpoint of its social value rather than merely from that of external success.

M42: (Advantages of scouting?) "I like to work with young people . . . satisfaction of helping someone. . . . It doesn't pay financially, but . . . you are happier . . . makes good friends. . . ."

M49: "Yes, and I've always been impressed by articles I've read in magazines . . . about a small company built up by the manager from himself and a helper . . . and just got in people that were very agreeable . . . and the ideal was lots of benefits and fellows felt they had a share in things, and each worker wasn't a machine, but an individual. . . ." Subject emphasizes personal relationship in this example of employer-employee setup, with a strong personal nurturance by the former, and gratefulness and cooperation of workers. "I think I'd be happy if I could find that kind of a company, and it wouldn't really matter too much what the actual job was, that is, within reason. I've always thought those (personal relationships) were the most important thing in a job."

M54: "At 17, wanted to be a doctor, but it didn't materialize because joined the service." Subject can't remember the origin of this interest. Perhaps some friends whose parents were doctors and subject liked to help bandage up other kids, minor scratches, etc.

M55: (What would a lot of money make possible for you?) "Do some charitable work, though not in established patterns, for example help some of my friends. Contribute to the March of Dimes, to end cancer, etc."

M56: "Security and a chance to do something for others. Seems to me now I have been helping others all my life."

M59: "To treat others as a person would wish to be treated himself and to help those less fortunate than oneself, and to be a part of the community or society that one is in, to take an active part in it, and being kind and generous and to more or less have a high regard for your fellow man. . . . The only happiness that we really know of is . . . here on earth, so why not try to enjoy the people and things on this earth, rather than a life somewhere else. . . . (What attracts you in a friend?) A person on the same intellectual level and one who has common ideas. You enjoy going out with him. You enjoy conversation and you like to do things for a friend."

F70: "If I had a lot of money I didn't know what to do with, I might run a small private hospital. For instance, for rheumatic fever patients. There are so many children with certain diseases that can't get the proper medical care, because their parents can't afford to have them hospitalized sufficiently long—like rheumatic fever patients. I wish to do a few altruistic things like my own private charity or something. I don't think I'd buy expensive objects of art; well, maybe I would. I might buy quite a few material things, go to a lot of concerts and plays. One seems to be able to spend a lot of money on those."

F75: (What do you like about public health nursing?) "You get to know people. You have to. You go into their homes and see them when they are well, help them prevent sickness instead of just seeing them in bed sick. I think it is a more useful occupation than bedside nursing, but that is important too."

The foregoing records also illustrate the ability, characteristic of low scorers to form *genuine object cathexis* (Category 32c), an ability probably due to the fact that they formed better identifications in early childhood. Thirteen low-scoring and only 1 of the high-scoring men show evidence in their interviews of this ability to form genuine, nonopportunistic object relationships. It is also found in the records of 8 low-scoring and 3 high-scoring women. Here, as in the case of most other ratings, it is very difficult to evaluate sex differences since—as was mentioned before—the ratings of the sample of women show considerably higher numbers of "Neutrals."

8. SOCIAL STATUS *VS.* INTRINSIC WORTH IN FRIENDSHIP

In line with all this, the traits which high-scoring subjects tend to desire most in their friends are that their *social or economic status* be prominent or at least "acceptable." Low scorers, on the other hand, tend to accept a friend more often on the basis of *intrinsic worth* or the companionship and common interests he offers. Theirs is an intellectual-aesthetic approach, and they appreciate in their friends "easy-going" traits, social awareness and insight, and generally "low" values (i.e., values in esteem with low scorers as defined in this volume). The difference is significant at the 1 per cent level for both men and women.

Examples of emphasis on status in high scorers follow.

M52: (How do you choose your friends?) "Well, I have a standard based along my own expectations in life. Somebody's got to have a goal in life, got to have manners, don't have to be a big shot, but I like 'em to have some position. I don't like these fly-by-nights. . . . A lot of my friends are social people."

M58: (What would more money make possible?) "Would raise our standard of living; probably buy better, or higher-priced automobile; move into better residential section; associations . . . to those in a bracket higher . . . with people on a higher level."

M4: "Picked a chum—usually one close chum." In high school he got into the ruling clique because he worked on the other boys' cars and radios. Apparently going into this "ruling clique" has made a great impression on him. Before, he felt uneasy around many people, uncertain of his appearance. The girls he asked out hadn't accepted him; he felt much more secure after he got into this clique—he felt that he amounted to something; it helped him get over his inferiority complex.

F31: "When I was a child, I was brighter than I am now. Moving up here may have retarded me. I was very unhappy when we first moved up here. I cried and cried. It was about a year and a half before I got in with the right crowd and joined a high school sorority."

F60 tells the interviewer that she has "been a 'governess' in the home of _____ and in _____'s family—first in the home of the older son, and then the younger. Talked to _____ on the phone when she was _____ at the time of the birth of the third child. Also worked for _____ (Southern California)." And her sister worked for _____, who later was _____.

F78 reports that she has "no really close girl friends." She looks for someone "I wouldn't have to make excuses for—someone well brought up, nice appearance, who dresses neatly."

The foregoing records manifest once more the desire of many high-scoring subjects to associate with the "right kind of people" and their tendency to judge people on the basis of such external criteria as "position" and "nice appearance."

Low-scoring subjects, on the other hand, not only tend to emphasize the intrinsic worth in their friends but tend explicitly to deny the importance of status. There may be, in some of these cases, an underlying concern with status, but the fact that they disclaim it shows that they have at least some inclination to resist conventionalism. There are, furthermore, other goals which take the place of conventional ones. There is more acceptance of passivity and relaxation, more emphasis on enjoyment and "fun." At the same time, there is active pursuing of intellectual goals. Examples follow.

M49: "There was one Chinese fellow, and we used to go swimming and play ping-pong . . . and he was married just after I got there and . . . his home was in an alley with no street address; just plain, simple people; and they could be serious, but if you wanted to have a lot of fun . . . and they seemed to be more understanding . . . more appreciative of little things and more sympathetic."

M42: "I like a person who doesn't think money is the most important thing . . . but wants to better himself and have a better education; who likes to get along with people . . . my friends are all kinds of people. . . . I have a friend who is a Catholic . . . who knows the criticisms of the Catholic Church better than I do . . . but who can argue intelligently for the Catholic Church. . . ."

M53: "People you cultivate are usually people you want to be with. (What do you like to do together?) Well, depends on the friend. My own friends seem to have a variety of interests. I guess . . . talk. Takes up more time than anything else . . . and sometimes drinking parties with a group of friends who are fun to see once in a while."

F62: "We four girls have many discussions about ideas. We had a professor who taught us to think about education and social conditions. We talk about all those things, and we hope to be socially-minded individuals. We try to think. My closest girl friend and I don't go out with boys, but the other two girls do, and we enjoy their experiences, about which they tell us. I was made to be a follower and not a leader. My girl friends are more dominant."

F65: "My best girl friend I still have from high school days. . . . We have the same interests. . . . Now my close friend is a Chinese girl." The interviewer senses a protective attitude on the part of the subject toward this friend. "In general I like intellectual girls who are nice and who have the same ideas."

Just as the high scorers frequently desire to have friends with "accepted" or even "admired" social status, they also tend to emphasize *conventional values* in their choice of friends. Their requirements for friends are that they be moral-conventional, "clean-cut," honest, have good manners, poise, and control (Category 33b). The predominance of such requirements in the records of high-scoring as contrasted with low-scoring subjects was found to be in the proportion of 11 to 4 in men and of 11 to 3 in women. Illustrations from the records of high-scoring subjects follow.

M41: (What attracts you in a friend?) "Well, their manner and behavior."

M11: (What do you like best in your boy friends?) "I like them clean-cut. . . . They're all swell fellows and they come from marvelous families."

F71: "Never stuck close to one—like girls who like a lot of clean fun—high ideals and morals, no drinking."

The emphasis, in the foregoing references, on "clean fun," "swell fellows," and the like, carries the connotation of an almost moral pride in the fact of having a good time. This type of exhibited or "official" optimism has been described previously in this book; it is entirely compatible, and often concomitant, with an underlying sense of despair and futility.

9. SUMMARY

The prejudiced thus seem to tend toward an externalized relation to other people, appreciating those who are higher up in the social hierarchy and who conform to conventional standards, and unrealistically condemning deviations from these standards. It seems likely that this moral condemnation serves the purpose of externalization of, and defense against, temptations toward immoral and unconventional behavior.

Hostile feelings are likewise externalized and projected by conceiving of others as threatening and dangerous. The persecutory ideas about threats in the environment apparently reinforce the wish to be strong; such power is to be obtained by falling in line with what is seen as the general pattern of social relationships, that is, by associating with those who have power. Fear of failure and of being overwhelmed by outside forces leads to an exaggerated preoccupation with such dichotomies as power vs. weakness, top vs. bottom.

The choice of friends is almost exclusively determined by the wish to get support in the compulsive striving for success. Often little attempt is made to disguise the resulting crude form of opportunism. As in the attitude toward parents, the focus seems to be on "getting things," on utilizing people for obtaining the necessary supplies and the help to overcome obstacles. The inclination to conceive of the world as a "jungle" seems to reveal a panic lest supply may run short and one may be helpless in view of dangers which are all too readily anticipated. It is easy to understand that in persons possessed by such fearfulness, the approach to people will tend to be manipulative and exploitive.

Similarly externalized is the relationship to work, as manifested in indifference toward its content and in the emphasis on work as a mere means to success and power. To succeed in the struggle of competition by roughness and by "outsmarting" the competitor seems often an important component of the ego-ideal of the prejudiced men (see the next section).

Since unprejudiced individuals are less apt to be anxiety-ridden than are the prejudiced, they are free to search in their friendships for affectionate companionship, enjoyment, and common interests such as intellectuality, social values, appreciation of art. As they did with their parents, they tend to form comparatively internalized and affectionate relations with people in general, focusing more on the specific characteristics of the other person. The greater capacity for such libidinization is closely related to a permissive and trusting attitude toward others. There is a tendency to conceive of the environment as congenial rather than as dangerous. Dependence on people thus tends to become focal and love-seeking rather than diffuse and ego-alien.

Often this search seems to be unrealistic and insatiable. This can be seen in the expression of longings for total acceptance and forgiveness for all one's faults as found in some of the low scorers. Such a high level of aspiration seems often the source of dissatisfactions with, and ambivalence toward, the object of love or of friendship.

Work seems likewise more libidinized in the low scorer than it is in the high scorer. There is often a persistent striving for intellectual achievement or for realization of productive social values. There is often concern with, and depression about, the possibility of failure along those lines rather than with respect to personal success. This is far from saying that the typical low scorer is indifferent toward success. But in him these tendencies are more often in conflict with, and partly inhibited by, a longing to be loved—a longing frequently crippled in the high scorer during early childhood.

At the same time there is more capacity for relaxation, passive enjoyment, and pleasure in general, as apparently due to the less rigid character of the defenses. Such values take the place of the external, conventional standards of the high scorers.

The tendency to focus on internal and intrinsic values of the individual must be seen as being directly connected with lack of prejudice. Rather than taking a stereotyped view of people and judging them on the basis of their place in the social hierarchy, low scorers are, in the manner described, more open to immediate experience and to an evaluation of people on the basis of individual and intrinsic merits.

C. ATTITUDE TOWARD PRESENT SELF

1. DEFINITION OF RATING CATEGORIES AND QUANTITATIVE RESULTS

The attitudes prejudiced and unprejudiced subjects assume toward themselves seem to be consistent with their attitudes toward family, sex, and people, as discussed in the foregoing pages. Thus the prejudiced tend toward self-glorification, conventionality of ego-ideal, and lack of insight; and at the same time they exhibit self-contempt which is not faced as such and which they try to deny. First, attitudes toward the "present self" will be discussed, followed by the conceptions of our subjects concerning their childhood personalities. The categories dealing with the first of these topics were defined as follows:

INTERVIEW SCORING MANUAL: ATTITUDE TOWARD PRESENT SELF
(to Table 3(XI))

PRESUMABLY "HIGH" VARIANT	PRESUMABLY "LOW" VARIANT
34a. *Self-glorification.* Positive traits mentioned, negative traits rationalized; has overcome weakness, handicaps, victimization, persecution; self-estimate and ego-ideal tend to be the same	34a. *Critical self-appraisal.* Self-estimate and ego-ideal separate; occasional morbid self-accusations
34b. *Ego-alien self-contempt* which is moralistic-authoritarian and semi-externalized. (Do not score unless there are some specific signs of self-rejection beyond compensatory self-glorification, etc.)	

35M. *Self-estimate traits, Men:*

a. *Pseudo-masculinity.* Determination, energy, industry, independence, decisivenes, will power. No admission of passivity	a. *Ego-accepted admission of passivity,* softness, weakness, etc.
b. *Conventionally moralistic.* Ideal of honesty, self-control; any violations regarded as essentially unexplained "break-through"	b. *Admitted fallibility of control,* not merely unexplained "break-through"

35W. *Self-estimate traits, Women:*

a. *Pseudo-femininity*	a. *Ego-accepted admission of nonfemininity*
b. *Conventionally moralistic.* Propriety, poise, self-control, unselfishness	b. *Admitted fallibility of control,* not merely unexplained "break-through." Admission of selfishness, etc.
36a. *Self as "average"* and therefore all right. Attempted denial or "forgetting" of deviations, past and present	36a. *Self as "different,"* individualized, or unconventional
	36b. *"World identification,"* equalitarian - brotherhood ideal

37M-W.	*Ego-ideal:* Same as self-estimate traits	37M-W.	*Ego-ideal:* Liberal values. Achievement, understanding, nurturance, affiliation; work for humanitarian values, to improve social relations, to improve self, etc.
38.	*Denial of psychological causes:* Explanations of self in terms of heredity, physical factors, accidental factors, etc.; or denial in effect of any casualty (e.g., of symptoms)	38.	*Sociopsychological explanations of self*
39.	*Property as extension of self*	39.	*Property as means to end*

Quantitative results concerning these categories are shown in Table 3(XI).

2. SELF-GLORIFICATION *VS.* OBJECTIVE APPRAISAL

The trend toward *self-glorification* in the prejudiced becomes evident in their tendency to ascribe to themselves predominantly positive traits and to rationalize whatever negative traits they are unable to deny. They are given to emphasizing that they have successfully overcome weakness, obstacles, and victimization. The opposite alternative, namely *objective self-appraisal*, is more common in low scorers. The difference between high- and low-scoring subjects, both men and women, is statistically significant at the 1 per cent level (Category 34a). Results already presented have indicated that prejudiced subjects tend to repress what may be unpleasant to face, and thus to narrow the scope of consciousness. One cause of these repressions may lie in the type of discipline to which these subjects were exposed, a discipline which required immediate submission. Apparently in a fearful attempt to please the parents, a "good" façade was presented and anything which did not fit in with this façade, such as, especially, resentment against the parents, was repressed and denied. This process very probably leads to self-deception, which may be of such crudeness that it seems obvious to anyone but the subject himself.

The following example illustrates the self-deception of a prejudiced man with respect to his will power and independence. He takes pride in certain decisions and actions of self-control which are obviously engineered by the father (see also Chapter II).

M13: "I grew up quickly. My father has allowed me to do as I pleased, although he forced some decisions upon me. About smoking, he said I must do it in front of him, if I must. He also provided wines and liquors in the ice chest. I soon tired of smoking and never took much to drinking. I have a stubborn nature, and if he had

TABLE 3 (XI)

INTERVIEW RATINGS ON ATTITUDE TOWARD PRESENT SELF FOR 80 SUBJECTS SCORING EXTREMELY "HIGH" OR "LOW" ON THE ETHNIC PREJUDICE QUESTIONNAIRE SCALE

Interview rating categories (abbreviated from Manual)	Sex	Number of "High"(H) and "Low"(L) ratings received by				Sums of instances		Level of statistical significance reached (percentage)
		20 men and 25 women "high scorers" H	L	20 men and 15 women "low scorers" H	L	"positive"	"negative"	
34a. Self-glorification(H) vs. objective self-appraisal(L)	Men	12	3	3	15	27	6	1
	Women	13	4	1	12	25	5	1
34b. Ego-alien self-contempt(H)	Men	10		1		10	1	
	Women	10		2		10	2	
35. Self-estimates of traits:								
aM. Pseudo-masculinity(H) vs. admission of passivity(L)	Men	13	1	2	14	27	3	1
aW. Pseudo-femininity(H) vs. admission of nonfemininity(L)	Women	7	1	2	7	14	3	
b. Conventional moralism(H) vs. admitted fallibility of of control(L)	Men	13	1	2	13	26	3	1
	Women	19	3	2	9	28	5	1
36a. Self as "average"(H) vs. self as "different"(L)	Men	14	2	5	14	28	7	1
	Women	2	0	5	9	11	5	
36b. "World identification," equalitarian-brotherhood ideal(L)	Men		2		5	5	2	
	Women		0		4	4	0	
37. Ego-ideal:								
aM. Pseudo-masculinity(H) vs. achievement(L)	Men	16	4	1	13	29	5	1
aW. Pseudo-femininity(H) vs. achievement(L)	Women	8	1	5	11	19	6	2
b. Conventional morality(H) vs. humanitarianism(L)	Men	14	4	3	15	29	7	1
	Women	16	5	2	11	27	7	1
38. Denial of genuine causality(H) vs. socio-psychological explanations of self(L)	Men	11	4	1	14	25	5	1
	Women	14	1	1	11	25	2	1
39. Property as: extension of self(H) vs. means to end(L)	Men	14	2	3	15	29	5	1
	Women	13	7	0	13	26	7	1

tried to stop me, I probably would have taken it up. . . . I have always tried to live according to His Ten Commandments. . . . (What disagreements have you had with your father?) There haven't been any to any great extent. I had a mind of my own at a very early age. He has too. We've had arguments but I can't remember any lickings by him. . . ."

A general satisfaction with one's self is expressed by the following high scorer:

M58: "Well, I'm the head operator—shift foreman—rotating schedules . . . (subject emphasizes 'head' position)—small department . . . five in department . . . five in shift . . . I get personal satisfaction that I have five people working for me, who come to me for advice in handling the production that we make, and that the ultimate decision is mine, and in fact that in that ultimate decision, I should be *right*—and am usually, and the knowledge that I am correct gives me personal satisfaction."

As previously mentioned, high-scoring subjects, especially men, tend to succumb to the temptation of displaying independence, ability for decisions, and leadership qualities, probably as a defense against a possible "breakthrough" of their underlying passivity and anxiety. In general, prejudiced subjects, in pointing out how well they overcame handicaps, sickness, and calamities, are prone to emphasize the use of will power. The tendency to cling to the belief that "will power and cheerfulness" can solve all problems seems of special importance.

Examples from the records of high-scoring women follow:

F71: "Child—nervous because of mastoid operations . . . terrible time getting started in school . . . afraid of kids . . . this in first half of kindergarten . . . by second half I was a leader. Think one of my best assets is my poise—learned from moving around so much. Remember hospital clearly at 3 years old."

F38, in telling how she conquered infantile paralysis by will power, continues: "I've always had a happy disposition, and I've always been honest with my family. I appreciate what they did for me. I've always tried to find a way so that I wouldn't be a burden to them. I've never wanted to be a cripple. I was always dependable in a pinch. I've always been cheerful and I'm sure I've never made anyone feel bad because of my handicap. Maybe one of the reasons I have been cheerful is because of my handicap. I wore a cast on my leg until I was 4 years old. . . . He (husband) compares me with his first wife. She was unfaithful to him. I'm not like that. She was a drinker. I've never done that. I've never done things behind people's backs. I've always done things in the open. . . . (Habits?) I didn't have any bad habits as a child, no nightmares. I rarely dream even now, night or day. (Q) My mother was the chief disciplinarian. I always got along well with my brothers and sisters. I was always honest with them and let them know where I stood. I believe that all the relations between my brothers and sisters and myself were better than average. I think I'm the favorite of the whole family. I know I'm the favorite niece of all my aunts and uncles. . . ."

Similar is this passage in the record of a high-scoring man who had been told, after having gone through infantile paralysis, that he would never walk again:

M4: "But you see, I can get around, because I made up my mind to. If I made up my mind, I can be in the upper crust too."

Low-scoring subjects, on the other hand, do not as a rule attempt to hide their feelings of insecurity, their shyness, and their dependence. For example:

M49 says about himself: "Well, I think social contact bothers me most. I could always talk with one person, but where there are several persons, I'll just stand there and not say 'boo.' I think that might have been due to our not having enough social contacts."

Or a low-scoring woman, *F63:* "I work best by myself—have difficulty working with other people. I get along with them all right, but it's a strain on me. I'm rather shy, don't like competition."

The fact that low-scoring men tend more often to admit their softness and their dependence on their mother is exemplified by the following quotation:

M50: "I don't mean I am in love with my mother, but I have a dependency complex . . . married a woman older than myself . . . and always depend on others . . . leave responsibility to others. . . . It seems on looking back that I have always done that . . . simply transferred my dependency on my mother and my wife and onto the (prison) authorities . . . now and in the future. . . ."

As was pointed out above, the dual phenomenon of surface admiration and underlying contempt revealed by the high scorers in their attitude toward the other sex, can sometimes be found in their attitude toward themselves as well. Statements of self-glorification are then followed by statements of self-contempt not faced as such. Such combinations indicate the profound doubt these subjects have about themselves, a doubt which they seem able to bear only by disclaiming responsibility for their own failures, projectively blaming instead other people, external circumstances, uncontrollable forces within oneself, or heredity. The trend of high scorers toward such an *ego-alien self-contempt* which is moralistic-authoritarian and semi-externalized (Category 34b) is distinct in both men (10 positive instances as compared with 1 negative) and women (10 positive vs. 2 negative instances). The difference between high scorers and low scorers, however, does not reach statistical significance on account of the large number of Neutral classifications in this category.

From ego-alien self-contempt there is a gradual transition to the self-condemnation of the typical low scorer. The latter is often characterized by a sober appraisal of intrinsic personality dynamics whereas the former is often warded off in thinly disguised attempts at self-justification in terms of factors beyond the control of the individual which are sometimes real, more often imaginary.

Examples of the type of self-rejection characteristic of high-scoring men follow. Although there is self-criticism in terms of conventional standards, the blame is being put on such factors outside of personality proper as heredity, other people, or external circumstances:

M40: "All the inheritance is all from the male side of the family for some reason or other. Except for my industriousness. That just doesn't exist. (Q) I guess I just got that from the other side of the family . . . just a black horse. . . . The whole trouble with me is I didn't grow up. I thought it was a big game of cops and robbers. I don't think any of . . . were malicious about it. We heard about others getting caught, but couldn't believe we would."

M57: "I'm kind of ashamed, I'm the only black sheep in the family . . . and I've made more money than all the others put together. Yes, a man of my intelligence let some damn broad put me behind bars."

In the following examples a weak ego is seen as possessed by alien forces within the personality, such as the "carnal self" or "weak flesh":

M52: "I've often stopped and more or less took an inventory of myself. I have let myself slip, let my carnal self get away from me. . . ."

M58: "Well, I'm a bad example—I don't live what I believe, possibly because the flesh is weak—don't have the stamina to stand up and live it—try not to harm somebody else. . . ."

Examples from the records of high-scoring women are:

F71: "I'm inclined to be nervous; haven't the confidence in myself. . . . I'm the clinging vine type and my sister is. My parents have always felt that I'm the backward one—need guidance. They gave me dancing lessons in grade school—knew I needed it. I made all B's in high school."

F77 says about the girl to whom she has a sexual attachment: "She is always the boss; although she's younger, she's mean, hurts my feelings awfully bad. I can't understand why I love a wicked girl so much."

The foregoing record of an otherwise conventional girl reflects rejection of an ego-alien part of herself, a part she is prone to link with an external temptation (see also Chapter XXII).

F79 is a good example of how derogatory the opinion about oneself can become: "I wanted to finish school after I got out of the SPARS, and I went to _____ Junior College although mother and father couldn't afford it. I didn't do much. I just ate and got fat and mother and father hit the ceiling. I was already neurotic, I guess. I didn't go out. I was in a rut and I got fatter. Mother and father made me do calisthenics by force. Then I went to _____ College summer school and was scared of the boys. Then I went to business school. I hated it; it was so boring just to sit and type. I could go to the University of _____ if I lost weight. My brother was going. I couldn't because I was too heavy. I felt out of place working in a jewelry store. I hated it and was awfully uncomfortable. I kept on eating; it was the only thing I could turn to, and mother and father got furious. Mother would get these terrific anger spurts. She would yell and I would yell, and then I would feel disgusted."

This is the same girl who at another place in her interview reported that she could get a sense of personal worth by reminding herself of her family background. The existing cleavage between pretense and reality is also revealed by her finding it a matter "of course" that her mother is "wonderful" (see the passages, quoted in Chapter X, concerning idealization of parents and other contexts).

3. MASCULINITY AND FEMININITY

We turn now to the more specific aspects of the self-image of the high-scoring subjects as contrasted with that of the low scorers. In line with previous discussion, especially in Section A of this chapter, one might expect high-scoring men to think of themselves as very masculine, and that this claim would be the more insistent the greater the underlying feelings of weakness. Low-scoring men, on the other hand, having actually more personal and masculine identity—perhaps by virtue of having had less threatening parental figures—can afford to admit failures and doubts along these lines.

In fact, there seems to be, in the high-scoring men, more of what may be called *pseudo-masculinity*—as defined by boastfulness about such traits as determination, energy, industry, independence, decisiveness, and will power —and less admission of passivity. An ego-accepted admission of passivity, softness, and weakness, on the other hand, is found predominantly in low-scoring men. The difference is significant at the 1 per cent level (Category 35a). Examples of these two different attitudes in the realm of sex have been quoted in Section A of this chapter.

Similar attitudes can be found in the vocational sphere and in the approach to life in general. Thus, one high-scoring man discussed his successful techniques of "driving sharp bargains." "Certain ordinary ways of doing business," he said, "are too damn slow for me." Being successful by outsmarting others in the competitive struggle is part of the ego-ideal of the prejudiced man. Low-scoring men, on the other hand, more often refer to their dependence, to their liking of cooking and to other tastes usually considered as feminine. They are, furthermore, more often described by the interviewer as "gentle," "mild," "soft-spoken."

An analogous trend—although statistically not significant—toward what may be called *pseudo-femininity* is found in evaluating the self-estimates given by high-scoring women. These women tend to think of themselves as feminine and soft; no masculine trends are being admitted ("being a housewife is definitely my career"). As is not surprising, a rather crude aggression, directed especially against men, seems to go with this attitude, as revealed indirectly in the interviews and directly in the Thematic Apperception Test stories.

Low-scoring women, on the other hand—as was mentioned in Section A— often profess to have a real conflict over their femininity. They sometimes show envy of men rather directly and often engage in so-called masculine activities. At the same time a certain real fondness for men and the wish to be with them and to participate in their activities is revealed. Extreme exam-

ples of openly expressed rejection of the feminine role in low-scoring women
are:

F62: "My mother always said that I would make a better boy than a girl. I was
always hammering, building, and constructing something. In my adolescence, I
was always wearing overalls. Today still when I am in despair, I build things—work
it out physically."

F23: Subject wished very much that she were a boy and elaborated on the prejudice against women in her profession. She does not like to cook or sew. "If I were a
man I could have a wife—that's what I really need, someone to cook and sew and
take care of me." She feels that she is really quite dependent in this respect. Therefore, she will either not marry, or else will continue to work after she is married.
Even if she had children she would want to go back to work and get someone else
to bring them up after the first year. "I don't think I could bring children up very
well anyway. . . . I liked everything the boys did and disliked everything the girls
did. I wanted to play baseball with the boys and I did go out and play baseball with
them. (What do girls do?) They sit around and talk about boys—and nothing bores
me more."

4. CONVENTIONALISM AND MORALISM

Likewise in line with some of the findings reported earlier is the tendency
of high-scoring men and women to think of themselves as basically highly
moral and controlled and to consider any conduct which contradicts this
norm as a "break-through" of tendencies which cannot be explained or
influenced. The above quotations illustrate the tendency these individuals
have to describe themselves as honest and as possessing high ideals and self-
control in the sense of a *conventional moralism.* Low-scoring subjects, on
the other hand, more readily admit *fallibility of self-control* without trying
to explain it away as a break-through of something foreign to their basic
nature. This difference is significant at the 1 per cent level for both men and
women (Category 35b). In the case of high-scoring women, the more detailed definition of the category, as given in the passages of the Scoring
Manual accompanying the table, indicates special emphasis on such traits
as propriety, poise, self-control, and unselfishness; these are contrasted with
admission of selfishness in low-scoring women.

The importance of conventional traits in the self-image of high-scoring
subjects may be considered as one of the aspects of their strong desire to
belong to the powerful majority. There is reason to believe that a certain
lack of personal identity is compensated for by a wish to "belong," and to
conceive of oneself as *average and therefore all right,* with attempted denial
or "forgetting" of deviations, may these deviations be past or present (Category 36a). A great deal of protection and security must be assumed to derive
from the feeling of being, in this sense, part of a group. However, as has been
mentioned before, this kind of belonging to a group is something quite different from genuine identification with other individuals and society. For
prejudiced subjects, then, the greater the deviation, the more stress must be

laid on denying its existence. This is especially marked in our prison sample, from which the following quotations are taken.

M51: Subject says he robbed just once and blamed this on drinking. "I still don't consider myself antisocial. . . ." He emphasizes that he doesn't consider himself perverted. He remarks that a while back he took some glandular treatments and feels that these have made him more masculine.

M57: Subject expresses the superficial desire to understand why he had gotten in so much trouble when his brothers have not, and to straighten out. He spontaneously denies "that there is anything the matter with me."

These passages from the interviews of high-scoring deviates illustrate at the same time the tendency of high-scoring subjects in general to see their deviations and lack of control as a break-through in the sense defined in the discussion of the preceding category.

In contrast to this, low-scoring subjects tend to see themselves as *different, individualized, or unconventional* (Category 36a, continued). This can be seen from records quoted in previous sections. The difference for the entire category is significant for men at the 1 per cent level; for women there is a trend in the same direction (11 positive vs. 5 negative instances).

Apparently, the greater "personal identity" of the low scorers facilitates establishment of genuine object relationships. In the few cases in which low scorers referred to identification in the present sense of "belonging" it tended to be in terms of mankind in general, that is, as a form of "*world identification*" with the stress on an equalitarian brotherhood ideal (Category 36b; for "humanitarianism" see the next subsection).

5. CONFORMITY OF SELF AND IDEAL

Lack of insight and of self-criticism on the part of the typical high scorers is revealed in their tendency to mention as the type of person they would wish to be, as their *self-ideal, the same set of traits which they actually ascribe to themselves*. There is hardly any discrepancy between their image of what they ought to be and their conception of what they really are.

Thus, high-scoring men tend to mention as their ego-ideal the combination of traits characterized above as "pseudo-masculine" (determination, energy, industry, independence, decisiveness, will power, no passivity) as well as the syndrome of "moralistic conventionalism," likewise mentioned above.

An example of a more worrisome adoption of this type of ego-ideal in a high-scoring man is the following:

M52: (Worries?) "Well, I had worries, I remember that. I think my greatest desire was to be somebody in life. I did a lot of reading as a kid. . . . I was sort of a hero worshipper—nobody particularly—I wanted to be a success in business. I used to plan, and sometimes worried about whether I would."

The following quotations illustrate the admiration high-scoring men have for men of action and success, such as MacArthur and Andrew Carnegie who "amounted to so much":

M47: "And then another one I like real well . . . this Patton. I like him for the same reason I like MacArthur. He went right up to the front. . . . He wouldn't send his men anywhere he wouldn't go himself."

M51: "Andrew Carnegie, I guess, I got from some of my relatives. . . . His coming over here with so little and amounting to so much. . . ."

High-scoring women likewise tend to list as the ideal the same traits which they mentioned in their self-description and which were summarized under the heading "pseudo-femininity" and "conventional moralism."

Low-scoring subjects, on the other hand, tend to mention, as their ideal, traits which are different from, or at least differently conceived from those which they ascribe to themselves. Being basically more secure, it seems, they can more easily afford to see a discrepancy between ego-ideal and actual reality. Seeing this discrepancy enables them to strive toward a better full-fillment of the ego-ideal. A study dealing with mechanisms of self-deception seems to indicate that the more aware subjects are of falling short of their ideals, the nearer they actually are to the realization of these ideals (see 33).

Specifically, the values listed as ideals by low-scoring men and women may best be summarized as *real achievement*. There is also an emphasis on humanitarian values such as understanding, *nurturance* (the latter especially emphasized by women), affiliation, or work for liberal values such as the improvement of social relations or self-improvement.

The difference between the two types of ego-ideal (as covered by the ratings on Categories 37a and 37b) is statistically highly significant for both men and women.

Since the ego-ideal of the low-scoring subjects is closely related to their tolerance, several illustrations of this point will here be given from their records. Their emphasis on achievement as a value in its own right rather than as a mere means for some ulterior end is shown in the following examples:

M55: (I see you would like to be a Congressman?) Subject laughs. He indicates this is not a realistic choice, but that he would like to be a Congressman. He emphasizes what he calls the "in-values" here, "not working just for money, etc. . . but for what you accomplish . . . and though are likely to be defeated, you have the satisfaction of trying." (Attractions?) Not adept at personal relations, but enjoys this more than statistics or research, but would rather be out in contact with people . . . one war job at Bethlehem Steel involved some personal relations work. . . . "I may be aiming too high. . . . I might be an interviewer at an employment agency."

F62: "I would like to teach drama in high school. The reason for this seems perhaps sort of queer. I have always enjoyed drama very much and I thought the world should know more about the theater. I want people to know about good entertainment, high-class art."

F63: "In my art work I have been very interested in abstract forms, not so much in representational forms. I have been very influenced by the Bauhaus kind of design." Now interested in writing. (Q) "I was at the _____ Art Gallery (school) and at that time there was a job open _____ art critic for the _____ which I took. I have also had other jobs for newspapers." Interested in experimental forms of writing.

F23: Subject has been employed as a junior chemist at _____ Development for a year and a half. She is disappointed in her job because she had hoped to do research, instead of which she is doing routine work such as could be done by a lab assistant. "You are not allowed to do things your own way, nor are you given any responsi- bility at _____ unless you have a Ph.D." Subject is also annoyed by the lack of honesty in her fellow workers: they practice what is known as "pencil chemistry"; i.e., if a reading fails to give the expected result, they will fake the result. She went and told the boss about this, but he did not do anything about it. "They won't do anything on your say-so, and he didn't even check the results for himself." In re- sponse to a question as to whether she had ever wished that she were a boy, subject replied: "Yes, I do very much because then I could do what I liked. When I first came here they asked me what I would like to do and I told them organic chemistry; so they asked me whether I would like to do organic analysis and I said, yes, without thinking very much about it. The work turned out to be simple filtrations which were interesting at first, but very easy to learn. . . . I want to quit next summer and get my Ph.D. because perhaps then I might have a better chance to do what I want."

M44: "One thing that I think was important, I always liked school and took pride in it. I was always afraid that I might lose out there."

Emphasis on humanitarian values is exemplified by the following records of interviewees scoring extremely low on the ethnocentrism questionnaire. Some of them refer to specific and concrete plans for help in the execution of a program with humanitarian implications, while others may do no more than pay lip-service in terms of vague generalities.

M53: (Satisfactions?) "Well, this is a little obscure . . . a certain justification of one's own existence . . . stocks and bonds never convinced me, because it didn't seem to me to make a damn bit of difference (to the public welfare). This work. . . . I can see results quickly . . . and honest-to-goodness results."

M59: "To help those less fortunate than oneself, and to be a part of the commu- nity or society that one is in, to take an active part in it, and being kind and generous and to more or less have a high regard for your fellow human being. . . ."

M15: "Started out in college with a strong interest in social studies, history. This interest is still strong, but now it is combined with a desire to work with people. Counseling appears to be my present choice. (Idea behind it?) Well, in our church I have observed how many people have problems. I think I would like to help them. (What kinds of probems?) Personal. . . . (Your religious point of view at present?) You might call it something like Social Religion. (Q) It is a sin to be indifferent to progress."

The statements just quoted are good examples of values important to low- scoring subjects: real achievement often accompanied by anxiety over pos- sible failure, intellectuality, and socially constructive goals.

6. DENIAL OF SOCIOPSYCHOLOGICAL CAUSATION

In high-scoring subjects the general lack of insight and the unrealistic view of oneself seem to be connected with a tendency toward a certain wishful *denial of genuine causality*—as revealed by easy explanations of one's own shortcomings in terms of heredity, physical or accidental factors, etc.—or the denial of the symptomatic character of one's behavioral manifestations. Thus, as will be discussed more fully in Chapter XXII, high-scoring subjects in the sample drawn from a psychiatric clinic tend to refer to their symptoms as something merely physical, or as caused by a "hereditary taint," or as otherwise alien to the ego of the subject.

On the other hand, low-scoring subjects tend in general toward *socio-psychological explanations*, conceiving of the present self in the context of its development under the influence of social and psychological factors. Thus, while talking about themselves, these subjects spontaneously refer back to their childhood, using explicitly such phrases as "it may go back to infancy" in describing the cause of behavioral deviations. One low-scoring subject relates his not having many fears to the fact that his "sister had a lot of fears." "I used that as a technique not to have any," he said. To be sure, all this should not be taken to imply that the low-scoring subjects in question necessarily possess the correct or full insight into themselves; it means only that there is a greater inclination to think in psychodynamic terms and to seek explanation of one's own behavior in these terms.

The difference between the two attitudes (encompassed in Category 38) is statistically highly significant (at the 1 per cent level) for both men and women.

7. PROPERTY AS EXTENSION OF SELF

The basic insecurity that lies beneath the overt denials and overconfidence of the high-scoring subjects may be a chief contributing factor in their exaggerated wish for property, in the sense of a conception of *property as an extension of the self*. There is an overlibidinization of money and property, per se. Low-scoring subjects, on the other hand, tend to have a more realistic attitude toward money, knowing fully its value as a means, yet not over-estimating it by making it an end in itself. They generally conceive of *property as means to an end*.

Differentiation between prejudiced and unprejudiced groups under this aspect (as covered by Category 39) is statistically highly significant.

The following quotations from high-scoring subjects are examples of their search for "basic security and independence" through money or through the accumulation of goods. It often seems that the need has become functionally autonomous, to use a term by Allport (9), and is as such insatiable.

F24: (How much is enough?) "Quite a bit—I have to make good—get lots of it and get it fast."

F32: The desire for $1000 a month or "all I could get" represents a wish for security. The more one earns, the more one can put aside.

M57: (What might a lot of money make possible for you?) "Buy more cattle, more land, that's my greatest ambition."

Records of low-scoring subjects, on the other hand, more often show emphasis on money as a means of obtaining some of the desirable things in life or else of achieving some socially constructive goal. They furthermore illustrate the greater casualness, passivity, and more pleasure-seeking attitude of the low scorers with respect to money and possessions. Enjoyment of music and books is often mentioned; and there is generally more emphasis on specific things to be obtained rather than on the more vague and perhaps imaginary goal of "security" as stressed by high scorers.

Examples are found in the following records of low-scoring subjects:

M42: "I think the best things are free, but lots of times . . . let's see . . . it takes a certain amount of money . . . to do a few things with friends, etc. (Saving vs. spending?) I don't believe in saving money to the point of a mania . . . but planning for the future is something. . . . I don't make a point of saving a certain amount of money every month . . . no use pinching pennies now, so that you can live better later. . . ."

M44: (What do you miss most that your present income doesn't permit?) "A good radio with a record player on it, but that's just an immediate thing. . . ."

M48: (What might a lot of money make possible for you?) "Mean just a good living. I like to go to plays, concerts, etc., to have a nice home, etc."

M49: (What do with $7500?) "Well, of course, it would give us a comfortable home, to begin with, and a good living, and my wife has always wanted to write, and she's started on several ideas, and that would give her enough to get materials and go ahead with her writing, and—if she did go into writing—we could hire the people to do the house cleaning and laundry, so as to give her more time . . . and she always likes to go to plays and concerts . . . and we could indulge in those things without jeopardizing. . . ."

F63: "Money has never meant much to me. Maybe it is stupid and unrealistic. But it is the work itself that gives me satisfaction."

F70: (If you had more, what would you do?) "I would probably spend it. (On what?) Well, maybe I would buy some more dishes and silver, although I have more than I can use now; probably not material things. If I had a lot of money I didn't know what to do with, I might run a small private hospital. . . . I don't think I'd buy expensive objects of art. Well, maybe I would. I might buy quite a few material things, go to a lot of concerts and plays. One seems to be able to spend a lot of money on those."

F27: "That isn't much, I guess. Neither of us wants much. (Is it enough for a family of six?) Well, what I meant was that we want a comfortable home without any worry, plenty of books, and a good record player with lots of records. We could be happy."

D. CONCEPTION OF CHILDHOOD SELF

1. DEFINITION OF RATING CATEGORIES AND
QUANTITATIVE RESULTS

The discussion of attitudes toward oneself thus far has concerned traits which our interviewed subjects ascribed to themselves as of the present. As a regular feature of the interview, subjects were further asked the question: "What were you like as a child?" Obviously, answers to this question must not necessarily be taken to reflect the actual nature of the subjects as children. The answers may well refer in part or predominantly to the subject's image of himself as a child. The two alternative interpretations of the material will have to be kept in mind throughout the discussion which follows. The results of a study on social discrimination in children, including interviews with their parents (30), give support to the assumption that the descriptions which our subjects give of themselves show at least a certain degree of correspondence with the actual facts.

The rating categories used in the evaluation of this part of the interview material are as follows:

INTERVIEW SCORING MANUAL: CONCEPTION OF CHILDHOOD SELF

(to Table 4(XI))

Presumably "High" Variants	Presumably "Low" Variants
40M. *Traits ascribed to childhood self by Men:*	
a. *Unmanageable, difficult*, stubborn, aggressive, spoiled, sensitive, etc.	a. *Quiet*, shy, self-conscious
b. *Bland childhood.* Happy, active, no worries, no shyness, etc.	b. *Adult-oriented, internalized standards.* Read a lot; interest in school and teachers; achievement striving
c. *"Gang"-oriented*	c. *Isolated* or sociable with few
40W. *Traits ascribed to childhood self by Women:*	
a. *Difficult child.* Nervous, frail, etc.	a. (1) *Quiet*, shy, self-conscious (2) *Tomboy*, independent
b. *Bland childhood*	b. *Adult-oriented, internalized standards*
41. *Discontinuity* between childhood self and now	41. *Continuity* between childhood self and now
	42. *Childhood habits* (Write in each habit mentioned, e.g., nail-biting, thumb-sucking, bedwetting, nightmares, fear of dark, fear of animals, etc.)
	43. *Time of earliest sex experience remembered* (Write in: *Childhood* [1-6]; *Prepuberty* [7-12]; *Adolescence* [13-19]; Adult life [20-])
	44. *Nature of earliest sex experience remembered* (Write in: e.g., homosexual or heterosexual sex play; dates; kissing; heterosexual or homosexual intercourse, masturbation)
	45. *Source of early sex information* (Write in: e.g., mother; father; male or female sib; other relative; other adult; books; the gang; etc.)
46. *Little spontaneous comment*	46. *Considerable spontaneous comment*

TABLE 4 (XI)

INTERVIEW RATINGS ON ATTITUDE TOWARD CHILDHOOD SELF

FOR 80 SUBJECTS SCORING EXTREMELY "HIGH" OR "LOW" ON THE ETHNIC PREJUDICE QUESTIONNAIRE SCALE

Interview rating categories (abbreviated from Manual)	Sex	Number of "High"(H) and "Low"(L) ratings received by				Sums of instances		Level of statistical significance reached (percentage)
		20 men and 25 women "high scorers" H	L	20 men and 15 women "low scorers" H	L	"positive"	"negative"	
40. Traits ascribed to childhood self:								
aM. Unmanageable, difficult(H) vs. quiet, shy(L)	Men	10	1	3	6	16	4	
aW. Difficult child(H) vs. quiet, shy, or tomboy; independent(L)	Women	9	5	2	7	16	7	
b. Bland childhood(H) vs. adult-oriented internalized standards(L)	Men	4	7	1	16	20	8	
	Women	6	5		7	13	5	5
41. Discontinuity(H) vs. continuity(L) between childhood self and now	Men	9	3	1	16	25	4	1
	Women	7	8	1	11	18	9	5
46. Little(H) vs. considerable (L) spontaneous comment	Men	11	4	4	13	24	8	2
	Women	10	5	1	10	20	6	2

Table 4(XI) presents the quantitative results of the analysis of the interviews. Categories 42 to 45 have been omitted from consideration since we gained the impression that there was a certain reluctance on the part of some subjects to talk freely about the topics concerned.

2. "DIFFICULT" CHILD

There is a tendency, though not a statistically significant one, for both high-scoring men and women to report more frequently than low scorers that they were "difficult" as children. Among the male interviewees, 10 high scorers as contrasted with only 1 low scorer describe themselves as *unmanageable, difficult, stubborn, aggressive, spoiled and/or sensitive* in childhood (Category 40a.M).

Aside from the possibility of this having actually been the case, it seems that some of the high-scoring subjects may seek in this way to justify the harsh discipline exerted by their parents by taking the blame themselves for any clashes that may have occurred. A further motive for this type of description may be the wish, known to be present in high-scoring men (see above, Chapter VII, to conceive of oneself as possessing "rugged masculinity." The following examples from the records of high-scoring men seem to support both of the latter alternatives offered here as explanations.

M40: (What were you like as a child?) "Rowdy, I guess. Typical fresh Irish kid. . . . Snot-nosed, they used to call it. (Q) Oh, steal Joe Blow's apples (and similar pranks). If there was any trouble, I was in it. (Q) Oh, just a kid—I mean, nothing serious."

M20: "I had a pretty mean streak in me, especially around ten, pretty mischievous. My grandparents tried to hold me back. See that I'd play with the right kind of children. When I was around 12, I began to be pretty snotty to them and run around any time I wanted to. Sometimes I didn't do my work. At times, I'd feel ashamed of myself. . . . Makes me feel bad now. . . . (Q) No money. I couldn't run around much without money. Always tried to make it some way. . . . Three or four of us ran around together. Pretty snotty. . . . Maybe they tried to hold me down too much when I was younger. Wouldn't let me play, only with certain children."

There is a corresponding though less pronounced trend in high-scoring women; they report that as children they were *difficult, nervous, frail* (Category 40a.W). Examples are:

F22: "All I can remember is that mother said I was very fussy and finicky especially about what I ate."

F31: "I used to cry all the time. I don't know why, but people hurt my feelings. My brother took that out of me. I fought with him, and it got to the point where I could dish it out."

F66: "I cried an awful lot when he died. Mother says I cried and ran out of rooms for years after he died because I didn't like to see her with any other man. She says I ruined her chances."

Low-scoring subjects, on the other hand, show a tendency to describe themselves as *quiet, shy, self-conscious,* or as *unpopular* in childhood. Low-scoring women, furthermore, relate somewhat more readily than do the high-scoring to have been *"tomboys"* and *independent* as children (Category 40a, continued). Examples from the records of low-scoring subjects follow:

M48: (What sort of a person were you?) "Hard for me to say—you mean, was I quiet? Well, would like to have been noisier, was always somewhat repressed by the other kids ... shunned by (the leading cliques in school) ... though I finally got in with my own gang about my own level. ..."

M53: (What sort of person were you?) "Hard to evaluate. ... I think I was fairly quiet. ... I was supposed to be pretty well behaved. Don't think I was remarkable in any respect."

M55: "Timid about dancing, afraid to dance; afraid to go out for sports for fear of being not a good player."

F27 "I was an awful drip really. I was a very unhappy child. I think it was because I was so fat. And I was abnormally shy. It used to make me mad when teachers would point me out as a model child for being so quiet. I knew I was only quiet because I was scared of everybody there. At home I was a noisy madcap. Of course, at home I was the center of the stage. Everyone thought I was wonderful. At school I guess I didn't feel appreciated. I knew I was very superior intellectually and was sort of a snob about that—but I didn't really care about that. I wanted to be liked and nobody liked me. So I just hurried home. All through grammar school I only had two friends—both girls. I never knew a boy well enough to really talk to. I guess those girls must have really tried to be friends with me because I never could have made any effort."

Floyd Allport and D. A. Hartmann (8) found similar results when they administered a scale to measure political attitudes as well as several personality schedules. They found that the liberals—to use our terminology—exceeded the conservatives in "tender-mindedness," awareness of inner motives and conflicts, touchiness in personal matters, sensitiveness to the opinions of others, and a retiring nature. They are less expansive and self-assertive.

3. BLANDNESS *VS.* ADULT-ORIENTATION

It was assumed, in line with their general tendency toward denial and toward reluctance to face difficulties, that high-scoring subjects would be inclined further to describe their childhood as *bland, happy, active,* and *without worries or shyness* (Category 40b). We were aware of the fact that this assumption is in apparent contradiction to the trend just referred to, namely that high scorers lean toward describing themselves as having been difficult children. However, it is quite common to find denial of difficulties in such subjects side by side with revelation of difficulties. In descriptions of the childhood self there seem to be on the whole fewer manifestations of denial than in any other field with which we have dealt so far. This might be due to the fact that childhood is a possible projection screen for undesirable traits, offering another possibility of rendering these traits "ego-alien." Obviously, there is comparatively little necessity to glorify one's childhood, a period so far away in time. On the contrary, some of our high-scoring subjects seem to find satisfaction in stressing handicaps, such as bad constitution, as something they had to overcome, thus making their success appear the more impressive.

Another aspect of childhood (referred to in the opposite variant of Category 40b) is found with considerable frequency in the reports of low-scoring subjects. It may be summarized as *orientation toward the adult and the espousal of internalized standards,* as manifested in reading a lot, an interest in school and teachers, and in achievement striving. This trend is especially typical of the group of low-scoring men, in which 16 interviewees give a picture of themselves as having been adult-oriented in childhood, as compared with only 1 high-scoring man who does so. In women the corresponding figures are 7 and 0.

This picture is substantiated in the direct study by the present author, referred to above (30), of children scoring low on a prejudice scale especially designed for them. Though such children show less submission to authority, they tend to be genuinely more oriented toward adult values, such as interest in work.

Examples from both low-scoring men and women follow:

M53: (Especially remarkable?) "I don't know. I don't think so. I was a pretty good student in school. Seemed to have a lot of friends. I don't remember any outstanding disappointments. (Worries as a child?) Oh, let's see, that's difficult. I don't know. I can't remember any recurring worries as a child. (What about little things?) Well, let me think. Shortly after my father's death, I worried about that for a while. Growing up without a father. . . . In high school I think I worried a lot about future occupation and how to earn a living."

M56: (What were you like as a child?) "Oh, very serious . . . read Rippants' 'History of the World' at nine. My grandfather, when I was nine or ten, gave me Washington Irving's 'Conquest of Granada,' which meant a great deal to me—gave me a sense of objectivity in history . . . he sometimes gave me temperance books."

F27: "I was reading Dickens and Thackeray when other children were on Brer Rabbit, and knew all about the symphonies and operas while they were on nursery rhymes."

Along the same line is a certain tendency on the part of the low-scoring subjects to report relative *isolation* in childhood, while high scorers refer to what may be defined as *gang-sociability* (Category 40c), including such aspects as popularity and the holding of offices in clubs and high school fraternities and sororities. No figures for this trend are given in Table 4(XI), but examples from records of low-scoring subjects describing shyness and relative isolation in childhood are given here:

M59: (What were you like as a child?) "Always shy and when I was around a large group it was quite a while before I would enter into the spirit of things."

F27: "I knew I was quiet because I was scared of everybody there. . . . I wanted to be liked and nobody liked me. So I just hurried home."

F75: "In a way we are all alike in our family—shy and afraid of people. We don't discuss it but I have noticed it in all of us, even my sister who doesn't act like it often.

My mother has always pushed us and wanted us to be different—go-getters—but she isn't. I was the worst—the sort who would cross the street rather than say hello to a friend. . . . I remember wishing my mother would leave me alone to do what I wanted. That would have been bad though. I guess, because I would have grown up a hermit. Even now, I prefer to curl up with a book or go for a walk by myself."

M49: "Well, when we were small, we spent all the time we possibly could out-of-doors, and when we came out here, we never associated with . . . never had any contact with other children outside of school time (worked, helping at home) . . . just played together at home. . . . Neither of us ever went out for any sports . . . ."

4. CONTRASTING PICTURE OF CHILDHOOD AND PRESENT

The last two categories to be discussed under attitude toward one's childhood help to support and to round out the impression gained so far. It was pointed out above that high-scoring subjects seem to use their childhood as a projection screen for traits now considered as undesirable. This should make for *discontinuity* between childhood and present self (Category 41). Actually, such is the case, significantly more often in the high scorers (at the 1 per cent level for men and at the 5 per cent level for women) than in the low scorers, the latter tending to show *continuity* between childhood and adult self. High scorers even may give the impression of an actual break by glorifying the present self and by finding fault with the past.

On the whole, finally, high scorers tend to make *little spontaneous comment* while the low scorers offer *considerable spontaneous comment* about their childhood (Category 46), the difference being significant at the 2 per cent level for both men and women. This is but one more among several manifestations of the greater intraceptiveness of the low scorers, and of their greater inclination to explain human behavior in psychological and social terms.

5. SUMMARY OF ATTITUDE TOWARD PRESENT SELF AND CHILDHOOD SELF

As in the evaluation of their parents and of the other sex, high scorers tend in their self-evaluation to stress the positive and desirable aspects; or at least this is so on the surface level. They are prone to point to their "will power" and determination in overcoming the handicaps and vicissitudes of life. Energy, decisiveness, aggressiveness in competition tend to be particularly prominent in the ego-ideal of high-scoring men.

However, there is evidence that the repeated assertions of independence are a defense against strong feelings of dependence, passivity, helplessness, and sometimes even self-contempt. These feelings are but rarely recognized or accepted as such without making an attempt at self-justification.

What is not acceptable to the ego tends in the further course of events to become externalized, thus rendering the ego narrow and constricted. In further consequence, prejudiced subjects tend to regard themselves as conventional, not different, and therefore "all right," and their descriptions of themselves have a definitely moralistic tone. Deviations from the commonly accepted pattern of conduct, if admitted at all, are regarded as a "break-through" of tendencies which are either beyond explanation or which are explained away by external factors and incidents over which the subject could not possibly have had control. Judicious explanations of the socio-psychological kind are avoided in this type of approach to the self. This makes for a comparative lack of experienced continuity between childhood self and present self. In line with this, high scorers are generally somewhat reluctant to make spontaneous reference to their childhood, thus trying further to disclaim for themselves and for their parents the responsibility for the outcome.

Unprejudiced individuals, on the other hand, seem to be on better terms with themselves, due perhaps to the fact that they have been more loved and accepted by their parents. Thus they are more ready to admit falling short of their ideals and of the roles they are expected to play by our culture. Impulses and tendencies which seem less desirable are nonetheless accepted as a part of the self, making for a richer, more complex, and more intraceptive content of the ego. Thus, as was pointed out in the first section of this chapter, low-scoring men prove themselves more able to afford frank admission of passivity and weakness without having to resort—to the same degree as high-scoring men may have to—to the use of rigid and counterphobic defenses against these feelings. In accordance with this, there is comparatively frequent evidence of open admission of conflict about the feminine role in low-scoring women, as well as of their genuine fondness of men.

Furthermore, low scorers tend to derive their security from recourse to their personal identity in addition to such external factors as group membership or property. Hence they tend to present themselves in their interviews as individualized and unconventional. Instead of trying to live up to conventionally defined rules and values, they tend to strive toward real achievement, toward understanding and affiliation, and toward the realization of humanitarian and liberal values such as the improvement of social relations or self-improvement. They seem to be interested in explanations of their present self in terms of their entire development. They make considerable spontaneous reference to their childhood. Their descriptions of themselves as children are often far from the picture of what would be generally called a well adjusted child. They report having been withdrawn, shy, and self-conscious; oriented toward work, reading, and an adult set of values. These reports are in accordance with direct findings, in an independent study, on the personality of extremely unprejudiced children.

As adults, low scorers often continue to manifest open anxieties and feelings of depression, due perhaps at least in part to their greater capacity of facing insecurity and conflict. Their greater readiness to introspect may be considered as an attempt to master these problems and to achieve a dependable and flexible form of adjustment. Sometimes it appears that they may succeed; in other cases it seems that there is but a morbid dwelling on psychological topics.

CHAPTER XII

DYNAMIC AND COGNITIVE PERSONALITY ORGANI-
ZATION AS SEEN THROUGH THE INTERVIEWS

Else Frenkel-Brunswik

A. DYNAMIC CHARACTER STRUCTURE

1. DEFINITION OF RATING CATEGORIES AND QUANTITATIVE RESULTS

Throughout the preceding discussion of interview material repeated reference was made to a variety of so-called defense mechanisms. Among them were repression of sex and aggression, overemphasis on cleanliness, various forms of defense against one's own passivity, and the like. Again and again it became evident that the difference between the ethnocentric and the non-ethnocentric extremes hinges more on the rejection vs. the acceptance of such depth factors as homosexuality, or aggression, or passivity, or anality than it does on the mere presence or absence of one or another of these tendencies. In other words, it was not primarily the relative strength of such tendencies that seemed to matter, but rather the way in which these tendencies were handled in the motivational dynamics of the subject in question. In the framework of these dynamics, defense mechanisms are the instruments of rejection of those tendencies which the subject is not ready to face and to incorporate.

The categories of the Interview Scoring Manual discussed in the present chapter are centered about such defense mechanisms, per se, along with other dynamic patterns fulfilling a related function. Thus, some of these categories cut across a variety of aspects investigated so far, and offer the possibility of providing synopses of previous observations. By the use of these categories direct support could be found for many assumptions made previously on the basis of more scattered or indirect evidence.

The list of categories related to dynamic character structure is as follows:

INTERVIEW SCORING MANUAL: DYNAMIC CHARACTER STRUCTURE

(to Table 1(XII))

PRESUMABLY "HIGH" VARIANTS	PRESUMABLY "LOW" VARIANTS
47. *Counter - cathectic rejection of "erotic" orality* (of zone-sensuality and/or its sublimations, i.e., of verbal-emotional-artistic expressiveness)	47. *Positive expressions of "erotic" orality* (of zone-sensuality, e.g., food cathexis, oral perversions, and/or sublimations, i.e., verbal-emotional-artistic expressiveness-expansiveness)
48. *Rigid-moralistic-anal reaction-formations* as ends-in-themselves; overemphasis on, and preoccupations with, totalitarian-moralistic (positive and negative) typologizing (e.g., two kinds of people, "clean" and "dirty"); emphasis on money and property	48. *Anal reaction-formations functional and nonmoralistic.* Means-end relationship retained; or anal sublimations; or relative absence of anal reaction-formations
49. *Diffuse, ego-alien dependence.* Escapism, dodging responsibility; underlying ego-alien passivity; helplessness-weakness (expressed openly in men only when overwhelmed or victimized—e.g. "foxhole religion"—with all-or-none character). Characterized by affective poverty and exchangeability of object	49. *Love-oriented succorance-nurturance,* acceptance of dependency and affect, specificity of object cathexis

50. *Aggression:*

a. *Diffuse, impersonalized;* sometimes replaced by ingratiation	a. *Focal, personal*
b. *Moralistic-authoritarian.* Totalitarian; punitive; often persecutory (pogrom frame of mind)	b. (1) *Principled - intellectualized*
	(2) *Love-oriented.* Especially in response to rejection by a cathected object
c. *Destructive-explosive.* Tending toward all-or-none, and toward physical expression	c. *Relatively mild, day-to-day.* Tending toward regular release, and toward verbal expression

51. *Ambivalence:*

a. *Ego-alien*	a. (1) *Sometimes admitted openly;* ego-accepted
	(2) *Conscious inhibition of affect*
b. *Solved by dichotomies and displacement*	b. *Expressed sometimes openly toward original objects* or

"reality representatives" of original objects (e.g. authority; mother figures)

52. Identification:

a. *Inverted Oedipal attachment*	a. *Normal Oedipal attachment*
b. *Underlying ego-alien identification with opposite sex parent's role.* Emphasis on dominance-submission conflicts	b. *Genuine, ego-integrated identification with either or both parents*
c/M. *Pseudo-masculinity*	c. *Ego-integrated masculinity and/or femininity.* Emphasis is on character traits and internalized values
c/W. *Pseudo-femininity*	

53. *Externalized superego, "social anxiety"; or rigid superego,* unconscious guilt

53. *Internalized superego,* sometimes severe and irrational; conscious guilt

54. *Rejection and countercathexis of ego-alien impulses,* especially of sex, of aggression against parents and authorities, and of feelings of weakness and passivity

54. *Acceptance and sublimation of id,* often with conscious conflict between competing impulses; sometimes conscious inhibition of id

55. *Ego weak;* often skillful in attaining success and determined in overt action; sometimes combined with opportunistic over-realism

55. *Ego moderate strength, or strong.* Criteria: sustained effort, ability to postpone pleasure for sake of internalized values; ability to assume responsibility; emotional maturity, etc. Sometimes drifting into impractical pursuits

Further mechanisms

56a. *Distortion of "reality"*	56a. *Realistic-objective* re world generally
56b. *Authoritarian moralism*	56b. *Intellectualization,* sometimes of the type of philosophical rationalization rather than of intellectual penetration
56c. *Denial of "negative things" in self, "official optimism"*	56c. *Open psychological conflict* concerning own adequacy, maturity, or the violation of liberal values, etc.
56d. *Concern with physical symptoms*	
56e. *Concern with physical appearance*	
56f. *Hysterical conversion symptoms* (especially in men)	

The quantitative results are shown, in the usual manner, in Table 1 (XII).

2. ORALITY AND ANALITY

We turn first to the so-called oral and anal trends, especially their acceptance vs. rejection whenever this occurs in the two groups scoring extremely high or low on the overt Ethnocentrism scale. As in the preceding discussion, the terms "anality" and "orality" do not refer here to the earlier psychogenetic stages but rather to special character syndromes found in the adult personality; these latter have been described, likewise by psychoanalysis, in terms of present symptoms assumed to be connected with their respective counterparts in childhood.

It was first expected that in line with the general tendency toward repression, high-scoring subjects would tend to defend themselves against both the direct oral urge, e.g., indulgence in food, drinking, smoking, etc., as well as against tendencies assumed to be related to this urge—indulgence in talking, artistic interests, etc. The low scorers, on the other hand, were expected to show more acceptance of and more liking for manifestations assumed to be directly or indirectly related to orality. On this basis, *orality* was incorporated in the Interview Scoring Manual in the form defined by Category 47.

Although there actually is within our material a trend in the expected direction, especially for women (see Table 1(XII)), it is far from being statistically significant. This may well be due to the presence of an "oral demandingness" in the high scorers as manifested, for example, in a dependence on getting "things," and a dependence on authorities and supernatural forces as discussed above. These specific manifestations were not fully anticipated at the time the definitions of the category were laid down, although they were given proper consideration throughout by the two raters, both being clinically trained and psychoanalytically oriented.

The original hypothesis proved most valid where rejection of drinking and smoking on the part of the typical high scorer was concerned, and this may well be seen as part of a general conventionalism.

As was expected, indulgence in what may be called direct orality is more often found in the low scorers. An illustration may be found in the following record:

F62: "For a while I wanted to be an actress but I love to eat and, strangely enough, the actresses seem not to eat. Because of not being able to reduce and because of the fact that the job of a teacher is more secure, I decided to become a teacher."

The various behavior forms assumed to be indirectly derived from orality do not show any pronounced differences, however. More detailed distinctions of the various levels and kinds of direct and devious manifestations of orality may well reveal striking differences between the ethnically prejudiced and unprejudiced.

In contrast to orality, the rejection vs. acceptance of tendencies customarily designated as *anal syndrome* (Category 48) proved significantly differentiating (at the 1 per cent level) for both men and women interviewees.

TABLE 1 (XII)

INTERVIEW RATINGS ON DYNAMIC CHARACTER STRUCTURE

FOR 80 SUBJECTS SCORING EXTREMELY "HIGH" OR "LOW" ON THE ETHNIC PREJUDICE QUESTIONNAIRE SCALE

Interview rating categories (abbreviated from Manual)	Sex	Number of "High"(H) and "Low"(L) ratings received by				Sums of instances		Level of statistical significance reached or surpassed (percentage)
		20 men and 25 women "high scorers" H	L	20 men and 15 women "low scorers" H	L	"positive"	"negative"	
47. Rejection(H) vs. positive expression(L) of "erotic" orality	Men	5	7	2	7	12	9	1
	Women	8	3	2	5	13	5	1
48. Anal reaction-formations rigid-moralistic (H) vs. functional and nonmoralistic(L)	Men	12	1	3	13	25	4	1
	Women	17	2	1	7	24	3	1
49. Diffuse, ego-alien(H) vs. love-oriented(L) dependence	Men	17	3	2	14	31	5	1
	Women	17	2	1	7	24	3	1
50. Aggression:								
a. Diffuse, depersonalized(H) vs. focal, personalized(L)	Men	17	2	2	13	30	4	1
	Women	13	3	0	11	24	3	1
b. Moralistic-authoritarian(H) vs. principled-intellectualized or love-oriented(L)	Men	15	2	2	12	27	4	1
	Women	16	1	2	10	26	3	1
c. Destructive-explosive(H) vs. relatively mild(L)	Men	9	2	2	10	19	4	5
	Women	6	3	3	9	15	6	
51. Ambivalence:								
a. Ego-alien(H) vs. sometimes admitted openly(L)	Men	15	2	4	12	27	6	1
	Women	16	4	2	9	25	6	1
b. Solved by dichotomies and displacement(H) vs. expressed openly toward original object(L)	Men	14	2	5	8	22	7	2
	Women	9	3	2	9	18	5	5

52. Oedipus complex:								
a. Inverted(H) vs. normal(L)	Men	6	4	3	12	18	7	
	Women	9	11	3	8	17	14	
b. Ego-alien identification with opposite sex parent's role (H) vs. ego-integrated identification with either or both parent(L)	Men	12	1	2	13	25	3	1
	Women	15	1	2	11	26	3	1
cM. Pseudo masculinity(H) vs. ego-integrated masculinity or "feminity"(L)	Men	15	1	2	10	25	3	1
cW. Pseudo femininity(H) vs. ego-integrated femininity or "masculinity"(L)	Women	4	5	2	11	15	7	
53. Externalized(H) vs. internalized superego(L)	Men	16	3	2	14	30	5	1
	Women	15	5	1	12	27	6	1
54. Countercathexis of ego-alien id(H) vs. acceptance and sublimation of id(L)	Men	14	1	5	10	24	6	1
	Women	21	1	4	7	28	5	1
55. Ego weak(H) vs. ego medium strength or strong(L)	Men	14	5	7	11	25	12	5
	Women	12	9	3	11	23	12	5
56a. Distortion of reality(H) vs. realistic-objective(L)	Men	8	3	4	10	18	7	
	Women	8	4	3	10	18	7	5
b. Authoritarian moralism(H) vs. intellectualization(L)	Men	14	3	3	12	26	6	1
	Women	16	1	3	9	25	4	1
c. Denial of negative things in self(H) vs. open psychological conflict(L)	Men	17	1	2	12	29	3	1
	Women	12	3	1	9	21	4	1
d. Concern with physical symptoms(H)	Men	7		3		7	3	
	Women	6		0		6	0	
e. Concern with physical appearance(H)	Men	3		5		3	5	
	Women	8		1		8	1	
f. Hysterical conversions(H)	Men	3		2		3	2	
	Women	7		3		7	3	

Thus it is that high-scoring subjects tend toward rigid-moralistic patterns of behavior, which are related in appearance to responses technically termed anal reaction-formations, and tend to conceive of them as ends-in-themselves; that they show overemphasis upon, and preoccupation with, such issues as money, neatness, "good clean life and hard work," etc.; and that they are given to totalitarian-moralistic typologizing (e.g., two kinds of people— "clean" and "dirty"), this typologizing being either positive or negative. These preoccupations may be considered as an outcome of a certain type of child training; thus, sociopsychological factors are brought into the picture. The affinity of these dynamic tendencies to the ideological issues in question seems evident on the basis of the above description.

Examples of this complex of attitudes in the records of high-scoring subjects are:

M41: "Lots of advantages . . . pensions. Put in 30 years and you retire. Good salary. Always something to see and learn in the army. Going different places. It's a good life in general. A clean life. . . . It makes a man of you. . . . (Main differences between Christians and others?) The Christian tries to live a Christian life and others go out and rob and steal, drink, carouse around, do a little of everything. . . . (What do you find most offensive in others?) Well, some people are more attractive than others. Some people have no attraction. (Interests, hobbies?) Well, I have no hobbies. I like fishing. I like hunting."

M51: (What is the core of your religious beliefs?) "No, I can't elaborate on that. I did answer that. That right thinking and right living. . . ."

F66: "Mother is a nurse, and I know the profession. I don't like dirty work. I don't like sick people. (About school.) They . . . wore dirty old plaid shirts."

F31: "I can't see a girl working in jeans and around grease and putting themselves on the same level as men."

F38: (What people have you disliked?) "I remember a man when I was 18 years old. I didn't like him because he was dirty and sloppy."

F78: She looks for similar interests, someone who enjoys the same things. "Someone I wouldn't have to make excuses for—someone well brought up, nice appearance, dressed neatly. I'm a very neat person."

Some of these findings corroborate earlier results by Krout and Stagner (65). They found that conservatives show more tendency to digestive disorders, more and an almost compulsive interest in washing and personal cleanliness.

Low scorers, on the other hand, tend toward anal reaction-formations which may be considered functional rather than moralistic, with the proper perspective upon their character as means to an end retained (Category 48, continued). More specifically, the more "central" attitude involved finds its expression on the functional level in a constructive inclination toward such frames of mind as planning, e.g., in scientific work; or else there is an absence of retentiveness altogether, as shown by a rather carefree, relaxed attitude. Examples of this latter subvariety from the records of low-scoring subjects are:

M42: "It may sound funny, but I don't particularly care to work really. . . . I like the independence of that kind of work. . . . I have the ability in such a job to simply go fishing on Saturdays or other days if I don't feel like working." Subject indicates that doing so was not a particularly rare occurrence with him. . . . "And I'm not as economical as my mother. I take after my dad probably in that respect more. In having a good time, I'm more like him. When I start out to have a good time, money doesn't matter. . . ."

M55: "I am inclined to be not very careful about spending money myself . . . my wife says so. . . . If I see something I like, I am inclined to buy it. . . . (About older sister:) However, a delightful person to live with. . . ."

M56: (Importance of money to father?) "Not important; never any money-grubbers in my family. My brother is a doctor who went to Ethiopia to help out as a doctor."

3. DEPENDENCE

Another "central" attitude which is not accepted and faced as such by the high-scoring subjects is "dependence." We made reference to this tendency in discussing the subjects' attitude toward their family, toward people, and toward themselves. Here we deal with dependence as a generalized trait in its various meanings and the ways in which it is handled by the subject. In Category 49, a *diffuse and ego-alien dependence* as manifested by escapism or the dodging of responsibility, a general underlying passivity, helplessness and weakness (in men expressed openly only when they are overwhelmed or victimized, as exemplified by "foxhole religion" and other all-or-none responses), accompanied by affective poverty, is contrasted with what has for the sake of brevity been labeled *love-oriented succorance-nurturance.* The first-named alternative is found significantly more often in high scorers (the difference being at the 1 per cent level of confidence) both in the case of men and women interviewees. Since the two patterns of dependence described have been discussed at length in previous chapters, it may suffice here briefly to remind the reader of the basic difference between affectionate love dependence and self-seeking dependence that is barren of affect.

The dependence on support in high-scoring subjects is furthermore clearly evident in their particular type of attitude toward religion. It is primarily when in need that they turn to the Bible; and it is support in the face of need rather than a system of ethics that they seek in religion. Frequently they become religious whenever "dependence on people" conflicts with suspicion, leading to isolation. Examples of this self-centered attitude toward religion from the records of high-scoring subjects are:

M13: (Under what conditions might you turn to religion?) "Yes, under some conditions I might. I have had a lot of sickness, stomach trouble ever since I was 12. I was in the hospital once for three months. During those periods, I like to turn to the Bible. I like the history and sayings of Christ, principally. . . . (What about your conception of God?) Well, I have none especially. The closest conception I got was when I was in the service, that is, God as strictly man, greater than any on this earth, one that would treat us as a father would his son. I don't think God is terrible in His justice."

M58: "Well, I'm not much on praying, myself, but instinctively . . . when a person needs something, when nothing else will help, the natural thing to do is turn to the Lord for help—whether prayers are answered, I dont know . . . but I believe prayers will be answered to those few who live and believe in religion, but to a person just to pray, no!"

F38: "Everyone should have a definite belief in a deity, instilled in childhood. Something to lean against, if you need it, for instance in case of a death in the family."

4. AGGRESSION

In considering the relationship of central dynamic tendencies to ethnic prejudice, the problem of "aggression" obviously calls for special attention. Indeed, prejudice seems to be but one of a number of manifestations of aggression. Thus a more detailed analysis of the degree and type of aggression found in the high scorer as compared with the low scorer seems appropriate. The subsequent distinctions of various aspects of aggression show a certain amount of overlapping. One of the foremost distinctions concerns whether aggression is an expression of a general and diffuse rage, with a tendency to be suppressed and to break through in an uncontrolled way, or whether there is a more specific reason for aggression, well integrated with the subject's ego, such as the violation of a principle or loss of love, in which case the expression of aggression is apt to be more specific and more channeled. A further distinction is as to whether the aggression tends to become displaced onto someone who is socially weaker or tends to be directed toward the actual source of frustration, even if this source should be found to be connected with those who are authoritative and powerful.

In accordance with these considerations, *three aspects of aggression* have been distinguished in the Scoring Manual for the interviews. In each case, the first of the two alternatives to be mentioned was actually found predominantly in the high scorers, the second predominantly in the low scorers, with the difference highly significant for the first two aspects, Categories 50a and 50b, in both men and women.

In particular, Category 50a distinguishes diffuse forms of aggression that are not integrated and have no personalized goal from an aggression that is both "focal" and personal. Reports about blind rage, temper tantrums, and bad temper in general, often found in the records of high-scoring subjects, are pertinent to the first of these two alternatives. The expression of aggression in low scorers shows, by contrast, greater awareness of the cause of aggression which thus tends to become more specific, and to be directed against a certain person or against violation of a general principle. At the same time there seems to be more open conflict and guilt over expressions or feelings of aggression in the low scorers.

Furthermore, aggression may be, on the one hand, moralistic-authoritarian, or totalitarian, or primitive, or even persecutory as in a pogrom frame-of-mind; or it may be, on the other hand, principled and intellectualized, or else love-oriented, especially in response to rejection by a sought-after ("cathexed") object (Category 50b). The clearest expressions of these forms of aggression can be found in those passages of the interviews which deal with social and political issues, i.e., those excluded in order to make "blind" scoring of the interviews possible. In addition to these passages, however, there are throughout the interviews, especially those of the high scorers, aggressive references to people who are considered as socially inferior, uneducated, not religious, etc. It is to such references that this subcategory applies. Expressions of generalized tolerance, on the other hand, can be found in many of the records of low scorers.

The distinction between an aggression that is destructive and explosive, tends toward the all-or-none and toward physical expression, and an aggression that is relatively mild, has a day-to-day character and tends toward regular release and toward verbal expression, is incorporated in Category 50c. There is less clear-cut statistical significance for this subcategory, but the trend in the expected direction is nonetheless present.

Statements about differences in the kind of aggression displayed do not imply that low scorers tend on the whole to have successfully overcome the vicissitudes inherent in this crucial aspect of human behavior. It may well be that while they succeed more often than do high scorers in avoiding manifestations of aggression which are destructive of others, they do so at the price of increased self-destruction.

5. AMBIVALENCE

The problem of ambivalence is related to that of aggression. In discussing attitudes toward parents and sex, the comparative inability of high-scoring subjects to verbalize aggression and thus to face ambivalence was pointed out in detail. It was also intimated that it may be precisely the inability to face ambivalence toward the powerful which leads to socially dangerous forms of displacement of aggression. The following *two aspects of ambivalence* seemed especially important and are thus covered in the Scoring Manual:

Category 51a deals with what may be called the degree of awareness of ambivalence. In the typical high-scoring subject ambivalence is not being faced but rather is rendered ego-alien, whereas it is more often openly admitted in the low scorers. The difference is quite significant in both sexes.

Category 51b deals with the mechanisms which help to circumvent ambivalence or to keep it on an unconscious level. The most outstanding of these mechanisms consist in a thinking in terms of dichotomies, i.e., in terms of pairs of diametrical opposites, and in an inclination toward displacement. Thus, glorification of the ingroup and rejection of the outgroup, familiar from the sphere of social and political beliefs, can be found as a general trend in some of our clinical data, predominantly in those relating to high scorers. Low scorers, on the other hand, tend toward openly expressing their ambivalence toward the original objects, or toward representatives of these objects in reality (e.g., toward authority, or toward mother figures, respectively.) The ability and the readiness to admit and to express aggression where it originates, instead of projecting and displacing it, provides one of the most important cornerstones of democracy, as was pointed out in parts of the previous discussion on the attitude toward the parents (Chapter X). Conscious aggression is apt to be less intensive than repressed aggression.

Quotations of records revealing underlying ambivalence in high scorers were given in one of the preceding chapters. We may repeat here only what seems a rather typical description of the mother, by one of our high-scoring woman interviewees. "Mother was, of course, a very wonderful person. She was very nervous. Irritable only when overdoing." There are, furthermore, indications in the records of high-scoring subjects of ambivalence toward members of professional groups who may be considered as parent substitutes, e.g., toward the priest, the doctor, the teacher, etc. To be sure, low-scoring subjects manifest a great deal of criticism toward such authoritative figures, but it is usually expressed more directly, and is characterized by a lesser degree of that type of anxiety which is not openly faced or admitted.

6. IDENTIFICATION

One of the aims of the present chapter is to take up topics, discussed in previous sections, under the aspects of personality dynamics as assumed by the school of psychoanalysis. In probing into what is called the "Oedipal" situation of the subjects and their "identifications" in general, we are seriously handicapped by the insufficiency of the data from which inferences about the psychogenetic picture could be made. It should be especially acknowledged and kept in mind therefore that in describing identifications in any particular subject we may well be wrong as to the ultimate interpretation. But since we are focusing on group trends, a certain neutralization of these sources of error is likely to be achieved.

The problems approached here in connection with the Oedipal situation coincide with those dealt with primarily in psychoanalysis: (1) the problem of cathexis, that is, of the choice of the parental love object, and (2) the problem of identification with one or the other parent. In Category 52a, the question was whether there is an "inverted" or a "normal" Oedipal situation, i.e., whether the subject has as his or her primary love object the parent of the same or of the opposite sex. Judgment in this respect involves a great deal of inference on the part of the rater. The hypothesis underlying the adoption of this category was that low-scoring subjects will reveal evidence of the normal trend of having more cathexis on the parent of the opposite sex. This would be in line with his more clear-cut heterosexual attitude as referred to in one of the previous chapters.

Due perhaps to the insufficient material on this score, or to the fact that the crucial difference has to be sought in the way of handling—rather than in the mere presence or absence—of the normal resolution of the Oedipal situation, this anticipated difference did not turn out to be statistically significant. For our women interviewees the difference is altogether negligible. For men, however, it may well reach significance in a somewhat larger sample, since 12 of our extreme low scorers and only 4 of the extreme high scorers report greater attachment to the mother, and since there are totals of 18 "positive" as against only 7 "negative" instances on the category as a whole. Again it must be emphasized that while such results may be interesting as a group trend, in any individual case the relationship to the parents may turn out to be very different, on a deeper level, from what it appears to be on the surface or in overt verbalization. This fact notwithstanding, much in the personality structure of the typical unprejudiced man induces us to believe that his attachment to the mother was indeed close and that it is a source of his favorable attitude toward women and his courage in opposing the father and authorities in general.

The closeness between mother and son is described in the following excerpt from the interview of one of the low-scoring men:

M55: (Which parent closer to?) "Closer to my mother quite a bit, confided more than with father, but mostly just about casual things. I think she made too much of me; told me how bright I was, etc., but I was just better adjusted (than older sister). I think they were awfully thoughtless and cruel to her."

While preference for the parent of the opposite sex does not differentiate significantly between high and low scorers, there is a significant difference with respect to acceptance of, or defense against, identification with the parent of the opposite sex or with the "weaker" parent (femininity in men and masculinity in women). The respective category, 52b, contrasts an underlying *ego-alien identification with the role of the parent of the opposite sex* (emphasizing the dominance-submission conflict) with a genuine ego-integrated identification with either parent or with both parents. The difference, significant at the 1 per cent level, indicates that high-scoring men tend to repress their "femininity," high-scoring women their "masculinity." The following examples show how little resistance, on the other hand, low-scoring men seem to have to discussing their similarities with their mothers and to showing their partial identifications with them:

M48: (Parents' feelings?) "Of course, my mother I imagine thinks it's a pretty good idea. My family have always had (artistic talents). Mother married a second time—stepfather would be against it. . . . (How do you take after your mother?) Well, very peculiar thing. I never thought mother was too bright or intellectual and I'm not either."

M59: (Similarities to mother?) "Well, both of us are a little sensitive in temperament, kind of quiet. I think we both like a certain amount of solitude. I used to like to take her out to dinner, to the theater quite often."

M42: (Which parent did you take after most?) "Well, I dont know.... I suppose I take after my mother's side of the family. I have a lot of traits like her father and brother ... but she, herself, is more like her mother ... although I have a lot of characteristics of my father. I have quick temper like he does."

Alongside the repression of feminine trends, high-scoring men tend to display what may be called "pseudo-masculinity" whereas low-scoring men tend to develop more ego-integrated masculinity and an acceptance of feminine tendencies in themselves, the emphasis being on character traits and internalized values rather than on a display of masculinity. The difference within this category, 52c.M, is significant at the 1 per cent level. For women, the corresponding difference does not reach statistical significance although there is a trend in the expected direction.

7. SUPEREGO

It seems to be the lack of genuine identification with, and the fear of, the parents which leads in the high scorers to an *externalization of the superego,* with the punishing and rewarding authority seen as being outside rather than inside of oneself. By contrast, low scorers tend toward an *internalized conscience;* their behavior is primarily oriented toward genuine, intrinsic values and standards rather than toward external authorities (Category 53). Rated directly and as such, this difference turns out in a statistically highly satisfactory manner, thus supporting the inferences made so far on the more specific aspects of this basic distinction.

Examples of the leaning on external authorities in the records of high-scoring men are:

M58: "If you don't harm anybody else, it's all right.... If you break a man-made law, it's OK if you don't harm someone else—the law is made to protect people.... If you harm yourself then also it could be wrong.... (Example?) Well, drinking ... if in your own home, nobody hurt and perfectly all right.... Law is broken every day in this respect. Adultery, as long as never found out, is OK—if found out, then it's wrong. Since some of the most respected people do it, it must be all right."

M41: (Views?) "Well, I believe a person should believe in religion.... Helps to protect society. (Q) A person that believes in religion, they're not apt to ... or pull off any kind of crime."

M51: "It's mostly a matter of disciplining yourself.... I never was so disgusted in my life(i.e., with Christian Science).... (What kind of things do you pray about?) I don't.... I ask whatever power there is to guide me—whether that power is divine mind or mortal mind—and I know that I'll be guided rightly."

M57: "Well, I believe ... there must be a power over us.... Always know if a man does something wrong, sooner or later he'll get punished for it, so there must be some power to punish us...."

The orientation toward inner standards can be seen in the following records of low scorers:

M42: (Views?) "Well, I think it's silly. (Laughs) Not silly, I wouldn't say that either. . . . I think they're ignorant people . . . have to be scared into the right kind of living . . . by fear of Hell . . . but I think a man can have his own religion without ever seeing a church . . . the Golden Rule . . . I think people feel that in themselves, but they're not changed by churches, etc. . . . I think religion, as the churches teach it, (is useless)."

M53: "Impulses suggest that you've given it some thought . . . and if you've given it some thought, you're going to control it, if you have any sense at all. . . . I don't think I have any desires that I have any difficulty in controlling."

F75: "About sex—it wasn't discussed. I don't know how we did find out. From friends I guess before we went into training and really learned. I think people should have standards within which they can give themselves leeway. If you don't have for yourself there is nothing to guide you. But it's just as bad to have them so rigid you can't break with them when you feel it is all right for yourself to do so."

The crucial difference between externalization and internalization of moral values has been discussed repeatedly and in various contexts throughout this volume. It may suffice to recall here the self-negating, fearful submission to the parents on the part of the ethnocentric subjects as described in Chapter X. The type of discipline used seems to prevent a genuine incorporation and assimilation of social values. The child had to renounce instinctual and other pleasures for an exchange of love which was given him only sparingly, inconsistently, and conditionally. Since the moral requirements must have appeared to the child overwhelming and unintelligible and the reward small, submission to them had to be reinforced by fear of, and pressure from, external agencies. This need for permanent reinforcement persisted, to become a constant state of affairs in the adult.

According to psychoanalytic theory, the development of ethical principles normally proceeds from outside values, as first represented by standards upheld by adults, to an internalization of these values. High scorers, due apparently to lack of genuine identification with the parents, do not succeed in making the important developmental step from mere "social anxiety" to real conscience. Fear of punishment by external authorities rather than self-chosen and ego-assimilated principles continue to be the primary determinant of their behavior. At the same time there is resentment against these authorities which are mainly experienced as restricting and punishing. Readiness to exchange these authorities mainly in the direction of a better bargain is one of the consequences of these attitudes. The preferred authority is the one who promises most in terms of material goods and backing to some release from restrictions which seem intolerable. Such persons have a longing to overthrow the troublesome moral restraints and to live fully according to the pleasure principle. The repressed, unsublimated, and unmodified tendencies are ready to break through and to flood the tenuously maintained social superstructure.

In contrast to the psychopath, the typical high scorer remains dependent on the blessing given by external authority. This makes for his accessibility to being manipulated by social forces, primarily those which give license for aggression, although he always stays potentially within reach of the more positively productive influences also, if they are powerful.

The internalization of the superego by the typical low scorer makes for more judicious and responsible citizenship in private and in public life. A certain proportion of the low scorers, however, tend to develop a harsh and irrational superego, with an effect not altogether dissimilar from the punitiveness and moral indignation frequent in high scorers, the difference being that the resulting guilt-feelings tend to be more conscious in the low scorers. Only very few of our subjects—all of them low scorers—seem to have succeeded in avoiding the "impasse" between an unduly severe super-ego, on the one hand, and an underdeveloped one, on the other.

Nonacceptance and repression of id-tendencies which have been rendered ego-alien, as found significantly more often in high-scoring subjects (Category 54), may be assumed to be the result of fearful submission to external authority. Under such conditions sex and aggression, not being integrated with the rest of the personality, continue to lead an independent existence. Although repressed, they tend to "break through" occasionally in an uncontrolled way.

Low scorers, on the other hand, tend significantly more often toward accepting and sublimating their id-tendencies (Category 54, continued). A greater ability for integrating and expressing aggression, for a successful fusion of sex and affection, for "love" in general, and for creative work seem to be among the many consequences of a not-too-drastic repression of instinctual tendencies as discussed before in this volume. Examples were given primarily in the section dealing with the attitude toward sex.

8. STRENGTH OF THE EGO

Since low scorers often tend toward a more successful integration of the various aspects of their personality, they tend to remain less immature and less infantile. They thus turn out to have more capacity for sustained effort, more ability to postpone pleasure for the sake of internalized values, more ability to assume responsibility, and more emotional maturity. The absence vs. presence of any or all of these characteristics may be summarized as a *"weak" vs. a "strong" ego.* Since it was not expected that low scorers would tend to exhibit superlative ego strength, Category 55 contrasts a weak ego with an ego of either moderate or great strength. As anticipated, the latter alternatives were found predominantly in low scorers, the first predominantly in high scorers, the differences between the two groups reaching the 5 per cent level of significance in both men and women. The fact that low scorers manifest relative strength of the rational tendencies as compared with the irrational may well be due to their attempt to master and sublimate rather than to escape the unconscious. Thus the low scorers' adaptation to reality is more flexible in spite of the more open conflict and anxiety which accompanies the greater awareness of existing problems.

This greater awareness, integration and, therefore, control of impulses is exemplified by the following record, quoted above, of a low-scoring subject:

M53: Subject questions the meaning of desires and impulses. "Impulses suggest that you've given it some thought . . . and if you've given it some thought, you're going to control it, if you have any sense at all. . . . I dont think I have any desires that I have any difficulty in controlling."

On the other hand, instinctual impulses are experienced as something overpowering and evil by the typical high-scoring subject. Repression of certain deeper tendencies on the part of the typical high scorer does not lessen their potential force. On the contrary, these frequently tend to find "projective" and other devious outlets. Excessive repression and counter-cathexis of unacceptable impulses requires inordinate expenditures of energy. This in turn contributes to the weakening of the ego, increasing the danger of a break-through of some of the repressed tendencies.

In spite of these over-all results, a certain type of ego-strength, that connected with the tenacious pursuit of success, is a frequent characteristic of the high scorer. On the other hand, low scorers sometimes dissipate their energies in internal conflicts or daydreaming. The Interview Scoring Manual concentrates on certain aspects of ego-strength; more detailed consideration of such further aspects as energy and determination in overt action may yield a somewhat different picture or even reveal a trend in the opposite direction than that noted in the preceding paragraphs (see also Chapter XI).

9. DISTORTION OF REALITY

One of the outlets for repressed instinctual tendencies is *distortion of outside reality*, as contrasted with a realistic and objective evaluation of reality (Category 56a). The difference between high- and low-scoring interviewees along this dimension is significant at the 5 per cent level for women, and there is a numerically similar trend—18 positive as against 7 negative instances —for men. (This, however, misses statistical significance due to the somewhat different proportion of interviewees in the two extreme groups as shown in the top portion of Table 1(XII)). In those parts of the interview that deal with political and social issues—omitted from the records as handed to the raters—this difference is more striking. It is there that we see most clearly the distortion of social reality, a reality which seems to serve primarily as a projection screen for repressed needs whenever repression transcends certain limits.

Less drastic but still apparent is the distortion manifested in the high scorers' evaluation of other people and of themselves. There also seems to be a paradoxical connection between distortion of reality and overrealism in the high scorer: The distortion in the conception of other people is built into the framework of an anxiety-ridden, overrealistic idea of a bitter, competitive struggle.

Awareness of the difficulties in judging distortion of reality of such controversial issues as the evaluation of social groups and social events led the author of this chapter to a series of experiments in children on perception and related cognitive problems which were to test distortion on a more neutral ground. Preliminary results indicate that there is more distortion of memory material and of perceptual stimuli in ethnically prejudiced than there is in ethnically unprejudiced children (see 37 and forthcoming reports).

Another expression of repression, this time primarily of sex and aggression, is *authoritarian moralism* (Category 56b). By this is meant a moral indignation about manifestations of what is considered improper behavior especially when it occurs in persons considered socially inferior. This mechanism gives opportunity both for the release of aggression toward someone who cannot very well retaliate, and for projecting repressed sexual needs onto an "alien" group. Since this mechanism, of which ethnic prejudice is but a part, is widespread and socially accepted, a kind of pseudoreality is thus constructed which helps to keep the individual unaware of his distortions.

The fact that the difference between high scorers and low scorers with respect to an authoritarian moralism is statistically highly significant is of course not to be construed as indicating that low scorers tend to have a fully integrated personality without undue repressions. In the preceding chapters the repressions and conflicts characteristic of the low scorers have been pointed out in some detail. But instead of crudely projecting these tendencies onto outgroups, low scorers seem to tend toward what may be called *intellectualization* (not necessarily intellectual penetration) of their conflicts (Category 56b, continued). That is to say, they make a serious attempt at understanding what is going on in themselves by thinking about it and thus getting some clarification and integration, a procedure that may or may not be entirely successful. Their approach in general tends to be cognitively less diffuse and more structured than that of the high scorers.

The further mechanism of *denial of "negative" things in oneself*, predominant in high scorers, is clearly related to what has just been discussed, in the context of repression, as well as repeatedly pointed out elsewhere in this volume. The responsibility for that which is considered bad is shifted away from the subject and from the ingroup in general. The contrasting variant, completing Category 56c, is described as open psychological conflict concerning one's own adequacy, maturity, or the violation of liberal values by oneself. It is significantly more often (1 per cent level) found in the low scorers.

Examples from the interview records illustrating the denial of negative traits, often manifested in a general, "official" optimism, have been quoted above (Chapter XI); a few further examples, again from the records of subjects scoring extremely high on the Ethnocentrism questionnaire, are:

M51: He does not feel that he has any serious problem except a tendency to get very drunk when discouraged, which he thinks he has conquered, pointing out that his recent drunkenness was purely a good-natured relaxation while he played juke boxes and had a pleasant evening before going to the hospital and that he wasn't arrested for that, but for being struck on the head.

M57: Though he expressed the superficial desire to understand why he had gotten in so much trouble when his brothers have not, and to straighten out, he spontaneously denied "that there is anything the matter with me." He also sought the interviewer's reassurance "that there is nothing the matter with me."

Admission of difficulties by low-scoring subjects is illustrated by the following quotations:

M16: During the interview he referred to himself wistfully "I guess I am a mature person now—or maybe not, otherwise I wouldn't be coming here," and "I guess I am a neurotic. . . . Well, that's just my trouble, I'm not at all aggressive. That's why I'm coming here. . . . I have reached a block in my work—something is hanging over me —always nervous—the sex problem."

M49: (What worry about most?) "Well, I think social contact bothers me most. I could always talk with one person, but where there are several persons, I'll just stand there and not say 'boo.' . . . Yeah, that's been one of my main problems. . . . I started here once in General Curriculum, and then stopped. I couldn't see any sense in going any further if I didn't know what I wanted to take."

10. PHYSICAL SYMPTOMS

The assumption that further manifestations of the repression tendencies typical of high scorers would be found in the more frequent occurrence of certain physical symptoms, as a type of *"projection onto the body,"* did not materialize to a statistically significant degree although there is a trend in this direction (see below). The absence of clear-cut results in this respect may be due to the very high number of "Neutrals" (small total of H and L ratings) on the categories concerned, 56d and 56f.[1] This in turn may have been occasioned by our refraining from making a special inquiry concerning this point, or else by the fact that these symptoms are not general enough. Or, perhaps, both high and low scorers tend to use this mechanism to about the same extent.

More evidence concerning these alternatives might be obtained by further scrutinizing the available data. Six high-scoring but none of the low-scoring women show particular *concern with physical symptoms* (Category 56d). Similarly, 7 high-scoring and 3 low-scoring men show this concern. Furthermore, 7 high-scoring and 3 low-scoring women reported what amounts to

[1] Significant differences were found in a group of psychiatric clinic patients (see Chapter XXII).

hysterical conversions (Category 56f). However, the corresponding difference in men is altogether negligible (3 to 2). In a larger sample such differences might turn out to be significant, especially those for women.

Examples of concern with physical symptoms in high-scoring subjects follow. Whether and how much the complaints have a basis in reality is of course difficult to decide in the individual case; the fact remains that high scorers seem particularly inclined to dwell on their symptoms or disease records.

F71: Wouldn't like to be a nurse or M.D.—admires anyone who does, but "I hate hospitals. . . . I've been in so many; two mastoid operations and heart murmur. I have a great fear of doctors' offices. My heart has been giving me trouble so I go to the doctor for checkups but haven't really been sick. Now I'm full of energy but they think its nervous energy. I tire easily. I had scarlet fever when I was 10."

F33: As a child subject had rickets. Later, the whole family with the exception of the mother came down with typhoid fever. Subject's sister caught it first, but it was not recognized at first and the doctor diagnosed it simply as a common cold, so that the subject was allowed to stay in the room with her and caught it from her as a result. In school the subject broke a leg. She suffers from severe menstrual cramps and menstruation has always been highly irregular. Her chief complaint, however, is a nervous stomach resulting in frequent stomach upsets with frightful nausea and vomiting. She is often unable to keep anything on her stomach for days at a time. She has always had a somewhat delicate stomach, but her first severe upset occurred the day after she announced her engagement to be married. Since her marriage she has had frequent severe upsets, some of which have necessitated hospitalization and intravenous injections of glucose. Subject does not smoke or drink but states that she does not mind being in the company of people who do, provided their drinking is moderate. There has been no thumb-sucking, nail-biting, or bed-wetting but there were feeding difficulties in early childhood because she could not take milk.

M13: "He (father) hasn't worked for thirty years. At the time he worked, the wage was around $75 a month. He had stomach trouble. . . . I have had a lot of sickness, stomach trouble ever since I was 12. I was in the hospital once for three months. During those periods I like to turn to the Bible. . . . They found I was anemic at the age of 12. I had my first hemorrhage from the stomach when I was 18. It always comes when I start working too hard. . . . I found out that she wasn't interested in money, but was interested in me in spite of my discharge from the army, my poor health and possibilities. . . . She is a good cook, and that is an asset, what with my stomach condition."

M45: "Always sick, always going to the doctor. (What was wrong with you?) Well, I don't think they ever knew."

M51: "Wasn't it Emily Brontë who wrote so much, with tuberculosis? . . . It's not laziness (with the subject)." Subject goes on about his tuberculosis and its enervating effects upon him and the restriction which this places on what kind of work he can do, etc. (Are you an active tubercular?) "I'm an arrested tubercular, inactive . . . still. . . ."

M45: "They thought it might be sugar diabetes. . . . In my childhood, something that held me back, my kidneys. . . . I wet the bed all the time, consequently couldn't visit other boys, etc. . . . Might have given me a kind of complex. . . . Though I couldn't help it. But I thought that other people might think that I could help it. . . . Finally stopped when I was about 12."

Within the general framework of preoccupation with one's body there is also some tendency, especially in high-scoring women, to put *exaggerated emphasis on physical appearance* (Category 56e). As many as 8 high-scoring women and only 1 low-scoring woman spontaneously refer to this aspect when describing people (see Chapters X and XI). The difference is, however, not significant, perhaps again due to the large number of "Neutrals." For men there is no trend in the direction indicated; in fact, there is even a slight reversal.

B. COGNITIVE PERSONALITY ORGANIZATION

1. DEFINITION OF RATING CATEGORIES AND QUANTITATIVE RESULTS

The last subsection of our Scoring Manual refers to those of the more general factors in personality orientation which are of a more specifically cognitive, or perceptual, character. Some of their special forms have been discussed repeatedly in the chapters dealing with the clinical aspects of the interviews. As in the preceding sections of this chapter, discussion can therefore again be brief and often will take the form of a summary.

The section of the Scoring Manual referring to cognitive factors follows:

INTERVIEW SCORING MANUAL: COGNITIVE PERSONALITY ORGANIZATION
(to Table 2(XII))

PRESUMABLY "HIGH" VARIANTS	PRESUMABLY "LOW" VARIANTS
57. *Rigid set and outlook;* preconceived categorizations, inaccessible to new experience	57. *Flexible:* more adaptable to changing circumstances, more open to rational argument
58. *Intolerant of ambiguity*	58. *Tolerant of ambiguity*
59. *Pseudoscientific or antiscientific;* implicit denial of personality dynamics; ready explanation by accidental factors, heredity, etc.; superstition	59. *Scientific-naturalistic* orientation toward social and psychological dynamics
60. *Anti-intraceptive*	60. *Intraceptive*
61. *Suggestible,* gullible	61. *Autonomous*
62. *Autistic* thinking in *goal-behavior;* unrealistic view of means-end relationships	62. *Realistic* thinking in *goal-behavior*

The quantitative results are shown in the usual manner in Table 2(XII).

2. RIGIDITY

The first two categories, *rigidity vs. flexibility* (Category 57), and *intolerance vs. tolerance of ambiguity* (Category 58) cover related personality trends. Most subjects received the same rating on the two variables. Differentiation between low scorers and high scorers in the anticipated direction

TABLE 2 (XII)

INTERVIEW RATINGS ON COGNITIVE PERSONALITY ORGANIZATION

FOR 80 SUBJECTS SCORING EXTREMELY "HIGH" OR "LOW" ON THE ETHNIC PREJUDICE QUESTIONNAIRE SCALE

| Interview rating categories (abbreviated from Manual) | Sex | Number of "High"(H) and "Low"(L) ratings received by | | | | Sums of instances | | Level of statistical significance reached or surpassed (percentage) |
| | | 20 men and 25 women "high scorers" | | 20 men and 15 women "low scorers" | | "positive" | "negative" | |
		H	L	H	L			
57. Rigid(H) vs. flexible(L)	Men	18	2	3	13	31	5	1
	Women	18	4	2	8	26	6	1
58. Intolerant of ambiguity(H) vs. tolerant of ambiguity(L)	Men	16	2	2	17	33	4	1
	Women	19	2	4	8	27	6	1
59. Pseudo- or anti-scientific(H) vs. scientific-naturalistic(L)	Men	12	3	1	15	27	4	1
	Women	16	1	0	14	30	1	1
60. Anti-intraceptive(H) vs. intraceptive(L)	Men	16	4	3	16	32	7	1
	Women	18	2	2	14	32	3	1
61. Suggestible, gullible(H) vs. autonomous(L)	Men	13	2	2	15	28	4	1
	Women	9	3	1	11	20	4	1
62. Autism(H) vs. realism(L) in goal-behavior	Men	13	5	7	8	21	12	
	Women	8	9	3	11	19	12	

is significant at the 1 per cent level throughout. High scorers show more rigidity and avoidance of ambiguity; low scorers tend toward greater flexibility and acceptance of ambiguity. The inability, on the part of typical high scorers, to face "ambivalence"—which is emotional ambiguity—has been discussed previously, mainly in connection with their attitude toward parents and toward the other sex: in these and other areas hostile emotions were found to have been repressed and hidden behind a façade of glorification. A rigid, and in most instances, conventionalized set of rules seems thus to determine the conception the typical high scorer has of his own and of other people's behavior. Values and religion are often taken over in their most dogmatic form. Quotations cited in the previous chapter revealed these rigid conceptions on the part of the high scorers in many a sphere of life.

On the other hand, the openness of conflicts and doubts in the case of low scorers likewise became obvious. Over and above the previous quotations the following records from the interviews of low-scoring subjects show their readiness to think over matters and to come to a solution through their own thinking as well as their unwillingness to take over traditional and fixed concepts and ideals without scrutiny:

M42: He shows much philosophizing about the purpose of it all, involving much questioning of prevailing values about work, success, etc. But, on the other hand, he keeps pulling back and is overcome with doubt and indecision about these things. He emphasizes the basic importance of happiness and the emptiness of "success" without any personal satisfaction.

M44: His speech abounds in qualifying phrases and overintellectualization. He seems repeatedly unable to verbalize a generalization before he is overwhelmed by a rush of qualifications. Further, his thinking is rich in philosophizing, psychologizing, and poetic statement. Moreover, these characteristics are not shallow but have much substance. ". . . Well, I don't think you should obey anyone or anything without question. I think it's man's unique function to question and when he ceases to question, he ceases to be man. (Have you ever had serious doubts about your religious beliefs?) Oh, not especially serious, I'd say, because I believe there should be changes."

M48: "I'm what they always call an agnostic. Sounds sort of prosaic. . . . I'm skeptical—though I believe Christ was a great man . . . persecuted. . . ."

M53: (How do you account for your growing away from the conventionalism of your background?) "I don't know. It wasn't simply a change of locale. I think, probably, through reading. From 15 to 16 I did a lot of reading and became rather dissatisfied with it (i.e., with conventional ideas with which brought up). (Were there any people who especially influenced you?) No, must have been a hell of a lot of people. (Q) I don't know. I think through reading. I enjoy reading for reading's sake as well as a means of securing information."

There is in the records of the low scorers a tendency to use a great deal of qualifying phrases and other devices characteristic of an approach that is judicious rather than prejudicial through dogma, convention or a fixed set. Impressionistic ratings based on synopsis as employed here are perhaps not the best means to nail down this difference. More concrete experimental studies on intolerance toward ambiguity now in progress (for an advance report see Frenkel-Brunswik, 37, and forthcoming papers dealing with the relationship between emotional ambivalence and perceptual ambiguity), and on rigidity (Rokeach, 98) point toward the relative prominence in ethnically prejudiced as compared with unprejudiced children of a tendency to impose, in a rigid manner, certain preconceived sets upon ambiguous perceptual data or upon the solving of reasoning problems.

There seems to be a general tendency on the part of low scorers to expose themselves to broad experience—emotional, cognitive, perceptual—even at the risk of having to modify one's preconceived notions and of having to sustain conflicts. Thus all the evidence seems to point toward a greater overall rigidity in the high scorers as compared with the low scorers. These results however, as many others, may well be valid only for the extreme groups. In the medium range, on the other hand, rigidity may be neither pervasive nor relatively absent throughout the personality as a whole, but may be differentially distributed over some areas of personality whereas other areas retain their flexibility.

Although low scorers seem in general to accept more realities even if complex and unstructured, there is a distinct sub-variety of the ethnically extremely unprejudiced who cling to the liberal ideology in a rigid and stereotyped manner. This often goes with a personality structure not dissimilar to that of the typical high scorer. (See also the characterization of the "rigid low" in Chapter XIX.)

Intolerance of emotional and cognitive ambiguity seems not only to be a characteristic of the personality of the ethnically prejudiced; it also appears as part of the explicitly stated ego-ideal of exponents of the Nazi ideology in professional psychology. The most notable case is that of E. R. Jaensch with his programatic glorification of a personality type characterized by fixed relationships between stimuli and perceptual responses, and with his rejection of the school of Gestalt psychology mainly on the ground of its stress on the concept of ambiguity. (For a summary on Jaensch see the paper by Boder, in Harriman, 47; see also 37.)

3. NEGATIVE ATTITUDE TOWARD SCIENCE. SUPERSTITION

The inability to "question" matters and the need for definite and dogmatic answers, as frequently found in high scorers, leads either to an easy acceptance of stereotyped, *pseudoscientific* answers, of which escape into ready-made hereditarian explanations is but one manifestation, or else to an explicitly *antiscientific* attitude. Explanations by accidental factors are likewise included under this general heading. Its opposite is a *scientific-naturalistic attitude,* found predominantly in the low scorers. The entire Category 59 encompassing these alternatives differentiates significantly (at the 1 per cent level) for both men and women. The difference in attitudes involved has been described previously, primarily in discussing the subjects' concepts of their "selves." It will be remembered that it was the low scorers who showed a tendency toward explanations in terms of sociopsychological dynamics.

The antiscientific thinking of the typical high scorer is closely connected with his tendency toward *superstition*, as discussed in Chapter VII. The tendency toward superstition is illustrated by the following records of high-scoring women:

F31: "I am not superstitious. Mother is a little bit superstitious. She believes in old-world customs and palmistry. I'm not a fatalist, either; what I do will control my life, what I make of it. But I don't know about that—there are the boys on the battle-field, for instance. They say a bullet has your name on it."

F36: Subject does not believe in formal religion; this is why she likes the Unitarians. She does not think the churches should have a narrow, strict creed and tell you exactly what you should believe. She has read a great deal of theosophy, Madame Blavatsky, etc. She believes in reincarnation and divine will: reincarnation in the sense that the soul goes from one body to another and that you will be subjected to those experiences that are necessary to learning, to enable the soul to reach a higher state.

F60: (Why did you come to _____?) "Why, I don't know! It just happened. Don't you think some things just happen to us?" (Superstition?) She was just "called" to do it. Once she was out walking in the early morning—the birds were singing—she raised her hands and her face to the sky, and they were wet. (What was it?) She considered it a supernatural phenomenon.

Along the same line Lentz (67) reports that conservatives are more antagonistic to science, especially with regard to its future activities, and, conversely, are more superstitious. They feel much more favorable toward the conventional, the traditional, and the routine. They are less tolerant and sympathetic towards the underdog, less aesthetic and less imaginative.

The fact that high scorers on ethnocentrism are more often given to stereotyping, pre-judgments and ready generalizations, or else to overconcreteness, should not blind us to the fact that there also are tendencies of this kind in the low scorers. The increasing complexity of the social realities and their partial unintelligibility to the individual sometimes may necessitate a falling back on stereotypes so that opaque events appear more comprehensible (see Chapter XVII). Ethnic prejudice is but one of many possible media for this tendency. It must be held in favor of the ethnically unprejudiced, however, that they make a serious effort to counteract such stereotyping in one of the areas of paramount social significance.

4. ANTI-INTRACEPTIVENESS AND AUTISM

Likewise previously discussed but rated here directly and in its own right is the tendency, found primarily in the high scorer, toward what may be called *anti-intraceptiveness* as contrasted with a greater readiness toward intraception in the low scorer (Category 60). The difference is significant at the 1 per cent level. The concept of intraception covers the tendency toward introspection, as well as a readiness toward gaining insights into psychological and social mechanisms. It is contrasted primarily with externalizations of various kinds as referred to above. The greater creativity, imagination, and ability for empathy of the low scorers just discussed is likewise related to their greater intraceptiveness.

It may suffice to cite here in addition to previous quotations only one record of a low-scoring woman and one of a low-scoring man in which the tendency toward reflection becomes apparent.

F70: Always wanted to work with people. . . . (What does religion give you?) "I suppose going to church takes a load off of me of thinking about things I should think about. I think it covers my social ideas, and it causes me to think about things I must think about for some reason. (What about?) Moral values, the relative value between peace and liberty in wartime, for instance. Pacifism and its ins and outs, interpersonal relationship as moral values. I don't think of those values as right or wrong, except as it has social implications."

. *M50:* (Future?) "I don't know. I just recently came of the opinion that it is not necessary for me to be a commercial artist. Important to do whatever I do well. Not important what I do any more (Q) Well, I was the prima donna type . . . built up myself into an idea that not suited for the work . . . now it doesn't matter any more . . . it began when I was here about a month . . . the child guidance center psychologist gave a speech . . . he gave the idea that (deviation in behavior has a cause). . . . It may go back to infancy. . . . I play around with it (leading to nothing) . . . until a friend also interested made a startling remark. . . . Then I thought a lot about it . . . put down reasons on both sides, on two sheets of paper and decided he was right. I don't mean I am in love with my mother, but I have a dependency complex . . . married a woman older than myself . . . and always depend on others . . . leave responsibility to others . . . it seems on looking back that I have always done that. . . ."

The absence of proper orientation toward social and psychological dynamics in the typical high scorer may be linked to a general tendency toward *autistic thinking in goal behavior* as contrasted with the somewhat more realistic attitude that might be expected to be present in the typical low scorer (Category 62). Though not significantly differentiating between the two extreme groups of interviewees, this category shows a distinct trend in the direction that we expected (21 positive as compared with 12 negative instances in men, and 19 positive as compared with 12 negative instances in women). The trend is particularly evident in the vocational choices and economic expectations of our subjects.

The somewhat adolescent and fantastic, glamour-seeking character of the vocational ambitions of high-scoring subjects is illustrated by the following records:

F66: "If you're good, you can get up to ambassador. I think there have been some women ambassadors. Or maybe there were only women ministers. I made the choice about three years ago. I just heard some friends of mine talking about it, and it sounded interesting. (Why vocational choice?) Well, salary had a little to do with it. I think if I could really put myself to it, I could do it. If I really wanted to and had nothing else to stand in the way. The times have much to do with my choice. I would like to know why they do what they do."

F34: Subject wants to be a journalist. This is purely utilitarian. She likes journalism, but her real desire is to do creative writing. She has imagined herself as a great actress. "But my acting is purely amateur stuff. I was always active in school dramatics as well as high school journalism. The family used to laugh because I was always play-acting. I always said I'd earn my living at either acting or writing. . . ."

5. SUGGESTIBILITY

Submission to authority and lack of independence and of critical judgment tend to lead the high scorer toward being *suggestible and gullible*, as contrasted with the greater *autonomy* of the low scorer (Category 61). Again, the difference is significant at the 1 per cent level for both men and women. The social implications of a tendency on the part of the gullible person to fall easy prey to unsound and destructive political propaganda are obvious. The high scorer's dependence, in his personal life, upon authority, conventionalized values, church dogma, public opinion, and prestige figures, and the low scorer's relative independence of, and occasional rebellion against, these authorities have been pointed out so often throughout this volume that no further comment seems necessary.

The present chapter will be summarized together with a general synopsis of the interview results at the conclusion of the chapter which follows.

CHAPTER XIII

COMPREHENSIVE SCORES AND
SUMMARY OF INTERVIEW RESULTS

Else Frenkel-Brunswik

A. THE DISCRIMINATORY POWERS OF THE MAJOR AREAS STUDIED

1. VERIFICATION OF ANTICIPATED TREND BY CATEGORIES

In the preceding four chapters (IX to XII), the technique of interviewing was described, and specific results of interviews with eighty subjects scoring extremely high or extremely low on the overt anti-Semitism or Ethnocentrism scales were presented and discussed in terms of the approximately ninety rating categories of the Scoring Manual used to classify the records of the subjects.

As shown in the tables of these chapters, a sizable proportion of the categories differentiated high scorers from low scorers to a statistically significant degree in the direction anticipated for either or both sexes. The vast majority of the remaining categories showed at least a trend in the expected direction. For men, there are only three out of the eighty-six categories for which the number of "positive" and "negative" instances is equal, and only one (Category 23c) which shows a slight trend in the direction opposite to the one expected. As can be seen from Tables 3(X), 1(XI), and 2(XI), to which the four exceptions are limited, the absolute number of ratings involved is very small in each case; the items involved deal with certain aspects of attitude toward siblings, sex, and people. For women there are two out of the ninety categories that show equality and four that show reversal, all six exceptions being confined to Tables 1(X), 2(X), and 3(X), and dealing with aspects of the relationships to parents and siblings. In no case does the reversal approach statistical significance; nor does it appear in the case of any category that yielded less than 50 per cent "Neutral" ratings and was thus included in the list of those for which intensive evaluation was undertaken (72 for men and 65 for women, see end of Chapter IX).

468

TABLE 1 (XIII)

COMPOSITE RATINGS (MEANS) FOR MAJOR AREAS OF STUDY FOR "HIGH" AND "LOW" SCORING GROUPS OF INTERVIEWEES

Based on categories presented in tables	Dealing with	Sex	Means of High(H) and Low(L) ratings received by				Sums of Means	
			20 men and 25 women "high scorers" H	L	20 men and 15 women "low scorers" H	L	"positive"	"negative"
1(X), 2(X), 3(X)	Parents and Childhood	Men	8.68	1.37	3.11	8.42	17.10	4.47
		Women	7.47	3.26	1.68	5.11	12.58	4.94
1(XI)	Attitude toward Sex	Men	10.57	2.86	2.57	5.86	16.43	5.43
		Women	10.43	1.86	2.29	9.00	19.43	4.14
2(XI)	Attitude toward People	Men	10.67	1.67	2.22	11.67	22.33	3.89
		Women	10.67	2.78	1.44	8.00	18.67	4.22
3(XI)	Attitude toward Present Self	Men	13.00	2.44	2.44	13.11	26.11	4.88
		Women	11.33	3.56	1.11	9.67	21.00	4.67
4(XI)	Attitude toward Childhood Self	Men	8.50	3.75	2.25	12.75	21.25	6.00
		Women	8.00	5.75	1.00	8.75	16.75	6.75
1(XII)	Dynamic Character Structure	Men	11.65	2.53	3.10	11.35	23.00	5.63
		Women	11.75	3.59	1.95	9.12	20.87	5.54
2(XII)	Cognitive Personality Organization	Men	14.67	3.00	3.00	14.00	28.67	6.00
		Women	14.67	3.50	1.83	11.00	25.67	5.33
All tables	All categories	Men	10.91	2.24	2.81	10.59	21.50	5.05
		Women	10.38	3.34	1.69	8.10	18.48	5.03

Thus there are no "negative validities" in the evaluation of the interviews. This result is not surprising in view of the fact that the categories of the Scoring Manual were derived from previous empirical evidence, including a preliminary inspection of the interview material; even so, the fact that the subsequent "blind" rating procedure supported most of the hypotheses with which the evaluation began is strong evidence of their validity.

2. COMPOSITE RATINGS FOR SEVEN MAJOR AREAS

Considering the almost universally confirmatory trend of the results just discussed, the computation of average ratings for larger groups of categories seems justified. The results of this procedure are presented in Table 1 (XIII) in the same manner as in the preceding tables except for the fact that indication of statistical significance is here omitted.

As can be seen by an inspection of the last two columns of the table, differentiation between high scorers and low scorers is consistently somewhat less clear-cut for women than for men. This may be due either to the unequal size of the two samples of women interviewees, or to the fact, repeatedly referred to above, that women were in the main interviewed at an earlier stage of the investigation than were men. It may also be that, in our culture at least, patterns of behavior and ideology are more coherent and consistent in men than they are in women.

Among all the areas studied, that of attitudes toward present self yields the most clear-cut differentiation between high scorers and low scorers. The ratio between "positive" (confirmatory) and "negative" instances is among the most favorable. At the same time, the absolute values of the positive instances are among the highest. This indicates, furthermore, that the number of "Neutral" ratings is relatively low for this area.

The categories pertaining to dynamic and, especially, cognitive personality organization likewise show excellent differentiation, a very high proportion of the differences being statistically significant.

Contrariwise, over-all results are least sharply defined in the area of attitude toward parents and siblings, for reasons outlined in Chapter X. This is in line with what was stated above concerning absence of reversal of the expected trend in the case of a few scattered categories pertaining to these topics. Even for this area, however, the ratio of positive to negative instances is, for the men, better than three to one, and thus the differentiation is quite satisfactory.

An explanation of the differences in discriminatory power among the various major areas covered by the ratings of interviews may be in the following. An adequate survey of the early family situation requires a great deal more specific information than could be obtained in our necessarily circumscribed interviews, and this made for the large proportion of "Neutral" ratings. Such aspects as cognitive organization and attitude toward self, on the other hand, may be inferred from expressions in a greater variety of fields, and thus the likelihood of insufficient information is reduced. Over and above this, the very nature of such formal variables permits the subject himself to choose from among a variety of "alternate" manifestations, many of them encompassed in a single rating category. This principle of shifting expression of identical motivational tendencies is apt to give an advantage to motivational categories regardless of how complete the specific information on any particular aspect of life may be. It is for the same reason that the value of generalized, synoptic ratings, as contrasted with specific or situationally limited quantification, was so much stressed at the beginning of the discussion of the problems connected with the evaluation of interviews (Chapter IX; see also 31, 32, 34, 36).

B. VALIDITY OF OVER-ALL SCORES AND RATINGS OF THE INTERVIEWS

1. INDIVIDUAL COMPOSITE SCORE BASED ON ALL AREAS OF RATING

Composite ratings, covering the entire range of the areas of rating, were also obtained for each individual interviewee. In a sense, these composite ratings define what may be called the "score" of the subject on the interview. (It was with a view to this final score that the manual was designated as the Interview Scoring Manual in spite of the fact that for each of the constituent categories ratings rather than scores were obtained.) Since, as was pointed out in the preceding section, there were no reversals of the expected discriminatory trend on any of the categories yielding less than 50 per cent "Neutral" ratings, all of these categories were included in the final score. These scores are shown, for all the 80 subjects interviewed, in Tables 1(IX) and 2(IX). The score itself is given in two parts, defined by the sums of the "High" and of the "Low" ratings received by the individual. The difference between the sum of these two parts and the fixed total (72 for men and 65 for women), not shown in the tables, indicates the number of "Neutral" ratings received by the individual on the categories in question.

The column referring to composite standing shows the letter H or L, depending on the preponderance of the High or the Low score in the preceding pair of columns.[1]

Means of the quantitative data are shown in the bottom rows of the tables. The ranges of the number of "high" and "low" interview scores for each of the four groups can be read directly from the two tables.

[1] Concerning the use of capital and lower-case symbols and other technical data pertinent to this section see Chapter IX, Section F, 3.

2. OVER-ALL INTUITIVE RATING
AND ITS AGREEMENT WITH THE COMPOSITE SCORE

The last column in Tables 1(IX) and 2(IX) adds what was briefly mentioned in Chapter IX as the intuitive rating of the interviewee. This is based on an informal synopsis and estimate after the blind interview-rating procedure had been completed, and it was made without the rater's making explicit to himself the quantitative results in terms of specific ratings on the single categories.

Composite scores and intuitive ratings agree very highly with one another. There is only one subject, F_{72}, among the 80 interviewees for whom there is a discrepancy between the two values. In her case the composite score (H) is correct; the over-all intuitive rating (L) is incorrect.

3. AGREEMENT WITH THE QUESTIONNAIRE RESULTS

It will be noted that while there is consistency as to "low" vs. "high" standing in the A-S and E columns of Tables 1(IX) and 2(IX)—this standing having been the very criterion of selection of the interviewees—the subsequent columns show a good deal of inconsistency. This inconsistency reaches major proportions in such cases as F_{21} or F_{39}, both overt low scorers who nonetheless score among the highest on the interview, with respect to both the composite score and the synoptic over-all ratings. Similar instances of opposition, though not all as striking ones, can be found among the high scorers. Various other kinds of inconsistency of trend may be noted upon inspection of the tables.

The general agreement between various columns in Tables 1(IX) and 2(IX) containing letter indices may be expressed conveniently in terms of percentage. "Percentage agreement" is then defined as the percentage of equal-letter combinations (HH or LL) in any pair of columns considered. The figures on percentage agreement could easily be transformed into tetrachoric correlation coefficients.

The defining criterion of selection, extremely high vs. extremely low standing on the overt anti-Semitism or Ethnocentrism scale, shows a percentage agreement of about 85 with both the over-all intuitive ratings and the composite standing on the interview. (This figure is an average of an agreement of about 95 per cent achieved by the rater whose material happened to include the most complete interviews, and of an agreement of 75 per cent achieved by the other of the two raters whose data were more fragmentary.)

Since composite ratings agree with intuitive ratings almost completely (see above), the figures for the agreement of overt ethnocentrism with the intuitive ratings are practically identical with those mentioned above for composite ratings.

Intuitive as well as composite interview ratings show slightly less agreement with standing on the F and the PEC scales, but even here the figures are between 75 and 80 per cent.

C. SUMMARY OF THE PERSONALITY PATTERNS DERIVED FROM THE INTERVIEWS

1. INTRODUCTION

The results of the "blind" ratings of the interviews, as discussed in the present and in the preceding four chapters, have shown that individuals extremely high on overt ethnic prejudice tend to differ with respect to a great variety of personality traits from those extremely low on prejudice. Some of the personality traits discussed were also measured by other techniques, especially the questionnaire. The results obtained by the various methods independently are very similar. However, rating by categories describes and substantiates in a more systematic, organized, and controlled way the impressions formed about the personality differences between high scorers and low scorers in the course of intensive study of individual cases.

It has to be emphasized, of course, that these differences are based on an analysis of group trends within statistical samples and do not imply that every individual will exhibit most or even a large proportion of the features belonging to either the "high" or the "low" syndrome, as the case may be. As can be seen from Tables 1(IX) and 2(IX), certain individuals seem to possess a relatively large number of either "high" or "low" features while others seem to have features of both patterns, with a relatively slight prevalence of one or the other. It should thus be kept in mind that the summary which follows deals with composite pictures of these patterns, abstracted from the study of groups, rather than with individual cases. Were we to lay greater stress on concrete personalities, the most frequent syndromes or combinations of trends within single individuals would have to be determined as an intermediate step, leading to the definition of subtypes within the prejudiced and the unprejudiced patterns. Some remarks pointing in this direction will be made in the following summary. The typology, as such, of the ethnically prejudiced, will be taken up more systematically in Chapter XIX.

The results are furthermore limited to trends found in individuals with extreme standing on the prejudice scale. How far the relations would hold for those with middle scores on prejudice has to be left open, since such individuals were not included in the present intensive investigation by means of interviews.

Finally, it remains for future investigation to ascertain how far the interrelationships found are interculturally valid or whether they are restricted to certain specific cultures or subcultures, such as the one from which our sample of subjects has been drawn; namely, an urban and suburban population on the West Coast of the United States.

In an attempt to summarize the social and psychological factors which, within our limited framework, have been found to be related to prejudice, we will proceed in the following manner: First, the aspects and "themes" of the personality structure of the high scorer as differentiated from the low scorer will be described in a synoptic fashion. Next, hypotheses concerning the genetic aspects of these two distinct patterns will be put forward. And finally, an attempt will be made to relate both patterns to the over-all cultural pattern.

2. REPRESSION *VS*. AWARENESS

In summarizing differences in the personality structure of our two groups, we may best start with the findings discussed in the preceding chapter under the heading of "defense mechanisms." Regardless of whether the specific topic was that of ambivalence, or aggression, or passivity, or some other related feature of personality dynamics, the outstanding finding was that the extremely unprejudiced individual tends to manifest a greater readiness to become aware of unacceptable tendencies and impulses in himself. The prejudiced individual, on the other hand, is more apt not to face these tendencies openly and thus to fail in integrating them satisfactorily with the conscious image he has of himself. The resultant break between the conscious and the unconscious layers in the personality of the high scorers, as compared with the greater fluidity of transition and of intercommunication between the different personality strata in the low scorers, appears to have the greatest implications for their respective personality patterns.

3. EXTERNALIZATION *VS*. INTERNALIZATION

Among the tendencies which the typical high scorer attempts to keep in a repressed state (but which nonetheless find indirect expression in the interview) are mainly fear, weakness, passivity, sex impulses, and aggressive feeling against authoritative figures, especially the parents. Among the rigid defenses against these tendencies there is, above all, the mechanism of projection, by which much of what cannot be accepted as part of one's own ego is externalized. Thus it is not oneself but others that are seen as hostile and threatening. Or else one's own weakness leads to an exaggerated condemnation of everything that is weak; one's own weakness is thus fought outside instead of inside. At the same time there is a compensatory—and therefore often compulsive—drive for power, strength, success, and self-determination.

Repression and externalization of the instinctual tendencies mentioned reduces their manageability and the possibility of their control by the individual, since it is now the external world to which the feared qualities of the unconscious are ascribed. As long as social conditions are conducive to and furnish acceptable outlets for compensatory tendencies, a relative mental balance within the individual may well be achieved in this manner.

Another aspect of externalization may be found in a tendency toward avoidance of introspection and of insight in general, thus rendering the content of consciousness relatively narrow. Since the energy of the person is in this case largely devoted either to keeping instinctual tendencies out of consciousness or to striving for external success and status, there appears to be relatively little left for genuine libidinization of one's interpersonal relationships, or of one's work, as ends in themselves. The comparatively impoverished potentialities for interpersonal relationships may exhibit themselves either in a relatively restricted, conventional, but dependable approach to people, as found primarily in the more conservative subgroup of the high scorers, or in a ruthless, manipulative approach, as found in the more delinquent subgroup.

There also seems to be relatively little enjoyment of sensuality or of passive pleasures such as affection, companionship, or art and music on the part of the typical high scorer. Instead of these internalized pleasures, there is an inclination toward mobility and activity, and a striving for material benefits.

The composite picture of the low scorer, on the other hand, not only reveals greater readiness to accept and to face one's impulses and weaknesses, but also to ruminate about them. While for the high scorer possible loss of energy is connected with his tendency toward rigid repressions, the low scorer is apt to waste energies by indulging in often unfruitful introspection and by placing the blame for mishaps too much upon himself. In contrast to the high scorer's tendency toward externalization, the typical low scorer is prone to internalize in an excessive manner, and this in turn may lead to open anxiety, feelings of guilt, and other neurotic features.

The positive aspects of this latter kind of orientation are a more closely knit integration within the individual and a more internalized and more intensive, though not conflict-free relation to others. The low scorer also tends to be oriented, more than is the high scorer, toward real achievement, toward intellectual or aesthetic goals, and toward the realization of socially productive values. His greater capacity for intensive interpersonal relationships goes hand in hand with greater self-sufficiency. He struggles for the establishment of inner harmony and self-actualization, whereas the high scorer is concentrated on an effort to adjust to the outside world and to gain power and success within it.

One of the results of greater internalization is the generally more creative and imaginative approach of the low scorer both in the cognitive and in the emotional sphere, as compared with a more constricted, conventional, and stereotypical approach in the high scorer.

4. CONVENTIONALISM *VS.* GENUINENESS

Conformity is one of the major expressions of lack of an internal focus in the high scorer. One of the outstanding characteristics to be found in both the conservatively inclined, as well as in the delinquent subvariety of the high scorer (see Chapter XXI), is the adoption of conventional values and rules. High scorers generally seem to need external support—whether this be offered by authorities or by public opinion—in order to find some assurance concerning what is right and what is wrong.

Conformity to externalized values in the extremely prejudiced can be observed in a variety of spheres of life. One of the earliest expressions of this conventionality is to be found, probably, in the high scorer's attitude toward his parents. It is one of stereotypical admiration, with little ability to express criticism or resentment. There are many indications that there actually is often considerable underlying hostility toward the parents which—though not always expressed—prevents the development of a truly affectionate relationship.

The greater genuineness of the low scorer is evident in his attitude toward the parents. His is an equalitarian conception of the parent-child relationship. This makes it possible for him to express criticism and resentment openly, and at the same time to have a more positive and affectionate relation with the parents. The descriptions of the parents given by the low scorers have an aspect of spontaneity: they depict real people with all their inherent assets and shortcomings.

External criteria, especially social status, are the yardsticks by which the high scorer tends to appraise people in general and the ground on which he either admires and accepts, or rejects them. Such values form the basis of a hierarchical order in which the powerful are seen at the top and the weak at the bottom. This may well be an over-all tendency in modern culture which, however, the high scorer displays to an exaggerated degree. The typical low scorer, on the other hand, seems to have developed for himself an image of other people which includes congeniality even with outgroups rather than conceiving of them mainly as a threat or danger. Feeling more secure, he searches in his relations with other people primarily for a realization of positive and individualized values rather than being oriented primarily toward getting support and help from the powerful as is the typical high scorer.

The high scorers' conception of the sex roles is likewise highly conventionalized. The high-scoring man tends to think of himself as active, determined, energetic, independent, rough, and successful in the competitive struggle. There is no room in this ego-ideal for passivity and softness, and thus strong defenses are erected against these attitudes in general, the effect being that only their opposites are established in consciousness. Nonetheless, inclinations toward dependency and a far-reaching passivity are evident in the interviews of high-scoring men although these remain unaccepted and ego-alien.

The role of the woman, as seen by the high-scoring man, is one of passivity and subservience. She is an object of solicitude on the part of the man. The hierarchical idea involved corresponds to the well-known conventional cliché and at the same time offers the high-scoring man the much-needed opportunity of asserting his superiority. There is, however, ample evidence that the high-scoring man wants to be on the receiving end in his relation to women; from them he wants material benefits and support more than he wants pure affection, for it would be difficult for him to accept the latter. There is relatively little genuine affective involvement in his non-marital sex relations, and of his wife he tends to require the conventional prerequisites of a good housewife. On the whole, sex is for him in the service of status, be this masculine status as achieved by pointing toward conquests, or be it social status as achieved by marrying the "right kind" of woman.

Low-scoring men, on the other hand, tend to look primarily for companionship, friendship, and sensuality in their relations to the other sex. They are able openly to take and to give nurturance and succorance in their relations with women. In fact, we often find a rather insatiable search for love and complete acceptance by the woman in low-scoring men, and this is often a source of open ambivalence toward her. Passivity and softness is thus an accepted part of the ego-ideal of the low-scoring man, who at the same time is often more capable of giving real protection and support in return. All degrees of expressiveness, ranging from extreme sexual inhibition, due to an overly developed and powerful superego, to a conscious tendency toward impulse-riddenness, may be found among low-scoring subjects.

The extremely unprejudiced woman likewise looks primarily for mutual interests and affection in her choice of a mate. As the low-scoring man shows greater readiness than does the high scorer to accept feminine features in himself, so the low-scoring woman tends not to repress but rather to accept and to sublimate her masculine tendencies by pursuing so-called masculine interests and activities. Though this often leads to open competition with, and envy of, men, there is at the same time more understanding and more genuine liking for them. There is more evidence of an open conflict about the feminine role, and at the same time evidence of more clearly focused heterosexuality and of more intensive maternal feelings.

The high-scoring woman, on the other hand, clings to a self-image of conventional femininity defined by subservience to, and adulation of, men. At the same time there is evidence of an exploitive and hostile attitude toward men, expressed only indirectly in the interviews and shown quite directly in the stories of the Thematic Apperception Test (see Chapter XIV). Since the high-scoring woman tends to renounce inclinations toward interests considered masculine in our culture, and since the home does not provide her with satisfactory forms of expression, her underlying bitterness often assumes deviously destructive forms. One way in which such a negative attitude is manifested is in her exaggerated demands on men as providers; another is the living out of her thwarted ambitions through the medium of the man. Again it may be that it is the general cultural plight of the woman that finds an exaggerated release in the high-scoring woman; indeed, low-scoring women seem by no means untouched by the difficult situation imposed upon them by our civilization. But whereas the high-scoring woman tends to give preference to the ideal of a restricted rather than a vaguely defined role for women, the low-scoring woman is more apt to take on the conflict and to face it openly.

As was anticipated above, the element of conventionality in the conception of sex roles is only part of a more general conventional self-image found to be characteristic of the high scorers. Good manners, attainment of success and status, self-control, and poise are some of the further requirements. Deviations from this ego-ideal are usually considered as inexplicable "breakthroughs" of forces that lie beyond the responsibility of the individual, such as external stress, heredity, etc.

Low scorers, on the other hand, are worried, in their self-evaluation, about attainment of goals in the realm of achievement, about the realization of socially constructive values, about success or failure in friendship, and about guilt resulting from aggression and ambivalence.

5. POWER VS. LOVE-ORIENTATION

The orientation toward conventional values in the high scorers as compared with orientation toward more intrinsic and basic values in the low scorers was found to extend over different areas of life. Related to conventionalism is the tendency toward admiration of, and search for, power, likewise more pronounced in the typical high scorer.

The comparative lack of ability for affectionate and individualized interpersonal relations, together with the conception of a threatening and dangerous environment, must be seen as underlying the prejudiced individual's striving for the attainment of power, either directly or by having the powerful on his side. In this vein, weakness is considered dangerous since it may lead to being "devoured" by the strong (see Simmel, 111), or at least to deprivation or starvation, dangers only too readily anticipated by the high scorer.

In this context we often find a frame of mind best characterized as "overrealism," a tendency to utilize everything and everybody as means to an end. Needless to say, such overrealism seems but rarely to lead to a real attainment of the goals involved and thus to ultimate satisfaction; it often involves strained interpersonal relations and possible or actual retaliation, of which there is much fear. The conflict arising between an unaccepted and un-recognized dependency on others for things and benefits, on the one hand, and the hostility stemming from distrust, envy, and feelings of being thwarted, on the other, cannot be resolved.

It is especially the prejudiced man who—as mentioned before—often considers ruthless opportunism as an essential attribute of masculinity. As a reaction to his fear of his passivity and dependency, he develops a propensity for power and success as the only measures of his value.

Modern authors have repeatedly stressed the fact that status as a measure of one's worth is a general phenomenon in American civilization. Assuming that this is the case, there still is a difference between the picture of the composite high scorer and of the composite low scorer in this respect. Whereas the striving for status and power, in their purely external aspects, seems to be the major concern of the extremely prejudiced, the unprejudiced individual—though as a rule by no means disinterested in status—still has a greater variety of other resources and pleasures at his disposal.

The search for affection and love in one's personal relationships is an important determinant of the behavior of the typical low scorer. To develop a satisfactory relation to one's mate and to friends is considered essential for happiness. In fact, much thought—often of an obsessional intensity—seems to be devoted to the striving for such ideal bonds, and to anxiety over the actual or potential failure of this striving. If successfully established, such intense relations constitute one of the most important sources of gratification. At the same time, the often insatiable wish for being fully accepted and loved leads to frustration and open ambivalence for the object of attachment. Thus it is that low scorers often manifest painful emotional dependence on others; this is a further way in which they may become maladjusted.

Not only contact with other people but also work tends to become more libidinized in the low scorers than in the high scorers. Though far from being indifferent to recognition, low scorers place comparatively little emphasis on their activities as means to an end; rather, these activities tend to become a source of pleasure and satisfaction in their own right, or else the emphasis lies on their social implications. Activity contributing to the realization of what may be called liberal values may also become important to the low scorer. Finally, interest and liking for art, music, literature, and philosophy are more often found in the low scorer. It may be considered that such interests contribute substantially to the greater resourcefulness, and to the comparative diversion from power and status, that is characteristic of the low scorer.

6. RIGIDITY *VS.* FLEXIBILITY. PROBLEMS OF ADJUSTMENT

One of the most pervasive formal aspects of the personality organization of the extremely prejudiced individual is his rigidity. This must be seen as a consequence of the features discussed so far. In order to keep unacceptable tendencies and impulses out of consciousness, rigid defenses have to be maintained. Any loosening of the absoluteness of these defenses involves the danger of a breaking through of the repressed tendencies. Impulses and inclinations repressed too severely, too suddenly, or too early in life do not lose their dynamic strength, however. On the contrary, abrupt or unsuccessful repression prevents rather than helps in their control and mastery. An ego thus weakened is more in danger of becoming completely overwhelmed by the repressed forces. Greater rigidity of defenses is necessary to cope with such increased threat. In this vicious circle, impulses are not prevented from breaking out in uncontrolled ways. Basically unmodified instinctual impulses lurk everywhere beneath the surface, narrowing considerably the content of the ego so that it must be kept constantly on the lookout. Rational control extends to a small sector of the personality only. As long as situational conditions of life draw on this sector only, and as long as our culture provides socially acceptable outlets for suppressed impulses, smooth functioning and fair adjustment can be achieved within the given framework.

But it must be kept in mind that the adjustment of the typical high scorer depends on conditions that are comparatively narrowly circumscribed. The idea of a sharp ingroup-outgroup dichotomy provided by our culture makes it possible for the high scorer to suppress the feared awareness of his hostility against the prestige figures, on which he is dependent, by displacing it onto weak outgroups from whom no retaliation need be feared. This mechanism enables him, furthermore, to remain relatively unaware of his own psychological weaknesses, since he now may feel superior to the socially weaker groups. Among other things, fear of one's own immoral tendencies can be alleviated by exaggerating and condemning the immorality of others, particularly outgroups.

As far as positive goals are concerned, the relative lack of individuation is compensated for by taking over conventional clichés and values. Rigid adherence to substitutes and crutches of this kind is found in various spheres of life. However, the tendency toward externalization, if kept within bounds, may often be in harmony with a healthy concern for external goals. Without such a tendency toward externalization, the individual might frequently go down in a competitive society.

In order to keep the balance under these conditions, a simple, firm, often stereotypical, cognitive structure is required. There is no place for ambivalence or ambiguities. Every attempt is made to eliminate them, but they remain as potentials which might interfere at any time. In the course of these attempts a subtle but profound distortion of reality has to take place, precipitated by the fact that stereotypical categorizations can never do justice to all the aspects of reality. As long as such distortions remain part and parcel of the cultural inventory, the removal of prejudice from the potentially fascist person may well endanger his psychological balance. The social implications of such a step have therefore to be carefully anticipated and preventive measures to be devised in advance.

The avoidance of ambiguities and the rigidity of mental sets in the ethnically prejudiced also becomes evident in the handling of perceptual and other cognitive materials free of immediate social and emotional implications (37; 98). The tendency to impose preconceived and often stereotypical categories upon experience may thus be envisaged as a more general trait in subjects scoring extremely high on Ethnocentrism. It must be reiterated, however, that there is a distinct sub-type among extreme low scorers in whom liberal ideology becomes a cliché that may include an undue glorification of the underdog, and who at the same time shows signs of rigidity in his personality makeup. On the other hand, it is primarily the conservative type of high scorer who displays rigidity, while the skillful manipulator among the high scorers is often characterized by a great deal of flexibility (see Chapter XIX). On the whole, however, it is in the low scorer that we find the more flexible emotional and cognitive adjustment; this is also reflected in his greater reluctance to "reify" concepts, in his more pronounced appreciation of the complexity of social and personal relations, as well as in his more profound sympathy with the psychological and social sciences studying these relations.

Whereas the extremely prejudiced person often exhibits a rigid form of superficial adjustment, interspersed with some measure of psychotic mechanisms stemming from the necessity of distorting reality, the extremely unprejudiced individual gives evidence of a more flexible kind of adjustment, although this goes with neurotic trends in a number of cases. An extreme tendency toward internalization can often be seen in the low scorer's preoccupation with his feelings and impulses, however unpleasant they may turn out to be. Far from escaping his emotional ambivalences and his feelings of inferiority, of guilt, and of anxiety, he even tends to dwell on them. This is not to say that he is free from self-deception. Dwelling on his feelings is often morbid and far removed from real insight. But the conscious consideration and comparative acceptance of instinctual impulses—especially in childhood —may well prevent the development of overly rigid defenses and disguises. Mechanisms of projection and displacement would thus be reduced to manageable proportions as far as cognitive mastery of reality is concerned.

Although the average unprejudiced individual in our culture is perhaps not free of some neurotic tendencies, it is in this same group that the relatively rare case of an individual, very well adjusted and mature, may also be found. It is only when conflicts, shortcomings, and unacceptable impulses are frankly faced that their mastery may be furthered to the point of perfection and the maximum potential for dealing adequately with varying conditions may be achieved. Temporarily, however, such frankness may well lead to increased anxieties and depressions, and some contestants may, for better or for worse, be left by the way.

7. SOME GENETIC ASPECTS

When we consider the childhood situation of the most prejudiced subjects, we find reports of a tendency toward rigid discipline on the part of the parents, with affection which is conditional rather than unconditional, i.e., dependent upon approved behavior on the part of the child. Related to this is a tendency apparent in families of prejudiced subjects to base interrelationships on rather clearly defined roles of dominance and submission, in contradistinction to equalitarian policies. Faithful execution of prescribed roles and the exchange of duties and obligations is, in the families of the prejudiced, often given preference over the exchange of free-flowing affection. The hypothesis may be offered that some of the traits of the prejudiced personality are an outcome of this family situation.

These as well as the other results concerning the family situations have been directly substantiated by a study of social discrimination in children which included an investigation of their parents. The remainder of this subsection is a summary taken, with minor modifications, from an advance report on that project (Frenkel-Brunswik, 30):

Forced into a surface submission to parental authority, the child develops hostility and aggression which are poorly channelized. The displacement of a repressed antagonism toward authority may be one of the sources, and perhaps the principal source, of his antagonism toward outgroups. That is to say, the prejudiced subject's ambivalence toward his parents, with a repression and externalization of the negative side of this ambivalence, may be a factor in determining his strongly polarized attitudes, such as his uncritical acceptance of the ingroup and violent rejection of the outgroup.

Fear and dependency seem to discourage the ethnocentric child from conscious criticism of the parents. It is especially the prejudiced man who seems intimidated by a threatening father figure. Display of a rough masculine façade seems to be a compensation for such an intimidation and the ensuing passivity and dependency. Rigid repression of hostility against parents may be accompanied by an occasional breaking through of drives in a crude and unsocialized form; under certain circumstances this may become dangerous to the very society to which there seems to be conformity.

The fact that the negative feelings against the parents have to be excluded from consciousness may be considered as contributing to the general lack of insight, rigidity of defense, and narrowness of the ego so characteristic of high scorers. Since the unprejudiced child as a rule does not seem to have to submit to stern authority—a fact supported by interviews with the parents—he can afford in his later life to do without strong authority, and he does not need to assert his strength against those who are weaker. The "antiweakness" attitude referred to above as characteristic of the prejudiced child seems thus to be directly related to the fearful submission to authority.

It may be noted that the parents of prejudiced subjects not only seem to have been rigid disciplinarians; they also tended toward preoccupation with problems of status, communicating to their children a set of rigid and externalized rules. Status-concern may well be assumed to be the basis of such a rigid and externalized set of values. What is socially accepted and what is helpful in the climbing of the social ladder is considered good, and what deviates, what is different, and what is socially inferior is considered bad. Quite often, the parents of the ethnocentric subject seem to be socially marginal. The less they were able to accept their marginality, the more urgent must have been the wish to belong to the privileged groups. The feelings of marginality involved do not seem to be related to the gross economic conditions of the families in question but rather to those more subtle factors which determine the relationship between social aspiration and effective social status.

The influence of the parents must be considered at least a contributing factor to the tendency, observed in the ethnocentric child, to be more concerned with status values than are low-scoring subjects. He expects—and gives—social approval on the basis of external moral values including cleanliness, politeness, and the like. He condemns others for their nonconformity to such values, conformity being an all-or-none affair. The functioning of his superego is mainly directed toward punishment, condemnation, and exclusion of others, thus mirroring the type of discipline to which he himself was apparently exposed. There is more moralistic condemnation on the part of the prejudiced and greater permissiveness toward people in general on the part of the unprejudiced. The difficulty which children growing up in such an environment as that pictured by our prejudiced subjects, seem to have in developing close personal relationships may be interpreted as one of the outcomes of the repression of hostile tendencies, which are not integrated or sublimated, but which become diffuse and free-flowing.

As was pointed out above, the low scorer seems more oriented toward love and less toward power than is the high scorer. The former is more capable of giving affection since he has received more real affection. He tends to judge people more on the basis of their intrinsic worth than on the basis of conformity to social mores. He takes internal values and principles more seriously. Since he fears punishment and retaliation less than does the ethnocentric person, he is more able really to incorporate the values of society imposed upon him.

As a child, he seems to have enjoyed the benefit of the help of adults in working out his problems of sex and aggression. He thus can more easily withstand propaganda which defames minorities or glorifies war. By virtue of the greater integration of his instinctual life, he becomes a more creative and sublimated individual. He is thus more flexible and less likely to form stereotyped opinions about others. He possesses a better developed, more integrated, and more internalized superego. He is able to express disagreement with, and resentment against, the parents more openly, thus achieving a much greater degree of independence from the parent and from authorities in general. At the same time, there is love-oriented dependence on parents and people in general which constitutes an important source of gratification. Possible frustration, however, may result from the exaggerated demand for affection sometimes found in individuals in this group.

8. CULTURAL OUTLOOK

Ethnic prejudice and its opposite have emerged, on the basis of the interviews, as two distinct patterns of life. Other kinds of approach have revealed these same patterns. In asking oneself how these two patterns may be related to general cultural trends, one may point toward the fact that by virtue of our evidence the outlook of the prejudiced individual, with his emphasis on status, power, and conventionality, seems to be the more salient of the two patterns. The outlook of the unprejudiced person, on the other hand, is characterized by relative absence of the undesirable features just listed. There is, furthermore, more basic uniformity in the prejudiced group, differences among them having more aspects of variations on the same theme. The unprejudiced group, on the other hand, shows greater diversity among its members.

It may be ventured that the greater uniformity of the prejudiced sample derives from their greater closeness to the broader cultural pattern of our society. There can be no doubt that our prejudiced group shows a more rigid adherence to existing cultural norms and that its emphasis on status is in line with what has been designated by several authors, such as especially Horney (54), Kardiner (59, 60), R. and H. Lynd (77), and Mead (82), as the general trend of Western civilization. More specifically, a feature especially emphasized by Mead as a characteristic of American culture, namely the "fear of being a sucker," is also typical of our high-scoring men.

On the other hand, the same author describes "identification with the underdog" as another outstanding characteristic of American culture; it represents one of the many influences of Christian ethics in general. Obviously, however, this is more common among the low scorers. It appears that both trends, as well as the conflict between them, are major characteristics of our civilization, with only relatively few individuals exhibiting the one or the other extreme in pure form.

The political and social ideology of the two personality structures differentiated throughout has been discussed in detail elsewhere in the volume. Here we shall confine ourselves to a summary of some of the consistencies that exist between personality structure and the social and political outlooks as assimilated from the possibilities available in our culture.

Admiration of power and a longing for strong leadership on the social scene as predominant in the high scorer may readily be interpreted as a carry-over from the hierarchical evaluation of interpersonal relations. Extreme personal opportunism is often, though not always, connected with ideological opportunism and indifference toward ideological content. Status anxiety, adherence to external criteria in value judgments, thinking in stereotypes, and the lack of a concept of equality is closely related to a contempt of what is allegedly socially inferior. Fear of one's own weakness and emasculation prevents the development of pity for the weak.

Rigid adherence to conventional values will render one inaccessible to groups and nations who deviate in some respect from one's own cultural norms. The striving toward being like the others and the shying away from being "different" lie in the same general direction.

Outside groups, on the other hand, also lend themselves as a projection-screen for wishes and fears, often so strongly repressed in the high scorer. Immoral tendencies are easier perceived in, or ascribed to, groups which seem not fully assimilated or are altogether foreign. Hostility and the fear of being victimized can be expressed against these groups without restraint or expectation of retaliation. Even if such outgroups as the Jews are described as powerful, it is the knowledge of their ultimate weakness which makes them suited for scapegoats. Toward the really powerful groups the ethnically prejudiced will more likely exhibit submission and suppress rather than manifest his hostility.

The high scorer's feeling of really belonging to the privileged group is highly tenuous. Due to his real or imagined social and psychological marginality he feels persistently threatened of being degraded in one way or another. It is as a defense against the possibility of being grouped with the outcast and underdog that he rigidly has to assert his identification with the privileged groups. This loud and explicit assertion of being on top seems to ensue from his silent and implicit conviction that he really is, or belongs, at the bottom (see the discussion concerning self-contempt, Chapters XI and XII). The obvious function of the mechanism described is in helping to keep existing anxieties and guilt-feelings in a repressed state.

All these repressed but no less turbulent inconsistencies and the conflicts resulting from them contribute to what may be called personalization of social issues which is so typical of the high scorer. Low scorers, on the other hand, tend to take their conflicts up where they originate: with their parents and with themselves. Thus there is less need for carrying them into the social sphere. There is greater accessibility to fact and to rational argument. Although confusion and biases are by no means excluded, they stem from a greater variety of sources and are less rigid than those typical of the high scorer. The greater readiness of the low scorers to face themselves goes with a greater readiness to look more objectively at man and society in general.

It is perhaps mainly the readiness to include, accept, and even love differences and diversities, as contrasted with the need to set off clear demarcation lines and to ascertain superiorities and inferiorities, which remains as the most basic distinguishing criterion of the two opposite patterns. Members of an outgroup representing deviations from the cultural norms of the ingroup are most threatening to one who must conceive of the cultural norms as absolute in order to be able to feel secure.

It would go beyond the scope of this volume to ascertain fully the determinants of this need for homogeneity and simplicity in all the various spheres of life. In some cases concern with the *status quo* and resistance to change might be a more primary need as determined by various social and psychological factors. In other cases it might be a secondary reaction to a situation that grew too complex for mastery by routine means of adjustment. As was pointed out by Fromm (42), this was probably the case with Nazism in Germany. Thus under certain socioeconomic conditions an entire nation may become inclined to "escape from freedom."

In our present-day struggle to achieve a strengthening of the tolerant, liberal point of view we may have to avoid presenting the prejudiced individual with more ambiguities than he is able to absorb and offer instead, in some spheres at least, solutions which are constructive and at the same time serve the general need for avoidance of uncertainties. Efforts to modify the "prejudiced" pattern may have to make use of authorities—though by no means necessarily of authoritarian authorities—in order to reach the individual in question. This follows from the fact that it is authority more than anything else that structures or prestructures the world of the prejudiced individual. Where public opinion takes over the function of authority and provides the necessary limitations—and thus certainties—in many walks of daily life, as is the case in this country, there will be some room for the tolerance of national or racial ambiguities.

It must be emphasized, however, that the potentially beneficial aspects of conformity are more than counterbalanced by the inherent seeds of stereotypy and pre-judgment. These latter trends are apt to increase in a culture which has become too complex to be fully mastered by the individual. The inevitability of certain developments toward stereotypy are being pointed out elsewhere in this volume. On the other hand, forces endeavoring to penetrate to the underlying causes of social trends in spite of their confusing manifestations are likewise as strong as never before, and they are rapidly spreading from the ivory tower of science to public opinion at large. The struggle between these opposing forces characterizes not only our culture as a whole, but every single individual as well. How this struggle will end does not hinge on psychological factors alone. As such factors are in the end manifestations of broader cultural influences, it is only by an understanding of the interplay of sociological and psychological phenomena in their entirety that a full appraisal of the relative potentials of the opposing trends can be achieved.

PART III

Personality as Revealed Through Projective Material

CHAPTER XIV

THE THEMATIC APPERCEPTION TEST IN THE STUDY
OF PREJUDICED AND UNPREJUDICED INDIVIDUALS

Betty Aron

The Thematic Apperception Test (T. A. T.) offers another avenue of approach to the study of the personality patterns of our high and low scorers, further substantiating some of the aspects that have been discussed in previous chapters and touching upon still others. This test was developed by Morgan and Murray (83) in 1934 and it has been the object of much study since that time (14, 81, 94, 99). It consists of a series of ambiguous pictures, about each of which the subject is asked to tell a story. It is assumed that in describing the characters depicted, in setting forth their actions and the stimuli which affect them, the subject indirectly tells something about himself.

By means of this indirect approach, areas of the personality that cannot be tapped by verbal questioning are sometimes revealed. Here the subject often allows himself a greater degree of freedom of expression because he is not openly telling about himself and giving his own ideas about real people and how they act. Although he is likely to identify himself with the content of the story, this is not usually apparent to him. Unlike the interview situation, in which the subject attempts consciously to defend himself against expressing feelings or desires which he would rather not recognize as belonging to himself, in the T. A. T., where the subject usually is motivated by the desire to succeed at a creative enterprise, he tends to be unaware of the significance of the content of his creation. Consequently, although much of the content produced in the T. A. T. is similar to that expressed in the interviews, other productions appear to differ, even to contradict, the interview data. These discrepancies can be understood only when the differences in defenses operating in each case are recognized. This relationship between expressions elicited through the interview and through the T. A. T. will become clearer with the comparisons in this chapter between the two types of data.

The theory behind the present technique assumes that the particular stories that the subject tells represent his fantasied environment and fantasied way of dealing with that environment. Various investigators of T. A. T. have pointed out the psychic determination of the individuality of these fantasies (14, 81, 106, 120). They have found that the content of these stories reveals desires or needs of the personality. Any person in the story with whose actions the subject concerns himself (we will speak of such persons as "heroes") represents a medium through whom the subject expresses his own inner tendencies, and the actions themselves are indicative of the nature of these tendencies.

When we speak of underlying desires or "needs," we do not refer to instinctual impulses nor do we wish to imply that these desires are innate. Rather, we refer to tendencies within the personality that result from the developmental pattern—from influences of the environment upon the basic psychic structure. We use the term "underlying" to refer especially to those tendencies which are not ordinarily allowed expression.

These underlying desires are, of course, not always revealed directly even in the T. A. T. They are transformed by unconscious ego defense mechanisms into acceptable expression. It is thus necessary to be familiar with the techniques of language that the individual learns to employ, in the service of ego defense mechanisms, in order to be able to understand the relationship between the verbalized expression of a particular desire and an underlying motivation. To give a simple example: Certain needs may be obscured by mechanisms of *denial*—the individual describes these needs in the story but condemns the hero for the actions representative of these needs or blames external forces for precipitating such action on the part of the hero. In fact, if certain desires are too anxiety-producing to be allowed expression, they may be inhibited altogether. In order, therefore, to get a clear picture of the motivations of our various subjects, we shall be concerned in the following pages not only with the expressed needs but also with cues indicative of motivation that is protected from open expression by defense mechanisms.

A.   TESTING PROCEDURE

1. THE SAMPLE TESTED

The test was administered to a group of 80 subjects, consisting of 20 high-scoring (prejudiced) and 20 low-scoring (unprejudiced) men, and 20 high- and 20 low-scoring women. In the main, these were the same subjects who were called for interviews (see Chapter IX). The groups from which the sample was drawn and the number in each group are given in Table 1(XIV).

It will be noted that all of the women in this sample either had a college education or were then taking classes, day or night, at the University. However, only a little more than half of our men were college educated. (The 16 men who were veterans or Maritime School officer candidates were not

TABLE 1 (XIV)

DISTRIBUTION OF THEMATIC APPERCEPTION TEST SAMPLE
AMONG THE SEVERAL GROUPS PARTICIPATING IN THE STUDY

Group	Men		Women	
	Low Scorers	High Scorers	Low Scorers	High Scorers
University of California Extension Psychology and Testing Classes	7	4	2	4
Employment Service Veterans and Maritime School Officer Candidates	8	8		
University of California Students	5	8	16	15
Professional Women			2	1
Totals	20	20	20	20

obtained from a college population, and most of them had not had any college training.) The lack of male students during wartime forced us to go outside of the University to find subjects. Although we were somewhat hesitant at first to consider in one group stories of people of different educational levels, we were interested to find that the veterans and officer candidates usually told stories that were similar in content to those of our other subjects and quite as representative of the high- or low-scoring group to which they belonged. Often their stories were less articulate, less literary, and less complete, but the main themes were not different from those found in our college group.

The ages of our female subjects ranged from 17 to 49, the bulk of the range falling between 17 and 27. Three low-scoring women, and 4 high-scoring women were over 27 years of age. The age range of the men was from 17 to 47, 5 low- and 5 high-scoring men being over 27. It will be observed from Table 2(XIV) that the women in our sample are slightly younger than the men.

The test was administered to most subjects by four examiners, two men and two women. Each of these examiners tested both men and women. It has not yet been established to what extent the sex of the experimenter affects the subject's responses. Whatever effect it might have had in this case, however, should have been canceled out by the fact that equal numbers of low-scoring and high-scoring men were tested by a male experimenter, and that approximately equal numbers from each group were tested by a female

TABLE 2 (XIV)

AGE DISTRIBUTION OF SUBJECTS RECEIVING THE THEMATIC APPERCEPTION TEST

Age	Men		Women	
	Low Scorers	High Scorers	Low Scorers	High Scorers
Under 20	3	3	9	7
20 - 27	12	12	8	9
Over 27	5	5	3	4
Total	20	20	20	20

experimenter. As will be noted in Table 3(XIV) below, there is a slightly greater discrepancy between the amount of testing done by male and female

TABLE 3 (XIV)

DISTRIBUTION OF THEMATIC APPERCEPTION TEST SUBJECTS
WITH RESPECT TO THE SEX OF THE EXAMINERS

Examiner	Men		Women	
	Low Scorers	High Scorers	Low Scorers	High Scorers
Men:				
Dr. W. M. Wickham	3	8	5	11
Dr. W. R. Morrow	6	7	1	
Dr. Alex Sherriffs	1		2	
Dr. Boyd R. McCandless	3			
Dr. D. J. Levinson	1			
Total subjects tested by men	14	15	8	11
Women:				
Dr. Suzanne Reichard	4	2	7	7
Betty Aron	1	3	5	2
Maria Levinson	1			
Total subjects tested by women	6	5	12	9
Over-all total	20	20	20	20

experimenters on each of the groups of women, but the discrepancy is still not great.

Further, it should be noted that on the whole the examiners who tested low-scoring men tested an almost equal number of high-scoring men and that those experimenters who tested women, tested an almost equal number of low- and high-scoring women. Thus, small differences in administration between individual testers should have affected high- and low-scoring groups of the same sex equally. Since our comparisons are always between high and low scorers in each sex group, such differences in administration will always be approximately equally distributed between compared groups.

2. TECHNIQUE OF ADMINISTRATION

Before the pictures are presented to the subject, he is given the following instructions:

You are going to be shown a series of pictures. I want you to tell a story about each picture, telling what's happening in the picture; what events led up to it; and how it will turn out; in other words, a complete story—the picture being an illustration to the story.

Each picture is presented in turn, and the subject has an opportunity to express his fantasies in story form, as a piece of fiction. The story is recorded verbatim by the examiner.

The examiner encourages the subject to explain more fully whenever it seems that valuable information can be elicited by elaboration of a particular idea that the subject has expressed. Under no circumstances is the examiner allowed to offer a remark or question that would be suggestive of a particular answer. The subject is always left free to invent his own story.

There was some variability in the amount of questioning that was done by different examiners. However, we have considered the variability in administration to be a small factor, since each experimenter tested both low- and high-scoring subjects, and since the responses resulting from questioning were given very little weight in scoring.

3. THE PICTURES USED

A set of ten pictures was used in the present study. Seven of these pictures were the same for men and women. In the cases of the first, the fifth, and the seventh pictures presented we used alternative pictures for the two sex groups, pictures that would call for a story with masculine identification being given to the men, and pictures that would call for a story with feminine identification being given to the women. We chose all our pictures, except two, four, six, and nine (numbered according to the order in which they were administered), from a group of Thematic Apperception Test pictures introduced by H. A. Murray. Analysis of stories given in response to these published pictures had already been made at the Harvard Psychological Clinic and by others using the T. A. T. technique (94, 99, 106), and it

TABLE 4 (XIV)

STIMULUS VALUES OF THE TEN THEMATIC APPERCEPTION TEST PICTURES

Active humans in picture usually represent:	Identification usually closest to:	Reveals relation to:	Environmental stimulus:	Mood of main character:
Pictures from the Murray Set				
M1 Father and son "Younger man and older man"	Son	Father	A[a]	Somber, sad, thoughtful, determined
F1 Father figure	?[b]	Father	A	Sad or thoughtful
3 A	Either person A man - for males A woman - for females	Love object	A	A
M5 Young man	Man	Female sex object	Common reaction to dark background and passivity of female figure as foreboding	Guilt, fear, shame, expressed
F5 Young girl	Girl	?	A	Guilt, fear, shame, expressed
M7 Mother and son	Son	Rejective mother	Mother with back turned to son (rejective)	Somber, sad, thoughtful, determined
F7 Old woman, young woman, mother and daughter	Young woman (sometimes old woman with older subjects)	Older woman (mother) Young woman with older subjects	Pressing old age	A

8 1. Dominant man 2. Passive man	A (either figure)	1. to passive submissive figure 2. to dominant aggressive figure		1. Dominant- sometimes aggressive 2. Passive
10 A (young boy, young girl, child)	A	Environmental stimuli	Religious, ethereal background	A
Special Pictures				
2 Adolescent boy and girl (zootsuiters or young jitterbugs)	Both or neither (identification stronger with same sex as subject)	A (sometimes opposite sex when identified)	Peculiar clothing A background	Gay
4 Man, woman in background	One, both, or neither	A	Slum area. Dark, somber. Heavy clothing-	A
6 Man (usually foreign, police suspect) Police	One or neither generally	A	Bars of prison	Suspect: fear Police: A
9 Negro mother or grandmother Young boy	Boy (older women sometimes identify with grandmother)	Mother figure	Home surroundings	A

a A: Ambiguous.
b ?: No clue in picture.

had been established that they were sufficiently ambiguous so that the subject could project his own personality into the story. Pictures two, four, six, and nine were selected by the study staff from current magazines. The people in these pictures were intended to suggest minority group members. We expected to obtain an expression of attitudes toward minority groups that was more spontaneous than that obtained through direct questioning.

We selected this particular set of ten pictures because we thought they would give us the maximum amount of pertinent material in approximately one hour's testing time, the amount of time that was allotted for this part of the clinical investigation of a subject.

We sought pictures that were dissimilar from one another, offering the subject a variety of possible story heroes and a diversity of suggested situations. We also wanted to make sure that each picture would allow for a variety of different themes, and hence provide a basis for comparing our different subjects. In short, we tried to find a series of pictures that would elicit as much information as possible about the individual's conceptualized environment, and his personality needs striving for expression.

Each picture has certain stimulus values that are fairly stable for all of our subjects (see Table 4(XIV)). Beyond these consistent similarities we found certain striking differences. The remainder of this chapter will be concerned with the methods by which the responses of high- and low-scoring subjects were compared, and the results obtained thereby.

B. METHOD OF ANALYSIS OF THE STORY PROTOCOLS

The T. A. T. stories were subjected to analysis by two separate techniques. First, they were scored according to Sanford's revised Murray need-press system (105). The second technique, based on Murray's concept of thema and adapted to the present study by the writer, was used to examine differences in the patterns of combinations of need-press variables.

A device for analysis of story outcomes was also applied. However, at the time this project was under way the outcome analysis technique was still in its undeveloped stages (12). Consequently, the results obtained added little to this investigation, and we shall, therefore, refer to them only briefly.

1. THE MURRAY-SANFORD SCHEME

a. EXPLANATION OF THE METHOD. The Murray-Sanford scheme for scoring Thematic Apperception Tests is a device by which the subject's stories are measured in terms of certain variables.[1] These variables are conceived as a kind of shorthand representation of psychologically meaningful content of the fantasy of an individual as expressed in response to the T. A. T. pictures. The variables fall into two groups, those that represent the direction

[1] The method and variables used in this study differ somewhat from those presented in the book referred to above.

of activity of the characters within the story and those that denote environmental (personal or physical) influences that act upon these characters. The former variables are termed *need* variables, the latter *press* variables. In a particular story, the hero's (or heroes') behavior (i.e., the actions of the central figure or figures) is noted by use of the proper need variable preceded by an "n." Reference to activity from external sources imposed upon the hero (or heroes) is noted by use of a press "p" variable. Secondary characters or central figures in the story who are openly rejected by the storyteller, and whose actions are not directed toward the hero, are termed *objects* and their behavior is recorded by use of need variables, preceded by the notation "on." Similarly, environmental impositions upon these characters are referred to by use of *object press* "op" variables. A list of these variables and an explanation of each follows:

Need Variables

(*These need variables are also used as press variables.)

n *Abasement:*	To comply, surrender, accept punishment. To apologize, condone, atone. To depreciate oneself. Masochism.
n *Achievement:*	To work intensely and persistently towards a goal.
*n *Acquisition:*	To take, snatch, or steal objects. Greedily to work for money or "goods." To bargain or gamble. To want possessions.
*n *Affiliation:*	To be sociable. To make friends. To love.
*n *Aggression:*	To fight. To criticize, blame, accuse, or ridicule maliciously. To injure or kill. Sadism.
n *Autonomy:*	To resist coercion. To be free and independent.
n *Blamavoidance:*	To avoid blame by inhibiting asocial impulses. To fear censure, ostracism, or punishment. To be well-behaved.
n *Blamescape:*	To escape blame by flight or by concealment of guilt.
*n *Cognizance:*	To observe, inquire, explore, and investigate. To acquire facts.
n *Construction:*	To organize and build things. To produce.
n *Counteraction:*	To restrive after failure and to overcome weakness.
n *Defendence:*	To defend the self verbally against blame or criticism.
*n *Dominance:*	To influence or control others. Leadership.
*n *Deference:*	To admire and follow a superior allied object.
n *Excitement:*	To seek adventure and excitement. To enjoy thrills, new sensations, drama.
*n *Exposition:*	To relate facts. To explain, judge, interpret.
n *Harmavoidance:*	To avoid or flee from danger. To fear injury, illness, or death. To hide or take protective measures.

n Infavoidance:	To avoid shame. To escape failure or humiliation.
*n Nurturance:	To nourish and protect a helpless object. To express sympathy. To mother a child.
n Nutriance:	To seek food and drink.
n Passivity:	To be relaxed and inactive. To receive benefits without effort. To allow others their way.
n Play:	To relax tension and alleviate stress by pleasurable and humorously irresponsible activity— motor, verbal, or mental.
n Recognition:	To seek attention, praise, appreciation, honor, fame.
*n Rejection:	To exclude or scornfully ignore inferior objects.
*n Retention:	To retain possession of objects. Economy, frugality, miserliness, to defend property.
n Seclusion:	To be alone or inconspicuous. To maintain privacy.
n Sentience:	To enjoy sensuous pleasures—sights and sounds.
*n Sex:	To participate in a heterosexual love relationship. To court, to enjoy intercourse.
*n Succorance:	To seek aid, protection, or sympathy. To indulge in self-pity.
n Understanding:	To think out explanations, develop logical relations, work out plans of procedure.

Press Variables

Psychological Press: These variables have the same meaning when used as need or press variables. When used as press variables they represent activity imposed upon the hero rather than expressed by the hero.

p Acquisition	p Exposition
p Affiliation	p Nurturance
p Aggression	p Rejection
p Cognizance	p Retention
p Dominance	p Sex
p Deference	p Succorance

Environmental Press:

p Affliction:	The hero is the victim of an illness or disease, is a dope fiend or chronic alcoholic.
p Bad Luck:	The hero experiences misfortune which he himself has not created.
p Claustrum:	The hero is forced into confinement.
p Death of Hero:	The hero dies.
p Death of Object:	Someone other than the hero dies.
p Failure:	The hero fails in his attempts to gain personal achievement.
p Gratuity:	The hero is endowed with money or personal success although he has not striven for this particular gain.

p *Inferiority:*	The hero is an "innately" inferior person.
p *Injury:*	The hero is physically injured.
p *Lack:*	The hero suffers from economic or environmental barrenness.
p *Loss:*	The hero loses something or someone (money, job, friend, opportunity).
p *Old Age:*	The hero is victimized by old age.
p *Physical Danger:*	The hero is exposed to physical danger from sources such as animals, a flood, a tornado, or by a warring national enemy.
p *Superiority:*	The hero is endowed with a superior personality.
p *Task:*	The hero is given something to do; practice on a violin, study. He is sent on a mission to serve his employer, a cause, or his country.
p *Uncongenial Environment:*	The hero's physical environment is unpleasant: ugly, sordid, noxious, dreary, or noisy.

Each story is analyzed separately and every variable reflected in the story content is noted and given a value of 1 to 5. The score thus assigned is based upon the degree of intensity of expression in the case of the particular variable and upon its importance to the story as a whole. We shall refer to these quantified scores as *intensity* scores. The following discussion will be concerned primarily with the comparison of scoring of a particular variable for all pictures in the case of unprejudiced men (or women) and in the case of prejudiced men (or women). In some cases reference will be made also to the number of times a variable is recorded for each of the two groups, regardless of the numerical intensity values that were assigned. These scores will be referred to as *frequency* scores.

b. RESULTS OF SCORING. The results of scoring by the Murray-Sanford scheme are given in Tables 5(XIV)A and 5(XIV)B. Twenty of the 80 records used in this sample were rescored by a second scorer for purposes of reliability testing. Rank order correlations of the two scorers' ratings of the stories of the twenty individuals for each variable varied between +.41 and +.83 except for one r (for n Rejection), which fell to .26. The fifteen variables with the highest reliability ratings (between +.63 and +.83) are designated in the tables.

The sum of the scoring of all variables was somewhat higher for the unprejudiced than for the prejudiced women (Low-scoring Women 4581/High-scoring Women 4186). However, this difference was not apparent in the case of the men (Low-scoring Men 4183/High-scoring Men 4254). In both cases, however, the subjects scoring low on ethnocentrism expressed more material that could be scored as needs (Low-scoring Women 2473/High-scoring Women 1966) (Low-scoring Men 2154/High-scoring Men 1896) but less that could be scored as object needs (*on*) (Low-scoring Women 276/High-scoring Women 333) (Low-scoring men 323/High-scoring Men 516). In our sample, both of men and of women, the total press

TABLE 5 (XIV) A

INTENSITIES OF NEED AND PRESS VARIABLES AS EXPRESSED IN STORIES TOLD BY MEN

	Picture 1				Picture 2				Picture 3				Picture 4				Picture 5				Picture 6			
	Low Scorers		High Scorers		Low Scorers		High Scorers		Low Scorers		High Scorers		Low Scorers		High Scorers		Low Scorers		High Scorers		Low Scorers		High Scorers	
Need Variables:	n	on	n	on	n	on	n	on	n	on	n	on	n	on	n	on	n	on	n	on	n	on	n	on
Abasement[a]	19	5	30	3	8	0	8	5	5	0	5	9	15	0	10	4	51	9	49	14	14	8	25	7
Achievement[a]	5	0	0	2	9	0	11	0	7	2	3	0	9	0	9	4	3	0	2	4	3	0	4	0
Acquisition[a]	2	0	13	0	10	3	5	4	3	0	4	0	37	8	24	14	9	3	9	3	5	9	14	5
Affiliation[a]	6	0	9	0	38	1	27	10	27	0	18	0	10	0	7	2	12	0	14	2	4	3	2	2
Aggression[a]	27	7	31	2	7	1	0	0	6	0	6	7	8	0	1	6	28	6	8	14	32	13	23	34
Autonomy	25	6	18	3	7	3	6	13	6	0	8	0	6	3	6	11	4	9	3	7	35	7	23	16
Blamavoidance	6	0	10	3	3	0	10	3	0	0	0	2	0	0	0	0	9	0	8	0	4	0	4	8
Blamescape	0	0	2	0	3	0	0	1	0	0	0	0	0	0	0	3	5	4	4	0	10	3	4	2
Cognizance	16	0	5	1	10	0	5	2	6	0	0	0	18	0	17	5	4	0	2	0	0	0	4	3
Construction	5	2	1	0	0	0	0	0	0	0	0	0	0	0	4	0	0	0	0	0	0	0	0	0
Counteraction	9	2	18	0	3	0	1	0	0	0	4	0	0	0	0	0	13	0	11	0	2	0	2	0
Deference	17	3	8	0	0	0	5	0	3	0	2	0	0	0	3	2	3	0	2	0	0	0	4	0
Defendance	0	0	2	0	0	0	0	0	0	0	0	0	0	0	0	0	0	0	0	0	0	0	0	0
Dominance	8	0	6	0	0	0	7	0	0	0	4	4	3	6	0	3	3	0	3	0	4	0	6	7
Excitance	0	0	0	0	16	2	5	14	1	0	5	0	3	0	0	0	3	0	6	0	2	0	0	0
Exposition	12	0	7	0	8	0	3	0	4	0	6	4	6	0	5	2	8	0	0	0	3	0	0	0
Harmavoidance	0	0	0	0	0	0	0	2	2	0	2	3	0	0	0	0	3	0	0	0	27	4	23	6
Infavoidance	3	0	0	0	0	0	1	0	0	0	1	0	0	0	0	0	0	0	0	0	0	0	1	0
Nurturance[a]	11	0	3	0	4	0	9	1	34	0	25	2	7	0	12	3	10	0	0	0	2	0	2	0
Nutriance	1	0	1	0	2	0	1	0	0	0	0	0	7	0	2	0	1	0	4	1	0	0	0	0
Passivity	2	0	1	0	2	2	3	0	9	0	3	0	9	0	9	3	3	2	6	2	3	0	0	0
Play[a]	0	0	0	0	34	0	21	10	4	0	4	0	0	0	6	1	13	0	3	0	3	0	0	0
Recognition[a]	3	0	0	0	29	3	25	13	0	0	3	0	0	0	9	0	9	0	3	0	1	0	0	0
Rejection	17	4	6	0	5	0	3	3	6	0	5	3	13	2	10	6	12	3	5	8	8	0	6	5
Retention	0	0	0	0	0	0	0	0	0	0	0	0	2	0	6	4	0	0	0	0	0	0	3	0
Seclusion	3	2	0	0	0	0	0	0	0	0	7	4	19	5	17	4	3	2	11	10	0	0	7	2
Sentience	0	0	0	0	0	0	0	3	2	0	0	0	5	0	0	0	17	0	0	0	0	0	0	0
Sex[a]	8	0	4	0	18	1	19	10	22	0	6	0	0	0	1	0	43	7	28	5	0	2	2	8
Succorance[a]	15	3	21	1	3	1	2	0	23	1	13	11	18	0	11	0	18	0	24	3	8	5	3	4
Understanding	10	0	1	0	3	0	2	0	1	0	0	0	3	0	2	0	2	0	0	0	0	0	0	0
Press Variables:	p	op	p	op	p	op	p	op	p	op	p	op	p	op	p	op	p	op	p	op	p	op	p	op
Abasement	0	0	0	0	0	0	0	0	0	0	0	0	0	0	3	0	0	0	0	0	0	0	0	0
Acquisition	0	0	0	0	0	0	0	0	2	0	0	0	0	0	8	0	0	0	0	0	0	0	0	2
Affiliation	3	3	10	0	34	1	27	8	29	0	21	0	7	0	6	3	10	0	13	2	0	2	0	3
Aggression[a]	23	5	26	0	5	2	0	6	7	0	7	4	10	4	4	6	58	8	42	16	19	6	11	3
Cognizance	1	2	6	0	13	0	11	2	3	0	4	0	3	3	0	3	7	0	3	0	0	0	13	3
Deference	5	0	0	0	5	0	9	0	2	1	3	3	3	0	6	3	4	0	3	0	0	0	6	2
Dominance	37	6	44	3	3	3	5	5	1	0	3	2	3	2	5	5	9	3	9	2	59	12	48	21
Excitance	0	0	0	0	3	0	0	0	2	0	0	0	0	0	0	0	0	0	0	0	2	0	2	3
Exposition	21	0	12	3	0	0	5	0	0	0	9	0	2	0	7	0	0	0	0	0	0	0	2	3
Nurturance[a]	18	2	33	2	9	0	4	6	9	0	8	1	6	0	9	0	3	0	9	2	4	0	3	5
Rejection[a]	11	3	2	0	13	0	13	4	2	0	7	0	11	0	13	3	20	3	24	8	13	3	5	1
Sex	3	0	2	0	17	0	18	9	21	0	5	0	0	0	1	0	24	2	20	0	0	0	0	0
Succorance	0	0	1	0	0	3	3	0	29	0	19	2	0	0	2	3	6	0	0	0	0	0	0	0
Affliction[a]	4	0	9	5	3	0	2	0	0	0	9	0	5	0	4	0	16	3	7	4	0	0	0	4
Birth-offspring	0	0	0	0	0	0	0	5	0	0	0	0	0	0	0	0	0	0	0	0	0	0	0	0
Bad Luck	0	0	6	0	0	0	3	2	0	0	0	0	0	0	9	3	0	0	3	0	0	0	0	0
Claustrum	11	2	5	0	0	0	0	0	0	0	0	0	0	0	0	0	6	0	1	1	14	0	16	9
Death of Hero	3	0	6	0	2	0	0	0	4	0	13	0	0	0	3	3	7	0	3	3	3	0	4	0
Death of Object	14	3	16	0	0	0	3	0	14	0	15	0	5	0	3	0	10	0	5	3	4	0	0	0
Failure	3	0	0	0	0	0	0	0	0	0	0	4	2	0	2	0	4	0	2	0	0	0	0	0
Gratuity	0	0	3	0	0	0	5	4	0	0	0	0	16	0	11	5	5	5	8	5	0	0	0	3
Inferiority	0	3	0	0	0	0	2	2	2	0	0	5	0	0	4	0	2	0	4	4	2	3	5	0
Injury	3	0	3	0	0	0	0	0	0	0	0	2	0	0	0	0	0	0	0	0	5	0	0	0
Lack	6	0	8	0	3	0	3	0	2	0	3	1	19	3	13	3	7	0	9	0	7	0	3	3
Loss	5	0	3	0	0	0	0	0	2	0	6	0	10	0	2	0	8	0	7	0	0	0	0	0
Old Age	0	0	0	0	0	0	1	0	0	0	0	0	5	0	6	0	0	0	0	0	0	0	0	0
Physical Danger	3	0	8	0	0	0	2	0	9	0	4	0	0	0	3	0	0	0	0	0	0	0	2	0
Superiority	4	0	2	2	8	0	5	0	3	0	0	0	0	0	0	0	0	0	3	0	0	0	2	0
Task[a]	0	0	2	2	13	0	2	5	13	2	19	2	18	0	14	3	11	3	2	0	7	0	2	6
Uncongenial Environment	4	0	0	0	0	0	0	3	0	0	0	0	27	0	25	8	5	2	5	6	0	0	0	3

[a]These fifteen variables showed the highest reliability (.63 to .83) between scores of two independent raters.

Note: Underlining indicates that there is a notable difference in total scores for the variable in question between subjects scoring low and those scoring high on the Ethnocentrism scale. Where a score is underlined once, the variable is more pronounced in stories of low scorers; where underlined twice, the variable is more pronounced in stories of high scorers.

TABLE 5 (XIV) A

INTENSITIES OF NEED AND PRESS VARIABLES AS EXPRESSED IN STORIES TOLD BY MEN

Need Variables:	Picture 7 Low Scorers		High Scorers		Picture 8 Low Scorers		High Scorers		Picture 9 Low Scorers		High Scorers		Picture 10 Low Scorers		High Scorers		Totals 10 Pictures Low Scorers		High Scorers	
	n	on	n	on	n	on	n	on	n	on	n	on	n	on	n	on	n	on	n	on
Abasement	24	10	32	6	12	1	9	4	6	3	13	0	4	0	19	0	158	36	200	57
Achievement	11	0	4	0	6	0	10	0	11	0	13	2	9	0	14	0	73	2	70	12
Acquisition	20	2	17	3	4	6	8	3	0	8	9	0	1	0	3	0	91	39	106	32
Affiliation	14	0	15	0	0	0	4	0	18	0	4	1	7	0	5	0	136	4	105	17
Aggression	16	0	13	6	18	10	15	9	6	3	14	2	5	0	3	4	153	40	114	84
Autonomy	41	0	33	0	0	5	5	0	4	3	14	2	3	0	2	0	131	36	118	52
Blamavoidance	9	7	17	3	0	0	0	0	4	6	9	1	0	3	6	0	35	16	64	20
Blamescape	8	0	14	0	0	0	4	0	0	0	3	0	0	0	0	0	29	7	31	6
Cognizance	4	0	6	0	13	0	9	0	21	3	13	0	29	0	14	0	121	3	75	11
Construction	2	0	1	0	0	0	1	0	0	0	0	0	2	0	2	0	9	2	9	0
Counteraction	14	0	10	0	0	0	0	0	5	0	5	0	5	0	3	0	51	2	54	0
Deference	26	5	21	4	9	0	15	0	21	3	17	0	19	3	28	0	98	14	105	6
Defendance	3	0	7	0	0	0	0	0	0	0	3	0	0	0	0	0	3	0	12	0
Dominance	0	0	4	0	20	3	27	3	4	0	0	1	0	0	0	0	42	9	57	18
Excitance	0	0	2	0	0	0	0	0	0	0	0	0	0	0	3	0	25	2	21	14
Exposition	10	0	16	0	13	0	4	3	0	0	2	0	19	3	14	0	83	3	57	9
Harmavoidance	0	0	2	0	0	0	3	0	3	0	4	0	0	0	0	0	35	4	34	11
Infavoidance	11	3	6	0	2	0	4	0	6	0	0	0	0	0	0	0	22	6	13	0
Nurturance	11	0	12	0	9	3	7	1	18	0	12	1	5	0	6	0	111	3	88	8
Nutriance	0	0	0	0	0	0	0	2	0	0	0	0	2	0	0	0	13	0	9	4
Passivity	2	4	4	2	12	3	8	2	9	5	5	3	8	0	6	0	59	16	45	12
Play	0	0	0	0	0	0	2	0	7	0	0	0	0	0	3	0	61	6	33	11
Recognition	2	0	5	0	22	3	8	0	19	0	18	0	6	0	8	0	91	6	79	13
Rejection	24	0	12	0	13	6	0	0	8	3	11	4	3	0	0	0	109	18	58	29
Retention	0	0	0	3	1	0	0	3	0	0	2	0	0	0	2	0	3	0	13	12
Seclusion	10	2	5	0	3	8	5	3	0	0	0	0	1	0	5	0	39	19	59	23
Sentience	0	0	0	0	0	0	0	0	9	0	2	0	37	0	16	0	70	0	18	3
Sex	18	0	14	0	0	0	0	1	3	0	0	0	2	0	2	0	114	10	76	24
Succorance	20	7	28	9	7	3	13	0	25	0	25	0	15	0	24	0	152	20	164	28
Understanding	2	0	0	0	5	0	1	0	6	0	0	0	5	0	3	0	37	0	9	0

Press Variables:	p	op	p	op	p	op	p	op	p	op	p	op	p	op	p	op	p	op	p	op
Abasement	0	0	0	0	5	0	4	0	0	0	0	0	0	0	0	0	5	0	7	0
Acquisition	3	0	0	0	0	0	0	0	0	0	3	0	2	3	0	0	7	3	11	5
Affiliation	10	0	13	0	2	0	5	0	14	0	5	0	3	0	3	0	112	6	103	16
Aggression	7	2	15	0	10	5	13	3	8	0	9	0	5	0	11	2	137	26	129	40
Cognizance	8	0	9	0	3	0	11	0	16	0	12	0	0	0	0	0	73	11	66	11
Deference	5	6	4	0	10	0	8	1	14	0	3	3	4	0	2	0	52	7	38	12
Dominance	33	0	33	5	20	0	22	3	13	0	22	0	7	3	5	0	184	30	196	54
Excitance	0	0	0	0	0	0	0	0	2	0	0	0	0	0	0	0	5	0	0	2
Exposition	6	0	11	0	5	0	0	0	9	0	13	0	16	0	13	0	61	0	72	6
Nurturance	17	4	12	0	9	2	7	0	10	0	8	0	10	0	12	0	95	8	105	16
Rejection	47	0	39	3	2	2	1	0	12	0	10	0	2	0	5	0	133	11	119	19
Sex	6	0	7	0	0	0	0	0	3	0	0	0	0	0	1	0	74	2	55	9
Succorance	9	0	9	0	2	0	5	0	4	0	3	0	0	0	0	0	50	0	45	5
Affliction	0	3	6	0	16	3	23	0	7	0	3	1	4	2	10	0	55	15	73	14
Birth-offspring	0	0	0	0	0	0	0	0	0	0	0	0	0	0	0	0	0	0	0	5
Bad Luck	0	0	0	0	0	0	0	0	0	0	2	0	2	0	0	0	2	0	23	5
Claustrum	6	0	2	0	0	0	7	0	2	0	0	0	0	0	2	0	39	2	32	10
Death of Hero	3	0	2	0	6	6	10	0	0	0	5	0	3	0	4	0	31	6	55	6
Death of Object	5	4	22	0	8	0	9	0	9	0	3	0	3	0	8	0	72	7	84	3
Failure	2	0	4	0	6	0	3	0	0	0	0	0	4	0	3	0	21	3	20	11
Gratuity	0	0	0	0	1	0	5	0	4	0	4	0	6	0	0	0	32	5	36	17
Inferiority	0	0	0	0	0	5	0	0	0	0	3	0	0	0	0	0	6	11	18	11
Injury	0	0	0	0	6	0	5	0	0	0	2	0	4	0	0	0	18	0	10	2
Lack	8	0	0	2	0	0	0	0	13	0	4	0	0	0	0	0	65	3	43	9
Loss	2	0	0	0	0	0	0	0	0	0	0	0	0	0	0	0	27	0	18	0
Old Age	0	0	0	0	0	0	0	0	0	0	0	0	0	0	0	0	5	0	7	0
Physical Danger	0	0	6	0	3	3	3	0	3	0	0	0	6	0	4	0	24	3	30	0
Superiority	0	0	2	0	2	0	0	0	5	0	3	0	4	0	3	0	28	0	17	5
Task	16	0	12	0	0	0	0	0	8	2	7	0	0	0	4	0	86	7	64	20
Uncongenial Environment	0	0	0	0	0	0	0	0	0	0	0	0	0	0	0	0	36	2	30	20

TABLE 5 (XIV) B

INTENSITIES OF NEED AND PRESS VARIABLES AS EXPRESSED IN STORIES TOLD BY WOMEN

	Picture 1 Low Scorers		Picture 1 High Scorers		Picture 2 Low Scorers		Picture 2 High Scorers		Picture 3 Low Scorers		Picture 3 High Scorers		Picture 4 Low Scorers		Picture 4 High Scorers		Picture 5 Low Scorers		Picture 5 High Scorers		Picture 6 Low Scorers		Picture 6 High Scorers	
Need Variables:	n	on	n	on	n	on	n	on	n	on	n	on	n	on	n	on	n	on	n	on	n	on	n	on
Abasement[a]	30	0	32	2	1	0	5	0	19	0	7	0	32	0	20	11	33	0	37	0	17	5	9	10
Achievement[a]	18	0	14	0	19	0	3	3	15	0	2	0	8	0	6	0	3	3	3	0	2	0	4	0
Acquisition[a]	8	3	10	0	13	0	0	3	6	0	3	0	37	0	20	10	8	0	3	0	15	7	14	4
Affiliation[a]	4	0	9	1	33	2	29	5	24	0	31	2	9	3	7	2	28	0	15	1	14	0	6	2
Aggression[a]	6	0	5	0	12	0	2	8	10	0	11	0	13	0	9	5	8	5	31	1	32	19	49	14
Autonomy	1	0	2	0	12	3	2	15	11	0	6	0	17	0	8	2	6	0	6	5	22	10	28	8
Blamavoidance	0	0	2	0	3	0	2	0	3	0	3	0	5	0	0	0	1	0	4	0	9	3	1	0
Blamescape	0	0	0	0	0	0	0	0	0	0	4	0	0	2	0	0	2	0	6	0	6	15	10	0
Cognizance	27	0	7	0	6	0	6	0	7	0	7	0	15	1	13	0	4	0	6	0	3	2	8	3
Construction	5	0	0	0	0	0	0	0	2	0	0	0	0	0	0	0	0	0	0	0	0	0	0	0
Counteraction	1	0	3	0	0	0	0	0	4	0	1	0	8	0	4	0	11	0	17	0	6	9	2	0
Deference	4	0	2	0	5	0	5	3	10	0	10	0	5	0	0	0	5	0	14	0	6	3	9	2
Defendance	0	0	0	0	0	0	0	0	0	0	3	0	0	0	0	0	0	0	3	0	6	0	0	0
Dominance	4	0	0	0	3	0	0	1	4	0	2	0	3	0	3	0	2	0	0	0	2	0	12	3
Excitance	0	0	0	0	18	1	18	2	1	0	0	0	4	0	0	0	2	0	0	0	0	4	0	0
Exposition	9	0	3	0	2	0	2	3	10	0	7	0	0	0	0	0	2	0	2	0	4	0	7	3
Harmavoidance	0	0	0	0	0	0	0	0	4	0	0	0	0	0	0	0	0	3	3	0	7	3	8	0
Infavoidance	0	0	0	0	0	0	2	0	3	0	2	0	0	0	5	0	3	0	2	0	0	0	0	0
Nurturance[a]	12	0	5	0	8	1	0	1	24	0	12	0	19	1	8	0	15	0	0	0	12	3	9	0
Nutriance	0	0	0	0	1	0	0	0	0	0	0	0	4	0	0	0	0	0	1	0	2	0	0	0
Passivity	2	0	0	0	1	2	0	3	5	0	2	0	15	0	2	0	5	1	0	0	4	0	0	0
Play[a]	0	0	0	0	40	1	22	3	1	0	1	0	2	0	0	0	2	0	0	0	2	0	0	0
Recognition[a]	2	0	13	0	25	2	14	14	4	2	3	0	8	0	6	0	6	0	7	0	2	0	2	0
Rejection	13	4	2	0	0	1	5	3	4	2	5	0	19	0	12	4	5	2	17	3	13	7	17	2
Retention	0	0	3	0	5	0	0	0	2	0	3	0	6	0	0	2	0	0	0	0	0	0	3	0
Seclusion	2	3	7	0	5	0	0	0	4	2	3	0	27	0	9	3	15	3	15	0	5	4	0	0
Sentience	5	0	8	0	3	0	0	0	0	0	3	0	1	0	0	0	0	0	0	0	0	0	0	0
Sex[a]	2	0	0	0	20	2	12	5	15	1	13	5	1	0	0	1	20	0	14	1	7	5	5	3
Succorance[a]	21	0	41	0	2	0	3	2	46	0	33	0	16	0	9	7	50	0	51	3	8	0	6	3
Understanding	19	0	13	0	5	0	0	0	2	3	8	2	8	0	8	0	2	0	6	0	2	0	0	0
Press Variables:	p	op	p	op	p	op	p	op	p	op	p	op	p	op	p	op	p	op	p	op	p	op	p	op
Abasement	0	0	0	0	0	0	0	0	0	0	0	0	0	0	0	0	0	0	0	0	0	0	0	0
Acquisition	0	0	3	0	0	0	0	0	0	0	0	0	3	0	0	0	7	0	3	0	0	0	3	3
Affiliation	1	0	11	0	32	1	27	4	19	0	34	0	7	0	2	2	19	0	7	1	12	0	6	0
Aggression[a]	4	0	6	0	7	1	2	7	1	0	7	0	11	0	5	3	27	3	21	8	41	14	43	14
Cognizance	0	0	0	0	12	0	4	2	3	0	0	0	1	0	3	3	2	0	12	3	14	9	22	7
Deference	6	3	5	0	8	0	6	0	0	3	5	0	5	0	7	2	8	0	6	0	0	0	9	0
Dominance	1	0	0	0	12	0	7	10	10	0	3	0	6	0	6	3	26	0	22	3	50	16	42	10
Excitance	0	0	0	0	0	0	0	0	0	0	0	0	4	0	0	0	0	0	0	0	0	0	0	0
Exposition	4	0	7	0	2	0	2	1	7	0	6	0	0	0	0	0	5	0	2	0	5	3	6	0
Nurturance[a]	0	0	9	0	6	0	4	3	16	0	23	0	1	0	8	3	17	0	10	0	5	2	3	0
Rejection[a]	9	0	15	0	10	1	8	6	18	0	8	0	17	0	13	0	14	3	20	3	15	3	11	2
Sex	1	0	0	0	20	1	11	5	15	0	14	0	0	0	0	0	17	0	10	1	2	0	4	0
Succorance	0	0	0	0	1	0	0	0	4	0	0	0	1	0	4	0	3	0	0	0	0	0	0	0
Affliction[a]	0	0	11	0	0	0	0	0	3	0	10	3	5	0	11	0	14	7	33	0	0	0	2	2
Birth-offspring	0	0	0	0	2	0	0	0	3	0	2	0	0	0	0	0	10	0	0	0.	0	0	0	0
Bad Luck	0	0	12	0	0	0	0	0	0	0	6	0	0	0	6	0	6	0	0	0	0	0	0	0
Claustrum	3	0	0	0	0	0	0	3	0	0	0	0	1	0	3	2	2	2	12	0	25	9	23	10
Death of Hero	16	0	27	0	0	0	0	0	3	0	0	0	3	0	12	3	3	0	7	0	0	0	0	0
Death of Object	18	0	19	0	0	0	0	0	13	0	14	0	6	0	2	0	33	0	30	0	0	0	3	0
Failure	8	0	9	0	0	3	0	0	1	0	0	0	4	0	7	0	0	0	0	0	0	0	0	0
Gratuity	2	0	13	0	0	0	0	0	0	0	4	0	3	0	4	3	4	0	5	0	0	0	3	3
Inferiority	2	0	0	0	2	3	2	11	0	0	0	0	0	0	0	4	0	0	4	0	0	0	0	0
Injury	0	0	0	0	0	0	0	0	0	0	0	0	0	0	0	0	0	0	0	0	0	0	0	0
Lack	10	0	15	0	7	0	0	3	6	0	5	0	19	0	10	0	9	0	11	0	2	3	5	0
Loss	10	0	17	0	0	0	0	0	3	0	2	0	6	0	4	0	3	0	3	0	2	0	0	0
Old Age	10	0	10	0	0	0	0	0	0	0	0	0	1	0	3	0	0	0	0	0	0	0	0	0
Physical Danger	0	0	0	0	0	0	0	0	6	0	16	3	3	0	3	0	14	3	3	1	0	0	0	0
Superiority	0	0	1	0	12	0	0	0	3	0	0	0	2	0	0	0	3	0	0	0	0	0	0	0
Task[a]	8	3	2	0	10	0	2	2	14	0	27	0	19	0	7	1	18	0	3	1	1	3	3	0
Uncongenial Environment	0	0	0	0	1	0	3	2	0	0	2	0	27	0	28	13	3	0	14	0	0	0	3	2

[a]These fifteen variables showed the highest reliability (.63 to .83) between scores of two independent raters.

Note: Underlining indicates that there is a notable difference in total scores for the variable in question between subjects scoring low and those scoring high on the Ethnocentrism scale. Where a score is underlined once, the variable is more pronounced in stories of low scorers; where underlined twice, the variable is more pronounced in stories of high scorers.

TABLE 5 (XIV) B

INTENSITIES OF NEED AND PRESS VARIABLES AS EXPRESSED IN STORIES TOLD BY WOMEN

	Picture 7				Picture 8				Picture 9				Picture 10				Totals 10 Pictures			
	Low Scorers		High Scorers		Low Scorers		High Scorers		Low Scorers		High Scorers		Low Scorers		High Scorers		Low Scorers		High Scorers	
Need Variables:	n	on	n	on	n	on	n	on	n	on	n	on	n	on	n	on	n	on	n	on
Abasement	19	4	19	3	18	0	7	0	6	0	4	0	9	0	12	0	184	9	152	26
Achievement	16	0	14	0	8	0	8	0	39	0	26	0	20	1	11	2	143	4	91	5
Acquisition	20	5	3	9	4	3	7	0	11	5	12	3	0	0	3	2	122	23	75	31
Affiliation	11	3	16	0	21	0	11	0	16	3	12	3	4	2	3	0	164	13	139	16
Aggression	11	5	8	8	6	12	8	6	3	5	6	3	0	0	9	0	101	46	138	45
Autonomy	16	3	7	12	6	0	7	3	14	4	10	2	8	0	4	0	113	20	80	47
Blamavoidance	0	5	5	0	2	0	0	0	11	0	14	0	0	0	4	0	34	8	35	0
Blamescape	5	0	0	0	2	0	0	0	0	0	0	2	0	0	0	0	15	17	20	2
Cognizance	12	0	9	3	16	2	15	0	28	0	14	0	24	0	27	0	142	5	112	6
Construction	6	0	2	2	4	0	3	0	2	2	0	0	0	0	0	0	19	2	5	2
Counteraction	5	0	10	0	4	0	6	0	6	0	3	0	3	0	7	0	48	9	53	0
Deference	12	1	14	2	10	0	8	0	34	2	18	0	37	0	20	0	128	6	100	7
Defendance	0	0	0	0	0	0	0	0	3	0	0	0	0	0	0	0	9	0	6	0
Dominance	17	0	3	2	16	8	34	4	5	0	6	3	4	0	2	0	60	8	62	13
Excitance	2	0	0	0	0	0	0	0	3	0	0	0	0	0	0	0	30	5	18	2
Exposition	20	0	14	3	17	3	9	5	19	4	7	0	16	0	19	0	108	7	70	14
Harmavoidance	0	0	0	0	0	0	0	0	0	0	0	0	0	0	0	0	11	6	11	0
Infavoidance	0	0	4	0	2	0	0	0	5	0	9	0	0	0	0	0	13	0	24	0
Nurturance	15	0	15	0	13	0	7	0	36	0	23	0	24	0	14	0	178	5	93	1
Nutriance	2	0	0	0	3	0	0	0	3	0	0	0	0	0	0	0	13	2	3	0
Passivity	0	0	2	0	14	5	3	0	0	2	0	3	5	0	0	0	51	10	9	16
Play	1	3	0	1	0	0	0	0	5	0	3	0	3	0	2	0	56	4	28	4
Recognition	20	2	15	0	14	0	11	6	15	0	16	0	8	0	8	0	104	6	95	20
Rejection	18	0	26	9	10	4	7	2	9	5	19	3	8	2	7	0	99	27	117	26
Retention	0	3	0	0	0	3	0	0	0	0	3	0	0	0	0	0	8	6	12	2
Seclusion	6	0	9	7	8	0	5	0	4	2	6	0	6	0	0	0	82	14	54	10
Sentience	6	0	1	0	0	0	0	2	6	0	2	0	33	0	11	0	54	0	25	2
Sex	1	3	8	0	4	0	0	0	0	0	0	0	0	0	0	0	73	11	52	15
Succorance	20	0	11	4	13	0	8	0	17	0	20	0	35	0	34	0	228	0	216	19
Understanding	2	0	3	0	11	0	18	0	15	0	3	0	12	0	7	0	78	3	71	2
Press Variables:	p	op	p	op	p	op	p	op	p	op	p	op	p	op	p	op	p	op	p	op
Abasement	0	0	0	0	2	0	11	1	0	0	0	0	0	0	0	0	2	0	11	1
Acquisition	0	0	6	0	0	3	3	0	0	0	0	0	0	0	4	0	10	3	22	3
Affiliation	6	1	12	0	18	0	7	2	13	0	17	0	3	0	0	0	130	2	123	9
Aggression	5	0	13	4	4	5	10	0	16	8	2	3	11	0	16	3	127	31	125	42
Cognizance	5	0	0	3	12	7	5	3	0	0	8	0	2	0	3	0	54	16	57	21
Deference	19	0	13	0	15	0	18	1	15	0	14	0	8	0	10	0	84	6	93	3
Dominance	27	0	22	4	13	7	15	0	17	4	18	3	17	0	14	0	179	27	149	33
Excitance	0	0	0	0	0	0	0	0	0	0	0	0	0	0	2	0	4	0	2	0
Exposition	5	0	13	0	2	0	0	0	9	0	10	0	12	0	21	0	51	3	67	1
Nurturance	12	2	13	4	14	0	14	0	19	0	7	0	24	0	20	0	114	4	111	10
Rejection	27	3	18	3	7	0	7	0	37	3	17	0	8	0	5	3	162	13	122	18
Sex	1	1	6	0	2	0	0	0	0	0	0	0	3	0	0	0	61	2	45	6
Succorance	0	0	2	0	1	3	4	0	7	0	1	0	2	0	0	0	19	3	11	0
Affliction	0	0	2	3	14	0	11	6	5	3	10	0	7	0	14	0	48	10	104	14
Birth-offspring	0	0	0	0	0	0	0	0	0	0	0	0	0	0	0	0	15	0	2	0
Bad Luck	6	0	0	0	0	0	0	0	0	0	3	0	0	0	0	0	12	0	27	0
Claustrum	0	0	2	0	0	3	0	3	0	3	0	0	4	0	2	0	35	17	42	20
Death of Hero	0	3	6	3	6	0	7	0	0	0	2	0	0	0	4	0	37	3	65	6
Death of Object	5	0	9	0	11	8	5	0	8	0	11	0	7	0	12	0	101	8	105	0
Failure	0	0	0	0	5	0	1	0	0	0	0	0	0	0	0	0	18	3	20	0
Gratuity	10	3	5	0	5	0	0	0	6	0	4	0	3	0	3	0	35	3	41	6
Inferiority	0	0	5	0	3	0	0	0	0	0	0	0	0	0	0	0	7	7	7	15
Injury	0	0	0	0	0	0	0	0	0	0	0	0	3	0	0	0	3	3	0	2
Lack	4	0	3	0	3	0	0	0	14	0	13	0	0	0	2	0	75	2	64	11
Loss	0	0	0	0	2	0	0	0	4	0	7	0	3	0	3	0	30	0	36	0
Old Age	12	0	9	0	0	0	0	0	0	0	0	0	0	0	0	0	26	0	19	3
Physical Danger	0	0	0	0	3	0	3	2	2	0	2	0	6	0	0	0	34	3	27	6
Superiority	8	0	8	0	0	0	5	0	11	0	10	0	8	0	0	0	47	0	24	0
Task	8	0	2	0	8	0	3	0	14	0	12	0	6	0	1	0	106	6	62	4
Uncongenial Environment	0	0	33	0	0	0	0	0	0	0	2	0	0	0	0	0	31	0	55	17

scored was about the same for unprejudiced and prejudiced subjects (Low-scoring Women 1657/High-scoring Women 1638) (Low-scoring Men 1538/High-scoring Men 1511), but press directed at characters with whom the subject did not identify—object press—was more common among prejudiced subjects (Low-scoring Women 175/High-scoring Women 249) (Low-scoring Men 168/High-scoring Men 331).

It is apparent from the data reported above that expressions which could properly be scored as *need* variables are scored more heavily for the stories of unprejudiced subjects while *object need* and *object press* variables have higher scores in the case of stories of prejudiced subjects. The *press* variables have about equal scoring in the case of the stories of each group. The question then remains as to which of the individual variables that go to make up the above summarized need and press scores differentiate the prejudiced and unprejudiced subjects.

An analysis of single variables on this basis follows. The variables are grouped in terms of certain similarities indicated in the headings below. Each notation of a variable, or of a group of variables, is followed by the mean per person (in the case of unprejudiced and of prejudiced subjects) of the total of the *intensity* scores (or, where indicated, frequency scores) for that variable or for each variable within the cluster being discussed.

Aggressive Rebellion Needs. The need variables of aggressive rebellion appear to be rated higher for low- than for high-scoring men. The ratio of the mean scores of unprejudiced to those of prejudiced men for these variables are: n Aggression 7.7/5.7, n Autonomy 6.5/5.9, n Rejection 5.5/2.9.

However, prejudiced men describe more aggressive and rebellious behavior by objects (on Aggression 2.0/4.2, on Autonomy 1.8/2.6, on Rejection .9/1.5).

This differentiation does not hold for women, except in the case of Autonomy (n Autonomy, Low-scoring mean 5.7, High-scoring mean 4.0; on Autonomy, Low-scoring mean 1.0, High-scoring mean 2.4). n Aggression and n Rejection both tend to have a slightly higher scoring in the case of "high" than of "low" stories (n Aggression 5.0/6.9; n Rejection 5.0/5.4). However, characters are often condemned by both groups for aggressive or rejective behavior (on Aggression: Low-scoring group 2.4/High-scoring group 2.3; on Rejection: Low-scoring group 1.3/High-scoring group 1.3).

In most cases the proportion of frequency of occurrence of a variable in stories of low- as compared to those of high-scoring men is about equal to the intensity proportions. The variables of n Aggression and n Autonomy are among the few whose *frequency* scores are worthy of special reference.

n Autonomy and on Autonomy appear as *frequently* in the stories of prejudiced as in the stories of unprejudiced men. Since the *intensity* scores of the two variables are differentiating for the two groups of subjects, we may conclude that the unprejudiced men identify with more intense expression of autonomy, whereas prejudiced men, when describing strong autonomous striving, tend to condemn the individual for his actions. We find also that the greater intensity of on Aggression in the stories of prejudiced men is due largely to higher scorings for each expression rather than to a greater frequency of expression (ratio of average intensity per expression: 2.5/3.8). Even the expressions of n Aggression, although less frequent, tend toward more intensity in stories of high-scoring men (ratio: 3.0/3.2). It would appear then that high-scoring men describe more intense aggression than do low-scoring men, although more often denying identification with the aggressive act.

The differences in scored autonomy—both needs and object needs—of prejudiced and unprejudiced women are due to its greater incidence in the stories of one group than in those of the other, rather than to its stronger expression. Although greater frequency but not intensity also accounts for a higher total rating of on Aggression, intensity ratings of n Aggression tend to be greater for prejudiced than for unprejudiced women (mean ratio of 3 to 2.5).

Submissive Withdrawal Needs. In contrast to the tendency of low-scoring men to describe more rebellion in their stories than do high-scoring men, the latter have a greater tendency toward expression of submissive, withdrawal needs (n Abasement: Low-scoring men 7.9/High-scoring men 10.0; n Blamavoidance: Low-scoring men 1.8/High-scoring men 3.2; n Seclusion: Low-scoring men 1.9/High-scoring men 2.5).

These differences do not hold for our female subjects. In fact, n Abasement appears to be somewhat higher for low- than for high-scoring women (Low-scoring mean 9.2/High-scoring mean 7.6), although scoring of on Abasement is greater for the prejudiced than for the unprejudiced women (Low-scoring mean .5/High-scoring mean 1.3).

Needs of Creative Expression. All the variables pertaining to constructive and creative behavior that differentiate high and low scorers indicate a predominance of expression on the part of the low scorers. The ratio of the mean scores of nonprejudiced to those of prejudiced men for these variables are: n Cognizance, 6.0/3.7; n Expression 4.2/2.9; n Understanding 1.8/.4; p Task 4.3/3.2. For the women the ratio is n Achievement 7.4/4.5; n Cognition 7.1/5.6; n Construction 1.0/.2; n Expression 5.4/3.5; p Task 5.3/3.1.

Needs of Sensual Expression. We found also that all the needs of sensual expression are scored higher in stories of low scorers than in those of high scorers. Men: n Excitance 1.25/1.05; n Passivity 2.95/2.25; n Play 3.05/1.65; n Sex 5.70/3.80; n Sentience 3.50/.90. Women: n Excitance 1.5/.9; n Passivity 2.6/.5; n Play 2.8/1.4; n Sex 3.7/2.6; n Sentience 2.7/1.2.

The scoring of object needs of sensual expression is greater for high- than for low-scoring men (mean of sum of sensual needs scored on: Low-scoring men 1.7/High-scoring men 3.2). The total scoring of object needs of sensual expression in the case of both groups of women is not appreciable.

Other Single Needs Differentiating Low and High Scorers. Two other variables have sufficiently greater scores for unprejudiced than for prejudiced women to deserve special mention: n Nurturance (Low-scoring mean 8.9/High-scoring mean 4.6) and n Acquisition (Low-scoring mean 6.1/High-scoring mean 3.7). The latter variable appears to be especially differentiating in stories told in response to Pictures 2 and 4, where the subjects often interpret the picture as indicating poverty, and in stories to Picture 7, where it appears to be related to the tendencies toward achievement and rebellion of the low-scoring women.

Press Variables from Human and Nonhuman Sources. Variables of press from human sources are expressed as often and with equal intensity by low and high scorers. Press from threatening nonhuman sources tends to be more common in stories of high- than in those of low-scoring subjects. The fantasies of permanent damage to the human body, scored as p Affliction and p Death-hero, are found to be especially differentiating between high and low scorers, both men and women (p Affliction: Women, Low-scoring mean 2.8/High-scoring mean 3.7; Men, Low-scoring mean 2.4/High-scoring mean 5.2) (p Death-hero: Women 1.5/2.8; Men 1.8/3.2).

Reference to undefined misfortune, p Bad Luck, is also more common in high-scoring subjects (Women: Low-scoring mean .1/High-scoring mean 1.2; Men: Low-scoring mean .6/High-scoring mean 1.4).

2. THEMATIC ANALYSIS

a. EXPLANATION OF THE METHOD. The thematic analysis, instead of measuring each separate variable, examines the variables in combination. Here we discover not how much of each individual variable is expressed, but rather how often certain *patterns* of variables occur. This type of analysis has the advantage of molarity with the disadvantage, often, of ambiguity.

The concept of thema is taken over from Murray (89). He defines it as "the dynamic structure of an event on a molar level," the "combination of a particular press or preaction or outcome and a particular need." When diagrammatically expressing a thema pattern, arrows are used to represent the direction of influence: e.g., p Dominance → n Deference means that press Dominance imposed upon the hero causes him to express Deference; n Sentience → n Sex means that need for Sentience causes the hero to express a need for Sex; n Succorance ←→ n Nurturance means that two equally important heroes express a mutual nurturance-succorance relationship.

We constructed hypothetical "low" and "high" thema categories after careful study of the differences in need and press scores shown in Tables

5(XIV)A and 5(XIV)B, and after observation of the stories told in response to each picture by each of the low and high scorers. Such categories were thought of as giving the general trends of the content of the stories. They were representative of differences in the more common variable constellation in the stories of our "high" as compared with our "low" subjects. We noted especially certain constellations in which one variable was equally weighted for "high" and "low" subjects. We noted also certain differences in the types of identifications with the heroes who expressed certain needs, and differences in the object toward which the action was directed. A list of "low" and "high" categories was thus compiled—one for men and one for women. There were several categories for each picture.

After the thema categories had been empirically derived in the fashion described above, each set of 40 stories (i.e., the stories told in response to each picture by the 40 men and by the 40 women tested) were scored "blindly" by two scorers, one staff member and one graduate student who had had no previous experience on our study. The scorers had only the derived categories as criteria by which to judge the "highness" or "lowness" of the subject who had told a particular story. Each story had been coded for identification, separated from other stories told by the same person, and randomly placed among the rest of the stories. Thus, judgments were based on the content of the single story. Every story thema was judged in terms of the thema category it most resembled. It should be pointed out that not all stories told conformed to patterns of the thema categories adopted as criteria. They were often more complex and sometimes included a combination of two or three themes. Scoring problems created by story complexity were dealt with by two methods. (1) The use of a neutral category when the theme of a particular story differed widely from any of the categories (about 10 per cent of the judgments fell in the neutral category); (2) scoring ½ or ⅓ to each of two or three included themes.

The percentage of agreement between the two scorers as to their "High," "Low," or "Neutral" judgments was higher on some pictures than on others. The mean percentage agreement of judgments on men's stories was 76, the range of percentages being from 70 to 80. The scorers had a mean percentage agreement of 79 on their ratings of the women's stories. Although the agreement was only 63 per cent for Picture 3, the range of percentages for the other nine sets of stories was from 74 to 91.

Examples of thema variables are included (in small print) in the following comparison of the stories told by low- and high-scoring subjects. Each example is followed by a notation, in parenthesis, of the picture concerned and of the number of times the given thema was found, by each of the two scorers, to occur in stories of subjects scoring low on the Ethnocentrism scale and by subjects scoring high on this scale. The practice of assigning scores of ½ or ⅓ to each of two or three themes found in a given story accounts for the fractional totals which appear in the following summaries of themes.

Within the discussion, notations are made also from time to time of the sum of intensity scores on a particular variable (reflected in the stories to the picture in question) in the case of low-scoring subjects and in the case of high-scoring subjects.

We have chosen to discuss stories told in response to Pictures 1 and 7 (dealing with parental figures) first; stories to 3 and 5 (relationships to opposite sex) next; and then stories to 8 and 10 (responses to nonfamilial press), considering the men's stories and then the stories of the women subjects. Stories of both men and women told in response to the special pictures portraying members of minority groups (2, 4, 6, 9) are discussed last. The reader is referred to the stimulus pictures reproduced on the insert opposite.

b. RESULTS

1. *Comparison of Stories Told by High- and by Low-scoring Men in Response to the Pictures from the Murray Series*

PICTURE M1.   Male subjects in both groups usually identify the characters as father and son or "older man" and "younger man." Identification tends to be mainly with the son, who is said to be somber, sad, distressed. Many of the themes told to this picture describe the older man in the capacity of advisor or counselor. There is a greater tendency for low- than for high-scoring men to describe the younger man's reaction to this supervision as respectful (n Deference: Low scorers 17, High scorers 8) and for high scorers to describe it as submissive (n Abasement: Low scorers 19, High scorers 30).

(p Dominance → n Submissive Abasement): The hero is reprimanded by the father for having committed an antisocial act. He responds with feelings of shame and submission to the instructions of the older man. The father figure acts as a restraining force, not just as an advisor or counselor. There is often a nurturant aspect to the father's dominance, but the dominance is the stronger press. (M1: Low scorers, 2, 1; High scorers, 8, 9.)

There appears to be a tendency for both groups to describe fantasies of rebellion against the older man's advice (n Autonomy, Low scorers 25; High scorers 18).

(p Nurturance-Dominance → n Autonomy-Rejection): The older man is advising the younger one. The younger man rejects the older man's advice. The father is deeply hurt, or in some way shows genuine concern over the action of the younger man—a concern other than a desire to dominate the boy. (M1: Low scorers 7, 6; High scorers 6, 7.)

However, there is a greater tendency for the high scorers to follow

MURRAY PICTURES GIVEN TO MEN AND WOMEN

MEN

WOMEN

MI

FI

3

M5

F5

M7

F7

MURRAY PICTURES GIVEN TO MEN AND WOMEN
(CONTINUED)

8

10

SPECIAL PICTURES GIVEN TO MEN AND WOMEN

2

6

4

9

Credits. Picture 2: Courtesy of *Life*, Copyright Time, Inc.
Picture 6: Courtesy of *Fortune* Magazine.
Photograph by Otto Hagel.

this theme with punishment for the rebellious younger man (3 of 7 high-scoring men, but no low-scoring men).

Another theme sometimes elicited by this picture is one in which both men are planning or plotting together. The low scorers more often than the high scorers describe a constructive enterprise (n Expression: Low scorers 12, High scorers 7; n Understanding: Low scorers 10, High scorers 1; n Cognizance: Low scorers 16; High scorers 5).

(n Understanding, n Nurturance): The hero strives for understanding and betterment of society. He attempts to right a wrong done to society. Rebellion is motivated by rational principle. There is close identification with the hero, who rebels against social injustice or who wants to right an injustice committed against a friend or relative. (M1: Low scorers 3, 6; High scorers 2½, 1⅓.)

The high- more often than the low-scoring men depict a father who acts as a moral control over the actions of the son and causes the son to conform to his demands or be punished. The low scorers are more inclined to portray a relationship in which the father acts as an advisor whom the son respects, but the son does not necessarily submit to his wishes. Although high and low scorers alike describe heroes who behave contrary to the wishes of the father, a principled, constructive purpose initiating the rebellion is more commonly described by "lows," whereas the rebellion in the stories of "highs" is more often of a criminal, impulsive nature. Furthermore, the revolt is more likely to be rejected or given up in stories of high scorers than in those of low scorers.

These differences in fantasied relationship between father and son remind one of the difference in the childhood memories of the father pointed out in Chapter X. The reader will recall that the stern father who represented a "moral-model" and who was respected out of fear, was more frequently described in the childhood memories of the high-scoring men than in those of the low-scoring men. On the other hand, the low scorers more often reported that their fathers were "relaxed and mild" and supported "principled independence," a similar picture to the one drawn in the T. A. T. stories.

To what extent either of these sources of portrayed relationships offers a true picture of family relationship is still an open question, but it is important to note that the needs expressed by the prejudiced men are in the direction of authoritarian relationships with father figures whereas those set forth by unprejudiced men tend to allow for individualized behavior. One may conclude from this that the low- as compared with the high-scoring men have less residual fears of punishment by their fathers, and that this accounts for their being better able to accept fantasies of constructive autonomy.

PICTURE M7. Most of our male subjects describe the people portrayed in this picture as mother and son, and the identification is mainly with the son.

The mother is usually said to be rejecting the son, and the mood expressed by the son is somber.

There are two main themes that appear more often in the stories of high-scoring men than in those of the low scorers. One of these, which deviates from the more common story of the rejecting mother, stresses tragic events leading up to the portrayed scene (p Aggression: Low scorers 7, High scorers 15; p Death: Low scorers 5, High scorers 22; p Physical Danger: Low scorers 0, High scorers 6).

(Environmental p Aggression, p Death-object, p Physical Danger → n Succorance): Environmental factors (a death or fire; a rejecting or erring child, or a demand from an external force that forces the man to leave home) threaten both of the portrayed figures. They both respond with dejection. (M7: Low scorers 1½, 0; High scorers 4, 6.)

In the other predominantly "high" theme more direct mother-son relationships are often described. In such cases the son is usually said to have committed a crime, and he is confessing or apologizing. (n Blamavoidance: Low scorers 9, High scorers 17; n Abasement: Low scorers 24, High scorers 32.)

(p Dominance → n Submissive Abasement): The mother rejects the son or the son fears she will reject him (for an act of theft, murder, or an affair with a girl). He responds with guilt and anxiety and subsequent submission to his mother's wishes. (He tries to make amends for what he has done by apologizing and/or complying with his mother's wishes from then on.) (M7: Low scorers, 4, 2; High scorers 4½, 9½.)

The mother-son conflict expressed by low scorers is most commonly said to arise out of the young man's demand for autonomy. He wants to do something of which the mother disapproves (leave home, marry, or plan for a particular career). In some stories she is said to be annoyed with him because he has committed a minor crime. These subjects often indicate that the son feels he is justified to some extent at least in what he has done or what he intends to do. He is determined to do what he thinks right, or defend what he has done. There is usually some sign of regret that he is disappointing his mother by defying her wishes, yet he insists on his independence. (n Autonomy: Low scorers 41, High scorers 33; n Rejection: Low scorers 24, High scorers 12.)

Autonomous striving receives high scores in both groups, but in the stories of our prejudiced subjects it is intense at first but is later given up, whereas nonprejudiced subjects describe less violent, less destructive autonomy that carries through to the conclusion.

(p Dominance → n Autonomy): A possessive mother rejects her son because of his past activities or plans for the future, of which she disapproves (leaving home, conflict over mode of achievement, intended marriage, a theft). The son feels that he is justified to some extent at least in what he has done or intends to do. He is determined to do what he thinks right or defend what he has done. There may be a note of regret that he must disappoint his mother by defying her wishes. (M7: Low scorers 11, 11; High scorers 4, 3.)

The fantasies of low-scoring and of high-scoring men centering about the mother figure tend to be distinguishable in much the same way as their fantasies about the father figure; that is, the high-scoring men tend to describe a hero who is morally dependent upon the mother while the hero of the low-scoring men more often considers her advice but finally acts according to his own judgment. This differentiation is in accordance with the analysis of the interview material, which indicated a more realistic, less awesome portrayal of the childhood mother by low than by high scorers.

Prejudiced subjects more often than the unprejudiced describe relations to parents, both fantasied and real (in the interviews), with more reference to the child's reacting because of fear or because of the compulsion of the parental demands for obedience. However, both the interviews and the T. A. T. indicate that the low-scoring subjects have a more critical attitude toward parental influences.

PICTURE 3. Male subjects in both groups tend to identify with a male hero in their stories to this picture. Usually the upper figure is so designated, the lower figure being described as his wife.

In the responses of low-scoring men to this picture there is much variability in the relationship between the two people portrayed. Often the woman is a nurturant mother figure who encourages and helps the man; sometimes he is the stronger and more dominant one who cares for her. In general, however, there is a clear affiliative relationship in which hero and love object show a mutual sensitivity to and concern over the mood and feelings of the other.

(Mutual Nurturance-Succorance Sex relationship—fusion of n Nurturance, n Succorance, n Sex, n Affiliation): Two people (husband and wife, usually) are embracing each other. They are glad to be together ("to see each other after a long separation") or both are sad (because they have to be separated). This theme is not preceded by an aggressive press such as an argument between them, the fear of death, affliction, or physical danger. Affiliation and Sex are expressed in the mutuality of the Nurturance-Succorance. (3: Low scorers 14, 16; High scorers 7, 2.)

Closer investigation of the stories of low scorers who produce this thema shows that when a joyful event such as a reunion is described, the woman usually plays the more active role. She is the one who protects and nurtures the man, the latter enjoying a more passive role. When the event is unpleasant or sad, a situation such as departure, the man is usually the one to give the woman support and reassurance and to deal forcefully with the situation.

The high-scoring men more often fantasy the man as the dominant person in the heterosexual relationship. They are inclined to identify with the role of a benevolent but despotic father, demonstrating no real dependence on the woman. The man is likely to be described as the master, while the woman is weak and dependent. This division of masculine and feminine roles is often sharply made, no overlapping of roles being allowed. At the same time the high-scoring man is likely to reject the woman because of her dependency. He describes her as being fickle, flighty or burdensome.

(Male n Dominance ⟷ Female n Succorance): There is no overlapping of roles. She is dependent and weak; he is the source of strength and he refrains from expressing any dependence on her. ("She is on the verge of hysterics; so he comforts her." "She is relying on strength from her husband to pull her through." "He comforts her and hides his own feelings.") (3: Low scorers 3, 2½; High scorers 7, 4.)

The woman becomes obstreperous. He comforts her in order to quiet her and subdue her aggression. ("He's comforting her. They have quarrelled, as they often do over some trivial matter." "She nagged at him. He got mad. Now he's comforting her.") (3: Low scorers 0, 0; High scorers 3, 2.)

Although the situational factor in the stories of high-scoring subjects is somewhat variable, reference to dangerous situations resulting in death and affliction are very common (p Death-hero: Low scorers 4, High scorers 13; p Affliction: Low scorers 0; High scorers 9). Usually the high scorers describe episodes which cause the woman to exhibit her weakness and the man his strength and superior capabilities. Even when the focus is on the husband's departure for war, ideas of fear are usually projected onto the woman. She is the one who "fears for his safety."

It appears, then, that the low- and high-scoring groups conceptualize different types of heterosexual relationship. The low-scoring men tend to identify mainly with a flexible male role that is varied with different situations, the heterosexual adjustment of hero and love object being on the basis of reciprocal dependency stemming from their mutual need of companionship and sympathy, and of someone to care for; whereas the high-scoring men characteristically identify with a dominant, heroic role, the woman being subservient. In contrast to stories of low-scoring men, in which women serve as helpful companions, the high-scoring men more often conceive of the woman's function as one of serving the man's needs, and he resents any demands placed upon him by her.

The implications derived from the differences in content of the stories told by low- and high-scoring men in response to Picture M1—that the "highs" tend to be more fearful of asserting themselves in the face of the father's opposition than are the "lows"—suggest one aspect at least of the differences in motivation behind the fantasied roles described in response to the present picture. The high-scoring men apparently can identify with the father's role in certain situations. They seem to compensate for feelings of inadequacy precipitated by the father, by adopting the role—at least in fantasy—of a dominant, authoritarian individual in relationships with people less threatening than the father.

From the interview material we would have reason to believe that the authoritarian sex role described by the prejudiced men in the T. A. T. is not limited to their fantasies. The quantitative results in Chapter XI, indicating that they tend to adhere to exploitive-manipulative and power-oriented attitudes toward sex objects, corroborate our findings here. The interview data for unprejudiced men are also in keeping with T. A. T. results. Their interviews reveal appreciation of more relaxed, equalitarian modes of love-seeking.

PICTURE M5. Except in rare cases there is consistent identification by all the male subjects with the man in the picture. The description of events leading up to the portrayed situation, in stories of low and high scorers alike, often involves an impulsive sexual act. Aggressive behavior on the part of the hero is described more often by low- than by high-scoring men; but the expression is more intense and more commonly rejected in stories of high than in those of low scorers (n Aggression: Low scorers 28, High scorers 8; on Aggression: Low scorers 6, High scorers 14). Some high-scoring subjects ignore the woman in the background and attribute the man's dejection to overindulgence in liquor.

The main difference between the stories of one group and those of the other lies in the story-teller's attitude toward what the hero has done and why he has done it. The more aggressive stories of murder and rape are often explained by low-scoring men on the basis of temporary maladjustments that could occur in the life of anyone, e.g., "He has difficulty in adjusting to civilian life after his army experiences." These story-tellers rarely condemn the hero. Rather they tend to identify with his problems, describing his feelings and thoughts about the situation. The hero is usually portrayed as dejected, guilt-ridden, and concerned about the welfare of the girl involved.

(n Sex, n Aggression → n Abasement-intrapunitive type): The hero is reproaching himself for having harmed the girl as the result of an impulsive sexual act. The girl is never rejected; in fact there is often an expression of affection for her. The hero is not rejected by the story-teller. Rather there are signs of sympathy for the hero's problems. (M5: Low scorers 8, 6; High scorers 2, 1½.)

The high scorers who describe the same situational factors as the above often attribute the action to inherent criminal tendencies, referring to the hero by such phrases as "a fiend" or a "sex maniac." Although detailed description of the crime may be given, references to the hero's feelings or thoughts about what has happened are comparatively rare. Suicide or punishment by authorities is the most common ending to these stories.

(on Aggression): The central character is rejected for being a criminal or a low character, and the picture is condemned as sordid. The story deals with an intense aggressive episode in which the story character has indulged preceding the pictured scene. He has committed a major crime (rape, murder, robbery) and the result is one of serious damage. (M_5: Low scorers 0, 1; High scorers 2, 4½.)

Subjects from both groups sometimes tell less aggressive stories dealing mainly with the sensual aspects of the picture. In these stories, the low scorers also tend to be more accepting of sensual indulgence than are high scorers. Three nonprejudiced men tell stories of the pleasures of "wine, women, and song," but none of the prejudiced men approach such a theme. There are, however, many stories by prejudiced men which center around a condemnation of passive sensuality.

(on Sex, Sentience → on Abasement, giving up of self-respect): The hero has yielded to sensual impulses because of innate weakness or a disappointing experience. (He has become a drunkard or indulged in sexual activities with a whore.) He is guilt-ridden, loses all self-respect, and becomes worthless to society. (M_5: Low scorers 6, 5; High scorers 12½, 10½.)

The low scorers, then, tend to identify with a hero who either finds no harm in a little overindulgence of sensuality or who blames himself for his transgressions, whereas the high scorers more often reject the hero for such behavior and predict for him a future of moral degradation.[2] The T.A.T. stories are in keeping with the evidence from the interviews (see Chapter XI) that the low-scoring men are better able to accept id impulses than are high-scoring men. They are, furthermore, consistent with interview data (see Chapter XII) indicating that intrapunitiveness tends to be more common in low than in high scorers.

PICTURE 8. The content of all the stories elicited by this picture implies a recognition, on the part of the subject, of the contrasting active and passive roles of the two figures presented. In most of the stories of high- and low-scoring subjects alike the situation described is either a hypnotic session or a scene of death or illness. Many of the subjects elaborate very little beyond a description of the setting. Where further content is offered, there is a tendency for high more often than for low scorers to attribute permanent affliction and death to their heroes (p Affliction: Low scorers, 16, High scorers, 23; Death-hero: low scorers, 6, High scorers 10) and to give emphasis to themes of exploitation by the dominant figure.

(n Coercive Dominance ⟷ n Submissive Abasement): The hypnotist uses his powers for the purpose of exploiting the hypnotized person. (He is trying to secure information that will be held against the hypnotized man, or he is hypnotizing him for the purpose of being able to control the man's actions.) Although there is usually some identification with the victim, and the hypnotist may be rejected, the story

[2] The variable n Abasement does not differentiate stories told by high- and low-scoring subjects in response to this picture (Low scorers 51; High scorers 49) because, according to the scheme of analysis used in this study, this variable includes both intragression and moral degradation.

ends without escape or counteraction on the part of the victim. (8: Low scorers 3, 1; High scorers 5, 5.)

The low-scoring men, on the other hand, tend to minimize the aggressive, dominant aspects usually suggested by the picture. Two low- but no high-scoring men tell stories in which hypnotism is used for purposes of aiding the psychological well-being of the patient.

Another predominantly "low" story is distinguished by the sequence of themes rather than by the content alone. The story-teller begins by indicating the possibility that the picture portrays an aggressive act on the part of the "hypnotist," but he does not elaborate this interpretation. Instead, he proceeds to minimize the intensity of the story content.

(Denial of n Aggression): The story-teller rejects the picture as unpleasant, or rejects the unpleasant possibilities for a story, or shows some confusion when the picture is first presented. He offers several suggestions of possible plots, involving aggressive intentions on the part of the hypnotist (death, an exploitive hypnotist, a potential crime), but these ideas are rejected. The intensity of the story content is then minimized. ("It is merely a stage demonstration of no consequence." "It is a doctor and a patient," or "It could be a priest saying a blessing over a sick man, or it may be a doctor and patient or most anything.") (8: Low scorers 5, 4; High scorers 1, 2.)

The elements which, in stories to Picture 8, appear to be more characteristic of high than of low scorers are similar to those that have already been seen to differentiate the story content of the two groups of subjects. The tendency of high- more often than low-scoring men to stress dominance-submission relationships was indicated in stories to Pictures M1, 3, M7, and it appears here again. Also, the greater incidence in "high" stories of references to death and affliction was noted before in the discussion of responses to Picture 3. The impunitive manner of dealing with the aggressive aspect of this picture, exhibited in stories of some low-scoring men, has not been apparent in their responses to the pictures discussed previously. The tendency of the low scorers to describe their heroes as intrapunitive, i.e., to tell stories in which the hero blames himself for his transgressions, was evident in the production of low scorers elicited by Picture M5. It will be remembered that the high scorers tended to condemn the characters instead. The difference in the way in which aggression is dealt with by these two groups of subjects—intra- or impunitively by low scorers and extrapunitively by high scorers—is reflected in the T.A.T. as well as in the interview data (see Chapter XI).

These findings may appear to be in contradiction to our previous remarks that the stories of low scorers describe more rebelliousness on the part of the hero. One might suspect that the trends toward obsessiveness suggested by the impunitive expressions would not be found in the same individual who describes fantasies of demands for independence. If the personality structure were essentially that of an obsessive nature, perhaps fantasies of decisive action could not be expressed. Apparently, however, the obsessiveness is limited to certain areas; the same group of men responding impunitively to Picture 8, almost without exception produce stories to Pictures M1 and M7 (father-son and mother-son) in which heroes demand their autonomous rights despite parental pressures. The type of hero reaction described apparently depends on the stimulus value of the picture. Perhaps the factor distinguishing Picture 8 from M1 and M7 is that the latter more readily allow for a choice of autonomy than does the former, in which the contrasting roles of dominance-submission are more clearly depicted.

As will be noted in the discussion of stories produced by men in response to Picture 6 (see page 527), low-scoring men are likely to refrain from describing rebellious activity when such action is not practical in view of the pictured situation.

PICTURE 10.   This picture was included in our series because it was expected that most of our subjects would make some kind of identification with a "religious" person and thereby add to our understanding of the comparative satisfactions derived from religious practices by our two groups. We anticipated differences similar to those found independently in the questionnaire and interview responses (see Chapters VI, XVIII), the low scorers being more concerned with principles, the high scorers with the authoritarian, conventional, and ritualistic aspects of religious practice. Although differences of this kind were found in the stories of those individuals who responded to the religious elements of the picture, many of our subjects, both high and low scorers (about half of the male subjects), appeared to be uninspired by the picture; they limited their responses to mere descriptions of the picture. It would seem that for these subjects there was not an adequate medium for identification. Of those men who elaborated their stories beyond what was given in the picture, a few in each of the two compared groups told stories in which a soldier in battle faced an immediate crisis and sought help from God.

The low scorers who actually projected a story with some content tended to interpret the scene portrayed as expressive of a hero thoughtfully evaluating life and religion and/or reacting with sensitive imaginative enjoyment to music or art. (n Sentience: Low scorers 37; High scorers 16.)

(n Sentence, n Cognizance): The hero is considering the problem of what religion, life, God really mean. Religion and/or music serves to give him emotional support, peace, and serenity. He is sensitive and imaginative, thoughtful, gets real enjoyment from playing the violin, and seeking the meaning of life. (10: Low scorers 2½, 4; High scorers 0, 2.)

The high scorers often identify with a hero who is afflicted with a disease such as infantile paralysis or suffering from the aggressions of an evil force such as "the Nazis," and who seeks refuge in religion (p Affliction: Low scorers 4, High scorers 10; n Abasement: Low scorers 4, High scorers 19; n Deference: Low scorers 19, High scorers 28).

(p Physical Danger → n Submissive Abasement): The hero is left totally helpless in the face of a crisis. Counteractive aggression is suppressed, taking the form of submissive abasement. (10: Low scorers 0, 0; High scorers 2, 4.)

(p Physical Danger, Affliction → Deference to supernatural forces): The hero, who is the victim of infantile paralysis or of some mysterious physical force, seeks refuge in religion. He becomes a believer. He "gets religion." (10: Low scorers 2, 0; High scorers 2, 5.)

These differences suggest patterns of reaction to the idea of God and the supernatural that are similar to those found in parent-child relationships. Those subjects who respond to the religious appeal of the picture generally depict the hero's behavior in the way that is most characteristic of their fantasied responses to parental dominance: the low scorers describe autonomous but deferent intellectual consideration, the high scorers apprehension and submission.

The more frequent reference by prejudiced than by unprejudiced men to death and affliction is apparent here as it was in stories to Pictures 8 and M7. One might say that the feelings of victimization so commonly expressed by high scorers in their interviews (see Chapter XI) are likewise an important feature of the fantasy life of these men. The finding from the interviews that subjects in this group tend, more often than the low scorers, to conceptualize the "world as a jungle" (see Chapter XI) is also borne out by the fact that in their T.A.T. stories, especially those elicited by the present picture and by Picture M7, they place more emphasis on the variable p Physical Danger.

2. Comparison of Stories Told by High- and by Low-scoring Women in Response to the Pictures from the Murray Series

PICTURE FI. Picture F1 elicited different types of themes than did M1. The stories for F1 center around the "old man" in the picture, but since he is the only figure present, the theme of parent-child relationship, so common in the case of M1, appears in only a few cases. Stories are mainly concerned with the father figure, with his attributes and interactions with his environment.

The high- more often than the low-scoring women tell stories about a man who is sad and completely defeated, who has been severely rejected or has lost all that he spent his life striving for. (p Rejection: Low scorers 9, High scorers 15; p Affliction: Low scorers 0, High scorers 11; p Bad Luck: Low scorers 0, High scorers 12; p Death of Hero: Low scorers 16, High scorers 27; p Lack: Low scorers 10, High scorers 15; p Loss: Low scorers 10, High scorers 17; n Succorance: Low scorers 21; High scorers 41.)

(p Failure, p Loss, p Lack, p Rejection, p Affliction and/or Death → n Succorance): The hero is sad, feels defeated because he has lost or never had money or status, because he is old and sick, or because he has been rejected by all his friends. (F1: Low scorers 8, 6; High scorers 16, 17½.)

The low-scoring women tend to describe a father figure who is a philosopher or scholar, one who is constructively thoughtful and sensitive to the broader aspects of his environment. (n Cognizance: Low scorers 27, High scorers 7; n Exposition: Low scorers 9, High scorers 3; n Nurturance: Low scorers 12, High scorers 5; n Understanding: Low scorers 19, High scorers 13).

(n Cognizance, n Understanding): The hero is a philosopher reflecting upon the ways of mankind, or upon life's pleasures and inconsistencies; or he is a scholar who desires to contribute to knowledge. He may be attempting to counteract injustice that has been directed at society as a whole, toward a particular social group or toward a friend—but not in response to personal press of aggression or dominance. (F1: Low scorers 8, 12; High scorers 1, 5½.)

It appears that the nonprejudiced women tend more to admire and accept elderly men—who might be termed "father figures"—than do the prejudiced women. The former usually make a more positive identification with the male figure presented in this picture, attributing to him positive successful striving, whereas the latter more often make a negative identification with the father figure, describing him as an unsuccessful, miserable individual.

PICTURE F7. This picture is regularly interpreted as portraying two women, one old and one young. The identification is most often with the younger woman.

Prejudiced women tend to reject the older woman in the picture as an unpleasant individual. She is often described as representing disagreeable characteristics that come with old age, and she is depicted as domineering, aggressive, selfish and manipulative of the younger woman, who is forced to submit to her demands. These trends are not clear in the scoring of need-press variables because many of the same variables are attributed to the older woman in stories of high scorers and to the younger person in stories of low scorers. Although total scores from some variables, e.g., n Aggression, are equally weighted for the F7 stories of high and low scorers, the constellation of variables in which they appear varies considerably. The following thema variables indicates that the high more often than the low scorers reject old age.

(op Old Age → on Aggression, Dominance): A story of contrast between youth and old age. The older woman is a product of the imagination of the figure in the foreground. The heroine is worrying about old age. Old women are conceived of as being mean and ugly. (F7: Low scorers 1, 1; High scorers 3, 5.)

The old woman is a dominant, aggressive mother or a witch who exploits others for her own gain. She dominates her daughter's life. She schemes to get her daughter married off. She forces others to submit to her. (F7: Low scorers 2, 2; High scorers 4, 5.)

Low scorers more often center their stories around the younger woman. The older woman in the picture is usually said to be either the same person as the younger one, portrayed later in life when she has gained the satisfaction of success, or the mother of the younger woman. Descriptions of mother-daughter relationship vary. The mother may be overprotective, causing the daughter to seek to escape from her; she may be a sympathizing, encouraging mother who aids the daughter in attempts for success; or she may be rejective of the daughter for the daughter's selfish behavior. Stories are often told of a woman seeking a successful career, attempting to compete with men, and sometimes even to dominate and exploit them (n Acquisition: Low scorers 20, High scorers 3; n Autonomy: Low scorers 16, High scorers 7; n Dominance: Low scorers 17, High scorers 3). In those stories of low-scoring women in which the central character (the young woman) is described as domineering, she is usually denounced for this quality. This rejection is particularly interesting in view of the fact that low scorers rarely condemn their characters. It would seem that although they are able to accept their fantasies of competition and professional success, the hostility, in the form of deceit and exploitation, that may be a part of these fantasies, is unacceptable.

(p Old Age → n Achievement, n Nurturance): The older woman is a product of the imagination of the younger woman or it is the same woman depicted at two stages of her career. She is often an artist or career woman for whom old age brings happiness and the satisfaction of success. (F7: Low scorers 4, 7; High scorers 1, 1.)

(on Dominance—toward men): The younger woman is sometimes rejected for her insincerity, her lack of understanding, or her attempts to exploit men. The older woman is sensitive to her environment and rejects the daughter's lack of sensitivity. (F7: Low scorers 5, 5; High scorers 1, 1.)

Low scorers differ from high scorers in their conceptions of both youth and old age. The low scorers tend to depict constructive striving as belonging to the period of youth, while the aged person enjoys the fruits of the earlier efforts. High scorers more often picture youth as a period of helplessness in which the girl is led by the aging mother, and old age as a period of life to be dreaded because with it comes loss of the personal charms of youth.

In stories told to this picture and to Picture F1, the high- more often than the low-scoring women describe parental figures as either weak and ineffective or as demanding and threatening. The hostility toward parental figures emphasized in these descriptions might well underlie the trend in these high-scoring subjects toward the comparative lack of genuine affection for their own parents that is described in Chapter X. Feelings both of hostility and love are more frankly expressed in the interviews of low scorers according to the data presented in Chapter X. However, parental figures appearing in the expressed fantasies of these subjects tend to be admired unambivalently. It is probably the greater ability to deal with hostile feelings that makes it possible for low- more than for high-scoring women to enjoy fantasies of the more pleasant aspects of parental behavior, rather than to dwell on, and to regard as characteristic of the parent, those aspects of the behavior which they regard as disagreeable.

PICTURE 3.   Women, for the most part, describe the characters portrayed in this picture in much the same way as do the men (upper figure, male; lower figure, female). Also like the men, the women usually interpret the expressions on both faces as somber and indicative of a crucial situation. The causative factor is often the man's departure for or return from the army.

Six low-scoring subjects and 3 high-scoring ones identify the characters as father and son. Stories of 3 low but no high scorers center around the boy's problem of breaking home ties and accepting the role of an independent adult. In these stories the father is sympathetic and encouraging. In the father-son stories of high-scoring women, the father tends to be more authoritarian and less nurturant.

Besides producing numerous stories in which departure and reunion is said to precipitate the immediate scene, the low-scoring women sometimes attribute the somberness depicted to the worry of parents over a child. In either case the reaction described involves sensitivity to the feelings of the other by each of the characters depicted. In most cases the more nurturant figure is the man, but in a few stories the woman is assigned a protective role.

(Female—n Succorance, n Affiliation): A description is given of the joy felt by a man and woman because they are together after a long separation: (or) They are sad because they have to be separated. There is no fear of death or affliction projected into the story. Although the man is usually the more nurturant, mutual dependency and strong affiliation are expressed. (3: Low scorers 6, 9; High scorers 4, 3.)

The man is sympathizing with the woman's joys or sorrows created by a crucial situation involving a child, close friend, or relative. (The situation is natural death, a child running away from home, or success achieved by their child.) Here the woman is the somewhat more dependent. (3: Low scorers 3½, 9; High scorers, 2½, 5.)

High-scoring women, like low-scoring women, tell stories in which the woman is the more dependent. However, the intensity of the personal relationships is usually not as great in "high" stories as in "low" stories. Prejudiced women more often elaborate descriptions of disastrous situational factors, such as personal affliction or threat from the physical environment, that prompts the woman to seek the aid of the man, or, sometimes, they imagine such dangers confronting the husband. Stories of a husband or son leaving for the army are often accompanied by an expression on the part of the woman of fearfulness lest the man be harmed. Several of the high scorers' stories of the man's return from war describe his afflictions. (p Affliction: Low scorers 3, High scorers 10; p Physical Danger: Low scorers 6, High scorers 16).

(p Death, p Affliction directed at male figure): The man is leaving for war. She fears that he will be killed or injured and that she will never see him again: (or) He has just come back from war, severely injured. (3: Low scorers 3, 5; High scorers 5, 11.)

Both prejudiced and unprejudiced women apparently fantasy a role of dependency upon their male partners. However, in the case of the high-scoring women, the relationships involve less intensity of personal feelings than is found in those of the low scorers. The commonly fantasied death and injury to the man, in stories of the prejudiced subjects, suggest that underlying hostilities are present that prevent expression of more genuine affection.

PICTURE F5. The woman in this picture is usually described as sad by both low- and high-scoring women. She is experiencing feelings of guilt, fear, and/or shame. There is a small group of subjects, mainly low scorers, who minimize the intensity of the disphoric tone by saying that the heroine is only putting on an act, or that she has a temporary illness which she will soon overcome (4 low scorers, 1 high scorer). (It is interesting to note the similarity of the defense used by these women against masochistic behavior to that used by some of the low-scoring men against aggressive behavior. See discussion of stories told in response to Picture 8, below.

Other low scorers relate the girl's unhappiness to deprivation of love from her family or from a male sex object.

The story-teller identifies with a girl who is unhappy or anxious because she is denied, or in danger of being denied, love and support from her husband or family. (F5: Low scorers 5, 4; High scorers 2, 0.)

Subjects from both groups attribute the unhappy mood to the natural or accidental death of a relative (4 low scorers, 6 high scorers). However, stories dwelling on the death scene are more often told by high scorers, themes of death or injury due to personal aggression are excessive among high as compared to low scorers (n Aggression: Low scorers 8, High scorers 31). Many prejudiced women tell stories describing feelings of guilt and fear resulting from an aggressive act committed impulsively. The object of the hostile act is, in most cases, the husband or lover.

(on Aggression toward men): The heroine is overcome with grief because she has killed her husband or lover in a fit of "passion" or "insanity" or she has just witnessed his death (the morbid details are elaborated). (F5: Low scorers 3, 3; High scorers 5, 11½.)

The low-scoring women again describe more real involvement in love relationships while the stories of high scorers are suggestive of the same underlying hostility toward men as was referred to previously. The identification of the latter subjects with the aggressor is obscured by techniques of rejecting the heroine for committing the act, attributing the cause to a temporary or permanent mental affliction, or by an outcome of punishment for the crime.

The results of analysis of stories to Pictures 3 and F5 corroborate the findings of the interview data. The tendency of low scorers to emphasize love in sexual relationships, and to describe unhappiness resulting from deprivation of love, is apparent in material from both sources. The open admission of fears of inadequacy by some low-scoring women, found in the interview data, may be related to fears of loss of love suggested by some of the T.A.T. stories of low-scoring subjects.

Responses in the interviews were interpreted by the interview raters as indicating underlying disrespect for and resentment against men significantly more often in the case of high-scoring women than in the case of low scorers. The fact that, in the T.A.T., high-scoring women more often than low scorers produce stories of aggressive action directed at men or of permanent injury or death imposed upon them, substantiates the interpretations of the interview responses. Although the hostility is not admitted directly in either case, both the T.A.T. and interview material strongly suggest that such a trend is latent in prejudiced women.

PICTURE 8.   As in stories told in response to this picture by men, both high- and low-scoring women describe an active and a passive figure. The low scorers identify more often with the submissive role, the high scorers with the dominant role (n Abasement: Low scorers 18, High scorers 7; p Abasement: Low scorers 2, High scorers 11; n Dominance: Low scorers 16, High scorers 34).

The themes produced by low-scoring men, referred to above, are not as common in stories of low-scoring women. Reference to aggressive intent is less often referred to in the themes of these women. When an aggressive act is described, the story-teller usually rejects the aggressor (n Aggression: Low scorers 6, High scorers 8; on Aggression: Low scorers 12, High scorers 6). More often, the active person is described as nurturant and helpful. He is a doctor or a priest, aiding a sick man (sometimes by hypnosis) or saying a prayer over a dying man.

(p Affliction, p Death of Object→ n Nurturance): A doctor is treating a patient in a psychoanalytic session or through hypnosis: (or) A priest blesses a dead or condemned man, emphasizing the dying man's virtues, his life achievements, and their meaning for the future world, and offering him hope for peace in the afterworld. (8: Low scorers 6, 6; High scorers 1, 3½.)

High- more often than low-scoring women condemn the passivity of the reclining figure or give him little consideration except in so far as he serves as a tool of the hypnotist (n Passivity: Low scorers 14, High scorers 3; on Passivity: Low scorers 5, High scorers 10). Instead, they tend to identify with the active figure, who is often described as an exhibitionist and trickster. He seeks to control the actions of the other man, or to seduce an audience into believing in his superhuman powers. Some low scorers also describe a stage demonstration (n Recognition: Low scorers 14, High scorers 11; on Recognition: Low scorers 0, High scorers 6) but the exploitive element is usually absent in their stories.

(n Dominance-Recognition): The hypnotist seeks the admiration of an audience, or of the man he is hypnotizing, for his powers to impose his will upon another. The audience is belittled as foolish for being "taken in." (8: Low scorers 1, 0; High scorers 6, 3½.)

These differences in story content again suggest that the low scorers are more likely to empathize in emotional situations than are the high scorers. The latter often appear to be disdainful of passive individuals or of those who react affectively. The comparative inability of the prejudiced women to deal with their own emotions (see Chapter XI) is probably basic to this rejection of emotion in others.

PICTURE 10. Identification is with the one portrayed figure, who is sometimes identified as a boy, sometimes as a girl, and in a few cases, as a woman. The religious theme is somewhat more readily responded to by low-scoring women than by low-scoring men. (The blandness of the responses by many of the men was discussed above.) However, aside from one type of "high" story which projects external aggressive force, stories by high-scoring women tend to reflect very little involvement in the story content.

The most common expression of low-scoring women concerns an internalized religion in which the hero appears humble and awed by the natural environment and stimulated to thought, creativity, and love of his fellow man (n Achievement: Low scorers 20, High scorers 11; n Deference: Low scorers 37, High scorers 20; n Nurturance: Low scorers 24, High scorers 14; n Sentience: Low scorers 30, High scorers 11; n Understanding: Low scorers 12, High scorers 7).

(n Sentience, n Deference, n Understanding): The hero is considering the problem of what religion, life, God really mean. Religion and/or music serves to give him emotional support, peace, and serenity. He is sensitive, imaginative, thoughtful, gets real enjoyment from playing the violin. (10: Low scorers 6, 12; High scorers 1, 3.)

The stories of high-scoring women are less intense. Many relate merely what is portrayed in the picture, sometimes making more concrete the vague picture structure.

The story is bland, consisting of picture description only, and being devoid of any creativity or sentience; e.g., it is stated that the hero is playing the violin in church. He imagines he sees a vision of Christ. (10: Low scorers 3, 2½; High scorers 9, 4½.)

Expressions of the meaning of religion to the individual are in terms of "giving oneself up to" religion rather than integrating it for everyday application. Stories are related in which the hero, as a result of inflicted suffering, becomes a believer, allowing religious direction to decide his actions (p Affliction: Low scorers 7, High scorers 14; p Death of Object: Low scorers 7, High scorers 12).

(p Affliction, p Death → n Succorance): The hero or a member of his family is afflicted by a dreaded disease. He turns to God in the crisis and is reminded of the suffering of Christ. (10: Low scorers 1½, 2; High scorers 3, 10.)

These findings offer further evidence of the greater sensitivity and need for understanding of the low scorers. That these qualities are incorporated into religious attitudes more often by low than by high scorers, was indicated by the differences between "high" and "low" responses to a questionnaire item concerning the importance of religion and the church (see Chapter VI), a finding which suggested a greater tendency in low scorers to have an internalized religion.

Findings from the questionnaire and from the interviews (see Chapter XVIII) suggest that the high scorers seek religion as something to which they can cling in defense against their own impulses and the threats of the mysterious supernatural.

3. *Comparison of Stories Told by Low and High Scorers (Men and Women) to Pictures Depicting Minority Group Members.* We expected Pictures 2, 4, 6, and 9 to elicit further information about the way in which high as compared with low scorers conceptualize the social roles of various group members. The results tend to substantiate other findings regarding attitudes of these two groups, but they did not differentiate the high and low scorers as sharply as did the pictures from the Murray series.

We had expected the low scorers to identify more closely with the characters shown in these pictures and to attribute more constructive behavior to them than would the high scorers. We had thought that the high scorers would view the characters more distantly, reject them more often, and tend to endow them with those traits of behavior for which these subjects had, in their interviews, condemned minority group members. As a matter of fact, since the pictures themselves were so expressive, both high and low scorers often *describe* the picture (the environmental situation) rather than tell a real story about it. They project less into the story than was the case with the stories elicited by the Murray pictures. In many cases there was no real clue as to what extent the subject identified with the person in the picture. There was often no clear-cut expression of acceptance or rejection of the heroes, because the test instructions did not call for expression of attitudes.

The problem of identification was complicated by the explicitness of the activity in the picture. It was clear in most cases that our subjects did not closely identify with the slum area in Picture 4 or the crime aspect of Picture 6. In response to Picture 6, description of antisocial behavior, more specifically of aggression, can hardly be called projective and is certainly "pulled" by the picture itself. Many low scorers as well as high scorers reject any aggressive acts. The difference between rejecting the act and rejecting the person committing the act was not always apparent in the short themes produced by our subjects. Pictures 2 and 9 also, because of their lack of equivocality, limit the amount of projectivity possible. However, the overlapping is more in the area of both low and high scorers' *identifying* with socially acceptable activity—activity that is clearly "pulled" by the picture.

PICTURE 2. Certain differences, however, are apparent. The most common story told to Picture 2 is one in which both figures are described as "zoot-suiters" or young "jitterbugs." Often our subjects, both high and low scorers, describe them as belonging to a minority group, usually Mexican or Negro. High scorers, men and women alike, more often than low scorers, reject the characters. They consider these people as immoral and antisocial. The men tend to reject them for their sensuality and for their carefree attitude, sometimes describing them as "too sexy" and "too playful" (on Sex: Low scorers 1, High scorers 10; on Play: Low scorers 0, High scorers 10.) The high-scoring women condemn them for their offensive exhibitionism (on Recognition: Low scorers 2; High scorers 14) and rebelliousness (on Aggression: Low scorers 0, High scorers 8; on Autonomy: Low scorers 3, High scorers 15).

(on Aggression, Autonomy): Because the parents have not been strict enough with the girl, have not given her a sufficient amount of direction and guidance, the girl has gotten into trouble, has done wrong. The story proceeds with an attempt to put her on the right path, to teach her to do the "right thing." (2: Low-scoring women 0, 1; High-scoring women 3, 5½.)

(on Play, Recognition, Excitance, Sex): The story-teller rejects the characters because of the clothes they are wearing (e.g., "I dont like people who wear that kind of clothes so that they can draw attention to themselves.") or they condemn them as an inferior kind of individual (e.g., "They are disrespectful citizens." "Typical zootsuiters," "criminal type," "typical jitterbugs who hang around the U.S.O." "They are the kind who won't ever accomplish anything.") They are accused of being noisy, antisocial, exhibitionistic, lacking seriousness. (2: Low-scoring men 2, 3; High-scoring men 4, 8; Low-scoring women 2, 2; High-scoring women 10½, 10½.)

Low scorers tell stories with similar content, but the men in this group more often identify with sensuality and playfulness and the women more often with the exhibitionistic and rebellious aspect of the picture than do the high scorers (Men—n Sex: Low scorers 18, High scorers 19, not differentiating; n Excitance: Low scorers 16, High scorers 5; n Play: Low scorers 34, High scorers 21. Women—n Autonomy: Low scorers 12, High scorers 2; n Aggression: Low scorers 12, High scorers 2; n Play: Low scorers 40, High scorers 22; n Recognition: Low scorers 25, High scorers 14).

(n Play, n Sentience, n Sex, n Affiliation): The couple in the picture are out on a date having a good time, and finding real enjoyment in dancing or watching others dance. The subject is identified with the heroes and the needs expressed. ("They love to dance." "They are happy together." "They are having fun." "This is a real pleasure for them.") This thema often is combined with success of n Recognition. They have won a dance contest, are happy that they were awarded the prize, and are having their pictures taken. (2: Low-scoring men 8, 11; High-scoring men 7, 6; Low-scoring women 9⅓, 7; High-scoring women 6, 4.)

A few high- and low-scoring subjects of both sexes place these characters in a situation in which social pressure demands that they give up their rebellious ways and conform. However, instead of condemning the rebellious youngsters, as the high scorers do, low scorers often attribute the behavior to a logical resistance to the demoralization that is likely to result from "racial" prejudice; and they usually conclude by saying, in effect, that in growing up the young people will learn to cope with the situation in more constructive ways.

Apparently the mechanism of projection operates in the T.A.T. situation in a fashion that is similar to what has already been suggested as a factor determining some of the interview responses. It is those more primitive, unsublimated forms of expression so often found in their fantasies (see stories told in response to Pictures M5 and F5) that the high scorers project onto members of minority groups. Those desires within themselves which remain unsatisfied tend to be magnified and rejected in others whom they suspect of satisfying the same desires. It also becomes understandable why high scorers, both men and women, should reject the independence and nonconformity of the young people in Picture 2 when we remember that these subjects employ submissiveness as a means for denying underlying hostile feelings. Thus, we often find the high scorers defending their own submissiveness by condemning as brazen the lack of submission suggested by the depicted clothing and by what they interpret to be a defiant smile of enjoyment.

PICTURE 4.   Stories told in response to Picture 4 by low scorers are, on the whole, more intense than stories told by high scorers. Low scorers tend to deal with realistic problems that face persons living in a slum area, such problems as how to earn a living, how to adapt to or to alter the poverty of the surroundings. Low-scoring women often describe thoughts and feelings of the hero regarding his own life and his relation to society and social goals.

(n Cognizance, n Nurturance): The hero is a philosopher thinking of mankind, of life's pleasures or inconsistencies. He strives to contribute to social betterment or to counteract social injustice directed at society as a whole or toward a particular social group or toward a friend. (4: Low-scoring women 4, 2½; High-scoring women 2½, 2.)

(n Cognizance, n Abasement—intrapunitive type): The hero is ashamed of his past actions and his past egocentrism. He envies the life of the poorer people who allow themselves to enjoy more sensual and passive activity. He decides that he, too, would like to enjoy such a life. (4: Low-scoring women 4, 5; High-scoring women ½, 0.)

The high scorers more often label the central character as a "typical East-sider" or as a "greedy Jewish businessman." They also tend to reject the lack of order and cleanliness in the presented environment.

(on Aggression, on Acquisition): The hero is rejected as a "typical Eastsider," a "greedy Jewish businessman," "a queer duck," or as a criminal, or a beggar. He is up to no good. The rejected hero is about to commit a crime or has just committed a crime. He is disguised or hiding out. (4: Low-scoring men 2½, 2½; High-scoring men 4, 3½.) (4: Low-scoring women 4, 2½; High-scoring women 8, 5.)

High-scoring women again exhibit a tendency to project failure, affliction, and death upon a father figure.

(p Failure, p Loss, p Death and/or p Affliction → n Succorance): The hero has spent his whole life seeking success. He is now very sad, feels defeated (because he has lost all his money, friends, status, or because he never had any money, status, friends, or because he is old and sick.) (4: Low-scoring women 0, 0; High-scoring women 2, 3.)

(p Physical Danger, p Aggression): The hero is a victim of an aggressive or rejective press, enforced on him by the human or physical environment. (4: Low-scoring women 0, 0; High-scoring women 3, 3½.)

These differences in the story content reflect the ethnic prejudice of the high scorer and the contrasting concern of the low scorer over the welfare of society and the individual's role in that society. That no further differentiation between the two groups was found in the present instance might well have been due to the comparative lack of ambiguity in the structure of the picture.

PICTURE 6. Picture 6 is commonly interpreted as a suspect caught by the police. High scorers often reject the suspect and identify more closely with the police authority. The high-scoring men, especially, describe the man in custody as a dangerous criminal, a Negro or Mexican with an innately weak character. (Men—on Aggression: Low scorers 13, High scorers 34; on Autonomy: Low scorers 7, High scorers 16.) He may have been involved in a strike or race riot for which he is condemned by the story-teller. Subjects telling stories in which the suspect is depicted in this manner usually identify with the dominant authoritarian figures who bring the situation under control and protect an imagined white victim.

(on Autonomy, on Aggression⟷n Dominance): The hero is rejected. He has committed a serious crime and the police have caught him. There is often some identification with the police. The suspect is described as a weak character, a Mexican or Negro, a dangerous person, or a person under the influence of alcohol; he is finally punished for his actions. (6: Low-scoring men 7, 7; High-scoring men 13, 13.)

Low scorers, in contrast, tend to identify more with the captured prisoner. They are more likely to attribute the cause of the act committed to a justified protest against social rejection or exploitation; i.e., the man has either been striking for higher wages or fighting race prejudice. The attitude of the hero is usually a combination of fear and defiant rebellion.

(p Dominance → n Autonomy, n Achievement, n Exposition): The story-teller identifies with a hero who has been involved in a strike or race riot or some petty crime. The police have caught him and have him under their control. The expression of Autonomy and Aggression by the hero is a counteractive measure, fighting against an explicitly defined or implied social dominance or rejection (i.e., employer exploitation, or race prejudice). (6: Low-scoring women 7, 9; High-scoring women 0, 3.)

(p Dominance, Aggression → n Harmavoidance, n Abasement or n Autonomy): The hero has been involved in a strike or race riot or some petty crime. The police have caught him and are unduly hard on him. He is afraid but tries to resist. However, he gives up his resistance when he finds that it would be of no value. (6: Low-scoring men 8, 7; High-scoring men 4, 4.)

Here again the most important differences between stories of high and those of low scorers reflect their attitudes toward minority groups. The projection of instinctual desires upon a rejected individual, one of the common defenses of the high-scoring individuals, is apparent in the T.A.T. as in their more direct verbalizations of prejudices.

PICTURE 9. The portrayed characters in Picture 9 are seldom openly rejected. The high scorers find it difficult to reject them because they appear as "clean," or "neat," and seem to be acting in a socially acceptable way. High scorers often state explicitly, or imply by the uniqueness they give to the story content, that these Negroes are different from most Negroes.

Both high- and low-scoring subjects customarily begin their stories by describing the characters as "grandmother" and "grandson." Both groups often say that the two people are having their picture taken. Although subjects from both groups attribute scholastic accomplishments to the boy, for the high scorers the accomplishments mean achieving a status that is only slightly above the slave position that they attribute to the other members of the family. The low scorers, who apparently identify more closely with the

Negro boy, project their own desires for success. They do not, as do the high scorers, limit the success to a minimum amount, implying inferior capacity on the part of the Negro.

Some of the low-scoring women emphasize the positive relationship between the grandmother and grandson.

(p Succorance⟷n Nurturance): The grandmother and grandson are fond of each other and are proud to be together. She is helping the boy to solve a problem or reach a decision. She is encouraging the boy to go on to further learning and achievement. She is teaching the boy or is explaining something to him. (9: Low-scoring women 2, 5; High-scoring women 0, ½.)

Some of the subjects, high and low scorers of both sexes, interpret Picture 9 as two people watching something. For the low scorers it is more commonly an enjoyable artistic performance. (Men—n Sentience: Low scorers 37, High scorers 16. Women—n Sentience: Low scorers 33, High scorers 11.) The high scorers emphasize unpleasant scenes involving death and affliction (Men—p Affliction: Low scorers 4, High scorers 10; p Death-object: Low scorers 3, High scorers 8; p Aggression: Low scorers 11, High scorers 16. Women—p Affliction: Low scorers 7, High scorers 14; p Death-object: Low scorers 7, High scorers 14; p Aggression: Low scorers 11, High scorers 16).

(p Physical Danger, p Dominance → n Abasement-Submission): An unpleasant scene presents itself; or an authoritarian figure representing police, a parent, or another socially dominant figure is demanding that the hero conform to his will. (9: Low-scoring men 4, 2½; High-scoring men 6, 3½.)

Here again, low scorers express greater involvement in interpersonal relationships and more sensitivity to pleasurable stimuli in the environment than do high scorers; whereas the high scorers tend to be more concerned with environmental threats.

C. THE T.A.T.s OF MACK AND LARRY

An examination of the T.A.T. stories produced by Mack and Larry will illustrate in detail the present approach to the scoring and interpretation of this material; it will show how, in concrete cases, some of the differences between high- and low-scoring men are manifest, and it will at the same time add something to the developing pictures of these two men.

These two cases were not chosen as those best suited for demonstrating the contribution of the T.A.T. to an understanding of "high" and "low" personality structures. The stories of Mack and Larry are used, rather, as a part of our plan for following these two men through all of our procedures; this means that from the point of view of one concerned solely with the T.A.T., the selection of illustrative cases is entirely random. This is probably a good thing, for it will be clear that we are not dealing here with dramatic instances of the T.A.T. at its best, but with virtues and faults and difficulties which appear in its ordinary application.

In the previous discussion we have spoken only of trends in the stories of low and high scorers; it is not to be expected that all of these trends will appear in the record of any one individual. In examining the stories of Mack and Larry we shall be concerned with the particular combinations of trends that appear to be consistent with the responses of these two subjects on the Ethnocentrism scale, and we shall point out those trends which appear to be inconsistent with the E-scale scores. This analysis will be carried out against the background afforded by the preceding pages of this chapter.

Presented below are the verbatim records of the stories produced by Mack and by Larry in response to our regular set of ten pictures. The two sets of stories were obtained by the same (male) examiner. The figure in parenthesis immediately following the number of the picture indicates the elapsed time, in seconds, between the presentation of the picture and the subject's beginning of his story. The examiner's questions are given in parenthesis within the body of the story. The notation (Q-o) refers to a question about the outcome of the story, e.g., "How does it turn out," (Q-m) to a request for elaboration or explanation of what the subject said immediately before, and (p) indicates a pause on the part of the subject.

After each story the ratings (on the 1–5 scale) of the needs and press in the story are given. Tabulation of these ratings appear at the end of each set of stories.

The analyses of the stories, which follow the presentation of the tabulated ratings, were "blind" in the sense that the analyst was not familiar with any of the other material on these two subjects. All that was known was that Mack scored high, and Larry low, on the E scale. If these analyses accord well with what is already known about these subjects, and, more particularly, with the clinical material to be given later, they will constitute evidence in favor of the validity of the T.A.T.

1.   LARRY'S STORIES

M1 *(5)* It looks like a father and son. The son is a criminal and the father is ashamed of him. He has a look of sympathy and not hatred. He is probably in prison and is facing the electric chair. The father thinks of how much he has done for the son and can't understand why the son did it. The son is in the death cell and the father is seeing him for the last time. They had been talking but have now reached the stage where all they can do is to just think. The guard comes along and leads the son away.

n Aggression	3	p Nurturance	2
n Nurturance	2	p Dominance	3
n Abasement	4	p Aggression	2
n Blamavoidance	2	p Exposition	2
n Deference	1	p Claustrum	2

n Cognizance	2	p Death of Object	2
n Exposition	2		
n Succorance	3		
on Rejection	1		

2 *(8)* This is a picture of zootsuiters. They seem to be in a prison line-up; they were involved in a crime. They are either confident or trying not to show fear. The latter is probably more true. A gang is standing around them. This gang got together and went to stealing and they are now being taken up for investigation. They are pretty sure of being released to go home because it will be hard for the police to get anything on them. (Are they guilty?) Yes, they are but they have been able to cover up. They continue with their petty crimes.

n Autonomy	2	p Aggression	2
n Affiliation	2	p Dominance	3
n Aggression	3	p Affiliation	2
n Acquisition	2		
n Blamescape	3		
on Succorance	1		

3 *(10)* This is a father and mother grieving over the loss of a son in the war. They have just received word of his death. He was their only son. They are just thinking and saying nothing. The mother thinks of the son, and the father thinks of the mother to comfort her. He thinks of their life together and how it will be changed now. They had been very happy about the accomplishments of their son. They can't bear to think of the tragic end. Neither are crying, so they will continue to make the best of it and will keep a stiff upper lip.

n Succorance	4	p Succorance	2
n Cognizance	2	p Death of object	4
n Passivity	3	p Affiliation	2
n Nurturance	3		
n Affiliation	2		
on Achievement	2		

4 *(12)* This woman is a peddler. The man is a rich banker who is walking through the slums of New York. He is on his way home. He doesn't want to be snobbish and not touch the people. He feels out of his neighborhood. The woman is right at home here. Each goes his own way in sort of contrast of two lives—the rich and the poor. He walks this way on his way home from work each day, and does his best not to be too personal with any of them. He just wants to know what's going on for business reasons.

n Acquisition	3	p Uncongenial Environment	3
n Seclusion	3	p Lack	3
n Rejection	1	p Gratuity	3
n Cognizance	3	p Task	2
on Rejection	2		

M5 *(6)* This is a young fellow who drinks a lot. His clothes are all messed up. In a dingy hotel room, he feels he has lost all of his friends. He thinks all of the troubles of the world are on his shoulders. He contemplates suicide. The trouble is with a woman he had an affair with. He doesn't know whether to injure her or destroy himself. (Q-m) To kill her or commit suicide. She isn't much good herself, and he isn't too much better. He is in a mixed up mental state. He is pausing there to make some decision. (p) (Q-o) He will try to get revenge on the woman. (Revenge for what?) He has been going with her and giving her money and thinks of marrying her. She fools him and is unfaithful, going around with other men. He kills her.

n	Abasement	4	p Uncongenital Environment	3
n	Succorance	3	p Sex	2
n	Aggression	4	p Rejection	4
n	Sex	4	p Death of Object	2
n	Affiliation	1		
n	Counteraction	2		
n	Nurturance	1		
n	Understanding	1		
n	Rejection	2		

6 (10) This is a man caught in an alley by the police, just before committing some crime. The police were called and he is surprised. He tries to get away but the police have the upper hand. He is frightened for fear they will use their sticks. He is probably a man with a family—a good wife and two or three children. He is a no good, just working once in a while. He steals when he can and keeps it from his wife. (Q-m) She is a good woman and doesn't know he is that type of person. Since he has been caught, he knows she will find it all out. For this reason, he would like to get away from the police, but is afraid if he tries he will get shot. He just backs against the wall and lets himself get caught.

on	Aggression	3	op Dominance	3
on	Autonomy	2	op Aggression	3
on	Acquisition	3	op Affiliation	2
on	Succorance	2	op Cognizance	3
on	Harmavoidance	4		
on	Blamescape	3		
on	Abasement	3		

M7 (8) This young fellow is going away to the army and his mother is very sad about it. She has been expecting this and they have talked it all over. Now that the moment is here, neither knows just what to say. In silence she thinks of his youth—his birth and what he used to do as a little boy. She thinks of his late teens and the honors he got in high school. He thinks less of the past than of the future—and what it will be like in the army. He determines to make the best of it, and try to get the war over with as soon as possible so he can come back. Both stand there for a few minutes, and when he leaves he kisses her and walks away without saying anything.

n	Exposition	2	p Task 4
n	Achievement	2	
n	Nurturance	3	
n	Succorance	3	
n	Passivity	2	
n	Counteraction	2	
n	Aggression	2	
n	Cognizance	2	

8 (15) This is a man lying on his death bed. The other man is an enemy of his. He has been the cause of his death and is glad he has gone because he hates him inwardly. He gave the impression that he was his friend. He has his hand in the air, not to touch him but as a relief of emotion—just clenching his fist over him. These were both respectable men. (How do you mean?) They were businessmen, not gangsters. They were competitors in business and were both from the same social group. The dying man has felt no tension between them; it's all in the other fellow. The dying man's wife had this fellow come in to sit with him for a few minutes. Now that his competitor has gone, he will have more confidence in himself and more esteem in the community.

n Aggression	3		p Affiliation	2
n Rejection	4		p Death of Object	4
n Achievement	3		p Deference	3
n Acquisition	3			
n Recognition	3			

9 (7) This is a mother and son at home; I say that because of the pictures on the wall. Both are sad. Something has happened in the family. It's a large family of ten or twelve children. (p) One of the brothers has just gotten in trouble; he stole something. This is a respectable, religious family. The mother makes them go to church. The boy is in jail and they have heard the news. The whole family is sitting around the living room, but in this picture we can see only the two. Both seem to have the same thoughts—the reputation of the family. The boy who committed the crime can't understand why he did it. Though not rich, they had a fairly nice home and enough food; there was just no reason why the boy should do a thing like that. Since he is one of the family they will of course try to help him. They try to punish him in some way, probably by being cool to him, not speaking. (How old is he?) He is about 25 and unmarried.

n Succorance	3		p Claustrum	2
n Blamavoidance	4		p Dominance	3
on Aggression	3		p Aggression	2
on Autonomy	3		p Gratuity	2
on Acquisition	3			
n Abasement	3			
n Affiliation	2			
n Nurturance	3			
n Rejection	3			

10 (12) This reminds me of a Biblical story. It is about Christ on the cross. This is a cloudy sky on a dull, stormy day. This woman is of the modern age; the picture in the background comes to her mind. She has had lots of troubles and doesn't know how to solve them. (p) (What kind?) It may have been the death of her husband. She is a very religious woman, and he has meant a lot to her. They always solved their problems together. All she knows now is to turn to Christ and the Bible to try to figure out a solution to her problems. She has been very religious from the time she was small. Now that the vision has come to her, she is more satisfied—she has found peace of mind and is now able to continue her life. She will be sad but will have the feeling that the Lord will care for her husband and will give her comfort.

n Abasement	3		p Bad Luck	2
n Succorance	3		p Death of Object	3
n Affiliation	2		p Affiliation	3
n Deference	4		p Gratuity	3
n Passivity	2		p Nurturance	3
n Counteraction	2			

2. MACK'S STORIES

M1   *(60)* This would indicate to me a man in distress and a comforting friend. Some accident may have happened, or a death in one of the younger man's family. (p) There is a certain dullness to the man's expression, probably from the great shock. (p) (Are the two men related?) It's possible, but I can't say; I think they may be just friends. I doubt if it's his father. The efforts of the older man to help the other fellow see the brighter side and get him on a steady course again will be successful. The young fellow is a deeply brooding type and maybe won't be too successful, or at best only temporarily. The young fellow indicates the type of person who might do violence if pushed too far. (Q-m) I think he could easily murder somebody on being oppressed. I think he will never completely get over the shock of the death and it affects him in such a way that it makes him hard to get along with from then on.

n Succorance	3	p Nurturance	3
n Affiliation	3	p Death of Object	3
n Counteraction	2	p Physical Danger	1
n Understanding	1	p Affiliation	3
n Abasement	1	p Dominance	3
n Aggression	3		

2   *(20)* This is a young fellow and his girl. They are all dolled up for the occasion. They are just starting out for the night. The style of his clothing is foreign to me; I never saw that sort of thing before. The girl looks to be about 17 and the man about 21—considerably older. After a show, they go some place and eat. Then he gets the girl home about ten or eleven o'clock. From the age of the girl they would get in at a reasonable hour. (Are they related?) No, I don't think they are; they are not the same type. I don't think they are husband and wife; they just go together. The girl has a nice, pleasant personality. He is not so deep, and he has a less full character than the girl. (p) The partial view of the other fellow gives me an idea of another story. This involves the same original setup except that they had their pictures taken at a party. This man stepped up and made a smart remark to make them smile for the picture. That fellows dress doesn't correspond to the girl's. He looks like he was from another period. It might be the early '30's. Maybe the suit was designed for a gag. (Q-o) They have other dates but they gradually drifted apart.

n Recognition	3	p Exposition	1
n Nutriance	2	p Affiliation	1
n Affiliation	1	p Superiority	2
n Excitance	1	p Cognizance	3
n Play	2		

3   *(10)* My first impression is from what I read in newspapers, you know, about the war. He is saying goodbye to his mother. He is of military age—about 23. His mother is about in her early 50's. He is advising her not to worry. He says he will write and asks her to keep him informed of the folks and his friends. He tries to lead her to believe he will see her again soon—like most men would. He seems to be a strong individual. He is clean-cut. Of course, we always like to hope they will all come back, but I can't help but guess that he will not come back. He was killed in the war. They are very close and yet are not the kind to show a lot of observable affection and make a lot of one another. They used to kid one another, and make fun of one another and yet if one got in trouble they all came to his rescue. That's the kind of family they were.

n Nurturance	3	p Task	3
n Dominance	2	p Succorance	2
n Affiliation	3	p Death of Hero	3
n Succorance	2	p Affiliation	3
n Deference	2	p Nurturance	3

4 (30) It looks something like a street off the main track in New York City. It's a run-down section of the city. These pictures are cleverly done—they don't tell you anything. (What preceded this picture?) Well, its perhaps on a Saturday or Sunday and this businessman is on his way home. I don't think he is very well, all bundled up like that. I think he must be a tailor. He isn't too well off, but is better off than most of his neighbors. He is a family man. As for the woman, it's difficult to give a motive for her. She has something to sell, is poor, and can just keep her family in food and clothes. (Q-o) There is no relationship between these people. It is just the end of the day and each is going home. Each represents a class—the well off and the poor. This is just a typical scene.

n Acquisition	3	p Uncongenial Environment	2
n Construction	1	p Affliction	2
n Nurturance	2	p Lack	2

M5 (70) Oh, oh! This is apt to be rather sordid. It doesn't represent a family scene to me! It may be a prostitute, and I see the old bottle there. This may be a young American down in the tropics; he is dressed in white because of the temperature. As for the woman, it's difficult to say because of the shadows, but she appears of darker skin. The place has crude furnishings. (p) (What preceded?) The natural assumption is that they had sexual intercourse. The fellow is about half drunk and is about to consume more. The fellow looks kind of "hang-dog"; perhaps he regrets his recent act or perhaps his station in life. He is down and out and liquor isn't much of a boon to him. He has sufficient depth of character to take himself out of a place like that and to genuinely regret what he did to the woman. She doesn't enter into the story, except to be the object of his lust. He is a better type than she. He can take care of himself. He finally drags himself out of such surroundings and gradually amounts to something. Do I take too long? I get quite involved in these stories.

n Excitance	1	p Sex	3
n Abasement	3	p Uncongenial Environment	1
n Blamavoidance	2		
n Sex	3		
n Blamescape	1		
n Counteraction	3		

6 (45) This is a public disturbance, perhaps a strike or a race disturbance. He has some Negroid features. He started a riot and has now been separated from the group he organized. The police have frightened him and he expects the worst. He is lodged in the local jail for a time and is scared out of such activities again. Maybe he was the fall guy for the group. Without the crowd influence he was pretty docile.

n Dominance	2	p Dominance	3
n Aggression	3	p Aggression	3
n Autonomy	2	p Claustrum	2
n Abasement	4		
n Succorance	2		

*M*7 *(45)* These people are related. They are mother and son since their features correspond. She is about 60 and he about 25. He has just told her something he has done which causes her grief and apprehension. She can't condone it, and is shocked. He's upset too, like he'd rather not have told her but had to. He doesn't look the type to get into trouble. (p) This picture gives me trouble. (Q-m) Well, it's the expressions on their faces. This man was responsible for the death of someone loved by both the mother and the man. It was not a crime, but an auto accident. It was sort of negligence on his part and he feels responsible. His mother turns away at first, then comes back to him and decides to help him. It was this way: this fellow in the picture and a friend went for a ride. There was an accident and this fellow (in the picture) was driving. He was negligent in some way or another, and caused the death of the person riding with him. He is now telling his mother all about it. He has a strong character, and feels badly about it all. He is serious. (p) (Q-o) Well, he and his mother talk it all over, and she helps him by giving him some good advice. (Q-m) She tells him it could have happened to anyone, and that the thing to do now is to forget it and just go right on living as usual. She tells him it is bad to keep thinking about it. (Does he?) Yes, he doesn't let it drag his life down. It finally passes out of his memory.

n Exposition	2		p Rejection	2
on Succorance	3		p Death of Object	3
n Abasement	3		p Nurturance	4
n Aggression	2		p Affiliation	2
n Affiliation	1		p Physical Danger	2
n Blamescape	2		p Exposition	2
n Passivity	2			

8 *(30)* Well, this suggests a doctor and his patient. Yet, the gesture gives me the idea it might be a hypnotist at work. I dont know much about the field of hypnosis. The patient is unconscious about the face, but his legs aren't relaxed. Usually such performances are put on on the stage, and this seems to be in a private home. Do people keep their clothes on while receiving hypnotic treatment? (I'm sure I don't know; let's just use our imagination.) I guess this is a scene on the stage of a theatre. This man is a hypnotist and is directing the performance along the lines that would be funny to the audience. The other fellow was taken from the audience and later joins his friends who ask him a lot of silly questions. The performance ends and all go home.

n Dominance	2		p Deference	2
n Play	2		p Affiliation	2
n Recognition	3		p Cognizance	3
n Affiliation	2			

9 *(30)* These people are Negroes, of course. It's the grandmother and the grand-son. I'm not very familiar with Negro features, but they look alike, these two. She is a kindly old lady. She looks toil-worn, and has had a hard life of work. She is dressed well. I guess it's a portrait in the home. Some Negroes carry their fortune on their back. These may be of a higher type and are better educated than most Negroes. She was a slave and was freed, and gradually accumulated some money. They are quiet folks. It may be they are enjoying a musical here. (Qo). After their picture is taken, they go back to their regular routine lives—he to school and she to helping their children to run their homes and just being generally useful.

n Recognition	1	p Task	3
n Acquisition	3	p Dominance	2
n Sentience	2	p Exposition	2
n Cognizance	2	p Cognizance	2
n Achievement	1		
n Nurturance	3		
n Deference	1		

10   (60) This is Christ on the cross, in the midst of flames or smoke. I can hardly reconcile myself to the fact that this is just a photo. It might be a trick picture. Jesus appears life-sized, and so does the cross, yet I don't know of a church with this sized crucifix. Here is a young boy of 8 or 9. In Sunday School he just received a vivid portrayal of Jesus on the cross by a very fine preacher and is very much impressed. That night he has trouble sleeping soundly and while in a semi-conscious state sees this image. He is just coming out of this dream when the image fades. This experience stays with him the rest of his life. I know I can remember a few dreams I had at about that age. (Do you think they influenced you?) I think they really did, all my life. This boy wakes up in the morning and tells his parents about it, and retains this memory the rest of his life.

n Deference	3	p Exposition	3
		p Dominance	1

3. ANALYSIS OF THE STORIES

The analysis of Larry's T.A.T. reveals a person who indulges actively in fantasy. (The total of the need and press scoring for this subject, 276, is much above the mean, 209, for the group of low-scoring men.)

His fantasies, however, exhibit a disphoric quality that is unusually marked in relation to other subjects tested. Death is often referred to in his stories and his heroes tend to be emotionally dependent and self-depreciating (p Death-object: Larry 15, Mean for low-scoring men 3.6; n Succorance: Larry 19, Mean for low-scoring men 7.6; n Abasement: Larry 14, Mean for low-scoring men 7.90). These depressive tones are accompanied by a greater concern over moral values than is usually apparent in stories of low-scoring men (n Blamavoidance: Larry 6, Mean for low-scoring men 1.75). The variable n Blamavoidance is found more often in stories of high- than in those of low-scoring men; but in the case of Larry the manner of dealing with moral values, which is revealed in the expression of succorance, of the intragressive type of abasement, and of n Cognizance (Larry 8, group mean 6.05), suggests an internalization of values that is more characteristic of low than of high scorers.

Larry expresses an excessive amount of aggressive fantasy (n Aggression: Larry 15, Mean for low-scoring men 7.65); it is of an impulsive, antisocial type, the type that is more often found in stories of high scorers. Were it not for the fact that the expressions of aggression are followed by evaluation of the act and acceptance of self-blame, the trend would be contradictory to the low E score. It has been noted often in this volume that one of the factors which most clearly differentiates prejudiced and unprejudiced subjects is the amount of intraceptiveness of the individual, a tendency which disposes him to evaluate, and sometimes even to be overly concerned with, his reactions in relation to other people. In the present case, if we accept the T.A.T. responses as representative of the subject's fantasy, it appears that Larry is preoccupied with a conflict over his rather generalized feelings of hostility. This conflict is reflected in the constant interplay between aggression and intragressive abasement and passivity. The fact that Larry's stories reveal a persistent attempt to evaluate and to deal with this conflict is consistent with a comparative lack of stereotyped projections of hostility, and, hence, with a low E score.

The summary of the scoring of Mack's stories is strikingly similar to the mean scores for the group of high-scoring men. Although he tends to be more restricted in amount of expression than many high-scoring men (Mack's total need and press scores 193, Mean for high-scoring group 213), the patterning of the scoring is rather typical of the group to which he belongs. As compared with low-scoring men, his fantasies exhibit less creative activity, less curiosity, and less independent striving. He describes the same type of impulsive aggressive behavior as did Larry although Mack does not do so as frequently as Larry. However, the variables which express an intraceptive mode of dealing with such behavior (n Cognizance, n Succorance, n Abasement) are also given considerably less weight by Mack than by our unprejudiced subjects.

In Mack's stories we find an excessive amount of n Affiliation and n Recognition, two variables which in our total group have higher mean scores for unprejudiced than for prejudiced subjects. However, Mack in contrast to Larry tends to express these variables through statements of relationship or status rather than through the description of personal interaction or active striving. In Mack's stories Affiliation is very rarely found in combination with n Nurturance or n Succorance or with n Recognition or n Cognizance.

Neither of these two men refers to more than a minimum amount of physical press. However, much of the n Abasement scored for Mack reflects story content that appears to describe submission to *implied* environmental demands.

From the stories told in response to Picture 1, we get the first indications of the differences in the quality of the fantasies of the two men. Although both express, through their heroes, strong underlying hostile feelings toward the world, Larry identifies more closely with these feelings and makes stronger attempts to understand them. Mack, on the other hand, describes a more primitive type of aggressive fantasy and tends to reject the hero of the story (although not directly enough to warrant the scoring of "object needs"), thereby disowning responsibility for the expression of hostility. In contrast to Larry, who attempts to understand the reasons for antisocial be-

TABLE 6 (XIV)

COMPARISON OF THE SCORES OF MACK AND LARRY ON THE THEMATIC APPERCEPTION
TEST WITH THE MEAN SCORES OF PREJUDICED AND UNPREJUDICED MEN

	Larry	Unprejudiced Men Mean Score	Mack	Prejudiced Men Mean Score
1. *Variables of Interpersonal Relationships:*				
n Affiliation	9	6.8	10	5.3
p Affilication	9	5.6	11	5.15
n Deference	5	4.9	6	5.25
p Deference	3	2.6	2	1.9
n Dominance	0	2.1	6	2.85
p Dominance	9	9.2	9	9.8
n Nurturance	12	5.55	8	4.4
p Nurturance	5	4.75	10	5.25
n Recognition	3	4.55	7	3.95
n Succorance	19	7.6	10	8.2
p Succorance	2	2.5	2	2.25
2. *Variables of Rebellion:*				
n Aggression	15	7.65	8	5.70
n Autonomy	3	6.55	2	5.90
n Rejection	3	5.45	0	2.90
3. *Variables of Positive Constructive Activity:*				
n Cognizance	8	6.05	2	3.75
n Construction	0	.45	1	.45
n Expression	4	4.15	2	2.85
n Understanding	1	1.85	1	.45
p Task	6	4.30	6	3.20
4. *Variables of Sensuality:*				
n Excitance	0	1.25	2	1.05
n Passivity	7	2.95	2	2.25
n Play	0	3.05	4	1.65
n Sex	4	5.70	3	3.80
n Sentience	0	3.50	2	.90
5. *Variables of Moral Control and Withdrawal:*				
n Abasement	14	7.90	11	10.00
n Blamavoidance	6	1.75	4	3.20
n Seclusion	3	1.95	0	2.95
6. *Variables of Environmental Press:*				
p Affliction	0	2.75	2	3.65
p Bad Luck	2	.10	0	1.15
p Death of hero	0	1.55	3	2.75
p Death of object	15	3.6	6	4.2

havior, i.e., why his own impulses cause him to have unacceptable thoughts, Mack seems to express the feeling that thinking about things too much causes a person to lose control of himself. He calls the hero a "deeply brooding type . . . who might do violence if pushed too far."

Mack is more sympathetic with the older man than with the younger one. The older man is a stronger individual who is able to withstand the stress of a difficult situation; the younger man is weak and dependent upon the direction of the older one. When Larry's hero gets into trouble, he seeks comfort and guidance from the father, but he nevertheless accepts the responsibility for his own acts. Larry fantasies a dependent relationship with the father that is based on respect and a need for sympathy, and he describes guilt resulting from action that is displeasing to the father. It is a dependence on love, not on power as in the case of Mack's story. The problem of the son and of the father is a mutual one for Larry; for Mack the responsibility for the impulsive act and the responsibility for restraint are separated. The one is "bad" and the other is "good," and there appears to be little reconciliation of the two.

In response to Picture 3, Larry describes the common "low" thema of mutual sympathy resulting from a crucial situation. He seems to identify with a nurturant father figure who is deeply concerned over his wife and family. However, Larry's tendency to exaggerate the morbid, as well as his preoccupation with self-destruction, is revealed in the description of the son who is killed in battle.

The story of Mack expresses little of the sensitivity and desire to be understood that is found in Larry's story. Rather, this subject describes in cliché phraseology the age and character of each of the people in his story. He identifies with the son, who is given a role of heroic bravery. In his story, as well as in Larry's, a man is killed in battle. However, concern about the dangers of war is restricted to the woman. The man is idealized as a "strong individual" behaving fearlessly, "like most men would."

The main difference between the stories told by Larry and by Mack to Picture 5 lies in the fact that the former accepts responsibility for his actions, whereas the latter projects most of the blame onto the woman. Both of these subjects reject the woman who freely enters into a sexual relationship. However, Larry appears to condemn her because she deceives the hero, with whom he is closely identified. The hostility that is directed at the woman does not appear to reflect a lack of respect for her as appears to be true in Mack's story, but rather it is the result of despair over her ability to frustrate him. Mack not only manifests a decided lack of respect for the woman in his story, but he blames her for causing his hero to act in an unbecoming manner; at the same time he defends the man's position and describes him as an individual with "depth of character," who allows himself to become a part of this "sordid" scene because of urges beyond a man's control.

These stories differ somewhat from the more common themes produced by low- and high-scoring men in response to Picture 5. The story of Larry is more hostile than those of most of his group. Mack is more rejecting of heterosexuality, and he projects more blame onto women, than is usually the case with high-scoring men. However, the lack of concern for the woman, and for her part in a sexual relationship, that we see in Mack's story, as contrasted with the more personal relationship in Larry's, fits closely the general difference in themes between high and low scorers described earlier.

The differing types of dependence expressed by these two subjects in their stories to Picture 7 are typical of those described by low and high scorers generally. Larry's hero seeks understanding and support, while Mack describes a hero who is dependent on external forces to direct his activity within acceptable channels.

Larry, however, refrains from giving the most common "low" theme of striving to act independently of the demands of the mother. Instead, he fantasies about a hero who performs unusual and wonderful deeds that please the mother and cause her to admire him.

Mack describes a theme commonly told by high-scoring men, one in which the son displeases the mother. She rejects him and he becomes dependent on her "good advice," forgiveness, and reassurance that he did not really do wrong. It is interesting how this man, who deprecates women in some of his other stories, and who usually describes his male heroes as "strong characters," describes a submissive relationship of son to mother. However, this relationship is as lacking in warmth as are the others. The forgiveness by the mother at the end lacks any real feeling of affiliation or nurturance.

In his story to Picture 8, Larry approaches a theme often produced by high-scoring men, the intense amount of hostility being more typical of high than of low scorers. The components that are consistent with the trends common to stories of low scorers are found in the extensive description of the feelings of each man and in the rationalization of the crime.

Mack appears severely disturbed by this picture. It is not the type of distress often evidenced in stories of low-scoring men, who apparently find it difficult to respond to the aggressive aspect of the picture. A real concern over homosexual attack appears to be expressed here, although it is perhaps not consciously recognized as such by the story-teller. The question, "Do people keep their clothes on while receiving hypnotic treatment?," the annoyance at being questioned by friends, as well as the symbolic description of the patient, are strongly suggestive of personally determined fantasies of a homosexual nature.

The concreteness of thinking exhibited in Mack's story in response to Picture 10, compared with the more intense creativity of Larry's expression, demonstrates well the difference with respect to this factor found in our two groups of subjects and described earlier in this chapter. Although Mack intellectualizes about the impression that the vision makes on the boy, he never describes what it actually means to him. Larry, on the other hand, discusses in detail his hero's problem, and his thoughts and feelings about the solution.

To Pictures 2, 4, 6 and 9 Larry tells stories of more intensity than does Mack. The former is able to identify more closely with the heroes drawn from minority groups and to describe their thoughts and feelings. In stories to Pictures 2 and 9 he identifies with the antisocial behavior of the character, and attempts to rationalize the action as he does in his story to Picture 1.

Mack makes no positive identifications with the "minority" heroes. In general, his stories consist of a statement of the immediate situation, the environmental surroundings, and the age, status, and costumes of the characters. The stories are almost completely devoid of any indications of the thoughts or feelings of the heroes.

Both Larry and Mack reject the man captured by the police in Picture 6. Larry rejects him because he is unworthy of his family and does not adequately care for them; Mack rejects him because he is weak, and at the same time dangerous and to be feared. Larry's story again expresses a strong empathy—in other individuals; in this case, the concern is for the woman.

Larry's T.A.T. stories then are essentially consistent with his low E score, although the patterning of scores in some instances deviates from that most commonly found in the records for unprejudiced men. However, as has been pointed out, these discrepancies reflect this individual's personal conflicts which he deals with in a manner distinctly representative of the unprejudiced men.

The features of stories of low scorers—intensity of story content, close identifications with the characters portrayed, description of personal interaction, and of reflective feelings and thoughts of the characters about their behavior—all are present in Larry's stories. However, it should be emphasized that the strength of the dependence upon sources of love, as described in this man's stories, and the intensity of reaction to frustration, is most extreme for our low-scoring men.

We would expect Larry to be sensitive to the feelings and thoughts of others, and capable of empathizing with them. At the same time he is probably unusually sensitive to signs of rejection from others. He appears to be a person who attempts to understand his own behavior, and to keep this behavior in line with a code of ethics that he has set up for himself despite impulses that are contradictory.

Mack's record reveals many of the trends that we have previously pointed out as being commonly found in stories of high-scoring men. The record is comparatively meager; there is a lack of intensity of identification, and partial rejections of story characters often occur in his stories. A dichotomy of roles characterizes the relationships depicted in his stories. Father, mother, husband are depicted as dominant and as determining the behavior of the wife or son, who are pictured in submissive roles. Little reference is made to introspectiveness or to consideration of underlying motivation. Behavior is often attributed to innate tendencies within the individual, over which he has no control.

Mack appears to be a person bound to conventional standards, attempting to ignore or deny unacceptable desires by projecting them onto others. He is unable to admit his own weakness, and he defends himself rigidly against revealing any feelings of inadequacy. This guarding causes a restriction of spontaneity and a limitation of the environmental stimuli to which he can allow himself to respond.

D. SUMMARY

We can conclude from the above discussion of data that certain types of expression in T.A.T. stories tend to differentiate our two groups of subjects. Although the differences can be considered as no more than trends, each variable having at least some degree of overlap between the two groups, a large percentage of our subjects demonstrate a sufficient number of these trends so that it is possible, by considering the content of their T.A.T. stories alone, to identify them as prejudiced or unprejudiced individuals.

We find that low scorers, as compared with high scorers, identify more closely with the heroes in their stories, and attribute to them more creative activity, more enjoyment of sensual pleasures, and more congenial relationships with other individuals. Aggression is expressed in more sublimated forms, most often being in the service of a goal of creativity, nurturance, or autonomy from imposed coercion. The activity described is more often determined by inner rational decision rather than by external forces. These subjects tend to emphasize autonomous behavior, and they often reject domination by authoritarian figures suggested by the pictures. Although the heroes in their stories often seek advice and sympathy from parents and friends, the ultimate decision is usually one of the hero's own choosing. Status relationships between man and woman, parent and child, or Negro and white, are more nearly equal in their stories than in those of high scorers.

The high scorers, as compared with the low scorers, tend to describe behavior of a less constructive nature. Expression of aggression is more often of a primitive, impulsive sort; it is condemned by the story-teller and is followed by an outcome of punishment of the hero.

High scorers tend more often to describe the motivation for the actions of their heroes in terms of external influence or innate tendencies over which the individual has no control. Their heroes more often appear as dependent upon the demands and rules and regulations of authority and are more often activated by parental demands and social custom. They are more frequently victimized by affliction or death.

Contrasting status relationships are more marked in the stories of high scorers. The male and female roles tend to be dichotomized, the man as the master, the woman as weak, dependent, and submissive. Parents are more often described as domineering and demanding, and their children as submissive and compliant.

CHAPTER XV

PROJECTIVE QUESTIONS IN THE STUDY
OF PERSONALITY AND IDEOLOGY

Daniel J. Levinson

A. INTRODUCTION

The Projective Question technique is an application of the general principles of projective techniques to the questionnaire method and to the study of the dynamics of ideology. A Projective Question is an open-ended question which is answered in a few words or lines and which deals with unusual events or experiences likely to have emotional significance for the individual. Care is taken to give the question a "homey," even humorous wording; also, an emphasis on the universal nature of certain emotional experiences (e.g., moods, embarrassment) may make the subject feel freer in giving an answer. The following eight questions were used in the present research:[1]

1. We all have times when we feel below par. What moods or feelings are the most unpleasant or disturbing to you?

2. We all have impulses and desires which are at times hard to control but which we try to keep in check. What desires do you often have difficulty in controlling?

3. What great people, living or dead, do you admire most?

[1] These questions were selected from among an original set of some thirty questions given to several groups of college students. The criteria for selection included statistical differentiation, theoretical significance, and nonduplication of content. It was necessary, for practical reasons, to eliminate many items which showed much promise. For example: What are your greatest weaknesses? Your greatest assets? What would you most like people to say of you after you have lived your life? What do you find most disgusting? Most annoying? As a parent, what would you try most to instill in your child? What would you protect your child against? What makes you lose your temper? What do you most admire in a person? Most dislike? Worst thing that could happen to anyone? Ingenious ways of committing murder? Why might a person commit suicide?

The instructions in all cases were as follows: The following questions give you a chance to express your ideas and opinions in your own way. *Please answer them all as fully as possible.*

We wish to thank the Graduate School of Western Reserve University for a grant-in-aid to cover certain phases of the analysis of data in this chapter.

4. There is hardly a person who hasn't said to himself, "If this keeps up, I'll go nuts!" What might drive a person nuts?

5. What do you consider the worst crimes a person could commit?

6. It seems that no matter how careful we are, we all sometimes have embarrassing moments. What experiences make you feel like sinking through the floor?

7. If you knew you had only six months to live, but could do just as you pleased during that period, how would you spend your time?

8. We get a feeling of awe when something seems to us wonderful, or impressive, or really important. What things would give you the greatest feeling of awe?

These items, considered as a technique, are similar in principle to the most intensive clinically used projective techniques such as the Thematic Apperception Test and the Rorschach, and to the various paper and pencil techniques. In general, all such techniques involve a standardized test situation uniform for all subjects, and a set of materials which (a) present a problem to be worked out, (b) are designed to bring out wide individual differences in response (that is, in the way the problem is worked out), and (c) elicit responses that are rich in meaning and in implications for deep-lying personality dynamics. The Projective Questions are sometimes called "indirect questions" because the subject is seldom aware of the implications of his responses and because the interpretations do not take the answers at face value, but rather go beyond the literal meaning of the response to look for deeper dynamic sources. The justification for such interpretation lies in the very nature of the technique; when the many psychologically important aspects of the situation and the problem-material are held uniform for all subjects, individual differences are attributed to *characteristics in the subject*, and the materials are so selected that the main difference-producing variables are likely to be personality trends of considerable importance in the individual's psychological functioning.

The various projective techniques differ in at least the following important respects: in the intensity of the relation of subject to tester, in the degree of structuring of the material as presented to the subject, and, as a result of these, in the interindividual variability of response and the intraindividual richness of response (expression of inner affect, impulses, deep-lying trends and conflicts). In traditional psychoanalytic therapy which is, in a sense, the model for all projective techniques, the relation of subject to therapist is the most intense and plays the greatest role in eliciting emotionally significant behavior. In the psychoanalytic technique, furthermore, the materials are as unstructured as possible; they include only the standardized situation and instructions, designed to produce a maximum of spontaneity, and the person of the analyst, who might also be considered an unstructured material on whom the subject can project whatever he wishes. Since transference and resistance are so crucial in psychoanalysis, the course of therapy might be regarded as a series of manipulations of the therapist by the subject, in much the same way as other projective materials are manipulated.

The use of the standardized play situation as a therapeutic projective technique probably comes closest to psychoanalysis with respect to the role of the therapist in eliciting and handling transference and resistance, and with respect to the range of self-expression stimulated by the relatively unstructured but behavior-inducing materials. It is possible here not only to elicit but also to record many aspects of the verbal and motor behavior of the subject. The major projective techniques used clinically for diagnostic rather than for therapeutic purposes, such as the T.A.T. and Rorschach, are more limited with regard to the role of the tester and the range of expression observed and recorded, but they have been of considerable value in clinical practice and personality research.

While the Projective Question technique involves almost none of the "relation between subject and tester" aspects of the therapeutic techniques, and while it is less intensive and more structured than the diagnostic clinical techniques, it has nevertheless a number of important advantages for large-scale sociopsychological research. The items are easily understood, they can be filled out quickly (8 items require only 10 to 15 minutes), and they require no "props" or detailed instructions. For these and other reasons they are ideally suited for questionnaire use.

One great value of the Projective Questions is that the variables derived from the scoring, as shown in the Scoring Manual which follows, are directly related to the variables expressed by many of the scale items in the questionnaire, especially those in the F scale. Thus, this technique not only adds important material about the individual, but it also partially validates the scale results, since the undirected, spontaneously given responses to the Projective Questions reflect trends similar to those involved in the channelized, agree-disagree responses to the scale items.

The Projective Questions were included in each form of the questionnaire (see Chapter IV). They contributed to the study of relationships between personality and ethnocentrism, and they were an important source of ideas for F-scale items. The high and low quartiles on the E scale were the groups compared. (The middle scorers constitute an important group for future study; preliminary perusal of their responses suggests that their intermediate position is more a matter of conflicting high and low trends than of simple neutrality or indifference.) The term "highs" or "high scorers" will be used to refer to the *high quartile as measured on the Ethnocentrism scale*, and conversely for the "lows," who constitute the *low quartile on E*.

As far as the writer is aware, this is the first attempt at systematic, "quantitative" analysis of Projective Questions as a formal technique. They were used previously in a nonquantitative manner on the Harvard Growth Study of School Children (106), and their use in the present research was suggested by R. N. Sanford, a member of that Study. Some of the questions as used here are taken directly from the Harvard Growth Study of School Children. Some of them were used subsequently by the United States Office of Strategic Services in their assessment program (116).[2] The content of the questions is, of course, hardly new; they have been asked, in one form or another, by clinical psychologists and others for some time.

B. QUANTIFICATION BY MEANS OF SCORING CATEGORIES

The problem of quantification has plagued everyone who works with projective tests, personal documents or other qualitative clinical material. Attempts at precise measurement and complex statistical treatment have usually resulted in quantification at the expense of meaning, in reliability without validity. Any quantitative mode of analysis, focusing as it does on aspects of response that occur with some frequency in larger groups, can hardly help but overlook those aspects which are more idiosyncratic, even though the latter may be crucial for understanding a given individual. Moreover, the more subtle and abstract qualities of response are difficult to formulate in a concrete, specific manner. These difficulties are particularly great when, as in the present case, one is interested in the primary *psychological content* of the response—in what the individual strives for or feels or values or experiences.

It seemed, however, that some middle ground between precise quantification and the total clinical gestalt might be found. The compromise chosen was scoring by means of *qualitative categories*. While each category is scored only in terms of present-absent—scoring in terms of quantitative degrees may yet be attempted—a measure of quantification is obtained by summing an individual's (or group's) scores on the several items. This method, while lacking a high degree of precision,[3] can, at the least, attempt to meet necessary standards of rigorous definition, controlled scoring, and scoring reliability. And, while neglecting much that the clinician may see intuitively in any single response, the categories can include numerous major trends

[2] See also Sanford and Conrad (108, 109), and Franck, K. (29) for other uses of the Projective Questions. A similar technique is that of Incomplete Sentences, as described by Rohde (97), Rotter (100) and Stein (114). For an example of the use of a slightly modified Projective Question technique in the study of antidemocratic personality trends —with results similar to those obtained here—see McGranahan (78).

[3] By "precision" is meant merely "the number of significant figures" in a score, e.g., the value 2.3689 is more precise than 2.4. However, a scoring system can be relatively imprecise, e.g., a wall clock as compared with a stop-watch, and yet be accurate and valid. Personality researchers may have to tolerate a low degree of precision until we are beyond the initial stage where significance and validity present the greatest methodological problems.

that define the dynamic framework within which further clinical differentiation is possible.

Thus the scoring of Projective Questions, like the scoring of interviews (see Chapter IX), requires a set of qualitative categories that meet various theoretical and technical standards. The categories should be carefully defined and illustrated to facilitate communication and interpretation. They should be literal enough to permit highly reliable scoring, yet sufficiently interpretive to have clinical significance and theoretical implications. A limited number of categories per item, preferably between two and six, is desirable and a minimum of responses should be ambiguous (unscorable) in terms of these categories. The degree to which these standards have been met can better be judged at the end of this chapter. Since the main personality trends of concern in the present research were those differentiating highs and lows on ethnocentrism, *high categories* and *low categories* were sought. The high categories incorporated those psychological qualities which were found to characterize the responses of the ethnocentric subjects, while the low categories appeared to characterize the anti-ethnocentric subjects.

The procedure in determining the specific categories for each item was as follows. The responses of the low scorers to that item were transposed by typing onto one or a few sheets, thus permitting easy inspection of group material; and similarly for the high scorers. Closer examination of the responses of each quartile as a whole revealed a few major trends characteristic of each group and differentiating it from the other group. These trends were formalized into categories which seemed both empirically differentiating and theoretically meaningful. The final step involved the preparation of a Scoring Manual (see below) in which each category is defined, discussed briefly, and illustrated with examples from the groups on which the Manual is based. The Manual, formed through examination of the first few groups studied, and on the basis of our over-all theory and results, was used with only minor modifications on all subsequent groups.

It should be noted that the determination and use of categories is not a purely mechanical and atheoretical procedure. The importance of an over-all personality theory, especially as applied to the understanding of differences between highs and lows, can hardly be overestimated as an aid in dealing with projective items. With regard to category determination, the general theory provides hypotheses before one sees the Projective Question material, and it is crucial in the selection of aspects of response which differentiate lows from highs. Furthermore, it gives the categories deeper and broader meaning by relating them to a larger theoretical frame and to results gained by other techniques. With regard to scoring, the general personality theory acts as a background factor making it easier for the scorer to decide on the appropriate category for a given response; it also facilitates the scoring of some idiosyncratic responses which do not directly fit any of the scoring categories used but which express low or high personality trends. Finally, by means of the over-all personality theory the categories of several items can be integrated into a single pattern involving several trends, thus permitting a more complex description of the high or low groups or of any individual subject. It is therefore of great value for the scorer to be familiar with the general personality theory involved, as a basis for competent scoring as well as for contributions to new theory, categories, and procedures.

C.　SCORING MANUAL: CATEGORIES OF PROJECTIVE QUESTION RESPONSE

There are three types of scores: *low* (L), *high* (H), and *neutral* (N). A neutral score is given when the question is left blank (Nb),[4] when the response is ambiguous with respect to the high and low categories (Na), or when high and low trends are present to equal degrees (Nhl). For the groups studied thus far there were relatively few Na and Nhl scores (8.8 per cent); the presence of many Na scores in future groups would necessitate modification or expansion of the present Manual. Each scorer assigns one of the above scores to each response. The scoring procedure will be discussed below (Section D). We may turn now to the Scoring Manual. It should be noted that the Scoring Manual has not only a *methodological* function but also a *descriptive* function, since it presents and even helps to interpret the differences between the responses of the ethnocentric and nonethnocentric groups.

QUESTION 1.　WHAT MOODS ARE UNPLEASANT OR DISTURBING?

Low Categories

1. *Conscious conflict and guilt.* Feelings of self-criticism, depression, frustration, insecurity, inadequacy, hopelessness, despair, lack of self-worth, remorse. The main conflict or sense of remorse is over violation of values referring to achievement, love-giving (nurturance), understanding, friendship, self-expression, and social contribution. This system of values, which the lows express in various forms in several of the projective questions, will be called *achievement values*. Important underlying variables are intrapunitiveness (the tendency to blame oneself rather than the world when things go wrong) and a well-internalized set of ethical standards. There is an inner orientation, an emphasis on the needs, strivings, and inner state of the individual; related to this is an intraceptive approach, a concern with self-understanding, and an acceptance of personal moral responsibility for one's actions.

[4] As it turned out, omissions on certain items, while recorded as Nb, were converted to scores of H in the statistical treatment. This was based on the discovery that the highs made appreciably more omissions than the lows (see below, Section D).

Examples: "Those times when I would like to give myself a swift kick in the pants." "A feeling of futility and pessimism." "When I don't do as well as I know I am capable of doing." "So much to do, so little time."

A response is scored here when external factors such as "lack of housing" or "lack of economic opportunity" are mentioned, as long as these external forces are represented as frustrating inner needs or achievement values. Thus, the lows refer to external difficulties as obstacles to self-expression and security, whereas the highs refer to external difficulties in themselves merely as a sign of general dissatisfaction, without indicating what inner needs or values are frustrated (see below).

2. *Focal dependency and love-seeking.* These responses reflect a desire for close personal relationships involving emotional warmth and exchange. The sense of lack of love and of focal relationships, often found in love (cf. Chapter XI), must be distinguished from the highs' feeling of aloneness and isolation in a generally barren world (see below). The loneliness of the highs represents, as it seems, underlying dependency which must remain ego-alien and which finds little or no positive, ego-satisfying expression.

Examples: "Moods where you feel like pouring out your soul to a person." "To love someone and not be loved back." "To feel alone when in the company of others; this can occur even after a period of congeniality." *Feelings of rejection* are scored low: "to appear ridiculous"; "to love but not be loved"; "to be laughed at unjustly." (However, a response is scored high if it involves a sense of active threat—rather than merely loss or lack of love—as well as extrapunitiveness and feelings of persecution. For example: "to be made a fool of"; "when a friend turns against me.") The dependency, self-blame, and depressive affect in lows may also take a more "cosmic" form (*Weltschmerz*): "When I feel what fools all we humans are." The highs are disturbed by the supposed stupidity or immorality of others rather than by any ideas of these trends in themselves; nor do they have a "world-identification."

3. *Open hostility, by self or others, toward love objects.* The lows are upset by feelings of hostility in themselves and by hostility and exploitiveness in others. The disturbing hostility may take two forms, *ideological* and *interpersonal.*

Ideologically, we find references to faults in our social system and social authority: discrimination, exploitation, insecurity, violations of democratic values.

Examples: "Thinking of the rotten, ruthless practices that go on under the name of rugged individualism and unrestricted initiative in the U.S.A." "Concern over the shortcomings of Americans and thus the nation." "The slowness of social progress; the stupidity of the powers that be." "Unemployment and lack of security for the average man or veterans."

In the sphere of interpersonal relations, hostile impulses or acts directed toward friends and love objects are a source of disturbing moods in low scorers.

Examples: "When I feel I have hurt a friend." "Envy, hatred, revenge, resentment." "When I feel a general dislike towards friends and the world in general." "Intolerance; cruelty to people." "Resentment toward parents." (It is characteristically low that *ambivalence* toward parents is more accessible to consciousness, though often conflict-producing.) "*Anger*" when it is the total response is scored Na. In connection with the thesis, presented in earlier chapters, that psychological themes can be found in the specific content of the individual's ideology, it is interesting to note that similar psychological content characterizes both the "ideological" and the "interpersonal" responses to this question.

In summary, the main trends expressed in the above categories are: violation of achievement values, resulting in conscious conflict, remorse, and self-criticism; intrapunitiveness; intraception; libidinized interpersonal relationships; focal, ego-assimilated dependency strivings; depressive affect focused on lack of achievement and on rejection by love objects; open ambivalence toward love objects and family members.

High Categories (Question 1)

1. *Violations of conventional values.* This category is the high equivalent to the "conscious conflict and guilt" category for the lows. These values are concerned with activity, success, upward mobility, and rugged masculinity in men, and with "sweetness and light" femininity in women. They also involve certain behavior formulae regarding etiquette and interpersonal relations, and an emphasis on conformity *per se*.

Examples: "Not making a success of life." "Not advancing in life." "Not doing something useful." "Lack of purpose" (i.e., not having aims, in contrast to the frustration of aims in lows). It is sometimes difficult to distinguish the high masculinity-status values, with their external criterion of success, from the low achievement values, with their inner orientation and their emphasis on self-expression. The difference in the examples above is in the use of the word "advancing" rather than "accomplishing," or "useful" rather than "contributing to the welfare of others." Another characteristic of certain high responses is their concern with *externally imposed tasks* or duties rather than with inner strivings. For example: "Not meeting expected requirements." What is implied here is shame over being caught and social anxiety over nonconformity, rather than guilt over value violations (violations that are felt internally whether or not they are observed by others).

Violations of conventional values (immorality) *by others* are included here. For example: "Seeing crude sexual behavior." "Drinking, breaking the law." "Anyone who displays bad habits publicly irritates all." "Disgust over filth and smut." "Disgust with human nature and people." These responses reflect trends mentioned previously: moral punitiveness, cynicism, the tendency to seek out, and to find, immorality in the world (especially in outgroups) rather than in oneself.

Finally, we find responses in which *hostility* toward friends and morality figures (parents, relatives, social authority, and the like) is implied though not explicitly stated or recognized.

Examples: "Little frictions with parents." "When my husband doesn't act right toward me." "Lack of harmony with friends." The emphasis is on the behavior or the situation in itself, without reference to motives or specific affect. Compare these responses with those of lows: "Resentment toward parents"; "When I feel I have hurt a friend." When an individual who is shown to be consistently high on other measures gives a response like "Worry over family members" or "Death of relatives" it is not difficult to infer that he or she feels hostility towards these people, hostility which is projected in the form of the idea that family members may be harmed by other people or by bad luck. Suffice it to say that responses of this sort are given predominantly by highs, and are scored H. The response "Fighting in Germany" is scored high because of its reference to motor aggression *per se* without specific psychological content (needs, affect, values); similarly in the case of "Long labor disputes."

2. *Threatening or nonsupporting environment:* focus on external obstacles, lacks, and threats, with an (implied) unconscious sense of helplessness and dependency. Theoretical discussion must be deferred until later; however, in order clearly to differentiate the high and low categories the following theoretical point must be made. As we know from the interviews and the T.A.T., highs and lows do not seem to differ in the amount of their underlying dependency (or other deep trends); the difference lies, rather, in the way such impulses are handled and integrated in the personality. Dependency is implied in the responses of many lows and many highs, but the form of expression differs systematically in the two groups. The emotional intensity, active sorrow, and focal conflict of the lows, as well as the intellectual and ideological strivings and the search for close relationship, are not difficult to distinguish from the emotionally shallow, ego-alien loneliness, and objectless passivity of the highs. The responses in the high categories for this question reveal an inner poverty, an external orientation, and a nonfocalized dependency on the outer world; these individuals are, so to say, glad when the world supports them and sad when their supports leave, with a minimum of self-determination and self-awareness.

One common type of response among the highs involves feelings of doubt, uncertainty, and momentary *lack of self-confidence*. These individuals are in doubt as to which is the more correct or success-producing act, whereas the lows feel intense inner conflicts between two impulses or between an impulse, e.g., hostility, and inner moral standards. The focus in the high responses is on the act itself or on the undependability of the environment. Interpretively, the lack of self-confidence seems primarily to be anxiety in a social situation which is unconsciously apperceived as threatening.

Examples: "The feeling that regardless of prearranged plans and ideas it is never possible to be sure of what a new day will bring." "The uncertainty of the future." "The feeling of people and places having changed so much that one feels lonely and loses self-confidence." "Unsure of taking the right step in business."

The highs are most disturbed by *lack of support* rather than lack of love, by isolation or threat rather than rejection. Their frustrations in regard to interpersonal relations seem to be experienced as a sort of undifferentiated "aloneness" without an aspect of active affection-seeking or focal relationship.

Examples: "To feel that I am not liked or wanted where I am." "To feel out of place in the company I am in and not be sure of my next move." "Being alone without company" (fear of solitude in this context is high). "When I feel alone and no one to turn to." These responses may also involve a sense of being persecuted or *victimized*, as well as a marked extrapunitive quality and feelings of self-pity. For example: "To feel cast aside." "The 'don't give a darn' feeling when you think nobody cares what happens to you." "When a friend turns against you." "Someone convicts you of something you never did." "Feeling the world is against me."

The affect of the highs is less clear-cut and focalized than that of the lows. It often takes the form of vague, *undifferentiated worry*, or of generalized dissatisfaction.

Examples: "Worry about the future." "Realization of impending danger." "Emotional moods." "When everything goes wrong." The single word "worry" is commonly given by highs. "Feeling absolutely lost." Responses such as "worry about the future" and "lack of money" are clearly high. However, the response "financial insecurity," with no clarifying context, should be scored Na, since its external orientation seems high, while its reference to insecurity as an inner state is low; not frequently given, it occurs almost equally in highs and lows.

While *fear* is implied by a number of the responses above, it is almost never given explicitly by highs, and evidence from other chapters suggests that they do not recognize these as fear experiences. Responses such as "fear" and "apprehension," though rare, are usually given by lows and should be scored L.

3. *"Rumblings from below."* These responses refer to situations or bodily conditions which, by inference though not explicitly, tend to bring out ego-alien trends such as passivity, anxiety, and hostility.

Examples: "Quietness, boredom, inactivity." "When at a party everything is quiet and dead as a morgue." "Lack of work or anything to do, causing restlessness and lack of self-confidence." The reference to *lack of work* is interesting in connection with the compulsive value for work commonly found in highs; work and "keeping busy" would appear, for some individuals at least, to have the psychological function of reducing anxiety and of aiding in the inhibition of unaccepted impulses. Perhaps this is the dynamic meaning of the slogan, "Keeping busy is the best way of staying out of mischief"; the mischievous impulses are conceived as "rumblings from below," as waiting only for an idle moment to force themselves through. Also evident in these responses are the anti-intraception and the opposition to leisure discussed in earlier chapters.

Another common source of disturbance is *poor bodily condition:* fatigue, hangover, sickness, headache, and the like. There may also be references to strain, external pressure, and overwork, that is, conditions which threaten the mind by harming the body. Once again there is no reference to inner needs, values, or emotions as such, but only a vague sense of threat, restlessness, or dissatisfaction. The underlying but unrecognized fear of body harm seems to be a major cause of anxiety. In addition, being "fatigued" or overworked is a condition in which defenses are lowered and unaccepted trends may break through. The person then has a "nervous breakdown"—something conceived as having a physiological rather than a psychological origin. It is of some interest that the highs are threatened by both lack of work and overwork; inactivity will turn one's mind to the wrong things, but overactivity—being too good for too long, so to speak—may intensify the bad impulses and weaken the defenses beyond the threshold of control. Work appears, therefore, to be a form of punishment as well as a value and a defense for these individuals.

4. *Omissions* are recorded as Nb but are considered as H in computing individual or group scores (agreement with E). While the total number of omissions is small (about 8 per cent), most of the omitters were highs; this is consistent with the greater anti-intraception and fear of "prying" in highs.

QUESTION 2. WHAT DESIRES ARE MOST DIFFICULT TO CONTROL?

Low Categories
All low categories for this question are bound up with violations of achievement values by oneself or others.

1. *Focal (usually verbal) hostility directed against violators of achievement values.* In the ideological sphere we find opposition to fascism, militarism, discrimination, suppression, exploitation, autocracy, and the like. In the sphere of interpersonal relations similar basic values are expressed in the form of opposition to hypocrisy, intellectual dishonesty, pompousness, narrowness, unfairness, and the like.

Examples: "To lash out at those people who voice an attitude of racial discrimination or an attitude of a dishonest intellect." "Getting mad at native fascists." "To walk out on people who are unmitigated boors or fools—usually I'm too curious to see everyone else's reaction to do so" (note also the psychological curiosity). "Upbraiding individuals having a 'don't give a damn' attitude in matters that are important; and those that fail to consider relative values." "The desire to devaluate men" (this is scored low for the focal hostility and competition with men). "The desire to deflate pompous, loud-mouthed people."

The response may also involve inner conflict over being hostile and rebellious (against oppressive convention or authority) as opposed to being tactful or submissive.

For example: "To express an opinion when it is more tactful to remain subordinate, as in the navy when you feel anything but subordinate; to accept militarism." "To disregard conventions and speak out of turn when I encounter hypocrisy." "Telling people about fallacies in our economic system and the impossibility of returning to prewar times; not to carry out the patriotic ballyhoo thrust on service men." "To express my feelings with people who wouldn't understand." (The last response should be distinguished from the high response, "Talk about my emotions"; in the latter there is a generalized, objectless need and inhibition, whereas in the former we find the desire for personal relationship as the basis for sharing of emotions.)

2. *The tendency to violate achievement values oneself.* These responses are concerned with interpersonal relations rather than ideology. They usually involve some degree of *inner conflict* between achievement values and pleasurable impulses (play, ego-satisfying passivity, intellectuality, sensuality). The main values involved are for nurturance and love-giving, as when one fails to realize an accepted obligation toward a friend, or for achievement, as when the individual does not actively strive toward serious goals but rather allows himself to be side-tracked into immediately pleasurable pursuits. That this is an *inner* conflict must be stressed: the conflict involves moral standards or obligations which the individual accepts as his own and which take the form of promptings from within, in contrast to the highs' reference to externally imposed tasks and duties. A further difference is that the passivity is ego-assimilated and satisfying for the lows, diffuse and ego-alien for the high scorers (see below).

Examples: "The desire to listen to music when I have work to do." "Self-indulgence" (note also the explicit self-criticism). "Being true to myself." "An impulse to procrastinate; to take the obvious easy course when a more direct facing of obstacles could enable me to obtain what I desire." "The wanderlust to see what the other part of the country is doing, or on a nice day, the desire to be enjoying it by fishing or hunting." "To be indifferent." "Be lazy and sleep." "Running away from trouble" (this is not the same as "forget my troubles," which is repressive rather than escapist and is scored H). Also scored here are responses involving guilt as a consequence of *hurting others* (emphatic focus on their feelings) or of violating other values. For example: "To blame rather than to understand." "Use the wrong means to achieve desirable aims."

3. *Miscellaneous.* Several relatively infrequent responses may be considered here. "*Fear*" is, as on Question 1, a low response. Most *sex* responses by *men* are scored H (see below). They are scored L when they are more personalized and subtle, or when they show some signs of surface inhibition. For example: "In my admiration of feminine beauty I find it hard at times to keep from staring." For *women*, however, most sex references are scored L, even when only the single word is given. Example: "Being too affectionate with the 'man in my life.'" "Amorous desires." "Falling in love." Conventionalized sex responses by women, e.g., "Going out on too many dates," are scored H.

Denial of hard-to-control impulses, e.g., the response "None," is more common in lows than in highs and is scored L. This empirical result was not anticipated; it is consistent with the apparently greater impulsivity of lows and their emphasis on independence and self-expression. (If high contextual features, e.g., anti-intraception, are present, a score of H is given.)

High Categories (Question 2)

1. *Nonfocal and/or motor aggression.* One of the most unequivocally high forms of response involves concrete, impersonal, aggressive acts, usually directed against "irritating" people.

Examples: "Spanking a very fresh or mean child." "Deliberately smashing into a foolish driver, the majority being women" (this response by a man who on other items shows a surface idealization of women). "The desire to slug the guy that talks for hours about the rough time he had in the service when you know he has been a U.S.O. Commando most of the time."

The high aggressive impulse tends to be cognitively blind and undifferentiated, and to have a symptomatic quality.

Examples: "The desire to beat my way out of a crowded place just to see how many persons I could overcome before I would be stopped." "The desire to keep moving so as not to slug somebody." "Temper." "The desire to blow my top when I get angry."

Verbal aggression in a context of low values is, as noted above, scored L. However, *undifferentiated verbal aggression*, without reference to values or to the nature of the object, is scored H.

For example: "Speaking my mind." "Tell people what I think of them." "Telling people off." Aggression against unconventional people or against liberal ideas may be included here; e.g., "To rebel against unionism." There is often an extrapunitive and projective element in the aggression of the highs; the idea of "being taken advantage of" is sometimes used to justify the hostile impulses. *Neutral scores* (Na): verbal aggression in which the values or context are unclear; "anger" alone without a qualifying context.

Responses which seem to represent more disguised forms of hostility, particularly in high women, may be mentioned here. These refer mainly to "impatience," to "stubbornness," or to domineering tendencies, usually without further qualification. They are occasionally given in a low context; for example: "The desire to 'lecture' and be too sure I am right." This is scored L because of the implicit self-criticism, the recognition of her own fallibility, and the recognition that the desire to help or teach may be tied up with dominance.

2. *Ego-alien passivity.* In contrast to the lows, the highs give relatively few responses involving passivity. Moreover, these responses do not refer to escapist enjoyment or to self-criticism and inner conflict. High passivity seems, rather, to involve mainly the idea of *task-avoidance*, of shirking an externally imposed duty (cf. also Chapter XIII).

Examples: "To procrastinate." "Not carry out what is expected of me." (Score

Na when the response involves the idea of running away from responsibilities and there is no indication as to whether the responsibilities have an internal or external origin.)

What seems also to express a primitive passive trend is the desire to "*forget everything*," to blot out the world and focus on cheerful things (as in Item 9, F scale, Form 45). Again we find a sense of threat from an overwhelming environment and an external orientation rather than an inner conflict and a conscious moral dilemma.

Examples: "Forgetting everything and traveling and looking for something more interesting." "The urge to run away and forget everything." "Going out on a real high bender and forget my troubles." (Note: "drink to forget" is high but "drink" alone is neutral.)

3. *Impersonal sex.* As noted above, most sex responses (even relatively crude ones) by women are scored L. More conventionalized responses, e.g., "Going out on dates," "Flirting," or "Getting married" are scored H. In men, on the other hand, most sex responses are given by highs. The most common response is simply "Sex" or "Sex matters." There is also a tendency to assume that sex impulses would "naturally" cause the most difficulty, e.g., "Desires relating to sex, *of course*." It would appear that some high men emphasize sex as part of their general emphasis on rugged masculinity, while some low women bring in sex as part of their rebellion against traditional nonsensual femininity. The sex responses of the high men have an impersonal, undifferentiated quality similar to that found in their aggression responses. For example: "Keeping my emotions in check when out with a beautiful blonde." "The desire to accompany women of the world." The lows tend to refer either to a love object with whom there is some psychological relationship, or to a love affair involving ego-accepted sensuality. It is certainly of theoretical interest that the latter form of response is more common in unprejudiced women than in unprejudiced men.

4. *Incidental pleasures and violations of conventional values.* The main qualities of these responses are their emotional diluteness, their lack of strong object-relationship, their concreteness (reference to specific acts), and their concern with minor conventions.

Examples: "Sweet tooth." "Overeating." "Use slang." "Travel." "Talking at the wrong time." "Break light bulbs in church." "Scream in church; scream when annoyed." "Have too much fun." References to "Too much activity" or to "Overindulging in sports" are sometimes given by high men; these desires appear to be related to concern with masculinity and may in some cases represent a defense against underlying passive impulses—impulses which find indirect expression on other items or techniques.

One of the more common forms of response in this category involves concern with *money*, particularly with spending it too freely rather than retaining it.

Examples: "Be extravagant." "Spending money wantonly and spending time wantonly." "Gambling." "I like to buy novels but I try not to as it costs so much money." There is sometimes self-idealization and/or self-pity. For example: "Desire to spend for others' benefits." "Help others at own expense." The highs' concern with money may well be related to their accusations of "money-mindedness" in outgroups.

There are several responses which are marginal to this category. While simple denial is scored L, denial in a context of "*will power*" or of anti-intraception is H. For example: "I don't have any difficulty controlling any desire if I make up my mind to a thing." Emphasis on will power is seen in the response, "Walking straight ahead when passing a cocktail bar." The idea of not planning or giving thought to decisions is also H; for example: "Jumping into something new without thinking of the consequences beforehand."

5. *Omissions* are recorded as Nb but are considered as H in the final scoring. The frequency of omissions was about 19 per cent—more than on any other item (see Table 2(XV)).

QUESTION 3.   WHAT GREAT PEOPLE DO YOU ADMIRE MOST?

Low Categories

Once again the concept of achievement values provides a unifying context for understanding the low responses. The several low categories represent various forms of expression of values for intellectual, aesthetic, and scientific achievement, for social contribution and for democratic social change. Usually the responses contain specific names of individuals representing these values. Occasionally, however—and this is more common in lows than in highs—a general abstract definition of admirable qualities is given.

Examples of general description: "Those people that I admire most are perhaps those that have at great personal risk and danger fought unstintingly against fascism —perfectly aware of all the implications of fascism." "Men who have had the courage to stand up against public opinion in order that some good might come of their position." "Those who have contributed most to the spiritual and social improvement of mankind." "Musicians and artists, any person with real creativeness." "I admire great writers, great thinkers, and people who really left mankind something of value."

Specific names fall into the following broad categories:

1. *The arts and philosophy.* Artists included here are writers, musicians, intellectuals, painters, architects, and so on. Examples: Shakespeare, Steinbeck, Robeson, Whitman, Pushkin, Beethoven, da Vinci, Bach, Voltaire. The writers tend to be liberal-radical and to write works of social and psychological significance, though this is not always so. There are a few high writers (see below).

The philosophers named include: Bertrand Russell, Comte, Mill, Dewey,

Spencer, Socrates, Maimonides. The lows occasionally—the highs almost never—admire individuals who are members of various minority groups (Jewish, Negro, Chinese, etc.). Certain *religious* figures are included in this category: Confucius, Buddha, St. Francis (see the neutral category below). Highs more than lows tend to mention Plato. Perhaps the reason for this is indicated by one high man who wrote: "Plato—the original personnel man." There are, so to speak, both low and high aspects to Plato's philosophy. If his name is given with others, one scores by context; if given alone, it is scored H.

2. *Physical and biological scientists.* (This does *not* include inventors or applied scientists or technologists, most of whom are scored H.) Sir William Osler, Newton, Washington Carver, Darwin, Einstein, Galileo, Pasteur, Madame Curie (particularly by men).

3. *Social scientists, liberal-radical political figures.* Jefferson, Marx, Tom Paine, Benjamin Franklin, Henry Wallace, Frances Perkins, Freud, Pestalozzi, Norman Thomas.

4. *Active denial of admiration.* For example: "I'm beholden to no man." "No one person stands out." However, omissions of this item are scored neutral.

Neutral Category.   Several names seem to be given equally often by highs and lows; they may apparently be admired for high reasons or for low reasons.

The most common examples are Lincoln, F. D. Roosevelt, and Christ. (Roosevelt's popularity with highs was probably limited to the war period.) Any of these names, alone or in combination with each other, are scored Na; if additional names are given, one scores by context. For example, the response, "Washington, Lincoln, F.D.R." is scored H because of the context of patriotism (see below). The response, "Jefferson, Paine, Lincoln, Roosevelt" is scored L. Ernie Pyle is given mainly by highs, but without a context is scored Na. Will Rogers, Woodrow Wilson, and Willkie are Na.

Omissions are scored Neutral.

High Categories (Question 3)

The main trends underlying the high responses are ones which recur throughout the projective questions as well as in the several other techniques of the study: authoritarianism, anti-intraception, "toughness"-power, militarism, and ultraconservatism. These are exemplified in the following categories.

1. *Power and control.* Emphasis here is on the strong, rugged, masculine leader.

One favorite source is the *military:* Halsey, Patton, Marshall, Byrd, Doolittle, Rickenbacker, Bismarck, Caesar, MacArthur, Lindbergh, Napoleon. A corollary of the emphasis on strength is an emphasis on *suffering:* being vicitimized, martyred, alone in a cruel world. For example: "The boys who died in the war for people who do not even appreciate it, as they show many times; being an ex-serviceman myself."

Among the high women *royalty* and nobility, particularly from past centuries, are quite popular. Certain *religious* leaders such as the Pope and Mary Baker Eddy are given predominantly by highs. Churchill seemed to have captured the imagination of many highs. A major source of names, particularly for the high men, is the area of practical invention, business, and technology, *industrial giants* being the most popular. Examples: Ford, Carnegie, Edison, leading manufacturers.

2. *Conservative Americana*. Men whose main distinction comes from being strong national leaders, usually in a military or politically conservative context. This category overlaps somewhat with the first.

Examples: Washington, Teddy Roosevelt, Herbert Hoover, Edgar Hoover, John Paul Jones, Dewey, "True Americans."

3. *Parents and relatives*. It is not uncommon for highs to list several family members, in addition to other individuals, in response to this question.

Example: "My mother who, although isn't famous or seemingly different from any other person, I think is one of the greatest persons alive today; you may think me prejudiced and childish, but I do have my reasons." It happens, though rarely, that a low mentions the parent of the opposite sex; this is scored L if the context is clearly low: "My Parents."

4. *Miscellaneous*. Responses expressing high trends but not in the above categories.

High women often mention actresses and movie stars, e.g. Kate Smith, Bing Crosby. Sabatini is a writer preferred by highs; best-seller authors are also included here for the most part. An example of a descriptive high response is: "My girl friends who live happily without any worry." (Superficial, anti-intraceptive.)

Scoring Procedure. Most subjects list several names in response to this question; the names may fall into more than one category, but they are usually uniformly high or uniformly low. In some cases, however, both H and L categories are represented. These cases are scored H, L, or Nhl according to the predominant trend.

Thus the response, "da Vinci, Ely Culbertson, Henry Ford" is scored H, while "Einstein, Edison, Carver" is scored L. One man gave a list of some 15 names representing most of the high and low categories above, with no apparent unifying theme or predominant trend; his response was scored Nhl. Clinically, he was a "conflicted low" who seemed to be struggling with opposing high and low trends, so that his score on this item was very meaningful.

QUESTION 4. WHAT MIGHT DRIVE A PERSON NUTS?

Low Categories

Both low and high categories for this question are similar to those for Question 1 (Moods). The lows tend to respond mainly in terms of psychological conflict and frustration. They have an intraceptive orientation and they emphasize the role of the individual himself in the neurosis. Once again we find a context of achievement values and active striving—striving which is made difficult by inner problems or by external blocks.

1. *Inner psychological states.* The main concepts here are focal conflict and anxiety. There is often a strong sense of failure, of self-blame, of helplessness or impotence.

Examples: "Inability to cope with problems; frustration." "Hardly anything that would make them express the above opinion (see the full statement of this question); sometimes complete suppression of a person's feelings, emotions, energies would do it." "Self-condemnation." "His own failure to put an end to the situation causing the disturbance or to stop thinking about it." "Despair caused by inability to cope with distressing situations; continual criticism without constructive suggestions." "Frustrations, pointlessness of existence, morbidity, sorrow, *violation of one's ego.*" "Insecurity." "Tension without release." "Being dishonest with oneself; wrong attitude toward life's problems." References to *fear* are low.

While undifferentiated "worry" or "brooding" are high, there is a kind of focal, *differentiated worry* or anxiety which is scored L. By this is meant not a vague anxiety in the face of a generally threatening world, but concern over specified personal frustrations.

Examples: "Continual worry about family problems, continual striving to earn a living." "Worry, emotional or economic." "Severe emotional strain, especially if combined with physical hardships or pain." (The highs often refer to physical hardships per se, but they seldom refer to the actual experience of emotion or pain.)

The inner life of the lows, while apparently relatively rich and satisfying in many ways, seems often to be stormy and conflictful. The sense of going too far, of being carried away by emotion, of having *too much inner life,* so to speak, may be expressed in responses to this item.

Examples: "Letting our emotional states wear us down." "Exaggerating one's personal problems." Obsessional trends are sometimes exhibited: "The man's mind is in a groove or rut; unless he has a varied interest, he will go insane from worry and thinking of one thing." "A person might become insane over too much interest in religion, love, money, etc.; any obsession carried too far might do it." The lows' references to inner life can be distinguished from those of the highs on the basis of their greater awareness, and acceptance, of emotion and of their more differentiated introspective experience. Compare the responses above with the high responses: "Worry" or "constant worry of a particular thing." Or compare the low response, "Too much self-analysis" with the high, "Talk oneself into it." (See high category 2, below.) In general, responses indicating rejection of inner life are more common in highs than lows.

2. *Dominating, blocking, rejecting environment.* These responses may take an "interpersonal" or an ideological form. In the former case, the individual is in a disturbing situation from which he cannot extricate himself, in part for inner reasons (explicit or implicit). Moral conflict and open *ambivalence* are

often expressed. There is not only hostility toward a dominating or rejecting person, but also some feeling of relationship or obligation. Surface conflict about hostility, especially toward love objects or those who represent both love and authority, is fairly common among lows. (The highs appear to resolve their ambivalence toward the ingroup by maintaining only the positive side in consciousness and by [unconsciously] redirecting the hostility toward outgroups, thus avoiding for the most part a clear-cut sense of inner conflict.)

Examples: "Living on intimate terms with people who insist on controlling every move." "Being mad or constantly irritated by one whom you must associate with." Compare these with the high response: "Worry, or have to live with and be nice to selfish or disagreeable or unpleasant people."

References to an *unhappy childhood*, to depriving parents, or to lack of love are low. However, references to bad parents in terms of poor discipline or lack of discipline, are scored H. While the idea of overwork or lack of *rest* is high, references to lack of *leisure* or of pleasant relaxation (ego-satisfying passivity) are low.

The more ideologized responses refer to the social system as creating insecurity and frustration, or as making complex and contradictory demands which the individual cannot meet. The imagery of the "social system" is similar to that of the family authority: dominating, rejecting, stifling.

References to "oppression" by lows and highs are sometimes difficult to distinguish. Thus, a low wrote: "Prolonged persecution could drive a person nuts, particularly if he felt un-united with anyone else and felt that he alone was subjected to the full brunt of the persecution." By way of contrast, note the following high response: "Constant oppression by employers, fellow-workers, or unions." In the high response we find not only the antiunion sentiment, but also a feeling of generalized threat and a strong extrapunitive quality with no self-orientation or intraception. The low, on the other hand, expresses intraception, an attempt at self-analysis, and a desire for strong emotional ties with his environment.

Neutral Responses. Facetious references to the questionnaire as a cause of going nuts are neutral. Presumably the highs' reasons for rejecting the test is their anti-intraception and opposition to "prying," whereas the lows are disturbed by the large number of scale items with which they strongly disagree. However, references to the projective items, and to this one in particular, are scored H. For example: "Trying to answer questions like this one" (see high category 2, below). References to *diet* and *nutrition* are neutral in themselves; they are given, usually as part of a larger response, more often by low than by high scorers.

High Categories (Question 4)

The main variables underlying these responses include anti-intraception, extrapunitiveness, external orientation, ego-alien passive-dependency, hostility, and anxiety; and an emotionally shallow diffuse inner life, These characteristically high variables also emerged from the analysis of interviews and of T.A.T. material.

1. *"Rumblings from below."* The rationale for this concept has been given above (Question 1: Moods). The orientation in these responses is toward the individual rather than toward the situation, but there is no reference to inner insecurities, conflicts, or affective states. On a more interpretive level, we find a superego-ridden ego with a rigid moral façade; "going nuts" involves break-through of the underlying impulses or anxieties and destruction of the façade. The popular expression, "blow your top" and "blow your cork" are literal representations of this underlying imagery. They refer primarily to quasi-psychotic episodes rather than to neurotic symptoms. The main ego defenses seem to be projection, denial, and reaction-formation (emphasis on work, opposition to leisure).

One common type of response involves the idea of *overwork*, strain, or pressure.

Examples: "Pressure." "Overwork, mental fatigue, or nervous strain." "Too much work (physical or mental)." "Undertaking too much." "Overtaxing your strength in business or social affairs." "Continual difficulties, suspense." "Too long hours at work; debt." "Long hours—16 or 18 hours a day for 7 days a week working on something that doesn't keep you busy constantly" (note the combined emphasis on overwork as well as boredom, and the fear of "having your mind unoccupied"). "Overwork—lousy physical conditions coupled with sudden shock." "The constant grind and routine of everyday life would drive me nuts if I couldn't find some way to lose myself; my books serve this purpose." In the last example, books apparently have a defensive, anti-intraceptive function rather than a creative or expressive one. Fear of overwork seems to exist most strongly in just those individuals who value work most. By inference—and this is supported by much clinical material—the overwork represents overconformity or "being too good for too long," something which leads to the break-through of passivity and/or hostility against external work-demanding authority.

Once again we find frequent references to *worry* with a minimum of elaboration or differentiation. Worry is often related to *body anxiety* and fear of physiological ("nervous") breakdown. Indeed, the references to overwork above often involve, implicitly or explicitly, the idea that mental breakdown is caused primarily by body breakdown. This underlying anxiety over body weakness and threat of body harm in the ethnocentric men stands in marked contrast to their surface emphasis on rugged masculinity which is expressed in other projective questions as well as in other techniques.

Examples: "Sickness, ill health, worry, trouble." "Insanity is (due) to several things, most of which are physical deteriorations; disease or sudden shock." "Loss of his senses (sight, etc.) or the fatigue of battle." "Unknown illness not treated in time."

Excessive *drinking* is included here because it represents a bodily rather than a psychological threat. Another common cause given is *heredity*. For example: "Wouldn't go mad without an innate streak of insanity." "Taxing self beyond innate ability." The hereditarian theory of neurosis is like the hereditarian theory of group differences and human nature; it helps to obviate the necessity for looking inward or for seeking psychosocial explanations of human behavior.

While *anti-intraception* is an aspect of many of the above responses, it is in many cases the primary theme. These responses are usually not difficult to differentiate from low category 2 ("too much inner life"). "Going nuts" is attributed to thinking about oneself or to straining one's mind.

Examples: "A strain on his nerves from overconcentration or something." "Intent concentration for a long period of time (years)." "Talk self into it." "Thinking too much about your own troubles and forgetting to let God help you." (Compare this with the low response: "Not learning to face problems squarely in the face and with courage.") "His imagination runs away with him." The response, "Trying to answer questions like this one," expresses both opposition to "prying" by others and a sense of discomfort and threat in the face of one's own emotions.

Individuals giving the above responses seem afraid to look inward at all, for fear of what they will find. Is this one basis for the tendency, at least in its more extreme forms, to regard extroversion as good, introversion as bad? A similar idea is expressed in Item 9 of the Form 45 F scale: One should concentrate on "cheerful things" and not think about "worries or problems." It seems also to be involved in the idea of leisure merely as rest from work or as escape rather than as a means of self-expression and self-understanding.

Responses referring to *"loss of loved ones"* or to worry over possible loss or harm, may be included here since they seem to express the rumbling of deep-lying hostility toward family and ingroup members.

As mentioned previously, the highs tend to handle their ambivalence toward family members by exaggerating the surface positive feelings (idealization, admiration, submission) and by deflecting the hostility by means of projection (imagery of outgroups and human nature), displacement and rationalization (hostility expressed directly but explained as moral indignation), and so on. The infrequent references by lows to concern over loved ones usually involve more explicit indications of strong personal relationship.

2. *Threatening, irritating, or nonsupporting environment.* These responses show a predominantly external orientation, with no reference to the individual's inner needs, strivings or values, and with no implication of surface inner conflict. Neurosis is, so to speak, imposed on the individual from without, by an invidious stimulus or idea that overwhelms his mind much as a germ infects the body.

Examples: "Continued irritating noises or lights, also pain or torture; depends on the person and his weaknesses; religion and alcohol are the two most frequent things in my belief." "Monotonous humdrum such as a quiet routine or just the opposite as a bombardment; from one extreme to the other." "Another war will drive most of the people nuts—mostly people who have been in World War II" (by a veteran).

"Constant noise of unpleasant nature, such as shrill whistles." "Continuous arguing, tedious work, lots of noise." "The current strikes, the uncertainty of the times, governments of the world constantly bickering." "A nagging wife, Harry James' Orchestra." "A continual series of things going wrong." "Financial troubles." "Loss of money."

The idea of aloneness, without reference to actual relationship or to strivings for love, is included here. For example: "Loneliness and departure from a nice manner of living; solitude, etc." *Fear of solitude* per se is high; it seems to represent, as do many of the examples above, underlying anxiety in the face of an environment unconsciously felt to be threatening. References to *self-pity* are fairly common and are consistent with the extrapunitive, projective trends in some of the other responses. For example: "Constant self-pity and imagination of a thousand ills." References to *sexual frustration* are usually high in men, low in women, although contextual qualities must be considered in scoring.

The idea of *monotony* or *tedious work* is high, particularly when the general context of the response indicates boredom, lack of stimulation, or other high trends; it is scored L when there is some indication of blocked inner (achievement) values and needs.

An example of a high response is: "Continuous repetition of a disliked subject or action." By way of contrast, consider the following response: "Frustration from lack of factors in the environment which will interest or inspire him in any way whatever." Despite the external orientation, this response is scored L because of the reference to frustration and the desire for inner satisfaction.

3. *Omissions* of Question 4 are statisticized as H. Omissions occurred in only 4 per cent of the cases, but three-fourths of these were highs (see Table 2(XV)). This result is consistent with the anti-intraception and other trends differentiating those high from those low in prejudice.

QUESTION 5. WORST CRIMES A PERSON COULD COMMIT?

Low Categories

The main inner problem to which these responses refer is aggression, the primary difference between lows and highs lying in the manner of handling this deep-lying need. Formal low categories have not been distinguished for this item, but certain general properties of the low responses may be indicated. *Achievement values* once again provide a moral frame of reference. Intraception, understanding, hesitancy in condemning, identification with the underdog, intense personal relationships, and the like are common qualities of the low responses. Concern with crimes against the personality is much more common than concern with crimes against the body; and bodily harm, when it is referred to, is described in a less primitive and a more object-related way. There is strong concern with the psychological development and integrity of the individual. It is convenient here as elsewhere to distinguish the ideological area from that of interpersonal relationships.

In the sphere of *ideology* we find references to exploitation and discrimination against minority groups, lower economic classes, "the common man," and other nations. Also references to crimes against "humanity" or "society" as a whole.

Examples: "The worst possible crime a person can commit would be that of true treason; by true treason I mean the motive or attempt to injure, impair, or jeopardize those things that are dear to the majority and of their best interests." "Race extermination and starting wars." "Hate, intolerance, narrowness; his crimes against society as a whole." "Selling out his fellow man for profit to himself." "Each crime is different—depends on motivation and result; in general, crimes against fellow man, Jew-baiting, etc." "Permit mob rule, economic exploitation." "Racial persecution and the enforced militarism of a country during peacetime." "Slavery, including mental slavery, warping and distorting the minds of children."

With regard to *interpersonal relationships* we find themes and qualities similar to those above.

Examples: "Tell a person's confidence; get personal gain from another's rights." "Graft, fraud, etc. at the expense of innocent victims; malicious slander" (while graft and fraud given alone are high, the focus on the victims and the last part of the response suggest a score of L). "The greater sins are committed by us who know the right and the needs of others but 'pass by on the other side'" (this response was given by a strongly religious low; compare with high religious responses). "Betrayal of principles, friends." "Avarice, intolerance." "Hypocrisy, deception; be untrue to oneself." There are frequent criticisms of *authority figures*. For example: "Abuse of authority." "Negligence on the part of a military commander or anyone that results in a loss of life."

While "murder" alone is scored Na, and brutality alone is H, responses involving *murder or physical attack* which bring in motivations and which describe more than the aggressive act itself are scored L.

Examples: "Murder for gain or envy." "Crimes done just to make people miserable." "Murder—because no man should have control over another's life" (intraception, achievement values). "Sadistically causing the suffering of others" (references to sadistic motives, to cruelty, and to resulting suffering are scored L, while the idea of "blind hate" implying breakdown of ego controls is scored H). "Brutality for the sake of seeing persons suffer." "Cruelty to helpless things." "Cause another to degenerate." "To take another's life" (more object-related than "murder"). References to crime as a *symptom* requiring psychological understanding also fall here.

A response involving *incest* and *matricide* was given once, by a low man and in a context meriting a score of L; "Incest with his mother or matricide, (crime against an individual); destroying world culture, that is books, sculpturing, etc. (crime against humanity)." (Parenthetical remarks by the subject.) This response seems to express, in a characteristically low form, deep ambivalence toward the mother in which love and hate motives are extremely strong. The ambivalence of the high men is not likely to be expressed in this way, and their erotic attachment to the mother is probably not as great (see the psychiatric clinic material, Chapter XXII). Note also how this man's relationship to his mother has become the image on which is built his relationship to humanity and culture. References to incest or matricide in a moralistic context would be scored H.

Neutral Responses. "Murder" alone is scored neutral; it is given seldom, and about equally often by highs and lows. References to murder are common, but in a context that is usually clearly high or low. "Create war' without further qualification is scored Na. *Omissions* are neutral for this item. They occurred in 8 per cent of the responses.

This is the only item which the lows omitted slightly more frequently than did the highs (9 per cent and 7 per cent respectively). The following hypothesis may help to explain this result. Whereas the highs are disturbed by looking inward, the lows are more disturbed by looking outward at major value-violations, particularly aggressive ones. (This hypothesis might be tested by determining high-low differences in reading reports of aggressive crimes, the highs being expected to read, to condemn, and to enjoy these more without recognizing that personal motives are at work.) To the extent that the highly ethnocentric subjects are more punitive than the others, they would be expected to show more interest in crime and other punishment-evoking activities. The disturbance of the lows may also be due in part to the tendency to identify with the victim.

High Categories (*Question 5*)

1. *Crude aggression and sex.* These responses suggest, as have responses to previous items, that for many highs there is a deep-lying, ego-alien fund of aggression and sex. These trends seem to have remained relatively primitive, destructive, unsocialized; and they are not well fused with or modified by other trends in the ego. The frequent association of sex with aggression suggests that sex is conceived as aggressive and threatening. Aggression is aimed at the body of the victim, without reference to personal relationships or to psychological meanings for aggressor or victim. It has the primitive quality commonly found in the fantasies and fears of small children. (The same impersonal, destructive, object-less quality is often found in the current flood of mystery detective fiction, in which the hero, finding a close friend or relative murdered, immediately responds not with sorrow or concern but with moral indignation and a list of suspects.) The responses often refer to bizarre, destructive acts one might commit in a psychotic episode when ego-control and cognitive structuring of the environment are eliminated and unsocialized impulses break through.

Examples: Probably the most popular high response is "*Murder and rape.*" In the group of Veteran men, for example, this was given, sometimes along with other crimes, by 15 out of 26 highs as compared with 4 out of 25 lows. "Torture." "Sex crimes." "Murder without sufficient reason." "Rape on juveniles." "Sex crimes on children, women; kidnapping; murdering of newly born babies." "Having been a prisoner of war in the Philippines, I would consider some of the sights I saw there truly unprintable, but to my knowledge the worst crime that is printable would be rape."

References to *attacks on children* are fairly common; this is perhaps related to the fact that in San Quentin the sex offenders, many of whom engaged in sexual activities with children, were extremely high on ethnocentrism (see Chapter XXI). Occasionally there are *detailed concrete descriptions of brutal acts*. For example: "Kidnap a person, starve them for two weeks, then strangle them; after they are finally dead, dissect their body, wrap up the pieces and mail them home to the victim's parents."

2. *Other immoral acts.* These responses fall within a context of ethnocentrism, pseudopatriotism, and moral values dealing with conventional masculinity-femininity and conformity.

Examples: "Treason, traitorism, sedition" (crimes against the *status quo*). "Dope peddling, failure of a politician to protect his country." "Heresy." "Traitorous acts against those who have faith in him, as well as sex crimes." (This is a matter of not living up to others' expectations rather than a matter of personal relationship or inner demands.) "Adultery." "Crimes against his person, sex crimes, and to willfully smear a woman's name." "Murder, immoral acts, dishonesty." "To neglect himself and family" (no reference to relationship, motivation). "The one against the Holy Ghost." "Willful passing on of dangerous disease to other person" (body anxiety, concern with contamination).

3. *Various legal offenses.* We note here the tendency to think in formal, external, legal terms. Again the concern with property and money is expressed.

The more common specific offenses include robbery, stealing, larceny, blackmail, kidnapping, "Destruction of property," arson, manslaughter, and so on. References to murder in legalistic terms are included here: "Willful first-degree murder." "Unjustifiable homicide."

QUESTION 6. MOST EMBARRASSING MOMENTS?

Low Categories

The defining context for the low responses includes violation of achievement values, self-blame and guilt, concern for the feeling of others, feelings of failure and inadequacy.

1. *Hurting another's feelings.* Both highs and lows often refer to acts which involve breaches of common courtesy. However, the highs ordinarily focus on the act per se and on the idea of etiquette, whereas the lows are concerned mainly with the problem of rejection and with the feelings of the other person. Also, there is often an element of self-reproach in the low responses.

Examples: "Forgetting things about others that I really should know" (explicit self-blame). "Unintentionally offending any person, but particularly any loved one or well-liked one." "When I have done anything tactless that may hurt someone, or any act of stupidity." "To see others suffer from embarrassment" (identification and empathy). "Walk into room at wrong moment, others are being intimate" (self-rejection for intruding, rather than rejection of others for behaving that way).

2. *Feelings of inadequacy, failure, being rejected.* In these responses the focus is mainly on oneself and there is explicit or implicit self-criticism.

Examples: "When I start talking, realize that I don't know what I'm talking about." "Ignorance—that is, not knowing well something I should know." "Meet someone and not know what to say." "Situations in which I am inadequate." "To be laughed at for failing to get off a presentable public speech; to be put in an embarrassing position by a person who outmaneuvers you mentally." ("Making a public speech" alone is Na.) "To find out that after taking a strong stand I was absolutely wrong." "People laugh at me, not with me." "Not go somewhere because I didn't have a date, then be asked how it was." "Asking someone something or some service" (scored L because of surface inhibition, inadequacy, implied fear of rejection).

The embarrassing situation may involve *moral obligation* and guilt. In some cases the individual does not meet his own inner standards; in other cases he does not want to do something or be with someone, but feels both obligation and open ambivalence.

Examples: "Not fulfilling promises I made." "When I feel I have neglected to do something I should have done." "Getting into some situation in which you had no desire to be but someone expected you to be there."

In general, references to *mistakes*, especially when they are described as silly or stupid, are scored L; they seem to be based on self-evaluation, inner focusing and intrapunitiveness.

Responses like "Exposure of my own weaknesses, I suppose" and "Being caught for the faker I am" are included here because of the explicit self-blame and the self-critical humor, although the idea of "exposure" or being caught, without this context, is high (see below).

High Categories (Question 6)

1. *Violations of convention and etiquette.* Probably the most common high response to this item refers to breaches of etiquette. The focus is on the behavior per se, on behavior which violates specific formulae of the Emily Post variety. There is almost never a reference to inner needs or faults, the violations usually being regarded as "slips" or unmotivated accidents. In this way guilt, self-blame, and ego-reference are made unnecessary. Whereas the embarrassment of the lows is primarily an inner matter, relatively independent of whether or not they were observed, the embarrassment of the highs depends almost entirely on being frowned upon by an external moral force. The idea of "being caught" is prominent in the high responses, and with it the implication that the same thing done without detection would not be embarrassing.

Examples: "Making a decided error in social etiquette would be the worst." "Forgetting names of people" (social anxiety, no reference to personal concern for person). "Faulty dress." "Saying something degrading of another person *within their hearing*" (author's italics). "To appear inefficient." "Saying the wrong thing at the wrong time." "When I talk about something and forget what I have been talking about" (compare with L response: "Discover I don't know what I am talking about"). "When the children pipe up in front of company with something I've said about the person or some other innocent thing which sounds evil and embarrasses me." "When my husband is rude to me in front of other people" (inhibited hostility?). "If I am found being lax about kindness, courtesy toward everybody" (the idea of kindness (not love) toward *everyone* as a kind of task is not uncommon among people who, in the details of their ideology, ethnocentrically reject the bulk of mankind). "Being disapproved of." "Get called down for an error in front of other people" (compare with the L response: "Being exposed for the faker I am"). "Mispronounce words." "Guests arrive and the house is dirty or I'm unkempt." "Be accidentally rude or impolite." "Do something out of the ordinary." The idea of being threatened, rather than being rejected, is often an undercurrent in high responses. So too is extrapunitiveness. For example: "Dirty jokes (by others)." "People's thoughtlessness." The response "Nothing I can write here" is scored H for its "antiprying" character.

2. *Blows at exhibitionism and narcissism.* Many of the violations in Category 1 imply unacceptable conspicuousness and loss of prestige. The same thing is expressed more directly in this category. Some of the main properties of the H responses are social anxiety, rigid conformity and fear of nonconformity, emphasis on appearance (apparently based on a combination of conventionality and exhibitionism, though the motives are largely unrecognized by the individual), nonintraceptive approach.

Examples: "Walking into a crowded room with my shorts on." "To stumble in public." "Fall off a horse in a riding exhibition." "Fall on a banana peel with men watching." "Have my slip showing or a hole in my sock." "I passed out waiting for an elevator one day and even now I can remember my humiliation when I opened my eyes and saw 'thousands' of people gazing at me." The humiliation over fainting lends itself to interpretation in terms of ego-alien, anxiety-producing passive needs covered over by a masculine façade. Some anxiety regarding women or regarding sexual impulses (or both) is implied in such responses as "Being alone with a crowd of women" and "Surrounded by women."

Neutral Responses. Omissions are scored Na. They occurred in 9 per cent of the cases and equally often in highs and lows.

When the response deals with errors of tact in personal relationships and it is not clear whether the subject is disturbed over hurting someone's feelings (L) or violating a rule of etiquette (H), the response should be scored Na. The superficial event is the same; it is the *meaning* of the experience that differentiates highs from lows, and the meaning is sometimes ambiguous.

Often, however, subtle cues can be used. Consider, for example, the response, "When I talk to a person, repeat his name wrong over and over, don't realize my mistake till later." The two scorers, working independently and "blindly," both correctly assigned a score of L primarily on the basis of the phrase, "realize my mistake" which seemed to imply introspection and self-blame. Similarly, they gave score of H to the response, "Speaking or acting out of turn," a score of L to "Barging in where I don't belong." Most of the responses are more clearly H or L.

QUESTION 7.   HOW WOULD YOU SPEND YOUR LAST SIX MONTHS?

Low Categories

1. *Achievement values: creativity and social contribution.*

Examples: "Conveying accumulated ideas to my fellow man." "I would like to spend such a time solely in creative endeavor." "Reading poetry, philosophy, studying psychiatry." "Fight intolerance and social wrongs." "Try to do something, anything, for mankind or at least help someone; will my eyes and nerves to medicine, find someone who could use them." (Words like *mankind* and *fellow man* are used frequently by lows, seldom by highs.) "Make people happy" (in contrast to H responses "try to be good" or "doing good deeds"). "If I were altruistic I would try to do as much as I could for the other person, but actually I would do everything possible to make my stay enjoyable" (scored L because of the surface conflict between social contribution and personal pleasure).

The general idea of "doing things for others" is expressed by both lows and highs, but in characteristically different forms. In the lows we find references to nurturance and love-giving which are either personalized towards a few love objects or else generalized to include all humanity.

Examples: "Try to make the world a better place for all to live in." "In doing the most I would be capable of for those of whom I am fond." In the highs, on the other hand, we find more moralized references to "doing good" rather than "making happy," and the generosity is usually directed toward individuals who are characterized as ingroup members rather than as love objects. For example: "Seeing if I could do the people I thought most of any good; my family, such as mother, father, sister and brother." In short, nurturance is scored L when it is found in a context of love, close relationship, and achievement values; it is scored H in a context of superficial conventionality and ingroup orientation. (It should be noted that there are many conventional lows, but their conventionality is expressed in a context of love-giving rather than conformity *per se*.)

2. *Open sensuality and active pleasure.* There were few references to sex, but most of these were by lows.

Examples: "Drinking and carousing around with women." "Making love." "Have a romantic love affair while touring South America." Sometimes a sexual-intellectual balance is sought: "Spend part of the time whoring around, most of the time trying to write 'the Great American Novel'—though I'm probably not good enough" (written by a low-scoring man).

The enjoyment of active sociability is characteristically low. It may occur in a sensual and/or intellectual context, or simply in the form of warmth and friendly interaction.

Examples: "Travel, enjoy life, take it easy with friends." "Spend the time with friends in a constant rush of vacation and work if they didn't know I had only 6 months; if they knew, I'd take off to spend the time with strangers—reading, playing, working." "I'd spend all that time with my friends, the people I know and like." "In the company of my wife and child, enjoying good shows, car rides, and doing things I now do in my leisure" (compare to the highs' references to their families, below; note also the reference to *leisure*, a strong indication for scoring L). The high's references to pleasure are characteristically more dilute and empty, e.g., "Have a good time" or "Do as I please" (see below).

Reference to *seclusion* in the sense of "rejecting the world" may be included because, though apparently the opposite of sociability, it seems to spring from similar deep sources.

Example: "I would go to some wild country region where I could just live and not be disturbed by anyone or anything." (In this man's interview, the desire for solitude seemed associated with depressive feelings of rejection by the mother.) This is in marked contrast to the objection to solitude in highs (see also Items 1 and 4); some high men, however, give "seclusion" responses in which the primary source seems to be passivity rather than ego-recognized rejection of others.

High Categories (*Question* 7)

An important aspect of many high responses is *constriction of fantasy*. Although the question allows complete freedom of choice—"if you could do just as you pleased, how would you spend your time?"—some highs (and no lows in the present groups) make their actions explicitly conditional on the presence of certain external conditions. It is as if they cannot allow themselves a completely uninhibited fantasy, as if they cannot get away from concrete "reality" even for a moment. This unimaginativeness, or rather circumscription of ego bounds, seems related to the barren inner life, the shallow emotions, and the "escape into reality" which are also revealed in the F scale and in the interview material.

Examples: "Probably quit my job—if I had a job." "Perhaps go fishing in the Sierras if the season was right." "That is a question that is impossible to answer, as I do not know how I would act under those circumstances."

1. *Conventional morality and inhibition.* The main theme in these responses is making peace with God and man (particularly ingroups), in the sense of being "good," of conforming, of denying oneself active pleasure. Many of the responses are in a religious context, but it must be stressed that there are also low religious responses. (To repeat a scoring slogan: It is not the event as such, but the meaning of the event to the individual, that determines whether the score is H or L.) Compare for example the high response, "Making peace with God," with the low equivalent, "Working toward spiritual realization in a monastery." The highs' emphasis is on inner peace and harmony, *on the absence of conflict rather than on positive achievement*. Religious responses having such qualities as self-expression, intraception, and self-blame should be scored L. (See also low category 1.)

Examples: "I would try and do as much good as I could." "Be nice to everyone." "I would live with God and prepare myself to meet Him." "I'd meet as many people as I could, go all over the world and above all, go to church." "With my wife" (devoid of content, no sign of pleasure or relationship). "Being normal." (The emphasis on *normality*, which is commonly expressed, suggests that the person is worried about "letting loose.") A recurrent high theme is that of "Getting my affairs in order," a sort of last-minute concern with compulsive detail. The response *"Commit suicide"* occurred in a few highs and no lows, and it was scored H. This response may reflect an authoritarian contempt for "cowards"; the individuals giving it would seem to regard death as more attractive than life—suicide being a temptation that "strong" men resist—something that the low scorers are not so likely to feel.

2. *Incidental, dilute pleasures.* These responses refer to pleasure-fun activities of a highly conventionalized, desensualized, and emotionally shallow nature. Interpretively, the individual is seeking satisfaction but his moral façade prevents the free, intense, ego-accepted expression of underlying impulses. *Travel* is probably the most common activity; whatever its other meanings (e.g., voyeuristic), it may also express the vague, undifferentiated desire for change (ego-alien rebellion?) which is also expressed in some of the interviews. These responses are distinguished from those in low category 2 by the lack of open sensuality and achievement values, and by the conventionalized quality.

Examples: "I would travel as far as possible, with a companion of the fair sex." "I think I would go the forest and wild life and enjoy some companionship, but be more or less reserved in my actions." "See interesting things, read books" (superficial, concrete, dilute). "I would spend the time at home and with my friends with a normal amount of recreation." "Marry—traveling around the world."
A "travel" response is scored L even when there is no explicit sensual quality, as long as there is some differentiation or detailed description. For example: "Traveling the world and visiting the countries to see their natural and man-made wonders and to see the natural habitats of the peoples of the world." "Travel to South America, Mexico and New York." There are, of course, transitional responses between the clearly high and the clearly low, but these are not numerous.

Included here also are responses in which there is no specific reference to what one would do but only to *empty pleasures,* e.g., "Have fun," "Spend money doing exactly what I please" (release of conventional inhibition), "Try to be happy."
All the references to *athletics* in the present groups were by highs, and were scored H. (Had athletics been mentioned in a clearly low context, it would have been scored L.)

Examples: "Probably quit my job—if I had a job; see as many sports events as I could; play golf and, I imagine, get drunk fairly often also" (by a "middle-class" man). "Traveling, playing golf, bowling; a great variety of activities and as little sleep as possible" (this is escape into reality rather than pleasure-sensuality). "Travel, adventure, general mischief, hazardous play." "Hunting and fishing."

When there is reference only to a single, specific behavior without a defining context, e.g., "go to camp," the response is scored *Neutral.* Also Na is the response, "Same as ever" when no qualifications are given.

3. *Passivity*. That many "high" men have considerable conflict between a surface emphasis on work-ambition-activity and an underlying, ego-alien passive-dependent trend, is suggested by several projective questions (1, 3, 4 especially), and it has been demonstrated by the material in other chapters. The passivity is occasionally expressed in the responses to this question. It is interesting that whereas the guiding (achievement) values of the lows come out more strongly than ever on this item, the guiding (work-success) values of the highs are less important, in the last six months—when one's individuality is at stake, so to speak—than are religious values,[5] passivity, or other pleasures. The main forms of passivity are sleep, fishing, and relaxing (in the sense of not working rather than of active leisure).

Examples: "Doing the things I like to do and *getting ten hours' sleep*" (underlining by subject). "I would go to a nice quiet place and just sit down by a stream and fish and think" (mainly passivity; insufficient evidence of intellectuality or intensity to merit a score of L). "Relaxing, but trying not to worry or I would die before my six months came up." "Not thinking about it" may be included here; it represents not only anti-intraception but also a high trend toward negative rather than positive solutions of inner problems.

4. *Omissions* are recorded as Nb, converted to H.

QUESTION 8. WHAT EXPERIENCES WOULD BE MOST AWE-INSPIRING?

Low Categories

1. *Realization of achievement values.* As discussed previously, these values may be expressed in terms of interpersonal relations, where they refer to personal achievement (intellectual, aesthetic, scientific), warm relationships and social contribution; or they may be expressed on an ideological level in the form of progressive social change, elimination of prejudice, and the realization of broad democratic values.

Examples: "To see the day when the people (collectively) really controlled their own destiny and would no longer be dictated to by special interests." "Mass emotion usually; awe that an emotion can be so uniform in so many people at the same time" (empathy, sense of unity with others). "The composition or fine performance of good music." "Impersonal and unselfish love for mankind." "The responsibility that a Negro friend of mine feels for 13 million people." "Birth of anything new—children, animals, seasons, scientific ideas" (references to *birth* and creativity are fairly common in lows). "A great work of art, poem, piece of sculpture, or symphony." "Certain manifestations of human personality where people are unexpectedly good, strong and beautiful, especially ordinary people who haven't had much chance; in people the two qualities which arouse my wonder are the power of courage and the power to accept defeat humbly and without bitterness and resentment." References to being *loved* are low, to being *praised* or popular are high.

[5] The sudden increase in the importance of religion to highs when they are faced with death reminds us of the acquiring of "fox-hole religion" during the war. These results, as well as the interview material on religion, suggest that such last-minute conversions occur more often in highs than in lows.

2. *Power as exemplified in man's achievements and in nature.* The idea of power is expressed by both low and high scorers, but again the same event seems to have systematically different meanings for the two groups. The highs' conception of power is extremely personalized (see below); they admire and are awe-inspired by powerful people, toward whom they show deference and submission. The lows, on the other hand, conceive of power in more impersonal terms; they see it mainly as a means toward socially beneficial ends (rather than an end in itself), as more universal in the sense of existing everywhere and for the over-all social good. The main kinds of admired power are material-technological achievements by man and examples of grandeur in nature.

Examples: "Watch a two-thousand-ton aircraft take off; the Golden Gate Bridge; the view of the Bay Area from Mt. Tamalpais on a clear night." "The great structures which man has built in this world." "Seeing a star explode or earthquakes—any extreme natural manifestation." "Great material achievements—building projects, etc." "The atomic bomb, Grand Canyon, Boulder Dam, etc." References to the *atomic bomb* in itself are neutral; it is scored L in a context of man-made power or material achievement, H in a context of destructiveness or other high trends.

3. *Intense nature experiences.* References to nature are scored L if there are explicit indications of a strong aesthetic, sensual-emotional experience, or if there is fairly specific description of what one would be looking at. Vague, empty references to nature in general or to "just looking" are scored H (see below).

Examples: "Natural phenomena such as Crater Lake, Grand Canyon." "Thoughts of God's infinite intelligence, power, etc., as shown in nature—the structure and physiology of living creatures, behavior of the universe, etc." (This is a good example of a low religious response; understanding, imaginative, universalistic, idea of God-in-universe rather than God-over-universe.) "Watching a beautiful sunset; seeing Frisco at night from a ferry boat in the middle of the Bay." "A descent into the center of the earth; a walk on the bottom of the ocean."

High Categories (Question 8)

1. *Realization of conventional values.* These are highly conventionalized responses referring to acquisition or possession of things, to peace of mind (in the sense of freedom from worry), to a vague, undefined sense of virtue, and to incidental, desensualized pleasures.

Examples: "Feelings of good, examples of good." "Marriage and happy family life; ownership of something important such as a home, new auto, business concern, etc." "Love, I guess; from what I understand, when it dawns a fellow he has met the right girl; this is something I imagine and I really believe will be true" (love as a completely strange emotion, more imposed from without than motivated from within). "To know that when I get married I would be able to live very comfortably in a home with my wife and child." "If my husband were home evenings" (no reference to relationship). "To get married." "Get rid of my stomach trouble." "Be in a good frame of mind all the time." "Possession of great wealth; outstanding accomplishment of any kind" (note the equating of wealth and accomplishment). "Knowing my husband loved me without a doubt; peace on earth" (this seems to refer more to freedom from anxiety than to emotional warmth and exchange). The responses in this category suggest a lack of inner emotional vitality.

2. *Power: deference and submission toward power figures.* The highs' references to power are in an *authoritarian* context: the power is personalized in a strong man toward whom the subject has, implicitly or explicitly, a deferent, submissive relation. The authority figure may come from various areas of social life: military, political, industrial, religious. There is often an emphasis on *ritual* and a concern with what is *external* rather than with intrinsic meanings and values.

Examples: "During the war: to sit in on a meeting of the German General Staff; to witness a V-2 bomb launching. For peacetime: a presidential conference with his aides and Cabinet; a meeting of the country's leading personnel men." "Watching politicians in action in Washington; talking with professional athletes." "A coronation, a college graduation, awarding of Nobel prizes" (emphasis on ritual and success, not an achievement in an inner sense). "Meeting a truly great man such as Admiral Halsey or General Patton, or President Truman."

The religious references by highs express the same underlying variables.

Examples: "Certain church services I have seen; religion in the midst of war, on battlefields I have seen." "A conversation or sight of God." "A picture of President Roosevelt, whom I admire; being in church during the service." Note the primary concern with religion as ritual rather than as ethics, and the conception of God in terms similar to those expressed above with regard to personnel men, athletes, military authorities, politicians. Again we find an indication of religion as a fox-hole phenomenon—something that one turns to only as a support against external threat and inner anxiety. A mystical, *superstitious* trend is illustrated by the following response: "The feeling relating to something that is supernatural, something that happens in a weird way and has no factual reasons about it."

In some cases the subject wants to play the power role *himself*, often with specific reference to someone else playing the deferent role.

Examples: "To be able to fly in the Army Air Corps" (gaining power through the plane; desire for military experience). "I have the mad desire to hear an audience screaming 'Author' for me when my play has been the greatest ever to see Broadway" (more emphasis on personal prestige, audience deference, than on achievement). "To know the basic actualities of electricity; to create something or see something created, heretofore considered impossible or unbelieveable" (not achievement values, but wanting to do what no one else is powerful enough to do).

3. *Destruction-harm of other persons.* Many of the military experiences in Category 2 have this aspect, but it is the focal one here.

Examples: "Death of a close relative; torture to reveal an important plan." "To see death" (this presumably means death in someone else; references to one's personal experience of death would be scored L). "To see San Francisco destroyed by an earthquake." "To see the results of the atomic bomb." "To watch a delicate stomach operation" (references to *surgery* are usually high; they seem related to the body-anxiety found in previous items). "To see an alcoholic who cannot help himself stay away from the cravings of liquor, a person who has been severely crippled by a disease, and to go to a funeral." (Note the associative sequence from dependency to disease to death.)

4. *Dilute experiences of nature and beauty.* These responses are matter-of-fact, general, superficial descriptions of aesthetic or "nature" experiences, with no detail and no indication of sensual-emotional involvement. The person is for the most part "just looking."

Examples: "Experiences in nature." "The sight of rare jewels and metals; the viewing of great natural wonders of the world." "Traveling to another planet-galaxy, though I doubt the probability of it" (note the "constriction of fantasy" observed also in Item 7). "The great natural beauties of nature have thrilled me and probably always will." "Trips through all the important nations of the world and not have to worry about the expenses involved" (note the limitation to "important" nations and the desire for gratuities). "Music." "Watching some unusual scientific event such as atomic energy" (merely watching, not participation or achievement). "Scenic grandeur." "Seeing something of real importance."

5. *Omissions* are recorded as Nb, scored as H. Of the 6 omissions (9 per cent), 5 were by highs.

Note: Due to various circumstances (see p. 580), only 65 of the total of 312 subjects received this question. It is likely, therefore, that further experience will suggest modifications and particularly additions to the present scoring scheme.

SUMMARY OF PROJECTIVE QUESTION CATEGORIES

High Categories	*Low Categories*

Question 1: What moods are unpleasant or disturbing?

High Categories	Low Categories
1. Violations of conventional values	1. Conscious conflict and guilt
2. Threatening or nonsupporting environment	2. Focal dependency and love-seeking
3. "Rumblings from below"	3. Open hostility, by self or others, toward love objects
4. Omissions	

Question 2: What desires are most difficult to control?

High Categories	Low Categories
1. Nonfocal and/or motor aggression	1. Focal (usually verbal) hostility directed against violators of achievement values
2. Ego-alien passivity	2. The tendency to violate achievement values oneself
3. Impersonal sex	3. Miscellaneous
4. Incidental pleasures and violations of conventional values	
5. Omissions	

Question 3: What great people do you admire most?

1. Power and control
2. Conservative Americans
3. Parents and relatives

4. Miscellaneous

1. The arts and philosophy
2. Physical and biological scientists
3. Social scientists, liberal-radical political figures
4. Active denial of admiration

Question 4: What might drive a person nuts?

1. "Rumblings from below"
2. Threatening, irritating, or non-supporting environment.
3. Omissions

1. Inner psychological states
2. Dominating, blocking, rejecting environment

Question 5: Worst crimes a person could commit?

1. Crude aggression and sex
2. Other immoral acts
3. Various legal offenses

1. Violation of achievement values

Question 6: Most embarrassing moments?

1. Violations of convention and etiquette
2. Blows at exhibitionism and narcissism

1. Hurting another's feelings.
2. Feelings of inadequacy, failure, being rejected

Question 7: How would you spend your last six months?

1. Conventional morality and inhibitions
2. Incidental, dilute pleasures

3. Passivity
4. Omissions

1. Achievement values: creativity and social contribution
2. Open sensuality and active pleasure

Question 8: What experiences would be most awe-inspiring?

1. Realization of conventional values
2. Power: deference and submission toward power figures
3. Destruction-harm of other persons
4. Dilute experiences of nature and beauty
5. Omissions

1. Realization of achievement values
2. Power as exemplified in man's achievements and in nature
3. Intense nature experiences

D. RESULTS

Practical considerations prevented quantification of the Projective Question material from every group to which the questionnaire was administered. (For a complete list and description of these groups, see Chapter IV.) The responses of the entire high and low quartiles of the following groups were analyzed. (The N's in the parentheses refer to the number of cases in the extreme high and low quartiles combined, on which the Projection Question analysis was made.)

1. *Psychology Women* (N = 63): the members of a Psychology class at the University of California. Initial forms of questionnaire, prior to Form 78.
2. *Employment Service Veteran Men* (N = 51): an unselected sample of the Veteran population going through an office of the United States Employment Service. Forms 45 and 40.
3. *Psychiatric Clinic Men* (N = 29); and 4. *Psychiatric Clinic Women* (N = 34): in- and out-patients at a local Community Clinic. Most of these subjects received Form 45, but some were given a shorter form which included only four projective questions.
5. *Middle-Class Women* (N = 70): A highly diversified sample from various middle-class groups: religious, political, business, and the like. Form 40.
6. *Middle-Class Men and Service Club Men* (combined) (N = 65): While the scale responses of these two groups were statisticized separately, it seemed feasible to combine them into a single group for the present purposes. The Middle-Class Men were obtained from largely the same groups as the Middle-Class Women. Form 40.

These groups constitute a fairly representative sample of all those studied. On the basis of the present results, it appears likely that similar quantitative differences between the highs and lows would have been obtained had we analyzed the Projective Question material of the remaining groups: The determination of qualitative differences among the highs from various groupings, and among the lows from various groupings, remains an interesting problem for future research.

Questionnaire Form 45 contained the eight Projective Questions in the order listed above (Section A). As part of the process of cutting Form 40 down to an absolute minimum (see Chapter IV), only the first five of these questions were used. Further complications occurred in the case of the initial form (taken by the Psychology Women), which contained only the first seven questions, and in the case of the Psychiatric Clinic Men and Women, some of whom received a shorter form which contained only Questions 3, 4, 5, and 6. The inconsistency is part of the general problem of working out a standard set of questions. However, the inconsistencies in Form 40 and in the form given to the clinic patients must be regarded as methodological errors, since complete data on all eight questions would have compensated for any possible increase in administrative difficulties. As a result of differences in the number of questions in each form of the questionnaire, there are also differences in the number of subjects receiving a given question. The number of subjects receiving each of the eight questions is indicated and explained in Table 1(XV), below. All 312 of the subjects received forms containing Questions 3, 4 and 5. The N varies for the other questions, reaching a low of 65 on Question 8, which was contained in Form 45 given to the Employment Service and Clinic groups.

The Scoring Manual presented above is a slight modification of the one used by the scorers. The original Manual contained the same categories with substantially the same definitions. It was based on an analysis of the responses of two large groups: University of California Students (male and female) and the University of California Summer Session Adults, Form 60 (adult men and women from various sections of the middle class). As the scoring proceeded, certain additional implications and theoretical points were brought out and incorporated as notes in the original Manual. Also, an attempt was made to clarify certain ambiguities pointed out by the scorers. These notes are in the text of the present Manual. The only further change is the addition of a number of examples from the groups on which the data below are based. While the present Scoring Manual is more articulate than the original, no essentially new theoretical points have been added.

1. RELIABILITY OF SCORING

The critical reader may, after going through the Scoring Manual above, legitimately ask whether the proposed differences between highs and lows are "really" there, or whether they are not imposed by the writer's bias. A partial answer to this question is offered by means of the controlled scoring procedure. In the last four groups (all but the Psychology Women and the Veteran Men), the following scoring procedure was followed.

The high and low quartiles from a given group were combined and their responses to each item typed in a single, randomly ordered series. Each response was identified by a code number, so that the scorer did not know whether it was given by an individual scoring high or by an individual scoring low on ethnocentrism. Moreover, the code numbers for each individual varied from item to item in order to prevent halo effect (e.g., the tendency to give an individual a score of H on Item 2 because he was scored H on Item 1). Each rater went through all responses of the combined-high-plus-low grouping for each item, recording her scores of H, L, Na, Nhl, or Nb (see Section A for key to symbols) for each code number. Only after all items had been scored were the code numbers taken away and the identity (with respect to standing on E) of each subject restored. The scorer was, therefore, entirely on her own in deciding whether each response fell into a high, low, or neutral category. This is what is meant by "blind" scoring.

In the case of the Psychology Women and the Employment Service Veterans the scoring was not done blindly. This was recognized as a methodological error and corrected on all subsequent groups. However, the advantage in knowing the subjects' standing on E may have been partially counterbalanced by the newness of the task for the scorers, and by the emphasis placed on caution.

As a further check on the dependability of scoring, it was always done independently by two raters. Their degree of agreement in assigning scores gives a measure of reliability, i.e., of the probability that these results can be duplicated by other raters with similar training. While high reliability does not in itself prove the correctness of the *interpretations* regarding the deeper meaning of the scoring categories, it does indicate that the scoring categories, *as specifically defined*, have been objectively measured and are not merely figments of the imagination. Scoring reliability is, then, one index of objectivity.

A word ought perhaps to be said about the training of the raters.[6] Both were, when the scoring started, at approximately the level of first-year graduate students in psychology. Their learning of the Scoring Manual was part of the process of becoming familiar with the general theoretical orientation of the present research. Neither had had any clinical experience or intensive training in dynamic personality theory, beyond a few undergraduate courses. In addition to studying the Scoring Manual, they had the benefit of several preliminary practice sessions on groups not included in the final statistical treatment. The nature of the scorers' background and training is stressed because it reveals that detailed familiarity with a particular psychological theory is not essential for scoring; theory is, of course, essential for an integrated understanding of the total pattern of data.

When the two raters had independently made and recorded their scores for a given group, a conference was held for the purpose of assigning a final score for each response. As has been noted above, each response was scored High, Low, or Neutral; the H or L scores did not specify which particular category (e.g., high category 3 or low category 1) the response represented. The reason for this is that a response might represent variables in more than one category; or it might express in abstract form an underlying high or low trend without falling into a specific category as described. A scoring disagreement was registered whenever the two original scores were not identical. Discussion of the disagreements usually convinced one rater or the other to change in the other's direction. Occasionally a response scored H by one rater and L by the other received a final score of Na or Nhl.

The scoring reliability, that is, the percentage of agreement between raters, was computed as follows. A full error was counted when one rater scored H, the other L. A half error was counted when one rater scored Na or Nhl and the other scored H or L. Thus, if in a group of 50 there are 8 full errors and 4 half errors, the percentage disagreement is 10/50 or 20 per cent, or in positive terms there is 80 per cent agreement.

The reliability data are presented in Table 1 (XV). The mean percentage agreement of 90 meets current standards for materials of this sort, and indicates that the two sets of scores, independently and blindly derived, agreed very well. In the case of Groups 1 and 2, which were scored independently but not blindly (the raters knowing which was the high-on-E subject, which

---

[6] We wish to express our thanks to Anne Morrow and Ellan Ulery for their work "beyond the call of duty" in learning and applying the scoring scheme.

TABLE 1 (XV)

SCORING RELIABILITY (PERCENTAGE INTERRATER AGREEMENT) FOR THE EIGHT PROJECTIVE QUESTIONS

Group	N	Percentage Agreement								Mean[b]
		1	2	3	4	5	6	7	8	
1. Psychology Women[c]	63	94	75	87	84	95	94	85	-	88
2. Employment Service Veteran Men	51 (24)[a]	100	96	95	95	94	90	100	87	) 95
3. Psychiatric Clinic Men	29 (17)[a]	76	82	91	71	90	90	59	71	) 80
4. Psychiatric Clinic Women	34 (24)[a]	96	79	94	88	87	84	81	88	) 87
5. Middle-Class Women[d]	70	91	82	96	92	97	-	-	-	92
6. Middle-Class and Business Club Men[d]	65	86	83	95	80	98	-	-	-	89
Mean Percentage Agreement[b]		93	85	94	88	95	90	83	83	90
Total N	312	290	290	312	312	312	150	128	65	1859

[a]The N for Groups 2, 3, and 4 is complicated by the fact that two questionnaire forms were given. Only 24 of the 51 highs and lows in Group 2 received Form 45, which contained all 8 questions; the remaining 27 received Form 40, containing only questions 1-5. Similarly, some of the subjects in Groups 3 and 4 filled out Form 45, while others received a modified form containing items 3, 4, 5, and 6 only. The differences between subgroups within each sample are random.

[b]The over-all group and item means are based on single item means weighted by N.

[c]Group 1 received Form 78, which did not contain question 8.

[d]Groups 5 and 6 received Form 40, which did not contain questions 6, 7, and 8.

[e]Key to questions: 1 (Moods), 2 (Desires), 3 (Great People), 4 (Drive Nuts), 5 (Crimes), 6 (Embarrassing), 7 (Last Six Months), 8 (Awe-inspiring).

the low), only Group 2, with 95 per cent agreement, is above the over-all mean. For only one group, the Psychiatric Clinic Men, does the reliability drop conspicuously below 90 per cent. This drop (to 80 per cent) seems due in part to certain intrinsic ambiguities in the responses of this group, and in part to the fact that this was the first group to be scored blindly.

The reliabilities for the individual items are also satisfactory, ranging from 83 to 95 per cent. Questions 1 ("Moods"), 3 ("Great people"), and 5 ("Crimes") were scored most consistently. The average agreement on Questions 7 ("Last six months") and 8 ("Awe-inspiring") might have been higher had they been filled out by Groups 5 and 6. In only 6 cases out of the total of 41 did an item have a reliability of less than 80 per cent. It would appear, therefore, that the present scoring scheme is relatively reliable, and in this sense "objective."

2. PROJECTIVE QUESTION SCORES IN RELATION TO STANDING ON THE E SCALE

To what extent are L scores on the Projective Questions characteristic of the anti-ethnocentric individuals, H scores characteristic of the extremely ethnocentric individuals? The Scoring Manual is based on the hypothesis that the low quartiles on the Ethnocentrism scale will give responses falling mainly in the low categories, whereas the responses of the high quartiles will fall mainly in the high categories.

Data bearing on this question are presented in Table 2(XV), which indicates the degree to which the Projective Questions differentiate the ethnocentric from the anti-ethnocentric subjects.

In order to obtain a quantitative measure of the relationship between Projective Question scores and standing on the E scale, the *percentage of PQ-E agreement* was computed for each quartile. This is called the *L%* in the case of the low quartile, *H%* for the high quartile, and *%A* for the two quartiles combined (average over-all agreement). Let us use L% to illustrate the procedure. Had scores of H and L been the only ones assigned, the L% would be simply the number of L scores divided by the total number of cases; thus, if all the low quartile members received L scores on a given item there would be 100 per cent agreement between PQ and E. But this procedure was not feasible because of the neutral scores.[7] Since a neutral score represents a half error, i.e., it signifies less agreement than an L score but more agreement than an H score, the L% was computed according to the following formula:

$$L\% = \frac{\text{Sum of L scores plus } \frac{1}{2} \text{ sum of neutral scores (Na, Nb, Nhl)}}{\text{Number of subjects in low quartile}}$$

[7] One possibility would have been not to consider subjects receiving scores of N, and to get a L/H ratio for the remaining subjects. This would have given higher L% values than those obtained by the method finally used, since in the latter method the N scores were used in such a way as to lower the L%. It was believed that all individuals taking the test should be included in the statistical treatment.

where Na means "ambiguous," Nb means "blank" (omitted), Nhl means "mixed high and low trends."

The only exception to this formula is in the case of Nb on Items 1, 2, 4, 7, and 8, where Nb is equivalent to H and is included among the H scores.

The computation of H% is based on an equivalent formula:

$$H\% = \frac{\text{Sum of H scores plus } \frac{1}{2} \text{ sum of neutral scores (Na, Nb, Nhl)}}{\text{Number of subjects in high quartile}}$$

Finally, %A is the average of L% and H%, weighted by N (number of cases in each quartile), and it indicates the over-all PQ-E agreement.

Table 2 (XV) gives the L%, H%, and %A for each group tested and for all groups combined. It also gives the number and percentage of Nb, Na, and Nhl responses. It may be noted first that the over-all PQ-E agreement (%A) is 74.9 per cent—a value which indicates a statistically significant relationship between Projective Question scores and high vs. low standing on the E scale. On a purely chance basis, the agreement would be only 50 per cent. The highs tend, however, to be more consistent in their PQ responses than do the lows: the highs have an over-all H% of 80.7, while for the lows the L% is only 69.1. In other words, the lows received more H scores than the highs did L scores. It is, so to speak, easier to make an H than an L score. The reason for this does not appear to lie primarily in the subjects themselves, for our general impression, based on other results and on clinical judgment, was that the low quartiles fitted the over-all conception of the "democratic" personality at least as well as the highs approximated the prototypic "authoritarian" personality. The preponderance of H scores is probably due to the conditions of testing. Since many of the groups were pressed for time, and since the instructions were not emphatic in suggesting that a fairly detailed answer be given, many of the responses were brief and superficial. It will be recalled from the Scoring Manual that references to "vague, dilute emotional experiences," as well as references only to "behavior or the situation *per se*, without consideration of inner meanings and motives," were important cues for assigning a score of H. It may be argued that if the instructions emphasized the giving of more detailed answers, both highs and lows would give more responses meriting a score of L. In the present groups, however, the elaborations of most lows took an L direction, of most highs an H direction. It might be expected, then, that the obtaining of longer responses would clarify and increase the differences between the low and high quartiles. It would also probably reduce somewhat the proportion (8.8 per cent) of responses scored Na and Nhl. We should not, of course, overlook the likelihood that numerous pressures in our culture, and perhaps the predominant ones, tend to make for authoritarianism in the individual. To the extent that this is true, we should expect some H trends even in individuals attempting to achieve a thoroughly democratic orientation.

TABLE 2 (XV)

PERCENTAGE AGREEMENT BETWEEN PROJECTIVE QUESTION SCORES AND E-SCALE SCORES

	N^a	Score	1	2	3	4	5	6	7	8	Mean[b]
1. Psychology Women											
Low quartile	32	L%	90.6	84.4	79.7	73.4	59.4	60.9	62.5	–	73.0
		N_b	0	1	0	0	3	3	0	–	7 $\big)$ 21.4%
		N_a-N_{HL}	2	4	7	13	1	10	10	–	41
High quartile	31	H%	91.9	79.0	72.6	79.0	91.9	88.7	82.3	–	83.6
		N_b	0	3	3	2	3	1	1	–	13 $\big)$ 14.3%
		N_a-N_{HL}	3	3	4	7	0	0	1	–	18
Total	63	%A	91.3	81.7	76.2	76.2	75.4	74.6	72.2	–	78.2
		N_b	0	4	3	2	2	4	1	–	20 $\big)$ 17.9%
		N_a-N_{HL}	5	7	11	20	1	11	11	–	59
2. Employment Service Men											
Low quartile	25 (10)	L%	78.0	66.0	76.0	82.0	66.0	80.0	65.0	80.0	73.9
		N_b	4	1	1	0	1	1	1	1	15 $\big)$ 15.5%
		N_a-N_{HL}	1	1	2	3	0	1	1	0	9
High quartile	26 (14)	H%	88.4	94.2	84.6	91.2	100.0	75.0	89.3	78.6	90.1
		N_b	1	1	1	3	0	0	0	2	12 $\big)$ 12.2%
		N_a-N_{HL}	3	1	5	3	0	1	1	2	9
Total	51 (24)	%A	83.3	80.4	80.4	91.2	83.3	77.1	79.2	79.2	82.6
		N_b	5	9	2	5	0	2	0	3	27 $\big)$ 13.8%
		N_a-N_{HL}	1	1	7	3	0	2	2	2	18

3. Psychiatric Clinic Men — 29

Low quartile 14 (9)

L%	55.6	38.9	82.2	50.0	53.6	46.4	50.0	88.9	58.1
N_b	0	2	1	0	2	1	1	0	6)16.3%
N_a-N_{HL}	0	1	2	0	3	2	2	0	9

High quartile 15 (8)

H%	75.0	83.3	86.7	83.3	66.7	93.8	50.0	77.7
N_b	0	0	1	0	1	0	0	4)13.1%
N_a-N_{HL}	0	3	0	3	1	1	0	8

Total 29 (17)

%A	64.7	55.9	82.8	69.0	69.0	56.8	70.6	70.6	67.9
N_b	0	4	1	2	1	2	0	0	10)14.7%
N_a-N_{HL}	0	1	5	6	0	3	2	0	17

4. Psychiatric Clinic Women — 34

Low quartile 17 (13)

L%	84.6	76.9	70.6	82.5	55.9	70.6	42.3	88.5	71.3
N_b	0	0	1	0	2	2	1	0	3)12.5%
N_a-N_{HL}	0	3	3	3	4	4	1	1	12

High quartile 17 (11)

H%	72.7	55.5	50.0	94.1	97.1	58.8	86.4	81.8	74.5
N_b	0	2	1	0	1	4	1	3	12)17.0%
N_a-N_{HL}	0	0	4	0	0	2	1	0	7

Total 34 (24)

%A	79.2	66.7	60.3	88.3	76.5	64.7	62.5	85.4	72.8
N_b	0	2	2	0	1	6	1	3	15)14.7%
N_a-N_{HL}	0	7	7	0	3	6	2	1	19

TABLE 5 (XX) (continued)

TABLE 2 (XV) (continued)

	N[a]	Score	1	2	3	4	5	6	7	8	Mean[b]
5. Middle-Class Women	70										
Low quartile		34									
		L%	72.1	60.2	76.5	60.2	76.5				69.1
		N_b	2	4	2	0	2				10
		N_a-N_{HL}	1	1	4	1	2				9 } 8.9%
High quartile		36									
		H%	82.0	80.5	56.9	79.2	76.4				75.0
		N_b	8	12	8	0	3				31
		N_a-N_{HL}	1	0	5	1	4				11 } 23.3%
Total		70									
		%A	77.1	70.7	66.4	70.0	76.4				72.1
		N_b	10	16	10	0	5				41
		N_a-N_{HL}	2	1	9	2	6				20 } 17.4%
6. Middle-Class Men	65										
Low quartile		33									
		L%	69.7	43.9	71.2	62.1	71.2				63.6
		N_b	3	7	3	1	6				20
		N_a-N_{HL}	4	1	4	3	3				15 } 21.2%
High quartile		32									
		H%	81.2	78.1	81.2	76.6	75.0				78.4
		N_b	6	10	4	3	8				27
		N_a-N_{HL}	0	0	6	1	8				15 } 26.3%
Total		65									
		%A	75.4	60.8	76.1	69.2	73.1				70.9
		N_b	9	17	7	4	10				47
		N_a-N_{HL}	4	1	10	4	11				30 } 23.7%

7. All groups combined

Score		1	2	3	4	5	6	7	8	Total	Mean
Low quartile	L%	76.7	63.0	75.8	68.4	65.8	63.0	57.0	85.9		69.1
	Nb	9	19	17	3	14	7	0	6	61	6.6%
	Na-NHL	8	8	22	20	15	11	13	3	95	10.3%
	ER	146	146	155	155	155	73	64	32	926	116
High quartile	H%	84.0	79.9	71.3	84.4	86.0	75.3	85.9	72.7		80.7
	Nb	15	33	17	9	11	7	2	6	99	10.6%
	Na-NHL	4	4	27	15	15	3	4	2	68	7.3%
	ER	144	144	157	157	157	77	64	33	933	117
Total	%A	80.3	71.4	73.6	76.5	76.0	69.3	71.5	79.2		74.9
	Nb	24	52	25	12	25	14	2	6	160	8.6%
	Na-NHL	12	12	49	29	27	14	17	3	163	8.8%
	ER	290	290	312	312	312	150	128	65	1859	232

aFor Groups 2, 3, and 4 the number of subjects varies somewhat from item to item because two questionnaire forms were used. The number indicated in the "N" column is the total N in each group or quartile. The N in parentheses refers to those subjects who received the complete set of projective questions. Thus, in Group 2 all 51 subjects received items 1 - 5 (Forms 45 and 40); only 10 Low and 14 High received all 8 questions (Form 45), so that the N's on items 6, 7, and 8 are 10 and 14 respectively, as indicated in parentheses in the "N" column. Similarly, of the 14 Lows in Group 3, only 9 received the full battery, the remaining 5 receiving a form which did not include items 1, 2, 7, and 8. For the high quartile in Group 3, there is an N of 8 on items 1, 2, 7, and 8. In Group 4, the N on these same items is 13 for Lows and 11 for Highs.

Group 1 received a form which did not include item 8 (see text).

Groups 5 and 6 received Form 40 which contained items 1-5 only.

Thus, while there were 312 subjects in all, the N per item varied. This is shown in the table under "All groups combined," where the row "ER" gives the number of subjects answering each item.

bIn the computation of all means, the component values are weighted by N.

Key to questions: 1 (Moods), 2 (Desires), 3 (Great People), 4 (Drive Nuts), 5 (Crimes), 6 (Embarrassing), 7 (Last Six Months), 8 (Awe-inspiring).

The average agreement varies among the six groups from 67.9 per cent for the Psychiatric Clinic Men to 82.6 per cent for the Employment Service Veteran Men. It appears that the scorers, try as they did to be unbiased, were systematically influenced by the fact that they knew the E-quartile standing of the Psychology Women and the Veteran Men. Thus, the %A for these two groups is about 80 per cent, whereas for the remaining four groups (scored blindly) it averages slightly over 70 per cent. The relatively low %A for the Clinic Men is consistent with the low scoring reliability for this group (see Table 1(XV)). The data for the Clinic Women and the Middle-Class Men and Women probably best represent what can be expected with the present Scoring Manual; the average agreement of about 72 per cent for these groups might have been slightly higher had all subjects received questions 6, 7, and 8.

The over-all average agreement for the individual items varies from 69.3 to 80.3 per cent. The poorest questions are 2 ("Desires"), 6 ("Embarrassing"), and 7 ("Last six months"). In all three of them the L% is particularly low (57–63 per cent), probably because of the brevity of the answers, as discussed above. Correction of this error should lead to considerably better results, particularly for Item 7. The agreements for the individual items reveal again the great consistency of the highs. Thus, the L% varied within a range of 29 points (57–86 per cent), whereas the H% covered a range of only 15 points (71–86 per cent). It is of some interest that the two most differentiating items, 1 ("Moods") and 8 ("Awe-inspiring"), deal with issues which, in their literal meanings, are completely removed from ideology about group interaction.

Table 2(XV) provides the empirical basis on which omissions (Nb) of Questions 1, 2, 4, 7, and 8 were converted into H scores in the statistical treatment. On each of these questions approximately two-thirds or more of the total number of omissions were made by the high quartiles. Moreover, it is consistent with the differential trends found that the highs should omit, more often than the lows, questions dealing with inner life (moods, desires, drive nuts) and with emotionally intense experiences (last six months, awe-inspiring). Question 3 might also have been scored in this way since some 70 per cent of the omissions were by highs. However, omissions on this item were not scored H because they did not appear to fulfill the requirement of theoretical consistency. Should the highs continue, in future groups, to make most of the omissions, Nb would have to be scored H and a theoretical rationale found. The scoring of Nb as H would, in the present groups, have raised the over-all agreement several points.

Having considered the degree to which groups are distinguished with respect to the H and L categories, we may consider briefly how the scoring scheme applies to the individual. It is possible to give each subject a total score which is the sum of his individual item scores. This total may be called the *L-H score*, and is computed as follows: One point is given for each H score, zero points for each L score, and one-half point for each Neutral score (except for Nb on Items 1, 2, 4, 7, and 8 where, as noted above, Nb is converted to H). Thus, the L-H scores may range, for eight questions, between 0 (all L scores) and 8 (all H scores), with a mid-point of 4.0. A subject receiving 4 H scores, 3 L's and 1 Na has an L-H score of 4.5, i.e., just on the high side of center. The over-all H% of 80.7 for the high quartiles can be converted to an average L-H score of 6.5 for the eight items. Similarly, the over-all L% of 69.1 for the low quartiles becomes an L-H score of 2.5.

The computing of L-H scores for each subject provides a means of determining the amount of overlap between the low and high quartiles. This has been done in the case of the Middle-Class Men and Women, who have a combined N of 135, and who received a battery of five Projective Questions. The L-H scores of the low quartile ranged between 0.0 and 4.5, those of the high quartile between 1.0 and 5.0, the mean for the total group being about 2.7 (slightly more H than L scores were assigned). Using 2.7 as a dividing point, we may then say that all L-H scores of 2.5 and below will be called "low," all scores of 3.0 and above will be called "high." On the basis of this criterion, 22 per cent of the low quartile members would be considered high in terms of Projective Question score, while 14 per cent of the high quartile members have a low L-H score. These are the exceptions. Or, to put it positively, 78 per cent of the anti-ethnocentric group, and 86 per cent of the ethnocentric group, would be correctly diagnosed on the basis of total Projective Question score.

The above data do not, of course, include the middle scorers on E. However, it is not unlikely that a longer Projective Question Test of perhaps fifteen or twenty items, applied to all subjects and not merely to the extreme quartiles, might yield correlations in the neighborhood of .7 between L-H score and E. The Projective Questions might then be used, like the F scale, as an indirect measure of ethnocentrism—a measure in which no reference to current social issues need be made. They also, like the F scale, permit one to go beyond the immediate limits of the scoring scheme and to make numerous inferences regarding individual dynamics. That the variables in the two techniques are so consistent is an important argument in favor of the validity of each.

In summary, the results indicate that the Projective Question Test meets current standards of reliability, under the most demanding of scoring conditions. It has also been demonstrated that the categories denoted as "high" are in fact characteristic of the high scorers on the Ethnocentrism scale, the "low" categories characteristic of the low quartile on E. There are, however, many highs who get L scores on single items, and many lows who get scores of H, the average PQ-E agreement being in the neighborhood of 75 per cent. In terms of individual L-H scores, the ethnocentrists and anti-ethnocentrists could, in the two groups considered, be diagnosed with approximately 82 per cent accuracy.

The present results can probably be improved in the future by modifications of the Scoring Manual, by an increase in the number of items (which, other things being equal, will improve the reliability of the L-H score), and by instructions which lay greater stress on full answers (two or three sentences would do). Moreover, in its practical application the test may be scored in a clinically more meaningful way, once the scorers have demonstrated their competence. If all the items for a given individual were scored at once, many apparently ambiguous responses might be interpreted in the light of the total pattern. This would not only improve the quantitative scoring but would also stimulate further differentiation and elaboration within the broad framework now conceived. There is also considerable research which needs to be done regarding additional categories, relative frequencies of specific categories, sex differences, various patterns among lows and among highs, differences among various religious, political, and other groupings, and so on.

3. VALIDATION BY MEANS OF CASE STUDIES: MACK AND LARRY

Throughout the present research the attempt has been made to develop techniques that would yield *statistically significant* relationships among numerous variables and that would, as well, provide *clinically meaningful* material regarding the individual. Accordingly, following the presentation of statistical (group) results for each technique, the protocols of the high man, Mack, and the low man, Larry, have been considered in relation to the group data. To the extent that their results on a given technique are consistent with those for the total sample, and to the exent that interpretations based on the technique are congruent with those derived from other techniques, further evidence of validity appears to be indicated.

The Projective Question responses of Mack and Larry are as follows (the scores being given at the end of each response):

MACK (High)	LARRY (Low)

1. Moods

| Physical weakness, perhaps due to ill health over the last 4 years. (H) | A lonesome mood, or a feeling that I am not progressing toward my goal, or a feeling that I have hurt someone. (L) |

2. Desires

| Anger. (Na) | When someone is persecuted unjustly, or to see a Negro serviceman endure unjust discrimination and prejudice. (L) |

3. Great people

Lincoln, Lee, Gen. Geo. C. Marshall, Edison. (H)

Lincoln, Willkie, Washington, Stalin, Chiang Kai Shek, Churchill, MacArthur, Eisenhower, and the great scientists of past and present. (H)

4. Drive nuts

It depends a lot on definition, but if crazy is meant, such a thing as losing my wife and children would most closely approximate it. (H)

A person might become insane over too much interest in love, religion, money, etc. Any obsession carried too far might drive a person insane. (L)

5. Worst crimes

Murder, rape. (H)

Murder, rape and a person that will incite hate toward another people, and groups that incite wars. (Nhl)

6. Embarrassing

Not included in this form.

7. Last six months

Seeing all of the world possible, with a particular person to see it with me. (H)

Trying to enjoy life as I have always wanted; travel, meet important people, have lots of friends, go to a lot of parties. All this without harming anyone. (L predominantly, despite some H trends.)

8. Awe-inspiring

The viewing of great natural wonders of the world, new scientific achievements, meeting really great men and women and the sight of rare jewels and metals. (H)

To see American people practice true democracy. Such incidents as a member of one race protects a member of another race. True comradeship between races. (L)

The scoring, done blindly and with complete agreement between two independent judges, gives Mack an L-H score of 6.5 out of 7 (or an H% of 93), Larry an L-H score of 1.5 (or an L% of 79). Mack's responses are relatively typical of those given by the high men; if he shows no bizarre features, neither does he show much individuality. Given an opportunity to be emotionally expressive (Items 7 and 8), he responds in a shallow, conventionalized manner; his concern with "looking," with a minimum of differentiation or focal affect, appears to be based on a deep but inhibited curiosity for which he has few constructive expressions. His tendency to align himself with power and success is expressed in Item 3 and again in Item 8 ("meeting really great men and women"). Item 1 reveals his anxiety over bodily harm and his conception of ill health as a form of weakness (rather than, for example, a barrier in the way of achievement). The equation of sickness with weakness is particularly interesting in the light of his mother's and his own weakness during childhood (see Chapters II and XX). It suggests, as does the material from other techniques, that his surface identification with powerful figures and groups is at least in part a means of maintaining his sense of mastery and of allaying his anxiety over bodily harm. It is not clear from his Projective Question responses alone whether Mack's aggression is more a surface defense against the admission of passive dependency or, rather, a strong underlying need. That he has aggressive impulses which he cannot easily assimilate into the ego is suggested by his "Murder, rape" on Item 5 and "Anger" on 2. Moreover, that these impulses are partially directed against family (ingroup) members is suggested by his response to Item 4: his fear of "losing my wife and children" (particularly since he is not yet married) would seem to be based on unconscious hostility toward them—hostility which is projected onto the "threatening world." (His fantasy, while he is still unmarried, of the death of wife and children may also be a projection of his own fear as a child that he might die when his mother did.) However, the over-all impression given is that of a conventional, deferent, pseudo-independent façade, and that what lies beneath the surface is primarily anxiety and dependency rather than active destructiveness.

Larry's responses, here as elsewhere, are less characteristically low than Mack's are high. Like Mack, Larry is attracted to those who have power, but his conception of power is different from Mack's. Thus, Larry can admire foreign as well as American leaders (Item 5: in 1945 Chiang Kai Shek was still conceived as a democratic leader). And his relationship to power figures seems to be based more on the open expression of dependency and need for support than on defense against fear of his own weakness. Indeed, Larry is openly and intensely identified with the weak and the helpless, and he can therefore be opposed to social authority when it mistreats Negroes and others (Items 2, 5, and 8). He is also characteristically low in his intraception, intrapunitiveness, achievement values, conscious guilt, and the like.

Larry's "timid dependency" is clearly expressed in his response to Item 7: what he wants most is to be loved and protected—"all this without harming anyone." The great fear of hurtng anyone, expressed also on Item 1, seems to imply deep-lying hostility which he must at all costs inhibit. Thus, his inhibition of aggression, combined with his tremendous love-seeking dependency, probably prevent Larry from fighting actively even for those things in which he believes most. He is disturbed by discrimination and he would be awe-inspired by the attaining of democratic group relations in America, but is not likely to be able militantly to oppose those who violate his basic values.

It cannot be said that the interpretations above were made in the absence of other clinical material on these two cases. However, the scoring was done in a controlled manner and many of the inferences follow fairly directly from the theory contained in the Scoring Manual. The conclusions reached here regarding Mack and Larry are in general agreement with those derived from other techniques, for example the F scale (Chapter VII) and the Thematic Apperception Test (Chapter XIV). It would seem, then, that the Projective Question technique may fruitfully be used not only for purposes of group research but also as an aid in the intensive study of the individual case.

E. CONCLUSIONS

It was apparent in the Scoring Manual that certain themes were repeated, with perhaps minor variations in form or content, in many of the Projective Question categories. There are, moreover, several instances in which two or more recurring themes, taken together, permit inferences regarding deeper-lying trends and processes. The results and theoretical constructions derived from the application of this technique are similar to those obtained from the other techniques used in the present research. In some cases there is almost exact duplication of variables; in others there is a more complementary or congruent relation, the variables from several techniques expressing diverse facets of a single, inclusive structure. Because the amount of duplication is considerable, a very brief discussion of the theoretical implications of the present results will suffice. Differential trends for high and low scorers on the E scale seem to exist in the following areas.

1. *General Ego Functioning.* Highs and lows differ markedly in their manner of handling deep-level trends such as aggression, sex, dependency, anxiety, and the like. We are not yet in a position to say whether one group or the other shows a greater total amount of any given trend; what is clear is that both groups exhibit all of these trends to a significant degree. The primary difference seems to lie in the ego functioning, and particularly in the relation of the ego to the deeper levels of personality. In the lows, as other techniques have shown, the underlying trends are more *ego-assimilated*, in the highs more *ego-alien*.

The lows appear to differ from highs in at least the following respects. The relations between the various levels of personality are more fluid, the boundaries more permeable. The ego defenses of the lows are relatively more impulse-releasing: at best we find considerable sublimation, to perhaps a greater degree we find that impulses have been assimilated into the ego without being fully integrated—witness the recurring Projective Question category, "Conscious conflict and guilt." In the highs, on the other hand—and the analysis of interviews led to the same conclusion—the ego defenses are characteristically more countercathectic; there is less sublimation and more use of defenses such as projection, denial, and reaction-formation, defenses which aid the individual in maintaining a moral façade at the expense of self-expression and emotional release.

These formulations are supported by many of the Projective Question results. Compare, for example, the low category, "Conscious conflict and guilt," with the contrasting high category, "Rumbling from below" (Questions 1, "Moods," and 4, "Drive nuts"). The former category refers to impulses which, disturbing though they may be, the individual at least to some extent recognizes and tries to handle. If there is conflict, there is also an attempt to integrate; if there is much that remains unconscious, there is also a willingness to look within and an attempt to assimilate. For most highs, on the other hand, there are few focal conflicts but there is a deep sense of anxiety and distress. The conflict is covered over by a moral façade or by symptomatic behavior; the disturbance is explained on the basis of a distressing (overdemanding, boring) external situation or of poor bodily condition, and the conflict is never faced in psychological terms. The difficulty of the highs in assimilating many important needs is shown by several other categories. Thus, when asked about highly satisfying emotional experiences ("Last six months" and "Awe-inspiring") they show much less intensity and inner vitality than the lows, that is, much less ability to utilize their psychic energies for constructive and ego-satisfying purposes. When the highs refer more directly to needs such as dependency, sex, and aggression ("Desires" and "Worst crimes"), they are more crude, impersonal, primitive, object-less and ego-less.

2. *Specific Properties of the Ego.* These properties are, of course, intimately bound up with ego functioning as discussed above. As might be expected from their use of primarily countercathectic defenses, the highs have comparatively narrow, circumscribed egos. One manifestation of this narrowness is *constriction of fantasy* (particularly in Question 6, see also Chapter XIV); this is probably related to the highs' emphasis on "sticking to the facts," to their extraceptiveness, and to their rejection of "imagination" and "emotion."

The highs also differ from the lows in their greater *concreteness of thinking* and in their *less differentiated emotional experience.* Thus, the responses of the highs characteristically refer to specific behavioral acts or situations, while the lows tend, to a greater degree, to describe more subtle experiences and more abstract, generalized situations. On Question 3 ("Great people"), for example, the lows, more than the highs, give the qualities that they admire in a person, with or without specific examples. The same is true for Question 5 ("Worst crimes"). Evidence of the greater complexity and abstractness of the lows has been given in the interview chapters (Part II) and in Chapter VIII (showing negative correlations between ethnocentrism and intelligence). These results are consistent with those showing the highs to be more stereotyped in their ideology (Chapters III, IV, XVI, XVII), more rigidly concrete in their solutions of arithmetical and spatial problems (Rokeach (98)).

The lows tend, in a frustrating situation, to blame themselves (*intrapunitiveness*), the highs to idealize themselves and to see the evil as existing in the external world (*extrapunitiveness*).

Finally, the greater *intraception* of the lows and the great *anti-intraception* of the highs is apparent in their responses to the Projective Questions as well as in the material elicited by the interviews, the T. A. T., and the F scale.

3. *Achievement Values vs. Conventional Values.* This distinction has been essential for the scoring of the Projective Questions. It is important not only because of the difference in the content of the values, but also because the values themselves express significant aspects of the personality dynamics of the two groups. It should be noted first that the two sets of values are not entirely mutually exclusive; few individuals will have only one set or the other. It is, rather, a matter of degree and of primacy. In most individuals one set of values is likely to be primary and most potent, the other to be of secondary importance. An individual who is struggling to decide between these two value orientations is, we believe, essentially struggling to decide, consciously or unconsciously, between conflicting needs and between conflicting conceptions of himself as a total person.

Achievement values found predominantly in the lows place primary emphasis on self-expression. Abstract and open-ended, they always leave room for further development and they can never be defined in terms of simple behavior formulae or rigid rules. Their main emphasis is on long-range goals, and the attainment of a given goal leads always to the formulation of new, higher goals expressing the same basic values. Examples of achievement values, taken from the Projective Question material as well as from the interviews and other material, include the following: Value for scientific, intellectual, and aesthetic achievement, and for understanding for its own sake, regardless of immediate practical application. Creativity is valued above efficiency, constructiveness above practicality; productive living, even if it involves inner conflict, is preferred over good adjustment at the expense of self-expression; richness and intensity of inner experience are valued more than "mere contentment." In personal relationships, as other techniques have shown, there is concern with giving as well as taking, and with the exchange of love rather than the exchange of things. What is particularly important here is that recognition of one's own individuality is the basis for recognition of the individuality of everyone, and for the democratic concept of the dignity of man.[8] These values are expressed ideologically in terms of opposition to all social structures (military, religious, educational, politico-

---

[8] This point has also been made by Fromm (43). His distinction between "humanistic" and "authoritarian" ethics corresponds very closely to the present one between "achievement" and "conventional" values, and is based on a similar attempt to distinguish two broad psychological approaches to man and society.

economic) which are based on the principle of absolute authority, which value power more than love, which engage in group suppression and exploitation, in short, which prevent man from developing his innate potentialities to a maximum degree. Once again we find anti-ethnocentrism as but one facet of a larger psychological framework.

What has been called "conventional values" might also have been called "*conditional values*," since their main function is to place limitations or conditions on the expression of needs rather than to stimulate need-experience. They might also have been called "*authoritarian values*," since they are based on the assumption of conformity to external authority rather than on inner moral responsibility. Whatever the name given, both of the above meanings, as well as others, belong to its definition. The prototypic examples of this value system are the Emily Post book of etiquette, the military "rules of behavior," and certain custom-ridden cultures, literate and nonliterate.[9] The main content of these values, at least for individuals with a strong middle-class identification, deals with conformity and loyalty to ingroup standards.

The difference between achievement values based on inner authority (internalized conscience), and conventional values based on external authority (and thus replaceable when the authority changes), results also in a difference in reaction to value-violations. This is the difference between *guilt* and *shame*.

It would be an exaggeration to state that the lows feel no shame, the highs no guilt. Nevertheless, there is considerable evidence from the Projective Questions, as well as from the ratings of interviews, that guilt is most characteristic of lows, shame of highs. The low categories for Questions 1, 2, 4, and 6 are for the most part concerned with personal violations of achievement values, with practically no reference to "being caught" or to external authority. For the same items there are high categories referring to violations of conventional values most of which require, almost by definition, an external observing and punishing agent. Indeed, the explicit idea of inner conflict in any form is practically lacking from the high responses. Moreover, it is much more common for the lows to refer to their own personal violations of values, whereas the highs refer either to violations by others, or, more often, to events which have, explicitly, neither moral nor motivational significance.[10]

These results are in keeping with the findings reported in earlier chapters that the highs, particularly those who are more conventional and "middle-class," have a punitive but poorly internalized superego. The ego, submitting

[9] See Kardiner (59, 60) and Benedict (15) for nonliterate societies, and Reich (96); these are but a few of many examples.

[10] We should have to predict—and there is already considerable supporting evidence—that studies of specific cultures will show a connection between shame as a predominant emotion, threat of punishment or isolation as a means of discipline in raising children, emphasis on ritual and custom, an authoritarian conception of God, relative lack of achievement values, and ethnocentrism in group relations within the culture and with other cultures. The higher E scale means made by the more ritualized, fundamentalistic religions in our own culture (see Chapter VI) may be cited in support of this hypothesis.

out of fear, must constantly forego conscious, constructive impulse gratification; instead, it finds morally acceptable ways of gaining indirect satisfaction (e.g., aggression by means of ethnocentrism and moral indignation, dependency through submission to powerful authority), and it "cheats" the superego when fear of detection is minimized (e.g., at conventions). Again we have a contradiction in levels: The highs, so moral on the surface, are essentially most concerned with underlying anxiety and with the gratification of impulses which, being ego-alien, have developed but little beyond their primitive, infantile form; whereas the lows, often so rebellious and so opposed to traditional morality on the surface, have more fully internalized moral *principles* and in their emotional functioning are more troubled with moral conflict.

4. *The Handling of Dependency as an Underlying Trend.* General differences in the ego functioning of lows and highs have been discussed above. We may turn now to a particular disposition, namely dependency, and see what light the Projective Questions shed on its differential ego-assimilation in lows and highs. It should be noted that there are certain sex differences here, since the expression of dependency is culturally permitted, even valued, in women, whereas in men it is opposed and inhibited. For convenience the following discussion will focus on high versus low *men*, with the understanding that for women some of these differences are somewhat reversed, while others hold equally well and still others are not found.

Dependency in lows is expressed mainly in the form of *concern with love*; many of their Projective Question responses deal with love-giving (nurturance) and love-seeking (active, focal dependency). They seem highly concerned with emotional exchange in their personal relationships.

Dependency plays a much different role in the personality of high men. It remains for the most part an ego-alien trend which can seldom be expressed directly because it violates the image (ego ideal) of the *normal, masculine man*: rugged, practical, realistic, earthbound, independent, "normally sexual and acquisitive, ready to take an active part in the bitter competition demanded by human nature, and eager to rise to the top of the ladder of success." It is apparent that not all men who have this self-ideal are high with respect to E or personality. Nevertheless, the present results indicate that most high men have this ideal, and that most men with this ideal are high.

Part of the high man's defense against ego-alien passive dependency—it is not the love-seeking dependency of the lows—is the rigid value for work, and anxiety over dependency is expressed in the idea that overwork would drive one nuts (Projective Questions 1 and 4).

If dependency promotes a concern with love in the lows, it promotes a *concern with power* in the highs. One of the more direct forms in which high dependency is expressed is *submission to power figures*. Whereas the ego-assimilated dependency of the lows is expressed in their value for equalitarian relationships and social structures, the ego-alien dependency of the highs leads to the acceptance of absolute authority and to a value for authoritarian forms of social interaction. As shown in Projective Question 3 ("Great people"), what the highs admire most in others is power, strength, authority, rugged masculinity. While the aggressive-assertive needs of authoritarian individuals are the most conspicuous ones, the dependent-submissive needs are equally if not more important. In the Projective Questions, particularly 7 ("Last six months") and 8 ("Awe-inspiring"), it was the highs' deference to authority which was expressed most strongly.

The ego-alien passive dependency of the highs is expressed in another form in Projective Questions 1 ("Moods") and 4 ("Drive nuts"). In Question 1, the most unpleasant moods are those involving a feeling of helplessness and dependency in the face of a threatening or barren environment. The dependency comes to the surface but meets an unwelcome reception in the weak, superego-ridden ego: there are no persons toward whom it can be satisfyingly expressed; there is no differentiated affect to make it an enriching experience; there is only a vague anxiety which is actually based not on the external situation but on a deep inner conflict between the superego and the upsurging primitive dependency. It is as if to express the impulse would be to lose one's masculinity or even to undergo bodily harm. Similar conflicts are expressed in Question 4. Again we find the inability to look inward and the vague rumblings of ego-alien trends, including body anxiety and aggression as well as dependency.

5. *The Handling of Other Trends.* There is evidence that aggression, sex, curiosity, homosexuality, and other trends are handled by highs and lows in ways similar to those discussed above. One additional point should be made regarding aggression. It appears not to have undergone much real socialization in highs but has, rather, remained relatively crude, destructive, punitive, unsoftened by ego-assimilation. If the term "hostility" be used for the aggression found in lows, then the term "destructiveness" seems most appropriate for what exists in highs, especially as revealed in Questions 2 ("Desires"), 5 ("Crimes"), and 8 ("Awe-inspiring").

The results and interpretations discussed above must not be applied in a stereotyped way. It should be understood that, while *most* highs show *most* of the high variables, and similarly for the lows, there are numerous exceptions and numerous variations on the central theme. The personality prototype above was that of the pseudodemocratic high, and other patterns, such as the "fascist leader" or the "psychopath" will be different in many respects. It is believed, nevertheless, that the Projective Question technique has yielded results comparable, and congruent, with those of other techniques, and that it may profitably be used for the study of other personality structures.

PART IV

Qualitative Studies of Ideology

INTRODUCTORY REMARKS

The present volume has so far offered findings from our research ranging from surface ideology to largely unconscious psychological traits of our subjects. The direction of research and the order of presentation were suggested by the nature of the ideological data themselves; they could not be derived solely from external factors, such as economic status, group membership, or religion; but rather the evidence pointed unmistakably to the role played by motivational forces in the personality. However, the study did not move mechanically from the ideological to the psychological; rather, we were constantly aware of the structural unity of the two. It thus seems permissible that we reverse the procedure now and ask: what is the meaning of the subjects' overt opinions and attitudes in the areas covered by the A-S, E, and PEC scales, when they are considered in the light of our psychological findings, particularly those deriving from the F-scale and the clinical sections of the interviews? By answering this question we may come closer to an integration of the various aspects of a study which is centered in the problem of the relationship between ideology and personality.

As was natural, the material for this task was mainly taken from the non-clinical parts of the interviews. Not only did these data promise to yield additional evidence bearing on the major issues discussed thus far, but the wealth of detailed and elaborate statements which our subjects had formulated spontaneously and in their own way, offered numerous psychological leads. There is good reason to believe that the non-clinical sections of the interviews constitute through their inherent structure a link between ideology and personality. However, attention was not limited to this interrelationship; at the same time an attempt was made to obtain a more colorful picture of the various ideologies themselves than was possible as long as we limited ourselves to the standard questionnaires.

Since the data from the questionnaire and from the Thematic Apperception Test and the clinical parts of the interviews had been subjected to thorough statistical treatment, quantification of the present material, though desirable, did not seem necessary. The aim, rather, was to develop for the problem areas under consideration, a phenomenology based on theoretical formulations and illustrated by quotations from the interviews. This procedure, it was hoped, would yield not only more information about the specific structure of the ideologies and the manner in which personality is expressed in them but also a further differentiation of the guiding theoretical concepts themselves.

The advantages of this supplementary procedure are several. It permits us to exploit the richness and concreteness of "live" interviews to a degree otherwise hardly attainable. What is lost for want of strict discipline in interpretation may be gained by flexibility and closeness to the phenomena. Rare or even unique statements may be elucidated by the discussion. Such statements, often of an extreme nature, may throw considerable light on potentialities which lie within supposedly "normal" areas, just as illness helps us to understand health. At the same time, attention to the consistency of the interpretation of these statements with the over-all picture provides a safeguard against arbitrariness.

A subjective or what might be called speculative element has a place in this method, just as it does in psychoanalysis, from which many of our categories have been drawn. If, in places, the analysis seems to jump to conclusions, the interpretations should be regarded as hypotheses for further research, and the continuous interaction of the various methods of the study should be recalled: some of the measured variables discussed in earlier chapters were based on speculations put forward in this part.

In view of the discussions in Chapters III and IV it was not deemed necessary to differentiate between A-S and E in the treatment of the interview material. While the generally close correlation of anti-Semitism and ethnocentrism could be taken for granted on the basis of previous results, more specific accounts of the nature of their interrelation, as well as of certain deviations, were incorporated into the first chapter of the present part (Chapter XVI).

The chapter which discusses various syndromes found in high and low scorers (XIX) is also included in this part. Although from a strictly logical point of view it may not belong here, it seemed nevertheless appropriate to include it, since it is based almost entirely on interview material and focused on the interconnection between ideology and personality. The syndromes evolved in this chapter should be followed up by quantitative investigation.[1]

---

[1] We have not deemed it necessary to establish cross references between interviewees' statements presented here—under interview numbers—and those given in Part II under code numbers (see Chapter X, p. 342). Therefore, some quotations may appear here which have already been given there, in a different connection. However, as twelve of the San Quentin inmates are dealt with as a special group in a later chapter (XXI), a Key linking the interview numbers used here with the fictitious names assigned to them there has been inserted on the bottom of Table 1 (XXI).

CHAPTER XVI

PREJUDICE IN THE INTERVIEW MATERIAL

T. W. Adorno

A. INTRODUCTION

Our study grew out of specific investigations into anti-Semitism. As our work advanced, however, the emphasis gradually shifted. We came to regard it as our main task not to analyze anti-Semitism or any other anti-minority prejudice as a sociopsychological phenomenon *per se,* but rather to examine the relation of antiminority prejudice to broader ideological and characterological patterns. Thus anti-Semitism gradually all but disappeared as a topic of our questionnaire and in our interview schedule it was only one among many topics which had to be covered.

Another investigation, carried through parallel to our research and partly by the same staff members of the Institute of Social Research, i.e., the study on anti-Semitism within labor (57b), concentrated on the question of anti-Semitism, but at the same time was concerned with sociopsychological issues akin to those presented in the present volume. While the bulk of the material to be discussed in this chapter is taken from the section on prejudice of the Berkeley interviews, an attempt was made to utilize, at least in a supplementary form, some of the ideas of the Labor Study as hypotheses for further investigation. This was done as a part of the work carried out in Los Angeles. In collaboration with J. F. Brown and F. Pollock we drew up an additional section of the interview schedule devoted to specific questions about Jews. These questions were derived for the most part from the material gathered through the "screened interviews" of the Labor Study. The aim of this new section of the interview schedule was to see if it was possible to establish certain differential patterns within the general structure of prejudice.

The list of questions follows. Not all of these questions were put to every subject, nor was the exact wording of the questions always the same, but most of the ground marked off by the questions was covered in each case.

List of Questions Pertaining to Jews

Do you think there is a Jewish problem? If yes, in what sense? Do you care about it?

Have you had any experience with Jews? What kind? Do you remember names of persons involved and other specific data?

If not, on what is your opinion based?

Did you have any contrary experiences (or hear about such experiences) with Jewish individuals?

If you had—would it change your opinion? If not, why not?

Can you tell a Jew from other people? How?

What do you know about the Jewish religion?

Are there Christians that are as bad as Jews? Is their percentage as high or higher than the percentage of bad Jews?

How do Jews behave at work? What about the alleged Jewish industriousness?

Is it true that the Jews have an undue influence in movies, radio, literature, and universities?

If yes—what is particularly bad about it? What should be done about it?

Is it true that the Jews have an undue influence in business, politics, labor, etc.?

If yes—what kind of an influence? Should something be done to curb it?

What did the Nazis do to the German Jews? What do you think about it? Is there such a problem here? What would you do to solve it?

What do you blame them most for? Are they: aggressive, bad-mannered; controlling the banks; black marketeers; cheating; Christ killers; clannish; Communists; corrupting; dirty; draft dodgers; exploiters; hiding their identity; too intellectual; Internationalists; overcrowding many jobs; lazy; controlling movies; money-minded; noisy; overassimilative; overbearing; oversexed; looking for privileges; quarrelsome; running the country; too smart; spoiling nice neighborhoods; owning too many stores; undisciplined; unethical against Gentiles; upstarts; shunning hard manual labor; forming a world conspiracy?

Do you favor social discrimination or special legislation?

Shall a Jew be treated as an individual or as a member of a group?

How do your suggestions go along with constitutional rights?

Do you object to personal contacts with individual Jews?

Do you consider Jews more as a nuisance or more as a menace?

Could you imagine yourself marrying a Jew?

Do you like to discuss the Jewish issue?

What would you do if you were a Jew?

Can a Jew ever become a real American?

The additional interview material taught us more about prevailing overt patterns of anti-Semitism than about its inner dynamics. It is probably fair to say that the detailed questions proved most helpful in understanding the phenomena of psychological *conflict* in prejudice—the problems characterized in Chapter V as "pseudo-democratism." Another significant observation has to do with the reactions of our interviewees to the list of "bad Jewish traits" presented to them. Most answers to this list read "all-inclusive," that is to say, very little differentiation takes place. The prejudiced subjects tend to subscribe to any reproach against the Jews, provided they do not have to produce these objections themselves but rather find them pre-established, as if they were commonly accepted. This observation could be interpreted in different ways. Either it may be indicative of the "inner con-sistency" of anti-Semitic ideology, or it may testify to the mental rigidity of our high scorers, and this apart from the fact that the method of multiple choice may itself make for automatic reactions. Although our questionnaire studies gave evidence of marked consistency within anti-Semitic ideology, it would hardly be enough to account for the all-inclusiveness of the present responses. It seems that one must think in terms of automatization, though it is impossible to say conclusively whether this is due to the "high" mentality or to the shortcomings of our procedure. In all probability, the presentation of extreme anti-Semitic statements as if they were no longer disreputable but rather something which can be sensibly discussed, works as a kind of antidote for the superego and may stimulate imitation even in cases where the individual's "own" reactions would be less violent. This consideration may throw some light upon the phenomenon of the whole German people tolerating the most extreme anti-Semitic measures, although it is highly to be doubted that the individuals themselves were more anti-Semitic than our high-scoring subjects. A pragmatic inference to be drawn from this hypoth-esis would be that, in so far as possible, pseudorational discussions of anti-Semitism should be avoided. One might refute factual anti-Semitic state-ments or explain the dynamics responsible for anti-Semitism, but he should not enter the sphere of the "Jewish problem." As things stand now, the acknowledgment of a "Jewish problem," after the European genocide, sug-gests, however subtly, that there might have been some justification for what the Nazis did.

The whole material on ideology has been taken from 63 Los Angeles in-terviews in addition to the pertinent sections of those gathered in Berkeley (see Chapter IX).

It should be stressed that once again the *subjective* aspect is in the fore-ground. The selection of our sample excluded an investigation into the role played by the "object"—that is to say, the Jews—in the formation of preju-dice. We do not deny that the object plays a role, but we devote our atten-tion to the forms of reaction directed towards the Jew, not to the basis of these reactions within the "object." This is due to a hypothesis with which we started and which has been given strong support in Chapter III, namely, that anti-Semitic prejudice has little to do with the qualities of those against whom it is directed. Our interest is centered in the high-scoring subjects.

In organizing the present chapter, we start with the general assumption that the—largely unconscious—hostility resulting from frustration and re-pression and socially diverted from its true object, *needs* a substitute object through which it may obtain a realistic aspect and thus dodge, as it were, more radical manifestations of a blocking of the subject's relationship to reality, e.g., psychosis. This "object" of unconscious destructiveness, far from being a superficial "scapegoat," must have certain characteristics in order to fulfill its role. It must be tangible enough; and yet not *too* tangible, lest it be exploded by its own realism. It must have a sufficient historical backing and appear as an indisputable element of tradition. It must be defined in rigid and well-known stereotypes. Finally, the object must possess features, or at least be capable of being perceived and interpreted in terms of features, which harmonize with the destructive tendencies of the prejudiced subject. Some of these features, such as "clannishness" aid rationalization; others, such as the expression of weakness or masochism, provide psychologically adequate stimuli for destructiveness. There can be hardly any doubt that all these requirements are fulfilled by the phenomenon of the Jew. This is not to say that Jews *must* draw hatred upon themselves, or that there is an absolute historical necessity which makes them, rather than others, the ideal target of social aggressiveness. Suffice it to say that they *can* perform this function in the psychological households of many people. The problem of the "uniqueness" of the Jewish phenomenon and hence of anti-Semitism could be approached only by recourse to a theory which is beyond the scope of this study. Such a theory would neither enumerate a diversity of "factors" nor single out a specific one as "the" cause but rather develop a unified framework within which all the "elements" are linked together consistently. This would amount to nothing less than a theory of modern society as a whole.

We shall first give some evidence of the "functional" character of anti-Semitism, that is to say, its relative independence of the object. Then we shall point out the problem of *cui bono:* anti-Semitism as a device for effortless "orientation" in a cold, alienated, and largely ununderstandable world. As a parallel to our analysis of political and economic ideologies, it will be shown that this "orientation" is achieved by stereotypy. The gap between this stereotypy on the one hand and real experience and the still-accepted standards of democracy on the other, leads to a *conflict* situation, something which is clearly set forth in a number of our interviews. We then take up what appears to be the resolution of this conflict: the underlying anti-Semitism of our cultural climate, keyed to the prejudiced person's own unconscious or preconscious wishes, proves in the more extreme cases to be stronger than either conscience or official democratic values. This leads up to the evidence of the destructive character of anti-Semitic reactions. As remnants of the conflict, there remain traces of sympathy for, or rather "appreciation" of, certain Jewish traits which, however, when viewed more closely, also show negative implications.

Some more specific observations about the structure of anti-Jewish prejudice will be added. Their focal point is the differentiation of anti-Semitism according to the subject's own social identifications. This survey of anti-Semitic features and dynamics will then be supplemented by a few remarks on the attitudes of low-scoring subjects. Finally, we shall offer some evidence of the broader social significance of anti-Semitism: its intrinsic denial of the principles of American democracy.

B. THE "FUNCTIONAL" CHARACTER OF ANTI-SEMITISM

The psychological dynamisms that "call for" the anti-Semitic outlet—most essentially, we believe, the ambivalence of authoritarian and rebellious trends —have been analyzed in detail in other sections of this book. Here we limit ourselves to some extreme but concrete evidence of the fact that anti-Semitism is not so much dependent upon the nature of the object as upon the subject's own psychological wants and needs.

There are a number of cases in which the "functional" character of prejudice is obvious. Here we find subjects who are prejudiced *per se*, but with whom it is relatively accidental against what group their prejudice is directed. We content ourselves with two examples. *5051* is a generally high-scoring man, one of a few Boy Scout leaders. He has strong, though unconscious, fascist leanings. Although anti-Semitic, he tries to mitigate his bias by certain semirational qualifications. Here, the following statement occurs:

"Sometimes we hear that the average Jew is smarter in business than the average white man. I do not believe this. I would hate to believe it. What the Jews should learn is to educate their bad individuals to be more cooperative and agreeable. Actually there is more underhandedness amongst Armenians than there is amongst Jews, but the Armenians aren't nearly as conspicuous and noisy. Mind you, I have known some Jews whom I consider my equal in every way and I like very much."

This is somewhat reminiscent of Poe's famous story about the double murder in the Rue Morgue where the savage cries of an orangutan are mistaken by bystanders as words of all kinds of different foreign languages, to wit, languages particularly strange to each of the listeners who happen to be foreigners themselves. The primary hostile reaction is directed against foreigners *per se*, who are perceived as "uncanny." This infantile fear of the strange is only subsequently "filled up" with the imagery of a specific group, stereotyped and handy for this purpose. The Jews are favorite stand-ins for the child's "bad man." The transference of unconscious fear to the particular object, however, the latter being of a secondary nature only, always maintains an aspect of accidentalness. Thus, as soon as other factors interfere, the aggression may be deflected, at least in part, from the Jews and to another group, preferably one of still greater social distance. Pseudodemocratic ideology and the professed desire to promote militantly what he conceives to be American ideals are marked in our Boy Scout leader, *5051*, and he considers himself not conservative but "predominantly liberal"; hence he tempers his anti-Semitism and anti-Negroism by referring to a third group. He summons the Armenians in order to prove that he is not "prejudiced," but at the same time his formulation is such that the usual anti-Semitic stereotypes can easily be maintained. Even his exoneration of the Jews with regard to their supposed "smartness" is actually a device for the glorification of the ingroup: he hates to think that "we are less smart than they." While anti-Semitism is functional with regard to the object choice on a more superficial level, its deeper determinants still seem to be much more rigid.

An extreme case of what might be called "mobile" prejudice is *M1225a*, of the Maritime School group. Though his questionnaire scores are only medium, the interview shows strong traces of a "manipulative" anti-Semite. The beginning of the minorities section of his interview is as follows:

(What do you think of the race-minority problem?) "I definitely think there is a problem. I'd probably be prejudiced there. Like the Negro situation. They could act more human. . . . It would be less of a problem."

His aggression is absorbed by the Negroes, in the "idiosyncratic" manner that can otherwise be observed among extreme anti-Semites, all of whose aggression appears to be directed against Jews.

"I wouldn't sail on a ship if I had to sail with a Negro. To me, they have an offensive smell. Course, the Chinese say we smell like sheep."

It may be mentioned that a subject of the Labor Study, a Negro woman, complained about the smell of the Jews. The present subject concentrates on the Negroes, exonerating the Jews, though in an equivocal way:

(What about the Jewish problem?) "I don't believe there is much of a problem there. They're too smart to have a problem. Well, they are good business men. (Too much influence?) I believe they have a lot of influence. (In what areas?) Well, motion picture industry. (Do they abuse it?) Well, the thing you hear an awful lot about is help the Jews, help the Jews. But you never hear anything about helping other races or nationalities. (Do they abuse their influence in the movies?) If they do, they do it in such a way that it is not offensive."

Here again, anti-Semitic sterotypy is maintained descriptively whereas the shift of actual hatred to the Negroes—which cannot be accounted for by the course of the interview—affects the superimposed value judgments. The twist with regard to the term "problem" should be noted. By denying the existence of a "Jewish problem," he consciously takes sides with the unbiased. By interpreting the word, however, as meaning "having difficulties," and emphasizing that the Jews are "too smart to *have* a problem," he expresses unwittingly his own rejection. In accordance with his "smartness" theory, his pro-Jewish statements have a rationalistic ring clearly indicative of the subject's ambivalence: all race hatred is "envy" but he leaves little doubt that in his mind there is some reason for this envy, e.g., his acceptance of the myth that the Jews controlled German industry.

This interview points to a way in which our picture of ethnocentrism may be differentiated. Although the correlation between anti-Semitism and anti-Negroism is undoubtedly high, a fact which stands out in our interviews as well as in our questionnaire studies (cf. Chapter IV), this is not to say that prejudice is a single compact mass. Readiness to accept statements hostile to minority groups may well be conceived as a more or less unitary trait, but when, in the interview situation, subjects are allowed to express themselves spontaneously it is not uncommon for one minority more than the others to appear, for the moment at least, as an object of special hatred. This phenomenon may be elucidated by reference to persecution mania which, as has been pointed out frequently, has many structural features in common with anti-Semitism. While the paranoid is beset by an over-all hatred, he nevertheless tends to "pick" his enemy, to molest certain individuals who draw his attention upon themselves: he falls, as it were, negatively in love. Something similar may hold good for the potentially fascist character. As soon as he has achieved a specific and concrete countercathexis, which is indispensable to his fabrication of a social pseudoreality, he may "canalize" his otherwise free-floating aggressiveness and then leave alone other potential objects of persecution. Naturally, these processes come to the fore in the dialectics of the interview rather than in the scales, which hardly allow the subject freely to "express" himself.

It may be added that subjects in our sample find numerous other substitutes for the Jew, such as the Mexicans and the Greeks. The latter, like the Armenians, are liberally endowed with traits otherwise associated with the imagery of the Jew.

One more aspect of the "functional" character of anti-Semitism should be mentioned. We encountered quite frequently members of other minority groups, with strong "conformist" tendencies, who were outspokenly anti-Semitic. Hardly any traces of solidarity among the different outgroups could be found. The pattern is rather one of "shifting the onus," of defamation of other groups in order to put one's own social status in a better light. An example is *5023*, a "psychoneurotic with anxiety state," Mexican by birth:

Being an American of Mexican ancestry, he identifies with the white race and feels "we are superior people." He particularly dislikes the Negroes and completely dislikes Jews. He feels that they are all alike and wants as little as possible to do with them. Full of contradiction as this subject is, it is not surprising to find that he would marry a Jewess if he really loved her. On the other hand he would control both Negroes and Jews and "keep them in their place."

5068 is regarded by the interviewer as representing a "pattern probably quite frequent in second-generation Americans who describe themselves as Italian-Americans." His prejudice is of the politico-fascist brand, distinctly colored by paranoid fantasies:

He is of pure Italian extraction and naturalized here at the time of the first World

War. He is very proud of this extraction and for a long time in the early days of Mussolini was active in Italian-American organizations. He still feels that the war against Italy was very unfortunate. Concerning the other minorities he is quite prejudiced. The Mexicans he feels are enough like the Italians so that if they were educated enough it would be all right. At the present time, however, he feels that they need much education. He believes that the California Japanese were more than correctly handled and that those about whom there is no question should be gradually allowed back. He described the Negro situation as a tough one. He believes there should be definite laws particularly with regard to racial intermarriage and that the color line should also be drawn "regarding where people can live." "Despite what they say, the Southern Negroes are really the happiest ones." "The trouble with Jews is that they are all Communists and for this reason dangerous." His own relations with them have only been fair. In his business relations he says they are "chiselers" and "stick together." Concerning a solution to this problem, he says, "The Jews should actually educate their own. The way the Jews stick together shows that they actually have more prejudice against the Gentiles than the Gentiles have against them." He illustrates this with a long story which I was not able to get in detail about some acquaintance of his who married into a Jewish family and was not allowed to eat off the same dishes with them.

We may mention, furthermore, *5052*, an anti-Semitic man of Spanish-Negro descent, with strong homosexual tendencies. He is a nightclub entertainer, and the interviewer summarizes his impression in the statement that this man wants to say, "I am not a Negro, I am an entertainer." Here the element of social identification in an outcast is clearly responsible for his prejudice.

Finally, reference should be made to a curiosity, the interview of a Turk, otherwise not evaluated because of his somewhat subnormal intelligence. He indulged in violent anti-Semitic diatribes until it came out near the end of the interview that he was Jewish himself. The whole complex of anti-Semitism among minority groups, and among Jews themselves, offers serious problems and deserves a study of its own. Even the casual observations provided by our sample suffice to corroborate the suspicion that those who suffer from social pressure may frequently tend to transfer this pressure onto others rather than to join hands with their fellow victims.

C. THE IMAGINARY FOE

Our examples of the "functional" character of anti-Semitism, and of the relative ease by which prejudice can be switched from one object to another, point in one direction: the hypothesis that prejudice, according to its intrinsic content, is but superficially, if at all, related to the specific nature of its object. We shall now give more direct support for this hypothesis, the relation of which to clinical categories such as stereotypy, incapacity to have "experience," projectivity, and power fantasies is not far to seek. This support is supplied by statements which are either plainly self-contradictory or incompatible with facts and of a manifestly imaginary character. Since the usual "self-contradictions" of the anti-Semite can, however, frequently be explained on the basis that they involve different layers of reality and different psychological urges which are still reconcilable in the over-all "*Weltanschauung*" of the anti-Semite, we concern ourselves here mainly with evidence of imaginary constructs. The fantasies with which we shall deal are so well known from everyday life that their significance for the structure of anti-Semitism can be taken for granted. They are merely highlighted by our research. One might say that these fantasies occur whenever stereotypes "run wild," that is to say, make themselves completely independent from interaction with reality. When these "emancipated" stereotypes are forcibly brought back into relation with reality, blatant distortions appear. The content of the examples of stereotyped fantasy which we collected has to do predominantly with ideas of excessive power attributed to the chosen foe. The disproportion between the relative social weakness of the object and its supposed sinister omnipotence is by itself evidence that the projective mechanism is at work.

We shall first give some examples of omnipotence fantasies projected upon a whole outgroup abstractly, as it were, and then show how the application of such ideas to factual experience comes close to paranoid delusion.

5054, a middle-aged woman with fairly high scores on all the scales, who is greatly concerned with herself and characterized by a "domineering" manner, claims that she has always tried "to see the other side" and even to "fight prejudice on every side." She derives her feelings of tolerance from the contrast with her husband whom she characterized as extremely anti-Jewish (he hates all Jews and makes no exceptions) whereas she is willing to make exceptions. Her actual attitude is described as follows:

> She would not subscribe to a "racist theory," but does not think that the Jews will change much, but rather that they will tend to become "more aggressive." She also believes that "they will eventually run the country, whether we like it or not."

The usual stereotype of undue Jewish influence in politics and economy is inflated to the assertion of threatening over-all domination. It is easy to guess that the countermeasures which such subjects have in mind are no less totalitarian than their persecution ideas, even if they do not dare to say so in so many words.

Similar is case *5061a*, chosen as a mixed case (she is high-middle on E, but low on F and PEC), but actually, as proved by the interview, markedly ethnocentric. In her statement, the vividness of the fantasies about the almighty Jew seems to be equalled by the intensity of her vindictiveness.

> "My relations with the Jews have been anything but pleasant." When asked to be more specific it was impossible for her to name individual incidents. She described them, however, as "pushing everybody about, aggressive, clannish, money-

minded. . . . The Jews are practically taking over the country. They are getting into everything. It is not that they are smarter, but they work so hard to get control. They are all alike." When asked if she did not feel that there were variations in the Jewish temperament as in any other, she said, "No, I don't think so. I think there is something that makes them all stick together and try to hold on to everything. I have Jewish friends and I have tried not to treat them antagonistically, but sooner or later they have also turned out to be aggressive and obnoxious. . . . I think the percentage of very bad Jews is very much greater than the percentage of bad Gentiles. . . . My husband feels exactly the same way on this whole problem. As a matter of fact, I don't go as far as he does. He didn't like many things about Hitler, but he did feel that Hitler did a good job on the Jews. He feels that we will come in this country to a place where we have to do something about it."

Sometimes the projective aspect of the fantasies of Jewish domination comes into the open. Those whose half-conscious wishes culminate in the idea of the abolition of democracy and the rule of the strong, call those antidemocratic whose only hope lies in the maintenance of democratic rights. *5018* is a 32-year-old ex-marine gunnery sergeant who scores high on all the scales. He is suspected by the interviewer of being "somewhat paranoid." He knows "one cannot consider Jews a race, but they are all alike. They have too much power but I guess it's really our fault." This is followed up by the statement:

He would handle the Jews by outlawing them from business domination. He thinks that all others who feel the same could get into business and compete with them and perhaps overcome them, but adds, "it would be better to ship them to Palestine and let them gyp one another. I have had some experiences with them and a few were good soldiers but not very many." The respondent went on to imply that lax democratic methods cannot solve the problem because "they won't co-operate in a democracy."

The implicitly antidemocratic feelings of this subject are evidenced by his speaking derogatorily about lax democratic methods: his blaming the Jews for lack of democratic cooperation is manifestly a rationalization.

One more aspect of unrealistic imagery of the Jew should at least be mentioned. It is the contention that the Jews "are everywhere." Omnipresence sometimes displaces omnipotence, perhaps because no actual "Jewish rule" can be pretended to exist, so that the image-ridden subject has to seek a different outlet for his power fantasy in ideas of dangerous, mysterious ubiquity. This is fused with another psychological element. To the highly prejudiced subject the idea of the total right of the ingroup, and of its tolerating nothing which does not strictly "belong," is all-pervasive. This is projected upon the Jews. Whereas the high scorer apparently cannot stand any "intruder"—ultimately nothing that is not strictly like himself—he sees this totality of presence in those whom he hates and whom he feels justified in exterminating because one otherwise "could not get rid of them." The following example shows the idea of Jewish omnipresence applied to personal experience, thus revealing its proximity to delusion.

6070, a 40-year-old woman, is high-middle on the E scale and particularly vehement about the Jews:

"I don't like Jews. The Jew is always crying. They are taking our country over from us. They are aggressive. They suffer from every lust. Last summer I met the famous musician X, and before I really knew him he wanted me to sign an affidavit to help bring his family into this country. Finally I had to flatly refuse and told him I want no more Jews here. Roosevelt started bringing the Jews into the government, and that is the chief cause of our difficulties today. The Jews arranged it so they were discriminated for in the draft. I favor a legislative discrimination against the Jews along American, not Hitler lines. Everybody knows that the Jews are back of the Communists. This X person almost drove me nuts. I had made the mistake of inviting him to be my guest at my beach club. He arrived with ten other Jews who were uninvited. They always cause trouble. If one gets in a place, he brings two more and those two bring two more."

This quotation is remarkable for more reasons than that it exemplifies the "Jews are everywhere" complex. It is the expression of Jewish *weakness*— that they are "always crying"—which is perverted into ubiquity. The refugee, forced to leave his country, appears as he who *wants* to intrude and to expand over the whole earth, and it is hardly too far-fetched to assume that this imagery is at least partly derived from the fact of persecution itself. Moreover, the quotation gives evidence of a certain ambivalence of the extreme anti-Semite which points in the direction of "negatively falling in love." This woman had *invited* the celebrity to her club, doubtless attracted by his fame, but used the contact, once it had been established, merely in order to personalize her aggressiveness.

Another example of the merging of semipsychotic idiosyncrasies and wild anti-Jewish imagery is the 26-year-old woman, *5004*. She scores high on the F scale and high-middle on E and PEC. Asked about Jewish religion, she produces an answer which partakes of the age-old image of "uncannyness." "I know very little, but I would be afraid to go into a synagogue." This has to be evaluated in relation to her statement about Nazi atrocities:

"I am not particularly sorry because of what the Germans did to the Jews. I feel Jews would do the same type of thing to me."

The persecution fantasy of what the Jews *might* do to her, is used, in authentic paranoid style, as a justification of the genocide committed by the Nazis.

Our last two examples refer to the distortions that occur when experience is viewed through the lens of congealed stereotypy. *M732c* of the Veterans Group, who scores generally high on the scales, shows this pattern of distorted experience with regard to both Negroes and Jews. As to the former:

"You never see a Negro driving (an ordinary car of which subject mentions a number of examples) but only a Cadillac or a Packard. . . . They always dress gaudy. They have that tendency to show off. . . . Since the Negro has that feeling that he isn't up to par, he's always trying to show off. . . . Even though he can't afford it, he will buy an expensive car just to make a show. . . ." Subject mentions that the brightest girl in a class at subject's school happens to be a Negro and he explains her outstandingness in the class in terms of Negro overcompensation for what he seems to be implying is her inherent inferiority.

The assertion about the Negro's Cadillac speaks for itself. As to the story about the student, it indicates in personalized terms the aspect of inescapability inherent in hostile stereotypy. To the prejudiced, the Negro is "dull"; if he meets, however, one of outstanding achievement, it is supposed to be mere overcompensation, the exception that proves the rule. No matter what the Negro is or does, he is condemned.

As to the "Jewish problem":

"As far as being good and shrewd businessmen, that's about all I have to say about *them*. They're *white* people, that's one thing. . . . Of course, they have the Jewish instinct, whatever that is. . . . I've heard they have a business nose. . . . I imagine the Jewish people are more *obsequious*. . . . For example, *somehow* a Jewish barber will entice you to come to *his* chair." Subject elaborates here a definite fantasy of some mysterious influence by Jews. . . . "They're mighty shrewd businessmen, and you don't have much chance" (competing with Jews).

The story about the barber seems to be a retrogression towards early infantile, magical patterns of thinking.

F359, a 48-year-old accountant in a government department, is, according to the interviewer, a cultured and educated woman. This, however, does not keep her from paranoid story-telling as soon as the critical area of race relations, which serves as a kind of free-for-all, is entered. (She is in the high quartile on E, though low on both F and PEC.) Her distortions refer both to Negroes and to Jews:

Subject considers this a very serious problem and she thinks that it is going to get worse. The Negroes are going to get worse. She experienced a riot in Washington; there was shooting; street-car windows were broken, and when a white would get into the Negro section of the car, the shooting would start. The white man would have to lie on the floor. She did not dare to go out at night. One day the Negroes were having a procession and some of them started pushing her off the sidewalk. When she asked them not to push, they looked so insolent that she thought they would start a riot, and her companion said, "Let's get out of here or we will start a riot." A friend of hers told her that she had asked her maid to work on a Thursday, but the maid had refused because she said it was "push and shove" day—the day they shoved the whites off the sidewalk. Another friend of hers in Los Angeles told her not to let her maid use her vacuum cleaner because they tamper with it in such a way as to cause it to tear your rugs. One day she caught the maid using a file on her vacuum cleaner and asked her what she was doing. The maid replied, "Oh, I'm just trying to fix this thing." They just want to get revenge on whites. One cannot give them equal rights yet, they are not ready for it; we will have to educate them first. Subject would not want to sit next to a Negro in a theatre or restaurant. She cited the case of a drugstore man who addressed a Negro janitor, a cleaner, as "Mr." You just can't do that to them or they will say, "Ah'm as good as white folks." (Outcome?) "I think there will be trouble." She expects riots and bloodshed.

(Jews?) "Well, they are to blame too, I think. They just cannot do business straight, they have to be underhanded—truth has no meaning for them in business." (What has been your personal experience?) She cited the case of a friend who is interested in photography and bought some second-hand cameras from pawn shops. One day when he was in one, a woman came in with a set of false teeth. She was told that they were not worth anything (there was some gold in them). Finally, the Jew gave her a few dollars for them. As soon as she had gone out, he turned to the man and said, "She didn't know it, but see that platinum under here?" In other words the teeth were worth many times what he gave for them. Subject's friend did not get gypped because he knew them and called their bluff.

It is often advocated as the best means of improving intercultural relations that as many personal contacts as possible be established between the different groups. While the value of such contacts in some cases of anti-Semitism is to be acknowledged, the material presented in this section argues for certain qualifications, at least in the case of the more extreme patterns of prejudice. There is no simple gap between experience and stereotypy. Stereotypy is a device for looking at things comfortably; since, however, it feeds on deep-lying unconscious sources, the distortions which occur are not to be corrected merely by taking a *real* look. Rather, experience itself is predetermined by stereotypy. The persons whose interviews on minority issues have just been discussed share one decisive trait. Even if brought together with minority group members as different from the stereotype as possible, they will perceive them through the glasses of stereotypy, and will hold against them whatever they are and do. Since this tendency is by no means confined to people who are actually "cranky" (rather, the whole complex of the Jew is a kind of recognized red-light district of legitimatized psychotic distortions), this inaccessibility to experience may not be limited to people of the kind discussed here, but may well operate in much milder cases. This should be taken into account by any well-planned policy of defense. Optimism with regard to the hygienic effects of personal contacts should be discarded. One cannot "correct" stereotypy by experience; he has to reconstitute the capacity for *having* experiences in order to prevent the growth of ideas which are malignant in the most literal, clinical sense.

D. ANTI-SEMITISM FOR WHAT?

It is a basic hypothesis of psychoanalysis that symptoms "make sense" in so far as they fulfill a specific function within the individual's psychological economy—that they are to be regarded, as a rule, as vicarious wish-fulfillments of, or as defenses against, repressed urges. Our previous discussion has shown the irrational aspect of anti-Semitic attitudes and opinions. Since their content is irreconcilable with reality, we are certainly entitled to call them symptoms. But they are symptoms which can hardly be explained by the mechanisms of neurosis; and at the same time, the anti-Semitic individual as such, the potentially fascist character, is certainly not a psychotic. The ultimate theoretical explanation of an entirely irrational symptom which nevertheless does not appear to affect the "normality" of those who show the symptom is beyond the scope of the present research. However, we feel justified in asking the question: *cui bono?* What purposes within the lives of our subjects are served by anti-Semitic ways of thinking? A final answer could be provided only by going back to the primary causes for the establishment and freezing of stereotypes. An approach to such an answer has been set forth in earlier chapters. Here, we limit ourselves to a level closer to the surface of the ego and ask: what does anti-Semitism "give" to the subject within the concrete configurations of his adult experience?

Some of the functions of prejudice may doubtless be called rational. One does not need to conjure up deeper motivations in order to understand the attitude of the farmer who wants to get hold of the property of his Japanese neighbor. One may also call rational the attitude of those who aim at a fascist dictatorship and accept prejudice as part of an over-all platform, though in this case the question of rationality becomes complicated, since neither the goal of such a dictatorship seems to be rational in terms of the individual's interest, nor can the wholesale automatized acceptance of a ready-made formula be called rational either. What we are interested in, for the moment, however, is a problem of a somewhat different order. What good does accrue to the actual adjustment of otherwise "sensible" persons when they subscribe to ideas which have no basis in reality and which we ordinarily associate with maladjustment?

In order to provide a provisional answer to this question, we may anticipate one of the conclusions from our consideration of the political and economic sections of the interview (Chapter XVII): the all-pervasive ignorance and confusion of our subjects when it comes to social matters beyond the range of their most immediate experience. The objectification of social processes, their obedience to intrinsic supra-individual laws, seems to result in an intellectual alienation of the individual from society. This alienation is experienced by the individual as disorientation, with concomitant fear and uncertainty. As will be seen, political stereotypy and personalization can be understood as devices for overcoming this uncomfortable state of affairs. Images of the politician and of the bureaucrat can be understood as signposts of orientation and as projections of the fears created by disorientation. Similar functions seem to be performed by the "irrational" imagery of the Jew. He is, for the highly prejudiced subject, extremely stereotyped; at the same time, he is more personalized than any other bogey in so far as he is not defined by a profession or by his role in social life, but by his human existence as such. For these reasons, as well as for historical ones, he is much better qualified for the psychological function of the "bad man" than the bureaucrats or politicians, who, incidentally, are often but handy substitutes for the real object of hatred, the Jew. The latter's alienness seems to provide the handiest formula for dealing with the alienation of society. Charging the Jews with all existing evils seems to penetrate the darkness of reality like a searchlight and to allow for quick and all-comprising orientation. The less anti-Jewish imagery is related to actual experience and the more it is kept "pure," as it were, from contamination by reality, the less it seems to be exposed to disturbance by the dialectics of experience, which it keeps away through its own rigidity. It is the Great Panacea, providing at once intellectual equilibrium, countercathexis, and a canalization of wishes for a "change."

Anti-Semitic writers and agitators from Chamberlain to Rosenberg and Hitler have always maintained that the existence of the Jews is the *key* to everything. By talking with individuals of fascist leanings, one can learn the psychological implications of this "key" idea. Their more-or-less cryptic hints frequently reveal a kind of sinister pride; they speak as if they were in the know and had solved a riddle otherwise unsolved by mankind (no matter how often their solution has been already expressed). They raise literally or figuratively their forefinger, sometimes with a smile of superior indulgence; they know the answer for everything and present to their partners in discussion the absolute security of those who have cut off the contacts by which any modification of their formula may occur. Probably it is this delusion-like security which casts its spell over those who feel insecure. By his very ignorance or confusion or semi-erudition the anti-Semite can often conquer the position of a profound wizard. The more primitive his drastic formulae are, due to their stereotypy, the more appealing they are at the same time, since they reduce the complicated to the elementary, no matter how the logic of this reduction may work. The superiority thus gained does not remain on the intellectual level. Since the cliché regularly makes the outgroup bad and the ingroup good, the anti-Semitic pattern of orientation offers emotional, narcissistic gratifications which tend to break down the barriers of rational self-criticism.

It is these psychological instruments upon which fascist agitators play incessantly. They would hardly do so if there were no susceptibility for spurious orientation among their listeners and readers. Here we are concerned only with the evidence for such susceptibility among people who are by no means overt fascist followers. We limit ourselves to three nerve points of the pseudocognitive lure of anti-Semitism: the idea that the Jews are a "problem," the assertion that they are all alike, and the claim that Jews can be recognized as such without exception.

The contention that the Jews, or the Negroes, are a "problem" is regularly found in our interviews with prejudiced subjects. We may quote one example picked at random and then briefly discuss the theoretical implications of the "problem" idea.

The prelaw student, *105*, when asked, "What about other groups?" states:

"Well, the Jews are a ticklish problem—not the whole race; there are both good and bad. But there are more bad than good."

The term "problem" is taken over from the sphere of science and is used to give the impression of searching, responsible deliberation. By referring to a problem, one implicitly claims personal aloofness from the matter in question—a kind of detachment and higher objectivity. This, of course, is an excellent rationalization for prejudice. It serves to give the impression that one's attitudes are not motivated subjectively but have resulted from hard thinking and mature experience. The subject who makes use of this device maintains a discursive attitude in the interview; he qualifies, quasi-empirically, what he has to say, and is ready to admit exceptions. Yet these qualifications and exceptions only scratch the surface. As soon as the existence of a "Jewish problem" is admitted, anti-Semitism has won its first surreptitious victory. This is made possible by the equivocal nature of the term itself; it can be both a neutral issue of analysis and, as indicated by the everyday use of the term "problematic" for a dubious character, a negative entity. There is no doubt that the relations between Jews and non-Jews do present a problem in the objective sense of the term, but when "the Jewish problem" is referred to, the emphasis is subtly shifted. While the veneer of objectivity is maintained, the implication is that the *Jews* are the problem, a problem, that is, to the rest of society. It is but one step from this position to the implicit notion that this problem has to be dealt with according to its own special requirements, i.e., the problematic nature of the Jews, and that this will naturally lead outside the bounds of democratic procedure. Moreover, the "problem" calls for a *solution*. As soon as the Jews themselves are stamped as this problem, they are transformed into objects, not only to "judges" of superior insight but also to the perpetrators of *an action;* far from being regarded as subjects, they are treated as terms of a mathematical equation. To call for a "solution of the Jewish problem" results in their being reduced to "material" for manipulation.

It should be added that the "problem" idea, which made deep inroads into public opinion through Nazi propaganda and the Nazi example, is also to be found in the interviews of low-scoring subjects. Here, however, it assumes regularly the aspect of a *protest*. Unprejudiced subjects try to restore the objective, "sociological" meaning of the term, generally insisting on the fact that the so-called "Jewish problem" is actually the problem of the non-Jews. However, the very use of the term may be partially indicative, even with unprejudiced persons, of a certain ambivalence or at least indifference, as in the case of *5047*, who scored low on the E scale but high on F and PEC.

"Yes, I think there is a so-called Jewish problem and a Negro problem, but essentially I believe that it is really a majority problem." He felt that there was a need for more education of the ignorant masses and for improving economic conditions so that there would not be a necessity for seeking a scapegoat. Generally, his understanding of the problems seemed to be quite sound, and he expressed disagreement with anti-Semitism and discrimination against Negroes. However, the manner in which he approached the matter and his tendency to treat it as a purely academic problem seemed to indicate that he was not thoroughly convinced of his statements and was merely using verbal clichés.

The term "problem" itself seems to suggest a too naive idea of common sense justice, following the pattern of democratic compromise in areas where decisions should be made only according to the merits of the case. The man who speaks about the "problem" is easily tempted to say that there are two sides to every problem, with the comfortable consequence that the Jews *must* have done something wrong, if they were exterminated. This pattern of conformist "sensibleness" lends itself very easily to the defense of various kinds of irrationality.

The statement that the Jews are all alike not only dispenses with all disturbing factors but also, by its sweep, gives to the judge the grandiose air of a person who sees the whole without allowing himself to be deflected by petty details—an intellectual leader. At the same time, the "all alike" idea rationalizes the glance at the individual case as a mere specimen of some generality which can be taken care of by general measures which are the more radical, since they call for no exceptions. We give but one example of a case where traces of "knowing better" still survive although the "all alike" idea leads up to the wildest fantasies. *F116* is middle on the E scale, but when the question of the Jews is raised:

(Jews?) "Now this is where I really do have strong feeling. I am not very proud of it. I don't think it is good to be so prejudiced but I can't help it. (What do you dislike about Jews?) Everything. I can't say one good thing for them. (Are there any exceptions?) No, I have never met one single one that was an exception. I used to hope I would. It isn't pleasant to feel the way I do. I would be just as nice and civil as I could, but it would end the same way. They cheat, take advantage. (Is it possible that you know some Jewish people and like them without knowing they are Jews?) Oh no, I don't think any Jew can hide it. I always know them. (How do they look?) Attractive. Very well dressed. And as though they knew exactly what they wanted. (How well have you known Jews?) Well, I never knew any in childhood. In fact, I never knew one until we moved to San Francisco, 10 years ago. He was our landlord. It was terrible. I had a lovely home in Denver and I hated to leave. And here I was stuck in an ugly apartment and he did everything to make it worse. If the rent was due on Sunday, he was there bright and early. After that I knew lots of them. I had Jewish bosses. There are Jews in the bank. They are everywhere—always in the money. My next-door neighbor is a Jew. I decided to be civil. After all, I can't move now and I might as well be neighborly. They borrow our lawn mower. They *say* it is because you can't buy one during the war. But of course lawn mowers cost money. We had a party last week and they called the police. I called her the next day because I suspected them. She said she did it so I asked if she didn't think she should have called me first. She said a man was singing in the yard and woke her baby and she got so upset she called the police. I asked her if she realized that her baby screamed for 3 months after she brought him home from the hospital. Ever since then she has been just grovelling and I hate that even worse."

"Knowing better" is mentioned not infrequently by high scorers: they realize they "should" not think that way, but stick to their prejudice under a kind of compulsion which is apparently stronger than the moral and rational counteragencies available to them. In addition to this phenomenon, there is hardly any aspect of the anti-Semitic syndrome discussed in this chapter which could not be illustrated by this quotation from a truly "all-out," totalitarian anti-Semite. She omits nothing. Her insatiability is indicative of the tremendous libidinous energy she has invested in her Jewish complex. Acting out her anti-Semitism obviously works with her as a wish-fulfillment, both with regard to aggressiveness and with regard to the desire for intellectual superiority as indicated by her cooperation in the present study "in the interests of science." Her personal attitude partakes of that sinister contempt shown by those who feel themselves to be "in the know" with respect to all kinds of dark secrets.

Her most characteristic attitude is one of pessimism—she dismisses many matters with a downward glance, a shrug of the shoulders, and a sigh.

The idea of the "Jew spotter" was introduced in the Labor Study, where it proved to be the most discriminating item. We used it only in a supplementary way, in work with the Los Angeles sample, but there can be no doubt that people who are extreme on A-S will regularly allege that they can recognize Jews at once. This is the most drastic expression of the "orientation" mechanism which we have seen to be so essential a feature of the prejudiced outlook. At the same time, it can frequently be observed that the actual variety of Jews, which could hardly escape notice, leads to a high amount of vagueness with regard to the criteria according to which Jews might be spotted; this vagueness does not, however, interfere with the definiteness of the spotter's claim. One example for this configuration will suffice. It is interesting because of the strange mixture of fantasy and real observation.

5039, a 27-year-old student at the University of Southern California and a war veteran, who scores high on E:

"Yes, I think I can . . . of course, you can't always, I know. But usually they have different features: larger nose, and I think differently shaped faces, more narrow, and different mannerisms. . . . But mainly they talk too much and they have different attitudes. Almost always they will counter a question with another question (gives examples from school); they are freer with criticism; tend to talk in big terms and generally more aggressive—at least I notice that immediately. . . ."

E. TWO KINDS OF JEWS

The stereotypes just discussed have been interpreted as means for pseudo-orientation in an estranged world, and at the same time as devices for "mastering" this world by being able completely to pigeonhole its negative aspects. The "problematizing" attitude puts the resentful person in the position of one who is rationally discriminating; the assertion that all the Jews are alike transposes the "problem" into the realm of systematic and complete knowledge, without a "loophole," as it were; the pretension of being able unfailingly to recognize Jews raises the claim that the subject is actually the judge in matters where the judgment is supposed to have been pronounced once and for all. In addition, there is another stereotype of "orientation" which deserves closer attention because it shows most clearly the "topographical" function and because it crops up spontaneously with great frequency in the interview material. It is even more indicative of the "pseudorational" element in anti-Semitic prejudice than is the manner of speaking about the "Jewish problem." We refer to the standard division of Jews into two groups, the good ones and the bad ones, a division frequently expressed in terms of the "white" Jews and the "kikes." It may be objected that this division cannot be taken as an index of subjective attitudes, since it has its basis in the object itself, namely, the different degrees of Jewish assimilation. We shall be able to demonstrate that this objection does not hold true and that we have to cope with an attitudinal pattern largely independent of the structure of the minority group to which it is applied.

It has been established in previous chapters that the mentality of the prejudiced subject is characterized by thinking in terms of rigidly contrasting ingroups and outgroups. In the stereotype here under consideration, this dichotomy is projected upon the outgroups themselves, or at least upon one particular outgroup. This is partly due no doubt to the automatization of black and white thinking which tends to "cut in two" whatever is being considered. It is also due to the desire to maintain an air of objectivity while expressing one's hostilities, and perhaps even to a mental reservation of the prejudiced person who does not want to deliver himself completely to ways of thinking which he still regards as "forbidden." The "two kinds" stereotype thus has to be viewed as a compromise between antagonistic tendencies within the prejudiced person himself. This would lead to the supposition that people who make this division are rarely *extreme* high scorers; a supposition which seems to be largely borne out by our data. In terms of our "orientation" theory we should expect that the "two kinds" idea serves as a makeshift for bridging the gap between general stereotypy and personal experience. Thus, the "good" outgroup members would be those whom the subject personally knows, whereas the "bad" ones would be those at a greater social distance—a distinction obviously related to the differences between assimilated and nonassimilated sectors of the outgroup. This again is at least partly corroborated, though it will be seen that the "two kinds" idea is in many respects so vague and abstract that it does not even coincide with the division between the known and the unknown. As a device for overcoming stereotypy the "two kinds" concept is spurious because it is thoroughly stereotyped itself.

5007, who scores high on all the scales, comments as follows:

"Most of the Jews I have known have been white Jews, and they are very charming people. Jews are aggressive, clannish, overcrowd nice neighborhoods, and are money-minded. At least the 'non-white Jews.' My experiences have been of two sorts. Some Jews are amongst the most charming and educated people I know. Other experiences have been less friendly. On the whole, I think Jews in the professions are all right, but in commerce they seem to be quite objectionable."

Here it can be seen clearly how the over-all stereotypy, as suggested by the list of "objectionable Jewish traits," struggles with the stereotype of a dichotomy, which in this case represents the more humanitarian trend. It is conceived in terms of acquaintances vs. others, but this is complicated by a second division, that between "professional" Jews (supposedly of higher education and morality) and "business" Jews, who are charged with being ruthless money-makers and cheats.

This, however, is not the classical form of the "two kinds" idea. The latter is expressed, rather, by the above-mentioned Boy Scout leader, *5051*, the man who brings the Armenians into play:

"Now take the Jews. There are good and bad amongst all races. We know that, and we know that Jews are a religion, not a race; but the trouble is that there are two types of Jews. There are the white Jews and the kikes. My pet theory is that the white Jews hate the kikes just as much as we do. I even knew a good Jew who ran a store and threw some kikes out, calling them kikes and saying he didn't want their business."

Research on anti-Semitism among Jews would probably corroborate this "pet" idea. In Germany at least, the "autochthonous" Jews used to discriminate heavily against refugees and immigrants from the East and often enough comforted themselves with the idea that the Nazi policies were directed merely against the "*Ostjuden*." Distinctions of this sort seem to promote gradual persecution of Jews, group by group, with the aid of the smooth rationalization that only those are to be excluded who do not belong anyway. It is a structural element of anti-Semitic persecution that it starts with limited objectives, but goes on and on without being stopped. It is through this structure that the "two kinds" stereotype assumes its sinister aspect. The division between "whites" and "kikes," arbitrary and unjust in itself, invariably turns against the so-called "whites" who become the "kikes" of tomorrow.

Evidence of the independence of the division from its object is offered by the all-around high scorer, *M1229m*, of the Maritime School group, who divides the Jews in a manner employed by other Southerners with regard to the Negroes. Here a certain break between general race prejudice and a relative freedom of more personal attitudes and experiences seems to exist.

(Jewish problem?) "Not a terrific problem. I get along with them. Jews in the South are different from those in the North. Not so grasping in the South. (Daughter marrying a Jew?) O.K.; no problem. Large number of Jewish families in Galveston. No prejudice against Jews in Texas."

This making of private exceptions is sometimes, as by the mildly anti-Semitic radio writer *5003*, expressed as follows:

"He doesn't know about Jews. 'Some of my best friends are Jews.'" In spite of the innumerable jokes, both European and American, about the "some of my best friends" cliché, it survives tenaciously. Apparently it combines felicitously the merits of "human interest"—supposedly personal experience—with a bow to the superego which does not seriously impede the underlying hostility.

Occasionally the concessions made to personal acquaintances are explained by the interspersion of racial theories, and thus a mildly paranoid touch is added. An example is the generally "high" woman, *F109:*

Father Scotch-Irish, mother English-Irish. Subject is not identified with any of these. "I have an age-old feeling against Jews, some against Negroes. Jews stick together, are out for money; they gyp you. Jews are in big businesses. It seems they will be running the country before long. I know some people of Jewish descent who are very nice, but they're not full-blooded Jews. Jews have large noses, are slight in stature, little sly Jews. The women have dark hair, dark eyes, are sort of loud."

This girl student, by the way, to whom the "education" idea is all-important, is among those who show traces of bad conscience.

Subject knows she's prejudiced; she thinks she needs educating too, by working with people of different races.

The intrinsic weakness of the "best friend" idea, which simulates human experience without truly expressing it, comes into the open in the following quotation, where the line between the friend and the "kikes" is drawn in such a way that even the "friend" is not fully admitted.

(Jews?) "There are Jews and Jews. I have a very good girl friend who is a Jew—never enters into our relationship except that she is in a Jewish sorority. (Would you want her in your sorority?) Well . . . (pause) . . . I don't think I'd have any objections. (Would you let in all Jewish girls?) No. One Jew is alright but you get a whole mob and . . . ! (What happens?) They get into anything and they'll control it—they'll group together for their own interests—the kike Jew is as dishonest as they come. Find them on Fillmore Street in San Francisco. I have had no experience with kike Jews. I think that's created in my family. Father feels strongly against them—I don't know why. (Nazis?) That's unnecessary—they have a right to exist—no reason for excluding them as long as they don't try to overstep the rights of others. I knew a lot of Jews in high school. They kept pretty much to themselves. Don't think I'm echoing. I would like Jews as long as they don't reflect typical Jewish qualities. Typical Jewish nose, mouth, voice. The presence of a

Jew creates feelings of tension. Squeaky voice, long, pointed nose. Couldn't name anti-Semitic groups in this country but think they exist."

Particular attention should be called to the statement of this girl, described by the interviewer as being "tight all over," that the presence of a Jew creates feelings of tension. There is reason to believe that this is a common experience. It would hardly suffice to attribute this uneasiness solely to repressed guilt feelings, or to the effect of some "strangeness" as such. At least the concrete aspects of this strangeness in social contacts needs further elucidation. We venture the hypothesis that it is due to a certain discomfort and uneasiness on the Jew's own part in non-Jewish company, and on a certain antagonism of the Jews, deeply rooted in history, against "genial" conviviality and harmless abandonment of oneself in order to enjoy the moment. Since this may be one concrete factor making for anti-Semitism, independent of traditional stereotypy, this whole complex should be followed up most carefully in future research.

As to the evidence for our assertion that the "two kinds" idea is not object-bound but rather a structural psychological pattern, we limit ourselves to two examples. The student nurse, *5013*, whose scale scores are generally high:

Feels towards the Japanese and the Mexicans and Negroes very much as she does toward the Jews. In all cases she holds to a sort of bifurcation theory, that is, that there are good Japanese and that they should be allowed to return to California, but there are bad ones and they should not. The Mexicans also fall into two groups, as do the Negroes. When it is pointed out to her that people of her own extraction probably also fall into good and bad groups, she admits this but feels that the line between the good and the bad is not as great in her case. She feels that the Negro problem is probably of greater importance than the other minorities but says that she speaks at the hospital to the colored nurses and doctors. At this point she related a long anecdote about taking care of a female Negro patient who had told her that the Negroes had brought their problems on themselves by aspiring to equality with the whites. She feels that this was a very wise Negress and agrees with her.

In the case of Southerners, the "two kinds" idea is frequently applied to the Negroes, those in the South being praised, and those who went away being denounced for demanding an equality to which they were not entitled. In so far as the Southern "white man's nigger" is more subservient and a better object of exploitation in the eyes of these subjects, this attitude, with its patriarchal and feudalistic rationalizations, can be called semirealistic. But the construct of "two kinds of Negroes" often results in quite a different connotation, as in the case of *F340a*. She is high on F and PEC and middle on E.

"The Negroes are getting so arrogant now, they come to the employment office and say they don't like this kind of a job and that kind of a job. However, there are some who are employed at the employment office and they are very nice and intelligent. There are nice ones and bad ones among us. The Negroes who have always lived in Oakland are all right; they don't know what to do with all those who are coming in from the South either. They all carry knives; if you do something they don't like, they 'will get even with you, they will slice you up.' "

Here, the "two kinds" idea results in plain persecution fantasies.

F. THE ANTI-SEMITE'S DILEMMA

If anti-Semitism is a "symptom" which fulfills an "economic" function within the subject's psychology, one is led to postulate that this symptom is not simply "there," as a mere expression of what the subject happens to be, but that it is the outcome of a conflict. It owes its very irrationality to psychological dynamics which force the individual, at least in certain areas, to abandon the reality principle. The conception of prejudice as a symptom resulting from a conflict has been elucidated in earlier chapters. Here, we are concerned not so much with the clinical evidence of conflict determinants as with the traces of conflict within the phenomenon of anti-Semitism itself. Some evidence bearing on this point has already been presented in the last sections. The "problem" idea as well as the dichotomy applied to the outgroup represent a kind of compromise between underlying urges and hostile stereotypes on the one hand, and the demands of conscience and the weight of concrete experience on the other. The subject who "discusses" the Jews usually wants to maintain some sense of proportion, at least formally, even though the content of his rational considerations is spurious and his supposed insight itself is warped by the very same instinctual urges which it is called upon to check.

The standard form under which conflict appears in statements of high-scoring subjects is, as indicated above, "I shouldn't, but. . . ." This formula is the result of a remarkable displacement. It has been pointed out that the anti-Semite is torn between negative stereotypy and personal experiences which contradict this stereotypy.[1] As soon as the subject reflects, however, upon his own attitude, the relation between stereotypy and experience appears in reverse. He regards tolerance as the general law, as the stereotype as it were, and personalizes his own stereotyped hostility, presenting it as the inescapable result either of experience or of idiosyncrasies which are stronger than he is himself. This can be accounted for partly by the officially prevailing democratic ideology which stamps prejudice as something wrong. It has also to be considered that the superego, being constituted as the psychological agency of society within the individual, regularly assumes an aspect of universality which easily appears to the subject, driven by wishes for in-

[1] The most drastic evidence for this hypothesis is, of course, the habit of differentiating between those Jews with whom the subject is acquainted, and who are "good," and the rest of them, who are the "kikes." In certain cases this contradiction is both concretized and cleared up etiologically. We refer here to case 5057, discussed in detail in Chapter XIX, where the subject's bias is practically explained by himself as the outcome of resentment aroused by a childhood experience with a Jewish delicatessen man.

stinctual gratification, as "rigid law." This, however, hardly tells the whole story. The discrepancy between experience and stereotype is put into the service of the prejudiced attitude. The prejudiced subject is dimly aware that the content of the stereotype is imaginary and that his own experience represents truth. Yet, for deeper psychological reasons, he wants to stick to the stereotype. This he achieves by transforming the latter into an expression of his personality and the antistereotypical elements into an abstract obligation. This displacement is enhanced by his innermost conviction that the supposed stereotypes of tolerance are not so strong socially as he pretends. He realizes that while he appears to rebel against the slogans of democracy and equality, for reasons that are strictly personal, he is actually backed by powerful social trends. And yet he will claim, at the same time, that he acts as a sincere and independent person who does not care what others think. Moreover, he relies on the idea that one's own feelings are always stronger than conventions, that he simply has to follow them, and that his prejudice is a kind of fatality which cannot be changed. This seems to be a common pattern by which the anti-Semite's conflict situation is rationalized in a way favorable to prejudice.

This pattern manifests itself objectively in a characteristic contradiction: that between general pretensions of being unbiased, and prejudiced statements as soon as specific issues are raised. *5056*, a 29-year-old housewife, with high scores on all the scales,

Stated that she and her husband have no particular dislike for *any* group of people. (This statement is interesting when contrasted with her very high E-score, and with the statements which follow.) "The Negro, however, should be kept with his own people. I would not want my niece marrying a Negro, and I would not want Negro neighbors." To subject there is quite a Negro problem—"it is probably the most important minority problem." She prefers "the way things are in the South; the Negroes seem so happy down there. Actually, they should have a separate state. This doesn't mean that we should snub them. The separate state would be very good, because, although we should govern them, they could run it themselves."

The underlying conflict could not be expressed more authentically than in the contradiction contained in the last statement. The subject tries to display an unbiased attitude toward Jews:

It is interesting to note that she objected rather strongly to discussing the Jews and the Negroes in the same context and protested when they were presented contiguously in the interview. "I would just as soon have Jews around—in fact, I have some Jewish friends. Some are overbearing, but then some Gentiles are overbearing too."

But as soon as it comes to her "personal" attitude, she falls for the stereotype and resolves the conflict by an aloofness which amounts for all practical purposes to an endorsement of anti-Semitism:

When asked about Jewish traits, she first mentioned "the Jewish nose." In addition, she believes Jews have a certain set of personality traits all their own, which will never change. "They want to argue all the time; some are greedy (though some aren't, in fact, some are generous); they talk with their hands and are dramatic in their speech." She believes the dislike of the Jews is increasing, to which trend she objects. "Think we're being selfish when we act that way, just as we accuse the Jews of being." She doesn't like to hear attacks on the Jews, but she wouldn't defend them by argument. This seems to be both a function of her dislike for argumentation as well as a certain attitude of noninvolvement in or detachment from the whole question of anti-Semitism.

The subjective mirroring of the conflict between stereotype and experience in reverse, resulting in rigidity of the supposed experience, is clearly exemplified in the statements of *M1230a*, a middle scorer of the Maritime School group:

(What do you think of the problem of racial minorities?) "Well, for the foreigners coming in, it's quite a question. This is supposed to be a melting pot. But shouldn't let too many of them in. . . . And then the Negro problem. . . . I try to be liberal, but I was raised in a Jim Crow state. . . . I don't think I would ever fall in with giving the Negroes equal rights in every way. . . . And yet, foreigners, you have a natural dislike for them. Yet, all of us were once foreigners. . . ."

The anti-Semite's dilemma may be epitomized by quoting verbatim the following statements of the girl student *5005*, who is high on both the E and F scales, but low on PEC.

"I don't think there should be a Jewish problem. People should not be discriminated against, but judged on their individual merits. I don't like it to be called a problem. Certainly I'm against prejudice. Jews are aggressive, bad-mannered, clannish, intellectual, clean, overcrowd neighborhoods, noisy, and oversexed. I will admit that my opinion is not based on much contact, however; I hear these things all the time. There are very few Jewish students in my school, and I have already referred to my good contact with the one girl."

Here the contradiction between judgment and experience is so striking that the existence of prejudice can be accounted for only by strong psychological urges.

G. PROSECUTOR AS JUDGE

In terms of ideology, the anti-Semite's conflict is between the current, culturally "approved" stereotypes of prejudice and the officially prevailing standards of democracy and human equality. Viewed psychologically, the conflict is between certain foreconscious or repressed id tendencies on the one hand and the superego, or its more or less externalized, conventional substitute, on the other. It is hard to predict or even to explain satisfactorily, on the basis of our data, which way this conflict will be decided in each individual case, though we may hypothesize that as soon as prejudice in any amount is allowed to enter a person's manifest ways of thinking, the scales weigh heavily in favor of an ever-increasing expansion of his prejudice. We are furthermore entitled to expect this result of the conflict in all cases where the potentially fascist personality syndrome is established. If the conflict within the individual has been decided *against* the Jews, the decision itself is almost without exception rationalized moralistically. It is as if the internal powers of prejudice, after the defeat of the countertendencies, would consummate their victory by taking the opposing energies, which they have defeated, into their own service. The superego becomes the spokesman of the id, as it were—a dynamic configuration, incidentally, which is not altogether new to psychoanalysis. We might call the urges expressing themselves in anti-Semitism the prosecutor, and conscience the judge, within the personality, and say that the two are fused. The Jews have to face, in the prejudiced personality, the parody of a trial. This is part of the psychological explanation of why the chances of the Jews making a successful defense against the prejudiced personality are so slim. It may be noted that the judiciary practice in Nazi Germany followed exactly the same pattern, that the Jews were never given a chance, in the Third Reich, to speak for their own cause, either in private law suits or collectively. It will be seen that the expropriation of the superego by the fascist character, with underlying unconscious guilt feelings which must be violently silenced at any price, contributes decisively to the transformation of "cultural discrimination" into an insatiably hostile attitude feeding upon destructive urges.

There is a clear index of the conquest of the superego by anti-Semitic ideology: the assertion that the responsibility for everything the Jews have to suffer, and more particularly, for the genocide committed by the Nazis, rests with the victims rather than with their persecutors. The anti-Semite avails himself of a cliché which seems to make this idea acceptable once and for all: that the Jews "brought it on themselves" no matter what "it" may be. *M107*, the young man who marked every question on the questionnaire scale either +3 or —3 but averaged high on all three scales, is a good example of this pattern of rationalization, following the dubious logic of "where there is smoke there must be fire":

"I never understood why Hitler was so brutal toward them. There must have been some reason for it, something to provoke it. Some say he had to show his authority, but I doubt it. I suspect the Jews contributed a great deal to it."

How the moralistic construct of Jewish responsibility leads to a complete reversal between victim and murderer is strikingly demonstrated by one subject, *5064*, another one of the Los Angeles Boy Scout leaders and a butcher by trade. He scores high on both the E and F scale although lower on PEC. While still officially condemning the German atrocities, he makes a surprising suggestion:

"No American can approve of what the Nazis did to the Jews. I really hope that the Jews will do something about it before we come to any such position here. The solution is in the education, particularly of the minority."

This type of mental perversion seems to utilize an idea taken from the stock of traditional liberalistic wisdom: God helps those who help themselves. The Jews are in jeopardy, therefore it is up to the Jews. In a cultural climate where success has come to be a major measuring rod for any value, the precarious situation of the Jews works as an argument against them. The affinity of this attitude and the "no pity for the poor" theme, to be discussed in the chapter on politics, can hardly be overlooked. The same line of thought occurs in the interview of another Boy Scout leader, the Austrian-born and somewhat over-Americanized 55-year-old *5044*, who is consistently high on all scales:

"The Jews should take the lead rather than the Gentiles. After all, the Jews are the ones who may get into serious trouble. They shouldn't walk on other people's feet."

While the Jews "bring it upon themselves," the Nazis' extermination policy is either justified or regarded as a Jewish exaggeration itself, in spite of all the evidence to the contrary. The high-scoring man, *M359*, departmental manager for a leather company, is one of those who have "a large number of very close Jewish friends." Despite this he is high on both the E and PEC scales, although lower on F. Nor does it prevent the following interview episode:

(Nazi treatment?) "Unable to convince myself that the treatment was limited to Jews. This seems to me to be Jewish propaganda to solicit sympathy and help by overemphasizing their hardships, though I have no sympathy for the Nazi's treatment of *peoples*."

The mercilessness accompanying the semi-apologetic attitude towards the Nazis can be seen in this subject's pseudorational statements on Palestine: while apparently wishing to "give the Jews a chance," he simultaneously excludes any prospects of success by referring to the Jews' supposedly unchangeably bad nature:

(Solution?) "Sending them to Palestine is silly because it's not big enough. A good idea to have a country of their own, but big enough so that they can go ahead with their daily pursuits in a normal way, but the Jews would not be happy. They are only happy to have others work for them."

The explanatory idea that the "Jews brought it upon themselves" is used as a rationalization for destructive wishes which otherwise would not be allowed to pass the censorship of the ego. In some cases this is disguised as a statement of fact; e.g., by *5012*, a 21-year-old discharged naval petty officer, who scores high on all scales:

"I don't want anything to do with them. They are a nuisance, but not a menace. They will get whatever they deserve as a result of their behavior."

The high-scoring woman *F103*, however, who used to be a social welfare student but has changed to decorative art, lets the cat out of the bag:

"I don't blame the Nazis at all for what they did to the Jews. That sounds terrible, I know, but if the Jews acted the way they do here, I don't blame them. I've never had any bad personal experiences with Jews, it's just the way they act. Don't help your fellow man; that's their creed."

Here the interrelation between death-wish and moralistic rationalization becomes truly terrifying. Particularly noteworthy is the subject's underscoring of her own irrationality, in spite of her rationalization concerning the Jews' innate badness. Her confession that she never had any bad experiences with Jews high-lights an important aspect of the whole phenomenon of anti-Semitic extremism. It is the fantastic disproportion between the Jewish "guilt" —even as conceived by the anti-Semite himself—and the judgment that is pronounced. In previous sections the role played by the theme of "exchange" in the mentality of the prejudiced person has been discussed. Frequently our high-scoring subjects complain that they never get their full share, that they are being exploited by everybody. This sense of victimization goes hand in hand with very strong underlying possessive and appropriative desires. Accordingly, when the subjects speak about the "justice" to be meted out to the Jews they express their own desire for an unjust state of affairs in which the exchange of equivalents has been replaced by distribution according to unmediated and irrational power relationships. This is expressed negatively towards the Jews: they should get *more* punishment—infinitely more—than they "deserve." Ordinarily, it would never occur even to a very aggressive person that somebody who is bad-mannered or even a cheat should be punished by death. Where the Jews are concerned, however, the transition from accusations which are not only flimsy but unsubstantial even if they were true, to suggestions of the severest kinds of treatment seems to work quite smoothly. This is indicative of one of the most pernicious features of the potentially fascist character.

The logical property of stereotypes, that is, their all-comprehensiveness which allows for no deviations, is not only well adapted to meet certain requirements of the prejudiced outlook; it is, by itself, an expression of a psychological trait which probably could be fully understood only in connection with the theory of paranoia and the paranoid "system" which always tends to include everything, to tolerate nothing which cannot be identified by the subject's formula. The extremely prejudiced person tends toward "psychological totalitarianism," something which seems to be almost a microcosmic image of the totalitarian state at which he aims. Nothing can be left untouched, as it were; everything must be made "equal" to the ego-ideal of a rigidly conceived and hypostatized ingroup. The outgroup, the chosen foe, represents an eternal challenge. As long as anything different survives, the fascist character feels threatened, no matter how weak the other being may be. It is as if the anti-Semite could not sleep quietly until he has transformed the whole world into the very same paranoid system by which he is beset: the Nazis went far beyond their official anti-Semitic program. This mechanism makes for the complete disproportion between "guilt" and punishment. The extreme anti-Semite simply cannot stop. By a logic of his own, which is of an archaic nature, much closer to associational transitions than to discursive inferences, he reaches, after having started from relatively mild accusations, the wildest conclusions, tantamount in the last analysis to the pronouncement of death sentences against those whom he literally "cannot stand." This mechanism was encountered in the "screened" interviews of the Labor Study where subjects frequently "talked themselves into anti-Semitism." Our interview schedule, more strictly standardized, prevented us from catching the latter phenomenon. Yet we have striking testimony of the disproportion between guilt and punishment in some of our cases. It is here that the "expropriation" of the superego by the anti-Semite's punitive moralism obtains its full significance. This removes the last obstacle to psychological totalitarianism. There are no inhibitions left by which the associational crescendo of destructive ideas could be checked. Hatred is reproduced and enhanced in an almost automatized, compulsive manner which is both utterly detached from the reality of the object and completely alien to the ego. It may be added that, viewed sociologically, the disproportion between guilt and punishment shows that to the extreme anti-Semite the whole idea of rational law has become a sham even though he dwells on orderliness and legalitarian niceties. He is ready to sacrifice his own ideology of equivalents as soon as he has the power to get the major share for himself. Psychologically, the idea of eternal Jewish guilt can be understood as a projection of the prejudiced person's own repressed guilt feelings; ideologically, it is a mere epiphenomenon, a rationalization in the strictest sense. In the extreme case, the psychological focal point is the wish to kill the object of his hatred. It is only afterwards that he looks for reasons why the Jews "must" be killed, and these reasons can never suffice fully to justify his extermination fantasies. This, however, does not "cure" the anti-Semite, once he has succeeded in expropriating his conscience. The disproportion between the guilt and the punishment induces him, rather, to pursue his hatred beyond any limits and thus to prove to himself and to others that he *must* be right. This is the ultimate function of ideas such as "the Jews brought it upon themselves" or the more generalized formula "there must be something to it." The extreme anti-Semite silences the remnants of his own conscience by the extremeness of his attitude. He seems to terrorize himself even while he terrorizes others.

The sham trial of rationalizations put on by the prejudiced person sometimes makes for a kind of defense of the Jews. But this psychological defense is all too reminiscent of the technique of the Nazi courts. It is permitted only in order to satisfy the formalized and hollow wish for legality, the empty shell of expropriated conscience. The defense must always remain impotent. Whatever good is said about the Jews sounds like an ironical or hypocritical variation of standard blames. Thus, reference is frequently made to the mythical "good family life" of the Jews, a comment which, however thinly, veils the accusation of conspiratorial clannishness; and this is accompanied by insincere protestations of envy of these Jewish qualities, the implication being that the anti-Semitic subject gets the worst deal in life because his noble nature prevents him from the practice of connivance. Still another type of mock-defense can be observed in our interviews. It is the assertion that the Jews are so clever; that they are "smarter" than the Gentiles, and that one has to admire them on this account. The mechanism at work here involves a double set of values which makes itself felt throughout contemporary culture. On the one hand, there are the "ideals" of magnanimity, unselfishness, justice, and love to which one has to pay lip service. On the other hand, there are the standards of achievement, success, and status which one has to follow in one's actual life. This double set of values is applied to the Jews in reverse, as it were. They are praised for their supposed or actual living up to the standards which the anti-Semite himself actually follows and simultaneously, they are condemned for their violation of the very same moral code of which he has successfully rid himself. The phraseology of conscience is used in order to take back the moral credit given to the chosen foe in order to appease one's own conscience. Even the praise apportioned to the Jews is used as supporting evidence for their pre-established guilt.

The point being developed here, as well as other features of the prejudiced mentality, is illustrated by the following description of *5039*, a 27-year-old veteran student, high on E and middle on the other scales, who is described by the interviewer as a "rather egocentric person."

In rebelling against his father's teachings, he has dissociated himself from the church, but nevertheless strongly identifies himself as a Gentile in contrast to the Jews. He explained this on the basis of having grown up in a neighborhood . . . where he was the only Gentile in a Jewish community and where he was made to feel that he was an "outsider." He feels that there is a basic conflict in the religious teachings and upbringing of Christians as against Jews, which is largely responsible for the incompatibility of the two groups. He stated that the Christian religion stresses the pacifistic teaching of "turning the other cheek," thus causing youth to become "maladjusted and submissive," whereas the Jewish religion spurs youth to achievement and aggression, on the basis that "your fathers have suffered, therefore it is now up to you to prove yourself." Therefore, he feels that a truly religious Christian is bound to be "outdone" by ambitious and aggressive Jews. . . . He did not seem aware that he was generalizing from his own particular experience and environment.

That the objectivity of these reflections about the supposedly realistic education instigated by Judaism is a mere fake and actually serves as a pretext for boundless hostility is shown by this subject's answer to the specific question referring to Hitler's atrocities:

"Well, if I had been in Germany, I think I would have done the same. . . . I suppose I could have been a Nazi. . . . I think discipline is a good thing. . . ."

Whereas this subject's statements on Jewish smartness are overtly hostile, and limited to the imagined disadvantages of Gentiles in competition with Jews, the smartness idea is sometimes expressed with an air of mock humbleness. An example is afforded by the high-scoring man $M104$, a former engineering student who has changed to law:

He said "you hear that our country is run by Jewish capitalists, that Jewish capitalists wield all the power here. If this is true, it means that our own people aren't smart enough. If our people know the way the Jews are, and can't do the same thing, more power to the Jews. If they know how the Jews work, they should be able to do it just as well." He doesn't "want to admit that the others aren't as smart as the Jews, and that's what it would mean if this country is run by Jewish capitalists. If they're smarter than we are, let them run it."

But the magnanimous ending of the quotation has sinister implications. A tiny shift of emphasis suffices to transform it into the idea that the Jews, because of their sinister cleverness, run the country, that we have to get rid of them and that, since Jewish smartness makes constitutional procedures ineffective, this can be done only by violent means. That the idea of Jewish omnipotence through smartness is a mere projection becomes nowhere clearer than in the case of the consistently high-scoring woman $F105$. She is crippled as a result of infantile paralysis in early childhood. She consummates the idea of Jewish smartness—of the Jews "taking over the business affairs of the nation" —by the expectation of a bloody uprising of the Jews which is but a superficially veiled projection of her own wish for anti-Jewish pogroms:

"The white people have decided that we're the thing—the white vs. black and yellow. I think there's going to be a Jewish uprising after the war. I'm not against the Jews. Those I've had contact with were very nice. Of course, I've seen some I didn't like, too. (What didn't you like about them?) They're loud and they seem to like attention. They're always trying to be at the top of something. I've heard stories about how they'll stab friends in the back, etc., but I have still to see to believe. (Uprising?) I think there will be bloodshed over it in this country. (Do you think it will be justified?) There's no doubt that they're taking over the business affairs of the nation. I don't think it's right that refugees should be taken care of the way they are. I think they should take care of their own problems."

It is noteworthy that when coming into the open with the "bloodshed" idea, this subject does not state clearly whose blood is going to be spilled. While putting the blame for the riots she wishes for upon nonexistent Jewish rioters, she leaves it open that it will be the Jews, after all, who are going to be killed. There may be more to this, however. To extreme anti-Semites the idea of bloodshed seems to become independent, an end in itself as it were.

On the deepest level, they do not differentiate so very strictly between subject and object. The underlying destructive urge pertains both to the enemy and to oneself. Destructiveness is truly "totalitarian."

As a summary of the structure of anti-Semitic extremism dealt with in this section, we present in some detail the comments on the Jews of the only interviewee who openly endorses the idea of genocide. This is *5006*, a dentistry student and contractor who scores high throughout the questionnaire. He suffers from color-blindness and from psychogenic sexual impotence, determined, according to the interviewer, by a severe Oedipus complex. His radical wishes for the extermination of the Jews are probably conditioned by severe, early childhood traumata: projections of his own castration fear. His exaggerated ingroup identification seems to be concomitant with an underlying feeling of weakness: he simply does not wish to become acquainted with what is different, apparently because he deems it dangerous.

He is a native-born American, and his grandfather was brought to this country at four. He has never been out of America, nor does he want to go out. Once he went to Tijuana and "that was enough." He has great pride in being an American.

To him, the minorities are characterized, above all, by their potential strength: "The trouble with the Jews is that they are too strong." The strength of the outgroups is expressed in symbols of potency—fertility and money:

"Of course, there is a problem. The Negroes produce so rapidly that they will populate the world, while the Jews get all of the money."

As to the basis of his anti-Semitism, he has the following to say:

"I have never had any good experiences with them." (This is qualified in a second interview where he remembers, as a college athlete, being taken on a private yacht to Catalina by Jews who were "very nice.") They have invariably attempted to cheat him and his family in business and are in every way inconsiderate. He tells a long story which I was not able to get verbatim about buying a fur coat as a Christmas present for his mother, at which time the Jewish salesman misread the price tag, quoting a price $100 cheaper than it actually was. They closed the sale and he insisted on taking the coat after the salesman's error had been noticed. This gave him considerable satisfaction, and he said, "That was a case where I out-Jewed a Jew."

His references to bad experiences are quite vague except in the case where he "out-Jewed the Jew"—another indication of the projective character of the "smartness" theme. The qualification in favor of the rich Jewish yacht owner shows the complication of anti-Semitism through class consciousness, particularly in cases of such strong upward social mobility as that found in this subject. It took even the Nazis some time to convince themselves, their followers, and the wealthiest Jewish groups that the latter should share the fate of poor cattle dealers and immigrants from Eastern Europe.

The tenets of individualism are altered by this subject as follows:

"They should be treated, I suppose, like individuals; but after all, they are all alike."

Of course, "everyone can tell a Jew." The distinction between in- and out-group obtains an almost metaphysical weight: even the imaginary possibility of the disappearance of the dichotomy is excluded:

"I couldn't be a Jew."

As to the relation between guilt and punishment and its outcome, he finds a formula which cannot be surpassed:

"I think what Hitler did to the Jews was all right. When I was having trouble with a competing contractor, I often thought, I wish Hitler would come here. No, I don't favor discrimination by legislation. I think the time will come when we will have to kill the bastards."

H. THE MISFIT BOURGEOIS

Our analysis has led us to the extreme consequence of anti-Semitism, the overt wish for the extermination of the Jews. The extremist's superego has been transformed into an extrapunitive agency of unbridled aggression. We have seen that this consequence consummates the intrinsic irrationality of anti-Semitism by establishing a complete disproportion between the "guilt" and the punishment of the chosen victim. Anti-Semitism, however, does not exhaust itself in the old formula by which it is characterized in Lessing's *Nathan der Weise*, "*tut nichts, der Jude wird verbrannt*"—the Jew is going to be burnt anyway, no matter how things are, or what could be said in his favor. Irrational and merciless wholesale condemnation is kept alive by the maintenance of a small number of highly stereotyped reproaches of the Jews which, while largely irrational themselves, give a mock semblance of justification to the death sentence. By constructing the nature of the Jew as unalterably bad, as innately corrupt, any possibility of change and reconciliation seems to be excluded. The more invariant the negative qualities of the Jew appear to be, the more they tend to leave open only one way of "solution": the eradication of those who cannot improve. This pattern of *quasinatural* incorrigibility is much more important to anti-Semites than is the content of the standard reproaches themselves, the latter being frequently quite harmless and essentially incompatible with the inferences to which they lead those who hate. While these reproaches are so widespread and well known that further evidence of their frequency and intensity is unnecessary, it is worthwhile to follow up some of their aspects which came out clearly in our interviews and which seem to throw some additional light on the phenomena concerned.

It is profitable to examine these reproaches from a sociological point of view. Our sample, in contrast to that of the Labor Study, was predominantly middle class. The San Quentin Group is the only striking exception, but its qualification of *Lumpenproletariat* as well as the prison situation, with its intrinsic emphasis on "official" moral values, makes it impossible to compare this group with the rest of the sample in terms of working-class identification. This identification is usually not very strong even among workers in this country. The general middle-class character of our sample colors the specific nature of the decisive accusations made against the Jews. If our basic hypothesis concerning the largely projective character of anti-Semitism is correct, the Jews are blamed, in social terms, for those properties which by their existence, sociologically ambiguous though it may be, impinge on sensitive spots in the class identification of the different prejudiced groups. To the true proletarian, the Jew is primarily the bourgeois. The working-man is likely to perceive the Jew, above all, as an agent of the economic sphere of the middle-man, as the executor of capitalist tendencies. The Jew is he who "presents the bill."

To the anti-Semitic members of the middle classes, the imagery of the Jew seems to have a somewhat different structure. The middle classes themselves experience to a certain degree the same threats to the economic basis of their existence which hang over the heads of the Jews. They are themselves on the defensive and struggle desperately for the maintenance of their status. Hence, they accentuate just the opposite of what workingmen are likely to complain about, namely, that the Jews are not real bourgeois, that they do not really "belong." By building up an image of the Jew out of traits which signify his failures in middle-class identification, the middle-class member is able subjectively to enhance the social status of his ingroup which is endangered by processes having nothing to do with ingroup-outgroup relations. To the middle-class anti-Semite, the Jew is likely to be regarded as the *misfit* bourgeois, as it were, he who did not succeed in living up to the standards of today's American civilization and who is a kind of obsolete and uncomfortable remnant of the past. The term "misfit" is actually applied to the Jew by some of our prejudiced subjects. The less the Jew qualifies as a legitimate member of the middle classes, the more easily can he be excluded from a group which, in the wake of monopolization, tends toward the *numerus clausus* anyway. If the usurper complex to be discussed in the section on politics and economics really belongs to an over-all pattern, the Jew functions, for the potentially fascist mentality, as the usurper par excellence. He is the peddler, impudently disguised as a respectable citizen and businessman.

The most characteristic anti-Jewish remarks appearing in our interviews fall within this frame of thinking, although motifs of a more "proletarian" anti-Semitism, such as the idea of the Jewish exploiter or of the Jews dodging hard manual labor, are not lacking. The division between proletarian and middle-class anti-Semitism should not be exaggerated. The traits ascribed to Jews by working men have often the aspect of the "misfit bourgeois" too. What appear to the worker as symptoms of capitalist exploitiveness can easily be transformed by the middle classes into the reproach of dishonesty, a flagrant violation of bourgeois ethics, one of the main tenets of which is, after all, the praise of good honest labor. The stereotypes here in question transcend the frontiers of the classes; it is only their function that changes, and hence the difference in emphasis.

The construct of the "misfit bourgeois" can easily be articulated according to three major groups of motifs: first, that of Jewish weakness and its psychological correlates, second, the middle-class identification of the Jews as an overcompensation that has essentially failed, third, the intrinsic disloyalty of the Jews to the class with which they vainly attempt to identify themselves, a disloyalty which is viewed as an expression of their abortive identification and of their nature as an objectionable, isolated, and "clannish" ingroup. The first two of these objections may have some basis in reality. There is considerable evidence, e.g., the recent studies by Anton Lourie, of Jewish masochism and its basis in religious psychology. The third objection seems to be predominantly projective and one of the major rationalizations of the wish to "get rid of the whole bunch."

The idea of Jewish weakness is epitomized by *F114*, a woman consistently high on all scales, who is a surgical nurse of partly Jewish descent:

"I have a cousin who was in love with me and wanted to marry me. He was more Jewish than I. I loved him, but wouldn't marry him. I told him why—because he's Jewish. He is now married to a Gentile with two children. He's more anti-Semitic than I. That's true of so many Jews—like they were lame or hunchback. They hate it or resent it."

It is perhaps characteristic that such overt statements on Jewish weakness are made frequently either by persons who are themselves being identified with the Jews or—with a more positive accent—by low-scoring subjects. The prejudiced individual, whose hatred is stimulated by weakness, rather tends to stress, on the surface, the strength of the Jews who "wield undue influence" and "own everything." An example of the low-scorer's attitude towards Jewish weakness is the statement of *5055*, an otherwise thoroughly liberal man of 73 years who scored low on all the scales. He feels

"that this protective philosophy of the Jews has led to a situation where they do stimulate antagonism in other people."

In cases of extreme low scorers the awareness of Jewish weakness sometimes leads to identification: they assume the role of Jews themselves, consciously in order to antagonize anti-Semitic acquaintances, unconsciously, possibly, in order to atone for anti-Semitism by at least figuratively suffering the same humiliations under which they know the Jews live. Here belongs the case of a 20-year-old, somewhat neurotic interior decorator, *5028*, who is in open rebellion against his father but strongly attached to his mother:

The subject and his sister are alike in that they both admire Jewish people. He told of jokes that they had played upon some of their father's relatives who are extremely anti-Semitic by pretending that a great grandfather on the maternal side was Jewish. The subject explained that many persons in his mother's family "look a little Jewish because they have long noses." The paternal cousin to whom they were talking "almost committed suicide" at the thought. The subject volunteered the comment that perhaps one reason he likes Jews is that he "has never known any who were objectionable."

To the prejudiced person, the imagery of Jewish weakness, combined as it is with the rationalization of strength, sometimes strikes a peculiar note, remarkable because of its close harmony with one of the standard themes of American fascist agitators. It is the image of the Jewish refugee who is depicted simultaneously as strong ("He takes the jobs away from our American boys") and as weak ("He is a dirty outcast"). There is reason enough to believe that the second motive is the decisive one. The high-scoring man *M105* makes the following statement:

"A lot of Jewish immigrants are coming to this country. They get a soft life, and they take over. You can't deal with one, and a lot of them are awful dirty, though they have money."

Aggressiveness against the refugees comes to the fore even in cases which are otherwise, according to the interviewer, only mildly anti-Semitic. *5036* is a jazz musician, at the present time drawing unemployment insurance. He is high on E and F, although lower on PEC.

Although he denies any outgroup antagonisms, many of these are implicit and at the surface level. He is most vehement in his belief that refugees should not assume citizenship and should be sent home when time and conditions permit it.

The psychological determination of this subject's hatred of the refugee competitors can be inferred the more safely since he acknowledges that

"There is no doubt that the Jews are talented in music."

He sets against this only the vague standard accusation:

"but they are so clannish and aggressive and loud that sometimes I can't stand them." On several occasions he claims that the aggressiveness and selfish demands of Jews within smaller bands he had tried to organize caused their failure. "These Jews would never really get a feeling of pride in the organization. They would always leave you the minute they had a better offer; and in trying to meet offers they had, I went broke twice." On the other hand, he says some Jews are undoubtedly outstandingly cultured people.

The refugees, as those who are objectively weak, are regularly blamed for having a domineering attitude and a drive for power. While there may be some basis for the objection of aggressiveness in certain institutionalized Jewish reaction formations, such as the Jewish habit of "pleading," this stereotype helps at the same time to alleviate the anti-Semite's discomfort about violating the principle of democratic asylum: it is not he but the fugitives who are supposed to disregard the rules of hospitality. *5043*, a middle-aged housewife with extremely high scores on all the scales, alleges that the Jews

are loud and often aggressive. (Here she gave an example of women at the market who push themselves forward.) She specifically distinguishes between "refugees" and other Jews and feels that the "type we have been getting in the neighborhood lately" is definitely clannish, unintelligent, and generally undesirable.

The stereotype of Jewish aggressiveness shows a characteristic of anti-Semitic thinking which deserves closer investigation. It is the mixing, in allegations against the Jews, of crudely physical acts of aggression with hypotheses of a more psychological nature. Just as the idea of "Jewish blood" ranges from the fear of "pollution of the race," where the term blood is used only figuratively, to the hysteria of bodily "poisoning" inflicted by Jewish blood donors, the imagery of aggressiveness ranges from the Jews using their elbows when standing in a queue to their allegedly ruthless business practices. This suggests the retrogressive, "mythological" feature of some anti-Semitism. Mental dispositions are translated into physical reality both in order to soothe the fear of the incomprehensible "alien mentality" and to add a sense of the real to that which is actually only projective. This retranslation probably throws some light on the over-all insistence of the anti-Semite on Jewish physical traits.

5067 "is a portly, rather maternal-looking woman who looks all of her forty-eight years." She was chosen as a mixed case with high E and PEC. She does not differentiate at all between the physical and the psychological aspect of Jewish "aggressiveness":

"I do not like their coercive aggression in business. They are not only aggressive, but they should also be segregated. They are always pushing people aside. I noticed nearly every time when there was pushing in the innumerable lines we had to wait in during the war, it was a Jew who started the pushing. I feel a real revulsion towards Jews."

In other cases, the idea of aggressiveness is used in the exclusively social sense of "intrusiveness." Sometimes one gets a glimpse into the mechanism behind this standard reproach. It probably has to do with the all-pervasive feeling of social isolation, which is overcompensated for in innumerable middle-class "social activities." Against this background of emotion the Jews, as the classic agents of circulation, are perceived and probably envied as those who are not isolated, but have "contacts" everywhere. This idea is closely associated with that of clannishness, which also implies the imagery of some kind of togetherness from which the members of the real ingroup pretend to be excluded. The aforementioned *F105* finds the formula:

"They seem to know everybody; they pull strings; they are like a clan, more united than any race. They have friends everywhere who can do the right thing."

Finally, it should be mentioned that there is some evidence in our material that the basis of the stereotype "aggressiveness" lies in repressed sexuality. The Jews are supposed to be unencumbered by the standards of Puritan morality, and the more strictly one adheres oneself to these standards, the more eagerly are the supposed sex habits of the Jews depicted as sordid. What goes uncensored in the case of Jewish "rich food" becomes intolerable in the sphere of supposedly uninhibited and therefore repulsive sensuality. Some insight into this matter is afforded by the 42-year-old woman, *F118*, a public health nurse—a person, incidentally, whose outgroup hatred is focused on organized labor rather than on minorities and whose score on A-S is middle, while she scores high on PEC and F.

She could not imagine herself marrying a Jew. She then proceeded to relate that actually she once had an opportunity to marry a Jew. One time, when she returned home for the summer after being in New York for a while, she met a very intelligent lawyer who worked in the same office as her brother. He was very well-educated and knew languages. She had dates with him and saw quite a lot of him for three weeks, until one day he said to her, "There is one thing I want to tell you about myself. You have never met my family and I had not intended that you should meet them. However, there is one thing that I want to ask you, and that is whether you would object to marrying a Jew?" She said that it was as if she had been struck a great blow. He did not look Jewish, his name was not Jewish, and he even sang in the choir of her church, so that she never suspected that he was Jewish. She just sat there without saying a word—and that was his answer. She then went on to add that it was very bad for him, because all the girls staying in her boarding house then found out that he was Jewish and it also became known at his place of work and made things bad for him there. Subject saw him again ten years later and felt that he did look more Jewish, but added that that was perhaps because she now knew that he was Jewish. The thing that is most impossible to her in the idea of marrying a Jew is the thought of bearing *Jewish children*.

It is noteworthy that the resistance of this woman was brought about only by her knowledge of the man's Jewish descent, not by any of his own characteristics. It is hardly going too far to assume that the stereotype has re-enacted old childhood taboos against sexuality and that it was only afterwards that these were turned against the Jew as an individual. Primary attraction is the basis for subsequent repulsion.

The close relations of the ubiquitous idea of clannishness to the reproach of aggressiveness has become obvious in previous examples. Suffice it to say here that clannishness appears as the justification for excluding the aggressive "intruder": he always "remains a Jew" and wants to cheat those by whom he wishes to be accepted. At the same time, the idea of clannishness consummates the imagery of Jewish togetherness, of a warm, family-like, archaic and very "ingroup-like" texture of the outgroup which seems to be denied to those who are thoroughly formed by American civilization and obey the rules of technological rationality.

The underlying attractiveness of the Jewish "clan" is accentuated by the statement of *M102*, a subject scoring high on all scales:

"The Jewish kids I knew in high school were the sons and daughters of the prominent Jewish businessmen, and they were very clannish. It's hard to say what ought to be done about it. It doesn't seem to bother them what people think. That is a natural characteristic. It doesn't do any good to try to exclude them from business because some of them are the smartest businessmen we have. Most of them are out of Germany by now, and I suppose they'll get back. Some are very crafty about sticking together and getting ahead in business, getting capital. People in Germany will feel the need of Jewish businessmen and they will pool their capital and make a start there. (What about Jewish women?) Some of them are very attractive, and some are very clannish. They are dominated by the men; it's all in their creed."

The more patriarchal structure of the Jewish family, whether it be real or imagined, seems to work as an element of sexual attraction. Jewish women are supposed "to do everything for men"—just what the Gentile American girl is expected not to do. At the same time, however, the idea of sexual fulfillment tends to diminish, in American culture, the social value of the women who offer this fulfillment. Here again, the praise of one Jewish quality is prone to tilt over into its opposite.

How the idea of clannishness can sometimes obtain features of an obsession laden with violent resentment is shown in the case of *F113*, a young woman who is high on the E scale but somewhat lower on F and PEC. She is an attractive, somewhat neurotic girl of 26, a subject from the Extension Class group. She resents both Jewish names and those who dared to change them. When speaking about Jewish acquaintances, she makes a point of their owning "a chain of burlesque houses," being rich as well as somewhat disreputable. In her statement about Jewish family life, it is remarkable how closely some observations which have a ring of truth are knit together with somewhat paranoid ideas about the selfishness determining the Jewish behavior in question and with a harsh evaluation of it as a "guilt":

"The worst experience with them I had was when I was overseas operator in Hawaii a couple of years ago. I had to monitor all the calls that went to New York so I listened to just thousands of conversations. And ninety percent of them were rich Jews calling up their families. That is the only really good thing I can say for them—their devotion to their families. But all purely selfish. The money they spent—and the time—on just purely selfish calls. (Business calls?) Well I worked mostly at night. But the other girls said it was the same people making business calls during the day. (How did you know they were Jews?) Their voices and the things they said. Selfish. (Could there have been Jews you didn't recognize?) I don't think so. You get so you always know a Jewish voice."

I. OBSERVATIONS ON LOW-SCORING SUBJECTS

Throughout this chapter, we have concentrated on the phenomena of anti-Semitism and their structural interconnections. We have abstained from a detailed discussion of the minority attitudes of the non-anti-Semite and of the anti-anti-Semite. Obviously, it is more difficult and less promising to analyze the absence of highly specific opinions and attitudes than it is to deal with their existence. We have been able, it seems, in the study as a whole to draw a fairly complete picture of the low scorers, ranging from surface ideology to characterological determinants. Their general tendency to be disinterested in so-called racial questions, however, limits the supply of pertinent information. Moreover, the pragmatic aspect of our study naturally requires a closer scrutiny of the danger zone than of areas which can be discounted as a potential for fascism. By and large, the attitudes of the high scorers suffice to define, *e contrario*, the attitudes of the "lows" which are, in many respects, set polemically against the anti-Semitic imagery prevailing in our cultural climate.

Yet a number of observations concerning the low scorers may be allowed, not only in order to round out the picture, but also because the low scorers, in their responses to questions about minorities, go beyond a simple negation of the prejudiced person's opinions and attitudes, and throw some additional light upon the nonfascist character.

An over-all characteristic of the low scorer's attitude towards Jews is emphatic rationality. This has a double aspect. On the one hand, the general tendency towards intraceptiveness so characteristic of low scorers expresses itself specifically in the racial area through self-reflection: anti-Semitism presents itself to the low scorers as the problem of the anti-Semite, not of the Jew. On the other hand, racial problems and minority traits are viewed within historical and sociological perspective and thus seen to be open to rational insight and change, instead of being hypostatized in a rigidly irrational manner.

An example of self-reflection in racial matters is *M910*, a student-minister, consistently low on all scales, who has strong intellectual leanings and, like most low scorers, a tendency toward hesitation, doubt, and qualifications of his own opinions. He traces back prejudice, in a plain-spoken though somewhat primitive manner, to the difficulties of the minority haters, not to the object of their hatred:

(What do you feel are the causes of prejudice?) "Probably the largest reason is the insecurity or fear of insecurity that the person has himself. The people in my community who have talked loudest about the Japs are the ones who have since taken over (the properties left by the Japanese) . . . and they're afraid they'll come back . . . and they're afraid of them as competitors because they work harder. . . . (You feel it's mainly an economic conflict?) Well, it isn't altogether economic, and I don't think it will be solved on an economic basis. . . . All people have some kind of insecurity. It may be pretty well concealed, and they may not know what it is, and it may not have anything to do with the Japanese, but they'll take it out on them. People are funny (laughs) and are cruel. (What ought to be done to combat prejudice?) I think one thing that could be done—kinda regimentation, is to get the facts, it would help, though it wouldn't solve the problem . . . e.g., that there is no necessity for separating Negro and white blood in blood banks, and there are a lot of people who think that the Japanese are a treacherous race, and that it's transmitted through heredity. . . . Of course, a lot of it is irrational."

As to the emphasis on dynamic factors versus supposedly innate qualities, the most striking illustration is provided by M203, a thoroughly liberal teacher, head of the English department in a junior college. He, too, is low on all scales. His whole philosophy is positivistic, with a strong interest in semantics, though he does not "think they should make a panacea out of semantics." His general outlook on minority problems is summarized by his statement on the Japanese:

"If the Germans were changed in one generation by the Nazis, then the Japanese can be changed in a democratic way in one or two generations. Anybody can become anything under the proper conditions."

Consequently, when discussing anti-Semitism, he chooses as an explanation a historical element, the maliciously superimposed Jewish names. The arbitrariness of the selection of this specific factor can probably be accounted for by the interviewee's semanticist hobby:

"Anti-Semitism is a little different. Semites are not so easily identified. I guess their name is about the main thing. For instance, from your name I guess you're Jewish though I wouldn't know to look at you. Are you?" (Yes.) (Subject is quite open about these things. The only sign of inhibition was that it was hard for him to use the word "Jew" as he preferred the word "Semite" at first, but later he used the word "Jew" also.)

This subject's readiness to discuss the interviewer's Jewishness is significant. To him, the word Jew is not a magic word, nor is being Jewish a disgrace: thus he does not feel inhibited about mentioning it in relation to the person with whom he is talking. It is hard to imagine that a high scorer would casually discuss the origins of an interviewer except on occasions when he feels on the defensive and wants to hurt the other fellow: "You are a Jew yourself, aren't you?"

The rationality of the unprejudiced subjects expresses itself, above all, in their rejection of anti-minority stereotypes. Frequently, this rejection is of a conscious, articulate nature: they take the concept of individuality seriously. We refer again to M910. His utterance shows a definite sense of proportion even in his rejection of stereotypy: he does not deny the existence of physical racial characteristics, but regards them as nonessential:

"Well, I wouldn't be tricked into making a statement about any people as a group. The Japanese I've known I've liked very well. I know there are some Japanese who aren't so nice. . . . We had a Japanese girl stand up with us at the altar and a Chinese girl too . . . in 1942 when there was some pretty tense feeling. (Do you feel that any racial group has certain distinguishing characteristics?) No, not at all. Of course you have biological characteristics, the height of the bridge of the nose or pigmentation."

A similar line is followed in the Los Angeles interview *5030*, of a 33-year-old Stanford graduate who served for four years in the navy, finally becoming a Lieutenant Commander. His scores on all scales are low. He is judged by the interviewer to be an extremely astute, successful individual:

"The Negroes, Jews, and all minority groups are having a very difficult time. I think many people dislike them because of their physical characteristics. They are really in a very bad spot. Such things as the FEPC help a lot and I favor both state and national laws concerning this issue. So many people are not willing to admit that many Negroes are intelligent, superior, and capable individuals. Their environment has held them back as a race. I have had both good and bad experiences with members of these groups but have never considered the people as belonging to a certain race or religion. I always take them for what they are worth as individuals. Yesterday I had a nice experience. There is a girl in one of my classes who is part Negro. She is a very superior and capable individual and I am sure the most intelligent member of the class. I have often thought I would like to visit with her but a suitable opportunity has never presented itself. Yesterday I, after much hesitation and fumbling, invited her to have a cup of coffee with me. Her acceptance was much more gracious than my invitation and we had a nice visit. I think the reason for my hesitation was simply a fear of what other people might think. I once had a Jewish roommate and he was the best roommate I have ever had."

An extreme example of fully conscious anti-stereotypy is *5046*, an executive secretary in the movie industry, in her late thirties, actively engaged in the labor movement. Her questionnaire scores are low for all scales. If some of her formulations suggest a "ticket low,"[2] it should be kept in mind that her rejection of stereotypy even prevents her from building up automatically a pro-Jewish stereotype. She is no "Jew lover," but seems truly to appraise people as individuals. As a matter of fact, she has just severed a relationship with a Jewish man:

When the interviewer began questioning subject on the Jewish problem, it became apparent immediately that she "knew all the answers." She stated: "Yes, there is a problem . . . but I don't think we should call it a Jewish problem; it really is a Christian problem . . . question of educating the Gentiles who practice anti-Semitism." When given the check list, she laughed and said: "Of course, one can't generalize . . . these are the stereotypes used by the anti-Semites to blame the Jews for certain faults . . . I don't think one should label any group like this . . . it is dangerous, especially in regard to the Jews, because one has to evaluate the individual on his or her own merits." None of the other questions brought out even a trace of anti-Semitism, and throughout, her answers indicated a consistent, almost

[2] See the "rigid low scorer" in Chapter XIX.

militant stand *against* anti-Semitism. She feels that anti-Semitism is one of the most dangerous trends in this country and feels that the only solution must be sought through widespread education along liberal lines and through extensive intermarriage. She feels rather optimistic about the process of assimilation, although she is quite alarmed about the increase of anti-Semitism during recent years. Hitler's race theory and persecution of the Jews should be combatted on every front, in whatever form it may appear. She stated: "I have also known some Jewish people whom I decidedly did not like, and some of them were quite aggressive, but I would never generalize that therefore 'all Jews' were aggressive . . . if only we could make people see that *some* people are aggressive for certain reasons, usually because of insecurity, and Jews are not aggressive because they are Jews."

As pointed out in great detail in the chapters on the personality aspects of the interview material, the low scorers' rationality, their rejection of projective imagery and automatized judgment, does not involve as a rule emotional coldness and detachment. Although they are more rational than the "highs" in so far as their judgment seems to be less determined by repressed unconscious factors, they are simultaneously less blocked in positive cathexes and in the expression of them. This refers not only to their general psychological make-up but also to their specific minority attitudes. The prejudiced person discusses the Jews as an "object" while he actually hates; the unprejudiced person displays sympathy even when he pretends simply to judge objectively. The link between this sympathy and rationality is the idea of *justice*, which has come to work, in certain people, spontaneously, almost as if it were instinctual. To the low scorer, racial discrimination violates the basic principle of the equality of all men. In the name of human rights he tends to identify himself with those who are discriminated against and who thus appeal to his own spontaneous feeling of solidarity with the oppressed.

Here are a few examples of this specific configuration. *M113*, a "religious low scorer" whose F scale shows higher trends and whose PEC scale was still higher:

(Minority problem?) "In a speech the other day in Public Speaking I said that democracy is mainly respect for minority groups." (Vague, little verbalized ideas.) "They have gotten a dirty deal, as most minorities do."

Similarly, in *M320*, a consistently low-scoring student of landscape architecture, protest against unfairness works as a "rationalization" for emotional identification which otherwise might not be allowed to come into the open:

"I'm very much pro-Negro, myself. I think I'm in favor of almost any minority that's discriminated against unfairly. . . . (What about the Jewish problem?) I don't see why it should be a problem at all. I think that in Europe the Jews should be allowed to live and have their businesses, etc., the same as anyone else."

Or the young woman *F129*, also low on all scales, a somewhat high-strung person who, according to the interviewer, is moved by any disturbing subject—including race prejudice—to tears and flushes:

(And how do you feel about Jews?) "Why, I don't feel any way about them except upset at the way they are treated. There are good and bad in all races but I am inclined to be even more tolerant about the shortcomings of people who are always persecuted and criticized. (Could you have married a Jew?) Why of course, if I had fallen in love with one. (Why do you think Jews are persecuted?) I don't know except some people have to hate."

There are indications that the low scorers' affect-laden sense of justice is not a mere surface ideology, or a means of narcissistic gratification in one's own humanitarianism, but that it has a real basis within the personality and is only presented afterwards, as it were, in theoretical terms. The sympathy for the underdog leads towards action, towards attempts to correct in concrete, individual situations what is felt to be general unfairness. A pertinent case was *5030* (see p. 646). We give one further illustration: *F126*, who is low on E and PEC and only slightly higher on F. She is a good-looking young woman, "very articulate and whimsical, with much charm and humor." She studies journalism and says that her real desire is to do "creative writing":

"I remember when I was in junior high, there was only one Jewish boy in our class. We were always having parties and affairs and he was left out. At first I didn't even understand why. He was a very nice boy, smart, and good-looking. But they left him out because he was a Jew. Well, I made it my business to be his special friend, not only invited him to my parties, but paid particular attention to him. That was one time it was really good to be one of the leading kids. The others began to treat him the same way, and he was just one of the crowd from then on. I never have been able to stand to see anyone be mean to anyone else. The same at the shipyards. I always made it a point to get acquainted with Negroes and Jews. They talked frankly with me, too, and I certainly found out what some of their problems are. Whenever I could, I would bring it into a story, too. Not directly about race prejudice, but nice stories about Negroes for instance. People have so many wrong ideas. I sometimes think it is just hopeless."

The general attitude of the low scorers towards the Jews profoundly affects their evaluation of so-called Jewish traits. It has been said above (pp. 612 ff.) that high scorers perceive the Jew altogether differently: their psychological make-up functions as a frame of reference even for their supposedly "immediate," everyday experiences. Something similar applies, in reverse, to the unprejudiced. Yet the diffuseness and inarticulateness of the objective "Jewish traits," complex as they are, is reflected by the low scorers' attitude no less than by the various projections of the high scorers. There is universal sympathy among the unprejudiced subjects, but no unanimity. Sometimes they try to *explain* Jewish traits; sometimes they simply deny their existence; sometimes they take an emphatically positive, admiring stand towards those traits.

The explanatory method is applied to the most widespread idea of a Jewish trait, that of clannishness, by *M202*, a 35-year-old construction engineer, with the lowest possible score on E, but with certain deviations from the usual picture of the low scorer with regard to PEC and also to F—a person who, according to the interviewer, "is conservative but not fascist."

In response to a question about how he would characterize the Jews, subject replied that they were a close-knit family with certain inborn characteristics like any other racial group. For instance, the Germans "must always be right," the English—here the interviewer interrupted, pointing out that she wished to know what he thought of the Jews. He replied that the Jews had not been accepted in a certain society and that this had led to their becoming a very close-knit family. The reason for this is that they have certain characteristics. On being asked to be more specific, his reply was they have a tendency to sharp dealing. Of course he doesn't blame them because he would probably do the same if he had the chance and if he were smart enough.

In this case, the wish to "explain," frequently an instrument for rationalizations, seems to mediate between broad-mindedness on the one hand and powerful anti-minority stereotypes, which are still there below the surface, on the other. As a matter of fact, the pro-Jewish apologies of the subject are followed by a rather unfriendly story about a supposed conspiracy among three Jewish bidders for a vast quantity of scrap-iron. The guess that the explanatory attitude may sometimes cover up ambivalence seems to be corroborated by M_{310}, an assistant manager for an advertising agency, who scored low on all scales. Nevertheless, his theorizing presupposes the acceptance of the stereotype of Jewish money-mindedness:

(Characteristic Jewish traits?) "Well, I think it is true that Jews, as a group, are more concerned with money. . . . Perhaps because persecuted for so long. . . . It's some small security in a money economy, that is, a money culture. Some security to be able to defend themselves with money. I also think they are better than average Gentiles at making money because forced to be usurers during the Middle Ages, etc."

Subjects whose scores are at the lowest extreme often tend simply to *deny* the existence of any Jewish traits, sometimes with a violence that seems to be due more to the impact of their own conscience than to an objective appraisal of the minority members. Here "neurotic" traits, which are often found in extremely unprejudiced subjects, may easily enter the picture. The vehicle by which they try to argue away Jewish traits is insight into the mechanisms of projectivity and stereotypy, i.e., into the subjective factors making for anti-Semitism.

M_{112}, a "quiet, reserved, well-mannered sophomore of 18 years," whose scale scores are all low, simply subscribes to the "envy" theory:

(Jews?) "Not an educational problem in this case. People just prejudiced. Want to keep them out of good positions, etc. People make up wild stories, like that the Jews have too much money, control the country, etc.; it's just to keep them back. (Your contacts?) No Negroes in my school. Jews were like anyone else. I'd never know they were Jewish if they hadn't told me."

5041 (whose scale scores are all low), a 59-year-old housewife who had studied to be a professional pianist, combines the denial of Jewish traits with reference to bygone ages and with the rejection of resentful generalizations:

"I think there is a Jewish problem—but I don't think that they are different . . . not that there is anything inherent in them that they should be set apart or treated differently. . . . There are historical reasons for their persecution . . . it is not their fault. Well, you can't apply any of these traits to the Jews as a group. Jews are not a race. . . . These terms might apply to some individuals, to Christians as well as Jews . . . you have some aggressive people, but they are not aggressive because they are Jewish . . . it's usually something that the other person does not like . . . say they appear to be more intellectual and some succeed, outdoing others, this causes resentment, and then they are called aggressive. . . ."

An extreme of denial is achieved by the "easy-going" low scorer, *M1206a*, of the Maritime School Group, who "is a highly introspective person and shows much inhibition against rejecting another person or group, even on the basis of principles founded in reality." His scores on all the scales are low:

(Most characteristic traits of Negroes?) "Well, I don't think there is such a thing. They have the same traits the white men have. . . . I don't believe any nationality has any characteristics. . . ."

Sometimes the intense emotions behind the denial of Jewish traits find a somewhat irrational expression. *F125* (low on E and F, but high on PEC) is a student who would like to become a drama teacher and who finds "the movies very stereotyped." Her indignation was stirred up by our own study.

"I was mad at some questions in your questionnaire, especially about the Jewish atmosphere. The Irish people and other national groups give an atmosphere to the place in which they live, but only the Jewish atmosphere is stamped as something bad. I don't find that the ways of living of the Jews are different at all."

If the prejudiced subjects, for reasons of general conformity and in order to obtain "social confirmation," frequently stress that practically everybody is anti-Semitic, some low scorers go so far as not only to deny the existence of Jewish traits, but even of anti-Semitism. A case in point is the somewhat muddle-headed *M115*, characterized as a typical conventional and conservative fraternity man who, however, is within the low quartile on the F scale though in the middle quartile on E and in the high quartile on PEC:

(What about the Jewish problem?) "There's not much persecution now in the United States. There shouldn't be any. The only reason for persecuting the Jew is that he is smarter than the next guy, as far as I can see."

As to the appreciation of the specific qualities of Jews and of other minorities, we content ourselves with two examples which may throw light on significant areas. *F128*, a 17-year-old girl, is low on F and PEC but slightly higher on E. She is studying social work and is interested in child welfare, but not "in any kind of a career":

"I guess I have had a better education than many people. We have entertained Negroes in our home as long as I can remember. I have known all sorts of people— lots of them very eccentric people—in music and art groups. The first good friends I ever had were Jewish boys and girls. I don't know why some people hate Negroes and Jews. With Jewish people perhaps they are a little afraid, because lots of Jews are smarter than other people."

The interesting element of this statement is contained in the word "eccentric." It refers to what is "different," to what is branded as slightly abnormal by standards of conformity, but which expresses individualization, the development of human traits which have not been preformed, as it were, by the social machinery of contemporary civilization. To this subject, the very "alienness" of minorities with respect to the rigid patterns of the highly organized mass society of today, represents the human, which she otherwise might feel to be lacking among the "right people." The Jewish "failure" to become completely absorbed by the American cultural climate presents itself to this subject as a merit, as a triumph of autonomy and resistance against the leveling impact of the "melting pot."

5050, a radio news commentator with progressive political affiliations, who is low on all three scales, denies the existence of Jewish traits but emphasizes a point rarely acknowledged: the patience of the minorities in the face of persecution. His praise of this attitude actually contains a critical element which may, by the implication of cowardice, be indicative of some hidden hostility. He blames the minorities for political reasons because they do not take a more energetic stand against American reaction:

He tries at all times to show that there are no so-called "Jewish traits," and that people such as described by Budd Schulberg in "What Makes Sammy Run" can and do occur quite as frequently among Gentiles. Then he usually points to a man like Rankin or Bilbo as an example of an obnoxious "Gentile." "I admire both the Negro and the Jewish people for their great patience in swallowing discrimination. . . . if I were in their shoes, I would start a really militant fight against the oppressors." He still feels that too many Jews and Negroes are too apathetic and rather let the other fellow do the fighting. . . . he feels that had the Jews been more alert, Hitler might have been stopped, or at least prevented from perpetrating the extreme atrocities. Again and again he stated that all forms of discrimination can and must be wiped out by *direct political action.*

One last characteristic of the unprejudiced attitude toward minority questions should be mentioned: the absence of fatalism. Not only do unprejudiced subjects, in the realm of their conscious convictions, appear to be set against ideas such as those of the inevitability of human badness or the perennial nature of any character traits, but on a deeper level, as suggested in Chapters XIV and XV, they appear to be relatively free of destructive urges and punitive fantasies. They look at things in a historical and sociological way rather than hypostatizing the existent as something ultimately given. This point of view expresses itself also in their concept of the future relationships between majority and minority. *5008*, low on E, in the middle quartile on F, and high on PEC, is a middle-aged woman who worked as a ghost writer, then as a literary agent, and is now employed as secretary to a radio show. In keeping with the low scorers' rejection of stereotypy, she sees the solution of the problem of anti-Semitism, however naively, in the establishment of personal contacts.

She holds nothing but good wishes for the intelligent immigrants and refugees who have come here recently, but feels that many of them have been undesirable. Concerning Negroes she reports that as a Republican she believes their position should be very much bettered, but says this is a difficult problem. Concerning Jews she says, "Before I went to work, I probably had a slight anti-Jewish feeling," but in several positions she has worked with and for Jews, and found them very charming, intelligent, and interesting people. She thinks the racial problem most in need of solution is that of anti-Semitism, and feels that if more "anti-Semites would mingle with Jews the way I have" it could be avoided. She believes in the FEPC and thinks that socioeconomic discrimination should be outlawed. When it was pointed out that this is a more New Deal type of political notion, she simply said, "Well, it can't all be bad."

This attitude, which stresses human spontaneity and freedom of action rather than rigid, authoritarian laws of nature, does not, however, lead toward "official optimism." The unprejudiced subjects' sensitivity to the suffering of human beings, their compassion, makes them keenly aware of the dangers of racial persecution. It is the high scorer who would say, "It can't happen here," thus apparently detaching himself from the "objective" course of history with which he actually identifies himself; the low scorer knows that it could happen, but wants to do something about it.

5058, low on all three scales, is a 29-year-old veteran of upper middle-class background whose main identification lies with "liberals" and "intellectuals."

He is very concerned about the problem of minority groups in this country. "I do a lot of talking about it—hoping to reduce prejudice and to encourage tolerance. In fact, I feel so concerned about this thing I would almost be willing to set myself up in Pershing Square. I tried to do a little crusading in the Navy but without much success." Subject is very pessimistic about the possibility of a solution to the "minority problem" which seems to stem largely from his failure to modify the opinions of the people with whom he has argued. He feels that dislike of the Jews is increasing because he has heard more talk against them lately. "Of course that might be because I am exposed to it more lately, both while I was in the Navy and in my present job." He does not feel that the Jews have too much influence in this country, nor does he believe that the Jews are a political force in America. He is certain that they did their part in the war effort. When asked about "basically Jewish traits," he was not able to respond since to him this term means practically nothing. "Jews are all so different from each other that we cannot speak of there being something 'basically Jewish' about them."

J. CONCLUSION

It has often been said that anti-Semitism works as the spearhead of anti-democratic forces. The phrase sounds a bit hackneyed and apologetic: the minority most immediately threatened seems to make an all-too-eager attempt to enlist the support of the majority by claiming that it is the latter's interest and not their own which really finds itself in jeopardy today. Looking back, however, at the material surveyed in this, and other, chapters, it has to be recognized that a link between anti-Semitism and antidemocratic feeling exists. True, those who wish to exterminate the Jews do not, as is sometimes claimed, wish to exterminate afterwards the Irish or the Protestants. But the limitation of human rights which is consummated in their idea of a special treatment of the Jews, not only logically implies the ultimate abolition of the democratic form of government and, hence, of the legal protection of the individual, but it is frequently associated quite consciously, by high-scoring interviewees, with overt antidemocratic ideas. We conclude this chapter with two examples of what appear to be the inescapable antidemocratic consequences of anti-Semitism. M106, a man high on the E, F, and PEC scales, still pretends to be democratic; but it is not difficult to infer what is in the back of his mind:

"Hitler's plan—well, Hitler carried things just a little too far. There was some justification—some are bad, but not all. But Hitler went on the idea that a rotten apple in the barrel will spoil all the rest of them." He doesn't approve of ruthless persecution. "If Hitler had handled the Jews as a minority group, had segregated them and set certain standards for them to live by, there would be less trouble for Hitler now. (Same problem in this country now?) Same problem, but it's handled much better because we're a democratic country."

While the suggestion that a minority be segregated is incompatible with the basic concepts of the same "democratic country" of which the subject professes to be proud, the metaphor of the rotten apple in the barrel conjures up the imagery of "evil germs" which is associated with appalling regularity with the dream of an effective germicide.

Perversion of a so-called democrat is manifested in 5019, another man whose scale scores are all high. He is a 20-year-old laborer, characterized above all, by his blind, authoritarian acceptance of his humble position in life. At the same time, he "dislikes timid people" and has "great admiration for real leaders":

Respondent believes that the "laws of democracy should favor white, Gentile people," yet he "would not openly persecute Jews in the way the Hitler program treated them."

The reservation of the second sentence is disavowed by the momentum of the convictions expressed in the first one.

CHAPTER XVII

POLITICS AND ECONOMICS IN
THE INTERVIEW MATERIAL

T. W. Adorno

A. INTRODUCTION

The questionnaire findings on political and economic ideology have been analyzed in Chapter V. It is now our task to study the interview material referring to the same topics. The purpose is, first of all, to concretize our insight into these ideologies. If we investigated, in Chapter V, into the responses of our subjects to a number of set, standardized political and economic ideas and slogans with which they are daily confronted, we shall now try to form a picture of "what they really think"—with the qualification that we shall also have to find out whether we are entitled to expect autonomous and spontaneous opinions from the majority of them. It is obvious that the answer to such problems, unless they should be made the very center of research, can be given only in a less rigorous way than was the case with the quantitative analysis of questionnaire responses, and that the results are of a more tentative nature. Their convincing power lies more in the consistency of specific interpretations with facts previously established than in any indisputable "proof" that one or the other of the ideological mechanisms under review prevail within a majority of subjects or within certain groups.

Again, our interpretations of ideology will go below the realm of surface opinion, and will be related to the psychological results of our study. It is not our aim merely to add some padding to our figures. As stated in the Introductory Remarks to this part, we would rather gain insight into the links between ideological opinions and psychological determinants. We do not pretend that psychology is the cause and ideology the effect. But we try to interrelate both as intimately as possible, guided by the assumption that ideological irrationalities just as other irrationalities of overt human behavior are concomitant with unconscious psychological conflicts. We combed through the interview material with particular attention to such irrationalities and to statements revealing something about the dynamics of personality. The establishment of plausible configurations involving both dynamic motivation and ideological rationalization seems to us the foremost means of achieving that consistency on which the evidence of the discussions to follow largely depends. The data discussed so far permit at least the assumption that personality could be regarded as *one* determinant of ideology.

Yet it is just the area with which we are now concerned that most strongly forbids any simple reduction to terms of personality. Our construct of the "potentially fascist character" was largely based on the division between high and low scorers. Whereas this division retains its value for numerous topics of political and economic ideology and can be substantiated, on a deeper level, probably for *all* ideological issues, there appears to be at work another determinant which, in numerous issues, blurs the distinction between high and low scorers and refuses to be stated unequivocally in terms of personality. This determinant may be called our general cultural climate, and particularly the ideological influence upon the people of most media for moulding public opinion. If our cultural climate has been standardized under the impact of social control and technological concentration to an extent never known before, we may expect that the thinking habits of individuals reflect this standardization as well as the dynamics of their own personalities. These personalities may, indeed, be the product of this very same standardization to a much higher degree than a naive observer is led to believe. In other words, we have to expect a kind of ideological "over-all pattern" in our interviewees which, though by no means indifferent to the dichotomy of high and low scorers, transcends its boundaries. Our data afford ample evidence that such an ideological over-all pattern exists in fact.

It is a major question for this chapter whether this over-all ideological pattern, perhaps even more than the specific susceptibility of our high scorers to fascist propaganda, does not entail the danger of a large-scale following of antidemocratic movements if they should get under way with powerful support.

The importance of this diagnosis, if it should be corroborated sufficiently by our data, is self-evident, its most immediate implication being that the fight against such a general potential cannot be carried through only educationally on a purely psychological level, but that it requires at the same time decisive changes of that cultural climate which makes for the over-all pattern. Methodologically, the importance of this aspect of our study lies in the fact that it relativizes, somewhat, the distinction between high vs. low scorers; this distinction, if taken as absolute, may easily lead to a "psychologizing" bias that would neglect the objective, supra-individual social forces operating in our society.

The introduction of the concept of an over-all pattern just in this ideological area may appear paradoxical at first glance. Since most political and economic issues are overt and relatively simple with reference to the blunt division between progressivism and reactionism, one should expect the difference to be particularly marked here. This, however, is not borne out by the facts. It is hard to escape the impression that there is much more actual similarity between high and low scorers in the political and economic section of the interviews than in more remote and complicated regions. To be sure, there are some topics which are as clearly discriminatory as some of the more extreme anti-Semitic ideas discussed in the preceding chapter. One hardly needs any research in order to establish that high scorers tend to be anti- and low scorers pro-Roosevelt, that high scorers more often want a "strong" foreign policy and low scorers favor reconciliation, that high scorers indignantly reject communism and low scorers tend to discuss it on a more discursive plane. However, there is a large number of what might be called more formal constituents of political ideology which seem to permeate the whole pattern while, by their own momentum, making for reactionary and potentially fascist persuasions. Here belong, as will be discussed in detail, general ignorance and confusion in political matters, the habits of "ticket thinking" and "personalization," resentment of unions, of government interference in business, of income limitations, and a number of other trends.

The existence of such an over-all pattern in politics need not be surprising, when the whole context of our study is considered. As a matter of fact, the problem itself is derived from our quantitative findings. After we once administered the PEC scale, no close relation between politics and anti-Semitism could be expected. Chapter V offered the evidence that the correlation of PEC with either anti-Semitism or ethnocentrism was never very high. There were some subjects high on PEC but low on E, others high on E but middle or low on PEC. This means that in this area particularly we cannot speak in categorical terms of high vs. low scorers. We shall see if this is borne out by a consideration of the interviews: both what the weakening of our basic distinction means qualitatively and whether and how we still can differentiate successfully in this area.

If a trend that differentiates statistically between high and low scorers on E—the "highs" being higher on it—appears very commonly in the interviews of all subjects, then we must conclude that it is a trend in culture itself. In this chapter we shall be particularly concerned with these outstanding features. The evidence that they are potentially fascistic is the fact that they "go" statistically, psychologically, and in every other respect with high scale scores; if they also occur with considerable frequency in interviews of low scorers it must be because we are living in potentially fascist times.

If a subject is low on *all* scales, but still shows trends which look potentially fascist, then one might say that the scales and other techniques do not cover everything, that the potential fascism of the trend is hypothetical as far as the statistical evidence goes, and that one might perform an empirical study to see if it really does go with what we know of the subject. We expect our discussion at least to shed some light on this methodological problem.

As far as the differentiation between high and low scorers goes, it is obvious that an over-all pattern would necessitate more differentiated characterizations than those previously employed. This can be hinted at only occasionally throughout this chapter. Sometimes high and low scorers are similar in what they say in politico-economic terms, but different in some more subtle way; just as sometimes they are superficially different but similar with respect to underlying trends.

Political and economic facts are subject to rapid change. This holds particularly true for the last few years. When our material was gathered, mainly throughout 1945, Russia was an ally; today, the tension between this country and the Soviet Union overshadows all other issues. Such changes make a valid interpretation of political ideology difficult and precarious. Thus, it might well be that anti-Russian sentiments, which were in 1945 part and parcel of a general pattern of reactionism, largely conditioned subjectively, would be of a much more "realistic" nature today, or at least they would fall to a greater extent within the "over-all pattern," being less differentiating *per se* between high and low scorers. Moreover, in all probability the typical high scorer has become even more articulate with regard to Russia. It is hard to imagine that Mack would still stick to his statement that "Joe" Stalin was all right. Our interpretation, of course, had to stick to the situation of 1945 in order to give an adequate picture of the relationship between ideology and personality factors. However, it should be emphasized that the PEC scale as well as its follow-up in the interviews depends to a much higher degree on external events than do the other scales. This is why we never expected that the correlations of PEC with E and F would be very high, and it is quite possible that under the new political circumstances the direction of some of the more superficial relationships might have changed. Ideology is so sensitive to political dynamics that even some interpretations formulated comparatively lately, when the bulk of the chapter had been written, should be qualified at publication time. Yet we may claim that the general trend of events has been entirely in accord with the general formulations reached in the discussion to follow.

With regard to the organization of the chapter we shall deal first with the more formal constituents of political and economic ideology and later with a number of specific political issues. The problem of cultural over-all pattern vs. psychological differentiation occurs in both sections, though the presuppositions of the over-all pattern belong mainly to the first one.

B. FORMAL CONSTITUENTS OF POLITICAL THINKING

1. IGNORANCE AND CONFUSION[1]

The evaluation of the political statements contained in our interview material has to be considered in relation to the widespread ignorance and confusion of our subjects in political matters, a phenomenon which might well surpass what even a skeptical observer should have anticipated. If people do not know what they are talking about, the concept of "opinion," which is basic to any approach to ideology, loses much of its meaning. This does not imply that the material becomes insignificant but rather that it cannot be interpreted in factual categories but must be related to the sociopsychological structure of the subject being investigated. In other words, the material itself calls for that personality analysis which marks the general strategy of our research. It is in the light of this analysis that the ideology of our subjects is now to be re-evaluated.

While ignorance and confusion marks the political statements of both high and low scorers, it is, nevertheless, by no means "neutral" with regard to the problem of susceptibility to fascist propaganda. Our general impression is that ignorance and confusion is more widespread among high than among low scorers. This would be consistent with our previous observations on the general "anti-intellectual" attitude of high scorers. In addition, the official optimism of the high scorer tends to exclude that kind of critical analysis of existent conditions on which rational political judgment depends. A man who is prone to identify himself *a priori* with the world as it is has little incentive to penetrate it intellectually and to distinguish between essence and surface. The "practical" bias of the high scorers, their emotional detachment from everything that is beyond their well defined range of action, is another factor contributing to their disinterestedness in, and lack of, political knowledge. However this may be, there is reason to believe that ignorance itself works in favor of general reactionary trends. This belief, based on consistent observations particularly in backward rural areas everywhere, has been epitomized by the old German social-democratic adage that anti-Semitism is the "socialism of the dolt." All modern fascist movements, including the practices of contemporary American demagogues, have aimed at the ignorant; they have consciously manipulated the facts in a way that could lead to success only with those who were not acquainted with the facts. Ignorance with respect to the complexities of contemporary society makes for a state of general uncertainty and anxiety, which is the ideal breeding ground for the modern type of reactionary mass movement. Such movements are always

---

[1] After completion of the study, the writer of this chapter became acquainted with the pertinent article by R. H. Gundlach (46).

"populist" and maliciously anti-intellectual. It is not accidental that fascism has never evolved any consistent social theory, but has persistently denounced theoretical thinking and knowledge as "alienation from the grass-roots." The existence of such ignorance and confusion as we find in the interviews of subjects, particularly when we consider the relatively high educational level which they as a group represent, has to be regarded as ominous, no matter whether the subjects in question score high or low on our scales. The configuration of technical skill and the "realism" of "looking after oneself" on the one hand, and of the stubborn refusal intellectually to penetrate reality on the other, is the very climate in which fascist movements can prosper. Where this outlook prevails, a critical situation may easily lead to the general acceptance of formulae which are today still regarded as prerogatives of the "lunatic fringe."

Sometimes ignorance is explicitly commented upon by our interviewers. But even if we do not regard their impression as sufficient proof, there is evidence enough within the material, be it that the statements betray a striking lack of information, be it that the interviewee confesses his disinterestedness in politics or his lack of knowledge. The latter attitude, incidentally, is particularly frequent with women, and often it is accompanied by self-accusing statements.

It is hard to distinguish between simple ignorance and confusedness, that is to say, between the state of simply not knowing the facts, and the state which exists when people without sufficient intellectual training grow muddle-headed under the incessant attack of all kinds of mass communication and propaganda and do not know what to make of the facts they have. It seems as if confusion were the effect of ignorance: as if those who do not know but feel somehow obliged to have political opinions, because of some vague idea about the requirements of democracy, help themselves with scurrilous ways of thinking and sometimes with forthright bluff.

The few quotations to follow are picked at random as illustrations of a phenomenon which is well-nigh universal, but for the very few exceptional cases of people who take a conscious and explicit interest in politics.

An example of ignorance, covered up by pompous phraseology, is the following statement by *M117*, a low-scoring man from the University Extension Group. He is a semi-educated sailor with high-school background and widely read, but generally muddle-headed.

(American political scene?) "We have a good basis for our political system. The majority of people are not interested or equipped enough to understand politics, so that the biggest proportion of U. S. politics is governed by the capitalistic system."

To this man, the existence or nonexistence of capitalism in this country is simply a matter of "education."

A "bluffer" is the veteran *M732c*, a high-scoring man with high-school education, who always starts with sentences which sound up-to-date but rarely finishes them:

(What does he think of political trends today?) "I would say that now we're in a very sad case. Worse off than two years ago—well, the situation with Russia in Iran—and these strikes that are coming on—quite a deal of good statesmanship to fix the world up. . . ."

The subject's statements abound with qualifications and evasions:

"I feel somehow that they (i.e., the unions) are progressing in a way but in other ways they are not. I think all things will work out for the best. But I really think they should not go into politics. . . . I am not very well versed on. . . ."

Asked about the most dangerous threats to present form of government:

"Well, let's see . . . well, we might have another war in the U. S. A. Since the U. S. itself is a huge melting pot. . . . I imagine in the U. S. there are a lot of people who hated to see Hitler die and are pro-German—and maybe one of these little groups will . . . catch on."

A San Quentin prisoner, *M621A*, who scores low on the E and PEC scales and middle on F, regards Russia as the most dangerous threat. When asked what ought to be done, he answers:

"Well, people should limit political parties to at least two groups and not have all these socialists and communists, etc. (What to do with socialists and communists?) Well, they could still believe in their own ideal . . . let them have a voice in the election but should not be allowed to have any power. (You mean they should not be allowed to put up any candidates?) No, unless they get a majority."

One of the most extreme examples is the high-scoring woman *F121*, who "was never good at school work" and apparently had very little general education.

Not interested, not informed. Thinks Roosevelt has been good and should see us through the war. Otherwise has no opinions. She had written on the side of the questionnaire, asking about political parties: "Don't know these parties."

Again, *5016*, a housewife, graduated from high school, high on F and E but middle on PEC, referred to by the interviewer as "being of moderately high intelligence," says

"I hear that communists and socialists are both bad."

By contrast, *5052*, the Spanish-Negro entertainer, high on F and PEC, middle on E, has an opinion of his own on communism and apparently some sympathy with communists, but his opinion is no less startling:

"All of the people in the entertainment world who are communists are good guys."

On further questioning it comes out that according to his opinion

Communism seems to be a sort of social club which holds meetings and raises money for worthy causes.

Somewhat exceptional is the statement of the moderately low-scoring call-house girl, *5035*, who, before she chose the profession of prostitute, was a graduate of the University of California. She is strongly interested in union activities and actually lost her former job as a dancing teacher because of such activities, but refused on the questionnaire to mark any questions with regard to political groups, for which she gives the following explanation:

"I am very confused about politics because I talk about them a great deal with our clients here and they all have different opinions. It was a struggle for me to get through economics in college."

In practical issues, however, her views are very liberal and even radical.

The self-accusing attitude of women with regard to political matters seems to be most common among medium and low scorers; this is consistent with the latter's general introspective and self-critical attitude.

An example is the 17-year-old student of social work, *F128*, who is middle on E and F but high on PEC:

"I am a little ashamed about this subject. I hate to be ignorant about anything but frankly, I don't know anything about politics. I am for Roosevelt, of course, but I don't think I have developed any ideas of my own. Mother and Jim talk about things, but it is mostly social work shop. I intend to read a lot and think a lot about things because I believe all intelligent people should have ideas."

Interesting also is the low scorer, *F517*, a 20-year-old freshman student majoring in music, who accuses herself of ignorance and dependence, though her general attitude, particularly with regard to minority questions, shows that she is rather articulate and outspoken and that she differs from her parents.

"I don't know much about it. I'm quite dependent—I get my opinions from my father. He is a die-hard Republican. He did not like Roosevelt but I think he did some good things (such as making things better for the poor people)."

It would go beyond the scope of the present study to attempt a full explanation of political ignorance so strikingly in contrast to the level of information in many other matters and to the highly rational way in which most of our subjects decide about the means and ends of their own lives. The ultimate reason for this ignorance might well be the opaqueness of the social, economic, and political situation to all those who are not in full command of all the resources of stored knowledge and theoretical thinking. In its present phase, our social system tends objectively and automatically to produce "curtains" which make it impossible for the naive person really to see what it is all about. These objective conditions are enhanced by powerful economic and social forces which, purposely or automatically, keep the people ignorant. The very fact that our social system is on the defense, as it were, that capitalism, instead of expanding the old way and opening up innumerable opportunities to the people, has to maintain itself somewhat precariously and to block critical insights which were regarded as "progressive" one hundred years ago but are viewed as potentially dangerous today, makes for a one-sided presentation of the facts, for manipulated information, and for certain shifts of emphasis which tend to check the universal enlightenment otherwise furthered by the technological development of communications. Once again, as in the era of the transition from feudalism to middle-class society, knowing too much has assumed a subversive touch, as it were. This tendency is met halfway by the "authoritarian" frame of mind of large sections of the population. The transformation of our social system from something dynamic into something conservative, a *status quo*, struggling for its perpetuation, is reflected by the attitudes and opinions of all those who, for reasons of vested interests or psychological conditions, identify themselves with the existing setup. In order not to undermine their own pattern of identification, they unconsciously do not *want* to know too much and are ready to accept superficial or distorted information as long as it confirms the world in which they want to go on living. It would be erroneous to ascribe the general state of ignorance and confusion in political matters to natural stupidity or to the mythological "immaturity" of the people. Stupidity may be due to psychological repressions more than to a basic lack of the capacity for thinking. Only in this way, it seems, can the low level of political intelligence even among our college sample be understood. They find it difficult to think and even to learn because they are afraid they might think the wrong thoughts or learn the wrong things. It may be added that this fear, probably often due to the father's refusal to tell the child more than he is supposedly capable of understanding, is continuously reinforced by an educational system which tends to discourage anything supposedly "speculative," or which cannot be corroborated by surface findings, and stated in terms of "facts and figures."

The discrepancy brought about by the absence of political training and the abundance of political news with which the population is flooded and which actually or fictitiously presupposes such training, is only one among many aspects of this general condition. With reference to the specific focus of our research, two aspects of political ignorance may be emphasized. One is that being "intelligent" today means largely to look after one's self, to take care of one's advantages whereas, to use Veblen's words, "idle curiosity" is discouraged. Since the pertinence of economic and political matters to private existence, however, is largely obscured to the population even now, they do not bother about things which apparently have little bearing on their fate and upon which they have, as they are dimly aware, not too much influence.

The second aspect of ignorance which has to be stressed here, is of a more psychological nature. Political news and comment like all other information poured out by the radio, the press, and the newsreels, is generally absorbed during leisure time and falls, in a certain way, within the framework of "entertainment." Politics is viewed in much the same way as sport or the movies, not as something directly involved with one's own participation in the process of production. Viewed within this frame of reference, however, politics is necessarily "disappointing." It appears to people conditioned by an industrial culture and its specific kinds of "entertainment values" as drab, cold, dry—as boring. This may be enhanced by that undercurrent of American tradition which regards politics somehow as a dirty business with which a respectable person should have but little to do. Disappointment in politics as a leisure-time activity which pays no quick returns probably makes for indifference, and it is quite possible that the prevailing ignorance is due not merely to unfamiliarity with the facts but also a kind of resistance against what is supposed to serve as a pastime and mostly tends to be disagreeable. A pattern most often to be observed, perhaps, among women, namely, skipping the political sections of newspapers, where information is available, and turning immediately to gossip columns, crime stories, the woman's page, and so forth, may be an extreme expression of something more general.

To sum up, political ignorance would seem to be specifically determined by the fact that political knowledge as a rule does not primarily help to further individual aims in reality, whereas, on the other hand, it does not help the individual to evade reality either.

2. TICKET THINKING AND PERSONALIZATION IN POLITICS

The frame of mind concomitant with ignorance and confusion may be called one of lack of political experience in the sense that the whole sphere of politics and economics is "aloof" from the subject, that he does not reach it with concrete innervations, insights, and reactions but has to contend with it in an indirect, alienated way. Yet, politics and economics, alien as they may be from individual life, and largely beyond the reach of individual decision and action, decisively affect the individual's fate. In our present society, in the era of all-comprising social organization and total war, even the most naive person becomes aware of the impact of the politico-economic sphere. Here belongs, of course, primarily the war situation, where literally life and death of the individual depend on apparently far-away political dynamics. But also issues such as the role of unionism in American economy, strikes, the development of free enterprise toward monopolism and therewith the question of state control, make themselves felt apparently down to the most private and intimate realms of the individual.

This, against the background of ignorance and confusion, makes for anxiety on the ego level that ties in only too well with childhood anxieties. The individual has to cope with problems which he actually does not understand, and he has to develop certain techniques of orientation, however crude and fallacious they may be, which help him to find his way through the dark, as it were.[2] These means fulfill a dual function: on the one hand, they provide the individual with a kind of knowledge, or with substitutes for knowledge, which makes it possible for him to take a stand where it is expected of him, whilst he is actually not equipped to do so. On the other hand, by themselves they alleviate psychologically the feeling of anxiety and uncertainty and provide the individual with the illusion of some kind of intellectual security, of something he can stick to even if he feels, underneath, the inadequacy of his opinions.

The task of how to understand the "ununderstandable," paradoxical in itself, leads toward a paradoxical solution, that is to say, the subjects tend to employ two devices which contradict each other, a contradiction that expresses the impasse in which many people find themselves. These two devices are *stereotypy* and *personalization*. It is easy to see that these "devices" are repetitions of infantile patterns. The specific interaction of stereotypy and prejudice has been discussed in detail in the preceding chapter. It may now be appropriate to review ideological stereotypy and its counterpart, personalization, in a broader context, and to relate it to more fundamental principles long established by psychology. Rigid dichotomies, such as that between "good and bad," "we and the others," "I and the world" date back to our earliest developmental phases. While serving as necessary constructs in order to enable us to cope, by mental anticipation and rough organization, with an otherwise chaotic reality, even the stereotypes of the child bear the hallmark of stunted experience and anxiety. They point back to the "chaotic" nature of reality, and its clash with the omnipotence fantasies of earliest infancy. Our stereotypes are both tools and scars: the "bad man" is the stereotype par excellence. At the same time, the psychological ambiguity inherent in the use of stereotypes, which are both necessary and constricting forces, stimulate regularly a countertendency. We try, by a kind of ritual, to soften the otherwise rigid, to make human, close, part of ourselves (or the family) that which appears, because of its very alienness, threatening. The child who is afraid of the bad man is at the same time tempted to call every stranger "uncle." The traumatic element in both these attitudes continuously serves as an obstacle to the reality principle, although both also function as means of adjustment. When transformed into character traits, the mechanisms involved make more and more for irrationality. The opaqueness of the present political and economic situation for the average person provides an ideal opportunity for retrogression to the infantile level of stereotypy and personalization. The political rationalizations used by the uninformed and confused are compulsive revivals of irrational mechanisms never overcome during the

[2] This has been pointed out with regard to the imagery of the Jews. See Chapter XVI, p. 618f.

individual's growth. This seems to be one of the main links between opinions and psychological determinants.

Once again, stereotypy helps to organize what appears to the ignorant as chaotic: the less he is able to enter into a really cognitive process, the more stubbornly he clings to certain patterns, belief in which saves him the trouble of really going into the matter.

Where the rigidly compulsive nature of the stereotype cuts off the dialectics of trial and error, stultification enters the picture. Stereotypy becomes—to use J. F. Brown's term—stereopathy. This is the case in the political area where a firm bulk of ignorance and lack of any relation to the objective material forbids any real experience. In addition, industrial standardization of innumerable phenomena of modern life enhances stereotypical thinking. The more stereotyped life itself becomes, the more the stereopath feels in the right, sees his frame of thinking vindicated by reality. Modern mass communciations, moulded after industrial production, spread a whole system of stereotypes which, while still being fundamentally "ununderstandable" to the individual, allow him at any moment to appear as being up to date and "knowing all about it." Thus, stereotyped thinking in political matters is almost inescapable.

However, the adult individual, like the child, has to pay a heavy price for the comfort he draws from stereotypy. The stereotype, while being a means of translating reality in a kind of multiple-choice questionnaire where every issue is subsumed and can be decided by a plus or minus mark, keeps the world as aloof, abstract, "nonexperienced" as it was before. Moreover, since it is above all the alienness and coldness of political reality which causes the individual's anxieties, these anxieties are not fully remedied by a device which itself reflects the threatening, streamlining process of the real social world. Thus, stereotypy calls again for its very opposite: personalization. Here, the term assumes a very definite meaning: the tendency to describe objective social and economic processes, political programs, internal and external tensions in terms of some person identified with the case in question rather than taking the trouble to perform the impersonal intellectual operations required by the abstractness of the social processes themselves.

Both stereotypy and personalization are inadequate to reality. Their interpretation may therefore be regarded as a first step in the direction of understanding the complex of "psychotic" thinking which appears to be a crucial characteristic of the fascist character. It is obvious, however, that this subjective failure to grasp reality is not primarily and exclusively a matter of the psychological dynamics of the individuals involved, but is in some part due to reality itself, to the relationship or lack of relationship between this reality and the individual. Stereotypy misses reality in so far as it dodges the concrete and contents itself with preconceived, rigid, and overgeneralized ideas to which the individual attributes a kind of magical omnipotence. Conversely, personalization dodges the real abstractness, that is to say, the "reification" of a social reality which is determined by property relations and in which the human beings themselves are, as it were, mere appendages. Stereotypy and personalization are two divergent parts of an actually nonexperienced world, parts which are not only irreconcilable with each other, but which also do not allow for any addition which would reconstruct the picture of the real.

a. CASES OF POLITICAL TICKET THINKING.   We limit ourselves to describing a few cases of political stereotypy.

M359 from the University Extension Testing Class is departmental manager for a leather company. He is high on E and PEC but middle on F. While imbued with authoritarian ideas he shows a certain imaginativeness and general disposition to discursive argumentation somewhat different from the typical high scorer's mentality. It is thus the more striking to find that the political section of his interview is completely abstract and cliché-like. Just because this subject is by no means a fanatic, his statements serve well to illustrate how ignorance is covered up by phraseology, and how the stereotypes, borrowed from the vernacular of current newspaper editorials, make for the acceptance of reactionary trends. In order to give a concrete picture of how this mechanism works, his political statements are given in full. This may also supply us with an example of how the various topics with which we shall have to deal in detail afterwards form a kind of ideological unit once a person is under the sway of political semi-information:

(Political trends?) "I am not very happy by the outward aspect of things, too much politics instead of a basis of equality and justice for all men. Running of the entire country is determined by the party in power, not very optimistic outlook. Under Roosevelt, the people were willing to turn entire schedule of living over to the government, wanted everything done for them. (Main problem?) No question but the problem of placing our servicemen back into employment, giving them a degree of happiness is a major problem. If not handled soon, may produce a serious danger. More firm organization of servicemen."

(What might do?) "Boycott the politicians and establish the old-time government that we should have had all along. (What is this?) Government of, by, and for the people." Subject emphasizes the moderate, average man is the serviceman. (Unions?) "Not satisfied with them. One characteristic is especially unsatisfactory. Theory is wonderful and would hate to see them abolished, but too much tendency to level all men, all standards of workmanship and effort by equalizing pay. Other objection is not enough democratic attitude by the membership, generally controlled by minority group." Subject emphasizes the compulsion imposed upon men to join but not to participate with the results of ignorant union leaders. He emphasizes the need to raise the standards of voting by members and to require rotation of office and high qualifications for officers. He compares these adversely with business leaders.

(Government control?) "There is too much tendency to level everything, doesn't give man opportunity to excel." Subject emphasizes the mediocrity of government workers, pay is insufficient to attract the best calibre of men and no incentive plans, etc.

(Threats to present government?) "Probably most dangerous threat to our government today, and that also applies to union organization, and life in general, is disinterest, the tendency to let the other fellow do it on the part of great numbers of people so that things go on the way a few selfish men determine."

The decisive twist is achieved by jumping from the very abstract idea of "equality and justice for all men" to the equally formalistic condemnation of "running the country by the party in power"—which happens to be the party of the New Deal. The vague cliché of an all-comprising democracy serves as an instrument against any specific democratic contents. It should not be overlooked, however, that some of his statements on unions—where he has some experience—make sense.

M1225a, a medium scorer who has been eighteen months at sea and is strongly interested in engineering, is a good example of stereotypy in politics employed by otherwise moderate people, and of its intimate relationship to ignorance. To this man one of the greatest political problems today is "the unions." Describing them, he applies indiscriminately and without entering into the matter three current clichés—that of the social danger, that of government interference, and that of the luxurious life of union leaders—simply by repeating certain formulae without caring much about their interconnection or their consistency:

"For one thing they have too much power. Cross between the socialistic part of the union and the government . . . seems to go to the other extreme. Government investigation . . . (subject seems rather confused in his ideas here). The unions . . . socialistic form in there. I know, I belonged to a few unions. They get up there and then call you brother and then drive off in a Cadillac. . . . Nine times out of ten the heads of the unions don't know anything of the trade. It's a good racket . . ."

Most of his subsequent answers are closely in line with a general pattern of reactionism, formulated mostly in terms of "I don't believe in it" without discussing the issue itself. The following passages may suffice as an illustration.

($25,000 limit on salaries?) "I don't believe in that."
(Most dangerous threats to present form of government?) "I believe it's in the government itself. Too many powers of its own."
(What ought to be done?) "Going to have to solve a lot of other problems first. Get goods back on the market."
(What about this conflict between Russia on the one hand and England and this country on the other?) "I don't particularly care for Russia and I don't particularly care for England."

In this case, clichés are manifestly used in order to cover up lack of information. It is as if each question to which he does not know any specific answer conjures up the carry-overs of innumerable press slogans which he repeats in order to demonstrate that he is one of those who do not like to be told and do like to think. Underlying is only a rigid pattern of yeas and nays. He is aware of how a man of his general political outlook should react to each political issue but he is not aware of the issues themselves. He therefore supplements his plus and minus marks by phrases which more often than not are mere gaucheries.

F139 belongs to the type which is to be characterized in Chapter XIX as "rigid low." Her most outstanding trait is her violent hatred of alcohol— which suggests deeper-lying "high" trends. Liquors are her Jews, as it were. She regards herself as a Christian Socialist and solves most problems not by discussing them but referring to what the religious socialist should think.

The break between her opinions and any kind of substantial experience is evidenced by the following statement:

"My favorite world statesman is Litvinov. I think the most dramatic speech of modern times is the one he made at the Geneva Conference when he pleaded for collective security. It has made us very happy to see the fog of ignorance and distrust surrounding the Soviet Union clearing away during this war. Things are not settled yet, though. There are many fascists in this country who would fight Roosevelt if they could."

She has a ready-made formula for the problem of nonviolence in international affairs:

"Of course, I am an internationalist. Would I be a true Christian if I weren't? And I have always been a pacifist. Wars are completely unnecessary. This one was. That is, it could have been avoided if the democratic people had recognized their own interest early enough and taken the proper steps. But they did not. And now we ask ourselves: would the interests of the people of the world be advanced by a fascist victory? Obviously they would not. So we must support this war completely because we are faced with a clear choice and cannot avoid it."

She offers a clear example of the association of stereotypy and personalization. Whereas her political persuasion should induce her to think in objective socioeconomic terms, she actually thinks in terms of favorite people, preferably famous ones, of humans who are public institutions as it were—of "human stereotypes."

"My second favorite world statesman is our own President although, perhaps, I should say Mrs. Roosevelt. I don't think he would have been anything without her. She really made him what he is. I believe the Roosevelts have a very sincere interest in people and their welfare. There is one thing that bothers me about them though— specially Mrs. Roosevelt—that is—liquor. She is not against it and it seems to me she should know how much we would be improved as a people without it."

She exhibits a significant characteristic of the low scorers' political stereotypy: a kind of mechanical belief in the triumph of progress, the counterpart to the high scorers' frequent references to impending doom which is also a keynote of the above-quoted political statements of *M359*.

"All one has to do is look backward to feel optimistic. I would not be a true

Christian if I did not believe that man's progress is upward. We are so much farther along than we were a century ago. Social legislation that was only a dream is an accomplished fact."

b. EXAMPLES OF PERSONALIZATION. The tendency towards personalization feeds on the American tradition of personal democracy as expressed most strikingly by the power delegated to the executive branch of the government by our Constitution, and also on that aspect of traditional American liberalism which regards competition as a contest between men, where the better man is likely to conquer. Cause and effect seem to be somewhat reversed: whereas in market economy the supposedly "better man" is defined by competitive success, people have come to think that success falls to the better man. Consistent with this is the highly personalized character of political propaganda, particularly in electioneering where the objective issues at stake are mostly hidden behind the exaltation of the individuals involved, often in categories which have but very little to do with the functions those individuals are supposed to fulfill. The ideal of a democracy, where the people have their immediate say, is frequently misused under conditions of today's mass society, as an ideology which covers up the omnipotence of objective social tendencies and, more specifically, the control exercised by the party machines.

The material on personalization is both abundant and monotonous. A few examples may suffice.

The low-scoring man, *M116*, prefers Wallace to Dewey because

"Wallace is the better man and I usually vote for the better man."

Here personalization is the more striking since these two figures are actually defined by objectively antagonistic platforms, whereas it is more than doubtful whether the interviewee, or, for that matter, the great majority of the American people, is in any position to say what they are like "as men."

The high-scoring man, *M102*, employs almost literally the same expression as *M116:*

". . . put down Democratic, but I never thought much about the party. I don't vote for the party but for the best man."

Professed belief in political theories is no antidote for personalization. *M117*, another "low" man, regards himself as a "scientific socialist" and is full of confidence in sociological psychology. But when asked about American parties, he comes out with the following statement:

"I don't know about that. I'm only interested in the man and his abilities. I don't care what party he belongs to. (What man do you like?) F. D. R. is one of the greatest. I did not like him when he was elected but I admit I was wrong. He did a marvelous job. He was concerned with the benefit of the country. Truman is doing a good job so far. The senators and congressmen are run-of-the-mill. Dewey is outstanding, I think; he has potentialities. He is apparently sincere and honest and concerned with the whole country. He did a good job as District Attorney."

More aspects of personalization will be described when our interviewees' attitudes towards Roosevelt are under consideration. Here, we content ourselves with suggesting two qualities which seem to play a great role in the personalization complex and which recur regularly in our high scorers' statements about Dewey: Honesty and Sincerity.

F114, a high-scoring woman, knows that Dewey "is strong, young, courageous, honest. He may have faults, but they're useful faults. I felt he was a strong, young person." Obviously, this statement is linked to the adulation of strength that plays so large a role in the psychology of our high scorers (cf. Chapter VII). The honesty of the former D.A. is derived from his much-advertised drive against political racketeering and corruption. He is supposed to be honest because he has exterminated, according to his propagandist build-up, the dishonest. Honesty seems largely to be a rationalization for vindictiveness. Speaking psychologically, the image of Dewey is a projection of the punitive superego, or rather one of those collective images which replace the superego in an externalized, rigid form. The praise of his honesty, together with the repeated emphasis on his strength and youth, fall within the "strong man" pattern.

F117, another high scorer, of the Professional Women group, has a maximal score on A-S and is generally extremely conservative. Her similarly personalized appraisal of Dewey strikes a slightly different note but fits within the same pattern:

She feels that Dewey knows the value of money better than Roosevelt, because he came from a family that did not have too much.

The punitiveness behind the praise of the honest man shows itself in this example as hatred against comfortable living, against the "snobbish upper class" who supposedly enjoy the things which one has to deny to oneself. Dewey, per contra, is the symbol of one's own frustrations and is unconsciously, i.e., sadomasochistically, expected to perpetuate frustration. What he seems to stand for within the minds of the high-scoring subjects is a state of affairs in which everybody has "learned the value of a dollar." Identification with him is easy because as a prospective President he has the halo of power whereas his frugality is that of the middle-class subject herself.

Perhaps it is not accidental that infatuation with honesty is particularly frequent among women. They see life from the consumer's side; they do not want to be cheated, and therefore the noisy promise of honesty has some appeal to them.

As to the differentiation between high and low scorers with regard to personalization, an impression may tentatively be formulated which is hard to substantiate but consistent with our clinical findings. The element of personalization that counts most heavily with the low scorers seems to be confidence, the idea that public figures are good, friendly fathers who take care of one, or of the "underdog." It seems to be derived from an actual life relationship to one's parents, from unblocked positive transference. This observation will be given relief when the attitude of our subjects towards Roosevelt is discussed. Conversely, the personal trait most appreciated by the high scorer seems to be strength. Social power and control, the ultimate focus of their identification, is translated by the personalization mechanism into a quality inherent in certain individuals. The symbols of the powers that be are drawn from the imagery of a stern father to whom one "looks up."

One last aspect of personalization may be mentioned. To know something about a person helps one to seem "informed" without actually going into the matter: it is easier to talk about names than about issues, while at the same time the names are recognized identification marks for all current topics. Thus, spurious personalization is an ideal behavior pattern for the semi-erudite, a device somewhere in the middle between complete ignorance and that kind of "knowledge" which is being promoted by mass communication and industrialized culture.

To sum up: ever more anonymous and opaque social processes make it increasingly difficult to integrate the limited sphere of one's personal life experience with objective social dynamics. Social alienation is hidden by a surface phenomenon in which the very opposite is being stressed: personalization of political attitudes and habits offers compensation for the dehumanization of the social sphere which is at the bottom of most of today's grievances. As less and less actually depends on individual spontaneity in our political and social organization, the more people are likely to cling to the idea that the man is everything and to seek a substitute for their own social impotence in the supposed omnipotence of great personalities.

3. SURFACE IDEOLOGY AND REAL OPINION

The alienation between the political sphere and the life experience of the individual, which the latter often tries to master by psychologically determined intellectual makeshifts such as stereotypy and personalization, sometimes results in a gap between what the subject professes to think about politics and economy and what he really thinks. His "official" ideology conforms to what he supposes he *has* to think; his real ideas are an expression of his more immediate personal needs as well as of his psychological urges. The "official" ideology pertains to the objectified, alienated sphere of the political, the "real opinion" to the subject's own sphere, and the contradiction between the two expresses their irreconcilability.

Since this formal structure of political thinking has an immediate bearing upon one of the key phenomena of susceptibility to fascism, namely upon pseudoconservatism, it may be appropriate to offer a few examples here.

F116, a prejudiced woman of the University Extension Group, offers an example of a conflict between surface ideology and real attitude through her somewhat deviate pattern of scale scores: she is middle on E and F but low on PEC. In her case, the deeper determinants are doubtless potentially fascist as evidenced particularly by her strong racial prejudice against both Negroes and Jews. In other political issues the picture is highly ambivalent. Characteristically, she classes herself as a Democrat, but voted for Willkie and then for Dewey. She "wasn't against Roosevelt," but her statement that "no man is indispensable" thinly veils her underlying hostility. She

"knew what Hoover stood for, and I had no use for him. But that didn't mean I had to worship Roosevelt. He was a good man, but when I heard people weeping and wailing over his death, I was just disgusted. As though he were indispensable."

The amazing irregularity is an emphatically pro-Russian statement and an outspokenly antifascist attitude in international politics:

"Now, I am a great admirer of Russia. Perhaps I shouldn't say it out loud, but I am. I think they are really trying to do something for all the people. Of course there was a lot of suffering and bloodshed but think of what they had to struggle against. My husband really gets disturbed about this. He says I ought to go to Russia if I like communism so much. He says that to admire communism is to want a change and he thinks it is very wrong for me to even sound as though I wanted any change when we have enough and are comfortable and are getting along all right. I tell him that is very selfish and also that some people under the Czar might have felt that way but when the situation got so bad there was a revolution they got wiped out too. (American Communists?) Well, I couldn't say because I don't really know anything about them.

"I don't hold the United States blameless. I think we have lots of faults. We talk now as though we had always hated war and tried to stop this one. That isn't true. There were ways to stop this war if they had wanted to. I remember when Mussolini moved on Ethiopia. I always think of that as the real beginning of this war. And we were not interested in stopping that. My husband doesn't like me to criticize the United States."

The frequent interspersion of this statement with reference to disagreements with her husband, from whom she is "very much different politically" and with whom she has "terrible arguments" leads us to assume that her "progressive" political views in areas apparently not highly affect-laden by her are rationalizations of her strong resentment of the man of whom she says "I don't think we can live for ourselves alone." One is tempted to hypothesize that she wants him to get mad at her when she speaks in favor of Russia. In her case, the broad-mindedness and rationality of surface opinion seems to be conditioned by strong underlying, repressed irrationalities:

Interviewer did not have much success with very personal data. She turned aside questions that came close to her deeper feelings. There was no depth to the discussion of her husband.

When it comes, however, to political topics which, for some reason unexplored in the interview, really mean something to this subject, she forgets all about her own rationality and gives vent to her vindictiveness though with a bad conscience, as evidenced by her previously quoted statement (Chapter XVI) that "she is not very proud of her anti-Semitic bias."

M320, of the University Extension Testing Class, is a low-scoring man, hesitant, apologetic, shy, and unaggressive. He wants to become a landscape architect. His political views are consciously liberal and definitely nonprejudiced. He struggles to maintain his liberalism continuously, but this is not easy for him with regard to certain political matters, his impulses in many instances disavowing what he states. He begins with the typical low scorer's statement:

"I am afraid I don't have as many ideas about politics and government as I should, but I think—a lot of people are more liberal now than they have been recently. Possibly some like the change that is taking place in England—I don't know."

He first takes a mildly antistrike attitude:

"I don't know, I cannot see that, as just a straight demand, without taking into consideration the company and its ties and all that. I have not read much about that but . . . in a large company . . . maybe they might be able to take it, all right, but in little shops . . . and if it did go through, and even if it did not have disastrous (effects) on business closing . . . price rises would make it come out even anyway. I guess I am really not in favor of strikes but I can see it just about. . . ."

Then he talks himself into a more definite stand against strikes, introduced by the still democratic "getting together" formula.

"They ought to get together and give, maybe, a 20 per cent or 30 per cent raise, then maybe kinda split it . . . and these strikes . . . just start at the wrong end . . . because if the strike is settled . . . they still have to come to some sort of agreement . . . and it's gonna be forced and men'll be driven . . . I guess human nature just is not that way but. . . ."

The last statement, rather confused, actually belongs to the high-scorer pattern concerning the inhert badness of human nature (cf. Chapter VII).

After he has made this turn, he goes on with the usual high scorer's condemnation of PAC, government control, etc., and ends up with an ambivalent statement about minimum wage-hour legislation:

"Well, things like that I guess if—I guess they are necessary—I guess maybe I am an idealist—I don't think there should have been a minimum wage law because I think the employer should pay his employee a living wage and if he cannot pay that, well, the person does not have to work there but if the employer cannot pay that, he is not going to stay in business. . . ."

It is the general trend rather than any specific statement which bears witness to the wish to be politically progressive and the very definite changes of mind as soon as concrete issues are raised. This man's "political instincts" —if this term is allowed—are against his official progressiveness. One might well infer from this observation that one can differentiate better between political potentials by looking at deeper psychological impulses than by looking at avowed ideology.

Something similar can be observed with the medium-scoring man $M118$, of the Extension Psychology Class group, a registered Democrat. He was middle on A-S but low on F and low-middle on E. It is the interviewer's impression that he is potentially "low" but that certain personality factors prevent him from going all the way. The exceptional aspect about him may well be explained through the conflict between different opinional layers. In terms of "big" and comparatively abstract political issues, he comes out with a "progressive" statement.

"There is a trend toward socialism, I don't know how modified. The conflict between labor and business will probably be mediated by the government. The government will probably hold the balance of power in labor-business conflicts. The emphasis now is on free enterprise but that often results in monopoly, the big concerns squeezing the little guys to death. There is too much of a gap between the rich and the poor. People climb up by pushing others down, with no regulation. For this reason, government should have more influence, economically, whether or not it goes as far as socialism."

The interviewer happened to ride with the subject from Berkeley to San Francisco and continued the discussion in a more informal, unofficial way, touching the subject matter of unionism. In this context a classic example of the gap between official ideology and political thinking in terms of one's own immediate interests occurred:

He thinks the C. I. O. is better than the A. F. of L. and he thinks that unions ought to extend their functions even more in political and educational and higher management brackets, but he himself won't join the Federal Workers Union which he would be eligible to join because he feels they are not enough concerned with the problems of the higher level incomes, that they are too much interested in keeping the wages of the poorer groups above a certain minimum. He wishes they would be concerned with promotions and upgrading and developing good criteria by which people could be promoted.

The Canadian $M934$, again a "medium" of the Public Speaking Class, is studying to become a minister. He calls himself "very far over on the left wing" but qualifies this immediately by the statement:

". . . I'm of a practical nature and I would not vote for the socialists . . . especially if I thought they would get in."

To him, the practical is irreconcilable with socialism. The latter is all right as an idea, as a stimulant, as it were, but heaven forbid that it should materialize.

"I would vote . . . only to maintain socialist opposition . . . to keep the existing government from going too far to the right . . . but don't think they have the experience to . . . put their socialist program into effect . . . and I think their program has to be modified."

He praises the British Labour Government but actually only because it has not carried through a socialist program, an abstinence interpreted by the interviewee as a sign of "political experience."

"Well . . . I think they were ready for the job . . . aren't trying to change social order in one fell swoop . . . I think that is an evidence of their maturity."

This subject wants to be endowed with the prestige of a left-wing intellectual while at the same time, as an empirical being, he is manifestly afraid of a concrete materialization of ideas to which he subscribes in the abstract.

It is hardly accidental that in these cases the overt ideology is always progressive, the real opinion of an opposite character. This would seem to have something to do with established democracy in this country, which makes the expression of democratic ideas the thing to be done, while the opposite is, in a certain way, unorthodox. There is reason to believe that the fascist potential today shows itself largely in the maintenance of traditional ideas which may be called either liberal or conservative, whereas the underlying "political instinct," fed largely by unconscious forces of the personality, is completely different. This will be elaborated in the following section.

4. PSEUDOCONSERVATISM

Our analysis of the questionnaire findings on PEC (Chapter V) has led to a differentiation between those who are high on PEC but low on E, and those who are high on both. This distinction was interpreted in terms of genuine and pseudoconservatives, the former supporting not only capitalism in its liberal, individualistic form but also those tenets of traditional Americanism which are definitely antirepressive and sincerely democratic, as indicated by an unqualified rejection of antiminority prejudices. Our interview material allows us to give more relief to this construct and also to qualify it in certain respects. Before we go into some details of the pseudoconservative's ideology, we should stress that our assumption of a pseudoconservative pattern of ideology is in agreement with the total trend of our psychological findings. The idea is that the potentially fascist character, in the specific sense given to this concept through our studies, is not only on the overt level but throughout the make-up of his personality a pseudoconservative rather than a genuine conservative. The psychological structure that corresponds to pseudoconservatism is conventionality and authoritarian submissiveness on the ego level, with violence, anarchic impulses, and chaotic destructiveness in the unconscious sphere. These contradictory trends are borne out particularly in those sections of our study where the range between the two poles of the unconscious and the conscious is widest, above all, where the T.A.T. is considered in relation to the clinical parts of the interviews. Traits such as authoritarian aggressiveness and vindictiveness may be regarded as intermediary between these antagonistic trends of the prejudiced personality. When turning to ideology which belongs in the context of psychological determinants here under discussion, to the realm of rationalization, it should be remembered that rationalizations of "forbidden" impulses, such as the drive for destruction, never completely succeed. While rationalization emasculates those urges which are subject to taboos, it does not make them disappear completely but allows them to express themselves in a "tolerable," modified, indirect way, conforming to the social requirements which the ego is ready to accept. Hence even the overt ideology of pseudoconservative persons is by no means unambiguously conservative, as they would have us believe, not a mere reaction-formation against underlying rebelliousness; rather, it indirectly admits the very same destructive tendencies which are held at bay by the individual's rigid identification with an externalized superego. This break-through of the nonconservative element is enhanced by certain supra-individual changes in today's ideology in which traditional values, such as the inalienable rights of each human being, are subject to a rarely articulate but nevertheless very severe attack by ascendent forces of crude repression, of virtual condemnation of anything that is deemed weak. There is reason to believe that those developmental tendencies of our society which point into the direction of some more or less fascist, state capitalist organization bring to the fore formerly hidden tendencies of violence and discrimination in ideology. All fascist movements officially employ traditional ideas and values but actually give them an entirely different, antihumanistic meaning. The reason that the pseudoconservative seems to be such a characteristically modern phenomenon is not that any new psychological element has been added to this particular syndrome, which was probably established during the last four centuries, but that objective social conditions make it easier for the character structure in question to express itself in its avowed opinions. It is one of the unpleasant results of our studies, which has to be faced squarely, that this process of social acceptance of pseudoconservatism has gone a long way—that it has secured an indubitable mass basis. In the opinions of a number of representative high scorers, ideas both of political conservatism and traditional liberalism are frequently neutralized and used as a mere cloak for repressive and ultimately destructive wishes. The pseudoconservative is a man who, in the name of upholding traditional American values and institutions and defending them against more or less fictitious dangers, consciously or unconsciously aims at their abolition.

The pattern of pseudoconservatism is unfolded in the interviewer's description of M109, another high-scoring man, a semifascist parole officer:

On his questionnaire, this man writes down "Republican" as the political party of his preference, and then scratches it out. He agrees with the anti-New Deal Democrats and the Willkie-type Republicans and disagrees with the New Deal

Democrats and the traditional Republicans. This is cleared up in his interview when he says that the party does not mean anything, the candidate is the thing.[3]

Asked what is his conception of the Willkie-type Republican, he says he thinks of the Willkie supporters as the same as the Dewey supporters. Big business favored both Willkie and Dewey.

The score 67 on PEC is high-middle. An examination of the individual items seems to show that he is not a true conservative in the sense of the rugged individual. True, he agrees with most of the PEC items, going to plus 3 on the Child-should-learn-the-value-of-the-dollar and the Morgan and Ford items, but marking most of the others plus 1 or plus 2, but, be it noted, he does not agree that depressions are like headaches, that businessmen are more important than artists and professors; and he believes the government should guarantee everybody an income, that there should be increased taxes on corporations and wealthy individuals, and that socialized medicine would be a good thing. He goes to plus 3 on the last item. Thus, it appears that he favors some kind of social function on the part of the government, but believes that the control should be in the proper hands. This is cleared up by the interview. Before becoming a policeman 6½ years ago, this man was in the hospital insurance business. He says he had first to battle with the A.M.A., who did not favor any kind of medical insurance; and later he thought it wise to give up the business because state medicine was in the offing.

In summing up his position concerning medical insurance, he says:

"I like the collectiveness of it, but believe private business could do it better than the government. The doctors have butchered the thing and the politicians would do worse. People need this sort of thing and I like it in theory if it is run right."

Thus it becomes clear, according to the interviewer, that he has some kind of collectivistic value system but believes that the control should be in the hands of the group with whom he can identify himself. This is clearly the Ford and Morgan sort of group rather than labor unions which he opposes.

The decisive thing about this man is that he has, in spite of his general reactionism and his all-pervasive ideas of power—which are evidenced by most of the other sections of the interview—socialistic leanings. This, however, does not refer to socialism in the sense of nationalizing the means of production but to his outspoken though inarticulate wish that the system of free enterprise and competition should be replaced by a state-capitalist integration where the economically strongest group, that is to say, heavy industry, takes control and organizes the whole life process of society without further interference by democratic dissension or by groups whom he regards as being in control only on account of the process of formal democracy, but not on the basis of the "legitimate" real economic power behind them.

This "socialist," or rather, pseudosocialist, element of pseudoconservatism, actually defined only by antiliberalism, serves as the democratic cloak for antidemocratic wishes. Formal democracy seems to this kind of thinking to

---

[3] Personalization, as indicated by these sentences, has an obvious fascist potential. It enhances the individual as against any objective anonymous system of checks and balances, against democratic control. Behind the adulation of the "great man" looms, in the present situation, the readiness to "follow the leader."

be too far away from "the people," and the people will have their right only if the "inefficient" democratic processes are substituted by some rather ill-defined strong-arm system.

M651A, another high-scoring man, a San Quentin prisoner, convicted of first-degree murder, is a good example of pseudodemocratism as a particular aspect of pseudoconservatism.

(What do you think of political trends today?) "We have got a persecutor in California for governor . . . don't put that in. They call it a democracy . . . democracy is the best type of government but (inefficient). . . ."

Subject criticizes President Roosevelt strongly, especially his NRA. He mentions his father's being pushed out of a job partly because of NRA, but he appears to be a little confused in this reference:

"Democracy is good when it is used right. I believe that too few people control the money in the country. I don't believe in communism . . . but there is so many *little* people who never have anything. . . ."
Subject mentioned his grandmother's only receiving $30 a month pension which, he says, she cannot live on . . . law ought to be changed in that respect . . . subject emphasizes the need of extending old-age insurance to people too old to benefit by recent legislation. . . .[4]

An exceedingly serious dynamics is involved here. It cannot be disputed that formal democracy, under the present economic system, does not suffice to guarantee permanently, to the bulk of the population, satisfaction of the most elementary wants and needs, whereas at the same time the democratic form of government is presented as if—to use a favorite phrase of our subjects—it were as close to an ideal society as it could be. The resentment caused by this contradiction is turned by those who fail to recognize its economic roots against the form of democracy itself. Because it does not fulfill what it promises, they regard it as a "swindle" and are ready to exchange it for a system which sacrifices all claims to human dignity and justice, but of which they expect vaguely some kind of a guarantee of their lives by better planning and organization. Even the most extreme concept of the tradition of American democracy is summoned by the pseudoconservative way of political thinking: the concept of revolution. However, it has become emasculated. There is only a vague idea of violent change, without any concrete reference to the people's aims involved—moreover, of a change which has in common with revolution only the aspect of a sudden and violent break but otherwise looks rather like an administrative measure. This is the spiteful, rebellious yet intrinsically passive idea which became famous after the former Prince of Wales visited the distressed areas of North England: the idea that "something should be done about it." It occurs literally in the interview of the high-scoring woman, *F105*, a 37-year-old crippled, frustrated housewife with

---

[4] This case is described in detail in Chapter XXI under the name of "Ronald."

strong paranoid traits. She had voted for Roosevelt every time because "I just decided I'd be a Democrat." Asked why, she continues as follows:

"I don't know. I'm just primarily against capitalism, and the Republicans are capitalistic. The Democrats have tried to give the working class a break. Father has voted for Thomas for years. He thinks eventually the world will come to that. But he's never made an issue of it. (Are your ideals a reflection of his attitude?) Oh, it could be. I'm not conscious of it. I voted as soon as I was able to. (What do you think will happen after the war?) Probably the Republicans will be in again. I think the American public is a very changing type. Probably I'll change too. The world's in such a chaotic mess, something should be done. We're going to have to learn to live with one another, the whole world."

The phoniness of this subject's supposed progressiveness comes out in the section on minorities where she proves to be a rabid anti-Semite.

In order to guess the significance of the dull wish of this woman for a radical change it has to be confronted with the stand another pseudoconservative takes, the violently anti-Semitic San Quentin inmate, *M661A*, a robber. He plays, according to the interviewer, the bored *décadent* satiated with "too much experience" and derives from this attitude a fake aristocratic ideology which serves as a pretext for violent oppression of those whom he deems weak. He pays "very little attention to politics, except that I think we are headed for communism, and I am thumbs down on it." Asked why, he comes forward with the following confession:

"For one thing, I have never forgiven the Russians for the revolution. . . . I consider them murders and not assassinations and I haven't forgiven Russia any more than I have forgiven France for her revolution, or Mexico . . . in other words, I still believe in the Old Order and I believe we were happiest under Hoover and should have kept him. I think I would have had more money under him too and I don't believe in inheritance taxes. If I earn $100,000 by the sweat of my brow, I ought to be able to leave it to whomever I please. I guess I really don't believe that all men are created free and equal."

While he still accepts the traditional critique of government interference in the name of rugged individualism, he would favor such government control if it were exercised by the strong. Here the criminal is in complete agreement with the aforementioned (p. 676) parole officer, *M109:*

(What about government controls over business?) "I half-approve. I certainly think that somebody should be over. . . . I believe in government control because it makes it less of—I really don't believe in democracy; if we know somebody's at the helm, we can't have revolutions and things. But I have never read much on politics and I don't think I have a right to say much."

That the idea of the "right people" is actually behind *M661A's* political philosophy is shown by his explanation of why he objects to all revolutions:

"They overthrow the established order . . . and they are always made by people who never had anything . . . I've never seen a communist who came from the right strata of society . . . I did read George Bernard Shaw's (book on socialism)."

One may differentiate between two kinds of pseudoconservatives: those who profess to believe in democracy and are actually antidemocratic, and those who call themselves conservative while surreptitiously indulging in subversive wishes. This differentiation, however, is somewhat rationalistic. It does not amount to much, either in terms of psychological motivations or of actual political decision. It seems to pertain merely to thin rationalizations: the core of the phenomenon is both times identical. The just-quoted *661A* belongs to the pseudoconservative group in the narrower sense and so does *M105*, a prelaw student high on all scales, who stresses his conservative background while admitting overt fascist leanings:

"Naturally, I get my Republican sentiments from my parents. But recently I have read more for myself, and I agree with them. . . . We are a conservative family. We hate anything to do with socialism. My father regretted that he voted for F.D.R. in 1932. Father wrote to Senator Reynolds of South Carolina about the Nationalist Party. It's not America First, it's not really isolationist, but we believe that our country is being sold down the river."

The overt link between father-fixation as discussed in the clinical chapters (Part II) and authoritarian persuasions in politics should be stressed. He uses a phrase familiar with fascists when they were faced with the defeat of Germany and the German system and yet somehow wished to cling to their negative Utopia.

"America is fighting the war but we will lose the peace if we win the war. I can't see what I can possibly get out of it."

Conversely, a striking example of pseudodemocratism in the narrower sense is offered at the beginning of the political section of the interview of the high-scoring man *M108*, a strongly fascistic student of insect toxicology, discussed in the chapter on typology as representative of the extreme "manipulative" syndrome. He is against Roosevelt, against the New Deal, and against practically any social humanitarian idea. At the next moment, however, he says he did feel that he was "somewhat of a socialist."

This is literally the pattern by which the German Nazis denounced the Weimar Republic in the name of authority unchecked by democratic control, exalted the sacredness of private property, and simultaneously inserted the word socialist into the vernacular of their own party. It is obvious that this kind of "socialism," which actually amounts merely to the curtailment of individual liberties in the name of some ill-defined collectivity, blends very well with the desire for authoritarian control as expressed by those who style themselves as conservatives. Here the overt incompatibility between private interests (what he "gets out of it") and objective political logic (the certainty of an Allied victory) is by hook and crook put into the service of profascist postwar defeatism. No matter how it goes, democracy must lose. Psychologically, the destructive "impending doom" pattern is involved.

This defeatism is characteristic of another trait of pseudoconservative political philosophy: sympathy with the fascist enemy, Hitler's Germany. This is easily rationalized as humane magnanimity and even as the democratic wish to give everybody a fair deal. It is the fifth-column mentality on which Hitlerian propaganda in democratic countries drew heavily before the war and which has by no means been uprooted.

M106, a college student high on all scales, fairly rational in many respects, seems at first sight to be critical of Germany. By tracing grandiloquently the sources of German fascism to supposedly profound historical roots, largely invented themselves by fascist propaganda, however, he slips into an apologetic attitude:

"German people have always been aggressive, have loved parades, have always had a big army. They received an unfair peace after the last war. The treaty of Versailles was obviously unfair to them, and because they were hard up, they were willing to listen to a young man like Hitler when he came along. If there had been a better peace, there'd be no trouble now. Hitler came along with promises, and people were willing to go for him. They had huge unemployment, inflation, and so on."

The legend of the "unjust" treaty of Versailles must feed on tremendous psychological resources—unconscious guilt feelings against the established symbol of prowess—in non-German countries: otherwise it could not have survived the Hitlerian war. That this subject's explanations of Hitler really mean sympathy is evidenced by a subsequent statement on Hitler's policy of exterminating the Jews, already quoted in Chapter XVI:

"Well, Hitler, carried things just a little too far. There was some justification—some are bad, but not all. But Hitler went on the idea that a rotten apple in the barrel will spoil all the rest of them."

Still, even this subject clings to the democratic cloak and refrains from overt fascism. Asked about the Jews in this country he answers:

"Same problem but it's handled much better, because we're a democratic country."

While pseudoconservatism is, of course, predominantly a trait of high scorers, it is by no means lacking among low scorers. This pertains particularly to the apologetic attitude toward the Nazis. Thus, *F133*, a woman low on prejudice though high on F, a young student of mathematics, calls herself "rather conservative." Her "official" ideology is set against bigotry. But referring to her Irish descent, she resents the English and this leads her to pro-German statements which, in harmony with her F score, more than merely hint at underlying fascist leanings:

"I am prejudiced against England. England gave a dirty deal to the Irish people. England says the Nazis are black and Russia is white, but I think England is black. She goes around conquering people and is not just at all; and I am opposed to

Russia. It is true that they took up the cause of the people, but on the whole they are not right, and their type of government is inferior to ours. (What about the Nazis?) The Germans lost everything; they just got hopeless. I don't believe in dividing Germany just in order to make Russia and England richer. It isn't true that Germany started the war—for war two people are necessary. It is not fair to put all the burden on one nation. The Germans will only feel more persecuted and fight more. One should leave the Germans to themselves. There is much too much emphasis on how cruel the Nazis are. The Germans did not have a just peace. We can't put our own Nazi regime in to run the Germans. The Russians will cause the next war. The devastation in Germany has been just too great. I am pessimistic because people believe that everybody is bad who is down, and those are good who are strong, and the strong ones cut in pieces the one who is down, and they are just practical and not just."

The decisive shift occurs when the subject, after demanding "fairness" with regard to the problem of war guilt, protests against "too much emphasis" on Nazi atrocities.

EXCURSUS ON THE MEANING OF PSEUDOCONSERVATISM.   The introduction of the term pseudoconservative which may often be replaced by pseudoliberal and even pseudoprogressive, necessitates a brief theoretical discussion of what is "pseudo" about the subjects in question and whether and to what extent the notion of genuine political ideologies can be upheld. All these terms have to be handled with the utmost caution and should never be hypostatized. The distinction between pseudo and genuine political ideologies has been introduced mainly in order to avoid the pitfall of oversimplification, of identifying the prejudiced person, and the prospective fascist in general, with "reactionism." It has been established beyond any doubt that fascism in terms of efficient organization and technological achievement has many "progressive" features. Moreover, it has been recognized long before our study that the general idea of "preserving the American way of living," as soon as it assumes the features of vigilantism, hides violently aggressive and destructive tendencies which pertain both to overt political manifestations and to character traits. However, it has to be emphasized that the idea of the genuineness of an attitude or of behavior set against its "overplaying," is somehow as problematic as that of, say, normality. Whether a person is a genuine or a pseudoconservative in overt political terms can be decided only in critical situations when he has to decide on his actions. As far as the distinction pertains to psychological determinants, it has to be relativized. Since all our psychological urges are permeated by identifications of all levels and types, it is impossible ever completely to sever the "genuine" from what is "imitation." It would be obviously nonsensical to call ungenuine those traits of a person which are based on the identification with his father. The idea of an absolute individual *per se*, completely identical with itself and with nothing else, is an empty abstraction. There is no psychological borderline between the genuine and the "assumed." Nor can the relation between the two ever be regarded as a static one. Today's pseudoconservative may become the genuine conservative of tomorrow.

In the light of these considerations, it will be of some methodological importance to formulate the distinction between "genuine" and "pseudo" with care. The simplest procedure, of course, would be to define both concepts operationally in terms of cluster relationships of the questionnaire and also of the interviews. One would have to call roughly pseudoconservative those who show blatant contradictions between their acceptance of all kinds of conventional and traditional values—by no means only in the political sphere—and their simultaneous acceptance of the more destructive clusters of the F scale, such as cynicism, punitiveness, and violent anti-Semitism. Yet, this procedure is somewhat arbitrary and mechanical. At its best, it would define the terms but never help to understand their implicit etiology. It would be more satisfactory to base the distinction on a psychological hypothesis that makes sense. An hypothesis that might serve is one that takes as its point of departure the differentiation between *successful or unsuccessful identification*. This would imply that the "genuine" conservative characters would be those who essentially or at least temporarily succeeded in their identification with authoritarian patterns without considerable carry-overs of their emotional conflicts—without strong ambivalence and destructive countertendencies. Conversely, the "pseudo" traits are characteristic of those whose authoritarian identification succeeded only on a superficial level. They are forced to overdo it continuously in order to convince themselves and the others that they belong, to quote the revolution-hater of San Quentin, to the right strata of society. The stubborn energy which they employ in order to accept conformist values constantly threatens to shatter these values themselves, to make them turn into their opposite, just as their "fanatical" eagerness to defend God and Country makes them join lunatic fringe rackets and sympathize with the enemies of their country.

Even this distinction, however, can claim only limited validity and is subject to psychological dynamics. We know from Freud that the identification with the father is always of a precarious nature and even in the "genuine" cases, where it seems to be well established, it may break down under the impact of a situation which substitutes the paternal superego by collectivized authority of the fascist brand.

Yet, with all these qualifications, the distinction still can claim some justification under present conditions. It may be permissible to contrast the pseudoconservatives so far discussed with a "genuine" conservative taken from the Los Angeles sample which, as pointed out in Chapter I, included—in contrast to the Berkeley sample—a number of actual or self-styled members of the upper class.

$F5008$ is low on E, middle on F, and high on PEC. She is a woman of old American stock, a direct descendant of Jefferson. She is apparently free of any vindictive sense of her social status and lays no emphasis on her good family or on her being a real member of the "right strata of society." She is definitely nonprejudiced. Her T.A.T. shows traits of a somewhat neurotic overoptimism which may or may not be a product of reaction-formation. One might venture that the "genuine" conservatives who still survive and whose number is probably shrinking, may develop an increasingly bad conscience because they become aware of the rapid development of important conservative layers of American society into the direction of labor baiting and race hatred. The more this tendency increases, the more the "genuine" conservative seems to feel compelled to profess democratic ideals, even if they are somewhat incompatible with his own upbringing and psychological patterns. If this observation could be generalized, it would imply that the "genuine" conservatives are more and more driven into the liberal camp by today's social dynamics. This may help to explain why it is so hard to find any striking examples for genuine conservatism among high scorers.

If our assumption is correct, that pseudoconservatism is based—as far as its psychological aspect is concerned—on incomplete identification, it becomes understandable why it is linked to a trait which also plays a considerable role within the pattern of conventionality: identification with higher social groups. The identification that failed is probably in most cases that with the father. Those people in whom this failure does not result in any real antagonism to authority, who accept the authoritarian pattern without, however, internalizing it, are likely to be those who identify themselves sociologically with higher social groups. This would be in harmony with the fact that the fascist movement in Germany drew heavily on frustrated middle-class people of all kinds: of those who had lost their economic basis without being ready to admit their being *déclassé;* of those who did not see any chances for themselves but the shortcut of joining a powerful movement which promised them jobs and ultimately a successful war. This socioeconomic aspect of pseudoconservatism is often hard to distinguish from the psychological one. To the prospective fascist his social identification is as precarious as that with the father. At the social root of this phenomenon is probably the fact that to rise by the means of "normal" economic competition becomes increasingly difficult, so that people who want to "make it"—which leads back to the psychological situation—are forced to seek other ways in order to be admitted into the ruling group. They must look for a kind of "co-optation," somewhat after the fashion of those who want to be admitted to a smart club. Snobbery, so violently denounced by the fascist, probably for reasons of projection, has been democratized and is part and parcel of their own mental make-up: who wants to make a "career" must really rely on "pull and climbing" rather than on individual merit in business or the professions. Identification with higher groups is the presupposition for climbing, or at least appears so to the outsider, whereas the "genuine" conservative group is utterly allergic to it. However, the man who often, in accordance with the old Horatio Alger ideology, maintains his own "upward social mobility" draws from it at least some narcissistic gratifications and felicitously anticipates internally a status which he ultimately hopes to attain in reality.

Here two examples of high scorers may be quoted, both again taken from the Los Angeles group.

5006, an extreme high scorer on all scales, one of the few of our interviewees who actually admitted that they want to kill the Jews (see his interview in Chapter XVI, p. 636), is the grandson of a dentist, whereas his father failed to become one, and he hopes fervently to regain the grandfather's social status. As to the problem of failure in identification, it is significant in this case that the image of the father is replaced by that of the grandfather—just as the idea of "having seen better times," of a good family background clouded over by recent economic developments, played a large role with the prefascist, postinflation generation in Germany.

5013, who is also extremely high on all scales, describes her father as a doctor, whereas he is actually a chiropractor—a habit which seems to be largely shared by the chiropractors themselves. If the German example teaches anything and if our concept of semierudition proves to be correct, one may expect that nonacademic "scientists" and "doctors" are strongly attracted by the fascist platform.[5]

5. THE USURPATION COMPLEX

The goal toward which the pseudoconservative mentality strives—diffusedly and semiconsciously—is to establish a dictatorship of the economically strongest group. This is to be achieved by means of a mass movement, one which promises security and privileges to the so-called "little man" (that is to say, worried members of the middle and lower middle class who still cling to their status and their supposed independence), if they join with the right people at the right time. This wish appears throughout pseudoconservative ideology in mirrored reflection. Government by representation is accused of perverting democracy. Roosevelt and the New Deal particularly are said to have usurped power and to have entrenched themselves dictatorially. Thus

[5] The role played by shady pseudo-medicine in Nazi Germany is sociologically linked to the ascendance of *déclassé* intellectuals under National Socialism, psychologically to the paranoid twist of Nazi ideology as well as of the personalities of many leaders. There is a direct interconnection between the doctrine of "purity of blood" and the glorification of sundry purifiers of the body. The first academic chair created by Hitler was one for "natural healing." His own physician was a quack, Himmler's a chiropractor, and Rudolf Hess encouraged all kinds of superstitious approaches to medicine. It should be noted that analogous tendencies make themselves felt in the American "lunatic fringe." One of our native crackpot agitators combines Jew-baiting with a "health food" campaign, directed against the *delikatessen* which are not only denounced as being Jewish but also as unwholesome. The imagery of Jewish food throughout the fascist ideology deserves careful examination.

pseudoconservatives accuse the progressives of the very thing which they would like to do, and they utilize their indictment as a pretext for "throwing the rascals out." They call for a defense of democracy against its "abuses" and would, through attacking the "abuses," ultimately abolish democracy altogether. Pseudoconservative ideology harmonizes completely with psychological projectivity.

One may well ask why people so concerned with power, if they really see the Roosevelt policy as a strong-armed dictatorship, do not endorse it and feel happy about it. The reasons, it would seem, are several. First, the social types representative of pseudoconservatism are not or do not regard themselves as beneficiaries of the New Deal. It appears to them as a government for the unemployed and for labor; and even if they themselves received some benefits from WPA or the closed shop, they are resentful about it because this demonstrates to them what they are least willing to admit: that their belonging to the middle classes has lost its economic foundation. Second, to them, the Roosevelt administration never was really strong enough. They sense very well the degree to which the New Deal was handicapped by the Supreme Court and by Congress; they know or have an inkling of the concessions Roosevelt had to make— he had to give conspicuous jobs to several men opposed to his political line, e.g., Jesse Jones; they cry "dictator" because they realize that the New Deal was no dictatorship at all and that it did not fit within the authoritarian pattern of their over-all ideology. Thirdly, their idea of the strong man, no matter in what glowing personalized terms it may be expressed, is colored by an image of real strength: the backing of the most powerful industrial groups. To them, progressives in the government are real usurpers, not so much because they have acquired by shrewd and illegal manipulation rights incompatible with American democracy, but rather because they assume a power position which should be reserved for the "right people." Pseudoconservatives have an underlying sense of "legitimacy": legitimate rulers are those who are actually in command of the machinery of production—not those who owe their ephemeral power to formal political processes. This last motif, which also plays a heavy role in the prehistory of German fascism, is to be taken the more seriously because it does not altogether contradict social reality. As long as democracy is really a formal system of political government which made, under Roosevelt, certain inroads into economic fields but never touched upon the economic fundamentals, it is true that the life of the people depends on the economic organization of the country and, in the last analysis, on those who control American industry, more than on the chosen representatives of the people. Pseudoconservatives sense an element of untruth in the idea of "their" democratic government, and realize that they do not really determine their fate as social beings by going to the polls. Resentment of this state of affairs, however, is not directed against the dangerous contradiction between economic inequality and formal political equality but against the democratic form as such. Instead of trying to give to this form its adequate content, they want to do away with the form of democracy itself and to bring about the direct control of those whom they deem the most powerful anyway.

This background of the dictatorship idea, that democracy is no reality under prevailing conditions, may be evidenced by two quotations from medium-scoring men. *M1223h* follows up his statement that the Democrats are going communistic and that the unions should be curbed, by the statement, "The people aren't running the country."

M1225a speaks cautiously about democracy: "It's supposed to be a government of the people by representation."

Asked whether we had it in this country he answers bluntly: No, but qualifies this immediately with the statement—a pretty standardized one— "We have as close to it as there is."

Similarly, *M1223h* qualifies his critique by the contention that "America is still fairly democratic but going away from democracy too fast."

The contradictory utterances of these two men, apart from wishful thinking, indicate that they are perturbed by the antagonism between formal political democracy and actual social control. They just reach the point where they see this antagonism. They did not dare, however, to explain it but rather retract their own opinions in order not to become "unrealistic." Conformism works as a brake on their political thinking.

A few examples of the usurpation fantasy proper follow.

M208, who obtained a middle score on E and F and a high score on PEC, insists, according to his interviewer,

that President Roosevelt lost the popular vote by several thousand votes, according to counts he and his father made following the news reports over the radio, implying that the official count had been incorrect.

While this man is for "initiative and competition, against government bungling and inefficiencies," he has boundless confidence in social control exercised by the proper organization:

"The best organizations for a citizen to belong to in order to influence the conditions in his community are local Chambers of Commerce. By improving your city, you make it attractive and create wealth." He said the San Francisco Chamber of Commerce was something he belonged to and his organization would send out postcards very soon to every single individual in the city in a huge membership drive.

M656, a high-scoring prison inmate (grand theft and forgery), was interviewed shortly after President Roosevelt's death and when asked what he regarded as the greatest danger facing this country, said

"the government we just had, the one that brought on the war, the Nazi-dictatorship."

The high-scoring man *M108,* the aforementioned insect toxicologist, is convinced that Roosevelt only carried out Hoover's ideas, a statement not infrequent among prejudiced subjects who regard the New Deal as usurpation in so far as it has "stolen" its ideas from its opponents. Asked further about Roosevelt, he goes on:

> "he usurped power that was necessary to do something—he took a lot more power than a lot. . . . He has been in too long, and there were deals on the fire that we don't know about with Churchill or Stalin."

In the end the usurper idea coincides with that of the conspirator who makes "secret deals" detrimental to his country.

The frequency and intensity of the usurper idea, together with the fantastic nature of many of the pertinent assertions in our material justifies our calling it a "complex," that is to say, looking for a widespread and stable psychological configuration on which this idea feeds. As far as we know, no attention has been given to this complex in psychological literature, though the frequency of usurpation conflicts throughout occidental drama warrants the assumption that there must be some deep-rooted basis in instinctual dynamics for it. Suffice it to recollect that Shakespeare's most famous tragedies: Hamlet, King Lear, Macbeth, Julius Caesar, and Richard III deal in one way or the other with usurpation, and that the usurper theme runs as a red thread through the whole dramatic work of Schiller, from Franz Moor in the "Robbers" to Demetrius. On a sociopsychological level, that is to say comparatively abstractly and superficially, an explanation is easy at hand. The existence of power and privilege, demanding sacrifices of all those who do not share in its advantages, provokes resentment and hurts deeply the longing for equality and justice evolved throughout the history of our culture. In the depth of his heart, everyone regards any privilege as illegitimate. Yet one is forced continuously, in order to get along in the world as it is, to adjust himself to the system of power relationships that actually defines this world. This process has been going on over the ages, and its results have become part and parcel of today's personalities. This means that people have learned to repress their resentment of privilege and to accept as legitimate just that which is suspected of being illegitimate. But since human sufferings from the survival of privilege have never ceased, adjustment to it has never become complete. Hence the prevailing attitude towards privileges is essentially ambivalent. While it is being accepted consciously, the underlying resentment is displaced unconsciously. This is done in such a way that a kind of emotional compromise between our forced acceptance of the existence of power, and resistance against it, is reached. Resentment is shifted from the "legitimate" representatives of power to those who want to take it away from them, who identify themselves, in their aims, with power but violate, at the same time, the code of existent power relations. The ideal object of this shift is the political usurper in whom one can denounce "greed for power" while at the same time taking a positive stand with regard to established power. Still, sympathy with the usurper survives at the bottom. It is the conflict between this sympathy and our displaced aggressiveness which qualifies him for dramatic conflict.

There is reason to believe, however, that this line of thought does not fully explain the usurper complex. Much more deep-lying, archaic mechanisms seem to be involved. As a rule, the usurper complex is linked with the problem of the family. The usurper is he who claims to be the member of a family to which he does not belong, or at least to pretend to rights due to another family. It may be noted that even in the Oedipus legend, the usurper complex is involved in so far as Oedipus believes himself to be the real child of his foster-parents, and this error accounts for his tragic entanglement. We venture, with all due reservation, the hypothesis that this has something to do with an observation that can be made not infrequently: that people are afraid of not really being the children of their parents. This fear may be based on the dim awareness that the order of the family, which stands for civilization in the form in which we know it, is not identical with "nature" —that our biological origin does not coincide with the institutional framework of marriage and monogamy, that "the stork brings us from the pond." We sense that the shelter of civilization is not safe, that the house of the family is built on shaky ground. We project our uneasiness upon the usurper, the image of him who is not his parents' child, who becomes psychologically a kind of ritualized, institutional "victim" whose annihilation is unconsciously supposed to bring us rest and security. It may very well be that our tendency to "look for the usurper" has its origin in psychological resources as deep as those here suggested.

6. F.D.R.

The usurpation complex is focused on Roosevelt, whose name evokes the sharpest differences between high and low scorers that are to be found in the interview material on politico-economic topics.

It hardly needs to be said that all the statements touching upon the late president are personalized. The political issues involved appear mainly as qualities of the man himself. He is criticized and praised because he *is* this or that, not because he stands for this or that. The most drastic accusation is that of war-monger. This accusation often assumes the form of those conspiracy fantasies which are so highly characteristic of the usurper complex.

The high-scoring man *M664c,* serving a San Quentin term of one year for forgery and check writing, professes to have been originally pro-Roosevelt.

"Hell, at that (election) I was strong for Roosevelt, we had an awful depression, one thing he'd done for that state he put that dam there. . . . We didn't need the war though. (Why did we get into it?) Started sending that iron over to Japan and then helping England...."

The idea of the "red Roosevelt" belongs to the same class of objections and paranoid exaggerations of political antipathies. Though much more common among subjects who score high on E and PEC, it can sometimes be found in the statements of low scorers. Note the remarks of F140, a young nursery school helper, rated according to her questionnaire score as low on E but high on A-S and PEC. She first refers to her father.

(Is your father anti-Roosevelt?) "Oh, sure he is. He just don't have any use for Roosevelt. It's all communism that is what he says. (And what do you think about it?) Oh, I don't know. I guess he's right. He ought to know. That's all he thinks about—politics—politics."

Sometimes the suspicion that Roosevelt was a Russophile war-monger is cloaked by legalistic argumentations, such as the statement that he left the country illegally during the war.

F101, a woman who stands high on all scales, a somewhat frustrated young college student, relates that her father is "extremely anti-Roosevelt," and, when asked why, answers:

"No president is supposed to leave the country without the consent of Congress, and he goes whenever he feels like it. He is being a little too dictatorial."

With regard to domestic politics, F359, the accountant in a government department who was quoted before (Chapter XVI, p. 616), states quite clearly and in fairly objective terms the contradiction which seems at the hub of anti-Roosevelt sentiment:

Subject did not like Roosevelt because of WPA. It creates a class of lazy people who would rather get $20 a week than work. She feels that Roosevelt did not accomplish what he set out to do—raise the standard of the poorer classes.

The conceptions of communist, internationalist, and war-monger are close to another one previously mentioned—that of the snob. Just as the fascist agitator persistently mixes up radicals and bankers, claiming that the latter financed the revolution and that the former seek financial gains, the contradictory ideas of an ultraleftist and an exclusive person alienated from the people are brought together by anti-Roosevelt sentiment. One may venture the hypothesis that the ultimate content of both objections is the same: the resentment of the frustrated middle-class person against those who represent the idea of happiness, be it by wanting other people—even the "lazy ones"—to be happy, be it that they are enjoying life themselves. This irrationality can be grasped better on the level of personality than on that of ideology.

M1223h, of the Maritime School, with medium scores on E and PEC, but high on F, does not like Roosevelt—"a socialite; got too much power." Similarly, the high-scoring married woman *F117*, 37 years old, employed in a Public Health Department,

feels that Roosevelt does not know how to handle money; he was born with a great deal. Now he throws it around—"millions here and millions there."

This is the exact opposite of the praise of Dewey, whose more humble origin is supposed to guarantee thriftiness. The "democratic cloak" of the pseudoconservative consists, in cases like these, in the assertion that measures taken for the benefit of the people cannot be approved because the one who carried them out is not one of the people and therefore, in a way, has no right to act in their behalf—he is a usurper. Really folksy men, one might suppose, would rather let them starve.

The idea that the late President was too old and too ill, and that the New Deal was decrepit plays a particular role among anti-Roosevelt arguments. The dark forebodings about Roosevelt's death have come true. Yet, one may suspect here a psychological element: the fear of his death often rationalizes the wish for it. Moreover, the idea of his supposed old age pertains to the illegitimacy complex: he should give way to others, to the "young generation," to fresh blood. This is in keeping with the fact that German Nazism often denounced the over-age of the representatives of the Weimar Republic, and that Italian fascism heavily emphasized the idea of youth *per se*. Ultimately, some light is shed on the whole complex of the President's age and illness by our clinical findings, pertaining to the tendency of our high scorers to praise physical health and vigor as the outstanding quality of their parents, particularly of the mother (pp. 340 ff.). This is due to the general "externalization" of values, the anti-intraceptiveness of the prejudiced personalities who seem to be continuously afraid of illnesses. If there is an interconnection between at least some syndromes of high scorers and psychotic dispositions, one may also think of the disproportionate role played by the concern with one's own body in many schizophrenics—a phenomenon linked to the mechanisms of "depersonalization"[6] which represents the extreme of the "ego-alienness" of the id characteristic of the high scoring subject. It should be remembered once again how large a role was played by ideas such as physical health, purity of the blood, and syphilophobia throughout fascist ideology.

M104, a high scoring young man of the Public Speaking Class, who changed from studying engineering to law is an example:

Subject would have voted for Dewey. The whole New Deal has become very stagnant, old, and decrepit. He feels Roosevelt has done some fine things, some of his experiments were about as good a cure as you could get for the depression, but it is now time for a change in party, a new President, younger blood.

As in most cases, the argument has, of course, a "rational" aspect too— the Roosevelt government held office for a longer period than any other

[6] Cf. Otto Fenichel (27).

one in American history. However, the complaints about "too long" are uttered only in the name of "changing the guard," not in the name of concrete progressive ideas which could be brought about by younger people.

Resentment against old people has a psychological aspect by which it seems to be linked to anti-Semitism. There is reason to believe that some subjects displace their hostility against the father upon aged persons and the notion of old age as such. Old people are, as it were, earmarked for death. In accordance with this pattern, the image of the Jew often bears features of the old man, thus allowing for the discharge of repressed hostility against the father. Judaism is regarded, not incidentally, as the religion of the father and Christianity that of the son. The most emphatic stereotype of the Jew, that of the inhabitant of the Eastern ghetto, bears attributes of the old, such as the beard or worn and obsolete clothes.

Hostility for the aged has, to be sure, a sociological as well as a psychological aspect: old people who cannot work any more are regarded as useless and are, therefore, rejected. But this idea, like those just discussed, has little immediate bearing upon the person of Roosevelt; rather, they are transferred to him after aggression has turned against him. The universally ambivalent role of the President as a father figure thus makes itself felt.

As to those who are *in favor* of Roosevelt, there are two clear-cut main motifs which are almost the reverse of those found in the Roosevelt haters. The man "who thinks too much of himself and assumes dictatorial powers" is now praised as a great personality; the leftist and initiator of the New Deal is loved as a friend of the underdog.

The "great personality" motif appears in the statement of the low-scoring man, *M711*, an interviewer in government employment, with many of the typical "low" characteristics of mildness, gentleness, and indecision.

(Roosevelt) "seemed to be the only man the country had produced that seemed to have the qualifications for the assignment (of war). . . . I'd say his ability to get along with other people . . . had been pretty responsible in the unification of our country."

The young woman, *F126*, scores low on A-S and E, middle on F, and high on PEC. She is studying journalism but actually is interested in "creative writing." She states

that her brother-in-law can find so many things to criticize and, of course, there are plenty. "But I think the President is for the underdog, and I've always been for the underdog."

The high-scoring man, *M102*, a student of seismology who went to college because he did not want to be "lined up as just an electrician," praises Roosevelt's "talent":

"Well, if another candidate had approached Roosevelt, I'd have voted for him. But, no other candidate approached his talent."

M106, another high-scoring man, again characterized by upward social mobility, is pro-Roosevelt for reasons that are just the opposite of those given by one group of his critics for disliking him, although he too suffers from the "old age" complex.

"Roosevelt has done a wonderful job but we should have a young man. Roosevelt stabilized the nation's currency, helped on unemployment, has handled foreign relations marvelously. He is a common man, goes fishing, takes time for relaxation—that's what I like. Mrs. Roosevelt has been active in political and social affairs."

The explanation of the deviation of this highly prejudiced man, who is beset by power ideas and objects to the Jews because they supposedly strive for power, is that he himself

"had infantile paralysis, and you appreciate what Roosevelt has done."

The inference may be allowed that if the same man is praised by some people as a "common man" and by others blamed as a "socialite," these judgments express subjective value scales rather than objective facts.

The established status of a President of the United States, the irrefutable success of Roosevelt, and, one may add, his tremendous impact as a symbolic father figure on the unconscious, seem in more cases than this particular one to check the usurper complex of the pseudoconservative and allow only for vague attacks about which there is something half-hearted, as if they were being made with a bad conscience.

7. BUREAUCRATS AND POLITICIANS

There is no mercy, however, for those to whom Roosevelt is supposed to have delegated power. They are usurpers, parasites, know nothing about the people, and should, one may well assume, be replaced by the "right men." The wealth of statements against bureaucrats and politicians in our interview material is tremendous. Although it comes mostly from high scorers, it is by no means confined to them, and may again be regarded as one of those patterns of political ideology which spread over the well-defined border lines of right vs. left.

It is beyond the scope of the present study to analyze the amount of truth inherent in American distrust of professional politics. Nor should it be denied that a tremendously swollen bureaucratic apparatus, such as that which was necessitated by war conditions and which was, to a certain extent, safe from public criticism, develops unpleasant features, and that the machinery has an inbound tendency to entrench itself and to perpetuate itself for its own sake. However, as one analyzes carefully the standard criticism of the bureaucrats and politicians, he finds very little evidence of such observations, very few specific indictments of bureaucratic institutions which prove them to be incompetent. It is impossible to escape the impression that "the bureaucrat," with the help of some sections of the press, and some radio commentators, has become a magic word, that he functions as a scapegoat to be blamed indiscriminately for all kinds of unsatisfactory conditions, somewhat reminiscent of the anti-Semitic imagery of the Jew with which that of the bureaucrat is often enough merged. At any rate, the frequency and intensity of antibureaucratic and antipolitician invectives is quite out of proportion with any possible experience. Resentment about the "alienation" of the political sphere as a whole, as discussed at the beginning of this chapter, is turned against those who represent the political sphere. The bureaucrat is the personalization of ununderstandable politics, of a depersonalized world.

Striking examples of this general attitude of high scorers are provided by the above-quoted political statements of Mack (p. 34) and of the markedly anti-Semitic manager of a leather factory, M359 (p. 666 of this chapter).

Sometimes the invectives against politics terminate in tautologies: politics is blamed for being too political.

M1230a is a young welder who wanted to study engineering. He scores high on E but low on F and PEC.

(What thinking of political trends today?) "Well, they're very disrupted. We discussed them a lot, and a lot of things we don't like. The administration seems to be so tied up in politics. . . . Statesmanship is gone completely. . . . Can't believe anything you read in the newspapers. We read the newspapers mainly to laugh. . . ."

The last passage is characteristic of the alienation from politics which expresses itself in a complete, and by no means altogether unjustified, distrust of the reliability of any news which has gone through the filter of a system of communications controlled by vested interests. This distrust, however, is shifted to the scapegoat, the bureaucrat and the politician, usually attacked by the same press which is this subject's laughing stock.

F120, a high-scoring woman, differentiates between Roosevelt and the bureaucracy.[7]

(Roosevelt and the New Deal?) "I admired him, in fact I voted for him, although I did not approve of a lot of things about the New Deal. All the bureaus. I would not have minded the spending if it had gone to help people. But I resented all the wasted motion—professional people digging ditches—and especially the expensive agencies stuffed with do-nothings, bureaucrats."

M1214b, a medium scorer of the Maritime School, is antipolitical in a traditionalistic way, the ultimate direction of which is still undetermined.

"No respect for politicians: bunch of windbags. They try to sound people out and follow along." (This is just the opposite of the usual argument according to which

[7] This observation is in accordance with experience in Nazi Germany where all kinds of criticism and jokes about the party hierarchy were whispered everywhere, whilst Hitler seems to have been largely exempted from this kind of criticism. One heard frequently the remark: "The Führer does not know about these things"—even when concentration camps were concerned.

the politicians are too independent. This particular twist may indicate the under-lying awareness of the *weakness* of the representatives of formal democracy.) "They are not sincere public servants. Roosevelt, Lincoln, Jefferson, and Bryan are exceptions. Wilson was also sincere." Subject has no respect for Harding or Coolidge.

Finally, an example from a low scorer. *M112*, asked about politics, simply states:

"I don't like it. We can get along without it. Don't think that people should be just politicians. Should have an ordinary life, just hold office at times. Not be trained for politics and nothing else, should know what people want and do it. Not control things for themselves or others."

The tone of this accusation is markedly different from the phraseology of the high scorers. This man seems really to be worried lest bureaucracy should become reified, an end in itself, rather than democratically expressing the wishes of the people.

The motivation of the low scorers' criticism of bureaucrats and politicians seems largely to vary from that of the high scorers; phenomenologically, however, it reminds so much of the latter that one is led to fear that in a critical situation quite a few antipolitical low scorers may be caught by a fascist movement.

8. THERE WILL BE NO UTOPIA

The political thinking of high scorers is consummated by the way they approach the ultimate political problem: their attitude toward the concept of an "ideal society." Their opinional pattern not only concerns the means but also the ultimate social ends.

According to the frame of mind which is being analyzed here, there is no utopia and, one may add, there should be no utopia. One has to be "realistic." This notion of realism, however, does not refer to the necessity of judging and accounting on the basis of objective, factual insight, but rather to the postulate that one recognizes from the very beginning the overwhelming superiority of the existent over the individual and his intentions, that one advocates an adjustment implying resignation with regard to any kind of basic improvements, that one gives up anything that may be called a day-dream, and reshapes oneself into an appendage of the social machinery. This is reflected by political opinion in so far as any kind of utopian idea in politics is excluded altogether.

It must be pointed out that an anti-utopia complex seems to occur in the interviews of low scorers even more frequently than in those of high scorers, perhaps because the former are more ready to admit their own worries and are less under the impact of "official optimism." This differentiation between the stand taken by high and low scorers against utopia seems to be corrob-orated by the study "Psychological Determinants of Optimism regarding the

Consequences of the War" by Sanford, Conrad, and Franck (108). Official optimism, the "keep smiling" attitude, goes with underlying traits of contempt for human nature, as expressed by the cynicism cluster of the F scale, which differentiates clearly between high and low scorers. Conversely, low scorers are much more ready to admit negative facts in general, and particularly with regard to themselves, on a surface level, being less spellbound by the conventional cliché that "everything is fine," but they show, on a deeper level of their opinions, much greater confidence in the innate potentialities of the human race. One may epitomize the difference dynamically by stating that the high scorers deny utopia because they ultimately do not *want* it to materialize, whereas anti-utopian statements of the low scorers are derived from a rejection of the official ideology of "God's own country." The latter are skeptical about utopia, because they take its realization seriously and therefore take a critical view of the existent, even up to the point where they acknowledge the threat exercised by the impact of prevailing conditions against just those human potentialities in which they trust in the depth of their hearts.

M345 is a high-scoring man of the University Extension Testing Class group. He scores high on E and PEC but low on F. When asked about what he thinks of an ideal society, his answer reads:

"I don't think there is such a thing without changing everything, including the people in it. Always some people unusually wealthy, always some unusually miserable economically."

This answer is significant in many respects. The denial of the possibility of an ideal society is based on the assumption that otherwise everything ought to be changed—an idea apparently unbearable to the subject. Rather than change everything, that is to say, to disobey ultimate respect for the existent, the world should be left as bad as it is. The argument that first the people should be changed before the world can be changed belongs to the old anti-utopian armory. It leads to a vicious circle, since, under prevailing external conditions, no such internal change can ever be expected, and, actually, those who speak in this way do not even admit its possibility, but rather assume the eternal and intrinsic badness of human nature, following the pattern of cynicism discussed in the chapter on the F scale. Simultaneously wealth and poverty which are obviously the products of social conditions are hypostatized by the subject as if they were inborn, natural qualities. This both exonerates society and helps to establish the idea of unchangeability on which the denunciation of utopia feeds. We venture the hypothesis that the brief statement of this subject bares a pattern of thinking which is exceedingly widespread, but which few people would epitomize as overtly as he does.

To the aforementioned *M105*, who comes as close to overt fascism as any of our subjects, the idea of natural qualities excluding an ideal society is related immediately to the most pressing issue: the abolition of war.

"Naturally, I like America best. The question is, is it worth while to give up what we have in order to have world trade? The Japs make cheap products and can undersell us. What I'm afraid of is a perpetual lend-lease. If we do trade with other nations we should have the cash. World trade would not prevent war. The fighting instinct is there."

The significant fact about his statement is that the assumption of a "fighting instinct," which apparently is never supposed to disappear, is related in an overrealistic manner to economic advantages, cash, sticking to what one has, and so on. Incidentally, this is the same man who speaks against the present war because he "can't see what he can possibly get out of it."

Self-contradictory is a statement by the executive secretary, *F340B*, a medium-scoring woman, whose personality as a whole, as well as her ready-made political opinions, come closer to the type of the high scorer than her questionnaire leads us to believe. In terms of surface opinion she wants to be "idealistic," in terms of her specific reactions she is under the spell of "realism," the cult of the existent.

"I'm not happy about our foreign policy here—it's not definite enough, and not idealistic enough. (What are your specific criticisms?) It is not much of anything: seems we haven't got any foreign policy. (What kind of foreign policy would you like to see?) I would like to see the four freedoms, the Atlantic Charter actually applied in other countries. Then we also have to be realistic about it, but we have to strive to be idealistic—to realize the ideals eventually."

There is something pathetic about this statement. For the contention that one has to be "realistic" in order ultimately to realize the ideals is certainly true. Taken *in abstracto*, however, and without specific concepts as to how this could be achieved, the truth becomes perverted into a lie, denoting only that "it cannot be done" while the individual still maintains the good conscience that she would be only too happy if it were possible.

Psychologically, the anti-utopian pattern of political thinking is related to sadomasochistic traits. They manifest themselves strikingly in the statement of the high-scoring San Quentin inmate, *M662A*, who comes fairly close to the "tough-guy" syndrome discussed in Chapter XIX. When asked "what is an ideal society like," he answers: "Plenty of work for everybody; have all the strikes stopped."

To the naïveté of this man, who certainly belongs to the poorest strata himself, the image of the present order has been petrified to such an extent that he cannot even conceive of a social system where, because of rational organization, each individual has *less* to work—to him the ideal is that everybody *can* work, which does not only include satisfaction of basic needs but also efforts which might easily be dispensed with today. The idea that some strict order should prevail is so overpowering to him that utopia becomes a society where no strikes are to be tolerated any more, rather than a society where strikes would be unnecessary.

It should be mentioned that the general denial of utopianism is sometimes reversed by the subjects whose statements we are scrutinizing here, when they speak about the United States.

Thus, *M619*, a low scorer of the San Quentin group, led by the prison situation to complete political resignation, still feels:

". . . I think part of the reason America has become the greatest country in the world is that because the dreams a man makes might come true."

Of course, this is to be understood primarily as an expression of the dream that can be measured by the dollars and cents an individual can make, but it should not be forgotten that among the ideological foundations of American liberalism there is also a utopian element which, under certain conditions, may break through and overcome the gospel of supposed realism.

Apparently, the anti-utopian somehow feels uneasy about his own "realism," and seeks an outlet by attributing to the reality with which he is most strongly identified, his own country, some of the utopian qualities he otherwise disavows.

Only the low- to medium-scoring San Quentin murderer, *M628B*, a man who has nothing to lose in life, says bluntly:

"This country educates people, but in the so-called American way. . . . I don't believe this is the best country. Maybe in a materialistic way. . . . I would not value my life by material things."

The undertone of this statement is, similar to *M619*, one of fatalistic resignation. Even low scorers who are not anti-utopian cannot think of utopia but in a quasi-fatalistic way: as if it were something preconceived, fixed once and for all; something which one has to "look up" rather than think and realize oneself. *M711*:

(What is ideal society like?) "That's an awfully difficult question. Isn't it based on the four freedoms?"

9. NO PITY FOR THE POOR

One should expect that a frame of mind which regards everything as basically bad should at least favor, in the area of politics and social measures, as much help for those who suffer as possible. But the philosophy of the anti-utopian pessimists is not tinged by Schopenhauerian mercy. The general pattern we are investigating here is characterized by an all-pervasive feature. These subjects want no pity for the poor, neither here nor abroad. This trait seems to be strictly confined to high scorers and to be one of the most differentiating features in political philosophy. At this point, the interrelatedness of some ideas measured by the PEC scale and certain attitudes caught by the

F scale should be stressed. Abolition of the dole, rejection of state interference with the "natural" play of supply and demand on the labor market, the spirit of the adage "who does not work, shall not eat" belong to the traditional wisdom of economic rugged individualism and are stressed by all those who regard the liberal system as being endangered by socialism. At the same time, the ideas involved have a tinge of punitiveness and authoritarian aggressiveness which makes them ideal receptacles of some typical psychological urges of the prejudiced character. Here goes, for example, the conviction that people would not work unless subject to pressure—a way of reasoning closely related to vilification of human nature and cynicism. The mechanism of projectivity is also involved: the potentially fascist character blames the poor who need assistance for the very same passivity and greediness which he has learnt not to admit to his own consciousness.

Examples: The extremely high-scoring San Quentin inmate, *M664C*, whose F score is outstanding, shows clearly the psychological aspect of this particular ideology. He regards as the "major problem" facing this country the fact that it might do something for the starving people abroad. His statement shows also the intimate interrelation between the "no pity for the poor" and the fatalism complexes.

"Christ, we licked those other countries and now we're gonna feed 'em. . . . I think we ought to let 'em starve, especially them Japs. . . . Lucky I don't have any relations killed in this war, I'd go out and kill me some Japs. . . . We're gonna have another depression and gonna have another war too in a few years."

By contrast, *M658*, another high-scoring convict with certain psychopathic traits, turn his affects against the unemployed rather than against the Japanese:

"I believe everybody should have an opportunity. Should not be any unemployment. Only reason they are unemployed, they are lazy like me."

This may be regarded as one of the most authentic examples of sadomasochistic thinking in our interviews. He wants others to be treated harshly because he despises himself: his punitiveness is obviously a projection of his own guilt feelings.

Women are freer of the "no pity for the poor" complex. They rather overcompensate for it in terms of social welfare and charity which is, as indicated previously, a "high" value anyway. The following statement may be regarded as characteristic of the woman who humiliates him whom she pretends to help, and actually does not help at all but just makes herself feel important.

F359, a high scorer who combines conventionality with somewhat paranoid ideas about the Negroes:

Subject thinks that the poorer people should be taken care of by state or community projects. People in the community should get together, like people, for instance, who are good at organizing boys' clubs; or they might organize dances and hold them at one person's house one week, and at somebody else's the next week. Everybody should contribute something; take up a small collection. In the case of a poor section it might get the funds from the city. One might also call on public funds for buildings, if needed.

The attitude of indifference to the lot of the poor together with admiration for rich and successful people sheds light on the potential attitude of the high scorers toward the prospective victims of fascism in a critical situation. Those who humiliate mentally those who are down-trodden anyway, are more than likely to react the same way when an outgroup is being "liquidated." This attitude has, of course, strong sociological determinants: upward social mobility, identification with the higher class to whom they wish to belong themselves, recognition of universal competition as a measuring rod for what a person is worth, and the wish to keep down the potential threat of the disinherited masses. These sociological motives, however, are inseparably bound up with the psychological mechanisms indicated above. The specific infantile implications may be indicated as follows: identification with the poor is quite enticing for children, since the world of the poor appears to them in many ways less restricted than their own, whilst they somehow sense the similarity between the social status of a child in an adult society and the status of the poor in a rich man's world. This identification is repressed at an early phase for the sake of "upward mobility," and also—even if the children are poor themselves—for the sake of the reality principle in general which tolerates compassion only as an ideology or as "charity" but not in its more spontaneous manifestations. They project the "punishment" they have received for their own compassion upon the downtrodden by regarding poverty as something the poor "brought upon themselves." The same formula, incidentally, plays a decisive role in anti-Semitism.

10. EDUCATION INSTEAD OF SOCIAL CHANGE

The complement of the "no pity for the poor" complex is the overemphasis given to the education of people within the political sections of our interviews. The frequent reference to this topic is the more significant since it does not appear in the interview schedule. Nobody will deny the desirability of political education. It is hard to overlook, however, that the ideal of education often serves as a rationalization for social privileges. People who do not want to confess to antidemocratic leanings prefer to take the stand that democracy would be all right if only people were educated and more "mature." This condition, naturally, would here and now exclude from political activities those who, on account of their economic situation, need most urgently a social change. This, of course, is never stated in so many words. If, however, as once happened, an overtly fascist man speaks in favor of the abolition of the poll tax in the South, and wants to replace it by an "intelligence test," there is little doubt about the ultimate purpose. The adulation of "education" occurs quite frequently among uneducated people—perhaps because, for some reason beyond the scope of the present study, education has come to be a kind of a panacea in American ideology. None of our subjects ever takes the trouble of defining to what the mysterious "education" should refer: whether it pertains to the general educational level or whether some special kind of political education is envisaged and how it should be carried out.

The education complex is not confined to high or medium scorers but seems to be more frequent with them than with low scorers. Some examples are given.

M1230A, a high-scoring man of the Maritime School Group, states,

(What is an ideal society like?) "It would take generations of breeding to bring everybody to the same educational standards . . . though not to have such *great* classes . . . although I think we should always have class distinction . . . some initiative to try to improve yourself."

Here it is obvious that the education idea serves as a subtle device by which the anti-utopian can act to prevent a change and yet appear progressive. It is also characteristic that the stress put on a long drawn-out educational process is concomitant with the idea that there always *should* be some class distinction.

Similarly, the Canadian *M934*, a medium scorer, endorses the education idea as a "brake," this time on the labor movement. He believes:

"The important thing in the labor movement today is education of the rank and file. I just don't think labor is ready to take more influence today."

It may be noted at random that the more production processes are standardized, the less special training is required, the more technological progress leads toward a certain enlightenment of the masses, the emptier the postulate of education becomes. Our subjects stick to it in a rather fetishistic way.

For the very high-scoring woman, *F104*, majoring in Spanish and interested in business, the political demarcation line between her ingroup, the Republicans, and the Democrats coincides with that of education.

"The type of people I have known who are Democrats are usually uneducated people who really don't know what is happening. The present administration has made a mess of things."

Thus the education ideology interprets the fact that the Democratic Party is more of a lower-class party than the Republicans.

Among low scorers the education idea is somewhat mixed up with the traditional socialist wish for enlightenment. Frequently, there occurs a complaint about the lethargy and the lack of political interest of the masses—from which, regularly, the subjects exempt themselves. In this context we may mention again the phraseological statement of our sailor, *M117:*

"We have a good basis for our political system. The majority of people are not interested or equipped enough to understand politics, so that the big proportion of U.S. politics is governed by the capitalistic system."

The education complex leads us back to where our analysis started, to the ignorance and confusion which clouds the political thinking of most of our sample. It is possible that the education complex somehow expresses the awareness that one really does not know what one talks about when one discusses politics—often enough the praise of education follows, with low scorers, self-accusations on account of their lack of knowledge. However, the vague idea of education takes care of the experience of ignorance rather summarily by a slogan and reliance on an isolated factor of cultural life, thus dispensing with the effort of political thinking. Moreover, it serves in most cases the purpose of projecting one's own ignorance onto others so that one may appear informed oneself.

One last observation may prove to be significant. Whereas the praise of education is heavily accentuated by high scorers, it is at the same time one of the most frequently heard anti-Semitic statements that "the Jews are all out for education"—generally associated with the assertion that they dodge hard manual labor. We may suspect that there is, at the hub of the education complex, the vague realization that this culture excludes the bulk of those whom it embraces from real participation in its more subtle gratifications. While the awkward talk about education expresses longing for a state of affairs where one is no longer stunted by the requirements of "being practical," fury about one's own educational frustration is projected upon the chosen foe who is supposed to possess what one has to deny to oneself.

C. SOME POLITICAL AND ECONOMIC TOPICS

Our previous discussion was, in accordance with the general approach of our study, formulated in subjective, rather than objective terms. That is to say, we have focussed our interest on the patterns of political thinking of our interviewees, rather than on the stand they take with regard to objective political issues. As a matter of course our approach led also to a discussion of numerous political topics such as, for example, the evaluation of Roosevelt, the problem of government "bureaucracy," attitudes taken toward "ideal society," etc. No strict dichotomy between the subjective and objective political issues could be made. What remains now to be discussed are the attitudes of our subjects toward those political topics of the interview schedule so far not covered, though some of them, particularly with regard to the bureaucrat complex and the problem of government control of business, have been touched upon.

1. UNIONS

The problem of unionism was heavily emphasized in our interview schedule because it is a very timely politico-economic topic, and because we expected it to be highly discriminatory. The questionnaire item, "Labor Unions should become stronger and have more influence generally," did indeed prove to be discriminating in the statistical sense (D. P., 3.16 for men and 3.49 for women on Forms 40–45), but the interview protocols offer ample warning against any such primitive formula as low-score = pro-union, high-score = anti-union. A certain amount of criticism of unions is universal and there is no lack of otherwise outspoken low scorers who deviate with regard to the union question. Unambiguously pro-union are only a small number of politically conscious and highly articulate left-wingers. Otherwise, there are strong reservations with respect to unions throughout our sample. High and low scorers differ more in the way these reservations are made than in the simple pro vs. anti dimension. A critical attitude is taken by people who do not belong to unions, as well as by those who are members.

Some differences between questionnaire and interview might be expected on the basis that the questionnaire calls for more or less forthright statements, whereas the interview allows the subjects to elaborate their ideas in all their complexity. Here, it would seem, the interview comes closer to the subjects' real opinion than does the questionnaire. Since the organization of labor and the issue of the closed shop affects the lives of most people in some immediate way, the factor of "alienation" and the accompanying ignorance and confusion plays a lesser part than it does, say, when people discuss "all those bureaus" far away in Washington.

Thus, the critical sentiment expressed with regard to the unions has to be taken very seriously. This criticism must not be identified automatically with reactionism. Here more than anywhere else, there is some basis in reality, and the complaints are, generally, much more reasonable, show much more common sense than when it comes to issues such as the politicians or the Jews. Labor organizations have more or less to adapt themselves to the prevailing conditions of an economic life ruled by huge combines, and thus they tend to become "monopolies." This means discomfort for innumerable persons who in their business are faced with a power which interferes with what they still feel to be their individual right as free competitors. They have to yield an extra part of their profit to what labor demands from them, over and above the price for the commodity which they buy, the laborer's working power. This appears to them as a mere tribute to the power of the organization. It is significant, however, that at least the high scorers resent labor monopolies but not their model, industrial monopolization as such. This is not surprising. The population has much more direct contact with the labor organizations than with the organizations of industry. People have to negotiate with their local unions about extra pay, overtime, wage increases, and working conditions, while Detroit, where their car is being made and priced, is far away. Of course, deeper-lying motives of social identification are also involved.

The monopolization of labor affects also the workers themselves who feel bossed by the huge organization upon which they exercise very little influence as individuals and who, if they are not admitted, feel hopelessly "outgrouped." This nucleus of experience in the critique of organized labor has to be recognized lest one rush to conclusions.

The element of partial truth in the critique of labor is among the most dangerous fascist potentials in this country. While there are quite a few points in the critique of labor which cannot be refuted, they are easily chosen as points of departure, in order to do away with unions altogether, replacing them by government-controlled corporations—one of the main economic objectives of fascists everywhere. No analysis of the fascist potential is valid which does not give account of the agglomerate of rational critique and irrational hatred in the people's attitude toward labor. Some characteristic reactions of our interviewees may, at least, illustrate the problem.

We begin with examples of an attitude toward labor which is very widespread among low scorers: the acceptance of unions with more or less incisive qualifications. Obviously, antilabor attitudes among otherwise "progressive" people are particularly important for broader issues of prognosis.

M310, a thoroughly liberal and progressive member of the University Extension Testing Class, speaks about the "so-called free enterprise system which really is monopoly." To the question about the 30 per cent wage increase demanded by labor, he answers:

"Well, don't like to see anybody set an arbitrary figure for any demand. At the same time very sympathetic to wage demands. E.g. the auto workers right now. On the other hand, the bakery workers in San Francisco are striking merely for a base rate, although all of them are making above that now: they are just thinking of the future. . . . I am for unions, but I think we should recognize that sometimes they become selfish-interest groups. . . . Disappointed in the labor movement as a reform vehicle, their only interest is in higher wages for their own small group, especially A.F. of L. craft unions or monopolies."

Behind this statement looms the dim consciousness that today's labor movement, instead of aiming at a better society, is satisfied with securing certain advantages and privileges within the present setup. This is just the opposite of the typical high scorer's complaint that unions have become too political, a matter to be discussed later.

M112, a low-scoring college sophomore, senses the danger that cumbersome, mammoth unions might become undemocratic. He is antimonopoly in the sense that he hopes to stop social trends by breaking down highly centralized units into smaller ones.

"I don't like large organizations. There should be local unions, local companies, never very large. There is Kaiser, but he's not so bad. Standard Oil is not good or I.G. Farben of Germany."

M620, a low-scoring convict, is typical of those who resent the interference of organized labor with the functioning of the machinery of production as a whole:

(What do you think of political trends today?) "Well, I believe seriously that labor is going to have to acquire a sense of responsibility. . . . Well, to me a contract is more or less sacred." Subject objects to strikes in general, especially to jurisdictional strikes. (What about 30% increase in wage demands?) "I believe if the unions are willing to work they should have it. But if they give no returns, completely unjustified. (What about G.M. strike?) Should be settled as quickly as possible, one way or the other. . . . I believe both labor and business sort of ignore the little fellow. . . . I am sort of bitter about this strike business. . . . I feel labor should have more responsibility."

M711, an extreme low scorer of the Employment Service Veterans group, mixes up the collectivistic power of unions with the threat of fascism and makes, by projection, Hitler a pro-union man:

(How do you feel about labor unions?) I don't know frankly on that. In theory I'm very much in favor of labor unions. (How do you feel about 30% wage increase demand?) Well, I do not approve . . . because I think any wage increase demand should be made in relation to living costs. (How do you mean that?) As a matter of fact, I just don't think about it . . . 30% wage increase won't mean a damn thing if living costs go up too. (What about G.M.'s labor union demand for increased wages, with no increase in prices?) "Yes . . . but I think wages and prices have to hit a stabilization. . . ." (Interviewer reads question #4, stating that labor unions should become stronger, and refers to subject's disagreeing a little with this item and asks for elaboration.) "Well, my disagreement on that—I'm perhaps thinking that labor unions becoming stronger would lead to a state of fascism. . . . After all, didn't Hitler use the labor unions in his early days, increasing labor unions and making them stronger. . . . I know we have labor unions in San Francisco which are simply little empires. On the other hand, we have others that are working for the general good. . . . I certainly don't think they should be controlled as some of our senators seem to want them."

F340B has been mentioned before. She is of the University Extension Testing Class and scores middle on E, low on F, and high on PEC. She differentiates between the positive function of unions and their inherent evils which she describes in personalistic terms as "capitalistic" themselves.

(What do you think of labor unions in general?) "I think they are necessary—as an idea they are fine, but in practice—I have had the misfortune to meet some of the labor leaders in this area, and it was very disillusioning to me. (In what way?) Well, if there ever were 'capitalists,' they were every bit of it, running their organization just like running a business—to squeeze everything out of it. (What do you think should be done about that?) Well, they should not object to having their financial statements audited—should be more open about it. (Do you think standards should be set up then, by the government perhaps?) Yes, I think I would rather see a strong public opinion do it—makes them realize they should be more fair-minded and open."

Although no scoring has been done, the impression created by careful perusal of the whole interview material is that the attitude which accepts unions as a necessary evil is the average one, at least among those who are not articulately reactionary.

There is an exceedingly small number of unqualified prolabor statements. The two examples to follow stem from San Quentin, both, of course, from low scorers.

M628B, a murderer:

(What do you think of labor unions?) "Definitely in favor of the closed shop. I don't believe in private enterprise as in this country. If it was what they say it is, I would be in favor of it.... I don't suppose the Constitution, but ... we don't live by it. ... This story of work hard, my boy, and you'll be great one day is fine ... but when you won't clothe and house, etc. the masses, I'll say that's an outrage...."

M619, a sex criminal characterized by the psychiatrist as "simple schizophrenic," is not altogether uncritical of labor but believes that the weaknesses of the unions are gradually disappearing: his unqualified acceptance is based on a somewhat empty general idea of progress.

(How do you feel about labor leaders today?) "The A.F. of L., I am in favor of it very much. The C.I.O., formerly I was not in favor of it, but as time moves on, the people seem to accept it more and more. I'm inclined to feel the faults of its inception have been ironed out ... of course, the unions in the beginning used pretty high-handed methods, but perhaps the end will justify the means they took."

One particular aspect of critical feelings toward labor should be stressed. It is the idea that unions should not engage in politics. Since this has nothing to do with those economic experiences with labor at which the complaints of many people aim, it is a matter of plain ideology, derived very probably from some belief that according to American tradition unions offer a means of "bargaining," of obtaining higher shares, and should not meddle in other issues. The anger about wage disputes and strikes is displaced and becomes rationalized by hasty identification of organized labor and communism. Since unions in this country are incomparably less political and class-conscious than anywhere else, this objection is of an entirely different order from those previously discussed: it is truly an expression of reactionism. However, in this area the reactionary ideology is so strongly backed by preconceived notions that it infiltrates easily into the opinion of people of whom it could hardly be expected.

M621A is serving a term in San Quentin for theft. He scores low on E and F but high on PEC.

"I admire unions, but they shouldn't agitate. (Evidently referring to any political activities.) They shouldn't try to get more money, but should help people more. They should want to keep prices down like anyone else ... unions have no business in politics."

M627, another San Quentin man, scores low on E and PEC but high on F.

He is a psychopathic alcoholic convicted for what seems to be a minor sex offense.

(What about the P.A.C. of the C.I.O.?) "No, politics should be let alone. Keep politics out of any organization. I just feel that labor and politics won't mix. (Do you think it ought to be prohibited?) Yessir."

Finally just one example from a San Quentin high scorer, *M656A*, who is by no means extreme:

(P.A.C.?) "Well, I don't say they should go into politics, they should work through their representatives ... as a whole they shouldn't enter into politics. (Why not?) If they go into politics, they're demanding a lot on the side, where rightfully they should take it to the lawful legislative body. ... As far as I am concerned, politics shouldn't enter into business, and these unions are a business."

That many statements of forthright hostility to labor can be found in our material is not astonishing. The striking fact, however, is that such statements occur not only among high scorers but again also among medium and low scorers.

We again limit ourselves to a few examples which will give an idea of the structure of unqualified anti-unionism.

M202, a construction engineer, scoring generally very low, is nevertheless strongly identified with the entrepreneurs. His interviewer, as was mentioned above (p. 649), called him "a person who is conservative but not fascist." His invectives against labor, however, make this evaluation appear to be a little too optimistic. As an interesting deviation, a full account of his antilabor stand should be given.

In connection with the discussion of his work subject was asked about his attitude toward labor unions. His response was, "I am hipped about unions; there you have a hole in me!" He joined a company as a strike-breaker in 1935. He took on a job as a chemist. At that time he was just out of California and there was a depression on. He had no strong feeling about unions then, but just wanted a job. However, he did feel that a man had a right to work if he wanted to, and he had no compunction about taking another man's job. He continued with the company after the strike was over. He described himself as a "company man," and, consequently, as having the company point of view. When he works for a company he is one hundred per cent for that company's interests, otherwise he would not stay with them. He has two objections to unions: (1) their policy of assuming that older men are better than younger men and giving the better jobs to them rather than to newcomers; (2) the closed shop. He thinks men should be allowed to "enjoy their work." If men know that they are going to be kept on a job even if they don't work hard, it does not encourage them to do their best. For example, he hired two shop stewards whom he found were no good, so he fired them; but the union demanded that he take them back, which he had to do, as otherwise he would have had no one to work for him. If a man sees that the fellow next to him goes slow on the job and yet makes the same wages, he will have no incentive to work hard and pretty soon he, too, will slow down. The unions should not prevent a man from working who does not want to join a union. The interviewer suggested that the main purpose of the closed shop was to bargain for rates of pay. Subject replied that if a group of men would band together to rate themselves and ask for more pay for the skilled workers, or to work out better means of production, that would be all right. If a company is not willing to pay for skilled work, they don't need to work there. By way of a summary, it may be pointed out that the subject's objections to unions boil down to a feeling that unions not only do not foster hard work, but even discourage it.

This case seems to be that of a man who, although politically unbiased, became highly antagonistic to labor through concrete experience. It should be emphasized that, in spite of his own description of himself as a "company man," he by no means admires businessmen, thinks that poverty could be done away with by changes in our social system, and favors government control in many respects. His views may be summarized as being torn by a conflict between very progressive general ideology and violent reactionary impulses within the sphere of his own immediate interests—a configuration that may be indicative of a dangerous pattern of potentialities in many "liberals." It seems, however, that the inconsistency of this subject is not so much due to psychological factors as to his professional position. His reactionary traits are derived from his function as a member of the technological hierarchy who has to look out for "efficiency" and finds that union interference tends to lower this efficiency rather than to enhance it. Thus his attitude is not really so inconsistent as it appears on the surface: one might rather say that his over-all progressiveness clashes with his technological progressiveness because the two kinds of progress by no means harmonize objectively under the present conditions of production.

The 22-year-old woman, *F316A*, is structurally similar. She is a low scorer who turns violently antilabor on account of some grudges she has developed in her work as a junior chemist in an oil development company.

Subject feels that the present labor situation is very bad because of all the strikes and that industry is really hamstrung. The big unions are asking too much. (What about the union at S.?) The S. union (C.I.O.) is undemocratic because the department heads and the junior chemists make all the decisions, then tell the members about it at meetings, and they are not even members of the union. (You also have a company union at S., don't you?) "You mean the Association of Industrial Scientists? It is not a company union (rather angrily). That was a dirty trick of the C.I.O.—or rather not a dirty trick but a ruse—to accuse it of being a company union, because then it could not be registered with the W.P.B. and so could not become a bargaining agent for the employees. They thought if they could prevent it from being registered for one or two years that it would die. Because it is not the bargaining agent it cannot make a contract for the workers, it can only hint to the company what it would like. Although the A.I.S. only has a chapter at S., I don't think it is company dominated, although I have no proof. (Don't the laboratory assistants get paid almost as much as the junior chemists?) Yes, when the junior chemists were getting only $170 a month and the C.I.O. secured a raise to $180 for the laboratory assistants, the company had to raise the junior chemists to $200 a mónth. The C.I.O. complains that they do all the work and yet the junior chemists won't join. (Was not the raise a good thing?) Yes, but I still would like to see what the A.I.S. could do if it were registered: maybe it wouldn't do anything."

As to the high scorers, the key theme of their antilabor ideology is that of the *racket*. They regard the pressure exercised by organized labor as illegitimate in a way comparable to organized crime and conspiracy—the latter being one of the high scorers' favorite topics anyway. To them, whose moralism has been emphasized from time to time in this book, the concept of the free market coincides with the moral law, and any factors which introduce, as it were, an extra-economic element into the business sphere are regarded by them as irregular. Incidentally, this suspicion does not pertain to industrial monopolies and their pricing agreements but merely to the supposedly monopolistic structure of unions. Here again the idea of "legitimacy"—of identification with the strong—comes into play. Industrial combines seem, according to this kind of thinking, to be the outgrowth of a "natural" tendency, labor organizations a banding together of people who want to get more than their due share.

Viewed from a purely psychological angle the idea of "labor racketeering" seems to be of a nature similar to the stereotype of Jewish clannishness. It dates back to the lack of an adequately internalized identification with paternal authority during the Oedipus situation. It is our general assumption that the typical high scorers, above all, fear the father and try to side with him in order to participate in his power. The "racketeers" are those who by demanding too much (though the subject wants as much himself) run the risk of arousing the father's anger—and hence the subject's castration anxiety. This anxiety, reflecting the subject's own guilt feelings, is relieved by projection. Thinking in terms of in- and outgroup, the high scorer who wants to "outgroup" the others is continuously prone to call them the ingroup. The more he tends himself, on account of his pretense to "status," to circumvent the "normal" channels of free competition, the more he is likely to blame those he deems weak for the very same thing. Workers become "racketeers," criminals to him as soon as they organize. They appear as the guilty ones after the pattern of "peddler bites dog." Such psychological tendencies are, of course, magnetically attracted by any elements of reality which fit into the projective pattern. Here, labor organizations afford a rare opportunity.

M352, a shift foreman who calls himself a "head operator," scores high on all scales.

"Well, at Standard Oil, no unions recognized. I've never been a union man. Through union there is strength, if it's run okay, but a lot of unions of today have developed into a racket, and a source of political influence. The C.I.O. Political Action Committee particularly . . . politics and unionism shouldn't become too involved. The unions shouldn't become a political organization; and the A.F.L. has developed into a racket for making money. The officers keep themselves in positions practically until they die, with no strings on how they use the money, and that should be controlled . . . but if the local organization can run itself in an orderly fashion, okay, if the officers are conservative, but the minute they get too liberal, use a strike as a first weapon instead of as a last resort . . . etc."

Here, as in many instances, critique is directed against the largeness of unions *per se;* with the romantic idea that purely local organization, being less institutionalized, would be better automatically.

M658, the San Quentin man quoted above, goes so far as plainly to advocate the abolition of unions:

(Political trends today?) "Oh, I think we are going to be ruled by a lot of clowns, by a lot of labor unions. . . . Look at all these working stiffs . . . that don't know anything else, but how to drive a nail . . . they try to run things, because a few hundred thousands of them get together. (What ought to be done?) Straighten them out, show them where they belong. . . . Take away their charters. (Meaning?) Well, every union has to have a charter. Abolish them. If necessary, abolish their meetings. (What about strikes?) That's what I'm thinking of . . . they're a detriment to the country. (How should strikes be handled?) Refuse to reemploy them, or fine them, I don't believe in sweat shops either, but this quittin' when you're making $150 a week anyway—kind of silly. Create inflation." (Subject had earlier made a remark in discussing vocation and income—which interviewer neglected to record—to the effect that he himself thinks in terms of saving perhaps $500 or so, e.g., by theatre work, and then quitting for awhile. Note subject's highly exaggerated fantasies of wartime wages.)

A few statements of extreme anti-unionism can be found among the Los Angeles sample. Perhaps the 20-year-old boy, *5014,* high on E and PEC and middle on F, represents a certain kind of war veterans' anti-unionism:

When asked about organized labor he says: "I am against it." He doesn't know the difference between the A.F.L. and the C.I.O. but he feels "like many of the veterans, we worked for nothing while the workers at home were on strike and making good money."

The contrast between this subject's hostility and his complete lack of information is striking.

5031–5032 are a husband and wife in a very high income group. Both are high on PEC, low on F, and low-middle on E. For them violent anti-unionism is concomitant again with contempt for human nature: they regard unionism simply as a device of the lazy ones to dodge labor.

Both of them are antilabor. The husband is quite vehement about this. Although he expects prosperity to continue he feels it will be at the cost of a continual fight against labor's demands. He feels that labor's demands are unreasonable and that with labor's recent victories that "even if one met labor's demands one certainly does not get a day's work out of carpenters, plumbers, etc." Both of them claim to be without prejudice with regard to various minorities. It is interesting, however, that they did raise the issue of the acceptance of Jewish children in the school where their son went.

F5043, an extremely high-scoring middle-aged housewife, belongs to that school of potential fascists who find that "everything is a mess." She first creates in true "we-the-mothers" style the imagery of a desperate crisis and then puts the blame on the labor situation.

"I have never seen anything like this," she lamented when asked about the labor situation. "What have our boys been fighting for? Why, they come back to find that they have to go without a lot of things . . . not even a place to live . . . all because of the strikes." Thus she blames labor for the present crises and resents the growth and strength of labor unions. She also feels that there is an irreconcilable breach between veterans and the workers and fears internal strife. She also blames the strikers for the growing trend of unemployment and is very pessimistic about the possibility of full employment. However, she does not feel that there is too much government interference and is rather vague about the role of big business and free enterprise. In fact, she seems to harbor only very strong antilabor and anti-strike feelings, without any strong convictions on other issues. "It's just a terrible mess," she repeated, and she does not think the layman should get his hands dirty by "messing with politics."

Whereas the low scorers who generally take a "pro, but" attitude toward unions insist on the soundness of the principle but object that unions are "going too far," getting more, as it were, than their share, the typical high scorers blame them indiscriminately for the supposedly critical social situation, for the standardization of life (*5001* and *5003*), and for forthright dictatorial aims. To the high scorers anti-unionism is no longer an expression of dissatisfaction with concrete conditions from which they might have suffered, but a plank in the platform of reactionism which also automatically includes anti-Semitism, hostility toward foreign countries, hatred of the New Deal, and all those hostile attitudes which are integrated in the negative imagery of American society underlying fascist and semifascist propaganda.

2. BUSINESS AND GOVERNMENT

As was to be expected, the general ideological pattern pertaining to government interference in business is highly consistent with that which pertains to labor. The average opinion—if such a term, without proper quantification, is allowed—seems to be that a certain degree of government control is indispensable, particularly in wartime, but that it contradicts basically the principle of economic liberalism. State interference still falls within the category of the necessary evil. To the high scorers in particular the government interference in business is just another aspect of the usurpation complex, a matter of dictatorial arbitrariness jeopardizing the rights of the hard-working money earners. But it should be noted again that there is no sharp line between high and low scorers with regard to government interference, whilst the *how*, the way in which both groups express their critical attitude, differentiates.

The following examples of a partly positive attitude toward government interference are chosen from medium and high scorers.

F340A, of the Extension Testing Class, a young clerk, is middle on E but high on F and PEC. She is interesting because of a certain attitude of intellectual fairness expressing itself in attempts to see also the other side of the picture: an "antiparanoid" trait of the American frame of mind which, incidentally, is among the strongest bulwarks against fascism as far as subjective factors are concerned.

> She doesn't believe in government control of industry. Maybe it would be all right for the government to take over transportation, gas, electricity, and water. (Why?) Maybe they could do it cheaper; she is not sure about that. Anyway, if there was a strike, like on the Key System they would be holding up everything and the government could make them go back to work. "When the government tells you to do something, you do it."

The quotation shows an ambiguous element in the affirmation of government interference: whereas the latter is resented as a violation of liberalism, it is, simultaneously, appreciated as a potential means to keep organized labor at bay. It should be remembered that the National Socialists always complained about the "Welfare State" of Weimar but later on surpassed by far any state interference ever attempted by German socialist governments.

The high-scoring parole officer, *M109*, is reminiscent of *F340A* in so far as his support for some kind of government interference is authoritarian rather than favorable to any restrictions on the anarchy of free enterprise or to rational planning for the sake of all. (Cf. quotations on pp. 676, 679.)

Those who are outspokenly set against government controls again comprise both low and high scorers. Here, of course, the low scorers are particularly interesting.

The already quoted *M711*, an "easy going" low scorer, is opposed to state interference simply because he feels a fascist potential in it, apparently unaware of the progressive function this interference had under Roosevelt:

> (Government control?) "I don't. There, again, that could be a road to a fascist state eventually. Certain controls would have to be exercised."

In spite of his leftist ideology this man shows symptoms of a confusion which may make him the prey of pseudoprogressive slogans of fascist propaganda: it is the same man who justifies his anti-union attitude with the spurious assertion that Hitler was in favor of unions.

M204, another low scorer, a young man of the Psychiatric Clinic group, suffering from anxiety neurosis, calls himself a socialist and feels that the New Deal was too conservative, but states, nevertheless:

> The government should not be completely in control of everything. Favors something like the Scandinavian system: CCF, full employment, labor government, favors cooperatives. "I think it will come that way in this country. Government control can be run wrong. Instead we should preserve individual freedom and work through education."

To sum up: the low scorers' criticism of government interference is based on the traditional idea of freedom, the fear of an authoritarian abolition of democratic institutions and an individualistic way of living. This makes for a potential resistance against any attempts at a planned economy. There is a possibility that a good many traditional values of American democratism and liberalism, if naively maintained within the setup of today's society, may radically change their objective functions without the subjects even being aware of it. In an era in which "rugged individualism" actually has resulted in far-reaching social control, all the ideals concomitant with an uncritical individualistic concept of liberty may simply serve to play into the hands of the most powerful groups.

The statements against government control of our high scorers are of a completely different kind. To them, unionism, New Dealism, government control are all the same, the rule of those who should not rule. Here resentment of government interference is fused with the "no pity for the poor" complex.

The San Quentin "tough guy," *M664b*:

(Political trends today?) "Well, the way it's agoing now, I think it's a detriment to our country. (How do you mean that?) I think a person should earn a living instead of expecting the government to give it to him. I don't believe in this New Deal and I don't believe in labor running the country. . . . If a man can't make a profit in his business, he'll close it down. . . ."

The San Quentin murderer, *M651a*, who is serving a life sentence, is set against government interference, his point of view being that of the business-man who talks "common sense."

(What about government controls over business?) "No, I believe in free enterprise. I believe that business should be able to conduct their own business, except during the war we had to have ceiling prices. . . . But competitive business makes low prices. . . ."

It may be noted that the feeling, even of the high scorers, with regard to government control as such, though it represents to them the hated New Deal, does not seem to be as "violent" as their anti-unionism. This may be partly due to the authoritarian undercurrent which, somehow, makes them respect, to a certain extent, any strong government, even if it is built on lines different from their own, partly from the rational insight into the necessity of some government interference. Many of our interviews were conducted during or shortly after the war, at a time when it was obvious that nothing could be achieved without government control, and it is this fact to which reference is frequently made, mostly as a qualification of the rejection of government control. This, however, certainly depends largely on the situation, and if interviews should be conducted today, the picture would very probably be different.

There is one particular issue which deserves some attention in this connection, the attitude of our subjects toward monopolism. On the one hand, monopolies are the outgrowth of free enterprise, the consummation of rugged individualism; on the other hand, they tend to assume that kind of noncompetitive control which is rejected when exercised by the government. Probably no "public opinion" concerning monopoly has crystallized so far, mainly because much fewer people are aware of the anonymous and objective power of big combines than are aware of official legal measures of the state. However, a few examples may illustrate how the problem of institutionalized superbusiness is reflected in the minds of some of our subjects.

M115, a conventional but nonfascistic fraternity man, who scores low on E and F but high on PEC, is set against "this Marxian stuff," but nevertheless, feels:

"Big business should be controlled when it gets too large. In some fields, like transportation, power, etc., large-scale organization is necessary. The main thing there is to prevent monopoly, and to have limitations on profits."

The unresolved contradiction between this man's strongly antisocialist and equally outspoken antimonopoly attitudes, is in all probability characteristic of a very large section of the population. In practice, it amounts to an artificial "holding up" of economic developmental tendencies, rather than to a clear-cut economic concept. Those layers of the European middle class which were finally enlisted by fascism were also not infrequently set, in ideology, against the big combines.

M118, a low-scoring man of the University Extension Testing Class, sees the problem but is still so deeply imbued with traditional economic concepts that he is prevented from following his logic to its conclusions.

"The emphasis now is on 'free enterprise,' but that often results in monopoly, the big concerns squeezing the little guys to death. There is too much of a gap between the rich and the poor. People climb up by pushing others down, with no regulation. For this reason, government should have more influence economically, whether or not it goes as far as socialism."

The same man criticizes Wallace for being "too impractical." One cannot escape the impression that monopolism is used as a vague negative formula but that very few subjects are actually aware of the impact of monopolization on their lives. The union issue, in particular, plays a much bigger role in over-all ideology.

3. POLITICAL ISSUES CLOSE TO THE SUBJECTS

It has been pointed out in the early part of this chapter that political confusion and ignorance, and the gap between surface ideology and concrete reactions, are partly due to the fact that the political sphere, even today, seems to most Americans too far away from their own experiences and their own pressing interests. Here we go briefly into a discussion of some political and economic topics of the interview schedule which, for imaginary or actual reasons, are *closer* to the hearts of our subjects, in order to form at least an impression on how they behave with regard to these matters, and whether their behavior differs markedly from that in the field of "high politics."

First, an illustration of what may be called "imaginary closeness." Our interview schedule contained at least one question which was, in the middle of its realistic surroundings, of a "projective" nature. It was concerned with the $25,000 income limit. Neither is this question a pressing political issue nor could many of our interviewees be expected to have any immediate personal interest in limitations of income on such a high level. The answers to this question, which would deserve a thoroughgoing analysis of its own, are indicative of an element of the American dream much more than of political attitudes. There were exceedingly few among our subjects who wanted to accept such an income limitation. The utmost concession they made was the acknowledgment that one can live on this amount. The prevailing view, however, was that, in a free country, every person should be allowed to earn as much as he can, notwithstanding the fact that the chance to make as much today has become largely illusory. It is as if the American kind of utopia was still much more that of the shoeshine boy who becomes a railroad king, than that of a world without poverty. The dream of unrestricted happiness has found its refuge, one might almost say its sole refuge, in the somewhat infantile fantasy of infinite wealth to be gathered by the individual. It goes without saying that this dream works in favor of the *status quo;* that the identification of the individual with the tycoon, in terms of the chance to become one himself, helps to perpetuate big business control.

Among those subjects who are outspokenly in favor of the income limit is the San Quentin check-writer, *M664C,* a high-scoring man, so full of fury and envy against everything that he does not even like the wealthy.

(What about $25,000 limit on salaries?) "What the hell is that for? That's no more than fair; hell, that's too much money anyway."

The apparent radicalism of this man can be appreciated only if one recollects that it is he who is outraged by the idea of feeding starving countries.

The very widespread feeling of our subjects on the $25,000 income limit can be summed up in the eager plea of *M621A,* of the San Quentin Group, a low scorer on E and F but a high scorer on PEC.

"They shouldn't do that. If a man has the ability, more power to him."

The next few topics are characteristic of the aforementioned tendency of our subjects to become more rational and "progressive" as soon as institutions or measures of a supposedly "socialistic" nature, from which the individual feels he can draw immediate benefits, are brought into the discussion. OPA and health insurance are examples.

Our interviews seem to show that OPA, also a "bureaucratic" agency of government interference, is very generally accepted. Here are a few examples, picked at random:

Again *M621A:*

(OPA?) "I think it's done a very wonderful thing in this country. May have gone too far, e.g., in the housing situation in San Diego." (Subject thinks the OPA should have solved the housing situation.)

One of the few exceptions is the wealthy Los Angeles couple, *5031* and *5032,* who are "disgusted and fed up with the New Deal, priorities, and all this damn red tape created by OPA."

Most others are in favor of OPA, sometimes, however, with a certain strain of punitiveness, such as the San Quentin low scorer, *M627,* already quoted:

"Well, the OPA is doing a good job if they control this black market."

This comes out most strongly in the interview of the San Quentin high scorer *M658,* the man who wants to abolish labor unions.

"If (the OPA) had an iron glove underneath their kid gloves, be all right. They fine a guy $100—for making $100,000."

The general appreciation of OPA is the more interesting since this institution has been under constant newspaper attacks for many years. But here the advantages, particularly with regard to the housing situation, are so obvious that ideological invectives apparently lose some of their impact on the population. To demand the abolition of OPA because of the "damn red tape" in Washington may mean that one has no roof over one's head.

Something similar holds true of health insurance. High and low scorers, with very few exceptions, concur in its appreciation. *M656A,* a high scorer of the San Quentin Group, serving a term for second-degree murder, after having stated that a person can live on $25,000 a year but should be allowed to make what he is capable of making, and who certainly cannot be called a socialist, answers to the question about public health insurance, "I'm for it."

The above quoted easy-going, low-scoring man, *M711,* is enthusiastic:

"Public health insurance? Unqualifiedly yes . . . important as almost any measure of ideal society."

Finally, our attention should be directed toward an economic area which is of the utmost importance for the formative processes of fascism. This is taxes. It is perhaps the point at which pent-up social fury is most freely given vent. With the high scorers, this fury is never directed overtly against basic conditions but has nevertheless the undertone of desired violent action. The man who bangs his fist on the table and complains about heavy taxation is a "natural candidate" for totalitarian movements. Not only are taxes associated with a supposedly spendthrift democratic government giving away millions to idlers and bureaucrats, but it is the very point where people feel, to put it in the words of one of our subjects, that this world does not really belong to the people. Here they feel immediately that they are required to make sacrifices for which they do not get any visible returns, just as one of our subjects complains that he cannot see what he can get out of the war. The indirect advantages each individual may draw from taxes paid are obscure to him. He can only see that he has to give something without getting anything back, and this, in itself, seems to contradict the concept of exchange upon which the free market idea of liberalism is built. However, the extraordinary amount of libido attached to the complex of taxes, even in a boom period, such as the years when our subjects were interviewed, seems to confirm the hypothesis that it draws on deeper sources of the personality as much as on the surface resentment of being deprived of a considerable part of one's income without visible advantages to the individual. The rage against the rational tax system is an explosion of the irrational hatred against the irrational taxation of the individual by society. The Nazis knew very well how to exploit the complex of the "taxpayer's money." They went so far as to grant, during the first years of their rule, a kind of tax amnesty, publicized by Goering. When they had to resort to heavier taxation than ever before they camouflaged it most skilfully as charity, voluntary donations, and so forth, and collected large amounts of money by illegal threats, rather than by official tax legislation.

Here are a few examples of the antitaxation complex:

The high-scoring man, *M105*, who is violently anti-Semitic and associated with the "lunatic fringe," says:

"It is the taxpayer's money that has been put into South America; other countries will think we are fools."

M345, a radar engineer of the Extension Testing Class, who scores middle on E, low on F, but high on PEC, believes:

(What about government control of business?) "It has gotten to the point where it is requiring too much of the citizens' tax money and time."

Again, the taxpayer's complex is not limited to high scorers. The low-scoring man, *M116*, the deviate case of a conformist, conventional conservative definitely opposed to prejudice, strongly identified with his father, accepts his Republican views:

". . . also because businessmen generally don't like the taxes."

In case of a new economic crisis, where unemployment would necessitate high taxation of people whose incomes have shrunk, this complex would undoubtedly play an exceptionally dangerous role. The threat is the more serious since, in such a situation, a government which would not impose taxes would fail, while one which would take steps in this direction would invariably antagonize the very same group from which totalitarian movements most likely draw their support.

4. FOREIGN POLICY AND RUSSIA

Lack of information on the part of our subjects prevails, even more than anywhere else, in the area of foreign politics. There are usually rather vague and misty ideas about international conflicts, interspersed with morsels of information on some individual topics with which the subjects either happen to be familiar or to which they have taken a fancy. The general mood is one of disappointment, anxiety, and vague discontent, as symbolically epitomized by the medium-scoring woman, *F340B:* "Seems we haven't got any foreign policy."

This may easily be a mere echo of newspaper statements frequently made at the time of the study by columnists such as Walter Lippman and Dorothy Thompson. Repeating them transforms the feeling of insecurity and disorientation of many of our subjects into the semblance of critical superiority. More than in any other political sphere, our subjects live "from hand to mouth" in the area of international affairs.

There is a striking lack of a sense of proportion, of balanced judgment, considering the importance or unimportance of topics of foreign politics.

One illustration, stemming from the "easy going" low scorer *M711:*

(Major problems facing country?) "Hard question to answer . . . Perhaps the main one is how we're going to fit in with the rest of the world. . . . I'm a little concerned about what we seem to be doing in China. . . . If we are a carrier of the torch of the Four Freedoms, I think we are a little inconsistent in our maneuverings in China and Indonesia."

This statement seems to be a "day residue" of continuous newspaper reading rather than the expression of autonomous thinking. Yet it should be noted that it remains within the anti-imperialist frame of reference of the low scorer.

The symbol of political uneasiness is the atom bomb which is dreaded everywhere. The stand taken toward the atom bomb seems to differentiate the high from the low scorers. As is to be expected, also for psychological reasons, the high scorers are all out for secrecy. Here, as elsewhere, "they want to keep what we have."

M662A, the San Quentin "tough guy," high on all scales:

(Threats to present form of government?) "Atom bomb. If these other countries get it, they're going to use it on us and we're going to have to look out for Russia. . . . I'm for Russia, but . . . I think sooner or later we're going to go to war with them."

As to the prospect of a devastating war, this man seems to take a fatalistic view as if it were a natural catastrophe rather than something dependent on humans. This is in keeping with our clinical knowledge of the male high scorers' psychological passivity (cf. p. 575).

The low scorers either want to outlaw the atom bomb or to make the secret public:

M627, the alcoholic sex-offender, low on E and PEC but high on F:

(Major problems facing this country?) "Well, I think this atom bomb. (Solution?) . . . Well, it ought to be outlawed and money appropriated to see if we can't use that power for good."

F515, the "genuine liberal" who is to be discussed in detail in Chapter XIX (p. 782), pleads for international atomic control:

"Truman doesn't want to give away the secret of the atom bomb—I think he should. It's already out anyway."

Although the over-all ideology is fear of war, the high scorer's attitude indicates that, while deeming war inevitable, they have some underlying sympathy for war-making, such as that found in the Los Angeles high-scoring radio writer 5003 characterized as highly neurotic:

As for the world state, he expects anything at the present time. "Why shouldn't we have further wars? We are animals and have animal instincts and Darwin showed us it is the survival of the fittest. I'd like to believe in the spiritual brotherhood of men, but it's the strong man who wins."

This kind of phrasing, "why shouldn't we have further wars," is indicative of his agreement with the idea, in spite of his talk of spiritual brotherhood. The use that is often made of the Darwinian slogan of the survival of the fittest in order to rationalize crude aggressiveness, may be significant of the fascist potential within American "naturalism," although it is supposedly linked to progressive ideals and enlightenment.

5009, a 32-year-old teaching principal in a small California town, who scores high on all scales, rationalizes his belief in a forthcoming war differently:

He expects no warless world and thinks that the next war will be with Russia. "The United States has always ranged itself against dictatorship."

While he shows the typical high scorers' attitude—psychologically linked to cynicism and contempt for man—of regarding war as unavoidable, he justifies a policy which actually may lead to war with a democratic ideal: the stand to be taken against dictatorships.

A third aspect of subscribing to the war idea comes up in the interview of the aforementioned 5031, a wealthy building contractor. He

feels that perhaps we had better go to war with Russia now and get it over with.

Here the high scorer's typical cynicism, a fusion of contempt for man, exaggerated down-to-earthness, and underlying destructiveness, is allowed uncensored expression. Whereas in the sphere of private morale such psychological urges are held at bay by the acceptance of more or less conventionalized humane standards, they are let loose in the sphere of international politics where there seems to be as little of a collective superego as there is of a truly powerful supranational control agency.

The all-too-ready assumption that war cannot be abolished—which, according to this man, could be hoped for only if military men ran the UNO—is fused with the administrative, quasi-technical, idea that one "should get it over with" as soon as possible, that Russia should be taken care of. War and peace become matters of technological expediency. The political consequence of this way of thinking is self-explanatory.

As with many other political topics, attitude toward Russia, whether for or against, does not by itself differentiate with any sharpness between high and low scorers. There is, first, a kind of "pseudo-low" attitude toward Russia. It falls in line with the general admiration of power in high scorers and is positive only as far as Russian military successes are concerned. It turns into hostility where Russian strength is presented as potentially dangerous. This happens with the San Quentin inmate *M621A*, who scores low on E and F but high on PEC. He expresses his true anti-Russian feelings by means of personalization:

(Major problems facing country today?) "I think Russia. . . . (Subject fears a war with Russia sooner or later over the atom bomb.) Russia wants control of territory in China, so do the United States and England. (What do you dislike most about Russia?) Well, a little bit too aggressive. Of course, they've done some wonderful things. Five year plan, educated themselves. (What good things about Russia?) Lots of stamina to stand up under hardship. (Objections?) I met quite a few Russians. Don't like them, because they seem to be overbearing. (How do you mean?) They like to have their own way. . . . (Subject met the Russians he has been exposed to in Shanghai, chiefly Russian merchants.) They really believe in 'taking' you. They are not very clean . . . I didn't have any very definite ideas before."

It may be noted how close this man's attitude toward the Russians comes to certain anti-Semitic stereotypes. However, he has nothing against the Jews; as a matter of fact his wife is Jewish. In this case anti-Russianism may be a phenomenon of displacement.

However, there is also a "genuine" low scorer's negative attitude against Russia, based on aversion to totalitarianism. Here, the Psychiatric Clinic patient *M204*, suffering from anxiety neurosis, a moderate socialist and militant pacifist, with low scores on all scales, fits in:

He is a little skeptical about the Soviet Union, disapproving of their totalitarian methods, but being interested in "their interesting experiment."

Another example is *M310*, a liberal of the Extension Testing Class with an unusually low score, assistant manager for an advertising agency, whose criticism touches upon formal democratism while at the same time he is repelled by the oligarchic aspects of Russian government:

(Your understanding of democracy?) "Government of, for, and by the people. Government by majority, directed to its achieving good results for the people. May be a difference between Nazi Germany and Soviet Russia, in that sense, may be democracy in Russia. I don't think it necessarily takes our voting system, although I like (democratic voting). . . . (You are critical of Soviet Russia?) I don't like the concentration of political power in so few hands."

Sometimes this kind of critique assumes, with low scorers, the aspect of disagreement with American communists because of their wholesale endorsement of Russian politics.

M203, a teacher, "liberal but not radical," with low scores on all scales:

"It is good to have intelligent, liberal leadership, rather than radical leadership, which would be bad. (Example?) Well, like the communists in this country: they are not intelligent, they are too radical, and there is too much line which is determined by Russia. For instance, Roosevelt was less rigid and learned more by his mistakes."

It should be noted that this man is an outspoken antifascist who finds it "disgraceful that Bilbo should be in Congress."

As to the pro-Russian attitude found among low scorers, it cannot be overlooked that it has sometimes a somewhat mechanical outlook. Here the element of stereotypy comes clearly to the fore in low scorers. As an example M713A may serve. He is a young veteran, studying landscape architecture, whose scores are all low.

(How do you feel about Soviet Russia?) "A very wonderful experiment. . . . I believe that if left alone will be the greatest power in a few years. (Disagreement with the communists' line?) Just in the matter of approach. Their approach is a little too violent, though I can see the reason for that. . . . I think we ought to approach it a little more gradually. . . . If went into communism would just be like the army. . . . Maybe take a hundred years—we are working gradually toward it."

It is a question whether the idea of a gradual development is compatible with the theory of dialectical materialism officially accepted in Russia, or whether it is indicative of a dubious element in the subject's appreciation of the "wonderful experiment." It should be noted that the idea of socialism as an "experiment" stems from the vernacular of middle-class "common sense" and it tends to replace the traditional socialist concept of class struggle with the image of a kind of joint, unanimous venture—as if society as a whole, as it is today, were ready to try socialism regardless of the influence of existing property relations. This pattern of thinking is at least inconsistent with the very same social theory to which our subject seems to subscribe. Anyway, he, like any of our other subjects, goes little into matters of

Marxian doctrine or of specific Russian issues, but contents himself with rather a summary positive stand.

And then there is the idea of the "greatest power." That this idea is not exceptional among low scorers, in other words, that a positive stand toward Russia may have something to do with the Russian successes on the battle-fields and in international competition, rather than with the system, is corroborated by the San Quentin inmate *M619*, who scores low on E and F but high on PEC, the man who does not believe in any real utopia:

"Well, Russia is undoubtedly one of the most powerful nations in the world today. They've risen to power in the last few years and made more progress than any other country."

Our general impression concerning our subjects' attitude towards Russia may be summed up as follows. To the vast majority of Americans, the very existence of the Soviet Union constitutes a source of continuous uneasiness. The emergence and survival of a system that has done away with free enter-prise seems to them a threat to the basic tenets of the culture of this coun-try, to the "American way," by the mere fact that it has shattered the belief in liberal economy and liberal political organization as a "natural" eternal phenomenon which excludes any other rational form of society. On the other hand, the success of Russia, particularly her performance during the war, appeals strongly to the American belief that values can be tested by the outcome, by whether they "work"—which is a profoundly liberalistic idea by itself. The way our subjects cope with this inconsistency of evaluation differentiates between high and low scorers. To the former, the Soviet Union, incompatible with their frame of reference, should be done away with as the extreme expression of the "foreign," of what is also in a psychological sense "strange," more than anything else. Even the fact that Russia has proved successful in some respects is put into the service of this fantasy: frequently, Russian power is exaggerated, with a highly ambivalent undertone com-parable to the stereotypes about "Jewish world power." To the low scorers Russia is rarely less "strange"—an attitude which has doubtless some basis in reality. But they try to master this sense of strangeness in a different way, by taking an objective attitude of "appreciation," combining understanding with detachment and a dash of superiority. When they express more out-spoken sympathies for the Soviet Union, they do so by implicitly translating Russian phenomena into ideas more familiar to Americans, often by present-ing the Russian system as something more harmless and "democratic" than it is, as a kind of pioneering venture somehow reminiscent of our own tradi-tion. Yet indices of a certain inner aloofness are rarely missing. The low scorers' pro-Russian sympathies seem to be of a somewhat indirect nature, either by rigid acceptance of an extraneous "ticket" or by identification based on theoretical thinking and moral reflections rather than on an immediate feeling that this is "my" cause. Their appraisal of Russia frequently assumes an air of hesitant, benevolent expectancy—let us see how they will manage. This contains both an element of authentic rationality and the potential of their swinging against Russia under the cover of handy rationalizations if pressure of public opinion should urge such a change.

5. COMMUNISM

The complex, Russia, is closely associated with the complex of communism in the minds of our subjects. This is all the more the case since communism has ceased to be in the public mind an entirely new form of society, based on a complete break in the economic setup, and has become bluntly identified with the Russian government and Russian influence on international politics. Hardly any reference to the basic issue of nationalization of the means of production as a part of the communist program has been found in our sample—a negative result which is significant enough with regard to the historical dynamics to which the concept of communism has been subjected during the last two decades.

Among the high scorers the only feature of the old idea that seems to have survived is the "bogy" of communism. The more the latter concept is emptied of any specific content, the more it is being transformed into a receptacle for all kinds of hostile projections, many of them on an infantile level somehow reminiscent of the presentation of evil forces in comic strips. Practically all features of "high" thinking are absorbed by this imagery. The vagueness of the notion of communism, which makes it an unknown and inscrutable quantity, may even contribute to the negative affects attached to it.

Among the crudest expressions of these feelings is that of our insect toxicologist *M108*, by whom the problem of communism is stated in terms of plain ethnocentrism:

(Why is he against communism?) "Well, it is foreign. Socialism, o.k.—you respect a man who is a socialist but a communist comes from a foreign country and he has no business here."

F111, who scores high on E, middle on F, and low on PEC, is a young girl who wants to become a diplomat because she is "mad at England and Russia." Her idea of communism has an involuntarily parodistic ring:

(Political outgroups?) "Fascists and communists. I don't like the totalitarian ideas of the fascists, the centralization of the communists. In Russia nothing is private, everything goes to one man. They have violent ways of doing things."

To the mind of this woman, the idea of political dictatorship has turned into the bogy of a kind of economic supra-individualism, just as if Stalin claimed ownership of her typewriter.

By a similarly irrational twist another high scorer, *M664B*, an uneducated and unintelligent sex offender of the San Quentin group, with high scores on all scales, simply associates communism with the danger of war:

"If labor keeps getting more power, we'll be like Russia. That's what causes wars."

The complete irrationality, not to say idiocy, of the last three examples shows what vast psychological resources fascist propaganda can rely on when denouncing a more or less imaginary communism without taking the trouble to discuss any real political or economic issues.

If representatives of this attitude enter upon any argumentation at all, it is, the last examples indicate, centered in the facile, though not completely spurious identification of communism and fascism which displaces hostility against the defeated enemy upon the foe to be.

Low scorers are not immune in this respect. Thus the low-scoring student-minister *M910* is of the following opinion:

(How do you feel about Russia's government?) "I think there is very little difference between fascism and communism as it's *practiced* in Russia. The 1936 Constitution is a marvelous *document*. I think it's five hundred years ahead of our Constitution because it guarantees *social* rights instead of individual rights but when man hasn't any rights except as a member of the Communist Party. . . . I think it's capitalistic. . . . (What is the nature of your objections to Russia?) Well, first of all, I think it was Russia that carried the ball in entering this veto power into the UNO which I think will be the death of the thing right now. . . . Russia has got the things right where she wants them. We think we're the leaders but we fool ourselves. . . ." (Subject objects strongly to deceitful diplomacy.)

High scorers who make less intellectual effort simply find communism not individualistic enough. The standard phraseology they employ contrasts nicely with the belief in spiritual independence which they profess. We quote as an example *F106*, a high scorer of the Public Speaking Class group, a young teacher:

(Political outgroups?) "Communists have some good ideas but I don't think too much of them. They don't give the individuals enough mind of their own."

Sometimes the identification of communism and fascism is accompanied by paranoid twists in the Elders of Zion style. *M345*, our radar field engineer:

(What do you think of the P.A.C.?) "Never found any definite information on the C.I.O. . . . but . . . C.I.O. seems the agency to turn international, certainly has got all the earmarks, not because of being labor union, but just because of the way they compare." (Subject compares communism to Hitler in *Mein Kampf*, telling exactly what planned to do and how, and then doing it.) "C.I.O. has followed the lines of action very similar to pronounced policies of Comintern—even their name, Congress for Industrial Workers; not much faith in the communists succeeding. Their aim is tight little control of their own group."

The mix-up of Comintern, CIO, and *Mein Kampf* is the appropriate climate for panic, and subsequent violent action.

But this climate by no means prevails. There is one quite frequently noted way of dealing with the problem of communism which safeguards the aspects of detached objectivity while allowing for good-natured rejection. It reminds one of the story of the boy who, when offered some very sour dish and asked whether he liked it answered: "Excellent—when I'll be grown up." Communism is a good thing *for the others*, particularly for "those foreigners," from whom it has been imported anyway. This technique is employed by both high and low scorers. *5008*, the liberal-minded Jefferson descendant:

"The communists may be able to do something in the Soviet Union, but they would utterly fail here."

In *M115*, the low-scoring fraternity man, the argument has a noticeable taint of contempt for the have-nots. This is the man who wants "none of this Marxian stuff."

". . . but in poorer countries, like in Russia, Germany, etc., it's necessary in some modified form; but not in America. We have too much here already, that is we are too developed already."

The subject is not struck by the idea that a collectivistic economy might be easier in an industrially highly advanced, mature country, rather than more difficult. To him, communism is simply identified with enhancement of material productive powers through more efficient organization. He seems to be afraid of overproduction as if this concept would still make sense in an economy no longer dependent upon the contingencies of the market.

Even the extreme low scorer *M1206a*, of the Maritime School group, who believes that America will eventually become a socialistic country,

thinks that Russia has a wonderful system of government—for Russia—"though I don't think we could transplant its system to this country . . . though we should watch her and get ideas to build our own country better."

In this case the argument is mitigated by an element of thoughtfulness which is in accordance with the stand taken by this subject with regard to the Communist Party in this country:

"Well, I don't know a great deal about it. I believe that if a man wants to be a communist, that's not only his privilege, but his duty . . . to try and convince as many people as he can. . . ." Subject objects vigorously to red-baiting tactics. . . . "I think that Russia will be the most democratic country in the world in time. . . . Joe has been a little ruthless at times, but. . . ."

Sometimes the argument is fused with the idea that socialism would not be "practical," for purely economic reasons which are mostly taken from the very sphere of a profit system which is supposed to be replaced under socialism by an economic organization moulded after the needs of the population. *F359*, the previously (pp. 616, 690) quoted high-scoring accountant in a government department:

Subject thinks that communism is all right for Russia, but not for this country, although the trend seems to be more and more that way. She believes in private ownership of property and the private enterprise system. She considers it more efficient. She is not so sure about government ownership of public utilities such as water, etc. She thinks that they probably operate better under private ownership, that the costs are lower.

The interviews of other subjects show an unmistakably condescending overtone of this same argument, such as *M107*, a medical student who scores high on E but middle on F and PEC:

"We can cooperate with Russia; if they want communism they have to have it."

This type of liberal approach, of which, incidentally, the Hitler regime profited during the whole Chamberlain era of noninterference, is not as broad-minded as it may appear. It often hides the conviction that there is no objective truth in politics, that every country, as every individual, may behave as it likes and that the only thing that counts is success. It is precisely this pragmatization of politics which ultimately defines fascist philosophy.

Obviously, the relationship between anticommunism and fascist potential as measured by our scales should not be oversimplified. In some of our earlier studies the correlation between anti-Semitism and anticommunism was very high,[8] but there is reason to believe that it would not be so high today, not, at least, at the surface level. During the last several years all the propaganda machinery of the country has been devoted to promoting anticommunist feeling in the sense of an irrational "scare" and there are probably not many people, except followers of the "party line," who have been able to resist the incessant ideological pressure. At the same time, during the past two or three years it may have become more "conventional" to be overtly opposed to anti-Semitism, if the large number of magazine articles, books, and films with wide circulation can be regarded as symptomatic of a trend. The underlying character structure has little bearing on such fluctuations. If they could be ascertained, they would demonstrate the extreme importance of propaganda in political matters. Propaganda, when directed to the antidemocratic potential in the people, determines to a large extent the choice of the social objects of psychological aggressiveness.

[8] Cf. Levinson and Sanford (71).

CHAPTER XVIII

SOME ASPECTS OF RELIGIOUS IDEOLOGY AS REVEALED IN THE INTERVIEW MATERIAL

T. W. Adorno

A. INTRODUCTION

The relationship between prejudice and religion played a relatively minor role in our research. This may be due in a large part to the nature of our sample. It did not include any specific religious groups nor was it drawn from geographical areas such as the Bible Belt or cities with a heavily concentrated Irish-Catholic population in which religious ideology has considerable social importance. If research along the lines of the present work should be carried through in such areas, the religious factor might easily come to the fore to a much greater extent than in the present study.

Apart from this limitation, there is another and more fundamental one. Religion does not play such a decisive role within the frame of mind of most people as it once did; only rarely does it seem to account for their social attitudes and opinions. This at least was indicated by the present results. The quantitative relationships obtained (Chapter VI) are not particularly striking, and although part of the interview schedule was devoted specifically to religion, it cannot be said that the material gathered in this part of the interviews is very rich. On an overt level at least, religious indifference seems to put this whole sphere of ideology somewhat into the background; there can be no question but that it is less affect-laden than most of the other ideological areas under consideration and that the traditional equation between religious "fanaticism" and fanatical prejudice no longer holds good.

Yet, there is reason enough to devote some close attention to our data on religion, scarce though they may be. The considerable part played by actual or former ministers in spreading fascist propaganda and the continuous use they make of the religious medium strongly suggest that the general trend toward religious indifference does not constitute altogether a break between religious persuasion and our main problem. Although religion may no longer stimulate open fanaticism against those who do not share one's own belief,

727

we are led to suspect that on a deeper, more unconscious level the religious heritage, the carry-over of old belief and the identification with certain denominations, still make themselves felt.

Our approach was guided by certain theoretical considerations inherent in our general frame of reference. In order to give relief to the focus of our observations, it is appropriate to indicate the more fundamental of these theoretical reflections.

It was expected from the very beginning that the relations between religious ideology and ethnocentrism would be complex. On the one hand the Christian doctrine of universal love and the idea of "Christian Humanism" is opposed to prejudice. This doctrine is doubtless one of the major historical presuppositions for the recognition of minorities as sharing equal rights with majorities "in the sight of God." The Christian relativization of the natural, the extreme emphasis on the "spirit," forbids any tendency to regard natural characteristics such as "racial" traits as ultimate values or to judge man according to his descent.

On the other hand, Christianity as the religion of the "Son" contains an implicit antagonism against the religion of the "Father" and its surviving witnesses, the Jews. This antagonism, continuous since St. Paul, is enhanced by the fact that the Jews, by clinging to their own religious culture, rejected the religion of the Son and by the fact that the New Testament puts upon them the blame for Christ's death. It has been pointed out again and again by great theologians, from Tertullian and Augustine to Kierkegaard, that the acceptance of Christianity by the Christians themselves contains a problematic and ambiguous element, engendered by the paradoxical nature of the doctrine of God becoming man, the Infinite finite. Unless this element is consciously put into the center of the religious conception, it tends to promote hostility against the outgroup. As Samuel (101) has pointed out, the "weak" Christians resent bitterly the openly negative attitude of the Jews toward the religion of the Son, since they feel within themselves traces of this negative attitude based upon the paradoxical, irrational nature of their creed—an attitude which they do not dare to admit and which they must therefore put under a heavy taboo in others.

It is hardly an exaggeration to say that many of the usual rationalizations of anti-Semitism originate within Christianity or at least have been amalgamated with Christian motives. The fight against the Jews seems to be modeled after the fight between the Redeemer and the Christian Devil. Joshuah Trachtenberg (119) has given detailed evidence that the imagery of the Jew is largely a secularization of the medieval imagery of the Devil. The fantasies about Jewish bankers and money-lenders have their biblical archetype in the story of Jesus driving the usurers from the Temple. The idea of the Jewish intellectual as a sophist is in keeping with the Christian denunciation of the Pharisee. The Jewish traitor who betrays not only his master but also the ingroup to which he has been admitted, is Judas. These motifs are enhanced by more unconscious trends such as are expressed in the idea of the crucifix and the sacrifice of blood. Although these latter ideas have been more or less successfully replaced by "Christian Humanism," their deeper psychological roots have still to be reckoned with.[1]

In attempting to evaluate the influence of such elements of religion upon the existence or absence of prejudice today, one has to take into consideration the position in which Christianity presently finds itself: it is faced with an "indifference" which often seems to make it altogether unimportant. The Christian religion has been deeply affected by the process of Enlightenment and the conquest of the scientific spirit. The "magical" elements of Christianity as well as the factual basis of Christian belief in biblical history have been profoundly shaken. This, however, does not mean that Christian religion has been abolished. Although largely emasculated in its profoundest claims, it has maintained at least part of the social functions acquired throughout the centuries. This means that it has largely become *neutralized*. The shell of Christian doctrine, above all its social authority and also a number of more or less isolated elements of its content, is preserved and "consumed" in a haphazard way as a "cultural good" like patriotism or traditional art.

This neutralization of religious beliefs is strikingly exemplified by the following statement of *M109*, a high-scoring Roman Catholic who attends church regularly. He writes on his questionnaire that he considers religion a

"thoroughly important part of existence, perhaps it should occupy 2 to 5 per cent of leisure time."

The relegation of religion, which was once regarded as the most essential sphere of life, to "leisure," as well as the time allotment made for it and, above all, the fact that it is subsumed under a calculated time schedule and referred to in terms of per cent is symbolic of the profound changes which have taken place with regard to the prevailing attitude towards religion.

It may be assumed that such neutralized residues of Christianity as that indicated in *M109's* statement are largely severed from their basis in serious belief and substantial individual experience. Therefore, they rarely produce individual behavior that is different from what is to be expected from the prevailing patterns of civilization. However, some of the formal properties of religion, such as the rigid antithesis of good and evil, ascetic ideals, emphasis upon unlimited effort on the part of the individual, still exercise considerable power. Severed from their roots and often devoid of any specific content, these formal constituents are apt to be congealed into mere formulae. Thus, they assume an aspect of rigidity and intolerance such as we expect to find in the prejudiced person.

[1] A detailed theoretical analysis of the relationship between Christianity and anti-Semitism has been contributed by Max Horkheimer and T. W. Adorno (53).

The dissolution of positive religion and its preservation in a noncommittal ideological form are due to social processes. While religion has been deprived of the intrinsic claim of truth, it has been gradually transformed into "social cement." The more this cement is needed for the maintenance of the *status quo* and the more dubious its inherent truth becomes, the more obstinately is its authority upheld and the more its hostile, destructive and negative features come to the fore. The transformation of religion into an agency of social conformity makes it fall in line with most other conformist tendencies. Adherence to Christianity under such conditions easily lends itself to abuse; to subservience, overadjustment, and ingroup loyalty as an ideology which covers up hatred against the disbeliever, the dissenter, the Jew. Belonging to a denomination assumes an air of aggressive fatality, similar to that of being born as a member of one particular nation. Membership in any particular religious group tends to be reduced to a fairly abstract ingroup-outgroup relationship within the general pattern brought out by the foregoing discussion of ethnocentrism.

These theoretical formulations are not intended as hypotheses for which crucial tests could be provided by our research; rather, they furnish some of the background against which the observations now to be reported may plausibly be interpreted.

B.   GENERAL OBSERVATIONS

There is much in the interview material to support the view, suggested by findings from the questionnaire, that the more religion becomes conventionalized, the more it falls in line with the general outlook of the ethnocentric individual. An illustration of this point is afforded by the following excerpt from the interview of *F5054,* a woman who scored high on the ethnocentrism scale.

The subject seems to have accepted a set of rather dogmatic moral codes which makes her regard people, especially "youngsters who call themselves atheists" as falling outside the circle in which she wants to move. She made a point of admitting (confidentially) that one of the main reasons she was looking forward to moving away from Westwood was that she could thereby get her youngest daughter away from the influence of the neighbor's boy, who is an atheist because his father tells him "religion is a lot of hooey." She is also distressed, because her eldest daughter "just won't go to church."

From the above it is evident that she is quite in agreement with organized religion and tends to be a conformist in religious matters. Christian ethics and its moral codes are regarded as absolutes; and deviations are to be frowned upon or punished.

This account suggests that there is a connection between conventional religious rigidity and an almost complete absence of what might be called personally "experienced" belief. The same holds for the high-scoring man

5057, a person who sticks to the Church although he "does not believe in a personal God."

The subject believes that most Protestant religions are very much the same. He selected Christian Science because "it is a quieter religion than most." He started going to Unity sunday school while living with his grandparents and liked the Unity Church, which, in his estimation, presents a mild form of Christian Science. He joined the Christian Science Church when he married, inasmuch as his wife's family and his wife are all Christian Scientists. "Religion should not be allowed to interfere with the ordinary essentials. However, religion should restrain you from overindulgences of any kind, such as drinking, gambling, or anything to excess."

A high-scoring young woman, *F103*, says "My parents let us make our own choice; just so we go to church." There we see the lack of any interest in the content of religion; one goes to church because "it's the thing to do" and because one wants to please one's parents. A final example is afforded by another prejudiced young woman, *F104*, who remarks "I have never known any people who were not religious. I have known one fellow who was wavering, and he was a very morbid person." The idea here seems to be that one goes to church in order to express one's normality or at least to be classed with normal people.

These examples help us to understand why persons or groups who "take religion seriously" in a more internalized sense are likely to be opposed to ethnocentrism. What proved to be true in Germany, where "radical" Christian movements, such as the dialectical theology of Karl Barth, courageously opposed Nazism, seems to hold good beyond the theological "élite." The fact that a person really worries about the meaning of religion as such, when he lives in a general atmosphere of "neutralized" religion, is indicative of a nonconformist attitude. It may easily lead toward opposition to the "regular fellow," for whom it is as much "second nature" to attend church as it is not to admit Jews to his country club. Moreover, the stress on the specific content of religion, rather than on the division between those who belong and those who do not belong to the Christian faith, necessarily accentuates the motives of love and compassion buried under conventionalized religious patterns. The more "human" and concrete a person's relation to religion, the more human his approach to those who "do not belong" is likely to be: their sufferings remind the religious subjectivist of the idea of martyrdom inseparably bound up with his thinking about Christ.

To put it bluntly, the adherent of what Kierkegaard, a hundred years ago, called "official Christianity" is likely to be ethnocentric although the religious organizations with which he is affiliated may be officially opposed to it, whereas the "radical" Christian is prone to think and to act differently.

However, it should not be forgotten that extreme religious subjectivism, with its one-sided emphasis on religious experience set against the objectified

Church, may also under certain conditions fall in line with the potentially fascist mentality. Religious subjectivism that dispenses with any binding principles provides the spiritual climate for other authoritative claims. Moreover, the sectarian spirit of people who carry this outlook to an extreme sometimes results in a certain affinity for the aggressive ingroup mood of movements generally condemned as "crack-pot," as well as for those underlying anarchical trends which characterize the potentially fascistic individual. This aspect of religious subjectivism plays an important role in the mentality of fascist agitators who operate in a religious setting.[2]

Among those who *reject* religion, a number of significant differences may be noted. As our quantitative results have shown, no mechanical identification of the non- or anti-religious person with the "low scorer" can be made. There are, to be sure, "agnostic" or "atheistic" persons whose persuasions are part and parcel of a universally progressive attitude which holds for minority questions. The actual meaning of this "progressiveness," however, may vary widely. Whereas anti-religious progressives are definitely opposed to prejudice under present conditions, when it comes to the question of susceptibility to fascist propaganda, it makes all the difference whether they are "ticket thinkers" who subscribe wholesale to tolerance, atheism, and what not, or whether their attitude toward religion can be called an autonomous one based on thinking of their own.

Moreover, it may turn out to be an important criterion of susceptibility whether a person is opposed to religion as an ally of repression and reaction, in which case we should expect him to be relatively unprejudiced, or whether he adopts an attitude of cynical utilitarianism and rejects everything that is not "realistic" and tangible, in which case we should expect him to be prejudiced. There also exists a fascist type of irreligious person who has become completely cynical after having been disillusioned with regard to religion, and who talks about the laws of nature, survival of the fittest and the rights of the strong. The true candidates of neo-paganism of the fascist extreme are recruited from the ranks of these people. A good example is the high-scoring man *5064*, the Boy Scout leader, discussed in Chapter XVI. Asked about religion, he confesses to "worshiping nature." He exalts athletics and camp collectivity, probably on the basis of latent homosexuality. He is the clearest example we have of the syndrome involving pagan pantheism, belief in "power," the idea of collective leadership, and a generally ethnocentric and pseudoconservative ideology.

It is against the background of these general observations on the structure of the relationship between religion and modern prejudice that the following, more specific observations may be understood.

---

[2] The interaction between revivalism, religious subjectivism, and fascist propaganda has been analyzed in detail by T. W. Adorno (3).

C. SPECIFIC ISSUES

1. THE FUNCTION OF RELIGION IN HIGH AND LOW SCORERS

Evidence in support of our hypothesis concerning "neutralized" religion is offered by a trait which seems to occur rather frequently in our interview material. It is the disposition to view religion as a means instead of an end. Religion is accepted, not because of its objective truth, but on account of its value in realizing goals that might also be achieved by other means. This attitude falls in line with the general tendency toward subordination and renunciation of one's own judgment so characteristic of the mentality of those who follow fascist movements. Acceptance of an ideology is not based upon understanding of or belief in its content but rather upon what immediate use can be made of it, or upon arbitrary decisions. Here lies one of the roots of the stubborn, conscious, and manipulative irrationalism of the Nazis, as it was summed up by Hitler's saying: "*Man kann nur für eine Idee sterben, die man nicht versteht.*" (One can die only for an idea which one does not understand.) This is by its intrinsic logic tantamount to contempt for truth *per se.* One selects a "*Weltanschauung*" after the pattern of choosing a particularly well advertised commodity, rather than for its real quality. This attitude, applied to religion, must necessarily produce ambivalence, for religion claims to express *absolute* truth. If it is accepted for some other reason alone, this claim is implicitly denied and thereby religion itself rejected, even while being accepted. Thus, rigid confirmation of religious values on account of their "usefulness" works against them by necessity.

Subordination of religion to extrinsic aims is common in both high and low scorers; by itself, it does not appear to differentiate between them. It seems, however, that prejudiced and unprejudiced subjects do differ with respect to the kinds of goals that are emphasized and the ways in which religion is utilized in their service.

High scorers, more often than low scorers, seem to make use of religious ideas in order to gain some immediate practical advantage or to aid in the manipulation of other people. An example of the way in which formalized religion is adhered to as a means for maintaining social status and social relationships is afforded by the highly prejudiced young woman, *F201*, who is very frankly interested in "a stable society" in which class lines are clearly drawn.

"I was brought up in the Episcopalian Church through going to a school for girls. It's nice. My friends go. It's more of a philosophy (than Christian Science); it raises your standards. The philosophy of the Episcopalian Church follows the pattern of all Protestant churches. It takes in the upper classes and gives them a religion or makes it a little nearer."

Ethnocentric subjects frequently think of religion as a practical aid in the mental hygiene of the individual. The statement of *F109* is characteristic.

"I don't understand religion. It's like a fairy tale to me. I don't know if I believe in God. There must be one but it is hard to believe it. Religion gives you something to hold on to, to base your life on."

If religion only serves the need for something "to hold on to," this need may also be served by anything which provides the individual with absolute authority, such as the fascist state. There is a strong probability that fascism played exactly the same role with German womanhood which was formally exercised by their belief in positive religion. Psychologically, fascist hierarchies may function largely as secularizations and substitutes of ecclesiastical ones. It is not accidental that Nazism arose in Southern Germany with its strong Roman-Catholic tradition.

M118, a moderately high scorer, shows clearly the element of arbitrariness in his religious belief, mixed up with pseudoscientific statements which take the stamina out of this belief.

"I am willing to believe in the existence of a God. Something I can't explain anyway. Was it Darwin who said the world started with whirling gas? Well, who created that? Where did the start of it come from? That of course has little to do with church ritual." (He has stated just before that the church "is pretty important.")

There is no logical interconnection between this reasoning and the subject's adherence to positive Christianity. Consequently the continuation of the passage reveals by its sophistry the aspect of insincerity in conventionalized religion which leads easily to malicious contempt for the values one officially subscribes to. *M118* goes on to say:

"I believe in the power of prayer even if it's just in the satisfaction of the individual performing it. I don't know if there is any direct communication but it helps the individual, so I'm for it. It's also a chance for introspection; to stop and look at yourself."[3]

The approach to religion for extraneous reasons is probably not so much an expression of the subject's own wants and needs as an expression of his opinion that religion is good for others, helps to keep them content, in short, can be used for manipulative purposes. Recommending religion to others makes it easier for a person to be "in favor" of it without any actual identification with it. The cynicism of the central European administrators of the

[3] This attitude, that of a homespun psychologist as it were, can also be found in low scorers. The characteristic configuration to be found in high scorers, however, seems to be the unresolved contradiction between a critical attitude toward religion as an objectivity and a positive attitude toward it for purely subjective reasons. It is characteristic of the prejudiced mentality as a whole that he stops thinking at certain contradictions and leaves them as they are, which implies both intellectual defeatism and authoritarian submissiveness. This mechanism of arbitrarily giving up processes by command of the ego, as it were, is often misinterpreted as "stupidity."

nineteenth century who taught that religion is a good medicine for the masses, seems to have been to a certain extent democratized. Numerous members of the masses themselves proclaim that religion is good for the masses, whereas they make for themselves, as individuals, a kind of mental reservation. There is a strong similarity between these appreciations of religion and a trait which played a large role in Nazi Germany. There, innumerable persons exempted themselves privately from the ruling ideology and talked about "they" when discussing the Party. The fascist-minded personality, it seems, can manage his life only by splitting his own ego into several agencies, some of which fall in line with the official doctrine, whilst others, heirs to the old superego, protect him from mental unbalance and allow him to maintain himself as an individual. Splits of this kind become manifest in the uncontrolled associations of uneducated and naive persons, such as the rather medium-scoring man *M629*, who is serving a life sentence in San Quentin prison. He makes the extraordinary statement:

"I believe, personally, I have a religion that hasn't been defined so far as I know in any books yet. I believe that religion has a value for people who believe in it. I think it's used as an escape mechanism by those who use it."

The illogical way in which this man has made a sedative of religion can be accounted for without much psychological interpretation by the fact that he spent nineteen months in condemned row.

More sophisticated persons sometimes have to deal with the same conflict. An example is the moderately high woman, *5059*, who rejects atheism because "an atheistic funeral was so cold." She simply denies any contradictions between science and religion, calling the idea of a contradiction a "malevolent invention," thus apparently projecting her own uneasiness about this conflict upon those who speak it out. This is similar to the mentality of the Nazi who puts the blame for social defects on the critique of our social order.

It must now be pointed out that low scorers also often accept religion, not because of any intrinsic truth that it may hold for them, but because it may serve as a means for furthering human aims. An example of such practical religion is the following excerpt from the interview with a woman student of journalism, *F126*, who obtained extremely low scores on both the A-S and the E scales.

Family were moderate church-goers. She rarely goes now. However, she has much respect for religion and seems to feel that it might be developed into something that would give people that faith and understanding for each other that is lacking. "I don't know what else could give people something to hold onto, some purpose in life. They seem to need something to believe in. Some of us seem to have a love for people without that, but not very many."

In one sense this way of looking at religion has something in common with the externalized attitudes described above. However, it is our impression that when the practical approach to religion appears in the thinking of the low scorer its content, or its context, can usually be distinguished from what is found in the thinking of the high scorer. Thus, although the young woman just quoted believes that religion is good for people, gives them "something to hold onto," she seems to mean that they need it at least for a humane and ideal purpose, that is, so that they may have more "understanding for each other," not simply in order to get along better or to function more efficiently. Low as well as high scorers are likely to consider that religion contributes to the mental hygiene of the individual; but whereas the high scorers characteristically indicate that it is good for other people because they are chronically weak, and possibly good for themselves in times of acute external stress ("fox-hole religion"), the low scorers are more likely to think of religion in internalized terms, as a means for reducing hatred, resolving inner conflicts, relieving anxiety, and the like. Practically never do we encounter a low scorer who conceives of religion primarily in terms of external practical utility—as an aid to success, to status and power, or to a sense of being in accord with conventional values.

2. BELIEF IN GOD, DISBELIEF IN IMMORTALITY

The neutralization of religion is accompanied by its dissection. Just as emphasis on the practical uses of religion tends to sever religious truth from religious authority, so the specific contents of religion are continually submitted to a process of selection and adaptation. The interview material suggests that the tendency to believe selectively in religion is a distinguishing feature of our prejudiced subjects. A fairly common phenomenon among them is belief in God accompanied by disbelief in immortality. Two examples follow. In the case of *5009*, a devout Baptist, the interviewer reports:

sincerely feels deeply religious, believes in God, but has, as an educated man, occasional doubts concerning the life after death.

And in the case of *5002*:

still is a "Christian," believes in God, would like to believe in life after death, but has doubts and thinks that a sincere religious revival or a new religious myth would be a good thing for the world.

Particularly common are statements to the effect that interviewees regard themselves as religious, as followers of the church, but disagree with "some of its teachings," which sometimes refers to miracles, sometimes to immortality. This outlook seems corroborative of an underlying pattern of considerable significance the elements of which have been established in our psychological analyses. The abstract idea of God is accepted as an expansion of the father idea, whereas general destructiveness makes itself felt in a reaction against the hope for the individual expressed by the dogma of immortality. Subjects with this point of view want a God to exist as the absolute authority to which they can bow, but they wish the individual to perish completely.

The concept of God underlying this way of thinking is that of the absolute essence of punitiveness. It is therefore not astonishing that religious leanings of this particular brand are frequent in the high scorers among our group of prison inmates (cf. Chapter XXI).

M627, who is serving a life sentence for rape, is "having trouble with religion" and does not believe that "there should be a set way of worship." But he believes, in spite of an undertone of religious rebelliousness,

"that every man should have his own way of worship as long as he believes in a power greater than himself."

This power has the form of external authority, but remains completely abstract, nothing but the projective concept of power as such.

"Well, I have heard so many fellows talk about the powers they believed in . . . and I tried to recognize the power in myself and just couldn't . . . read all kinds of religious books . . . but still kind of foggy."

The same line of thought is expressed by *M656A*, who is serving a term for forgery, "Robert" in Chapter XXI.

"Well, I'm not a man to discuss religion a great deal, because I don't know a lot about it. I believe in the Bible, I believe there is someone a lot bigger and stronger than anyone on this earth. . . . I don't attend church often but . . . try to live the right way."

For this man all specific religious content is negligible compared with the idea of power and the closely related rigid, moralistic stereotypes of good and bad:

"The Catholic religion, for example, is just as good as the one I believe in. They all are patterned after the same type of living, right or wrong. I'm the type of person that doesn't believe in any particular denomination."

This "abstract authoritarianism" in religious matters easily turns into cynicism and overt contempt for what one professes to believe. *M664 C*, asked about his religious views, answers:

"Oh, I don't pay much attention . . . I believe in God and all that stuff but that is about all."

The choice of the word "stuff" refutes the statement in which it occurs. One effect of neutralization in such cases is that little is left of God but the object of swearing.

The nihilistic aspect of the configuration here under consideration is clearly indicated in the case of the murderer *M651*.

"The part I like about it is the fact that it makes other people happy, though it doesn't concern me, and you see so much hypocrisy. . . ."

Asked what is most important in religion, he says:

"Belief, I think that belief is everything. That is the thing that holds you together."

When this is pursued by the interviewer who wants to find out something about the subject's own religious feelings, he answers:

". . . I believe when you die you are through. . . . Life is short and eternity is forever. How could God send you to Hell for eternity, just on the basis of a short lifetime's record . . . it doesn't seem to be either merciful or just."

This material is indicative of relationships among abstract belief in power, rejection of the more concrete and personal aspects of religion, particularly the idea of an eternal life, and thinly veiled impulses toward violence. As this violence is taboo within the individual, particularly in situations such as a prison, it is projected upon a Deity. Moreover, it should not be forgotten that an entirely abstract idea of the almighty Deity, as it prevailed during the eighteenth century, could be reconciled much more easily with the "scientific spirit" than could the doctrine of an immortal soul, with its "magical" connotations. The process of demythification liquidates traces of animism earlier and more radically than it does the philosophical idea of the Absolute.

It may be noted, however, that just the opposite tendency can be observed among addicts of astrology and spiritualism. They often believe in the immortality of the soul, but strongly deny the existence of God, because of some kind of pantheism which ultimately results in exaltation of nature. Thus, case M651, not quite consistently with his previous confession of religiousness for extraneous reasons, comes out with the statement that he:

believes in astrology because he doesn't believe in God.

There is reason to believe that the ultimate consequence of this attitude is sinister.

3. THE IRRELIGIOUS LOW SCORER

The difference beteen irreligious and religious low scorers may correspond to a difference between rational and emotional determinants of freedom from prejudice. Subject M203 is characteristic of the former. He may be regarded as a genuine liberal with a somewhat abstract, rationalistic mentality. His anti-religious attitude is based not so much on political persuasions as on a general positivistic outlook. He rejects religion for "logical reasons" but differentiates between "Christian ethics," which he regards as falling in line with his progressive views, and "organized religion." Originally, his anti-religious attitude may have been derived from anticonventional rebellion: "I went to church because I was expected to."

This rebellion is somewhat vaguely rationalized as being of a purely logical nature, perhaps on account of some unconscious guilt feelings. (He is unemotional and apathetic in a way suggesting neurotic traits, possibly a disturbance in his relation to objects.) His rational critique of religion is formulated as follows:

"But I was always pretty skeptical of it; I thought it kind of phony, narrow, bigotted and snobbish, hypocritical . . . unsemantic, you might say. It violates the whole Christian ethics."

Religion is here experienced both as a humanizing factor (Christian ethics) and as a repressing agency. There can be no doubt that this ambiguity has its basis in the double function of religion itself throughout history and it should, therefore, not be attributed solely to subjective factors.

The term hypocritical, used by *M203*, occurs very frequently in the interviews of low scorers, and sometimes in those of high scorers, usually with reference to the organization of the church in contrast to "genuine" religious values. This expresses the historical emancipation of subjective religious experience from institutionalized religion. The hatred of the hypocrite, however, may work in two ways, either as a force toward enlightenment or as a rationalization of cynicism and contempt for man. It seems that the use of the term hypocrite, like that of the term "snob" obtains more and more the connotation of envy and resentment. It denounces those who "regard themselves as something better" in order to glorify the average and to establish something plain and supposedly natural as the norm.[4] The struggle against the lie is often a mere pretext for coming into the open with destructive motives rationalized by the supposed "hypocrisy" and "uppishness" of others.

This phenomenon can be understood against the background of democratized culture. The critique of religion as "hypocritical," a critique which in Europe was either confined to small intellectual layers or countered by metaphysical philosophy, is in this country as widespread as Christian religion itself. Part of the ambivalence toward religion can be accounted for by the simultaneous ubiquity of both the Christian heritage and the "spirit of science." This double cultural ubiquity may favor an inconsistent attitude toward religion without necessarily involving the individual's psychological make-up.

The fact that America, for all its interest in science, is still close to a religious climate may help to explain a more general trait of irreligious low scorers: their actual or fictitious "negative" conversion. Thus, for example, *5028* and *5058*, like *M203*, report that they "broke away" from religion. In American culture one is rarely "born" as an irreligious person: one becomes irreligious through conflicts of childhood or adolescence, and these dynamics favor nonconformist sympathies which, in turn, go with opposition to prejudice.

That a subject is consciously irreligious under the prevailing cultural conditions suggests the existence of a certain strength of the ego. An example is

---

[4] Cf. the section on F.D.R. in Chapter XVII.

M202, our "conservative but not fascist" person (see pp. 649, 707), who scores extremely low on the E scale.

As a child subject was very religious. He went to church with his family every-Sunday and he would "fall on my knees in the street" to pray for something. At the age of 19 he changed. He became disgusted by the gossip in church. They would tell him things about someone that were "none of their damned business." Also these people would come and testify in church and do bad things again. He could not understand this inconsistency in their actions.

In this case the anti-religious attitude, as far as it goes, is overtly derived from resentment against outside interference with individual liberty and this, be it noted, is hardly less an element in American ideology than is Christianity itself. Here, as in many other respects, individual, psychological ambivalence toward religion on the part of the subject reflects objective antagonism in our culture.

M310, a genuine liberal, offers another example of the rebellious feature in irreligiousness. The subject, who rejects Christian tradition altogether, is the child of religious parents. He admits no open conflict with them, although relations with them were apparently very cool. In all probability he displaced his rebellion against the family upon their religion, thus avoiding the trouble of undergoing difficulties of a more personal kind. Often enough, strong ideological attachments or oppositions can be understood as such displacements of family conflicts, a device which allows the individual to express his hostilities on a level of rationalization and so dispense with the necessity of deep emotional entanglements—and which also allows the youngster to remain within the family shelter. It may also be in some respects more gratifying to attack the infinite father than to attack the finite one. It should be emphasized, however, that the term rationalization does not imply, here or elsewhere, the allegation *untrue*. Rationalization is a psychological aspect of thinking which by itself decides neither truth nor untruth. A decision on this matter depends entirely on the objective merits of the idea in which the process of rationalization terminates.

In contrast to those irreligious low scorers who underwent a "negative" conversion are *easy-going* low scorers such as *M711*. His negative attitude toward religion is marked not so much by opposition as by an indifference that involves the element of a somewhat humorous self-reflection. This subject professes rather frankly a certain confusion in religious matters but in a way which suggests that his apparent weakness is allowed to manifest itself on the basis of some considerable underlying strength of character. With people like him it is as if they could afford to profess intellectual inconsistencies because they find more security in their own character structure and in the depth of their experience than in clear-cut, well-organized, highly rationalized convictions. When asked about his attitude toward religion, he answers:

"I don't really have any (laughs). More or less an absence of views. On organized religion I suppose I am confused (laughs) if anything."

He does not need to reject religion because he is not under its spell; there are no traces of ambivalence, and therefore no signs of hatred, but rather a kind of humane and detached understanding. The religious idea he accepts is tolerance, in a characteristically nonconventional way demonstrated by his choice of negative expressions rather than high sounding "ideals." "I think I became aware of intolerance." But he does not use this awareness for ego enhancement but is rather inclined to attribute his religious emancipation to external accidental factors:

"If I'd stayed in Denver, I'd probably attended a church. I don't know. I don't think of it; I don't feel the need of organized religion particularly."

Interesting is this subject's discussion of prayer. He admits the psychological efficacy of prayer, but is aware that this "therapeutic" aspect of religion is incompatible with the idea of religion itself. He regards prayer as a kind of autosuggestion, which could "accomplish results" but "I certainly don't see there is anyone on the receiving end."

This subject makes the bizarre but strangely profound statement:

"My religious curiosity did not last very long. Probably took up photography (laughs) about that time."

Only an interpretation making full use of psychoanalytic categories would do justice to this sentence. The link between his early interest in religion and the later one in photography is apparently curiosity, the desire to "see" things—a sublimation of voyeurism. It is as if photography in a somewhat infantile way would fulfill the wish for "imagery" which underlies certain trends in religion and is at the same time put under a heavy taboo by both Judaism and Protestantism. This may be corroborated by the fact that the subject during his religious phase was attracted by theosophy, by religious ways of thinking which promised to "lift the curtain."

It should be noted that this subject's attitude toward atheism is no more "radical" than is his opposition to religion.[5] He says:

"Well, I don't think any more about atheists than anything else. As a matter of fact I talked with several people who profess to be atheists and they don't even seem to agree. Perhaps I am an atheist (laughs) . . . you get into semantics, really. Professional atheists . . . just impress me as doing it because it seems to be a stunt. Don Quixote battling windmills."

This may be indicative of the easy-going person's suspicion of the "ticket,"

[5] The "easy-going" low scorer is rarely radical in any respect. This, however, does not make him a middle-of-the-roader. He is persistently aware of the nonidentity between concept and reality. He is fundamentally nontotalitarian. This is behind his specific idea of tolerance.

his awareness of the tendency of any rigid formula to degenerate into a mere piece of propaganda.[6]

Incidentally, the subject senses clearly what was formulated one hundred years ago in Baudelaire's Diary: that atheism becomes obsolescent in a world the objective spirit of which is essentially areligious. The meaning of atheism undergoes historical changes. What was one of the decisive impulses of the eighteenth century Enlightenment may function today as a manifestation of provincial sectarianism or even as a paranoid system. Half-mad Nazis such as Mathilde Ludendorff fought, besides the Jews and the Free Masons, the Roman-Catholics as an *ultra-montan* conspiracy directed against Germany, transforming the tradition of Bismarck's *Kulturkampf* into a pattern of persecution mania.

4. RELIGIOUS LOW SCORERS

A clear-cut example of a religious low scorer is the somewhat sketchy interview of *F132*, a young woman brought up in India where her parents are missionaries. Her combining positive Christianity with an outspoken concrete idea of tolerance ("equality for everyone") is derived from "life experience with the Indians." She is passionate in matters of racial understanding. However, her church affiliations make it impossible for her to draw the political consequences from her tolerance idea:

"I don't like Ghandi. I don't like radical people. He is a radical. He has done much to upset and disunite the country."

Her association with the church involves an element of that religious conventionalism which is usually associated with ethnocentrism. In spite of her closeness to the church and to theological doctrine, her religious outlook has a practical coloring.

"It (religion) means a great deal. It makes a person happier—more satisfied. Gives them peace of mind. You know where you stand and have something to work for—an example to follow. Hope for an after-life. Yes, I believe in immortality."[7]

This girl is probably atypical in many ways because of her colonial upbringing as well as because of the mixture of "official" religiosity and more spon-

[6] More material on this subject is presented in Chapter XIX.

[7] It would be a tempting task to analyze the change of meaning undergone by the word "belief." It illustrates most clearly religious neutralization. Formerly the idea of belief was emphatically related to the religious dogma. Today it is applied to practically everything which a subject feels the right to have as his own, as his "opinion" (for everybody is entitled to have opinion) without subjecting it to any criteria of objective truth. The secularization of "believing" is accompanied by arbitrariness of that which one believes: it is moulded after the preferences for one or the other commodity and has little relation to the idea of truth. ("I don't believe in parking," said a conventional high-scoring girl in her interview.) This use of belief is almost an equivalent of the hackneyed, "I like it," which is about to lose any meaning. (Cf. the statement of Mack, given in Chapter II, "I like the history and sayings of Christ.")

taneous religious humanism. Her particular attitude is probably due, on the surface level at least, to her insight into ingroup-outgroup problems. However, this example seems to offer some support for the hypothesis that only fully conscious, very articulate, unconventional Christians are likely to be free of ethnocentrism. At any rate, the rareness of religious low scorers in our sample is significant. As indicated above, the composition of the sample itself may be responsible for this. However, this rarity suggests something more fundamental. The tendency of our society to become split into "progressive" and "*status quo*" camps may be accompanied by a tendency of all persons who cling to religion, as a part of the *status quo*, also to assume other features of the *status quo* ideology which are associated with the ethnocentric outlook. Whether this is true or whether religion can produce effective trends in opposition to prejudice, could be elucidated only after much extensive research.

CHAPTER XIX

TYPES AND SYNDROMES

T. W. Adorno

A. THE APPROACH

Hardly any concept in contemporary American psychology has been so thoroughly criticized as that of typology. Since "any doctrine of types is a halfway approach to the problem of individuality, and nothing more," (9) any such doctrine is subject to devastating attacks from both extremes: because it never catches the unique, and because its generalizations are not statistically valid and do not even afford productive heuristic tools. From the viewpoint of general dynamic theory of personality, it is objected that typologies tend towards pigeonholing and transform highly flexible traits into static, quasi-biological characteristics while neglecting, above all, the impact of historical and social factors. Statistically, the insufficiency of twofold typologies is particularly emphasized. As to the heuristic value of typologies, their overlapping, and the necessity of constructing "mixed types" which practically disavow the original constructs, is pointed out. At the hub of all these arguments is aversion against the application of rigid concepts to the supposedly fluid reality of psychological life.

The development of modern psychological typologies, as contrasted, for example, with the old scheme of "temperaments," has its origin in psychiatry, in the therapeutic need for a classification of mental diseases as a means of facilitating diagnosis and prognosis. Kraepelin and Lombroso are the fathers of psychiatric typology. Since the clear-cut division of mental diseases has in the meantime completely broken down, the basis of typological classifications of the "normal," derived from the former, seems to vanish. It is stigmatized as a remnant of the "taxonomic phase of behavior theory" the formulation of which "tended to remain descriptive, static and sterile" (80). If not even the mentally diseased, whose psychological dynamics are largely replaced by rigid patterns, can be sensibly divided according to types, how, then, is there any chance of success for procedures such as the famous one of Kretschmer, the *raison d'être* of which was the standard classification of manic-depression and dementia praecox?

744

The present state of the discussion on typology is summed up by Anne Anastasi (11) as follows:

"Type theories have been most commonly criticized because of their attempt to classify individuals into sharply divided categories. . . . Such a procedure implies a multi-modal distribution of traits. The introverts, for example, would be expected to cluster at one end of the scale, the extroverts at the other end, and the point of demarcation between them should be clearly apparent. Actual measurement, however, reveals a unimodal distribution of all traits, which closely resembles the bell-shaped normal curve.

"Similarly, it is often difficult to classify a given individual definitely into one type or the other. The typologists, when confronted with this difficulty, have frequently proposed intermediate or 'mixed' types to bridge the gap between the extremes. Thus Jung suggested an ambivert type which manifests neither introvert nor extrovert tendencies to a predominant degree. Observation seems to show, however, that the ambivert category is the largest, and the decided introverts and extroverts are relatively rare. The reader is referred, for example, to the distribution curve obtained by Heidbreder with an introversion questionnaire administered to 200 college students. . . . It will be recalled that the majority of scores were intermediate and that as the extremes of either introversion or extroversion were approached, the number of cases became progressively smaller. The curve, too, showed no sharp breaks, but only a continuous gradation from the mean to the two extremes. As was indicated in Chapter II, the same may be said of all other measurable traits of the individual, whether social, emotional, intellectual, or physical.

"It is apparent, then, that insofar as type theories imply the classification of individuals into clear-cut classes, they are untenable in the face of a mass of indisputable data. Such an assumption, however, is not necessarily inherent in all systems of human typology. It is more characteristic of the popular versions and adaptations of type theories than of the original concepts. To be sure, type psychologists have often attempted to categorize individuals, but this was not an indispensable part of their theories; their concepts have occasionally been sufficiently modified to admit of a normal distribution of traits."

In spite of such concessions to more satisfactory categorizations, the "nominalistic" exclusion of typological classifications has triumphed to such a degree that it is almost tantamount to a taboo, no matter how urgent the scientific and pragmatic need for such classifications may be. It should be noted that this taboo is closely related to the notion, still taught by numerous academic psychiatrists, that mental diseases are essentially inexplicable. If one would assume, for the argument's sake, that psychoanalytic theory has really succeeded in establishing a number of dynamic schemata of psychoses, by which the latter become "meaningful" within the psychological life of the individual in spite of all their irrationality and the disintegration of the psychotic personality, the problem of typology would be completely redefined.

It cannot be doubted that the critique of psychological types expresses a truly humane impulse, directed against that kind of subsumption of individuals under pre-established classes which has been consummated in Nazi

746 THE AUTHORITARIAN PERSONALITY

Germany, where the labeling of live human beings, independently of their specific qualities, resulted in decisions about their life and death. It is this motive which has been stressed particularly by Allport (9); and Boder has demonstrated in great detail in his study of "Nazi Science" the interconnections of psychological *pro et contra* schemes, the repressive function of categories such as Jaensch's *"Gegentypus"* and the arbitrary manipulation of empirical findings (47). Thus, enquiries devoted to the study of prejudice have to be particularly cautious when the issue of typology comes up. To express it pointedly, the rigidity of constructing types is itself indicative of that "stereopathic" mentality which belongs to the basic constituents of the potentially fascist character. We need only to refer, in this connection, to our high scorer of Irish descent who attributes his personal traits unhesitatingly to his national extraction. Jaensch's "anti-type," for example, is an almost classic case of the mechanism of projection, the effectiveness of which in the make-up of our high scorers has been established, and which in Jaensch's has wormed its way into the very same science whose task it would be to account for this mechanism. The essentially undynamic, "antisociological," and *quasi*-biological nature of classifications of the Jaensch brand is directly opposed to the theory of our work as well as to its empirical results.[1]

Yet all these objections do not dispose altogether of the problem of typology. Not all typologies are devices for dividing the world into sheep and buck, but some of them reflect certain experiences which, though hard to systematize, have, to put it as loosely as possible, hit upon something. Here one has to think primarily of Kretschmer, Jung, and Freud. It should be particularly emphasized that Freud, whose general emphasis on psychological dynamics puts him above the suspicion of any simple "biologism" and stereotypical thinking, published as late as 1931 (39) a rather categorical typology without bothering much about the methodological difficulties of which he must have been aware very well, and even, with apparent naïveté, constructing "mixed" types out of the basic ones. Freud was too much led by concrete

[1] It should be remembered that Jaensch's anti-type is defined by synaesthesia, that is to say, the supposed or actual tendency of certain people "to have color experiences when listening to a tone, or to music in general, and to have tone experiences when looking at colors or pictures" (Boder, in (47), p. 15). This tendency is interpreted by Jaensch as a symptom of degeneracy. It may well be assumed that this interpretation is based on historical reminiscence rather than on any factual psychological findings. For the cult of synaesthesia played a large role within the lyrical poetry of the same French authors who introduced the concept of *décadence*, particularly Baudelaire. It can be noted, however, that synaesthetic imagery fulfills a specific function in their works. By clouding the division between different realms of sense perception, they simultaneously try to efface the rigid classification of different kinds of objects, as it is brought about under the practical requirements of industrial civilization. They rebel against reification. It is highly characteristic that an entirely administrative ideology chooses as its archfoe an attitude which is, above all, rebellion against stereotypy. The Nazi cannot stand anything which does not fit into his scheme and even less anything which does not recognize his own reified, "stereopathic" way of looking at things.

insights into the matters themselves, had too intimate a relationship to his scientific objects, to waste his energy on the kind of methodological reflections which may well turn out to be acts of sabotage of organized science against productive thinking. This is not to say that his typology has to be accepted as it stands. Not only can it be criticized by the usual antitypological arguments to which reference was made at the beginning of this chapter; as Otto Fenichel has pointed out, it is also problematic from the viewpoint of orthodox psychoanalytic theory. What counts, however, is that Freud found such a classification worthwhile. One has only to look at the relatively easy and convincing integration of different kinds of twofold typologies in Donald W. MacKinnon's *Structure of Personality* (in 55) to gain the impression that typologies are not altogether arbitrary, do not necessarily do violence to the manifoldness of the human, but have some basis in the structure of psychological reality.

The reason for the persistent plausibility of the typological approach, however, is not a static biological one, but just the opposite: dynamic and social. The fact that human society has been up to now divided into classes affects more than the external relations of men. The marks of social repression are left within the individual soul. The French sociologist Durkheim in particular has shown how and to what extent hierarchical social orders permeate the individual's thinking, attitudes, and behavior. People form psychological "classes," inasmuch as they are stamped by variegated social processes. This in all probability holds good for our own standardized mass culture to even higher a degree than for previous periods. The relative rigidity of our high scorers, and of some of our low scorers, reflects psychologically the increasing rigidity according to which our society falls into two more or less crude opposing camps. Individualism, opposed to inhuman pigeonholing, may ultimately become a mere ideological veil in a society which actually *is* inhuman and whose intrinsic tendency towards the "subsumption" of everything shows itself by the classification of people themselves. In other words, the critique of typology should not neglect the fact that large numbers of people are no longer, or rather never were, "individuals" in the sense of traditional nineteenth-century philosophy. Ticket thinking is possible only because the actual existence of those who indulge in it is largely determined by "tickets," standardized, opaque, and overpowering social processes which leave to the "individual" but little freedom for action and true individuation. Thus the problem of typology is put on a different basis. There is reason to look for psychological types because the world in which we live is typed and "produces" different "types" of persons. Only by identifying stereotypical traits in modern humans, and not by denying their existence, can the pernicious tendency towards all-pervasive classification and subsumption be challenged.

The construction of psychological types does not merely imply an arbitrary, compulsive attempt to bring some "order" into the confusing diversity of human personality. It represents a means of "conceptualizing" this diversity, according to its own structure, of achieving closer understanding. The radical renunciation of all generalizations beyond those pertaining to the most obvious findings would not result in true empathy into human individuals but rather in an opaque, dull description of psychological "facts": every step which goes beyond the factual and aims at psychological meaning—as it has been defined in Freud's basic statement that all our experiences are meaningful ("*dass alle unsere Erlebnisse einen Sinn haben*")—inevitably involves generalizations transcending the supposedly unique "case," and it happens that these generalizations more frequently than not imply the existence of certain regularly recurring *nuclei* or syndromes which come rather close to the idea of "types." Ideas such as those of orality, or of the compulsive character, though apparently derived from highly individualized studies, make sense only if they are accompanied by the implicit assumption that the structures thus named, and discovered within the individual dynamics of an individual, pertain to such basic constellations that they may be expected to be representative, no matter how "unique" the observations upon which they are based may be. Since there is a typological element inherent in any kind of psychological theory, it would be spurious to exclude typology *per se*. Methodological "purity" in this respect would be tantamount to renouncing the conceptual medium or any theoretical penetration of the given material, and would result in an irrationality as complete as the arbitrary subsumptiveness of the "pigeonholing" schools.

Within the context of our study, another reflection of an entirely different nature points in the same direction. It is a pragmatic one: the necessity that science provide weapons against the potential threat of the fascist mentality. It is an open question whether and to what extent the fascist danger really can be fought with psychological weapons. Psychological "treatment" of prejudiced persons is problematic because of their large number as well as because they are by no means "ill," in the usual sense, and, as we have seen, at least on the surface level are often even better "adjusted" than the non-prejudiced ones. Since, however, modern fascism is inconceivable without a mass basis, the inner complexion of its prospective followers still maintains its crucial significance, and no defense which does not take into account the subjective phase of the problem would be truly "realistic." It is obvious that psychological countermeasures, in view of the extent of the fascist potential among modern masses, are promising only if they are differentiated in such a way that they are adapted to specific groups. An over-all defense would move on a level of such vague generalities that it would in all probability fall flat. It may be regarded as one of the practical results of our study that such a differentiation has at least to be *also* one which follows psychological lines, since certain basic variables of the fascist character persist relatively independently of marked social differentiations. There is no psychological defense against prejudice which is not oriented toward certain psychological "types."

We would make a fetish of the methodological critique of typology and jeopardize each attempt of coming psychologically to grips with prejudiced persons if a number of very drastic and extreme differences—such as the one between the psychological make-up of a conventional anti-Semite and a sado-masochistic "tough guy"—were excluded simply because none of these types is ever represented in classic purity by a single individual.

The possibility of constructing largely different sets of psychological types has been widely recognized. As the result of the previous discussions, we base our own attempt on the three following major criteria:

a. We do not want to classify human beings by types which divide them neatly statistically, nor by ideal types in the usual sense which have to be supplemented by "mixtures." Our types are justified only if we succeed in organizing, under the name of each type, a number of traits and dispositions, in bringing them into a context which shows some unity of meaning in those traits. We regard those types as being scientifically most productive which integrate traits, otherwise dispersed, into meaningful continuities and bring to the fore the interconnection of elements which belong together according to their inherent "logic," in terms of psychological understanding of underlying dynamics. No mere additive or mechanical subsumption of traits under the same type should be permitted. A major criterion for this postulate would be that, confronted with "genuine" types, even so-called deviations would no longer appear as accidental but would be recognizable as meaningful, in a structural sense. Speaking genetically, the consistency of meaning of each type would suggest that as many traits as possible can be deduced from certain basic forms of underlying psychological conflicts, and their resolutions.

b. Our typology has to be a *critical* typology in the sense that it comprehends the typification of men itself as a social function. The more rigid a type, the more deeply does he show the hallmarks of social rubber stamps. This is in accordance with the characterization of our high scorers by traits such as rigidity and stereotypical thinking. Here lies the ultimate principle of our whole typology. Its major dichotomy lies in the question of whether a person is standardized himself and thinks in a standardized way, or whether he is truly "individualized" and opposes standardization in the sphere of human experience. The individual types will be specific configurations within this general division. The latter differentiates *prima facie* between high and low scorers. At closer view, however, it also affects the low scorers themselves: the more they are "typified" themselves, the more they express unwittingly the fascist potential within themselves.[2]

---

[2] It should be stressed that two concepts of types have to be distinguished. On the one hand, there are those who are types in the proper sense, typified persons, individuals who are largely reflecting set patterns and social mechanisms, and on the other hand, persons who can be called types only in a formal-logical sense and who often may be characterized just by the *absence* of standard qualities. It is essential to distinguish the real, "genuine" type structure of a person and his merely belonging to a logical class by which he is defined from outside, as it were.

c. The types must be constructed in such a way that they may become productive pragmatically, that is to say, that they can be translated into relatively drastic defense patterns which are organized in such a way that differences of a more individual nature play but a minor role. This makes for a certain conscious "superficiality" of typification, comparable to the situation in a sanatorium where no therapy could ever be initiated if one did not divide the patients into manic-depressives, schizophrenics, paranoiacs, and so forth, though one is fully aware of the fact that these distinctions are likely to vanish the deeper one goes. In this connection, however, the hypothesis may be allowed that if one could only succeed in going deep *enough*, at the end of the differentiation just the more universal "crude" structure would reappear: some basic libidinous constellations. An analogy from the history of the arts may be permitted. The traditional, crude distinction between Romanesque and Gothic style was based on the characteristic of round and pointed arches. It became apparent that this division was insufficient; that both traits were overlapping and that there were much deeper-lying contrasts of construction between the two styles. This, however, led to such complicated definitions that it proved impossible to state in their terms whether a given building was Romanesque or Gothic in character though its structural totality rarely left any doubt to the observer to which epoch it belonged. Thus it ultimately became necessary to resume the primitive and naive classification. Something similar may be advisable in the case of our problem. An apparently superficial question such as "What kind of people do you find among the prejudiced?" may easily do more justice to typological requirements than the attempt to define types at first sight by, say, different fixations at pregenital or genital developmental phases and the like. This indispensable simplification can probably be achieved by the integration of *sociological* criteria into the psychological constructs. Such sociological criteria may refer to the group memberships and identifications of our subjects as well as to social aims, attitudes, and patterns of behavior. The task of relating psychological type criteria to sociological ones is facilitated because it has been established in the course of our study that a number of "clinical" categories (such as the adulation of a punitive father) are intimately related to social attitudes (such as belief in authority for authority's sake). Hence, we may well "translate" for the hypothetical purposes of a typology a number of our basic psychological concepts into sociological ones most closely akin to them.

These considerations have to be supplemented by a requirement prescribed by the nature of our study. Our typology, or rather, scheme of syndromes, has to be organized in such a way that it fits as "naturally" as possible our empirical data. It should be borne in mind that our material does not exist in an empty space, as it were, but that it is structurally predetermined by our tools, particularly the questionnaire and the interview schedule. Since our hypotheses were formulated according to psychoanalytic theory, the orientation of our syndromes toward psychoanalytic concepts is reinforced. Of course, the limitations of such an attempt are narrow since we did not "analyze" any of our subjects. Our characterization of syndromes has to concentrate on traits that have proved to be psychoanalytically significant rather than on the ultimate dynamic patterns of depth psychology.

In order to place the following typological draft into its proper perspective, it should be recalled that we have pointed out in the chapter on the F scale that all the clusters of which this scale is made up belong to one single, "over-all" syndrome. It is one of the outstanding findings of the study that "highness" is essentially *one* syndrome, distinguishable from a variety of "low" syndromes. There exists something like "the" potentially fascist character, which is by itself a "structural unit." In other words, traits such as conventionality, authoritarian submissiveness and aggressiveness, projectivity, manipulativeness, etc., regularly go together. Hence, the "subsyndromes" which we outline here are not intended to *isolate* any of these traits. They are all to be understood within the general frame of reference of the high scorer. What differentiates them is the emphasis on one or another of the features or dynamics selected for characterization, not their exclusiveness. However, it seems to us that the differential profiles arising within the over-all structure can readily be distinguished. At the same time, their interconnection by the over-all potentially fascist structure is of such a nature that they are "dynamic" in the sense that transitions from one to the other could easily be worked out by analyzing the increase or decrease of some of the specific factors. Such a dynamic interpretation of them could achieve more adequately—that is to say, with a better understanding of the underlying processes—what is usually done in a haphazard way by the "mixed types" of static typologies. However, theory and empirical substantiation of these dynamic relations among the syndromes could not be touched upon within the present research.

The principle according to which the syndromes are organized is their "type-being" in the sense of rigidity, lack of cathexis, stereopathy. This does not necessarily imply, however, that the order of our syndromes represents a more dynamic "scale of measurement." It pertains to potentialities, and accessibility to countermeasures, but not to overt prejudice—basically to the problem of "over-all highness" vs. "lowness." It will be seen, for example, that the case illustrating the psychologically relatively harmless syndrome at the bottom of our scheme is extremely high in terms of overt antiminority prejudice.

Pragmatic requirements as well as the idea that the high scorers are generally more "typed" than the low scorers seem to focus our interest on the prejudiced person. Yet, we deem it necessary also to construct syndromes of low scorers. The general direction of our research leads us to stress, with a certain one-sidedness, psychological determinants. This, however, should never make us forget that prejudice is by no means an entirely psychological, "subjective" phenomenon. It has to be remembered what we pointed out in Chapter XVII: that "high" ideology and mentality are largely fomented by the objective spirit of our society. Whereas different individuals react differently, according to their psychological make-up, to the ubiquitous cultural stimuli of prejudice, the objective element of prejudice cannot be neglected if we want to understand the attitudes of individuals or psychological groups. It is therefore not sufficient to ask, "Why is this or that individual ethnocentric?" but rather: "Why does he react positively to the omnipresent stimuli, to which this other man reacts negatively?" The potentially fascist character has to be regarded as a product of interaction between the cultural climate of prejudice and the "psychological" responses to this climate. The former consists not only of crude outside factors, such as economic and social conditions, but of opinions, ideas, attitudes, and behavior which appear to be the individual's but which have originated neither in his autonomous thinking nor in his self-sufficient psychological development but are due to his belonging to our culture. These objective patterns are so pervasive in their influence that it is just as much of a problem to explain why an individual resists them as it is to explain why they are accepted. In other words, the low scorers present just as much of a psychological problem as do the high scorers, and only by understanding them can we obtain a picture of the objective momentum of prejudice. Thus the construction of "low" syndromes becomes imperative. Naturally, they have been chosen in such a way as to fit as well as possible with our general principles of organization. Yet it should not come as a surprise that they are more loosely interconnected than the "high" ones.

The syndromes to be discussed have been developed gradually. They go back to a typology of anti-Semites worked out and published by the Institute of Social Research (57). This scheme was modified and extended to the low scorers during the present research. In its new form, which emphasized the more psychological aspects, it was applied particularly to the Los Angeles sample; the interviewers here tried as far as possible to ascertain the relation between their case findings and the hypothetical types. The syndromes which are presented here are the result of the modifications which this draft underwent on the basis of our empirical findings, and of continuous theoretical critique. Still, they have to be regarded as tentative, as an intermediate step between theory and empirical data. For further research, they need redefinition in terms of quantifiable criteria. The justification of presenting them now lies in the fact that they may serve as guides for this future research. Each syndrome is illustrated by a profile of one characteristic case, mainly on the basis of the interview protocol of each person selected.

B. SYNDROMES FOUND AMONG HIGH SCORERS

A rough characterization of the several types may precede their detailed presentation. *Surface Resentment* can easily be recognized in terms of justified or unjustified social anxieties; our construct does not say anything about the psychological fixations or defense mechanisms underlying the pattern of opinion. With the *Conventional* pattern, of course, acceptance of conventional values is outstanding. The superego was never firmly established and the individual is largely under the sway of its external representatives. The most obvious underlying motive is the fear of "being different." The *Authoritarian* type is governed by the superego and has continuously to contend with strong and highly ambivalent id tendencies. He is driven by the fear of being weak. In the *Tough Guy* the repressed id tendencies gain the upper hand, but in a stunted and destructive form. Both the *Crank* and the *Manipulative* types seem to have resolved the Oedipus complex through a narcissistic withdrawal into their inner selves. Their relation to the outer world, however, varies. The cranks have largely replaced outward reality by an imaginary inner world; concomitantly, their main characteristic is projectivity and their main fear is that the inner world will be "contaminated" by contact with dreaded reality: they are beset by heavy taboos, in Freud's language by the *délire de toucher*." The manipulative individual avoids the danger of psychosis by reducing outer reality to a mere object of action: thus he is incapable of any positive cathexis. He is even more compulsive than the authoritarian, and his compulsiveness seems to be completely ego-alien: he did not achieve the transformation of an externally coercive power into a superego. Complete rejection of any urge to love is his most outstanding defense.

In our sample, the conventional and the authoritarian types seem to be by far the most frequent.

1. SURFACE RESENTMENT

The phenomenon to be discussed here is not on the same logical level as the various "types" of high and low scorers characterized afterwards. As a matter of fact, it is not in and of itself a psychological "type," but rather a condensation of the more rational, either conscious or preconscious, manifestations of prejudice, in so far as they can be distinguished from more deeply-lying, unconscious aspects. We may say that there are a number of people who "belong together" in terms of more or less rational motivations, whereas the remainder of our "high" syndromes are characterized by the relative absence or spuriousness of rational motivation which, in their case, has to be recognized as a mere "rationalization." This does not mean, however, that those high scorers whose prejudiced statements show a certain rationality *per se* are exempt from the psychological mechanisms of the fascist character. Thus the example we offer is high not only on the F scale but on all scales: she has the *generality* of prejudiced outlook which we have taken as evidence that underlying personality trends were the ultimate determinants. Still, we feel that the phenomenon of "Surface Resentment," though generally nourished by deeper instinctual sources, should not be entirely neglected in our discussion since it represents a sociological aspect of our problem which might be underestimated in its importance for the fascist potential if we concentrate entirely on psychological description and etiology.

We refer here to people who accept stereotypes of prejudice from outside, as ready-made formulae, as it were, in order to rationalize and—psychologically or actually—overcome overt difficulties of their own existence. While their personalities are unquestionably those of high scorers, the stereotype of prejudice as such does not appear to be too much libidinized, and it generally maintains a certain rational or pseudorational level. There is no complete break between their experience and their prejudice: both are often explicitly contrasted one with the other. These subjects are able to present relatively sensible reasons for their prejudice, and are accessible to rational argumentation. Here belongs the discontented, grumbling family father who is happy if somebody else can be blamed for his own economic failures, and even happier if he can derive material advantages from antiminority discrimination, or the actually or potentially "vanquished competitors," such as small retailers, economically endangered by chain stores, which they suppose to be owned by Jews. We may also think of anti-Semitic Negroes in Harlem who have to pay excessive rents to Jewish collectors. But these people are spread over all those sectors of economic life where one has to feel the pinch of the process of concentration without seeing through its mechanism, while at the same time still maintaining one's economic function.

5043, a housewife with extremely high scores on the scales who "had often been heard discussing the Jews in the neighborhood," but is "a very friendly, middle-aged" person who "enjoys harmless gossip," expressed high respect for science and takes a serious though somewhat repressed interest in painting. She "has fears about economic competition from zootsuiters" and "the interview revealed that similar attitudes are strongly held about Negroes." She "has experienced quite a severe comedown in terms of status and economic security since her youth. Her father was an extremely wealthy ranch owner."

Although her husband was making a good living as a stock broker when she married him in 1927, the stockmarket crash and the ensuing depression made it necessary for her to grapple with economic problems, and finally it even became necessary for them to move in with her wealthy mother-in-law. This situation has caused some friction while at the same time relieving her of a great deal of responsibility. In general, the subject seems to identify herself with the upper middle-class, thus striking a balance between her upper-class background and her present precarious middle-class position. Although she does not admit this into her ego, the loss of money and status must have been very painful to her; and her strong prejudice against Jews infiltrating the neighborhood may be directly related to her fear of sinking "lower" on the economic scale.

The consistently high scores of this subject are explained by the interviewer on the basis of a "generally uncritical attitude" (she always "agrees very much" on the questionnaire) rather than by an active, fascist bias, which does not come out in the interview. Characteristic is the relative absence of serious family conflicts.

She was never severely disciplined; on the contrary, both parents tended to give in to her wishes and she was ostensibly their favorite. . . . There was never any serious friction and, continuing through the present, the relationship among the siblings and the family in general is still very close.

The reason why she was chosen as a representative of "Surface Resentment" is her attitude in race questions. She "shows a very strong prejudice towards all minority groups" and "regards the Jews as a problem," her stereotypes following "pretty much the traditional pattern" which she has taken over mechanically from outside. But "she does not feel

that *all* Jews necessarily exhibit all the characteristics. Also she does not believe that they can be distinguished by looks or any special characteristics, except that they are loud and often aggressive.

The last quotation shows that she does not regard those features of the Jews which she incriminates as inborn and natural. Neither rigid projection nor destructive punitiveness is involved:

With regard to the Jews she feels that assimilation and education will eventually solve the problem.

Her aggressiveness is evidently directed against those who might, as she fears, "take something away from her," either economically or in status, but the Jews are no "countertype."

Hostility is openly expressed toward the Jews who have been moving into the neighborhood as well as toward those Jews who she believes "run the movies." She seems to fear the extension of their influence and strongly resents the "infiltration" of Jews from Europe.

She also expresses the above-mentioned differentiation between "outside" stereotypy and concrete experiences, thus keeping the door open for a mitigation of her prejudice, though, according to the interviewer, if a fascist wave should arise, "it seems likely that she would display more hostility and quite possibly accept fascist ideology":

Experiences with Jews have been limited to more or less impersonal contacts with only one or two closer acquaintances, whom she describes as "fine people."

It may be added that if there is any truth in the popular "scapegoat theory" of anti-Semitism, it applies to people of her kind. Their "blind spots" are at least partly to be attributed to the narrow, "petty bourgeois" limitations of experience and explanation on which they have to draw. They see the Jew as the executor of tendencies actually inherent in the total economic process, and they put the blame upon him. It is a postulate necessary for the equilibrium of their ego that they must find some "guilt" responsible for their precarious social situation: otherwise the just order of the world would be disturbed. In all probability, they primarily seek this guilt within themselves and regard themselves, preconsciously, as "failures." The Jews relieve them superficially of this guilt feeling. Anti-Semitism offers them the gratification of being "good" and blameless and of putting the *onus* on some visible and highly personalized entity. This mechanism has been institutionalized. Persons such as our case *5043* probably never had negative experiences with Jews, but simply adopt the externally pronounced judgment because of the benefit they draw from it.

2. THE "CONVENTIONAL" SYNDROME

This syndrome represents stereotypy which comes from outside, but which has been integrated within the personality as part and parcel of a general conformity. In women there is special emphasis on neatness and femininity, in men upon being a "regular" he-man. Acceptance of prevailing standards is more important than is discontent. Thinking in terms of ingroup and outgroup prevails. Prejudice apparently does not fulfill a decisive function within the psychological household of the individuals, but is only a means of facile identification with the group to which they belong or to which they wish to belong. They are prejudiced in the specific sense of the term: taking over current judgments of others without having looked into the matter themselves. Their prejudice is a "matter of course," possibly "preconscious," and not even known to the subjects themselves. It may become articulate only under certain conditions. There is a certain antagonism between prejudice and experience; their prejudice is not "rational" inasmuch as it is little related to their own worries but at the same time, at least on the surface, it is not particularly outspoken, on account of a characteristic absence of *violent* impulses, due to wholesale acceptance of the values of civilization and "decency." Although this syndrome includes the "well-bred anti-Semite," it is by no means confined to upper social strata.

An illustration of the latter contention, and of the syndrome as a whole, is *5057*, a 30-year-old welder, "extremely charming in manner," whose case is summarized by the interviewer as follows:

He presents a personality and attitudinal configuration encountered rather frequently among skilled workers, and is neither vicious nor exploitive, but instead merely reflects the prejudices of his own ingroup in the fashion of the "Conventional" anti-Semite.

His acceptance of his own situation as well as his underlying concern with status is evidenced by the description of his occupational attitude:

The subject likes his work very much. He expressed absolutely no reservations about his present job. It was clear from the outset that he sees himself as a skilled craftsman, and finds in welding a chance for creative and constructive activity. He did say that one limitation is that welding is certainly not a "white-collar" job; it is physically dirty and carries with it some hazards. His satisfaction with his present work is further corroborated by his questionnaire statement that if he were not restricted in any way his occupation would be in the same line of work, perhaps on the slightly higher level of welding engineer.

His professional outlook is optimistic in a realistic way, with no indications of insecurity. His conventionalism is set against "extremes" in every respect: thus he

selected Christian Science because "it is a quieter religion than most . . . religion should restrain you from overindulgences of any kind, such as drinking, gambling, or anything to excess." . . . He has not broken away from his grandparents' teachings and hasn't ever questioned his religious beliefs.

Most characteristic of the subject's over-all attitude are the following data from his questionnaire:

Replying to the projective question, "What moods or feelings are the most unpleasant or disturbing to you?" the subject mentioned "disorder in my home or surroundings" and "the destruction of property." The impulse which he finds hard to control is "telling people what is wrong with them." In answering the question, "What might drive a person nuts?" he said, "Worry—A person should be able to control their mind as well as their body."

With regard to ethnocentrism he is, in spite of his general moderateness and seeming "broad-mindedness," in the high quartile. The specific color of his antiminority attitude is provided by his special emphasis upon the ingroup-outgroup dichotomy: he does not have, or does not like to have, "contacts" with the outgroup, and at the same time he projects upon them his own ingroup pattern and emphasizes their "clannishness." His hostility is mitigated by his general conformity and his expressed value for "our form of government." However, a certain rigidity of his conventional pattern is discernible in his belief in the unchangeability of the traits of the outgroup. When he experiences individuals who deviate from the pattern, he feels uneasy and seems to enter a conflict situation which tends to reinforce his hostility rather than to mitigate it. His most intense prejudice is directed against the Negroes, apparently because here the demarcation line between in- and outgroup is most drastic.

Concerning other minorities his remarks are as follows:

The biggest minority problem right now, according to the subject, is that of the Japanese-Americans "because they are coming back." Subject feels they should be "restricted in some way and their parents deported." As for their traits: "I have had no personal contact with them except in school where they always seemed to be good students. I have no personal dislike for them."

When questioned as to the "Jewish problem" subject commented, "They certainly stick together. They support each other a lot more than the Protestants do." He thinks they should not be persecuted just because they are Jewish. "A Jew has just as much right to freedom in the United States as anyone else." This was followed by the statement: "I hate to see an excessive amount of them coming in from other countries. I favor complete exclusion of Jewish immigrants."

His rejection of the Jews is primarily based on their difference from the subject's conventional ingroup ideal, and the Jews themselves are differentiated according to degrees of assimilation:

Subject can recognize a Jew by the "kinkiness" of his hair, his heavy features, his thick nose, and sometimes by his thick lips. As for Jewish "traits," the subject remarked that there are "different types of Jews just as there are different types of Gentiles." He spoke of the "kikey type, like those at Ocean Park," and the "higher type, like those in Beverly Hills."

As to the relation between stereotypy and experience,

"What contacts I have had have all been on the good side. When I was running the gas station in Beverly Hills I had to deal quite a bit with them, but I cannot remember any unfortunate experiences with them. All the experiences were rather pleasant in fact." At this point, the subject recounted an experience with a Jewish delicatessen owner in Ocean Park. At the time the subject was 8–10 years old. He was selling magazines in this area, and went into the store to try to sell a magazine to the owner. While waiting to get the owner's attention he spied a wonderful-looking coffee cake and wished that he could have it. The man bought the magazine and noticed the longing look on the boy's face. Apparently thinking that the boy did not have enough money to buy it, he took it out of the case, put it in a bag, and gave it to the boy. From the respondent's account of this incident, it was apparent that this gesture was both humiliating and gratifying at the same time. He recalls how embarrassed he was that the man should think that he was "poor and hungry."

Subject believes that there are some "good" Jews as well as "bad" Jews—just as there are "good" and "bad" Gentiles. However, "Jews as a whole will never change, because they stick together close and hold to their religious ideals. They could improve the opinion that people have of them, nevertheless, by not being so greedy." ... Would permit those Jews already here to remain, though he adds, "Jews should be allowed to return to Palestine, of course." Further, "I would not be sorry to see them go." With respect to the educational quota system the subject expressed his approval, though he suggested the alternative of having "separate schools established for the Jews."

3. THE "AUTHORITARIAN" SYNDROME

This syndrome comes closest to the over-all picture of the high scorer as it stands out throughout our study. It follows the "classic" psychoanalytic pattern involving a sadomasochistic resolution of the Oedipus complex, and it has been pointed out by Erich Fromm under the title of the "sadomasochistic" character (56). According to Max Horkheimer's theory in the collective work of which he wrote the sociopsychological part, external social repression is concomitant with the internal repression of impulses. In order to achieve "internalization" of social control which never gives as much to the individual as it takes, the latter's attitude towards authority and its psychological agency, the superego, assumes an irrational aspect. The subject achieves his own social adjustment only by taking pleasure in obedience and subordination. This brings into play the sadomasochistic impulse structure both as a condition and as a result of social adjustment. In our form of society, sadistic as well as masochistic tendencies actually find gratification. The pattern for the translation of such gratifications into character traits is a specific resolution of the Oedipus complex which defines the formation of the syndrome here in question. Love for the mother, in its primary form, comes under a severe taboo. The resulting hatred against the father is transformed by reaction-formation into love. This transformation leads to a particular kind of superego. The transformation of hatred into love, the most difficult task an individual has to perform in his early development, never succeeds completely. In the psychodynamics of the "authoritarian character," part of the preceding aggressiveness is absorbed and turned into masochism, while another part is left over as sadism, which seeks an outlet in those with whom the subject does not identify himself: ultimately the outgroup. The Jew frequently becomes a substitute for the hated father, often assuming, on a fantasy level, the very same qualities against which the subject revolted in the father, such as being practical, cold, domineering, and even a sexual rival. Ambivalence is all-pervasive, being evidenced mainly by the simultaneity of blind belief in authority and readiness to attack those who are deemed weak and who are socially acceptable as "victims." Stereotypy, in this syndrome, is not only a means of social identification, but has a truly "economic" function in the subject's own psychology: it helps to canalize his libidinous energy according to the demands of his overstrict superego. Thus stereotypy itself tends to become heavily libidinized and plays a large role in the subject's inner household. He develops deep "compulsive" character traits, partly by retrogression to the anal-sadistic phase of development. Sociologically, this syndrome used to be, in Europe, highly characteristic of the lower middle-class. In this country, we may expect it among people whose actual status differs from that to which they aspire. This is in marked contrast to the social contentment and lack of conflict that is more characteristic of the "Conventional" syndrome, with which the "Authoritarian" one shares the conformist aspect.

Interview *M352* begins as follows:

(Satisfaction?) "Well, I'm the head operator—shift foreman—rotating schedules. . . . (Subject emphasizes "head" position)—small department—5 in department—5 in a shift—I get personal satisfaction . . . that I have 5 people working for me, who come to me for advice in handling the production that we make, and that the ultimate decision . . . is mine, and in the fact that in the ultimate decision, I should be *right*—and am usually, and the knowledge that I am correct gives me personal satisfaction. The fact that I earn a living doesn't give me any personal satisfaction. It's these things that I have mentioned . . . knowing that I am pleasing someone else also gives me satisfaction."

The denial of material gratifications, indicative of a restrictive superego, is no less characteristic than the twofold pleasure in being obeyed and giving pleasure to the boss.

His upward social mobility is expressed in terms of overt identification with those who are higher in the hierarchy of authority:

(What would more money make possible?) "Would raise our standard, automobile; move into better residential section; associations with business and fraternal, etc., would be raised . . . to those in a bracket higher, except for a few staunch friends which you keep always; and naturally, associate with people on a higher level—with more education and more experience. After you get there, and associate with those people . . . that fires you on to the next step higher. . . ."

His religious belief has something compulsive and highly punitive:

"My belief is that, just according to the Bible, there is a God—the world has gone along and needed a Savior, and there was one born—lived, died, risen again, and will come back some time; and the person who has lived according to Christianity will live forever—those who have not will perish at that time."

This overt rigidity of conscience, however, shows strong traces of ambivalence: what is forbidden may be acceptable if it does not lead to social conflict. The over-rigid superego is not really integrated, but remains external.

"Adultery, as long as never found out, is o.k.—if found out, then it's wrong—since some of the most respected people do it, it must be all right."

The subject's concept of God is plainly identical with such an externalized superego or, to use Freud's original term, with the "ego ideal," with all the traits of a strong, but "helpful" father:

"Well, when it comes down to the fundamentals, everybody has an idea of some sort: may not call Him God, but an ideal that they live up to and strive to be like. . . . Heathens or anybody else has some sort of religion, but it is something that they put their faith in that can do things for them—can help them."

The genetic relation between the "Authoritarian" syndrome and the sado-masochistic resolution of the Oedipus complex is borne out by some statements of the subject about his own childhood:

"Well, my father was a very strict man. He wasn't religious, but strict in raising the youngsters. His word was law, and whenever he was disobeyed, there was punishment. When I was 12, my father beat me practically every day for getting into the tool chest in the back yard and not putting everything away . . . finally he explained that those things cost money, and I must learn to put it back." . . . (Subject explains that his carelessness led to a beating every day, as promised by the father, and finally after several weeks, he simply quit using the tools altogether, because "I just couldn't get 'em all back") . . . "But, you know, I never hold that against my father—I had it coming. He laid the law down, and if I broke it, there was punishment, but never in uncontrolled anger. My father was a good man—no doubt about that. Always interested in boys' activities.

"My father was a great fraternal man; was out practically every night. Took an active part always on committees—a good mixer, everybody liked him . . . a good provider. We always had everything we needed, but no unnecessary luxuries . . . no whims provided for. . . . Father felt they were luxuries that probably—felt they were unnecessary. . . . Yes, rather austere. . . . (Which parent closest to?) I think my father. Although he beat the life out of me, I could talk to him about anything." . . . (Subject emphasizes that his father always gave everyone, including himself, a square deal.)

The subject has been "broken" by the father: he has been overadjusted. It is exactly this aspect which bears the main emphasis in his anti-Semitism. He who admires brute force blames the Jews for their recklessness in practical matters.

"The Jews seem to be taking advantage of the present-day situation, I think. Now, they want to—they're bringing these Jews in from Europe, and they seem to click together, somehow, and they seem to be able to corner capital. They're a peculiar people—no conscience about anything except money." (Subject apparently meant, here, no conscience about money, although maybe about other things.) "If you stand in the way of their making money, they'll brush you aside."

Rigidity of the image of the Jew, visible already in the "Conventional" syndrome, tends to become absolute and highly vindictive:

"To me a Jew is just like a foreigner in the same class as—say, oh, I was gonna say a Filipino. You would be pointed out . . . they observe all these different religious days that's completely foreign to me—and they stick to it—they don't completely Americanize. . . . (What if there were less prejudice against them?) I don't know—I can't help but feel that a Jew is meant to be just the way he is—no change possible—a sort of instinct that will never lose—stay Jewish right straight through. (What ought to be done?) They have the ability to get control—now, how we're gonna stop 'em . . . probably have to pass some regulation prohibiting them."

Again the idea of authority is the focal point: the Jews appear dangerous to him as usurpers of "control."

One last feature of the "Authoritarian" syndrome should be mentioned. It is the psychological equivalent of the "no-pity-for-the-poor" ideology discussed in Chapter XVII. The identification of the "authoritarian" character with strength is concomitant with rejection of everything that is "down." Even where social conditions have to be recognized as the reason for the depressed situation of a group, a twist is applied in order to transform this situation into some kind of well-deserved punishment. This is accompanied by moralistic invectives indicative of strict repression of several desires:

He went on to emphasize that you should segregate Negroes and whites, that by all means give equal opportunities and everything instead of "evading the problem" as he called it. He refers to high prevalence of venereal disease among Negroes, which he blames on their low morals and, under further questioning by the interviewer, he finally attributes it to "congested conditions of living" and tries very hard to explain what he means. This leads to a lack of modesty and respect for privacy—everybody's thrown together—"lose the distance that is supposed to be between people," etc., etc.

The emphasis on "distance," the fear of "close physical contacts" may be interpreted as corroborative of our thesis that, for this syndrome, the ingroup-outgroup dichotomy absorbs large quantities of psychological energy. Identification with the familial structure and ultimately with the whole ingroup becomes, to this kind of individual, one of the main mechanisms by which they can impose authoritarian discipline upon themselves and avoid "breaking away"—a temptation nourished continuously by their underlying ambivalence.

4. THE REBEL AND THE PSYCHOPATH

The resolution of the Oedipus complex characteristic of the "Authoritarian" syndrome is not the only one that makes for a "high" character structure. Instead of identification with parental authority, "insurrection" may take place. This, of course, may in certain cases liquidate the sadomasochistic tendencies. However, insurrection may also occur in such a way that the authoritarian character structure is not basically affected (56).[3] Thus, the hated paternal authority may be abolished only to be replaced by another one—a process facilitated by the "externalized" superego structure concomitant with the over-all picture of the high scorer. Or masochistic transference to authority may be kept down on the unconscious level while resistance takes place on the manifest level. This may lead to an irrational and blind hatred of all authority, with strong destructive connotations, accompanied by a secret readiness to "capitulate" and to join hands with the "hated" strong. It is exceedingly difficult to distinguish such an attitude from a truly non-authoritarian one and it may be well-nigh impossible to achieve such a differentiation on a purely psychological level: here as much as anywhere else it is the sociopolitical behavior that counts, determining whether a person is

[3] Cf. also in this connection Erikson, E. H., *Hitler's Imagery and German Youth* (25).

truly independent or merely replaces his dependency by negative transference.

The latter case, when it is combined with an urge to take pseudorevolutionary actions against those whom the individual ultimately deems to be weak, is that of the "Rebel." This syndrome played a large role in Nazi Germany: the late Captain Roehm, who called himself a *"Hochverräter"* in his autobiography, is a perfect example. Here we expect to find the "Condottiere" which was included in the typology drafted by the Institute of Social Research in 1939, and described as follows:

This type has arisen with the increased insecurity of post-war existence. He is convinced that what matters is not life but chance. He is nihilistic, not out of a "drive for destruction" but because he is indifferent to individual existence. One of the reservoirs out of which this type arises is the modern unemployed. He differs from former unemployed in that his contact with the sphere of production is sporadic, if any. Individuals belonging to this category can no longer expect to be regularly absorbed by the labor process. From their youth they have been ready to act wherever they could grab something. They are inclined to hate the Jew partly because of his cautiousness and physical inefficacy, partly because, being themselves unemployed, they are economically uprooted, unusually susceptible to any propaganda, and ready to follow any leader. The other reservoir, at the opposite pole of society, is the group belonging to the dangerous professions, colonial adventurers, racing motorists, airplane aces. They are the born leaders of the former group. Their ideal, actually an heroic one, is all the more sensitive to the "destructive," critical intellect of the Jews because they themselves are not quite convinced of their ideal in the depths of their hearts, but have developed it as a rationalization of their dangerous way of living (57, p. 135).

Symptomatically, this syndrome is characterized, above all, by a penchant for "tolerated excesses" of all kinds, from heavy drinking and overt homosexuality under the cloak of enthusiasm for "youth" to proneness to acts of violence in the sense of *"Putsch."* Subjects of this type do not have as much rigidity as do those who exhibit the orthodox "Authoritarian" syndrome.

The extreme representative of this syndrome is the "Tough Guy," in psychiatric terminology the "Psychopath." Here, the superego seems to have been completely crippled through the outcome of the Oedipus conflict, by means of a retrogression to the omnipotence fantasy of very early infancy. These individuals are the most "infantile" of all: they have thoroughly failed to "develop," have not been moulded at all by civilization. They are "asocial." Destructive urges come to the fore in an overt, nonrationalized way. Bodily strength and toughness—also in the sense of being able to "take it"—are decisive. The borderline between them and the criminal is fluid. Their indulgence in persecution is crudely sadistic, directed against any helpless victim; it is unspecific and hardly colored by "prejudice." Here go the hoodlums and rowdies, plug-uglies, torturers, and all those who do the "dirty work" of a fascist movement.

Robert M. Lindner's extensive case study, *Rebel Without a Cause* (74), offers a description and dynamic interpretation of the "Tough Guy" which establish the affinity of this type to the "Rebel" as well as to the "Authoritarian" character. According to Lindner:

The psychopath is not only a criminal; he is the embryonic Storm-Trooper; he is the disinherited, betrayed antagonist whose aggressions can be mobilized on the instant at which the properly-aimed and frustration-evoking formula is communicated by that leader under whose tinseled aegis license becomes law, secret and primitive desires become virtuous ambitions readily attained, and compulsive behavior formerly deemed punishable becomes the order of the day.

The psychopath is described as a "rebel, a religious disobeyer of prevailing codes and standards" whose main characteristic is that he cannot wait, "cannot delay the pleasures of gratification"—an inability suggesting that, together with the failure to build up a superego, the formation of the ego has been crippled, in spite of the bridled "egotism" of such persons. As to the masochistic component, the following passage from Lindner may be quoted:

That the psychopath is burdened with guilt and literally seeks punishment has been observed by the author in countless cases. The clue to this strange situation lies, as one would suspect, in the Oedipus situation. Deprived of an avenue to satisfactory post-Oedipal adjustment and continuously beset by the consequent incest and parricidal fantasies, the mergent guilt can be assuaged only through expiation. "I have sinned against my father and I must be punished" is the unverbalized theme of psychopathic conduct: and for this reason they very often commit crimes free from acquisitional motives, marry prostitutes or, in the case of women, apportion their charms occupationally in an attempt at self-castigation. That such activities constitute a species of "neurotic gain" is also to be considered. The fact of punishment sought, received and accepted does not complete the tale: there is in addition a narcissistic "yield" which derives directly from the punitive act and mediates the original need. This is naturally on a subliminal level of apprehension, unreportable directly but always noticeable.

Examples of the rebel-psychopath are to be found in our San Quentin sample. We think mainly of the psychopath, *Floyd,* our *M658,* and the "Tough Guy," *Eugene,* our *M662A,* dealt with extensively in Chapter XXI. If the traits under consideration here do not appear so vividly there, it should be borne in mind that the guiding interest of the San Quentin study was defined by our over-all variables rather than by psychological subgroups among the high and low scorers. Moreover, it has to be kept in mind that the prison situation works as a heavy check on the expression of the decisive traits of the psychopath who, after all, is not a psychotic and behaves, in a certain sense, quite "realistically." In addition, his completely living "for the moment," his lack of ego identity enables him to adapt himself successfully to a given situation: when talking to an interviewer, he is likely not to display directly the attitudes indicative of his "toughness." Rather, the latter have to be inferred indirectly, particularly from certain speaking habits, such as the frequency of references to bodily violence. It is with an eye to such indices that the statements of those two San Quentin interviewees should be read. Neither the widespread existence of the "Tough Guy" syndrome, particularly in marginal spheres of society, nor its importance for some of the most sinister aspects of the fascist potential can be doubted.

5. THE CRANK

In so far as the introjection of paternal discipline in the "Authoritarian" syndrome means continuous repression of the id, this syndrome can be characterized by frustration in the widest sense of the term. However, there seems to be a pattern in which frustration plays a much more specific role. This pattern is found in those people who did not succeed in adjusting themselves to the world, in accepting the "reality principle"—who failed, as it were, to strike a balance between renunciations and gratifications, and whose whole inner life is determined by the denials imposed upon them from outside, not only during childhood but also during their adult life. These people are driven into *isolation*. They have to build up a spurious inner world, often approaching delusion, emphatically set against outer reality. They can exist only by self-aggrandizement, coupled with violent rejection of the external world. Their "soul" becomes their dearest possession. At the same time, they are highly projective and suspicious. An affinity to psychosis cannot be overlooked: they are "paranoid." To them, prejudice is all-important: it is a means to escape acute mental diseases by collectivization, and by building up a pseudoreality against which their aggressiveness can be directed without any *overt* violation of the "reality principle." Stereotypy is decisive: it works as a kind of social corroboration of their projective formulae, and is therefore institutionalized to a degree often approaching religious beliefs. The pattern is found in women and old men whose isolation is socially reinforced by their virtual exclusion from the economic process of production. Here belong organized war mothers, ham-an'-eggers, and regular followers of agitators even in periods when racist propaganda is at a low ebb. The often-abused term "lunatic fringe" has a certain validity with regard to them: their compulsiveness has reached the stage of fanaticism. In order to confirm to each other their pseudoreality, they are likely to form sects, often with some panacea of "nature," which corresponds to their projective notion of the Jew as eternally bad and spoiling the purity of the natural. Ideas of conspiracy play a large role: they do not hesitate to attribute to the Jews a quest for world domination, and they are likely to swear by the Elders of Zion. A significant social trait is semi-erudition, a magical belief in science which makes them the ideal followers of racial theory. They can hardly be expected above a certain educational level, but also rarely among workers. *F124* is a woman over 50 years of age, tall, heavily built, with sharp features, prominent gray-blue eyes, a pointed nose, thin lips, straight mouth line. She had a bearing which was meant to be impressive.

This "impressiveness" actually implies a pathological sense of inner superiority, as if she belonged to a secret order, at the same time being surrounded by people whose names she does not want to mention, since otherwise she might divulge too vulgar or dangerous implications:

She doesn't care for her fellow-workers. Some have all the degrees but no common sense. She wouldn't like to mention names, but she'd like to tell me what goes on. Some just spend their time gossiping together. She doesn't believe she could do more than just speak to her fellow-workers. Very scornful of them, feels superior and aloof. . . . They don't know her at all—no indeed—implies she's a very special somebody and could reveal her gifts to them but doesn't.

Her interest in internal and as far as possible external status is strongly colored by an overemphasis on "connections," which suggests "ideas of reference":

She has been a "governess" in the home of President X's family . . . and in President Y's son's family—first the older son, then the younger. Talked to Mrs. Y on the phone when she was in the White House at the time of the birth of the third child. And her sister worked for S. who later was governor of a southwestern state.

As to her spurious "inner world," semi-erudition, and pseudointellectuality, the following account is highly characteristic:

She reads a great deal—"good" books—went through the schools in her Texas home town about equal to seventh grade now. She also draws and writes and was learning to play an instrument. One picture she drew here at school but never showed it to anyone. It was of two mountains and the sun in between shining on the valley in which the mist was rising. This just "came" to her, too, though she had never had any training. It was really beautiful. She writes stories, too. When she was left a widow, instead of chasing after men like some women, she wrote stories. One was a fantasy for Mary Pickford. It would have been just right for her to play in, but of course, she'd never shown it to anyone. It was called *Little May and O'June* and had come to her once when she had her children on a picnic. A love fantasy about Little May (the girl) and O'June (the boy). Her daughter was very gifted, too. An artist . . . who drew Texas Blue Bonnets—"the state flower, you know." —— saw her daughter's work and said, "You've got a real genius there." He wanted to give the daughter lessons, but she refused, saying, "No, Mother, he would just spoil my style; I know how to draw what I want to draw."

With regard to race questions, her hatred shows the paranoid tendency towards stopping nowhere—in principle she would be willing to stigmatize every group she can lay her hands on and only reluctantly confines herself to her favorite foes.

She thinks the "Japs, Jews, and Niggers should go back where they came from." . . . "Of course, then the Italians should go back where they belong in Italy, but—well, the three main ones who don't belong here are the Japs, Jews, and Niggers."

Her anti-Semitism shows strong traces of projectivity, of the fake mysticism of the "blood," and of sex envy. The following statement reveals her attitudinal pattern:

"The Jews feel superior to Gentiles. They wouldn't pollute their blood by mixing it with Gentiles. They would bleed us of our money and use our women for mistresses, but they wouldn't marry among us, and they want their wives spotless. The Y's entertained Jews quite often. I don't know if it was their money or what. That's why I didn't vote for Y the second time. I'd seen too many fat Jew women and hooked-nose men at their house. Of course, I've heard Pres. Roosevelt's mother had some Jewish blood, too." Left the B's because they were Jews. They had a home like a palace and wanted her to stay. They said, "We knew it was too good to be true" . . . when she was leaving.

Striking is the similarity between the subject's way of thinking and a certain kind of crackpot religious movement, based on readiness to hear "inner voices" which give both moral uplifting and sinister advice:

The Catholics have been wonderful to her, and she admires them but wouldn't join their church. There was something inside her that said "No." (She gestures her rejection.) She has an individualistic religion. Once she was out walking in the early morning—the birds were singing—she raised her hands and her face to the sky, and they were wet. . . . (She considered it a supernatural phenomenon.)

6. THE "MANIPULATIVE" TYPE

This syndrome, potentially the most dangerous one, is defined by stereotypy as an extreme: rigid notions become ends rather than means, and the whole world is divided into empty, schematic, administrative fields. There is an almost complete lack of object cathexis and of emotional ties. If the "Crank" syndrome had something paranoid about it, the "Manipulative" one has something schizophrenic. However, the break between internal and external world, in this case, does not result in anything like ordinary "introversion," but rather the contrary: a kind of compulsive overrealism which treats everything and everyone as an object to be handled, manipulated, seized by the subject's own theoretical and practical patterns. The technical aspects of life, and things *qua* "tools" are fraught with libido. The emphasis is on "doing things," with far-reaching indifference towards the content of what is going to be done. The pattern is found in numerous business people and also, in increasing numbers, among members of the rising managerial and technological class who maintain, in the process of production, a function between the old type of ownership and the workers' aristocracy. Many fascist-political anti-Semites in Germany showed this syndrome: Himmler may be symbolic of them. Their sober intelligence, together with their almost complete absence of any affections makes them perhaps the most merciless of all. Their organizational way of looking at things predisposes them to totalitarian solutions. Their goal is the construction of gas chambers rather than the pogrom. They do not even have to hate the Jews; they "cope" with them by administrative measures without any personal contacts with the victims. Anti-Semitism is reified, an export article: it must "function." Their cynicism is almost complete: "The Jewish question will be solved strictly legally" is the way they talk about the cold pogrom. The Jews are provocative to them in so far as supposed Jewish individualism is a challenge to their stereotypy, and because they feel in the Jews a neurotic overemphasis on the very same kind of human relationships which they are lacking themselves. The ingroup-outgroup relationship becomes the principle according to which the whole world is abstractly organized. Naturally, this syndrome can be found in this country only in a rudimentary state.

As to the psychological etiology of this type, our material sets us certain limitations. However, it should be borne in mind that compulsiveness is the psychological equivalent of what we call, in terms of social theory, reification. The compulsive features of the boy chosen as an example for the "Manipulative" type, together with his sadism, can hardly be overlooked—he comes close to the classical Freudian conception of the "anal" character and is in this regard reminiscent of the "Authoritarian" syndrome. But he is differentiated from the latter by the simultaneity of extreme narcissism and a certain emptiness and shallowness. This, however, involves a contradiction only if looked at superficially, since whatever we call a person's emotional and intellectual richness is due to the intensity of his object cathexes. Notable in our case is an interest in sex almost amounting to preoccupation, going with backwardness as far as actual experience is concerned. One pictures a very inhibited boy, worried about masturbation, collecting insects while the other boys played baseball. There must have been early and deep emotional traumata, probably on a pregenital level. *M108*

  is going to be an insect toxicologist and work for a large organization like Standard Oil or a university, presumably not in private business. He first started in chemistry in college but about the third term began to wonder if that was what he really wanted. He was interested in entomology in high school, and while hashing in a sorority he met a fellow worker in entomology, and in talking about the possibility of combining entomology and chemistry, this man said he thought it would be a very good field to investigate a little further. He found out insect toxicology had everything that combined his interests, wasn't overcrowded, and that he could make a good living there, and that there wasn't likely to be a surplus as there would be in chemistry or engineering.

Taken in isolation, the professional choice of this subject may appear accidental, but when viewed in the context of the whole interview, it assumes a certain significance. It has been pointed out by L. Lowenthal (75) that fascist orators often compare their "enemies" to "vermin." The interest of this boy in entomology may be due to his regarding the insects, which are both "repulsive" and weak, as ideal objects for his manipulation.[4]

The manipulative aspect of his professional choice is stressed by himself:

Asked what he expects to get from the job other than the economic side, he said that he hopes to have a hand in organizing the whole field, that is, in organizing the knowledge. There is no textbook, the information is scattered, and he hopes to make a contribution in organizing the material.

His emphasis on "doing things" goes so far that he even appreciates people whom he otherwise hates, though in a terminology with destructive over-tones. Here belongs his statement about Roosevelt, which was quoted in part in Chapter XVII:

Asked about the good points of Roosevelt, he said, "Well, the first term he was in office he whipped the U.S. into shape. Some people argue he only carried out Hoover's ideas, but actually he did a good job which was badly needed . . . he usurped power that was necessary to do something—he took a lot more power than a lot." . . . Asked whether his policies were good or bad, subject replied, "Well, at any rate, he was doing something."

His political concepts are defined by the friend-foe relationship, in exactly the same way as the Nazi theoretician Karl Schmitt defined the nature of politics. His lust for organization, concomitant with an obsession with the domination of nature, seems boundless:

"There will always be wars. (Is there any way of preventing wars?) No, it's not common goals but common enemies that make friends. Perhaps if they could dis-cover other planets and some way of getting there, spread out that way, we could prevent wars for a time, but eventually there'd be wars again."

The truly totalitarian and destructive implications of his dichotomous way of thinking become manifest in his statement about the Negroes:

(What can we do about the Negroes?) "Nothing can be done. There are two factions. I'm not in favor of interbreeding because this would produce an inferior race. The Negroes haven't reached the point of development of Caucasians, arti-ficially living and absorbing from the races." He would approve of segregation, but that's not possible. Not unless you are willing to use Hitler's methods. There are only two ways of handling this problem—Hitler's methods or race mixture. Race mixture is the only answer and is already taking place, according to what he has read, but he's against it. It wouldn't do the race any good.

[4] This, of course, covers only a superficial aspect. It is well known from psychoanalysis that insects and vermin serve frequently as symbols for siblings. The fantasies involved here may be traces of the little boy's wish to beat his little brother until he "keeps quiet." Manipulativeness may be one form in which death wishes for the siblings are allowed to come to the fore. "Organizers" are frequently persons who want to exercise domineering control over those who are actually their *equals*—substitutes for the siblings over whom they wish to rule, like the father, as the next best thing, if they cannot kill them. Our insect toxicologist mentions frequent childhood quarrels with his sister.

This logic allows only for one conclusion: that the Negroes should be killed. At the same time, his way of looking at the prospective objects of manipulation is completely unemotional and detached: although his anti-Semitism is marked he doesn't even claim that you can

"tell the Jews by their appearance, they're just like other people, all kinds."

His administrative and pathologically detached outlook is again evidenced by his statement on intermarriage:

He said that if he were an American businessman in Germany or England he'd probably marry first an American woman if he could, then he might marry a German or an English woman.

However, "swarthy" people like Greeks or Jews have no chance in this experimental setup. It is true, he has nothing against his Spanish brother-in-law, but expresses his approval by the phrase that "you couldn't tell him from a white person."

He takes a positive attitude towards the church for manipulative purposes:

"Well, people want church; there is a purpose, it sets standards for some people, but for other people, it is not necessary. A general sense of social duty would do the same thing."

His own metaphysical views are naturalistic, with a strong nihilistic coloring:

Asked about his own beliefs he said he's a mechanistic—there is no supernatural entity, not concerned with us as humans; it goes back to a law of physics. Humans and life are just an accident—but an inevitable accident. And then he tried to explain that—that there was some matter accrued when the earth was started and it was almost by accident that life started and it just kept on.

As to his emotional structure:

His mother is "just Mom"; he seems to have some respect for his father and father's opinions, but there was no real attachment any place. He said as a child he had a lot of friends, but on further questioning, he couldn't mention any closer friends. He did a lot of reading as a child. Didn't have many fights—couldn't remember them—didn't have any more than any other boys. He has no real close friends now. His closest friends were when he was in the 10th or 11th grade, and he still keeps track of some of them, he said. (How important are friends?) "Well, they're especially important in younger years, and in your older years you don't enjoy life as much without them. I don't expect my friends to help me get along." They're not needed so much at present age, but he supposed that at the interviewer's age it would be very important to have friends.

Finally it should be mentioned that the only moral quality that plays a considerable role in the thinking of this subject is loyalty, perhaps as a compensation for his own lack of affection. By loyalty he probably means complete and unconditional identification of a person with the group to which he happens to belong. He is expected to surrender completely to his "unit" and to give up all individual particularities for the sake of the "whole." *M108* objects to Jewish refugees not having been "loyal to Germany."

C. SYNDROMES FOUND AMONG LOW SCORERS

The following schematic observations may help towards orientation among the "low" syndromes. The *Rigid* low scorers are characterized by strong superego tendencies and compulsive features. Paternal authority and its social substitutes, however, are frequently replaced by the image of some collectivity, possibly moulded after the archaic image of what Freud calls the brother horde. Their main taboo is directed against violations of actual or supposed brotherly love. The *Protesting* low scorer has much in common with the "Authoritarian" high scorer, the main difference being that the further-going sublimation of the father idea, concomitant with an undercurrent of hostility against the father, leads to the conscientious rejection of heteronomous authority instead of its acceptance. The decisive feature is opposition to whatever appears to be tyranny. The syndrome of the *Impulsive* low scorer denotes people in whom strong id impulses were never integrated with ego and superego. They are threatened by overpowering libidinous energy and in a way as close to psychosis as the "Crank" and the "Manipulative" high scorer. As to the *Easy-Going* low scorer, the id seems to be little repressed, but rather to be sublimated into compassion, and the superego well developed, whereas the extraverted functions of the otherwise quite articulate ego frequently do not keep pace. These subjects sometimes come close to neurotic indecision. One of their main features is the fear of "hurting" anyone or anything by action. The construct of the *Genuine Liberal* may be conceived in terms of that balance between superego, ego, and id which Freud deemed ideal.

In our sample the "Protesting" and the "Easy-Going" low scorers apparently occur most frequently. Emphasizing, however, once again that the low scorers are as a whole less "typed" than the high scorers, we shall refrain from any undue generalization.

1. THE "RIGID" LOW SCORER

We may start with the "low" syndrome that has most in common with the over-all "high" pattern, and proceed in the direction of sounder and more durable "lowness." The syndrome which commands first attention is the one which shows the most markedly stereotypical features—that is to say, configurations in which the absence of prejudice, instead of being based on concrete experience and integrated within the personality, is derived from some general, external, ideological pattern. Here we find those subjects whose lack of prejudice, however consistent in terms of surface ideology, has to be regarded as accidental in terms of personality, but we also find people whose rigidity is hardly less related to personality than is the case with certain syndromes of high scorers. The latter kind of low scorers are definitely disposed towards totalitarianism in their thinking; what is accidental up to a certain degree is the particular brand of ideological world formula that they chance to come into contact with. We encountered a few subjects who had been identified ideologically with some progressive movement, such as the struggle for minority rights, for a long time, but with whom such ideas contained features of compulsiveness, even of paranoid obsession, and who, with respect to many of our variables, especially rigidity and "total" thinking, could hardly be distinguished from some of our high extremes. All the representatives of this syndrome can in one way or another be regarded as counterparts of the "Surface Resentment" type of high scorer. The accidentalness in their total outlook makes them liable to change fronts in critical situations, as was the case with certain kinds of radicals under the Nazi regime. They may often be recognized by a certain disinterestedness with respect to crucial minority questions *per se*, being, rather, against prejudice as a plank in the fascist platform; but sometimes they also see *only* minority problems. They are likely to use clichés and phraseology hardly less frequently than do their political opponents. Some of them tend to belittle the importance of racial discrimination by labeling it simply as a byproduct of the big issues of class struggle—an attitude which may be indicative of repressed prejudice on their own part. Representatives of this syndrome can often be found, for example, among young, "progressive" people, particularly students, whose personal development has failed to keep pace with their ideological indoctrination. One of the best means for identifying the syndrome is to note the subject's readiness to deduce his stand towards minority problems from some general formula, rather than to make spontaneous statements. He also may often come forward with value judgments which cannot possibly be based on any real knowledge of the matter in question.

F139 is a religious educator.

For the past ten years she has considered herself very progressive. Lately she has little time to read, but her husband reads and studies constantly and keeps her up to date by discussion. "My favorite world statesman is Litvinov. I think the most dramatic speech of modern times is the one he made at the Geneva conference when he pleaded for collective security. It has made us very happy to see the fog of ignorance and distrust surrounding the Soviet Union clear away during this war. Things are not settled yet though. There are many fascists in our own country who would fight Russia if they could."

The hollowness of her enthusiasm about Litvinov has already been noted in our discussion of stereotyped thinking in politics (Chapter XVII). The same seems to be true of her assertion that she is an internationalist, followed up by her rhetorical question, "Would I be a true Christian if I weren't?" This is typical of the "deductive" way of thinking which seems to characterize the rigid low scorer. The present subject seems to proceed in the same way as she approaches minority questions.

Subject believes that all people are one, and again she feels that is the only point of view possible for a true Christian.

The somewhat sweeping expression "that all people are one" should be noted: a person free of stereotypy would rather tend to acknowledge differences and to take a positive stand towards differentiation. What is meant is probably "equal in the sight of God" and she deduces her tolerance from this general assumption.

As mentioned in the chapter on politics, the superficiality of her progressivism is indicated by her highly aggressive attitude towards alcoholism, called by herself "one of her pet subjects," which plays almost the same role as do certain paranoid ideas in the "Cranks" among the high scorers. It may be recalled in this connection, that Alfred McClung Lee has demonstrated the close connection between prohibitionism and prejudiced ways of thinking. As a matter of fact, there is evidence enough that this "Rigid" low scorer has more than a sprinkling of the "high" mentality. There is the emphasis on "status," with reference to her daughter:

"I feel badly about her school too—(names the school). The influx of people with lower educational and cultural standards than ours has had effect on the schools of course."

There are destructive fantasies, thinly veiled by "sensible" moral reflections:

"The same with smoking. I am not really worried about it though. No one of either side of our family ever smoked or drank, with one exception. My husband's sister smoked. She is dead now."

There is a rationalization of punitiveness:

"If I could bring about Prohibition tomorrow I would do it. I believe in preventing everything that doesn't make man better—that makes him worse. Some people say if you forbid something it makes people do it on the sly. Well, I say, how about murder, and robbery, and dope? We have prohibited them and some people still commit crimes, but we do not think of taking off the ban on them."

And there is, finally, official optimism, a characteristic reaction-formation against underlying destructiveness:

"If one didn't always have hope and believe everything was moving upwards, one's Christianity wouldn't mean anything, would it?"

Under changing conditions she might be willing to join a subversive movement as long as it pretended to be "Christian" and to "move upwards."

2. THE "PROTESTING" LOW SCORER[5]

This syndrome is in many respects the counterpart of the "Authoritarian" high scorer. Its determinants are psychological rather than rational. It is based on a specific resolution of the Oedipus complex which has deeply affected the individuals in question. While they are set against paternal authority, they have at the same time internalized the father image to a high degree. One may say that in them the superego is so strong that it turns against its own "model," the father, and all external authorities. They are thoroughly guided by *conscience* which seems to be, in many cases exhibiting this pattern, a secularization of religious authority. This conscience, however, is quite autonomous and independent of outside codes. They "protest" out of purely moral reasons against social repression or at least against some of its extreme manifestations, such as racial prejudice.[6] Most of the "neurotic" low scorers who play such a large role in our sample show the "Protest" syndrome. They are often shy, "retiring," uncertain about themselves, and even given to tormenting themselves with all kinds of doubts and scruples. They sometimes show certain compulsive features, and their reaction against prejudice has also an aspect of having been forced upon them by rigid superego demands. They are frequently guilt-ridden and regard the Jews *a priori* as "victims," as being distinctly different from themselves. An element of stereotypy may be inherent in their sympathies and identifications. They are guided by the wish to "make good" the injustice that has been done to minorities. At the same time they may be easily attracted by the real or imaginary intellectual qualities of the Jews which they deem to be akin to their desire to be "aloof" from worldly affairs. While being nonauthoritarian in their way of thinking, they are often psychologically constricted and thus not able to act as energetically as their conscience demands. It is as if the internalization of conscience has succeeded so well that they are severely inhibited or even psychologically "paralyzed." Their eternal guilt feelings tend to make them regard *everyone* as "guilty." Though they detest discrimination, they may find it sometimes difficult to stand up against it. Socially, they seem usually to belong to the middle class, but it is hard to define their group membership in more precise terms. However, our material seems to indicate that they are frequently to be found among people who underwent serious family troubles, such as a divorce of their parents. *F127*

is extremely pretty in the conventional "campus girl" style. She is very slight, blond, fair-skinned, and blue-eyed. She wears a becoming "sloppy Joe" sweater, daintily fixed blouse, and brief skirt, with bobby socks. She wears a sorority pin. She

[5] This term was suggested by J. F. Brown.

[6] It was pointed out in Chapter XVIII that religion, when it has been internalized, is an effective antidote against prejudice and the whole fascist potential, notwithstanding its own authoritarian aspects.

is very friendly and interested, seems to enjoy the discussion, but is quite vague in her answers about family life until the interview is quite well along. Then she suddenly decides to reveal the most important single fact in her life—her parents' divorce which she usually hides—and from that point on speaks with apparent freedom about her own feelings.

She shows the characteristic neurotic concern with herself, indicative of a feeling of impotence: she has a somewhat magical belief in psychology, apparently expecting that the psychologist knows more about her than she does herself:

What she would like above all is to be a psychiatrist. (Why?) "Because psychiatrists know more about people. Everyone tells me their troubles. I don't think there is anything more satisfying than to be able to help people with their problems. But I don't have the brains or the patience to be a psychiatrist. That is just an idea."

Her attitude towards the father is hostile:

Father is a lawyer. At present he is enlisted in the army and is somewhere in the Pacific, in charge of a Negro battalion. (What does he think about that?) "I don't know what he thinks about anything."

Her social attitude is a combination of conformist "correctness," the emphatic and self-confessed desire for "pleasure" (almost as if her conscience would order her to enjoy herself), and a tendency towards retiring internalization. Her indifference to "status," though perhaps not quite authentic, is noteworthy.

(Interests?) "Oh fun—and serious things too. I like to read and discuss things. I like bright people—can't stand clinging vines. Like to dance, dress up, go places. Am not much good at sports, but I play at them—tennis, swimming. I belong to a sorority and we do lots of war work as well as entertaining service men. (Subject names sorority.) (That is supposed to be a good house isn't it?) They say so. I didn't think there was anything very special about it."

Her social progressiveness is characterized by both an element of fear and a conscientious sense of justice:

(What do you think about poverty?) "I hate to think of it. And I don't think it is necessary. (Who is to blame?) Oh, I don't mean the poor people are. I don't know, but you would think that by now we could work out a way so that everyone would have enough."

Her anxiety makes her more aware of the fascist potential than most other low scorers are:

"It would be terrible to have Nazis here. Of course there are some. And they would like to have the same thing happen. . . . Lots of Jewish kids have a hard time—in the service, and in going to medical school. It isn't fair. (Why the discrimination?) I don't know unless it is the Nazi influence. No, it went back before that. I guess there always are some people who have ideas like the Nazis."

Her indignation is primarily directed against "unfairness." The notion that "there are always people with ideas like the Nazis" is remarkable: a highly developed sense of responsibility seems to give her an understanding in social matters that goes far beyond her purely intellectual insight. Psychologically, the complete absence of prejudice in her case seems best understood as a superego function, since the girl relates a rather unpleasant experience which otherwise might well have made her prejudiced: she was kidnapped, as a child of four, by a Negro but

"He didn't hurt me. I don't think I was even scared."

As to the genetic background of her attitude, the following clinical data are pertinent:

"I am more like my father I am afraid and that isn't good. He is a very impatient man, overbearing, and everything for himself. He and I didn't get along. He favored my sister because she played up to him. But both of us suffered with him. If I even called my sister a name as kids will do when they fight, I got spanked, and hard. That used to worry my mother. For that reason she hardly ever punished us, because he did it all the time, and mostly for nothing. I was spanked constantly. I remember that better than anything. (Do you think your mother and father loved each other?) No, perhaps they did at first, but my mother couldn't stand the way he treated us. She divorced him." (She flushes and her eyes fill with tears as she says this. When interviewer commented that she had not realized the parents were divorced she says—"I wasn't going to say anything. I hardly ever do.")

As to neurotic traits: there are indications of a strong mother-fixation:

"I don't want mother to ever get married again. (Why?) I don't know. She doesn't need to. She can have friends. She is very attractive and has lots of friends but I couldn't stand to have her marry again. (Do you think she might anyway?) No. She won't if I don't want her to."

And there are symptoms of sexual inhibition, based on her experience of the breakdown of her parents' marriage.

(Boys?) "Oh, I don't get serious and I don't want them to. I neck a little of course, but nothing to give them any idea I am cheap. I don't like cheap fellows either."

Her statement that she does not want to commit herself because she is afraid of war marriages is probably a rationalization.

3. THE "IMPULSIVE" LOW SCORER

The case of an "impulse-ridden" low scorer has been described by Frenkel-Brunswik and Sanford (38). They write:

The most markedly pathologial case from among our low scorers showed in an extreme degree a pattern that was different from that which we have regarded as most typical of our low extremes. This girl was clearly impulse ridden. Her ego was lined up with her id, so that all kinds of excesses were made to seem permissible to her. In stating why she liked Jews she gave much the same reasons that the high extremes had given for hating them.

There is reason to assume that this case represents a syndrome of its own, being in some respects the counterpart of the psychopathic high scorer. This syndrome stands out in all-adjusted people who have an extremely strong id, but are relatively free of destructive impulses: people who, on account of their own libidinous situation, sympathize with everything they feel to be repressed. Moreover, they are those who respond so strongly to all kinds of stimuli that the ingroup-outgroup relation has no meaning to them—rather, they are attracted by everything that is "different" and promises some new kind of gratification. If they have destructive elements, these seem to be directed against themselves instead of against others. The range of this syndrome seems to reach from *libertines* and "addicts" of all kinds, over certain asocial characters such as prostitutes and nonviolent criminals, to certain psychotics. It may also be noted that in Germany very few Nazis were found among actors, circus folk, and vagrants—people whom the Nazis put into concentration camps. It is difficult to say what are the deeper psychological sources of this syndrome. It seems, however, that there is weakness both in the superego and in the ego, and that this makes these individuals somewhat unstable in political matters as well as in other areas. They certainly do not think in stereotypes, but it is doubtful to what extent they succeed in conceptualization at all.

Our illustration, *F205*, is selected from the Psychiatric Clinic material:

She is a pleasantly mannered, attractive young college girl who is obviously seriously maladjusted and who suffers from great mood swings, tension, who cannot concentrate on her school work and has no goals in life. . . . Sometimes she is extremely upset, comes crying and "mixed up," complains that she is not being helped fast enough. Therapist feels that she cannot stand any deeper probing, that therapy will have to be mostly supportive, because of her weak ego, possibility of precipitating a psychosis. Schizoid tendencies.

She is set against prejudice with a strong accent on "interbreeding," probably an expression of her own impulse for promiscuity: there should be no "boundaries":

(Prejudices?) "If there were interbreeding between races it might help in the combining of cultures—it may internationalize culture. I think there should be one system of education everywhere. It may not be practical—but perhaps selective breeding would be possible—an accumulation of good traits might come out. And the imbeciles could be sterilized." (Quotes some study on heredity subject has learned about.) "It seems improvements aren't made fast enough. The whole society is ill and unhappy."

The last sentence indicates that her own discontent leads her, by the way of empathy, towards a rather radical and consistent critique of society. The keenness of her insight as well as her being attracted by what is "different" comes out even more clearly in her statement on minority problems:

"There is a terrific amount of minority oppression—prejudice. There is a fear of minorities, a lack of knowledge. I would like to assimilate all groups—internationally. Would want the education of the world unified. The minorities themselves also keep themselves apart. It's a vicious circle. Society makes them outcasts and they react this way." (Differences?) (Interviewer tried hard to have subject describe differences between groups, but subject insisted): "All differences that exist are due to conditions people grow up in and also to the emotional responses (to discrimination). (Jews?) I don't see how they are different as a *group*. I have Jewish friends. . . . Maybe they are more sensitive because of prejudice against them. But that's good."

According to the clinical data the girl is a genuine Lesbian, who was severely reprimanded because of her homosexuality, and became afterwards "rather promiscuous to determine whether she did react sexually to men." "All emotionally upset in one way or the other," she said. Her later history indicates that the Lesbian component is stronger than anything else.

It may be added that the Los Angeles sample contains three call-house girls, all of them completely free of prejudice and also low on the F scale. Since their profession tends to make them resentful about sex altogether, and since they profess symptoms of frigidity, they do not seem to belong to the "Impulsive" syndrome. However, only much closer analysis could ascertain whether the ultimate basis of their character formation is of the "impulsive" kind and has only been hidden by later reaction-formations, or whether their low score is due to a purely social factor, namely the innumerable contacts they have with all kinds of people.

4. THE "EASY-GOING" LOW SCORER

This syndrome is the exact opposite of the "Manipulative" high scorer. Negatively, it is characterized by a marked tendency to "let things go," a profound unwillingness to do violence to any object (an unwillingness which often may approach, on the surface level, conformity), and by an extreme reluctance to make decisions, often underscored by the subjects themselves. This reluctance even affects their language: they may be recognized by the frequency of unfinished sentences, as if they would not like to commit themselves, but rather leave it to the listener to decide on the merits of the case. Positively, they are inclined to "live and let live," while at the same time their own desires seem to be free of the acquisitive touch. Grudging and discontent are absent. They show a certain psychological richness, the opposite of constrictedness: a capacity for enjoying things, imagination, a sense of humor which often assumes the form of self-irony. The latter, however, is as little destructive as their other attitudes: it is as if they were ready to confess all kinds of weaknesses not so much out of any neurotic compulsion as because of a strong underlying sense of inner security. They can give themselves up without being afraid of losing themselves. They are rarely radical in their political outlook, but rather behave as if they were already living under nonrepressive conditions, in a truly human society, an attitude which may, sometimes, tend to weaken their power of resistance. There is no evidence of any truly schizoid tendencies. They are completely nonstereopathic —they do not even resist stereotypy, but simply fail to understand the urge for subsumption.

The etiology of the "Easy-Going" syndrome is still somewhat obscure. The subjects in whom it is pronounced seem not to be defined by the preponderance of any psychological agency, or by retrogression to any particular infantile phase though there is, superficially seen, something of the child about them. Rather, they should be understood *dynamically*. They are people whose character structure has not become "congealed": no set pattern of control by any of the agencies of Freud's typology has crystallized, but they are completely "open" to experience. This, however, does not imply ego weakness, but rather the absence of traumatic experiences and defects which otherwise lead to the "reification" of the ego. In this sense, they are "normal," but it is just this normality which gives them in our civilization the appearance of a certain immaturity. Not only did they not undergo severe childhood conflicts, but their whole childhood seems to be determined by motherly or other female images.[7] Perhaps they may best be characterized as those who know no fear of women. This may account for the absence of aggressiveness. At the same time, it is possibly indicative of an archaic trait: to them, the world has still a matriarchal outlook. Thus, they may often represent, sociologically, the genuine "folk" element as against rational civilization. Representatives of this syndrome are not infrequent among the lower middle-classes. Though no "action" is to be expected of them, one may count on them as on persons who, under no circumstances, ever will adjust themselves to political or psychological fascism. The aforementioned M711

is very amiable, mild, gentle, casual, slow, and somewhat lethargic in both voice and manner. He is quite verbal, but very circumstantial. His statements are typically surrounded with qualifications to which he commonly devotes more attention than to the main proposition. He seems to suffer from pervasive indecision and doubt, to be pretty unsure of his ideas, and to have great difficulty in committing himself to positive statements on very many matters. In general, he tends to avoid committing himself to things, either intellectually or emotionally, and in general avoids getting involved in things.

He describes his choice of profession as accidental, but it is interesting that he was originally a landscape architect—which may imply a desire for the restitution of nature rather than its domination—and later became an interviewer in government employment, a job that gives him the gratification of helping other people without his stressing, however, this aspect narcissistically. He is not indifferent to wealth and admits his wish for "security," but is, at the same time, totally unimpressed by the importance of money *per*

---

[7] The subject chosen as an illustration of this type "was brought up in a household of women—mother and grandmother."

se. His religious attitude has been described in Chapter XVIII, and it fits psychologically, in every detail, into the make-up of the "Easy-Going" syndrome. It may be added that he "does not believe in the Immaculate Conception" but doesn't think "it makes any difference."

When asked about discipline in childhood, he answers "practically none," "very undisciplined." His strong attachment to his mother is emphasized without any inhibition: the only period of his childhood when there were any "bones of contention" was when his mother "exhibited her possessiveness. She didn't like the gals I went with." What he himself likes about women is described as follows:

"Awfully hard to say when you're pretty sold on a gal. . . . Seems to have all the things I like—fun to be with, brains, pretty. She likes me, which is important. We share things together. (What enjoy doing together?) Music, reading, swimming, dancing. Most of the things which don't require too much energy, which makes it good."

It is remarkable that there is no trace of hostility against the father—whom he lost very early—in spite of the mother-fixation. It is the imaginative gift of the father which lingers in his memory:

(Pleasant memories of father?) "Lots of pleasant memories, because he spoiled us when he was home, always cooking up wonderful ideas for things to do. (Mother and father got along?) I think very well. (Which parent take after?) I don't know, because I didn't know my father very well. (Father's faults?) Don't know."

Most significant are his statements on race issues:

(What think of minority group problems?) "I wish I knew. I don't know. I think that is one problem we should all be working on. (Biggest problem?) Negroes, in terms of numbers. . . . I don't think we've ever faced the problem squarely. . . . Many Negroes have come to the West Coast. . . . (Have you ever had Negroes as friends?) Yes . . . Not intimately, though have known a number that I've liked and enjoyed. (What about intermarriage?) I think it's a false issue. . . . They say, 'What if your sister married a Negro?' I wouldn't have any feelings about it, frankly. . . . (Negro traits?) No."

As to the Jews, he does not come to their "defense," but actually denies that they are a "problem":

(What about the Jewish problem?) "I don't think there is a Jewish problem. There again, I think that's been a herring for agitators. (How do you mean?) Hitler, Ku Klux Klan, etc. (Jewish traits?) No . . . I've seen Jewish people exhibit so-called Jewish traits, but also many non-Jewish people." . . . (Subject emphasizes there is no distinction along racial lines.)

The danger implicit in the "Easy-Going" syndrome, i.e., too great reluctance to use violence even against violence, is suggested by the following passage:

(What about picketing Gerald K. Smith?) "I think Gerald K. Smith should have an opportunity to speak, if we are operating under a democracy. (What about picketing as registering a protest?) If a certain group wants to, they have a right to. . . . I don't think it's always effective."

That the subject's attitude of noncommitment to any "principle" is actually based on a sense of the concrete and not purely evasive is indicated by the following highly elucidating passage:

(Interviewer reads question . . . about tireless leader and refers to subject as agreeing a little, asks for elaboration.) "I agree a *little*. However, the opposite of that, Huey Long, was a courageous, tireless leader and Hitler (laughs). It depends. (How do you mean?) Well, I admired Willkie; I admired Roosevelt; I admired Wallace. But, I don't think we should ever have leaders in whom the people put their faith and then settle back. People seem to seek leaders to avoid thinking for themselves."

This subject's interview concludes with the dialectical statement that "power is almost equivalent to the abuse of power."

5. THE GENUINE LIBERAL

By contrast to the pattern just described, this syndrome is very outspoken in reaction and opinion. The subject in whom it is pronounced has a strong sense of personal autonomy and independence. He cannot stand any outside interference with his personal convictions and beliefs, and he does not want to interfere with those of others either. His ego is quite developed but not libidinized—he is rarely "narcissistic." At the same time, he is willing to admit id tendencies, and to take the consequence—as is the case with Freud's "erotic type" (39). One of his conspicuous features is moral courage, often far beyond his rational evaluation of a situation. He cannot "keep silent" if something wrong is being done, even if he seriously endangers himself. Just as he is strongly "individualized" himself, he sees the others, above all, as individuals, not as specimens of a general concept. He shares some features with other syndromes found among low scorers. Like the "Impulsive," he is little repressed and even has certain difficulties in keeping himself under "control." However, his emotionality is not blind, but directed towards the other person as a *subject*. His love is not only desire but also compassion—as a matter of fact, one might think of defining this syndrome as the "compassionate" low scorer. He shares with the "Protesting" low scorer the vigor of identification with the underdog, but without compulsion, and without traces of overcompensation: he is no "Jew lover." Like the "Easy-Going" low scorer he is antitotalitarian, but much more consciously so, without the element of hesitation and indecision. It is this configuration rather than any single trait which characterizes the "Genuine Liberal." Aesthetic interests seem to occur frequently.

The illustration we give is a girl whose character of a "genuine liberal" stands out the more clearly, since, according to the interviewer, she is politically naive like the majority of our college women, regardless whether they are high or low.

No "ticket" is involved. *F515*

is a 21-year-old college student. She is a handsome brunette with dark, flashing eyes, who exudes temperament and vitality. She has none of the pretty-pretty femininity so frequently seen in high subjects, and would probably scorn the little feminine wiles and schemes practiced by such women. On the contrary, she is extremely frank and outspoken in manner, and in build she is athletic. One senses in her a very passionate nature and so strong a desire to give intensely of herself in all her relationships, that she must experience difficulty in restraining herself within the bounds of conventionality.

Apart from a semiprofessional interest in music she also "enjoys painting and dramatics." As to her vocation, however, she is still undecided. She

has taken nurses' aid training. She liked helping people in this way. "I enjoyed it. I feel that I could now take care of a sick person. It didn't bother me to carry bed-pans and urinals. I learned that I could touch flesh without being squeamish. I learned to be tactful about certain things. And then it was patriotic! (slightly joking tone). People liked me. (Why did they like you?) Because I smiled, and because I was always making cracks—like I'm doing now."

Her views with regard to minorities are guided by the idea of the individual:

"Minorities have to have just as many rights as majorities. They are all people and should have just as many rights as the majority. There should be no minorities; there should only be individuals and they should be judged according to the individual. Period! Is that sufficient?"

(Negroes?) "Same thing! Still as individuals. Their skin is black, but they are still people. Individuals have loves and sorrows and joys. I don't think you should kill them all or liquidate them or stick them in a corner just because they are different people. I would not marry one, because I should not want to marry a person who has a trait I don't like, like a large nose, etc. I would not want to have children with dark skins. I would not mind if they live next door to me." (Earlier in the interview subject had brought out the fact that she had also to care for Negro patients during her nurses' aid work, and that she had not minded at all having to give baths to them, etc.)

(Jews?) "Same! Well I could marry a Jew very easily. I could even marry a Negro if he had a light enough skin. I prefer a light skin. I don't consider Jews different from white people at all, because they even have light skins. It's really silly. (What do you think are the causes of prejudice?) Jealousy. (Explain?) Because they are smarter and they don't want any competition. We don't want any competition. If they want it they should have it. I don't know if they are more intelligent, but if they are they should have it."

The last statement shows complete absence of any aspect of guilt feelings in her relation to the Jews. It is followed up by the joke:

"Maybe if the Jews get in power they would liquidate the majority! That's not smart. Because we would fight back."

Her views on religion, with a slightly humorous touch, are centered in the idea of Utopia. She mentions the word herself, when referring to her reading of Plato. The gist of her religion is contained in the statement: "Perhaps we will all be saved." This should be compared with the prevailing "anti-Utopian" attitude of our subjects.

The description of both her parents contains elements of her own ego ideal, in quite an unconventional way:

"Father has been employed for 25 years in the freight complaint department of the ———— R.R. Co. His work involves the hiring of many men. He has about 150 people working under him." (Subject described her father as follows:) "He could have been vice-president by now—he has the brains—but he does not have the go-get-in nature; he is not enough of a politician. He is broad-minded—always listens to both sides of a question before making up his mind. He is a good 'argumenter' for this reason. He is understanding. He is not emotional like mother. Mother is emotional, father factual. Mother is good. She has a personality of her own. She gives to all of us. She is emotional. She keeps Daddy very satisfied. (In what way?) She makes a home for him to come home to—he has it very hard at the office. It's living. Their marriage is very happy—everybody notices it. Their children perform too—people notice them! Mother is very friendly. Understanding. She gives sympathy. People love to talk to her. Someone calls her up on the telephone and they become lifelong friends just from having talked on the telephone! She is sensitive; it is easy to hurt her."

Her attitude towards sex is one of precarious restraint. Her boy friend

wants to have sexual intercourse everytime that they have a date—in fact he wanted it the first time he dated her—and she doesn't want it that way. She cries every time he tries something, so she supposes it cannot be right for her. She thinks that friendship should precede sexual relations, but he thinks that sex relations are a way of getting to know each other better. Finally she broke with him three days ago (said with mock tearfulness). He had said, "Let's just be friends," but she didn't want that either! The sex problem bothers her. The first time she danced with him he told her that he thought she wanted intercourse; whereas she just wanted to be close to him. She is worried because she didn't mean it the other way, but perhaps unconsciously she did!

It is evident that her erotic character is connected with a lack of repression with regard to her feelings towards her father: "I would like to marry someone like my father."

The result of the interview is summed up by the interviewer:

The most potent factors making for the low score in this case are the open-mindedness of the parents and the great love subject's mother bore all her children.

If this can be generalized, and consequences be drawn for high scorers, we might postulate that the increasing significance of the fascist character depends largely upon basic changes in the structure of the family itself (see Max Horkheimer, 53a).

PART V

Applications to Individuals and to Special Groups

C H A P T E R X X

GENETIC ASPECTS OF THE AUTHORITARIAN PERSONALITY: CASE STUDIES OF TWO CONTRASTING INDIVIDUALS

R. Nevitt Sanford

A. INTRODUCTION

As Mack and Larry have been followed through the various techniques of the study each of these subjects has shown striking consistency of response, and numerous differences between them have been found. The consistency embraces personality as well as ideology, and the differences have appeared in each area of investigation, from surface attitudes to the deep-lying needs explored by the T.A.T. Evidence has accumulated in support of the view that the differing ideological patterns are closely associated with differences in personality structure. The present task is to describe these personality structures, to see how they are expressed in ideological trends and, above all, to learn as much as possible about how they developed. Numerous personality characteristics of the two subjects have already been brought to light, and the T.A.T. has given strong indications of what the central forces in each case might be; over-all formulation, however, has had to wait upon an examination of the material from the clinical section of the interview. This material obviously leaves much to be desired, but when it is brought into relation with what has gone before and interpreted with the freedom which the background afforded by the foregoing clinical chapters now permits, reasonably complete and meaningful pictures emerge.

Many of the variables discussed in the chapters dealing with data from the clinical interviews will appear again as we consider these two cases. It is hoped that by paying more attention to specific detail than has been possible when the concern was with groups of subjects, we may come to closer grips with some of the concrete phenomena from which our variables were abstracted and that they will thus gain something in meaningfulness. The concern here, however, is not so much with particular variables as with the patterning of variables within a single individual. The aim is to achieve as lifelike a portrait of one authoritarian personality, in its genetic aspects, as our frag-

787

mentary material permits, and to point up the contrasts with a nonauthoritarian personality.

Most consideration will be given to the case of Mack: Here, as throughout the book, prejudice, rather than the relative lack of it, is in the focus of attention. Larry's case is used mainly for purposes of contrast—contrast both with respect to the broad outlines of personality structure and with respect to certain turning points of development which seem to have been crucial for prejudice.

B. THE CASE OF MACK

The clinical part of Mack's interview follows.

"Mother was sick in bed a great deal of the time. I remember her reading and singing to us. She devoted her last strength to us kids. I don't have those early recollections of my father. My first recollection of him as a father was one spring morning, when mother passed away. He came back to tell us. Of course, there is such a disparity between his age and mine. He is 77 now. Mother had 3 operations. The third time she left I was very distressed. It was like a premonition. The aunt across the street helped take care of us, when we got sick. Father spent all of his time with us after mother died.

"My sister is 4 years older than I. She has been married about 3½ years. She is a housewife, has a 2-year-old boy, and is expecting another. I have had very good relations with her, a few arguments, but not like other brothers and sisters I have seen. She took care of the family cooking and took care of me. They called her 'the little old lady.' That has kept up. She helped put me through school and to buy my clothes. She is an accomplished stenographer and bookkeeper. She loaned me money to get started in the East. I have repaid her. No, she has not influenced me much in ideas. She's like myself in that. She doesn't take religion very seriously; she never drinks or smokes, has high ideals. But father was more responsible for that.

"Up to high school I didn't do much thinking about anything. When I entered high school, my sister had left. The four years in high school I spent mostly with my father. When I graduated, he was living with us in _____."

(What things did you admire especially in your father?) "Mostly, his attention to us kids was very admirable. He's very honest, so much so that he won't condone charge accounts. He's known throughout the country as a man whose word is as good as his bond. His greatest contribution was denying himself pleasures to take care of us kids. (What disagreements have you had with your father?) There haven't been any to any great extent. I had a mind of my own at a very early age. He has too. We've had arguments, but I can't remember any lickings by him. He scolded but usually talked things over. Our arguments were usually about things I wanted that he didn't want me to have—like the 22 rifle I wanted when I was 10, or a bicycle. He had to be very careful about money. He wouldn't let me work—he thought it was beneath me. He was afraid I would hurt myself with the rifle. But he never denied me anything I needed. (What have been the effects of the age discrepancy?) Well, I've had to shift for myself a lot. I would have welcomed instruction that he wasn't able to give me. My first venture socially was in the DeMolay. I was a charter member and later a master counselor. I was vice-president of the student body in high school and president of the student body at business school. He was pleased and encouraged me.

"Bud, my cousin, and I were always together. He is 2 months younger. We played baseball and went hunting, etc. We're still close, though we write seldom. He is in India."

(What are your most pleasant memories of childhood?) "Those good times Bud and I had, and with other groups. Skiing and tobogganing. My real pleasures are very simple and always have been. But I like nice equipment, for example, a good rifle. Bud and I had good help from father. He used to spend his winters alone in the mountains, and made his own skis and snowshoes. He showed us how to make them."

(What did you worry most about as a kid?) "Well, mostly about being held back by lack of funds. I worried about such things. In the 7th grade, I was the best speller, but I remember a defeat by a girl at the county spelling bee. Often I was just a little under the top. Just like in the service. I went to OCS, and got sick just before getting my commission. Usually I tried too hard, like in football. I was not as good an end as I should have been. I dropped passes because I tried too hard and so I was mediocre. Now, when I'm relaxed I have no trouble at all.

"They found I was anemic at the age of 12. I had my first hemorrhage from the stomach when I was 18. It always comes around when I start working too hard."

(Where did you get your sex instruction?) "I never had any from my parents, though I did get some suggestions from my aunt; no real instruction. What I know I have picked up from reading. I've listened to men talk, but accepted little of it; I weighed it in the light of what I have read."

(What was your first sex experience?) "It was in 1940–41, the aftermath of a New Year's party in Washington. There was liquor. I was always the backward boy. I hope to get married to the girl I'm going with now. She is an awfully nice companion. Most girls are interested only in a good time and want fellows with lots of money to spend. I didn't have the money for giving them a swell time. The girl I'm in love with now lived 9 miles from me. She attended a rival high school. I dated her once in high school. When I got back from the army, I worked in a lumber mill. This girl had graduated from ____ and started teaching. Her uncle is the vice-president of the bank. I talked to him about buying an automobile that she was interested in. I looked it over for her, since I knew something about cars, and told her it was in good condition. I got started going with her that way. I found out that she wasn't interested in money, but was interested in me in spite of my discharge from the army, my poor health and prospects. She's just very good—not beautiful, but a tremendously nice personality. She is French with some Irish in her. She has a nice figure and is very wholesome. When we get married depends on circumstances. It's quite a responsibility. She wants to get married now; she is teaching in ____. I'm under the GI Bill. If I get assurance of four years in college, I might get married this spring. We're well suited; I know she's interested in me, because I have so little to offer. We're both at the proper age. I intend to work part time. I don't like her teaching; I like to support my wife. I've always had that idea. But maybe under the circumstances, that won't be fully possible. She is a good cook, and that is an asset, what with my stomach condition. When I tell her that you approve of our marriage, she will be pleased, but of course, I'm always a man to make my own decisions."

1. ENVIRONMENTAL FORCES AND EVENTS

a. SOCIOECONOMIC FACTORS. Mack is not very informative with respect to the socioeconomic status of his family—partly because he was not questioned closely enough and partly, as it seems, because he is sometimes tempted to distort the facts. We learned from his questionnaire, it may be recalled, that the father is a "retired lumberman" with an annual income of $1,000. In the interview we are told that the father has not worked for thirty years (this would mean that he stopped working when he was 47, approximately six years before Mack was born) and that his present income is from "stocks and bonds." At the time he *did* work the wage, we are told, was $75 a month, hardly enough to have accumulated stocks and bonds the income from which is $1,000 a year. The most plausible hypothesis, it seems, is that Mack is merely guessing at the time since the father retired, that it was actually not so long as thirty years, and that the major portion of the income is from a pension. ("He owned some lumber lands, but he mostly preferred working for other people.") That the father owned his home probably helped to give the family an aspect of stability, but there seems little reason to doubt that Mack was indeed "held back by lack of funds" or that this was a cause for worry.

The status of the family would seem to have been lower middle-class, bordering on lower class. There was certainly little upward mobility in the sense of actual social or economic advancement. Whether or not the family was concerned with status is a question. The mother and the aunt appear to have tried to keep the children in Sunday School, but the father, whom Mack regards as his major guide, seems not to have participated in this endeavor. We are told that the father wanted his son to go into business, which is not remarkable; but that he did not want Mack to work as a boy because "he thought it was beneath me" sounds definitely status-minded. It also sounds somewhat dubious. We are led to wonder whether we are not dealing here with the status-mindedness of the son rather than with that of the father. It seems that part of the time Mack would like to gain prestige by giving the impression that his father was a man of parts—a retired lumberman who was "known throughout the country as a man whose word was as good as his bond"—and that part of the time he would attain the same end by showing that he had done well despite the economic handicaps with which he had to contend. A man who retired on $1,000 a year at the age of 47, or when his two children were in infancy—or not yet born—could hardly be described as a go-getter or as a man who was deeply concerned to secure advantages and status for his children. That Mack does not deliberately tell us this may probably be put down as an aspect of his general inability to criticize his father.

b. FATHER. Although the father seems not to have been status-driven in the ordinary sense, there is no evidence that he was relaxed or easy-going with respect either to traditional morality or the values of a business community. While Mack undoubtedly exaggerates the virtuous aspects of his father, some of the remarks about his moral strictness have the ring of truth.

He "followed the church rules" although he did not go to church, he "drank but little, and never smoked," he was "very honest and strict in his dealings —so honest that he wouldn't condone charge accounts"; even when considerably discounted, these remarks still give a picture of a rigidly moral man or at the least, of a man who held up this type of standard for his son. That he did so without showing by example that such standards led to satisfying goals—he himself did not work or provide adequately for his family—may well have been the cause for resentment in Mack.

But Mack only hints at this state of affairs. Each time he describes an authoritarian trait or behavior pattern of his father he seems constrained to deny it or to cancel it out by mentioning something of an opposite character: although "he forced some decisions on me," he "allowed me to do as I pleased"; arguments were about "things he didn't want me to have," but "he never denied me anything I needed"; "he scolded but usually talked things over"; "I've had to shift for myself a lot," but "his attention to us kids was very admirable." It is possible, of course, that these statements should be taken at their face value, for such inconsistency as Mack describes is certainly not uncommon among parents. In this case the conclusion would be that our subject had to deal both with authoritarian discipline and with kindly solicitude on the part of his father. This circumstance would not have prevented the discipline from being resented but it would have made open rebellion against it very difficult, if not impossible. With the father in the position of both disciplinarian and love object it would have been necessary for Mack to submit to the discipline in order not to lose the love.

There is reason enough to believe that after the death of the mother[1] Mack's father did have the central role which is here assigned to him, but it is doubtful that Mack got as much from his father as he seems to want us to believe or that the father's dominance was always as easily excused. Mack seems entirely unambiguous when it comes to the matter of his father's distance from himself. Not only does he appear to have been genuinely troubled by the father's advanced age and to feel that this by itself made the latter inaccessible, but the nearest he comes to uttering a complaint against the father is when he refers, repeatedly but as it seems reluctantly, to the old man's retiring nature. It is easy to believe that a man who "used to spend his winters alone in the mountains" was deeply introverted, and it is easy to imagine that after the death of his wife he used to spend a great deal of time brooding at home, rousing himself now and then to issue a categorical command and telling himself occasionally that he ought to take more interest in "the kids." This picture is unlike that found most commonly among the fathers of

[1] It should be borne in mind, as the effects of the mother's death upon Mack's development are discussed in this chapter, that of the 7 subjects in our sample of interviewees who suffered the same misfortune, all were high on the E scale.

prejudiced men; one might even go so far as to speculate that Mack's father was himself unprejudiced; but even so, his silence and reserve could have been of decisive importance in impelling Mack in the direction of prejudice. If this father possessed such human qualities as suggested above, they were certainly lost on Mack, who says he "can't understand" his father's withdrawal. It is likely that after the mother's death Mack turned to his father for love and comfort, but there is no evidence that he received it in adequate measure. There is no hint of warmth or demonstrativeness on the father's part; instead he is assigned those empty virtues—moral strictness and kindness—which prejudiced subjects characteristically ascribe to parents with whom they were not on good terms. Silence and distance, no less than meaningless aggression, on a father's part may be a sufficient stimulus for fear and hostility in the son.

In summary, it seems that the nearest we can come to an estimate of what the father was like in reality is to say that he was a defeated man who, in an authoritarian manner, held up conventional moral standards for his son without being able to show by example that adherence to these standards actually led to worthwhile ends; after the death of his wife he seems to have tried to take over some of the maternal functions in his relations with his children but because of his own personality problems he was unable to be understanding or affectionate toward his son.

c. Cousin Bud. Although very little is known about Bud, the cousin two months younger than our subject, it must be noted that he seems to have supplied more or less constant male companionship for Mack. There is a hint that Bud was the stronger and more assertive of the two boys; Mack was sick much of the time and finally failed in Officer Candidate School because of his stomach condition, while Bud, at the time of our interview, was overseas as a member of the armed services.

d. Mother. In approaching the question of what Mack's mother was actually like, in her relations with her own son, we face the same difficulty that arose in the case of the father: our subject tends to glorify his parents, and, in assigning traits to them, to express so well his own personality needs that we cannot accept his appraisal at face value. When Mack tells us that his mother was kind and self-sacrificing ("she devoted her last strength to us kids") and that she was morally strict ("she brought us up very strictly in this [church] guidance") our first thought is that this is what the great majority of our prejudiced subjects—in contrast to the unprejudiced ones—report. The question is whether Mack's mother, and the mothers of most high-scoring men, was actually as he describes her—in which case we should understand the relations of this type of maternal influence to prejudice in the son—or whether the personality needs of the subject are such that he has to describe the mother as he does, even though she may have been quite different in reality.

There seems little reason to doubt that the mother was strict in much the way that Mack describes. She tried to bring up her children according to the moral principles of the Methodist Church and she, no more than the father, could give sex instruction to the subject. This general pattern of strictness seems to have been carried forward by the aunt and by the sister after the mother's death. It can well be imagined that the sister especially, who was cast so prematurely into the role of mother—"the little old lady"—overdid in her attempts to enforce conventional moral standards. But there is no basis for thinking of Mack as a victim of "maternal domination"; the strictness which we may envision here seems no more than what is ordinary among mothers of the lower middle-class.

That Mack may have felt imposed upon by these women, however, is another matter. He may well have felt that the amount of love he received was far from being enough to make up for the restrictions that were placed on him. True, Mack undoubtedly received *some* genuine love from his mother. When he remembers "her reading and singing to us" and notes that he does not have such recollections of his father, when he reports his distress on learning of her death, and when he says—at the conclusion of his T.A.T. session— "there were times when I would have gone to a mother had I had one," it seems clear that he at the least knew what it was to be loved by his mother. But Mack lost this love, and the indications are that it went hard with him. The sense of deprivation and of injustice that this loss may have aroused in him could easily have made later restrictions seem unfair; if at the time of the mother's death Mack harbored some resentment because of her real or imagined strictness, there would be sufficient reason why he, out of guilt feelings, should idealize her.

The mother's illness, which seems to have been a lingering one ("she was sick in bed a great deal of the time" and had three operations), was probably also a significant factor in our subject's development. It could have meant that although he received a certain amount of love, he did not feel secure about it; there must have been many times when he wanted more than she was able to give, and because she was sick in bed he could not be demanding or give vent to the anger which his frustration must have aroused in him.

e. MACK'S ILLNESS. Mack's illness as a boy may be regarded both as an event which had important effects upon his later behavior and attitudes and as something which itself may have been, in large part, psychologically determined. That the illness must have been severe and of long standing seems clear from the following: "I have had a lot of sickness; stomach trouble ever since I was 12. I had my first hemorrhage from the stomach when I was 18" and "I went to OCS and got sick just before getting my commission." An indication of how much this illness has meant to Mack is found in his statement on his questionnaire that "physical weakness, perhaps due to ill health continued over the last four years" is the mood or feeling most disturbing to him.[2]

2. DEEPER PERSONALITY NEEDS

The concern here is with those needs in Mack's personality which were aroused with particular intensity early in his life and which were later inhibited so that their present activity becomes manifest only in indirect ways. These needs do not form a part of his "better self"; they are not accepted by his ego, and he would conceal them from himself as well as from other people. To appraise these needs, therefore, it is necessary to use special techniques for getting below the surface, to call into play what psychological insight we can, and to rely rather heavily upon inference. The T.A.T. and the Projective Questions offer some evidence bearing fairly directly upon inhibited trends in the personality; analysis of the interview material with special attention to "giveaways" of hidden motives can provide further understanding. When the results of this analysis are integrated with the projective material, and when the conclusions reached are viewed in the light of what is known from psychoanalytic investigation of similar cases,[3] a meaningful formulation of the most important deeper personality needs may be achieved.

a. DEPENDENCE. After a reading of Mack's interview, one might be inclined to say that his dependence—his wish to be taken care of, to have someone to lean upon—is hardly below the surface. He tells us straight out that he missed his mother very much, that he relied upon his sister's care, that there have been times when he has turned to the Bible for comfort; and when he speaks of his approaching marriage it seems plain that he is attracted by the prospect of having someone take care of him. Yet there is sufficient indication that Mack does not really accept his present dependence. It is only under special conditions that the need for love and support comes into the open. The first condition is that this need be made to appear as belonging to the past, as an aspect of his former self that he has, as it were, got over: There *were* times when he would have turned to a mother. The second condition is that the need be justified by the fact of illness. It is as if he felt that being physically ill is beyond one's control and that in this circumstance one cannot be blamed, or accused of being weak, if he accepts help from others. Thus, it is during periods of illness that he likes to turn to the Bible and it is because of his stomach condition that he can tolerate the idea

---

[2] The greater incidence of "concern with physical symptoms" in high- than in low-scoring subjects has been discussed in Chapter XII. It is especially interesting to note in the present connection that of the 7 subjects from our sample of Psychiatric Clinic Patients (Chapter XXII) who, like Mack, suffered from stomach ulcers, 4 were high and none was low on the E scale.

[3] Cf. in this connection Ackerman and Jahoda (1), E. Jones (58), and Sanford (104). A study of a case very similar to Mack, based entirely on questionnaire and projective material, has been reported by Sanford and Conrad (107).

of his wife's working and cooking for him. And even when these conditions are met, Mack does not seem to feel comfortable about being dependent; it is necessary for him to assert that, as a matter of fact, he is, and was, quite independent. This defensive procedure seems to go on unconsciously. Mack is not in the least aware of the bid for sympathy implicit in his recounting of his illnesses and handicaps.

There is, to be sure, nothing particularly remarkable about a young man's having feelings of dependence which he tries to suppress because they do not accord with his ideal of masculinity. But in Mack it seems that we are dealing with dependent impulses which are unusually strong, and which come to the surface in spite of his unusual pains to hold them in check. One might say that one reason he cannot allow himself openly to express these impulses is that they are childish, and that the reason they are so is because they were repressed in childhood and, hence, could not be transformed into more mature forms of expression. It is here that the mother's illness and death would seem to have played a crucial role. As noted above, there is reason to believe that during the early years of his life Mack received considerable love and attention from his mother and felt close to her. Her illness intensified his need, and her death must have been a severe trauma for him. With the main source of love and comfort thus lost it is natural that he would make every attempt to repress his longings for dependence. His sister and his aunt were hardly adequate substitutes. And, as has also been noted above, his attempts to get "mother's love" from the father were frustrated by the latter's "distance." Mack's references to his father's devotion and attention can be better understood as expressions of a wish rather than as statements of what the father was like in actuality.

The manifestations of dependence contained in Mack's responses on the T.A.T. seem to have more to do with the father than with the mother. As the examiner points out, the need is for direction and advice rather than for love and understanding and it appears to be aroused by the fear of rejection. This would seem to reflect certain aspects of Mack's relations with his father, in later childhood, more than it reflects the early tie to the mother. The hypothesis would be that after the mother's death the father became both disciplinarian and love object, and it became necessary for Mack to go strictly according to his father's wishes in order to avoid the danger of a further loss of love. It was not, however, that he expected, or even dared to seek, the kind of warmth and care that he had experienced at his mother's hand. This aspect of the dependence need had been firmly repressed. Both the father-dependence and the mother-dependence conflict, at the present time, with Mack's ideal of masculinity and can be admitted only when sufficiently rationalized, but it is the mother-dependence that lies deeper and has resulted in the building up of the more elaborate defenses. One way in which this deeper dependence seems to find indirect expression is through the use of symbols. The enjoyment of music and singing in church could have this significance. The same interpretation might be given to several of Mack's responses to the Projective Questions: his desire to see all of the world, his fascination with natural wonders and with rare jewels and metals. As substitutes for "mother" these cathected objects have the advantage of being sufficiently removed from the human, so that the forces of repression, originally directed against the need for mother, are not brought into play. Mack's dependence upon "things," e.g., food, the Bible, might conceivably be explained in the same way. The special importance of illness, as a condition under which dependence can be admitted and gratified, has already been discussed. It remains only to point out that Mack's stomach ulcer was very probably psychogenic and that in this case it could be regarded, in accordance with generally accepted theory,[4] as an expression par excellence of unconscious dependence.

b. Hostility against the Father. If the above attempt to reconstruct the actual behavior of Mack's father was successful then one might say that there was reason enough why our subject should feel hostile toward him. Silence and distance on the father's part when the son wants to be loved, authoritarian discipline without any demonstration of its purpose—these are stimuli which regularly arouse aggression, and there is no reason to suppose that Mack was an exception. But if Mack has such impulses they must be severely inhibited, for at no time does he allow himself freely to blame or to criticize his father. Indeed, the underlying hostility here hypothesized is very well concealed and it is only by the maximum use of subtle cues that we become convinced of its existence.

In responding to the Projective Questions Mack tell us that "anger" is the emotion which he finds most difficult to control. This is in keeping with his references, in the interview, to his "hot temper" and "stubborn nature." These expressions might be understood in the light of his need to impress us with his masculinity, to present himself as a man who is not to be trifled with. They might be dismissed as the whistling in the dark of a young man who in his overt behavior is—far from being aggressive—rather timid and deferential. But in another response to the Projective Questions—"murder and rape" are the worst crimes—we are given a hint that aggression might indeed be one of Mack's preoccupations, and when we come to the T.A.T., evidence that this is true accumulates. Here the analysis seems to reveal "underlying hostile feelings toward the world," "crude aggressive fantasies," and a tendency to "impulsive antisocial acts." A striking figure in the stories is that of a young man "who might do violence if pushed too far." We are given no direct indication of what might be the form of the violence or against whom it might be directed. The responses are like the bare and unqualified "anger" of the Projective Questions. But in the present light it seems clear that in that in-

---

[4] Cf. for example, F. Alexander, et al. (5).

stance Mack was doing more than protesting his toughness; he was probably telling us the truth. Not that he frequently becomes angry and gets into trouble; it is rather that he is afraid he might become angry and release forces which, though not familiar to him, are vaguely imagined to be primitive and chaotic and likely to provoke disastrous retaliation.

What are the reasons for believing that this deep-lying hostility is directed primarily against the father? We have already seen that the father is the central figure in Mack's imagery of his childhood and that the father was the source of major frustrations. The T.A.T. stories contain no instances in which heroes express aggression against father figures, but the T.A.T. analysis contains indications that it is precisely this type of aggression that our subject is most concerned to control. Whereas hostility against women is clearly manifested by T.A.T. heroes and can be regarded as a tendency that is accepted by Mack's ego, the primitive impulsive aggression of which we speak is exhibited only by characters whom the story-teller has been at pains to reject and it may be regarded, therefore, as ego-alien. This ego-alien aggression is directed against powerful figures, against "oppressors." "The young man looks as if he might commit murder if oppressed." But the heroes do not fight oppression; instead, to quote the T.A.T. analysis, they "identify themselves with the restraining force." Thus, the T.A.T. material favors the hypothesis that underlying aggression against the father has immediately to be countered—disclaimed, redirected, or smothered—because the father is conceived as too strong and dangerous. And in this circumstance the aggression itself is felt to be dangerous.

In this light, a rereading of Mack's interview seems to show clearly the ambivalence of his feelings about his father. It is entirely necessary for Mack that every implied criticism of the father be taken back or counterbalanced by "good" traits; otherwise the hostility might come too much into the open, and with it, images of disastrous consequences. A rather poignant illustration of what Mack is up against is afforded by one of his responses to the Projective Questions. He gives as one of his two greatest assets, "ability to enjoy people's company." At first glance this might not seem to be much to be proud of, but in Mack's case it represents a real achievement. After telling us, in the interview, of his father's social withdrawal he says, "I looked at my father and saw that I had to do differently," and "I have gone in for social things in spite of a great dread of them." Going in for social things is an expression of rebellion against the father, and hence the "great dread." In no other instance, as far as our material goes, has Mack made so bold; and even here it must have been a comfort to him to know that "he (the father) was pleased and he encouraged me."

c. Submission, Passivity, and Homosexuality. With the single not very striking deviation just described, the general picture of Mack's surface attitudes toward his father is one of submission and admiration. And this despite the subject's claim to stubbornness and independence. One might say that his only recourse in the face of what he conceived to be the father's irresistible power was to submit—and then to gain a sense of adequacy by participating psychologically in the father's power. This, in the last analysis, is the homosexual solution of the Oedipus problem.[5] It is not surprising, therefore, to find in Mack's T.A.T. productions clear indications of his fear of homosexual attack. (This is made manifest, primarily, in his treatment of the "hypnotist" picture.)

Even without this piece of direct evidence we would be led to hypothesize repressed homosexuality in order to explain some of the outstanding features of Mack's personality development. The material is replete with manifestations of authoritarian submission. As clear a manifestation as any, perhaps, is the conception of God "as strictly a man, one who would treat us as a father would his son." There would seem to be no doubt that Mack has longed for his father's love—as we should expect in a boy who lost his mother when he was 6 years old. He has tried to replace the imagery of a bad, dangerous father with imagery of a good father who would spend "*all* of his time with us." But Mack is not able to admit this need. Even while *acting* in a submissive and deferential manner he seems to cling to the belief that he is very manly and self-sufficient. The reason for this self-deception, we can well believe, is that, for this subject, to submit to a man and so to gain his love has definite sexual implications. It may be connected with very primitive imagery of passivity and emasculation. One might say that Mack's homosexuality, repressed in childhood in a setting of sadomasochistic relations with the father, has remained on an infantile level; insufficiently sublimated, it cannot find gratification in friendly, equalitarian relations with men but, instead, it determines that most such relations have to be on a dominance-submission dimension.

d. FEAR OF WEAKNESS. It is Mack's repressed homosexuality, very probably, that is mainly responsible for his compelling fear of weakness. If weakness means emasculation, if it means being at the mercy of an irresistibly strong man, then it is not difficult to see why this subject should exert every effort to make himself appear impregnable.

Fear of weakness, and the need to conceal any signs of it, comes almost to the surface in Mack. As we shall see in a moment it seems to lie immediately behind a number of his most pronounced manifest traits and attitudes. But just because Mack is so concerned to cover up his fear, direct evidence of its existence is not easy to obtain. Perhaps the closest he comes to an open admission is when he writes, in response to the Projective Question, "What mood or feelings are most disturbing?": "Physical weakness, perhaps due to ill health continued over the last four years." If the weakness is clearly physical and can be excused on the ground of ill health, then it can be fully admitted. But

[5] Cf. S. Freud (41), E. Jones (58), and, for a recent discussion, C. Thompson (117).

it is not physical weakness alone, but a general sense of inadequacy which seems to be expressed indirectly in Mack's response to the Projective Question pertaining to greatest assets: "A definite desire to raise myself physically, financially, and socially." Not that a desire to raise oneself is necessarily based upon an underlying sense of inadequacy; the argument that it is so based in Mack's case rests upon what appears to be the extraordinary emphasis that he places upon this desire and upon supporting indications from the T.A.T. It may be recalled that the analysis of Mack's stories gave considerable emphasis to the "underlying fears and feelings of inadequacy behind the desire to 'be a strong individual' or to 'be like most men.'"

The T.A.T. throws rather direct light upon the sexual aspects of the fear of weakness. The manifest attitudes of contempt and distrust toward women seem clearly to derive from the idea that they will drag a man down or deprive him of his "strong character." It is because women are weak that they are not to be trusted; they are out to exploit the man and to reduce his manliness by involving him in the "sordid" business of sex.

The role of Mack's physical illness, particularly in childhood, in determining the fear of weakness should not be underestimated. We can well imagine that the experiences of illness rearoused the infantile anxiety of helplessness. More than this, the sense of being a "sickly boy" might have put Mack at a disadvantage in his relations with his Cousin Bud, so that homosexual feelings were aroused—with the consequences that have been discussed above. Again, the weaker Mack was in actuality the stronger would the father appear to him; and it was the idea that the father was too strong and dangerous, we may suppose, that prevented any basic identification with him. This failure in identification would, by itself, be sufficient ground for the fear that he was not quite a man. The mother's illness and death was probably a factor here also. As suggested above, there is some reason to believe that in the early years of his life Mack tended rather strongly to identify with his mother. (His illness may, indeed, have been in some part an identification with her.) He still has his "softer side," as it were. But following her death this identification could hardly have remained as a source of inner security; on the contrary, Mack had had an experience well calculated to promote terrifying ideas of what it might mean to be feminine, and we should expect him to regard any feminine traits within himself primarily as areas of vulnerability.

This consideration of Mack's fear of weakness seems to throw further light on his struggle with dependence. It is very likely that he regards his dependent needs as signs of weakness—the same kind of weakness that has just been discussed—and that this is another reason why he cannot freely admit the existence of these needs. It is as if accepting help or love or comfort from a woman meant being somehow identified with her, and hence open to the dangers with which women have to contend. Accepting help or love or comfort from a man suggest being treated like a woman by that man, and hence threatened with the loss of masculinity. But because in his innermost self Mack would like to be treated in just this way, the sense of weakness is constantly stimulated, and no amount of counteractive striving can entirely dispel it.

3. DYNAMICS OF SURFACE BEHAVIOR AND ATTITUDES

Given these underlying trends—dependence, hostility against the father, submission, passivity and homosexuality, and fear of weakness—it is possible to offer reasonable explanations for most of Mack's characteristic traits and attitudes. These surface trends can be understood in large part as derivations or transformations of the deep-lying needs we have discussed. Surface and depth are connected by means of well-known psychological mechanisms.

An abstract formulation of Mack's personality, in its genetic aspects, is sketched in its general outlines in Figure 1(XX). Genetically early forces and events appear at the bottom of the chart, and the course of development is followed by reading upward, arrows indicating the directions of determination and the points at which it is applied. No attempt is made to indicate the nature of the causation in the various instances. A rough correspondence between order in the genetic sequence and degree of depth within the contemporary personality structure is assumed, the earliest reaction tendencies being regarded as those which now lie deepest within the personality.

It may be noted at once that fear of weakness occupies the most central position on the chart. Deriving, as we have seen, chiefly from the deep-lying tendencies toward dependence on the one hand and toward submission, passivity and homosexuality on the other, this fear necessitates several protective devices which lead to a variety of behavior patterns and general attitudes at the surface level. The fear has to be denied, allayed, and if possible, overcome. We observe in Mack, therefore, attempts to conceal weakness by verbal denial and by presenting a façade of toughness, to get rid of weakness by projecting it onto other people, chiefly outgroups, and then condemning them on this score, to overcompensate for weakness by strivings for power and status and to allay the sense of weakness by aligning himself with powerful individuals and groups.

Little more need be said, it seems, concerning Mack's straightout verbal denial of weakness. It is simply that all through his interview he is at pains to tell us that he is not weak but strong and that if at any time he has appeared to be weak, then this was entirely justified by external circumstances. Of particular importance for Mack's susceptibility to fascist propaganda is the fact that the need to excuse weakness sometimes leads him into distortions of reality; he exaggerates the power and misreads the intentions of outgroups according to the formula, "If I appear to be weak, it is because they are so

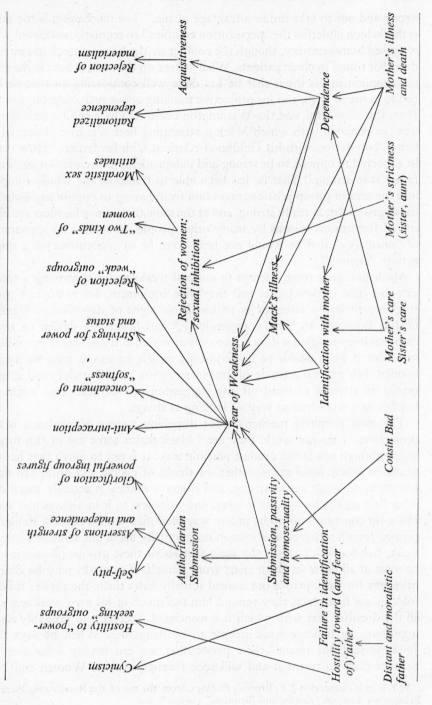

FIGURE 1 (XX)

THE GENETIC ASPECTS OF MACK'S PERSONALITY

strong and out to take unfair advantage of me." The mechanism is the same as that which underlies the "persecution complex" so regularly associated with repressed homosexuality, though the conflict in Mack seems much less intense than that found in clinic patients. What we see on the surface here is the self-pity implicit in his thesis that he has done well considering all that he has had to contend with, and his projective thinking about such outgroups as the Jews, the New Deal, and the Washington bureaus. There can be little doubt that the problem with which Mack is struggling here was first presented to him in connection with his childhood relations with his father: "How can I be expected to oppose, to be strong and independent, to become a man, when father is so strong." That he has been able to transpose the whole complex into the area of group relations saves him from having to oppose any individual or group that is really strong, and at the same time—since his ideas are now shared for various reasons by many other people—to achieve an appearance of "normality" that he would not have were he to concentrate on a single private "enemy."

Mack has made some attempt to conceal weakness by contriving a tough exterior. The leather jacket and the "nice equipment, for example a good rifle" are probably intended as unmistakable signs of masculinity. Mack is unable, however, to behave aggressively,[6] and hence the device of over-compensatory toughness does not serve him as well as it does many prejudiced men. But if he is unable to be physically tough, he can at least be tough-minded. His general attitude of anti-intraception can be understood as primarily an attempt to ward off any suggestion of "softness" that might be implicit in a more human way of looking at things.

The most primitive mechanism for dispelling a sense of weakness is the projection, "I am not weak, they are." Mack makes some use of this mechanism, though not in the crudest possible way. It is not so much that he sees weakness where none exists; rather, he thinks of people and groups in rigid categories of weak versus strong, and if any weakness is actually there it is what first strikes his eye, as it were, and he reacts to it in a particular way. His main concern is not to be in any way identified with weakness. Religious people, Jewish refugees, and women may actually be, in one sense or another, weak, but for Mack this is the *main* fact about these groups of people and he must at all costs set them apart from himself. If one asks why he cannot have pity for weak people but instead actually hates them, the answer is two-fold. In the first place, they remind him too much of his own weakness and all the dreadful fear with which it is associated. Second, and probably more important, he believes weak people to be dangerous. When he says that Jews "should not resent" their persecution we can readily infer that he believes they *do* resent it and will seek revenge in time. Women and Ne-

---

[6] Cf. in this connection J. F. Brown's findings, from the use of the Rosenzweig Picture-Frustration Test, on "passive anti-Semitism" (16).

groes, as the T.A.T. analysis made clear, are regarded in this same way. It is to be granted that the strictness of Mack's mother, and later attempts of the sister and the aunt to carry out her policy, helped to teach Mack that women could be aggressive, but there is reason to believe that his notions about the dangerous aspects of "weak" people are based primarily upon a projection. The feeling of being persecuted aroused in him the strongest impulses to violence ("the young man looks like he might commit murder if oppressed") and he imagines that "downtrodden" people are similarly motivated.

Fear of the weak woman, as has been pointed out, would largely explain Mack's sexual backwardness, and this in turn offers sufficient basis for the moralistic sex attitudes expressed on the questionnaire and in the interview. How is the rejection of women to be reconciled with the fact that Mack idealizes his mother and intends to marry a girl with a "tremendously nice personality"? Here it must be considered that Mack actually has two conceptions of women: the "bad," weak, dangerous, exploitive, sexual woman who drags one down, and the good, wholesome, asexual one who gives. It is the former with whom one dares to have sex relations as "the aftermath of a New Year's party"; the latter is described mainly contrasting her with the former; she is not interested primarily in "a good time" or "in spending fellows' money" or in anything "sordid." Undoubtedly the imagery of this "good" woman derives in part from the imagery of the mother "who devoted her last strength to us kids." Certainly Mack would like to recapture some of the love and comfort that he received from his mother, provided this motive on his part can be adequately rationalized. It must be pointed out, however, that his appreciation of his mother seems somewhat overdone, enough so to suggest that his idealization of her is based partly on bad conscience and is an attempt to undo hostility that was directed against her. One cannot be very optimistic about the prospects for Mack's forthcoming marriage. While on the one hand he wants more than any woman can give him, on the other hand, he feels it would be weak to ask his wife for anything at all. And this is not to mention the problem of how sex is to be introduced into the picture without spoiling it altogether.

It has already been suggested that Mack's strivings for power and status—his desire to "raise" himself—may be regarded as largely overcompensatory. Indeed, it would be very surprising if some kind of counteractive activity did not have a place among the devices he employs for overcoming the sense of weakness. From this point of view we can understand why it is that the needs for affiliation and recognition when they appear in the T.A.T. are expressed mainly as a desire for having the members of his group look up to him, and why being an officer in the DeMolay and in his class at business school is important to him. The crucial role of the status drive in determining Mack's general ideology was first indicated in the analysis of his remarks concerning vocation and income. There it seemed clear that for him "going up" meant going up in a hierarchy; in his mind the existence of dominant groups and submerged groups was "natural" and, far from being concerned with changing this state of affairs, his aim was to have membership in the groups that were dominant. This is something different from the ordinary, everyday desire to improve one's lot in a sociological sense. It seems that here again Mack's thinking about group relations is dominated by the rigid categories of "strong" and "weak." In the light of the foregoing personality analysis we may say that, once again, Mack brings to his interpretation of group relations images and attitudes which have remained unchanged since their genesis in the childhood relations with his father. That one was weak and the other strong was then the salient fact, and the persistence of this idea is a part of the fixation upon the traumatic situation of childhood. Since Mack could not conceive of himself opposing the irresistibly strong father, his attempt at a solution was to convince himself that his father was "good" and so to align himself with him. This corresponds exactly with Mack's present approach to group relations. He does not oppose any group that is, in actuality, strong; instead, he argues that the strong ones are the good ones, and even while admiring and being subservient to them he overcomes weakness through gaining a sense of participation in their power.

This last is, of course, one aspect of the general attitude which we have termed authoritarian submission, and which we have previously seen to be an outstanding feature of Mack's manifest personality. To say that this attitude rests upon an attempt to overcome weakness through identification with power is to mention only one of its major sources. In so far as authoritarian submission is a means for overcoming weakness it stands as a kind of defense against the underlying homosexual submission and passivity; it remains to be pointed out that this surface trend offers at the same time gratification for these very same needs. In glorifying strong groups and individuals —"father figures"—he is expressing the need for a father's love and support and guidance, for a God who is "strictly man, greater than any on this earth, one that would treat us as a father would his son." Whereas most channels for the expression of this need are closed because they pass too close to weakness, it can in certain circumstances come into the open and be gratified: Chiefly when the strong man or strong group is *strong enough*, strong enough so that there is a chance for participation in real power and strong enough so that submission can be readily excused. If one should ask why Roosevelt, who was almost universally experienced in this country as a father figure, was not happily accepted and admired by Mack instead of being rejected as a "dictator," the answer would seem to be that he was not strong enough:[7] he "would come off second best in a contest with Winnie," while as for General Marshall, "nobody could alter his position."

How authoritarian submission promotes political conservatism and moral

[7] This point has been elaborated in Chapter XVII.

conventionalism in this subject has been described in sufficient detail in Chapter II. Lacking a firmly internalized superego, a result of the failure to achieve a basic identification with the father, Mack looks outside of himself for guidance as to what to do and what not to do, and turns naturally to the authorities that seem strongest and most commonly accepted. He cannot, however, admit that this is the case, but clings to the illusion that he has a stubborn nature and is a man to make his own decisions.

This last suggests that Mack's relations with his authorities are not entirely harmonious, that he is not altogether comfortable with the arrangements that he has made. This is no more than we should expect from a consideration of the sources of his authoritarianism. It springs originally, as we have seen, from hostility toward his father. This hostility led to submission based on fear and, although submission offers other rewards as well, the element of fearful necessity still has an important role in Mack's attitude toward authority. It is this circumstance that gives his adherence to conventional standards the aspect of rigidity; since they have never been fully integrated with the ego, it is necessary to adhere to them strictly lest they be thrown overboard altogether.

Mack's hostility against minority groups and other groups and individuals is almost always justified by him on moral grounds. And the morality to which he appeals is that of the external authorities to which he is subservient. His manifest aggression is, so to speak, in the name of authority. He arranges things so that his conscience and his deepest antisocial impulses operate in collaboration. But if we ask what is his conception of the outgroup and why it provokes him so we are led back to the same sources that gave rise to his conceptions and attitudes concerning ingroup authorities. Outgroups are hated, as we saw in Chapter II, for being selfishly and ruthlessly aggressive. (That outgroups are also "weak" may be a logical contradiction, but it is not a psychological one; Mack's thinking about social and political matters is dominated by unconscious processes and, hence, cannot be expected to conform with the rules of logic.[8]) The power-seeking features of the outgroup, no less than the admirably strong aspects of the "good" ingroup, can be understood as derivatives of the infantile imagery of the father. Since Mack dared not oppose his father but could only submit to him, it became necessary to convince himself that the father was good. But this did not dissipate the original hostility against the father. Nor did Mack attempt to handle it by turning it against himself; one of the outstanding features of his case is the relative absence of self-criticism. What he did was *displace* the hostility onto outgroups; or better, the frustrating, punishing, persecutory features which had to be denied in the father were seen as originating in outgroups who could then be hated in safety, because they were not strong in actuality, and in good conscience, because the traits ascribed to them were those which the

[8] Cf. Freud's discussion of "exemption from mutual contradiction" as one of the characteristics of unconscious processes.

ingroup authorities would condemn. Thus it is that each "good" trait that the father is said to have is the opposite of a "bad" trait which belongs to the image of the Jew: while the father's "greatest contribution was denying himself pleasures to take care of us kids" the Jews are not "interested in humanity," while the father was renowned for his "honesty," one has to be careful of Jewish clothiers. At the same time, when it comes to the one trait in the father which Mack is almost inclined to criticize, that is, social withdrawal, one finds that it too looms large in the imagery of the Jew: they refuse "to mingle and become a part of our people," "they would rather be alone." If the Jews have thus to bear the brunt of Mack's ambivalent feelings toward his father, there might be some comfort for them in the fact that his feelings toward them are also somewhat ambivalent. It may be recalled that Mack's explanation for what he supposes to be Jewish pressure on Congress and for the fact that Jews have been "fully repaid" for their part in the war effort is that "they are businessmen," and we know that he has nothing but admiration for businessmen, especially those who represent a "concentration of wealth in a certain class," i.e., "the big capitalists." Unfortunately, however, it is very doubtful that the Jews could ever benefit from the positive phase of Mack's ambivalence, for their supposed inability makes them more dangerous to him. The separation of the good father image from the bad is an essential of Mack's personality adjustment and he could no more see "good" in his image of the Jew than he can see "bad" in his father.

As far as our material goes the only outlets for the expression of aggression that Mack has is through his ethnocentrism, that is, through authoritarian aggression against various kinds of outgroups. There is, however, one other manifestation of underlying aggression which may afford some vent for his feelings, and that is cynicism. This prominent tendency in our subject has been described in Chapters II and VII. It seems clear enough now that its major source is the bottled-up resentment with which the present analysis has been so largely concerned. We must understand, however, that in cynicism the destructiveness is directed against the self as well as against the world.[9] It is not only that the subject's own aggressiveness is projected onto other people, who are then accused of being acquisitive and warlike, but contempt for other people seems to be closely related to contempt for himself. In Mack's case—and this probably holds generally for authoritarian personalities—the self-contempt derives from his sense of weakness and this, as we have seen, is the aftermath of his surrender to his father. This surrender cannot be wholly excused, and as long as he cannot permit himself to feel aggressive toward those who are actually strong, there will be a nagging reminder that he, in reality, is weak. He tries to free himself from this thought

[9] On the topic of cynicism Sanford, Conrad, and Franck (108) have published findings based on a questionnaire similar to those employed in the present study.

by projecting the contemptibleness onto mankind, and thus there is some basis for saying that he hates others because he hates himself.

To complete the picture it is necessary to return now to the topic of Mack's dependence. The sense of deprivation that followed the loss of his mother, and the growing feelings that because of his weakness people might leave him out or take advantage of him, seem to have generated in him a general attitude of acquisitiveness and, more specifically, a feeling that somebody ought to give him something. The highest praise of mother, father, sister, or fiancée is that they gave or will give to him, and one of the major characteristics of "bad" people is that they are selfish or "not interested in humanity." It is not difficult to infer that his concern with justice is primarily concern with getting something. A man who can speak sentimentally of justice in one breath and almost in the next speak of barring Hitler's victims from this country on the ground that they are "Europe's misfits" is hardly employing the term "justice" in its basic sense. But apparently his acquisitiveness encounters his conventional moral standards and has to be reacted against. He is very careful to assure us that he has "repaid" what he got from others, and he is moralistically temperate in stating his objectives with respect to income. The importance of this conflict about acquisitiveness for Mack's social outlook lies in the fact that it supplies the basis for another accusation against outgroups. They are said to be "materialistic" and "money-minded." This seems to be in part a projection, since outgroups are accused of doing exactly what he and his own group do but would like to deny, and in part a mere complaint about the fact that the world goes its own way without paying much attention to him and his wants.

A remarkable feature of Mack's dependence is that although it has been rendered ego-alien and as an unconscious force leads to the misjudgment and rejection of other people, so much of it still finds expression in behavior. (This has been brought out in the above discussion of underlying dependence.) This is testimony to his outstanding facility in rationalization, something that is made possible, as it seems, by his unwillingess to look at himself.

This brings us to a place where we must consider Mack's stereotypy, a characteristic of his thinking that is highly pronounced and, clearly, of the greatest significance for his prejudice. In one sense, his stereotyped thinking about social phenomena seems to be related to his general attitude of antiintraception and to be dependent, in part at least, upon the same underlying conditions. It might be said that one reason why Mack's explanations of social phenomena are so primitive and oversimplified (for example, differences among ethnic groups are categorical and due to differences in blood strain) is that he is unable to make any use of social or psychological theories of determination. This can hardly be due to a lack of intelligence or of information, for an examination of his interview leaves a strong impression that with regard to those factors he is above the average for college students. A stronger argument could be made for the view that his is an educational deficiency, that he simply has not been subjected to instruction about man and society. But this is such a widespread phenomenon in this country that it can hardly be used to explain why Mack stands out from the group. Besides, he could have made some use of the social and psychological viewpoints that are available, but he chose not to. And, for that matter, the fact that anti-intra-ceptive education is so widespread has itself to be explained, and we can well believe that factors of individual psychology have an important role to play. In Mack's case at least there is a strong suggestion that he cannot reckon with either the sociology or the psychology of other people because he cannot examine the conditions or determinants of his own behavior. Ideas or observations that would be necessary to lend breadth or depth to his view of the world or of himself cannot enter the picture, because they would arouse too much anxiety. It is as if—to put it somewhat dramatically—*he can see only what he has seen before and learn only what he already knows*. In our consideration of Mack's anti-intraception we were given reason to believe that he has to avoid introspection or attention to human factors in order to maintain his sense of being tough-minded. The fuller analysis of his personality shows that his problem is much more serious: he has to deal with a variety of strong unconscious impulses which are not integrated with the ego and which he feels—not without good cause—might get out of hand. In short, the task of maintaining his repressions imposes a heavy burden upon him. This state of affairs has been described, in previous chapters, as ego weakness, and Mack's case offers an excellent illustration of this concept. The problems with which he was faced as a child—problems centering around the loss of his mother and the necessity for making an adjustment to the "distant" father —were too much, they were more than the undeveloped ego could handle. Primitive defenses, chiefly repression and countercathexis, were necessary; and since that time, the ego has had to devote so much energy to maintaining these defenses that it could not develop normally. It remains narrow and con-stricted, in danger of being overwhelmed by emotional impulses from within or authoritative commands from without. Since the inner impulses are more to be feared than the outer authorities there is rigid adherence to the stand-ards of the latter, but since these authorities are not accepted in any funda-mental way this adherence could be given up altogether in circumstances that made it safe to do so. Since the traumatic experiences of childhood have not been integrated with the ego, the categories with which the child struc-tured the world have persisted, in more or less unmodified form, to dominate contemporary thinking. Since there is little that is truly *inside* the personality, there can be little tolerance of inner conflict and little self-criticism; instead there is an attitude of hostile watchfulness toward a world that is largely alien.

C. THE CONTRASTING CASE OF LARRY

We may now turn to the case of Larry. A final appraisal of Mack and a judgment of the implications of his case can better be made after the two cases have been compared.

At the time of recording Larry's interview, the interviewer made the following observations:

Larry is conventional, conservative, well-mannered, deferent, quiet, and a conformist. Overtly he could be described as a passive, feminine type. He is a good example of the weak, unadjusted man who reads Dale Carnegie and becomes well-mannered, friendly, articulate, outgoing, but empty.

In appearance, he is slight, short, becoming bald-headed, rather feminine in general. He is openly dependent, highly articulate, and highly involved in the interview, making great effort, and appearing to enjoy it very much, remarking so especially at the end and being concerned with the general nature and purpose of the study. In spite of his highly conservative politics and his big-business personal goal, there is something very naive and unworldly about him.

The clinical section of Larry's interview follows.

(What were you like as a child?) "I seldom got any spankings. I was very active and played a lot of games. I don't want to brag, but I was well liked, like by the neighborhood women, who said I was a nice boy, if you know what I mean. That was until I was about 10. But outside the home, like in school and the neighborhood, away from home, I was more mischievous. I got into little difficulties. My brother, who is two and a half years older than I, and I were always together. We were fighting, jealous of each other, then friendly, going to the show or something. He was huskier, more athletic; I was always small, still am. My brother was more studious, conservative, wouldn't take chances, quiet. I admired him for this, for being a good big brother; for having a nice build, being nice looking, having good judgment; I admired him a lot, but I always maintained my own independence."

(Early experiences?) Age 3—an uncle passed away. "I remember his body in the house; it stayed there all day; then the hearse came and took it away. He used to hold me on his knee; I liked him a lot. I was the baby of the family. And his wife was especially nice. She used to pet me and play with me a lot. Then, another time— I guess about age 3 also—I remember wandering into the bull pen on the farm; and then the bull came for me, and the hired man just barely saved me, and I was really scared to death. I remember my mother's being there nearby and how scared she was too. Another memory I have, age 3 or 4, I remember how my brothers would catch rabbits on the farm. The rabbits would get into a lot of long pipes that we had in the back yard and my brothers would force the rabbits out with long poles and catch them as they came out the other end of the pipe. They would either knock them over the head as they came out, or sometimes they would catch them alive. What impressed me particularly was being able to touch a wild animal, and it couldn't run away, and I would rub its fur. Then, at the same period, on the farm, I have another memory, of sitting on a horse which belonged to my brothers and being held on it, half afraid and half jubilant over riding."

(Larry is extremely effortful here and apparently has thought about these things considerably. They come out fairly easily.)

(Experiences with father?) "I remember at age 2½ my father whipped my oldest brother very severely and my mother took all the children and went into town to separate from my father. I remember we went to the lawyer's office and had to stay there overnight because there was nowhere else. The next morning my father came in and found us, and he and my mother settled their differences. That's the only difficulty that I've ever known between them. There's never been an argument since, they've gotten along swell. I've had a wonderful home. (Is father very severe?) He wasn't strict in the sense of many rules, but when he told us to do something, we had to do it. We got few whippings, but when we did, they were plenty bad. (What about you?) I didn't get as many as my brothers did. I'd maneuver out of them. I didn't get any after the age of 12. I remember my brother got one even when he was 15. That was when I learned how to maneuver out of things—I just kept out of his way. When I was younger, I did whatever might avoid his punishment. My mother spanked us more often, but not so severely. We feared our father through our mother, that is, we feared she'd tell him and he'd punish us. Her main threat was not 'I'll spank you,' but 'I'll tell your father.' Her own spankings were so mild that we almost enjoyed them."

(Fears?) "I was afraid of the dark till age 16 or 18, my last years of high school, but I overcame it. I don't fear animals, except snakes, which I still fear and dislike."

(Nightmares?) "I had them, but I don't recall any particular ones." (Larry brought up nightmares himself, asking if that were a fear.) "One fear I had was in a big farmhouse we lived in when I was a kid, and it creaked in the wind, and I'd lie awake for an hour or more, thinking someone was there and being afraid. I remember lying awake sometimes most of the night; sometimes I'd go into my mother's bed.

"I still have unpleasant dreams; I don't know if they're nightmares. One was that my heart was stopping; or that I was sick and wouldn't get well. One was that my leg was getting amputated; I'd have to feel it just to see that it was still there. That was probably on account of the war, though. Recently I dreamed I was awake, in bed, and someone was just about to grab me. I couldn't move or yell; I was just completely paralyzed there, but at the last minute I woke up. Or I'll dream that I can't see people or writing around me; it's like being blind. They can see, but I can't quite make things out."

(Adolescence?) "I went through it smoothly into manhood. I didn't notice any great change in my life. (Sex?) No great problem. I thought about girls all the time, as boys will, and I looked at them. I started going out with them at about 15. I liked them a lot and associated with them at school and in the neighborhood. You know, you have the usual sexual desires, but you don't let them bother you. (Sex morals?) I feel a girl should remain a virgin until 21 or 22 anyway. If she expects to marry soon after that, she should wait until after marriage, but if she is a career girl or doesn't want to get married, then an affair with an unmarried man is O.K. if they keep it quiet and secluded so the moral standards of others are not lowered. She should pick out one fellow to have a sex relation with, and not carry on with several." (This is another example of Larry's highly articulate and theorized views on a subject.)

(You?) "Not until after I came out of the hospital, when I was 23 or 24. Since then I've had several affairs, lasting a few weeks or a month. I won't marry until I have more security. She almost has to be a virgin, though not necessarily. I lost respect for the women I slept with. I know that's selfish, but I guess that's the way most fellows are."

(Ideal wife?) "She shouldn't work, no career. She should stay at home, love me, raise a family, not expect too much in the way of fine clothes and a good time. She should have a good reputation, be attractive, not taller than I, nor too short, say 2 or 3 inches shorter; she should be intelligent and a college graduate; congenial, easy to get along with, sympathetic, a good mother, stick with me through thin and thick, even if I get sick. She shouldn't drink to excess, but drinking moderately is all right. She shouldn't get too friendly with other men—you know how some married women put their arms around other men, and things like that—but she should be friendly with men. She should have a good home background, come from a good family. Wealth is immaterial."

(Ideal husband?) "He should give her happiness, through security, home, car, enjoyment and entertainment; money to travel, and so on. He should be a good father to the children, shouldn't give the wife any worries; he shouldn't get drunk, and he should be faithful to his wife."

(Good father?) "He should be devoted to his children, give them the proper clothing, food, education; he shouldn't spoil them, give them cars in high school, and like that; but be good to them; he should take them on vacations; discipline them in a kind but firm way, teach them the proper morals when they are young, and give them the right environment."

(What were you good at in school?) "History and economics. I wasn't very good or very bad at anything. I had a C plus average. I didn't work hard in high school; I just slid along. I liked sports, and I played basketball for four years in high school, although I was too slight and light to get very far. Languages were especially difficult, and math. Then I went to junior college for a year; then I got sick and was in a sanitarium for four years. I got out, worked, and I've been back in school for a semester now. I'm living at a cooperative house."

Most of the outstanding features of Larry's personality seem to belong to one or the other of two syndromes: the one centering around dependence, passivity, and feminine identification, the other around subservience to an internalized but relatively narrow and restricting superego. Both of these patterns are more pronounced in this subject than in most unprejudiced men. Whereas some acceptance of dependence, passivity, and femininity appears regularly in men who score low on the scales, Larry's "softness" would seem to be fairly extreme by any standard. His conservatism, conventionalism, and authoritarian aggression—trends which in his case can be attributed mainly to the superego—are sufficiently pronounced so that he exhibits a number of features which are found more commonly among high than among low scorers. He actually scores high on the PEC scale, and there is reason to believe that his liberal sentiments with respect to minority issues are of fairly recent origin. The contrasts between Larry and Mack are nevertheless marked. The fact that the two men are similar in certain respects—passivity and conventionalism have loomed large in the discussion of Mack's case—should help us to see what circumstances made the crucial differences.

Numerous manifest traits of Larry's can be grouped on the basis that they express a general pattern of dependence, passivity, and feminine identification. He quite openly expresses his desire for understanding and support, and his readiness to accept the material help which he expects will be offered to him. He wants to be liked, and to this end he is prepared to inhibit aggression and to be generally pleasing in his relations with others. More than this, he wants pleasure and comfort and relaxation—and he wants to be assured of a bountiful and dependable source of supply. He has a basic "taking in" attitude toward the world. What prevents him from being grasping, it seems, is his conviction that there is plenty for everybody. This conviction even permits him to be generous. He *wants* everybody to have plenty and to be happy—himself included. What holds for material supplies holds also for people: he is ready to take them in too, that is, to be identified with them and to share their feelings, just as he is ready to give out his own feelings. This attitude leaves him sensitive to rejection, but at the same time able to sympathize with those whom he conceives as downtrodden—an essential feature of his positive attitudes toward minority groups. Relatively free from the idea that softness might leave him open to attack, he is able to indulge in tendencies which in men like Mack are automatically associated with dangerous weakness: he can experience the human, emotional aspects of things; he can be subjective and introspective, enjoy fantasy life and "philosophizing," admit having fears, anxieties, and doubts. Consistent with all this is the fact that he can have close relationships with women, whom he conceives to be not very different from himself.

These trends are on the surface in Larry; they are directly expressed in his overt behavior. The contrast with Mack lies in the fact that in him trends of this very same kind operate below the surface and he is very concerned to deny and counteract them. What is it that has made the difference? Most important, it would seem, were the differing circumstances connected with the childhood relationships with the mother. It was in this area that Mack was subjected to severely traumatic experiences, whereas Larry's early relationship with his mother was close and for the most part highly gratifying. Indeed the mother looms as the central figure in Larry's childhood. There is reason to believe that she took good care of him and that he became strongly attached to her. The attitude of love-seeking was carried over into his relations with other women, whose love he sought to obtain and to hold by being a "good boy." It seems that he is still bent on obtaining the kind of gratification he received as a child, and that to a considerable extent he succeeds in doing so—through having found modes of behavior that are more or less acceptable socially. (Mack, for his part, was forced to repress his dependent needs in childhood, and so was not able to find suitable modes for their expression; hence, he remains comparatively frustrated, unhappy, and self-pitying.) Larry is not, however, altogether secure with respect to the needs under discussion. He did not receive enough gratification in childhood, nor does he receive enough now, so that he can take love and support for granted. He is still susceptible to frustration and sensitive to rejection. The circumstance of there being much but still not enough gratification would account, in large part, for Larry's identification with his mother in childhood. Identification was a means for getting close to her and holding on to her, and of protecting himself from having to feel rejected and hostile. It seems, however, that the identification is a comfortable one, and that it must have been based more upon love than upon fear.

An additional reason why Larry is able to be comfortable and relaxed with his feminine identification lies in the fact that his mother was to a sufficient extent strong and protective. We are told that when the father was too hard on one of the boys, the mother took all the children and went to see her lawyer. She thus made it plain that she was not afraid to oppose the father and that she was a real source of protection. Larry could be on the side of this woman, be identified with her, without feeling that he was placing himself in a hopelessly weak position. This is in crucial contrast to Mack and many other prejudiced men, who cannot possibly come close to or be identified with the mother, no matter how "sweet" or "devoted" she might be, because she is conceived as too weak or inconsequential. Apparently, it is easier for a boy to identify himself with a feminine role, which he associates with the weakness and suffering of the underdog, when the weakness is not seen as hopeless nor the suffering as intolerable.

But if Larry's passivity and amiability is mainly a derivative of his childhood dependence on the mother, it has at the same time another function within the personality. It serves as a defense against his underlying aggressive impulses. Several of his responses in the interview and to the Projective Questions seem to show a particular concern with the inhibition of aggression, e.g., after describing the good time he would have if he had only six months to live, he adds "all this without hurting anyone"; and "a feeling that I have hurt someone" is one of the moods or feelings most disturbing to him. His concern with "true comradeship" and his solicitude for persecuted people suggest that, to some extent at least, he loves in order that he might not hate. The hypothesis of underlying aggression is supported by the T.A.T., which gives evidence of "strong underlying hostile impulses." These impulses are directed both against women and against men. Hostility against women is aroused by rejection or the threat of it, and can be understood as an aspect of the mother-dependence discussed above. (This is different from Mack, whose aggression against women is aroused by the fear that they might drag him down to their level.) Hostility against men is fused with antisocial rebellion, and the conflict between these tendencies on the one hand and the demands of conscience on the other is much more intense than is common among low-scoring men. Here, it appears, Larry is expressing attitudes built up on the basis of experiences with his father. There is nothing in the interview material to indicate that the father was unusually provoking, but he certainly enforced his will, administered some whippings, and was cast by the mother in the role of feared disciplinarian. This would be reason enough why Larry should have hostile and rebellious feelings. More than this, the T.A.T. offers the strong suggestion that Larry reproaches his father for not loving him enough, and that part of the interview in which Larry tells what a father *should* be seems to be in keeping with this suggestion. But what is particularly important, Larry must also have loved his father and become to some extent identified with him. This would account for the fact that rebellious aggression goes against Larry's conscience and leaves him feeling guilty and remorseful. It is to ward off such feelings that he must praise his father, remain subservient to his family's ideals, and exhibit other conservative tendencies more characteristic of high-scoring men. This brings us to the most crucial differences between Larry and Mack. The two subjects differ in the quality and intensity of their aggression and in the way of dealing with it. Larry takes responsibility for his aggression; though it is not conscious now, it seems to have been conscious at one time so that he could actually imagine himself taking revenge in one way or another upon his father. With Mack, as we have seen, the aggression appears to be out of touch with the rest of the personality; it is something which is entirely disclaimed, but which might suddenly explode in a blindly impulsive way. We have attributed these aspects of Mack's aggression to his extreme fear of the father. With Larry this fear seems not to have been so great. He tells us that he was afraid of his father's punishment, it is true, while Mack does not admit such fears; but Larry acted as if he were afraid of being merely whipped while Mack acted as if he were afraid of being torn limb from limb. There seems to have been two reasons for this: first, Larry's father was in an objective sense less dangerous; he was more human and understandable; and second, Larry had his mother to support him; she did not come off so badly in her quarrels with the father, and though "she would tell father" if Larry did not behave, she would protect him if the father was unjust.

These differences in the real situations with which the two subjects had to deal seem to have determined also their differing ways of handling their aggression. Whereas in Mack it is immediately repressed and displaced onto outgroups, in Larry it is turned against the self, giving rise to guilt feelings and self-depreciation. It is this state of affairs in Larry that makes it impossible for him to indulge in wholesale condemnation of other individuals or groups; there is a readiness to take blame himself, to suspect that the fault might lie within him. This is the work of a fairly normal conscience, a conscience built up through identification with the father as well as with the mother. Larry was willing to accept and to internalize their punishment or disapproval because he received enough love to make it seem that his sacrifices were worthwhile. In the case of Mack, the father has remained "out there," a source of actual danger, rather than become an inner source of guilt or conflict; instead of striving to live up to principles in order to feel loved and free of guilt, Mack acts like a man who has made a bad bargain; he feels that he has somehow been "gypped" and it is mainly fear that keeps him in line.

But Larry can hardly be regarded as a model of personality integration. There is too great a discrepancy between what he feels he must be and what he believes himself to be capable of. Since he is still dependent on his parents for love and support, he must constantly exert himself lest he "fall from grace" and lose their good will. And since his underlying aggressive tendencies are not fully integrated with the ego, it is necessary for him to maintain careful defenses against them. These defenses include masochism, passivity, and oversolicitude for possible victims of aggression. Thus it is that his positive attitudes toward minority groups are based in part upon neurotic trends. But this does not mean that these attitudes are unstable. It would be as difficult to induce Larry to attack a minority group member (just because he belonged to such a group) as it would be to get Mack to see that there might be some evil in himself or in his group. It would take a series of severe disappointments to divert Larry from his present course; he would have to be shown that it is not true that virtue and good work lead to the rewards of love and material support and then, instead of becoming overtly aggressive, he would probably suffer a depression.

It must be noted, however, that Larry is capable of further growth. The fact that he is willing to look at himself and to inquire into his motivations indicates that he may achieve a higher degree of personality integration. And should he continue to gain understanding of himself, we should expect his understanding of the world to increase.

We should not expect Larry to become militantly outspoken in the interests of his democratic beliefs, nor would he be likely to assume any leadership in a moment of acute crisis. He is too weak, that is to say, he finds it too difficult to be overtly aggressive, for that. His tendency, rather, would be to try in an inoffensive way to smooth troubled waters, to get everybody to "cooperate"—a contribution not to be altogether despised.

Larry is a rather ordinary young man. His case, though not typical of our low scorers, seems to show that among the determinants of relative freedom from prejudice are a willingness to accept one's own softness and to take responsibility for one's own "badness." But, as the results from our clinical sample as a whole have shown, accepting one's softness does not require that one *be* as soft as Larry or that one overadjust to it as he has done; and one can certainly take responsibility for one's own "badness" without remaining caught like Larry in the dilemma of parental dependence, with its underlying hostility and overlying guilt feelings.

Turning back now to Mack, it would appear that therapy in his case would have to consist, first of all, in showing him that the sources of his frustrations and unhappiness are mainly *in him*. (Only after attaining this insight could he approach a true appraisal of the conflicts and dislocations within society.) He would have to learn to accept more of his own softness and to come to terms with his own aggression. Since, however, the sources of these trends lie, as we have seen, very deep within the personality it is doubtful that anything short of individual therapy would effect any important change in him. Would individual therapy work? Since he is a relatively mild case and since he showed in his interview that he is able to make a positive transference to an older man, it probably would—but it is highly doubtful that he would ever seek it. But if it seems unlikely that his *personality* will change, there is good reason to believe that his *behavior* can be controlled. Indeed he can be *too easily* controlled, and therein lies one of the major troubles. There is little in his make-up to render him resistant to fascist propaganda or to fascist leadership. He too, in his own way, is weak and afraid to be overtly aggressive. He could never on his own initiative be an aggressive leader, but given strong direction from above he could pass it along to those who, in an organizational sense, were below him. He would be unlikely on his own initiative openly to attack a minority group member, not because of conscience but because of fear that he might get hurt or be disapproved of; but given the safety and influence of a crowd or the backing of someone he regarded as an authority, he could be violently aggressive. However regrettable from the democratic point of view this susceptibility to external control might be, the fact remains that it offers the best basis for preventing his antidemocratic tendencies from expressing themselves in action. The appeal should be not to his sympathy or his conscience, but to his fear and submissiveness. He must be convinced that arrayed against the overt expression of his prejudices are the law, overwhelming numbers of people, numerous conventional authorities and prestige figures. If those who stand for democracy want to win him to their side, they must do more than show him that they have high ideals and realistic plans for social improvement; they must convince him that they also have strength. Such a program, unfortunately, involves an essential paradox: in inducing him to *behave* in accordance with democratic principles, one is likely to strengthen his authoritarianism and, hence, his antidemocratic *potential*. One could not, therefore, undertake so to influence the contemporary behavior of individuals like Mack unless one exerted as much effort toward insuring that antidemocratic leadership did not gain the ascendancy in the future.

CHAPTER XXI

CRIMINALITY AND ANTIDEMOCRATIC TRENDS: A STUDY OF PRISON INMATES

William R. Morrow

A. INTRODUCTION

1. THE PROBLEM

If, as the foregoing chapters have indicated, failure in superego integration, inability to establish emotional relationships with others, and overcompensatory reactions to weakness and passivity are among the important sources of potentially fascist trends within the personality, should we not expect that a group of prison inmates would score particularly high on our scales? This, at any rate, was the thought which led us to consider our subjects from the San Quentin Prison[1] as a key group.

The most extreme failures in superego integration are found in the psychopathic personality (see Chapter XIX), a type of character structure which has been given an important role in criminality by many authorities, e.g., Karpman (61), Lindner (74), and Glueck and Glueck (44). Traits which some writers assign to criminals in general, e.g., egocentricity, absence of sense of guilt, inadequate emotional control, are often regarded as aspects of the psychopathy syndrome. Inability to establish emotional relationships with other people is probably a mark of psychopathy, though it is a trait often assigned to the delinquent personality in general, e.g., by Lowrey (76). That the inordinate longing for status and power, the readiness for aggression against weaker or relatively defenseless people, and the demands for immediate recognition so common among criminals usually spring from underlying weakness, passivity, and homosexuality has often been noted, e.g., by Aichorn (4) and by Alexander and Healy (6). These considerations are in accord with the well-known role of criminal types in fascist movements; they are the "plug-uglies" who are assigned the task of terrorizing minority group members, active labor unionists, liberals, and radicals.

[1] This study was made possible by the extended cooperation and assistance of Dr. David G. Schmidt, Chief Psychiatrist, San Quentin, California, and his staff.

At the same time, however, it was considered that there might be certain types of criminals who, exhibiting trends quite different from those noted above, would obtain relatively low scores on our scales. Thus in the "normal criminal" of Alexander and Staub (7) and in the "antisocial offender" of Sanford (103) rebellion against the *status quo* seems to be an important feature. This suggested that we might expect to find in some of the San Quentin subjects certain manifestations of a trend which in our major sample had appeared to favor low scores on the scales. Finally, in the "pre-social offender" described by Sanford, the need for love and the sense of love deprivation are outstanding features, and it was considered possible that in some cases these trends might outweigh the displaced hostility that is basic to prejudice. There was no information concerning the frequency with which these anti-authoritarian and love-oriented patterns appear in the general population of penal inmates, though it seemed fairly certain that it was small compared with that of the authoritarian personality trends noted above.

2. SAMPLING AND ADMINISTRATION

The sample of inmates on whom the questionnaire statistics are based was selected as follows. The prison psychiatric department provided, upon request, a sample of the inmate population subject to the following conditions: (a) A sampling of offense-groups should be obtained, roughly in proportion to their ratios in the total inmate population.[2] (b) Inmates beyond maximum age of 55 should be excluded. (c) Feebleminded inmates should be excluded.[3] (d) As far as possible, inmates with less than eight years of schooling should be excluded.[4] In addition to these restrictions, about twenty of the questionnaires obtained were subsequently excluded because: (e) they were incomplete (eight or more items left unanswered); or (f) they belonged to Negro or Jewish inmates; or (g) they belonged to inmates in the prison psychotic ward. These exclusions left a working sample of 110, on which the statistics were obtained.

The inmates filled out the questionnaire (Form 45) in groups of six or eight

[2] The ratios of different offense-groups in the questionnaire sample are as follows: "check-writing" 40%; "robbery," "burglary," and "theft" 28%; "homicide" 11%; "sex offenses" 21%. The corresponding ratios for the prison population (1945) are as follows: "check-writing" 14%; "robbery," "burglary," and "theft" 54%; homicide 7%; "sex offenses" 11%. The chief difference between the questionnaire sample and the prison population is that the latter includes 26% fewer cases of "check-writing," and 26% more cases of "robbery," "burglary," and "theft." The E- and F-scale means for these two offense-groups in the sample are not significantly different. (See Table 5 (XXI).) All of the ratios given in this note, it should be remembered, refer only to the "present" offense; many inmates have committed previous offenses in different categories.

[3] One subject included in the sample violated this condition; he obtained a Wechsler-Bellevue I.Q. of 48.

[4] Actually, sixteen subjects included in the sample (including the feebleminded subject referred to in footnote 3) violated this condition.

at a time, in the prison psychiatric department. Instructions given were the same as for other groups, with one addition: An attempt was made to get across the idea not only that anonymity would be maintained,[5] but also that this task had no relation to prison routine or authority. Such verbal reassurance could not, of course, alter the general atmosphere of the prison, which stresses compulsion and conformity. And it cannot be denied that such an environment is conducive to agreement with many of the conventional, authoritarian values represented in the questionnaire items. That this factor had a relatively minor effect upon the responses, however, is indicated by the wide inter- and intra-individual differences in answering the questionnaire. These differences appear in the fairly wide dispersion of scores obtained for most items considered separately, in patterns of agreement and disagreement for all except a few ultra-high scorers, and above all in some patterns of predominant disagreement (i.e., low scorers). There is also validating interview material. It deserves emphasis, moreover, that submission to surrounding authoritarian pressures is itself an index of authoritarian trends in the personality, of inability to maintain individualistic values in the face of counterpressure.

It is probable that items were sometimes misunderstood and answered incorrectly on account of external distraction, i.e., noise and crowded conditions. For inmates of low educational status, the possibility of misunderstanding would naturally be increased. It was discovered in follow-up interviews that some inmates had in fact misunderstood some items, and had answered them in a manner opposite to their intentions. This type of distortion appears to have been a minor (i.e., only occasional) factor, however.

Fifteen of the inmates were interviewed. Of these, eight scored high, four low, and three had scores placing them in what is, for most groups studied, the middle range. To avoid overcomplicating the picture, the interviews of these "middles" are not included in the discussion. Subjects were selected for interviews on the basis of E score (high or low), offense-group (to get some sampling of each major group), intellectual level (average or better, as estimated roughly from the data on the front page of the questionnaire and from the language used),[6] and the suggestiveness of their responses to the Projective Questions. A further selection was imposed by the fact that a few of the inmates sought for interviews were in the sick ward at the time or could not conveniently be seen because of conflicting prison routine.

The interviewees did not come voluntarily to be interviewed, but were summoned by the psychiatric department. The examiner tried as best he

---

[5] This anonymity was violated to the extent necessary to follow up certain inmates in interviews. It will of course be preserved here. To connect the names given to interviewees here with the numbers used in Part IV, see Key on the bottom of Table 1 (XXI).

[6] This was before the prison I.Q. test data had been made available to us.

TABLE 1 (XXI)

IDENTIFYING DATA FOR INTERVIEWEES IN THE PRISON INMATES GROUP

Pseudonym	Age[a]	Marital Status	Family[b] Class Status	Years of Schooling	I. Q.[c]	Pre-Prison Occupation
Pseudodemocratic						
Ronald	30	Divorced 3 times	UL	9	126	Cook
Robert	32	Separated	LM	12	115(est.)	Grocery manager
Eugene	28	Single	LL	10	115	Plumber
Wilbur	42	Married	LL	0	86	Truck driver
Clarence	63	Widower	LM	3	94	Farmer; soldier-pensioner
Fascist						
Floyd	23	Single	LM	11	125	Irregular odd jobs
Adrian	30	Single	LU	14	122	Homosexual prostitute; occasional clerk
Buck	32	Divorced twice	LM	6	83	"Cattleman"
Low Scoring						
Jim	28	Single	LL	11	117	Messenger; clerk
Don	42	1st wife died; 2nd wife divorced	UM	12	128	Salesman
Dick	26	Divorced; now engaged	UL	12	112	Clerk
Art	31	Married 2nd time	UM	14	130	Commercial artist

[a]As of November, 1945.

[b]These ratings are estimates by the examiner, using Lloyd Warner's categories: "Upper Upper," "Lower Upper," "Upper Middle," "Lower Middle," "Upper Lower," "Lower Lower."

KEY FOR CONNECTING NAMES GIVEN TO INTERVIEWEES IN THIS CHAPTER WITH NUMBERS USED IN PART IV:

Ronald:	M651A	Robert:	M656A	Eugene:	M662A	Wilbur:	M662B
Clarence:	M664B	Floyd:	M658	Adrian:	M661A	Buck:	M664C
Jim:	M619	Don:	M620	Dick:	M621A	Art:	M621B

Present Offense	Previous Delinquencies	Typical Self-characterizations
Murder during gang robbery	Numerous thefts and burglaries	Robbed "as a business"; "I always get married spectacularly."
Killed mistress in quarrel	Check-writing; robbery	Was "a good boy"; "hard-working.... self-made...business-success."
Check-writing	Eight drunk sentences; battery; robbery	"I like to fight"; "I'm a little wild."
Killed landlord in knife fight	None	One of the "poor people" whom "the Greeks like to punish."
Attempted rape (girl 12)	"Molesting" children; attempted rape (child)	Was "a good boy"; "a follower"; "framed by the people in politics."
Gang robberies	Drunk-and-disorderly; several Army AWOL's	"Everything I do is an act"; "my industriousness just doesn't exist"; "only one help I've got...my father."
Robbery with cap pistol	Numerous drunk and (homosexual) "soliciting" sentences; others	"Men irritate me...by...a superior attitude"; "I've got to have a God"; "my father haunts me."
Check-writing while drunk	Fraud; statutory rape (girl 13); "failure to provide"; "molesting" own children	"Money is the main object", "you don't think I'm a sex maniac, do you?"
While drunk, clubbed elderly woman to death	Several thefts: to buy necessities for mother	"The only happiness we really know of is ... here on earth"; "I look on God as mostly the goodness in all peoples."
Bank robberies (alone): to pay mother's debts	None	"Helping others all my life, it seems"; "beset by all sorts of emotional problems."
Stole auto while drunk	None	"I never did like to argue"; "when we were separated, I got a little wild."
Check-writing while drunk	Check-writing while drunk	Doing an "autopsychoanalysis" of own "Oedipus complex" to improve social adjustment.

cThis column gives the full-scale I.Q. score obtained on a Wechsler-Bellevue test administered by an inmate working in the prison psychiatric department.

could to dissociate himself from prison authority. Some of the interviews suffered, like the questionnaire sessions, from external noise and interruptions. But except for one interview (with Wilbur, a high scorer), which for lack of space had to be conducted in an office where another person was working, it is believed that these factors did not seriously interfere with rapport or with smooth conduct of the interview (as compared with interviews held in freer circumstances).

3. PLAN OF DISCUSSION

As elsewhere in the book, the general order of presentation is from surface attitudes to successively deeper dynamic factors. The bulk of the discussion is concerned with interview material, although in each section relevant questionnaire statistics are given. The concepts developed earlier in the book, especially in Chapters IX–XIII, are here applied systematically to a group of key importance for understanding fascism, namely criminals.[7] The more adequate interviews obtained for this group permit detailed exemplification of differentiating variables, combined with case studies of individuals who are followed as such throughout the chapter. An attempt is made to indicate in what respects the inmates are similar to other groups studied, and also what features seem to distinguish them. To help keep the interviewees in mind as individuals, Table 1 (XXI), which summarizes a few salient facts about each one, is presented.

One notable way in which the prison group is distinguished is the fact that some of the high scorers express openly fascistic attitudes. Three of the high-scoring interviewees differ sufficiently from the others in this respect to warrant special consideration. For each general topic, therefore, the interviewees are discussed in three groups: pseudodemocratic high scorers, fascists, and low scorers. For variables in which there is no notable difference between the two kinds of high scorers, some quotations from the fascists are often included under discussion of the pseudodemocratic high scorers. The distinction between these two differently organized types of mentality among the interviewees emerged empirically; it is developed inductively as various aspects of the fascist syndrome are taken up in successive sections of the chapter. The term fascist (as distinguished from pseudodemocratic, potential fascist) is used here to characterize anyone who expresses open hostility toward minority groups and endorses the use of force where "necessary" to suppress such groups; and who explicitly favors a "strong" government to protect business power against demands of labor unions and progressive political groups—even to the point of suppressing them by force.

[7] The twelve interviewees considered in this chapter were a part of the total sample which formed the basis for the quantitative analysis presented in Chapters IX–XIII. This fact no doubt accounts in part, but only in part, for the similarity of the clinical results to be reported here and those which emerged from the analysis of our clinical material taken as a whole.

B. ETHNOCENTRISM

1. GENERAL QUESTIONNAIRE STATISTICS AND THEIR SIGNIFICANCE

A statistical summary of E-scale results for the prison group is presented in Table 2 (XXI). *The prison inmates obtained a higher group mean on the*

TABLE 2 (XXI)

RESULTS ON THE E SCALE FROM THE GROUP OF PRISON INMATES

Item	High Quartile Mean/Person	Low Quartile Mean/Person	D.P.	Over-all Mean/Person
5. (Zootsuiters)	6.17	3.22	2.95	5.18
10. (Negro rights)	6.86	2.70	4.16	5.26
15. (Foreign ideas)	5.90	3.11	2.79	4.78
20. (Negro foremen)	6.79	2.78	4.01	5.16
24. (Jewish businessmen)	5.69	2.63	3.06	4.06
28. (Marry a Jew)	5.07	1.30	3.77	3.20
32. (Negroes live)	5.72	1.67	4.05	3.49
36. (Jews alike)	6.52	2.70	3.82	4.63
40. (Jewish neighborhood)	6.03	1.78	4.25	3.92
45. (World organization)	6.59	5.93	0.66	6.38
Total mean/person	61.34	27.82	33.52	46.06
Mean/person item	6.13	2.78	3.35	4.61
Range	5.5–7.0	1.6–3.6		1.6–7.0

Standard Deviation: 1.28
Reliability: .65

E scale (45)—4.6 per item—than did any other group tested.[8] Although there are a number of extreme high scorers, there are no extreme low scorers,[9] and the low end of the frequency distribution is truncated. This truncation produces the lowest Standard Deviation for the E scale (Form 45) distribution found in any group studied.[10] In terms of E-scale item means, the bulk of the differences between the inmates and other groups is accounted for by the inmates' high means on non-Jewish items—a result to be discussed later.

These gross findings point immediately to an important conclusion. The general run of criminals are *not* to be thought of as genuine rebels who act according to some principle, however dissident, and whose conflict with authority is accompanied by some consideration for the weak or oppressed.

[8] See Table 17 (IV).
[9] The four lowest scores, in terms of mean per item, are 1.6, 1.8, 1.9, and 2.0.
[10] See Table 17 (IV).

On the contrary, they would appear to be full of hate and fear toward under-dogs. Themselves disfranchised, prisoners and social outcasts, a kind of ulti-mate outgroup, they are yet unable to identify with other outgroups. This is in accordance with the common observation that most inmates do not iden-tify with other inmates, but make moralistic distinctions between themselves and "ordinary criminals." The predominant tendency is for each inmate to be "an island, entire in itself." One of the high-scoring interviewees, Eu-gene, expressed this isolationism succinctly in his general attitude to the "race problem": "I'm strictly for havin' all of 'em segregated."

A second general result is that the (Form 45) E-scale reliability of .65 is somewhat lower than that for other groups.[11] This can probably be attributed in part to misunderstanding of items and incorrect recording of responses, related to inadequate education and to environmental distractions. More of the reduction, however, is probably traceable to two statistical characteristics of the group results. One is the relative truncation of the lower end of the distribution. It is well known that cutting off either extreme portion of a bivariate distribution (including, of course, a split-half reliability distribution) tends to reduce the correlation. Secondly, the particular split of E-scale items used in computing reliability is such that one of the halves—the A items— includes precisely the five items on which the prison group means are most distinctively higher than those for other groups. The A set, moreover, in-cludes the three items with the poorest D.P.'s (see Table 2 (XXI)). With these "handicaps," a reliability coefficient as high as .65 would seem to be all that could be expected (see Chapter IV).

The pattern of E-scale item means for the group is interesting (see Table 2 (XXI)). A very high mean was obtained on Item 45, which states that Amer-ica must maintain complete independence in any world organization. Al-though this proposition always yields a high mean, the unusually high value for the inmates suggests that low scorers in prison may submit almost as much as high scorers to sufficiently strong nationalistic propaganda. This item would appear to lend itself particularly well to projection of the most severely frustrated strivings of prison inmates—their need to be free of re-straint. Aside from this statement opposing world organization, the three items with the highest means (numbers 5, 10, and 20) have one thing in common: each expresses strong status anxiety with respect to outgroups per-ceived as submerged, namely "zootsuiters" or Negroes. The significance of this feature is indicated in the following discussion of interview material on Negroes (the only truly submerged outgroup specifically inquired about).

2. IDEOLOGY CONCERNING NEGROES: A SUBMERGED OUTGROUP

a. HIGH SCORERS. The content of anti-Negro ideology seems to be related to the fact that Negroes are almost universally perceived as a very submerged

[11] See Table 17(IV).

outgroup—as contrasted with an imagined "dominant" outgroup such as Jews are thought to be. In the interviews, the principal traits ascribed to Negroes by high scorers are uninhibited sexuality, "laziness," "dirtiness," crude aggression, asocial acquisitiveness (petty thievery), pathological (infantile) lying, and exhibitionism. In a word, Negroes are held to be characterized by "untamed instincts," which keep them "primitive" and "childish." This imagery is partly expressed in questionnaire Item 32: Negroes are "lazy, ignorant, and without self-control."

The most conventional of the prejudiced interviewees, Robert, summarizes this idea in general terms: "They have more of a primitive nature . . . just want to *exist* as the cannibal type of man." The fascists tend to be more picturesque: "They're very closely linked with the jungle. They're built for it" (Floyd). Or, Negroes "originated from the apes" (Buck), and are "still half-African savage, no matter how dressed up they get" (Adrian).[12]

Implicit in these statements is the hereditarianism that pervades so much of potentially fascist thinking.

One of the most persistent preoccupations of the prejudiced interviewees has to do with the allegedly unsocialized sexuality of Negroes:

"There is more animalism in them. . . . (Animalism?) Well, a bitch dog runs down the street and five dogs jump on top of her. . . . Like the Latin race, they're hot-blooded" (Ronald). One of the fascists, though less graphic, seems more bitter: Negroes are "bestial, like animals. Wonder they don't have seasons for their heat" (Floyd). Another fascist affirms that Negroes are "very prolific" (Adrian).

More specific anxiety is expressed about sexual approach to "white women" by Negroes:

"One thing I can't stand is to see a white girl with a nigger" (Ronald). "In here, when they have shows, the colored boys holler out about white women on the screen, 'Oh, what a babe!' . . . That don't set right with me" (Eugene). "Under no circumstances," of course, should *any* member of "the white race . . . marry into the colored race" (Clarence). "Don't think a white person should marry one" (Wilbur).

The other traits stressed vary in specific content. They have in common some reference to asocial instincts, and to Negroes' alleged failure to develop superego restraints and ego-ideal drives. Thus Robert, who has struggled so hard to "make good" in business, is much concerned over the "laziness" of Negroes: "I don't think they try to satisfy their ego." Then, pulling back—apparently because this phrasing touches a conflict between Robert's own drive to get "up there" and his need to mask this power-seeking behind a pretense of "service"—he qualifies: "Not their ego, but their

---

[12] Throughout the chapter, more than one quotation is generally given to illustrate each point. This is done not merely to multiply illustrations but because each interviewee is followed as an individual case study, on which some material is presented in each section.

fellow man. . . . They don't have a goal in life." It is Robert also who expresses distaste for Negroes' alleged failure to conform to cultural ideals of cleanliness: "They don't wash themselves as cleanly." Other characteristics assigned include the following:

Asocial acquisitiveness: "The majority of them have sticky fingers. They can't let things alone" (Clarence). Aggressiveness: Negroes are "troublesome," always starting trouble. . . . They get smart, start a lot of fights. . . . They always try to cause so much trouble—fight, trying to be big shots" (Eugene, who admits to a long record of getting in petty "trouble," especially "fighting" when drunk). Pathological lying: "You can't depend on him. . . . He'll lie to you every chance he gets" (Buck, one of the fascists, whose protocol was discovered on checking with his social history chart to be filled with boastful lies on a grand scale). Being over-verbal and grossly exhibitionistic: "Chatter like a bunch of apes when you get three or four in a crowd. Strut around like peacocks. . . . Take a look at their clothes" (Floyd, another fascist, who speaks in abrupt, blurted sentences and might be called "underverbal," is exceptionally vain and preoccupied with his appearance, and even admits that, "Everything I do is an act").

The prejudiced interviewees' attitudes toward Negroes, as distinguished from their stereotypes of what Negroes are like, betray intense *status anxiety* —a fear lest "the black" rise up and challenge the right of "the white" to suppress him. Negroes must constantly be kept "in their place," i.e., submerged, in order to save the high scorers from feeling severe anxiety. This status fear appears both in invidious comparisons of Negroes vs. whites, and in direct insistence upon Jim Crow policies. The following expressions are typical:

"I don't believe in associating with them. I believe they should have their own schools. I don't believe we should have to eat with them" (Clarence). "I figure they're black and I'm white. . . . I won't work with them. . . . Let them stay in their place" (Eugene). Negroes "should stay in their place . . . not mix with whites" (Wilbur). Robert wants to be "tolerant" by reducing discrimination in employment and living standards, but "by that I don't mean that we should intermingle"; "there should be a separate section of town" for Negroes; and we "ought to do away with public office-holding" by Negroes.

Ronald complains: "The hardest thing for me to stomach is (Southern Negroes coming North) and taking advantage of opportunities. . . . They try to get themselves into a spot, not because they want it but just to annoy other people." He goes on to describe an incident in the Negro section of a midwestern city, in which he forced a Negro to move from the "spot" next to him on a street car, was arrested by a Negro policeman, and subsequently fined. He expresses resentment against "the overbearing attitude they get when the odds are all in their favor."

Ronald's bitterness toward the "overbearing attitude" of Negroes also illustrates another feature commonly found in prejudiced subjects: an inability to conceive of genuine equality. This anxiety-laden blind spot leads to some curious distortions by the prejudiced interviewees:

"(Negroes) feel themselves better than the white person" (Clarence). "They think they're better than we are" (Eugene). More fully elaborated: "When white people give them a little rope, they just think they are a little better than whites ... take a bit too far advantage if you give them a chance" (Wilbur).

Despite the highly antidemocratic attitudes outlined above, 5 of the high-scoring interviewees present the type of pseudodemocratic façade described in Chapters III and XVII. To convince themselves and others that they conform to the democratic values of "The American Creed," they try to disguise or deny their authoritarian hostility. They show reluctance to approve openly that violence against Negroes to which their inner anxieties predispose them.

"They're human, just as we are. . . . I don't believe we should hold racial hate" (Clarence). "There's a few good ones (who) go out of their way not to cause trouble" (Eugene).

Robert would even like to equalize some opportunities for Negroes—up to a certain point—so that they may be encouraged to suppress passive wishes and acquire a "goal in life." It is as if Negroes symbolize for Robert his own suppressed desires to be more passive and pleasure-seeking, desires that he feels compelled to inhibit so as to drive himself to "get up there" and prove his masculinity. Even Ronald admits "there are a few good ones"; and when asked what might have to be done if Negroes continue to demand more equality, he wistfully restrains his vigilante impulses: "It isn't so much what will have to be done as that nothing *will* be done under our democratic system." When pushed further, he sums up an attitude implicit in many of the quotations so far—the high scorers' ultimate pessimism as to any real solution of group tensions: "Well, there's a problem I don't think will ever be solved."

Wilbur, however, shows a kind of transition stage between pseudodemocratic façade and open fascist readiness to abandon pretense of democracy. On the one hand he insists, "I have nothing against them if they stay in their place." But if Negroes organize to demand equal rights, "plenty would have to be done . . . battle just like with the Japs." Underdogs' demands for equality seem to arouse in Wilbur a persecutory fear of being overwhelmed, so that he feels driven to "fight back" in paranoid desperation.

b. Fascists. The three fascist high scorers, Adrian, Buck, and Floyd, reveal essentially the same kinds of anti-Negro stereotypes, with even more intense status-anxiety. In addition, they show two interrelated characteristics that are more openly antidemocratic: undisguised hate combined with explicit readiness to suppress the outgroup by physical force "if necessary."

Buck rages: "Goddam nigger, he's no good at all. . . . I don't want any near me. . . . They ought to be kept in their place. Shouldn't let 'em come over here in the first goddam place! . . . Floyd is even more virulent: "Ignorant _____! . . . What ought to be done, but won't be done, is to ship 'em back to Haiti or to Liberia. (What may happen if they continue to encroach on white men?) There'll be bloodshed if it keeps up!"

Adrian's protective pattern of submissiveness prevents this blustering type of expression of his tremendous hate. But he leaves no doubt as to his approval of violent fascist suppressions: Negroes "keep their place and that's that. (What if the Negro doesn't keep his place?) He *does* keep his place. (But if not?) They *learn* their place." Further probing elicits the assertion that if Negroes should insist on seeking political representation, there would have to be "another civil war" to suppress them. Adrian makes clear the symbolic equivalence for him of Negroes and other submerged groups: (Should Negroes work in the same factory with whites?) "Yes, because if they're working in a factory with whites, they're poor whites anyway."

c. Low Scorers.   Despite the unusually high means obtained by the prison group on the three items expressing status-anxiety toward submerged groups, these items have fairly low means for the low quartile and therefore have quite high Discriminatory Powers (Table 2 (XXI)). This indicates the relative freedom of most low scorers from strong anti-Negro prejudice. Of the 4 low-scoring interviewees, however, none were found to be entirely free of prejudice against Negroes. But their attitudes are distinguished from those of the high scorers in several ways.

In the first place, they are much less hostile and far less rigid in such prejudice as they do disclose. In particular, they exhibit less status-anxiety toward Negroes. Three of them emphasize that "there should be no discrimination in jobs"; the other, Jim, expresses guilt feelings over his present prejudice on this issue (see below). On the basis of an individualized attitude toward people, these men tend to be more willing to accept Negroes as friends and equals. Thus Don, who was brought up in a Southern state, declares that he chooses friends "mostly on the basis of the individual, not the race." Dick, raised in another Southern state, describes two Negro doctors whom he enjoys "talking to." He hesitates "as far as having close friends goes," but decides that "that would be all right, too, if they had the same education I had." (Art's and Jim's views on this matter will be indicated in ensuing paragraphs.) All four protocols, however, contain evidence of some barriers against complete freedom of social relations with Negroes. The clearest barrier, subscribed to in some degree by all four, is that they "don't believe in intermarriage." But even here these men are more relaxed and flexible than the high-scoring inmates. They typically ascribe to external social pressure the main basis of their own social distance in this respect:

This barrier is a custom "brought down from years and years in history" (Dick). "I am thinking mostly of the children" who might be "socially ostracized" (Don). "It isn't socially accepted" (Art). The barrier is not regarded as rigid and eternal: "If I'd been raised in New York City (instead of in the South), I might have felt different" (Dick). In countries where intermarriage is generally accepted, it is "okay—not myself, perhaps; but I certainly wouldn't want to be dogmatic about it" (Don). (How would you feel about intermarriage if it were generally accepted socially?) "I don't know. It isn't now. . . . I never thought about it" (Art).

Most of these men would appear to have genuinely democratic values and yet, as mentioned before, none of them is entirely free of anti-Negro prejudice. One reason for this is suggested by a feature of their ideology itself. This is a tendency to discount somewhat the seriousness and extent of antidemocratic oppression; a reluctance to assign blame in intergroup conflict—especially reluctance to identify and to blame those who are more powerful for antidemocratic attitudes or actions toward those who are weaker; and a tendency to adopt a "harmonizing" attitude that urges *both* sides to be "reasonable" and to avoid impatient extremism—as if both sides were equally at fault. Inferentially, it is as if these men experience a conflict between democratic values and the fear of actively resisting the antidemocratic behavior of "respectable" groups "on top." One way of justifying an inability to mobilize aggressiveness toward what is strong and established is to "play down" conflicts between stronger and weaker groups, by a kind of false impartiality. Thus, Art declares: "The (Negro-white) problem is highlighted out of all proportion to what it is." Unable actively to resist conventional antidemocratic sanctions (though he refers to having known a few Negroes casually), he prefers not to "conduct my social life with them—only from one standpoint: It is not socially accepted." This explains why the "impartiality" is called false: it seems to give way, under pressure, to submission to antidemocratic *status-quo* values and policies. In order to justify this appeasement and maintain self-respect, such a person may turn around to blame the outgroup for being a source of "trouble"—as if it caused the trouble by not submitting quietly. The fact that democratic rights are being denied to the outgroup may be conveniently glossed over or denied. Thus, Art declares: Negroes "have equal rights with me, (but) many of them have set themselves apart." Asked to elaborate, he pulls back to a more "impartial" position: "I don't feel that they have set themselves apart; publicity has set them apart." "Publicity" is sufficiently anonymous so that he can avoid blaming anyone at all. . . . Thus it is clear that even the lowest scorers in the inmate group are not free of "high" trends.

Where definite rejection of Negroes is expressed by the low scorers, they show a readiness to examine their own attitudes with some degree of intraceptive and self-critical objectivity. An example is Dick's statement that, "If I'd been raised in New York City (instead of in the South), I might have felt different." Jim illustrates this trait more clearly. He verbalizes open guilt over having undemocratic attitudes toward Negroes, and describes these attitudes objectively as a psychological part of himself. "I have a kind of natural, instinctive dislike for working with them. My mind tells me that's wrong, not fair ... but I just feel that way." Jim sees the conflict as in himself, and conceives the solution as requiring a change not in the outgroup (as the high scorers tend to do) but in the attitudes of himself and the ingroup: "It's certainly unfair according to all human concepts. We just seem to have a natural antipathy toward them that will eventually have to be worked out, because a person can't help being born a Negro any more than a white man can a white man." Implicit in this last observation is another feature of unprejudiced thinking in this area: these men seem to have an ultimate optimism as to the solution of intergroup conflict—it will "eventually have to be worked out." Further: "As far as coming to the time when they won't be segregated, I think that would have to come naturally. . . . I believe it's becoming solved more and more" (Jim).

Like other low scorers, these men tend, when they do attribute certain character traits to Negroes, to offer sociopsychological explanations for such traits in terms of environmental pressures. (As might be expected, this is intimately linked with their ultimate optimism, just as the prejudiced men's hereditarianism is associated with their ultimate pessimism.) This capacity for sociopsychological thinking is usually combined with a readiness for empathy with the outgroup member's inner feelings. Thus, Dick: "If (a Negro is) kept under supervision, suppressed, naturally he's not going to have any initiative, not going to care."

3. IDEOLOGY CONCERNING JEWS: A SUPPOSED "DOMINANT" OUTGROUP

a. HIGH SCORERS.   Anti-Semitic stereotypes differ markedly from the qualities ascribed to Negroes. Specifically, they seem to reflect the notion of Jews as a "dominant" outgroup. One of the questionnaire items (number 24) which clearly differentiates high and low scorers, condemns Jews for monopolizing business (see Table 2(XXI)). This expresses the core of the prejudiced men's typical imagery of "the Jew" and their attitudes toward the latter. Jews are seen as embodying to a singular degree what seems to be a central value-complex of our culture. This set of values revolves around acquisitiveness and drive for "success" conceived in terms of "getting on top" and staying there—that is, compulsive drive for status and power. Every high-scoring interviewee gave spontaneous fantasies about extreme acquisitiveness as a supposed Jewish trait. The following are typical examples:

"They like to be where there's money and take all the money and hang on to it" (Wilbur). "You put (a Jew) on a rock and he'll make money. . . . He's thrifty and tries to get ahead" (Clarence). Jews have a "special drive" and "have always been after money and capable of making it" (Robert).

This drive is imagined to lead to Jewish dominance and power:

"I guess they run most of the things in this country," and "They run an awful lot of politics" (Eugene). "I believe that the Jews control a lot of the money in this country" (Ronald). Jews have "put themselves up there, where what they say counts" (Robert).

This power is secured, so the fantasies go, by combining acquisitive drive with "clannishness":

Jews are thought of as "stickin' together" (Eugene); as being "self-centered" and acting so that "when one Jews gets in, first thing you know there are about fifty of them" (Ronald); as being "good mixers among their own people, but don't mix much with other people" (Clarence).

It is noteworthy that none of the pseudodemocratic inmates ascribed to Jews a single id (primitive instinct) trait, of the sort described above in the anti-Negro stereotype. This striking difference in fantasies about an outgroup imagined to be "dominant," as contrasted with an outgroup perceived as "submerged," was a matter of the spontaneous emphasis of the inmates themselves.

The prejudiced men's attitude toward Jews also differs clearly from their attitude toward Negroes. Their attitude toward Jews seems to be associated with the image of Jewish dominance combined with exclusiveness. This attitude centers around fantasies of victimization by Jewish power, and a fear of being overwhelmed by that power. Here the personalization of ideology is even more striking than in the anti-Negro attitudes.

Thus, Eugene: "Say I have a grocery store. They'll come in and start a bigger one." They "get in a small town" (Eugene was raised in a small town) and "take over the grocery stores." Or Ronald: "You put a Jew in an office. First thing you know, you haven't got a job. You've got five Jews instead. . . . They act like they're better than anyone else, and anyone that doesn't think they are is nothing but a fool."

Of special interest is the anti-Greek ideology of Wilbur. He shows the usual anti-Semitic fantasies, but without as intense feelings as those characterizing his anti-Greek ideology, which serves a similar function and is more focal.[13] This fact appears to have been precipitated by a specific experience with a Greek landlord. Following an argument over the rent, the landlord evicted Wilbur's family while Wilbur was at work. Wilbur sought him out in a rage, started a fight, and gave him a fatal wound (leading to Wilbur's imprisonment). Wilbur's emotional conflicts (to be discussed later) prevented him from merely rejecting the particular individual. Instead he de-

[13] Cf. the discussion in Chapter XVI of the functional character of anti-Semitism.

veloped rigid delusions about "the Greeks," imagining them as "all alike" and as having deliberately "come over here" to "punish the poor people, pay low wages, make you work too hard," etc.

Significant is the fact that the prejudiced men's anti-Semitic resentment seems to have an ambivalent aspect, to be combined with a secret envy of, and longing to be accepted into, the supposedly "dominant" outgroup. Observe in the following examples the reluctant admiration of and implied wish to share in "Jewish power":

"God knows they're good businessmen, but all for the Jew" (Adrian). " 'Course they've got to stick together, but why at the expense of others" (Ronald). "Smart people, ain't they?" (Buck). "Still, if they can do it . . ." (Eugene). "Trouble is, they're so goddam clannish . . . won't mix and mingle like other people" (Floyd).

More positive (surface) identification with "Jewish" drive to "get up there" is illustrated in Robert, who seems to have experienced a severe struggle to internalize this same goal in the face of desires to relax and enjoy life (see p. 858). With a kind of inverted anti-Semitism, he expresses admiration for Jews' "knack to earn money, to control something," and for their having had "the foresight and drive and ambition to get there." His envy is plain: "I think it would be better if some white men had something put on their backs to get that drive." Floyd, a fascist who expresses contempt for himself for never having held a job for more than a few weeks at a time, stresses Jewish "industriousness" which he consciously envies: "They believe in working for what they get. . . . Talk to a little Yid kid, and he is studying for what he's gonna be ten years from now."

Despite the antidemocratic hostility implicit in their anti-Semitic fantasies, the same five men again maintain a pseudodemocratic façade. They ward off attention to their own hostility as such by focusing rigidly on "what is wrong with the outgroup."

Hence, it is often possible for them to believe that they are "strictly not prejudiced" (Robert); to declare that Jews have "got to have some place to live—can't run them out of the country" (Clarence); or that "however, I don't think they should be persecuted" (Ronald); or assert that "I don't have no trouble with a person (such as a Jew) if he don't bother me" (Wilbur); or that "I guess they're all right, I never had no run-in. They stay in their place" (Eugene).

Although these men may feel that perhaps Hitler faced a "real problem . . . with this domineering type" who "possibly controlled Germany quite a bit through big business" (Robert), they reject Nazi persecution of Jews as brutal and unwarranted.

The pseudodemocratic character of this façade is seen not only in the hostile stereotypes of Jews but also in responses to questioning about "what might have to be done if Jewish control goes too far?"

For example: "There might be no way to get them out except by revolution"

(Ronald). Wilbur reveals, rather pathetically, a similar pogrom mentality in his attitude toward "the Greeks": "If they don't stop (punishing the poor people), there's going to be more American people in the penitentiary." He feels "they" ought to be sent back to Greece.

b. FASCISTS. The anti-Semitic stereotypes of the three fascists are fairly similar to those of the pseudodemocratic high scorers. They focus on acquisitiveness as well as clannishness and monopolization of power. The fascist subjects stress a further trait attributed to Jews, however, which is not mentioned by the other high scorers, viz., excessive sensuality.

Buck refers especially to sexual obsessions and homosexuality among Jewish men: (What are Jews like?) "Most all of them Jews talk about sex mostly, or beatin' a guy out of his money. . . . (What do they talk about sex?) About what they're gonna do when they get out, or they're gonna get a _____[14] tonight." . . . Floyd, whose ambivalence is peculiarly clear-cut, complains that Jews "won't intermarry." An underlying orientation toward Jewish *men* is suggested by his phrasing: "Some of *their* women are really all right" (italics supplied). . . . Adrian does not himself introduce the topic of Jewish sensuality but does verbalize such fantasies quite readily: (Are Jews somewhat different sexually?) "They are more amorous than other people. Yes, and I know whereof I speak! More passionate, more romantic. Not that I like it, but they are."

Like the other high scorers, the fascists reveal a fear of being victimized by Jewish power, along with an ambivalent wish to be accepted into the supposedly "dominant" outgroup. As in their anti-Negro ideology, the fascist inmates' attitudes are distinguished by undisguised hate and by explicit readiness to suppress the outgroup by physical force. This goes along with open approval of specifically fascist aggressions against underdogs.

Buck feels that Hitler "done the right thing" to the Jews, who are "lower than a goddam snake." In this country "they'll have to watch out if they want to eat." . . . Floyd grimaces with disgust as he speaks of "that harsh guttural voice." If Floyd had been in Hitler's place, "I'd have done the same thing he did!" . . . Adrian is again too ingratiating to bluster in this way, but is quite open as to his authoritarian hostility: (Is dislike for Jews increasing?) "No, just the opposite, and I deplore it personally!" He is willing to support fascist persecution in the form of arbitrary deportation of all Jews in America—"send them all to Palestine"—even though he feels compelled to "disapprove of the *means* (Hitler) took to rid Germany of the Jewish problem. Because they *did* monopolize industry, and *something* had to be done." And "the Jews are just as apt to monopolize industry in this country." While he justifies persecution of Jews for being allegedly *too* aggressive and powerful, Adrian also "wanted to let the Japs go into Manchuria" because the Chinese are "not aggressive enough!" "They have enough resources and could be a great nation if they had the aggressiveness of the Japs."

This contradiction throws into relief a further aspect of fascist ideology that can be described as ideological opportunism. By this term is meant a disregard for ethical principles and truth-values, which are replaced by

[14] Profane term meaning to have fellatio performed upon oneself.

opportunistic manipulation of ideas and "facts" in the service of *Realpolitik* ends. The contexts in which such opportunistic thinking appears are characteristically those involving dominance-submission conflicts. The aim of such opportunism is to maintain identification with those on top—whoever they are, whatever they represent—and to avoid at all cost the anxiety of being identified with those below. There is an essential indifference to content, i.e., indifference to any goals of human happiness. Power for power's sake is the ultimate end; ideological opportunism is one of the means. Such opportunism appears also in the thinking of pseudodemocratic high scorers, but in more disguised forms. (See Chapter XVII.)

Another facet of Adrian's opportunism is revealed by a superficial shift in his identifications which occurred "after the war began in Europe." His explicit sympathy with the aggressions of fascist Germany and Japan was modified, as American opinion became crystalized against the Axis. He rationalizes that Hitler's aggressions during the war "seemed to be more a matter of conquest than protecting against communism"; and "I certainly didn't expect (the Japanese) to go beyond China." That Adrian experienced no change in heart but only a superficial realignment so as to avoid conflict with a more dominant ingroup (America), is suggested by his present explicit approval of all aggressions by the Axis nations carried out prior to their open war with the stronger Allied powers.

Floyd's ideological opportunism is even clearer. He summarizes (and plainly approves) the "harmony" technique exploited by German industrialists, through Hitler, to "solve" class conflict: Hitler's "object wasn't the Jew. He wanted a scapegrace (sic) to get the different classes and provincials together, to fight one thing.... To get together instead of having all this bickering and split power. (Was his cause just?) In the eyes of the German people, yes. (In your eyes?) Every man for his own country."

Buck, besides supporting Nazi persecution of Jews, exhibits an interesting mode of ideological opportunism in his behavior toward the interviewer. The first three inquiries about his views on "the Jewish problem" and "the most characteristic Jewish traits" elicited only pseudodemocratic denials of hostility. For example: "They got a right to make a living as much as anybody else. ... They got a way to make money is all I know. More power to 'em is all I can say. . . . I don't know much about 'em." But with the fourth question he apparently sensed that he would not be punished for expressing hostility and might (judging from the interviewer's noncommittal attitude) even gain approval for having the "right" view of things: (Can you tell a Jew usually?) "You're damn right I can tell 'em as soon as I talk to 'em." From this point on, Buck drops his façade and exhibits intense aggressiveness toward Jews.

c. Low Scorers. The low scorers tend to reject anti-Semitic stereotypy as such. Thus Dick retorts that "it doesn't hold true" that there are any "characteristic Jewish traits"; for "the Jews, in my opinion, are not a race but a religion." Jim declares: "I don't see why they should be picked out as being any different from anyone else." More positively, these men actively condemn anti-Semitism.

"When a person gets too far off the base about the Jews or Negroes, I am liable to step in and tell him off" (Don). Art interprets the hostility concealed behind pseudodemocratic anti-Semitism; his own equalitarian ideology is apparent: "I have often heard the expression, 'Some of my best friends are Jews.' Well, hell, some of my best friends are *people!* It sounds like you are making a concession to them." It is of interest that Art's father is described as "a rabid Jew-hater."

Further, in contrast with the narrow, personalized mythologies that dominate the thinking of the high scorers, these men exhibit a broader perspective. They seem to show a greater capacity for surveying human relationships in a detached way, which at the same time reveals compassion and respect for other human beings. One form this takes is empathy with Jews' psychological problems as an outgroup and a tendency to construct sociopsychological interpretations of anti-Semitism.

Jim remarks that Jews may be "inclined to be egotistical"; and at first a typical anti-Semitic projection is expected, until he goes on to clarify his meaning: "Not exactly a trait, but I think a good many of them feel that they're discriminated against. I think, in view of that, that they strive harder than most people do, and as a race they stick together and cooperate with each other to a large extent." This is quite unlike Ronald's complaint that "they act like they're better than anyone else, and anyone that doesn't think they are is nothing but a fool." Don believes that "if they have any objectionable features" as a group (which he doubts), it is because they are "stepchildren of history" in the sense of having been restricted to certain occupations and living conditions. Art is more explicit: "The Jews way back in history were other than Christians, and were limited (by the Christians) in their spheres of endeavor. . . . So they became sharpies in the money department as a defense mechanism. . . . So they had attributed to them those traits that are most despicable: craftiness, greed about money, etc."

Art says that he is inclined to regard the Jews' "reputation for sharp dealing" as unfounded, but "I don't know whether it is true or not." The important point is that the matter is not vital to him: he is not driven by inner conflicts to an insistence on projecting ruthless acquisitiveness onto Jews. Dick is more at a loss for ideas to account for anti-Semitism. He can only suggest that it is "just brought down from history."

C. POLITICO-ECONOMIC ATTITUDES

1. GENERAL QUESTIONNAIRE STATISTICS

A statistical summary of results from the PEC scale for the prison group is presented in Table 3(XXI). On this scale, the prison group obtained the highest mean, 4.68, of all groups taking Form 40 or 45 except the Service

TABLE 3 (XXI)

RESULTS ON THE PEC SCALE FROM THE GROUP OF PRISON INMATES

Item	High Quartile Mean/Person	Low Quartile Mean/Person	D.P.	Over-all Mean/Person
3. (Labor unions)	5.93	2.74	3.19	4.16
7. (American Way)	6.80	5.22	1.58	5.87
11. (Government control)	5.30	2.67	2.63	4.52
14. (Ford and Morgan)	6.07	3.33	2.74	4.94
17. (Economic security)	4.93	3.04	1.89	3.90
Total mean/person	29.03	17.00	12.03	23.39
Mean/person/item	5.80	3.40	2.41	4.68
Range	5.4–7.0	1.0–4.0		1.0–7.0

Standard Deviation: .96

Club Men.[15] It would seem that criminals tend in general to be conservative in their politics. With respect to the PEC scale quartiles, Table 3(XXI) reveals that not only is the high quartile mean fairly high, but the low quartile mean is definitely higher than in other groups—so high as to indicate that there could be few if any extreme low scorers on the PEC scale. As a matter of fact, only one inmate (out of 110) obtained a PEC score of 5, i.e., 1.0 per item. The two next lowest scores were, respectively, 2.2 and 3.0 per item. It is not surprising, then, to find that the average D.P. for the PEC scale is only 2.41, the lowest for any group which took Forms 40 or 45. (See Table 9(V).) Moreover, the correlation between the E and PEC scales for the prison group is only .14.

How can these results—the inmates' general conservatism, and the low correlation between E and PEC scores—best be explained? First, as to the general conservatism, interview material suggests that antidemocratic emotional attitudes play an important determining role. Another factor, partially "caused" by such attitudes, which may favor conservatism, is the lack of an informed and adequate frame of reference within which to evaluate politico-economic events.[16] This phenomenon, the general significance of which has been discussed in Chapter XVII, seems on the basis of interview material more extreme in the inmates than in most other groups. Such a lack could be influenced partly by prison isolation, but also by disinterestedness deriving from preoccupation with private emotional conflicts as well as from the low educational level of many of the inmates.

[15] See Table 8(V).

[16] The relationship between lack of an informed and adequate frame of reference, on the one hand, and receptiveness to reactionary ideas on the other, has been discussed particularly by Cantril (17).

Since the reliability and validity of the PEC scale depends upon at least a minimal information and interest on the part of the subjects, the factor just discussed might help to account also for the low correlation obtained between PEC and E scores. Another factor that would reduce this correlation is the truncation of both distributions at their lower ends—i.e., the near-absence of very low scores. In addition, two special features of some high-scoring inmates might have helped to lower the E-PEC correlation by lowering their scores on certain items. One is superficially liberal attitudes among some high scorers (exemplified in interview material). These would seem to be related in part to reality factors such as marginal socioeconomic status, greater first-hand experience of economic insecurity, and so forth. The lack of genuineness in these attitudes is revealed in their personalized-persecutory tone, and in a readiness for antidemocratic approaches to politico-economic conflicts. A second special feature is the greater frequency among these high-scoring inmates of openly fascist politico-economic attitudes. Not only are these not measured directly by the PEC scale (see Chapter V) but to the extent that they are consistently fascist, they actually tend to lower scores on PEC Item 11. For while fascists share the conservative antilabor, pro-business approach, they differ from traditional laissez-faire conservatives in desiring "strong" government control (not, of course, social control over business, but control by business over labor).

The pattern of specific PEC item means and D.P.'s is consistent with the above interpretations of general conservatism among the inmates and of the slight relationship between PEC and E scores (see Table 3(XXI)). The reactionary implications of Item 7 (American way) are probably not easy to grasp without a rather positive liberal-internationalist political orientation. This item, as might be expected, has an exceptionally high mean and a rather low D.P. On the other hand, Item 17, condemning economic security, would be expected to have a relatively low mean because it touches the personal experience of both high- and low-scoring inmates; and this factor should also lower its D.P. These expectations are borne out. Finally, Item 3, urging stronger labor unions, should discriminate most clearly between high and low scorers: it presents in a fairly pure form the issue of political liberalism-conservatism and little sophistication is required to understand what it implies. This PEC item is in fact the most differentiating of all.

2. INTERVIEWEES GENERALLY

The interviews tend to confirm the supposition that most of the inmates are politically uninformed. The above-average intelligence and education of most of the particular inmates interviewed makes this fact even more striking. In addition to revealing general ignorance and confusion in discussing politico-economic affairs, a number of the interviewees directly admit their ignorance and lack of interest in this area.

"I don't know about politics. I never studied that much and I never talk about it. . . . I don't think much—only what I hear over the radio" (Wilbur). "That's something I don't know nothing about: politics" (Eugene). "I'm not a political-minded man" (Robert). "Don't know much about" the Roosevelt New Deal (Floyd). "I never did pay much attention about political things" (Buck). "I pay very little attention to it"; "I don't understand those things, but I prefer to do what the Republicans do, whatever that is" (Adrian). "A subject I never gave a lot of attention to" (Dick).

There are nonetheless important differences among the interviewees in their degree of political awareness (or lack of it), as well as in some of their general attitudes.

3. HIGH SCORERS

Differences between the politico-economic attitudes of the low-scoring interviewees and those of the pseudodemocratic prejudiced interviewees are not clear-cut. Four of the 5 pseudodemocratic men—Robert, Eugene, Wilbur, and Ronald—exhibit some pro-labor attitudes, though these are not consistent. For instance, in late 1945 or early 1946, all of these men believed that wage increases were justified by high prices and by the ability of employers to pay more wages. Each of them, however, revealed indecision as to how far trade union activity should go, especially where strikes might be involved. Typical is Robert's view that "the unions demand just a little more than they have a right to." All of these men condemned political activity by organized labor. In varying degrees, however, they support some social security legislation. Robert even endorses such measures as public health insurance and the general idea of government economic planning. But all of them oppose such equalizing restrictions as wartime salary limitations.

Clarence, on the other hand, is consistently reactionary. He seems to support the more hard-boiled policies of big business. Objecting strenuously to trade union activity and identifying with employer "toughness," he declares with satisfaction: "If a man can't make a profit in his business, he'll close it down." He complains that "it's the corporation they blame all the trouble on." Ronald asserts a similar view: "I believe in free enterprise. I believe that business should be able to conduct their own business." Clarence, Ronald, and Eugene, despite their own (pre-prison) submerged economic status, express marked status anxiety toward politico-economic outgroups and a persecutory fear of being overwhelmed by such groups becoming dominant—specifically, organized labor, "the Communists," and Russia. (Recall the problem of status-anxiety toward Negroes, and the fear of being overwhelmed by the latter if they should succeed in rising nearer to democratic equality.)

Clarence is afraid that "if labor keeps getting more power we'll be like Russia. That's what causes wars! . . . You take the C.I.O. The majority of the C.I.O. is communism (*sic*)! . . . Anyone who believes in communism ought to be deported!"

Ronald complains that labor unions are "so strong now that they're trying to run the government." Eugene fears that our government could become threatened by "the strikes" but even more by Russia: "We're going to have to look out for Russia. . . . I think sooner or later we're going to go to war with them."

For 4 of these men (all except Robert), there is definite evidence that such liberal attitudes as they do express may be undependable. For these attitudes seem to be based not on genuinely democratic principles but on the same kind of personalization of ideology that was seen in their racism. On one side are fantasies of actual or threatened victimization, in which politico-economic processes are oversimplified into an imagined, purely personal conflict between forces of "good" and forces of "evil." Thus, Clarence's attitude toward unions seems to be determined by his fear of criticizing business power and by an overcompensatory "rugged individualism": "I've worked all my life and I wouldn't let no organization tell me when I worked and when I couldn't." His ambivalent attitude toward what he calls "the best form of government" is equally devoid of any reference to issues, and reflects a "good man, bad man" theory of society: "Of course, sometimes we get rotten politicians." . . . Ronald's paranoid interpretations of political events are suggestive of the kind of thinking we came to expect from Hitler and Mussolini. His first response to inquiry about his political views is that "We've got a persecutor in California for governor." Declining to explain this, he goes on instead to attack President Roosevelt as another "persecutor." He tells of how his father was "pushed out of a job" by the N.R.A. Then, making it clear first that "I don't believe in communism," he complains that "there's so many *little* people who never have anything." This prefaces another personal story—of his grandmother's inadequate old-age pension, from which he concludes that the law ought to be changed to grant more liberal allowances. (He objects, however, to public health insurance because "there are plenty of private insurance companies.") Asked his opinion of the then current 30 per cent wage increase demands, Ronald again personalizes the matter by referring bitterly to high prices in the prison canteen. He attributes these to prison "graft" and hints darkly at various people "getting theirs." Prompted to return to the question, in one breath he denounces unions, rejects the idea of any government controls over business, and concludes that by "agreement" with business "the government should arrange higher wages without the union." This is an unwitting description of the "impartial," big-business-controlled fascist state. It is consistent also with his feeling that while "democracy is the best type of government," it is "inefficient."

Intimately linked with feelings of victimization by "forces of evil" are similarly personalized attitudes to the "forces of good," viz., submissive-dependent leader worship. This is well exemplified by Eugene's conception of President Roosevelt as a paternal hero who single-handedly saved America: "Just everything good about him. Took this country out of a rut. He took guys on the street without a job and put them in the C.C.C.[17] In other words, he's just tops, that's all." . . . Wilbur, who is one of "the poor people," also admires Roosevelt in a personalized way because "he fixed it so that people could have jobs and get food for their families." Neither of these men shows any conception of the New Deal as a social reform movement induced by mass democratic pressure. Wilbur expressed as follows his concern (in December, 1945) over high prices and relatively low wages: "They're trying to cut the little fellow off." On the face of it this sounds like a strong identification with the economically oppressed. Such an identification is rendered suspect, however, by the personalization of Wilbur's attitudes toward Roosevelt and by his lack of any generalized democratic philosophy. His persecutory anti-Greek delusions and general ethnocentrism increase this suspicion. It is not any economic circumstance but "the Greeks" which "punish the *poor* people, pay low wages, make you work too hard." This suggests that Wilbur's reaction to economic frustrations could easily be diverted into the fascist pattern of vigilante attacks against scapegoats.

A final comment on the dependability of Robert's somewhat liberal views may be permitted. Doubt is raised on this point first by the authoritarian hostility of his racism, but also by his behavior at the close of the interview. Consistent with his seemingly universal reputation in childhood and youth as a "good boy" (according to social service reports), Robert submissively asks the interviewer, "Do you think I have the right view on things?" He repeatedly rejects the interviewer's explanation that it is not a matter of "right" or "wrong" but of individual evaluations, and insists on being given "the answer." This excessive need to conform with "the right views" implies a lack of internalized values and a readiness to change his opinions to accord with "the right views" of "the right people." Such a "detachable" ethic does not augur well for his ability to resist fascist ideology.

4. FASCISTS

The politico-economic ideology of the fascists is consistently reactionary. It also differs from the "politics" of the pseudodemocratic high scorers in the same general way that the fascists' racism was seen to differ from the pseudodemocratic men's racism. This is, namely, in being openly antidemocratic. The fascists show an *explicit readiness to use force against labor*, toward whom they reveal intense status-anxiety. They also display contempt for ideals of equality; the concept of an élite, implicit in the thinking of the pseudodemocratic inmates, is made articulate by these men.

Floyd's contempt for working men and his persecutory fantasies about unions show the violent anxiety of these attitudes. He fears that "we are going to be ruled by a lot of clowns, by a lot of labor unions. (How do you mean?) Look at all these

[17] Eugene was in a C.C.C. camp for a year.

working stiffs, that don't know anything else but how to drive a nail. . . . They try to run things, because a few hundred thousand of them get together. (What ought to be done about it?) Straighten them out, show them where they belong. . . . Take away their charters. . . . Abolish them." Strikes should be handled by "refusing to employ them or fine them." Characteristically, Floyd wants to "get tough" with other nations, feeling that "we deal too loosely with other powers. (Which ones?) Oh, Russia, England—communism on the whole. I don't like any place where free enterprise is not." . . . Adrian, whose contempt for "poor whites" has been noted earlier, states openly that "I really don't believe in democracy." Again: "I think the powers should be in a few hands. I'm not a democrat." He makes clear the antidemocratic meaning of his obsessive fear of "communism": "I've never seen a Communist who came from the right strata of society." His readiness to support authoritarian aggression is not limited to approval (see pp. 833–34) of Nazi and Japanese-fascist aggressions: "I'd like to do to the Bolsheviks what the Bolsheviks did to the Russians" (i.e., the Czarists). . . . Buck is less articulate but leaves little doubt as to his élite identifications: he "never did figure much about" labor unions, because "you can't make no money unless you have guys workin' for *you*. . . . I expect in ten years or so I can retire. As long as I got the money, I can go out and buy cattle and make it (i.e., money)." His readiness for fascist aggression is plain: "Christ, we licked those other countries and now we're gonna feed 'em. . . . I think we ought to let 'em starve, especially them Japs. . . . Lucky I don't have any relations killed in this war, I'd go out and kill me some Japs!"

These men are consistently fascist in their longing for a "strong" antidemocratic government, to maintain monopolistic "free enterprise" by force if necessary against the challenge of democratic equalitarianism. The underlying wish to submit to antidemocratic "strength" and "leadership" is implicit in the pseudodemocratic ideology of the other high scorers. In the questionnaire, it appears most clearly in Item 30 (see Table 4(XXI)), which hints that "force may be necessary" to preserve the *status quo*. This item is quite discriminating even though its group mean is lower than that for most items. Very few low scorers agree with it. Two other items reflect similar attitudes much more indirectly, and discriminate either poorly (Item 23) or insignificantly (Item 22) (see Table 4(XXI)). But the idea is expressed more directly by the fascist inmates. The aspect of authoritarian suppression was illustrated in the previous paragraph. The *Führer* idea is also made explicit by these men:

Thus, Adrian: "I believe in government control because . . . if we know somebody's at the helm, we can't have revolutions and things." He longs to go "back": "I still believe in the Old Order, and I believe we were happiest under Hoover and should have kept him in"; "I'll always thumbs down anything new!" "I have never forgiven France for her Revolution, or Mexico." . . . Buck's authoritarian mentality requires no political sophistication to reach a similar conclusion. Concerning government controls, he has this to say: "You got to have somebody at the head of things to keep it organized." . . . Floyd's cynical approval of Nazi "coordination" was described earlier in discussing racism.

These men's racism can be isolated only by artificial analysis from their "politics." The examples given above for ideological opportunism in the race attitudes could serve almost equally well to exemplify politico-economic opportunism. Here are some additional examples, however, which do not directly involve racism:

Floyd's preoccupation with "toughness," power, and "efficiency" for their own sake—without respect for human aims or purposes—drives him into a striking self-contradiction. His submissive respect for business power leads him to say of government controls over business: "Modified form, approve of. Too stringent, no." But in the next breath his need for "strength" combines with his political confusion to produce this contradictory attitude toward O.P.A. price control (in December, 1945): "If they had an iron glove underneath their kid glove, be all right. They fine a guy (only) $100 for makin' $100,000." . . . Buck, who is intellectually duller than Floyd or Adrian, reveals directly the egocentrism behind his ideological opportunism. He evaluates public policies in terms of benefit to his local ingroup (in this case his home state): "Hell, at that, I was strong for Roosevelt. One thing he done for that state, he put that dam there. We didn't need the war, though!" . . . Adrian's views on inheritance taxes betray a similar egocentric motivation: "I think I would have had more money under (Hoover), too, and I don't believe in inheritance taxes. If I earn $100,000 by the sweat of my brow, I ought to be able to leave it to whomever I please. I really don't believe that all men are created free and equal." (At the age of 31, Adrian has by his own admission earned less than $2,000 in his lifetime "by the sweat of my brow," aside from the returns of homosexual prostitution.)

5. LOW SCORERS

None of the low-scoring interviewees obtained a low PEC score, and all of them displayed rather conservative attitudes when interviewed. Art and Jim are less conservative than Dick and Don. The latter two conceive themselves as ambitious young entrepreneurs in an expanding economy—a fact which definitely affects their politico-economic views. These individual differences will be somewhat neglected, however, in favor of what the four men show in common. Their present orientation is by and large conservative, although they seem to be less power-oriented than the high scorers and more willing to reconcile conservatism with democratic values. They appear to share the traditional belief in an expanding capitalist economy, conceived as largely self-governing and as "individualistic" rather than monopoly-dominated. They show some willingness to carry out "free enterprise" principles by controlling or nationalizing monopolies that destroy "economic freedom."

Typical is Jim's view that "I'd much rather see private industry control things than the government," but "in big organizations, monopolies . . . I think (the government) should control them." Dick expresses the same idea: "If a business gets out of hand, (government) should take it over. But if the business is run okay, they should keep hands off."

These men's conservatism poses a dilemma for their democratic values.

Faced with the conflict between business and labor, they are caught between their inclination to identify with labor and their conservative fear of resisting *status quo* power. This leads to the same gesture of impartiality which appeared in Art's views on "the Negro problem." Art says, "I don't like to divide people into classes." What he seems to mean is that he is reluctant to "see" existing conflicts between business and labor. For to "see" such conflicts exerts an implicit pressure to take sides; specifically, for a democrat such as Art, on the side of the underdog. But this arouses his anxiety about carrying through democratic resistance against established power. He protects himself from such anxiety by trying to deny the existence of economic power conflicts. This denial can only mean implicit support of the *status quo* and consequent resentment of what he perceives as "troublemakers" who stir up his anxiety by resisting the *status quo*.

Thus he objects to the C.I.O. Political Action Committee because "I don't believe they should . . . set themselves off as a class." About the then current 30 per cent wage increase demands he declares: "Whether they are right or wrong is unimportant. The important thing is that they are grouping together." But Art is made uneasy by the fact that "grouping together" involves resisting powerful employers, and concludes: "As far as these demands, or uncalled-for strikes, they have set back their own cause." . . . Don is also upset by the then current strikes, which "should be settled as quickly as possible, *one way or the other*." (Italics supplied.) By thus opposing conflict as such and ignoring issues, Don tries hard to maintain an appearance of impartiality; he pictures both employers and employees as giants and as equals. "I believe both labor and business sort of ignore the little fellow." More generally, "I am against special interests and pressure groups." But the illogicality of this position combines with the difficulty of avoiding sides, to push him into attacking labor and implicitly supporting the employers: "I am sort of bitter about this strike business. . . . I feel labor should have more responsibility." . . . Dick becomes even more conservative in his fear of "agitation": "I admire unions, but they shouldn't agitate. . . . They shouldn't try to get more money, but should help people more (by trying) to keep prices down." Of the then current strikes, he decides that the employers should pay the wage demands if they can, but hints that they probably cannot "afford to." . . . Jim's views seem to express a kind of transition stage. Fundamentally conservative in his laissez-faire orientation, he is nonetheless concerned that "politics are not really controlled by the people." Moreover, his conception of an ideal society reflects a tendency to identify with the economic needs of *all* people: "An ideal society would provide employment for all able-bodied citizens, and it would also take care of all those that weren't able to work, as well as the aged, and it would give every family a home and a car and a salary in sufficient quantities so that they might enjoy the privileges that we are aware of." Yet, despite his recognition that "the majority of the people do come under . . . labor," he is made a little uneasy by the militancy of some C.I.O. unions: "The A. F. of L., I'm in favor of it very much. The C.I.O., formerly I wasn't in favor of it, but as time goes on, the people seem to accept it more and more. . . . The (C.I.O.) unions in the beginning used pretty high-handed methods." His final conclusion hints at an inner struggle to accept C.I.O. resistance to established power: "But perhaps the end will justify the means."

The above examples indicate that these men suffer from inner conflicts in relation to authority and power, which are similar to the power conflicts of the high scorers. Their difference from the high scorers seems to be mainly a matter of degree. The democratic identifications of the low scorers are stronger. Their ability to resist authoritarian power is somewhat greater, and aggressiveness toward unjust authority seems closer to conscious acceptance. Their relative freedom from ethnocentrism renders them less susceptible to fascist pressures.

D. MORALS AND RELIGION

1. GENERAL QUESTIONNAIRE STATISTICS: THE F SCALE

Since questionnaire results on some of the F-scale items, as well as corresponding interview material, are introduced in this section, it may be helpful at this point to present the general statistical findings for the F scale. Item means and D.P.'s are given in Table 4 (XXI). The over-all group mean per person per item for the F scale is 4.73, the *highest mean obtained for any group studied*. This provides further support for the implications drawn from the E-scale results, viz., that the types of criminals most frequently found in a state prison are antidemocratically repressive toward themselves as well as others. Moreover, there are *no extremely low scorers* and only a handful of moderately low scorers: The low quartile range of F scores, in terms of mean per person per item scores, extends from 2.0 to 4.1, with a mean of 3.7. This suggests that nearly all forms of criminal behavior tend to be incompatible with the kind of liberalism reflected in very low scores on the F scale.

The F-scale reliability coefficient of .87 is satisfactory. That it is considerably higher than the E-scale reliability of .65 may be attributed in good part to the fact that the F scale is three times as long, so that factors like attenuation of the lower end of the distribution affect the reliability much less.

The E-F correlation is .59, somewhat lower than that obtained for other groups. This might be interpreted as due mainly to the factors responsible for the inadequate E-scale reliability, discussed in Section B of this chapter. Similarly, the very low F-PEC correlation of .23 might be attributed mainly to the factors discussed in Section C, regarded as impairing the validity of the PEC scale for the Prison Group.

2. HIGH SCORERS

In discussing the prejudiced inmates' moral-religious ideology, attention is centered upon their moral repressiveness toward themselves and others. Discussed more briefly are feelings of distrust-victimization toward people, and submissiveness to religious authority.

It has been indicated above how these men's ideology is distorted by conceiving broad social processes in narrow, personalized terms. By contrast, as the rest of this chapter attempts to show, they tend to impersonalize relationships which a healthy person might be expected to personalize, namely, personal relationships with other individuals and with themselves. In fact, it has been repeatedly indicated in this book that the failure to become solidly identified with other people and with one's real self is the basic cause of receptiveness to authoritarian ideology. Such ideology, instead of being an objective appraisal of social reality, tends to resemble a fantasy world in which unconscious impulses and fears are projected in personified form.

The tendency to impersonalize human relations takes an ideologized form in anti-instinctual moralism which has two aspects: authoritarian hostility toward "moral outgroups"; and moralistic repressiveness toward much of one's own feelings and impulses. Moralism has been exemplified earlier in discussing anti-Negro ideology. Examples from the questionnaire results include items expressing moralistic condemnation of "zootsuiters" (Item 5); rejection of people with "bad manners, habits, and breeding" (Item 12); and authoritarian aggression against "sex criminals" (Item 25), "immoral, crooked, and feebleminded people" (Item 34), and homosexuals (Item 39). (See Tables 2(XXI) and 4(XXI). For all questionnaire items referred to in the remainder of the chapter, see Table 4(XXI) unless otherwise specified.) A related item reflects obsessive fears of contamination by "so many different kinds of people" (Item 18), who may symbolize dangers of instinctual contagion. All of these items are clearly discriminating except for Item 12, which yields one of the highest over-all means in the F scale. A possible interpretation is that Item 12 is especially calculated to appeal to the eagerness of most inmates to be accepted again by "decent people."

Similar moralism appears in the interviews with prejudiced inmates. In some of these men, the moralism has a religious coloring.

For example, Clarence asserts a rigid dichotomy between "good Christians" and "bad non-Christians": "The Christian tries to live a Christian life, and others go out and rob and steal, drink, carouse around, do a little of everything." When Clarence became a professional soldier, this meant for him living a "clean life." Wilbur has an equally moralistic conception: Being a Christian means "not to swear, use bad words, or down the other fellow," and "to behave and do right, live a clean life." Wilbur regards atheists as "pretty bad people." Robert, too, emphasizes submission to extrahuman absolutes: "Christians are people that at all times strive to do what is right, and abide by God's word."

The religious formulation is, however, incidental to the moralistic approach to life. This manner of thinking appears as a general characteristic in various personality topics yet to be discussed. Here are some examples of antisexual righteousness in the prejudiced men.

Clarence moralizes that "I don't think it's a very good subject to teach" children, for "they learn it soon enough." He speaks with approval of the fact that "when I was a kid . . . if you met a girl on the street, you'd blush." . . . Likewise, Wilbur,

TABLE 4 (XXI)

RESULTS ON THE F SCALE FROM THE GROUP OF PRISON INMATES

	Item	High Quartile Mean/Person	Low Quartile Mean/Person	D.P.	Over-all
1.	(Obedience and respect)	6.66	5.75	0.91	6.45
2.	(Will power)	6.62	4.93	1.69	5.81
4.	(Science)	6.00	3.64	2.36	4.93
6.	(War and conflict)	6.17	4.82	1.35	5.68
8.	(Supernatural power)	5.93	3.43	2.50	4.44
9.	(Cheerful things)	5.38	2.79	2.59	3.92
12.	(Bad manners)	6.14	5.68	0.46	5.85
13.	(Discipline and determination)	6.69	4.50	2.19	5.51
16.	(Born with urge)	5.24	3.07	2.17	4.07
18.	(Infection and disease)	6.66	4.64	2.02	5.68
19.	(Honor)	5.52	2.46	3.06	3.91
21.	(Rebellious ideas)	6.52	5.39	1.13	6.07
22.	(Germany)	5.76	5.32	0.44	5.48
23.	(Devoted leaders)	5.59	4.57	1.02	5.45
25.	(Sex crimes)	5.86	2.32	3.54	4.49
26.	(Weak and strong)	6.28	2.64	3.64	4.24
27.	(Undying love)	6.79	4.07	2.72	5.75
29.	(Astrology)	5.72	3.25	2.47	4.69
30.	(Force to preserve)	5.10	1.86	3.24	3.44
31.	(Prying)	6.07	4.21	1.86	5.31
33.	(Earthquake)	4.00	2.25	1.75	3.07
34.	(Immoral people)	4.83	2.64	2.19	3.37
35.	(Wild sex life)	6.07	3.25	2.82	4.62
37.	(Talk less)	6.69	5.36	1.33	5.94
38.	(Plots)	5.97	2.82	3.15	4.45
39.	(Homosexuals)	5.14	2.21	2.93	3.45
41.	(Artists)	4.38	2.36	2.02	3.08
42.	(No sane, normal person)	6.41	4.11	2.30	5.42
43.	(Familiarity)	5.17	3.93	1.24	4.34
44.	(Suffering)	4.79	2.04	2.75	2.95
	Total mean/person	174.15	110.31	63.84	141.86
	Mean/person/item	5.80	3.68	2.13	4.73
	Range	5.4–6.8	2.0–4.1		2.0–6.8

Standard Deviation: .86
Reliability: .87

asked what things annoy him most in others, expresses concern about "doing things before little children that you shouldn't," "doing anything out of the way to a little nine-year-old girl." . . . Ronald is alarmed by the "sexual perversion that you'll find in this country today: it's pretty bad. (Q.) . . . fellatio . . . sodomy." Robert's focus is somewhat less extrapunitive but reveals an equally externalizing attitude toward his own sexuality: Sometimes, he admits, "I have let myself slip, let my carnal self get away from me"; but in general he feels that he has "always lived up to" his mother's precept that "a woman is the most perfect thing in the world."

Similar nonreligious moralism appears in *nonsexual* contexts.

Eugene believes that "good persons . . . won't smoke or drink," and is "going to lay off drinking." His moralistic hostility against Negroes for "fighting" and "causing trouble" has already been described. . . . Ronald finds himself disturbed by "petty habits" involving nose, muscles, or skin, such as "snorting," "twitching their shoulders," or "my wife's habit of picking at things with her fingernails." He is also upset by "greed": "I can't stand anyone who will take something without thinking about the other person." And he makes repeated references to "politeness," complaining that "it's changed around here (in the prison) now—getting so many of these young kids, zootsuiters: don't have any tact at all."

All 5 of these high-scoring men express generalized moralizations about money or work or both.

Several of them show inhibitions about enjoying money: Its importance is in having "just enough to get along on"; beyond that "it can bring a lot of unhappiness" (Eugene). "If it's not too *much* money, it can give you happiness. If it's too much, it won't." "To me the only thing you need money for is to satisfy your basic needs: food, clothing, shelter" (Robert). . . . Work for the sake of "discipline" and "control" is exalted by all but Ronald: "I don't think you enjoy things as much when you work for them" (Robert). "I think it's a special privilege for a man to have some special handicap: it gives him a special drive" (Robert). "Work don't hurt no people. These child labor laws, I believe, are makin' more trouble than anything else" by preventing children from working to keep themselves "out of trouble" (Clarence). Asked how he and his wife are most alike, Wilbur declares: "Well, she don't like to run around so much and I don't either. We both like to work." Eugene, although he adds other similarities, says the same thing of his mother and himself: "She likes to work and so do I." . . . This antipleasure submission to work and hardship as desirable is expressed also in questionnaire Item 44, which exalts the value of "suffering." This item has a fairly high Discriminatory Power.

The moralism just described appears to be an anxious attempt by these men to keep instinctual impulses repressed and externalized. Their anxiety toward their own impulses is suggested by their responses to the projective question, "What desires do you often have difficulty in controlling?" Their answers reveal efforts to separate their impulses from their conscious selves and to avoid awareness of inner feelings by focusing on external behavior and situations. Three "desires" thus externalized recur with monotonous regularity: "drinking;" "fighting" or "temper"; and "when I'm out with a lady" or "intercourse."[18]

It is not necessary to rely on inference in stating that the prejudiced men's conscience is externalized and therefore undependable. Evidence for this appears in their violations of their own moralism.

Clarence's moralism about sex and drinking may be contrasted with his history of three separate offenses of attempted rape on pre-adolescent girls after getting them drunk. His insistence on the virtue of hard work, and overconcern about people who "rob and steal" is quite interesting in view of the prison medical examiner's opinion that he was "wrongly drawing Army compensation for years" on a claim of tuberculosis, and thus avoiding work. . . . The only gross moral violation revealed in Wilbur's interview protocol is his panicky homicidal attack upon his landlord. Despite his defensive paranoid rationalizations about this, he gives evidence of regarding it, in another compartment of his thinking, as "immoral" in his own terms: "Don't think I would be in so much trouble if I lived up to the church." . . . Robert, with his moralistic "respect" for "woman" as "the most perfect thing in the world," has let his "carnal self get away" from him in relation to "the most perfect thing": While ostensibly still "in love" with his wife, he engaged in a violent affair with an extremely promiscuous woman whom he finally shot in a quarrel. And despite his insistence that one must work for things as a condition of "enjoying them," he served an earlier prison term for "enjoying" several hundred dollars' worth of forged checks. . . . Ronald's condemnation of "greed" may be compared with his long record of thefts and gang robberies which he engaged in, by his own description, "as a business." Also after condemning "sexual perversion" and especially homosexuality, he confessed to having had fellatio performed upon him occasionally in prison, but denied that this was homosexuality by disclaiming any emotional involvement in it. . . . Eugene's moralism against "drinking," "fighting," and "causing trouble," and his statement that he "likes to work," stand in contrast with his long history of "trouble," including eight jail sentences for drunkenness and one for battery, frequent fights, an earlier term for robbery, and the present term for a series of forged checks.

Relevant here are some suggestive statistical data for the 23 inmates whose present term is for a sex offense (rape, "molesting" children, etc.). The lowest E score obtained by any sex offender is 3.4 per item;[19] the E-scale mean for all sex offenders is 5.1 per item, as compared with the general group mean of 4.7. This high degree of ethnocentric hostility toward outgroups is of particular interest, when it is considered that these men themselves are generally scorned as an outgroup by other inmates. But of even greater significance

[18] In contrast, of the 7 inmates whose E scores fall in what would be the low quartile for most other groups (below 2.6 per item), none gives this type of response. Instead, all of them express *inner* conflict—especially over passivity strivings—e.g., "the impulse to say 'to hell with it' when confronted by a difficult problem."

[19] This is excluding one sex offender who scored 2.7 per item on the E scale, but who was discovered in an interview (not reported here) to have answered the questionnaire rather carelessly. He indicated on questioning that on three E items (and several other items) he had inadvertently recorded "—3" where he had intended "+3."

is the fact that two-thirds of these men (15 out of 23) agree with Item 25, which states that "Sex crimes . . . deserve more than mere imprisonment; such criminals ought to be publicly whipped, or worse." Half of them (12 out of 23) agree with Item 39, which expresses punitive hostility toward homosexuals. Three-fourths of them (17 out of 23) agree with Item 35, which reflects projective fantasy preoccupations concerning the prevalence of "wild" sexual "goings-on." All but 2 (21 out of 23) sex offenders agree with at least one of these items; 16 agree with two items; 7 agree with all three items. These findings provide further evidence that moralism often involves a desperate attempt to keep one's own repressed impulses under tight control. Two of the interviewees (Clarence and a middle scorer not reported here) deny their (repeated) sex offenses, and insist that they were "framed." It is possible that they actually believe the memory distortions by which they seek to maintain a precarious self-respect. Prison authorities report that the majority of sex offenders deny their offenses, and, further, that such offenders are generally self-righteous and "good."

Evidence has accumulated in this volume to show that impulses which are moralistically condemned in others symbolize the feared impulses of the moralizer himself. Corresponding, on the other hand, to ethnocentric fears of being abused by fantasied "dominant" outgroups such as Jews, are feelings of distrust, victimization, and cynicism toward the world. Some examples have already been mentioned, such as Wilbur's feelings of being victimized by "the Greeks"; and the personal bitterness of Ronald (a recidivist) toward the governor of the state as "a persecutor"—associated with his resentment at not having been released because of the parole system's "nine thousand restrictions. . . . It stinks."

Analogous are Clarence's delusions about having been "framed" by "the people in politics" (his defense-rationale against remembering his sex offenses). Clarence expresses succinctly his suspicious conception of the world as a jungle: "Nowadays it's get the other fellow before he gets you." He seems to want to avoid the necessity of having to trust others, by avoiding dependence on anyone; thus the main value of having a lot of money is that a person "don't have to depend on anybody or anything." Associated with this diffuse distrust of people is a fear of "prying," resentment against people's "not being able to attend to their own business" (Ronald), against "a guy trying to butt in my business" (Eugene). . . . Robert, whose life goal is to "own three —— stores," feels especially abused by "spongers . . . these so-called shoppers who . . . pick over all the —— and pick out the one on the bottom."

This suspiciousness is expressed in several questionnaire items, such as those betraying a cynical view of "human nature" as inherently warlike (Item 6), fears of "prying" (Item 31), and fantasies about secret "plots" which "control our lives" (Item 38). The last item, which reflects the victimization theme most directly, has much the highest Discriminatory Power.

A further aspect of the high scorers' moral-religious ideology is their dependence and submission to authority in religion and morals. Such basic submission is in striking contrast with their exaggerated fears of having to submit to domination by outgroups—Jews, Negroes, labor, "Reds," Russia, etc. Authoritarian submission in the moral-religious sphere is expressed in three main ways. In every prejudiced interviewee, as the foregoing discussion has emphasized, there seems to be a submissive self-negating overconformity to externalized, conventional moralism. This requires no further elaboration here.

A second aspect is the submissive emphasis on unquestioning belief in religious authority. Questionnaire Item 8, which is clearly discriminating, expresses the core of this attitude: Everyone should submit "without question" to the "decisions" of "some supernatural power" in whom he has "complete faith." In the interviews, the three most conventional high scorers are definitely traditionalists in religion.

Robert reiterates the point that "I believe pretty strongly along the lines of the Bible." Both Clarence and Wilbur declare categorically that they have never questioned any of the (fundamentalist) religious teachings of their parents. . . . Religion is more remote for Eugene, who confesses that "I don't know" the Ten Commandments or Christ's teachings. But he states that the most important thing in religion is "belief . . . in Jesus Christ, the Bible," and "I've always believed in it." Even Ronald, who says that he no longer "believes," reveals that his is not the integrated philosophy of "a staunch free-thinker" who has no need for external props of "faith." Rather, he suffers from a hollow cynicism, and longs to surrender himself dependently to "God." The most important thing in religion, he declares, is "belief." "I think that belief in anything—that's the thing that holds you together." More personally: "It seems as if I want to believe in the Supreme Being, but try and keep it suppressed." The source of this conflict is suggested later in discussing Ronald's relations with his father.

The third aspect of authoritarian submission in religion on the part of these men is their submissive relationship to their deity, conceived as a dominating "supreme" power.

God is "someone a lot bigger and stronger than anyone on this earth (Robert), who "rules all things" (Clarence), and whose "word" in the Bible one is called upon to "live up to" (Wilbur) and "abide by" (Robert). Ronald's longing for such submission has just been mentioned. It is of interest that Eugene, who never knew his father, is the only one of these men whose conception of God appears to be quite blank: "Just believe in it and that's about all."

The prejudiced men's repression of a large part of their selves, their intellectual-emotional submissiveness in the moral-religious sphere, their anti-intraceptive narrowing of inner freedom—all these trends weaken their intellectual strength. Loss of conscious awareness of so much of one's self tends to undermine one's confidence in human ability to understand the world in general, and to render one susceptible to various forms of mysticism—especially mystical interpretations of human behavior. These trends are thus conducive to agreement with such questionnaire items, all clearly discriminating between high and low quartiles, as those stressing the limitations of human understanding (Item 4), admitting belief in astrology (Item 29), and assuming a mystical-hereditarian (externalized) explanation for some people's "urge to jump from high places" (Item 16). The general tendency toward mysticism and intellectual defeatism appears as a formal characteristic of many quotations from the present high scorers.

3. FASCISTS

Certain attitudes implicit in the approach of the pseudodemocratic high scorers break through explicitly in the fascists. To begin with, the authoritarian hostility toward people implicit in moralism appears in the fascists as open hate and contempt for people, directed especially toward moral-outgroups. The attempt to bolster up self-esteem by identifying oneself with an (hereditarian) élite, is also more openly expressed by these men.

Floyd shows the hatred for people in its most extreme form, when asked what things irritate him most in others. "Just that they're people! (How do you mean?) Oh, the majority are ignorant, close to animals as anything else. I mean *dumb* animals! (Can you elaborate on that?) They haven't got sense enough to see things as they are, they are easily swayed, crude, uncouth, they are like a pack. Show 'em a leader and they will go anywhere." . . . Buck's authoritarian hate is not "systematized" into an explicit ideology like Floyd's, but his interview protocol is filled with expressions of hate and contempt for "slummy women" and "goddam ch——"; for "j—— o—— happy idiots," "sex maniacs," "goddam syphilitic people" (homosexuals); "people that go around stealin' "; other inmates—"Hell, you can't have real friends in here. . . . Stab you in the back. Can't trust many of them"— and everyone else regarded as outside "my own class of people." . . . Adrian is too deferential to use the same strong language as these men, but his antidemocratic hatreds seem clear. His contempt for "people who never had anything" and for workers generally has already been mentioned. Interesting is his emphatic dichotomy between men and women, and his authoritarian hostility toward both. It is men who evoke his deepest anxiety and hate: "A lot of people irritate me, a lot of *men* irritate me by what I think is a superior attitude that women don't usually have"; "*all* men are more or less supercilious." Having self-protectively identified himself with what he conceives as the submissive-dependent role of women vis-à-vis men—"I identify myself with the dependent kind" of woman—Adrian adopts an essentially paranoid attitude toward *all* men in terms of this identification: "I don't think men respect women, or anything about women, the way they ought to. . . . Women aren't inferior to men. If anything, they are superior!" (The possibility of equality is alien to his thinking; the only choices he knows are to submit or to dominate, to be superior or inferior.) Yet, in his role as would-be aristocrat, Adrian shares the same chauvinistic attitudes toward women which (in his paranoid submissive-"feminine" role) he ostensibly criticizes. As a persecuted "woman" he protests that "women make better business women than men do"; but as an aristocrat, "I don't approve of women in business." He even mentions an episode in which he was strongly condemned by a woman for his "supercilious" attitude toward her and toward women who work.

The lack of a genuine conscience is scarcely even concealed by a moralistic façade in the fascists. They display an externalized, undeveloped superego. One aspect of this is an absence of inner guilt over violation of values; no ethical values have really been incorporated into the self. What superego activity exists is almost entirely limited to fear of external punishment or social ostracism.

Buck suggests in almost so many words that his superego is merely an external mystical "power": "There must be some power over us to punish us. . . . He's sure givin' me hell, bein' in here." This "hell" is not the torture of a guilty conscience. On the contrary, Buck explains that being in prison "hurts my pride" and "hurts my business," when "I could be out there makin' money all the time." The cause of his delinquency (a long trail of bad checks, passed on an extended spree with a woman) is for him purely external: Lying about many details, he bemoans that "a man of my intelligence[20] let some damn broad put me behind bars." . . . Floyd, too, shows no signs of actual guilt over his long record of delinquencies. On his admission to prison he is described by an interviewer as feeling "that his present series of violent robberies doesn't mean a thing." To the present examiner, he mentions these as "just something that happened." He is reported to have said on admission: "We heard about others getting caught but couldn't believe we would." . . . Adrian attributes his various delinquencies to drinking: "That's all my trouble is." According to the initial prison interview report, "he does not feel that he has any serious problem except a tendency to get very drunk when discouraged." Adrian's conscience, too, is organized chiefly around fears of ostracism and of punitive agencies mystically assigned to an "intangible something" outside himself: "I *do* believe in retribution. We pay right here. I've proved that in my own life. We think we can get away with things. It's an illusion." (Adrian has spent "most of my life" in jails, prison, or "on probation.") With respect to ostracism: "I have always been greatly concerned with what other people thought about me." As will be elaborated later, he is especially apprehensive over rejection by his father, who "haunts me" and whose approval is required to allay Adrian's anxiety: "I'm always wondering if he would approve of this or approve of that."

A second aspect of the fascists' undeveloped superego is its domination by the pleasure principle. They are quite unable to postpone gratification. Unable to pursue any integrated long-term achievement goals, they are at the mercy of an imperious oral-demandingness.

Describing with much braggadocio his sharp dealings in cattle trading (actually, he lost a sizeable inheritance by mismanagement and drunken neglect), Buck bemoans openly that ordinary ways of doing business are "too damn slow for me." (Recall his anti-Semitic projection about Jews' "beatin' a guy out of his money.") Admittedly, "money is the main object. . . . Can't buy nothin' without money. . . . Can't buy whiskey."

These attitudes are part of an essentially egocentric conception of reality. The following is one of many similar remarks made by Buck in his discussion of politico-economic affairs:

"I never paid no attention to that ———; get me out of here and out on that damn

[20] Buck obtained a Wechsler-Bellevue Full-Scale I.Q. of 83.

range is all I want." . . . Similarly, Floyd states that the $59 a week he received on his last job (which he held for a month) was "too slow" because "I started from scratch." "Had to acquire everything: clothes, quarters, the fundamentals." Detailing on admission to the prison some of the robberies and orgies of his gang, Floyd explains that "We had to have money to operate on. We spent $40 or so for our dinner parties." . . . Adrian admits that from infancy he "usually got my way." "In fact, all I ever had to do was cry about anything." At the several boarding schools where his father placed him after his mother's death (when he was 5), "I was incorrigible, left school when I pleased. I overdrew my charge account . . ." His self-centered definition of reality is made explicit: "When things don't *personally* concern me, they just don't *exist* for me."

Implicit in these men's weak conscience, their infantile-demanding impulses, and their egocentric view of the world, is a trait which governs their entire behavior. This is their extreme (personal) opportunism. The disregard of principle in their personal behavior corresponds with the ideological opportunism of their racism and reactionism. The personal opportunism is usually expressed in the service of infantile attitudes of omnipotence, and of trying to deny personal weakness.

Buck's pathological lying has been mentioned. As for his other offenses, he has served time for obtaining money on false pretenses, and for failure to provide for his children. He was arrested on one occasion for "molesting" his own children (girl then age 2-3, boy age 4-5), but it is reported the charges were dropped because the children were too small to testify. . . . Floyd's delinquencies are less dramatic, but equally capricious. They include two jail sentences for disturbing the peace; an Army record of alternating between the guardhouse and repeated A.W.O.L.'s until he was discharged; and a series of armed gang robberies undertaken as an easy way of making a lot of money "to operate on." Relevant here is Floyd's stated desire to marry a "wealthy woman," who should have "fair physical attractions" but whose personality he will "take as it comes." . . . Adrian's delinquencies include his self-styled "incorrigibility" at boarding schools (truancy, repeatedly overdrawing his charge accounts, etc.); numerous jail sentences for drunkenness and homosexual prostitution; and robbery. "I had probation, it seems to me, most of my life." He supported himself mainly by prostitution, and by his own statement "never had any (sexual) relations with anyone that didn't have money connected with it." He admits that some men attract him more than others, but "I never let preferences stand in the way. . . . The only thing I was ever interested in was the rent."

The essentially frantic nature of these men's approach to life suggests a desperate inner emptiness and lack of moorings. This hollowness may provide part of the basis for their wish to submit to "strong" political "leadership." Further, any religious leanings of these men might be expected to express cravings for authoritarian submission. This would be expected to differ from the religious authoritarian submission of other high scorers in two interrelated aspects. As in other conflicts in the fascists, the craving for religious submission might very well be explicit rather than implicit; and since dominance-submission conflicts are involved, this craving might be expressed with open ideological opportunism. It happens that Buck "never did think much about religion," but Adrian and Floyd reveal these very characteristics clearly. Floyd's opportunism takes the form of highly egocentric (as well as confused) "criteria" for belief, with no apparent interest in considerations of evidence or truth-falsity.

Floyd states that before he was shot (almost fatally) in his last gang robbery, he was "reaching for something" and "wanted" to believe in God. (He had never had any religious training; his father was a free-thinker, and he had never known his mother.) But "I just couldn't feature that a human being, an intelligence, could be obliterated so easily." Having been thus let down "personally" by the God he was "reaching for" (in that his delinquency led to disaster), he could no longer "believe." . . . Adrian's religious training consisted of very early exposure to the Christian Science of a governess and living in Episcopal boarding schools from the ages of 8 to 15. At 15 he tried to submit to what for him seemed clearly to represent religious totalitarianism and voluntary self-emasculation: "I very seriously went into the Church of Rome at 15" to become a priest—not because of any specific religious convictions, but "because I believed and still do . . . that the Catholic Church is the only true church," since "she *was* the church founded by Christ." "She was the first" and therefore "the other churches had no real excuse to break away." His fascistic inclinations are stated openly: "I respect her as a political organization. I think it would be better to have everything under one head. It would save dissension." Adrian's father forcibly interfered, however, to prevent his entry into the priesthood. Adrian drifted until he became "very interested in Christian Science" with quite practical motives: "I'm not positive I believe in Christian Science, but there's much in it that seems to help me. . . . I don't try to apply Christian Science to physical things . . . but my worries, mental things—there's where it helps me most." In anticipation of parole, he wrote to two Christian Science practitioners for aid in lining up a job (a prerequisite to being granted parole). When both of them criticized him for "trying to *manifest* a job" instead of relying mystically upon "the Divine Employer," Adrian was "never so disgusted in my life." But Adrian admittedly has "got to have a God" to submit to, "So what do you think I took up!" The answer is "Hinduism," which "teaches you *discipline*" such as "cutting down on cigarettes." Adrian summarizes his approach to his latest ideological "manipulandum" in this way: "It's *practical*. That's the main thing."

4. LOW SCORERS

The moral-religious ideology of the low-scoring interviewees is quite different from that of the prejudiced men. They are relatively free of moralism, and sometimes verbalize explicitly antimoralistic sentiments.

Thus, for Art religion has "nothing to do with keeping laws, except the Golden Rule." Highly objectionable to Don is the idea of religion as "abiding by a certain set of rules." Probing reveals no sign of rejection in any of the 4 low scorers toward atheists or non-Christians.

They speak of religion primarily in terms of ethical values. Religion is "whatever spiritual qualities you have within yourself" (Art). This orientation is embedded in more individualized relationships to themselves and other people, as compared with the high scorers' impersonalization of such relationships. Different features of this ethical approach are stressed by each. Jim expresses most clearly the aspect of nurturant-affiliative attitudes toward people:

"I look on God as mostly the goodness in all peoples. . . . If everyone . . . carried out the principles that religion expounds, it would be a better world. (How do you mean?) To treat others as a person would wish to be treated himself, and to help those less fortunate than oneself, and to be a part of the community or society that one is in, to take an active part in it, and being kind and generous, and to more or less have a high regard for your fellow human being." Art, too, conceives of God, not as a person, but "more a power of good. . . . God is a force."

Another aspect is the emphasis on full expression of the individual personality and "happiness on earth."

Don declares that his concept of a hereafter was nicely expressed by a girl-friend who said that "if she believed in a hereafter it would mean developing one's undeveloped talents." For Jim "the only happiness that we really know of is here on earth; so why not try to enjoy the people and things on this earth, rather than a life somewhere else."

Further, a rich inner life is a religious value.

Religion "gives you some access to your thoughts" (Dick). Prayer is conceived not as a mode of securing gratification of personal desires or of paying obeisance to a parent-substitute God. Rather, prayer is something which in and of itself "can help a person" (Dick); which "helps form what you're to be" (Don); "a personal thing that happens when the lights are out before you retire. Not 'I want something or other,' but consciously putting into words so as to place whatever you are looking for into a positive plane" (Art).

Opposed to the prejudiced men's authoritarian submission in moral-religious matters is the insistence upon individuality in the credos of the low scorers.

"Religion is a personal thing. . . . Religion is as individual to me as my fingerprints, or as yours are to you" (Art). Dick explains his change from a Baptist to a Christian Scientist partly in terms of his objection to the teachings of a Navy chaplain, and especially the chaplain's efforts to "*force* us to come to church . . . I believe it's a man's personal affair." It happened that Dick "got hold of a Christian Science textbook, liked the ideas . . . the idea that they had an explanation for almost everything that happened." (Contrast Dick's emphasis on "ideas" and the implied internalization of Christian Science, with Adrian's externalized, opportunistic-manipulative approach.) Dick adds another value, however, which suggests some of that antiweakness drive that is usually typical of high scorers: "And another idea—they claimed that if you try to attain a goal, nothing can stop you."

It will be recalled that those who "believe" show submissiveness toward a God who is essentially dominating (whose "word" they must "abide by") and punitive (toward those who violate his "word"). The low scorers, on the other hand, show an optimistic and trusting dependence toward a God conceived as kind and nurturant.

Although spoken of as "kind of an infinite being" rather than directly anthropomorphic, God is "something there you can turn to in case you need someone to turn to" (Dick); "someone to cling to in times of emergency or stress" (Jim). Actually, "I don't know if there is a God," but the most important thing in religion is "a genuine belief and a faith that things would always turn out all right" (Jim). Religion involves "a belief, without academic proof, of a higher power—of something you can depend on, of dependency" (Art).

The *ultimate* optimism hinted in these statements is consistent with findings about low scorers generally. However, the lack of inner self-reliance implied by their dependence on a supernatural power resembles certain trends found to be more typical of high scorers generally. This latter aspect is consistent with the fact that none of the low-scoring interviewees scored extremely low on any of the questionnaire scales.

E. DEFENSES AGAINST WEAKNESS

1. HIGH SCORERS

Defenses against weakness seem to be especially pronounced in the prejudiced inmates. All of the high-scoring interviewees show deep-seated fears of weakness in themselves. The meaning of weakness to these men seems to be tied up with intense fears of nonmasculinity. To escape these fears they try to bolster themselves up by various antiweakness or pseudomasculinity defenses. These can be grouped into four general themes, each of which may be expressed in a certain formula: (1) *Power-strivings:* "I am not on the bottom, I am one of those on top"; or, "I do not weakly submit, I dominate and control, I have power." (2) *"Toughness":* "I am not weak, I am strong"; "I am not soft, I am tough"; "I am not passive and feminine, I am active and masculine." (3) *Flight into heterosexual activity:* "I am not homosexual, I am heterosexual"; or "I do not love him, I love her." (4) *Paranoid reactions:* "I do not love him, I hate him because he persecutes me"; i.e., "I do not feel submissive-homosexual desires, I feel aggressive resentment toward men because they persecute me."[21]

The questionnaire item which reflects defensive masculinity attitudes (specifically, "toughness" and power) in purest form is number 26, which stereotypically divides the world into "the strong" (ingroup) and "the weak" (outgroup). This item has the highest D.P. in the F scale. Other items containing antiweakness themes are those exalting "will power" (Item 2), "discipline" and "determination" (Item 13), an exaggerated notion of "honor"

---

[21] The formulae (3) and (4) are adapted from Freud (40).

(Item 19), as well as items already mentioned in another context, especially 14 (PEC), 23, 30, and 45 (E).

The relative emphasis placed on different aspects of masculinity façades, in relation to the fears underneath, differs from individual to individual. Therefore, instead of proceeding variable by variable, we shall discuss the weakness-antiweakness complex separately for each inmate.

Robert has centered his efforts to "prove" his "masculinity" around compulsive status-power strivings. He declares that from an early age "my greatest desire was to be somebody in life. . . . I wanted to be a success in business . . . and sometimes worried whether I would. . . . The future goal that I have set up is to own at least three . . . stores of my own . . . I was on my first store at the time of my arrest." This concern with status and power gives meaning to his anxious fantasy that Negroes "don't have a goal in life" but "just want to *exist*," and his envious stereotype of Jewish "drive and ambition to get there." Robert projects this compulsive power-drive onto others and reveals his inability to imagine any alternative to dominance or submission: "Every man has a certain ego that he has to satisfy. You like to be on top. If you're anybody at all, *you don't like to be on the bottom*." (Italics supplied.)

The submissive dependence behind Robert's power-seeking is shown in his attitudes toward friends and family. (What do friends offer a person?) "To me, friends offer satisfaction to myself that I've been doing a job well done, that I'm satisfying those people of their expectations. . . . (Q.) Well, I was referring to the business viewpoint." (Note the impersonalized use of people as primarily an external prop for what Robert calls his "ego.") His main satisfaction with his younger brother was "the satisfaction he gave my ego. . . . He's patterned his life after mine. He's in the —— business, too." Robert further expresses pride that "my folks have always classed me as a success in the —— business." The deference toward the examiner ("Do you think I have the right view of things?") has been mentioned before.

Robert's power drive has apparently not stopped his fears of femininity, of heterosexual impotence, and possibly of latent homosexuality. Underlying identification with a feminine *role* is suggested by his own admission that "up until the time I left home, (my mother) always referred to me as her best daughter." The possibility of conflict over latent homosexuality is raised by several cues: e.g., by Robert's insistence, despite instructions not to bother with details, on exhibitionistically giving to the examiner (a man) a minutely detailed account of his first experience of intercourse; and by indirect "contact" with other men via a hostile affair with a highly promiscuous woman. This last behavior, which finally broke up Robert's marriage, suggests a common type of defense against homosexual wishes, viz., compulsive flight into heterosexual relationships which are extremely impersonal and hostile.

Ronald's ego-alien weakness is more transparent than Robert's. Mentioned earlier was his unsatisfied dependent longing for authoritarian religious belief as "the thing that holds you together." Similar extreme dependence is shown in his conception of "friends" as "someone that you can . . . talk to about your troubles, and vice versa" and "know that he's there at all times, and if you need any help at any time." Also, like Robert, he asked the examiner to reassure him at the close of the interview that he is not "too radical" in some of his ideas. This "too radical" was apparently a euphemism for "too aggressive" toward outgroups. Ronald has a history of severe chronic bed-wetting until the age of 12, for which he has no explanation to offer beyond an externalization of the symptom onto "my kidneys." He has no idea why his enuresis suddenly stopped at the age of 12. That bed-wetting may have represented in part a passive mode of sexual gratification is suggested by his homosexual conflicts. Earlier mention has been made of his righteous condemnation of "sexual perversion" including, explicitly, fellatio. He denies that he has ever "felt any desire of any kind" for homosexual relations, yet subsequently admits to having several times had such relations with a fellow inmate. He implicitly denies any "real" homosexuality in this (blaming it exclusively on prison sex deprivation), and says that he had no special reaction to the experiences except to lose respect for the *other* man. Ronald's paranoid "toughness" toward Negro men might perhaps be a defense against homosexual excitement aroused by them. Ronald's promiscuous heterosexuality, including several impersonalized, unusual marriage ceremonies, may also be understood as an attempt to deny homosexual impulses. "I always get married spectacularly"—e.g., "in a taxicab" or "my partner in a dance walkathon—married on the floor—no love, but received money for it from the spectators." Both weakness and compensatory "toughness" seem to be combined in Ronald's thefts and gang robberies carried out "as a business."

The chief prop of *Eugene's* defenses is a façade of toughness. He has repeatedly been involved in petty trouble, especially by fighting when drunk. "I've got quite a temper," and "I like to fight once in a while . . . usually when I'm drinking." Moreover, "I'm proud of my people," the "Scotch-Irish," whose most prominent characteristic, according to Eugene, is that "most of them like to fight." When the examiner points out that this is precisely what Eugene resentfully says about Negroes, he differentiates on the basis that Negroes "go around looking" for fights, while he himself merely "likes" to fight (and does so frequently). The psychological reason why he likes to fight and has "quite a temper" seems to be largely unconscious; he "can't explain it." He explains, however, that Negroes "go around picking trouble" because they've "got an inferiority complex" and "try to be big shots"—which may be a projection of his own inferiority feelings and the "big shot" way he tries to compensate for them. The situations which evoke Eugene's temper suggest possibly more specific causes, namely homosexual impulses, against which his impulsive aggressiveness may be a paranoid defense: "I was with a girl at a bar, and a guy got a little out of line . . . talkin' dirty—not to her, but he was talkin' loud. . . ."; or "maybe some guy calls me a name." Eugene himself associates his propensity for "trouble" with fear of heterosexual adjustment: "I'm just a little too wild to get married. I'm scared of it."

Clarence shows more obvious signs of ego-alien "weakness," and has less effective defenses against it. The army, he declares, "makes a man of you," but it did not succeed in overcoming Clarence's fear of rising above a private, because that would have meant "too much responsibility"— although "I'm pretty good at *takin'* orders." Discharged for tuberculosis, he drew government compensation for seventeen years and then lived "on the county." According to the prison physician, Clarence "claimed he still had T.B., but . . . we failed to find any evidence of any active T.B. whatever. . . . We felt that he was wrongly drawing government compensation for years." This avoidance of work contrasts strikingly with Clarence's moralistic glorification of the disciplinary value of hard work. Moreover, to the prison physician Clarence appeared "very neurasthenic and enlarged on minor and rather normal aches and pains; was very feministic." He did not marry until he was 38, to a woman 39, toward whom he was apparently quite submissive. Although "we weren't much alike in any way . . . we got along good" because "I let her have her own way. Takes two to start an argument." It was only a few months after her death, eleven years later, that he was arrested for "molesting" four girls, ages 8 to 10, who testified that he felt of their genitals. Such behavior could well be a panicky attempt to deny homosexual impulses by "proving" heterosexual masculinity. Clarence claimed that the girls made up the entire story just to "get even" with him because he "wouldn't give them candy." Three years later, he was again arrested on a charge of getting two little girls drunk and attempting intercourse with one of them. He escaped conviction on these two occasions, but two years later the half-sister (age 12) of one of the last two little girls was picked up by the police at Clarence's home. This time he was convicted of attempted rape. Clarence seems to have denied this episode to himself by developing a system of persecutory delusions: He protests that he "worked for the people in politics in order to clean up the city," and that when his candidates were not elected the police "went after" him. This paranoid reaction is consistent with the interpretation that his heterosexual delinquency was a defense against homosexual panic.

Wilbur has also worked out a rigid system of paranoid delusions, but shows less obvious signs of underlying weakness than Clarence. For him, as for Robert and Ronald, friends mean primarily dependence; they offer "help in lots of needs, sickness, money—well, a friend can just help you in most any way." He indicates that, like Clarence, he has a very submissive relationship to his wife: His wife manages finances, gives the discipline to the children, and, when he and his wife disagree, "I usually do just what she asks me to do." In view of his reactions to the landlord, Wilbur may well have experienced a deep threat to his masculinity and possible homosexual panic directed toward a "persecuting" father figure, when he and his family were evicted following a controversy. He felt compelled to "fight back" in desperation; he sought out the landlord, who happened to be of Greek descent, and attacked him fatally. Apparently unable to face emotional conflicts stirred up by this episode, Wilbur stereotypically impersonalized the relationship by imagining himself as an unfortunate victim of "the Greek people, who like to punish the poor people."

These men are distinguished not only by the intensity of their conflicts about weakness, but also by a special feature of their defenses against weakness in themselves: In addition to the pseudomasculine *attitudes* which they share with prejudiced men in other groups, the high-scoring inmates express antiweakness themes overtly in delinquent behavior. This behavior has a superficial appearance of being an uninhibited expression of basic impulses. But closer observation reveals that the acts referred to are by no means free or expressive; they have an aspect of desperate compulsion, and can be understood as a defensive attempt to deny weakness. This defensiveness actually conceals intense inhibitions (as is shown elsewhere in this chapter) against genuine heterosexuality and against straightforward aggression against real authority and parent figures. It seems as if these men's uninternalized conscience combines with especially intense disturbance about weakness to produce delinquency, as an extreme type of antiweakness defense. Such actions are perhaps even more unrestrained in those interviewees we have called openly fascist.

2. FASCISTS

The antiweakness defenses appear in more extreme form in the fascists, with more unconcealed anxiety about inner weakness. *Buck's* deep fear that he may be a "sex maniac," his delinquent heterosexual behavior toward a 13-year-old girl and toward his own small children, have been discussed. Further hints of an obsessive fear of homosexuality are given in his reply to the questionnaire item asking what are the worst possible crimes. Besides rape and murder, Buck lists homosexual intercourse per anum. In the interview, he reveals graphic fantasies suggesting preoccupation with "any man that abuses any part of another man's body. . . . I could never see (he refers in profane language to sodomy and fellatio). Buck exhibits vain blustering in almost complete disregard of reality. He repeatedly interrupted the interview to protest, inappropriately, that "I can make money as well as the next guy." His emotional involvement in these unreal fantasies is suggested by his asking the examiner, "Do you think I can make it?"; and by his interview explanation of his response "worry" to the questionnaire item asking "What might drive a person nuts?": "Well, I'm worryin' here, I gotta make it *now*, or I'm not gonna make it. I'm gettin' pretty old. Well, not old—but it can't be done by foolin' around in the penitentiary." His greatest ambition, he declares, is to "buy more cattle, more land." Buck, as will be recalled, "made it" by leaving a trail of bad checks up and down the state.

Floyd says "I laugh at homosexuals," and he agrees very much with the questionnaire item that "homosexuals . . . ought to be severely punished." His promiscuous sexuality has already been described. Nonetheless, his feminine identifications are almost conscious. Asked on the questionnaire what great people he admires most, he lists "Salome, Madame DuBarry, Mata Hari." In the interview, he reveals that what he identifies with is their opportunistic rise from feminine submergence to positions of power. "Yeh, they did their share. (How do you mean?) I am particularly fond of women. . . . I like a woman who is capable. . . . DuBarry came up from a courtesan to be the indirect ruler of the country." Floyd's feminine-submissive-homosexual identifications appear also in his attitude toward his "crime partner," to whom he is deeply attached. Note the peculiar context in which status considerations irrelevantly intrude: "He's 30, but I guess we are *intellectual* equals if nothing else." And observe the preoccupation with physical relationships, with a consequently inappropriate response: (What sort of *person* is he?) "Well, he is short and heavy and light. I'm tall and lean and dark. We're physical opposites." Floyd is so preoccupied with his dependent role toward the other man that even further probing fails to elicit any real description of the latter's personality: (What sort of a guy is he?) "The best. (Can you give an example?) If he says something, he means it. And the thing that I thought most about him: the night—well, we walked into a police trap. The other fellow ran off, but *he* tried to come back and get me. . . . He's loyal." Thus, Floyd's devoted "lieutenant" relationship to his crime partner possibly enabled him indirectly to gratify submissive-homosexual wishes, at the same time as he was bolstering his masculinity as a "big operator" engaged in armed robberies.

For *Adrian*, the feminine-submissive-homosexual identifications require no inference. Since leaving school, he has lived as a homosexual prostitute, and "I look at all things from a feminine viewpoint." There is abundant evidence that his homosexuality is an acting-out of hate-filled power conflicts. Not only do "men irritate me by what I think is a superior attitude," but "I never did like homosexual affairs. . . . The actual physical act always repelled me and still does." It is as if Adrian is driven by some inner compulsion to "prove" to men again and again, by ingratiating effeminate behavior, that he is submissive and self-emasculated. He "could pet all night." But since he "found you can't get away with that," he submits further by doing "just whatever they want to." Adrian's resentment against such utter submission is expressed in opportunistic exploitation of the men who "kept" him: "I wasn't interested in anything except clothes and the rent." Frequent disagreements arose "about money—I never had as much money as I thought I ought to have. I'd always threaten to leave and go somewhere else. I usually got my way." The underlying wish to turn the tables and dominate the very men to whom he submitted is plain: "I ruled those roosts. (How do you mean?) I cooked what *I* wanted to cook and did what *I* wanted to do."

Adrian's "feminine viewpoint" is thus fundamentally sexless and loveless. He presents an extreme caricature of the façade which helps greatly to distinguish certain high-scoring women (see Chapter XI): exaggerated effeminacy of manner, ingratiating coyness, flirtatiousness, excessive attention to dress, ostentatious display of physical weakness with vague hypochondriacal complaining and appeal for pity, etc. The cynical exploitiveness hidden behind this façade is further exemplified in his favorite heroes of fiction—"Becky Sharp, Madame Bovary, and Ivy Lashton. . . . I don't *admire* anything in any of them. You asked me who I *liked* the best. Because they were all decidedly—what do you call it?—designing women." The power motif is even clearer in his identification with Mary Baker Eddy, whom he regards as "neurotic" and "I don't have much faith in (her) personally," but "I admire (her) immensely" as a "shrewd business woman."

Even Adrian, with his self-emasculated homosexual submission, made a stab at compensatory "toughness" in his present offense. While drinking in a bar, "I read in True Detective Stories about a girl who got herself up a bunch of hoodlums and raised herself a lot of hell. . . . And I figured if a little tiny thing like this girl could, I could." He proceeded to pick out from the customers at the bar the man who seemed "the most mean looking and corrupt," and suggested they do a robbery together. "I didn't intend to play the active role." "I thought he would do the dirty work but he wouldn't. So I had to." The man got Adrian a cap pistol and, by standing outside, gave him the moral courage to enter a store, where he held up "a very big man" and escaped with the cash register contents. Referring to this incident in discussing Hitler, Adrian himself formulates its fascistic implications: "I'm no leader, but I can follow. . . . Though I led when I had that gun, didn't I? . . . When you make people lead you, that means the same thing, doesn't it?"

Implicit in the "moralism-immorality" and "weakness-antiweakness" complexes of the pseudodemocratic high scorers, is a feature that becomes explicit in the fascists, namely, externalized self-contempt. This is termed externalized because what is despised is not regarded as really a part of the self but as somehow alien or accidental, something for which the subject does not really accept responsibility. *Floyd's* self-contempt is expressed in such remarks as "Only reason (anyone is) unemployed is they're lazy like me," and "My industriousness . . . just doesn't exist . . . just a black horse." He speaks of this as if it were an isolated trait unrelated to his personality as a whole—an accident of heredity "from the other (maternal) side of the family." Floyd says he was as a child "a typical fresh Irish kid. . . . Snot-nosed they used to call it"; "I didn't grow up"; "Everything I do is an act." . . . Buck, even in the same breath in which he blames all his troubles on "some damn b_____," declares that "I'm kind of ashamed; I'm the only black sheep in the family." Mention has been made earlier of his concern that "You don't think I'm a sex maniac, do you?" and "Do you think I can make it?" (i.e., money). This anxiety, combined with Buck's previous sex offenses, his gross financial mismanagement and fabricated financial exploits, suggests intense, externalized self-contempt. *Adrian* exhibits the most profound self-contempt of all. He describes himself as "spoiled," "selfish," "neurotic," dominated by "moral laxness," etc. Further, "I get along very well with old maids. I guess *I'm* kind of an old maid in my mental make-up." About homosexuality: "The whole subject is *repulsive* to me now. I'd just as soon forget I ever lived that sort of life." This last statement was made just before a short-lived parole, in which he quickly reverted to drinking and to homosexual prostitution.

3. LOW SCORERS

As mentioned before, the low-scoring interviewees, too, show some signs of conflicts about "weakness," but usually with this difference: Such conflicts are in these men more ego-accepted, instead of being denied by the anti-weakness pretenses appearing in the prejudiced men. The greater capacity of the low scorers to face these emotional problems seems to facilitate more constructive attempts at solving them, especially through persistent achievement-strivings (not a quest for external success only, but a striving to satisfy inner standards of self-expressive attainment). Related to this is a more general feature of their approach to life: the development of self-expressive interests that seem to be more than escapist distractions or ways of gaining status. Likewise, these men's more relaxed attitude toward masculinity (as compared with the prejudiced men) seems to have permitted them to develop soft-passive-feminine character traits and sublimated expressions of love-oriented homosexual impulses (not the ego-alien, hostile-submissive homosexual conflicts of the prejudiced men).

Art's "weakness" has been expressed primarily in his search for a nurturant mother figure on whom he could be dependent. When frustrated in this, he "arranged" to get himself into prison by writing bad checks and taking no precautions against being caught—in order to satisfy his dependency needs by using the prison as "mother." This is his own interpretation—worked out by consciously trying to understand his behavior in retrospect—by "auto-psychoanalysis." Art also verbalizes openly his "feeling of inferiority." His compensatory ambition is expressed in striving to satisfy inner values, to demonstrate his inner "abilities and capacities," to an extent that seems neurotically insistent: "I don't like to think of limits . . . on my own abilities and capaci-

ties." Deeply admiring his mother's "intellectual ability," Art was "very conscientious" in school and "was disappointed one time when I got a 'B' instead
of all 'A's.' " Having been "imbued" by his mother "with the idea that my
body was a precious possession and that I should take care of it," he trained
himself rigorously as "an athlete" and set a world's _____ record while
still in high school. A leg injury at this time interrupted his further athletic
career and prevented his entry into Annapolis; he was in bed with a cast on his
leg for nine months. Significantly, during this period of enforced, and complete, dependency on his mother (and to a lesser extent an older sister), Art
"broke training" by "smoking for the first time in my life" and also "started
drinking." It was as if, unable to accept this dependence and deprived of an
important part of his male ego identity as "an athlete," he needed to assert
his independence of maternal moral precepts and to prove that he was a
"big guy." . . . Art prefers "fine art" to his (and his father's) vocation of
commercial art. The former arouses real enthusiasm in him: "I'm immensely
happy in that type of work . . . tremendously interested in it." His main
interests are (as he describes them) explicitly intellectual and aesthetic.

Jim has a more disorganized background. His father, after years of violently maltreating the entire family, deserted them when Jim was 13. The
main burden of supporting the family now fell upon Jim. Although he had
done well enough in school to skip a grade, he now played truant for two
semesters, while struggling along on a paper route, odd jobs, and relief allot-
ments. The mother reports that when a doctor urged that she eat more fruit
for the sake of her health, Jim sometimes went without eating in order to buy
fruit for her. It was during this period that he engaged in several petty thefts;
he was arrested once, but the case was dismissed. Not long after the father
returned, following an eight-year absence, Jim began to work for him. But
when the father "scolded and nagged him one day," according to the
mother's report, "he refused to work for his father any more." This may help
to explain Jim's apparent resistance to the two employers he has had: the one
private employer he worked for (as a messenger-clerk, for about fifteen
months) reported a generally uncooperative work adjustment. Also, Jim
was discharged from a C.C.C. camp for refusing to work (no details available). In contrast with this resistance to father-figure authorities, is behavior suggesting a quest for a "good father" who might deserve his love: a
government relief investigator refers to Jim's "disposition to stay with a man
much older . . . than himself. This man . . . supposedly took an interest in
(Jim) and was attempting to lend every aid at his disposal . . . was somewhat
of a drinking man, but according to (Jim), during (Jim's) stay with (him)
he stopped drinking; and so the living together was considered mutually beneficial." In prison, where Jim has been given increasing responsibility, his work
adjustment is reported as "excellent." When last seen, he was working as a
kind of counselor to other inmates coming to the psychiatric department

for advice. He declared that most of them seemed to feel much better after releasing their feelings to a sympathetic person (such as himself), and expressed the feeling that he himself had grown in self-insight and maturity as a by-product of listening to other inmates' problems. Meanwhile, his earlier expressed wish to achieve success as a "business executive" has given way to a desire to do some sort of personnel work when he is paroled.

The conventional "drive for success" motive has played a larger role in the thinking of Don and Dick, even though this seems to be integrated into an internalized value-system. From the time *Don's* parents were divorced, when he was 12, he has been fully self-supporting. Through high school he lived with a group of other youngsters who were also working, and somehow found time to play in the school band and on the football team. Meanwhile, having earned the grades necessary for entering college, he had saved $4,000 with the intention of working toward a medical degree. A three-year siege of meningitis "busted" this goal. His subsequent work-history, he says, has been "more or less accidental." Going to work in his stepfather's business, Don became a _____ salesman. This has been his main occupation, for a period of some years as manager of his own business, in which he was "very successful." His primary goal was "security," which he lost when he began to loan money heavily to his mother, and finally to steal for her—an episode to be described later. Since being in prison, he has seriously developed a boyhood hobby of photography, which he now plans to continue as a vocation in partnership with his son-in-law. As an inmate he has worked into a position that involves photographic work with some supervisory capacity. Photography represents "a form of salesmanship—meet people and analyze them"; it has a "terrific future" as a result of technical advances accomplished during the war. Don's other interests include a variety of sports and reading a great deal. He is described in the initial prison psychiatric interview as "one of the most talkative inmates to cross this interviewer's desk," as showing "a genuine curiosity" and continually "interrupting the interview to ask questions . . . regarding prison life, inmates, and characteristics of various officials."

Through the interview with *Dick* there seems to run the theme of being what he calls "too easy-going" (suggesting open passivity as an inhibitory defense against expressing aggression). He "never did like to argue with anyone." (This may well be related to his fear of "agitators" and his anxiety that unions "shouldn't agitate.") Thus, Dick avoided having "any fights with other kids." Later, when his parents objected strenuously to his marrying a girl with whom he was in love, because she had a crippled leg, he "didn't argue —just listened to them and told them my side. I couldn't agree with them." Apparently unable to withstand their pressure, he subsequently married another girl while he was in the Navy. Despite continuous conflict, they stayed together seven years for the sake of their child, and then separated. Dick then "broke loose" from some of his inhibitions and "got a little wild . . . doing a lot of drinking" which led up to the present term in prison. (More of this later.) Dick might have been better able to sublimate his inhibited aggressions if his early ambition to become a doctor had not been blocked by financial difficulties: he "used to dream I was a doctor delivering babies and cutting people open." While in prison, however, he has developed a thoroughgoing interest in watchmaking as both vocation and hobby. It is interesting to speculate whether the focus on close detail in such work may serve as a compulsive means of holding down certain (aggressive) feelings—perhaps allowing less (indirect) expression of those feelings than medicine, but nonetheless a highly sublimated form of control. It is of interest that Dick has learned watchmaking during his spare time from "one real close friend," who is a sex offender. His accepting attitude to the latter contrasts with the prejudiced men's hostile righteousness on such matters. At the same time, the question may be asked whether this friendship involves some indirect satisfaction of latent homosexual impulses, as was suggested for Jim's close friendship with an older man. Such impulses are hinted in a slip that Dick made in describing his childhood friendship with the crippled girl whom he later wanted to marry: "She always used to come to me for advice. . . . If a boy asked her for a date, she would come to me to ask whether I—or rather *she* should go out with him." (Italics supplied.)

F. HETEROSEXUALITY

1. HIGH SCORERS

As was to be expected from their antisexual moralism, their anxious imaginings about the "animalism" of Negroes, and their intense fears of sexual approach to "white women" by Negroes, the prejudiced men show an impaired ability to combine sexual and tender feelings toward the same woman. Moreover, they exhibit signs of underlying resentful disrespect for women generally. These men tend to keep both sexual and hostile feelings toward "respectable" women partly split off from conscious awareness. They do this by making a rigid distinction between two stereotypes, in terms of which they classify all women: "pure," "sweet" (unsexual) women (like "mothers"), and "bad" (sexual) women. Toward "pure" women there are superficial gestures of respect; the artificiality of such attitudes suggests that they may be based on defenses which hold down sexual and aggressive feelings underneath. This inference is partly confirmed by expressions of open disrespect and hostility toward "bad" women, along with impersonalized sexual attitudes toward them. Further confirmation appears in some direct break-throughs of hostility to "pure" women, and in the fact that all heterosexual relationships tend to be distant, stereotyped and either dominating or submissive-dependent. (See Parts III and IV.)

In one form or another, this pattern appears in every prejudiced inter-viewee. *Robert* formulates succinctly the stereotyped notion of two kinds of women. His mother, he declares, taught him "something that stuck with me all my life, that a woman is the most perfect thing in the world"; he reveals the split-off resentment behind this seeming respect by adding, "that is, the right kind of woman." His sexually frigid wife, whom he calls "the sweetest wife in the world," apparently represented the "perfect thing" stereotype. What Robert admired most about her, he indicates, was her submissiveness toward him: "that she was willing to do whatever I did." Their life together is revealed, in his descriptions, as a constant round of mutual accusations of spending money carelessly, jealousy on her part over his going out alone, and "every little thing . . . she'd immediately run to mother and stay all night." She filed suit for divorce on discovering an affair he was having with a waitress, who seemed to represent "the other kind" of woman. The latter relationship was characterized by extreme hostility, exploitation, and dis-respect. The woman was quite promiscuous with other men, Robert says, during the affair with him. Further, "she was often drunk, and liked to battle and fight and argue and fuss. . . . Once this woman climbed a pole and got in my window, and another time she threw whiskey through the window at me in bed." On discovering his former prison record (for forgery), she began to blackmail him. He finally shot her (unpremeditatedly) in a vio-lent quarrel.

Clarence and Wilbur describe a still more distant, empty relationship to their wives than does Robert, with the difference that they rather than their wives were the more submissive. Although *Clarence* had "quite a few" ex-periences with prostitutes, he remained unmarried until the age of 38. He was attracted to his wife, he says, mainly by such external features as "her looks and manners." "We weren't much alike in any way" and were "a little different in taste about things. (Q.) Most anything!" But Clarence and his wife "got along good," by virtue of his submissiveness: "I let her have her own way . . . in most anything." Shortly following his wife's death, Clarence, who as a boy would "blush" if he "met a girl on the street," began to "molest" young girls, getting them drunk and attempting rape on them. . . . *Wilbur's* relationship to his wife has likewise been that of a subordinate. He indicates that she managed the finances, the children, and usually made the family decisions. When they disagreed—e.g., "she likes to stay home on Sun-day and I don't"—Wilbur would "usually do just what she asks me to do." A few minutes later in the interview, however, when asked in what ways he and his wife are alike, he says: "Well, she don't like to run around so much, and I don't either." A further, equally external "commonalty" is that "we both like to work."

Ronald's sexual history is more colorful. In addition to a number of "one-night relationships," he has been married three times—each time quite briefly.

With the first wife "the sex relationship was more enjoyable," he declares, "*because* there was nothing deep between us." (Italics supplied.) He left the second wife after a week, because "I just got tired of her"; although he "went back to her after seven or eight months" and stayed with her for a short time until the police caught up with his trail of robberies. The third wife was "pure"—a business woman who "didn't know anything about life. . . . We didn't get along too good sexually, because she was kind of on the frigid line." But whereas Ronald had been unable to feel tender toward more "sexual" women, this frigid "purity" seemed to attract something in him. He decided that he was "actually in love with her, and I still am," although "I don't know if she was in love with me. . . . I'd like nothing better than to go back to her."

Eugene's sexual relationships have been "mostly here or there." One lasted six months and was characterized by frequent "disagreements." "She tried to get me to quit drinking, and I wouldn't and didn't." There was much mutual jealousy, Eugene indicates, with charges such as "in a nightclub, she might keep staring at another guy." Also, sometimes "I'd make a date to take her some place and not show up." The inhibitory respect for female "purity" is expressed in Eugene's statement that "I have a bad temper when I'm drinking, except toward a woman," and in his report of how some of his fights start—e.g., going out of his way to pick a fight with a stranger at a bar, for "talking dirty" near Eugene when he was with a girl.

2. FASCISTS

The fascists reveal a heterosexual orientation which is even more externalized, contemptuous, exploitative, and dichotomistic than that of the other high scorers. *Buck* scarcely disguises his contemptuous use of women as mere physical objects. "I always thought," he declared, after having described his own rather promiscuous sexual activities "that _____ was meant to be tampered with." He shows an obsessive bitterness toward prostitutes and "loose" women, with whom he indicates he has had a good many experiences. Likewise he expresses resentment of his first wife's efforts to obtain financial support for their children. His second wife he curses as being extremely promiscuous during their marriage; and as mentioned before, he blames "that damn _____" entirely for his present situation. Also mentioned before was his statutory rape of a neighbor's 13-year-old girl, because he "had to have some sex" and "it was there to get." Toward "good" women, however, Buck manifests an inhibitory respect. He "never did try to play around with" his first wife before marriage, because "she comes from a pretty good family." Nor did he have intercourse before marriage with his second wife, who "seemed pretty respectable." He later decided, after falling out with her, that "she was playin' good to get me to marry her." Buck formulates his stereotypic dichotomy between "good" and "bad" women in a phrase: "Funny as hell—I always marry —————, my brothers all got good women."

Floyd, who was only 21 at the time he was apprehended, refers to "a few" passing heterosexual relationships "here and there," typically with "a married woman as usual." He describes as an example "one (who) was about 22 years old, married, beautiful, dumb." But, like Ronald and Robert, Floyd seems to require frigidity in a woman before he can feel respect and become attached to her. As reported in the prison case file, "his principal interest has been a supposed passionate devotion to one who is almost sexless." This was again a married woman, whom he wanted to marry if she would divorce her husband. When she "rediscovered her loyalty" to her husband, however, Floyd "got fed up from her sheer stupidity." Now he wants to marry a "wealthy woman . . . preferably anywhere between 28 and 30 . . . (of) fair physical attractions" whose personality he is satisfied to "take as it comes." Specifically, he is "looking forward" to marrying a Jewish actress "I got my eye on," whom he claims to have met once at a party in Hollywood. Her appeal for him he characterizes as only "physical." (What else?) "I don't know. She's just 'it,' that's all." This appears to be stereotypic fantasy expressing inverted anti-Semitism about "their women," who as Floyd says in referring to the Jewish actress "are really all right"; he admittedly has not "communicated" with her and doesn't know what her feelings toward him might be.

Adrian's few heterosexual relationships have been with women "all older than me, and they weren't anything but physical." "I never get romantic or emotional over a woman." With women as well as men, "I never had any relations with anyone that didn't have money connected with it." This applied to the business woman of 30 to whom he was married for a few weeks at the age of 18: "she had money and I didn't." Like the frigid "pure women" to whom other prejudiced men seem to become attached, she was "cold as a clam sexually." After an annulment, Adrian continued to correspond with her (as he still does also with his childhood governesses) for over a decade, "until she got married a year ago"; although (or because) "she treats me like a two-year-old." Adrian's deep-seated inhibitions against expressing genuine sexuality are revealed directly in response to a question whether he has any present heterosexual fantasies: "I don't have fantasies in the sexual sense. . . . I am a lot more sentimental than I am sexy."

3. LOW SCORERS

All 4 of the low-scoring inmates reveal definite disturbance in their heterosexual adjustment. Specifically, they appear to suffer conflicts based on unsatisfied love-dependency longings directed toward women as mother figures. These longings are associated with reciprocal love-nurturance toward women. At the same time, these men show ambivalence toward women that is near-consciously inhibited (instead of being split off and denied by moralistic dichotomies, as is the high scorers' power-ridden ambivalence to women). Such ambivalence seems in their case to stem primarily from frustration of the love-dependency longings rather than from fear-hate, dominance-submission conflicts as in the case of the prejudiced men. Moreover, in contrast with the latter's underlying contempt for women, the low scorers show greater basic respect for women as individuals and as essential equals. Their relationships with women stress common values and interests.

Art partially interprets his "dependency complex" himself. As the result of his "autopsychoanalysis" during his present term in prison, he spontaneously refers to this problem in the first minutes of the interview. All of the women with whom he has been intimate, he points out, have been older than himself, "business women, wage-earners, and providers," like his mother. He "simply transferred my dependency on my mother" to "my wife" and then "onto the (prison) authorities." After getting himself fired from his job, he made only half-hearted efforts to secure another one, until his first "wife as provider and support was no longer a tolerable condition consciously." Then he "got plastered" and wrote some bad checks as "unconsciously a way of transferring dependency." After a six-months jail term, she took him back. He was "repentant, but soon got plastered and did it again." This time she divorced him, though apparently on friendly terms. Art reports complete amnesia for his second wife, a woman twelve years older than himself, whom he also put in the position of supporting him. He lived with her only a short time when this situation became intolerable to him: another check-writing episode then landed him in prison. Unlike Buck, who led the authorities a merry chase before being caught for his check-writing, Art "knew I was going to get caught" and had unconsciously "arranged" to "transfer my dependency" to the prison "mother." . . . Despite Art's conflicts over "dependency," in describing his first marriage he emphasizes shared experiences and expressed genuine respect for his former wife: She was "an artist also, and a really thoroughgoing individual. She had a tremendous amount of scope, both intellectually and individually. . . . I liked her interests, her intellect." He is self-critical of his role in the marriage: "I wasn't in love with her . . . though I wouldn't admit it to myself. . . . Though I was very fond of her. . . . At that time I was too self-centered to be in love with anyone. . . . I did admire and respect and like her. . . . Today, I think we could have a better chance of making a go of it . . . because I have grown up sufficiently." Art's second wife continues to correspond with him, despite his "amnesia," and he is grateful for her "loyalty." Her letters, he says, indicate that she stresses "social functions" and the like, which are "of little consequence to me." Although they plan to reunite, he says that he will not remain with her if their interests and attitudes should prove uncongenial.

Art's continued "amnesia" for his second marriage suggests that he has by no means resolved the conflicting feelings involved in his "dependency complex." *Jim's* offense illustrates more directly, if gruesomely, the negative side of such an ambivalent attachment. His history includes one extended sexual affair in high school with a girl a year older than himself. When she finally broke off the affair because of his poor prospects (he was struggling to support his mother), he became very despondent and, according to the mother's report, attempted suicide with gas (the mother stopped him). This turned-inward aggression suggests reproachful inhibited hostility toward the girl for withholding love and frustrating his love-dependency needs. Both the emotional dependence and the inhibited hostility are revealed in one of Jim's prison "Progress Reports" when he speaks of "life goals": "Secondly I would like more than anything on this Earth to meet the girl of my dreams. . . . I desire to provide for her and take care of her with Love and Charity in my heart and with a real understanding of *whatever little faults she may have.* We all have many defects, but it takes a good man to minimize the defects in others and search his own conscience for *whatever bad thoughts dwell in him.* When I do meet the one girl for me, I shall explain all my past life to her, because I do not believe that happiness can be based on lies." (Italics supplied.) It is interesting that Jim was "out with an older woman with whom he was drinking (as reported in the prison case file), when at the age of 20 he stole an auto for the night. (This led to a year in a reformatory.) His inhibited, oral-dependent hostility to ambivalently regarded mother-figures was expressed directly in his present offense, committed at the age of 21. According to the case record, he "attacked a woman, 50, out for a walk . . . hit her on the head with a club, causing two skull fractures which resulted in her death. The victim's body showed also that he kissed and chewed her breasts. . . . She was totally unknown to him." This act was committed while Jim was very drunk and apparently in a dazed, fugue-like state—i.e., while his defenses were weakened to permit a *direct* expression of near-consciously inhibited impulses: subsequently he seemed to become at least partially amnesic for the episode.

Don, too, shows signs of strong emotional dependence toward loved and respected women. His first wife's death "was quite a blow. I never recovered from it, until I got this jolt" (i.e., the present incarceration); "I'm getting over it now." He "got along fine" with his second wife, "until I got involved in Mother's affairs," which broke up the marriage. Don refers here to his series of bank robberies to obtain money for his mother in her neurotic involvements; these will be discussed in the section on parents. "I have always felt guilty about it towards my wife." Although "I was fortunate in being perfectly mated to my wife—sexually, that is," Don admits directly what might be expected from his continuing overattachment to his mother (see below, page 885): "I have always been rather inhibited about sex."

Dick, whose "Mother was much more free about (sex) than Father" and with whom he was "pals more than Father," also verbalizes sexual inhibitions directly in discussing his former wife: "She's very hot-blooded and I'm just the opposite. . . . Sexual intercourse once a month would be okay for me." Parental pressure had prevented his marrying the boyhood sweetheart to whom he had been engaged (because she was crippled). Dick had then "married the first white woman I saw," on three weeks' acquaintance, after returning from overseas, because he was "lonesome." This didn't work out "worth a darn." In particularly they "argued about how to take care of the child, mainly . . . she always nagged the kid—wanted to use force on the kid." When they finally broke up, Dick escaped "into the Marines" where, disconsolate, he "got into the habit of doing a lot of drinking." While drinking with a girl-friend, he "picked up a car" (like Jim) and drove with her to Reno, where he "got married again while drunk." They sold the car. In the aftermath, Dick made civil restitution for the theft and had the marriage annulled; he is making additional restitution in prison. Meanwhile, when the crippled girl "back home" had "found out I was married," she too had sought emotional consolation by doing "the same thing: married the first man who came along. It turned out equally badly" and also ended in divorce. Now, she and Dick are corresponding again and plan to marry on his release—at last with parental approval. His attitude toward her seems to be genuinely nurturant: "She always used to come to me for advice. At a dance, I was about the only person she would dance with. And we studied together." At the same time she seems to represent for Dick (who is in other ways, too, more conventional than the other low-scoring men) a somewhat inhibitory mother figure with conventional moral values, on whom he can depend to "steady" him: she is "sort of refined. Not wild—steady. . . . Quiet, settled, doesn't get mad or express her views. . . . Very particular who she associates with."

4. SUMMARY

The contrasting sexual orientations of the prejudiced and unprejudiced interviewees suggest certain crucial personality differences. The unprejudiced men seem to seek, above all, love—which they also have some capacity to give. Despite frustration and conflict their approach to life is influenced by basic respect for themselves and other people. This makes for democratic identifications with other people, and for an inclination to identify with underdogs. The prejudiced men, on the other hand, seem to feel basically rejected and to have almost given up hope of experiencing genuine love. They speak as if they dislike and fear themselves as well as others. Their main energies seem to be devoted to defending themselves against any sense of weakness, chiefly by striving for external status and power and "proofs" of masculinity. The result is a power-oriented character structure driven to attack outgroups as symbols of their own suppressed characteristics.

G. ANTI-INTRACEPTIVENESS AND CHILDHOOD

1. HIGH SCORERS

All of the material so far presented supports what was stated earlier: that the high scorers anxiously avoid letting themselves think and feel freely, especially about psychological matters. For such inner freedom might lead them to "see" things they are afraid of in themselves. So they externalize their feared impulses, weakness, and conflicts with other people, onto outside situations and events and onto scapegoats. To the extent that these men let themselves feel their real feelings and impulses at all, they tend to keep them undifferentiated and to experience them as alien, as coming from outside their conscious self. Above all, what seems to be the emotional origin of their deepest conflicts—namely childhood and relations with parent figures—tends to be split off by them and regarded as discontinuous with their adult personality.

Thus, *Robert* declares that, "As far as home environment, I've had the best." He was "a good child" and "a good boy up until the age of 16." It was his "carnal self," he believes, that made him commit a few forgeries and thefts at the age of 18 and later engage in the hostile affair which led to his present term in prison. He regards these actions as quite "accidental," with no relation to life-history conflicts such as ambivalence toward parentally coerced· "goodness."

Wilbur even more clearly denies to himself the childhood roots of his present personality and behavior: (Which one influenced you more—your uncle or your aunt?[22]) "Well, that which I have today is that which I have made of my own self. (Q.) Well, as far as givin' me my own disposition, ... I more learned it since I have been on my own." Asked what he was like as a child, his answer is moralistically empty of personal content: He was "just a working boy . . . never in no trouble."

Eugene, like Robert, was "pretty good up to the time I was about 17 years old—never in trouble, never smoked or drank." He sees no connection between his submission to self-suppressive "goodness" in childhood and youth and his long history of "trouble" since then. He "can't explain" his violent "temper" or frequent drunken "benders." Concerning his gambling, he declares mystically that "I haven't got that in my blood."

Clarence, too, describes himself in childhood as "a good boy" who "didn't run wild" but "started to work" at a very early age. Not only does he deny any causal connection between this moralistic childhood self-suppression and his later avoidance of work (by probably "wrongly drawing government

[22] Wilbur's parents separated when he was an infant, and he never knew either of them. He was raised by an uncle and an aunt.

compensation for years") and attacks on little girls; his panic makes him deny, by means of paranoid delusions, that he ever exhibited such behavior.

In *Ronald's* case the splitting off of crucial aspects of childhood is more equivocal. For instance, he does criticize the severity of childhood discipline by his father: "They say, 'Spare the rod and spoil the child,' but I don't think it worked out in my case." It is shown in the next section, however, that Ronald is unable to carry through this criticism in a principled way but only in a paranoid-victimization context and by capricious rebellion.

2. FASCISTS

The fascist inmates reveal a similar "split" between childhood and later personality. *Adrian* shows some "break-through" of childhood conflicts in what sounds at times like the beginnings of insight. But this is negated by lack of emotional realization and by failure to accept responsibility for his own personality. Instead he feels only cynical, ego-alien self-contempt, with no real interest in changing what he despises in himself. Thus, Adrian observes at one point that "my selfishness is something I can almost blame (my father) for. His attitude and that of the whole family led me to believe that I was . . . the whole universe." In a later discussion, the cynical nature of this superficial "insight" is clearer: "All I want to know is how to put the best into *this* life. I should say *get* the best *out, not* put *in*, since I *am* selfish." Adrian's "explanation" for parental "influence" on deeper impulses behind his symptoms is mystically hereditarian: "If I ever did anything wrong, it was the Latin in me, which is the side I have more of an affinity for—my mother's side: I *look* more like them."

Floyd also avoids identifying with his own personality development as a life-experience process. Instead, he adopts hereditarian explanations: "All the inheritance is from the male side of the family for some reason or other. Except for my industriousness . . . that just doesn't exist. . . . I guess I just got that from the other side of the family."

Buck, when questioned rather persistently by the examiner as to what he was like as a child, just "doesn't know." Asked which of his parents had the most influence on his personality, he becomes very defensive, assuming falsely that the examiner must be moralizing about his delinquencies. Ignoring the examiner's efforts to correct this misunderstanding, he persists in his own obsessive moralism: Both parents, he protests, "always tried to teach me the right thing"; being in prison is "not my folks' fault."

3. LOW SCORERS

More characteristic of the "low" interviewees, with whatever partial inhibitions, is a general readiness to accept the causal continuity between present emotional problems and childhood emotional conflicts with parents. This has been previously exemplified in Art's self-interpretation of the effect of his dependence toward his mother upon his marriages and upon his delinquence. Similarly, *Don* volunteers that "in prison this is the first time that I haven't been beset by all sorts of emotional problems" centering around "my mother and father." No such striking single quotations are available for *Jim* and *Dick*, although the "inner continuity" of their lives is implicit in some of the discussion of parents, to be presented shortly.

H. ATTITUDES TO PARENTS

1. HIGH SCORERS

Certain critical aspects of the prejudiced inmates' ideology—"racial," politico-economic, and moral-religious—have been explained as attempts to deny personal dispositions by displacing them onto things outside. Their ideology seems to express fearful oversubmissiveness to authority and power, "antiweakness" façades, and displaced hatred of imaginary power figures (e.g., Jews); as well as desperate fear of their own impulses, especially sexual aggression toward "respected white women." These men's unconscious, split-off anxieties may in turn be traced to deeper sources, namely fear-ridden attitudes to parents.[23] All of them reveal, above all, a loss of inner integrity by self-negating oversubmissiveness-out-of-fear to parental authority. Such an attitude is shown especially toward the parent who is regarded as "stronger," typically the father. This submission is betrayed by a striking inability to criticize parents' basic values; by inhibitions against making principled criticisms of parental harshness; by acceptance of suppression imposed by parents; and by stereotypic overidealization of parents. The last feature seems to be an anxious attempt to suppress hostility by showing the opposite—awed "respect." The false quality of this "respect" is revealed by its empty clichés, referring mostly to external stereotypes such as the parents' status, the "sacrifices" they made for the family, etc. Positive feelings tend to be oriented not toward "lovable" personal qualities of parents but rather toward what parents have "done" for them, or "given" to them; i.e., they reflect an exploitative dependence-for-external-things. Self-negating submission and dependence toward parents may well be the ultimate origin of that "weakness" in themselves which these men so frantically try to deny. But fear prevents their resentment from leading to real self-assertion or to independence of their parents or other established authority. Sometimes they express feelings of victimization toward parents and other authorities (recall Ronald's "persecutor for a governor"). But these feelings are overpersonalized: the prejudiced men cannot really criticize antidemocraticness as such; instead, they feel themselves singled out—as individuals, as "the poor people" or

[23] The statistical comparison of high- and low-scoring interviewees generally, with respect to attitudes toward parents, is reported in Chapter X.

whatnot—for "persecution." Their furtive resentment of parents and other authorities can be expressed only in pseudo rebellion, often delinquent or fascist; and in prejudice against mythically "dominant" groups such as Jews, who symbolize the hated parental power and values—i.e., by "growling" defiantly while expressing the very authoritarianism "growled" against. There are signs that, to bolster their weakened masculinity and independence, these men have tried to identify with the external aspects of the resented parents—i.e., parental authoritarianism, status and power, especially that of the father. This involves, not solidly internalized character traits, but only vicarious participation as a "lieutenant" in the parent-leader's strength. This narcissistic identification is also a way of disguising masochistic submissiveness to the parent-leader.

A further consequence of the prejudiced inmates' submission to parents is splitting-off of sexual impulses toward the first heterosexual figure, the mother. These are kept split off by developing reverence for the mother's imagined asexual "purity." By emphasizing the mother's "sweetness" and "goodness," she is in fantasy deprived of sexuality. Such distortions help to protect these men against their own feared sexual impulses, and provide a basis for their later inability to fuse love and sex. Their fear of Negroes' approach to "white women" may well be a projection of their own repressed impulses toward the mother.

Several questionnaire items indirectly reflect submissiveness to parental authority and denial of any hostility to family figures. These include an overemphasis on "obedience and respect for authority" (Item 1), rejection of "rebellious ideas" (Item 21), condemnation of those who do not feel "love, gratitude, and respect" for parents (Item 27), and rejection of any hostile impulses toward "a close friend or relative" (Item 42). While these items are differentiating, even the low quartile means on them are rather high. It may be suspected that prison has stirred up considerable guilt over rebellion and hostility, in both low and high scorers.

Robert's submissiveness is underlined by his insistent repetition that he was "a perfect son to my parents, a perfect brother to my sisters and brothers." His mother is the "most terrific person in the world to me," and he is quite unable to evaluate her objectively: "I truthfully can't say she has any definite shortcomings." Yet his conception of her is empty and distant. Probing as to what sort of person she is draws a complete blank, except for references to her antisexual moralism (about "woman" as "the most perfect thing") and her "self-sacrificing" gratification of dependence: "I think she has devoted her life to making her mate. (my father) and her children very happy. Has never taken much interest in outside social affairs; is concerned with her family." Even this "devotion" is regarded with mixed feelings: "I don't really think she has any (shortcomings)—except maybe too wound up in her home and didn't take more interest in social affairs." Robert overidealizes his father

in an equally empty way as "very good—I couldn't ask for a better father."
He then proceeds furtively to "undo" this praise by expressions of feeling
victimized: "He was a little strict at times," and "I haven't had *everything* I
might have wanted from him." (Note the dependence-for-things.) "I would
have liked to have a nicer home, better position." His underlying submission,
however, impels him to pull back and "apologize": "Possibly at the time I
couldn't realize" the reasons for punishment, and "all in all, I was very happy
to be one of his boys." Most interesting are Robert's comments about his
father's economic status: "Not a successful businessman. . . . Instead of improving himself, I think he went down a bit. . . . Since I got out of school,
he's always worked for wages." Thinking of the family's frequent moves
which deeply upset his mother, Robert has "often tried in later years to
analyze my father's wanderlust." Robert decided that in moving so often, his
father was "apparently seeking business success." In this respect, "My
mother," who "always referred to me as her best daughter" because "I've always tried to do everything to make her happy"—(note the submissive
feminine identification)—"has remarked that I'm just the opposite of him."
According to Robert, his mother in no way criticized the father's obsession
with external status; she objected only that he did not "stay put" in seeking
it and was not "successful" enough. But this seems to have provided a rationale for Robert, while submitting to his father's notion of economic "success" as the end-all of existence, to assert: "To me, looking back now, he's not
the type of a man that I want to pattern my business after." Robert's ambivalent ego-ideal of "business success" is, so he likes to think, "the opposite" of
his father's ideal. This might help to explain the inversion of his anti-Semitism,
in which he expresses mainly envy of Jewish "drive and ambition to get
there," with only furtive signs of his hostility against "the Jew." "The Jew"
perhaps symbolizes less his father directly than it does a superficially differing father-ideal toward which Robert's resentment is even more repressed
than toward his actual father. This father-ideal is difficult for him to rebel
against even by way of displaced resentment against the symbol of "the Jew,"
because under moralistic pressure from his mother he is deceived into thinking that his submission to this ideal is itself an assertion of independence
from his father's values.

Ronald's resentment has broken through more openly. After the divorce
of his parents when he was 3, he lived with his (paternal) grandmother. He
was "taught . . . that (my mother) had deserted my father and brother and
I." Upon his father's remarriage, Ronald went, at the age of 7, to live with
his father and stepmother. From the beginning there seemed to be "a mutual
understanding between my brother and myself that we didn't like her." Her
position as only a secondary mother figure seemed to enable Ronald to
express resentments toward her directly. His stepmother, he says, "didn't take
any interest at all" and "resented us": "We always felt that we were in the

way." A hint of possible homosexual fixation on the father is suggested by jealousy that his father "was more interested in her than in me or my brother." Ronald expresses much disappointment in the father, and feelings of being victimized by him: The father "*was* dependable, but he changed"; "worked his way up . . . then drinking caused him to go down." "He never shirked at the idea of anyone helping him, especially financially. . . . I know he used some of my grandmother's money to buy real estate with. And I know he lost it, and it didn't seem to bother him." The father gave Ronald an allowance of only fifteen cents a week, which Ronald still resents: "I'll never forget that." For the most part, however, he blames his stepmother for being "never satisfied" and "greedy." Even here, his guilt makes him pull back, as if sensing that he may be projecting onto her some of his own feelings: "*I* thought she was greedy. 'Course it might have been for other reasons—wanting to save something." Most striking is his almost complete displacement of hate for the father's harsh discipline, onto the stepmother. Telling how his father "didn't believe in sparing the rod" and "laid it on pretty thick," he declares: "The hard part about it was that my stepmother would tell him that my brother or I had done things, and he wouldn't give us a chance to explain." Ronald actually "ran off twice," but "it didn't cause me to hate *him*. I held it mostly against *her*." (Just as Ronald now "holds it mostly against" those of lesser status and weak position, not those who represent real power.)

Wilbur's parents died in his infancy. He was raised by an aunt and uncle, with whom his main satisfactions, he says, were limited to "board and room, a place to sleep." The aunt was a "good woman" (i.e., "pure"). Specifically, she gratified Wilbur's dependency-for-things; she was "good to the children: clothed, fed, took care of us when sick." "I couldn't think of any" faults in her, except perhaps that "she would never like to go no place—stayed at home all the time" (like the woman Wilbur later chose to marry). He is unable to make his "idealization" of his aunt meaningful by any details; she was "just a good woman," "good to me." He "never did" confide in her. Wilbur's monosyllabic answers to the examiner's inquiry indicate that his childhood was dominated by the harsh rule of his uncle, whose regime he was apparently too submissive to think of questioning. He says that his uncle whipped him several times a month: (Did you ever question whether he was right about it?) "No." The uncle, he declares, "treated me okay," but from a very early age "made me work pretty hard. (Q.) Sun-up to sun-down. (Q. How did you take that?) We did what the elders told us to. (Q. Did you ever question that?) Well, I never questioned." Wilbur was able to rebel only when he could create a persecutory rationale by feeling singled out: "Only one disagreement—he wanted me to do more work than his own children." Wilbur reacted to this rationale with explosive defiance—still submissively unable to criticize his uncle's authoritarianism as such—by abruptly leaving home at the age of 15. With all this, Wilbur in another context describes his uncle as "pretty easy to get along with." Then, in almost the next breath he reveals that "he would stay away at night and drink, sometimes come home drunk. My aunt went off in a corner." Wilbur indicates that he didn't dare to think seriously of criticizing the uncle or of protecting the aunt: (What was your reaction?) "Didn't think much about it."

Clarence, too, describes his (real) father as "easy to get along with." What he admired most about the father was "the way he treated me. (Q.) Never did abuse me or scold me." Later, Clarence betrays the reason for his freedom from physical discipline, namely, his own cowed submission to stern parental authority. Although the father would "tell us what we should do, what he wanted us to do, and what he expected us to do," "there wasn't much (discipline) to exercise," simply because "we just did what they said." A moment later, Clarence unwittingly reveals the parental intimidation that forced such utter submission from him: bemoaning the independence of children today, he declares that if he had ever answered his parents back the way he thinks children do now, "I wouldn't be able to sit down!" Clarence has justified his parents' intimidation of him by adopting the same general philosophy of authoritarianism: "Children didn't run wild in those days like they do nowadays. . . . If they have to whip them, I believe in whipping them. I don't believe in sparing the rod and spoiling the child." This submissive acceptance of parental authoritarianism helps to explain Clarence's inability to evaluate his father objectively: he "didn't know (my father) had any weaknesses." His description of his mother is equally superficial and moralistic: "She was a nice, easy-going woman—good mother." What he admired most about her, he states, was the "way she handled me—always tell me how good I was." Clarence's distant, stereotyped attitude to his mother is further suggested by his purely physical conception of the way in which "I take after my mother more than my father. (Q. In what ways?) Well, in my complexion. (Q. What about personality traits?) That I couldn't answer."

After *Eugene's* father "ran away when I was 2 years old," his mother went to work as a waitress and "took care of me all my life." Thus she was both mother and father to Eugene. His remarks about her suggest the fear which forms the basis of his "idealizing" her—namely a desperate dependence on her to "do things" for him: (Note the similarity in phrasing with Eugene's submissive-dependent "idealization" of Roosevelt, who "did things" for Eugene via the C.C.C.). "She's good. In fact, the best. In other words, she's just tops with me. . . . Does everything for me she can. Writes me all the time. (Q. What do you admire most about her?) Just about everything. (Q.) Well, I guess her being so good and friendly to everybody, especially me. (Q. What's an example?) Well, always trying to do everything for me. Very seldom go uptown without bringing something back for me. (Q. What else?) When Father went away, Mother took care of me all her life, where she could have put me in a home some place. She always stayed with me in trouble." This dependence, this fear of loss of support, may have been a powerful force driving Eugene to submit to his mother's righteous repression. She is described as having taught him not values but absolutistic moral rules: "She always taught me the difference between right and wrong, the things I should do and shouldn't." Her moralism, as he describes it, smothered any chance of answering the implicit hostility behind it, because the hostility was veiled by a fog of self-righteousness: She would characteristically "just bawl us out" in a way that "made it seem like it was hurting *her* more than it did us." "She'd look hurt," with the result that "it just hurt. I never sassed her back or said a mean thing." The implied struggle to hold a desire to "sass her back" is illustrated further in a striking contradiction. The only thing Eugene can imagine that might have prevented his long record of "getting in trouble" is *more* strict moral repression by his mother: "To tell the truth, I don't think she was strict enough with us." As evidence for this, he mentioned that he sometimes "came home later than I was supposed to." A minute later, unaware of the contradiction, he declares: "She was pretty strict about that being home on time!" Eugene submitted to his mother's moralism by being "pretty good, up to the time I was 17 years old." His subsequent "trouble"—gambling, drinking, fighting, and sexual promiscuity—suggests a belated reaction against this submission. Meanwhile, the hostility which her "hurt" moralism made him suppress causes him to feel guilty and therefore obligated to "do things" for her. Asked what his main satisfactions were in the relationship with his mother, this guilt evokes the inappropriate response that "I guess I haven't made her very happy, but when I'm out there and going straight, I'll always take care of my mother. . . . I feel I've never treated her like I really should."

2. FASCISTS

The 3 fascist men show, in more extreme form, essentially the same pattern of attitudes to parent figures as do the other prejudiced men. Especially notable is their fearful submission to the father, in which homosexual aspects are hardly even disguised.

Buck verbalizes fairly directly his fear of sexuality in relation to his mother: "I'd kinda feel embarrassed if my mother ever brought up a subject like (sex)." His conception of her seems to be exclusively that of an agent to "do things" to gratify his dependence: "She was a hard-workin' lady, took care of us kids." In fact, when asked what were his main satisfactions in his relationships with his parents, his response is limited to the purely external fact that "they gave me most anything I wanted." As for his parents' personalities, Buck's orientation toward the external leads him to ask: "You mean the people they associated with?" He cannot go beyond the most superficial references to their external roles, such as giving things to himself, being "hard-working" or a "businessman," "got drunk," "gave orders," etc.

This inhibitory block against any personal relation to them is consistent with the absolute submission which his father forced upon him. Buck "never did see any weaknesses in him." His blind acceptance of his father's "rightness" about everything explains why: His father, he protests repeatedly, was "generally right when he says something," "always trying to show us the right view of things," "always right in the things he said." Buck "always figured I had it comin'" when he was "licked," and in his fright "knew right from wrong right away" as an absolute distinction never to be questioned. Hence his father usually needed only to "give us one look and we'd know what he meant." Buck's fear leads him to say that his parents "never argued . . . even when he (the father) got drunk." A moment later he naively reveals the reason for the lack of arguments, with no apparent awareness of the contradiction: "Mother didn't say anything." "If they did" have any disagreements, "they never did let us kids know." This denial is followed a few sentences later by a description of how sometimes "Dad would go into a rage and walk away . . . and Mother would go into a room and cry; but she'd get over it right away." Of particular interest, in connection with Buck's fantasy that "most all of them Jews talk about sex mostly . . . about they're gonna (have fellatio performed on them) tonight," are some remarks about the ways in which his father (symbolized by Jews?) used to "talk about sex." The only sex instruction Buck had, he declares, consisted in his father's frequent warnings to "watch out for these ch____" in order not to be exploited. In another context he relates how his father began, during his middle 'teens, to give him money for the express purpose of visiting prostitutes. Whether truth or fantasy, this is highly suggestive. It is not difficult to imagine that Buck may have been sexually overstimulated, rather crudely, by his father.

After *Floyd's* parents separated in his infancy, he rarely saw either of them. Until he was 7 he was raised by a foster mother who boarded children. From age 7 to 14 he lived with his father and a newly acquired stepmother, until he was sent away to boarding school. Floyd describes himself as grossly neglected by the foster mother: "Those people always had something to do from dawn to dusk, and as a kid I never had anything to say." He "didn't get along too well" with the other children. Discipline was "more corporeal than anything else . . . for any infraction of her so-called rules." The stepmother he scornfully resented as "just another woman, I guess," "just somebody that was there," and as "mean" and rejective toward himself as "that other woman's child." He jealously contrasts her with his father as different "in every way. She wasn't his equal in anything—intellectually." This phrasing raises a suspicion that Floyd wanted to replace his stepmother and adopt the same "lieutenant" role toward his father as he seems to have adopted toward his crime partner. Indirect evidence for this hypothesis is to be found in his "mixed-up loyalty" to his real mother, suggesting definite identification with her feminine role: "I wish she had a husband, and that's the pitiful part of it—a woman shouldn't be alone." There is much further evidence of Floyd's intense, if ambivalent homosexual father fixation. He describes his father as a "very, very fine man, intelligent, understanding. Excellent father . . . in every way . . . a man everybody in the community looked up to." As to what he admires most about his father, he "couldn't singularize on that. Just all of him." The one shortcoming which he can think of in his father is aggressive abruptness in criticizing: "Well, he was outspoken. . . . If he thought you were no good or doing something wrong, he didn't hesitate to tell you." But Floyd's fear of his father compels him to justify even this: "That's as much of an asset in ways." In fact, Floyd cannot mobilize sufficient aggression toward his father to make a single criticism of him, not even of the father's virtual abandonment of him during the first seven years of his life: "Just always been away, that's all." He denies that his father ever punished him unjustly. A significant reason for Floyd's anxious splitting-off from conscious awareness of all negative feelings toward his father may be similar to the preoccupation of Eugene toward his mother—fear of complete abandonment. This is suggested by Floyd's description of the quarrels between his father and stepmother. These were "very sharp, and their remarks were lasting and bitter, like, 'We never should have taken him home.' And Father would be confused. . . . Then he would punish me, once very hard; then he would talk to me until I went to sleep." This dependence, as well as further signs of homosexual attachment, would seem to be expressed in the following remarks: "There's only one help I've got, and that's my father"; although "he's never been close to me," he "has stood by me. . . . This affair has brought us closer together than before"; and "he has written me a beautiful letter."

Adrian's case reveals in rather pure form the dynamics of a power-ridden type of inverted Oedipus complex: fear-driven homosexual submission to a hated father, and underlying identification with the mother's role as subordinate. His mother, who died in her early twenties when he was only 5, seems to have been a very infantile person with "no sense of humor." She neglected Adrian entirely except for flaunting her sexuality in his face, and then terrifying him by her "way of punishing me." She was "a very beautiful woman," "very vivacious," "came out in——society . . . spent most of her life going out to dinners. . . . She mostly ignored me, but she always came to show me how she looked before she went out. . . . Except that my nurse said I was this or that, she didn't seem to know personally what I was about." Her punishments, "usually for something petty" such as "stealing fudge off a shelf," were capricious and deeply traumatic: "She locked me in dark closets —scared me to death," or "threatened to give me to a neighborhood woman whom she said was a witch." Yet the fearful dependence of a little child apparently forced Adrian to repress the hate such treatment must have excited: for in the same breath in which he reveals her self-centered cruelty, he idealizes her and is unable to criticize her for these things. (How did you feel toward your mother when she punished you?) "I *loved* my mother. I was very crazy about my mother. (Did your mother ever punish you unjustly?) No. She lost her temper unjustly. She was very vacillating—up one minute and down the next; never knew what she was going to do next. People just had to stay out of her way when she was that way." Questioned about her weaknesses or faults, Adrian declares: "In my memory, she just doesn't have any faults." His mother's intimidation alone might be thought to have discouraged Adrian's heterosexual development. But fear of a stern father appears to have combined with this to "stampede" Adrian into complete homosexual submission to the father and adoption of the mother's manipulative techniques. The father, who died several years ago, was a military officer who was "not the least bit demonstrative. . . . He disapproved of any show of emotion of *any* kind." Adrian was awed by "his consistency." "He was a stickler for rules. . . . I thought of him as a sort of tyrant.". Yet, though he seemed "hard as nails with everyone else," he was "very easy with me," because "if my father punished me, (my mother) was so upset that it didn't go." Adrian describes specific episodes that would seem to have encouraged a fearful "feminine" attitude toward the father: "Incidentally, whenever she cried, I cried, too. . . . She often threw tantrums, and father just put on his hat and went out, which only made her all the madder. And I would always cry with her. . . . I always felt when he scolded her, he was scolding me." Adrian indicates that from earliest infancy he adopted his mother's techniques for manipulating the father: "I hollered . . . usually got my way. In fact, all I ever had to do was cry about anything, and he'd do whatever it was that upset me." "And remember," says Adrian in explaining his father's coddling him as the father coddled Adrian's mother, "that I look like my mother." Note the continuing father fixation: "I missed him very much when I was at the boarding house. . . . When I was sick, I used to . . . daydream about his coming to see me. . . . I've saved all my letters to him. . . . He very dramatically returned all my letters, like to an old love. I loved my father very much." Quite unable to assert any genuine inner independence, Adrian's furtive resentment broke through his weak superego in the form of delinquent rebelliousness: "I became such a worry to him . . . left school when I pleased. I overdrew my charge accounts, and he was ill." This was followed by an endless succession of delinquencies as an adult. "When he died," however, "and when I realized I could never see him again," Adrian began to feel intense shame over his delinquencies and to feel even more deeply submissive to his father: "I put him on a pedestal now he wasn't on for me as a child. . . . He haunts me: I'm always wondering if he would approve of this or approve of that. . . . His judgment was always right. . . . And when I hear opinions expressed, I wonder if they would be *his* opinion." Adrian has even made a belated stab at catching up with father-masculinity identifications. Before his short-lived parole, he asserted that he was through with his "repulsive" homosexuality, and that although he would have been "happier as a woman," he had "more determination than I am given credit for" and "can live a man's life, since this is a man's world." As we have seen before, his "determination" lasted for only about two weeks.

3. LOW SCORERS

In contrast with the high scorers' submission, the low-scoring interviewees exhibit more underlying independence toward parents, especially toward the father. This includes some capacity for objective evaluation of parents, as well as some ability to resist parental authority on the basis of principle. In each case the preferred parent is definitely the mother, who is loved and respected as an individual. At the same time, each of these men reveals a deep ambivalence toward the mother, which is (almost consciously) inhibited, but not denied by masks of overidealization and reverence. The ambivalence appears to center around frustrated love-dependency longings. It is this primary love-orientation, however, which forms the basis of genuine liking for people and for democratic identifications. And to the extent that these men carry out identifications with underdogs and show resistance to *status quo* injustice, a basis was formed in early assertions of independence as underdogs in relation to parental authority. Their failure to carry out such identification fully may be due to inhibitions against asserting *full* independence from parents.

By his "autopsychoanalysis," *Art* has made partly conscious his "Oedipus complex"; or, as he says he prefers to call it (denying specifically sexual feelings toward his mother)—his "dependency complex," later displaced onto mother substitutes. After the death of the father when Art was 9, several factors combined to intensify this complex. His sister and (paternal) half-brother went to stay with relatives. This left Art alone "at home with Mother, who had an advertising job." Their relationship, he indicates, was quite close, but with himself in a dependent role (though with reciprocating nurturance) toward his mother-provider: "I stayed at home and cooked the meals and did the housework." She apparently overstimulated his sexual fantasies, in a way that made it harder for him to overcome the mother fixation, by glorifying his body as a "precious possession." And when he was "about 14" she presented to him "the business of childbirth and conception . . . in a very cold-blooded way" (note the almost-conscious ambivalence toward the mother) including an arrangement for him to watch several childbirth operations surreptitiously. Withal, Art's image of her stresses inner, psychological values: "An intellectual and a very well-educated person. Her principal gift seems to be that of perception. And a musician—pianist— . . . not by trade but certainly by nature." Her frailties include "a psychological disturbance as great as mine. Fortunately didn't cause her as much trouble, but certainly caused her as much anguish." The mother's emotional support seemed to help Art assert considerable independence of his father: e.g., explicitly rejecting the latter's anti-Semitism; evaluating him with some criticalness as "spoiled" by his "rich parents" as "an only child"; criticizing his discipline as having "not much consistency"; and rejecting his father's discipline when it seemed unfair, in which case "you got nothing but a lot of argument from me." The mother was in some ways a better model: her discipline "deprived us of privileges" but "had more effect" because of her greater consistency—"she meant what she said." The father's capriciousness, as a masculine model to identify with, seemed to confuse Art's conception of his own ego-identity. For instance, in pursuing the career of artist and having to compromise by becoming a commercial artist, Art was following his father, who "of course was fostering any particular art ability I had." But "curiously enough, I don't think I have any particular art ability" though "no one else thinks it is either ordinary or mediocre." Instead, "I think I could become a good musician, pianist" (like his mother); although he admits on questioning that "I don't play the piano at all." Art even makes explicit his conflict over internalizing the father as a masculine model: though the father "championed my causes. . . . I didn't like my father as champion—preferred my mother as champion." Art recognizes that his father was "temperamental," "running away from something, too . . . managed to dissipate a rather large fortune" by drinking and gambling which caused "considerable domestic strife: I didn't like it." Yet having himself "started drinking," done some gambling, chafed against "commercializing" his artistic bent by getting fired from several jobs, and "transferred my dependency" onto prison by check-writing —Art senses that he has "probably got some of (my father's) extravagant qualities."

Don's life, too, has been dominated by a neurotic overattachment to his mother. His underlying love-dependency has been masked, however, by his reciprocal role of nurturant protector to his mother. In pre-adolescence he became actively involved in the "bitter quarrels" between his parents concerning the father's "going with women." He took the mother's side, strongly criticizing the father, who repeatedly "licked my pants off" for intervening. "At the same time, I tried to bring them back together; they still care for each other." But his efforts at mediation were unsuccessful: his parents were divorced when he was 12, and from then on Don supported himself, living with several other boys. (One wonders if Don's experience of being squeezed between his two adult giants partly determines his opinion that "both labor and business sort of ignore the little fellow.") Years later, in the mother's third marriage, her husband "took her" for a great deal of money, which he lost in a succession of wildcat schemes. Eventually she went into debt, mortgaging the old family farm. Don, having tried in vain to persuade her to divorce the man, and inhibiting conscious wishes to kill him, borrowed heavily to keep her in funds. He then carried out a series of bank robberies (by himself) to make these debts good, and to continue supplying money to his mother. On the last one, after a wild automobile and foot chase by a bank manager, he let himself be caught rather than shoot the unarmed man with his loaded gun. Don recognizes that his mother is "governed by emotional biases," by "willingness to accept and believe too much ... generous to a fault ... not too practical, forbearing to a fault ... not assertive enough." But he respects her deeply as "quite a person" who "has taken up something every year of her life. ... She has recently learned to play the accordion; she studied music all her life." Don's ego-identity, like Art's, seems to be confused with respect to mother-versus father-identifications: he feels that he takes after his father in *not* being "governed by emotional biases as Mother is." This conflicts sharply with his statement that prison is "the first time that I haven't been beset by all sorts of emotional problems." Ambivalence toward his mother's "emotional biases" is indicated by his first, abrupt response to questioning about his mother's weaknesses: "Let's call it emotional and let it go at that."

Jim's involvement with his mother is still deeper, with respect to both love-dependency feelings and nurturant protection of her, as well as strong hostility close to the surface. Conflict with the father is also more violent. Jim has been very close to his mother, as to an intimate sweetheart: "I could talk to my mother about any subject under the sun. No embarrassment there. I was interested in the same things. . . . Both of us are a little sensitive in temperament, kind of quiet. I think we both like a certain amount of solitude. I used to like to take her out to dinner, to the theatre quite often." During the depression, as he struggled against poverty to support his mother, she says that he was "a prince, and went without eating himself to buy fruit for me." Jim is able to criticize her as "not social enough ... by herself too much" and as "having a little temper," but he formulates his near-conscious ambivalence: "It's a little difficult to find weaknesses in one's mother. ... We usually tend to overlook a mother's weaknesses. ... I find it difficult to find very many frailties." At another point Jim indicates unmistakably the process of consciously struggling to inhibit, by what he calls "insight," resentments toward his mother. Citing, in response to questioning, an occasion on which she had spanked him impulsively for something that wasn't his fault, he declares: "At the time I resented it. Today I don't. I know she did things the best she could. ... I didn't have enough insight then." Of the father, who deserted the family for eight years during the 'thirties, Jim says: "My dad used to get drunk quite often, and he would beat (my mother) physically. ... He's a little crude, socially. He's very happy-go-lucky. He likes to fish. He's very egotistical, I think a little too much so. Very stubborn in argument. If he believes a thing, why that's it. He probably has an inferiority complex which he never admits to himself." The mother expresses the view that Jim was reduced to "a hopeless state of mind . . . due to his father's hardness and cruelty." But note

Jim's love-oriented wish to believe that his relation to his father was nonetheless "a very friendly relationship. He was pretty much of a pal. We liked to go places together, fishing, play cards, etc. We had a lot of good times." (Recall Jim's close relationship with an older man whom he persuaded to stop drinking, and who was in turn kind to him.)

Dick, too, was closer to his mother than to his father. "I always like to putter around the house with Mother. Mother and I were pals more than Father. . . . I confided in Mother a good deal. (What's an example?) Well, sex. Mother was much more free about it than Father." Nonetheless, Dick's conception of her is more "moral" and conventional than that of the other low-scoring interviewees, and reflects some dependence-for-things: He describes her as a "good housekeeper, always interested in the kids' welfare. Liked to putter around the house." He admired most in her "the fact that she's always looked after the kids the best she could, and kept a very nice household and dresses nice. Personal appearance always kept up to snuff. Doesn't smoke and doesn't drink." Dick is also unable to criticize her directly: (Weaknesses?) "Well, might say my dad is her principal weakness. He can talk her out of most anything. . . . (Other weaknesses?) By golly, I don't know. I can't think of a one." His hostility toward her for her greater strictness, as compared with the father, is not difficult to infer: "Dad tried to" exercise the discipline, "but he was too easy-going, so Mother did. . . . Never had a whipping. She used to take privileges away . . . for not coming home on time. That was the main thing. . . . I got a wild streak for about six months before I went into the service. First got the use of a car then. Neglected my studies for picnics and dates in the evenings." (One may wonder if this was not in protest against his mother's moral strictness). As for the father, who "always found something to laugh at—very easy to get along with," Dick mentions his main weaknesses as violations of the mother's strictness: "Might say he's a sucker for anybody's sob story," and "pretty lenient with his kids . . . would let us play hookey, would let me have the car a bit too often; too easy with money for us kids," whereas the mother was a "little more careful about money." (Recall that Dick's fiancée, the crippled girl "back home," is "not wild—steady"; she might be a mother figure who could help him to inhibit resentment against his mother's strictness.)

I. "CRIMINALITY" IN HIGH AND LOW SCORERS

1. GENERAL

What relations may exist between "criminality" and the antidemocratic trends? Two kinds of data are available: mean scores on the scales for subgroups composed of legally defined offense categories, and certain interview material. Table 5 (XXI) presents the E- and F-scale means for the legally

TABLE 5 (XXI)

MEAN E- AND F-SCALE SCORES OF THE PRISON INMATES,
GROUPED ACCORDING TO OFFENSE

Offense Group	Number of Cases	E Scale Mean/Person/Item	F Scale Mean/Person/Item
Check-writing	44	4.45	4.76
Robbery, burglary, theft	31	4.63	4.39
Murder	12	4.31	4.33
Sex offenses	23	5.02	5.33
	110	4.61	4.73

defined offense categories—murderers, robbers, etc. None of the differences
between means of different offense groups are statistically significant. As for
the relevant interview material, the heterogeneity of offenses combined with
the small number of cases would seem to discourage general conclusions. But
perhaps if an appropriate level of generalization can be found, a brief review of this material might be rewarded with further insight. Such a review
is now presented, considering the interviewees one by one.

2. HIGH SCORERS (INCLUDING FASCISTS)

Complete details are not available as to the exact circumstances of each of
the interviewees' offenses and their attitudes toward these offenses. Nonetheless the material obtained is highly suggestive.

Robert's murder of his hostile, despised mistress was the climax of a flight
into sexual promiscuity which has been interpreted as an unconscious attempt to quiet fears of nonmasculinity that his wife's frigidity may have
intensified. *Ronald's* habitual gang robbery "as a business" appears to have
represented an easy way of obtaining money as well as an effort to "prove"
himself a "big operator." *Eugene's* delinquencies consist of a long history of
"trouble": getting easy money by check-writing, gambling, drinking, and
especially fighting, of which he is both proud because of its manliness and
ashamed because of being "a little wild." In contrast with his submissiveness
to his moralistic mother, by being "good, up to the time I was 17 years old,"
this behavior sounds like a belated protest of "masculinity." *Wilbur's* murder of his landlord following eviction, and his development of paranoid
anti-Greek delusions, appears to have been a desperate defiance of an emas-
culating father figure, in order to reassert his own threatened masculinity.
Clarence's sexual assaults on children, with his accompanying paranoid delusions of being "framed by the people in politics," seem to be attempts to

"prove" masculinity and suppress homosexual panic. *Buck's* statutory rape of a young girl and molesting of his own small children probably have similar meanings. His drunken check-writing spree with a despised prostitute seems to have been an attempt to bolster his masculinity by means of heterosexual promiscuity and "big-shot financier" behavior. *Floyd's* gang robberies were undisguised attempts to be a "big operator," to be "tough," and to gain easy power. Similarly for his disturbing the peace by drunken brawls, and his repeated Army A.W.O.L.'s, which characteristically involved a spree with "a married woman as usual." *Adrian's* cap-pistol robbery was, by his own statement, an attempt to "prove" that he could "lead." He himself attributes this act in part to some glandular treatments he had just completed a week before, which he feels made him "more masculine."

The one feature which all of these offenses have in common is that they represent *attempts to "prove"* something. What they seek to "prove" is toughness, strength, power, all of which signify *"masculinity."* More significantly, they are *attempts to deny* something, namely, what to the subject means psychologically *"weakness" and "nonmasculinity"*—whether this be nonheterosexuality, impotence, homosexual impulses, submissiveness, dependence, softness, or passivity. In a word, the high scorers' crimes express the emotional complex that seems to dominate their lives: desperate fear of their own "weakness," which they try to deny by a façade of masculinity. Thus what superficially looks like direct, uninhibited expression of impulses in these men, turns out to be a cover-up for intense inhibition and fear.

3. LOW SCORERS

Art has himself interpreted his check-writing, in which he made no efforts to avoid getting caught, as an unconscious attempt to transfer his ambivalent dependency from his wife onto the prison "mother." He ascribes the origin of this complex to his attachment to his mother. *Don's* bank robberies for his mother express a similar mother attachment, in which his own love-dependence is closely associated with nurturance toward his mother. Near-conscious ambivalence is verbalized toward the emotional biases by which her behavior is governed. *Jim's* clubbing of a middle-aged woman and then kissing and chewing her breasts—all carried out while drunk and in a dazed, fugue-like state, with later partial amnesia—suggests a direct expression of primitive mother-oriented ambivalence. His earlier theft of an auto for a joy ride with an older woman may well have been related to the same general conflicts. *Dick's* theft of an auto to drive a woman to Reno to marry, while both were drunk, seems to have been part of his near-conscious search for consolation, after the frustration of his love-dependent-nurturant desire to marry the crippled girl "back home."

Each of these men's offenses suggests different aspects of a common constellation which dominates their lives: longing to be loved by and to love a mother figure who will both "mother" them and let them "father" her—with near-conscious ambivalence to women, caused by frustration of this striving.

The crimes of the high and low scorers thus seem to express their different central strivings or life-themes: antiweakness defenses versus ambivalent quest-for-love. They do not appear to be differentiated, with respect to the manifest violence of their offenses. It seems that the same legal offense, and the same degree of violence, may spring from quite different underlying personality structures; accordingly, as other writers have noted (51, 103), the legal offense per se is a poor index of susceptibility to rehabilitation. There is a strong suggestion, however, that low scorers offer considerably more promise of rehabilitation than do high scorers. This follows from the apparent greater capacity of the former to establish genuine relationships with other people; just as their criminal behavior seems to have followed upon frustration of the need for love, or upon some crisis in their love relationships, so would the establishment of new relationships offer the basis for changed behavior. In the high scorers, on the other hand, relationships based primarily upon love would seem to be very difficult of achievement; rather, we should expect new relationships in their case to conform with the old pattern of dominance-submission, something which, though it might induce conforming behavior for the moment, would in the end only strengthen those personality structures which are basic to their criminality—and to their fascist potential.

CHAPTER XXII

PSYCHOLOGICAL ILL HEALTH IN RE-LATION TO POTENTIAL FASCISM: A STUDY OF PSYCHIATRIC CLINIC PATIENTS[1]

Maria Hertz Levinson

A. INTRODUCTION

If differences in ideology are significantly related to personality differences, then one would expect ideology to be related also to various kinds of mental disturbance. It is the contention of modern psychiatry that the experiences and behavior of mentally disturbed persons differ only in degree from those of normal people, and that the disturbances which any given individual develops depend in very large part on his personality structure. Indeed, most of the concepts of modern psychology of personality were first developed on the basis of material from psychologically unhealthy people. The reasons for this were similar to the reasons, given below, which prompted the present study of ideology and personality in psychiatric patients.

In the first place, it is usually easier to describe and to explain the more pathological personality patterns than the more "healthy" ones. "Healthy" people, to be sure, also have problems, i.e., areas in which their adjustment to outer and inner stresses is not entirely smooth. They have, however, to a large extent "solved" these problems. They have succeeded in sublimating or successfully controlling their primitive impulses and, to the extent that inner problems still exist, they are able to achieve life situations which help to minimize their conflicts and anxieties. Those who need therapy, have, on the other hand, whether they are aware of the need or not, failed to achieve the proper balance, and the nature and degree of their imbalance is usually plain to be seen. The primitive impulses break through in more or less undisguised forms, the defensive struggles against them can often be

[1] The writer wishes to thank Dr. Karl Bowman, head of the Langley Porter Clinic, for making the Clinic facilities available. She also is indebted to Dr. Robert E. Harris, Chief Psychologist, for his generous support and numerous helpful suggestions, and to various members of the Clinic staff for their aid and cooperation.

clearly observed, and the conflicts with the environment are often still in progress. Thus, the "elements" and adjustment mechanisms of the personality are here more clearly discernible than in psychologically healthy individuals.

In the second place, an advantage in using the psychiatric clinic as a laboratory lies in the fact that here, more than in the usual research interview, people are willing to disclose the more intimate details of their lives. Thus, studies on patients who are strongly motivated to tell the truth about themselves may help to validate the methods used for the study of other groups.

Thirdly, the present investigation sought an approach to the very difficult problem of the relation between ideology and the dimension of psychological health-ill health. Are people with psychological disturbances—severe enough to make them seek psychiatric help—more prejudiced or less prejudiced than other groups of people? What is the general relation between neurosis and psychosis, on the one hand, and ideology on the other? Are particular patterns of ideology significantly related to any of the common psychiatric diagnostic groups?

In an attempt to answer these and other questions, 121 psychiatric patients were studied by means of our questionnaire and other methods. Data bearing on such factors as intelligence level, education, type of complaint, and psychiatric diagnosis were obtained from the Clinic records. In addition, 16 cases were studied intensively by means of interviews and the Thematic Apperception Test, and all material previously collected by the Clinic workers was brought into the picture. A majority of the subjects also took a standardized test known as the Minnesota Multiphasic Personality Inventory. In analyzing and interpreting these data, concepts and findings from the other areas of the study as a whole were employed to the full.

B. THE NATURE OF THE SAMPLE

The subjects, 71 women and 50 men, were all patients at the Langley Porter Clinic in San Francisco, a state institution for the diagnosis and treatment of psychiatric disorders. Violent cases and cases for permanent commitment are not admitted. At the time of the study reported in the present chapter, the inpatient department had three wards (about 45 beds) for patients requiring temporary hospitalization. Most of these cases can be classed as severe neuroses or mild psychoses. The majority of the patients are treated in the outpatient department, where adults are seen regularly for therapeutic interviews and various psychological procedures.

The hospital facilities are open to everyone, regardless of income. Fees range from $0 (gratis) to $2 per interview and are graded according to ability to pay. In terms of income, occupation, and residence, most Clinic patients could be said to fall into the urban lower middle class, though in some cases the lower class or the educated middle class are represented. Most upper-class and upper middle-class individuals who wish psychiatric help go to private psychiatrists.

One may ask to what extent patients, of whatever social class, who seek help from a public psychiatric clinic are different from those people with psychological disturbances who do not seek such help. One important trait distinguishing the two groups is acceptance of psychiatry and of the idea that one's illness might have important psychological sources. This is true particularly of many persons who come to the Clinic of their own accord or at the instigation of relatives or friends. Almost as large a proportion of the patients, however, are referred by social agencies or by physicians to whom they have usually turned because of physical symptoms. Most of these people have little or no idea about psychiatry and many drop out of treatment after a few interviews have shown them that their "mind" is involved.

Another selective sampling factor is the admission policy of the hospital. The outpatient clinic arranges at least one interview for every person applying, except in cases which should properly be handled by other agencies. The outpatients are selected therefore only on the basis of their wishing psychiatric help from a clinic. The inpatient department, on the other hand, is so small that only a limited portion of applications can be considered. The only cases admitted are those requiring immediate attention, those presenting special diagnostic problems, and those which could best profit from temporary hospitalization. The judgment regarding prognosis rests, of course, on age and the nature of the disturbance, but also to a large extent on such factors as the patient's cooperativeness, desire to be helped, degree of insight, intelligence, and education. The staff's judgment as to whether the patient is a particularly worthwhile person also plays a role. This latter judgment rests in part on the personal impression the patient makes, that is, on his conformity with middle-class or upper middle-class standards of dress, occupational and educational level, and speech, manners, and so forth. The Langley Porter patients are referred from a great variety of sources: many kinds of agencies, army, navy, physicians, private individuals. About 20 per cent of the applicants are self-referred; this group contains many college graduates and other younger people who feel that they can be helped in making better life choices and who are extremely receptive to psychological procedures.

For these combined reasons the Langley Porter Clinic patients are on the whole younger, more intelligent, better educated, and more receptive to psychological procedures than the general population.

In selecting subjects for the present investigation, an attempt was made to get a random sample of the Clinic population, exclusive of those who were under 20 years of age,[2] Jewish, non-white, or foreign-born. Questionnaires were given to all ward patients who were able to cooperate and to the 7 subjects of a special research study on stomach ulcers. In the outpatient de-

[2] A few subjects slightly younger than 20 were actually included in the final sample.

partment, most cases were selected on a random basis by approaching all patients coming into the waiting room on certain days and by having questionnaires administered by Clinic staff members who were instructed in the principles of random selection. Most subjects filled out the blanks on the spot. A few (less than 5 per cent) refused altogether. Some took the questionnaire home; of these, more than half returned the completed forms. Care was taken to preserve the anonymity of the subjects, and this further increased willingness to cooperate. Unfortunately, there is no exact record of what proportion of the blanks distributed were returned. It is estimated that the return was 85 to 90 per cent.

Thus, although degree of cooperativeness played some part in the selection of subjects, this factor was probably no larger than in many other groups studied. The sample is probably fairly representative of the Langley Porter Clinic population as a whole, within the limits stated above.

The 50 men and 71 women selected for study may be further characterized as follows:

Age. A majority were between 20 and 40 years—very few being under 20.

Sex. There were more women than men, due to the greater number of women patients in the Clinic as a whole. Most results were computed for men and women separately.

Marital status. Of the men, 58 per cent were married, 36 per cent unmarried, and 6 per cent divorced. In the case of the women, 62 per cent were married, 31 per cent unmarried, and 7 per cent divorced. Of the men who were married or who had been married, 56 per cent had children, 44 per cent had no children. Of the women who were married or who had been married, 67 per cent had children, 33 per cent no children.

Education. Records were available on 46 of the men and 66 of the women. These records are probably not entirely accurate, since many people with little schooling try to conceal this fact. On the whole, however, the figures are well confirmed by inspection of the data on occupation. The majority of the group had completed high school, all had completed grammar school, and some had college educations. In computing averages, 1 year was added to the number of grades completed when there was additional vocational training such as nursing, business college, music conservatory, and so forth. The mean number of years of schooling for the men was 12.2, for the women 12.5.

Intelligence. Usable intelligence quotients were available on only one-third of the group. The only scores considered were those obtained by means of the Wechsler-Bellevue Test of Adult Intelligence. Among these, the only subtests included were those judged as most probably valid, that is, as not much affected by temporary disturbance due to the neurotic or psychotic condition. Since all cases showing wide discrepancies between two subtests, and many others with low scores, were excluded, the obtained average I.Q.

of 115 (for men and women combined, N = 37) seems spuriously high, the true average for the group probably being closer to 110. This agrees pretty well with an estimate made by the Chief Psychologist regarding the Langley Porter Clinic population as a whole. It is slightly but significantly above the average of 100 for the population at large.

Parents' birthplace. A considerable number of subjects had foreign-born parents. In the case of the men 70 per cent said both parents were born in the U.S., 12 per cent gave both parents as foreign born, 16 per cent had one foreign-born parent, and 2 per cent gave no answer. In the case of the women, there were 65 per cent with both parents born in the U.S., 18 per cent with both parents foreign born, 13 per cent with one foreign-born parent, and 4 per cent gave no answer.

Income. The data here (obtained on the questionnaire) are very incomplete because a great many subjects left the question unanswered or put "none"— either because of a sense of privacy or because they were temporarily unemployed due to their illness. In the case of the women the data are less complete than for the men, because on some of the questionnaire blanks used there was no question about husband's income. For the 33 men who indicated their income, the figures are as follows:

> under $2,000 a year: 18 per cent
> $2,000 to $2,900 a year: 42 per cent
> $3,000 to $3,900 a year: 28 per cent
> $4,000 or above, a year: 12 per cent

Of the women, only 19 reported their own income and 29 gave the husband's income. None of the women earned $4,000 or more; only 5 husbands earned $4,000 or more. Most of the stated incomes fell between $2,000 and $3,900.

Occupation. Of the 50 men, 22 per cent classed themselves as unemployed, students, etc., 41 per cent could be classed as skilled workers, 21 per cent as white collar, and 10 per cent as professional workers. There were one unskilled worker and two seamen. Of the 60 women who gave an occupation, 58 per cent were housewives, 23 per cent clerical or sales personnel, 8 per cent held other nonprofessional jobs, 5 per cent had professions, and 6 per cent were students.

Religion. Many religious denominations were represented in this group. They are discussed more fully in relation to political and social ideology, as revealed by the questionnaire, in Chapter VI. About one-half were Protestants and one-fifth to one-fourth were Catholics; the rest were agnostic or declined to state a preference.

Politics. With respect to political group membership the men were distributed as follows: Blank, undecided, 16 per cent; Republicans, 24 per cent; Democrats, 54 per cent; Socialists and Communists, 6 per cent. The women were grouped in the following way: Blank, undecided, 25 per cent; Republicans, 17 per cent; Democrats, 54 per cent; Socialists and Communists, 4 per cent.

These socioeconomic characteristics of our group were similar to those of several other groups in the study as a whole. Attempts to compare our sample with other *clinic* groups with regard to socioeconomic characteristics and psychiatric diagnostic groupings would have been rather difficult and was not necessary for our purpose. Since the Clinic draws its patients from a wide variety of sources, and attempts to serve as many applicants as possible, the Langley Porter population as a whole and our sample in particular is probably fairly characteristic of groups of patients from similar public psychiatric clinics in large American cities.

C. STATISTICAL RESULTS FROM THE QUESTIONNAIRE

The scales used included the 10-item E scale from Form 60, a 28-item F scale, and two different PEC scales—a 5-item one and a 12-item one. One-third of the questionnaires had been collected when the new and improved Form 45 was completed, and it seemed advisable to use it because it had better statistical properties, and because better comparisons between the Langley Porter group and other, nonpsychiatric groups could be made.

The main concern in the present chapter is with the characteristics of subjects scoring high and of subjects scoring low on the E scale. The statistical properties of the E scale, for the Langley Porter groups of men and women are shown in Table 1 (XXII).

TABLE 1 (XXII)

RELIABILITY DATA ON THE E SCALE FOR PSYCHIATRIC CLINIC MEN AND WOMEN

	Men (N=50)	Women (N=71)
Reliability	.75	.84
Mean (total)	3.67	3.65
Mean (Part A)	3.92	4.23
Mean (Part B)	3.42	3.06
S.D. (total)	1.59	1.60
S.D. (Part A)	1.78	1.81
S.D. (Part B)	1.70	1.64
Mean D.P.	4.11	4.21
Range	1.00–6.20	1.00–7.00

The reliability of the scale is as high as that found in most other groups, and the mean D.P. is somewhat higher. (The mean scores show the Clinic men and women to be slightly—but not significantly—less prejudiced than the average for other groups.) The mean scores (men: 3.67; women: 3.65) are close to the figures obtained by averaging the results for all groups studied (Chapter IV). The means for men and for women are practically the same.

That both men and women score higher on Part A (the non-A-S part) of the scale than on Part B is consistent with findings in other groups. In general there is very little in the E-scale responses of the Langley Porter group that would distinguish them from most of the other groups studied.[3]

As we have shown above, the Clinic sample was somewhat selected for age, intelligence, education, and cooperativeness. All these factors are correlated to some extent with ethnocentrism. Therefore, the average ethnocentrism score of psychiatric patients in general or of all "neurotic and psychotic persons" in the general population could be expected to be somewhat higher.[4]

D. RELATIONSHIP OF ETHNOCENTRISM TO VARIOUS PSYCHIATRIC CLASSIFICATIONS

We undertook first to investigate the following questions: (1) Is ethnocentrism related to the two major psychiatric groupings, "neurotic" and "psychotic"? (2) Is it related to any of the specific psychiatric classifications? With these questions in mind, E scores were compared with the official psychiatric diagnoses assigned by the staff psychiatrists. Psychiatric diagnoses were available for 114 out of our total of 121 subjects. Of the remaining 7 cases, 2 had not yet been diagnosed, 5 had been given questionnaire forms without the usual identifying code number so that it was not possible to look up the appropriate files.

Table 2 (XXII) shows the proportion of subjects falling into various psychiatric classifications. These classifications represent the official diagnoses entered by the Clinic staff into the subjects' case records. The definitions of the psychiatric categories and the manner in which they were assigned will be discussed in the next section.

Twenty-four per cent of our diagnosed group had been classed as psy-

[3] See Chapters V, VII, and XV for results obtained from the Langley Porter Clinic group by means of the PEC and F scales and the projective items.

[4] See Chapter VIII for the relationship of ethnocentrism to intelligence; Chapter IV for ethnocentrism and education; Chapters I, XII and XV for resistance of high scorers to psychological procedures and explanations. Further support is given by the fact that a group of psychiatric patients (largely non-self-referred and emphasizing organic causes of their problems) in a Veterans' Administration hospital obtained a mean of nearly 5.0 on both the E and F scales (unpublished material of D. J. Levinson).

TABLE 2 (XXII)

INCIDENCE OF VARIOUS PSYCHIATRIC DIAGNOSES IN THE SAMPLE OF PSYCHIATRIC CLINIC PATIENTS[a]

	No.	Percentage	OPD[b] as a whole (percentage)
Psychoses:			
Schizophrenia	15	13.2	9.2
Manic depressive	10	8.8	5.2
Other psychoses	2	1.8	
Total psychoses	27	23.7	
Psychoneuroses:			
Psychoneurosis mixed	34	29.8	
Reactive depression	2	1.8	
Anxiety state	20	17.5	
Anxiety hysteria	3	2.6	
Hysteria	6	5.3	
Hypochondriasis	1	0.9	
Psychasthenia (obsessive-compulsive neurosis)	3	2.6	
Obsessive-compulsive ruminative state	2	1.8	
Total neuroses	71	62.3	43.6
Other disorders:			
Psychopathic personality	3	2.6	
Alcoholism	2	1.8	
Ulcers	7	6.1	
Miscellaneous	4	3.5	
Total other disorders	16	14.0	

[a]N is 114; of these 29% are inpatients, 65% outpatients, and 6% (ulcer cases) are from the research project in psychosomatic medicine.

[b]OPD = outpatient department.

chotic, 62 per cent as psychoneurotic. The remaining 14 per cent were considered to have "other disorders" such as "psychopathic personality," "alcoholism," and so forth. For our purposes, only those categories were included which appeared with some frequency. Thus, among the psychoses we have included only schizophrenia and manic-depressive psychoses. The remaining 2 cases, 1 "epilepsy with psychosis," 1 "undiagnosed psychosis," have been placed together under the heading "other psychoses."

The cases appearing together under the heading "other disorders" include: (1) 7 male patients suffering from stomach ulcers who had come to the

Clinic not for psychiatric help but to serve as subjects in a study in psychosomatic medicine. These cases were officially classed as "mixed neurosis," but were so different from the group here classified "psychoneurosis, mixed type" that they were considered separately for the purposes of the present investigation; (2) several cases classified as "psychopathic personality" and "alcoholism without psychosis"; (3) 4 cases, grouped under the heading "miscellaneous." These include 2 cases diagnosed "schizoid personality," 1 case of "primary behavior disorder," and 1 "post-traumatic personality disorder."

Our list of diagnostic categories covers only the main headings (or names of disorders) used for psychiatric classification. Often these were the only categories assigned. Usually, however, the cases were further described in terms of their particular symptomatology (e.g., psychoneurosis, mixed; anxiety and depressive features; or schizophrenia, paranoid type). The number of cases from our sample in each of the resulting finer subgroups was too small to be considered here.

No figures on the distribution of the various groups in the Clinic population as a whole were available for comparison with our figures. In Table 2 (XXII) we have included a few figures covering the outpatient department alone. These show that our group contains more psychotics and psychoneurotics (and consequently fewer cases falling into the "other disorders") than the outpatient clinic as a whole. This is to be expected, because 29 per cent of our group came from the inpatient department where most cases have a diagnosis of psychosis or neurosis.

In making the formal diagnoses, the physicians were supposed to follow the official list of mental disorders, set up by the American Psychiatric Association. (Condensed Form of New Classification Adopted by the Committee on Statistics and Approved by the Council, December 27, 1933.)

The classifications in this list are based on symptomatology rather than on personality dynamics. Thus, a "psychoneurosis" is a mental disorder in which the main symptoms are hysterical, compulsive, or anxiety manifestations. In the absence of such symptoms, many peculiarities of behavior, e.g., sexual perversions, alcoholism, delinquency, would not be considered "neurotic," but would be categorized as "primary behavior disorder," "alcoholism," "psychopathic personality."

In most of our cases, a preliminary diagnosis was assigned by the patient's psychiatrist. In a conference with the director of the department (outpatient or inpatient) an official diagnosis was then worked out on the basis of the case history presented by the physician. We had no way of actually measuring the reliability of the psychiatric diagnoses. It is our guess, however, that there was considerable unreliability. One source of unreliability probably lies in the categories themselves, which are rather broadly defined. Also it is often unclear whether a case should be classed as a "mixed neurosis" or whether one type of symptom stands out sufficiently to warrant a diagnosis such as "hysteria" or "hypochondriasis." Then also, there is sometimes the question of which symptoms are the predominant ones.

The categories, then, leave a great deal to the subjective judgment of each physician. And it is possible for the physicians to use the classification scheme in various ways, according to their predilections and theoretical orientations. Thus, unreliability of the classifications is no doubt further increased by the fact that the Langley Porter Clinic, at the time of the present research, had a great number of therapists varying greatly in training, experience and theoretical outlook. They ranged in training from supervised medical students to staff psychiatrists with many years of experience. In theoretical orientation they included strictly (Freudian) psychoanalytic, Jungian, and other dynamic and nondynamic points of view.

Because of these sources of unreliability, one would expect to find only slight relationships between the psychiatric diagnostic categories and other variables. Furthermore, on theoretical grounds one cannot expect very clearcut relationships between categories based entirely on symptomatology rather than on personality dynamics, and variables like ethnocentrism which seem to be directly related to certain dynamic factors. Lastly, the division of our total group into several small subgroups according to sex and diagnosis further decreased the chances of obtaining significant statistical relationships with ethnocentrism. The relationships that were nevertheless obtained seem even more significant in the light of these considerations.

The total group was divided into 8 subgroups, on the basis of sex and E quartile. The proportion of each subgroup having any given psychiatric diagnosis was then obtained (Table 3 (XXII)). Thus, the percentage of low quartile women diagnosed as schizophrenic can be compared with the proportion of schizophrenics in any other quartile or in the total sample.

In addition, the same percentages were computed for the two *halves* of the E distribution (Table 4 (XXII)). (This was done by combining the figures for the low and low middle quartiles, on the one hand, and those for the high middle and high quartiles, on the other.) This increased the number of cases in each subgroup and made it possible to obtain more dependable critical ratios for the differences between high and low groups in terms of the incidence of various diagnoses within them.

Many cases, in addition to being roughly classified, were further described according to finer differentiating features. Because of the small number of cases, the additional features of only the largest single group, namely, the neurotics, were tabulated. Table 5 (XXII) shows the percentage of neurotics in each quartile who had been diagnosed as presenting various additional "features." It should be remembered that these percentages are not based on the

TABLE 3 (XXII)

PERCENTAGE OF EACH E-SCALE QUARTILE FALLING INTO VARIOUS PSYCHIATRIC CATEGORIES

	MEN					WOMEN					MEN AND WOMEN
	Low N=12	Low Middle N=12	High Middle N=13	High N=11	Total N=48	Low N=16	Low Middle N=18	High Middle N=14	High N=18	Total N=66	Total N=144
Psychoses:											
Schizophrenia	8.3	8.3	15.4	9.1	10.4	6.3	22.2	35.7	-	15.2	13.2
Manic depressive	8.3	-	15.4	-	6.2	-	16.7	7.1	16.7	10.6	8.8
Other	-	8.3	-	-	2.1	-	-	0	5.6	1.5	1.8
Total	16.7	16.7	30.8	9.1	18.7	6.3	38.9	42.9	22.3	27.3	23.7
Neuroses:											
Psychoneurosis mixed	25.0	33.3	15.4	9.1	20.8	68.8	33.3	28.6	16.7	36.4	29.8
Reactive depression	-	-	7.7	-	2.1	6.3	-	-	-	1.5	1.8
Anxiety state	33.3	33.3	15.4	27.3	27.1	-	5.6	7.1	27.8	10.6	17.5
Anxiety hysteria	-	-	-	-	-	-	5.6	-	11.1	4.5	2.6
Hysteria	8.3	-	7.7	-	4.2	-	5.6	7.1	11.1	6.0	5.3
Hypochondriasis	-	-	-	-	-	-	5.6	-	-	1.5	.9
Psychasthenia (obsessive-compulsive)	-	-	7.7	-	2.1	12.5	-	-	-	3.0	2.6
Obsessive-compulsive ruminative state	-	-	-	-	-	-	-	-	11.1	3.0	1.8
Total	66.7	66.7	53.8	36.4	56.2	87.5	55.6	42.9	77.8	66.7	62.3
Other Disorders:											
Psychopathic personality	8.3	-	-	18.2	6.2	-	-	7.1	-	1.5	2.6
Alcoholism	-	8.3	-	-	2.1	-	5.6	-	-	1.5	1.8
Stomach ulcers	-	8.3	15.4	36.4	14.6	-	-	-	-	-	6.1
Miscellaneous	8.3	-	-	-	2.1	6.3	-	7.1	-	3.0	3.5
Total	16.7	16.7	15.4	54.5	25.0	6.3	5.6	14.3	-	6.0	14.0
Over-all total	100.1	100.1	100.0	100.0	99.9	100.1	100.1	100.1	100.1	100.0	100.0

TABLE 4 (XXII)

PERCENTAGE OF THE UPPER AND OF THE LOWER HALVES OF THE E-SCALE DISTRIBUTION FALLING INTO VARIOUS PSYCHIATRIC CATEGORIES

	Men		Women	
	Low Half N = 24	High Half N = 24	Low Half N = 34	High Half N = 32
Psychoses:				
Schizophrenia	8.3	12.5	14.6	15.7
Manic depressive	4.2	8.3	8.9	12.2
Other psychoses	-	-	-	3.1
Total psychoses	12.5	20.8	23.5	31.0
Psychoneuroses:				
Psychoneurosis mixed[a]	29.2	12.5	50.0	22.0
Reactive depression	-	4.2	2.9	-
Anxiety state[a]	33.3	20.8	2.9	18.8
Anxiety hysteria	-	-	2.9	6.3
Hysteria	4.2	4.2	2.9	9.4
Hypochondriasis	-	-	2.9	-
Obsessive-compulsive	-	4.2	5.9	-
Obsessive-compulsive ruminative state	-	-	-	6.3
Total neuroses	66.7	45.9	70.4	62.8
Other disorders:				
Psychopathic personality	-	8.3	-	3.1
Alcoholism	4.2	-	2.9	-
Ulcers	4.2	25.0	-	-
Others	12.5	-	2.9	3.1
Total other disorders	20.9	33.3	5.8	6.2

[a]In only 2 cases are the differences between the high and low halves statistically significant. For the "psychoneurosis mixed type" there are significantly more low-scoring than high-scoring women (C.R. = 2.4; 2% level). There are significantly more high-scoring than low-scoring women with "anxiety state" (C.R. = 2.1; 5% level).

total number of cases in each quartile but only on the number of psychoneurotic cases in each quartile. Not all cases had such finer descriptions and many cases had more than one of these features. Therefore, the vertical columns in Table 5 (XXII) do not add up to 100. Table 6 (XXII) gives the same results as Table 5 (XXII), but for the upper and lower halves of the E distribution rather than for the four quartiles.

The relation between ethnocentrism and psychiatric diagnosis, as summarized in Tables 3–6 (XXII), may now be considered under two main headings: (1) ethnocentrism in relation to neurosis vs. psychosis, and (2) ethnocentrism in relation to specific diagnostic categories.

TABLE 5 (XXII)

PERCENTAGE OF NEUROTIC PATIENTS IN EACH E-SCALE QUARTILE SHOWING VARIOUS NEUROTIC FEATURES

	MEN				WOMEN			
	Low N=8	Low Middle N=8	High Middle N=7	High N=4	Low N=14	Low Middle N=10	High Middle N=6	High N=14
Depressive	50.0	12.5	28.5	-	50.0	10.0	33.3	7.1
Anxiety and phobias	25.0	-	28.5	50.0	64.3	30.0	50.0	7.1
Obsessive-compulsive	-	-	-	50.0	-	10.0	-	-
Neurasthenic	-	-	-	-	14.2	-	-	-
Hysterical conversion	-	-	-	25.0	7.1	20.0	16.6	-
Hypochondriacal	-	12.5	-	-	-	10.0	-	7.1
Psychopathic	-	-	-	-	7.1	-	-	7.1
Schizoid	25.0	12.5	-	-	-	-	33.3	14.2
Paranoid	-	-	-	-	-	-	16.6	-
Homosexual (or perversion)	25.0	25.0	-	50.0	7.1	-	16.6	7.1

TABLE 6 (XXII)

PERCENTAGE OF NEUROTIC PATIENTS IN THE UPPER AND LOWER HALVES
OF THE E-SCALE DISTRIBUTION SHOWING VARIOUS NEUROTIC FEATURES

| | Men | | Women | |
	Low Half N = 16	High Half N = 11	Low Half N = 24	High Half N = 20
Depressive	31.3	18.1	33.3	20.0
Anxiety and phobias	12.5	36.2	50.0	20.0
Obsessive-compulsive	-	18.1	4.2	5.0
Hysterical conversion	-	-	12.5	5.0
Hypochondriacal	-	9.1	4.2	5.0
Psychopathic	6.3	-	4.2	5.0
Schizoid	12.5	-	-	20.0
Paranoid	6.3	-	-	5.0
Neurasthenic	-	-	8.4	-
Homosexual (or perversion)	25.0	18.2	4.2	10.0

1. ETHNOCENTRISM IN RELATION TO NEUROSIS AND PSYCHOSIS

In our total group, there was a preponderance of psychoneurotics over psychotics, the ratio being 62:24 per cent. Table 4 (XXII) shows that this ratio is somewhat greater in the low than in the high half of the E distribution. The trend appears even more markedly in Table 3 (XXII), especially in the figures for the women. There are practically no psychotics, but a relatively very large number of neurotics in the low quartile, with the proportion of psychotics increasing, that of neurotics decreasing, in the low middle and high middle quartiles. The largest number of psychotics is in the high middle quartile, but relatively few are in the high quartile. The same trends appeared in the male and female groups.

Several hypotheses can be offered to explain the drop in the proportion of psychotic subjects from the high middle to the high quartile. One hypothesis is that the drop is caused entirely by certain factors of sampling. It can be argued that the proportion of psychotics in the high quartile would actually be equal to or even higher than that in the high middle quartile were it not that many of the very high-scoring individuals were eliminated from the group through certain external circumstances. We know from experience at the Clinic and from work with other groups that high scorers are in general less cooperative, because they are relatively more suspicious and more afraid of any infringement of their privacy. Thus, they often left unanswered parts of the questionnaire dealing, for instance, with income or father's income and other "private" topics, even when their anonymity was assured. By these and similar means high scorers avoid dealing with topics which might remind them of problems and emotions they are trying to keep in repression or which might expose their weaknesses to others.

It is probable, therefore, that a great many extremely prejudiced people could never be induced to go to a psychiatric clinic for help. Perhaps this holds particularly for those ethnocentric individuals who are most disturbed, that is, for those with psychotic or near-psychotic disturbances. If it is true that there are relatively many potential high scorers among severely psychotic patients, the relatively low incidence of psychotics in the high quartile could be caused by the fact that the Clinic excludes violent psychotic cases and many of the cases with very poor prognosis.

Lastly, there were a few ward patients who were either too disturbed to fill out a questionnaire properly or who refused to do so. But there were not enough cases like this to explain entirely the decrease of psychotics from the high middle to the high quartile. Another line of speculation, to which we shall return later, is that prejudice in its extreme degree may be an expression of certain ego-defenses which the person has invested with a great deal of energy, because without them he would suffer a psychotic breakdown. Perhaps the high scorers are very similar to our "high middles" except for somewhat greater ego-strength and better working defenses.

Another hypothesis is that the decrease in the proportion of psychotics from the high middle to the high quartile is a true one, and that it can be explained by certain features of the psychotic process itself which would tend to produce middle rather than extreme scores. In support of this hypothesis some observations on psychotic clinic patients should be mentioned here.

Several of the psychotic subjects were interviewed, and it was found that only one of them had even some slight knowledge of current events and of the social issues of the present. Even this one case, a professional person, was concerned mainly with abstract ideology and never talked in terms of political reality. It seemed as if these psychotic subjects—all mild cases in their first psychotic episode—were emotionally too removed from social reality to pay much attention to it or to form any strong and consistent ideology about it. Apparently this did not produce enough inconsistency of response to have much lowering effect on scale reliabilities, but enough to produce various deviant patterns and unintense responses, resulting in "middle" scores.

A related hypothesis would be that the tendency toward "middle" E scores in our psychotic group was due in largest part to certain special, temporary factors arising out of the circumstance that these patients were all in acute psychotic episodes—or had just recovered from one. Here, too, we have some supporting observations. One patient, for instance, responded only in terms of $+1$ and -1. When released from the hospital, greatly improved and free from delusions, the patient said in an interview that he thought his constricted responses had been due to his extreme lack of self-confidence at the time, which prevented him from expressing himself in a more definite fashion, and that he might respond differently now.

Another subject, who at the time suffered from paranoid delusions and who showed great hostility towards his hospital environment and resentment toward the test procedure, answered only in terms of +3 and —3 (further emphasized by exclamation marks, underlinings or negativisitic comments). Such a pattern of responses would also lead to a score closer to the mean than the subject's actual attitude would warrant.

Temporary characteristics of the illness itself may be important in some cases, but it is the author's impression that they are not likely to influence the E scores of most subjects to any considerable extent. The subjects who at the time the scale was administered were very much out of contact with reality usually refused to participate or produced records which could be immediately recognized as invalid. These either had many omissions or bizarre comments, or they showed that the person was not able to follow the directions properly.

Assuming that the trends obtained with the present small sample are valid, the data show a negative relationship between psychosis and strong opposition to prejudice, a positive relationship between psychosis and moderate prejudice, but a relatively low incidence of psychosis among the extremely high scorers.

To explain this trend we favor the following hypothesis, which fits in with many of the findings discussed in previous chapters and which is supported also by the clinical findings to be discussed later: Strong opposition to prejudice, as measured by the E scale, appears to be related to certain personality structures which, under stress, are more likely to lead to psychoneurotic than to psychotic disturbances. This hypothesis will be discussed in more detail later in the present chapter.

2. ETHNOCENTRISM IN RELATION TO SPECIFIC DIAGNOSTIC CATEGORIES

Our sample does not contain enough cases, in each of the more frequent diagnostic categories, to draw very specific conclusions. On the whole, however, it appears that ethnocentrism is not correlated very highly with any given psychiatric syndrome, at least as the latter was defined at Langley Porter Clinic. There were both high and low scorers among the schizophrenics, manic depressives, anxiety states, hysterias, obsessive-compulsives, and, of course, "mixed neuroses." However, *certain quantitative relationships* between E and psychiatric diagnosis, as well as *qualitative differences between high and low scorers within the same diagnostic category,* were found.

The quantitative relations may be considered first. (1) The low scorers, especially those in the low quartile, were concentrated mostly in the "mixed neurosis category," and distinguished most often by depression and conscious anxiety, and sometimes by neurasthenic features. This was particularly true of the women. The difference between percentages of women with mixed neurosis falling into the high and low halves of the E-scale distribution is statistically significant above the 2 per cent level of confidence (Table 4 (XXII)). (2) There were many more high-scoring than low-scoring women classified as "anxiety state." This difference is significant above the 5 per cent level of confidence (Table 4 (XXII)). The trend is less marked in men, where many low scorers were considered "anxiety states." As will be seen below, important qualitative differences exist between the high- and low-scoring men with anxiety state. (3) Seven of our subjects were men with stomach ulcers, taken from a research project in psychosomatic medicine. Not one of these made a low score. One had a low middle score, but turned out to be strongly prejudiced against Negroes, although not in regard to other groups. Two were "high middles," and four fell into the high quartile. This is a very marked trend, though of course not conclusive because of the small number of cases. However, this result is interesting because the modern psychoanalytic theory concerning the dynamics of ulcer has much in common with the dynamic formulations about the character structure of highly prejudiced men, as advanced in this book. This theory emphasizes underlying dependency which is held in repression by counteractive defenses, a masculine façade, much drive for activity, and so forth.

We may now consider the qualitative differences between high and low scorers in the same psychiatric category.

a. "MIXED NEUROSIS." This seemed to be the most frequent single diagnosis of our low-quartile women. It also occurred in one-third of the "low middle" women. There were eleven low-scoring and only three high-scoring women with the diagnosis "mixed neurosis." Among the low scorers, eight reported feelings of depression and inferiority, mood swings, crying; the rest complained of tiredness and/or dysmenorrhea and difficulties in social relationships. One case had other physical symptoms—probably on an hysterical basis—and inhibitions in group situations. Of the three high-scoring women, none reported depressed feelings, two denied all psychological difficulties. One was a psychopath, who also complained of menstrual difficulties. She was brought in by her husband for drinking, spending money excessively, and going out with men from bars. She did not feel any need of help. Two were psychosomatic cases: one an extremely tense young woman who had had a thyroidectomy and denied psychological problems; the other originally came in for a chronic (psychosomatic) skin rash, but soon admitted sexual (marital) maladjustment of long standing.

When the cases of stomach ulcer are not included, there are fewer men with the diagnosis "mixed neurosis." But the trend is similar to that in the women, with 25 per cent and 33 per cent in the two lower groups, only 15 per cent and 9 per cent in the two higher quartiles. There were three cases of "mixed neurosis" in the low quartile, one in the high. Two of the three low scorers were reported as suffering from neurotic depression. All three seemed to be soft, openly dependent characters whose difficulties had been precipitated by rejection by a love object. This was recognized by the subjects and brought out in the first interview. The one high scorer in this category was depressed but also showed obsessive-compulsive and anxiety symptoms. The anxiety centered on the idea that he might harm himself and his baby. It had appeared suddenly and left him subject to recurrent attacks.

b. ANXIETY STATE

Women: Of all single categories, this one contains the largest percentage of high scorers (28 per cent)—no low scorers, with few cases in the middle quartiles. (C. R. between percentage falling in the high and in the low halves of the E distribution is significant at the 5 per cent level). Five high scorers were classed as "anxiety state," and two very similar ones were classed as "anxiety hysteria." Five of these seven suffered from "spells" of tension, irritability, or hyperventilation symptoms often including dizziness and fainting. There was characteristic hypochondriacal concern, fear of death, of heart attack, and so on. Two women were afraid they would harm their children during the spells; one actually had choked her children on such occasions. In the picture of the two cases which did not have "spells," the hypochondriacal preoccupations with physical symptoms stood out and were combined with some depressed affect, in one case with schizo-affective reaction. There were no low scorers in this category.

Men: The numerical trend was less clear here, with a slightly greater proportion of cases in the low and low middle quartiles. There were four low scorers, three high scorers. One of the low scorers suffered from hyperventilation symptoms and fainting spells in certain situations of friction with a brutally aggressive father. The other three were similar to the low-quartile cases classed as "mixed neurosis," except for clinically more marked anxiety, with signs of much self-dissatisfaction, depression, social and sexual maladjustment, work disturbances, and some schizoid withdrawal.

The three high scorers showed physical anxiety symptoms with little conscious content. In one case this was coupled with much hypochondriacal concern, and in another, with some paranoid trends involving anxiety dreams and fear of attack by a certain person. Two of the three attributed the onset of symptoms to accidents.

c. SCHIZOPHRENIA

Women: There were high- and low-scoring schizophrenics. None of the high-quartile women fell into this group. The "high middles" that were classed as "schizophrenia" did not fall into any of the schizophrenic "types" (e.g., hebephrenia, paranoia). They showed paranoid, catatonic, obsessive-compulsive, and other features. The difference between the high and low scorers seems to be similar for men and for women. The high scorers appear to be very infantile, constricted, narrow personalities, often classed as "schizophrenia, simple type." Among the "high middle" women, several sudden post-partum psychoses of withdrawal in previously schizoid or compulsive + schizoid personalities, were found. The low-scoring schizophrenics were more of the hypersensitive, introspective sort, with relatively much interest in their own and others' psychological lives, and with relatively much insight into their own illness.

With regard to *paranoia*, the following observations have been made. Our group did not include any cases diagnosed as "true paranoia," but it included several schizophrenics (and others) with paranoid ideas. Among these were high, low, and middle scorers. However, the paranoid symptoms of the low scorers appeared to be qualitatively different from those of the high scorers, in that the low scorers more often combined ideas of being persecuted with severe inferiority feelings—"others are threatening, rejecting, or ridiculing me because of my symptoms, because I am inferior." The "devil" is not only threatening from outside, but is largely perceived as inside the person. The high scorers, on the other hand, tended towards more highly projective types of fantasies, sometimes accompanied by bragging, self-aggrandisement, and self-righteousness. Consciously, at least, the "devil" or evil forces were seen as only *outside*.

d. OBSESSIVE-COMPULSIVE NEUROSIS. There were only 1 man and 4 women in this group. The man fell into the high-middle quartile on E. Of the 4 women, 2 were low, 1 was high middle, and 1 was high. One of the two obsessive-compulsive cases appearing in the low group was just on the borderline between the low and low-middle group and had an F score slightly above the mean. The other case, an all-round low scorer, showed no typical obsessive-compulsive pattern, but had a phobic tendency and much conscious anxiety and feeling of inadequacy. The 2 high-scoring women (1 high middle, 1 high) were both classed as "obsessive-compulsive ruminative state" because of particularly rigid preoccupations, and constant ruminative thinking of schizoid quality. Extensive data are available only on the high-scoring case, a fifteen-year-old girl with preoccupations of a sexual character. She was worried because of fantasies about intercourse and pregnancy. During her stay at the hospital most of her conscious anxiety and ruminative thinking were centered about her physiological functions, particularly constipation, and imagined somatic changes (enlargement of abdomen).

From the above description it can be seen that a number of psychological trends differentiate the ethnocentric from the non-ethnocentric patients, regardless of formal classification. These and other trends will be studied more directly, and interpreted in relation to our general theory, below.

E. ETHNOCENTRISM IN RELATION TO THE MINNESOTA MULTIPHASIC PERSONALITY INVENTORY

The question of possible relationships between ethnocentrism and psychiatric diagnoses was approached in a preliminary way also by means of a test procedure known as the Minnesota Multiphasic Personality Inventory (from now on referred to as MMPI). This is an improved inventory of the Bernreuter type which has been validated against psychiatrists' diagnoses of carefully studied cases. It contains several scales, each made up of items which differentiate statistically between patients showing a given clinical syndrome —such as conversion hysteria, paranoid conditions, or schizophrenia—and the general population. It was thought that the test scores might provide more valid and more reliable criteria than the diagnoses that had been made of our subjects by many different physicians with varying orientations, training, and experience.

Test results were available for 34 men and 48 women, that is, for 68 per cent of our total group. Because of the fact that men and women had to be treated separately, the number of subjects is far too small to lead to conclusive results.

Comparison of average scores on the various MMPI scales for the four E quartiles, and preliminary inspection of individual and group test profiles, failed to show large or consistent relationships between E and psychiatric syndromes as measured by this inventory. The results show a few trends suggesting that further research along the same lines might be well worth while.

The following are the names of the scales and brief descriptions of the principal psychological or psychiatric dimensions they are supposed to measure. The descriptions are condensations of those given in the far more detailed test manual. For a description of the test and its interpretations see Hathaway and McKinley (50).

1. *Hypochondriasis*—Scales I (HCh) and II (Hs). Both scales purport to measure the degree of abnormal concern about bodily functions; many of the symptoms mentioned are vague or belong among the list of common physical expressions of anxiety. Scale I is more valid because it is less highly correlated with Sc and also contains an age correction.

2. *Hysteria* (Hy). A preliminary scale, measuring the degree of similarity between the subject (S) and patients who have developed conversion-type hysteria symptoms.

3. *Depression* (D). "Measures depth of clinically recognized symptom

complex, depression." "A high score indicates poor morale (of the emotional type) with a feeling of uselessness and inability to assume the normal degree of optimism regarding the future."

4. *Hypomania* (Ma). "Measures the personality factor characteristic of persons with marked overproductivity of thought and action."

5. *Psychasthenia* (Pt). "Measures the similarity of subject to psychiatric patients who are troubled by phobias or compulsive behavior." Mild degrees of this tendency may "be manifested merely in a mild depression, excessive worry, lack of confidence or inability to concentrate."

6. *Paranoia* (Pa). The preliminary scale, differentiating normals from a group of clinic patients characterized by suspiciousness, oversensitivity and delusions of persecution with or without expansive egotism. Their diagnoses were usually paranoia, paranoid state or paranoid schizophrenia.

7. *Schizophrenia* (Sc). Preliminary scale measuring similarity of subject's responses to those of patients who are characterized by bizarre and unusual thoughts or behavior.

8. *Psychopathic Deviate*—Scale I (Pd). Measures "absence of deep emotional response, inability to profit from experience and disregard of social mores." (Revised) Scale II (Pd$_r$) contains in addition a rather large group of items expressing a feeling of estrangement from the self and others, and is more highly correlated with Sc than is Scale I (Pd).

9. *Mf$_r$*. Measures masculinity or femininity of interest pattern.

The scales are arranged in such a way that the means are 50 with Standard Deviations of 10. Deviations from 50 in the direction of 0 are usually disregarded. Scores around 70 (i.e., 2 S.D. above the mean), are usually considered of borderline significance, scores above 80 as high. Elevations to 60 can be regarded as clinically significant when occurring in individual profiles in which most scores are close to 50 (or below).

Individuals with sufficient degrees of maladjustment to seek psychiatric help usually score high (2 S.D. above the average) on more than one of these scales. Recent clinical experience with the inventory seems to indicate that profiles or patterns of scores have more diagnostic significance than the single scores taken by themselves. In general, cases falling into the psychoneurotic group have their maximal scores on the HCh, Hs, Hy, D, and Pt scales (with secondary elevations on any of these), whereas psychotics on the whole have profiles with peaks on D, Sc, Ma, Pa, Pd, and Pd$_r$.

Slight borderline elevations on the "psychotic" scales occur frequently in a great variety of conditions without clinical evidence of psychotic manifestations. At present, their significance is not quite clear. Harris and Christiansen (48), in a study on the effect of short psychotherapy, have found that patients showing elevations on the psychotic scales and Pd, but without clinical evidence of psychotic tendencies, responded less well to psycho-therapy than others who did not have such scores.

Means for each of the MMPI scales were computed for each E quartile, with men and women being treated separately. These means are shown in Tables 7 and 8(XXII). The number of cases in each of these subgroups was so small that no measure of variability was computed. However, profiles for individual cases were drawn for high and low quartile. They showed great variability with regard to magnitude of score as well as to type of profile. This means (1) that differences between means would have to be very large to be statistically significant, and (2) that even significant differ-ences between means for single scales would be hard to interpret, if one takes the view that only profiles, and not single scale values, have much psy-chological meaning. (a) On the whole, the low scorers made somewhat less abnormal scores. (b) This was especially true for the men on the scales Hypochondriasis I, II and Depression, and for men and women on Psychas-thenia, Paranoia, and Schizophrenia. The low-scoring women were some-what higher on Hysteria; the low-scoring men on Femininity of Interests. Because of the nature of the differences mentioned under (b), it was thought necessary to determine whether some of these trends were caused by pres-ence of psychotic cases in the group, especially since there were somewhat more psychotics among the high half (especially "high middles"). When the means for nonpsychotic subjects were computed separately, the average pat-terns and differences remained much the same. Because the number of cases was again reduced by this procedure, and also because the patterns for high and high-middle scorers and those of low and low-middle scorers were similar in most respects, the figures for the two low quartiles and the two high quartiles, respectively, were combined (Figure 1 (XXII)).

The average profiles for the high scorers—especially for the men—re-semble most closely the "severe neurotic" pattern described by Harris and Christiansen in their study of the effects of brief psychotherapy; whereas the means for the low scorers resemble a more mildly neurotic pattern. The "severe neurosis" pattern, in which HCh and/or Hs, Hy, and D stand out as a pattern, with definite secondary elevation in Pd and with Pa, Sc approach-ing significance, but below the means for the first four scales, was found to be correlated with relatively poor prognosis for brief psychotherapy (of the sort administered at Langley Porter Clinic).

One difference between our high's average pattern and Harris and Christian-sen's poor prognosis pattern lies in the prominence in their group of second-ary elevated scores on Pd I, II. In our group there is little difference on these scales between our high- and low-scoring women and, for the men, the high scorers exceed the low scorers only on Pd II.

In the Harris and Christiansen study a question was raised concerning the

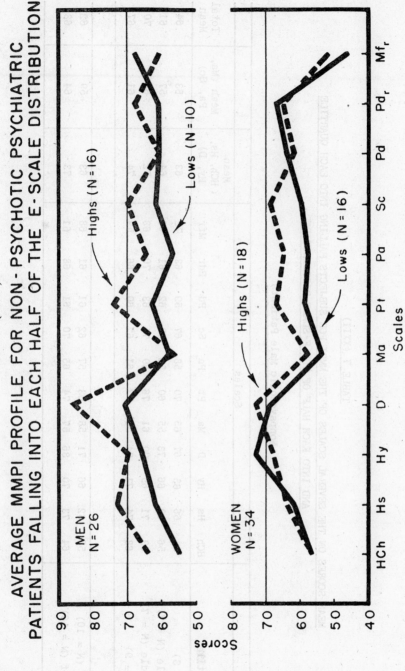

FIGURE 1 (XXII)

AVERAGE MMPI PROFILE FOR NON-PSYCHOTIC PSYCHIATRIC PATIENTS FALLING INTO EACH HALF OF THE E-SCALE DISTRIBUTION

TABLE 7 (XXII)

MEAN SCORES ON THE SEVERAL SCALES OF THE MMPI FOR SUBJECTS FALLING INTO EACH QUARTILE
AND INTO EACH HALF OF THE E-SCALE DISTRIBUTION

Nonpsychotic Male Patients

Quartile	Scales											Mean (HCh, Hs, Hy, D)	Mean (Ma, Pa, Sc)	Total Mean
	HCh	Hs	Hy	D	Ma	Pt	Pa	Sc	Pd	Pdr	Mfr			
Low (N = 3)	54	66	65	67	65	70	58	67	59	63	72	63	63	64
Low middle (N = 7)	56	60	66	73	55	60	56	60	62	61	66	64	57	61
High middle (N = 7)	59	71	69	90	61	76	69	75	63	70	63	72	68	70
High (N = 9)	68	74	71	84	54	73	61	67	60	66	59	74	61	67
Half														
Low half (N = 10)	55	62	66	71	58	63	57	62	61	61	68	63	59	62
High half (N = 16)	64	73	70	86	57	74	65	70	61	68	61	73	64	68

TABLE 8 (XXII)

MEAN SCORES ON THE SEVERAL SCALES OF THE MMPI FOR SUBJECTS FALLING INTO EACH QUARTILE AND INTO EACH HALF OF THE E-SCALE DISTRIBUTION

Nonpsychotic Female Patients

Quartile	HCh	Hs	Hy	D	Ma	Pt	Pa	Sc	Pd	Pdr	Mfr	Mean (HCh, Hs, Hy, D)	Mean (Ma, Pa, Sc)	Total Mean
Low (N = 10)	53	59	72	71	52	58	59	58	60	65	47	64	56	59
Low middle (N = 6)	64	67	74	66	58	60	58	62	70	71	46	68	59	63
High middle (N = 7)	54	55	67	71	62	65	62	65	61	62	49	62	63	61
High (N = 11)	59	70	69	75	56	68	67	71	63	67	54	68	65	65
Half														
Low half (N = 16)	57	62	73	69	54	59	58	60	64	67	46	65	57	61
High half (N = 18)	57	64	68	73	58	67	65	69	62	65	52	66	64	64

psychological meaning of elevations on such scales as Ma, Pa, and Sc in the absence of clinically discernible psychotic trends. Therefore the items on each scale were (arbitrarily) grouped into *subscales*, each of which was designed to measure some common general attitude. None of the subscales for the so-called neurotic scales (HCh, Hs, D, Hy) differentiated between the poor and good prognostic groups. The subscales that did differentiate came from Pd and Ma, Sc, Pa. Their content revealed a common "feeling of being victimized," a "tendency towards perceiving one's problems as imposed from outside and resulting in a feeling of lack of control of senses and motorium."

The difference between the neurotic and psychotic scales—apart from items referring to specific symptoms (e.g., delusions)—seems to lie in the relationship of the ego to the world, and to the body.

Perhaps the finding that our high scorers are somewhat higher on the psychotic scales may be interpreted in the same way. It would certainly fit in with trends described earlier in this book, e.g., the tendency to externalize and project unacceptable impulses, ideas, and affects. However, in order to test such an interpretation, an analysis of our data in terms of the Harris-Christiansen subscales would have to be made. This was not thought worth while mainly because of the small number of cases in our sample. Further study along these lines should prove rewarding.

One very unexpected result was that the high-scoring men obtained extremely high scores on the depression scale, whereas clinically the low scorers, and especially the low-scoring women, showed the greatest tendency towards neurotic depressive symptoms. On the MMPI, the low-scoring women did not make particularly high D scores. (See also the discussion of the clinical material in Section G of the present chapter.)

These apparently contradictory results suggest that the D scale does not measure the same psychological tendencies as were observed clinically in our low scorers, who characteristically suffer from subjective depressions, feelings of inferiority and failure. Therefore, the items of the D scale were examined and put in groups according to content. Out of the 60 items, only 23 clearly referred to the kind of feelings reported by our low subjects, these were:

1. Signs of inferiority feelings, easily hurt, unhappy, self-criticisms.
2. Opposition to cruelty and aggressiveness, lack of extrapunitiveness.
3. Submissive reactions in social situations.
4. Admission of uneasiness in social situations.
5. Lack of energy, and work inhibition.
6. Rejection of religious ideas (possibly).

The other 37 items referred to: impairment of mental functioning and of body functions; brooding and "worrying"; perception of the environmental forces as threatening or mistreating the subject; and general expressions of "not feeling well," "don't care about anything." Many of these items, pertaining as they do to very vague and nonspecific ideas, are clinically more consistent with *anxiety* or with anxious rumination of the more obsessive-compulsive variety than with neurotic depression. This leads to the supposition that "depression" as measured by this scale is not a unitary process; that there may be qualitatively different types of depression which occur in individuals with different personality structures.

F. PERSONALITY TRENDS AS REVEALED BY PATIENTS' "STATEMENT OF PROBLEM" IN THE FIRST PSYCHIATRIC INTERVIEW

The attempt to relate ethnocentrism to type of psychological disturbance, using only the conventional psychiatric classifications, produced some statistical trends, but it did not in itself allow inferences about personality dynamics in high and low scorers. The particular problem posed at the beginning of the present chapter seemed to call for extensive clinical material. Therefore, a greater proportion of subjects from the total Clinic group, than from other groups in the study as a whole, were studied by means of interviews and T.A.T.'s. However, due mainly to limitations of time, it was not possible to study intensively a large proportion of subjects from the high and low quartiles. This proportion was further decreased by the inclusion ·of some "middles" in the group to be interviewed. This was done for reasons of availability and out of special interest in certain individual cases. The total number of fairly complete case studies, including T.A.T. and interviews covering ideology as well as personal data and history, was 21—11 men and 10 women. These subjects represented a great variety of clinical pictures. Some types of cases, particularly needed for purposes of comparison, such as high-scoring obsessive-compulsives, high-scoring paranoids or low-scoring men with stomach ulcers, were not represented. Due to the limited number of cases interviewed and to the manner of their selection, no quantitative statements as to the relationships of ethnocentrism to personality structure, type of disturbance, and genetic factors can be made from our case material by itself. Most of the interviews gathered at the Clinic were, however, included in the larger sample of interviews employed in the quantitative analysis reported in Chapters IX through XIII.

In the absence of a sufficient number of case histories on psychiatric patients for quantitative comparisons, the material gathered by the Clinic staff and recorded in the patients' charts was examined for its usefulness for the present purpose. This material turned out to be very variable in amount and quality. Only in rare instances was sufficient material recorded in the charts to permit relatively complete dynamic formulation of the case. Each physician's notes varied with regard to length, completeness, amount, and type of interpretation included in the recorded material. Also, the material from later contacts between patient and physician was obviously colored in uncontrollable amounts and directions by the patient's relationship to the therapist, the latter's personality and approach (number and kind of questions asked), and by the therapeutic process (e.g., increasing insight).

One part of the case records appeared relatively less variable in most of these respects. This was the *first psychiatric interview* in which the patient stated his reasons for seeking help at the Clinic. Here, the patient, confronted with an unknown but friendly clinic worker, was invited by a very general question to state his problem. The response was often recorded in the patient's own words and often included the worker's observations regarding emotional concomitants. Here, then, was a sample of rather spontaneous behavior in response to a more or less constant situation and relating directly to the patients' problems. This material was thought particularly suitable for a comparison of high and low scorers with regard to their views of and attitudes toward their psychological disturbance and its possible causes.

1. SELECTION OF MATERIAL

A patient first entering the Clinic is usually interviewed by a psychiatric social worker, and later by a physician. The social worker's "intake interview" is recorded in an approximately standard order of topics, starting with social status, then "patient's story," followed by a few inquiries about "past history" and ending with an appraisal of the patient's understanding of and attitude toward the clinic service. In some cases of referral from other hospitals and agencies, a referral letter giving a similar but less standardized account takes the place of this interview. After a patient is admitted for clinic care, he sees a physician who usually begins by asking the patient to tell about the condition for which he seeks help. Often, the physician also asks how long the condition has existed and whether there are any other problems. After this there is usually an attempt at taking a case history.

The section preceding the questions as to past history is headed "chief complaint" and varies from a verbatim account of the patient's story, with behavioral description, to a list of the main symptoms.

In selecting our material, the part of the intake interview (or referral letter) headed "patient's story" and the physician's first notes of "chief complaints" were read. Whenever the two duplicated each other, the one that was more complete or that contained more of the patient's own words was used. Whenever one record contained a statement missing in the other, that statement was included along with the other material. Material relating to past history or other topics was included only when the record seemed to indicate that the patient brought it up spontaneously when asked about his symptoms, without a preceding question from the interviewer. These sections of the case records, usually only a paragraph in all, were transcribed verbatim along with the patient's sex, questionnaire scores, and official diagnosis.[5]

These interview samples were obtained for all subjects falling into the high and low E quartiles.

Analysis of the data showed certain striking differences between the statements of the high and low scorers regarding *type of complaint* and *general attitudes*. To describe these differences a number of categories—very similar to some of those described in Chapter IX—were defined. All cases were then rated on these categories (variables) by independent raters who knew only the subject's sex and interview samples, but not the diagnoses or the questionnaire scores.

The variables thought to be differentiating between high and low scorers in their intake interviews are described below. These descriptions were included in a manual that was employed by the raters. For each category we here note the variants which were presumed to be associated with high and with low scores on the E scale, but this information was, of course, withheld from the raters' manual itself.

2. THE SCORING MANUAL: DESCRIPTION OF VARIABLES

There were seven categories, some broader and more interpretable than others. They are defined in terms of behavior cues and should be regarded as various expressions of more general underlying dynamic trends. Thus, the variables overlap (in content) to a certain extent.

I. *Emphasis on Somatic Symptoms.* As was to be expected from earlier findings (Chapter XII) it appeared that in the story of their complaints *more high than low scorers tended to put the main emphasis on somatic symptoms.* The majority of persons neurotic enough to seek psychiatric help have some psychogenic somatic complaints. Patients vary both in amount and severity of these somatic symptoms and in the subjective importance these symptoms have for the patient. There was a considerable number of low scorers who had somatic problems, but these tended, for the most part, to state their problems in terms of faulty adjustment or emotional difficulties. Some of the high scorers, on the other hand, showed a particularly strong preoccupation with body processes, and anxiety about the integrity of bodily and nervous functioning. In some cases this focus on the physical aspect seemed related to fear of admitting the existence of *psychological problems*, which carried the connotation of "being crazy." Attributing the symptoms to something physical could, in some cases, be due less to anxiety about the body itself than to the need for a device for removing a deficiency from the threatened

---

[5] The material from the research on stomach ulcers did not include regular intake interviews; instead there were very condensed research interviews in which the patient was questioned regarding certain precipitating factors. We took from the records of these interviews those statements which seemed relevant to our scoring categories.

ego. (Probably, however, the two motives usually occur in the same persons, mainly in those with obsessive-compulsive character traits, or in certain men with particularly strong castration fears.)

The raters were instructed to use the following criteria in deciding on presence or absence of the trait.

Presence: Patient may state numerous problems, including physical and psychological ones. *Main emphasis* is put on physical symptoms when these are: (1) mentioned as the main trouble; (2) mentioned first; (3) emphasized in some other way, as, for example, when other problems are stated only after the interviewer had brought them out.

Absence: Patient puts main emphasis on a psychological disturbance: (1) disturbance of mood; (2) in interpersonal relations; (3) impairment of work adjustment; (4) specific conflicts (about drinking, homosexuality, enuresis . . .); (5) more specific fears; (6) compulsions.

II. *Intraception.* This trait has been discussed in earlier chapters (VII, XII, XIV, XV), where it was seen to be a common correlate of low scores on E. It may be recalled that it expresses the tendency to think in terms of psychological experience. This involves a certain familiarity with one's inner life (especially in its content aspect) and a corresponding readiness to perceive others in the same terms (psychological insight, understanding).

Presence: The patient is aware of the fact that he has problems of a psychological nature (not purely physical problems). In addition, he states these problems with some appreciation of their psychological content.

Patient complains of *specific* difficulties: specific fears, conflicts, or environmental problems; conflicts about sexual or aggressive impulses, problems in interpersonal relations. Sometimes the statements include the description of certain situations which seem connected with the symptoms. In this case the emphasis is not so much on the situation as *the cause*, but there is some insight into the psychological significance of the situation for the patient. (Not merely: "I feel this way when I do heavy work; when something or somebody bothers me." Statement has to have more specific psychological content.)

Absence: (a) denial of any psychological difficulty; (b) emphasis is not on the content of the problem (conflict with family member; struggle with certain impulses, etc.) but rather on the "malfunctioning" itself (the lack of mental energy, inability to concentrate, to think, to do this or that). The complaints are made in general vague terms: "I don't get along with people," "I don't feel well," "I am nervous." Statement often seems to imply the idea of "a machine part" having broken down. Often the "machine" is the body, sometimes "the mind," "the head," "nerves." Often it includes the idea of "going crazy."

Sometimes the statement of the problem appears more specific (e.g., "can't do such and such work") but the main thing about it is the idea that "one cannot do one's duty" (for instance, as a good wife or mother) due to this unwelcome illness. The concern is not so much with the task itself or the feeling of failure involved in the present inability to carry it out, but rather with the violation of conventions and morals. But there is little awareness of specific conflicts, fears, frustrated desires, or life failures.

III. *"Ego-alienness"*

Presence (goes with high score): The symptoms and the patients' attitudes toward them give evidence of particularly strong repressions. The repressed problems and also some of the symptoms have a strong ego-alien quality. Certain impulses, problems, and even some symptoms are experienced as completely *"foreign" to the self*. They cannot be accepted or admitted. They "belong to the body," or they are the "breaking through" of a completely unacceptable part of the personality. The person "cannot understand what makes me do that." There is fear of something "devilish inside" that overwhelms the normal accepted self. Fear of "losing control." Examples: "Fear I'll kill someone during one of my spells; fear I'll lose my mind."

When certain impulses have broken through and have been expressed in behavior, this ego-alienness is expressed sometimes in *moralistic statements and self-accusations* ("Can't understand how I could do this"). Another criterion might be the *blandness of the interview*, stemming from the patient's inability to admit socially unacceptable impulses, either because of repression or because of fear of disapproval from the interviewer.

Absence: The symptoms are experienced as *belonging to one's personality and life history*. There may be severe conflict over some impulses, but the latter are admitted to consciousness and understood as part of one's self and life experiences. There is *relative frankness and freedom from "moralism."*

In the case of obsessions, compulsions, delusions, and other psychotic manifestations, which usually have *some* ego-alien quality, the rating will have to be based on the relative emphasis on the ego-alienness itself ("Something makes me do it; someone influences me; can't control it," etc.), or on the degree to which the content of the symptom is consciously divorced from or related to the patient's past or present inner life.

IV. *Externalized Theory of Onset and Causation of the Illness*

Presence (goes with high E scores): Attempts at externalization of the symptoms by: (a) *denying any and all precipitating factors*. Tensions, depressions, etc., appear "without any reason at all." "*It* just appeared." (b) *dating the illness back to a very definite event or moment:* an operation, a "spell," a death, a particular day—sometime during the last few weeks or years. "Before that I was well . . . happy . . . ." (c) making no attempt to relate the illness to one's past, especially *not* to childhood. No spontaneous references to childhood unless specifically questioned, during this first interview.

Absence: Spontaneously, or when asked about onset, states that the problems have been present "for a long time"—for years, always or since childhood, but perhaps in milder form.

V. *Spontaneous Mention of Unhappy Childhood or Family Relationships*
Presence (goes with low E scores): Patient spontaneously refers to his unhappy childhood. Often elaborates in great detail on a history of frustrations (often with a clearly masochistic attitude). Complains of parents' present or past attitudes and is critical of them.

Absence: No spontaneous reference to childhood. Childhood, if discussed at all, is pictured as "happy and normal." No criticism or other sign of hostility towards family members is expressed (except in "spells" and psychotic episodes), in spite of admission of friction. Sometimes there is clearly compensatory great concern for family members and their welfare.

VI. *Cues Referring to the Patient's Character Structure*
Obviously the interview fragments cannot be used to construct complete pictures of the subject's personality structure. It was found, however, that they often contained some important hints as to the nature of this structure. Formulation of categories listed below was, of course, guided by the concepts found most useful for distinguishing high and low scorers in the rest of the study. But only those categories were included which would be applied to the particular interview material at hand. The raters were asked to state for each case whether cues from List A or List B predominated in a record, or whether the record was "neutral" (meaning he could discern equally as many cues from "A" as from "B" or none at all).

List A (goes with high degree of ethnocentrism):
1. "Countercathectic" defenses. Men: counteraction against passivity. Women: Anal reaction-formations. No mention of a love object or relationship (other than spouse).
2. Extrapunitive or impunitive.[6] If self-criticism occurs, it is couched in moralistic terms, "I am bad, have done wrong." "God is punishing me." Tendency either hysterically to dramatize certain physical symptoms, spells, etc., or to minimize all complaints of a psychological nature.
3. Externalized superego. Religion: God is seen as an external judge of one's action. Illness is a punishment from God. Or religious standards are part of the conventional ideology. Religious reasons are given for refraining from divorce or suicide.

List B ("low" characteristics):
4. Absence of "countercathectic" defenses:
   Direct expressions of orality: dependent character traits; eating, drinking, drugs. Dependency problems, *nurturance.* Open admission of weak-

[6] Further research on impunitiveness is indicated. Here it seemed preferable to classify it "high;" it was "low" in Chapter XI (p. 406).

ness, passivity, femininity in men. Love-seeking attitude. References to rejections by specific love-objects.

Sublimations: form an important part of the ego; references to achievement. When symptoms interfere particularly with patient's work, this is stated in such a way as to suggest concern with the particular work he is doing. Emphasis on ideals. Concern with helping others, society; artistic activity and interest.

5. Intrapunitiveness, masochism: "I was mistreated as a child." Identification with suffering; self-criticism ("I am a failure").
6. Internalized superego: guilt feelings, true depressions, religious ideas as part of the inner life of the person.

VII. *Predominant Types of Symptoms*

List A ("high"):

1. Physical anxiety symptoms and other emotional equivalents: "hyperventilation syndrome"; dizziness, sweating, tingling sensations, numbness, tachycardia, breathlessness, fainting, tremors. Anxiety has no conscious content.
2. Emotional outbursts, tantrums and "spells," in women.
3. Hypochondriacal fears: fear of death, heart attack, etc.
4. Hysterical conversions.[7]
5. "Rigid compulsive rumination": repetitious complaints, self-accusations, self-reassurances, "thinking around and around in a circle."
6. Depersonalization (sense of estrangement from self and world) in a person who emphasizes that heretofore he had had no tendency toward timidity and withdrawal.
7. Suspiciousness, fear of people or aversion to people is stated in somewhat externalized terms: "They irritate me," "I can't stand them. They make me nervous." (To be distinguished from hypersensitiveness and withdrawal when described in a more intraceptive way.)
8. Psychopathic tendencies, not in the sense merely of unconventional behavior (as the term is sometimes used) but rather in the sense of a really defective and not sufficiently internalized superego. Antisocial and destructive behavior, callousness, emotional shallowness.
9. Stomach ulcers in men, especially in subjects who emphasize their masculinity.

List B:

10. Depressed mood, hopelessness, lack of self-confidence, verbalized feelings of inadequacy, suicidal ideas, guilt. Often patients complain of

[7] This item was included in the manual used by our raters; but later analysis of case material suggested that there may be more frequent hysterical conversions in low scorers. The trends are as yet not clear. Perhaps there is also a sex difference here. Two of the low-quartile men had conversion symptoms.

"depression," but the "true" depressions as described above have to be distinguished from the more schizoid type of mood disturbance.

11. Tiredness. "Neurasthenia."
12. Dismenorrhea.
13. Conscious rejection of feminine role by women.
14. In men, expression of traits opposite to the culturally emphasized masculine pattern. Withdrawal, timidity, shyness, sometimes coupled with feelings of unreality or with physical anxiety symptoms or hysterical conversion. The patient's attitude toward all these "weaknesses" is to some degree accepting.
15. Conscious anxiety and conflicts.

3. THE METHOD OF QUANTIFICATION

Inspection of the statements of complaint led to the impression that the high and low quartile groups were clearly differentiated with regard to the variables just discussed. In order to check this impression in a more rigorous manner, it was decided to use a method of "blind ratings," similar to that used on the interview, T.A.T. and Projective Question Test material (Parts II and III). At least two judges who are not acquainted with the subjects (and in this case did not know which were high and which were low scorers) independently rate each subject on certain characteristics. These ratings can then be compared with other data on the subjects. The problem of blind ratings has been discussed in other chapters dealing with interview scoring and projective questions. If these ratings turn out to be highly correlated with some trait of the subjects (in this case ethnocentrism) on which the judges had no information, it is very probable that relationships between the former and latter traits exist in reality and could be demonstrated by other methods. (This holds only if the rating procedure is so controlled as to prevent the raters from utilizing cues other than those to be experimentally tested.) There are, however, various possible pitfalls inherent in the rating method. Such "errors of measurement" could arise, for instance, from material which did not contain sufficient information from which to judge the subject on a certain trait. Other errors might arise from the manner in which the characteristics were defined and described for the judges; from the ability of the judges to apply the instructions to the material to be judged —depending in turn on the judges' training, theoretical bias, and personality— and from other factors. Use of a rating technique, therefore, requires not only the determination of certain relationships between the ratings and other data, but also a careful consideration of various factors which could have influenced the results either in the positive or in the negative direction.

a. THE RATERS. The two *primary raters* were staff members of the major study and will be referred to as raters (or judges) A and B. In addition to much clinical training and experience, these two raters had a strong psychoanalytic orientation. Both were familiar with all concepts, hypotheses, data, and results of the total study. Both had had opportunity to interview high- and low-scoring subjects, and were therefore acquainted with the behavior and material usually obtained from such subjects in interview situations.

Each of the judges independently rated each record on all seven categories and then assigned an "over-all" intuitive estimate of "highness" or "lowness."

After these primary ratings had been completed, 7 independent raters (they are referred to hereafter as the control raters, their ratings as control ratings) were used, each rating one category only.[8] Six of the control raters were clinical psychologists (of these, 1 was a senior clinician, 5 junior clinicians at the level of internes, working at the Langley Porter Clinic). They were not acquainted with the concepts and data of the over-all study. This was important for reasons to be discussed below. One of the more narrowly defined categories (Onset and cause of illness are explained by subject in externalized terms) was rated by our office secretary who had had no formal training in psychology or psychiatry, but who had much intuitive psychological insight and who had absorbed a great deal of the research material and hypotheses. The 7 judges varied greatly in age, training, and theoretical orientation.

b. THE RATING TECHNIQUE.   The instructions for the control raters were as follows:

The material to be rated consists of "Statements of Complaint" by Langley Porter Clinic patients in a first intake interview or in the first interview with a therapist. Only the section "patient's story" or "chief complaint" was included. The interviews are here reproduced verbatim, although a few have been slightly condensed by the writer. Each numbered paragraph refers to one case. There are 26 men, 33 women.

Each case is to be rated on *one variable* (or syndrome) as described in the manual. Each rater will be assigned one variable and will not know about other variables until he has completed his ratings.

The ratings are to be made in terms of presence ($\sqrt{}$) or absence ($-$) of the trait. A few of the variables permit of a "mixed" judgment. Assignment of such a "mixed" (M) rating should be avoided if possible. But occasionally it may have to be used. Sometimes (due to the fragmentary way in which some of these interviews are recorded) there will be insufficient material to rate. In this case mark (o).

Each primary rater (A and B) first rated each record in terms of all seven individual categories. They knew which categories were expected to be related to high or to low ethnocentrism. They therefore tried to assign each record a "high" or "low" rating for each category. Often a record did not contain enough material to permit the rater to reach a decision on a given variable, e.g., a given topic was not discussed, or there were few cues permit-

[8] We wish to thank Dorothy Bomberg, Janet Gist, Carole Horne, Virginia Patterson, Dr. Claire W. Thompson, Anne Vollmar, and Elaine Wesley Barron for the patience and care with which they carried out, on short notice, the task of doing the control ratings.

ting inferences regarding character structure. In this case no rating was assigned. When there were about an equal number of cues pointing in the high and in the low directions, a "mixed" rating was assigned. The raters then went over the records a second time, trying to guess in each case whether the subject had made a high or low score on the E scale. The guesses were to be based on the decisions reached regarding the individual categories. However, no mechanical formula was set up to convert the individual ratings into "over-all" ratings. The raters arrived at the latter by a new rating process in which any or all of the categories could be used and weighted as the rater saw fit.

Two types of data were obtained from this rating material: (1) Inter-rater scoring agreement for each category and for the over-all ratings. (2) Relationship between ratings and scores on the E scale. These will now be discussed.

4. THE RELIABILITY OF THE MEASURES

When several persons agree considerably more than half of the time that certain subjects in a group do, others do not, possess a given trait, the chances are good that these various raters knew what they were supposed to look for, had a similar conception of the trait, understood this concept, and could clearly recognize something in the interview data to which this concept could be applied; and that personality, training, and other differences between the raters influenced the ratings only to a relatively small degree.

All rating notations (high, low, presence, absence, omission, mixed) were converted into "high," "low," and "neutral" scores. E.g., a rating of "presence" on variable I—Main emphasis on subject's physical complaints—was considered a "high" score, "absence" a "low" score; "mixed" notations and omissions were considered "neutral" scores.

Scoring reliability was then obtained by computing the percentage of times 2 raters had assigned the same scores to the same records. Whenever both raters had assigned exactly the same score (high, low, or neutral) to the same record, this was considered one agreement. When one of the raters had given either a high or a low, the other a neutral score, this was considered one-half an agreement. When one rater gave a high score, the other a low, this was counted a full disagreement. The number of agreements, divided by the total number of records rated, yielded the percentage agreement between 2 raters. There were very few instances in which both judges gave a neutral score.

Table 9(XXII) shows the percentage agreements between Raters A and B as well as the scores on which these figures are based. All of the percentage agreements, except one (category III, "lows"), are above 70, statistically higher than could have been obtained by chance (1 per cent level).

Raters A and B agreed best, 91 per cent, on variable V (Subject spon-

TABLE 9 (XXII)

THE AMOUNT OF AGREEMENT BETWEEN TWO RATERS IN ESTIMATING A SUBJECT'S STANDING ON THE E SCALE FROM AN ANALYSIS OF HIS INTAKE INTERVIEW

PSYCHIATRIC CLINIC PATIENTS: MEN AND WOMEN COMBINED
(N = 59: High scorers: N = 28; Low scorers: N = 31)

	Actual Standing on E Scale	No. scored High (H)		No. scored Neutral (N)		No. scored Low (L)		Interrater Agreement[a]			
								No. of Agreements		Percent Agreements	
		(1) Rated H by Both	(2) Rated H by One; N by Other	(3) Rated N by Both	(4) Rated H by One; L by Other	(5) Rated L by Both	(6) Rated L by One; N by Other	(7) High or Low	(8) H and L Combined	(9) High or Low	(10) H and L Combined
Over-all rating of highness or lowness on E Scale	High	21	-	-	5	2	-	23	51	82.1	86.4
	Low	4	-	-	3	24	-	28		90.3	
Single Variables:											
I. Main emphasis on somatic complaints	High	15	5	1	-	2	5	23	45	82.1	76.3
	Low	3	2	2	1	9	14	22		71.0	
II. Intraception	High	15	7	2	1	-	3	22	48	78.6	83.1
	Low	1	4	3	1	18	4	26		83.9	
III. Ego-alienness	High	14	11	1	-	-	2	21.5	41.5	76.8	70.3
	Low	3	2	1	5	10	10	20		64.5	
IV. Externalized theory of onset and causes	High	13	8	3	2	-	2	21	45	75.0	76.3
	Low	4	2	6	2	9	8	24		77.4	
V. Spontaneous mention of unhappy childhood and family relations	High	23	2	-	2	1	-	25	53.5	89.3	90.7
	Low	15	-	-	2	13	1	28.5		91.9	
VI. Cues regarding character structure	High	10	7	2	2	2	5	20	46	71.4	78.0
	Low	3	2	-	2	20	4	26		83.9	
VII. Predominant type of symptoms	High	18	4	1	3	1	1	22.5	48	80.3	81.4
	Low	4	-	1	4	19	3	25.5		82.3	
Mean agreement on the variables	High	15.4	6.3	1.4	1.4	0.9	2.6	22.2		79.3	79.5
	Low	4.8	1.7	1.9	2.4	14.0	6.3	24.7		79.7	

[a] Number of agreements for a given variable is the sum of the values, opposite that variable, in Columns 1, 3, and 5.

taneously and explicitly mentions unhappy childhood and family relationships). This result was to be expected because this variable is so unambiguous and requires little subjective evaluation. Besides, most subjects did not bring up this subject when first asked about their symptoms.

The next highest agreement was reached on the "over-all" guess regarding the subject's standing on ethnocentrism; then came Intraception, Types of Symptoms, and Character Traits, with agreements around 80 per cent.

The average agreement for all seven variables was 80 per cent.

There are several possible reasons why the over-all rating had so high a reliability. One reason is that the instructions prohibited "neutral" ratings in this instance. Another is that the category "over-all" highness-lowness, is a broad one, and the raters are thus given the opportunity to utilize a great variety of explicit or nonexplicit cues and impressions; that they should do this was favored by the fact that both A and B had had experience interviewing high and low scorers, possibly developing thereby a "feeling for" a general "high" or "low" personality factor.

Analysis of the ratings assigned by the two judges showed that rater B had a relatively greater number of omissions (meaning "I can't tell from the data given") whereas rater A had tried hard to come to a decision, even when the data offered only one subtle cue. As can be seen from Table 9(XXII), what lowered the agreements between A and B were usually instances in which one rater gave a neutral score; there were very few cases in which one gave a high, the other a low rating.

Because the ratings of A and B were so similar, and because of B's consistently greater number of neutrals, which lowered all reliability (and validity) figures somewhat, only rater A's ratings were compared with those made by the 7 control raters.

Table 10(XXII) shows the percentage agreements between the ratings by A and those made by the 7 control judges, each of whom rated only one category. As the control raters made no "over-all" guesses of highness or lowness on E, no agreement with A's over-all rating could be obtained. Instead, a composite "high" or "low" score for each subject was derived from the 7 control ratings of single variables. A rating of "high" on a given variable was counted as one point, a "neutral" rating was given ½ point, a "low" rating, 0 points. By adding the points for each subject, scores ranging from 0 to 7 were obtained. All subjects receiving such a composite score of 4 or more were then classed as "high," those with scores below 4 as "low." The agreement between A's "over-all" rating with these composite ratings is shown near the bottom of Table 10(XXII).

The composite high-low score agreed with A's over-all estimate of highness or lowness 85 per cent of the time. Practically the same figure was obtained when comparing A's and B's over-all guesses.

The average agreement between A and the control raters for the single variables was only very slightly lower (77 per cent) than the average agreement between A and B (80 per cent). On the whole, the reliabilities obtained were quite acceptable.

In general, those variables which had the highest reliability when the ratings of A and B were compared also had a relatively high percentage agreement in the comparison between A and the control raters, and conversely with the variables of relatively low reliability. The two categories in which this relationship was almost reversed were: categories I (Emphasis on Physical Symptoms) and II (Intraception). The reliability of the former ranked second best in the case of A and the control raters, about fifth in the case of A and B. The reliability of the latter ranked sixth with A and the controls, second best with A and B.

The relatively low agreement between A and B on category I was caused not so much by disagreements but by a relatively large proportion of "neutral" scores (omissions) on the part of B (see Table 9(XXII)). While the control raters and A felt able to judge the presence or absence of certain cues in the record, rater B frequently felt that the subjects' attitudes toward their symptoms were not sufficiently brought out in the interviews.

The relatively low agreement between the control rater and A on Intraception was due mainly to a larger number of disagreements. The control rater was in this case particularly dissatisfied with her ratings, feeling that she did not have a sufficient grasp of the concept of intraception nor enough acquaintance with the cues by which the trait could be recognized. In the case of A and B the concept and manifestations of intraception had been made the object of special study and played an important part in their thinking. Rater A thought that her ratings of any given case—on over-all highness-lowness and on all other variables—had been more influenced by her impression of the subject's intraceptiveness than by any other cue. It is reasonable to assume that this difference in training is the cause of the difference in reliability between the two sets of raters. This becomes even more probable when the reliability figures are compared with the agreements between ratings and actual E score. Here, A's and B's ratings of presence or absence of intraception were related to high and low E score (in the expected direction) 80 to 83 per cent of the time, while the control rater's judgment agreed with E only 65 per cent of the time (see Table 12(XXII)).

The highest reliabilities (91 per cent and 95 per cent) were obtained for variable V (Patient Mentions Unhappy Childhood, etc.). It is clear that there is not much room for disagreement here.

The lowest reliabilities were obtained for variable III (Ego-alienness). Here the agreement between A and the control rater was only 65 per cent, that between A and B 70 per cent. The former figure barely meets the standard of acceptable reliability of measurement. There was an unusually large discrepancy between A's and the control rater's estimate for the high scorers,

TABLE 10 (XXII)

THE AMOUNT OF AGREEMENT BETWEEN A SINGLE RATER (A) AND SEVEN OTHER RATERS IN ESTIMATING VARIABLES IN INTAKE INTERVIEWS

PSYCHIATRIC CLINIC PATIENTS: MEN AND WOMEN COMBINED (N = 59)

Variable	Actual Standing on E Scale	Rated H by Both	Rated H by One; N by Other	Rated N by Both	Rated H by One; L by Other
I. Main emphasis on somatic complaints	High	12	4	-	2
	Low	4	1	1	4
II. Intraception	High	18	1	2	6
	Low	4	2	1	8
III. Ego-alienness	High	9	4	1	10
	Low	4	2	2	5
IV. Externalized theory of onset and causes	High	14	6	1	4
	Low	4	4	4	2
V. Spontaneous mention of unhappy childhood and family relations	High	26	-	-	1
	Low	17	1	-	1
VI. Cues regarding character structure	High	11	5	1	4
	Low	3	2	1	2
VII. Predominant type of symptoms	High	22	-	-	3
	Low	4	1	-	7
Agreement between A's overall H-L rating and composite score based on ratings of 7 independent raters, each rating a single variable	High	21			5
	Low	5			4
Averages	High	16.0	2.9	0.7	?
	Low	5.7	1.9	1.3	?

PSYCHIATRIC CLINIC PATIENTS: MEN AND WOMEN COMBINED (N = 59)

Rated L by Both	Rated L by One N by Other	No. of Agreements		Percentage Agreement	Total Percentage Agreement
		H and L Respectively	H and L Combined		
6	4	18 + 4 = 22	48	78.6	81.4
20	1	25 + 1 = 26		83.9	
-	1	20 + 1 = 21	42.5	75.0	72.0
15	1	20+1.5=21.5		69.4	
2	2	12 + 3 = 15	38.5	53.6	65.3
15	3	21+2.5=23.5		75.8	
1	2	16 + 4 = 20	43.5	71.4	73.7
10	7	18+5.5=23.5		75.8	
1	-	27	56	96.4	94.9
11	1	29		93.5	
2	5	14 + 5 = 19	43.5	67.9	73.7
16	7	20+4.5=24.5		79.0	
1	2	24	47	85.7	79.7
18	1	23		74.2	
2		23	50	82.1	84.7
22		27		87.1	
1.9	2.3	21.1	45.5	75.5	77.2
15.0	3.0	24.5		78.8	

there being only 54 per cent agreement. This figure is the result of a rather large number of disagreements between the two raters. The control rater said that she was quite unsure of her ratings because she felt that the interview material reflected more the physician's than the patient's attitude toward the complaints. Also, she conceived of "ego-alienness" as something unfavorable from the mental hygiene point of view and was therefore more often willing to score "absence" of the trait than "presence." Possibly the most important factor, which lowered both sets of reliabilities, is the relative broadness with which this variable was defined, including few behavioral criteria but leaving much to the rater's intuition.

With the exception of variable III, the ratings for all variables, as well as the over-all estimates, proved to be reliable measures.

5. RELATIONSHIP BETWEEN RATINGS AND ETHNOCENTRISM SCORE

The idea of the present rating method is the following: If the "blind" ratings of a given trait correlate significantly with another trait about which the raters had no information (in this case ethnocentrism), it is likely that the two traits are correlated in reality. The relationships to be described below are probably valid because we have eliminated many of the factors inherent in the rating process which could have influenced the results.

There are, however, many factors inherent in the rating method which can still influence the "blind" ratings in such a way that statistical relationships of two traits are artificially raised or lowered. The possibility of artificially high correlations is present particularly when several traits are rated at the same time. Here, the rating of one trait can easily influence the ratings of other traits. This factor (called halo effect) could have influenced the ratings of judges A and B. It was primarily for this reason that control raters, each of whom was trained to pay attention to and to recognize only one of the seven single traits, were used.

The ratings of (1) over-all highness and lowness, and (2) of the single traits, were related to ethnocentrism in the following manner: For a given trait, we counted the number of subjects in the high E quartile who were judged to be "high" by the raters. To these were added half of the high-scoring subjects receiving a "neutral" rating. This sum, divided by the total number of high scorers in the group, yielded the percentage of high scorers rated in the high direction. By the same procedure the percentage of low scorers rated in the low direction was obtained. The weighted average of these two percentages was then computed; this indicated the percentage of subjects related "correctly," that is, the percentage whose ratings were related to E score in the expected way.

a. THE OVER-ALL RATINGS.   Table 11 (XXII) gives the agreements between the subject's standing on E and A's ratings. Rater A's guesses as to highness and lowness agreed with the subject's actual E score 86 per cent of the

TABLE 11 (XXII)

THE AMOUNT OF AGREEMENT BETWEEN RATER A'S ESTIMATE OF HIGH OR LOW ETHNOCENTRISM, BASED ON ANALYSIS OF INTAKE INTERVIEWS, AND ETHNOCENTRISM AS MEASURED BY THE E SCALE

PSYCHIATRIC CLINIC PATIENTS: MEN AND WOMEN COMBINED (N = 59)

Variable	Actual Standing on E Scale	Rated H	Rated L	Rated N	No. of Agreements	No. of Agreements Combined	Percentage Agreement	Total Percentage Agreement
I. Main emphasis on somatic complaints	High	15	6	7	18-1/2	43	66.1	72.9
	Low	5	23	3	24-1/2		79.0	
II. Intraception	High	24	2	2	25	49	89.3	83.1
	Low	5	22	4	24		77.4	
III. Ego-alienness	High	23	2	3	24-1/2	45-1/2	87.5	77.1
	Low	9	20	2	21		67.7	
IV. Externalized theory of onset and causes	High	17	4	7	20-1/2	39-1/2	73.2	66.9
	Low	7	14	10	19		61.3	
V. Spontaneous mention of unhappy childhood and family relations	High	27	1	0	27	40-1/2	96.4	68.6
	Low	17	13	1	13-1/2		43.5	
VI. Cues regarding character structure	High	19	2	7	22-1/2	47	80.4	79.7
	Low	5	23	3	24-1/2		79.0	
VII. Predominant type of symptoms	High	25	1	2	26	50	92.9	84.7
	Low	6	23	2	24		77.4	
Over-all	High	25	3	0	25	51	89.3	86.4
	Low	5	26	0	26		83.9	
Averages	High						83.7	
	Low						69.3	

TABLE 12 (XXII)

THE AMOUNT OF AGREEMENT BETWEEN ESTIMATES OF ETHNOCENTRISM, BASED ON RATINGS OF SINGLE VARIABLES FROM INTAKE INTERVIEWS, AND ETHNOCENTRISM AS MEASURED BY THE E SCALE

Psychiatric Clinic Patients: Men And Women Combined (N = 59)

Variable	Actual Standing on E Scale	No. Rated H	No. Rated L	No. Rated N	No. of Agreements	No. of Agreements Combined	Percentage Agreement	Total Percentage Agreement
Composite Rating[a]	High	22	6	0	22.0	44.0	71.0	74.6
	Low	9	22	0	22.0		78.6	
Single Variables:								
I. Main emphasis on somatic complaints	High	15	12	1	15.5	38.0	55.4	64.0
	Low	8	22	1	22.5		72.6	
II. Intraception	High	19	5	4	21.0	38.5	75.0	65.3
	Low	13	17	1	17.5		56.5	
III. Ego-alienness	High	9	14	5	11.5	33.0	41.1	55.9
	Low	6	18	7	21.5		69.4	
IV. Externalized theory of onset and causes	High	21	4	3	22.5	42.0	80.4	71.2
	Low	7	15	9	19.5		62.9	
V. Spontaneous mention of unhappy childhood and family relations	High	26	2	0	26.0	37.5	92.9	63.6
	Low	19	11	1	11.5		37.1	
VI. Cues regarding character structure	High	12	11	5	14.5	36.5	51.8	61.9
	Low	5	18	8	22.0		71.0	
VII. Predominant type of symptoms	High	22	6	0	22.0	43.0	78.6	72.9
	Low	10	21	0	21.0		67.7	
Means	High	17.71	7.7	2.6	19.0	38.4	67.9	65.0
	Low	9.71	17.4	3.9	19.4		62.5	

[a]Composite rating based on ratings by 7 independent raters on the variables listed. A "High rating" received 1 point, a "Neutral rating" ½ point; 4 points or more constituted a composite "High" score; everything below 4 a "Low" score.

time. For the high scorers alone the agreement was 89 per cent, for the low scorers 84 per cent. These figures show again how closely ethnocentrism is related to personality factors, although the relationships are by no means perfect.

The remaining problem now is: How did raters A and B arrive at their rather accurate guesses about ethnocentrism from a short paragraph of interview material dealing almost exclusively with the subjects' complaints? Did they base their guesses mainly on the variables described in the manual, or did they inadvertently use other cues, such as type of language used and other cues that have not been made explicit but which they learned to associate with highness or lowness while interviewing subjects with known ethnocentrism scores?

The results obtained from the control raters, who had had no such previous experience with high- and low-scoring subjects, should help to decide this question. These results are shown in Table 12 (XXII).

As discussed above, a composite "high" or "low" score was computed, based only on the ratings of the seven single variables by the different raters. This composite rating agreed with E score 75 per cent of the time, indicating a statistically significant relationship. This figure is 11 points lower than the validity figure obtained by rater A. Some of this difference could undoubtedly have been eliminated by more extensive training of the control raters regarding the concepts and the cues in the material they had to use. Nevertheless, in view of the control raters' unfamiliarity with the over-all theory, and their knowledge of only the single variable being rated in each case, their achievement of 75 per cent accuracy takes on added significance.

Prediction of ethnocentrism score (high or low) from clinical material was made more accurate (86 per cent for rater A) when the rater had more training, was acquainted with the concepts and materials of the total study, and could form a picture of the subject by looking for a whole pattern or syndrome of responses.

b.   The Single Variables.   For purposes of this discussion all results for each of the single variables have been summarized in Table 13 (XXII). This table shows: (1) Percentage agreements between rater A and each control rater; (2) Percentage agreements between raters A and B; (3) Percentage agreements between A's ratings and E score; (4) Percentage agreements between each control rater and E score.

Variable I: Main Emphasis on Somatic Complaints Rather than on Psychological Problems.   Among the reliabilities between rater A and the control raters, this variable had the second highest, 81 per cent. Among the reliabilities between raters A and B this variable ranked only about fifth best (76 per cent). This relatively low, but still acceptable agreement between A and B was caused not so much by disagreements but by a relatively large number of "neutral" scores (omissions) on the part of B.

TABLE 13 (XXII)

SUMMARY OF DATA FROM THE RATING OF INTAKE INTERVIEWS

A. RELIABILITY: PERCENTAGE AGREEMENT AMONG RATERS FOR SEVEN VARIABLES

B. VALIDITY: PERCENTAGE AGREEMENT BETWEEN RATINGS AND SCORE ON THE E SCALE

Psychiatric Clinic Patients: Men and Women Combined (N = 59)

Variable	Actual Standing on E Scale	A. Reliability			B. Validity			
		Percentage Agreement: Rater A and Control Raters	Percentage Agreement: Raters B and Control Raters	Percentage Agreement: Raters B and A	Percentage Agreement: Rater A and E Score	Percentage Agreement: Rater A and E Score	Percentage Agreement: Control Raters and E Score	Percentage Agreement: Control Raters and E Score
I. Main emphasis on somatic complaints	High	78.6	82.1	76.3	66.1	72.9	55.4	64.0
	Low	83.9	71.0		79.0		72.6	
II. Intraception	High	75.0	78.6	83.1	89.3	83.1	75.0	65.3
	Low	69.4	83.9		77.4		56.5	
III. Ego-alienness	High	53.6	76.8	70.3	87.5	77.1	41.1	55.9
	Low	75.8	64.5		67.7		69.4	
IV. Externalized theory of onset and causes	High	71.4	75.0	76.3	73.2	66.9	80.4	71.2
	Low	75.8	77.4		61.3		62.9	
V. Spontaneous mention of unhappy childhood and family relations	High	96.4	89.3	90.7	96.4	68.6	92.9	63.6
	Low	93.5	91.9		43.5		37.1	
VI. Cues regarding character structure	High	67.9	71.4	78.0	80.4	79.7	51.8	61.9
	Low	79.0	83.9		79.0		71.0	
VII. Predominant type of symptoms	High	85.7	80.3	81.4	92.9	84.7	78.6	72.9
	Low	74.2	82.3		77.4		67.7	
Averages	High	75.5	79.3	79.5	83.7	76.1	67.9	65.0
	Low	78.8	79.7		69.3		62.5	
Over-all rating	High	82.1[a]	82.1[a]	86.4	89.3	86.4	71.0[b]	74.6[b]
	Low	87.1[a]	90.3		83.9		78.6[b]	

[a]Percentage agreement between Rater A's "over-all rating" and a composite score based on 7 independent ratings by control raters.

[b]Percentage agreement between E score and composite rating.

There was a significant relationship between variable I and ethnocentrism. According to rater A, 66 per cent of the high scorers emphasized their physical complaints, whereas about 79 per cent of the low scorers failed to do so. The control rater's figures are lower: 55 per cent for the high scorers, 73 per cent for the low scorers. In addition, case studies indicated that this variable is important for differentiating subjects high and low on E.

To be sure, there were some cases of low scorers with tendencies toward conversion symptoms or other psychogenic somatic disturbances. But such symptoms, together with marked anxious concern about bodily integrity was characteristic of high scorers. This anxiety is often extended to the functioning of the nervous system or "mind." Thus, high-scoring patients complain and have anxious concern about headaches, various sensory disturbances, loss of memory, nervousness, and "going crazy." There is also a tendency on the part of the high scorers to develop somatic rather than psychological symptoms. Many of these somatic symptoms, on closer examination, turn out to be expressions of repressed affects. Thus, the tendency to develop and to focus on somatic complaints can be considered part of the defensive activity of the high scorer's narrow ego, which shuts out extensive parts of the individual's inner life and, as an additional defensive measure, causes rejection of any thinking in psychological terms and, instead, an emphasis on thinking in terms of physical causation. Thus, variable I may be an expression of the same processes which underlie variable II, and, in a sense, all the other variables as well.

Variable II: Intraception. This variable had the highest reliability with raters A and B (83 per cent). Among the agreements of A with the control raters, this variable ranked only sixth (72 per cent). As noted above, a difference in training between raters A and B on the one hand and the control rater on the other is probably the cause of the difference in the reliabilities of the two sets of ratings. The fact that A's and B's ratings agreed more closely with E score (83 per cent) than did those of the control rater (65 per cent) is probably to be explained in the same way.

From these data it appears that (1) adequately trained raters can arrive at very reliable ratings of intraception, using patients' statements about their complaints in a first psychiatric interview; (2) intraception is highly correlated with lack of ethnocentrism. The latter proposition is supported by a great deal of evidence from other material presented in this volume, in connection with the F scale, the Projective Questions, and particularly the Thematic Apperception Test and the interviews.

In the Clinic the difference between high and low scorers on intraception became very clear when any kind of psychotherapy was attempted. Some of the high-scoring subjects whom we interviewed were almost unable to accept the notion of psychological causation of their disturbances, and it took a great deal of time to make them see some very obvious connections between their symptoms, on the one hand, and some anxiety-producing factors in their life situation and events in the past, on the other. The low scorers either knew these more obvious connections before coming to the Clinic (often reporting about their inner and outer lives with a great deal of awareness of their own and other's psychological processes) or were quick in grasping the therapist's interpretations. Many of these latter patients, at least at first sight, appear to be especially good subjects for psychotherapy. They are cooperative, perceptive, and give excellent histories. But often it is difficult to effect changes in their symptoms because of their characteristic defenses: isolation of affect and intellectualization. It is as if they "can afford" to know more about their inner lives because, among other things, their egos, used to admitting impulses, have developed certain intellectual ways of dealing with drives and emotions.

Variable III: Ego-alienness. This variable had the lowest reliabilities. The agreement between A and the control rater was only 65 per cent; the agreement between A and B was 70 per cent. The control rater, as noted above, was quite unsure of her ratings and expressed misgivings about the way in which the variable had been defined. Indeed, it seems likely that the breadth of the category and the absence from it of behavioral criteria lowered the reliability of both sets of ratings. Thus it happened that the control rater tried mainly to judge ego-alienness from the degree of conscious acceptance or rejection of the symptoms as revealed by the interview. Raters A and B also included in their judgments the nature of the symptoms themselves, regardless of the patient's expressed attitude toward them. Thus they judged the presence of predominantly psychosomatic symptoms, or of vague anxiety without content, as more ego-alien than conscious conflicts or feelings of failure.

As was to be expected, the control rater's judgment did not agree very well with E score (56 per cent). Rater A's ratings, however, showed a fairly high relationship (77 per cent). Examination of the data revealed that some of the low-scoring patients, who on the basis of this variable were judged to be ethnocentric, showed psychotic manifestations. Such manifestations actually have much more ego-alien quality than the neurotic symptoms which generally predominated in our group. The variable probably works better for the high- than for the low-scoring group.

Variable IV: Externalized Theory of Onset and Causes of the Illness. The reliabilities here are quite good—74 per cent for A and the control rater, and 76 per cent for A and B. Rater A's agreement with E is her lowest (67 per cent); the control rater agreed more highly with E (71 per cent). In general, the variable seemed to work better for the high scorers. It is possible that this has to do with the fact that more "neutrals" were scored for this category than for any other, and there were a few more "neutrals" in the low-scoring group. The large number of neutral ratings seemed to be due to the circumstance that not all subjects talked about (or were even asked about) the onset of their illness in this interview but confined themselves to describing their present difficulties. The high scorers more often brought up the onset and causes of their symptoms because they felt as if these symptoms had come about mysteriously "all of a sudden" on a certain day and that "everything had been quite all right before."

This is another example of the high scorers' unfamiliarity with their inner lives, their need to be like everyone else, and their strenuous efforts at keeping less acceptable impulses and emotions completely out of consciousness. When these impulses finally do break through in the form of symptoms, they are felt as ego-alien intruders, which appear "suddenly" and often "without any reason at all."

Variable V: Spontaneous Mention of Unhappy Childhood or Unhappy Family Relationships. The least ambiguous category, and therefore the one receiving the highest agreement scores (91 per cent and 95 per cent) is variable V. Here the rater simply had to state whether the patient spontaneously mentioned unhappy childhood or family relationships. The relationship between this variable and ethnocentrism was found to be very close in the case of the high scorers (93 per cent, 96 per cent) but not in the case of the low scorers (44 per cent, 37 per cent). This result seems connected with the fact that, in general, few subjects mentioned anything about their childhood in the intake interview, which dealt primarily with the patient's symptoms. Practically none of the high scorers did so. Whenever such a reference was made, the subject was usually a low scorer on ethnocentrism. The figures for this variable, for the low scorers, are actually spuriously low.

The results here agree with the general finding of the study as a whole that low scorers freely admit friction with and negative feelings towards their families, and in general are more aware of and more frank about conflict and affect. The high scorers gave smooth, bland histories and had idealized pictures of their families. This would rarely allow them to admit feelings of unhappiness and loneliness in childhood such as arise from sibling jealousy and disappointment in parents. Such feelings were often reported in the interviews of low scorers at the Clinic.

Variable VI: Cues Referring to the Patient's Character Structure. The reliabilities here were 74 per cent (rater A with control rater) and 78 per cent (for rater A with rater B). These agreements are statistically quite acceptable. Rater A also achieved quite high agreement with E score (80 per cent), while the control rater's agreement with E was only 62 per cent. The control rater's judgments of the low scorers showed much higher agreement (71 percent) than did her ratings of the high scorers (52 per cent). Her reliability was also lower for the high group. This could be related to the fact that the manual gave more detailed and concrete instructions and examples for the "low" characteristics than for the "high" ones. This probably penalized the control rater much more than rater A, because the latter was already very familiar with the concepts and their application to interview material. It seems likely that the control rater's judgments would have shown much greater relationship to E had she had more training (in applying psycho-analytic concepts in general and the present variables in particular).

The syndrome of traits to be included in rating variable VI, were discussed in the scoring manual above (Section F, 2). They included:

For high scorers	*For low scorers*
1. countercathectic defenses: re-action formations, projection, particularly anal reaction forma-tions for women, counteraction of passivity for men	1. other defenses: particularly sub-limations into artistic, intellec-tual, humanitarian interests and activities
2. lack of concern with love-objects	2. oral-dependent-love-seeking at-titude; nurturance, concern about being rejected
3. extra- and impunitiveness	3. intrapunitiveness; masochism
4. externalized superego	4. internalized superego

These variables, of course, are identical with some of those used in the study of personality by means of the questionnaire and clinical techniques described earlier in the book. The detailed case studies of Clinic patients, the results of the Projective Questions for our group, and many of the State-ments of Complaint showed that these variables were just as valuable for dis-tinguishing high and low scores in this group as they were in the case of other groups. It is, of course, impossible to form, on the basis of the short Statements of Complaint alone, a personality picture of patients in which all of these characteristics appear. Therefore the reader, going over the examples of these Statements and a few selected case studies in the following section, may not be convinced, particularly since only brief outlines of the cases were given to illustrate the symptomatology, important genetic factors, and a few other characteristics common to a whole group of patients in the high and low quartiles. Many of the details about the patients' relationships to others and to their work were omitted there. Still, the reader will find striking differ-ences between low and high scorers by paying attention to the cues as defined above. Perhaps the first group of variables, namely the nature of defenses, will not become so apparent from the interview fragments selected for presentation. They will be illustrated primarily by the brief case examples included also in the following section. The complete material, as given to the raters, did offer more cues in this direction. Particularly striking was the frequency with which the low-scoring subjects (but hardly ever high-scor-ing ones) spoke about the interference of their symptoms with their work, which was in this connection described in such a way that one could infer the patient's true involvement in his work. A striking proportion of the low scorers had artistic occupations or interests.

The most frequent sign of trait no. 2 in our examples, lies in the frequency with which the low scorers refer in some way to their relationships to other people, to concern about being rejected, and to their own shortcomings in interpersonal relationships, quite in contrast to the high scorers.

The character syndrome intrapunitiveness-masochism-strong internalized superego is illustrated by several of the examples of low scorers, particularly the cases with neurotic depressions and inferiority feelings, but also by the self-critical attitude with which the low scorers report their difficulties. The great frankness with which many of them expose their weaknesses or spontaneously talk about their childhood sufferings also perhaps expresses their (dependent) wish to receive sympathy from the interviewer, as well as a desire to appease their strict superegos ("If I confess everything now, I won't have to feel quite as guilty as I would if you discovered these things about me later.")

Variable VII: Predominant Types of Symptoms. The two lists of symptoms are given in Section F, 2. The reliabilities for this category were statistically acceptable (around 80 per cent) and the relationship to E was relatively high with all raters (73–85 per cent). According to these findings, the symptoms in List A characterize the high-scoring group, those in List B predominate in the low-scoring group. The symptomatology of the high- and low-scoring groups will be presented and discussed in more detail in the following section which deals with the clinical pictures and personalities of the subjects. There, material gathered by the various techniques employed in this study will be utilized and the discussion illustrated by a number of case examples.

6. SUMMARY

Before turning to the clinical section, however, we may summarize and discuss the findings of the rating technique.

1. It was possible to predict standing on the E scale from a small section of a subject's first psychiatric interview, dealing almost exclusively with the subject's symptoms. This shows again how strongly ethnocentrism is correlated with personality dynamics.

2. In order to test the thesis that the differences between the high- and low-scoring groups could be described by means of the variables described above, 7 control raters, each rating only one variable, were employed. Unfortunately, these raters were not quite familiar enough with the meaning and application of psychoanalytic concepts. In spite of this, an average reliability of 77 per cent between rater A (a staff member of the study) and

the control raters was obtained. This figure is statistically acceptable for our purpose and indicates that the ratings by raters A and B were not based merely on comparisons of the interviews with a general "apperceptive mass" acquired in their experience with high and low scorers, but were actually based on the variables as here described. The average agreement for A (and also for B) between ratings of the single variables and E score was around 77 per cent; the corresponding figure for the control raters was only 65 per cent. However, when composite scores of highness-lowness were computed (derived from all 7 independent control ratings), the agreement with E was 75 per cent. This indicates that the variables show significant relationships to E, although we cannot say just how well one could predict E from any one of the single variables. The percentage-agreements of A's ratings with E score may have been raised somewhat by previous experience with high- and low-scoring subjects and by the halo effect. The control raters' predictions are certainly not as good as they could be, due to relative lack of training. From a theoretical point of view, the actual degree to which the relationships between E and each of the single variables exceed chance, is of little importance. Obviously all of the variables overlap. They probably represent various aspects of one or of a very few more basic personality factors.

G. CLINICAL PICTURES AND PERSONALITIES OF HIGH AND LOW SCORERS

1. THE HIGH SCORERS

Probably any one of the symptoms listed under A ("high") in Category VII, such as physical anxiety symptoms, hypochondriacal fears, stomach ulcers (men), could be found in low-scoring subjects—and depression, tiredness, conscious conflict, and the like, in high scorers. However, the manifestations in List A and in List B seem to form syndromes which differentiated well between our two groups. The various symptoms in each syndrome have certain common characteristics. Even the control rater who had little training in psychoanalytic or other dynamic theories sensed this relatedness. It helped her in the rating task because it was possible for her to form "whole impressions" of the patients, using the various single symptoms as alternative cues.

In comparing the various symptoms mentioned in one list with those mentioned in the other, it becomes clear that the main difference between them consists in the way less acceptable parts of the personality are handled by the ego. In the high scorers the sources of disturbance—aggressive impulses, for instance—are seen as "outside" the self or other means are used to deny their true significance. Anxiety is displaced from the inner conflicts themselves to the body, or it appears in consciousness without the conflicts to which it belongs; or countercathective defenses are used, producing compulsive features or psychosomatic manifestations such as stomach ulcers (men). When impulses do begin to break through, they often do so in the form of violent outbursts, "spells," or tantrums, or they lead to a feeling of not being oneself.

It is this strenuous denial of many of one's impulses and the attempt at seeing everything unacceptable as outside the self, which seems to be the common denominator for most of the content of List A in Category VII. This is, in essence, the tendency—so common in high scorers—to keep things ego-alien. The same general character tendency, it seems, is expressed in extra-punitiveness and in other ways described elsewhere in the present volume. Once again, the findings on Clinic patients confirm what was found to be true in the Study's sample of the general population (Chapter XII).

a. HIGH-SCORING MEN. In order to illustrate the clinical pictures in high-scoring men a few case examples will be given here.

The first patient is a middle-aged businessman. In his first psychiatric interview he stated that he had "been fighting a nervous breakdown." He complained of tremors, sweating, fatigue, polyuria, intestinal gas, spells of panic, and a tendency to cry. He said that his symptoms first appeared when he heard how much temporary alimony he had to pay. Then "something snapped in my head." This condition had improved for a while, after some medical treatment, but reappeared after the patient's business license was suspended for a short time because of certain irregularities.

In the course of psychotherapy the patient was superficially cooperative, came on time, and was particularly polite to the therapist but could not enter into the therapeutic relationship. He offered several times to take the woman therapist to an elegant place for dinner. When speaking about himself, the patient dwelled merely on his somatic complaints in a hypochondriacal way and refused to give up the idea that his trouble was of physiological origin, requiring medical treatment. At the therapist's request, the patient told about his life experiences. He used this situation mainly to impress the therapist with stories of his business success and of his successful and influential friends, but it became apparent that he had no genuine attachments to anyone. After some months both patient and therapist felt that treatment should be discontinued for lack of progress.

This patient's character and history point towards anal problems (retention). Castration anxiety is experienced in terms of a fear of "losing something" or "having to give up something." His strong anxiety and underlying weakness is unsuccessfully cloaked by a masculine façade which, in this case, centers around the idea of being a "successful businessman." His relations to others are weak and egocentric. His externalized superego does not prevent him from trying slightly illegal means for reaching success. When his ego is threatened by some "loss" or lack of success, his anxiety is increased.

In such a situation he becomes aware of anxiety without much content. He focuses on the physiological symptoms of anxiety, becomes even more anxious, then seeks medical treatment.

This particular type of high-scoring man was not very frequent in the Clinic group. Probably it is more frequent in medical clinics or in the practice of private physicians. The same pattern of underlying weakness and castration anxiety covered by a masculine façade was, however, found in most other high-scoring men patients, some with more, some with less compulsive characters. In some, unconscious homosexual conflicts were especially important. And paranoid trends were not uncommon. One group of high-scoring patients had few or no compulsive features but more marked phobic trends. These cases, too, had much "vague anxiety," were focused often on the physical anxiety symptoms such as tremors, and so forth, and showed some hypochondriacal concern.

An example of this latter type is a young veteran who suffered from a common type of combat neurosis consisting of severe tremors and vague anxiety whenever he engaged in the least strenuous activity. This patient's ship had been torpedoed and the patient (who could not swim) had had to spend an hour on a leaky raft. At the time he had felt little fear. A month later, when on shore in a hotel, symptoms appeared suddenly, apparently without any precipitating cause. The patient had always suffered from mild phobias— being afraid of guns, bumblebees, snakes, hypodermics and, occasionally, of crowds and gatherings of strangers. However, "toughness" stood out in his personality. He had always had "crazy dreams," lately severe nightmares. In a recent one, four men in full military gear, including guns, had taken a blood test on him and a group of friends. They did it roughly and blood streamed down his arm.

This dream makes one wonder whether the battle incident in itself precipitated the acute anxiety state. It seems more likely that the actual danger situation on the raft only contributed by temporarily decreasing the ego's ability to deal with other conflicts, possibly of a homosexual nature, that were activated by the situation in the service.

As in the case of several high-scoring male interviewees, the parents died when the patient was young. From the age of 12 on, the subject and his older brother were raised by the two older sisters. Little material on childhood history was recorded by the therapist. Of the family relationships we know only that the patient had, at the time of his treatment, warm feelings for his brother who, he said, bullied him in childhood to some extent. The patient still spoke with resentment of his sisters, who "dominated" him and whose guardianship he resented.

The patient's symptoms disappeared after six interviews in which his family relationships were discussed. He was also given explanations of the psychological and physiological mechanisms in fear and read some mental hygiene literature on this point. This, he said, had been helpful because it showed him "what our minds are made up of."

Our last example is concerned with another type of case with a very infantile personality, who had had a schizophrenic episode in the service and was diagnosed as a "schizophrenia, simple type." He said in his statement of complaint that he came to the Clinic "because I want to be natural again." He felt that a few years ago he had "a good personality, but that is gone now." He complained of lack of interest in anything, inability to concentrate or to enjoy anything, of "nervousness," "restlessness," and a "depressed and dazed feeling." He couldn't "make friends or get acquainted." He found it very hard to keep a job.

The patient, a 26-year-old man who lived at home with his father, had no friends, no girl friend, and no idea what he would like to do. He felt timid, very discouraged, empty, and utterly lonely. His relationships to his family were shallow and frustrating. The patient was the second of six siblings—he had one older brother, four younger sisters. His mother was committed to a mental institution when the patient was 10 years old. The children were raised in different foster homes and had little contact with one another. He felt lonely and unhappy. When interviewed, the patient could not even give the exact ages of his younger sisters, but said, "I miss my family." The relationship to his father was very disturbing to the patient, who found it somewhat hard to admit this. The father was a strict Catholic and a punitive person with a bad temper, who had little understanding of the patient. He told his son that he would leave him if he could not stay at his present job. He also advised the subject to avoid psychiatrists and consult the priest instead. The patient seemed to be afraid of, and submissive to, his father in most respects, and had much underlying hostility toward him.

This man made high scores on the E and F scales, a middle score on PEC. The interview disclosed that the patient had no idea about most current issues. His prejudice, as expressed in the questionnaire, seemed to be related in part to his uncritical acceptance of all kinds of clichés about outgroups and to a general underlying hostility and a feeling of futility and threatening chaos. One of his main ideas was the importance of segregation of all kinds of minority groups "to avoid fights." He felt "there will be trouble" and that "the country is going to the dogs." Almost his only specific accusation against outgroups was that Negroes are inferior and aggressive. (At the same time, the patient said that he was the only white orderly in the military hospital who did not mind waiting on Negro patients. Perhaps this was due to an "ingratiation mechanism" which also made it possible for the patient to "get along" with his father.)

The following statements of complaint by high-scoring men may serve to illustrate further the personality trends discussed earlier.

One subject came to the hospital for gastro-intestinal study in connection with a project in psychosomatic medicine. He said he had suffered from stomach ulcers for fifteen years, complained of "nervousness and depressed attitude." He had done much worrying about his stomach. His nervousness had markedly increased since his wife was operated on for thyroid trouble. Also, living with in-laws had been trying.

Another patient, who had been diagnosed as a "psychopathic personality with homosexuality and psychosomatic features," gave the following story in his first interview. Tension, headaches, "peculiar feelings," jumpiness, gas pains, and fear of being attacked. The symptoms appeared after an appendectomy a year earlier. Since then he had been afraid that a certain person would do him physical harm. "Shortly after that I was in a car accident and the same fellow tried to harm me. I didn't feel strong enough to protect myself."

A third case was diagnosed "psychopathic personality with pathological sexuality and neurotic trends." He was suspected of having duodenal ulcers, but no diagnosis had been made. The court had committed this patient to the hospital because he had exposed himself sexually to a small girl. The record of the first interview runs as follows:

The patient doesn't know why he does it. Relates a long history of sexual preoccupations after being warned by his brother about masturbation and relations with girls. Has had fights when he has felt that someone was making fun of him or that something was due him and was being refused. Says he has always been rather close-mouthed, doesn't like to ask favors of anyone, and doesn't want to be indebted to anyone. Three years ago he noticed that his ability to concentrate and to think fast was somewhat impaired. His job as an oil driller necessitated keen coordination and he was responsible for several injuries to the ground crew for which he subsequently blamed himself and felt that he could have prevented them if he had been more on his toes. Decided to give up oil drilling, became a welder. The patient confessed and stated that he was guilty of sexual exposure on one occasion but vigorously denied the others. The incident occurred when he was driving to work early in the morning, and the next thing he remembers was sometime in the afternoon. He recalls having exposed himself to a young girl on the corner, offering her a nickel to play with his penis. He became violently upset over this, felt that he had been working too hard, and took a week's vacation. Had been working fifteen or sixteen hours daily.

A fourth example is afforded by a high-scoring man diagnosed as "psychoneurosis, anxiety state" whose statement of complaint was as follows:

Rapid breathing, pain over precordium, anxiety, and tension. Patient states he does not know when his trouble started but has never felt well since a car accident five years ago, when he fractured two ribs and struck his head. Developed headaches which came on if he had been worrying. His work, and especially the union men working under him have irritated him greatly. An increasing source of aggravation has been trouble with the production in the factory. Since the last summer vacation in the mountains he has developed more breathlessness, vomiting, diarrhea, some headaches, dreams of a senseless, disagreeable character. Symptoms reappear when he returns to work.

In the final example the diagnosis was "psychoneurosis, mixed, obsessive, compulsive and anxiety features, alcohol addiction," and the statement of complaint:

Being nervous and drinking too much. "I am afraid I'm going crazy." Patient says that prior to four years ago he was perfectly well. Following a ball game, when he was home alone, minding the baby, he suffered a sudden onset of fear with profuse perspiration, palpitation, and trembling. He was afraid that he might harm himself or the child in some way. The doctor told him it was just nervousness and gave him phenobarbitol. Since that time he has had many such attacks, but not as severe. Can't account for the episodes. About one year ago he found that one shot of whiskey would make him "normal again." This progressed slowly, building up to a pint a day and ever since. Since taking alcohol, he has been able to cut down the phenobarbitol almost entirely. He says he never gets completely drunk, but cannot get along without drinking. Realizes he is taking more and more and that this is quite expensive. The patient is anxious to stop drinking and to work out his problem. States there is no problem in his family relations.

b. HIGH-SCORING WOMEN. The high-scoring women showed the same types of anxiety and hypochondriacal symptoms as did the men; sometimes these appeared in more compulsive, sometimes in "phobic," sometimes in schizoid personalities. Many of them suffered from "spells," either of anxiety and/or of hyperventilation symptoms and loss of consciousness or of tension and temper outbursts. In some, all of these features were present.

The following statements of complaints are typical:

Nervous attacks, easily upset. For three years. Attacks of confusion, tingling, tremors for eighteen months. The nervous spell consists of dizzy feeling in her head leading almost to unconsciousness, numbness, and tingling in her extremities. Breathing at the onset is fast and the heart starts beating fast. The symptoms began to appear after husband was shipped overseas. Husband is described as personally and sexually compatible. Questioning brought out, however, that there is some friction because he is not considerate enough of the children.

(Essentially the same physical symptoms as in the first example were related.) Also, the patient was terrified of dying of heart failure during her spells. She got very tense and irritable at the children and occasionally squeezed their throats until she regained composure. Alarmed at these tendencies, the patient sought help.

(Same physical symptoms as above.) Panic, crying spells, sexual difficulties, and jealousy of husband. Spells started three and a half years ago, when she felt "an electric shock passing from the bottom of her feet to her head." After this followed the first "spell." They have recurred two or three times a day since. The patient is afraid of death during a spell, of heart trouble, of cancer, of "losing my mind," and of harming her children during a spell.

The following case is the only one of this type that was interviewed. The patient was a young, lower middle-class housewife with two children. Her husband was a semi-skilled worker who had been on the night shift since their marriage ten years ago. Patient feared the dark as a child and had never liked staying home at night alone, but a few months ago her anxiety became acute. She locked all windows and doors at night, for fear someone might come in and attack her and the children. Two months ago, while dozing off at night, she awoke with a sudden anxiety attack and then lost consciousness. Every day since then she has become very tense and has had pains in the cords of her neck. She has had a feeling of being hot and cold at the same time, and a queer sinking feeling. Occasionally she has had spells of shaking and fainting. She has been able to call someone to help her each time just before losing consciousness. At such times she also has had fits of screaming. Afterwards, she has had amnesia for part of the event. The following history material and personality picture was gleaned from interviews, T.A.T. stories, and from a series of dreams reported during her therapy.

The symptoms refer primarily to a present conflict about the patient's dissatisfaction with her marriage. This conflict is patterned after an earlier one involving her relationships to her family, particularly one brother.

The patient and her two older brothers were raised on a rather isolated farm. They had few friends and even in adolescence the patient was not permitted to go out much nor to have dates or witness boys' athletic events unchaperoned. The parents were Swiss Catholic immigrants who adhered strictly to their old-world mores. The mother seems to have been particularly severe with regard to toilet and cleanliness training—as indicated also by her present treatment of the grandchildren—and to have completely suppressed the children's noisiness and overt hostility. The sexual taboos were strictly observed; the children were trained to be extremely modest and were given no sex instruction. This type of training has produced a number of reaction formations in the patient, e.g., excessive concern with neatness, punctuality, obedience, and modesty. Aside from these facts, it is difficult to form a concrete realistic picture of the personalities and relationships in the subject's family, as her descriptions were so extremely idealized. She described the father as an old-fashioned but very jovial and mild man; the mother as a nervous and somewhat ailing but hard-working, generous, and kind woman and good mother; the brothers as particularly nice and good natured. The patient claimed she "had a lot of fun" in childhood, and "never fought" with the two brothers. Similarly, she insisted that there was nothing wrong in her relationship with her husband except for his working nights, for which he is not to blame. She said that sexual relations, though often somewhat hurried, were usually satisfactory—though she occasionally did not achieve an orgasm.

The dreams and T.A.T. revealed, however, that the patient had a great deal of unconscious hostility towards her husband, as well as towards her mother, her favorite brother, and men in general, who were represented as aggressive and sexually brutal. This unconscious imagery of men as "attackers" was expressed consciously in her thinking about certain outgroups such as Negroes and Mexicans. The dreams also suggest a conflict over sexual and oral-aggressive impulses directed towards men. The contexts in which the orality and aggression appeared (smashing snakes, biting into chicken drumsticks, etc.) suggest infantile wishes to bite, destroy and incorporate a penis. Dangerous, electrically charged wire fences belonging to an enclosure for chickens (such as existed on her parents' farm) formed a recurrent theme; the patient unwittingly climbed a fence or touched it, with the resulting sensation of "being shaken" and of inability to tear herself away from the fence until the current was shut off. Here, it seems, there is reenactment of fears connected with the gratification of infantile wishes—probably sexual ones. This is likely also to be the meaning of her shaking and fainting spells, of which the dream scene is reminiscent.

To this subject, the expression of hostility represented a special problem. She could not admit any aggression towards her husband or family, inhibiting most expressions of anger and irritation behind a façade of submissive compliance and somewhat forced cheerfulness. In therapy it was revealed that her shaking and fainting spells always followed incidents in which a man provoked her anger by acting in a deprecating and implicitly aggressive and demanding manner, while she retained a calm and good-humored attitude. Thus, the first spell occurred after a card game in which her husband called her attention to an ace she had overlooked. She said that ordinarily she would have become angry with her husband, but this time she "laughed it off." Other spells have occurred after she was asked to pay a bill which had already been paid and after she was told she would have to pay more for an article than the price previously agreed upon. In both cases she felt no anger at the time but had a "spell" later.

This case can be described as an anxiety hysteria in which compulsive trends play a role, and in which conflicts about hostile impulses are particularly important. The other cases with anxiety and "nervous spells" are probably dynamically similar. There was one case with a psychogenic paralysis of the right arm and face. This woman had a very rigid character and some compulsive traits. She, too, had extreme unconscious hostility towards men, particularly her former husband. The symptom appeared after she had struck her brother, to whom she had an ambivalent erotic attachment, when he made sexual advances towards her.

Another personality pattern found among the ethnocentric subjects might be called the *constricted infantile schizoid* type. Here, too, compulsive traits are an important part of the picture. Some of these cases, when acutely disturbed, had feelings of depersonalization and apathy. The following case is an example:

The patient was a 27-year-old college graduate who had been married about a year and had just had a baby. She looked and acted younger than her age, and generally made the impression of a naive, very "good little girl." She was very inhibited—in the expression of both sensuality and aggression—

and her ego was occupied to a very large extent with maintaining order, cleanliness, control, and a good façade. She did this by limiting her interests and concentrating on religion and her duties. The latter were carried out efficiently, and this gave her a sense of satisfaction. Before her marriage she achieved this kind of satisfaction through secretarial work; at the time of admission to the Clinic she was interested exclusively in housekeeping.

The patient described her father as a "stern disciplinarian" whom she had always feared. She resented his treatment of her husband of whom he did not approve, but she was unable to admit this resentment. She described her mother in the familiar idealized terms and said: "I have always respected her." She had several brothers with whom she competed for love and approval, and, like many of our high-scoring women, she ended this competition by accepting—on the surface—a completely feminine and submissive role.

The husband, a social service worker, was still in the army, and so was not with the patient after the birth of the child. It was at this time that the patient began to feel "peculiar like in a fog" and as though she were "not quite myself." She was oriented in space and time but could not carry out some of the simplest tasks, in spite of very superior mental ability which, according to tests, had not been affected by her illness. Her physicians thought it best to have the patient join her husband at the earliest possible moment. She was thought well enough to travel alone with the baby. Unexpectedly, during the trip she had to change plans. This stumped her completely. She just sat down with her baby in the waiting room at the airport, quite lost and not able to ask for information nor to make arrangements for herself. She did not improve much after she had joined her husband. In going shopping, for instance, she would stand before the grocery shelves, unable to think of things to buy. The patient was very alarmed and depressed about her condition. In the hospital she kept repeating her complaints over and over, and said she feared she was going crazy and that she could not be helped.

The husband reported that the patient had changed in other respects too. Whereas she had been sexually rather frigid before the delivery, she all of a sudden became very passionate.

Hospitalization and psychotherapy seemed to do little good. So the patient was discharged and brought in by her husband at intervals for electric shock treatments. After very few treatments the patient felt normal and both she and her husband felt that she was now less inhibited, warmer, and able to enjoy herself more.

At the present time the psychological meanings and effects of shock treatments are not sufficiently understood to permit theorizing concerning its role in this case. Its evaluation is rendered the more difficult by the fact that the patient had received and was receiving psychotherapy. The doctors' and husband's acceptance of her newly awakened sensuality may have helped the patient to accept this part of herself, and this may have been an important factor in her improvement.

Another case of the same general type was a 24-year-old mother of two children. She too had an episode of depersonalization and forgetfulness following the birth of the first child. This woman could have been taken for a naive high school girl. Her usual submissive and conventional "good girl" behavior occasionally alternated with outbursts of anger and spite. She was a very dependent person with no ideas and opinions of her own and without interests outside of the domestic sphere. When her husband's support was withdrawn (because of illness) just after she had her second child, she suffered a paranoid schizophrenic episode, became afraid someone would harm her and the children, that her husband or relatives would take one of her daughters out and not bring her back.

Still another case was that of a girl who had always been a particularly conscientious worker and who was completely submissive to her rigid, unsympathetic parents and aggressive older sister, without ever becoming aware of any resentment. When this girl was promoted to a job of considerable responsibility she developed extreme headaches and entered a state of depression and anxiety, in which she accused herself of being bad, thought people were looking at her, and feared she would lose her mind.

This girl and several other high-scoring women suffered, during the acute stages of their illness, from a mood disturbance which could only be described as "agitated depression." (In some cases this was accompanied by suicidal ideas.) These depressions, however, were different from those seen in the patients who were subject to periodic neurotic depressions. They were often accompanied by somewhat bizarre ideas and in general showed schizoid qualities. For this reason they were sometimes labeled schizo-affective reactions.

Few of these cases had the slightest idea of or interest in current issues and were very unsure of the few ideas they could voice during the interviews. Their ideologies about outgroups were meager, less elaborated, and even more naive and stereotyped than those of less disturbed high-scoring subjects. Their rejection of outgroups—in the abstract at least—was extremely strong, leading to very high prejudice scores and often to emotionally charged responses during interviews such as "You wouldn't want to have a black baby, would you?" This is an expression of their particular ego weakness, necessitating special efforts at creating and maintaining countercathexes.

2. THE LOW SCORERS

The pattern formed by the symptoms in List B of Category VII is different. The unacceptable impulses—although not all conscious nor undisguised—are more ego-assimilated and are perceived as part of the self. The low-scoring patients generally came to the Clinic with a particular psychological problem they wanted to solve. They complained of certain conflicts or anxieties about some more or less definite idea or situation or were consciously dissatisfied with their sex role. Many of these are character neuroses. The "evil" was not sought outside but in the self. Elsewhere in the present volume it has been shown that high scorers on E are typically extrapunitive, while low scorers are intrapunitive. Intrapunitiveness has been understood as a sign of a strict but *internalized* superego and probably also of a somewhat masochistic character structure. The psychologically ill low scorers seem to show this tendency in exaggerated form: in (neurotic) depression, suicidal ideas, inferiority, and guilt feelings.

Their greater acceptance of their instinctual and fantasy lives and their relative independence from conventional restrictions give great variety, individuality, and even bizarreness to the pathological ideas and behavior of these patients.

In some ways many of these patients (although by no means all of them) behaved in a way that is opposite to the cultural norm for their sex. Some of the men were shy, timid, passive, and dependent and had some interests more often found in women. Some of the women were aggressive, less interested in home and family than in some occupational achievement. Homosexuality and sexual perversions were more freely admitted, and conflicts about such impulses were often quite conscious and undisguised. (This does not mean that the low scorers have more homosexual tendencies. There are probably just as many if not many more high scorers with such impulses. But in the latter case, these impulses and fantasies are strongly disguised and repressed.)

a. LOW-SCORING MEN. The low scorers on E presented such a variety of complaints and clinical pictures that it is almost impossible to fit them into a few "types." While some had psychoses or classical neuroses with anxiety-hysterical and compulsive symptoms, many cases presented character disorders which had come to the fore or were accentuated because of situational factors. An example of this type was a very dependent man, married to a more aggressive woman to whom he was very much attached and sexually attracted. The relationship, always problematic, had become intolerable since the wife had a second child whom she rejected. The Clinic suggested foster-home placement for the child. The patient could not accept this nor could he decide to leave his famliy.

Broadly speaking, the low-scoring men were generally unaggressive, nurturant, often somewhat withdrawn and inhibited socially. They came to the Clinic with depressions and conscious anxieties relating to problems of sex, work, or general adjustment. In contrast to the high-scoring men, the problems as stated by these patients referred directly to their relationships to others. During the war a few of them suffered acute conflict about the problem of participation, leading, in a few cases, to self-inflicted injuries to avoid the draft, in others to conscientious objection. This was not primarily because of fear of physical injury or death but because of ideological reasons and a horror of being forced to kill.

An illustrative case is that of a young man of college age who had been in a camp for conscientious objectors. He was short and slight. His manner and speech betrayed much tension and self-consciousness. He was very unsure of himself and suffered somewhat from compulsive doubt and indecision. He had well-formed opinions about some subjects—such as the problems of minorities and pacifism—but in most areas he was quite uncertain, mentioning one opinion and then retreating when challenged by the interviewer, saying "I really don't know much about it yet—I have to read a lot more." He was keenly interested in politics and concerned about social progress. He realized that his occupational choice—to counsel people about their personal problems —stemmed from awareness of his own inner struggles and from his own desire to be helped.

The patient voluntarily sought help because of restlessness, anxiety, occasional depression, and inability to concentrate. He also had severe feelings of inadequacy, stage-fright, social anxiety, and several fears—of the dark, of physical injury, and of graveyards and mental institutions.

The patient's father was of lower-class origin with a grade-school education, who became a carpenter, then a farmer and minister in a fundamentalist church. He was a stern, dominating and punitive man with narrow, fundamentalist and puritanical ideas, who made the children work hard on the farm and dealt out severe corporal punishment. The mother, a church singer, would have liked to push the father into a higher ministerial position. She was ashamed of her husband's fire and brimstone sermons and his denunciation of vices he himself possessed. Though not punitive herself, she did not actively take the children's part. She tried to appease the father by conformity to his demands, and she tried to influence the children to do the same. There was much discord between the parents which was painful to the patient. He usually sided with the mother, who had made him her special confidant. Although he had been close to his mother in his earlier life, the patient was, at the time of the interview, rather critical of her.

The patient had one brother, several years his senior, with whom he was never close but whom he liked and respected and wanted to know better. He was quite close, however, to his twin brother, taller, stronger, and more aggressive than the patient, and admired him for his poise and school achievement. The patient let his brother play the socially aggressive role and also let the brother go ahead in football while the patient remained in the background, doing the chores on the farm. The brother submitted to the father, did not resist the corporal punishment and, so far, remained a conformist. The patient, on the other hand, always resisted the father's punishment to some extent, though often in fantasy only; he felt the father was doing him a wrong, often broke the father's rules, and finally tried to break completely with the parental ideology with regard to religion, mores, and politics. This process caused the patient a great deal of conscious anxiety and conflict. The core of the neurosis was undoubtedly the partly repressed hostility against the father, complicated by the relationship to the twin brother.

The following are excerpts from the first psychiatric interviews of low-scoring men:

The patient says that since childhood he has been somewhat withdrawn, making very few social contacts, remaining in his room for days at a time. Never has had any particular interests, heroes, or ideals other than the vague feeling that he should somehow get a good job and become a respectable member of society. But he "loses interest and becomes bored with a job as soon as he finds out that he can handle it." He has had a variety of positions from laborer to personnel interviewer. When the job becomes intolerable, feelings of anxiety and frustration are at their height. He will feel very dissatisfied with himself as well as with the job and then try to change jobs. He shot off the middle finger of one hand "in a hysterical effort to escape the draft." He feels that psychotherapy is his "last chance" to straighten out and settle down mentally.

The patient complained of acute anxiety, depression, suicidal thoughts, and present inability to work or make decisions. He said the problem worrying him was whether he was a homosexual and if so, how could he make a happy adjustment to it? While in the army, the patient had formed a strong attachment to a homosexual man of his own age who, for a long time, encouraged and courted, then suddenly rejected him. When the relationship had become very strained, the patient was very angry and thought of killing the friend, but instead made a suicide attempt, wounding himself quite severely with a gun.

The patient suffers from feelings of depression, primarily in reaction to receiving a letter from his girl friend stating that she had married someone else. They had been friends on a purely platonic basis, sharing intellectual interests. Also he feels bitter and hopeless about his recent transfer from a public service camp to a government camp where he has no opportunity for constructive activity. He feels the C.O. camps should provide more public service, not be there merely for purposes of detention.

There were two cases with hysterical symptoms: One pianist, with a history of various mild hysterical conversion symptoms while in the service, who complained of numbness and partial loss of function of the right index finger; one student who suffered from anxiety nightmares and fainting spells, particularly during examination times. The fainting spells had first appeared in situations in which he had felt attacked by his very aggressive, brutal father.

Finally, there were a few low-scoring men with mild cases of schizophrenia. Actually, their E scores were in the low end of the low middle quartile. But interviews revealed that timidity had inhibited the questionnaire responses in one case in which the subject was really strongly opposed to prejudice. This patient had always been a seclusive, somewhat compulsive, obviously schizoid person. Although all his relationships were weak and ego-centric, he gave a history of having been somewhat closer to his mother than to his father, whom he described as particularly puritanical, stern, and co-ercive. He expressed much hatred for his father, but there was evidence that some of these sentiments were actually expressions of unconscious fantasies of homosexual submission to the father. While an officer in the army, he suffered from feelings of jealousy regarding his wife, hopelessness and rest-lessness, finally ending in a schizophrenic episode in which he imagined that a number of his subordinates were criticizing his work and were spying on him and talking about him. He became so angry he wanted to kill these individuals. In spite of these tendencies towards projection, the parent was strongly intrapunitive, as shown by the ideas just cited as well as by his responses to the questionnaire and projective items.

The other schizophrenic from the low middle quartile, a young seaman, claimed that he experienced sexual satisfaction only when he deliberately soiled his trousers. He reported various bizarre fantasies, usually of sadistic actions directed against women. He imagined that his shipmates knew about his secret sexual practice and that they looked down on him and rejected him for it. He sought help voluntarily.

In the projections of this and the previous case, both intrapunitive char-acters, the superego seems to play a different role than it does in the charac-teristic projections of the high scorers, where the self is seen as the virtuous one, the "others" as the representatives of the id. While undoubtedly the two psychotic cases just cited projected some of their repressed impulses, e.g., homosexual and sadistic ones, onto their environment, they did this to a smaller degree than did the high scorers. In addition, they projected their own superego strivings onto the environment, feeling that others—more or less justifiably—rejected and punished them.

b. Low-scoring Women. It was brought out in Section D that a great many of the low-scoring women were classified as "mixed neurosis." This is partly due to the fact that in the classification scheme used, no separate category was available for neurotic depression, one of the main complaints of our low-scoring group. Also, the diagnosis of mixed neurosis was usually resorted to in the case of character disorders. These also were prevalent among the low-scoring women.

The following excerpts from the first psychiatric interviews are typical of the low-quartile women. Feelings of depression were given as main com-plaints by low-scoring patients with a great variety of other problems. Even the one schizophrenic scoring in the low quartile complained of the charac-teristic depression and feelings of inadequacy. The prevalence of passivity and orality is also to be noted.

Main concern is "that I have failed repeatedly with everything I do." Complains of lack of self-confidence in her abilities and in her work. States "I have built up such a resentment toward myself that I am afraid I will commit suicide."

Several of these women, suffering from depression, felt that their symptom was related to their difficult relationship to their mothers. One young woman said she felt "a great deal of hatred" for her mother and got sleepy and irritable whenever her mother was around.

She is depressed, with loss of appetite, lassitude, and suicidal thoughts, wants to lie down all the time, requires an abnormal amount of sleep—fifteen to sixteen hours—but without gaining a feeling of vitality afterwards.

Another woman stated that she felt "things are too hard"—she'd rather go to bed. Felt depressed, weak, irritable.

In two women, the central problem was their conscious struggle with homosexual impulses. One young girl with strong intellectual interests had had a violent crush on a female teacher during adolescence. Later she formed crushes on men.

She is aware of some homosexual tendencies. She has a strong desire for friendship and love relationships. Depending on the satisfaction and frustration of this need, she alternates between periods of elation and depression.

The other had crying spells, the desire to sleep all the time, and also suffered from vomiting and cramps.

Some of the women sought help mainly because they felt they were harming their children by their neurotic behavior. All of these were rather active women with interests outside the home, and with a great desire for achievement and for playing a more or less masculine role.

One woman had married an invalid man whom she admired for his intellectual talents. She worked to support him and their child, waiting on her husband hand and foot when at home. She continually drove herself to undertake too much, felt nervous, did not sleep well, and felt she "wasn't a decent mother." She often got spells of excessive eating, followed by depression. Formerly she had had the same "spells" of drinking.

Another case is that of a married woman about 30 years of age who had one child of a previous marriage. She had felt extremely depressed and unable to work since she discovered that she was pregnant again. She did not want the baby because it would mean giving up a career she had just started with much satisfaction, but could not think of offering it for adoption because her husband very much wanted a child. She wanted to have help so that she would either be able to accept the child or decide to give it up. She said, "I bitterly resent having been born a female." From her history, it appeared that she had always actively competed with boys or men. As a kindergarten child she picked fights with little boys—"I liked to beat them to a pulp to show them who was really something." She was married twice previously, each time to a brilliant and successful man with whom she would compete bitterly. These marriages were unsuccessful. At the time of her treatment, she was happily married to a more passive man who admired her and encouraged her professional ambitions. The patient was a serious, sensitive, tense person who was uncomfortable and shy in groups and preferred to be or work alone. Asked about her early life, she described herself as a thoroughly undisciplined, nonconforming child, who in spite of very high intelligence could not do well in school because she got bored and refused to do work she disliked. She did not get along with other children, and preferred to do art work by herself. In later childhood she wanted to be a cowgirl. In adolescence she went through a very rebellious period, then took art training and became a radical. She was talented and had had some success in various artistic fields. She was interested in modern experimental art forms and in the representation of psychological moods. She was politically left-wing but felt she could not be of great use to any political movement because of her shyness and inability to function in groups or to approach people. She described herself and her history with much psychological perceptiveness, frankness, and insight. In spite of this, psychotherapy was difficult because everything was told in a very intellectualized fashion. Instead of letting herself feel the appropriate emotions, the patient usually managed to keep quite aloof, carefully choosing her words to describe her early environment and history.

The patient had had previous periods of depression, each time when something blocked her professional ambitions. The last episode was very severe: She became afraid there was a man in the house who could harm her, and she developed such a loathing for herself that she felt her skin was covered with repulsive fish scales.

The history revealed that she was the only child of two rather neurotic people, who in her early childhood gave the girl a good deal of freedom and individual attention. In spite of this, she often felt lonely and "left out." Through the circumstance of the parents' separation when the patient was 5, the patient came to feel that her mother had caused the beloved father much suffering and was responsible for the separation. She began to feel great disgust for and hostility towards her mother, who became the prototype for her image of the "shallow, pretty, exploiting woman." Her professional interests and activities were based on identification with her professionally successful father, and perhaps also her stepmother.

It is not necessary for our purpose to go into a detailed discussion of the dynamics of this woman's personality and development. The case was presented merely as a description of one type of female patient found among the low scorers. Though too extreme to be representative, the case has many characteristics typical of a whole group of low-scoring women, usually political radicals or militant liberals: the masculine identification (which is unusually strong here), the competition with men and striving for professional achievement, the rejection of femininity and inability to accept the role of a mother. The latter two are exceptionally pronounced here. In most of our low-scoring women there were strong feminine identifications also which were in conflict with the "masculine" strivings. In contrast to the high-scoring women, there is—as with low-scoring women generally—little compulsiveness, less constriction, greater richness of fantasy life—here expressed in artistic and other professional fields—introversion (here particularly strong), and concern with ideas and inner experience. The patient tried to handle her conflicts by seeking rational explanations (therapy) and by sublimations.

In a few of the low-scoring women anxiety symptoms predominated. In these cases, feelings of inadequacy were quite prominent and there was anxiety and shyness in certain social situations. One woman felt so uneasy in groups that she frequently broke into a sweat. She was also jealous of her husband's interest in other women and afraid she might retaliate by having an affair, as she did once before. Another patient, an unmarried woman who was embarrassed in social situations, had developed tremors whenever she had to hold a cup or stemmed glass, or when filling out application blanks. After having fallen down the stairs at a party where she was very uncomfortable, she developed a panic of going down stairs. Also, the patient thought she was always attracted by the wrong men—usually very neurotic men. One very inhibited young girl came to the Clinic because she was afraid her former enuresis might return. She thought she would use the symptom to avoid social engagements, of which she was somewhat afraid. She felt very guilty about her adolescent sexual interests. She had night terrors about a half hour after going to sleep, in which she saw something coming down on her—sometimes a net, sometimes a swarm of bugs. Sometimes an abstract shape of a person would crawl into her bed. She would scream and jump out of bed. One case was of a more phobic character. The girl had had an animal phobia. When seen at the Clinic she was in a "confused anxious state," afraid of entering graduate school, particularly of going to see her graduate advisor. She could not bring herself to go to him and discuss her work. She felt that she had not accomplished much. She was also worried because she did not feel warmly towards anyone, because she felt rather hostile—particularly toward her mother.

There was one case with obsessive-compulsive symptoms, a woman with a previous depressive episode. At the time of her treatment she was unable to do her (clerical) work for fear she might write down something that would embarrass her or damage someone else. The trouble began at 17 when she feared to write down "darn" or "damn." (Swearing was severely condemned by her strict father, whom she reported she hated.) Years later, after she read about rape in the papers she began to worry about the word "rape." Now she was afraid of writing down something pertaining to her current employer's raping or attacking her. She was never certain whether she had not by chance inserted these ideas into a letter, or into other products of her typing work. For the last few years she had found that sedatives and alcohol would relieve her condition.

One of the low-scoring women was classified as a paranoid schizophrenic. Yet her complaints, except for a few bizarre ideas, were similar to the ones reported by other low-scoring women suffering primarily from depression. The patient described with much insight her extreme sensitivity to other people's reactions, her concern lest she be rejected by others, her early feelings of insecurity and of being unwanted. She said her illness started with nervousness, indecision, and fears "of not being able to keep a job, that I might harm people, of dying of a cerebral hemorrhage (her mother had died in this way); afraid I was going to die and none knew about it or cared." When first interviewed she complained of being depressed and lacking in the ability to concentrate on her work. She was afraid people were "questioning her motives" and had tried to read her mind by saying things to elicit her reactions. She felt a change in the attitude of her family towards her. She had been weak and tired, attributing this to a drug which she believed was used in the food at the previous hospital. She said "there is a barrier between me and other people erected by myself. Last week I felt closer to people."

Finally, there were two cases who were referred by physicians to whom they had turned because of physical symptoms. In one case the main complaint was a headache and "hypersensitivity to light, necessitating wearing of dark glasses." The other case complained mainly of dismenorrhea, also of nausea and of muscular pains simulating her mother's arthritis. Both cases traced their symptoms to accidents. Although little material on these patients was available, it seemed very likely that they were cases of conversion hysteria.

3. THE "MIDDLES"

Most of the data just presented pertain only to patients receiving E scores within the high or low quartiles. We have, of course, collected some data on "middle scorers." First, there were the questionnaire data, including responses to Projective Questions, and second, the psychiatric diagnoses and Minnesota Multiphasic scores. These indicated that, on the whole, "low middles" resembled the low scorers more, the "high middles" showed more resemblance to the high scorers.

In addition, several clinical case studies were made of patients with middle scores. In these cases one could clearly discern both "high" and "low" personality trends and, sometimes, curious inconsistencies in ideology and behavior. This was true of some of our most disturbed patients. Most of the psychotic patients made middle scores—a few were "low middles," but most of them made high middle scores. Some explanations of this trend have been advanced in Section D above; it seemed to be related in these patients to ego weakness and unconcern with social reality. There were, of course, people with middle scores who were relatively little disturbed, but we have very little information concerning them.

The total sample of Clinic subjects contained 27 cases diagnosed as psychotic. Of these, 70 per cent (19 cases) made scores in the middle quartiles. This percentage is considerably greater than chance (which would be 50 per cent) and is significant at the 5 per cent level. However, little weight can be given this result because of the small number of cases.

The clinical case studies also indicate that many of the most disturbed patients tended to make middle rather than extreme scores. In these cases it can often be shown that the over-all personality picture is either "high" or "low" but that the neurotic or psychotic processes lead to certain contradictory opinions, or attitudes that are the opposite.

An example of such a picture is a schizophrenic man, a strongly intrapunitive person, thoroughly opposed to any kind of prejudice against minorities, usually a pacifist (and believer in a vague humanitarianism) who at certain times expressed marked chauvinism and destructive ideas directed against other nations. He developed these ideas when control of his own homosexuality and hostility was threatening to collapse. Another case is that of a man with a strongly paranoid character who had the most outspoken fascist ideology. This man's character structure and his scores on the F and PEC scales revealed that in most respects this man was very much like our high-scoring subjects. Great hostility and fear of his father had prevented genuine identifications. But the subject spent all his efforts in a fruitless attempt to prove to himself and the world that *he* was more powerful, capable, intelligent, and virtuous than his father. This manifested itself, among other ways, in continual though unrealistic and unsuccessful strivings for positions of power, in a grandiose conception of himself, in a verbose manner of speech and continual orientation toward making an impression on others. In many ways this man could be described as a psychopathic character. Still, he made only a low-middle score on E. Interviews revealed that this was related to a certain opposition to the father's prejudiced ideology, although in other areas this subject had very conventional values. Also, the mild opposition to prejudice seemed to rest on a certain amount of identification with deprived groups. For instance, he considered the differences between whites and Negroes to be primarily due to a difference in education; in fact he would like to solve all problems in the area of group relations by giving educational opportunities to all. He also considers the basis for all his own failures to be his lack of a college education due to the fact that his father lost his money just when the patient was of college age. Needless to say, this subject's ideology differed qualitatively from that of low-middle subjects whose characters were more typical of low scorers. These differences, however, were revealed only in the interview.

H. CONCLUSIONS

In this concluding section we shall discuss the problem of the relationship between ethnocentrism and psychological ill health in the light of the findings just reported. First, however, it will be necessary to make a statement about the degree to which conclusions drawn on the basis of findings from the Langley Porter Clinic group can be generalized. In our description of the sample (Section B) we have defined the Langley Porter Clinic population as a group coming mainly from the urban lower middle-class and, on the average, somewhat younger and slightly more educated and more intelligent than the general population, and more cooperative than average. In these respects Langley Porter Clinic patients are probably similar to patient groups from other psychiatric clinics in large American cities. Within the limits set by our selection procedure, the sample studied was thought to be fairly representative of the Clinic population as a whole, although an exact comparison with the clinic population at large could not be made for want of available data. Results of the present investigation which were found to be statistically significant probably hold for similar clinic groups. A question then arises as to how representative these clinic groups are of the psychologically disturbed (neurotic-psychotic) population as a whole. This question cannot be answered, because no one knows just what this population is like. There are countless individuals who have severe psychological disturbances but never come to the attention of clinics or private psychiatrists. On the other hand, a public clinic such as the one described probably covers a wider range of clinical pictures and social backgrounds than any other agency, certainly a much wider one than could be found among patients going to private therapists and institutions.

As far as the statistical significance of most of the results is concerned, much is left to be desired. The scope of the investigation did not permit the use of many more than 120 subjects. For many of our comparisons this group had to be divided into many small subgroups. Taken one by one, most of the numerical results therefore are not statistically significant, nor otherwise impressive. Whatever value there is in the present investigation lies more in the consistency of all of our findings with one another and with the findings of the study as a whole.

Now an attempt will be made to bring our findings to bear on several questions regarding the relationships between ethnocentrism and psychological ill health. All of the following questions have been raised in connection with the research findings reported in this book: (1) Are people with relatively severe psychological disturbances on the average more or less prejudiced than "normal" people? (2) Are people making extreme (high or low) scores on the E scale also extreme on the dimension of mental health-mental illness? (3) Are high or low scorers prone to develop certain specific kinds of psychological disturbances? (4) Did the study of neurotic and psychotic subjects lead to new hypotheses about the character structure and its possible genetic sources in high and low scorers? (5) Is there any evidence that one of the two groups, at the opposite extremes of the E scale, was more severely disturbed than the other? Is there a relationship between ethnocentrism and psychosis?

1. *Are people with relatively severe psychological disturbances on the average more or less prejudiced than "normal" people?* When the average ethnocentrism scores of the Langley Porter men and women were compared with scores obtained by averaging all other groups, the Clinic group turned out to be slightly, but not significantly, less prejudiced than average. The scores showed a wide range and great variability, indicating that the group contained subjects of greatly varying ideologies and personalities. If one would like to generalize to a wider group of psychologically disturbed people, the Langley Porter Clinic mean is probably too low. As we have shown, the Clinic group was younger, somewhat more educated, intelligent, and cooperative than average. All these selective factors are known to show slight negative correlations with ethnocentrism. On these and other grounds it seems reasonable to assume that a large group of disturbed persons taken at random from the general population would on the average make prejudice scores similar to those of a group of nondisturbed people.

2. *Are people making extreme (high or low) scores on the E scale also extreme on the dimension of mental health-mental illness?* Most of the dynamic formulations in this book have been derived from comparisons of subjects scoring in the high and low quartiles. An objection to this procedure has been that perhaps high and low scorers are both deviant groups, that they are "marginal and neurotic," and that "normal people" in our society are "middles," that is, mildly in agreement with the stereotypes prevalent in our culture. In order to answer the above question conclusively one would first have to establish a reliable measure of *degree* of psychological disturbance. This could then be correlated with ethnocentrism in a large group of subjects. No such measure was available for the present investigation. However, there were some indications that the subjects receiving middle scores on E were at least as disturbed—if not more so—than the patients making extreme scores. This statement is based on some clinical case studies of neurotic and psychotic middle scorers and on the finding that 70 per cent of our psychotic subjects scored in the middle quartiles.

3. *Are high or low scorers prone to develop certain specific kinds of psychological disturbances?* On the whole our data seem to show that the clinical

pictures of subjects in the high quartile resemble each other and differ systematically from the clinical pictures shown by patients from the low quartile. These trends cannot be completely described in terms of the conventional psychiatric classifications as they were used at Langley Porter Clinic. In these terms, the trends were partially expressed in a predominance of "mixed neurosis" with "depressive and anxiety features" in low-scoring women, of "anxiety states" in high-scoring women. The relationships were less marked in the men. However, clinically defined similarities among high-scoring cases, on the one hand, and low-scoring cases, on the other, cut across the lines drawn by these diagnostic classifications. There are high as well as low scorers in each of the major psychiatric categories (e.g., schizophrenia, manic-depressive psychosis, anxiety state, hysteria, obsessive-compulsive, and "mixed neurosis"). It cannot be decided here whether this is due to the essentially nondynamic nature of the classification system or to the way in which the classifications were applied by the physicians. Probably both factors are responsible. More detailed study of the complaints as described by the patients in a first psychiatric interview revealed the following differences in clinical pictures of high and low scorers.

The subjects scoring high on ethnocentrism usually displayed very little awareness of their own feelings and psychological problems. What is more, they tended to resist psychological explanations and to suppress emotion. Their complaints were very often devoid of any psychological content. The most common symptoms in both men and women were vague anxiety or physical signs of anxiety and rage. The more disturbed patients suffered from feelings of depersonalization, lack of interest, and depressed affect of a more schizoid type. Very many high-scoring men and women came to the Clinic with somatic complaints—some of them psychosomatic symptoms which could be understood as expressions of suppressed affects such as fear or rage. They were inclined to dwell at length on these symptoms to the exclusion of other problems. Some showed pathological fear of sickness, physical injury, or death.

The most frequent physical complaints of the high-scoring men in our group were stomach ulcers and physical expressions, such as tremors, sweating, etc., of tension and anxiety. Some of the cases had markedly compulsive characters, others appeared to be more "phobic" or to have characters built around defenses against passive homosexuality. In some of these cases fears of being injured or attacked, or other paranoid trends, were part of the picture. Other types of cases were primarily psychopathic (one of these had admitted sexual exposure to a child) and still others were overt homosexuals. All of them, except for one case of simple schizophrenia, showed to some extent the "toughness" and masculine façade together with various signs of extreme castration anxiety and underlying passivity. The majority of the high-scoring women complained of irritability, anxiety or hyperven-

tilation symptoms; many also had temper outbursts or attacks of trembling, screaming, or fainting (probably equivalents of attacks of rage)
and fear of dying during such an attack. When one of these cases was studied
in detail, it was found that her attacks of panic, trembling, fainting, and
screaming were expressions of extreme rage precipitated by an incident
earlier in the day but suppressed at the time. There was one case of hysterical
conversion in a woman with a very rigid character, and there were several
very infantile schizoid cases with different features such as agitated depression, depersonalization, and paranoid fears. All of these women, however,
resembled each other in the following ways: their main problems seemed to
center around the inability to express strong hostilities directed against some
member of their family; their personalities were rigid and very constricted;
most of them had marked compulsive traits. Rigidity of personality and the
tendency to use countercathective defenses seem to be characteristic of both
high-scoring men and high-scoring women.

The low scorers were found to exhibit a wide variety of clinical pictures
and complaints. They were much more familiar with themselves, more aware
and accepting of emotional experiences and problems. The complaints of
low-scoring patients very rarely consisted of vague anxiety or physical
symptoms alone. If anxiety without content appeared at all, the patient also
reported being concerned about other problems. Usually, the patients stated
their problems in terms of specific impulses, fears, or adjustment difficulties.
The most common single symptom characteristic of low-scoring men and
women was neurotic depression with feelings of inadequacy. Most of these
patients had inhibitions in some area—sexual, work, social—and felt uneasy
in group situations.

Summarizing these findings, then, one might say that some statistical relationship was found for the women between high E score and the classification
"anxiety state," on the one hand, low E score and a classification which was
labeled "mixed neurosis" (which probably should have been called "neurotic
depression"), on the other. It became clear, however, that ethnocentrism
was much more strongly related to certain very general personality trends
which cut across the lines drawn by the psychiatric classifications. It has
therefore been impossible to speak of symptoms or "types of disturbance"
without some reference to the personality syndromes in which they occurred. These personality syndromes will be discussed more fully, more
interpretatively in the following section.

4. *Did the study of neurotic and psychotic subjects lead to new hypotheses about the character structure and its possible genetic sources in high and
low scorers?* All the important variables in which high- and low-scoring
patients differed, were identical with those found to differentiate high and
low scorers in groups of people who were relatively little disturbed. In the

disturbed group, however, these characteristics were seen in more exaggerated form. In the first student group studied by the questionnaire and clinical techniques, Frenkel-Brunswik and Sanford (38) found that the high-scoring women more often mentioned health problems, in spite of the fact that their health histories appeared to be quite similar to those of the low scorers. These few, often casual, remarks about health were related to certain themes in the T.A.T. stories, where many characters suffered mutilating injuries and accidents. On the basis of these data, a tentative interpretation was made to the effect that high-scoring women characteristically show concern about their physical well-being because they are unconsciously afraid of being hurt as a punishment for strong hostile impulses. This hypothesis was confirmed and extended by the data furnished by the Clinic group. In the Langley Porter Clinic women, references to physical symptoms were not confined to a few more or less casual remarks but often formed the most emphasized part of the patient's statement of complaint. Intensive study of several cases supported the hypothesis, developed on the basis of earlier findings (Chapter XII), that the tendency to focus on one's physical condition in this particular way not only expresses strong unconscious (castration) anxiety but also represents the way in which a person with a very constricted ego defends himself against becoming aware of large areas of his emotional life.

Similarly, some of the "normal" subjects in the over-all sample of the study mentioned tendencies towards depressed feelings. The data on the low-scoring Clinic patients confirmed the hypothesis that tendencies toward feelings of inferiority and guilt and depression were consistent with a type of character structure found commonly in low scorers and would appear to some degree under conditions of inner or outer stress. In the "normal" subjects, however, these tendencies appeared to be relatively mild, while some of the Clinic patients were incapacitated by them.

Thus, the material from the Clinic group supported and, in some instances shed additional light upon, the dynamic hypotheses advanced in Chapters IX through XIII. Also, our data strongly bore out our hypothesis that the relationships between ethnocentrism and personality variables would be essentially the same for "normal" and for psychologically disturbed groups, but that some of these personality trends would, in the disturbed group, appear in pathological forms and degrees.

Taking the evidence from the various techniques with which our group was studied, and recalling major conclusions from earlier chapters, we can make the following general formulation regarding the character structure of high and low scorers.

The high scorers have rigid, constricted personalities, as shown by their stereotyped, conventionalized thinking and acting and their violent and categorical rejection of everything reminding them of their own repressed impulses. Their egos appear to be not only very constricted but also quite undifferentiated: their range of experience, emotionally and intellectually, is narrow. It is as if they can experience only the one conventionally correct attitude or emotion in any given situation. Everything else is suppressed or denied, or if another impulse breaks through, it is experienced as something which is completely incompatible with the conception of the self, and which suddenly overwhelms the ego. In part, this high degree of ego-alienness probably derives from the fact that the impulses emerging from repression are so primitive and, especially in the women, so very hostile. Compare, for example, the ways in which two high-scoring women on the one hand, and one low-scoring woman, on the other, expressed their ambivalence towards their children. The two high-scoring women had "spells" of excitement, trembling, and various physical manifestations which they did not recognize as expressions of rage. One woman actually choked her children during such attacks, the other had had the impulse but could control it. Both tried to convince the interviewer and themselves that they "really" loved their children. The low-scoring woman was quite aware of rejecting her child, of her habitual impatience and inability to give enough love to the child. She recognized the effects of her behavior on the child, tried to make up for it at times and hoped that after therapy she would be able to be a better mother. The high-scoring mothers were not able to admit any deviation from the conventional idea that a mother, unless she is utterly depraved, can feel anything but tenderness and devotion for her children. In these, and in all of the other cases of high scorers, it seemed as if the person's ego had usually been able to keep the unacceptable impulses completely out of consciousness, by means of countercathexes, and that this prevented modifications of the impulse, such as channelization into milder and more adult forms, sublimations and the like. The T.A.T. stories of the high scorers showed the ego's constriction and lack of differentiation particularly clearly. Even subjects of high intelligence, with excellent vocabularies, told stereotyped, unimaginative stories. The repressed impulses appeared in very primitive, crude forms, giving rise to stories of crime and punishment very much like those of high scorers in other groups (see Chapter XIV). The stories of the low scorers were much richer in content and often less primitive, giving evidence that the person had experienced in himself or through empathy with others a wide range of emotions and that he had found relatively mature ways of expressing his impulses. Besides this channelization, sublimations and intellectualization seemed to play a larger role in low scorers as expressed in their intellectual and artistic interests, their attitudes towards their work, and their attempts to solve their neurotic problems by intellectual analysis and understanding.

It is our general impression that the high scorers, more than the low scorers, are dominated by castration anxiety and more often show anal character traits such as hostile rejectiveness, retentiveness, and anal reaction formations. The last trend was found to be particularly strong in the women. High scorers—particularly men—also seem to have strong but repressed passive-dependent desires, but these appear to be differently organized in the personality than is the case with the low scorers. Whereas in the low scorers these tendencies are expressed directly in interpersonal relationships, in the desire to be loved and in the fear of being rejected in a very personalized way, the high-scoring men's passivity and dependency probably is mainly a reaction to their extreme castration anxiety. The high-scoring men often seek protection from this anxiety in a motherly woman, but without having a very differentiated relationship to this woman as a person.

This brings us to the problem of interpersonal relationships in high and low scorers. The relevant information comes from the detailed case studies (including T.A.T.'s) and the first psychiatric interviews. The frequency with which the low scorers discussed their relationships to others was striking; though often quite disturbed, they tend to behave toward others in a very personal way. Furthermore, the low scorers' relationships, as expressed in their lives as well as in their fantasies, often were of a combined nurturant-dependent type. The same tendency was also shown in their occupational interests (social service, physician, psychological counselor). The interpersonal relationships of high scorers appeared to be much weaker, less personal, more conventional, and more often expressed in terms of dominance-submission.

5. *Is there any evidence that one of the two groups, at the opposite extremes of the E scale, was more severely disturbed than the other? Is there a relationship between ethnocentrism and psychosis?* Two kinds of hypotheses regarding possible relationships between ethnocentrism and mental ill health have been advanced by people who were more or less familiar with the results reported on throughout this book. Some, usually those strongly interested in fighting prejudice, have focussed their attention on the personality descriptions of high scorers. Because these include so many variables (e.g., constriction, projectivity, self-deception, etc.) usually considered unfavorable from a mental-hygiene point of view and because of the fact that our low-scoring subjects do not have these characteristics to any great extent, the conclusion has been drawn that highly prejudiced people are simply mentally disturbed people, those opposed to prejudice are the "normals." The difference in ideology is then explained by the hypothesis that the ethnocentric ideology of the high scorers is based on irrational attitudes which in turn spring from their neurotic conflicts, while the ideology of the "normal" low scorers is developed entirely in a rational, reality-adapted manner.

Others, however, have pointed out that of our two groups, the low scorers deviate more from the culture pattern of their environment. They are more often "socially maladjusted" and seem to suffer more from feelings of depression, anxiety, and inadequacy—all characteristic of a popular conception of the neurotic pattern. According to this hypothesis, then, people who are prejudiced are the "normals" because they are well adjusted in their culture. They have taken over the prejudices along with other ideologies of the culture to which they conform. The low scorers, who rebel against their parents and often against many of the cultural mores, are psychologically ill.

Both of these hypotheses assume that one of the groups scoring at the extremes of the E scale is a "normal," the other an "abnormal" group. Our investigation shows that one is likely to find people with more or less severe psychological disturbances in the high, low, and middle quartiles although we cannot say in what proportions. It even suggests the possibility that the most disturbed people will be found in the middle quartiles.

But there are more basic theoretical reasons for objecting to both of the above hypotheses. The first one, commonly found in liberal thought, assumes that "rational" behavior, in contrast to "irrational" behavior, is entirely independent of deeper-lying personality dynamics. Finding obvious irrational qualities in ethnocentric ideology, some individuals have concluded that prejudiced people think "emotionally" whereas unprejudiced people think "rationally"—that is, without being influenced by their needs and emotions. Our results indicate, however, that the way a person thinks is always conditioned, to a greater or lesser degree, by emotional dispositions. The capacity for rational functioning, in which needs and affects play a *positive* rather than a negative (distorting, inhibiting) role, is part of what we and others have called a *strong ego*. While ego strength seems higher, on the average, in the low than in the high scorers, it must be emphasized that irrationality has been found to some degree in both; however, it is qualitatively different in the two groups and impels the individuals in antipodal directions.

We must object even more strenuously to the second of the above hypotheses—which equates conformity with psychic health, nonconformity with psychic disturbance—because it represents a way of thinking which is all too common in the social sciences as well as in everyday life. It is true, as our results and others show, that ethnocentric individuals are frequently more conforming and more "adjusted" to the prevailing pressures and ideas of our culture. These individuals are thus more "normal" in the sense of approximating the behavior- and ideology-demands of the culture. However, to see *normality* (in this external sense) as identical with psychic *health* (a concept involving inner integration, sublimation, and the like) is to maintain a thoroughly behavioristic, nondynamic conception of the individual. If good external adjustment is to be psychologically healthy, it must be in response to an environment which sufficiently gratifies the most important needs of the individual; being "well-adjusted" under other conditions, e.g., in the face of severe suppression or denial of self-expression, can only be achieved at tremendous inner expense. The "cost" of adjustment to most high scorers has been demonstrated throughout this book. Similarly, rebellious and nonconforming behavior must also be understood in relation to external forces and inner demands. That they may occur, though with different meanings, in both democratic and authoritarian personalities showing various degrees of disturbance, is shown by data from the Clinic group, the San Quentin group (Chapter XXI), and the over-all study sample (Parts II and III).

What, then, can we say regarding our original question of the relation of ethnocentrism to the degree of psychological disturbance? Although no really conclusive answer is at hand, we can, however, try to make certain hypotheses based on (1) our data regarding the incidence of neuroses and psychoses in the various E quartiles for the Clinic group; and (2) the evidence, presented throughout this book, regarding personality characteristics of high and low scorers.

As pointed out in Section D of this chapter, we found a consistent increase in the proportion of psychoses going from the low to the high middle quartiles, with a drop from the high middle to the high quartile. The figures are presented in Tables 3(XXII) and 4(XXII). Because of the small numbers of cases in each quartile, this trend is not statistically significant. Supposing that this result were found to be generally valid, and if psychosis is regarded as a more severe disturbance than neurosis, one could say that there is a slight relationship between severity of mental disturbance (psychosis) and ethnocentrism. The possible reasons why there were fewer psychotics in the extreme high quartile have already been discussed.

Is there a relationship between ethnocentrism and psychosis, anti-ethnocentrism and neurosis? The following discussion is meant as a mere speculation on our findings and presented only to stimulate further discussion and research. It seemed to all of us, who discussed and made formulations about the character structures of high and low scorers, that there were personality trends in the high scorers which would make them more prone to develop psychotic manifestations, while the low scorers seemed to tend more towards neurotic disturbances. (See also Simmel, 111.)

In spite of the fact that we found some low scorers with very disorganized and weak egos (among them at least one schizophrenic), comparison with the high scorers still gave the impression that the low scorers had relatively much stronger egos—that is, they appeared to us to be able to handle their impulses much more successfully due to relatively less extensive repressions and countercathexes and to greater capacity for sublimation and other modifications. Also, the low scorers appeared capable of more genuine relationships to other people, whereas the interpersonal relationships of the high scorers were much more shallow and founded less on personal experiences and feelings than on conventions and stereotypes. These character trends are more consistent with the formation of neurotic traits rather than with the formation of psychotic ones. In pathological forms, these tendencies are less alien and less overwhelming to the ego. Just exactly what the deeper dynamics and the genetic sources of these trends are, we cannot say. Perhaps the clue to the type of character found most commonly among low scorers is a very early inhibition of aggressions which are then turned upon the self; or the early relationships to parents lead to strong identifications and a well-internalized—though often disturbing—conscience.

In the high scorers, extensive repressions and countercathexes have hindered the ego's development. The ego remains rather primitive, undifferentiated, and completely isolated from a large portion of the deeper layers. When the unresolved unconscious conflicts become intensified and come closer to consciousness, the ego, totally unprepared, feels overwhelmed and shocked. This may lead merely to strong anxieties with or without somatic symptoms. In more extreme form, however, it may lead to depersonalization, withdrawal from reality, denial, projections, and other psychotic manifestations. Given a sufficiently supporting environment, highly ethnocentric individuals achieve a sense of "comfort" and "adjustment"; but they frequently lack the productiveness, the capacity for love, and, in times of stress, the grip on reality, which are more characteristic of the anti-authoritarian individuals.

CHAPTER XXIII

CONCLUSIONS

The most crucial result of the present study, as it seems to the authors, is the demonstration of close correspondence in the type of approach and outlook a subject is likely to have in a great variety of areas, ranging from the most intimate features of family and sex adjustment through relationships to other people in general, to religion and to social and political philosophy. Thus a basically hierarchical, authoritarian, exploitive parent-child relationship is apt to carry over into a power-oriented, exploitively dependent attitude toward one's sex partner and one's God and may well culminate in a political philosophy and social outlook which has no room for anything but a desperate clinging to what appears to be strong and a disdainful rejection of whatever is relegated to the bottom. The inherent dramatization likewise extends from the parent-child dichotomy to the dichotomous conception of sex roles and of moral values, as well as to a dichotomous handling of social relations as manifested especially in the formation of stereotypes and of ingroup-outgroup cleavages. Conventionality, rigidity, repressive denial, and the ensuing break-through of one's weakness, fear and dependency are but other aspects of the same fundamental personality pattern, and they can be observed in personal life as well as in attitudes toward religion and social issues.

On the other hand, there is a pattern characterized chiefly by affectionate, basically equalitarian, and permissive interpersonal relationships. This pattern encompasses attitudes within the family and toward the opposite sex, as well as an internalization of religious and social values. Greater flexibility and the potentiality for more genuine satisfactions appear as results of this basic attitude.

However, the two opposite types of outlook must by no means be regarded as absolutes. They emerge as a result of statistical analysis and thus have to be considered as syndromes of correlating and dynamically related factors.[1]

---

[1] There is marked similarity between the syndrome which we have labeled the authoritarian personality and "the portrait of the anti-Semite" by Jean-Paul Sartre (110). Sartre's brilliant paper became available to us after all our data had been collected and analyzed. That his phenomenological "portrait" should resemble so closely, both in general structure and in numerous details, the syndrome which slowly emerged from our empirical observations and quantitative analysis, seems to us remarkable.

They consist in accumulations of symptoms frequently found together but they leave plenty of room for variations of specific features. Furthermore, various distinct subtypes are found within each of the two major patterns. Above all, two subvarieties of the ethnically prejudiced must be distinguished: the conventional and the psychopathic. Many more subvarieties can be distinguished on the basis of differential preoccupation with this or that particular trait that is alleged to exist in an ethnic minority. Our prejudiced subjects, however, are on the whole more alike as a group than are the unprejudiced. The latter include a great variety of personalities; many, on the surface at least, have no more extreme variants in common than the absence of a particular brand of hostility.

Indications are that there may be more similarity, within the major types, at the core than at the surface. This holds especially for the highly prejudiced subject, with his great variety of rationalizations and behavioral manifestations of prejudice.

Furthermore, our findings are strictly limited to the psychological aspects of the more general problem of prejudice. Historical factors or economic forces operating in our society to promote or to diminish ethnic prejudice are clearly beyond the scope of our investigation. In pointing toward the importance of the parent-child relationship in the establishment of prejudice or tolerance we have moved one step in the direction of an explanation. We have not, however, gone into the social and economic processes that in turn determine the development of characteristic family patterns.

Finally, the present study deals with dynamic potentials rather than with overt behavior. We may be able to say something about the readiness of an individual to break into violence, but we are pretty much in the dark as to the remaining necessary conditions under which an actual outbreak would occur. There is, in other words, still plenty of room for action research. Actually such additional research is necessary for all practical purposes. Outbreaks into action must be considered the results of both the internal potential and a set of eliciting factors in the environment. No action research can, however, be complete without analysis of the factors within the individual, an analysis to which this volume endeavors to contribute, so that we should be enabled to anticipate who would behave in a certain way under given circumstances.

All this is, of course, subject to the over-all limitation which lies in the character of our sample of subjects. It is our opinion that a study of a topic of such crucial social significance could well deserve to be conducted on a statistical basis comparable to that of nation-wide opinion polls. The present study has chosen to be an intensive rather than an extensive one. In spite of the fact that part of it has been conducted with subjects numbering over two thousand, its major aim is penetration into underlying patterns of factors rather than exhaustive representativeness in covering the entire population.

Broadening of the factual basis in this respect undoubtedly will lead to reformulation of many specific questionnaire items and technical revisions. Actually, only in a truly representative study would it become possible to appraise quantitatively the amount of prejudice in our culture, to determine the general validity of the personality correlates outlined in this volume, and to assess the various possibilities of a mutual overlapping of the two major patterns that we have described.

Although it is not a part of our task to prescribe or to plan programs for countering prejudice we may be permitted some remarks concerning the general implications of our research.

It follows directly from our major findings that countermeasures should take into account the whole structure of the prejudiced outlook. The major emphasis should be placed, it seems, not upon discrimination against particular minority groups, but upon such phenomena as stereotypy, emotional coldness, identification with power, and general destructiveness. When one takes this view of the matter it is not difficult to see why measures to oppose social discrimination have not been more effective. Rational arguments cannot be expected to have deep or lasting effects upon a phenomenon that is irrational in its essential nature; appeals to sympathy may do as much harm as good when directed to people one of whose deepest fears is that they might be identified with weakness or suffering; closer association with members of minority groups can hardly be expected to influence people who are largely characterized by the inability to have experience, and liking for particular groups or individuals is very difficult to establish in people whose structure is such that they cannot really like anybody; and if we should succeed in diverting hostility from one minority group we should be prevented from taking satisfaction by the knowledge that the hostility will now very probably be directed against some other group.

So it is with various other measures which from our point of view are concerned with the treatment of symptoms or particular manifestations rather than with the disease itself. Yet we certainly do not wish to belittle, or to ask for any reduction in, such activities. Some symptoms are more harmful than others, and we are sometimes very glad to be able to control a disease even though we cannot cure it. Indeed it may be hoped that knowledge of what the potential fascist is like—knowledge of the kind that this book has attempted to supply—will make symptomatic treatment more effective. Thus, for example, although appeals to his reason or to his sympathy are likely to be lost on him, appeals to his conventionality or to his submissiveness toward authority might be effective. (But it should be clearly understood that such activity would in no way reduce his conventionality or authoritarianism or his fascist potential.) Similarly it is consistent with what we know of the potentially fascist personality to suppose that he would be impressed by legal restraints against discrimination, and that his self-restraint would increase as minority groups became stronger through being protected. (But it must be remembered that it is the usual practice of the fascist to dress his most antidemocratic actions in a legalistic cloak.) Again, since acceptance of what is like oneself and rejection of what is different is one feature of the prejudiced outlook, it may be that members of minority groups can in limited situations and for some period of time protect themselves and gain certain advantages by conforming in outward appearance as best they can with the prevailing ways of the dominant group. We say this cautiously because it is necessary continuously to be aware that the same tendencies to conformity which are praised in the ingroup may be condemned in the outgroup. (Furthermore, aside from the fact that such conformity works against the values of cultural diversity, it is a necessary conclusion from the present study that the ultimate fate of any minority group does not depend primarily upon what that group may do, and moreover, once the minority group member has conformed in this way there is little reason to suppose that he would not adopt the prevailing ingroup attitudes toward those who have not been able to conform.)

Thus it appears that when we address ourselves to symptoms, here as in any disease, we have to face the fact that a "cure" of one manifestation is likely to be followed by a breaking out in some other area. Yet there is sufficient reason why there can be no letup in the kinds of activity just described: so great is the over-all fascist potential that any withdrawal on any front might make it even more difficult than it now is for groups discriminated against to secure their rights.

It would be most unfortunate if a grasp of the true enormity of the fundamental problem should anywhere lead to a diminution of effort. It is impossible to conceive of any way of attacking the problem that does not involve a multiplicity of subgoals—to be attained by individuals or by groups. Any act, however limited in time and place, that serves to counter or diminish destructiveness can be regarded as a microcosm, as it were, of a total effective program.

What can be done about the disease itself? If, as the present study has shown, we are dealing with a structure within the person it seems that we should consider, first, psychological techniques for changing personality. Yet, a moment's reflection will show that the therapeutic possibilities of individual psychology are severely limited. How could one "cure" one of our high scorers? This probably could be done by proceeding along the lines indicated in our clinical and genetic chapters. But when one considers the time and the amount of arduous work that would be required and the small number of available therapists, and when he considers that many of the main traits of the ethnocentrist are precisely those which, when they occur in the setting of a clinic, cause him to be regarded as a poor therapeutic risk, it appears at once that the direct contribution of individual psychotherapy has to be regarded as negligible.

Confronted with the rigidity of the adult ethnocentrist, one turns naturally to the question of whether the prospects for healthy personality structure would not be greater if the proper influences were brought to bear earlier in the individual's life, and since the earlier the influence the more profound it will be, attention becomes focused upon child training. It would not be difficult, on the basis of the clinical and genetic studies reported in this volume, to propose a program which, even in the present cultural pattern, could produce nonethnocentric personalities. All that is really essential is that children be genuinely loved and treated as individual humans. But all the features of such a program would have the aspect of being more easily said than done. For ethnocentric parents, acting by themselves, the prescribed measures would probably be impossible. We should expect them to exhibit in their relations with their children much the same moralistically punitive attitudes that they express toward minority groups—and toward their own impulses. In children then, as in the case of the adult ethnocentrist, we cannot expect psychology, by itself, to produce the desired result; one is too familiar with cases of young parents with the fullest intellectual understanding of modern theories whose need to do the "correct" thing prevents the very warmth and spontaneity which those theories prescribe. But more serious, because much more widespread, is the case of parents who with the best will and the best feelings are thwarted by the need to mould the child so that he will find a place in the world as it is. Few parents can be expected to persist for long in educating their children for a society that does not exist, or even in orienting themselves toward goals which they share only with a minority.

It seems obvious therefore that the modification of the potentially fascist structure cannot be achieved by psychological means alone. The task is comparable to that of eliminating neurosis, or delinquency, or nationalism from the world. These are products of the total organization of society and are to be changed only as that society is changed. It is not for the psychologist to say how such changes are to be brought about. The problem is one which requires the efforts of all social scientists. All that we would insist upon is that in the councils or round tables where the problem is considered and action planned the psychologist should have a voice. We believe that the scientific understanding of society must include an understanding of what it does to people, and that it is possible to have social reforms, even broad and sweeping ones, which though desirable in their own right would not necessarily change the structure of the prejudiced personality. For the fascist potential to change, or even to be held in check, there must be an increase in people's capacity to see themselves and to be themselves. This cannot be achieved by the manipulation of people, however well grounded in modern psychology the devices of manipulation might be; and it is a judgment which finds support in the present study that the man who is first to seize power will be the last to give it up. It is safe to assume, however, that fascism is imposed on the people, that it actually goes against their basic interests, and that when they can be made fully aware of themselves and their situation they are capable of behaving realistically. That people too often cannot see the workings of society or their own role within it is due not only to a social control that does not tell the truth but to a "blindness" that is rooted in their own psychology. Although it cannot be claimed that psychological insight is any guarantee of insight into society, there is ample evidence that people who have the greatest difficulty in facing themselves are the least able to see the way the world is made. Resistance to self-insight and resistance to social facts are contrived, most essentially, of the same stuff. It is here that psychology may play its most important role. Techniques for overcoming resistance, developed mainly in the field of individual psychotherapy, can be improved and adapted for use with groups and even for use on a mass scale. Let it be admitted that such techniques could hardly be effective with the extreme ethnocentrist, but it may be remembered that the majority of the population are not extreme but, in our terminology, "middle."

It is the fact that the potentially fascist pattern is to so large an extent imposed upon people that carries with it some hope for the future. People are continuously molded from above because they must be molded if the over-all economic pattern is to be maintained, and the amount of energy that goes into this process bears a direct relation to the amount of potential, residing within the people, for moving in a different direction. It would be foolish to underestimate the fascist potential with which this volume has been mainly concerned, but it would be equally unwise to overlook the fact that the majority of our subjects do not exhibit the extreme ethnocentric pattern and the fact that there are various ways in which it may be avoided altogether. Although there is reason to believe that the prejudiced are the better rewarded in our society as far as external values are concerned (it is when they take shortcuts to these rewards that they land in prison), we need not suppose that the tolerant have to wait and receive their rewards in heaven, as it were. Actually there is good reason to believe that the tolerant receive more gratification of basic needs. They are likely to pay for this satisfaction in conscious guilt feelings, since they frequently have to go against prevailing social standards, but the evidence is that they are, basically, happier than the prejudiced. Thus, we need not suppose that appeal to emotion belongs to those who strive in the direction of fascism, while democratic propaganda must limit itself to reason and restraint. If fear and destructiveness are the major emotional sources of fascism, *eros* belongs mainly to democracy.

REFERENCES

1. ACKERMAN, N., and JAHODA, M.: *Anti-Semitism and Emotional Disorder*, New York, Harper & Brothers, 1950.
2. ADORNO, T.W.: Anti-Semitism and fascist propaganda. In Simmel, E., ed.: *Anti-Semitism: A Social Disease*, New York, International Universities Press, 1946.
3. ADORNO, T.W.: The psychological technique of Martin Luther Thomas' radio speeches. (In the files of the Institute of Social Research, New York.)
4. AICHORN, A.: *Wayward Youth*, New York, The Viking Press, 1935.
5. ALEXANDER, F., BACON, C., LEVEY, H.B., LEVINE, M., and WILSON, G.W.: The influence of psychological factors upon gastrointestinal disturbances; a symposium. *Psychoanalytic Quarterly* 3:501–588, 1934.
6. ALEXANDER, F., and HEALY, W.: *Roots of Crime*, New York, Alfred A. Knopf, 1935.
7. ALEXANDER, F., and STAUB, H.: *The Criminal, the Judge and the Public*, New York, The Macmillan Company, 1931.
8. ALLPORT, F.H., and HARTMANN, D.A.: Measurement and motivation of atypical opinion in a certain group. *American Political Science Review* 19: 735–760, 1925.
9. ALLPORT, G.W.: *Personality: A Psychological Interpretation*, New York, Henry Holt & Company, 1937.
10. ALLPORT, G.W.: *The ABC's of Scapegoating*, Chicago, Central YMCA College, 1942.
11. ANASTASI, ANNE: *Differential Psychology*, New York, The Macmillan Company, 1937.
12. ARON, BETTY: *A Manual for Analysis of the Thematic Apperception Test*, Berkeley, Willis E. Berg, 1949.
13. ASHLEY-MONTAGUE, M.F.: *Man's Most Dangerous Myth: The Fallacy of Race*, New York, Columbia University Press, 1942.
14. BALKEN, E.R., and VANDER VEER, A.H.: The clinical application of the T.A.T. to neurotic children. *American Journal of Orthopsychiatry* 12:68–80, 1942; 14:421–440, 1944.
15. BENEDICT, RUTH: *The Chrysanthemum and the Sword*, Boston, Houghton Mifflin Company, 1946.
16. BROWN, J.F.: A modification of the Rosenzweig picture-frustration test to study hostile interracial attitudes. *The Journal of Psychology* 24:247–272, 1947.
17. CANTRIL, H.: *The Psychology of Social Movements*, New York, John Wiley & Sons, 1941.

977

18. CHISHOLM, G.B.: The reestablishment of peacetime society. *Psychiatry* 9:3–21, 1946.

19. CONRAD, H.S., and SANFORD, R.N.: Scales for the measurement of war-optimism: I. Military optimism. II. Optimism on the consequences of the war. *The Journal of Psychology* 16:285–311, 1943.

20. CONRAD, H.S., and SANFORD, R.N.: Some specific war attitudes of college students. *The Journal of Psychology* 17:153–186, 1944.

21. DE SALES, R. DE ROUSSY: *The Making of Tomorrow*, New York, Reynal & Hitchcock, Inc., 1942.

22. EDWARDS, A.L.: A critique of "neutral" items in attitude scales constructed by the method of equal appearing intervals. *Psychological Review* 53:159–169, 1946.

23. EDWARDS, A.L.: The signs of incipient fascism. *Journal of Abnormal and Social Psychology* 39:301–316, 1944.

24. EDWARDS, A.L.: Unlabeled fascist attitudes. *Journal of Abnormal and Social Psychology* 36:575–82, 1941.

25. ERIKSON, E.H.: Hitler's imagery and German youth. *Psychiatry* 5:475–493, 1942.

26. FENICHEL, O.: The psycho-analysis of anti-Semitism. *American Imago* 1:24–39, 1940.

27. FENICHEL, O.: *The Psychoanalytic Theory of Neurosis*, New York, W. W. Norton & Company, 1945.

28. FISHER, R.A.: *Statistical Methods for Research Workers*, New York, G.E. Stechert & Company, 1944 (9th ed.).

29. FRANCK, KATE: Preferences for sex symbols and their personality correlates. *Genetic Psychology Monographs* 33:73–123, 1946.

30. FRENKEL-BRUNSWIK, ELSE: A study of prejudice in children. *Human Relations* 1:295–306, 1949.

31. FRENKEL-BRUNSWIK, ELSE: Dynamic and cognitive categorization of qualitative material: I. General problems and the Thematic Apperception Test. *The Journal of Psychology* 25:253–260, 1948.

32. FRENKEL-BRUNSWIK, ELSE: Dynamic and cognitive categorization of qualitative material: II. Interviews of the ethnically prejudiced. *The Journal of Psychology* 25:261–277, 1948.

33. FRENKEL-BRUNSWIK, ELSE: Mechanisms of self-deception. *The Journal of Social Psychology (S.P.S.S.I. Bulletin)* 10:409–420, 1939.

34. FRENKEL-BRUNSWIK, ELSE: Motivation and behavior. *Genetic Psychology Monographs* 26:121–265, 1942.

35. FRENKEL-BRUNSWIK, ELSE: Personality and prejudice in women. (Abstract) *American Psychologist* 1:233, 1946.

36. FRENKEL-BRUNSWIK, ELSE: Psychoanalysis and personality research. *Journal of Abnormal and Social Psychology* 35:176–197, 1940.

37. FRENKEL-BRUNSWIK, ELSE: Tolerance toward ambiguity as a personality variable. (Abstract.) *American Psychologist* 3:268, 1948.

38. FRENKEL-BRUNSWIK, ELSE, and SANFORD, R.N.: Some personality correlates of anti-Semitism. *The Journal of Psychology* 20:271–291, 1945.

39. FREUD, S.: Libidinal types. *Psychoanalytic Quarterly* 1:3–6, 1932.

40. FREUD, S.: Psycho-analytic notes upon an autobiographical account of a case of paranoia (dementia paranoides). In *Collected Papers*, Vol. III. London, Hogarth Press, 1943.

41. FREUD, S.: The passing of the Oedipus complex. In *Collected Papers*, Vol. II. London, Hogarth Press, 1943.

42. FROMM, E.: *Escape from Freedom*, New York, Farrar & Rinehart, Inc., 1941.

43. FROMM, E.: *Man for Himself*, New York, Rinehart & Company, 1947.

44. GLUECK, S. and GLUECK, E.: *500 Criminal Careers*, New York, Alfred A. Knopf, 1930.

45. GUILFORD, J.P.: *Psychometric Methods*, New York, McGraw-Hill Book Company, Inc., 1936.

46. GUNDLACH, R.H.: Confusion among undergraduates in political and economic ideas. *Journal of Abnormal and Social Psychology* 32:357–367, 1937.

47. HARRIMAN, P.H., ed.: *Twentieth Century Psychology*, New York, Philosophical Library, 1946.

48. HARRIS, R.E., and CHRISTIANSEN, C.: Prediction of response to brief psychotherapy. *The Journal of Psychology* 21:269–284, 1946.

49. HARTLEY, E.: *Problems in Prejudice*, New York, Kings Crown Press, 1946.

50. HATHAWAY, S.R., and McKINLEY, J.C.: A multiphasic personality schedule (Minnesota): I. Construction of the schedule. *The Journal of Psychology* 10:249–254, 1940.

51. HEALY, WILLIAM: *Mental Conflict and Misconduct*, Boston, Little, Brown & Company, 1923.

52. HITLER, A.: *Mein Kampf*, New York, Reynal & Hitchcock, Inc., 1940.

53. HORKHEIMER, M., and ADORNO, T.W.: Elemente des Antisemitismus. In *Dialektik der Aufklärung*, Amsterdam, Querido Verlag N. V., 1947.

53a. HORKHEIMER, M.: Authoritarianism and the family today. In Anshen, R.N., ed.: *The Family: Its Function and Destiny*, New York, Harper & Brothers, 1949.

54. HORNEY, KAREN: *The Neurotic Personality of Our Time*, New York, W.W. Norton & Company, 1937.

55. HUNT, J. McV., ed.: *Personality and the Behavior Disorders*, New York, The Ronald Press Company, 1944.

56. Institute of Social Research, Horkheimer, M., ed.: *Studien über Autorität und Familie*, Paris, Felix Alcan, 1936.

57. Institute of Social Research, Horkheimer, M., ed.: *Studies in Philosophy and Social Science*. Vol. IX, 1941.

57a. Institute of Social Research: *Studies in Anti-Semitism: A Report to the American Jewish Committee* (4 vols., August 1944, unpublished).

57b. Institute of Social Research: *Anti-Semitism within American Labor: A Report to the Jewish Labor Committee* (4 vols., May 1945, unpublished).

58. JONES, E.: On Quislingism. *International Journal of Psychoanalysis*, 22:1–6, 1941.

59. KARDINER, A.: *The Individual and His Society: The Psychodynamics of Primitive Social Organization*, New York, Columbia University Press, 1939.

60. KARDINER, A.: *Psychological Frontiers of Society*, New York, Columbia University Press, 1945.

61. KARPMAN, B.: *Case Studies in the Psychopathology of Crime*, Washington, D. C., Mimeoform Press, 1933.

62. KATZ, D., and CANTRIL, H.: An analysis of attitudes toward communism and fascism. *Journal of Abnormal and Social Psychology* 35:356–366, 1940.

63. KERR, W.A.: Correlates of politico-economic liberalism-conservatism. *The Journal of Social Psychology* 20:61–77, 1944.

64. KLINEBERG, O.: *Social Psychology*, New York, Henry Holt & Company, 1940.

65. KROUT, M.H., and STAGNER, R.: Personality development in radicals: a comparative study. *Sociometry* 2:39–46, 1939.

66. LASSWELL, H.D.: *Psychopathology and Politics*, Chicago, University of Chicago Press, 1930.

67. LENTZ, T.F.: Generality and specificity of conservatism-radicalism. *Journal of Educational Psychology* 29:590–596, 1938.

68. LENTZ, T.F.: Personage admiration and other correlates of conservatism-radicalism. *The Journal of Social Psychology* 10:81–93, 1939.

69. LERNER, M.: *It Is Later Than You Think*, New York, The Viking Press, 1938.

70. LEVINSON, D.J.: A scale for the measurement of political-economic conservatism. (Abstract) *American Psychologist* 1:451, 1946.

71. LEVINSON, D.J., and SANFORD, R.N.: A scale for the measurement of anti-Semitism. *The Journal of Psychology* 17:339–370, 1944.

72. LEWIS, SINCLAIR: *Babbitt, New York*, Harcourt, Brace & Company, 1922.

73. LIKERT, R.: A technique for the measurement of attitudes. *Archives of Psychology* 140:55 pp., 1932.

74. LINDNER, R.M.: *Rebel without a Cause*, New York, Grune & Stratton, Inc., 1944.

75. LOWENTHAL, L., and GUTERMAN, N.: *Prophets of Deceit*, New York, Harper & Brothers, 1949.

76. LOWREY, L.G.: Delinquent and criminal personalities. In HUNT, J. McV., ed.: *Personality and the Behavior Disorders*, New York, The Ronald Press Company, 1944.

77. LYND, R.S., and LYND, H.M.: *Middletown*, New York, Harcourt, Brace & Company, 1929.

78. McGRANAHAN, D.V.: A comparison of social attitudes among American and German youth. *Journal of Abnormal and Social Psychology* 41:245–258, 1946.

79. MASLOW, A.H.: The authoritarian character structure. *The Journal of Social Psychology* 18:401–411, 1943.

80. MASSERMAN, J.H.: *Principles of Dynamic Psychiatry*, Philadelphia, W. B. Saunders Company, 1946.

81. MASSERMAN, J.H., and BALKEN, E.R.: The psychoanalytic and psychiatric significance of fantasy. *Psychoanalytic Review* 26:343–379, 535–549, 1939.

82. MEAD, MARGARET: *And Keep Your Powder Dry*, New York, William Morrow & Company, Inc., 1942.

83. MORGAN, C.D., and MURRAY, H.A.: A method for investigating fantasies: the

Thematic Apperception Test. *Archives of Neurology and Psychiatry* 34:289–306, 1935.

84. MURPHY, G., and LIKERT, R.: *Public Opinion and the Individual*, New York, Harper & Brothers, 1938.

85. MURPHY, G., MURPHY, L.B., and NEWCOMB, T.M.: *Experimental Social Psychology*, New York, Harper & Brothers, 1937.

86. MURRAY, H.A.: *The Thematic Apperception Test*, Cambridge, Harvard University Press, 1943.

87. MURRAY, H.A.: *The Thematic Apperception Test Manual*, Cambridge, Harvard University Press, 1943.

88. MURRAY, H.A., and MORGAN, C.D.: A clinical study of sentiments. *Genetic Psychology Monographs* 32:3–311, 1945.

89. MURRAY, H.A., et al.: *Explorations in Personality*, New York, Oxford University Press, 1938.

90. MYRDAL, G.: *An American Dilemma*, New York, Harper & Brothers, 1944 (2 vols.).

91. NEWCOMB, T.M.: *Personality and Social Change*, New York, Dryden Press, 1943.

92. PARRINGTON, V.L.: *Main Currents in American Thought*, New York, Harcourt, Brace & Company, 1927, 1930 (3 vols.).

93. PROUST, M.: *Remembrance of Things Past*, New York, Random House, Inc., 1934.

94. RAPAPORT, D.: *Diagnostic Psychological Testing*, Vol. II, Chicago, The Year Book Publishers, 1946.

95. RAUSCHNING, H.: *The Revolution of Nihilism*, New York, Garden City Publishing Company, Inc., 1942.

96. REICH, W.: *The Mass Psychology of Fascism*, New York, Orgone Institute Press, 1946.

97. ROHDE, A.: Explorations in personality by the sentence completions method. *Journal of Applied Psychology* 30:169–180, 1946.

98. ROKEACH, M.: Generalized mental rigidity as a factor in ethnocentrism. *Journal of Abnormal and Social Psychology* 43:259–278, 1948.

99. ROTTER, J.B.: Studies in the use and validity of the T.A.T. with mentally disordered patients. I. Methods of analysis and clinical problems. *Character and Personality* 9:18–34, 1940.

100. ROTTER, J.B., and WILLERMAN, B.: The incomplete sentences test as a method of studying personality. *Journal of Consulting Psychology* 11:43–48, 1947.

101. SAMUEL, M.: *The Great Hatred*, New York, Alfred A. Knopf, 1940.

102. SANFORD, R.N.: American conscience and the coming peace. *Journal of Abnormal and Social Psychology* 38:158–165, 1943.

103. SANFORD, R.N.: A psychoanalytic study of three types of criminals. *Journal of Criminal Psychopathology* 5:57–68, 1943.

104. SANFORD, R.N.: Identification with the enemy: case study of an American Quisling. *Journal of Personality* 15:53–58, 1946.

105. SANFORD, R.N.: *Procedure for Scoring the T.A.T.*, Cambridge, Harvard Psychological Clinic, 1939 (mimeographed and privately distributed).

106. SANFORD, R.N., ADKINS, M.M., MILLER, R.B., COBB, E.A., et al.: Physique, personality and scholarship. *Monographs of the Society for Research in Child Development* 8, 1:705 pp., 1943.

107. SANFORD, R.N., and CONRAD, H.S.: High and low morale as exemplified in two cases. *Character and Personality* 13:207–227, 1944.

108. SANFORD, R.N., CONRAD, H.S., and FRANCK, K.: Psychological determinants of optimism regarding the consequences of the war. *The Journal of Psychology* 22:207–235, 1946.

109. SANFORD, R.N., and CONRAD, H.S.: Some personality correlates of morale. *Journal of Abnormal and Social Psychology* 38:3–20, 1943.

110. SARTRE, JEAN-PAUL: Portrait of the antisemite. *Partisan Review* 13:163–178, 1946.

111. SIMMEL, E., ed.: *Anti-Semitism: A Social Disease*, New York, International Universities Press, 1946.

112. STAGNER, R.: Fascist attitudes: their determining conditions. *The Journal of Social Psychology* 7:438–454, 1936.

113. STAGNER, R.: Studies of aggressive social attitudes. III. The role of personal and family scores. *The Journal of Social Psychology* 20:129–140, 1944.

114. STEIN, M.I.: The use of a sentence completion test for the diagnosis of personality. *Journal of Clinical Psychology* 3:47–56, 1947.

115. SUMNER, W.G.: *Folkways*, Boston, Ginn & Company, 1906.

116. The O.S.S. Assessment Staff: *Assessment of Men*, New York, Rinehart & Company, 1948.

117. THOMPSON, CLARA: Changing concepts of homosexuality in psychoanalysis. *Psychiatry* 10:183–190, 1947.

118. THURSTONE, L.L., and CHAVE, E.J.: *The Measurement of Attitude*, Chicago, University of Chicago Press, 1931.

119. TRACHTENBERG, J.: *The Devil and the Jews*, New Haven, Yale University Press, 1943.

120. WHITE, R.W.: Interpretation of imaginative productions. In HUNT, J. McV., ed.: *Personality and the Behavior Disorders*, New York, The Ronald Press Company, 1944.

121. WOODWORTH, R.S.: *Experimental Psychology*, New York, Henry Holt & Company, 1938.

INDEX

This index was compiled from listings supplied by the various authors. To make it as concise as possible, they included only those subject matters, names, and passages which they deemed sufficiently significant for indexing.

I. SUBJECTS

II. NAMES

Ackerman, N., 794
Adorno, T. W., 338, 729, 732
Aichorn, A., 817
Alexander, F., 796, 817, 818
Allport, F., 438, 746
Allport, G., 370, 433
Anastasi, A., 745
Barth, K., 731
Benedict, R., 598
Boder, D. P., 464, 746
Brown, J. F., 132, 605, 665, 774, 802
Cantril, H., 109
Chisholm, M. B., 231
Christiansen, C., 911
Conrad, H., 548, 794, 806
Durkheim, E., 747
Edwards, A., 109, 152
Erikson, E. H., 231, 370, 376, 762
Fenichel, O., 370, 747
Fisher, R., 261
Franck, K., 548, 806
Frenkel-Brunswik, E., 293, 338, 348, 358, 458, 464, 481, 776, 965
Freud, S., 5, 308, 382, 683, 746ff, 753, 760, 768ff, 779ff, 798, 805
Fromm, E., 231, 370, 376, 411, 414, 416, 486, 597, 759
Glueck, S. and Glueck, E., 817
Gundlach, R. H., 109, 658
Harriman, P., 464
Harris, R. E., 912
Hartman, H., 308, 438
Hathaway, S., 910
Healy, W., 817
Hitler, A., 733, 832ff, 862
Horkheimer, Max, 729, 759, 783
Horney, K., 484
Institute of Social Research, 225, 605, 752
Jaensch, E. R., 464, 746
Jahoda, M., 794
Jones, E., 794, 798
Jones, H. E., 338
Jung, C. G., 746
Kardiner, A., 414, 485, 598
Karpman, B., 817

Katz, D., 109
Kerr, W., 281
Kretschmer, E., 746
Krout, M., 405, 448
Lasswell, H., 376
Lee, A. McClung, 773
Lentz, T., 152, 465
Levinson, D., 152, 192, 897
Likert, R., 58, 77, 104, 109, 152
Lindner, R., 764, 817
Lourie, A., 639
Lowenthal, L., 768
Lowrey, L., 817
Lynd, R. and H., 484
MacKinnon, D. W., 747
Maslow, A., 231, 411
McGranahan, D., 548
McKinley, J., 910
Mead, M., 414, 484
Morgan, C., 489
Murphy, G., 77, 109, 152, 192, 281
Murphy, L., 152, 192, 281
Murray, H. A., 235, 489, 493, 506
Newcomb, T., 152, 192, 281
Pollock, F., 605
Reich, W., 231, 598
Rohde, A., 548
Rokeach, M., 280, 464, 596
Roosevelt, F. D., 46ff, 164, 688ff, 804, 839ff, 842
Rosenzweig, S., 409, 802
Rotter, J., 548
Samuel, M., 728
Sanford, R. N., 152, 192, 496, 548, 776, 794, 806, 818, 965
Sartre, Jean-Paul, 971
Schmitt, Karl, 769
Simmel, E., 478
Stagner, R., 109, 152, 405, 448
Staub, H., 818
Stein, M., 548
Sumner, W. G., 102, 104
Thompson, C., 798
Thurstone, L. L., 58
Trachtenberg, J., 728
Wylie, P., 368

990